S0-BYA-826

ADULT PSYCHOPATHOLOGY
AND DIAGNOSIS

Adult Psychopathology and Diagnosis

Third Edition

Edited by

Samuel M. Turner
Michel Hersen

JOHN WILEY & SONS, INC.

New York · Chichester · Weinheim · Brisbane · Singapore · Toronto

This text is printed on acid-free paper.

Copyright © 1997 by John Wiley & Sons, Inc.
Published by John Wiley & Sons, Inc.

All rights reserved. Published simultaneously in Canada.

Reproduction or translation of any part of this work beyond that
permitted by Section 107 or 108 of the 1976 United States Copyright
Act without the permission of the copyright owner is unlawful.
Requests for permission or further information should be addressed
to the Permissions Department, John Wiley & Sons, Inc.

This publication is designed to provide accurate and authoritative
information in regard to the subject matter covered. It is sold with
the understanding that the publisher is not engaged in rendering
professional services. If legal, accounting, medical, psychological,
or any other advice or other expert assistance is required, the services
of a competent professional person should be sought.

Library of Congress Cataloging-in-Publication Data

Adult psychopathology and diagnosis / Samuel M. Turner and Michel
   Hersen, editors. — 3rd ed.
       p.   cm.
   Includes bibliographical references and index.
   ISBN 0-471-11716-1 (alk. paper)
   1. Psychology, Pathological.   2. Mental illness—Diagnosis.
I. Turner, Samuel M., 1944–   . II. Hersen, Michel.
   [DNLM: 1. Mental Disorders—diagnosis. 2. Mental Disor-
ders—in adulthood.   WM 141 A244 1997]
RC454.A324   1997
616.89—dc20
DNLM/DLC
for Library of Congress   96-42980
                                                                    CIP

Printed in the United States of America

10 9 8 7 6 5 4 3 2 1

Contributors

RONALD ACIERNO, Ph.D., RESEARCH ASSOCIATE, Department of Psychiatry and Behavioral Sciences, Medical University of South Carolina, Charleston, South Carolina

PATRICIA A. AREÁN, Ph.D., ASSISTANT PROFESSOR, Department of Psychiatry and Langley Porter Psychiatric Institute, University of California, San Francisco, California

DEBORAH C. BEIDEL, Ph.D., ASSOCIATE PROFESSOR, Department of Psychiatry and Behavioral Sciences, Medical University of South Carolina, Charleston, South Carolina

F. CURTIS BRESLIN, Ph.D., ASSISTANT PROFESSOR, Department of Behavioral Medicine, Addiction Research Foundation and University of Toronto, Toronto, Ontario, Canada

ETZEL CARDEÑA, Ph.D., ASSISTANT PROFESSOR, Department of Psychiatry, Uniform Services University of Health Sciences, Bethesda, Maryland

BRIAN L. COOK, Ph.D., ASSOCIATE PROFESSOR, Department of Psychiatry, College of Medicine and Veterans Affairs Medical Center, University of Iowa, Iowa City, Iowa

JACK D. EDINGER, Ph.D., ASSOCIATE PROFESSOR, Department of Psychiatry and Behavioral Sciences, Duke University Medical Center, Durham, North Carolina

GERALD GOLDSTEIN, Ph.D., DIRECTOR, Neuropsychology Program, Veterans Affairs Medical Center, Pittsburgh, Pennsylvania

MICHEL HERSEN, Ph.D., PROFESSOR, Center for Psychological Studies, Nova Southeastern University, Fort Lauderdale, Florida

BILL N. KINDER, Ph.D., PROFESSOR, Department of Psychology, University of South Florida, Tampa, Florida

LAURENCE J. KIRMAYER, M.D., PROFESSOR AND DIRECTOR, Division of Transcultural Psychiatry, Culture and Mental Health Research Unit, Institute of Community and Family Psychiatry, Sir Mortimer B. Davis–Jewish General Hospital, Montréal, Québec, Canada

W. L. MARSHALL, Ph.D., PROFESSOR, Department of Psychology, Queen's University, Kingston, Ontario, Canada

NATHANIEL McCONAGHY, M.D., ASSOCIATE PROFESSOR OF PSYCHIATRY, University of New South Wales, Prince Henry Hospital, Little Bay, New South Wales, Australia

JOHN McQUAID, Ph.D., ASSISTANT PROFESSOR, Department of Psychiatry, University of California, San Diego, La Jolla, California

JESSE B. MILBY, Ph.D., CHIEF, Psychology Service, Veterans Affairs Medical Center, Birmingham, Alabama

CHARLES M. MORIN, Ph.D., ASSOCIATE PROFESSOR AND DIRECTOR OF CLINICAL TRAINING, School of Psychology, Laval University, Quebec City, Canada

KIM T. MUESER, Ph.D., ASSOCIATE PROFESSOR, Department of Psychiatry and Community and Family Medicine, Dartmouth Medical School, Hanover, New Hampshire

RICARDO F. MUÑOZ, Ph.D., PROFESSOR, Department of Psychiatry, Latino Mental Health Research Program, University of San Francisco and San Francisco General Hospital, San Francisco, California

BARBARA M. ROHLAND, M.D., ASSISTANT PROFESSOR, Department of Psychiatry, College of Medicine, University of Iowa, Iowa City, Iowa

JOSEPH E. SCHUMACHER, Ph.D., Veterans Affairs Medical Center, Birmingham, Alabama

DANIEL L. SEGAL, Ph.D., ASSISTANT PROFESSOR, Department of Psychology, University of Colorado at Colorado Springs, Colorado Springs, Colorado

R. SERIN, Ph.D., ADJUNCT ASSOCIATE PROFESSOR, Department of Psychiatry, Queens University, Kingston, Ontario, Canada

LINDA C. SOBELL, Ph.D., PROFESSOR, Center for Psychological Studies, Nova Southeastern University, Fort Lauderdale, Florida

MARK B. SOBELL, Ph.D., PROFESSOR, Center for Psychological Studies, Nova Southeastern University, Fort Lauderdale, Florida

ROBERT D. STAINBACK, Ph.D., Veterans Affairs Medical Center, Birmingham, Alabama

SUZANNE TAILLEFER, M.Sc., Culture and Mental Health Research Unit, Institute of Community and Family Psychiatry, Sir Mortimer B. Davis–Jewish General Hospital, Montréal, Québec, Canada

SVENN TORGERSEN, Ph.D., Department of Psychology, Oslo University, Oslo, Norway

WARREN W. TRYON, Ph.D., PROFESSOR, Department of Psychology, Fordham University, Bronx, New York

SAMUEL M. TURNER, Ph.D., PROFESSOR, Department of Psychiatry and Behavioral Sciences, Medical University of South Carolina, Charleston, South Carolina

VINCENT B. VAN HASSELT, Ph.D., PROFESSOR, Center for Psychological Studies, Nova Southeastern University, Fort Lauderdale, Florida

THOMAS A. WIDIGER, Ph.D., PROFESSOR, Department of Psychology, University of Kentucky, Lexington, Kentucky

GEORGE WINOKUR, M.D., PROFESSOR AND HEAD, Department of Psychiatry, University of Iowa College of Medicine and Veterans Affairs Medical Center, Iowa City, Iowa

Preface

This is the third edition of *Adult Psychopathology and Diagnosis.* The publication of this volume was necessitated primarily by the rapid advancement in knowledge about psychopathological states and their assessment and treatment. These new findings have been incorporated into DSM-IV, the latest version of the *Diagnostic and Statistical Manual of Mental Disorders,* which was published in 1994. This revision reflects the refinement of some diagnostic categories and the inclusion of others for the first time. Additionally, there is an emerging body of data describing similarities and differences in the manifestation of psychiatric disorders among ethnic and racial minority groups and differences associated with gender. This latter information is highlighted within a special section of each chapter.

As in previous editions, the text is arranged to provide a discussion of the major adult psychiatric disorders using DSM nomenclature (now DSM-IV). Our intention in all three editions of this text was to present an integration of the empirical data and diagnostic criteria in order to provide the reader with the empirical underpinnings of the specific disorder and its diagnosis, while at the same time illuminating ambiguities and inconsistencies. Chapters are organized such that each presents a discussion of the clinical picture of the disorder, the diagnostic criteria, major theories of etiology, issues of assessment and measurement, and as noted above, a discussion of issues pertaining to ethnic and racial minority status and gender. Treatment is discussed only insofar as it contributes to the understanding of the psychopathology of a specific condition.

In this, our third edition, we have included 18 chapters, one more than in the second edition. We have deleted a number of chapters and added new ones not heretofore included. These additions reflect major emerging trends in psychopathology and issues of particular importance, controversy, or both. In other cases, new diagnostic categories were added due to development of important new information and/or refinement of the diagnostic category. Part One (Overview) has chapters entitled "Mental Disorders as Discrete Clinical Conditions: Dimensional versus Categorical Classification," "Structured Interviewing and DSM Classification," and "Genetic Basis and Psychopathology." Part Two (Specific Disorders) addresses individual psychiatric syndromes and represents the "heart" of the book. This section includes two diagnostic categories new to the volume in chapters on "Somatoform Disorders" and "Sleep Disorders." Finally,

Part Three (Special Topics) includes chapters on "Motor Activity and DSM-IV" and "DSM-IV and Multidimensional Assessment Strategies."

We are indebted to many individuals for their contributions to bringing this volume to fruition. First, and foremost, we thank the many authors who endeavored to meet our specifications for the chapters. Second, we thank Agnes Seibert and Burt Bolton for their technical assistance. Third, we thank Herb Reich, the editor at John Wiley & Sons under whom each of the editions of this text was conceived. Fourth, we acknowledge the contribution of many who assisted us with various aspects of the manuscript. These include Christine Apple, Christopher Brooks, Stacy Sanders, and Brenda G. Turner, Ph.D. Finally, we express our sincere thanks to Jo Ann Miller, our current editor, who has taken over the reins of editorship at John Wiley & Sons.

SAMUEL M. TURNER
MICHEL HERSEN

Charleston, South Carolina
Fort Lauderdale, Florida
July 1996

Contents

PART ONE   OVERVIEW

1. Mental Disorders as Discrete Clinical Conditions: Dimensional versus Categorical Classification
   Thomas A. Widiger   3

2. Structured Interviewing and DSM Classification
   Daniel L. Segal   24

3. Genetic Basis and Psychopathology
   Svenn Torgersen   58

PART TWO   SPECIFIC DISORDERS

4. Delirium, Dementia, and Amnestic and Other Cognitive Disorders
   Gerald Goldstein   89

5. Substance-Related Disorders: Alcohol
   Linda C. Sobell, F. Curtis Breslin, and Mark B. Sobell   128

6. Psychoactive Substance Use Disorders: Drugs
   Jesse B. Milby, Joseph E. Schumacher, and Robert D. Stainback   159

7. Schizophrenia
   Kim T. Mueser   203

8. Mood Disorders: Depressive Disorders
   Patricia A. Areán, John McQuaid, and Ricardo F. Muñoz   230

9. Mood Disorders: Bipolar Disorders
   Barbara M. Rohland, George Winokur, and Brian L. Cook   256

10. Anxiety Disorders
    Deborah C. Beidel and Samuel M. Turner   282

11. Somatoform Disorders
   Laurence J. Kirmayer and Suzanne Taillefer   333

12. Dissociative Disorders: Phantoms of the Self
   Etzel Cardeña   384

13. Sexual and Gender Identity Disorders
   Nathaniel McConaghy   409

14. Eating Disorders
   Bill N. Kinder   465

15. Sleep Disorders: Evaluation and Diagnosis
   Charles M. Morin and Jack D. Edinger   483

16. Personality Disorders
   W. L. Marshall and R. Serin   508

PART THREE   SPECIAL TOPICS

17. Motor Activity and DSM-IV
   Warren W. Tryon   547

18. DSM-IV and Multidimensional Assessment Strategies
   Ronald Acierno, Michel Hersen, and Vincent B. Van Hasselt   578

Author Index   595

Subject Index   621

PART ONE

Overview

CHAPTER 1

Mental Disorders as Discrete Clinical Conditions: Dimensional versus Categorical Classification

THOMAS A. WIDIGER

"In DSM-IV, there is no assumption that each category of mental disorder is a completely discrete entity with absolute boundaries dividing it from other mental disorders or from no mental disorder" (American Psychiatric Association [APA], 1994, p. xxii). This carefully worded disclaimer, however, is somewhat hollow, as it is the case that "DSM-IV is a categorical classification that divides mental disorders into types based on criteria sets with defining features" (APA, 1994, p. xxii). Researchers and clinicians, following this lead, diagnose and interpret the disorders presented in DSM-IV (*Diagnostic and Statistical Manual of Mental Disorders; APA 1994*) as clinical conditions that are distinct from normal human functioning and from one another.

The question of whether mental disorders are discrete clinical conditions or arbitrary distinctions along various dimensions of functioning is a longstanding issue (Kendell, 1975). However, the controversy is escalating with the increasing difficulties of the categorical model. For example, an issue that predominates much of the concern and interest of clinicians and researchers today is the substantial comorbidity among mental disorders (Caron & Rutter, 1991; Clark, Watson, & Reynolds, 1995; Klein & Riso, 1993; Lilienfeld, Waldman, & Israel, 1994; Sher & Trull, 1996). Very few patients fail to meet the criteria for a number of seemingly different mental disorders. A fundamental question is whether this apparent comorbidity represents the co-occurrence of multiple mental disorders or the presence of one disorder that is being given multiple diagnoses.

Stoking the fire is the inadequacy of the diagnostic categories to fully cover many of the persons within clinical treatment (Clark et al., 1995; Frances et al., 1991). Each of the recent editions of the DSM has added many new diagnoses, subtypes, and modifiers. However, these additions rarely concern newly discovered forms or domains of psychopathology. Their purpose is instead to fill in holes and gaps along boundaries of existing categories.

The purpose of this chapter is to review the categorical model of diagnosis of DSM-IV. The chapter begins with a discussion of the primary categorical distinctions, including the boundaries with normality, with physical disorders, and among different mental disorders. The discussion will indicate the arbitrary nature of and problems created by these categorical distinctions. The reasons for maintaining the categorical model will then be considered. The chapter concludes with a recommendation for a gradual (and perhaps inevitable) conversion to a more quantitative, dimensional classification of mental disorders.

BOUNDARY WITH NORMALITY

"In DSM-IV, each of the mental disorders is conceptualized as a clinically significant behavioral or psychological syndrome or pattern that occurs in an individual and that is associated with present distress (e.g., a painful symptom) or disability (i.e., impairment in one or more important areas of functioning) or with a significantly increased risk of suffering death, pain, disability, or an important loss of freedom" (APA, 1994, p. xxi). This definition of mental disorder nowhere states, or even implies, that a mental disorder is distinct from normal human functioning. In fact, if one considers the fundamental, defining features of a mental disorder, it is apparent that there is no qualitative distinction from normal functioning. This will be illustrated with respect to dyscontrol and impairment.

Dyscontrol

Central to the concept of a mental disorder is that the behavior is not within the person's control. A mental disorder is an *"involuntary* organismic impairment in psychological functioning"* (Widiger & Trull, 1991, p. 112; my emphasis). Persons who freely choose to engage in harmful or impairing behavior would not be said to have a mental disorder. The maladaptive, harmful, or impairing behaviors of persons with mental disorders are compelled or caused by the disorder.

It is difficult, however, to imagine a qualitative distinction or discrete break between the presence and absence of self-control. It is not even clear how much control a "normal" person has over behavior that is adaptive (Howard & Conway, 1986; Rachlin, 1992). Both normal and abnormal human functioning is the result of a complex interaction of apparent volitional choice with an array of biogenetic and environmental determinants (Barton, 1994). It does not appear to be the case that people either have full volitional control or absolutely no control of their behavior, but that persons vary in the extent to which they are in control of particular aspects of their behavior. Some persons may have more control than others, and some may have more control over certain aspects of their behavior than other aspects, but even those persons who have recognized mental disorders will have some measure of control over the maladaptive behavior pattern (Peterson & Stunkard, 1992).

The continuum of dyscontrol is particularly evident in those disorders that involve behaviors that have immediate benefits or pleasures to the person, such as pedophilia, intermittent explosive disorder, transvestic fetishism, kleptomania, bulimia nervosa, anorexia nervosa, pathological gambling, and substance-related disorders such as alcohol abuse, cocaine abuse, anabolic steroid abuse, and nicotine dependence. These disorders are difficult to diagnose and are often controversial precisely because there is no distinct point at which dyscontrol occurs (Widiger & Smith, 1994).

Persons can choose to consume alcohol, take anabolic steroids, shoot heroin, gamble, steal, assault, or engage in deviant sexual acts. Such acts can be harmful and maladaptive, but the occurrence of a harmful (or deviant) act does not itself constitute a mental disorder (Gorenstein, 1984; Wakefield, 1992; Widiger & Trull, 1991). It is only when the person lacks sufficient control of the harmful behavior pattern that he or she would be diagnosed with a mental disorder (Frances, Widiger, & Sabshin, 1991).

For example, each of the diagnostic criteria for pathological gambling represent valid but fallible indicators of dyscontrol (Lesieur & Rosenthal, 1991). It is possible that the presence of just one of the criteria indicates the presence of a maladaptive dyscontrol of gambling behavior. A person who has displayed "repeated unsuccessful efforts to control, cut back, or stop gambling" (APA, 1994, p 618) is not in control of his or her behavior, and if this person has also "lost a significant relationship, job, [and] educational or career opportunity because of gambling" (APA, 1994, p. 618), it would not be unreasonable to suggest that he or she has suffered clinically significant maladaptive consequences. However, DSM-IV requires at least 5 of the 10 diagnostic criteria. It is the case that it is much more likely that a person who has all 10 criteria lacks adequate control than a person who has just one, but there is no distinct point at which the diagnosis could ever be certain or infallible, such that all persons below the threshold have adequate control over their gambling behavior and all persons above the threshold do not (Rosenthal, 1989).

The lack of a distinct boundary is evident in other mental disorders. For example, the DSM-III-R (APA, 1987) criteria for substance dependence and pathological gambling were made isomorphic because the dyscontrol is comparable across these disorders (Bradley, 1990; Goodman, 1990). At one time, persons with alcohol dependence were thought to have a discrete pathology that rendered them incapable of any control of their drinking behavior. However, there is now substantial research to indicate that persons vary in the extent to which they are able to control their drinking (Peele, 1984; Widiger & Smith, 1994). Treatment for controlled drinking is controversial in part because there is no absolute point of demarcation and persons who lack sufficient control often deny the extent of their dyscontrol.

Impairment

An additional fundamental feature of mental disorders is impairment (APA, 1994; Wakefield, 1992; Widiger & Trull, 1991). "The definition of mental disorder in the introduction to DSM-IV requires that there be clinically significant impairment" (APA, 1994, p. 7). The purpose of this requirement is to distinguish between a mental disorder and simply a problem in living. "The ever-increasing number of new categories meant to describe the less impaired outpatient population raises the question of where psychopathology ends and the wear and tear of everyday life begins" (Frances, First, & Pincus, 1995, p. 15).

To highlight the importance of considering this issue, the criteria sets for most disorders include a clinical significance criterion (usually worded ". . . causes clinically significant . . . impairment in social, occupational, or other important areas of functioning"). This criterion helps establish the threshold for the diagnosis of a disorder in those situations in which the symptomatic presentation by itself (particularly in its milder forms) is not inherently pathological and may be encountered in individuals for whom a diagnosis of "mental disorder" would be inappropriate. (APA, 1994, p. 7)

DSM-III-R (APA, 1987) failed to include this requirement within the diagnostic criteria sets for many of the individual mental disorders, contributing to a confusion of harmless deviances, eccentricities, peculiarities, or annoyances with the presence of a mental disorder (Frances et al., 1991). For example, the attention-deficit hyperactivity and oppositional defiant disorders were diagnosed even if the behaviors resulted in "only minimal or no impairment in school and social functioning" (APA, 1987, pp. 53, 58) as long as the behaviors were "more frequent than that of most people of the same mental age" (APA, 1987, pp. 52, 57). Statistical deviance alone, however, is insufficient for the presence of a mental disorder (Frances et al., 1991; Gorenstein, 1984).

Similarly, a diagnosis of transvestic fetishism could be made in DSM-III-R if the person simply had recurrent intense sexual urges, fantasies, and behaviors involving cross-dressing for longer than 6 months (APA, 1987). A man who engaged in this behavior for longer than 6 months and experienced no impairment in marital, social, or occupational functioning (e.g., was able to limit the behavior within tolerable or acceptable limits) would be considered in DSM-III-R to have been mentally ill, simply because he did it for longer than 6 months. It is possible that a 6-month duration is a valid (but fallible) indicator for impairment (as well as dyscontrol), if most persons who engage in this deviant sexual behavior longer than 6 months usually experience clinically significant social, occupational, or legal consequences, but deviant sexual preferences can be egosyntonic, controlled, and harmless. Therefore, DSM-IV now requires that "the fantasies, sexual urges, or behaviors cause clinically significant distress or impairment in social, occupational, or other important areas of functioning" (APA, 1994, p. 531).

However, nowhere in DSM-IV is a "clinically significant" impairment defined, not even within the section of the manual identified by the heading "Criteria for Clinical Significance" (APA, 1994, p. 7). It is stated only that this "is an inherently difficult clinical judgment" (APA, 1994, p. 7), and it is advised that the clinician consider information obtained from family members and other third parties. Frances et al. (1995) in fact state that "the evaluation of clinical significance is likely to vary in different cultures and to depend on the availability and interests of clinicians" (p. 15), an acknowledgment of no absolute (or perhaps even valid) basis for the threshold. The absence of a clear basis for this distinction helps fuel the considerable controversy of premenstrual dysphoric disorder, which is essentially a clinically significant variant of the "normal" premenstrual syndrome that occurs in 20%–40% of adult women (Caplan, McCurdy-Myers, & Gans, 1992; Gallant & Hamilton, 1990).

Spitzer and Williams (1982), the original authors of the DSM-IV definition of mental disorder, defined a clinically significant impairment as that point at which the attention of a clinician is indicated. "There are many behavioral or psychological conditions that can be considered 'pathological' but the clinical manifestations of which are so mild that clinical attention is not indicated" (Spitzer & Williams, 1982, p. 166). They provided three examples: caffeine withdrawal, jet lag syndrome, and insomnia due to environmental noise. The impairments in each case would be too small to be "justified as syndromes that were clinically significant to mental health professionals" (Spitzer & Williams, 1982, p. 166). Persons do not seek or need the intervention of a clinician to treat these conditions. Nevertheless, jet lag syndrome was actually included within DSM-III-R as a variant of sleep-wake schedule disorder (APA, 1987, p. 306), caffeine withdrawal was subsequently included in the appendix to DSM-IV (APA, 1994), and a strong case has been made for the inclusion of caffeine dependence (Hughes, Oliveto, Helzer, Higgins, & Bickel, 1992).

The threshold of impairment that is used by most persons who seek treatment is that point at which they desire to overcome their dysfunction (Widiger & Corbitt, 1994). People seek the intervention of a clinician when they are sufficiently troubled or distressed by their condition or when they are compelled by others when these persons are sufficiently troubled. This is not to suggest that the attribution of impairment is inaccurate or illusory, just that the threshold point is not absolute.

The degree of impairment that is sufficiently distressful to seek treatment varies substantially across patients and clinicians, and it appears to be well below the threshold of many of the DSM-IV criteria sets. Clark et al. (1995) document well the reliance of clinicians on the category of "not otherwise specified" (NOS) to diagnose subthreshold cases. Whenever this catchall diagnosis is included within a study, it is often the most frequent diagnosis, as in the case of mood disorders (Angst, 1992), dissociative disorders (Spiegel & Cardena, 1991), and personality disorders (Widiger & Sanderson, 1995).

The purpose of many of the new diagnoses added to DSM-IV is to fill the gap between an existing category and normal functioning. For example, acute stress disorder is essentially posttraumatic stress disorder with a shorter duration (Spiegel & Cardena, 1991), recurrent brief depressive disorder is major depression with shorter episodes (Merikangas, Hoyer, & Angst, 1996), mixed anxiety-depressive disorder concerns subthreshold cases of mood and anxiety disorders (Zinbarg & Barlow, 1991), binge eating disorder concerns subthreshold cases of bulimia nervosa (Devlin, Walsh, Spitzer, & Hasin, 1992), and mild neurocognitive disorder concerns subthreshold cases of dementia, delirium, or amnestic disorder (Gutierrez, Atkinson, & Grant, 1993). A fundamental difficulty shared by all of these diagnoses is the lack of a clear distinction with normal human functioning. Two illustrative cases are minor depressive disorder and age-related cognitive decline.

Minor depressive disorder is a new addition to DSM-IV that attempts to plug the gap between DSM-III-R mood disorder diagnoses and normal sadness. It has been estimated that up to 50% of depressive symptomatology is currently being treated by primary care physicians without any consultation or involvement of a psychiatric clinician in part because the depression is below the threshold of a mood disorder diagnosis (Munoz, Hollon, McGrath, Rehm, & VandenBos, 1994). Many of these persons would meet the DSM-IV criteria for minor depressive disorder. However, it is acknowledged in DSM-IV that "symptoms meeting . . . criteria for minor depressive disorder can be difficult to distinguish from periods of sadness that are an inherent part of everyday life" (APA, 1994, p. 719). Only two distinctions are provided. One is a 2-week duration. If one is sad for less than 2 weeks, it is normal sadness. If it lasts longer than 2 weeks, it is a mental disorder. This is comparable to indicating that normal cross-dressing becomes transvestic fetishism if it is done longer than 6 months (APA, 1987). The second distinction is that "the depressive symptoms must cause clinically significant distress or impairment" (APA, 1994, p. 719), but, again, clinical significance is left undefined.

Age-related cognitive decline is a new addition to the section of the manual for other conditions that may be the focus of clinical attention. "Cognitive decline in the elderly can be considered dimensionally . . . , involving aging-associated cognitive decline, mild cognitive impairment, and dementia" (Caine, 1994, p. 335). "It may be very difficult to establish an arbitrary or numerical level where a disease state should be proclaimed" (Caine, 1994, p. 334). The DSM-IV diagnosis of age-related cognitive decline involves an objectively identified decline in cognitive functioning, such as "problems remembering names or appointments or . . . difficulty in solving complex problems" (APA, 1994, p. 684). Persons with this condition often seek the professional assistance of clinicians who specialize in the treatment of dementia. The DSM-IV Task Force decided that it should not be classified as a mental disorder because the decline in cognitive functioning is the result of "the aging process that is within normal limits given the person's age" (APA, 1994, p. 684). It does involve a clinically significant impairment but this level of impairment is considered to be normative for that time in life. One might question, however, whether being close to the norm is any more relevant to the issue of maladaptivity than being deviant from the norm (Frances et al., 1991; Gorenstein, 1984). The fact that it is the result of the normal process of aging does not indicate that it is adaptive, healthy, or even acceptable. The aging process is simply the etiology for the deterioration in functioning. Fortunately, physicians do not apply the same reasoning by judging that a deterioration in the functioning of one's vision, liver, bladder, or other organs is not a disorder because it is normal process of aging and common to persons within one's age group.

BOUNDARY WITH PHYSICAL DISORDERS

An additional defining feature of mental disorder is that it involves an involuntary organismic impairment to *psychological* functioning. A mental disorder is analogous to a physical disorder, but it is not equivalent to a physical disorder. This is the reason that the DSM-IV definition of mental disorder specifies that it is a "behavioral or psychological syndrome or pattern" (APA, 1994, p. xxi).

In DSM-IV, mental disorders are placed on Axes I and II, whereas physical disorders (or general medical conditions, as they are termed in DSM-IV) are placed on Axis III. However, it is also noted that this is not meant to imply that "mental disorders are unrelated to physical or biological factors or processes, or that general medical conditions are unrelated to behavioral or psychosocial factors or processes" (APA, 1994, p. 27). In fact, DSM-IV disavows any "fundamental differences in their conceptualization" (APA, 1994, p. 27) or "any fundamental distinction between mental disorders and general medical conditions" (APA, 1994, p. xxv). They overlap, shade into one another, and are at times impossible to disentangle.

A section of DSM-III-R had been devoted to "organic" mental syndromes and disorders, including such diagnoses as organic personality disorder and organic mood disorder, along with delirium, dementia, and amnestic disorders. "The essential feature of all these disorders is a psychological or behavioral abnormality associated with transient or permanent dysfunction of the brain" (APA, 1987, p. 98). However, the inclusion of a section of the manual for mental disorders secondary to central nervous system ("brain") dysfunction suggested that the pathology of the disorders contained elsewhere was largely nonorganic, perpetuating an archaic, illusory and often quite false distinction (Spitzer et al., 1992). A mood disorder due to thyroid disease can be as much of a mood disorder as a mood disorder due to the dysregulation in serotonin, and dysregulation in neurotransmitter monoamines can be as much a matter of a brain dysfunction ("organic") as thyroid disease. Therefore, the term "organic" was deleted from the manual in DSM-IV and most of the disorders that were within this section were moved to their phenomenological group (Frances et al., 1995). For example, DSM-III-R organic mood disorder is now within the mood disorder section as a mood disorder due to a general medical condition.

On the other hand, DSM-III-R also included a mental disorder diagnosis of psychological factors affecting a physical condition (APA, 1987). In DSM-IV, it became psychological factors affecting a medical condition (PFAMC) and, more important, was moved out of the mental disorders section to the section for other conditions that may be the focus of clinical attention (APA, 1994). PFAMC is a diagnosis often used by health psychologists for persons with physical disorders (e.g., ulcer, obesity, or headaches) for which psychological factors have contributed to their development, maintenance, or exacerbation. However, there are a multitude of psychological factors that may contribute to the development or exacerbation of a physical disorder, including a sedentary lifestyle and religious values. It is unclear if or when such behavior patterns or belief systems should constitute a mental disorder. More important, it is difficult to find a physical disorder for which psychological factors have not or could not make an important contribution to its development or exacerbation (Adler & Matthews, 1994). PFAMC could be diagnosed in such physical diseases as AIDS and cancer (Stoudemire et al., 1996). To the extent that PFAMC is a mental disorder, then almost any person with a physical disorder would have this mental disorder. In sum, the disorder that is clearly present in persons with PFAMC is a physical disorder. The impetus for and focus of treatment in cases of PFAMC concerns the physical pathology or dysfunction, or both. Psychological factors may contribute to its development, its exacerbation, and (it is hoped) its amelioration, but the phenomenology and pathology are largely physical. Therefore, PFAMC is no longer considered to be a mental disorder (Frances et al., 1995).

However, this same argument could, and perhaps should, be made for many of the other diagnoses within DSM-IV. For example, pain disorder is a mental disorder diagnosis given to persons when psychological factors are judged to have an important role in the onset, severity, exacerbation, or maintenance of pain, even when there is also a physical basis for the pain (APA, 1994, p. 458). There is perhaps no meaningful distinction between PFAMC and pain disorder, other than that pain disorder refers to a specific variant of PFAMC. In fact, a compelling proposal for DSM-IV was to delete all reference to psychological factors in the definition of pain disorder because there may be no meaningful distinction between psychological and physical pain (Trief, Elliott, & Stein, 1987). Both are mediated by the central nervous system. It may be as meaningful to distinguish between psychological pain and physical pain as it is to distinguish between an organic mood disorder and a mood disorder due to the dysregulation of serotonin (King & Strain, 1996).

Similar arguments could be made for female sexual arousal disorder and male erectile disorder. Female sexual arousal disorder is a "persistent or recurrent inability to attain, or to maintain . . . an adequate lubrication-swelling response to sexual excitement" (APA, 1994, p. 502), and male erectile disorder involves a "persistent or recurrent inability to attain, or to maintain . . . an adequate erection" (APA, 1994, p. 504). Both disorders are defined by a physical dysfunction, not a psychological dysfunction. In female sexual arousal disorder, "the arousal response consists of vasocongestion in the pelvis, vaginal lubrication and expansion, and swelling of the external genitalia" (APA, 1994, p. 500), not a psychological experience of inadequate arousal. It may be appropriate to consider female sexual arousal disorder as a mental rather than a physical disorder, but the same rationale should then apply to PFAMC.

The most heated controversy in the development of DSM-IV involved premenstrual dysphoric disorder (Ross, Frances, & Widiger, 1995). Those who opposed the inclusion of the diagnosis in DSM-IV did not argue that it did not exist. They argued instead that it is a physical rather than a mental disorder. "Few people question whether or not some women experience mild, moderate or severe mood or behavior changes at certain times in their menstrual cycle. . . . In other words, almost everyone agrees there is such a thing as what is often called 'PMS'" (Caplan et al., 1992, p. 28). However, one should not "rush to consider these physiologically based changes a psychiatric disorder" (Caplan et al., 1992, p. 28). Consistent with this argument is that premenstrual dysphoric disorder is directly related to the menstrual cycle, and effective treatment includes suppression of ovulation. Classifying premenstrual dysphoric disorder as a physical rather than a mental disorder would also help avoid the substantial stigmatization, misattributions, and other social repercussions that accompany its classification as a mental disorder (Caplan et al., 1992; Gallant & Hamilton, 1990). However, it is classified in DSM-IV as a depressive disorder NOS (not even as a mood disorder due to a general medical condition). Supporting this classification is that its symptomatology is predominantly that of a mood disorder (e.g., depressed mood, affective lability, irritability, decreased interest in activities, sleep difficulties, difficulty concentrating, and lethargy), its differential diagnosis in ambiguous cases will concern mood disorders rather than physical (gynecological) disorders, and effective treatment will often include an antidepressant medication (Gold & Severino, 1994). The seasonal pattern specifier for episodes of major depression is also related to a hormonal cycle and often involves a unique form of treatment that is focused directly on this cycle (i.e., light therapy), yet there is little controversy concerning its classification as a mental disorder.

Perhaps the most problematic boundary with a physical disorder is provided by the new DSM-IV diagnosis of breathing-related sleep disorder (APA, 1994). Breathing-related sleep disorder is classified as a mental disorder in DSM-IV, but its most common variant is obstructive sleep apnea due either to an upper airway narrowing secondary to the excessive bulk of soft tissues in overweight persons, or to an upper airway obstruction secondary to localized structural abnormalities in normal or below weight individuals (e.g., adenotonsillar enlargement). There was substantial opposition to its inclusion in DSM-IV, as there is very little that is psychological in its etiology, phenomenology, pathology, or treatment (Thorpy, 1994). The final compromise is almost amusing. One is instructed in DSM-IV to also diagnose the physical disorder of sleep-related breathing disorder on Axis III whenever the mental disorder of breathing-related sleep disorder is diagnosed on Axis I (APA, 1994, p. 573). It is to be hoped that nobody will study the comorbidity of these two "distinct" disorders.

BOUNDARIES AMONG MENTAL DISORDERS

The final categorical distinction to consider in this chapter concerns the boundaries among the mental disorders. DSM-IV is replete with unresolvable boundary distinctions and, as noted earlier, many of the new additions to DSM-IV represent efforts to fill gaps between existing categories. Notable examples include bipolar II (filling the gap between DSM-III-R bipolar and cyclothymic mood disorders), mixed anxiety-depressive disorder (anxiety and mood disorders), depressive personality disorder (personality and mood disorders), and postpsychotic depressive disorder of schizophrenia (schizophrenia and major depression). Only a few illustrations of problematic distinctions can be provided here, but many more exist, including the distinction between oppositional defiant, attention-deficit (with and without hyperactivity-impulsivity), and conduct disorder (Caron & Rutter, 1991; Loeber, Lahey, & Thomas, 1991), anorexia and bulimia (Wilson & Walsh, 1991), trichotillomania and obsessive-compulsive anxiety disorder (Liebowitz, 1992), depressive personality disorder and dysthymia (Phillips, Gunderson, Hirschfeld, & Smith, 1990), conversion disorder and dissociative disorder (Kihlstrom, 1992), bipolar and unipolar disorder (Blacker & Tsuang, 1992), and body dysmorphic disorder and anxiety disorder (Hollander, Neville, Frenkel, Josephson, & Liebowitz, 1992).

Generalized Social Phobia

Social phobia was a new addition to DSM-III (Spitzer, Williams, & Skodol, 1980; Turner & Beidel, 1989). It was considered to be a distinct, circumscribed condition, consistent with the definition of a phobia, or a "persistent, irrational fear of a *specific* object, activity, or situation" (APA, 1994, p. 770, my emphasis). However, it became apparent to anxiety disorder researchers and clinicians that the behavior of many of their patients was rarely so discrete and circumscribed (Spitzer & Williams, 1985). Therefore, the authors of DSM-III-R developed a generalized subtype for when "the phobic situation includes most social situations" (APA, 1987, p. 243).

DSM-III-R generalized social phobia, however, merged into the diagnosis of avoidant personality disorder. Both involved a pervasive, generalized social insecurity, discomfort, and timidity. Efforts to distinguish them have indicated only that avoidant personality disorder tends to be, on average, relatively more dysfunctional than generalized social phobia (Turner, Beidel, & Townsley, 1992; Widiger, 1992b).

DSM-IV provided no solution. In fact, it is now acknowledged that generalized social phobia emerges "out of a childhood history of social inhibition or shyness" (APA, 1994, p. 414), consistent with the definition of a personality disorder. An argument for considering this condition to be an anxiety rather than a personality disorder is that many persons with the disorder benefit from pharmacologic interventions (Liebowitz, 1992). "One may have to rethink what the personality disorder concept means in an instance where 6 weeks of phenelzine therapy begins to reverse long-standing interpersonal hypersensitivity as well as discomfort in socializing" (Liebowitz, 1992, p. 251). If so, one might have to rethink what the anxiety disorder concept means when an antidepressant is an effective form of treating an anxiety disorder. On the other hand, it is unclear why a maladaptive personality trait should not be responsive to a pharmacologic intervention (Siever & Davis, 1991), particularly when the response is confined to simply the beginning of a reversal in hypersensitivity and discomfort. In any case, DSM-IV provides no indication on how these two disorders could be distinguished, acknowledging that "they may be alternative conceptualizations of the same or similar conditions" (APA, 1994, pp. 663–664).

Acute Stress Disorder

Spiegel and Cardena (1991) proposed a new diagnosis for DSM-IV titled "brief reactive dissociative disorder" to be included within the dissociative disorders section, as indicated in the 1991 DSM-IV Options Book (Task Force on DSM-IV, 1991). The predominant symptomatology were symptoms of dissociation, including derealization, depersonalization, detachment, stupor, and amnesia.

Brief reactive dissociative disorder, though, resembled closely posttraumatic stress disorder (PTSD), which was classified as an anxiety disorder (APA, 1987). The major distinction was simply that brief reactive dissociative disorder was of a shorter duration (2 days to 4 weeks, whereas PTSD requires a duration of longer than 4 weeks). However, there are many arguments for considering PTSD a dissociative disorder (Spiegel & Cardena, 1991). The etiology and treatment of persons suffering from PTSD resembles more closely the etiology and treatment of dissociative disorders than most anxiety disorders (e.g., panic disorder, social phobia, obsessive-compulsive anxiety disorder, and specific phobia). Dissociative identity disorder and dissociative amnesia are almost invariably in response to having experienced, witnessed, or been confronted with a PTSD stressor. The pathology of PTSD and dissociative disorders involves the difficulties accepting, absorbing, or integrating a severe trauma (expressed through gross denial, avoidance, or recurrent recollections, or all of these). The theories, treatment techniques, and concerns of persons who specialize in crisis intervention, trauma, victimization, and abuse may overlap more with specialists in dissociative disorders than with specialists in anxiety disorders.

On the other hand, there are arguments to support the conceptualization of PTSD as an anxiety disorder (Davidson & Foa, 1991). Dissociative symptomatology is often seen in persons with PTSD, but dissociation could be understood as a cognitive avoidance of anxiety. In addition, dissociative symptoms are not as certain or predominant as anxious, avoidant symptoms in cases of PTSD. Finally, animal models can reproduce much of the PTSD symptomatology without invoking the notion that the animal is experiencing depersonalization or derealization (March, 1990).

The final decision for DSM-IV was to classify brief reactive dissociative disorder within the anxiety disorders section and to rename it as acute stress disorder (i.e., subthreshold PTSD). The best solution might have been to classify it as both an anxiety and as a dissociative disorder so that clinicians would recognize the importance of considering the presence of both a dysregulation of anxiety and dissociation in their understanding of the pathology and treatment of the condition. In any case, it is evident that the boundary between these conditions is uncertain, at best.

Schizoaffective Disorder

Schizoaffective disorder may be the prototypic boundary condition. It was included in DSM-III (APA, 1980) with no diagnostic criteria because it represented the gray area between schizophrenia and mood disorders (Spitzer et al., 1980). There are many cases that are clearly a mood disorder or schizophrenia, but these two major classes of disorder do appear to shade into one another, due perhaps to an overlap in their etiology and pathology (Blacker & Tsuang, 1992; Taylor, 1992). The DSM-III diagnosis of schizoaffective disorder represented those cases in which it was unclear whether it was more accurate to characterize the disorder as schizophrenic or mood (APA, 1980).

Researchers, though, had difficulty studying a condition with no diagnostic criteria. Therefore, specific and explicit diagnostic criteria were developed for DSM-III-R (APA, 1987). However, it may be paradoxical to create a distinct clinical entity to define a gray area between two other disorders. The diagnostic criteria for schizoaffective disorder have been notably complex and confusing (Frances et al., 1995). The solutions have been to develop increasingly more narrow definitions of the disorder, hoping to eventually identify a distinct clinical entity (Aubert & Rush, 1996). However, these efforts may serve primarily to create even more gray areas, including schizoaffective disorder versus schizophrenia, and schizoaffective disorder versus mood disorder. Yet, there have been proposals to create more categorical distinctions to identify the "distinct" clinical conditions along these new borders (Blacker & Tsuang, 1992).

Hypochondriasis

Hypochondriasis is classified as a somatoform disorder, but it may also be considered as an illness phobia (Liebowitz, 1992). Hypochondriasis involves the preoccupation with a fear of or belief that one has a serious physical disease based on the misinterpretation of one or more bodily signs or symptoms (APA, 1994). It shares with the other somatoform disorders "the presence of physical symptoms that suggest a general medical condition" (APA, 1994, p. 445). Persons with this disorder will initially seek treatment by a physician, and there is the need to exclude the presence of an actual physical disorder. As in the case of the somatization, pain, conversion, and body dysmorphic disorders, they may continually return to physicians in their belief that the disorder is physical rather than psychological.

However, persons with hypochondriasis also share the rumination, doubt, and worry that is central to obsessive-compulsive anxiety disorder, the continuous and daily anxiety seen in persons with generalized anxiety disorder, and the avoidant behavior seen in persons with specific phobias. Many persons with a phobia of getting a major disease ruminate over possibly having contracted a disease, and many persons who are hypochondriacal are phobic of contracting a disease (Task Force on DSM-IV, 1991). It is specified in DSM-IV that a disease phobia is the fear of contracting a disease (without the belief that it is already present), whereas hypochondriasis is the fear of having a disease (APA, 1994, p. 410). This distinction is seemingly discrete, but it is evident that hypochondriasis and specific phobia shade into one another.

Personality Disorders

"The diagnostic approach used in this manual represents the categorical perspective that Personality Disorders represent qualitatively distinct clinical syndromes" (APA, 1994, p. 633). However, many patients will meet the DSM-IV diagnostic criteria for more than one personality disorder, and the co-occurrence of just two personality disorders is problematic to their validity as distinct clinical conditions (Widiger, 1993). Persons have only one personality. It is unclear how they could have multiple personality disorders that comorbidly exist and interact, each with its own distinct etiology and pathology (Lilienfeld et al., 1994).

Much of the effort of the DSM-III-R Personality Disorders Advisory Committee was to reduce the overlap and co-occurrence among the categories by increasing the specificity of the diagnostic criteria. However, they were unsuccessful, as co-occurrence increased with DSM-III-R rather than decreased (Morey, 1988). It is unlikely that the DSM-IV Personality Disorders Work Group will be any more successful (Livesley, Schroeder, Jackson, & Jang, 1994; Widiger & Sanderson, 1995).

Several studies have attempted to identify empirically a clear distinction among the personality disorders, but none have been successful (Livesley et al., 1994; Widiger & Sanderson, 1995). The authors of these studies have maintained that their findings were more consistent with a dimensional model, and most personality disorder researchers favor a recognition that personality disorders are not categorically distinct conditions (Widiger, 1992a). It may be more accurate to say that a person has one personality disorder, characterized by a variety of maladaptive personality traits, than to choose only one category that fails to be fully or adequately descriptive.

RATIONALE AND JUSTIFICATION FOR THE CATEGORICAL MODEL

There are a number of reasons that diagnostic categories are used rather than clinical spectra or dimensions of functioning (Frances, 1990; Kendell, 1975), including tradition, simplicity, utility, and validity. Each of these reasons will be considered in turn.

Tradition

The diagnosis of mental disorders has been largely within the domain of medicine, which has itself used a categorical model of classification since Hippocrates (Kendell, 1975). It would be a major departure from this tradition to convert to a dimensional form of describing and diagnosing psychopathology (Frances, 1990). Many clinicians identify themselves as being within a branch of medicine, treating pathologies that are qualitatively distinct from normal functioning. A reformulation of mental disorders as shading imperceptibly into normal functioning could complicate the identity and credibility of the profession (Guze & Helzer, 1987).

Simplicity

It is human nature to categorize (Cantor & Genero, 1986). It is difficult, and often impossible, to be cognizant of all of the shades of gray. Typologies are created in large part to render information into a more simple, succinct form (Frances, 1990; Frances et al., 1995). However, "there is a tendency, once having categorized, to exaggerate the similarity among nonidentical stimuli by overlooking within-group variability, discounting disconfirming evidence, and focusing on stereotypic examples" (Cantor & Genero, 1986, p. 235). Mental disorder categories often are frustrating and troublesome to clinicians precisely because they suggest a uniformity of presentation and homogeneity of pathology that rarely seem to be present in actual cases.

To the extent that diagnostic categories are imposed upon underlying dimensions, they will be inaccurate and misleading when the information that is lost is relevant and informative to understanding the etiology, pathology, and treatment of the condition. For example, describing the extent of one's nearsightedness by the single diagnosis of myopia is succinct and informative, but ophthalmologists recognize that a more accurate and precise description of the extent of near-sightedness is necessary for clinical research and treatment decisions. DSM-IV diagnostic categories may be problematic and difficult to use in part because the information that is lost is important and relevant to understanding etiology, pathology, and treatment.

Utility

Clinical decisions are themselves categorical. Whether to provide a medication, hospitalization, or insurance coverage are categorical decisions. Knowing that a person is somewhere within the clinical spectra of unipolar depression is insufficient. Cutoff points will need to be placed along dimensions to guide clinical decisions. If these categorical distinctions will inevitably occur, then it might be more useful to provide them in the first place.

However, the cutoff point that is optimal for one clinical decision (e.g., hospitalization) will not be optimal for another (e.g., medication). Kendler (1990) indicates how the threshold for the diagnosis of schizophrenia that is associated with a family history of the disorder is different from the threshold that is associated with course. That point at which medication, hospitalization, insurance coverage, or disability is provided will not all be equivalent to that point at which a diagnosis of major depression is made. As a result, the diagnosis of major depression may not be as informative as indicating the extent to which the person suffers from depression.

Validity

The major reason for retaining the categorical model should be its validity, and there is indeed the concern that dimensional models mask underlying latent class taxons (Kendell, 1975; Lilienfeld et al., 1994). "Tuberculosis means a great deal more to the clinician than does a profile of measurements of fever, joint pain, energy level, and symptoms like coughing, expectorating, and so on" (Benjamin, 1993, p. 92).

Dimensional models, however, vary in their level of analysis (Widiger & Costa, 1994). There could be a dimensional model at the level of individual symptoms, but the most valid and useful model would probably be at a level that is consistent with the existing categorical system. For example, a dimensional model of psychopathology might begin at the broad levels of mood, anxiety, personality, and other classes of disorders included within the DSM-IV (APA, 1994). Each of these fundamental dimensions would then be divided into finer differentiations. Blacker and Tsuang (1992) suggest that degree of affectivity, psychosis, chronicity, and impairment could be used for the mood and schizophrenic spectrum (along with perhaps degree of bipolarity and negative symptomatology). The end result would resemble the DSM-IV quite closely. The difference would be the provision of more precise descriptions of the extent to which each domain of dysfunction is evident and the avoidance of the proliferation of arbitrary diagnostic categories that are misunderstood as distinct and comorbidly interacting clinical entities.

For example, schizophrenic pathology is currently subdivided into the paranoid, disorganized, catatonic, undifferentiated, and residual diagnostic categories (APA, 1994). However, patients often meet the criteria for more than one category and change categories over time (McGlashan & Fenton, 1994). The appendix to DSM-IV provides an alternative dimensional classification, wherein one indicates the extent to which there have been 1. psychotic (hallucinations or delusions) symptoms, 2. disorganized speech, disorganized behavior, or inappropriate affect, and 3. negative (deficit) symptoms (i.e., affective flattening, alogia, and avolition). It is not a new categorical system because "various combinations of severity on the three dimensions are encountered in clinical practice, and it is relatively uncommon for one dimension to be present in the complete absence of both of the others" (APA, 1994, p. 710).

There are substantial data to indicate that the DSM-IV diagnostic categories provide useful information, but not that they represent distinct clinical entities. For example, the categorical diagnoses of cyclothymia and bipolar I are indeed valid distinctions, but the research is more consistent with cyclothymia being simply a milder variant of bipolar I (Blacker & Tsuang, 1992). There does not appear to be any distinct, nonarbitrary point of demarcation between a hypomanic and a manic episode, nor between a dysthymic and a major depressive episode. At what specific point does a hypomanic episode become a manic episode? How much faster is the pressured speech of mania versus hypomania; how much greater is the self-esteem; how much less is the need for sleep? Prototypic cases of each variant are very distinct, but typical cases fall in between. Clinicians and researchers fill in the gaps with such new diagnostic entities as bipolar II, recurrent brief depressive disorder, and double depression, but once sufficient experience with these new "distinct" clinical entities has occurred, there will probably be the need to create further diagnostic entities to fill in the additional gaps and boundaries created by them. It would be more accurate and precise to simply indicate where along a continuous spectra of unipolar-bipolar dysfunction each particular patient falls.

There have been surprisingly few studies concerned specifically with the question of whether findings are more consistent with a dimensional or a categorical model of classification. These studies assess for evidence of bimodality, discrete breaks within distributions, reproducibility of factor analytic solutions across groups, and incremental validity of categorical versus dimensional classifications. More elaborate statistical efforts include the use of maximum covariance analysis, assessment of discontinuous regression, latent class analyses, and admixture analysis (Klein & Riso, 1993; Meehl, 1992). Such studies have at times obtained results that were more consistent with a categorical than a dimensional model of classification, but the body of research tends to be more consistent with a dimensional model (Blacker & Tsuang, 1992; Klein & Riso, 1993; Livesley et al., 1994; Sher & Trull, 1996; Widiger & Trull, 1991).

It may be that no distinct break will ever be found unless the mental disorder in question is shown to have a single and discrete biological etiology and pathology (Lilienfeld & Marino, 1995). The success of the categorical model within general medicine is in large part because medical conditions often have a quite specific etiology, pathology, and even phenomenology that allows for relatively homogeneous, uniform groups to be defined and diagnosed. Physical disorders and diseases will often have a specific, discrete event, pathogen, or lesion that provides the condition with validity as a discrete clinical condition. This is not the case for most mental disorders. Mental disorders are typically the result of a complex interaction of an array of biological factors and environmental, psychosocial events, as indicated in each of the chapters presented in this volume. No mental disorder has been or likely will be reduced to a specific biological event. It is not that there are no specific physiological and environmental determinants worth identifying (e.g., sex abuse in the etiology of dissociative identity disorder) but that in order for there to be a meaningful categorical diagnosis the disorder would have to be largely unaffected by most to all of the other physiological and environmental determinants that will have significant effects on human behavior. It may be unrealistic to expect such multifactorially determined behavior patterns to be discrete or distinct clinical conditions.

A useful illustration is provided by the disorder of mental retardation, a disorder for which much is known regarding its etiology, pathology, and classification. Mental retardation is currently defined in large part as the level of intelligence below an IQ score of approximately 70 (APA, 1990). The point of demarcation is not unreasonable, random, or meaningless, but it is arbitrary. Persons below an IQ of 70 will experience a variety of significant impairments. However, this point of demarcation does not carve nature at a discrete joint. It is simply that point at which clinicians have decided is a meaningful or useful point at which to characterize the limitations to intelligence as a retardation. Most points of possible demarcation along the continuous distribution of intelligence will be equally successful in identifying clinically significant maladaptive functioning secondary to a relatively lower intelligence. Persons with a level of intelligence of approximately 79 (i.e., borderline intellectual functioning; APA, 1994) will also experience significant impairments in their efforts to succeed in school, careers, and relationships (i.e., social and occupational functioning). These impairments will not be as severe as those with levels of intelligence of 72, but the distinction between an IQ of 72 and 79 concerns the number or degree of limitations and impairments. It is not a qualitative distinction.

There are persons below an IQ of 70 for whom a qualitatively distinct disorder is evident. However, the disorder in these cases is not mental retardation, it is a physical disorder (e.g., Down's syndrome) that can be traced to a specific biological event (i.e., trisomy 21). "In approximately 30%–40% of individuals seen in clinical settings, no clear etiology for the Mental Retardation can be determined" (APA, 1994, p. 43). There is substantial research to indicate that intelligence is distributed as a continuous variable, consistent with a normal distribution, because the level of intelligence of most individuals is the result of a complex array of multiple genetic, fetal and infant development, and environmental influences. There are no discrete breaks in this distribution that provide an absolute distinction between normal intelligence and abnormal intelligence.

Recognizing the continuous nature of the distribution of intelligence and the arbitrary nature of any particular point of demarcation to identify retardation does not suggest that the disorder of mental retardation is illusory or invalid, as suggested by Gorenstein (1984) and Lilienfeld and Marino (1995). Mental retardation is an involuntary organismic impairment to psychological functioning (Widiger & Trull, 1991) or a harmful dysfunction (Wakefield, 1992). Intelligence is highly correlated with adaptive functioning. As one's level of intelligence increases, the potential for optimal, successful functioning in a variety of domains (particularly occupational) increases. Likewise, as one's level of intelligence decreases, the likelihood of experiencing clinically significant impairments to one's functioning also increases. Lower levels of intelligence do retard (limit) social and occupational functioning. It is very helpful and in fact necessary to identify a particular level of intelligence at which one will or should provide professional intervention to treat the impairment to psychological functioning, but the disorder itself exists along a continuum.

CONCLUSIONS

The modern effort to demarcate a taxonomy of distinct clinical conditions is often traced to Kraepelin (1917). Kraepelin (1917), however, acknowledged that "wherever we try to mark out the frontier between mental health and disease, we find a neutral territory, in which the imperceptible change from the realm of normal life to that of obvious derangement takes place" (p. 295). It would be an overreaction to the many limitations and problems of the categorical model to suggest abandoning altogether the categorical distinctions contained within DSM-IV. The DSM-IV diagnostic categories do provide valid and useful information (as indicated in the chapters herein). However, it is likely that many researchers and clinicians will gradually convert to more quantitative or dimensional forms of classification as the inadequacies of the categorical distinctions become increasingly problematic and unwieldy. The initial signs of this conversion are already evident within the DSM-IV itself: in the dimensional classification of schizophrenia provided in an appendix, the acknowledgment of the dimensional classification of personality disorders, and the use of more quantitative terms to characterize certain categories (e.g., the "predominantly" hyperactive-impulsive subtype to attention-deficit hyperactivity disorder; APA, 1994, p. 85). Perhaps by the time of DSM-V, further demonstrations that more quantitative and dimensional classifications of mental disorders increase rather than decrease the validity and credibility of mental disorder diagnosis will result in even more acceptance and recognition.

REFERENCES

Adler, N., & Matthews, K. (1994). Health psychology: Why do some people get sick and some stay well? *Annual Review of Psychology, 45,* 229–259.

American Psychiatric Association. (1980). *Diagnostic and statistical manual of mental disorders* (3rd ed.). Washington, DC: Author.

American Psychiatric Association. (1987). *Diagnostic and statistical manual of mental disorders* (3rd ed., rev. ed.). Washington, DC: Author.

American Psychiatric Association. (1994). *Diagnostic and statistical manual of mental disorders* (4th ed.). Washington, DC: Author.

Angst, J. (1992). Recurrent brief psychiatric syndromes of depression, hypomania, neurasthenia, and anxiety from an epidemiological point of view. *Neurological, Psychiatric, and Brain Research, 1,* 5–12.

Aubert, J. L., & Rush, A. J. (1996). Schizoaffective disorder. In T. A. Widiger, A. J. Frances, H. A. Pincus, R. Ross, M. B. First, & W. W. Davis (Eds.), *DSM-IV sourcebook* (Vol. 2). Washington, DC: American Psychiatric Association.

Barton, S. (1994). Chaos, self-organization, and psychology. *American Psychologist, 49,* 5–14.

Benjamin, L. S. (1993). Dimensional, categorical, or hybrid analyses of personality: A response to Widiger's proposal. *Psychological Inquiry, 4,* 91–95.

Blacker, D., & Tsuang, M. T. (1992). Contested boundaries of bipolar disorder and the limits of categorical diagnosis in psychiatry. *American Journal of Psychiatry, 149,* 1473–1483.

Bradley, B. P. (1990). Behavioral addictions: Common features and treatment implications. *British Journal of Addiction, 85,* 1417–1419.

Caine, E. D. (1994). Should aging-associated memory decline be included in DSM-IV? In T. A. Widiger, A. J. Frances, H. A. Pincus, M. B. First, R. Ross, & W. W. Davis (Eds.), *DSM-IV sourcebook* (Vol. 1, pp. 329–337). Washington, DC: American Psychiatric Association.

Cantor, N., & Genero, N. (1986). Psychiatric diagnosis and natural categorization: A close analogy. In T. Millon & G. Klerman (Eds.), *Contemporary directions in psychopathology* (pp. 233–256). NY: Guilford.

Caplan, P. J., McCurdy-Myers, J., & Gans, M. (1992). Should "premenstrual syndrome" be called a psychiatric abnormality? *Feminism and Psychology, 2,* 27–44.

Caron, C., & Rutter, M. (1991). Comorbidity in child psychopathology: Concepts, issues, and research strategies. *Journal of Child Psychology and Psychiatry, 32,* 1063–1080.

Clark, L. A., Watson, D., & Reynolds, S. (1995). Diagnosis and classification of psychopathology: Challenges to the current system and future directions. *Annual Review of Psychology, 46,* 121–153.

Davidson, J. R. T., & Foa, E. B. (1991). Diagnostic issues in posttraumatic stress disorder. *Journal of Abnormal Psychology, 100,* 346–355.

Devlin, M. G., Walsh, B. T., Spitzer, R. L., & Hasin, D. (1992). Is there another binge eating disorder? A review of the literature on overeating in the absence of bulimia nervosa. *International Journal of Eating Disorders, 11,* 333–340.

Frances, A. J. (1990, May). *Conceptual problems of psychiatric classification.* Paper presented at the annual meeting of the American Psychiatric Association, New York.

Frances, A. J., First, M. B., & Pincus, H. A. (1995). *DSM-IV guidebook.* Washington, DC: American Psychiatric Press.

Frances, A. J., First, M. B., Widiger, T. A., Miele, G., Tilly, S., Davis, W. W., & Pincus, H. A. (1991). An A to Z guide to DSM-IV conundrums. *Journal of Abnormal Psychology, 100,* 407–412.

Frances, A. J., Widiger, T. A., & Sabshin, M. (1991). Psychiatric diagnosis and normality. In D. Offer & M. Sabshin (Eds.), *The diversity of normal behavior* (pp. 3–38). New York: Basic Books.

Gallant, S. J., & Hamilton, J. A. (1990). Problematic aspects of diagnosing premenstrual phase dysphoria. *Professional Psychology, 20,* 60–68.

Gold, J. H., & Severino, S. (Eds.). (1994). *Premenstrual dysphorias: Myths and realities.* Washington, DC: American Psychiatric Press.

Goodman, A. (1990). Addiction: Definition and implications. *British Journal of Addiction, 85,* 1403–1408.

Gorenstein, E. (1984). Debating mental illness. *American Psychologist, 39,* 50–56.

Gutierrez, R., Atkinson, J. H., & Grant, I. (1993). Mild neurocognitive disorder. A needed addition to the nosology of cognitive impairment (organic mental) disorders. *Journal of Neuropsychiatry and Clinical Neurosciences, 5,* 161–177.

Guze, S. B., & Helzer, J. E. (1987). The medical model and psychiatric disorders. In R. Michels & J. Cavenar (Eds.), *Psychiatry* (Vol. 1, pp. 1–8). Philadelphia: Lippincott.

Hollander, E., Neville, D., Frenkel, M., Josephson, S., & Liebowitz, M. R. (1992). Body dysmorphic disorder: Diagnostic issues and related disorders. *Psychosomatics, 33,* 156–125.

Howard, G. S., & Conway, C. G. (1986). Can there be an empirical science of volitional action? *American Psychologist, 41,* 1241–1251.

Hughes, J. R., Oliveto, A. H., Helzer, J. E., Higgins, S. T., & Bickel, W. K. (1992). Should caffeine abuse, dependence, or withdrawal be added to DSM-IV or ICD-10? *American Journal of Psychiatry, 149,* 33–40.

Kendell, R. C. (1975). *The role of diagnosis in psychiatry.* Oxford: Blackwell.

Kendler, K. S. (1990). Toward a scientific psychiatric nosology: Strengths and limitations. *Archives of General Psychiatry, 47,* 969–973.

Kihlstrom, J. F. (1992). Dissociative and conversion disorders. In D. J. Stein & J. Young (Eds.), *Cognitive science and clinical disorders* (pp. 247–270). San Diego, CA: Academic Press.

King, S. A., & Strain, J. J. (1996). Somatoform pain disorder. In T. A. Widiger, A. J. Frances, H. A. Pincus, R. Ross, M. B. First, & W. W. Davis (Eds.), *DSM-IV sourcebook* (Vol. 2). Washington, DC: American Psychiatric Association.

Klein, D. N., & Riso, L. P. (1993). Psychiatric disorders: Problems of boundaries and comorbidity. In C. G. Costello (Ed.), *Basic issues in psychopathology* (pp. 19–66). New York: Guilford.

Kraepelin, E. (1917). *Lectures on clinical psychiatry* (3rd ed.). New York: William Wood.

Lesieur, H. R., & Rosenthal, R. L. (1991). Pathological gambling: A review of the literature. *Journal of Gambling Studies, 7,* 5–40.

Liebowitz, M. R. (1992). Diagnostic issues in anxiety disorders. In A. Tasman & M. B. Riba (Eds.), *Review of psychiatry* (Vol. 11, pp. 247–259). Washington, DC: American Psychiatric Press.

Lilienfeld, S. O., & Marino, L. (1995). Mental disorder as a Roschian concept: A critique of Wakefield's "harmful dysfunction" analysis. *Journal of Abnormal Psychology, 104,* 411–420.

Lilienfeld, S. O., Waldman, I. D., & Israel, A. C. (1994). A critical examination of the use of the term "comorbidity" in psychopathology research. *Clinical Psychology: Science and Practice, 1,* 71–83.

Livesley, W. J., Schroeder, M. L., Jackson, D. N., & Jang, K. L. (1994). Categorical distinctions in the study of personality disorder: Implications for classification. *Journal of Abnormal Psychology, 103,* 6–17.

Loeber, R., Lahey, B. B., & Thomas, C. (1991). Diagnostic conundrum of oppositional defiant disorder and conduct disorder. *Journal of Abnormal Psychology, 100,* 379–390.

March, J. S. (1990). The nosology of posttraumatic stress disorder. *Journal of Anxiety Disorders, 4,* 61–82.

McGlashan, T. H., & Fenton, W. S. (1994). Classical subtypes for schizophrenia. In T. A. Widiger, A. J. Frances, H. A. Pincus, M. B. First, R. Ross, & W. W. Davis (Eds.), *DSM-IV sourcebook* (Vol. 1, pp. 419–440). Washington, DC: American Psychiatric Association.

Meehl, P. E. (1992). Factors and taxa, traits and types, differences of degree and differences in kind. *Journal of Personality, 60,* 117–174.

Merikangas, K. R., Hoyer, E. B., & Angst, J. (1996). Recurrent brief depressive disorder. In T. A. Widiger, A. J. Frances, H. A. Pincus, R. Ross, M. B. First, & W. W. Davis (Eds.), *DSM-IV sourcebook* (Vol. 2). Washington, DC: American Psychiatric Association.

Morey, L. C. (1988). Personality disorders under DSM-III and DSM-III-R: An examination of convergence, coverage, and internal consistency. *American Journal of Psychiatry, 145,* 573–577.

Munoz, R. F., Hollon, S. D., McGrath, E., Rehm, L. P., & VandenBos, G. P. (1994). On the AHCPR depression in primary care guidelines. *American Psychologist, 49,* 42–61.

Peele, S. (1984). The cultural context of psychological approaches to alcoholism. *American Psychologist, 39,* 1337–1351.

Peterson, C., & Stunkard, A. J. (1992). Cognates of personal control: Locus of control, self-efficacy, and explanatory style. *Applied and Preventive Psychology, 1,* 111–117.

Phillips, K. A., Gunderson, J. G., Hirschfeld, R. M. A., & Smith, L. E. (1990). A review of the depressive personality. *American Journal of Psychiatry, 147,* 830–837.

Rachlin, H. (1992). Teleological behaviorism. *American Psychologist, 47,* 1371–1382.

Rosenthal, R. J. (1989). Pathological gambling and problem gambling: Problems in definition and diagnosis. In H. Shaffer, S. A. Stein, & B. Gambino (Eds.), *Compulsive gambling: theory, research, and practice* (pp. 101–125). Lexington, MA: Lexington Books.

Ross, R., Frances, A. J., & Widiger, T. A. (1995). Gender issues in DSM-IV. In J. M. Oldham & M. B. Riba (Eds.), *Review of psychiatry* (Vol. 14, pp. 205–226). Washington, DC: American Psychiatric Press.

Sher, K. J., & Trull, T. J. (1996). Methodological issues in psychopathology research. *Annual Review of Psychology, 47,* 371–400.

Siever, L. J., & Davis, K. L. (1991). A psychobiological perspective on the personality disorders. *American Journal of Psychiatry, 148,* 1647–1658.

Spiegel, D., & Cardena, E. (1991). Disintegrated experience: The dissociative disorders revisited. *Journal of Abnormal Psychology, 100,* 366–378.

Spitzer, R. L., First, M. B., Williams, J. B. W., Kendler, K., Pincus, H. A., & Tucker, G. (1992). Now is the time to retire the term "organic mental disorder." *American Journal of Psychiatry, 149,* 240–244.

Spitzer, R. L., & Williams, J. B. W. (1982). The definition and diagnosis of mental disorder. In W. Gove (Ed.), *Deviance and mental illness* (pp. 15–31). Beverly Hills, CA: Sage.

Spitzer, R. L., & Williams, J. B. W. (1985). Proposed revisions in the DSM-III classification of anxiety disorders based on research and clinical experience. In A. H. Tuma & J. Maser (Eds.), *Anxiety and the anxiety disorders* (pp. 759–773). Hillsdale, NJ: Erlbaum.

Spitzer, R. L., Williams, J. B. W., & Skodol, A. E. (1980). DSM-III: The major achievements and an overview. *American Journal of Psychiatry, 137,* 151–164.

Stoudemire, A., Beardsley, G., Folks, D. G., Goldstein, M. G., Levenson, J., McNamara, M. E., Moran, M., & Niaura, R. (1996). Psychological factors affecting physical condition (PFAPC). In T. A. Widiger, A. J. Frances, H. A. Pincus, R. Ross, M. B. First, & W. W. Davis (Eds.), *DSM-IV sourcebook* (Vol. 2). Washington, DC: American Psychiatric Association.

Task Force on DSM-IV. (1991, September). *DSM-IV options book: Work in progress.* Washington, DC: American Psychiatric Association.

Taylor, M. A. (1992). Are schizophrenia and affective disorder related? A selective literature review. *American Journal of Psychiatry, 149,* 22–32.

Thorpy, M. J. (1994). Breathing-related sleep disorder. In T. A. Widiger, A. J. Frances, H. A. Pincus, M. B. First, R. Ross, & W. W. Davis (Eds.), *DSM-IV sourcebook* (Vol. 1, pp. 639–642). Washington, DC: American Psychiatric Association.

Trief, P. M., Elliott, D. J., & Stein, N. (1987). Functional versus organic pain: A meaningful distinction? *Journal of Clinical Psychology, 43,* 219–226.

Turner, S. M., & Beidel, D. C. (1989). Social phobia: Clinical syndrome, diagnosis, and comorbidity. *Clinical Psychology Review, 9,* 3–18.

Turner, S. M., Beidel, D. C., & Townsley, R. M. (1992). Social phobia: A comparison of specific and generalized subtypes and avoidant personality disorder. *Journal of Abnormal Psychology, 101,* 326–331.

Wakefield, J. C. (1992). Disorder as harmful dysfunction: A conceptual critique of DSM-III-R's definition of mental disorder. *Psychological Review, 99,* 232–247.

Widiger, T. A. (1992a). Categorical versus dimensional classification: Implications from and for research. *Journal of Personality Disorders, 6,* 287–300.

Widiger, T. A. (1992b). Generalized social phobia versus avoidant personality disorder: A commentary on three studies. *Journal of Abnormal Psychology, 101,* 340–343.

Widiger, T. A. (1993). The DSM-III-R categorical personality disorder diagnoses: A critique and an alternative. *Psychological Inquiry, 4,* 75–90.

Widiger, T. A., & Corbitt, E. M. (1994). Normal versus abnormal personality from the perspective of the DSM. In S. Strack & M. Lorr (Eds.), *Differentiating normal and abnormal personality* (pp. 158–175). New York: Springer.

Widiger, T. A., & Costa, P. T. (1994). Personality and personality disorders. *Journal of Abnormal Psychology, 103,* 78–91.

Widiger, T. A., & Sanderson, C. J. (1995). Toward a dimensional model of personality disorders. In W. J. Livesley (Ed.), *The DSM-IV personality disorders* (pp. 433–458). New York: Guilford.

Widiger, T. A., & Smith, G. T. (1994). Substance use disorder: Abuse, dependence, and dyscontrol. *Addiction, 89,* 267–282.

Widiger, T. A., & Trull, T. J. (1991). Diagnosis and clinical assessment. *Annual Review of Psychology, 42,* 109–133.

Wilson, G. T., & Walsh, B. T. (1991). Eating disorders in the DSM-IV. *Journal of Abnormal Psychology, 100,* 362–365.

Zinbarg, R. E., & Barlow, D. H. (1991). Mixed anxiety-depression: A new diagnostic category? In R. M. Rapee & D. H. Barlow (Eds.), *Chronic anxiety: Generalized anxiety disorder and mixed anxiety-depression* (pp. 136–152). New York: Guilford.

CHAPTER 2

Structured Interviewing and DSM Classification

DANIEL L. SEGAL

Assessment of psychiatric signs, symptoms, and disorders has undergone significant change and maturation over the last three decades. More specifically, the ability of clinicians and researchers to *accurately* assign psychiatric diagnoses and classify mental illness has improved with quantum leaps. During this time, numerous structured diagnostic interviews have been developed for clinical, research, and training applications, and these instruments have strongly contributed to the advancement in diagnostic clarity and precision. Structured interviews have been devised to assist in the diagnosis of most major Axis I (clinical syndromes) and all standard Axis II (personality) disorders. Most structured interviews are linked to DSM criteria and subsequently have been revamped to match refinements in that classification system as it has also evolved. Overall, such structured interviews have improved clinical and research endeavors by providing a more standardized, scientific, and quantitative approach to the evaluation of psychiatric symptomatology. The purpose of this chapter is to review the prominent structured interviews designed to assess psychopathology and enhance diagnosis of Axis I and Axis II disorders. For each instrument, the purpose, construction, psychometric properties, and clinical applications will be discussed. First, however, some general issues about the development and evaluation of structured interviews are examined.

METHODOLOGICAL ISSUES IN INTERVIEW DEVELOPMENT

Historical Problems in Achieving Adequate Diagnostic Reliability

In general, psychiatric research has historically been hampered by the lack of agreement between two raters concerning presence or absence of a psychiatric diagnosis. Early landmark reports in the 1950s and 1960s documented consistently poor and unacceptable interclinician agreement (reliability) results (see Frank, 1975; Grove, Andreason, McDonald-Scott, Keller, & Shapiro, 1981; Hersen & Bellack, 1988; Spitzer, Endicott, & Robins 1975). Indeed, credible findings from most early investigations were lacking for even the best-known and most prevalent diagnostic categories, such as major depression, manic-depression (now bipolar disorder), and schizophrenia (Grove, 1987; Grove et al., 1981; Hersen & Bellack, 1988). This notorious and disheartening unreliability of the DSM-I (*Diagnostic and Statistical Manual of Mental Disorders;* American Psychiatric Association [APA], 1952) and DSM-II (APA, 1968) classification systems has been a grave cause of concern for psychiatric clinicians and researchers alike. Pervasive lack of agreement between clinicians and researchers when diagnosing patients is particularly troublesome, given that reliability is a necessary, but insufficient, prerequisite for validity (Grove, 1987). In fact, psychometric theory dictates that reliability sets the upper limit on validity.

Two primary reasons have been identified to account for this historically lamentable state of affairs. The first targets the diagnostic criteria themselves, suggesting that inadequate nosology and poorly defined criteria play a substantial role in poor reliability (Ward, Beck, Mendelson, Mock, & Erbaugh, 1962). In the classic report by Ward et al., 80% of all diagnostic disagreements were attributed to inadequate diagnostic criteria. Spitzer, Endicott, and Robins (1975) labeled this source of disagreement "criterion variance." To elaborate, disagreement about a diagnosis could result when two interviewers have different interpretations about the same criteria for a disorder. Indeed, early classification systems, such as the original DSM (APA, 1952) and its revision, DSM-II (APA, 1968), lacked explicit diagnostic criteria for many disorders, provided a theoretical (often psychoanalytic) focus with respect to etiology, contained many inconsistencies, and confounded etiology with symptomatology. Interviewers faced the formidable task of rating general or vague symptoms that often represented a theoretical construct that was difficult to operationalize. As a consequence, these two early systems had poor reliability and highly questionable validity. This particular problem of nebulous and unclear criteria was partially addressed with publication of the DSM-III (APA, 1980), which greatly operationalized criteria and took a more descriptive, objective, and theoretically neutral approach regarding signs and symptoms of mental disorders. Empirical findings from clinical researchers were also included, while the psychoanalytic influence was lessened (Hersen, 1988). Additionally, the current multiaxial diagnostic system was introduced in DSM-III, which provided five separate axes upon which more comprehensive diagnostic data could be recorded. Most notably here, clinical syndromes, such as bipolar disorder and generalized anxiety disorder, were recorded on Axis I, while personality disorders reflecting chronic interpersonal and self-image deficits were denoted separately on Axis II. Inclusion and exclusion criteria for many disorders were also more objectively defined in clear behavioral terms. These innovations have continued to be refined in subsequent versions of DSM including DSM-III-R (APA, 1987) and DSM-IV (APA, 1994). Overall, these improvements in diagnostic criteria have greatly reduced criterion variance.

A second factor accounting for historically poor agreement rates between clinicians concerns the lack of standardization of questions that are asked to patients to evaluate psychiatric symptomatology and ultimately to arrive at a formal diagnosis. Prior to standardized structured interviews, the unstructured psychosocial interview format prevailed. With unstructured interviews, clinicians were entirely responsible for asking whatever questions they decided were necessary for them to reach a diagnostic conclusion. The amount and kind of information gathered, as well as the way clinicians probed and assessed psychiatric symptoms during an interview, was largely determined by their theoretical model, view of psychopathology, training, and interpersonal style, all of which can vary widely from clinician to clinician. The source of error involved when different clinicians obtain different information from the same patient is referred to as "information variance" (Spitzer et al., 1975). The impetus for development of structured interviews was generated by the need to standardize questions asked of patients and provide guidelines for categorizing or coding responses. Adoption of such procedures served to 1. increase coverage of many disorders that previously might have been ignored, 2. enhance the diagnostician's ability to accurately determine if a particular symptom is present or absent, and 3. reduce variability among interviewers (i.e., reduce information variance). Clearly, introduction of operationalized, specified, empirically derived, and standardized criteria for mental disorders in conjunction with construction of standardized structured diagnostic interviews has served to revolutionize the diagnostic process and improve reliability and validity.

Reliability Strategies and Validity for Structured Interviews

Reliability and validity are important psychometric qualities to consider when critically evaluating diagnoses generated by structured interviews, or any assessment device for that matter. In general terms, reliability refers to *replicability* and *stability.* If a structured interview does not provide reproducible data when readministered under identical conditions (i.e., poor reliability), what the instrument purports to measure is inconsequential (Magnusson, 1966). Indeed, it is commonly noted in introductory statistics classes that acceptable levels of reliability must be confirmed *before* conclusions about validity can be drawn. Reliability constrains validity but does not guarantee it. For example, with structured interviews, even if high reliability is attained, validity is not guaranteed, as two clinicians can have perfect agreement but still be incorrect about all cases.

Two strategies have generally been implemented to ascertain reliability of a structured interview. The most commonly employed method is referred to as the *joint interview* or *simultaneous rating* design. In this type of study, the same interview is scored by at least two different raters who make independent diagnoses. This may be done "in vivo" when multiple raters simultaneously observe the same interview. Or, one rater may conduct the interview while additional raters are present and making judgments. A common variation involves audio- or videotaped interviews with post hoc analyses. Whether ratings are made live or post hoc, second or additional raters are always "blind" to diagnoses obtained on the basis of the original evaluation, thus yielding an independent diagnostic appraisal. In many cases, the initial interviewer's diagnosis is included as a data point, which then is compared to judgments from at least one rater who made simultaneous live ratings or used taped interviews for post hoc ratings.

The type of variance encountered in simultaneous or joint interviewer designs is referred to as "rater variance," since raters are presented with the same responses from subjects, but may *score* responses in different ways. For example, one rater may judge a symptom criterion for generalized anxiety disorder to be present (i.e., excessive unrealistic worrying), while another may judge the same response to indicate a subthreshold or clinically insignificant level of the symptom.

The second, and more stringent, reliability strategy has been referred to as the *test-retest* method. In such a study, two (or more) clinicians interview the same patient on separate occasions, with clinicians formulating independent diagnoses. Reliability in test-retest investigations refers to the extent of agreement between multiple raters as to presence or absence of a disorder. A major source of variance in this type of study is "information variance," in which separate interviewers elicit conflicting information from the same respondent. For example, a subject may deny experiencing suicidal thoughts to one interviewer, but admit such concerns to another. Obviously, there is a great potential for information variance when unstructured formats are used. However, information variance can also occur when structured interviews are employed. For example, there can be differences in the manner in which clinicians phrase questions, probe about symptoms, or form a therapeutic alliance with the patient. Patients themselves can also contribute to information variance by responding inconsistently from one interview to the next. Indeed, much anecdotal evidence supports the notion that many patients report inconsistent information from day to day and interview to interview.

In test-retest reliability investigations, there typically is a specified time period by which the second interview must be completed in order to decrease the probability that the respondent will change his or her symptom picture between interviews. For most conditions, second reliability interviews usually are conducted at least 24 hours, but no longer than 2 weeks, after the initial interview. For personality disorders, however, where there is an assumption of longstanding, inflexible, and enduring character traits, reliability intervals typically are longer, sometimes up to 1 year.

An advantage of the test-retest method is that it approximates "true clinical practice," in that patients in some settings can be examined by several clinicians with distinct orientations and interviewing styles. However, this may be burdensome for the client, especially if completion of a lengthy assessment battery is desirable. Conversely, an advantage of the simultaneous rating design is that it fits well with a normal flow of patients and does not cause any sort of clinical disruption, as can be the case with a test-retest design. A drawback is that reliability estimates derived from this method are generally somewhat inflated and less conservative compared to other reliability procedures. Given that both reliability strategies have particular advantages and shortcomings, it has been pointed out that the ideal procedure would be to combine both methods in one study (Grove, 1987). This would involve test-retest of subjects with different interviewers in short-term and long-term intervals, while other raters make independent simultaneous or post hoc ratings of each interview. Despite the expense and effort required, use of such a procedure appears justified by the potential quality of data obtained.

Whether the test-retest or joint interviewer design is utilized, results of reliability studies are typically reported by statistics of percentage agreement, the kappa index, or both. Kappa is a better choice, however, because unlike percentage agreement kappa corrects for chance levels of agreement (Fleiss, 1981). Kappa coefficients range from -1.00 (perfect disagreement) to $+1.00$ (perfect agreement), with 0 indicating agreement no better or worse than chance. Although there are no definitive guidelines for the interpretation of the kappa index, Landis and Koch (1977) have provided the following benchmarks: values above .81 are considered almost perfect, values from .61 to .80 suggest substantial agreement, values between .41 and .60 indicate moderate agreement. Kappa values between .21 and .40 denote fair agreement, values below .20 are slight, and values below 0.0 reflect less than chance disagreement. For structured interviews, many researchers deem kappas of .40 or .50 to denote the lower limits of acceptability. Values below this cutoff suggest serious limitations of the instrument, diagnostic criteria, or possibly a combination of the two.

Whereas reliability refers to reproducibility and stability, validity of a structured diagnostic interview refers to how well it measures the psychiatric conditions it purports to measure. The issue here is one of *accuracy*. Unfortunately, validity is much harder to accurately gauge and document and thus represents a formidable challenge for psychiatric researchers. A common strategy employed is to compare diagnoses generated by a structured interview with diagnoses from another source, such as a clinical interview, chart review, or other testing. However, such an endeavor is fraught with difficulties because these other diagnostic measures often suffer from questionable reliability and validity in the first place. Indeed, a major problem encountered by clinical researchers interested in validity is the lack of a solid criterion diagnosis with which to compare an interview generated diagnosis. Lack of the so-called gold standard severely restricts conclusions drawn from many previous validity investigations.

While reliability of a structured interview can be enhanced by improved training of raters and refinement of items, it appears that no "quick fix" is currently available to ameliorate our currently severe validity problems. In fact, lack of diagnostic validity is considered to be among the most serious issues facing the mental health community. This problem is especially noteworthy as to Axis II personality disorders, which since their introduction in DSM-III have been plagued with even poorer reliability and validity coefficients than most Axis I conditions (Mellsop, Varghese, Joshua, & Hicks, 1982). Indeed, there is currently a strong debate among clinical researchers as to validity of categorical diagnosis of personality disorders (Frances, 1982) and usefulness of the three clusters (odd-eccentric, dramatic-erratic, anxious-fearful) proposed by the DSM system.

In his seminal and often quoted paper, Spitzer (1983) proposed a method to establish procedural validity of a diagnostic instrument in the absence of clear-cut or flawed external validators. This type of validity refers to agreements between diagnoses made by structured interviews and expert clinicians. As such, Spitzer has postulated a LEAD standard, and that acronym denotes diagnoses made on the basis of a thorough *clinical* assessment with three components: Longitudinal information, Expert clinicians, and use of All Data. Use of the LEAD standard methodology will no doubt result in a better criterion measure against which to ascertain validity. Despite many potential gains, this method has not been frequently applied in empirical work to date. Indeed, the time-consuming and thorough nature of such a methodology may be both a strength and limitation.

Another issue to consider here is that reliability and validity are not tied to an interview in any direct way and are not constants. Therefore, it is a mistake to talk about the reliability or validity of a structured interview as a permanent attribute. Indeed, reliability and validity of interviewer-administered instruments are affected by many factors, such as the characteristics of the interviewers and the subject sample, type of reliability assessed (e.g., interrater or test-retest), true reliability of the diagnostic criteria, and the criterion measure. Also, for validity, structured interviews are tied to specific diagnostic criteria. Unfortunately, these interviews do not provide an estimate of how good the criteria actually are, and no diagnostic assessment device can compensate for poor criteria. Indeed, each new version of a particular instrument requires its own full evaluation in studies with diverse interviewers, patient populations, reliability designs, and comparison groups. Moreover, each particular study requires that some form of reliability and validity be established with the particular interviewers and patient population.

STRUCTURED DIAGNOSTIC INTERVIEWS FOR AXIS I

This section is limited to discussion of the major structured instruments that cover a wide range of DSM Axis I disorders, yield categorical diagnoses, and are employed with adult respondents. Diagnostic interviews covered are the Schedule for Affective Disorders and Schizophrenia (SADS), the Diagnostic Interview Schedule (DIS), and the Structured Clinical Interview for DSM-IV (SCID).

Schedule for Affective Disorders and Schizophrenia (SADS)

The Schedule for Affective Disorders and Schizophrenia (SADS; Endicott & Spitzer, 1978) is a semistructured diagnostic interview designed to evaluate symptoms of psychiatric disorders as specified by the Research Diagnostic Criteria (RDC; Spitzer, Endicott, & Robins, 1978). Indeed, the SADS was developed in conjunction with the RDC, which provided specific inclusion and exclusion criteria for many psychiatric disorders. In fact, the RDC predated publication of the DSM-III and was a significant predecessor of that system. Although not directly affiliated with DSM conceptualizations, the SADS is included here because many of the specified criteria outlined in the RDC were adopted for inclusion in DSM-III. As such, much information derived from SADS interviews can be applied to make DSM-based diagnoses. It should be noted, however, that while some sections of the SADS can be easily modified to accommodate DSM diagnoses, this is not easy or possible for some disorders as the systems do differ in coverage and conceptualizations of some disorders. Because of its ties to the RDC system, the SADS is not currently being revised to match new DSM-IV criteria, although many such disorders are covered by traditional SADS items.

The SADS is intended to be used with adult psychiatric respondents and to be administered by trained mental health professionals. It focuses heavily on the differential diagnosis of affective and psychotic disorders but also covers anxiety, alcohol, and drug use disorders. The full SADS is divided into two parts, each focusing on a different time period. Prior to those sections, a brief overview of the respondent's background and psychiatric problems is elicited in an open-ended inquiry. Then, Part I provides for a thoroughly detailed evaluation of *current* psychiatric problems and concomitant functional impairment. Psychosocial functioning during the week *preceding* the interview is also assessed. A unique feature of the SADS is that for the current episode, symptoms are rated when they were at their worst levels to increase diagnostic sensitivity and validity. In contrast, Part II evaluates *past* episodes of psychopathology and treatment. Overall, the SADS covers over 20 RDC diagnoses in a systematic and comprehensive fashion, and provides for diagnosis of both current and lifetime RDC psychiatric disorders. Some examples include schizophrenia (with six subtypes), schizoaffective disorder, manic disorder, hypomanic disorder, major depressive disorder (with 11 subtypes), minor depressive disorder, panic disorder, obsessive-compulsive disorder, phobic disorder, alcoholism, and antisocial personality disorder. In addition to collecting information to diagnose specific RDC disorders, the SADS also yields scores for eight clinically relevant dimensional "Summary Scales" that were identified through factor analysis: depressive mood and ideation, endogenous features, depressive-associated features, suicidal ideation and behavior, anxiety, manic syndrome, delusions-hallucinations, and formal thought disorder (Endicott & Spitzer, 1978).

In the SADS, questions are clustered according to specific diagnoses, which enables administration to simulate the natural flow characteristic of skilled unstructured interviews. Indeed, for each disorder, standard probes are specified to evaluate specific symptoms of that disorder. Questions are either dichotomous, or rated on a Likert scale which allows for uniform documentation of levels of severity, persistence, and functional impairment associated with each symptom. For example, the mania syndrome criteria of "grandiosity" is rated from "(1) not at all or decreased self-esteem" to "(6) extremely preoccupied with grandiose delusions." Items are rated "0" if no information is available or the item is not applicable. To supplement patient self-report and obtain the most accurate symptom picture, the SADS allows for consideration of all available sources of information (e.g., chart records and relatives' input). Additionally, SADS interviewers are instructed to ask as many general and specific probes and gently challenge as necessary to accurately rate the symptom. To reduce length of administration and evaluation of symptoms that are not diagnostically significant, many diagnostic sections begin with screening questions, which provide for "skip-outs" to the next section if the respondent shows no evidence of having the disorder. Administration of the SADS typically takes between 1.5 and 2.5 hours, but can be extended if the respondent is currently severely mentally impaired or has an extensive psychiatric history. After all symptoms are rated and the interview is completed, interviewers consult the RDC and make diagnostic appraisals according to specified criteria. At present, no reliable computer scoring applications have been designed due to the complex nature of the diagnostic process and the SADS' strong reliance on clinical judgment.

As noted, the SADS was designed for use by trained clinicians. Indeed, considerable clinical judgment, interviewing skills, and familiarity with diagnostic criteria and psychiatric symptoms are requisite for competent administration of the SADS. As such, it is recommended that the SADS be given only by professionals with graduate degrees and clinical experience, such as clinical psychologists, psychiatrists, and psychiatric social workers (Endicott & Spitzer, 1978). Training in the SADS is intensive and can encompass several weeks. The process includes reading articles about the SADS and the RDC, and the most recent SADS manual. Then, practice is provided in rating written case vignettes and videotaped SADS interviews. Additionally, trainees typically watch and score live interviews as if participating in a reliability study with a simultaneous rating design. Throughout, discussion and clarification with expert interviewers regarding diagnostic disagreements or difficulties add to the experience. Finally, trainees conduct their own SADS interviews, which are observed and critiqued by the expert trainers.

Numerous additional versions of the SADS have been devised, each with a distinct focus and purpose. Perhaps the most common is the SADS-L (Lifetime version), which can be used to make both current and lifetime diagnoses but has significantly less detail about current psychopathology than the full SADS. The SADS-L generally is used with nonpsychiatric samples, where there is no assumption of a significant current disturbance. Reduced emphasis on current symptoms of the SADS-L results in a quicker administration time. Two offshoots of the SADS-L are the SADS-LA and SADS-LB, for comprehensive and detailed evaluation of anxiety and bipolar disorders, respectively. Also popular is the SADS-C (Change version), which provides for measurement of change in symptom levels over time that can be used in treatment planning and outcome studies. For family studies, the Family History-RDC (FH-RDC) version elicits diagnostic data from family members about other relatives who are not present. The Family Informant Schedule and Criteria (FISC) is a revision of the FH-RDC with expanded coverage of anxiety disorders.

Early psychometric data on the SADS came from its developers, who evaluated interrater reliability of SADS summary scales in two samples (Endicott & Spitzer, 1978). In the first study, 150 inpatients were jointly evaluated by two raters who made independent diagnostic appraisals. Reliability was excellent, with intraclass correlation coefficients (ICC) ranging from .82 (formal thought disorder) to .99 (manic syndrome). Similarly, internal consistency was high for all composite scales except formal thought disorder and anxiety. In the second study, which employed a test-retest design with 60 hospitalized subjects, agreement rates were slightly lower than in the joint evaluations but still substantial for all summary scales except formal thought disorder (ICC = .49). With the same sample, Spitzer et al. (1978) reported test-retest concordance rates for many major diagnostic categories of the RDC. Agreement rates (kappa coefficients) were high for all eight current disorders, ranging from .65 for schizophrenia to 1.00 for alcoholism, while kappas for lifetime diagnoses tended to be lower, ranging from .40 for bipolar I to .95 for alcoholism. In a similar test-retest project with a nonpatient sample, reliability generally was good for the SADS-L (Andreason et al., 1981). Later, in a small multicenter investigation, Andreason et al. (1982) used a videotape design with eight patients selected from five centers. Overall, a total of 36 raters viewed and rated the tapes. Their results indicated excellent agreement rates for schizophrenia (ICC = 1.00) and major depressive disorder (.84), while a moderate value was found for manic disorder (.64). Also, subtypes of major depression (such as psychotic, endogenous, agitated) were also generally rated with acceptable reliability. Taken together, these studies suggest that sufficiently high diagnostic reliability can be achieved for summary scales and most major diagnoses of the SADS.

The SADS has been translated into several languages, has been widely used in clinical research over the past three decades, and subsequently has a large body of empirical data associated with it. As such, it is often the instrument of choice for clinical researchers interested in depression, schizophrenia, and anxiety. The extensive subtyping of disorders provided by the SADS is also highly valued by clinical researchers. However, because of its length and complexity, the SADS is less often chosen for use in pure clinical settings.

For information on SADS materials, training, and related procedures, the interested reader should contact Jean Endicott, Ph.D., Department of Research Assessment and Training Unit 123, New York State Psychiatric Institute, 722 West 168th Street, New York, New York, 10032; telephone (212) 960-5536.

Diagnostic Interview Schedule (DIS)

The Diagnostic Interview Schedule (DIS; Robins, Helzer, Croughan, & Ratcliff, 1981) is a *fully structured* diagnostic interview specifically designed for use by lay, nonprofessional interviewers. It was originally developed by Robins et al. at Washington University Department of Psychiatry in St. Louis at the request of the National Institute of Mental Health (NIMH) Division of Biometry and Epidemiology. The DIS was designed for use in a set of large-scale epidemiological investigations of mental illness in the general adult population (age 18 and older), as part of the Epidemiological Catchment Area (ECA) Program. Variables to be assessed included incidence and prevalence of specific mental disorders and utilization profiles of health and mental health services. With this purpose in mind, development of a structured interview that could be administered by nonclinicians was imperative due to the prohibitive cost of using professional clinicians for these expansive community studies. The original DIS collected information to make psychiatric diagnoses according to three different, but popular, sets of criteria: the "Feighner criteria," associated with the St. Louis group (Feighner et al., 1972), the Research Diagnostic Criteria (Spitzer et al., 1978), and the DSM-III (APA, 1980).

Since its early beginnings as a draft version in 1978, there have been several revisions and adaptations of the original DIS. While the original DIS covered criteria for over 30 DSM-III diagnoses, three added disorders (posttraumatic stress, generalized anxiety, and bulimia), and a comprehensive set of training materials were among the refinements in the DIS-III-A (Robins et al., 1987). More recently, DIS questions and diagnostic algorithms were revamped to match new criteria presented in DSM-III-R (DIS Version III-R; Robins, Helzer, Cottler, & Goldring, 1989). Complete computerized administration, computer-prompted administration (interviewer uses computer program as a guide), as well as Quick computerized versions of the DIS (Marcus, Robins, & Bucholz, 1991) are also now available, and have been applied successfully (Blouin, Perez, & Blouin, 1988; Erdman et al., 1992). Similarly, modifications have recently been completed to establish compatibility with DSM-IV, and the updated version (DIS-IV) will surely add to the researcher's arsenal for large-scale community-based psychiatric research. Like all revised instruments, this new DIS version will require its own reliability and validity evaluation.

To compensate for administration by nonclinical lay interviewers, the DIS is a fully structured interview. Indeed, the exact wording of all symptom questions and follow-up probes is delineated in an interview book, items are read verbatim to the respondent in a standardized order, and clarification or rephrasing of questions is discouraged, although DIS interviewers can repeat any question as necessary to ensure that it is understood by the respondent. Further, all questions are written to be closed-ended, and replies are coded with a forced choice yes/no format, which eliminates the need for clinical judgment to rate responses. Given the yes/no format, clarification of responses is neither needed nor required. Unlike other structured interviews, the DIS gathers all necessary information about the subject from the subject, and collateral sources of information are not used, which again obviates the need for advanced clinical skills.

As the DIS was designed for epidemiological research with normative samples, DIS interviewers do not elicit a presenting problem or chief complaint from the subject, but rather begin by asking questions about symptoms in a standardized order. Like other structured interviews, the DIS has sections that cover different disorders. Once a symptom is reported to be present, further closed-ended questions are pursued to assess additional diagnostically relevant information such as severity, frequency, time frame, and possibility of organic etiology of the symptom. The DIS includes a set of core questions that are asked of each respondent, which are followed by contingent questions that are administered only if the preceding core question is endorsed. DIS interviewers use a Probe Flow Chart that indicates which probes to use in which circumstances. Because of its highly structured format, administration of the DIS interview typically requires between 60 and 75 minutes, with a 3 hour maximum for severely ill or loquacious subjects.

For each symptom, the respondent is asked to state whether it has ever been present, and how recently. All data about presence or absence of symptoms and time frames of occurrence are coded and then entered into a computer for scoring. Indeed, consistent with its use of lay interviewers who may not be familiar with the DSM or psychiatric diagnosis, diagnostic output of the DIS is generated by a computer which analyzes the coded data from the completed interview. Output of the computer program provides estimates of prevalence for two time periods: current and lifetime.

Although designed for use by lay administrators, training for competent administration of the DIS is intensive and includes several components. Trainees typically attend a 1-week training program at Washington University, during which they review the DIS manual, listen to didactic presentations about the format, structure, and conventions of the DIS, and view videotaped vignettes. Additionally, many role-play practice interviews are conducted with extensive feedback and review to ensure that trainees master the material. Finally, a supplemental week of supervised practice is also recommended.

The psychometric properties of the original DIS and its revisions have been evaluated in numerous investigations. Initial reliability results from St. Louis were encouraging (Robins et al., 1981), as concordance between lay administration and psychiatrist administration was assessed in a test-retest design with 216 patients. Psychiatrist interviews were employed as the criterion measure. For DSM-III diagnoses, mean kappa was .69, mean sensitivity was 75%, and mean specificity was 94%. In a more recent study (Blouin et al., 1988), 80 psychiatric patients and 20 normal controls completed a self-administered computerized version of the DIS (C-DIS) on two occasions. Results showed generally acceptable test-retest reliability for the computerized DIS. With a similar test-retest design, Semler et al. (1987) examined 60 psychiatric inpatients on two occasions with a mean interval 1.7 days. Results indicated respectable agreement values (kappa over .5) for 11 DSM-III lifetime diagnoses, with lower values found for dysthymic disorder (.47) and generalized anxiety disorder (.41). Further, Semler et al. noted that their results were improved over earlier versions of the DIS, especially for anxiety disorders. More recently, Vandiver and Sher (1991) investigated the temporal stability of the DIS by administering it to 486 college students at baseline and again approximately 9 months later. Findings suggested that the DIS is a moderately reliable instrument for evaluating lifetime psychopathology, although reliability estimates tended to be lower for 12-month and 6-month diagnoses than for lifetime diagnoses. Unreliability was attributed to "borderline" cases, which historically have complicated reliability in categorical diagnostic systems.

Validity of the DIS has been evaluated in several studies that typically compare DIS diagnoses to clinician-generated diagnoses. Taken together, results have generally been variable depending on the sample, diagnosis, and criterion measure. An early study by Robins, Helzer, Ratcliff, and Seyfried (1982) compared DIS diagnoses to medical chart diagnoses, with generally poor concordance. With lay administration, mean agreement was 55%, while psychiatrist-administered DIS resulted in a 63% success rate. Anthony et al. (1985) compared lay-administered DIS diagnoses to standardized DSM-III diagnoses made by psychiatrists in a sample of 810 community residents. Their results also were discouraging, with agreement rates (kappa) ranging between −.02 (panic disorder) to .35 (alcohol use disorder), with a mean of .15. In another study, psychiatrist-administered DIS diagnoses were examined in relation to clinical diagnoses from a DSM-III checklist (Helzer et al., 1985). Subjects were 370 community residents. Results were generally higher in this report, as kappas ranged from .12 to .63, with an average unweighted kappa of .40.

More recently, Erdman et al. (1987) used clinical diagnosis based on chart review and case staffing as the criterion measure to compare against DIS-generated diagnosis. Agreement (kappas) between clinical diagnoses and current DIS diagnoses for 220 psychiatric patients ranged from −.03 (social phobia) to .39 (obsessive-compulsive disorder), with 9 of 14 diagnoses achieving kappas below .20. Rates for lifetime DIS diagnoses were similarly poor, with a range from −.03 (schizophreniform) to .39 (bipolar disorder). Application of the DIS in pure clinical settings (as opposed to epidemiological research) has been a cause for some concern because of the rather poor relationship between DIS diagnoses and clinical diagnosis (Erdman et al., 1987). It should be reiterated here, however, that chart or psychiatrist diagnoses are not the "gold standard" with which to compare DIS diagnoses to assess validity, as problems with diagnoses from unstructured interviews precipitated development of structured interviews in the first place. Given our present knowledge, though, it recommended that DIS data be supplemented with other clinician-generated data to make clinical diagnoses and treatment planning decisions in individual cases.

Overall, the DIS and its numerous versions and adaptations have proven to be popular and useful diagnostic assessment tools for large-scale epidemiological research. The DIS has been translated into numerous languages, is used in many countries for epidemiological research, and served as the basis for the Composite International Diagnostic Interview (CIDI/DIS) employed by the World Health Organization. Presently, it is the only well-validated case finding strategy that can make DSM-based diagnoses in large-scale epidemiological research. It is anticipated that the new DIS-IV will have similar popularity, success, and worldwide application for these purposes.

For information on DIS materials, training, and related procedures, the interested reader should contact Lee Robins, Ph.D., Department of Psychiatry, Washington University School of Medicine, 4940 Children's Place, St. Louis, Missouri, 63110; telephone (314) 362-2469.

Structured Clinical Interview for DSM-IV (SCID)

The Structured Clinical Interview for DSM-IV (First, Spitzer, Gibbon, & Williams, 1995) is a flexible, interviewer-administered, diagnostic interview designed for use by trained administrators to diagnose most adult Axis I DSM-IV mental disorders. Like the other interviews reviewed, the current version is the product of many prior editions that were updated and modified over time. The original Structured Clinical Interview for DSM-III (Spitzer & Williams, 1984) was the first comprehensive *semistructured* diagnostic interview that was specifically designed to generate psychiatric diagnoses based on DSM-III criteria for mental disorders. The SADS (Endicott & Spitzer, 1978), in contrast, was published prior to DSM-III and was based on Research Diagnostic Criteria (RDC; Spitzer et al., 1978) which for many disorders are quite different than the DSM conceptualizations. While the DIS (Robins et al., 1981) provided for diagnostic evaluations based on DSM-III criteria, its fully structured format, administration by nonclinicians, and computer scoring has caused debate over whether obtained diagnoses are valid (see Spitzer, 1983). Indeed, the oft-quoted report by Spitzer (1983) suggested that clinicians were still necessary to the diagnostic process, thus highlighting some potential limitations of the DIS.

Four years after its debut in the literature, the SCID was revised (Spitzer, Williams, Gibbon, & First, 1988) to reflect modifications that appeared in DSM-III-R. And, as noted above, a version keyed to DSM-IV has recently been published (First et al., 1995). With each revision, the SCID has been broadened to encompass Axis I disorders that were not evaluated in the original instrument and reworked to enhance ease of use. Interestingly, a computer-administered screening version for the SCID for DSM-IV, the Mini-SCID, is available. Complementary versions have also been designed to diagnose personality disorders according to DSM-III-R (SCID-II, version 1.0; Spitzer, Williams, Gibbon, & First, 1990), and DSM-IV (SCID-II, version 2.0; First, Spitzer, Gibbon, Williams, & Lorna, 1994), located on Axis II (reviewed later). Additionally, specialized editions of the SCID have been developed to specifically evaluate panic disorder and panic subtypes (SCID-Upjohn version; Williams, Spitzer, & Gibbon, 1992) and to provide a two-tiered categorical and dimensional exploration of psychotic disorders (SCID-PANSS; Kay et al., 1991). Since its inception, the SCID has enjoyed widespread popularity as an instrument to obtain reliable and valid psychiatric diagnoses for clinical, research, and training purposes. It is available in several foreign languages and has been successfully applied in transcultural investigations.

Two standard versions of the SCID exist for assessment of Axis I disorders, each targeting a different population: patients and nonpatients (Spitzer, Williams, Gibbon, & First, 1992). The SCID-P (patient version) is used with psychiatric inpatients and outpatients and includes full coverage of psychotic disorders. For settings where psychotic disorders are unlikely to be seen, an abridged version (SCID-P with psychotic screen) can be employed which screens for hallucinations and delusions but does not provide for a differential diagnosis of psychotic disorders. The SCID-NP (nonpatient) is designed for application with normal control subjects or community surveys where no assumption of mental illness is made. Logically, this version does not ask for a chief complaint and employs the shorter psychotic screen format. The SCID is primarily used with adult respondents due to the language, format, coverage, and type of responses needed for administration. Note, however, that it may be appropriately modified for older adolescents.

Both standard versions of the SCID (patient and nonpatient) contain broad "modules" of major diagnostic categories (e.g., mood disorders, anxiety disorders, somatoform disorders, and eating disorders) under which specific disorders (e.g., major depression, obsessive-compulsive disorder, somatoform pain, and bulimia nervosa) are subsumed. Disorder coverage of the SCID-P and SCID-NP are similar, except that for the SCID-NP version, the Psychotic Module is replaced by the Psychotic Screening. The modular design is a major innovation of the SCID as administration can be customized to meet unique needs of the user. For example, the SCID can be shortened or lengthened to include only those categories of interest, and the order of modules can be altered. Most of the major Axis I disorders for adults are covered in the DSM-IV version, and these are shown in Table 2.1.

The format and sequence of the SCID was designed to approximate the flowchart and decision trees followed by experienced diagnostic interviewers. As such, questions are grouped by major diagnostic category (e.g., Mood, Anxiety, and Somatoform) under which specific disorders are covered independently. Most disorders are evaluated for two time periods: current (meets criteria for past month) and lifetime (ever met criteria), although a few conditions (e.g., dysthymia and generalized anxiety disorder) are only considered in their current context. The SCID begins with an "overview" portion, during which the development and history of the present psychological disturbance are elicited and tentative diagnostic hypotheses are generated. Then, the SCID systematically presents modules that allow for assessment of specific disorders and symptoms. Consistent with its anchor in DSM, formal diagnostic criteria are embedded in the context of the SCID, thus permitting interviewers to make direct queries about specific features that contribute to the overall diagnostic picture. This unique feature also makes the SCID an excellent training device for administrators because it facilitates the learning of diagnostic criteria and appropri-

TABLE 2.1 Diagnoses Covered by the Structured Clinical Interview for Axis I DSM-IV Disorders, Patient Edition (SCID-I/P), by Modules

Mood disorders
    Bipolar I disorder
    Bipolar II disorder
    Other bipolar disorder (includes cyclothymic disorder, intermittent hypomanic episodes, and
       manic or hypomanic episode superimposed on psychotic disorder)
    Major depressive disorder
    Dysthymic disorder
    Other depressive disorder (includes postpsychotic depressive disorder of schizophrenia,
       premenstrual dysphoric disorder, minor depressive disorder, recurrent brief depressive
       disorder)
    Mood disorder due to a GMC
    Substance-induced mood disorder

Psychotic disorders
    Schizophrenia
    Schizophreniform disorder
    Schizoaffective disorder
    Delusional disorder
    Brief psychotic disorder
    Psychotic disorder due to a GMC
    Substance-induced psychotic disorder
    Psychotic disorder NOS

Psychoactive substance use disorders (abuse or dependence)
    Alcohol
    Sedative-hypnotic-anxiolytic
    Cannabis
    Stimulant
    Opioid
    Cocaine
    Hallucinogen/PCP
    Polysubstance (dependence only)
    Other substances

Anxiety disorders
    Panic disorder
    Agoraphobia without history of panic disorder
    Social phobia
    Specific phobia
    Obsessive-compulsive disorder
    Posttraumatic stress disorder
    Generalized anxiety disorder
    Anxiety disorder due to a GMC
    Substance-induced anxiety disorder
    Anxiety disorder NOS

Somatoform disorders
    Somatization disorder
    Pain disorder
    Undifferentiated somatoform disorder
    Hypochondriasis
    Body dysmorphic disorder

Eating disorders
    Anorexia nervosa
    Bulimia nervosa
    Binge eating disorder

Adjustment disorder

ate probes. Unlike the fully structured DIS, the SCID has many open-ended prompts that encourage respondents to freely elaborate about their symptoms. At times, open-ended prompts are followed up by closed-ended questions to fully clarify a particular symptom. While the SCID provides structure to cover criteria for each disorder in each module, its flexible semistructured format provides for significant latitude for interviewers to restate questions, ask for further clarification, probe, and challenge if the initial prompt was misunderstood by the interviewee or clarification is needed to fully rate a symptom. SCID interviewers are encouraged to use all sources of information about a respondent, and gentle challenging of the respondent is encouraged if discrepant information is suspected.

Each symptom criterion is rated 1, 2, 3, or "?." The 1 indicates that the criterion was clearly absent, 2 refers to subthreshold levels of the symptom, 3 means that the symptom criterion was clearly present and clinically significant, and the question mark (?) denotes that inadequate information was obtained to code the criterion. Like the SADS, the SCID flowchart instructs interviewers to "skip out" of a particular diagnostic section when essential symptoms are judged to be absent or false. These skip-outs result in decreased time of administration, as well as the passing over of items with no diagnostic significance. Administration of the SCID typically involves between 60 and 90 minutes, although coverage of the Psychotic Module or use with a subject manifesting extensive current or past psychopathology, or both, can add considerable length.

Spitzer et al. (1992) suggest that the SCID is optimally administered by trained interviewers who have knowledge about psychopathology, DSM criteria, and diagnostic interviewing. Indeed, with its semistructured format, proper administration often requires that interviewers restate or clarify questions in ways that are sometimes not clearly outlined in the manual in order to accurately judge if particular symptom criteria have been met. The task requires that SCID assessors have working knowledge of psychopathology, DSM-III-R, and DSM-IV, as well as basic interviewing skills. Standard procedures for training to use the SCID include carefully reading the SCID, consulting an instruction manual (Spitzer, Williams, Gibbon, & First, 1989), role-playing practice administrations, and viewing videotape training materials that are available from the SCID authors at Biometrics Research Department. Following this, trainees administer the SCID to representative subjects who are jointly rated so that a discussion about sources of disagreements can ensue. Finally, a test-retest reliability study should be completed, with further discussion and remediation of problem areas.

The reliability of the SCID in adult populations with diverse disorders has been evaluated in a number of investigations. A recent review of this literature indicated generally high reliability values for most major disorders, despite widely varied subject samples and experimental designs (see Segal, Hersen, & Van Hasselt, 1994), and these data will be summarized here. Most impressive is an extensive multisite project, which involved test-retest reliability interviews of 592 subjects in four patient and two nonpatient sites in the United States and one patient site in Germany (Williams et al., 1992). Randomly matched pairs of two professionals independently evaluated and rated the same subject within a 2-week period. The sample was divided into patient ($n = 390$) and nonpatient ($n = 202$) subjects for whom levels of agreement for current and lifetime disorders were reported. Results for the patient sample indicated that kappas for current and lifetime disorders ranged from a low of .40 (dysthymia) to a high of .86 (bulimia nervosa). Kappas were above .60 for most of the major disorders (e.g., bipolar disorder = .84, alcohol abuse or dependence = .75, schizophrenia = .65, and major depression = .64). Combining all disorders yielded mean kappas of .61 for current and .68 for lifetime disorders. Results for the nonpatient sample suggested poorer concordance, with an overall weighted kappa of .37 for current and .51 for lifetime disorders. Overall, obtained kappas were judged to be comparable to data from other structured interviews (Williams et al., 1992), namely the SADS and DIS.

Riskind, Beck, Berchick, Brown, and Steer (1987) videotaped 75 psychiatric outpatients to assess interrater reliability of DSM-III major depression and generalized anxiety disorder. Results showed that the SCID can reliably differentiate between the two disorders (major depression, kappa = .72; generalized anxiety disorder, kappa = .79). In another study, Skre, Onstad, Torgerson, and Kringlen (1991) investigated reliability using audiotaped SCID interviews of 54 adults participating in a larger Norwegian twin family study of mental illness. Excellent interrater agreement (kappa above .80) was obtained for many disorders (e.g., schizophrenia, major depression, dysthymia, generalized anxiety disorder, panic disorder, alcohol abuse, and other nonalcohol abuse disorder), while moderate levels (kappa between .70 and .80) were found for most other major conditions (e.g., cyclothymia, PTSD, social phobia, simple phobia, bipolar disorder, and adjustment disorder). Poor reliability was indicated for obsessive-compulsive disorder (kappa = .40), agoraphobia without history of panic disorder (.32), and somatoform disorder (−.03). Interestingly, Skre et al. (1991) also tested reliability for combinations of diagnoses (e.g., mood and anxiety disorders). As could be expected, reliability was generally favorable for combinations of two disorders (range = .53 to 1.00), and poorer but still decent for most combinations of three disorders (range = .38 to .87).

Reliability of the Upjohn version of the SCID (panic disorder and subtypes) has been appraised in a large, multinational, test-retest project (Williams, Spitzer, & Gibbon, 1992). Of the 72 patients who participated in the investigation, 52 (72%) were retested within 1 week of the initial administration. Agreement on the diagnosis of panic disorder was very good (kappa = .87), although this base rate was very high (86%). Agreement was only fair to good for subtypes of panic disorder: uncomplicated (.73), panic disorder with limited phobic avoidance (.61), and agoraphobia with panic attacks (kappa = .66).

In our earlier review (Segal et al., 1994), we called for increased evaluations of the reliability of the SCID in minority populations, including older adults. Our research group has conducted two such reliability studies with elderly individuals. In the first study (Segal, Hersen, Van Hasselt, Kabacoff, & Roth, 1993), subjects consisted of older psychiatric inpatients and outpatients ($N = 33$, age range = 56 to 84 years, mean = 67.33 years). SCID interviews were administered by masters-level clinicians and audiotaped for retrospective review by an independent rater. Reliability estimates (kappa) were calculated for current major depression (47% base rate, kappa = .70), and the broad diagnostic categories of anxiety disorder (15% base rate, kappa = .77) and somatoform disorder (12% base rate, kappa = 1.0).

The second investigation (Segal, Kabacoff, Hersen, Van Hasselt, & Ryan, 1995) targeted older outpatients exclusively ($N = 40$, age range = 55 to 87 years, mean = 67.05 years) and evaluated a larger number of diagnoses. Diagnostic concordance was determined for the general groupings of mood disorder (60% base rate), anxiety disorder (25% base rate), somatoform disorder (9% base rate), and psychoactive substance use disorder (9% base rate). Three specific disorders were evaluated: major depressive disorder (58% base rate), dysthymia (9% base rate), and panic disorder (15% base rate). Agreement for the broad diagnostic group of somatoform disorder (kappa = .84) was almost perfect, while concordance was slightly lower, but still substantial, for mood disorder (kappa = .79) and anxiety disorder (kappa = .73). Psychoactive substance use disorder (kappa = .23) had the lowest rate, reflecting poor agreement. For specific disorders, kappas were high for major depressive disorder (kappa = .90) and panic disorder (.80), while agreement for dysthymia (.53) was moderate. Taken together, these two studies suggest that reliability of the SCID administered by graduate-level clinicians to older adults appears very promising, although additional research with larger samples obviously is warranted.

The latest and most comprehensive version of the SCID (First, Spitzer, Gibbon, & Williams, 1995b) mirrors diagnostic refinements made in the recently published DSM-IV (APA, 1994) classification system. This new DSM-IV version of the SCID has been divided into two components, research and clinical. The research version covers more disorders, subtypes, and course specifiers than the DSM-III-R version, and as such takes longer to complete. The benefit, however, is that it provides for a wealth of diagnostic data that is particularly valued by clinical researchers. Like its predecessor, the DSM-IV research SCID has a patient version (SCID-P), a shorter patient version with psychotic screen, and a nonpatient version (SCID-NP). The new clinical SCID has been trimmed down to encompass only those DSM-IV disorders that are most typically seen in clinical practice and can further be abbreviated on a module-by-module basis. Undoubtedly, the DSM-IV SCID can be expected to enjoy widespread application in psychiatric research, service, and training for many years to come, and studies are needed to evaluate and document its psychometric properties. At this time, however, no data on the latest version have been published.

For information on SCID materials, training, and related procedures, the interested reader should contact Miriam Gibbon, M.S.W., Biometrics Research Department, Unit 74, New York State Psychiatric Institute, 722 West 168th Street, New York, New York, 10032; telephone (212) 960-5524.

STRUCTURED DIAGNOSTIC INTERVIEWS FOR AXIS II

This section focuses on evaluation of instruments that are consistent with DSM conceptualizations and yield as part of their output a clinical wide range of personality disorder diagnoses located on Axis II. Interestingly, the separation of clinical disorders from personality disorders is a relatively new idea, which first occurred in the new multiaxial format of DSM-III (APA, 1980). Development of structured diagnostic interviews for personality disorders was somewhat behind, but as a consequence, research on diagnosis of character

TABLE 2.2   DSM-IV Personality Disorders Diagnoses Covered by the SCID-II, IPDE, and SIDP-IV

Personality Disorders	Instrument		
	SCID-II	IPDE	SIDP-IV
Cluster A			
Paranoid	X	X	X
Schizoid	X	X	X
Schizotypal	X	X	X
Cluster B			
Antisocial	X	X	X
Borderline	X	X	X
Histrionic	X	X	X
Narcissistic	X	X	X
Cluster C			
Avoidant	X	X	X
Dependent	X	X	X
Obsessive-compulsive	X	X	X
Other personality disorders			
Mixed or personality disorder NOS	X	X	X
Sadistic	No	No	No
Self-defeating	No	No	X
Depressive	X	No	X
Negativistic	X	No	X

pathology is more recent and relatively less comprehensive than for some Axis I conditions. Instruments reviewed include the Structured Interview for DSM-IV Personality (SIDP-IV), the International Personality Disorder Examination (IPDE), and the Structured Clinical Interview for DSM-IV Axis II (SCID-II). Personality disorders covered by the DSM-IV version of each instrument are presented in Table 2.2.

Structured Interview for DSM-IV Personality (SIDP-IV)

The Structured Interview for DSM-IV Personality (SIDP-IV; Pfohl, Blum, & Zimmerman, 1995) is a comprehensive semistructured diagnostic interview for personality disorders as conceptualized by the DSM-IV system. The SIDP-IV covers 14 DSM-IV Axis II diagnoses, including the 10 standard personality disorders, mixed personality disorder, as well as self-defeating, depressive, and negativistic personality disorders that are proposed for further study in DSM-IV. The current edition of this popular instrument (SIDP-IV) has its roots in earlier versions that date back over a decade. Indeed, the original Structured Interview for DSM-III Personality Disorders (SIDP; Stangl, Pfohl, Zimmerman, Bowers, & Corentahl, 1985) was the *first* structured interview designed to diagnose the full range of DSM-III personality disorders. Impetus for development of such an instrument was to improve reliability of Axis II disorders, which were exceedingly difficult to accurately assess at that time (Mellsop et al., 1982). With publication of DSM-III-R in 1987, the SIDP was subsequently revised to match the new criteria for personality disorders and renamed the Structured

Interview for DSM-III-R Personality Disorders (SIDP-R; Pfohl, Blum, Zimmerman, & Stangl, 1989).

Prior to the SIDP-IV structured interview, a full evaluation of current mental state or Axis I conditions is required (Pfohl et al., 1995). This is not surprising given that self-report of enduring personality characteristics can be seriously compromised in a respondent experiencing acute psychopathology. Indeed, the aim of all personality assessment measures is to rate the respondent's typical, habitual, and lifelong personal functioning rather than acute or temporary states.

Interestingly, the SIDP-IV does not cover DSM personality categories on a disorder-by-disorder basis. Rather, DSM-IV personality disorder criteria are reflected in items that are grouped according to "topical sections" that reflect a different dimension of personality functioning. Such topical areas have been slightly altered over time as the instrument has been revised; however, it should be noted that these categories are not scored or rated in any way. Rather, they reflect broad areas of personal functioning under which personality disorder items can logically be subsumed. The original SIDP consisted of 160 standardized questions arranged into 16 domains (e.g., egocentricity, overdramatic or overreacts, ideas of reference and magical thinking, hostility or anger, and perception of threat). While the DSM-III-R version contained 189 probe queries, the design and organizational structure was similar to the original, and many of the items were identical across the two instruments (Blashfield, Blum, & Pfohl, 1992). Likewise, the DSM-IV edition maintains a comparable format, but with updated questions and only 10 functional categories. Some examples of these new groupings include: interests and activities, close relationships, emotions, self-perception, and social conformity (Pfohl et al., 1995).

Each SIDP-IV question corresponds to a unique DSM-IV Axis II criterion, except that one item addresses two criteria. In fact, an improvement of the SIDP-IV relative to the SIDP and SIDP-R is that the specific DSM criterion associated with each question is provided for interviewers to easily see and reference. All questions are always administered to the patient and there are no skip-out options. Most questions are conversational in tone and open-ended to encourage respondents to talk about their *usual* behaviors and long-term functioning. In fact, respondents are specifically instructed to focus on their typical or habitual behavior when addressing each item and are prompted to "remember what you are like when you are your usual self." It is possible, however, that this distinction may be difficult for some psychiatrically impaired patients to make. Based on patient responses, each criterion is rated on a scale with four anchor points. A rating of 0 indicates that the criterion was not present, 1 corresponds to a subthreshold level, where there is some evidence of the trait but it is not sufficiently prominent, 2 refers to the criterion being present for most of the last 5 years, and 3 signifies a strongly present and debilitating level. The SIDP-IV requires that a trait be prominent for most of the last 5 years to be considered a part of the respondent's personality. This "5-year rule" helps ensure that the particular personality characteristic is "stable and of long duration" as required by the General Diagnostic Criteria for a Personality Disorder described in DSM-IV.

A strong point of the organizational format by personality dimensions (rather than by disorders) is that data for *specific* diagnoses are minimized until final ratings have been collated on the summary sheet. This feature can potentially reduce interviewer biases, such as the halo effect or changing thresholds, if it is obvious that a subject needs to meet one additional criteria to make the diagnosis. Like the SADS and SCID, significant clinical judgment is required to properly administer the SIDP-IV as interviewers are expected to ask additional questions to clarify patient responses when necessary. Also data are not limited to self-report; rather, chart records and relatives and friends who know the patient well should be consulted when available, and a standard informed consent is included for informant interviews. Such collateral information is particularly prized when evaluating personality-disordered individuals, who tend to lack insight into their own maladaptive personality traits and distort facts about their strengths and limitations. Moreover, informants can also provide diagnostic data that can help resolve the state/trait distinction about specific criterion behaviors. If discrepancies between sources of information are noted, interviewers must consider all data and use their own judgment to determine veracity of each source. Making this distinction can be one of the challenges faced by SIDP-IV administrators. Given the multiple sources of diagnostic data, final ratings are made *after* all sources of information are considered. Then, such ratings are transcribed onto a summary sheet that lists each criterion organized by personality disorder, and formal diagnoses are assigned. As required by the DSM, diagnoses are made only if the minimum number of criteria (or threshold) has been met for that particular disorder.

Minimum qualifications for competent administration consist of an interviewer with an undergraduate degree in the social sciences and 6-months experience with diagnostic interviewing. Moreover, SIDP-IV developers note that such an interviewer requires an additional 1-month of specialized training and practice with the SIDP to become a competent interviewer (Pfohl et al., 1995). Administrators are required to possess an understanding of manifest psychopathology and the typical presentation and course of Axis I and II disorders. Training tapes and workshop information are available from the instrument authors. Overall, the SIDP typically requires 60–90 minutes for the patient interview, 20 minutes for interview of significant informants, and approximately 20 minutes to fill out the summary score sheet.

Early interrater reliability values for the SIDP were reported by its developers (Stangl et al., 1985). In their study, 63 adult psychiatric inpatients were independently rated by two interviewers ($n = 43$ with simultaneous ratings, $n = 20$ with test-retest ratings). Kappas for specific disorders diagnosed at least five times varied widely: avoidant (.45), schizotypal (.62), histrionic (.75), borderline (.85), and dependent (.90). Such values indicate excellent agreement with the exception of avoidant personality disorder. Evidence for convergent validity between SIDP diagnoses and appropriate MMPI subscales was also adequately documented (Stangl et al., 1985). Other investigators have examined the psychometric properties of the SIDP. For example, van den Brink et al. (cited in Reich, 1989) reported data from a 6-month test-retest study with 73 subjects. Results (kappas) were disappointing for schizotypal (.14), passive-aggressive (.40), dependent (.44), and histrionic (.46), but good for borderline (.70) and any personality disorder (.62).

Using a joint interview design, Nazikian, Rudd, Edwards, and Jackson (1990) investigated reliability of the SIDP in a sample of 10 inpatients and reported an overall kappa of .50. In contrast, high agreement was found when SIDP ratings were converted into trait percentage scores. Hogg, Jackson, Rudd, and Edwards (1990) studied personality disorders in recent-onset schizophrenics and reported an overall kappa of .59 and a similarly adequate figure for the only specific disorder evaluated, schizotypal (.54). Their analysis of trait ratings (rather than categorical diagnoses) revealed widely discrepant results. Also employing a joint-reliability design, Brent, Zelenak, Bukstein, and Brown (1990) examined reliability of the SIDP in a sample of 23 depressed adolescents. Weighted kappas ranged from .24 for borderline to 1.0 for schizoid, with a mean kappa of .49. Jackson, Gazis, Rudd, and Edwards (1991) assessed interclinician agreement of the SIDP in a subset of 27 out of 82 psychiatric inpatients, reporting excellent kappas for histrionic (.70) and borderline (.77), moderate kappas for paranoid (.61) and schizotypal (.67), and a tolerable result for dependent (.42).

Validity of the SIDP has been assessed in several studies in which SIDP diagnoses typically were compared to diagnoses from self-report Axis II instruments. Generally poor diagnostic concordance has been documented between the SIDP and the self-report MCMI with varied settings and methodologies (Hogg et al., 1990; Jackson et al., 1991; Miller, Streiner, & Parkinson, 1992; Nazikian et al., 1990; Turley, Bates, Edwards, & Jackson, 1992). It should be noted, however, that these studies may not be a fair test of the validity of the SIDP due to the differing nature of the instruments (interview vs. self-report) and the questionable validity of self-report personality disorder measures. Unfortunately, few studies exist in which SIDP diagnoses are compared to findings from other validated structured interviews or diagnoses made according to Spitzer's (1983) LEAD standard. Such studies are needed to fully document the validity of the SIDP for Axis II diagnoses and will undoubtedly enhance our understanding of the instrument. Moreover, as the DSM-IV version is only recently available, most of the literature regarding this instrument pertains to the earlier versions. Consequently, new studies investigating reliability and validity must be conducted.

As noted above, the latest and most sophisticated version of the instrument (SIDP-IV) has recently been produced. Several additional versions are currently under development and deserve mention. The SIDP-IV Modular Edition employs the same items as the standard SIDP-IV but organizes them by diagnoses that are covered one at a time rather than by thematic area. This format lends itself to easy tailoring and shortening of the instrument as users can assess only those specific disorders of interest. The Self-Report Supplement for the SIDP-IV, a paper-and-pencil test, can provide research data that are not influenced by interviewers and can allow comparisons between different raters. Finally, the Super SIDP is a comprehensive version that allows clinicians and researchers to make diagnoses according to three diagnostic systems: DSM-III-R, DSM-IV, and the International Classification of Disease, 10th edition (ICD-10). This Super SIDP will allow for useful comparisons between older and current DSM criteria to empirically evaluate the results of changes in disorder conceptualization and criterion operationalization. Further, its ties to the ICD system will enhance its application in international research on character disorders. Although studies are required to formally test the psychometric properties of each of these new devices, it is likely that such instruments will enhance psychiatric research on personality disorders for many years to come.

For information on SIDP-IV materials, training, and related procedures, the interested reader should contact Bruce Pfohl, M.D., Department of Psychiatry, University of Iowa Hospitals and Clinics, 200 Hawkins Drive, No. 2887 JPP, Iowa City, Iowa 52242–1775; telephone (319) 356-1350, fax (319) 356-2587.

International Personality Disorder Examination (IPDE)

The International Personality Disorder Examination (IPDE; Loranger et al., 1994) is an extensive, semistructured diagnostic interview administered by experienced clinicians to evaluate personality disorders. The 1994 version is compatible with the DSM-III-R and ICD-10 diagnostic schemes and was developed for the worldwide study of personality disorders. Notably, a version keyed to DSM-IV has recently been produced by the World Health Organization (WHO, 1995). The IPDE is an outgrowth of the Personality Disorder Examination which was developed and refined over a 5 year period from 1983 to 1988 (Loranger, Hirschfeld, Sartorius, & Regier, 1991). The first pilot version was tied to the DSM-III classification system and was successfully field tested by Loranger, Susman, Oldham, and Russakof (1987). A revision of that early instrument was soon updated for draft criteria of the DSM-III-R and also favorably evaluated in a larger clinical trial. While some pilot items remain intact in the current version, others were replaced, refined, or dropped (Loranger et al., 1991), and the IPDE is substantially different than its predecessors. Impetus for the development of the IPDE came from the WHO and the U.S. Alcohol, Drug Abuse, and Mental Health Administration (ADAMHA) in their joint effort aimed at producing standardized assessment instruments to measure mental disorders on an worldwide basis. The PDE was chosen as the basis for an international instrument capable of diagnosing personality disorders. The IPDE was subsequently produced to tap all DSM-III-R and ICD-10 personality disorders, while the most recent edition incorporates DSM-IV and ICD-10 criteria.

Items reflecting personality disorder criteria according to the DSM and ICD systems are grouped into six thematic headings: Work, Self, Interpersonal Relationships, Affects, Reality Testing, and Impulse Control (Loranger et al., 1991). Like the SIDP-IV, disorders are not covered on a one-by-one basis. Also similar to the SIDP-IV, respondents are encouraged to report their typical or usual functioning rather than their often altered personality functioning during times of acute psychiatric illness. Prior to the structured interview, a screening of Axis I conditions and the respondent's personal history is recommended.

IPDE sections typically begin with open-ended prompts to encourage respondents to elaborate about themselves in a less structured fashion. Then, specific questions are asked to evaluate each DSM and ICD criterion. In the DSM-III-R version, the disorder name, criterion, and criterion number are printed above the question or questions designed to tap that criterion (Loranger et al., 1991, 1994). Some items tap a similar DSM and ICD criterion, while others only relate to one particular system. The recently released DSM-IV version maintains the same format in terms of principles of administration and organization as the DSM-III-R IPDE, with the exception that there are separate modules for the DSM-IV and ICD-10 classification systems. This change was implemented because clinical researchers typically followed one system or the other but rarely required diagnoses according to both. This modification also serves to reduce length and administration time of the interview.

The IPDE requires that a trait be prominent during the last 5 years to be considered a part of the respondent's personality. Information about age of onset of particular behaviors is also explored to determine if a late-onset diagnosis is appropriate. When a respondent acknowledges a particular trait, interviewers follow-up by asking for examples and anecdotes to clarify the trait or behavior, gauge impact of the trait on the person's functioning, and fully substantiate the rating. Such probing requires significant clinical judgment and knowledge about each criterion on the part of interviewers. Moreover, some items are rated based on observation of the respondent's behavior during the session, and this too requires a certain level of clinical expertise. To supplement self-report, interview of informants is encouraged, and clinical judgment is needed to ascertain which source is more reliable if inconsistencies arise. Data from informants are recorded on a separate column, and final ratings on the scoresheet are marked to indicate that they were obtained by informants. Overall, all items are rated on a three-point scale with the following definitions: 0 indicates that the behavior or trait is denied or within normal limits, 1 refers to present to an accentuated degree, and 2 signifies pathological/meets criterion (Loranger et al., 1994). A comprehensive item-by-item scoring manual is available, which clarifies the intent of each criterion and provides guidelines for scoring. At the end of the interview, final impressions are recorded on a summary scoresheet. Then, such ratings are collated either by hand or computer. The ultimate output is quite extensive including: presence or absence of each criterion, number of criteria met for each disorder, a dimensional score (sum of individual scores for each criterion for each disorder), and a categorical diagnosis (definite, probable, or negative); see Loranger et al. (1994). Such comprehensive output is quite valued by clinical researchers, who can analyze such data in multitude and creative ways.

Given that the DSM-III-R IPDE evaluates approximately 150 different diagnostic criteria according to two different diagnostic systems, administration time is longer than other interviews and typically requires 3 to 4 hours. As such, it is recommended that administration be divided into at least two separate sessions to reduce lethargy and incomplete exploration of later items (Loranger et al., 1991). Separation of the DSM and ICD systems in the DSM-IV edition will surely reduce interview length, but time estimates are currently unavailable. The IPDE is intended to be administered by experienced clinicians, such as clinical psychologists and psychiatrists, who have also received specific training in the use of the IPDE. Such training typically involves a 2-day workshop with demonstration videotapes, discussions, and practice. The WHO has established approximately 15 training centers around the world, and questions about IPDE training in the United States should be directed to Dr. Loranger. As noted, this instrument was selected by the WHO for international application, and as such has been translated into numerous languages to facilitate transcultural research.

Reliability of the original PDE was first assessed by the instrument developers (Loranger et al., 1987) in a sample of 60 nonpsychotic adult inpatients. This report focused on DSM-III personality disorders that were diagnosed at least five times. Kappas were quite impressive: antisocial (.70), histrionic (.77), schizotypal (.80), compulsive (.88), and borderline (.96). Later, Standage and Ladha (1988) examined the PDE in a clinical sample, reporting generally lower, but still acceptable interclinician concordance rates that ranged from .38 to .78, and averaged .63. Also, Loranger and colleagues (1991) reported data from the field trial of the 1985 pilot version of the PDE, which was tied to DSM-III-R criteria. In a sample of 136 patients, diagnostic concordance between the PDE examiner and a silent independent observer ranged from .55 to .93, with a median of .83. Stability of diagnosis based on second interviews 1 to 6 months later in a subsample of the original population ($n = 86$) ranged from .52 to .57.

As noted above, the IPDE was selected by the WHO/ADAMHA for use in a international pilot study to assess personality disorders in different languages, cultures, and countries, and data from this comprehensive study are now available. In this large-scale, multinational, reliability project (Loranger et al., 1994), the IPDE was administered by 58 experienced clinicians to 716 patients being treated at 14 field trial centers in 11 countries in North America, Europe, Africa, and Asia. One-hundred forty-one interviews were simultaneously rated by a second clinician to evaluate interrater reliability. Agreement rates were calculated for five definite (met full criteria) and nine probable or definite (met one criteria less than required number) DSM-III-R diagnoses. This strategy was employed to increase base rates of some disorders so that more kappas could be computed. Results for the definite or probable diagnoses were higher than the definite cases (as can be expected) and generally were quite strong. Kappa values ranged from a low of .51 for paranoid to a high of .87 for schizoid. Moreover, kappas were above .70 (indicating excellent agreement) for six out of nine diagnoses. Overall weighted kappas for definite and probable or definite diagnoses were .57 and .69, respectively. Most impressively, these values are similar to those reported for many Axis I disorders, which previously were found to be substantially easier to accurately classify. Temporal stability of the IPDE was also assessed in 243 cases who were reexamined with mean interval of 6 months between administrations. Results for stability were somewhat more variable than those for interrater reliability, ranging from .28 for paranoid to .68 for both schizoid and schizotypal. For temporal stability, overall weighted kappas for definite and probable or definite diagnoses were .50 and .53, respectively. Interestingly, interrater reliability and temporal stability concordance rates were also reported for *dimensional* scores and the number of criteria met for each disorder. In fact, these rates were consistently higher than those obtained with categorical diagnoses, which suggests that the dimensional approach to personality disorder diagnosis and taxonomy may have some advantage over the existing scheme. Indeed, a clear strong point of the IPDE is that the output always includes both dimensional and categorical scores for each disorder.

Two studies evaluated validity of the PDE by utilizing the LEAD technique proposed by Spitzer (1983). Skodol, Oldham, Rosnick, Kellman, and Hyler (1991) compared the PDE with SCID-II, as well as with consensus diagnosis according to the LEAD technique in a sample of 100 inpatients. Agreement between the PDE and SCID-II was modest, ranging from schizoid (.14) to dependent (.66), with a mean of .45. When compared to LEAD diagnosis, positive predictive, negative predictive, and overall diagnostic power were calculated for each PDE diagnosis, with modest results. Overall diagnostic power ranged from .47 (passive-aggressive) to .97 (schizoid), with 6 of 11 disorders having values of .70 or greater. However, kappas were consistently lower and moderate to poor. Pilkonis, Heape, Ruddy, and Serrao (1991) reported on the validity of PDE diagnosis in 40 depressed patients who were also diagnosed according to the LEAD standard. Use of the LEAD standard as the validity diagnosis resulted in high sensitivity (.71) but only fair specificity (.58) for the PDE. Relative to the LEAD method, the PDE diagnosed considerably fewer patients with personality dysfunction, and resulted in 8 false negatives and 5 false positives out of 40 cases. Overall agreement (kappa) between the two sets of diagnoses about presence or absence of any personality disorder was poor at intake (.28) and follow-up (.29), with false negatives again prominent.

In other validity studies, Hunt and Andrews (1992) reported poor diagnostic concordance between the PDE and the self-report Personality Diagnostic Questionnaire-Revised (PDQ-R), while similarly disappointing results were found when the PDE and MCMI-II were administered to 34 wife assaulters (Hart, Dutton, & Newlove, 1993) and 97 psychiatric outpatients (Soldz, Budman, Demby, & Merry, 1993). However, these studies most likely suggest limitations of the self-report inventories rather than of the structured interviews, because the former tend to result in substantial false positives. The PDE has been also contrasted with another popular semistructured interview, the SCID-II, with better but still only fair concordance rates (see elaboration below in SCID-II section). Overall, while reliability of past and recent versions of the IPDE is firmly established for most disorders, validity remains to be firmly established, and this topic will undoubtedly receive focused research attention in the near future.

The most recent version of this IPDE is updated for DSM-IV personality disorders, and publication is expected soon by the American Psychiatric Press. Due to its ties to the most recent DSM and ICD classification systems, and adoption by WHO, the IPDE appears to be a valuable instrument for international and transcultural investigations of personality pathology.

For information on IPDE materials, training, and related procedures, the interested reader should contact Armand W. Loranger, Ph.D., The New York Hospital–Cornell Medical Center, Westchester Division, 21 Bloomingdale Road, White Plains, New York 10605; telephone (914) 997-5922, fax (914) 946-5859.

Structured Clinical Interview for DSM-IV Axis II (SCID-II)

To complement the Axis I version of the SCID, Spitzer and colleagues endeavored to develop a semistructured interview that would facilitate improved diagnosis of Axis II personality disorders. Their efforts resulted in publication of the SCID-II (Spitzer, Williams, Gibbon, & First, 1990), which targeted Axis II personality disorders according to the then-current DSM-III-R system. Indeed, this early version had a semistructured format and covered the 11 standard

DSM-III-R personality disorders, personality disorder NOS, and the proposed self-defeating personality disorder. In 1994, the SCID-II was updated (SCID-II, version 2.0; First, Spitzer, Gibbon, Williams, & Lorna, 1994) so that all of the questions correspond to the new diagnostic criteria in DSM-IV. In this DSM-IV version, self-defeating and passive-aggressive personality disorder have been deleted, while the depressive and negativistic personality disorders have been added (see Table 2.2).

The SCID-II is usually employed in conjunction with the SCID-I, which typically is administered prior to personality assessment. This is encouraged so that the respondent's present mental state can be considered when judging accuracy of self-reported personality traits. If the SCID-I is not administered, it is recommended that an unstructured interview be provided beforehand to evaluate the major Axis I conditions (First, Spitzer, Gibbon, & Williams, 1995b). The basic structure and conventions of the SCID-II closely resemble those of the SCID-I described above. One unique feature of the SCID-II is that it includes a brief self-report forced-choice yes/no screening component (called the Personality Questionnaire) that is completed prior to the interview portion and requires about 20 minutes to complete. While the DSM-III-R version of the Personality Questionnaire contained 113 items, the DSM-IV version is slightly longer with 117 questions. The purpose of this screening measure is to reduce overall administration time. In the questionnaire, initial diagnostic items for each personality disorder are presented, so that later sections of the structured assessment can be omitted if particular personality traits are denied. All items are negatively worded so that a "Yes" response requires further investigation.

During the structured interview component, only positively endorsed screening responses are further pursued to ascertain whether the symptom criteria is actually at clinically significant levels. Here, the respondent is asked to elaborate about each suspected personality disorder criteria, and specified prompts are provided. Like the Axis I SCID, the DSM diagnostic criteria are printed on the interview page for easy review, responses are coded similarly (i.e., ? = inadequate information, 1 = absent, 2 = subthreshold, and 3 = threshold), and each disorder is assessed completely and diagnoses are made before proceeding to the next disorder (First, Spitzer, Gibbon, & Williams, 1995b). The modular format permits researchers and clinicians to tailor the SCID-II to their specific needs and reduce administration time. SCID-II administrators are expected to use their clinical judgment to clarify responses, gently challenge inconsistencies, and ask for additional information as required to accurately rate each criterion and disorder. Collection of diagnostic information from ancillary sources is permitted. Complete administration of the SCID-II typically takes under 50 minutes, which is substantially shorter than other structured measures, and is a major attractive feature of the instrument along with availability of the screening questionnaire. Training requirements and interviewer qualifications are similar to that of the SCID-I.

Numerous studies have reported reliability data for the SCID-II. The largest and most recent study to date was a multisite, test-retest reliability project that utilized 284 subjects in four psychiatric and two nonclinical sites (First, Spitzer, Gibbon, Williams, Davies, et al., 1995). At all sites, two raters independently evaluated the same subject at separate times, with intervals ranging from 1 day to 2 weeks. Agreement rates (kappa) for the patient sample ($n = 103$) ranged from a low of .24 for obsessive-compulsive to a high of .74 for histrionic. Kappas were above .50 for 5 of 10 disorders, with a mean kappa of .53. Similar to the Axis I project (and as expected with lower base rates and milder threshold cases), agreement rates for nonpatient subjects were poorer, with an overall weighted kappa of .38. When compared to test-retest data from other structured interviews (SIDP and PDE), findings for the SCID-II were roughly comparable, but achieved in a shorter administration time.

Two additional studies added to our current knowledge about test-retest reliability of the SCID-II. O'Boyle and Self (1990) examined reliability of personality disorders in a subsample of five inpatients participating in a larger validity study. Mean interval between administrations was 1.7 days. Agreement (kappa) for presence of any personality disorder was .74, but rates for specific disorders were not reported due to the small sample size. Also employing a test-retest design (second interview within 48 hours), Malow, West, Williams, and Sutker (1989) reported excellent reliability of borderline (kappa = .87) and antisocial (.84) personality disorders in a subsample of 29 out of 117 male veteran inpatients diagnosed with either cocaine or opioid dependence.

Several other studies have deployed the less stringent joint interview design. Fogelson, Nuechterlein, Asarnow, Subotnik, and Talovic (1991) evaluated interrater reliability of the SCID-II in a sample of 45 first-degree relatives of probands with schizophrenia, schizoaffective, or bipolar disorder. Intraclass correlation coefficients (ICC) for five disorders found in the sample were moderate to excellent: avoidant (ICC = .84), borderline (.82), schizotypal (.73), paranoid (.70), and schizoid (.60). Two similar investigations used a joint interviewer design to evaluate personality disorders in anxious outpatients. Renneberg, Chambless, and Gracely (1992) administered the SCID-II to 32 anxious outpatients. Audiotaped interviews were scored post hoc by a second rater, and reliability estimates (kappa) were calculated for four specific DSM-III-R disorders: avoidant (.81), obsessive-compulsive (.71), borderline (.63), and paranoid (.61). Interrater reliability for diagnosis of any personality disorder was .75. Similarly, personality disorders were rated in a sample of 30 outpatients with panic disorder with agoraphobia (Brooks, Baltazar, McDowell, Munjack, & Bruns, 1991). Audio- and videotaped SCID-II interviews were assessed retrospectively by two additional independent raters. Their findings indicated respectable agreement for 10 personality disorders, with generalized kappas ranging from .43 for histrionic to .89 for schizotypal personality disorder. Kappas were not computed for schizoid and antisocial personality disorder, as neither disorder was diagnosed by any rater. A unique feature of this study is that interrater agreement was also evaluated for every criterion item for each personality disorder, and results revealed acceptable agreement (alpha less than .05) for 110 of 112 criteria. Similarly, Wonderlich, Swift, Slotnick, and Goodman (1990) retrospectively rated 14 audiotaped interviews of patients suffering from eating disorders. Kappas were obtained for five personality disorders: obsessive-compulsive (.77), histrionic (.75), borderline (.74), dependent (.66), and avoidant (.56), suggesting acceptable reliability.

In a larger scale project carried out in Holland by Arntz, van Beijsterveldt,

Hoekstra, Eussen, and Sallaerts (1992), two raters observed the same interview to compare diagnoses of 70 outpatients suffering primarily from anxiety disorders. Interrater reliability (kappa) was moderate to excellent, ranging from .65 for schizotypal to 1.00 for dependent, self-defeating, and narcissistic personality disorders, with an impressive overall kappa of .80. Similar to the procedure utilized by Brooks et al. (1991), Arntz et al. (1992) also calculated reliability levels for each DSM-III-R criteria for all personality disorders. Out of a total of 116 criteria, results (using intraclass correlation coefficient) suggested "excellent" reliability for 84 ($r > .75$) and "good" reliability for 14 ($r > .65$); only 6 criteria showed disappointing levels ($r < .60$).

Considerably less empirical attention has been devoted to validity of SCID-II diagnoses, although several reports have been published. In an early study, SCID diagnoses were compared to those generated by Spitzer's (1983) LEAD standard (i.e., a longitudinal, expert, evaluation using all data) in a sample of 20 psychiatric inpatients (Skodol, Rosnick, Kellman, Oldham, & Hyler, 1988). Positive predictive, negative predictive, and overall diagnostic power were calculated for each diagnosis, although kappas were not reported. Overall diagnostic power ranged from .45 (narcissistic) to .95 (antisocial), with 8 of 12 disorders having values of .70 or greater. It was noted that the SCID appeared to more accurately diagnose disorders with clear-cut behavioral descriptors (i.e., antisocial, schizotypal) compared to less behaviorally defined disorders (i.e., narcissistic, self-defeating).

More recently, the SCID-II has been compared to the PDE in two studies (O'Boyle & Self, 1990; Skodol, Oldham, Rosnick, Kellman, & Hyler, 1991). In the O'Boyle and Self study, both measures were administered to 20 depressed inpatients. Diagnostic agreement between the two devices for any disorder was fair (kappa = .38). Rates for specific disorders diagnosed at least five times were poor for paranoid (.18) and dependent (.23), but moderate for borderline (.62). In the investigation by Skodol et al., 100 applicants for long-term inpatient treatment of personality pathology were independently assessed with both measures. Their results indicated better, but still modest agreement, as kappa was over .50 (indicating acceptable levels) for 6 of 11 disorders, with a mean of .45. When compared to LEAD diagnoses, the SCID-II had slightly higher validity coefficients than the PDE for 8 of the 11 disorders studied, although values for both measures were moderate at best.

As noted above, the SCID-II has recently been modified to match DSM-IV criteria for personality disorders (SCID-II, version 2.0; First et al., 1994). As this instrument has only recently been available, no data currently are available. It is anticipated, however, that reports will soon be forthcoming describing the application and psychometrics of this interview. It is likely that the new SCID-II will soon be established as a valuable and popular tool for DSM-IV-based character pathology assessment.

For information on SCID-II materials, training, and related procedures, the interested reader should contact Miriam Gibbon, M.S.W., or Michael B. First, M.D., Biometrics Research Department, Unit 74, New York State Psychiatric Institute, 722 West 168th Street, New York, New York, 10032; telephone (212) 960-5524.

SUMMARY

This chapter suggests that application of structured interviews in clinical and research endeavors has greatly facilitated the task of psychiatric diagnosis and DSM classification. Current reliability estimates derived from the various Axis I interviews (SADS, DIS, and SCID) are highly promising for a broad range of clinical disorders. For personality disorders, reliability values for the SIDP, PDE, and SCID-II interviews generally indicate modest to excellent agreement with diverse patient populations and experimental designs. Most important, values from these structured interviews greatly surpass results from early investigations with unstructured interviews (Mellsop et al., 1982). In fact, prior efforts to classify personality disorders without structured interviews resulted in the lowest reliability rates in the entire DSM system (Mellsop et al., 1982; Reich, 1987). Improved criteria in combination with structured assessment instruments have no doubt combined to create this significant advancement.

For both Axis I and Axis II categories, however, it should be underscored here that reliability in the absence of validity is meaningless. Indeed, Grove (1987) cogently examined this issue and articulated that "reliability studies can never be more than a necessary first step in diagnostic research. Given the amorphous and overlapping nature of many psychiatric syndromes, one must be suspicious of highly reliable diagnoses until they are proven to be highly valid, too" (p. 116). Regrettably, while reliability rates are now more acceptable, relatively little has been written about the validity of diagnoses, especially for personality disorders. Most studies in this area have focused on basic reliability, differentiation of separate personality disorders from each other, and description of these conditions. Establishment of construct validity for these disorders is definitely lacking, and investigation in this area should be the major focus of future research attention. Clearly, structured interviews will be of great assistance in this endeavor. It is hoped that once these diagnostic constructs are well validated, comparisons between structured interviews can be carried out to assess the strengths and limitations of each instrument relative to each other for each personality disorder. Unfortunately, as noted above, validity studies are more complex and difficult to conduct than pure reliability investigations, and it is apparent that lack of validity is the paramount issue facing psychiatric researchers at present. Indeed, in the extant literature for Axis I and Axis II categories, there are too few studies in which diagnoses from one structured interview are compared to other structured interviews or Spitzer's LEAD standard for assessing validity. Now that reliability of diagnosis has been firmly established, enhancement of diagnostic validity appears to the logical next area for active investigative attention.

The information in this chapter is intended to provide a broad overview of the many standardized structured interviews that are available to the clinician and researcher. Basic descriptions, guidelines for use, and evidence for reliability and validity have been summarized for each instrument. It is hoped that this review will enable clinicians and researchers to choose an instrument that will most appropriately suit their needs. It is also hoped that awareness of the thorny and troubling issue of diagnostic validity of structured interviews will stimulate state of the art research in the future to move the field of psychiatric diagnosis ahead.

REFERENCES

American Psychiatric Association. (1952). *Diagnostic and statistical manual of mental disorders*. Washington, DC: Author.

American Psychiatric Association. (1968). *Diagnostic and statistical manual of mental disorders* (2nd ed.). Washington, DC: Author.

American Psychiatric Association. (1980). *Diagnostic and statistical manual of mental disorders* (3rd ed.). Washington, DC: Author.

American Psychiatric Association. (1987). *Diagnostic and statistical manual of mental disorders* (3rd ed., rev. ed.). Washington, DC: Author.

American Psychiatric Association. (1994). *Diagnostic and statistical manual of mental disorders* (4th ed.). Washington, DC: Author.

Andreason, N. C., Grove, W. M., Shapiro, R. W., Keller, M. B., Hirschfeld, R. M. A., & McDonald-Scott, P. (1981). Reliability of lifetime diagnosis. *Archives of General Psychiatry, 38,* 400–405.

Andreason, N. C., McDonald-Scott, P., Grove, W. M., Keller, M. B., Shapiro, R. W., & Hirschfeld, R. M. A. (1982). Assessment of reliability in multicenter collaborative research with a videotape approach. *American Journal of Psychiatry, 139,* 876–882.

Anthony, J. C., Folstein, M., Romanoski, A. J., Von Korf, M. R., Nestadt, G. R., Chahal, R., Merchant, A., Brown, C. H., Shapiro, S., Kramer, M., & Gruenberg, E. M. (1985). Comparison of the lay Diagnostic Interview Schedule and a standardized psychiatric diagnosis. *Archives of General Psychiatry, 42,* 667–675.

Arntz, A., van Beijsterveldt, B., Hoekstra, R., Eussen, M., & Sallaerts, S. (1992). The interrater reliability of a Dutch version of the Structured Clinical Interview for DSM-III-R Personality Disorders. *Acta Psychiatrica Scandinavica, 85,* 394–400.

Blashfield, R., Blum, N., & Pfohl, B. (1992). The effects of changing Axis II diagnostic criteria. *Comprehensive Psychiatry, 33,* 245–252.

Blouin, A. G., Perez, E. L., & Blouin, J. H. (1988). Computerized administration of the Diagnostic Interview Schedule. *Psychiatry Research, 23,* 335–344.

Brent, D. A., Zelenak, J. P., Bukstein, O., & Brown, R. V. (1990). Reliability and validity of the Structured Interview for Personality Disorders in adolescents. *Journal of the American Academy of Child and Adolescent Psychiatry, 29,* 349–354.

Brooks, R. B., Baltazar, P. L., McDowell, D. E., Munjack, D. J., & Bruns, J. R. (1991). Personality disorders co-occurring with panic disorder with agoraphobia. *Journal of Personality Disorders, 5,* 328–336.

Endicott, J., & Spitzer, R. L. (1978). A diagnostic interview: The Schedule for Affective Disorders and Schizophrenia. *Archives of General Psychiatry, 35,* 837–844.

Erdman, H. P., Klein, M. H., Greist, J. H., Bass, S. M., Bires, J. K., & Machtinger, P. E. (1987). A comparison of the Diagnostic Interview Schedule and clinical diagnosis. *American Journal of Psychiatry, 144,* 1477–1480.

Erdman, H. P., Klein, M. H., Greist, J. H., Skare, S., Husted, J., Robins, L. N., Helzer, J. E., Goldring, E., Hamburger, M., & Miller, J. P. (1992). A comparison of two computer-administered versions of the NIMH Diagnostic Interview Schedule. *Journal of Psychiatric Research, 26,* 85–95.

Feighner, J. P., Robins, E., Guze, S. B., Woodruf, R. A., Winokur, G., & Munoz, R. (1972). Diagnostic criteria for use in psychiatric research. *Archives of General Psychiatry, 26*, 57–63.

First, M. B., Spitzer, R. L., Gibbon, M., & Williams, J. B. W. (1995a). *Structured Clinical Interview for Axis I DSM-IV Disorders-Patient Edition (SCID-I/P, ver. 2.0)*. New York: New York State Psychiatric Institute, Biometrics Research Department.

First, M. B., Spitzer, R. L., Gibbon, M., & Williams, J. B. W. (1995b). The Structured Clinical Interview for DSM-III-R Personality Disorders (SCID-II): Part I. Description. *Journal of Personality Disorders, 9*, 83–91.

First, M. B., Spitzer, R. L., Gibbon, M., Williams, J. B. W., Davies, M., Borus, J., Howes, M. J., Kane, J., Pope, H. G., & Rounsaville, B. (1995). The Structured Clinical Interview for DSM-III-R Personality Disorders (SCID-II): Part II. Multisite test-retest reliability study. *Journal of Personality Disorders, 9*, 92–104.

First, M. B., Spitzer, R. L., Gibbon, M., Williams, J. B. W., & Lorna, B. (1994). *Structured Clinical Interview for DSM-IV Axis II Personality Disorders (SCID-II, ver. 2.0)*. New York: New York State Psychiatric Institute, Biometrics Research Department.

Fleiss, J. L. (1981). *Statistical methods for rates and proportions* (2nd ed.). New York: Wiley.

Fogelson, D. L., Nuechterlein, K. H., Asarnow, R. F., Subotnik, K. L., & Talovic, S. A. (1991). Interrater reliability of the Structured Clinical Interview for DSM-III-R, Axis II: Schizophrenia spectrum and affective spectrum disorders. *Psychiatry Research, 39*, 55–63.

Frances, A. (1982). Categorical and dimensional systems of personality diagnosis: A comparison. *Comprehensive Psychiatry, 23*, 516–527.

Frank, G. (1975). *Psychiatric diagnosis.* Oxford: Pergamon.

Grove, W. M. (1987). The reliability of psychiatric diagnosis. In C. G. Last & M. Hersen (Eds.), *Issues in diagnostic research* (pp. 99–119). New York: Plenum.

Grove, W. M., Andreason, N. C., McDonald-Scott, P., Keller, M. B., & Shapiro, R. W. (1981). Reliability studies of psychiatric diagnosis. *Archives of General Psychiatry, 38*, 408–413.

Hart, S. D., Dutton, D. G., & Newlove, T. (1993). The prevalence of personality disorder among wife assaulters. *Journal of Personality Disorders, 7*, 329–341.

Helzer, J. E., Robins, L. N., McEvoy, M. A., Spitznagle, E. L., Stoltzman, R. K., Farmer, A., & Brockington, I. F. (1985). A comparison of clinical and diagnostic interview schedule diagnoses: Physician reexamination of lay-interviewed cases in the general population. *Archives of General Psychiatry, 42*, 657–666.

Hersen, M. (1988). Behavioral assessment and psychiatric diagnosis. *Behavioral Assessment, 10*, 107–121.

Hersen, M., & Bellack, A. S. (1988). DSM-III and behavioral assessment. In A. S. Bellack & M. Hersen (Eds.), *Behavioral assessment: A practical handbook* (pp. 67–84). New York: Pergamon.

Hogg, B., Jackson, H. J., Rudd, R. P., & Edwards, J. (1990). Diagnosing personality disorders in recent-onset schizophrenia. *Journal of Nervous and Mental Disease, 178*, 194–199.

Hunt, C., & Andrews, G. (1992). Measuring personality disorder: The use of self-report questionnaires. *Journal of Personality Disorders, 6*, 125–133.

Jackson, H. J., Gazis, J., Rudd, R. P., & Edwards, J. (1991). Concordance between two personality disorder instruments with psychiatric inpatients. *Comprehensive Psychiatry, 32*, 252–260.

Kay, S. R., Opler, L. A., Spitzer, R. L., Williams, J. B. W., Fiszbein, A., & Gorelick, A. (1991). SCID-PANSS: Two-tier diagnostic system for psychotic disorders. *Comprehensive Psychiatry, 32,* 355–361.

Landis, J. R., & Koch, G. G. (1977). The measurement of observer agreement for categorical data. *Biometrics, 33,* 159–174.

Loranger, A. W., Hirschfeld, R. M., Sartorius, N., & Regier, D. A. (1991). The WHO/ADAMHA International Pilot Study of Personality Disorders: Background and purpose. *Journal of Personality Disorders, 5,* 296–306.

Loranger, A. W., Sartorius, N., Andreoli, A., Berger, P., Buchleim, P., Channabasavanna, S. M., Coid, B., Dahl, A., Diekstra, R. F. W., Feguson, B., Jacobsberg, L. B., Mombour, W., Pull, C., Ono, Y., & Regier, D. (1994). The International Personality Disorder Examination: The World Health Organization/Alcohol, Drug Abuse, and Mental Health Administration international pilot study of personality disorders. *Archives of General Psychiatry, 51,* 215–224.

Loranger, A. W., Susman, V. L., Oldham, J. M., & Russakof, L. M. (1987). The Personality Disorder Examination: A preliminary report. *Journal of Personality Disorders, 1,* 1–13.

Magnusson, D. (1966). *Test theory.* Stockholm: Almqvist and Wiksell.

Malow, R. M., West, J. A., Williams, J. L., & Sutker, P. B. (1989). Personality disorders classification and symptoms in cocaine and opioid addicts. *Journal of Consulting and Clinical Psychology, 57,* 765–767.

Marcus, S., Robins, L. N., & Bucholz, K. K. (1991). Computerized Quick Diagnostic Interview Schedule (QDIS 3R). St. Louis, MO: Washington University.

Mellsop, G., Varghese, F., Joshua, S., & Hicks, A. (1982). The reliability of Axis II of DSM-III. *American Journal of Psychiatry, 139,* 1360–1361.

Miller, H. R., Streiner, D. L., & Parkinson, A. (1992). Maximum likelihood estimates of the ability of the MMPI and MCMI personality disorder scales and the SIDP to identify personality disorder. *Journal of Personality Assessment, 59,* 1–13.

Nazikian, H., Rudd, R. P., Edwards, J., & Jackson, H. J. (1990). Personality disorder assessment for psychiatric inpatients. *Australian and New Zealand Journal of Psychiatry, 24,* 37–46.

O'Boyle, M., & Self, D. (1990). A comparison of two interviews for DSM-III-R personality disorders. *Psychiatry Research, 32,* 85–92.

Pfohl, B., Blum, N., & Zimmerman, M. (1995). *Structured Interview for DSM-IV Personality SIDP-IV.* Iowa City, IA: University of Iowa.

Pfohl, B., Blum, N., Zimmerman, M., & Stangl, D. (1989). *Structured Interview for DSM-III-R Personality (SIDP-R, rev.).* Iowa City, IA: University of Iowa.

Pilkonis, P. A., Heape, C. L., Ruddy, J., & Serrao, P. (1991). Validity in the diagnosis of personality disorders: The use of the LEAD standard. *Psychological Assessment, 3,* 46–54.

Reich, J. (1987). Instruments measuring DSM-III and DSM-III-R personality disorders. *Journal of Personality Disorders, 1,* 220–240.

Reich, J. (1989). Update on instruments to measure DSM-III and DSM-III-R personality disorders. *Journal of Nervous and Mental Disease, 177,* 366–370.

Renneberg, B., Chambless, D. L., & Gracely, E. J. (1992). Prevalence of SCID-diagnosed personality disorders in agoraphobic outpatients. *Journal of Anxiety Disorders, 6,* 111–118.

Riskind, J. H., Beck, A. T., Berchick, R. J., Brown, G., & Steer, R. A. (1987). Reliability of DSM-III-R diagnoses for major depression and generalized anxiety disorder using the Structured Clinical Interview for DSM-III-R. *Archives of General Psychiatry, 44,* 817–820.

Robins, L. N., Helzer, J. E., Cottler, L. B., & Goldring, E. (1989). *The Diagnostic Interview Schedule Version III-R.* St. Louis, MO: Washington University School of Medicine.

Robins, L. N., Helzer, J. E., Cottler, L. B., Works, J., Goldring, E., McEvoy, L., & Stoltzman, R. (1987). *The Diagnostic Interview Schedule Version III-A Training Manual.* St. Louis, MO: Veterans Administration.

Robins, L. N., Helzer, J. E., Croughan, J., & Ratcliff, K. S. (1981). National Institute of Mental Health Diagnostic Interview Schedule: Its history, characteristics, and validity. *Archives of General Psychiatry, 38,* 381–389.

Robins, L. N., Helzer, J. E., Ratcliff, K. S., & Seyfried, W. (1982). Validity of the Diagnostic Interview Schedule, version II: DSM-III diagnoses. *Psychological Medicine, 12,* 855–870.

Segal, D. L., Hersen, M., & Van Hasselt, V. B. (1994). Reliability of the Structured Clinical Interview for DSM-III-R: An evaluative review. *Comprehensive Psychiatry, 35,* 316–327.

Segal, D. L., Hersen, M., Van Hasselt, V. B., Kabacoff, R. I., & Roth, L. (1993). Reliability of diagnosis in older psychiatric patients using the Structured Clinical Interview for DSM-III-R. *Journal of Psychopathology and Behavioral Assessment, 15,* 347–356.

Segal, D. L., Kabacoff, R. I., Hersen, M., Van Hasselt, V. B., & Ryan, C. F. (1995). Update on the reliability of diagnosis in older psychiatric outpatients using the Structured Clinical Interview for DSM-III-R. *Journal of Clinical Geropsychology, 1,* 313–321.

Semler, G., Wittchen, H. U., Joschke, K., Zaudig, M., von Gieso, T., Kaiser, S., von Cranach, M., & Pfister, H. (1987). Test-retest reliability of a standardized psychiatric interview (DIS/CIDI). *European Archives of Psychiatry and Neurological Sciences, 236,* 214–222.

Skodol, A. E., Oldham, J. M., Rosnick, L., Kellman, H. D., & Hyler, S.E. (1991). Diagnosis of DSM-III-R personality disorders: A comparison of two structured interviews. *International Journal of Methods in Psychiatric Research, 1,* 13–26.

Skodol, A. E., Rosnick, L., Kellman, H. D., Oldham, J. M., & Hyler, S. E. (1988). Validating structured DSM-III-R personality disorders assessments with longitudinal data. *American Journal of Psychiatry, 145,* 1297–1299.

Skre, I., Onstad, S., Torgerson, S., & Kringlen, E. (1991). High interrater reliability for the Structured Clinical Interview for DSM-III-R Axis I (SCID-I). *Acta Psychiatrica Scandinavica, 84,* 167–173.

Soldz, S., Budman, S., Demby, A., & Merry, J. (1993). Diagnostic agreement between the Personality Disorder Examination and the MCMI-II. *Journal of Personality Assessment, 60,* 486–499.

Spitzer, R. L. (1983). Psychiatric diagnosis: Are clinicians still necessary? *Comprehensive Psychiatry, 24,* 399–411.

Spitzer, R. L., Endicott, J., & Robins, E. (1975). Clinical criteria for psychiatric diagnosis and DSM-III. *American Journal of Psychiatry, 132,* 1187–1192.

Spitzer, R. L., Endicott, J., & Robins, E. (1978). Research diagnostic criteria. *Archives of General Psychiatry, 35,* 773–782.

Spitzer, R. L., & Williams, J. B. W. (1984). *Structured Clinical Interview for DSM-III disorders (SCID-P 5/1/84 rev.).* New York: New York State Psychiatric Institute, Biometrics Research Department.

Spitzer, R. L., Williams, J. B. W., Gibbon, M., & First, M. B. (1988). *Structured Clinical*

Interview for DSM-III-R-patient version (SCID-P 6/1/88 rev.). New York: New York State Psychiatric Institute, Biometrics Research Department.

Spitzer, R. L., Williams, J. B. W., Gibbon, M., & First, M. B. (1989). *Instruction manual for the Structured Clinical Interview for DSM-III-R (SCID, 5/1/89 rev.)*. New York: New York State Psychiatric Institute, Biometrics Research Department.

Spitzer, R. L., Williams, J. B. W., Gibbon, M., & First, M. B. (1990). *Structured Clinical Interview for DSM-III-R Personality Disorders (SCID-II, ver. 1.0)*. Washington, DC: American Psychiatric Press.

Spitzer, R. L., Williams, J. B. W., Gibbon, M., & First, M. B. (1992). The Structured Clinical Interview for DSM-III-R (SCID): History, rationale, and description. *Archives of General Psychiatry, 49,* 624–629.

Standage, K., & Ladha, N. (1988). An examination of the reliability of the Personality Disorder Examination and a comparison with other methods of identifying personality disorders in a clinical sample. *Journal of Personality Disorders, 2,* 267–271.

Stangl, D., Pfohl, B., Zimmerman, M., Bowers, W., & Corentahl, C. (1985). A structured interview for the DSM-III personality disorders. *Archives of General Psychiatry, 42,* 591–596.

Turley, B., Bates, G. W., Edwards, J., & Jackson, H. J. (1992). MCMI-II personality disorders in recent-onset bipolar disorders. *Journal of Clinical Psychology, 48,* 320–329.

Vandiver, T., & Sher, K. J. (1991). Temporal stability of the Diagnostic Interview Schedule. *Psychological Assessment, 3,* 277–281.

Ward, C. H., Beck, A. T., Mendelson, M., Mock, J. E., & Erbaugh, J. K. (1962). The psychiatric nomenclature: Reasons for diagnostic disagreement. *Archives of General Psychiatry, 7,* 198–205.

Williams, J. B. W., Gibbon, M., First, M. B., Spitzer, R. L., Davies, M., Borus, J., Howes, M. J., Kane, J., Pope, H. G., Rounsaville, B., & Wittchen, H. (1992). The Structured Clinical Interview for DSM-III-R (SCID): Multisite test-retest reliability. *Archives of General Psychiatry, 49,* 630–636.

Williams, J. B. W., Spitzer, R. L., & Gibbon, M. (1992). International reliability of a diagnostic intake procedure for panic disorder. *American Journal of Psychiatry, 149,* 560–562.

Wonderlich, S. A., Swift, W. J., Slotnick, H. B., & Goodman, S. (1990). DSM-III-R personality disorders in eating-disorder subtypes. *International Journal of Eating Disorders, 9,* 607–616.

World Health Organization. (1995). *The International Personality Disorder Examination (IPDE) DSM-IV Module*. Washington, DC: American Psychiatric Press.

CHAPTER 3

Genetic Basis and Psychopathology

SVENN TORGERSEN

Attitudes toward genetics have been rather ambivalent in the fields of clinical psychology and psychiatry. Everyday experiences and clinical observations suggest that relatives resemble each other not only in physical attributes but also in personality and psychological strengths and weaknesses. Sometimes the similarity is understood as a consequence of imitation and identification. However, it appears that even children who have never met their biological parents seem similar to them. Sibs who were separated at an early age and met each other as adults feel that they are similar to each other. Can all this be due to distorted perceptions, wishful thinking, attributions, or resolutions of cognitive dissonance—or is there more to it? Is it possible that cognitive distortions, rather, make us explain away than invent heredity factors that influence the development of behavior tendencies?

It is easy to see reasons for the difficulty of maintaining rationality in questions concerning genetics. The existence of genetic factors that influence personality, development, and conduct may affect our views about basic values, political ideas, optimism or pessimism about changing the world, and the human condition. Professional interests may be threatened, as well as our views about which attitude to adopt in therapy.

By and large, most of these ideas about the eventual consequences are based upon misunderstandings, simplifications, the confusion of cause and effect, etiology, and therapy. It is possible to prevent strongly hereditary disorders like phenylketonuria (Fölling's disease) entirely by an appropriate diet in childhood. On the other hand, it may be difficult to reverse consequences of concentration camp experiences, physical or sexual abuse, or massive neglect in childhood. Nongenetic factors are not solely psychological; physical or environmental factors such as head traumas, intoxications, and injuries can be decisive for development. Furthermore, questions about genetic versus environmental factors are largely erroneous. Usually, we are dealing with both genetics *and* environment. No behavior is independent of inborn endowments, and any behavior requires an environment in order to take place. We shall see that the question asked in behavior genetics is: To what extent is variation in behavior due to variation in genetic factors, to variation in environment, or to a joint effect of genetic and environmental factors?

The basic mechanisms, concepts, models, and theories in human behavior genetics will first be presented. Methods in genetic research will be described next. Finally, some results pertaining to psychopathological conditions will be examined.

BASIC PREMISES

It is usually held that certain behavior patterns can be inherited. In reality, however, behavior cannot be inherited. What is inherited are certain molecular chains located on the chromosomes. The genetic code influencing the development of human behavior is situated on 23 pairs of chromosomes. One of these pairs contains the sex chromosomes: two X-chromosomes for females and one X- and one Y-chromosome for males. Spread around the chromosome pairs we find the sites or loci for different *genes*. Genes may exist in different versions, or *alleles*. Such allelic diversification creates the variation among human individuals. With more than 100,000 genes with alternative alleles, we can easily imagine how unlikely it is to find two people with the same genetic endowment. The exception is the case of identical twins, who stem from the same fertilized egg cell. Sometimes, both alleles of the chromosome pair are identical (homozygous), but often they are different (heterozygous).

The allele's variation is due to differences in their building blocks: the DNA molecules (deoxyribonucleic acid). The DNA molecule is composed of four different nucleotides; the *nucleotide* is a base attached to sugar as bonding material. The sequence of these four different nucleotides and the strands of different nucleotides define the property of the allele. The allele may influence behavior by means of the DNA structure, which is stamped on a molecule of RNA (ribonucleic acid). The RNA molecule monitors the construction of a polypeptide: a protein. The sequence of specific amino acids in the polypeptide is dependent on the base sequence in RNA, which in turn depends on the base sequence in DNA. In this way, DNA in the allele determines the polypeptides. These peptides can then eventually influence the central nervous system and our behavior. Genes are transmitted to the offspring in a way that make them partly similar and partly dissimilar to their parents and sibs. Sex cells in the parents are created by the process of meiosis. Without going into detail, we can emphasize the following: One cell consists of 23 pairs of chromosomes, one of each pair inherited from the mother and one from the father. The cell is divided into two new cells, each containing only 21 single chromosomes, partly maternal and partly paternal. One cell will never be identical to another cell. The two new cells are again split into four cells, with 23 single chromosomes: the sex cells. Two pairs of these four cells are generally identical. However, often a so-called crossing over takes place. A part of the chromosome in the new sex cells stems from the mother's chromosome in the original allele; a part stems from the father's chromosome. This phenomenon is the basis for the *linkage method,* which will be presented later.

Offspring and parents share 50% of the genes. On the average, the same is true for siblings. Identical or *monozygotic* (MZ) twins are an exception because they stem from the same fertilized egg. Fraternal or *dizygotic* (DZ) twins, on the other hand, are the result of two different fertilized eggs. Genetically they are no more similar than any other two sibs.

Genes may affect behavior in different ways. We may have simple *Mendelian inheritance,* in which one gene is responsible for the development of a disorder. If the disorder-producing allele is dominant, the individual needs only one such allele in the gene pair in order to develop the disorder. He or she can be *heterozygotic* for the disorder. If the allele is recessive, however, the individual must have the disorder-producing allele on both chromosomes. He or she must be *homozygotic* in order to develop the disorder.

Usually, genetic transmission is not that simple. Several separate genes may be independently responsible for the disorder (*oligogenic inheritance*). In that case, the disorder is heterogenous. There could be an interaction or epistatis among the genes. For instance, one gene may be important in creating the biochemical basis for the disorder. However, unless another gene also occurs, the disorder-producing gene will have no effect. On the other hand, some genes may be protective. It is possible that a person must both have the disorder-producing gene and lack the protective one in order to develop the disorder.

Most common behavior patterns may be due to several additive, independent genes: a *polygenic inheritance.* Each gene is replaceable, and the sum total of genes determines whether a behavior pattern is likely to develop. Finally, we may have a complex inheritance, whereby the presence of any of a variety of single rare genes could be a necessary but not a sufficient condition for the development of the disorder. In addition, other more common genes must occur together, and perhaps even a sufficient number of independent additive genes are necessary for development of the disorder.

If some specific or general provocation is necessary in addition to the genes, we then get a multifactorial-polygenic inheritance. We may also assume that some individuals will develop the disorder without any genetic basis. If the disorder is phenomenologically identical to the disorder created by genes, we call it a *phenocopy* or a sporadic disorder.

To add even more complexity, one and the same gene may be responsible for many different disorders: a *pleiotropy.* In many instances, we have to assume that more or less qualitatively different variants of the same disorder of varying severity might be due to a variation in the same genetic background. We will deal with this in more detail in connection with quantitative genetics.

So far we have discussed genetic transmission by means of chromosomes other than sex chromosomes: *autosomal inheritance.* However, genes may also be located on the sex chromosomes. This has important implications for genetic transmission. If the locus of the gene is on the Y-chromosome, the only transmission is from father to son. A recessive X-linked transmitted disorder is much more likely to occur among men because women must be homozygous for the allele to cause the disorder. If the disorder is lethal in early age and is X-linked, recessive, it can be transmitted only from the mother. She can be heterozygous and thus unaffected, whereas a man will not survive with the allele. With an X-linked recessive inheritance, the genetic basis for the disorder is generally transmitted from a healthy mother to the offspring, with consequences only for the son. However, a healthy heterozygous daughter may cause the disorder in her future son.

Quantitative Genetics

Geneticists have increasingly turned away from descriptions of specific genetic disorders in individuals and toward calculation of the impact of genetic variation on populations. The reason is that one can assess the effects of the allele on the individuals only for single-gene transmitted disorders. Because most disorders and behaviors are considered to be polygenetic, it would be better to speak about genetic variation in a population. This has important implications. It means that we speak about heredity as a percentage of the variance of the behavior or disorder accounted for by genetic factors. The rest has to be due to environmental variance. Environmental variance is usually divided in two parts. One part is a variance that affects only all first-degree members of a family to the same degree. This is called *common family variance* or *shared-in-families variance.* The other environmental part is a variance due to factors that make close family members dissimilar; a *unique* or *nonshared-in-families variance.* These three types of variance may change over time and may become different from culture to culture. This means that it is not possible to speak about heritability as a fixed attribute of a disorder. If the environmental variance increases, then the genetic variance, heredity, must decrease, because the sum total is unity, or 100%.

Recently, several quantitative models have been developed to make assumptions about monogenetic or polygenetic inheritance, dominance, epistases, and so on. The concept of *penetrance,* which says something about the likelihood that the disorder will emerge, is also of importance. Another important point is *selective mating* (the tendency of a person to choose a similar or dissimilar spouse). This has important implications for the kind of offspring they will produce. If spouses often are dissimilar with respect to a specific behavior pattern, then their children can be more dissimilar than unrelated children. By means of chi-square tests, it is possible to test which models will fit the data and which will have to be rejected.

The *multithreshold model* of disease transmission is particularly interesting. This model states that all individuals in a population are liable to develop a certain disorder. The liability is the sum total of all genetic and environmental influences on the disorder. If the liability is greater than a certain threshold, then the individual will have the disorder. Milder variants of the disorder may occur at lower thresholds, and the most severe variants require that a high threshold of liability be passed. Relatives of individuals with a severe variant will have a higher frequency of the disorder and are also more likely to have the more severe subtypes of the disorder. Relatives of individuals with a milder variant of the disorder have the disorder less frequently and have a milder type of the disorder. Exact mathematical predictions can be made and tested.

Recently, models have been developed that describe alternative joint effects of genotype and environment. It is assumed that the genetic influence is monogenetic and that the environment contributes to development of the disorder. There may be three possibilities:

1. Genotype and environmental provocation are simply additive. If the genotype is severe, then less provocation is required for the disorder to develop.

An individual who has a benign genotype needs a strong stressor to develop the disorder.

2. The gene determines the sensitivity of the individual to a certain negative environment. If he has both sensitive alleles, he will be vulnerable in a provocative environment but safe in a protective one. If he has one sensitive allele, he will show the same tendency to a lesser degree. If he lacks both sensitive alleles, however, the environment is of no importance for his likelihood of developing the disorder.

3. The gene may be unrelated to the development of the disorder in itself because the disorder is due to a certain life event, but the genotype affects the likelihood of experiencing the live event. Thus, without the provocation, no disorder develops irrespective of genotype, and given the provocation, disorder occurs independently of genotype. However, the genotype makes the provocation more or less likely.

Given frequency of the allele and the provocative environment, it is possible to make precise predictions of the frequency of the disorder among relatives who are exposed to a protective or provocative environment and then to test which of the models best fits the data.

RESEARCH METHODS

Having presented the basic principles of human behavior genetics, I will now turn to research methods in genetics.

The Family Method

The most straightforward method in genetic studies is the family method, whereby one simply records the frequency of a disorder among the biological relatives of the proband (identified case). It is important to differentiate between first-, second-, and third-degree relatives. First-degree relatives share, on average, half of the genetic variation, second-degree relatives 25%, and so on. Pedigree studies, in which family trees are studied, may provide valuable information about the mode of inheritance.

There are many ways to collect data about relatives. The easiest way, the family history method, is to ask the proband about the relatives. Although the proband may be well informed about emotional problems among his children, he may not know as much about parents, older sibs, cousins, aunts, uncles, and grandparents. Although this method may give some underestimation, it has proved to be more accurate than one might expect, especially for the more serious psychiatric disorders.

The best method, however, is the family interview method, in which relatives are interviewed directly. In that way, one can apply the same structured interview methods to the relatives as to the probands. The biggest problem with the direct family interview is that it is expensive and time consuming, especially in countries where people move a lot. One way to reduce the costs can be to conduct the interviews by telephone. Then, however, some information about the relatives' emotional reactions and contact abilities will be lost.

Frequency of a certain disorder among relatives may be compared to its frequency in the general population. However, the best strategy is also to study the relatives of a control group. The control group can be patients with another mental disorder, patients with a medical disease, random individuals from the general population, or screened individuals without any disorder or disease.

It is important to match the control group for age, sex, education, and rural versus urban living, but multivariate techniques can also be applied to rule out these third variables. In any case, morbidity risk is better than mere frequency of a disorder. *Morbidity risk* means the risk for an individual of developing a disorder in his lifetime. If he is young, he still has the chance, but as he ages, the chance decreases. If the disorder usually has an early debut, the chance decreases more rapidly. Most commonly, number of individuals at risk is calculated. This means that the individual is counted as less than one if he is younger than the age of the end of the risk period for the disorder, and the fraction is smaller, the younger the person is. In this way the number of relatives at risk will usually be lower than the actual number of relatives. Hence, morbidity risk—number of cases divided by the number at risk—will usually be higher than the frequency of cases among the relatives.

The sampling procedure is important in family studies. Most studies deal with probands who have been treated in psychiatric facilities. The possibility exists that the likelihood of seeking help for treatment may be related to the number of relatives with psychiatric disorders. In that case, the morbidity risk will be too high in studies of this kind. The best would be a study of the common population. Because only 10% of the individuals with nonpsychotic mental disorders attend psychiatric facilities, however, the possibility of biased results is considerable.

Even though the family method seems straightforward, it is not easy to draw conclusions about genetic factors. One might say that if no higher morbidity risk is observed among relatives of probands with a certain disorder, then genetic factors cannot be of any importance, but this is not certain. Selective mating can cause individuals with opposite characteristics to marry. This means that offspring can be very different even if genetic factors contribute to the development of the characteristics. The wish to be different from parents and sibs might also counteract an eventual genetic tendency to be similar. That this is not a trivial objection is shown by many twin studies in which the correlations between MZ twins can be considerable, while the DZ twin correlations are zero or even minus. Even when a higher morbidity risk is obtained among relatives, evidence does not prove that genetic factors are important in the etiology of the disorder. Results may be due to common environment, identification, imitation, or learning.

Why then perform family studies? In part, family studies are interesting in themselves. To find a similarity between family members can tell us something about risk factors for disorders. Furthermore, establishment of a familial link can provide an impetus to go further with more powerful genetic methods. Finally, given that importance of genetic factors is established, pedigree studies can tell us something about the mode of inheritance.

If we find that the morbidity risk is halved every time we move one degree away from the proband, the inheritance might be a simple Mendelian one, with only one gene. If it decreases more rapidly, then we probably are dealing with interacting genes. If the morbidity risk is lower among parents than among sibs, recessive genes are likely. We have earlier commented on how family studies can reveal sex-linked inheritance.

A modern technique made possible by frequency of divorces today is to study so-called blended families (families in which not only the spouses but also some of the children are not biologically related). Some children may be half-sibs, whereas other are full sibs. The family method has been applied more frequently not to study genetic factors but to examine environmental factors and the interaction between genetic and environmental influences.

I have discussed the family method in detail because it illustrates many of the problems that are also found in the application of the other methods.

The Twin Method

The blended family design gives several opportunities to study the effect of having a different amount of genetic similarity while growing up in the same family. However, half-sibs and social sibs who are genetically unrelated have usually not lived together for very long. Twins are more like ordinary sibs in that respect. They usually grow up together. If they are monozygotic (MZ) twins, they not only have a very similar environment but are genetically identical as well. Dizygotic (DZ) twins are no more similar genetically than ordinary sibs. Given that the environment is not more similar for MZ than for DZ twins, an eventual higher similarity or concordance in MZ twins compared to DZ twins is considered a proof of the influence of genes.

However, studies uniformly show that MZ twins spend more time together, are closer, and more frequently have the same friends and the same activities. So the equal environment similarity premise in the twin study is not true. Then how can the twin method be applied? It is argued that more similar environments for MZ twin partners do not make the MZ twins more similar than DZ twin partners. Furthermore, one way to solve the problem is to see whether similarity in environment is related to similarity in the characteristics studied within the group of MZ twins.

Another problem with twin studies is the extent to which twins are representative of the population at large. A twin delivery is a physical risk event, and twins are more prone to head injuries than singletons. So perhaps environmental factors, less important to singletons, might be important to twins. To grow up with a sib of the same age, to compete for attention, to share everything, to be able to develop your dependency or reclusiveness to a greater degree than other children, to be dominated and bullied, or to express your own domineering tendencies, all may make the environment of twins very special.

Even so, most of what we know about genetic factors comes from twin studies. The usual formula for expressing the relative contribution of heredity and environment is

$$H + V_c + V_u = 1,$$

where H is heredity, V_c is common or shared environment, and V_u is unique or nonshared environment.

These three variances are usually calculated from the correlation R_{MZ} between MZ twins and the correlation R_{DZ} between DZ twins, in this way:

$$H = 2(R_{MZ} - R_{DZ}), \quad V_C = 2R_{DZ} - R_{MZ}, \quad V_U = 1 - R_{MZ}.$$

We observe that if the twin relationship makes the MZ twins too similar, the hereditability H will be too high and V_c and V_u too low. If, in addition, DZ twins are pushed in the direction of being dissimilar in order to develop their separate identities, V_c will be even more reduced. A twin relationship where one of the MZ twins has a strong tendency to domineer the other may increase V_u unduly.

Generally, these factors most likely lead to an overestimation of H and V_u, heredity and nonshared environment, and an underestimation of V_c; in other words, individual and not collective factors are the source of variance.

It is also important to note that this model is based on an assumption of additive genes. If the genetic etiology is based on a single recessive gene or on several genes that all have to be there, R_{DZ} will be very small compared to R_{MZ}, and again H will be overestimated and V_c underestimated.

The Adoption Method

One limitation of the twin method is the fact that although genetic factors vary, the family environment is more constant. The adoption method makes it possible to study also the effect of the family variation.

Two procedures are employed. One consists of starting with an adopted-away proband with a certain disorder and then looking at the disorders among the biological and social relatives. A higher frequency or morbidity risk among the biological than the social adoptive relatives speaks for the stronger effect of heredity than of family environment for the development of the disorder.

Another approach is to start with parents who have given away their offspring for adoption. One proband group consists of parents without the disorder. Frequency of the disorder among the adopted-away offspring of disordered parents is contrasted to frequency among the adopted-away offspring of the normal controls.

The adoption method may demonstrate the effects of heredity by showing a striking similarity among relatives even if they never have lived together. However, some limitations do exist. The method is perhaps less effective in studying the effect of variation in environment, because the adoption homes may be relatively similar. Requirements for being accepted as adoptive parents are rather severe, and the home must meet at least current middle-class standards.

Furthermore, characteristics of the adoptive home often are not recorded thoroughly. In this way, the design disregards important information. Another problem is that many children have been in residential placement before adoption, often with bad care. One can also imagine that conditions in pregnancy and shortly after birth are not always optimal for children of mothers with severe psychiatric disorders. To give up a child for adoption means that parents are far from average in the first place, and adoptive children may not be representative of the population at large. A lack of genetically determined personality match between adoptive child and adoptive relatives may also create problems.

Many of these shortcomings of the adoption method are solved by using an adequate control group. Even so, one has to make a careful search for alternative explanations for the often striking findings in adoption studies.

Twins Reared Apart

An interesting design is a combination of the twin method and the adoption method, whereby one studies twins who are reared apart. It is particularly interesting to look at MZ twins reared apart. An eventual positive correlation or a concordance between twin partners cannot be due to common upbringing. Theoretically, prenatal and perinatal factors may contribute. However, the twins-reared-apart design may solve some problems of the classical twin design. One problem is to find enough twins reared apart who have rare disorders. Another problem is the fact that twins reared apart cannot give us the opportunity to study the effect of shared environment in a positive way. Rather, this method may tell us what we find when the possibility of shared environment does not exist.

An alternative design that is much more feasible is to study twins with variable contact. In that way the shared environment will be a gradual variable, and its effect on behavior can be studied more reliably.

Linkage Methods

All these methods are indirect ways of studying genetics by estimating the effects of genetic variance. The direct method is to study the gene itself. The linkage studies seem to make this possible.

As mentioned before, frequent recombinations during meiosis make it possible to trace the site of the gene for a specific disorder. A positive result of a linkage study tells two things: that a simple gene is important for development of the disorder and that the gene has a specific location on a certain part of the chromosome. The first achievement may be the most important for understanding the etiology for the disorder and the second for treatment of the disorder. The exact location of the gene may in future make it possible to study the biochemical process from the DNA molecule, via RNA and amino acids, and eventually the central nervous system effects of the allele. This may make it possible to create the right therapeutic drug for the disorder. Today, however, this goal is far from being achieved.

Basically, the linkage method requires either large pedigrees with many affected individuals or a number of sibships. Here there is a source of nonrepresentation, in that many individuals with severe mental disorders have few sibs.

The claim of monogeneity is more problematic. Although positive confirmed results do tell us that a major gene is in operation, negative results may tell either that we have not located the gene or that it is not any single that is responsible for the disorder. Many believe that psychopathology seldom is due to only one major gene. This means that the ability of the linkage method is limited.

Another problem has to do with the statistics. Although the logic of the linkage studies is relatively simple, the statistical models and assumptions behind the calculation of LOD (logarithm of the odds ratio) scores are very complicated. The robustness of the calculation methods seems questionable.

In the following section I shall discuss the relative importance of genetic factors in the development of different types of psychopathology.

ROLE IN PSYCHOPATHOLOGY

Personality Disorders

Modern empirical personality research has shown that commonly studied personality traits are clustered in five general factors or dimensions—the *Big Five.* They are usually named *neuroticism, extraversion-introversion, openness to experience, agreeableness,* and *conscientiousness.* These dimensions seem to be correlated to the various personality disorders (PDs), either being assessed by interview (Soldz, Budman, Demby, & Merry, 1993; Trull, 1992) or questionnaire (Costa & McCrae, 1990; Soldz et al., 1993; Trull, 1992).

In absence of genetic research on most of the PDs it may be of interest to look at the genetic and environmental contribution to development of these personality dimensions.

All five dimensions are studied in a Swedish study of twins reared apart and together (Bergeman et al., 1993; Pedersen et al., 1991). In an American study, three dimensions that are close to three of the Big Five have been studied: *negative affectivity,* which is close to neuroticism; *Positive affectivity,* which is similar to *extraversion;* and *constraint,* which is analogous to conscientiousness (Tellegen et al., 1988). If we look at the results together, we find evidence of heredity for all dimensions, except agreeableness. The nonshared-in-families environmental variance is, however, higher than the genetic variance, and the shared-in-families environmental variance very low. However, the nonshared variance also includes error variance due to unreliability of the personality scales. Such unreliability decreases the calculated genetic and shared environmental variance to the same degree as it inflates the nonshared variance. Fortunately, the articles state the reliability of the instruments. If we control for unreliability, we find a heritability close to 50% for four of the dimensions, excluding agreeableness. The shared environmental variance is around 10%, and the nonshared variance is around 40%. These results are in accordance with other twin and adoption studies of similar personality dimensions and represent probably the truth concerning the development of these broad personality dimensions. Agreeableness is an exception. The heritability is probably only 10% to 20%, shared environment 33%, and nonshared environment more than 50%.

However, even if the regression correlations between the Big Five and PDs, measured by interview are around .40, and around .60 when PDs are measured with questionnaires, PDs may have a somewhat different etiology from the personality dimensions.

Because PDs measured by questionnaires are strongly correlated to the broad personality measures, one may expect a similar etiology for personality disorders measured in that way.

Livesley, Jang, Jackson, and Vernon (1993) have measured (by means of a questionnaire) personality deviances that are similar to the PDs in DSM-III

(*Diagnostic and Statistical Manual of Mental Disorders;* American Psychiatric Association [APA], 1980). They observed that most of their types of personality deviances showed heritability. The heritability (when additive and nonadditive was combined) ranged from .64 to 0 with a median of .49. Narcissism, identity problems (analogous to borderline) and social avoidance (similar to avoidant-schizoid), callousness (antisocial), and oppositionality (passive-aggressive) were most heritable. Conduct problems did not show heritability. Submissiveness (dependent), self-harm (borderline), insecure attachment (dependent), and intimacy problems (avoidant) showed a relatively low heritability. Correspondingly, conduct problems showed a very high shared environment variance; submissiveness also had such high variance. The nonshared environmental variance was highest for self-harm, followed by intimacy problems. As is the case for most twin studies, only 7 of the 18 traits displayed any shared-in-families variance. These estimates are probably too low, due to more similar environments for MZ twin partners compared to DZ twin partners and possibly to gene/environment interaction.

The pattern of heritability does not follow that of the PDs in the study by Livesley et al. (1993). Personality deviance (close to borderline, antisocial, and avoidant) shows both high and low heritability. The reason may be the heterogeneity of the PDs defined by DSM (Torgersen, Skre, Onstad, Edvardsen, & Kringlen, 1993a). Another reason may be that Livesley et al. (1993) used a questionnaire, and thus other delineation of disorders may appear than proposed in the clinical DSM approach.

Very few additional twin studies exist. Kendler, Heath, and Martin (1987) used four items from Eysenck's personality inventory (intending to measure suspiciousness) in a large Australian sample. They obtained a heritability of .41, nonshared environment variance, as common in twin studies, so the rest, .59, was nonshared-in-families variance.

More recently, Kendler and Hewitt (1992) studied heritability of schizotypal features using nine scales intended to measure schizotypi. They found that for seven of the scales, heritability was relatively high, from .40 to .68, and with no-shared environmental variance. The highest heritability was found for anhedonia, picturing the *negative* features of schizotypi. On the other hand, for two scales measuring perceptual aberration and *positive* schizotypi, no heredity was observed. There was a high shared environmental variance (.25–.29) and a very high nonshared variance (.71–.75).

These studies suggest, as expected from the high correlations between the Big Five and PDs measured by questionnaires, that heritability contributes considerably to development of PDs. However, as correlations between PDs measured by questionnaires and by interviews are moderate to low (Zimmermann, 1994), we do not know whether interview PDs are also genetically transmitted.

Most of the genetic research which has to do with personality disorders assessed by interview or records has applied to antisocial personality disorder or an important aspect of this disorder: namely, criminal behavior. In 1976, Dalgard and Kringlen published a twin study of criminality. With a very broad definition of criminality, they observed only a slightly higher concordance for MZ twin pairs compared to DZ pairs. A more strict concept of crime yielded a concordance of 26% for MZ and 15% for DZ twin pairs. Some will consider this difference as impressive, others will be more skeptical, taking into account the fact that MZ partners spend more time together than DZ twins. To study the effect of similarity in environment, the authors analyzed separately twin pairs who were close and pairs who were distant. They then made the surprising discovery that the closer MZ twins showed lower concordance and the closer DZ twins showed higher concordance. Thus, the concordance difference appeared only among twin pairs who were distant. In disagreement with Dalgard and Kringlen, I do not think that this result disproved genetic influence. However, results may show that an environmental factor in the twin relationship modifies the effect of genes in criminality.

McGuffin and Gottesman (1984) reviewed a number of relatively systematic ascertained twin studies of crime. They concluded that a fairly high difference in concordance was found between MZ and DZ twin pairs. However, the same was not true for juvenile delinquency. An American study of discharges for dishonesty in the American army also showed a clearly higher concordance for MZ twin partners compared to DZ partners. (Centerwall & Robinette, 1989). All these studies share the problem that MZ twins often make offenses together. Consequently, some data from the Minnesota Study of Twins Reared Apart are important. By applying the Diagnostic Interview Survey (DIS) to twins reared apart, the investigators observed a heritability for child antisocial features of .41 and adult antisocial features of .28 (Grove et al., 1990). Thus, this study did not find that the genetic influence is higher for antisociality in older age.

Several adoption studies of antisocial features and criminality have been performed. Crowe (1974) studied offspring of female offenders that were given up for adoption in infancy. Offspring of the offenders more often had antisocial personality (but not other personality deviations or psychiatric disorders) when compared with control adopted-away offspring. Length of time spent in temporary care prior to final placement was important for development of antisocial personality, pointing to the interaction between genetic factors and environment.

Cadoret has published a number of articles from his adoption study of antisocial personality. In a more recent article (Cadoret & Stewart, 1991), it is shown that not only antisocial personality but also attention-deficit hyperactivity disorder (ADHD) were found among adopted-away offspring of criminals. However, this was true only when offspring had been placed in lower socioeconomic status homes. Psychiatric problems in the adoptive home were related to aggressivity in the offspring, and such aggressivity syndrome in its turn predicted antisocial adult personality. The study does show important interaction between environment and genetics in the development of antisocial personality. In addition, ADHD seems to be an alternative outcome of genetic factors influencing development of antisociality.

Other adoption studies (Cloninger, Sigvardson, & Bohman, 1982, Sigvardson, Cloninger, & Bohman, 1982) have also shown that prolonged institutional care before adoption and the socioeconomic status of the adoption home influences the likelihood of criminality in the adopted-away offspring of criminals.

In addition to antisocial disorder, schizotypal disorder is the most studied personality syndrome in the realm of genetics. An early twin study of 25 MZ and 34 DZ twin pairs showed a concordance of 28% for the MZ twins and 3%

for the DZ twin partners (Torgersen, 1984). Genetic factors seem to play a part in the development of schizotypal personality disorder. A more recent twin study has demonstrated the heterogeneity of the schizotypal personality disorder. Only the odd, eccentric, and affect-constricted features of the schizotypal personality disorder seem to be genetically influenced (Torgersen et al., 1993a).

Kendler, Walters, Truett, et al. (1994) have recently updated the famous Danish Adoption Study of Schizophrenia. Among their adopted-away probands were also some (13) they diagnosed (based on interview) as having a schizotypal personality disorder. It turned out that five (21.7%) of their first-degree biological relatives and two (8.3%) of their second-degree biological relatives also had schizotypal personality disorder. Frequencies were significantly higher than biological relatives of control adoptees (respectively 3.7% and 1.6%).

Therefore, an adoption study also confirms the genetic influence on development of schizotypal PD.

As to other types of personality disorders, very little genetic research has been performed. A twin study did not find any concordance for borderline personality disorder among seven MZ pairs (Torgersen, 1984). On the other hand, two of 18 DZ pairs were concordant, pointing to some shared-in-families environmental variance.

A more recent twin study yielded moderate genetic influence on PD features (Torgersen et al., 1993a). Syndromes close to the self-defeating PD seemed to be genetically influenced, in addition to affect-constricted, eccentric schizotypal syndrome. A tendency was also observed for genetic factors influencing development of passive-aggressive, obsessive, paranoid, and narcissistic features. On the other hand, histrionic, borderline, and avoidant traits were more influenced by shared-in-families environmental variance. All in all, the median genetic variance for the 12 personality disorder syndromes was around 20%, the shared-in-families variance 10%, and the nonshared-in-families environmental variance around 70%. Using a reliability factor of about .70, we would have to conclude that around 30% of the variance may be accounted for by heredity, 15% by shared environment and 55% by unshared environment. Shared-in-families environmental variance may be more important, and heredity less important in development of personality disorders, compared to common personality dimensions. However, to date, we know too little about the genetic transmission of personality disorders other than antisocial and schizotypal disorders.

Given the power of studies of twins reared apart, one has to conclude that most broad personality dimensions are genetically influenced. Perhaps half the variance is explained by genes. Studies of twins reared together have usually disconfirmed that shared-in-families environmental variance has any importance. The reason may be that the higher similarity in environment for MZ twins compared with DZ twin partners inflates estimates of heredity at the expense of shared family environment. A tendency to show opposite behavior in DZ twin pairs may also be the reason. The studies of twins reared apart demonstrate that at least 1/10 of the variance in the personality dimensions may be due to shared family environment.

As to the personality disorders proper, we may be able to state firmly that genes influence development of antisocial personality disorder. The adoptive studies clearly demonstrate the importance of environment. Whether aspects by the family environment, indicated in the adoption studies, interact with genes, constitute unique nonshared environmental influence, or represent shared environmental influence, is difficult to determine. To make that evaluation, we should have explicit information about whether eventual adoptive siblings also develop antisocial traits. No adoption study has evaluated this factor.

Schizotypal personality disorder, especially the eccentric and affect-constricted aspects of the disorder, also seems to be influenced by genes. Yet we do not know enough about the kind of environmental influence that exists. To adduce information about aggregation of schizotypal cases in the Danish adoption families would have been informative.

As to the other personality disorders, we do not have sufficient data. We know that borderline and also some fearful personality disorders (Cluster C) co-occur in families, but we can only speculate whether such aggregation is due to genes or shared environment. If the scattered evidence that exists today is taken as a point of departure, it would appear that genes influence development of personality disorders a little less than is the case for most broad personality dimensions and influence shared-in-families environment a bit more. However, the less than ideal reliability of the assessment of personality disorders may deflate estimates of familial transmission of such disorders.

Substance Abuse and Dependency

Family studies uniformly show that relatives of individuals with problems involving alcohol and drug use also show substance abuse and dependency. The question arises whether such familial aggregation is due to genes or shared environment. Twin studies may provide the answer.

In the Virginia Twin Study, more than 1,000 female twin pairs and most of their biological parents were investigated (Kendler, Neal, Heath, Kessler, & Eaves, 1994). The study yielded an estimate of heritability of more than 50% and no evidence of shared-in-families environmental variance for alcoholism in females. Genetical vulnerability was equally transmitted to daughters from their fathers and from their mothers.

Another twin study showed results at variance with the Virginia study (McGue, Pickens, & Svikis, 1992). This study showed that females did not display a heritability for alcohol. However, men showed a heritability of more than 50%. Furthermore, early onset alcoholism yielded a heritability of above 70%, against 30% for later onset alcoholism. Moreover, shared-in-families environmental variance was substantial: around 30% for males and 60% for females.

A problem of twin studies is that MZ twins spend more time together than DZ twin partners; therefore, the higher concordance in MZ pairs compared to DZ pairs may be due to common twin environment and not identified genes. Rose, Kaprio, Williams, Viken, and Obrenski (1990) showed that MZ twins having much contact seem to have more similar alcohol consumption than twins seeing very little of each other. Studies of twins reared apart have yielded mixed results in American and Scandinavian studies (Grove et al., 1990; Kaprio, Koskenuvo, & Langinvaino, 1984; Pedersen, Friberg, Floderins-Myrhed, McClean, & Plomin, 1984). So, without completely ruling out results from twins reared together, the evidence is questionable.

It is fortunate, then, that we have some adoption studies of alcoholism. A Swedish adoption study demonstrated some effect of genetic factors in the development of alcoholism (Bohman, Sigvardsson, & Cloninger, 1981). The same held true for an American adoption study (Cadoret, Yates, Woodworth, & Stewart, 1995). The latter study showed through a path analysis that alcohol abuse and dependency in adoptees were also influenced by alcohol problems and other psychiatric conditions in the adoptive family.

As for drug abuse, the Minnesota Study of Twins Reared Apart observed a heritability of 45% for this kind of substance abuse (Grove et al., 1990). The American adoption study mentioned before (Cadoret et al., 1995) indicated that genes also were of importance for development of drug problems in combination with adverse adoption family environment.

Alcohol abuse and dependency in biological parents, as well as disturbed adoptive parents, contribute to development of alcohol problems in adoptees. In fact, the study showed the alcohol problems development via drug abuse and dependency. Thus, drug problems and alcohol problems may have the same genetic roots.

In DSM-III and IV (APA, 1994), smoking also is classified as a substance disorder. The Virginia twin study also investigated smoking in females, and the authors observed a heritability above 50% (Kendler et al., 1993). In this case, the shared-in-families environmental variance was above 25%, unusual in twin studies.

Taken together, the various methods applied to study the genetics of alcohol problems suggest that heritability does play a role in the development of abuse, dependency, or both. However, the fact that more of the studies are negative indicates that the genetic etiology in some populations may be weak. Cultural factors play a large role in alcohol consumption and may reduce the potential effects of genes in some populations. If Muslim and Christian families were mixed in the same samples, heritability of alcohol abuse would tend to be close to zero, because of the high between-family variance in alcohol consumption. Furthermore, some twin studies showing no effect of shared-in-families environmental variance are very likely biased by the close ties between MZ twin partners. Studies of twins reared apart and adoption studies document the importance of the family environment.

The same limitations that have been noted about alcohol disorders may also hold true for drug abuse and dependency. These two groups of disorders seem to be genetically and family environmentally linked. Smoking as well seems to be influenced by hereditary and family environmental factors.

Somatoform Disorders

Little is known about genetic factors in the development of somatoform disorders. Family studies have shown a weak aggregation of somatization or multiple-somatic-symptom disorders in families.

While some older twin studies have included cases with what they called hysteria, only one twin study has applied DSM-III criteria for somatoform disorders (Torgersen, 1986b). Both the older study and the new one show relatively similar results, however, with a moderately high concordance in MZ twin pairs

(29%–21%) and a clearly lower concordance (10%–0%) in DZ twin pairs. The concordance difference between MZ and DZ pairs suggests a genetic etiology; the relatively moderate concordance in MZ pairs speaks for the limits of such genetic influence. The twin study also showed that the more the MZ twins had been together in childhood, the more concordant they were. The same was true for DZ twins. Thus, environmental factors that influence sibs in a similar way seem to contribute to development of somatoform disorders.

Indirect evidence for inheritance of somatoform disorders is also observed in a Swedish adoption study, where female offspring of antisocial and alcoholic biological fathers had an increased risk of developing somatoform disorders (Bohman, Cloninger, von Knorring, & Sigvardson, 1984). However, these results will be discussed more thoroughly under the section about the genetic relationship between different psychiatric disorders.

Anxiety Disorders

Today, we know more about the influence of genetic factors on the development of the various anxiety disorders than is the case for any other group of psychiatric disorders. Several family studies have shown that anxiety disorders run in families. The question arises: Is this familial transmission genetic, environmental, or both? A Norwegian twin study from the early 1980s (Torgersen, 1983) suggested that genetic factors have a role in the development of anxiety disorders.

However, more interesting than the etiology of anxiety disorders in general are the genetics of the specific anxiety disorders. The Norwegian twin study suggested that panic disorders and anxiety disorders with panic attacks were more strongly influenced by genetic factors. For generalized anxiety disorder, when strict criteria were applied (the individual had never experienced any other anxiety or affective disorder higher in the hierarchy), genetic factors were of no importance.

The Virginia Twin Study comprising more than 1,000 female twin pairs from the general population made it possible to study the genetics of a number of anxiety disorders (Kendler, Neale, Kessler, Heath, & Eaves, 1993c). Study of panic disorders revealed a heritability above .40 when a strict definition of the disorder was applied and below that when subclinical cases also were included. A multiple-threshold model with panic disorders with phobic avoidance as a more severe variant yielded a heritability a little below .40. As Kendler et al. note, their results are very much in agreement with the Norwegian study.

What about the generalized anxiety disorders in the Virginia Twin Study? Different definitions of generalized anxiety disorders and different hierarchies yielded heritabilities of .30 and lower. Applying a hierarchy with major depression reduced heritability with 6-month duration to zero (Kendler, Neale, Kessler, Heath, & Eaves, 1992a). However, a multiple-threshold model with 1- and 6-months' duration evaluating generalized anxiety disorders without major depression yielded a heritability of 19%.

Kendler, Neale, Kessler, Heath, and Eaves (1992b) also studied the etiology of phobias in women. They obtained a heredity of .32 for any phobia, .39 for agoraphobia, .32 for animal phobia, and .30 for social phobia. The rest of the variance was explained by a nonshared environment. Situational phobias (claustrophobia, nature, etc.) constitute an exception, as heredity seemed to be of no importance, but surprisingly there was a shared-in-families environmental variance of 27%. The investigators, however, viewed this as a chance finding.

Especially interesting was an analysis disclosing common and specific genetic and nonshared-in-families environmental variance. Agoraphobia was the phobic disorder that shared most etiology with other phobias, but the common variance was almost exclusively nonshared-in-families variance. Social phobia and animal phobia were in a middle position. For social phobia, the common variance was environmental, and for animal phobia, genetic. Situational phobia was mainly due to specific nonshared-in-families environmental variance, but little etiology was shared with other phobias. As for all results from the Virginia Twin Study, the fact that MZ twins seem to spend more time together in childhood and later did not influence the results.

An exceptional study of 4,000 male twin pairs who served in the armed forces during the Vietnam War has evaluated the etiology of posttraumatic stress symptoms (True et al., 1993). Although intuitively one would think posttraumatic stress disorder to be environmentally determined, the twin study shows that heredity contributes. MZ twins were more often concordant for posttraumatic stress symptoms than DZ twin partners. However, MZ twin partners were also more concordant for combat exposure. So, some might think that here was the explanation. However, difference in concordance for PTSD between MZ and DZ partners survived the connection for such exposure. After such correction, the adjusted heritability varied between .13 and .35, with a median of .30, for 15 symptoms. Thirteen of the 15 showed a heritability of .26 or higher. Shared-in-families environmental variance only slightly influenced symptoms.

Taken together, genetic factors seem to be of importance for all types of anxiety disorders. The exception is obsessive-compulsive disorders, where we have insufficient data. The difference is small between the various anxiety disorders. Maybe panic disorder is most strongly influenced by heredity, followed by agoraphobia, animal phobia, social phobia, and posttraumatic stress disorder. Generalized anxiety disorder also seems to be influenced by genes. However, if a strict hierarchy is applied, the influence becomes trivial. The genetic contribution to development of situational phobias seems questionable.

Most of the genetic variance lies between .30 and .40. As reliability problems reduce the genetic variance, a qualified guess may be that the "real" genetic variance for these disorders is between .40 and .55. Shared-in-families environmental variance, such as social class, parental upbringing methods, neighborhood, and so on, does not seem to be of much importance.

Mood Disorders

It is well known that mood disorders run in families. Furthermore, major depression is observed among biological relatives of individuals with bipolar disorder and dysthymic disorder among relatives of individuals with major depression.

A twin study confirms that bipolar depression is genetically transmitted in families. As for dysthymic disorder, the evidence is less compelling (Torgersen,

1986a). Moreover, results of this study suggest a genetic relationship between bipolar disorder and major depression and between major depression and dysthymic disorder. Heritability for major depression was calculated to more than 50%.

Recently, the large population-based Virginia Twin Study indicated a heredity of more than 40% when the DSM-III-R (APA, 1987) definition of major depression was applied (Kendler, Neale, Kessler, Heath, & Eaves, 1992d). As in the Norwegian twin study, shared-in-families environmental variance was of little importance.

In an additional sample of close to 20,000 individuals, twins and their relatives were also studied (Kendler et al., 1994). Both samples yielded a heritability between 30% and 40%. Correction for unreliability brought heritability up to 50% (Kendler, Neale, Kessler, Heath & Eaves, 1993a).

Results from the twin studies are confirmed by a Danish adoption study that showed a higher morbidity risk of bipolar disorder major depression among the biological relatives of adopted-away mood disorder probands (Wender et al., 1986). A Swedish adoption study yields weak evidence for genetic transmission among milder nonpsychotic mood disorders (von Knorring et al., 1983). On the other hand, depression in the adoptive father seemed to be related to depression in the adopted child, pointing to importance of environmental familial transmission of minor depression.

Linkage studies offer a more direct evidence of the genetic influence on the development of mood disorders. A linkage study among the so-called Amish people in the United States showed promising clues to the location of a gene for bipolar disorder on chromosome 11 (Egeland et al., 1987). However, as new cases appeared among the studied families, such evidence was no longer apparent. Other linkage studies have not been able to confirm a site for such a gene on chromosome 11.

Twin and adoption studies suggest that genetic factors are of importance in the transmission of bipolar depression. Twin studies also point to a high—possibly 50%—heritability of major depression. As to the milder dysthymic disorder, the evidence is weak.

The possible genetic relationship between bipolar disorder and major depression, and between major depression and dysthymic disorder, may be understood in two ways: either by a multiple-threshold theory or by heterogeneity. A multiple-threshold theory would state that all three mood disorders are due to the same continuous liability for mood disorders. A severe condition such as bipolar disorder is more likely to appear if the liability is high, major depression if the liability is moderate, and dysthymic disorder if the liability is low. Among relatives, especially MZ co-twins of individuals with bipolar disorder, distribution of liability includes both high, moderate, and low levels. Distribution of liability is somewhat more restricted among relatives of individuals with major depression. Consequently, bipolar disorder occurs less frequently. However, dysthymic disorder, in addition to major depression, will often be observed. Finally, among relatives of individuals with dysthymic disorder, the low average liability will preclude other disorders than dysthymic disorder.

Against this theory speaks the fact that we do not find more major depression among the relatives (especially MZ co-twins) of individuals with bipolar disorder than among other relatives. Neither do we find more dysthymic disorder among the relatives of individuals with more severe mood disorders than among relatives of dysthymic individuals.

The heterogeneity theory seems more promising; among the major disorder cases, some are in reality bipolar disorders who have not yet experienced the manic phase. The rest are "true" unipolar major depressives. Correspondingly, among the dysthymic disorders, some are in the prodromal stage of major depression. Further research, of course, will confirm whether this heterogeneity hypothesis is right.

Nothing is known about the mode of genetic transmission, whether it is additive, polygenetic, nonadditive with one or more genes, or mixed. In the case of additive heritability, linkage studies are very difficult, as it is unlikely that one of many genes has a major impact. To locate a series of genes at the same time is not possible with known linkage methodology.

Schizophrenia

It has been known for many years that schizophrenia, to some extent, runs in families. Relatives of individuals with a schizophrenic disorder have an increased risk of developing schizophrenia. The risk for first-degree relatives is around 10%, half of that for second-degree relatives and half for third-degree relatives. The risk for parents of individuals with schizophrenia is somewhat lower than the risk for siblings and children. Individuals who are schizophrenic, or about to become schizophrenic, are less likely to marry and in general have less contact with the opposite sex. To the extent that schizophrenia is genetically transmitted, parents of schizophrenics may sometimes "transfer" some genes to the offspring without themselves being influenced by those genes. However, almost 9 of 10 individuals who become schizophrenic have no relatives with schizophrenia.

Is it true that schizophrenia is genetically transmitted? Family studies cannot confirm this; twin studies may be more informative. Modern studies with good sampling techniques, interview methods, and DSM-III/DSM-III-R criteria show that half of the MZ co-twins of individuals with schizophrenia also develop schizophrenia, compared to about 13% of DZ co-twins (Farmer, McGuffin, & Gottesman, 1987; Onstad Skre, Torgersen, & Kringlen, 1991). With a population risk under 1%, these results yield a heritability between 80% and 90%, with the rest being nonshared environment.

However, twin studies have a tendency to produce too high a heritability factor. The reason can be attributed to nonadditive genetic transmission. MZ twins will have all the necessary genes, DZ twins will not, especially if the genes are rare. Another reason can be attributed to interaction between genes and environment. If schizophrenia is caused by an interaction between some genes and specific environmental factors, twin studies show us only the product of these genes and environment. We do not see the cases where only the genes are present or only the adverse environment, as the separate set of factors does not lead to schizophrenia. This fact will exaggerate concordance in MZ pairs determined through a schizophrenic index twin and decrease concordance in DZ pairs. Furthermore, MZ twin partners, in fact, experience more similar environment than DZ twins. When twin and family studies are combined, a more likely estimate of heritability is 60%–70% (McGue, Gottesman, & Rao, 1985).

However, the best strategy to avoid the problem of correlation between similarity in genes and environment in twin pairs is to apply the adoption method. The best adoption study of schizophrenia is the Danish Adoption Study. It started in the 1960s, looking at the adopted-away children of schizophrenic mothers and the biological and adoptive relatives of adoptees with schizophrenia. Recently, results for the total sample, comprising the whole of Denmark, were published (Kendler, Gruenberg, & Kinney, 1994). DSM-III diagnoses were applied to the interview material, collected 40 years ago. Investigators observed a high frequency of schizophrenia among biological relatives of adopted-away individuals with schizophrenia. This frequency was in fact the same as one observes among relatives of schizophrenics who are not adopted away and living with their biological families (Onstad Skre, Torgersen, & Kringlen, 1991). No schizophrenia was observed among adoptive relatives. Biological relatives of adoptees without schizophrenia displayed a very low rate of schizophrenia. Therefore, the most likely interpretation is that schizophrenia is genetically and not environmentally transmitted in families.

Different subtypes of schizophrenia show both different symptomatology, different age of onset, and different course and progression. The question arises as to whether these subtypes have the same or different etiology. A way to answer this question is to look at biological relatives of probands with schizophrenia and see whether subtypes of schizophrenia breed true in families and whether the various schizophrenic members of the family have the same type of schizophrenia. If one looks at ordinary first-degree relatives, one does not find such a pattern. However, among MZ twin partners, the same subtype of schizophrenia is displayed (Onstad, Skre, Edwardsen, Torgersen, & Kringlen, 1991).

Furthermore, nonparanoid disorganized and catatonic schizophrenia showed more evidence of genetic influence than paranoid schizophrenia. One may interpret these results in two ways. One interpretation may be according to a multiple-threshold theory. Nonparanoid schizophrenia appears when the highest threshold of liability for schizophrenia is passed. Nonparanoid schizophrenia is on a lower threshold of liability. If an index twin has nonparanoid schizophrenia, the high liability will then predict a high degree of schizophrenia among the MZ co-twins. Some of them will have the same subtype of schizophrenia. If the index twin has paranoid schizophrenia, the MZ co-twin is less likely to have schizophrenia and very seldom nonparanoid schizophrenia. Another explanation may be that different genes are responsible for the inheritance of schizophrenia generally and the subtype specifically.

The delineation between schizophrenia and other psychoses has been debated. A way to solve the problem is to see whether schizophrenia and other psychoses have similar etiology. Kendler, McGuire, Gruenberg, and O'Hare (1993c) investigated the familial relationship between schizophrenia and other nonaffective psychoses and affective illness in the Roscommon Family Study. Their conclusion was that schizophrenia shares a familial predisposition with schizoaffective disorder and other nonaffective psychoses (schizophreniform and delusional disorder, atypical psychoses) and probably psychotic affective disorder, but not nonpsychotic affective disorder.

One twin study (Farmer et al., 1987) suggested a genetic relationship between schizophrenia and affective psychoses, but another one did not (Onstad, Skre Torgersen, & Kringlen, 1991). The Danish Adoption Study confirmed a genetic relationship between schizophrenia and schizophrenic-like schizoaffective disorder, but no other kind of psychoses or affective disorders.

The genetic linkage studies have proved to be useful in detecting the site of the genes for some somatic and neurological disorders. Several researchers hoped that the same would happen for schizophrenia. One promising study was published by Sherrington et al. (1988). Strong evidence was observed for a site for a schizophrenia gene on chromosome 5. However, other studies have disconfirmed such localization of a gene for schizophrenia (McGuffin et al., 1990). Either the Sherrington et al. results appeared by chance or some few cases of schizophrenia have such an etiology.

There is little doubt that genetic factors influence development of schizophrenia. However, we do not know the mode of transmission, whether there is one dominant or recessive gene, more nonadditive genes, or a number of additive genes. One gene is unlikely (a factor that also makes it difficult to perform linkage studies).

The different subtypes of schizophrenia may possibly have some specific genetic etiology. The schizophrenic-like schizoaffective disorder may share genetic etiology with schizophrenia. Other types of psychoses may have environmental factors, possibly familial, in common with schizophrenia.

Genetic Relationship between Disorders

An interesting question is whether different disorders have some similarity in etiology. Different disorders may be variants of the same underlying pathology, genetical or environmentally. Some milder disorders may be within the spectrum of more serious disorders. Genetic research methods are a good way to identify such relationships.

The Virginia Twin Study also has made a great contribution in this area. Kendler, Neale, Kessler, Heath, and Eaves (1992c) showed that the same genetic factors seemed to influence the development of major depression and generalized anxiety disorders. Their conclusion was that environmental nonshared experiences determine whether a genetically vulnerable woman shall develop major depression or generalized anxiety disorder or both. However, if the diagnosis of generalized anxiety disorder is applied only if no major depression exists, then the genetic factors (which were the same as those for major depression) were *unimportant* in the development of generalized anxiety disorder (i.e., less than 20%). Generally, the study demonstrated how much more important genetic variables are for major depression as contrasted to generalized anxiety disorder.

Kendler, Neale, Kessler, Heath, and Eaves (1993b) also looked at the genetic relationship between major depression and phobias. They found that the common genetic influence was modest—and perhaps nonexistent—for simple situational phobias. On the other hand, shared-in-families environmental variance seemed to be common for major depression and situational phobias. Nonshared environmental variance seemed to some extent to be common for major depression and agoraphobia.

In addition, smoking (Kendler et al., 1993) and alcoholism (Kendler, Heath, Neale, Kessler, & Eaves, 1993) shared to some extent genetic vulnerability with major depression.

Kendler, Walters, Neale, and Kessler (1995) finally attempted to delineate the genetic and environmental relationship between major depression and all of the aforementioned anxiety disorders plus bulimia. By means of multivariate genetic analyses they discovered two common genetic factors and one disorder-specific factor. The first factor apparently influenced development of phobias, panic disorder, and bulimia. The second is mainly responsible for development of major depression but also contributes to development of generalized anxiety disorder. Both factors have a modest influence on development of alcoholism. However, the disorder-specific factor was the really important one in the etiology of alcoholism. One shared-families environmental factor had a strong influence on bulimia, which is rarely confirmed in genetic research. Furthermore, one nonshared-in-families factor was of importance both for major depression and generalized anxiety disorder and to a lesser extent phobias and panic disorder. All disorders had some specific nonshared-in-families variance. We see that major depression and generalized anxiety have a common etiology, which may account for high comorbidity between these disorders.

The Swedish adoption study shows a genetic and environmental relationship between antisociality, alcoholism, and somatization disorders (Bohman et al., 1984). The investigators observed a genetic relationship in females between what they called "high-frequency somatizers" and antisociality. Antisociality, on the other hand, was genetically related to what they named "diversiform somatizers" in females. In addition, alcohol abuse in the adoption family contributed to the development of "diversiform somatizers." Names of these disorders were based on discriminant analysis of information from health registers. Therefore, it is difficult to say for sure what kind of disorders the name subsumes, except that both groups suffered from abdominal pain, back-ache, and nervous complaints. The "diversiform" group had more headaches and the "high-frequency" group had greater sick-leave. The study is in accordance with an early family study, showing the relationship between antisocial personality disorder and somatization disorder (Cloninger, Reich, & Guze, 1975).

Other adoption studies have demonstrated a genetic relationship between substance abuse and antisociality. Cadoret et al. (1995) discovered a pathway from antisocial personality in biological parents to aggressivity in adoptees. If the adoptive parents were psychiatric disturbed, such aggressivity had a higher likelihood to develop into antisocial personality as well in adoptees. The antisocial personality may develop further to drug abuse/dependency in adoptees, especially if also the biological parents suffered from alcohol abuse or dependency. Drug abuse and dependency may finally lead to alcohol abuse and dependency in the adoptees, the so-called early onset alcoholism. Thus, a genetic tendency to antisociality combined with a disturbed family environment seems to increase the risk for substance abuse and dependency.

In the last decade we have seen a growing interest in studying the genetic relationship between personality disorders and schizophrenia. Kendler et al. (1994) discovered in the Danish Adoption Study a genetic relationship between schizotypal personality disorder and schizophrenia. A twin family study has shown the same (Torgersen, Skre, Onstad, Edvardsen, & Kringlen, 1993b). However, it seems as if only the affect-constricted, eccentric aspects of the schizotypal personality disorder are related to schizophrenia. The schizotypal personality disorder is highly heterogeneous, and it is likely that most cases of schizotypal personality disorder are completely outside the realm of the schizophrenia spectrum.

We see that the same genes seem to affect the development of a large range of various psychiatric disorders.

SUMMARY

In the course of the last decade we have been able to detect the genetic contribution to many psychiatric disorders. The more severe disorders, such as schizophrenia and bipolar disorder, seem to be highly influenced by genes. Major depression and panic disorder may be in a middle position, while the rest of the mood and anxiety disorders seem to be influenced to a lesser degree by genes. Least genetically influenced are dysthymic disorder and generalized anxiety disorder without a life history of major depression. The strength of the genetic determination of alcoholism is a bit unclear, but the confirmative twin and adoption studies suggest that genes may be of importance.

Less is known about the personality disorders, with the exception of the antisocial and schizotypal disorders, where the genetic influence is established. However, the marked genetic influence on development of broad personality dimensions as well as a few studies of relevance for the other personality disorders suggest that at least some of the other personality disorders are also influenced by genes.

Twin studies generally show little effect of shared-in-families environmental variance. (Bulimia seems to be an exception. This disorder seems to be highly influenced by familial variance.) The reason may be that the equal environmental assumptions which state that MZ and DZ twins have similar environment are often violated. Adoption studies evince more effect of shared family environmental variance. However, even these studies, together with studies of twins reared apart, suggest that such environmental variance is seldom more than 10%. That means that socioeconomic factors, living conditions, rural/urban environment, parental rearing practice, and so on, are of less importance. However, it is likely that sampling limitations (which may mean that individuals from most adverse childhood environments have not agreed to participate in the studies) may deflate the family environmental variance.

The nonshared-in-families environmental variance may sometimes be estimated too high, leaving too little to the other types of variance, because of unreliability of the measurement instruments.

We know very little, if anything, about the mode of inheritance—additive or nonadditive. Interaction effects between genes or between genes and environment are also unidentified at this juncture.

Linkage studies have not yet yielded what we once expected in the field of psychiatric disorders. One reason may be the painstaking work of searching through the whole geneme, given the numerous possible sites for genes. Another reason may be the likely fact that the disorders are influenced by a number of genes, each of limited importance. Even so, there is reason to believe that in the future the locations of genes for some disorders will be identified. This is likely to happen if new technology is able to handle many genes at the same time in linkage or microbiological genetic studies. When this technology materializes, studies of the interaction between genes and environment will take place with increased speed.

The fact that disorders are genetically influenced does not mean that the children with a parent who has a disorder will evidence it. Indeed, in schizophrenia, only 5%–10% of children of a parent with schizophrenia will also develop that disorder. The reason is that a rare combination of genes is difficult to inherit from the parents. However, studies of the genetics of psychiatric disorders tell us that an individual can develop the disorder without any adverse childhood environment. Unique experiences are of much higher importance than experiences shared by the rest of the family. It is likely that such experiences may be of little importance for other individuals without the requisite genetic vulnerability. The experience may be psychological but also could be somatic (i.e., physical trauma or virus in pregnancy).

Genetic research points clearly to the fact that adverse experiences do not necessarily eventuate in psychiatric disorders. If a person with a disorder reports adverse experiences in childhood, one often thinks that such experiences may be the *cause* of the disorder. However, the possibility may be that the events which lead to the experiences are the *consequences* of disorders in the parents. The child inherits the genes from his/her parents, and that may be the most important cause of the disorder in the offspring. The disorder might have appeared in any case, as some adoption studies suggest. Furthermore, adverse experiences may be created by the individual. Genes may be both the cause of the eliciting event and of the disorder. For example, a man's alcoholism may be elicited by termination of a relationship. However, the girlfriend possibly left him because of his antisociality. And both antisocial traits and alcoholism are influenced by the same genes.

Thus, genetic research forces us to stop thinking automatically that events lead to a disorder, or a disorder is a consequence of events. Existence of genes represents a third factor that we should not ignore if we truly wish to fully comprehend development of a disorder.

REFERENCES

American Psychiatric Association. (1980). *Diagnostic and statistical manual of mental disorders* (3rd ed.). Washington, DC: Author.

American Psychiatric Association. (1987). *Diagnostic and statistical manual of mental disorders* (3rd ed., rev. ed.). Washington, DC: Author.

American Psychiatric Association. (1994). *Diagnostic and statistical manual of mental disorders* (4th ed.). Washington, DC: Author.

Bergeman, C. S., Chipuer, H. M., Plomin, R., Pedersen, N. L., McClearn, G. E., Nesselroade, J. R., Costa, P. T., Jr., & McCrae, R. R. (1993). Genetic and environmental effects on openness to experience, agreeableness, and conscientiousness: An adoption/twin study. *Journal of Personality, 61,* 159–178.

Bohman, M., Cloninger, R. C., von Knorring, A. L., & Sigvardson, S. (1984). An adoption study of somatoform disorders: III. Cross-fostering analysis and genetic relationship to alcoholism and criminality. *Archives of General Psychiatry, 41,* 872–878.

Bohman, M., Sigvardsson, S., & Cloninger, C. R. (1981). Maternal inheritance of alcohol abuse: Cross-fostering analysis of adopted women. *Archives of General Psychiatry, 38,* 965–969.

Cadoret, R. J., & Stewart, M. A. (1991). An adoption study of attention deficit/hyperactivity/aggression and their relationship to adult antisocial personality. *Comprehensive Psychiatry, 32,* 73–82.

Cadoret, R. J., Yates, W. R., Woodworth, G., & Stewart, M. A. (1995). Adoption study demonstrating two genetic pathways to drug abuse. *Archives of General Psychiatry, 52,* 42–52.

Centerwall, B. S., & Robinette, C. D. (1989). Twin concordance for dishonorable discharge from the military: With a review of the genetics of antisocial behavior. *Comprehensive Psychiatry, 30,* 442–446.

Cloninger, C. R., Reich, T., & Guze, S. B. (1975). The multifactorial model of disease transmission: III. Familial relationship between sociopathy and hysteria (Briquets syndrome). *British Journal of Psychiatry, 127,* 11–22.

Cloninger, C. R., Sigvardson, S., & Bohman, M. (1982). Predisposition to petty criminality in Swedish adoptees. III. Cross-fostering analysis of gene-environment interaction. *Archives of General Psychiatry, 39,* 1242–1253.

Costa, P. T., Jr., & McCrae, R. R. (1990). Personality disorders and the five-factor model of personality. *Journal of Personality Disorders, 4,* 362–371.

Crowe, R. R. (1974). An adoption study of antisocial personality. *Archives of General Psychiatry, 31,* 785–791.

Dalgard, O. S., & Kringlen, E. (1976). A Norwegian twin study of criminality. *British Journal of Criminology, 16,* 213–232.

Egeland, J. A., Gerhard, D. S., Pauls, D. L., Susser, J. N., Kidd, K. K., Allen, C. R., Hostetter, A. M., & Housman, D. E. (1987). Bipolar affective disorders linked to DNA markers on chromosome 11. *Nature, 325,* 783–787.

Farmer, A. E., McGuffin, P., & Gottesman, I. I. (1987). Twin concordance for DSM-III schizophrenia: Scrutinizing the validity of the definition. *Archives of General Psychiatry, 44,* 634–641.

Grove, W. M., Eckert, E. D., Heston, L., Bouchard, T. J., Jr., Segal, N., & Lykken, D. T. (1990). Heritability of substance abuse and antisocial behavior: A study of monozygotic twins reared apart. *Biological Psychiatry, 27,* 1293–1304.

Kaprio, J., Koskenuvo, M., & Langinvaino, H. (1984). Finnish twins reared apart: IV. Smoking and drinking habits: A preliminary analysis of heredity and environment. *Acta Geneticae Medicae et Gemellologiae, 33,* 425–433.

Kendler, H. S., Gruenberg, A. M., & Kinney, D. K. (1994). Independent diagnoses of adoptees and relatives as defined by DSM-III in the provincial and national samples of the Danish Adoption Study of Schizophrenia. *Archives of General Psychiatry, 51,* 456–468.

Kendler, K. S., Heath, A., & Martin, N. G. (1987). A genetic epidemiologic study of self-report suspiciousness. *Comprehensive Psychiatry, 28,* 187–196.

Kendler, K. S., Heath, A. C., Neale, M. C., Kessler, R. C., & Eaves, L. J. (1993). Alcoholism and major depression in women: A twin study of the causes of comorbidity. *Archives of General Psychiatry, 50,* 690–698.

Kendler, K. S., & Hewitt, J. K. (1992). The structure of self-report schizotypi in twins. *Journal of Personality Disorders, 6,* 1–17.

Kendler, K. S., McGuire, M., Gruenberg, A. M., & O'Hare, A. (1993). The Roscommon Family Study: I. Methods, diagnosis of probands, and risk of schizophrenia in relatives. *Archives of General Psychiatry, 50,* 527–540.

Kendler, K. S., Neale, M. C., Heath, A. C., Kessler, R. C., & Eaves, L. J. (1994). A twin-family study of alcoholism in women. *American Journal of Psychiatry, 151,* 707–715.

Kendler, K. S., Neale, M. C., Kessler, R. C., Heath, A. C., & Eaves, L. J. (1992a). Generalized anxiety disorder in women: A population-based twin study. *Archives of General Psychiatry, 49,* 267–272.

Kendler, K. S., Neale, M. C., Kessler, R. C., Heath, A. C., & Eaves, L. J. (1992b). The genetic epidemiology of phobias in women. The interrelationship of agoraphobia, social phobia, situational phobia, and simple phobia. *Archives of General Psychiatry, 49,* 273–281.

Kendler, K. S., Neale, M. C., Kessler, R. C., Heath, A. C., & Eaves, L. J. (1992c). Major depression and generalized anxiety disorder: Same genes, (partly) different environments? *Archives of General Psychiatry, 49,* 716–722.

Kendler, K. S., Neale, M. C., Kessler, R. C., Heath, A. C., & Eaves, L. J. (1993a). The lifetime history of major depression in women: Reliability of diagnosis and heritability. *Archives of General Psychiatry, 50,* 863–870.

Kendler, K. S., Neale, M. C., Kessler, R. L., Heath, A. C., & Eaves, L. J. (1993b). Major depression and phobias: The genetic and environmental sources of comorbidity. *Psychological Medicine, 23,* 361–371.

Kendler, K. S., Neale, M. C., Kessler, R. L., Heath, A. C., & Eaves, L. J. (1993c). Panic disorder in women: A population-based twin study. *Psychological Medicine, 23,* 397–406.

Kendler, K. S., Neale, M. C., Kessler, R. C., Heath, A. C., & Eaves, L. J. (1992d). A population-based twin study of major depression in women: The impact of varying definitions of illness. *Archives of General Psychiatry, 49,* 257–266.

Kendler, K. S., Neale, M. C., MacLean, C. J., Heath, A. C., Eaves, L. J., & Kessler, R. C. (1993). Smoking and major depression: A casual analysis. *Archives of General Psychiatry, 50,* 36–43.

Kendler, K. S., Walters, E. E., Neale, M. C., & Kessler, R. C. (1995). The structure of the genetic and environmental risk factors for six major psychiatric disorders in women: Phobia, generalized anxiety disorder, panic disorder, bulimia, major depression, and alcoholism. *Archives of General Psychiatry, 52,* 374–383.

Kendler, K. S., Walters, E. E., Truett, K. R., Heath, A. C., Neale, M. C., Martin, N. G., & Eaves, L. J. (1994). Sources of individual differences in depression symptoms: Analysis of two samples of twins and their families. *Archives of General Psychiatry, 151,* 1605–1614.

Livesley, W. J., Jang, K. L., Jackson, D. N., & Vernon, P. A. (1993). Genetic and environmental contributions to dimensions of personality disorder. *American Journal of Psychiatry, 150,* 1826–1831.

McGue, M., Gottesman, I. I., & Rao, D.C. (1985). Resolving genetic models for the transmission of schizophrenia. *Genetic Epidemiology, 2,* 99–110.

McGue, M., Pickens, R., & Svikis, D. (1992). Sex and age effects on the inheritance of alcohol problems: A twin study. *Journal of Abnormal Psychiatry, 101,* 3–17.

McGuffin, P., & Gottesman, I. I. (1984). Genetic influence on normal and abnormal development. In M. Rutter & L. Hersou (Eds.), *Child psychiatry: Modern approaches* (2nd ed.). London: Blackwell.

McGuffin, P., Sargeant, M., Hetti, G., Tidmarsh, S., Whatley, S., & Marchbanks, R. M. (1990). Exclusion of a schizophrenia susceptibility gene from the chromosome 5Q11–Q13 region: New data and a reanalysis of previous reports. *American Journal of Human Genetics, 47*, 524–535.

Onstad, S., Skre, I., Edvardsen, J., Torgersen, S., & Kringlen, E. (1991). Mental disorders in first-degree relatives of schizophrenics. *Acta Psychiatrica Scandinavica, 83*, 463–467.

Onstad, S., Skre, I., Torgersen, S., & Kringlen, E. (1991). Twin concordance for DSM-III-R schizophrenia. *Acta Psychiatrica Scandinavica, 83*, 395–401.

Pedersen, N. L., Friberg, L., Floderins-Myrhed, B., McClean, G. E., & Plomin, R. (1984). Swedish early separated twins: Identification and characterization. *Acta Geneticae Medicae et Gemellologiae, 33*, 243–250.

Pedersen, N. L., McClearn, G. E., Plomin, R., Nesselroade, J. R., Berg, S., & De Faire, U. (1991). The Swedish Adoption/Twin Study of Aging: An update. *Acta Geneticae Medicae et Gemellologiae, 40*, 7–20.

Rose, R. J., Kaprio, J., Williams, C. J., Viken, R., & Obrenski, K. (1990). Social contact and sibling similarity: Facts, issues, and red herrings. *Behavior Genetics, 20*, 763–778.

Sherrington, R., Brynjolfsson, J., Pettersen, A., Potter, M., Dadlesten, K., Barrachlough, B., Wasmuth, J., Dobbs, M., & Gruling, H. (1988). Localization of a susceptibility locus for schizophrenia on chromosome 5. *Nature, 336*, 164–167.

Sigvardson, S., Cloninger, C. R., & Bohman, M. (1982). Predisposition to petty criminality in Swedish adoptees: III. Sex differences and validation of the male typology. *Archives of General Psychiatry, 39*, 1248–1253.

Soldz, S., Budman, S., Demby, A., & Merry, J. (1993). Representation of personality disorders in circumplex and five-factor space: Exploration with a clinical sample. *Psychological Assessment, 5*, 41–52.

Tellegen, A., Lykken, T. D., Bouchard, T. J., Wilcox, K. J., Segal, N. L., & Rich, S. (1988). Personality similarity in twins reared apart and together. *Journal of Personality and Social Psychology, 54*, 1031–1039.

Torgersen, S. (1983). Genetic factors in anxiety disorders. *Archives of General Psychiatry, 40*, 1085–1089.

Torgersen, S. (1984). Genetic and nosological aspects of schizotypal and borderline personality disorders. A twin study. *Archives of General Psychiatry, 41*, 546–554.

Torgersen, S. (1986a). Genetic factors in moderately severe and mild affective disorders. *Archives of General Psychiatry, 43*, 222–226.

Torgersen, S. (1986b). Genetics of somatoform disorders. *Archives of General Psychiatry, 43*, 502–505.

Torgersen, S., Skre, I., Onstad, S., Edvardsen, I., & Kringlen, E. (1993a). The psychometric-genetic structure of DSM-III-R personality disorder criteria. *Journal of Personality Disorders, 7*, 196–213.

Torgersen, S., Skre, I., Onstad, S., Edvardsen, I., & Kringlen, E. (1993b). "True" schizotypal personality disorder: A study of co-twins and relatives of schizophrenic probands. *American Journal of Psychiatry, 150*, 1661–1667.

True, W. R., Rice, J., Eisen, S. A., Heath, A. C., Goldberg, J., Lyons, M. J., & Nowak, J. (1993). A twin study of genetic and environmental contributions to liability for posttraumatic stress symptoms. *Archives of General Psychiatry, 50*, 257–264.

Trull, T. J. (1992). DSM-III-R personality disorders and the five-factor model of personality: An empirical comparison. *Journal of Abnormal Psychology, 101*, 553–560.

von Knorring, A. L., Cloningen, C. R., Bohman, M., & Sigvardson, S. (1983). An adoption study of depressive disorders and substance abuse. *Archives of General Psychiatry, 40,* 943–950.

Wender, P. H., Kety, S. S., Rosenthal, D., Shalzinger, F., Oreman, J., & Lund, I. (1986). Psychiatric disorders in the biological and adoption families of adopted individuals with affective disorders. *Archives of General Psychiatry, 43,* 923–929.

Zimmermann, M. (1994). Diagnosing personality disorders. A review of issues and research methods. *Archives of General Psychiatry, 51,* 225–242.

PART TWO

Specific Disorders

CHAPTER 4

Delirium, Dementia, and Amnestic and Other Cognitive Disorders[1]

GERALD GOLDSTEIN

Since the writing of the last revision of this chapter, developments in treatment and cure of neurological disorders continue to be slow. However, massive research efforts made during the past 5 years in numerous areas have raised hope for improved treatment and management. A new drug, called tacrine hydrochloride, has received Food and Drug Administration approval for use in treatment of patients with Alzheimer's disease. It works on the cholinergic system and has been shown to be associated with cognitive improvement in patients with Alzheimer's disease of mild to moderate severity. In the last edition, we reported that the marker for the Huntington's disease gene had been discovered on chromosome 4 (Gusella et al., 1983); while the gene itself had not been identified, geneticists were apparently coming close to doing so. The gene has now been isolated. It is IT15, a region containing a polymorphic trinucleotide (CAG) repeat. CAG encodes glutamine, an amino acid. The length of the repeat is substantially increased in Huntington disease chromosomes, and apparently, an unstable trinucleotide repeat is the Huntington's disease mutation. Discovery of the gene opens treatment possibilities for this currently incurable illness, probably through methods involving recombinant DNA.

We also reported on the appearance of AIDS or human immunodeficiency virus (HIV) dementia in the last edition. AIDS dementia is a consequence of human immunovirus infection and apparently represents an illness that has not appeared on the planet previously. It has been characterized as a progressive "subcortical dementia" of the type seen in patients with Huntington's disease and other neurological disorders in which the major neuropathology is in the subcortex. The syndrome itself has not been completely described, but there is substantial evidence of neuropsychological abnormalities. The first papers in this area appeared circa 1987, with the most well known study being that of Grant et al. (1987). An extensive review of the available literature was accomplished by Van Gorp, Miller, Satz, and Visscher (1989), and a large recent study done by Heaton and collaborators (1995) confirmed presence of neuropsychological deficits in AIDS patients, varying in severity with the stage of the infec-

The author thanks the Department of Veterans Affairs for support of this work.

[1] This diagnostic category was called "Organic Mental Syndromes and Disorders" in DSM-III-R.

tion. We are gaining extensive knowledge concerning the associations between HIV infection and brain function, and new medications have become available, but the treatment problem remains formidable.

There has been a major conceptual change made within the psychiatric profession in the description of the organic mental disorders. Indeed, they are no longer described by that term in the new *Diagnostic and Statistical Manual* (DSM-IV; American Psychiatric Association [APA], 1994), in which there is a rather radical reorganization of what used to be called the organic mental disorders. The criteria for the individual disorders have not changed greatly, but their organization and related terminology reflect substantial change from the earlier manuals.

The modifications made in DSM-IV, and the abandonment of the term "organic mental disorder" in particular were accomplished for two purposes: to remove the implication that "nonorganic disorders" do not have a biological basis and to diminish the commonly made distinction between "mental" and "general medical" disorders. The philosophy of DSM-IV is clearly that there is no fundamental distinction between mental and general medical conditions. Thus, the traditional distinction made in psychopathology between the so-called organic and functional disorders has been modified by DSM-IV within the context of a more biological orientation.

Implementation of this philosophy produced a number of important organizational and terminological changes in DSM-IV. The DSM-III-R (APA, 1987) chapter on organic mental disorders has been changed to three chapters called "Delirium, Dementia, and Amnestic and Other Cognitive Disorders"; "Mental Disorders due to a General Medical Condition"; and "Substance-related Disorders." DSM-III-R had a section of the organic mental disorders chapter devoted to "Psychoactive Substance–induced Organic Mental Disorders" and a full chapter on "Psychoactive Substance Use Disorders." DSM-IV has incorporated these two separate components into a single chapter on "Substance-related Disorders." The DSM-IV chapter on "Mental Disorders due to a General Medical Condition" is the equivalent of the DSM-III-R section of the organic mental disorders chapter, "Organic Mental Disorders Associated with Axis III Physical Disorders or Conditions, or Whose Etiology is Unknown," but with some important changes in diagnostic terminology. We will return to modifications of DSM-IV as we provide more detailed descriptions of the individual disorders themselves. In these descriptions, we will follow the lead of DSM-IV and abandon use of such terms as "organic mental disorders" and "organic brain syndrome."

Delirium, dementia, amnesia, and related cognitive disorders are those conditions that can be more or less definitively associated with temporary or permanent dysfunction of the brain. It is clear that recent developments in psychopathological research and theory have gone a long way toward breaking down the distinction between such patients and those with other disorders. It is becoming increasingly clear that many of the schizophrenic, mood, and attentional disorders have their bases in some alteration of brain function. Nevertheless, the clinical phenomenology, assessment methods, and treatment management procedures associated with patients generally described as brain damaged are sufficiently unique that the traditional functional versus organic distinction is probably worth retaining. However, in order to delineate the subject matter of this chapter as precisely as possible, we would nevertheless prefer to say that we will be concerned with individuals having structural brain damage resulting from some medical condition or use of a substance.

The theoretical approach taken here will be neuropsychological in orientation, in that it will be based on the assumption that clinical problems associated with brain damage can be understood best in the context of what is known about the relationships between brain function and behavior. Thus, attempts will be made to expand our presentation beyond the descriptive psychopathology of DSM-IV in the direction of attempting to provide some material related to basic brain-behavior mechanisms. There are many sources of brain dysfunction, and the nature of the source has a great deal to do with determining behavioral consequences: morbidity and mortality. Thus, a basic grasp of key neuropathological processes is crucial to understanding the differential consequences of brain damage. Furthermore, it is important to have some conceptualization of how the brain functions. There is really not a great deal known about this matter yet, and so it remains necessary to think in terms of brain models or conceptual schema concerning brain function. For example, it is still not known how memories are preserved in brain tissue. However, there are several neuropsychological models and hypotheses concerning memory, portions of which have been supported by neurochemical and neurophysiological research.

In recognition of the complexities involved in relating structural brain damage to behavioral consequences, clinical neuropsychology has emerged as a specialty area within psychology. Clinical neuropsychological research has provided a number of specialized instruments for assessment of brain-damaged patients, and more recently, a variety of rehabilitation methods aimed at remediation of neuropsychological deficits. This research has also pointed out that "brain damage," far from being a single clinical entity, actually represents a wide variety of disorders. Initially, neuropsychologists were strongly interested in the relationship between localization of brain damage and behavioral outcome. In recent years, however, localization has come to be seen as only one determinant of outcome, albeit often a very important one. Other considerations include such matters as the age of the individual, the individual's age when the brain damage was acquired, the premorbid personality and level of achievement, and the type of pathological process producing the brain dysfunction. Furthermore, neuropsychologists are now cognizant of the possible influence of various "nonorganic" factors on their assessment methods, such as educational level, socioeconomic status, and mood states. Thus, this chapter will concern itself with concepts of brain dysfunction in historical and contemporary perspectives, the various causes of brain dysfunction, and the clinical phenomenology of a number of syndromes associated with brain damage in relation to such factors as localization, age of the individual, age of the lesion, and pathological process.

CHANGING VIEWS OF BRAIN FUNCTION AND DYSFUNCTION

Concepts of how mental events are mediated have evolved from vague philosophical speculations concerning the "mind-body problem" to rigorous scientific theories supported by objective experimental evidence. We may recall from our studies of the history of science that it was not always understood that the "mind" was in the brain and mental events were thought to be mediated by other organs of the body. Boring (1950) indicates that Aristotle thought that the mind was in the heart. Once the discovery was made that it was in the brain, scientists turned their interest to how the brain mediates behavior, thus ushering in a line of investigation that to this day is far from complete. Two major methodologies were used in this research: direct investigations of brain function through lesion generation or brain stimulation in animal subjects, and studies of patients who had sustained brain damage, particularly localized brain damage. During the past decade, neuroimaging has come into its own as a method of investigating brain function, since the brain, brain pathology, and brain function can now be clearly visualized and investigated through such relative new methods as magnetic resonance imaging (MRI) and positive emission tomography (PET). The method of studying patients with various forms of brain damage can be reasonably dated back to 1861 when Paul Broca produced his report on the case of a patient who had suddenly developed speech loss. An autopsy done on this patient revealed that he had sustained an extensive infarct in the area of the third frontal convolution of the left cerebral hemisphere. Thus, an important center in the brain for speech had been discovered, but perhaps more significantly, this case produced what many would view as the first reported example of a neuropsychological or brain-behavior relationship in a human. Indeed, to this day, the third frontal convolution of the left hemisphere is known as Broca's area, and the type of speech impairment demonstrated by the patient is known as Broca's aphasia. Following Broca's discovery, much effort was devoted to relating specific behaviors to discrete areas of the brain. Wernicke (1874) made the very important discovery that the area that mediates the comprehension as opposed to the expression of speech is not the Broca area but in a more posterior region in the left temporal lobe: the superior temporal gyrus. Other investigators sought to localize other language, cognitive, sensory, and motor abilities in the tradition of Broca and Wernicke, some using animal lesion and stimulation methods and others using clinical autopsy investigations of human brain-damaged patients. Various syndromes were described, and centers or pathways whose damage or disconnection produced these syndromes were suggested. These early neuropsychological investigations not only provided data concerning specific brain-behavior relationships but also explicitly or implicitly evolved a theory of brain function, now commonly known as classical localization theory. In essence, the brain was viewed as consisting of centers for various functions connected by neural pathways. In human subjects, presence of these centers and pathways was documented through studies of individuals who had sustained damage to either a center or the connecting links between one center and another such that they became disconnected. To this day, the behavioral consequences of this latter kind of tissue destruction is referred to as a "disconnection syndrome" (Geschwind, 1965). For example, there are patients who can speak and understand, but who cannot repeat what was just said to them. In such cases, it is postulated that there is a disconnection between the speech and auditory comprehension centers.

From beginnings of the scientific investigation of brain function, not all investigators advocated localization theory. The alternative view is that rather than functioning through centers and pathways the brain functions as a whole in an integrated manner. Views of this type are currently known as mass action, holistic, or organismic theories of brain function. While we generally think of holistic theory as a reaction to localization theory, it actually can be seen as preceding localization theory, in that the very early concepts of brain function proposed by Galen and Descartes can be understood as holistic in nature. However, what is viewed as the first scientific presentation of holistic theory was made in 1824 by Flourens, who proposed that the brain may have centers for special functions (*action propre*). But there is a unity to the system as a whole (*action commune*), and this unity dominates the entire system. Boring (1950) quotes Flourens's statement, "Unity is the great principle that reigns; it is everywhere, it dominates everything." The legacy of holistic theory has come down to us from Flourens through the neurologist Hughlings Jackson (1932), who proposed a distinction between primary and secondary symptoms of brain damage. The primary symptoms are the direct consequences of the insult to the brain itself, while the secondary symptoms are the changes that take place in the unimpaired stratum. Thus, a lesion produces changes not only at its site but throughout the brain. In contemporary neuropsychology, the strongest advocates of holistic theory were Kurt Goldstein, Martin Scheerer, and Heinz Werner. Goldstein and Scheerer (1941) are best known for their distinction between abstract and concrete behavior, their description of the "abstract attitude," and the tests they devised to study abstract and concrete functioning in brain-damaged patients. Their major proposition was that many symptoms of brain damage can be viewed not as specific manifestations of damage to centers or connecting pathways but as some form of impairment of the abstract attitude. The abstract attitude is not localized in any region of the brain but depends on the functional integrity of the brain as a whole. Goldstein (1959) describes the abstract attitude as the capacity to transcend immediate sensory impressions and consider situations from a conceptual standpoint. Generally, it is viewed as underlying such functions as planning, forming intentions, developing concepts, and separating ourselves from immediate sensory experience. The abstract attitude is evaluated objectively primarily through the use of concept formation tests that involve sorting or related categorical abilities. In language it is evaluated by testing the patient's ability to use speech symbolically. Often this testing is accomplished by asking the patient to produce a narrative about some object that is not present in the immediate situation.

Heinz Werner and various collaborators applied many of Goldstein's concepts to studies of brain-injured and mentally retarded children (e.g., Werner & Strauss, 1942). His analyses and conceptualizations reflected an orientation toward gestalt psychology and holistic concepts, dealing with such matters as figure-ground relationships and rigidity. Halstead (1947) made use of the concept of the abstract attitude in his conceptualizations of brain function, but in a modified form. Like most contemporary neuropsychologists, Halstead viewed abstraction as one component or factor in cognitive function among many and did not give it the central role attributed to it by Goldstein and his followers. Correspondingly, rather than adhering to an extreme position concerning the absence of localization, Halstead provided evidence to suggest that the frontal lobes were of greater importance in regard to mediation of abstract behavior than were other regions of the brain. Goldstein (1936) also came to accept the view that the frontal lobes were particularly important in regard to mediation of the abstract attitude.

The notion of a nonlocalized generalized deficit underlying many of the specific behavioral phenomena associated with brain damage has survived to some extent in contemporary neuropsychology, but in a greatly modified form. Similarly, some aspects of classical localization theory are still with us, but also with major changes (Mesulam, 1985). None of the current theories accepts the view that there is no localization of function in the brain, and correspondingly, none of them would deny that there are some behaviors that cannot be localized to some structure or group of structures. This synthesis is reflected in a number of modern concepts of brain function, the most explicit one probably being that of Luria (1973), who developed the concept of functional systems as an alternative to both strict localization and mass action theories. Basically, a functional system consists of a number of elements involved in the mediation of some complex behavior. For example, there may be a functional system for auditory comprehension of language. The concept of pluripotentiality is substituted for Lashley's (1950/1960) older concept of equipotentiality. Equipotentiality theory suggests that any tissue in a functional area can carry out the functions previously mediated by destroyed tissue. Pluripotentiality is a more limited concept suggesting that one particular structure or element may be involved in many functional systems. Thus, no structure in the brain is involved in only a single function. Depending on varying conditions, the same structure may play a role in several functional systems.

Current neuropsychological thought reflects some elements of all of the general theories of brain function briefly outlined above. In essence, it is thought that the brain is capable of highly localized activity directed toward control of certain behaviors, but also of mediating other behaviors through means other than geographically localized centers. Indeed, since discovery of the neurotransmitters (chemical substances that appear to play an important role in brain function), there appears to have been a marked change in how localization of function is viewed. To some authorities at least, localization is important only because the receptor sites for specific neurotransmitters appear to be selectively distributed in the brain. As we will see later, neuroscientists now tend to think not only in terms of geographical localization but of neurochemical localization as well. With regard to clinical neuropsychology, however, the main point seems to be that there are both specific and nonspecific effects of brain damage. Evidence for this point of view has been presented most clearly by Teuber and his associates (Teuber, 1959) and by Satz (1966). The Teuber group was able to show that patients with penetrating brain wounds that produced very focal damage had symptoms that could be directly attributed to the lesion site, but they also had other symptoms that were shared by all patients studied, regardless of their specific lesion sites. For example, a patient with a posterior lesion might have an area of cortical blindness associated with the specific lesion site in the visual projection areas, but he or she might also have difficulties in performing complex nonvisual tasks such as placing blocks into a formboard while blindfolded. Most of Teuber's patients had difficulty with formboard type and other complex tasks regardless of specific lesion site. In clinical settings we may see brain-damaged patients with this combination of specific and nonspecific symptoms as well as patients with only nonspecific symptoms. One of the difficulties with early localization theory is that investigators tended to be unaware of the problem of nonspecific symptoms and so only reported the often more dramatic specific symptoms.

An old principle of brain function in higher organisms that has held up well and that is commonly employed in clinical neuropsychology involves contralateral control: the right half of the brain controls the left side of the body and vice versa. Motor, auditory, and somatosensory fibers cross over at the base of the brain and thus control the contralateral side of the body. In the case of vision the crossover is atypical. The optic nerve enters a structure called the optic chiasm, at which point fibers coming from the outer or temporal halves of the retinas go to the ipsilateral side of the brain, while fibers from the inner or nasal halves cross over and go the contralateral cerebral hemispheres. However, the pattern is thought to be complete, and all fibers coming from a particular hemiretina take the same course. In the case of somesthesis, hearing, and motor function, the crossover is not complete, but the majority of fibers do cross over. Thus, for example, most of the fibers from the right auditory nerve find their way to the left cerebral hemisphere. The contralateral control principle is important for clinical neuropsychology because it explains why patients with damage to one side of the brain only may become paralyzed on the opposite side of their body or may develop sensory disturbances on that side. We see this condition most commonly in individuals who have had strokes, but it is also seen in some patients who have head injuries or brain tumors.

While aphasia, or impaired communicative abilities, as a result of brain damage was recognized before Broca (Benton & Joynt, 1960), it was not recognized that it was associated with destruction of a particular area of one side of the brain. Thus, the basic significance of Broca's discovery was not the discovery of aphasia, but of cerebral dominance. Cerebral dominance is the term that is commonly employed to denote the fact that the human brain has a hemisphere that is dominant for language and a nondominant hemisphere. In most people, the left hemisphere is dominant, and left hemisphere brain damage may lead to aphasia. However, some individuals have dominant right hemispheres, while others do not appear to have a dominant hemisphere. What was once viewed as a strong relationship between handedness and choice of dominant hemisphere has not held up in recent studies. But the answers to questions regarding why the left hemisphere is dominant in most people and why some people are right dominant or have no apparent dominance remain unknown. In any event, it seems clear that for individuals who sustain left hemisphere brain damage, aphasia is a common symptom, while aphasia is a rare consequence of damage to the right hemisphere. Following Broca's discovery, other neuroscientists discovered that just as the left hemisphere has specialized functions in the area of language, the right hemisphere also has its own specialized functions. These functions all seem to relate to nonverbal abilities such as visual-spatial skills, perception of complex visual configurations, and, to some extent, appreciation of nonverbal auditory stimuli such as music. Some investigators have conceptualized the problem in terms of sequential as opposed to simultaneous abilities. The left hemisphere is said to deal with material in a sequential, analytic manner, while the right hemisphere functions more as a detector of patterns or configurations (Dean, 1986). Thus, while patients with left hemisphere brain damage tend to have difficulty with language and other activities that involve sequencing, patients with right hemisphere brain damage have difficulties with such tasks as copying figures and producing constructions since these tasks involve either perception or synthesis of patterns. In view of these findings regarding specialized functions of the right hemisphere, many neuropsychologists now prefer to use the expression "functional asymmetries of the cerebral hemispheres" rather than "cerebral dominance." The former terminology suggests that one hemisphere does not really dominate or lead the other. Rather, each hemisphere has its own specialized functions.

As indicated above, localization alone is not the sole determinant of the behavioral outcomes of brain damage. While age, sociocultural, and personality factors make their contributions, perhaps the most important consideration is the type of brain damage. Some would argue that neuropsychological assessment is rarely the best method of determining type of brain damage because other techniques such as the CT scan, cerebral blood flow studies, and, more recently, MRI are more adequate for that purpose. That view has been reinforced since the writing of the previous version of this chapter by substantial advances in neuroimaging including development of new procedures such as functional MRI by means of which activated brain function can be observed during the MRI procedure, and magnetic resonance spectroscopy (MRS), a procedure that allows for generation of neurochemical spectra reflecting brain metabolism at a molecular level.

While this point may be well taken, the problem remains that different types of lesions produce different behavioral outcomes even when they involve precisely the same areas of the brain. Thus, the clinician should be aware that the assessment methodology he or she uses may not be the best one to meet some specific diagnostic goal, and it is often necessary to use a variety of methods coming from different disciplines to arrive at an adequate description of the patient's condition. In the present context, an adequate description generally involves identification of the kind of brain damage the patient has as well as its location. In order to point out the implications of this principle, it is necessary to provide a brief outline of the types of pathology that involve the brain and their physical and behavioral consequences.

NEUROPATHOLOGICAL CONSIDERATIONS

The brain may incur many of the illnesses that afflict other organs and organ systems. It may be damaged by trauma or it may become infected. The brain can become cancerous or can lose adequate oxygen through occlusion of the blood vessels that supply it. The brain can be affected through acute or chronic exposure to toxins, such as carbon monoxide or other poisonous substances. Nutritional deficiencies can alter brain function just as they alter the function of other organs and organ systems. Aside from these general systemic and exogenous factors, there are diseases that more or less specifically have the central nervous system as their target. These conditions, generally known as degenerative and demyelinating diseases, include Huntington's disease, multiple sclerosis, Parkinson's disease, and a number of disorders associated with aging. From the point of view of neuropsychological considerations, it is useful to categorize the various disorders according to temporal and topographical parameters. Thus, certain neuropathological conditions are static and do not change substantially; others are slowly progressive, and some are rapidly progressive. With regard to topography, certain conditions tend to involve focal, localized disease, others multifocal lesions, and still others diffuse brain damage without specific localization. Another very important consideration has to do with morbidity and mortality. Some brain disorders are more or less reversible, some are static and do not produce marked change in the patient over lengthy periods of time, while some are rapidly or slowly progressive, producing increasing morbidity and eventually leading to death. Thus, some types of brain damage produce a stable condition with minimal changes, some types permit substantial recovery, while other types are in actuality terminal illnesses. It is therefore apparent that the kind of brain disorder the patient suffers from is a crucial clinical consideration in that it has major implications for treatment, management, and planning.

Head Trauma

While the skull affords the brain a great deal of protection, severe blows to the head can produce temporary brain dysfunction or permanent brain injury. The temporary conditions, popularly known as concussions, are generally self-limiting and follow a period of confusion, dizziness, and perhaps double vision. However, there seems to be complete recovery. In these cases, the brain is not thought to be permanently damaged. More serious trauma is generally classified as closed or open head injury. In closed head injury, which is more common, the vault of the skull is not penetrated, but the impact of the blow crashes the brain against the skull and thus may create permanent structural damage. A commonly occurring type of closed head injury is the subdural hematoma in which a clot of blood forms under the dura: one of the protective layers on the external surface of the brain. These clots produce pressure on the brain that may be associated with clear-cut neurological symptoms. They may be removed surgically, but even when that is done there may be persistent residual symptoms of a localized nature, such as weakness of one side of the body. In the case of open head injury, the skull is penetrated by a missile of some kind. Open head injuries occur most commonly during wartime as a result of bullet wounds. They sometimes occur as a result of vehicular or industrial accidents, if some rapidly moving object penetrates the skull. Open head injuries are characterized by the destruction of brain tissue in a localized area. There are generally thought to be more remote effects as well, but usually, the most severe symptoms are likely to be associated with the track of the missile through the brain. Thus, an open head injury involving the left temporal lobe could produce an aphasia, while similar injury to the back of the head could produce a visual disturbance. A major neuropsychological difference between open and closed head injury is that while the open injury typically produces specific, localized symptoms, the closed head injury, with the possible exception of subdural hematoma, produces diffuse dysfunction without specific focal symptoms. In both cases, some of these symptoms may disappear with time, while others may persist. There is generally a sequence of phases that applies to the course of both closed and open head injury. Often, the patient is initially unconscious and may remain that way for an extremely varying amount of time, ranging from minutes to weeks or months. After consciousness is regained, the patient generally goes through a so-called acute phase during which there may be confusion and disorientation.

Very often a condition called posttraumatic amnesia is present, in which the patient cannot recall events that immediately preceded the trauma up to the present time. Research has shown that length of time spent unconscious as well as length of posttraumatic amnesia are reasonably accurate prognostic signs; the longer either persist, the worse the prognosis. During this stage seizures are common, and treatment with anticonvulsant drugs is often necessary. When the patient emerges from this acute phase, the confusion diminishes, amnesia may persist but may not be severe as previously, the seizures may abate, and one gets a better picture of what the long-term outcome will be. The range of variability here is extremely wide, extending from patients remaining in persistent vegetative states to essentially complete recovery of function. In general, the residual difficulties of the head trauma patient, when they are significant, represent a combination of cognitive and physical symptoms. With regard to the latter, these patients are often more or less permanently confined to wheelchairs because of partial paralysis. Frequently there are sensory handicaps such as partial loss of vision or hearing.

Trauma to the head not only can do damage to the brain but to other parts of the head as well, such as the eyes and ears. Additionally, there is sometimes substantial disfigurement in the form of scars, some of which can be treated with cosmetic surgery. The cognitive residual symptoms of head trauma are extremely varied since they are associated with whether the injury was open head or closed head and whether there was clear tissue destruction. Most often, patients with closed head injury have generalized intellectual deficits involving abstract reasoning ability, memory, and judgment. Sometimes marked personality changes are noted, often having the characteristic of increased impulsiveness and exaggerated affective responsivity. Patients suffering from the residual of open head injury may have classic neuropsychological syndromes such as aphasia, visual-spatial disorders, and specific types of memory or perceptual disorders. In these cases, symptoms tend to be strongly associated with the lesion site. For example, a patient with left hemisphere brain damage may have an impaired memory for verbal material such as names of objects, while the right hemisphere patient may have an impaired memory for nonverbal material such as pictures or musical compositions. In these cases there is said to be both modality (e.g., memory) and material (e.g., verbal stimuli) specificity. Head trauma is generally thought to be the most frequently seen type of brain damage in adolescents and young adults. It therefore generally occurs in a reasonably healthy brain. When the combination of a young person with a healthy brain exists, the prognosis for recovery is generally good if the wound itself is not devastating in terms of its extent or the area of the brain involved. For practical purposes, residual brain damage is a static condition that does not generate progressive changes for the worse. While there is some research evidence

(Walker, Caveness, & Critchley, 1969) that following a long quiescent phase, head-injured individuals may begin to deteriorate more rapidly than normal when they become elderly, head-injured individuals may nevertheless have many years of productive functioning.

There is increasing interest in outcome following mild head injury (Levin, Eisenberg, & Benton, 1989), as well as in the specific problems associated with head injury in children (Goethe & Levin, 1986). It has been frequently pointed out in recent years that trauma is the major cause of death in children, and head trauma among children is not uncommon. The issue of the residual effects of mild head injury has become increasingly controversial, with some authorities claiming that there is no significant residual effect that can be directly attributed to the injury itself, with others taking the opposite position (Beers, 1992). The Beers review provides a persuasive case for the conclusion that mild head injury can have significant cognitive, emotional, and social consequences.

Brain Tumors

Cancer of the brain is a complex area, particularly since cancer in general is not as yet completely understood. However, the conventional distinction between malignant and nonmalignant tumors is a useful one for the brain as it is for other organs and organ systems. Thus, some brain tumors are destructive, rapidly progressive, and essentially untreatable. Generally, these tissue structures are known as intrinsic tumors since they directly infiltrate the parenchyma of the brain. The most common type is a class of tumor that is known as glioma. Other types of tumors grow on the external surface of the brain and produce symptoms through the exertion of pressure on brain tissue. This type of tumor is described as being extrinsic, and the most common type is called a meningioma. Aside from these two types, there are metastases in which tumors have spread to the brain from some other organ of the body, often the lung. The extrinsic tumors are often treatable surgically, but metastases are essentially untreatable. The clinical symptoms of tumor include headache that frequently occurs at night or on awakening, seizures, and vomiting. There are often progressive cognitive changes, perhaps beginning with some degree of confusion and poor comprehension and progressing to severe dementia during the terminal stages. Since tumors often begin in quite localized areas of the brain, the symptoms associated with them tend to depend on the particular location affected. For example, there is a large literature on frontal lobe tumors in which impairment of judgment, apathy, and general loss of the ability to regulate and modulate behavior are the major symptoms. As in the case of head injury, patients with left hemisphere tumors may develop aphasia, while patients with right hemisphere tumors may have visual-spatial disorders as their most prominent symptoms. The difference from head injury is that short of surgical intervention, the severity of symptoms increases with time, sometimes at a very slow and sometimes at a very rapid rate, depending on the type of tumor. On rare occasions, the clinical psychologist or psychiatrist may see patients with tumors that affect particular structures in the brain, thereby generating characteristic syndromes. Among the most common of these are cranial pharyngiomas, pituitary adenomas, and acoustic neuromas.

Cranial pharyngiomas are cystic growths that lie near the pituitary gland and often depress the optic chiasm so that the primary symptoms may involve delayed development in children and waning libido and amenorrhea in adults, in combination with weakening of vision. Pituitary adenomas are similar in location but the visual loss is often more prominent, frequently taking the form of what is called a bitemporal hemianopia: a loss of vision in both peripheral fields. Acoustic neuromas are tumors of the auditory nerve and thereby produce hearing loss as the earliest symptom. However, because the auditory nerve also has a vestibular component, there may be progressive unsteadiness of gait and dizziness. Clinicians may also see patients who have had surgically treated tumors. When these patients demonstrate residual neuropsychological symptoms, they look like patients with histories of open head injury. Perhaps that is because the brain lesion has, in a manner of speaking, been converted from a mass of abnormal tissue to a stable, nonmalignant wound. When neurosurgery has been successful, the changes are often rapid and very substantial. One is normally concerned about recurrence, and these patients should remain under continued medical care. However, successful surgical treatment may leave the patient with many years of productive life.

Brain Malformations and Early-Life Brain Damage

Perhaps nowhere among the brain disorders is the type of lesion issue as significant as it is in the case of the developmental disorders of brain function. The crux of the matter here is that there is a great deal of difference between destruction of a function already acquired and destruction of the brain mechanisms needed to acquire that function before it has been developed. Thus, consequences of being born with an abnormal brain or acquiring brain damage during the early years of life may be quite different from consequences of acquiring brain damage as an adult. On the positive side, the young brain generally has greater plasticity than the older brain, and it is somewhat easier for preserved structures to take over functions of impaired structures. On the negative side, however, when the brain mechanisms usually involved in acquisition of some function are absent or impaired, that function is often not learned or not learned at a normal level. While the relationship between age and consequences of brain damage remains an intensively researched area (Satz, 1993), for practical purposes it can be said that there is a population of individuals born with abnormal brain function, or who have sustained structural brain damage at or shortly after birth, who go on to have developmental histories of either generalized or specific cognitive subnormality. Those with generalized deficit, when it is sufficiently severe, are frequently described with a variety of terms such as minimal brain damage, learning disability, and attention-deficit disorder.

One common subclass of this specific group consists of children who fail to learn to read normally despite adequate educational opportunity and average intelligence. These children are described as having dyslexia or developmental dyslexia. With regard to neuropathological considerations, there are several types of brain disorder that may occur during the prenatal period. Some of them are developmental in nature in the sense that either the brain itself or the skull does not grow normally during gestation. When the skull is involved, the brain is damaged through the effects of pressure on it. Sometimes a genetic factor is present as is clearly the case with Down's syndrome. Sometimes poor prenatal care is the responsible agent, the fetal alcohol syndrome perhaps being an extreme case of this condition. Sometimes an infection acquired during pregnancy, notably rubella (German measles), can produce severe mental retardation in the embryo. Probably most often, however, the cases of the developmental abnormality are unknown.

Damage to the brain can also occur as the result of a traumatic birth. Such conditions as cerebral anoxia, infection, and brain dysfunction associated with such ongoing conditions as malnutrition or exposure to toxic substances are the major agents. Children have strokes and brain tumors, but they are quite rare. In essence, brain damage can occur in the very young before, during, and after birth. While the neuropathological distinctions among the various disorders are quite important, the life span development of individuals from all three categories share some common characteristics. And retrospectively, it is often difficult to identify the responsible agent in the school-age child or adult. Thus, it is sometimes useful to think in terms of some general concept, such as perinatal or early-life brain damage, rather than to attempt to specifically relate a particular developmental course or pattern of functioning to a single entity.

While early-life brain damage is usually a static condition in the sense that the lesion itself does not change, it may have varying consequences throughout life. During the preschool years, the child may not achieve the generally accepted landmarks, such as walking and talking at the average times. In school, these children often do not do well academically and may be either poor learners in general or have specific disabilities in such areas as reading, arithmetic, or visual-spatial skills. These academic difficulties may be accompanied by some form of behavior disorder, often manifested in the form of hyperactivity or diminished attentional capacity. During adulthood, it is often found that these individuals do not make satisfactory vocational adjustments, and many researchers now feel that they are particularly vulnerable to certain psychiatric disorders, notably alcoholism (Tarter, 1976) or schizophrenia (Mednick, 1970).

We would note that, while this volume does not address itself to child psychopathology, there are several disorders that would now be classed as neurobehavioral disorders that begin during childhood but persist into adulthood. There is growing evidence (McCue & Goldstein, 1991; Spreen, 1987) that learning disability frequently persists into adulthood. Autism, which is now generally viewed as a neurobehavioral disorder (Minshew & Payton, 1988a, 1988b) also persists into adulthood. A recent study (Rumsey & Hamburger, 1988) that followed up some of Kanner's (1943) original cases demonstrated persistence of neuropsychological deficit in these autistic adults. There is also increasing acknowledgement that attention-deficit hyperactivity disorder, also traditionally viewed as a disorder of childhood, may persist into adulthood (Hallowell & Ratey, 1994).

Diseases of the Circulatory System

Current thinking about the significance of vascular disease has changed in recent years from the time when it was felt that cerebral arteriosclerosis or "hardening of the arteries" was the major cause of generalized brain dysfunction in the middle-aged and elderly. While this condition is much less common than was once thought, the status of the heart and the blood vessels is significantly related to the intactness of brain function. Basically, the brain requires oxygen to function, and oxygen is distributed to the brain through the cerebral blood vessels. When these vessels become occluded, circulation is compromised and brain function is correspondingly impaired. Such impairment occurs in a number of ways, perhaps the most serious and abrupt way being stroke. A stroke is a sudden total blockage of a cerebral artery caused by blood clot or a hemorrhage. The clot may be a thrombosis formed out of atherosclerotic plaque at branches and curves in the cerebral arteries or an embolism, which is a fragment that has broken away from a thrombus in the heart that has migrated to the brain. Cerebral hemorrhages are generally fatal, but survival from thrombosis or embolism is not at all uncommon. Following a period of stupor or unconsciousness, the most common and apparent postacute symptom is hemiplegia: paralysis of one side of the body. There is also a milder form of stroke known as a transient ischemic attack (TIA), which is basically a temporary, self-reversing stroke that does not produce severe syndromes or may be essentially asymptomatic.

A somewhat different picture emerges in another cerebral vascular disorder that was called multi-infarct dementia in DSM-III-R. As opposed to the abruptly rapid onset seen in stroke, multi-infarct dementia is a progressive condition based on a history of small strokes associated with hypertension. Patients with multi-infarct dementia experience a stepwise deterioration of function, with each small stroke making the dementia worse in some way. There are parallels between multi-infarct dementia and the older concept of cerebral arteriosclerosis, in that they both relate to the role of generalized cerebral vascular disease in producing progressive brain dysfunction. However, multi-infarct dementia is actually a much more precisely defined syndrome that, while not rare, is not extremely common either. As we will see, many of the patients that used to be diagnosed as having cerebral arteriosclerosis would now be diagnosed as having one of the degenerative diseases associated with the presenile or senile period of life. Since the previous version of this chapter was written, the concept of multi-infarct dementia has been questioned, and the diagnosis has been abandoned by DSM-IV. The disorder is now called vascular dementia, and there is no requirement for a stepwise deteriorative course, although that may occur. The major requirements are that criteria for dementia are met and that there is evidence for cerebral vascular disease such as multiple strokes.

Other relatively common cerebrovascular disorders are associated with aneurysms and other vascular malformations in the brain. An aneurysm is an area of weak structure in a blood vessel that may not produce symptoms until it balloons out to the extent that it creates pressure effects or it ruptures. A ruptured aneurysm is an extremely serious medical condition in that it may lead to sudden death. However, surgical intervention in which the aneurysm is ligated is often effective.

Arteriovenous malformations are congenitally acquired tangles of blood vessels. They may be asymptomatic for many years, but can eventually rupture and hemorrhage. They may appear anywhere in the brain, but commonly they occur in the posterior half. The symptoms produced, when they occur, may include headache and neurological signs associated with the particular site.

There are major neuropsychological differences between the individual with a focal vascular lesion, most commonly associated with stroke, and the patient with generalized vascular disease such as vascular dementia. The stroke patient is not only characterized by the hemiplegia or hemiparesis, but sometimes by an area of blindness in the right or left visual fields and commonly by a pattern of behavioral deficits associated with the hemisphere of the brain affected and the locus within that hemisphere. If the stroke involves a blood vessel in the left hemisphere, the patient will be paralyzed or weak on the right side of the body; the area of blindness, if present, will involve the right field of vision and there will frequently be an aphasia. Right hemisphere strokes may produce left-sided weakness or paralysis and left visual fields defects but no aphasia. Instead, a variety of phenomena may occur. The patient may acquire a severe difficulty with spatial relations, a condition known as constructional apraxia. The ability to recognize faces or to appreciate music may be affected. A phenomenon known as unilateral neglect may develop in which the patient does not attend to stimuli in the left visual field, although it may be demonstrated that basic vision is intact. Sometimes affective changes occur in which the patient denies that he or she is ill and may even develop euphoria. In contrast with this specific, localized symptom picture seen in the stroke patient, the individual with vascular dementia or other generalized cerebral vascular disease has quite a different set of symptoms. Generally, there is no unilateral paralysis, no visual field deficit, no gross aphasia, and none of the symptoms characteristic of patients with right hemisphere strokes. Rather there is a picture of generalized intellectual, and to some extent physical, deterioration. If weakness is present, it is likely to affect both sides of the body, and typically there is general diminution of intellectual functions including memory, abstraction ability, problem-solving ability, and speed of thought and action. In the case of the patient with vascular dementia, there may be localizing signs, but there would tend to be several of them, and they would not point to a single lesion in one specific site.

The more common forms of cerebral vascular disease are generally not seen until at least middle age and for the most part are diseases of the elderly. Clinically significant cerebral vascular disease is often associated with a history of generalized cardiovascular or other systemic diseases, notably hypertension and diabetes. There are some genetic or metabolic conditions that promote greater production of atheromatous material than is normal, and some people are born with arteriovenous malformations or aneurysms, placing them at higher than usual risk for serious cerebral vascular disease. When a stroke is seen in a young adult it is usually because of an aneurysm or other vascular malformation. Most authorities agree that stroke is basically caused by atherosclerosis, and so genetic and acquired conditions that promote atherosclerotic changes in blood vessels generate risk of stroke. With modern medical treatment there is a good deal of recovery from stroke with substantial restoration of function. However, in the case of the diffuse disorders, there is really no concept of recovery since they tend to be slowly progressive. The major hope is to minimize the risk of future strokes through such means as controlling blood pressure and weight.

An area of recently developed interest has to do with the long-term effects of hypertension on cerebral function, as well as the long-term effects of antihypertensive medication. Based on literature reviews, Elias and Streeten (1980) and King and Miller (1990) have suggested that hypertension in itself, as well as antihypertensive medication, can impair cognitive function, but there are no definite conclusions in this area as yet, with studies reporting mixed as well as benign outcomes associated with prudent use of antihypertensive medication (Goldstein, 1986).

Degenerative and Demyelinating Diseases

The degenerative and demyelinating diseases constitute a variety of disorders that have a number of characteristics in common, but that are also widely different from each other in many ways. What they have in common is that they specifically attack the central nervous system, they are slowly progressive and incurable, and while they are not all hereditary diseases, they appear to stem from some often unknown but endogenous defect in physiology. Certain diseases, once thought to be degenerative, have been found not to be so or are thought not to be so at present. For example, certain dementias have been shown to be caused by a "slow virus," while multiple sclerosis, the major demyelinating disease, is strongly suspected of having viral etiology. Thus, in these two examples, the classification would change from degenerative to infectious disease.

The term "degenerative disease" simply means that for some unknown reason the brain or the entire central nervous system gradually wastes away. In some cases such wasting, or atrophy, resembles what happens to the nervous system in very old people, but substantially earlier than the senile period—perhaps as early as the late forties. These diseases are known as presenile dementia, the commonest type being Alzheimer's disease. Alzheimer's disease also occurs in a senile form, but there is some controversy as to whether the senile and the presenile forms are in actuality the same disease. Senile dementia is generally diagnosed in elderly individuals when the degree of cognitive deficit is substantially greater than one would expect with normal aging. In other words, not all old people become significantly demented before death. Most of those who do, but do not have another identifiable disease of the central nervous system, are generally thought to have Alzheimer's disease. Indeed, Alzheimer's disease is now thought to account for more senile dementia than does cerebral arteriosclerosis.

There is another disorder related to Alzheimer's disease call Pick's disease, but it is difficult to distinguish from Alzheimer's disease in living individuals. The distinction only becomes apparent at autopsy, since the neuropathological changes in the brain are different. There has been a recent change within psychiatry with regard to the attempt to differentiate clinically among Alzheimer's, Pick's, and some rarer degenerative diseases. DSM-III (APA, 1980) describes these disorders with the single term "primary degenerative dementia." DSM-III-R uses the term "primary degenerative dementia of the Alzheimer type." DSM-IV has separate codes for dementia due to HIV disease, head trauma, Parkinson's disease, Huntington's disease, Pick's disease, Creutzfeldt-Jakob disease, and other general medical conditions. We would assume that these changes are based on recent developments in assessment procedures including major advances in structural and functional neuroimaging, genetic testing, particularly with regard to Huntington's disease, and new procedures such as MRS.

There is another frequently occurring degenerative disease found in younger adults called Huntington's chorea or Huntington's disease. The disease is characterized by progressive intellectual deterioration and a motor disorder involving gait disturbance and involuntary jerky, spasmodic movements. It has definitely been established as a hereditary disorder, and there is a 50% chance of acquiring the disease if born to a carrier of the gene for it. Symptoms may begin to appear during the second or third decade, and survival from the time of appearance of symptoms is generally about 8 years. The intellectual deterioration is characterized by progressively profound impairment of memory, with most cognitive functions eventually becoming involved. There is often a speech articulation difficulty because of loss of control of the musculature involved in speech.

While much is still not known about the degenerative disorders, much has been discovered in recent years. The major discovery was that Alzheimer's and Huntington's diseases are apparently associated with neurochemical deficiencies. In the case of Alzheimer's disease, the deficiency is thought to be primarily in the group of substances related to choline, one of the neurotransmitters. The disease process itself is characterized by progressive death of the choline neurons, the cells that serve as receptor sites for cholinergic agents. Huntington's disease is more neurochemically complex because three neurotransmitters are involved: choline, GABA, and substance P. As indicated above, the gene for this disorder has been identified. The reasons for these neurochemical deficiency states remain unknown, but the states themselves have been described, and treatment efforts have been initiated based on this information. For example, some Alzheimer's patients are being given the new drug tacrine hydrochloride in the hope of achieving symptomatic improvement. There is extensive ongoing research with related drugs.

Multiple sclerosis is the most common of the demyelinating diseases and is described as such because its pathology involves progressive erosion of the myelin sheaths that surround fibers in the central nervous system. Both the brain and the spinal cord are involved in this illness. Nerve conduction takes place along the myelin sheaths and therefore cannot occur normally when these sheaths erode. This abnormality leads to motor symptoms, such as paralysis, tremor, and loss of coordination, but there are characteristic changes in vision if the optic nerve is involved and in cognitive function. Obviously, cognitive skills that involve motor function tend to be more impaired than those that do not. Until its final stages, multiple sclerosis does not have nearly as devastating an effect on cognitive function as do the degenerative diseases. The crippling motor disorder may be the only apparent and significantly disabling symptom for many years. Less often, but not infrequently, progressive loss of vision also occurs. Multiple sclerosis acts much like an infectious disease, and some authorities feel that it is, in fact, caused by some unknown viral agent. Symptoms generally appear during young adulthood and may be rapidly or slowly progressive, leading some authorities to differentiate between acute and chronic multiple sclerosis. Individuals with this disorder may live long lives; there are sometimes lengthy periods during which no deterioration takes place. Sometimes temporary remission of particular symptoms is seen. In recent years, there have been extensive neuropsychological studies of multiple sclerosis (reviewed in Allen & Goreczny, 1995; Peyser & Poser, 1986), and a particular interest in differences between relapsing-remitting and chronic-progessive forms of the disease (Heaton et al., 1985).

Alcoholism

The term "alcoholism" in the context of central nervous system function involves not only the matter of excessive consumption of alcoholic beverages, but a complex set of considerations involving nutritional status, related disorders such as head trauma, physiological alterations associated with the combination of excessive alcohol consumption and malnutrition, and possible genetic factors. All of these elements, and perhaps others as well, may influence the status of the central nervous system in alcoholic patients. What is frequently observed in long-term chronic alcoholics is a pattern of deterioration of intellectual function not unlike what is seen in patients with primary degenerative dementia. However, it is not clear that the deteriorative process is specifically associated with alcohol consumption per se. Thus, while some clinicians use the term alcoholic dementia, this characterization lacks sufficient specificity since it is rarely at all clear that the observed dementia is in fact solely a product of excessive use of alcohol. DSM-IV does not use the term "dementia associated with alcoholism," substituting "substance-induced persisting dementia." The diagnosis is recorded by indicating the substance, followed by that term. Thus, if the substance is alcohol, the diagnosis would be "alcohol-induced persisting dementia." This terminology change may be in recognition of the numerous substances that can be associated with dementia (inhalants, sedatives, industrial solvents, etc.) and the increasing incidence of polysubstance abuse, dependency, or exposure.

Looking at the matter in temporal perspective, there first of all may be a genetic propensity for acquisition of alcoholism that might ultimately have implications for central nervous system function (Goodwin, 1979). Second, Tarter (1976) has suggested that there may be an association between having minimal brain damage or a hyperactivity syndrome as a child and acquisition of alcoholism as an adult. These two considerations suggest the possibility that at least some individuals who eventually become alcoholics may not have completely normal brain function anteceding development of alcoholism. Third, during the course of becoming chronically alcoholic, dietary habits tend to become poor and multiple head injuries may be sustained as a result of fights or accidents. As the combination of excessive alcohol abuse and poor nutrition progresses, major physiological changes may occur particularly in the liver and to some extent in the pancreas and gastrointestinal system. Thus, the dementia seen in long-term alcoholic patients may well involve a combination of all of these factors in addition to the always present possibility of other neurological complications.

While most alcoholics who develop central nervous system complication manifest it in the form of general deterioration of intellectual abilities, some develop specific syndromes. The most common of these is the Wernicke-Korsakoff syndrome. The Wernicke-Korsakoff disorder begins with the patient's going into a confusional state accompanied by difficulty in walking and controlling eye movements, and by polyneuritis, a condition marked by pain or loss of sensation in the arms and legs. The latter symptoms may gradually disappear, but the confusional state may evolve into a permanent, severe amnesia. When this transition has taken place, the patient is generally described as having Korsakoff's syndrome or alcohol amnestic disorder and is treated with large dosages of thiamine, since the etiology of the disorder appears to be a thiamine deficiency rather than a direct consequence of alcohol ingestion. There is now evidence (Blass & Gibson, 1977) that thiamine deficiency must be accompanied by an inborn metabolic defect related to an enzyme that metabolizes thiamine. It should be noted that amnesic and intellectual disorders found in chronic alcoholics are permanent and present even when the patient is not intoxicated. The acute effects of intoxication or withdrawal (e.g., delirium tremens [DTs]) are superimposed on these permanent conditions. These disorders are also progressive as long as the abuse of alcohol and malnutrition persist. Other than abstinence and improved nutrition, there is no specific treatment. Even thiamine treatment for the Korsakoff patient does not restore memory; it is used primarily to prevent additional brain damage.

It is probably fair to say that a major interest in recent years has been the genetics of alcoholism. Findings have been impressive thus far, and there is a growing, probably well-justified belief that presence in an individual of a positive family history of alcoholism puts that individual at increased risk for becoming alcoholic if exposed to beverage alcohol. The research done has been broad ranging, including extensive family adoption studies (Goodwin, Schulsinger, Hermansen, Guze, & Winokur, 1973), neuropsychological studies of relatives (Schaeffer, Parsons, & Yohman, 1984) and children of alcoholics (Tarter, Hegedus, Goldstein, Shelly, & Alterman, 1984), psychophysiological studies, emphasizing brain event-related potentials in siblings (Steinhauer, Hill, & Zubin, 1987) and children (Begleiter, Porjesz, Bihari, & Kissin, 1984) of alcoholics, and laboratory genetic studies. In summary, there is an extensive effort being made to find biological markers of alcoholism (Hill, Steinhauer, & Zubin, 1987), and to determine transmission of alcoholism in families. One reasonable assumption is that alcoholism is a heterogeneous disorder and there may be both hereditary and nonhereditary forms of it (Cloninger, Bohman, & Sigvardsson, 1981).

Toxic, Infectious, and Metabolic Illnesses

The brain may be poisoned by exogenous or endogenous agents or it may become infected. Sometimes these events occur with such severity that the person dies, but more often, the individual survives with a greater or lesser degree of neurological dysfunction. Beginning with the exogenous toxins, we have already discussed the major one: alcohol. However, excessive use of drugs such as bromides and barbiturates may produce at least temporary brain dysfunction. This temporary condition, called delirium, is basically a loss of capacity to maintain attention with corresponding reduced awareness of the environment. Tremors and lethargy may be accompanying symptoms. Delirium is reversible in most cases, but may evolve into a permanent dementia or other neurological disorder.

In psychiatric settings a fairly frequently seen type of toxic disorder is carbon monoxide poisoning. This disorder and its treatment are quite complex because it usually occurs in an individual with a major mood or psychotic disorder who attempted to commit suicide by inhaling car fumes in a closed garage. The brain damage sustained during the episode may often be permanent, resulting in significant intellectual and physical dysfunction in addition to the previously existing psychiatric disorder. Other toxic substances that may affect central nervous system function include certain sedative and hypnotic drugs, plant poisons, heavy metals, and toxins produced by certain bacteria leading to such conditions as tetanus and botulism. The specific effects of these substances themselves, as well as on whether exposure is acute (as in the case of tetanus or arsenic poisoning) or chronic (as in the case of addiction to opiates and related drugs).

There is a very large number of brain disorders associated with inborn errors of metabolism. In some way, a fault in metabolism produces a detrimental effect on the nervous system, generally beginning in early life. There are so many of these disorders that we will only mention two of the better known ones as illustrations. The first of them is phenylketonuria (PKU). PKU is an amino acid uria, a disorder that involves excessive excretion of some amino acid into the urine. It is genetic and, if untreated, can produce mental retardation accompanied by poor psychomotor development and hyperactivity. The treatment involves a diet low in a substance called phenylalanine. The second disorder to be mentioned is Tay-Sach's disease. The enzyme abnormality here is a deficiency in a substance called hexasaminidase A, which is important for the metabolism of protein and polysaccharides. It is hereditary, occurs mainly in Jewish children, and is present from birth. The symptoms are initially poor motor development and progressive loss of vision, followed by dementia, with death usually occurring before age 5. These two examples illustrate similarity in process, which is basically an inherited enzyme deficiency, but variability in outcome. PKU is treatable, with a relatively favorable prognosis, while Tay-Sachs is a rapidly progressive, incurable terminal illness.

Bacterial infections of the brain are generally associated with epidemics, but sometimes are seen when there are no epidemics at large. They are generally referred to as encephalitis, when the brain itself is infected, or meningitis, when the infection is in the membranous tissue that lines the brain, known as the meninges. Infections, of course, are produced by microorganisms that invade tissue and produce inflammation. During the acute phase of the bacterial infections, the patient may be quite ill, and survival is an important issue. Headaches, fever, and a stiff neck are major symptoms. There may be delirium, confusion, and alterations in state of consciousness ranging from drowsiness, through excessive sleeping, to coma. Some forms of encephalitis used to be popularly known as "sleeping sickness." Following the acute phase of bacterial infection, the patient may be left with residual neurological and neuropsychological disabilities and personality changes. Sometimes infections are local, and the patient is left with neurological deficits that correspond with the lesion site. The irritability, restlessness, and aggressiveness of postencephalitic children are mentioned in the literature. Jervis (1959) described them as overactive, restless, impulsive, assaultive, and wantonly destructive.

Neurosyphylis is another type of infection that has a relatively unique course. Most interesting, aside from the progressive dementia that characterizes this disorder, there are major personality changes involving acquisition of delusions and a tendency toward uncritical self-aggrandizement. While neurosyphilis or general paresis played a major role in the development of psychiatry, it is now a relatively rare disease and is seldom seen in clinical practice. Similarly, the related neurosyphilitic symptoms, such as tabes dorsalis and syphilitic deafness, are also rarely seen.

While incidence and perhaps interest in the bacterial infections and neurosyphilis have diminished, interest in viral infections has increased substantially during recent years. There are perhaps four reasons for this phenomenon: Jonas Salk's discovery that poliomyelitis was caused by virus and could be prevented by vaccination, the recent increase in the incidence of herpes simplex, which is a viral disorder, the appearance of AIDS, and the discovery of the "slow viruses." The latter two reasons are probably of greatest interest in the present context. With regard to slow viruses, it has recently been discovered that certain viruses have a long incubation period and may cause chronic degenerative disease, resembling Alzheimer's disease in many ways. Thus, some forms of dementia may be produced by a transmittable agent. One of these dementias appears to be a disease known as kuru, and another is known as Creutzfeldt-Jakob disease. The importance of the finding is that the discovery of infection as the cause of disease opens the possibility of the development of preventive treatment in the form of a vaccine. As indicated above, AIDS or HIV dementia is another form of viral encephalopathy. HIV dementia is thought to be produced by the human immunodeficiency virus and has been characterized as a subcortical dementia. The tissue destruction is mainly to white matter and subcortical structures.

Epilepsy

Despite the usual manner in which this condition is described, epilepsy is a symptom of many diseases and not really a disease in itself. Patients are generally diagnosed as "epileptics" when seizures are the major or only presenting symptoms and the cause cannot be determined. However, seizures are commonly associated with diagnosable disorders such as brain tumors, alcoholism, or head trauma. Furthermore, the view that epilepsy means that the patient has "fits" or episodes of falling and engaging in uncontrolled, spasmodic movements is also not completely accurate. These fits or convulsions do represent one form of epilepsy, but there are other forms as well. There have been several attempts made to classify epilepsy into subtypes, and we will mention only the most recent one generally accepted by neurologists (Gastaut, 1970).

The major distinction made is between generalized and partial seizures. In the case of the generalized seizures there is a bilaterally symmetrical abnormality of brain function, with one of two things generally happening. One of them is a massive convulsion with a sequence of spasmodic movements and jerking, while the other is a brief abrupt loss of consciousness with little in the way of abnormal motor activity. There may be some lip smacking or involuntary movements of the eyelids. The former type used to be called a grand mal seizure, while the latter type was called a petit mal seizure or absence. The partial seizures may have what is described as a simple or complex symptomatology. In the simple case, the seizure may be confined to a single limb and may involve either motor or sensory function. When motor function is involved, there is often a turning movement of the head, accompanied by contractions of the trunk and limbs. There is a relatively rare form of this disorder called a Jacksonian motor seizure in which there is a spread of the spasmodic movements from the original site to the entire side of the body. The phenomenon is referred to as a march. In the case of sensory seizures, the epileptic activity may consist of a variety of sensory disorders such as sudden numbness, "pins and needles" feeling, seeing spots of light, or even a buzzing or roaring in the ears.

The complex partial seizures involve confused but purposeful appearing behavior followed by amnesia for the episode. In this condition, sometimes known as temporal lobe or psychomotor epilepsy, the patient may walk around in a daze, engage in inappropriate behavior, or have visual or auditory hallucinations. From this description, it is clear that not all seizures involve massive motor convulsions. What all of these phenomena have in common is that they are based on a sudden, abrupt alteration of brain function. The alteration is produced by an excessive, disorganized discharge of neurons. Thus, if one were looking at an epileptic individual's brain waves on an electroencephalograph (EEG), if a seizure occurred, there would be a sudden and dramatic alteration in the characteristics of the EEG. The presence and particular pattern of these alterations are often used to identify and diagnose various forms of epilepsy.

The question of whether there is an association between epilepsy and intellectual impairment is a complex one. According to Klove and Matthews (1974), individuals having complex partial (temporal lobe) seizures demonstrate little in the way of intellectual impairment. However, individuals with generalized seizures of unknown etiology that appear early in life are likely to have significant intellectual deficit. The matter is also complicated by the cause of the seizure. If an individual has seizures related to a brain tumor, it is likely that the neuropsychological deficits generally associated with the lesion sites involved can be expected to appear as well as the seizures. The question of intellectual deficit seems to arise primarily in the case of individuals who are just epileptic and have no other apparent neurological signs or symptoms. This condition is known as recurrent seizures of unknown cause or as idiopathic epilepsy. Our tentative answer to the question appears to be that there is a higher probability of significant intellectual deficit when the disorder involves generalized seizures and appears early in life.

The mental health practitioner should be aware that while epilepsy is an eminently treatable disorder through the use of a variety of "anticonvulsant" medications, the epileptic patient may have many difficulties of various types. There still appears to be some degree of social stigma attached to the disorder, either in the form of superstitious beliefs or the inaccurate stereotype that epileptics tend to be violent or impulsive people. More realistically, epileptics do have difficulties with such matters as obtaining drivers' licenses or insurance coverage that allows them to work around potentially hazardous equipment. It is possible that during a complex partial seizure an individual can perform an antisocial act over which he or she honestly has no control and cannot remember. Epileptic seizures may be symptoms of some life-threatening illness. Children with petit mal epilepsy may have school difficulties because of their momentary lapses of consciousness. Individuals with motor seizures may injure their heads during the seizure and produce additional brain dysfunction through trauma. Thus, the epileptic may have many problems in living that are not experienced by the nonepileptic and frequently may be assisted through an understanding of the nature of the condition, and counseling and support in coping with it.

Myslobodsky and Mirsky (1988) have edited an extensive work on petit mal epilepsy that covers its genetic, neurophysiological, neuropsychological, metabolic, and electrophysiological aspects. There is a growing interest in psychosocial aspects of epilepsy. Having seizures clearly produces an impact on one's environment, and people in the environment may maintain the older superstitions and false beliefs about epilepsy. Furthermore, modifications of behavior in epileptics may be largely biologically determined because of the cerebral dysfunction associated with the disorder. Dodrill (1986) has recently reviewed the extensive literature on psychosocial consequences of epilepsy and provided a useful outline of the types of psychosocial difficulties epileptics commonly experience, the relationship between psychosocial and neuropsychological functions, and treatment-related issues. An issue that has emerged recently with regard to treatment relates to the use of surgery. While surgery for epilepsy is limited to patients with identifiable epileptogenic foci who do not respond to medication, when it is used there is concern for decrements in cognitive function following such surgery. A comprehensive consideration of the potential risk of performing such surgery is provided by Chelune (1995).

SOME COMMON SYNDROMES

In this section we provide descriptions of the more commonly occurring disorders associated with structural brain damage. It is clear that what is common in one setting may be rare in another. Thus, we will tend to focus on what is common in an adult neuropsychiatric setting. The neuropsychological syndromes found in childhood are often quite different from what is seen in adults and deserve separate treatment. Furthermore, the emphasis will be placed on chronic rather than acute syndromes since, with relatively rare exceptions, the psychologist and psychiatrist encounter the former type far more frequently than the latter. However, initially acute conditions such as stroke that evolve into chronic conditions will be dealt with in some detail.

Thus far, we have viewed matters from the standpoints of general concepts of brain function and of neuropathological processes. Now we will be looking at the behavioral manifestations of the interaction between various brain mechanisms and different types of pathology. It is useful to view these manifestations in the form of identified patterns of behavioral characteristics that might be described as neuropsychological syndromes. While there are admittedly other ways of describing and classifying neuropsychological deficit, the syndrome approach has the advantage of providing rather graphic phenomenological descriptions of different kinds of brain-damaged patients. However, it runs the risk of suggesting that every brain-damaged patient can be classified as having some specific, identifiable syndrome—something that is not at all true. It is therefore important to keep in mind that we are discussing classic types of various disorders that are in fact seen in some actual patients. However, there are many brain-damaged patients that do not have classic-type syndromes, their symptomatology reflecting an often complex combination of portions of several syndromes.

Heilman and Valenstein (1993), in the way in which they outlined their recently revised clinical neuropsychology text, have suggested a useful and workable classification of syndromes. There are first of all the communicative disorders, which may be subdivided into aphasia and the specialized language or language-related disorders including reading impairment (alexia), writing disorders (agraphia), and calculation disorders (acalculia). Second, there are the syndromes associated with some aspect of perception or motility. These include the perception of one's body (the body schema disturbances), the various visual-spatial disorders (which may involve perception, constructional abilities, or both), the gnostic disorders (impairment of visual, auditory, and tactile recognition), the neglect syndromes, and the disorders of skilled and purposeful movement, called apraxias. Third, there are the syndromes that primarily involve general intelligence and memory: dementia and the amnesic disorders. Associated with this latter type are the relatively unique syndromes associated with damage to the frontal lobes. These three general categories account for most of the syndromes seen in adults, and our discussion here will be limited to them.

The Communicative Disorders

In general, aphasia and related language disorders are associated with unilateral brain damage to the dominant hemisphere, which in most individuals is the left hemisphere. Most aphasias result from stroke, but it can be acquired on the basis of left hemisphere head trauma or from brain tumor. While the definition has changed over the years, the most current one requires the presence of impairment of communicative ability associated with focal, structural brain damage. Thus, the term is not coextensive with all disorders of communicative ability and does not include, for example, the language disorders commonly seen in demented individuals with diffuse brain damage. The study of aphasia has in essence become a separate area of scientific inquiry, having its own literature and several theoretical frameworks. The term aphasia itself does not convey a great deal of clinically significant information since the various subtypes are quite different from each other. Numerous attempts have been made to classify the aphasias, and there is no universally accepted system. Contemporary theory indicates that perhaps the most useful major distinction is between fluent and nonfluent aphasias. To many authorities, this distinction is more accurate than the previously more commonly made one between expressive and receptive aphasias. The problem is that aphasics with primarily expressive problems do not generally have normal language comprehension, and it is almost always true that aphasics with major speech comprehension disturbances do not express themselves normally. However, there are aphasics who talk fluently and aphasics whose speech is labored, very limited, and halting, if present at all in a meaningful sense. In the case of the former group, while speech is fluent, it is generally more or less incomprehensible because of a tendency to substitute incorrect words for correct ones; a condition known as verbal paraphasia. However, the primary disturbance in these patients involves profoundly impaired auditory comprehension. This combination of impaired comprehension and paraphasia is generally known as Wernicke's aphasia. The responsible lesion is generally in the superior gyrus of the left temporal lobe. In nonfluent aphasia, comprehension is generally somewhat better, but speech is accomplished with great difficulty and is quite limited. This condition is generally known as Broca's aphasia, the responsible lesion being in the lower, posterior portion of the left frontal lobe (i.e., Broca's area).

There are several other types of aphasia that are relatively rare and will not be described here. However, it is important to point out that most aphasias are mixed, having components of the various pure types. Furthermore, the type of aphasia may change in the same patient particularly during the course of recovery. The disorders of reading, writing, and calculation may also be divided into subtypes. In the case of reading, our interest here is in the so-called acquired alexias in which an individual formerly able to read has lost that ability because of focal, structural brain damage. The ability to read letters, words, or sentences may be lost. Handwriting disturbances or agraphia might involve a disability in writing words from dictation or a basic disability in forming letters. Thus, some agraphic patients can write, but with omissions and distortions relative to what was dictated. However, some can no longer engage in the purposive movements needed to form letters. Calculation disturbances or acalculias are also of several types. The patient may lose the ability to read numbers, to calculate even if the numbers can be read, or to arrange numbers in a proper spatial sequence for calculation. The various syndromes associated with communicative disorders, while sometimes existing in pure forms, often merge. For example, alexia is frequently associated with Broca's aphasia, and difficulty with handwriting is commonly seen in patients with Wernicke's aphasia. However, there is generally a pattern in which there is a clear primary disorder, such as impaired auditory comprehension, with other disorders, such as difficulty with reading or writing, occurring as associated defects. Sometimes rather unusual combinations occur, as in the case of the syndrome of alexia without agraphia. In this case, the patient can write but cannot read, often to the extent that he or she cannot read what he or she has just written. Based on recent research, we would add that in adults academic deficits are frequently seen that are not the product of brain damage acquired during adulthood or of inadequate educational opportunity. Rather, people with these deficits have developmentally based learning disabilities that they never outgrew. The view that learning disability is commonly outgrown has been rejected by most students of this area (McCue & Goldstein, 1991).

Disorders of Perception and Motility

Disorders of perception can involve perception of one's body as well as perception of the external world. In the case of the external world, the disorder can involve some class of objects or some geographical location. Disorders of motility to be discussed here will not be primary losses of motor function as in the cases of paralysis or paresis, but losses in the area of the capacity to perform skilled, purposive acts. The set of impairments found in this area is called apraxia. There is also the borderline area in which the neuropsychological defect has to do with the coordination of a sense modality, usually vision, and purposive movement. These disorders are sometimes described as impairment of constructional or visual-spatial relations ability. In some patients the primary difficulty is perceptual, while in others it is mainly motoric. The body schema disturbances most commonly seen are of three types. The first of them has to do with the patient's inability to point to his or her own body parts on command. The syndrome is called autotopognosia, meaning lack of awareness of the surface of one's body. A more localized disorder of this type is finger agnosia in which, while identification of body parts is otherwise intact, the patient cannot identify the fingers of his or her own hands, or the hands of another person. Finger agnosia has been conceptualized as a partial dissolution of the body schema. The third type of body schema disturbance is right-left disorientation, in which the patient cannot identify body parts in regard to whether they are on the right or left side. For example, when the patient is asked to show you his or her right hand he or she may become confused or show you his or her left hand. More commonly, however, a more complex command is required to elicit this deficit, such as asking the patient to place his or her left hand on his or her right shoulder. The traditional thinking about this disorder is that both finger agnosia and right-left disorientation are part of a syndrome, the responsible brain damage being in the region of the left angular gyrus. However, Benton (1985), and later Benton and Sivan (1993), pointed out that the matter is more complicated than that, and the issue of localization involves the specific nature of these defects in terms of the underlying cognitive and perceptual processes affected.

The perceptual disorders in which the difficulty is in recognition of some class of external objects are called gnostic disorders or agnosias. These disorders may be classified with regard to modality and verbal or nonverbal content. Thus, one form of the disorder might involve visual perception of nonverbal stimuli and would be called visual agnosia. By definition, an agnosia is present when primary function of the affected modality is intact, but the patient cannot recognize or identify the stimulus. For example, in visual agnosia, the patient can see but cannot recognize what he or she has seen. In order to assure oneself that visual agnosia is present, it should be determined that the patient can recognize and name the object in question when it is placed in his or her hand, so that it can be recognized by touch, or when it produces some characteristic sound, so that it can be recognized by audition. The brain lesions involved in the agnosias are generally in the association areas for the various perceptual modalities. Thus, visual agnosia is generally produced by damage to association areas in the occipital lobes. When language is involved, there is obviously a great deal of overlap between the agnosias and the aphasias. For example, visual-verbal agnosia can really be viewed as a form of alexia. In these cases, it is often important to determine through detailed testing whether the deficit is primarily a disturbance of perceptual recognition or a higher level conceptual disturbance involving language comprehension. There is a wide variety of gnostic disorders reported in the literature involving such phenomena as the inability to recognize faces, colors, or spoken works. However, they are relatively rare conditions and when present may only persist during the acute phase of the illness. In general, agnosia has been described as "perception without meaning." It is important to remember that it is quite a different phenomenon from what we usually think of as blindness or deafness.

Sometimes a perceptual disorder does not involve a class of objects but a portion of geographical space. The phenomenon itself is described by many terms, the most frequently used ones being neglect and inattention. It is seen most dramatically in vision, where the patient may neglect the entire right or left side of the visual world. It also occurs in the somatosensory modality, in which case the patient may neglect one side or the other of his or her body. While neglect can occur on either side, it is more common on the left side, since it is generally associated with right hemisphere brain damage. In testing for neglect, it is often useful to employ the method of double stimulation, for example, in the form of simultaneous finger wiggles in the areas of the right and left visual fields. Typically, the patient may report seeing the wiggle in the right field but not in the left. Similarly, when the patient with neglect is touched lightly on the right and left hand at the same time, he or she may report feeling the touch in only one hand or the other. As in the case of the gnostic disorders, neglect is defined in terms of the assumption of intactness of the primary sensory modalities. Thus, the patient with visual neglect should have otherwise normal vision in the neglected half field, while the patient with tactile neglect should have normal somatosensory function. Clinically, neglect may be a symptom of some acute process and should diminish in severity or disappear as the neuropathological condition stabilizes. For example, visual neglect of the left field is often seen in individuals who have recently sustained right hemisphere strokes but can be expected to disappear as the patient recovers.

The apraxias constitute a group of syndromes in which the basic deficit involves impairment of purposive movement occurring in the absence of paralysis, weakness, or unsteadiness. For some time, the distinction has been made among three major types of apraxia: ideomotor, limb-kinetic, and ideational. In ideomotor apraxia, the patient has difficulty in performing a movement to verbal command. In the case of limb-kinetic apraxia, movement is clumsy when performed on command or when the patient is asked to imitate a movement. In ideational apraxia, the difficulty is with organizing the correct motor sequences in response to language. In other words, it may be viewed as a disability in regard to carrying out a series of acts. In addition, there are facial apraxias in which the patient cannot carry out facial movements to command. These four types are thought to involve different brain regions and different pathways. However, they are all generally conceptualized as a destruction or disconnection of motor engrams or traces that control skilled, purposive movement. Certain of the visual-spatial disorders are referred to as apraxias, such as constructional or dressing apraxia, but they are different in nature from the purer motor apraxias described above.

The basic difficulty the patient with a visual-spatial disorder has relates to comprehension of spatial relationships, and in most cases, coordination between visual perception and movement. In extreme cases, the patient may readily become disoriented and lose his or her way when going from one location to another. However, in most cases the difficulty appears to be at the cognitive level and may be examined by asking the patient to copy figures or solve jigsaw or block design type puzzles. Patients with primarily perceptual difficulties have problems in localizing points in space, judging direction, and maintaining geographical orientation, as tested by asking the patient to describe a route or use a map. Patients with constructional difficulties have problems with copying and block building. So-called dressing apraxia may be seen as a form of constructional disability in which the patient cannot deal effectively with the visual-spatial demands involved in such tasks as buttoning clothing. While visual-spatial disorders can arise from lesions found in most parts of the brain, they are most frequently seen, and seen with the greatest severity, in patients with right hemisphere brain damage. Generally, the area that will most consistently produce the severest deficit is the posterior portion of the right hemisphere. In general, while some patients show a dissociation between visual-spatial and visual-motor or constructional aspects of the syndrome of constructional apraxia, most patients have difficulties on both purely perceptual and constructional tasks.

Dementia

Dementia is probably the most common form of organic mental disorder. There are several types of dementia, but they all involve usually slowly progressive deterioration of intellectual function. Deterioration is frequently patterned, with loss of memory generally being the first function to decline, and other abilities deteriorating at later stages of the illness. One major class of dementia consists of those disorders that arise during late life, either during late middle age or old age. In the former case, they are known as presenile dementias, while those that occur during old age are known as senile dementia. As the term is used now, dementia may occur at any age. In children it is differentiated from mental retardation on the basis of the presence of deterioration from a formerly higher level. Dementia may result from head trauma or essentially any of the neuropathological conditions discussed above. One common cause of dementia appears to be alcoholism and the nutritional disorders that typically accompany it. A specific type of dementia that generally appears before the presenile period is Huntington's disease. The term "dementia," when defined in the broad way suggested here, is not particularly useful and does not really provide more information than do such terms as "organic brain syndrome" or "chronic brain syndrome." However, when the term is used in a more specific way, it becomes possible to point out specific characteristics that may be described as syndromes. This specificity may be achieved by defining the dementias as those disorders in which for no exogenous reason, the brain begins to deteriorate and continues to do so until death. DSM-III-R described these conditions as progressive degenerative dementia. DSM-IV has abandoned this general categorization and describes the varying dementias on the basis of etiology (e.g., Alzheimer's type and Parkinson's disease). The most common type of progressive dementia is Alzheimer's disease, but sufficient diagnostic methods are not yet available to diagnose Alzheimer's disease in the living patient. That is why it is called dementia of the Alzheimer's type. However, its presence becomes apparent on examination of the brain at autopsy. Clinically, the course of the illness generally begins with signs of impairment of memory for recent events, followed by deficits in judgment, visual-spatial skills, and language. In recent years, the language deficit has become a matter of particular interest, perhaps because the communicative difficulties of dementia patients are becoming increasingly recognized. Generally, the language difficulty does not resemble aphasia but can perhaps be best characterized as an impoverishment of speech, with word finding difficulties and progressive inability to produce extended and comprehensible narrative speech. Basically, the same finding is noted in the descriptive writing of Alzheimer's disease patients (Neils, Boller, Gerdeman, & Cole, 1989). Patients write shorter descriptive paragraphs than age-matched controls and also make more handwriting errors of various types.

The end state of dementia is generalized, severe intellectual impairment involving all areas, with the patient sometimes surviving for various lengths of time in a persistent vegetative state. The progressive dementia seen in Huntington's disease also involves significant impairment of memory, with other abilities becoming gradually affected through the course of the illness. However, it differs from Alzheimer's disease in that it is accompanied by the choreic movements described earlier and by the fact that the age of onset is substantially earlier than is the case for Alzheimer's disease. Because of the chorea, there is also a difficulty in speech articulation frequently seen, which is not the case for Alzheimer's patients. A form of dementia that does not have an unknown etiology but that is slowly progressive is vascular dementia. This disorder is known to be associated with hypertension and a series of strokes, with the end result being substantial deterioration. However, the course of the deterioration is not thought to be as uniform as is the case in Alzheimer's disease but rather is generally described as stepwise and patchy. The patient may remain relatively stable between strokes, and the symptomatology produced may be associated with the site of the strokes. It may be mentioned that while these distinctions between vascular and primary degenerative dementia are clearly described, in individual patients it is not always possible to make a definitive differential diagnosis. Even such sophisticated radiological methods as the CT scan and MRI do not always contribute to the diagnosis. During the bulk of the course of the illness, the dementia patient will typically appear as confused, possibly disoriented, and lacking in the ability to recall recent events. Speech may be very limited and, if fluent, likely to be incomprehensible. Thus, these patients do not have the specific syndromes of the type described above surrounded by otherwise intact function. Instead, the deficit pattern tends to be global in nature, with all functions more or less involved. Some investigators have attempted to identify syndromal subtypes, with some having more deficit in the area of abstraction and judgment, some in the area of memory and some in the areas of affect and personality changes. However, this proposed typology has not been well established, with most patients having difficulties with all three areas. While there are some treatable dementias, particularly dementias associated with endocrine disorders or normal pressure hydrocephalus, there is no curative treatment for progressive degenerative dementia. Current research offers the hope that pharmacological treatment may eventually be able to ameliorate the course of Alzheimer's disease, but thus far only one medication, tacrine hydrochloride, has received FDA approval. Even its effect, however, is modest.

There is a type of dementia that appears to be specifically associated with frontal lobe brain damage. The damage may occur as a result of a number of processes such as head trauma, tumor, or stroke, but the syndrome produced is more or less the same. Indeed, clinicians speak of a "frontal lobe syndrome." The outstanding features all may be viewed as relating to impaired ability to control, regulate, and program behavior. This impairment is manifested in numerous ways, including poor abstraction ability, impaired judgment, apathy, and loss of impulse control. Language is sometimes impaired, but in a rather unique way. Rather than having a formal language disorder, the patient loses the ability to control behavior through language. There is also often a difficulty with narrative speech that has been interpreted as a problem in forming the intention to speak or in formulating a plan for a narrative. Such terms as lack of insight or of the ability to produce goal-oriented behavior are used to describe the frontal lobe patient. In many cases, these activating, regulatory, and programming functions are so impaired that the outcome looks like a generalized dementia with implications for many forms of cognitive, perceptual, and motor activities.

Amnesia

While some degree of impairment of memory is a part of many brain disorders, there are some conditions in which loss of memory is clearly the most outstanding deficit. When loss of memory is particularly severe and persistent, and other cognitive and perceptual functions are relatively intact, the patient can be described as having an amnesic syndrome. Dementia patients are often amnesic, but their memory disturbance is embedded in significant generalized impairment of intellectual and communicative abilities. The amnesic patient generally has normal language and may be of average intelligence. As in the case of aphasia and several of the other disorders, there is more than one amnesic syndrome. The differences among them revolve around what the patient can and cannot remember. The structures in the brain that are particularly important for memory are the limbic system, especially the hippocampus, and certain brain stem structures including the mammilary bodies and the dorsomedial nucleus of the thalamus. There are many systems described in the literature for distinguishing among types of amnesia and types of memory. With regard to the amnesias, perhaps the most basic distinction is between anterograde and retrograde amnesia. Anterograde amnesia involves the inability to form new memories from the time of the onset of the illness producing the amnesia, while retrograde amnesia refers to the inability to recall events that took place before the onset of the illness. This distinction dovetails with the distinction between recent and remote memory. It is also in some correspondence with the distinction made between short-term and long-term memory in the experimental literature. However, various theories define these terms somewhat differently and perhaps it is best to use the more purely descriptive terms *recent* and *remote* memory in describing the amnesic disorders. It then can be stated that the most commonly appearing amnesic disorders involve dramatic impairment of recent memory with relative sparing of remote memory. This sparing becomes greater as the events to be remembered become more remote. Thus, most amnesic patients can recall their early lives, but may totally forget what occurred during that last several hours. This distinction between recent and remote memory possibly aids in explaining why most amnesic patients maintain normal language function and average intelligence. In this respect, an amnesic disorder is not so much an obliteration of the past as it is an inability to learn new material.

Probably the most common type of relatively pure amnesic disorder is alcoholic Korsakoff's syndrome. These patients, while often maintaining average levels in a number of areas of cognitive function, demonstrate a dense amnesia for recent events with relatively well preserved remote memory. Alcoholic Korsakoff's syndrome has been conceptualized by Butters and Cermak (1980) as an information processing defect in which new material is encoded in a highly degraded manner leading to high susceptibility to interference. Butters and Cermak (1980), as well as numerous other investigators, have accomplished detailed experimental studies of alcoholic Korsakoff's patients in which the nature of their perceptual, memory, and learning difficulties have been described in detail. The results of this research aid in explaining numerous clinical phenomena noted in Korsakoff's patients, such as their capacity to perform learned behaviors without recall of when or if those behaviors were previously executed, or their tendency to confabulate or "fill in" for the events of the past day that they do not recall. It may be noted that while confabulation was once thought to be a cardinal symptom of Korsakoff's syndrome, it is only seen in some patients.

Another type of amnesic disorder is seen when there is direct, focal damage to the temporal lobes and most importantly to the hippocampus. These temporal lobe or limbic system amnesias are less common than Korsakoff's syndrome but have been well studied because of the light they shed on the neuropathology of memory. These patients share many of the characteristics of Korsakoff's patients but have a much more profound deficit in regard to basic consolidation and storage of new material. When Korsakoff's patients are sufficiently cued and given enough time, they can learn. Indeed, sometimes they can demonstrate normal recognition memory. However, patients with temporal lobe amnesias may find it almost impossible to learn new material under any circumstances. In some cases, amnesic disorders are modality specific. If one distinguishes between verbal and nonverbal memory, the translation can be made from the distinction between language and nonverbal abilities associated with the specialized functions of each cerebral hemisphere. It has in fact been reported that patients with unilateral lesions involving the left temporal lobe may have memory deficits for verbal material only, while right temporal patients have corresponding deficits for nonverbal material. Thus, the left temporal patient may have difficulty with learning word lists, while the right temporal patient may have difficulty with geometric forms. In summary, while there are several amnesic syndromes, they all have in common the symptom of lack of ability to learn new material following the onset of the illness. Sometimes the symptom is modality specific, involving only verbal or nonverbal material, but more often than not it involves both modalities. There are several relatively pure types of amnesia, notably Korsakoff's syndrome, but memory difficulties are cardinal symptoms of many other brain disorders; notably the progressive dementias and certain disorders associated with infection. For example, people with herpes encephalitis frequently have severely impaired memories, but they have other cognitive deficits as well.

ALTERNATIVE DESCRIPTIVE SYSTEMS

As has been indicated, not all clinicians or researchers associated with brain-damaged patients have adopted the neuropsychologically oriented syndrome approach briefly described above. There are many reasons for the existence of these differing views, some of them methodological and some substantive in nature. The methodological issues largely revolve around the operations used by investigators to establish the existence of a syndrome. Critics suggest that syndromes may be established on the basis of overly subjective inferences as well as on incomplete examinations. The alternative method proposed is generally described as a dimensional approach in which patients are measured on a variety of neuropsychologically relevant dimensions such as intellectual function, language ability, and memory rather than assigned categories. Advocates of this approach are less concerned with determining whether the patient has a recognizable syndrome and are more involved with profiling the patient along a number of continuous dimensions and relating that profile to underlying brain mechanisms. Rourke and Brown (1986) have clarified this issue in a full discussion of similarities and differences between behavioral neurology and clinical neuropsychology.

Utilizing a dimensional philosophy, there is no need to develop a classification system except perhaps in terms of certain characteristic profiles. For purposes of providing an overview of the descriptive phenomenology of structural brain damage, however, the substantive matters probably are of more relevance. In essence, the disciplines of neurology, neuropsychology, and psychiatry have all developed descriptive classificatory systems that differ in many respects. We have already discussed the ways in which brain damage is described and classified by neurologists and neuropsychologists. However, the psychiatric descriptions are also quite important, because they point to problems not uncommonly seen in brain-damaged patients that are not always clearly identifiable in the neurological and neuropsychological systems. There is an area of overlap in regard to dementia and the amnesias, but DSM-III-R and DSM-IV contain a number of categories that are not clearly defined neurologically or neuropsychologically. We will briefly describe them here.

We will recall that DSM-III and DSM-III-R used such terms as organic delusional syndrome and organic anxiety syndrome. These specific terms are not contained in DSM-IV, but some equivalents are now contained in the chapter called "Mental Disorders due to a General Medical Condition." Thus, patients previously characterized as having an organic delusion disorder would now be diagnosed as having a psychotic disorder due to a general medical condition. The specific diagnosis would be psychotic disorder due to (specify medical condition; e.g., malignant brain neoplasm) with delusions. Patients with this disorder have delusional beliefs while in a normal state of consciousness as the primary symptom. It must be established that the delusions have an organic basis and the patient is not actually delusional because of a paranoid or schizophrenic disorder. The neurological basis for this syndrome is varied and may involve drug abuse, right hemisphere brain damage, or in some cases Huntington's disease or other dementias. A related diagnosis was formerly described as organic hallucinosis and is now described in DSM-IV with several separate diagnoses including alcohol-induced psychotic disorder with hallucinations, other substance-induced psychotic disorder with hallucinations, a number of specific substance-induced psychotic disorders with hallucinations, and psychotic disorder (specify general medical condition) with hallucinations. Here, hallucinations rather than delusions are the primary symptoms, but again, the disorder must have an organic basis. DSM-III and DSM-III-R also describe an organic affective and an organic personality syndrome, in which the primary symptoms are, respectively, a mood disturbance (either mania or depression), or a personality change. The personality changes noted generally involve increased impulsiveness, emotional lability, or apathy. Perhaps these are really mainly frontal lobes syndromes, but the syndrome may also be seen in conjunction with temporal lobe epilepsy. In DSM-IV, these disorders are called mood disorder due to a general medical condition or personality change due to a medical condition. These disorders can also be substance induced (e.g., substance-induced mood disorder.) The personality change diagnosis is divided into labile, disinhibited, aggressive, pathetic, paranoid, other, combined, and unspecified types. A disorder called organic anxiety disorder in DSM-III-R is now called anxiety disorder due to a general medical condition.

DSM-III, DSM-III-R, and DSM-IV all classify substance-induced intoxication, withdrawal states, and other symptom complexes associated with various sympathomimetic and hallucinogenic drugs. Typically, these conditions are acute phenomena and do not persist beyond a matter of days. However, certain of them, notably those associated with alcohol abuse, may eventually evolve into permanent disorders, notably dementia. Their behavioral correlates generally involve personality changes such as euphoria, agitation, anxiety, hallucinations, and depersonalization. Cognitive changes might include impairment of memory and inability to concentrate. Within the context of psychopathology, the commonality between these conditions and those related to more permanent, structural brain damage is that they all have an identified or presumed organic basis and are therefore distinct from the functional psychiatric disorders.

The phraseology used throughout the organic mental disorders section of DSM-III and DSM-III-R was "Evidence, from the history, physical examination, or laboratory test, of a specific organic factor that is judged to be etiologically related to the disturbance." The DSM-IV phraseology is "Evidence from the history, physical examination, or laboratory findings that the disturbance is the direct physiological consequence of a general medical condition." Again, the word "organic" has been abandoned, and the phrase "general medical condition" has been substituted for it. The term "general medical condition" means that an Axis III diagnosis should be specified if possible. Clearly, DSM-IV aims toward encouraging use of more specific terminology when making diagnoses in the areas of delirium, dementia, amnesia, other cognitive disorders, and mental disorders that are substance-induced or due to general medical illness.

This psychiatrically based categorization can perhaps be most productively viewed as supplemental to the type of neuropsychological system used by Heilman and Valenstein (1993) rather than as an alternative to it. It plays a major role in describing the noncognitive kinds of symptomatology that are often associated with structural brain damage, particularly for those cases in which these personality and mood changes are the predominant symptoms. These considerations are of the utmost clinical importance because the failure to recognize the organic basis for some apparently functional symptom such as a personality change may lead to the initiation of totally inappropriate treatment or the failure to recognize a life-threatening physical illness.

While alterations in brain function can give rise to symptoms that look like functional personality changes, the reverse can also occur. That is, a nonorganic personality change, notably acquisition of a depression, can produce symptoms that look like they have been produced by alterations in brain function. The term generally applied to this situation is "pseudodementia," and is most frequently seen in elderly people who become depressed. The concept of pseudodementia or depressive pseudodementia is not universally accepted, but it is not uncommon to find elderly patients diagnosed as demented when in fact the symptoms of dementia are actually produced by depression. The point is proved when the symptoms disappear or diminish substantially after the depression has run its course, or the patient is treated with antidepressant medication. Wells (1979, 1980) has pointed out that this differential diagnosis is a difficult one to make and cannot be accomplished satisfactorily with the usual examinational, laboratory, and psychometric methods. He suggests that perhaps the most useful diagnostic criteria are clinical features. For example, patients with pseudodementia tend to complain about their cognitive losses, while patients with dementia tend not to complain. Caine (1986) pointed to the many complexities of differential diagnosis in the elderly, referring in particular to the abundant evidence for neuropsychological deficits in younger depressed patients, and to the not uncommon coexistence of neurological and psychiatric impairments in the elderly. Recent formulations of pseudodementia suggest that what we are really dealing with are disorders of mood, cognition, and motor function in the elderly. These disorders are now thought to have anatomical substrates, and while the depression may recover, it nevertheless may also be an early indicator of progressive dementia (Nussbaum, 1994).

GENDER, RACIAL, AND ETHNIC ISSUES

Gender

While the biological disorders that produce delirium, dementia, amnesia, and other cognitive disorders are seen about equally in women and men, we can note some prominent exceptions. The issue is not so much gender difference as it is an interaction between gender and developmental level. Thus, head trauma occurs with greater prevalence in young men than it does in women of all ages, and older men. Several of the pervasive developmental disorders, namely autism and attention-deficit hyperactivity disorder, are more prevalent in males than in females. In most inpatient settings, with such obvious exceptions as Veterans Administration facilities, it is common to have a higher population of female than male Alzheimer's disease patients. This phenomenon seems to be largely attributable to the typically longer life span of women relative to men. In the case of the substance-related disorders, gender differences in occurrence of neurological disorder exist in rough correspondence to the gender differences found for the disorder in general. The case literature on Wernicke-Korsakoff's syndrome is largely restricted to men, but it is interesting to note that one of Wernicke's original three cases was a woman.

Racial and Ethnic Considerations

The differing prevalences of various neurobehavioral disorders are predominantly related to health and social practices among different cultures. In countries, largely in the Orient, where beverage alcohol has limited accessibility, such alcohol-related neurobehavioral disorders are not commonly found. The reverse is true in cultures in which there are patterns of relatively heavy alcohol ingestion. Disorders related to malnutrition become more prevalent as the availability of an adequate diet becomes limited. Dietary and recreational drug use patterns have important implications for cardiovascular and neoplastic disorders. Availability of high-speed vehicles has implications for traumatic injury.

There are some rare disorders that appear to be specifically related to an ethnic group, notably Tay-Sachs disease in Eastern European Jewish children. Black individuals are at less risk for multiple sclerosis than are white individuals, but both ethnic groups show the peculiar geographic pattern of the disorder in which prevalence increases with distance from the equator, mainly in the northern hemisphere. Another complex pattern occurs in Huntington's disease, in that while the disease is always genetic, age of onset of illness is somewhat earlier in black families, and when the father is the affected parent. The epidemiology of the various neurobehavioral disorders is obviously a complex phenomenon, receiving contributions from genetics, health maintenance practices, varying customs and mores of socioethnic groups, and environmental influences, as in the example given of high-speed vehicles.

SUMMARY

Delirium, dementia, amnestic, and other cognitive disorders, and mental disorders due to a general medical condition, all of which were previously called the organic mental disorders, are a large number of conditions in which behavioral changes may be directly associated with some basis in altered brain function. While the general diagnostic term "organic brain syndrome" has commonly been used to describe these conditions, the wide variability in the manifestations of brain dysfunction make this term insufficiently precise in reference to clinical relevance. It was pointed out that the variability is attributable to a number of factors, including the following considerations: 1. the location of damage in the brain, 2. the neuropathological process producing damage, 3. the length of time brain damage has been present, 4. the age and health status of the individual at the time damage is sustained, and 5. the individual's premorbid personality and level of function.

The neuropsychological approach to the conceptualization of the organic mental disorders has identified a number of behavioral parameters along which manifestations of brain dysfunction can be described and classified. The most frequently considered dimensions are intellectual function, language, memory, visual-spatial skills, perceptual skills, and motor function. Some important concepts related to brain function and brain disorders include the principle of contralateral control of neuroimaging. There have been important technological advances, notably major increases in the sophistication of magnetic resonance imaging and capacities to measure cerebral activity through various cerebral blood flow techniques, positron emission tomography, and magnetic resonance spectroscopy (see Bigler, Yeo, & Turkheimer, [1989], for a comprehensive review). The capacity to visualize the brain with increasingly fine resolution, and to measure brain function at rest and under activation conditions, is growing rapidly.

REFERENCES

Allen, D. N., & Goreczny, A. J. (1995). Assessment and treatment of multiple sclerosis. In A. J. Goreczny (Ed.), *Handbook of health and rehabilitation psychology* (pp. 389–429). New York: Plenum.

American Psychiatric Association. (1980). *Diagnostic and statistical manual of mental disorders* (3rd ed.). Washington, DC: Author.

American Psychiatric Association. (1987). *Diagnostic and statistical manual of mental disorders* (3rd ed., rev. ed.). Washington, DC: Author.

American Psychiatric Association. (1994). *Diagnostic and statistical manual of mental disorders* (4th ed.). Washington, DC: Author.

Beers, S. R. (1992). Cognitive effects of mild head injury in children and adolescents. *Neuropsychology Review, 3,* 281–320.

Begleiter, H., Porjesz, B., Bihari, B., & Kissin, B. (1984). Event-related potentials in boys at high risk for alcoholism. *Science, 225,* 1493–1496.

Benton, A., & Sivan, A. B. (1993). Disturbances of the body schema. In K. M. Heilman & E. Valenstein (Eds.), *Clinical neuropsychology* (3rd ed., pp. 123–140). New York: Oxford University Press.

Benton, A. L. (1985). Body schema disturbances: Finger agnosia and right-left disorientation. In K. H. Heilman & E. Valenstein (Eds.), *Clinical neuropsychology* (2nd ed., pp. 115–129). New York: Oxford University Press.

Benton, A. L., & Joynt, R. J. (1960). Early descriptions of aphasia. *Archives of Neurology, 3,* 205–222.

Bigler, E. D., Yeo, R. A., & Turkheimer, E. (1989). *Neuropsychological function and brain imaging.* New York: Plenum.

Blass, J. P., & Gibson, G. E. (1977). Abnormality of a thiamine-requiring enzyme in patients with Wernicke-Korsakoff syndrome. *New England Journal of Medicine, 297,* 1367–1370.

Boring, E. G. (1950). *A history of experimental psychology* (2nd ed.). New York: Appleton-Century-Crofts.

Broca, P. (1861). Perte de la parole. Ramollissement chronique et destruction partielle du lobe antérieur gauche du cerveau. *Bulletin de ia Société de l'Anthropologie, 2,* 235–238.

Butters, N., & Cermak, L. S. (1980). Alcoholic Korsakoff's syndrome. New York: Academic Press.

Caine, E. D. (1986). The neuropsychology of depression: The pseudodementia syndrome. In I. Grant & K. M. Adams (Eds.), *Neuropsychological assessment of neuropsychiatric disorders* (pp. 221–243). New York: Oxford University Press.

Chelune, G. J. (1995). Hippocampal adequacy versus functional reserve: Predicting memory functions following temporal lobectomy. *Archives of Clinical Neuropsychology, 10,* 413–432.

Cloninger, C. R., Bohman, M., & Sigvardsson, S. (1981). Inheritance of alcohol abuse: Cross-fostering analysis of adopted men. *Archives of General Psychiatry, 38,* 861–868.

Dean, R. S. (1986). Lateralization of cerebral functions. In D. Wedding, A. M. Horton, Jr., & J. Webster (Eds.), *The neuropsychology handbook: Behavioral and clinical perspectives* (pp. 80–102). New York: Springer.

Dodrill, C. B. (1986). Psychosocial consequences of epilepsy. In S. B. Filskov & T. J. Boll (Eds.), *Handbook of clinical neuropsychology* (Vol. 2, pp. 338–363). New York: Wiley.

Elias, M. F. & Streeten, D. H. P. (1980). *Hypertension and cognitive processes.* Mount Desert, ME: Beech Hill.

Flourens, M. J. P. (1824). *Recherches experimentales sur les propriétés et les fonctions du système nerveux dans les animaux vertèbres.* Paris: Crevot.

Gastaut, H. (1970). Clinical and electroencephalographical classification of epileptic seizures. *Epilepsia, 11,* 102–103.

Geschwind, N. (1965). Disconnection syndromes in animals and man. *Brain, 88,* 237–294.

Goethe, K. E., & Levin, H. S. (1986). Neuropsychological consequences of head injury in children. In G. Goldstein & R. E. Tarter (Eds.), *Advances in clinical neuropsychology* (Vol. 3, pp. 213–242). New York: Plenum.

Goldstein, G. (1986, February). *Neuropsychological effects of five antihypertensive agents.* Poster presented at annual meeting of International Neuropsychological Society, Denver.

Goldstein, K. (1936). The significance of the frontal lobes for mental performance. *Journal of Neurology and Psychopathology, 17,* 27–40.

Goldstein, K. (1959). Functional disturbances in brain damage. In S. Arieti (Ed.), *American handbook of psychiatry* (pp. 770–794). New York: Basic Books.

Goldstein, K., & Scheerer, M. (1941). Abstract and concrete behavior: An experimental study with special tests. *Psychological Monographs, 53* (2, no. 239).

Goodwin, D. W. (1979). Alcoholism and heredity: A review and hypothesis. *Archives of General Psychiatry, 36,* 57–61.

Goodwin, D. W., Schulsinger, F., Hermansen, L., Guze, S. B., & Winokur, G. (1973). Alcohol problems in adoptees raised apart from alcoholic biological parents. *Archives of General Psychiatry, 28,* 238–243.

Grant, I., Atkinson, J. H., Hesselink, J. R., Kennedy, C. J., Richman, D. D., Spector, S. A., & McCutchan, J. A. (1987). Evidence for early central nervous system involvement in the acquired immunodeficiency syndrome (AIDS) and other human immunodeficiency virus (HIV) infections. *Annals of Internal Medicine, 107,* 828–836.

Gusella, J. F., Wexler, N. S., Conneallly, P. M., Naylor, S. L., Anderson, M. A., Tanzi, R. E., Watkins, P. C., Ottina, K., Wallace, M. R., Sakaguchi, A. Y., Young, A. B., Shoulson, I., Bonilla, E., & Martin, J. B. (1983). A polymorphic DNA marker genetically linked to Huntington's disease. *Nature, 306,* 234–238.

Hallowell, E. M., & Ratey, J. J. (1994). *Driven to distraction.* New York: Pantheon.

Halstead, W. C. (1947). *Brain and intelligence.* Chicago: University of Chicago Press.

Heaton, R. K., Grant, I., Butters, N., White, D. A., Kirson, D., Atkinson, J. A., Taylor,

M. J., Kelly, M. D., Ellis, R. J., Wolfson, T., Velin, R., Marcotte, T. D., Hesselink, J. R., Jernigan, T. L., Chandler, J., Wallace, M. Abramson, I., and the HNRC Group (1995). The HNRC 500–Neuropsychology of HIV infection at different disease stages. *Journal of the International Neuropsychological Society, 1,* 231–251.

Heaton, R. K., Nelson, L. M., Thompson, D. S., Burks, J. S., & Franklin, G. M. (1985). Neuropsychological findings in relapsing-remitting and chronic-progressive multiple sclerosis. *Journal of Consulting and Clinical Psychology, 53,* 103–110.

Heilman, K. M., & Valenstein, E. (Eds.). (1993). *Clinical neuropsychology* (3rd ed.) New York: Oxford University Press.

Hill, S. Y., Steinhauer, S. R., & Zubin, J. (1987). Biological markers for alcoholism: A vulnerability model conceptualization. In C. Rivers (Ed.), *Nebraska Symposium on Motivation: Vol. 34. Alcohol and addictive behavior* (pp. 207–256). Lincoln, NE: University of Nebraska Press.

Jackson, J. H. (1932). In J. Taylor (Ed.), *Selected writings.* London: Hodder and Stoughton.

Jervis, G. A. (1959). The mental deficiencies. In S. Arieti (Ed.), *American handbook of psychiatry* (Vol. 2, pp. 1289–1314). New York: Basic Books.

Kanner, L. (1943). Autistic disturbances of affective contact. *Nervous Child, 2,* 217–250.

King, H. E., & Miller, R. E. (1990). Hypertension: Cognitive and behavioral considerations. *Neuropsychology Review, 1,* 31–73.

Klove, H., & Matthews, C. G. (1974). Neuropsychological studies of patients with epilepsy. In R. M. Reitan & L. A. Davison (Eds.), *Clinical neuropsychology: Current status and applications* (pp. 237–265). New York: Winston-Wiley.

Lashley, K. S. (1960). In search of the engram. In F. A. Beach, D. O. Hebb, C. T. Morgan, & H. W. Nissen (Eds.), *The neuropsychology of Lashley* (pp. 478–505). New York: McGraw-Hill. (Original work published in 1950)

Levin, H. S., Eisenberg, H. M., & Benton, A. L. (1989). *Mild head injury.* New York: Oxford University Press.

Luria, A. R. (1973). *The working brain.* New York: Basic Books.

McCue, M., & Goldstein, G. (1991). Neuropsychological aspects of learning disability in adults. In B. P. Rourke (Ed.), *Neuropsychological validation of learning disability subtypes* (pp. 311–329). New York: Guilford.

Mednick, S. A. (1970). Breakdown in individuals at high risk for schizophrenia: Possible predispositional perinatal factors. *Mental Hygiene, 54,* 50–63.

Mesulam, M. M. (1985). *Principles of behavioral neurology.* Philadelphia: Davis.

Minshew, N. J., & Payton, J. B. (1988a). New perspectives in autism: Part 1. The clinical spectrum of infantile autism. *Current Problems in Pediatrics, 18,* 561–610.

Minshew, N. J., & Payton, J. B. (1988b). New perspectives in autism: Part 2. The differential diagnosis and neurobiology of autism. *Current Problems in Pediatrics, 19,* 615–694.

Myslobodsky, M. S., & Mirsky, A. F. (1988). *Elements of petit mal epilepsy.* New York: Lang.

Neils, J., Boller, F., Gerdeman, B., & Cole, M. (1989). Descriptive writing abilities in Alzheimer's disease. *Journal of Clinical and Experimental Neuropsychology, 11,* 692–698.

Nussbaum, P. D. (1994). Pseudodementia: A slow death. *Neuropsychology Review, 4,* 71–90.

Peyser, J. M., & Poser, C. M. (1986). Neuropsychological correlates of multiple sclerosis. In S. B. Filskov & T. J. Boll (Eds.), *Handbook of clinical neuropsychology* (Vol. 2, pp. 364–397). New York: Wiley.

Rourke, B. P., & Brown, G. G. (1986). Clinical neuropsychology and behavioral neurology: Similarities and differences. In S. B. Filskov & T. J. Boll (Eds.), *Handbook of clinical neuropsychology* (Vol. 2, pp. 3–18). New York: Wiley.

Rumsey, J. M., & Hamburger, S. D. (1988). Neuropsychological findings in high-functioning men with infantile autism, residual state. *Journal of Clinical and Experimental Neuropsychology, 10,* 201–221.

Satz, P. (1966). Specific and nonspecific effects of brain lesions in man. *Journal of Abnormal Psychology, 71,* 65–70.

Satz, P. (1993). Brain reserve capacity on symptom onset after brain injury: A formulation and review of evidence for threshold theory. *Neuropsychology, 7,* 273–295.

Schaeffer, K. W., Parsons, O. A., & Yohman, J. R. (1984). Neuropsychological differences between male familial and nonfamilial alcoholics and nonalcoholics. *Alcoholism: Clinical and Experimental Research, 8,* 347–351.

Spreen, O. (1987). *Learning disabled children growing up: A follow-up into adulthood.* Lisse, The Netherlands: Swets and Zeitlinger.

Steinhauer, S. R., Hill, S. Y., & Zubin, J. (1987). Event related potentials in alcoholics and their first-degree relatives. *Alcoholism, 4,* 307–314.

Tarter, R. E. (1976). Neuropsychological investigations of alcoholism. In G. Goldstein & C. Neuringer (Eds.), *Empirical studies of alcoholism* (pp. 231–256). Cambridge, MA: Ballinger.

Tarter, R. E., Hegedus, A., Goldstein, G., Shelly, C., & Alterman, A. I. (1984). Adolescent sons of alcoholics: Neuropsychological and personality characteristics. *Alcoholism: Clinical and Experimental Research, 8,* 216–222.

Teuber, H.-L. (1959). Some alterations in behavior after cerebral lesions in man. In A. D. Bass (Ed.), *Evolution of nervous control from primitive organisms to man* (pp. 157–194). Washington, DC: American Association for the Advancement of Science.

Van Gorp, W. G., Miller, E. N., Satz, P., & Visscher, B. (1989). Neuropsychological performance in HIV-1 immunocompromised patients: A preliminary report. *Journal of Clinical and Experimental Neuropsychology, 11,* 763–773.

Walker, A. E., Caveness, W. F., & Critchley, M. (Eds.). (1969). *Late effects of head injury.* Springfield, IL: Thomas.

Wells, C. E. (1979). Pseudodementia. *American Journal of Psychiatry, 136,* 895–900.

Wells, C. E. (1980). The differential diagnosis of psychiatric disorders in the elderly. In J. O. Cole & J. E. Barrett (Eds.), *Psychopathology in the aged* (pp. 19–31). New York: Raven.

Werner, H., & Strauss, A. (1942). Experimental analysis of the clinical symptom "perseveration" in mentally retarded children. *American Journal of Mental Deficiency, 47,* 185–188.

Wernicke, C. (1874). *Der aphasiche symptomencomplex.* Breslau, Germany: Cohn and Weingart.

CHAPTER 5

Substance-Related Disorders: Alcohol

LINDA C. SOBELL, F. CURTIS BRESLIN, and MARK B. SOBELL

Problems related to alcohol abuse impose a staggering cost to society (e.g., medical, work, and family problems and highway fatalities). The estimated fiscal cost of alcohol problems in the United States in 1988 was $85.8 billion (National Institute on Alcohol Abuse and Alcoholism, 1990), and the costs in human suffering are incalculable.

Present views about the nature of alcohol use disorders are a mix of concepts derived from research and from clinical anecdote. To understand modern views about alcohol problems, it is necessary to understand how approaches have changed over several decades. Public opinion about individuals with alcohol problems has ranged from viewing them as being morally wrong to being victims of a disease. In the United States, early views of alcohol problems as a disorder developed after the repeal of Prohibition and focused on individuals who were severely dependent. This probably occurred because such individuals not only were highly visible but also had experienced the most severe consequences. One intent of the early views was to shift responsibility for dealing with alcohol problems from the criminal justice system to the health care system. These views, referred to as traditional conceptualizations of alcohol problems (Pattison, Sobell, & Sobell, 1977), stemmed primarily from Alcoholics Anonymous (AA; Bacon, 1973), and E. M. Jellinek (1960).

Alcoholics Anonymous viewed alcoholics as suffering from a biological aberration, an "allergy" to alcohol (i.e., it was stated that with repeated exposure to alcohol, alcoholics would change so as to quickly become physically dependent on alcohol if they started drinking), and once dependent they would continue to drink to avoid withdrawal symptoms. This, however, does not explain why people who stopped drinking for some time would return to drinking. To explain a return to drinking, AA stated that alcoholics had an "obsession" to drink like normal drinkers (nonalcoholics). Alcoholism was also thought to be a progressive disorder (i.e., if alcoholics continued to drink, their problem would inevitably worsen, even following a long abstinence period).

Jellinek, a scientist, attempted to bridge the gap between lay views and the slight scientific knowledge available by postulating a disease concept of alcoholism. He and others felt that the medical profession should be responsible for the care of persons with alcohol problems (Bacon, 1973). Although he alluded to genetic components, he did not speculate about why only some drinkers develop alcohol problems. He conjectured that alcoholics 1. use alcohol to cope with emotional problems, 2. over time develop tolerance to alcohol, thereby leading to increased consumption to achieve the desired effects, and 3. at some point in their drinking careers develop "loss of control." By loss of control, Jellinek (1960) hypothesized that consumption of even small amounts of alcohol would initiate physical dependence, which would then motivate continued drinking. Jellinek also hypothesized that there were many different types of alcohol problems. The type described above he called *gamma* alcoholism. He felt it was most common in the United States and was a progressive disorder.

Since these early views, research has been conducted that requires traditional concepts to be modified or abandoned. Although the research literature suggests that some individuals may be genetically predisposed to develop alcohol problems, a large proportion of persons with alcohol problems do not have a positive family history. Research also shows that social and cultural factors play a large role in the development of alcohol problems (Sigvardsson, Cloninger, & Bohman, 1985). For most cases, research shows that the natural history of the disorder is not progressive. Rather, it includes periods of alcohol problems of varying severity separated by periods of either nondrinking or of drinking limited quantities without problems (Cahalan, 1970). Epidemiological studies have also demonstrated that individuals with less serious alcohol problems outnumber those that have severe problems (Institute of Medicine, 1990). As will be discussed in the next section, alcohol use patterns lie along a continuum ranging from no problems to highly serious problems, and conceptualizations of alcohol problems must explain *all* forms of the problem, not just severe cases.

The treatment implications of the epidemiological findings are profound. Treatment approaches grounded in traditional conceptualizations have considered persons who are mildly dependent on alcohol as in the "early stages" of the progressive development of alcoholism, thus needing the same treatment as those who are severely dependent. By labeling everyone who experiences problems with alcohol an "alcoholic," it follows that such individuals must never drink again. Considerable research, however, shows that those who are mildly dependent on alcohol not only respond well to brief treatments but often recover by reducing rather than totally ceasing their alcohol consumption (Bien, Miller, & Tonigan, 1993; M. B. Sobell & Sobell, 1993).

With regard to loss of control, research has demonstrated that even in very severe cases, physical dependence is not initiated by a small amount of drinking (Marlatt, 1978; Pattison et al., 1977). This suggests that other factors, such as conditioned cues (Niaura et al., 1988), are necessary to explain why some people continue drinking despite having repeatedly suffered adverse consequences.

Another research finding of interest is the phenomenon of natural recoveries. Recent reports indicate that recovery from alcohol problems in the absence of treatment is more prevalent than once thought (American Psychiatric Association [APA], 1994; Fillmore, Hartka, Johnstone, Speiglman, & Temple, 1988; Institute of Medicine, 1990; L. C. Sobell, Cunningham, & Sobell, 1996). From a public health standpoint, this suggests that community interventions might facilitate natural recoveries (e.g., by prompting people to identify that they have a problem and to attempt to recover on their own).

EPIDEMIOLOGY

General population surveys provide information on rates of alcohol consumption as well as prevalence rates of problem drinking. Next to caffeine, alcohol is the second most used psychoactive substance (APA, 1994). In North America, per capita consumption has been declining for several years, particularly for spirits (Adams, Brown, & Flom, 1976). This decline is consistent with patterns observed in other developed countries (Adams & Celentan, 1975). This trend is thought to be due to either an aging population (i.e., older people tend to decrease use) or increased adoption of healthy lifestyles over the past decade (National Institute on Alcohol Abuse and Alcoholism, 1993). Per capita consumption and drinking patterns, however, can provide only a rough estimate of the rate of alcohol abuse or dependence.

Operational definitions of alcohol abuse and dependence are of concern because drinking problems have been reported as either diagnosis based or symptom based. Reporting the prevalence of abuse and dependence using current DSM definitions has the advantage that those definitions are accepted by both the research and clinical communities. However, a symptom-based approach where rates of specific types of problems (e.g., physiological vs. psychosocial) are reported is more congruent with a conceptualization of alcohol problems as lying along a severity continuum (Institute of Medicine, 1990). Although the exact ratio of problem drinkers to severely dependent drinkers varies depending on the definitions used and the populations sampled, on the problem severity continuum the population of persons with identifiable problems but no severe signs of dependence is many times larger than the population with severe dependence (M. B. Sobell & Sobell, 1993). Problem drinkers comprise between 15% and 35% of individuals in the adult population, whereas severely dependent drinkers only account for between 3% and 7% (Adamec & Phil, 1978; Institute of Medicine, 1990).

Alcohol problems are quite prevalent. Drinking problems are not distributed equally across sociodemographic groups. Further, male alcohol abusers greatly outnumber females (Fillmore, 1988; Hilton, 1987). Alcohol-related problems also appear to be inversely related to age, with the highest problem rates occurring for people between 18 and 29 years of age (Adams, Brown, Flom, & Jones, 1975; Fillmore, 1988). Several epidemiological studies have suggested that women have a later problem onset than men (reviewed in: Adamec & Phil, 1978; Fillmore, 1988). Marital status is also related to problem drinking, with single individuals experiencing more physiological symptoms of dependence and more psychosocial problems than married individuals (Adamec & Phil, 1978).

CLINICAL PICTURE

Individuals who present with alcohol problems in clinical settings can show impairment ranging from very mild symptoms (e.g., repeated hangovers) to severe symptoms (e.g., major withdrawal symptoms, cirrhosis). Recent evidence has shown that there is a significant incidence of psychiatric comorbidity with alcohol abuse (Anthony, Warner, & Kessler, 1994; Regier et al., 1990).

Chronic alcoholics—those who are severely dependent on alcohol—represent but the tip of the iceberg of all persons with alcohol problems (Cahalan, 1987; Room, 1977). In this regard, clinicians need to learn to recognize individuals with mild alcohol problems, and they should be aware that such individuals often respond well to brief interventions that allow reduced drinking as a goal (Bien et al., 1993; Heather, 1990; M. B. Sobell & Sobell, 1993).

COURSE AND PROGNOSIS

Traditional concepts of alcohol problems, based on Jellinek's work on progressivity (Jellinek, 1952), postulated that alcohol problems typically develop in early adulthood (i.e., 20 to 30 years of age) and increase in severity for several years thereafter. As noted earlier, research has not supported the notion of progressivity, although some individuals' problems do worsen over time. Research has also demonstrated that alcohol problems can have their onset at any age (Atkinson, 1994; Schonfeld & Dupree, 1991; Wilsnack, Klassen, Schur, & Wilsnack, 1991). The temporal pattern of problems can be variable, with problems sometimes remitting, worsening, or improving (Cahalan & Room, 1974; Hasin, Grant, & Endicott, 1990; Mandell, 1983). If an individual is experiencing alcohol problems at one point, it is not possible to predict that in the absence of treatment the problem will continue to worsen. It has been found, however, that men whose alcohol problems are severe are likely to continue to worsen over time (Fillmore & Midanik, 1984).

Alcohol problems are well known as a recurrent disorder (Polich, Armor, & Braiker, 1981). This characteristic has perhaps given the disorder a reputation as being difficult to treat and seldom "cured." Recent research, however, has found that the probability of relapse in persons who have been in remission for several years is fairly low (De Soto, O'Donnell, & De Soto, 1989; L. C. Sobell & Sobell, 1992a). Clinically, the high likelihood of recurrence has led to the development of relapse prevention procedures (Marlatt & Gordon, 1985). These procedures include advising clients that setbacks may occur during the course of recovery from the disorder and that they should use these setbacks as learning experiences to help prevent future relapses rather than interpret them as evidence that recovery is impossible. Finally, the presence of psychiatric comorbidity is associated with a more guarded prognosis for recovery (McLellan, 1986).

INDIVIDUAL DIFFERENCES

Minorities and Drinking Patterns

Even though epidemiological studies provide information on ethnic and racial differences in relation to alcohol use and abuse, the methods for categorizing respondents' cultural/ethnic backgrounds have been rudimentary. Consequently, data on ethnic differences must be considered preliminary. Across ethnic/racial groups, heavy drinking patterns occur at different points in the lifespan (Caetano & Kaskutas, 1995; National Institute on Alcohol Abuse and Alcoholism, 1993; Robins, 1991). Among white males, frequency of heavy drinking typically peaks in the twenties and decreases in the late thirties to forties, whereas heavy drinking among young black males is relatively low (Caetano, 1984; Herd, 1989; Russell, 1989), but does increase during middle age. This later onset in heavy drinking may explain why, despite similar overall rates of heavy drinking among black and white males, alcohol-related health problems (e.g., liver cirrhosis) were more common among black males. Such age-related differences have not been observed between black and white females.

The U.S. Hispanic population is very heterogeneous and includes individuals from Mexico, Puerto Rico, Cuba, and other Latin American countries. Acculturation appears to be associated with increased rates of heavy drinking among Hispanics (Caetano, 1985; Cahalan & Room, 1974). Some reports show Hispanics with lower rates of heavy drinking than other Americans (National Institute on Drug Abuse, 1991; Welte & Barnes, 1995), while others show Hispanics with higher rates (Caetano, 1989; Caetano & Kaskutas, 1995). These latter studies have found increased prevalence of alcohol-related problems among Hispanic males, especially those who are young to middle aged.

Among Asian Americans, alcohol problem rates are generally lower than the U.S. norms (National Institute on Alcohol Abuse and Alcoholism, 1993). As with other ethnic groups, there is marked variation in drinking patterns and problems among different Asian groups. Surveys of Hawaiians found that Caucasians report drinking significantly more alcohol than Japanese, Chinese, or Filipinos, and reports of alcohol problems paralleled use patterns (Ahern, 1985; Murakami, 1985). Across several studies, Chinese men and women report the lowest levels of alcohol use and abuse, with a large proportion reporting no drinking (Ahern, 1985; Yu, Liu, Xia, & Zhang, 1985). Low use has been attributed both to cultural norms and to sensitivity to alcohol (Clark & Hesselbrock, 1988).

Gender and Drinking Patterns

Numerous epidemiologic studies report that in every age category, men drink more than women and experience more adverse consequences of drinking (National Institute on Alcohol Abuse and Alcoholism, 1993). For example, there are almost nine times the number of young male heavy drinkers as females (Collins, 1993). Besides gender differences in prevalence, problem drinking tends to occur later in life for women (Fillmore, 1987). Women also appear to be more vulnerable to the adverse physical consequences of heavy alcohol use (Dawson & Grant, 1993). For example, alcohol-dependent women may be at higher risk of dying of alcohol-related causes such as hypertension and liver disease (Ashley & Rankin, 1979; Hill, 1984). Even nonfatal medical problems such as gynecological and obstetric problems appear to occur more frequently among female problem drinkers (Collins, 1993). Compared to nonalcoholic women, female alcoholics have a higher incidence of menstrual irregularities, have more difficulty becoming pregnant, and have more prenatal complications (Beckman, 1979; Wilsnack & Wilsnack, 1995). This increased vulnerability to alcohol's health effects may be due to the fact that body composition differences between men and women result in women having higher blood alcohol levels given an equivalent amount of alcohol.

GENETIC AND FAMILY INFLUENCES

Although genetic studies provide some support for a biologic influence on the development of alcohol problems, additional research is needed to clarify these findings. Several twin studies have found higher concordance rates for monozygotic than dizygotic twins, suggesting a positive relationship between degree of genetic overlap and risk of alcohol problems (Hrubec & Omenn, 1981; Kaij, 1960). Other twin studies, however, have shown little effect, and although twin studies are necessary, they do not provide sufficient support for a genetic model given the inevitable confounding of heredity and environment (Fillmore, 1988; Peele, 1986; Searles, 1988). Adoption studies constitute a clearer test of a genetic transmission of alcohol abuse because they allow for an independent assessment of genetic and environmental factors. Goodwin, Schulsinger, Hermanse, Guze, and Winokur (1973) examined adopted sons with and without parental alcohol problems and found that being a biological son of an alcoholic increased the likelihood of alcoholism fourfold. Adoption studies from Cloninger, Bohman, and Sigvardsson (1981) suggest that only a subpopulation of alcohol users show a genetic vulnerability for alcohol problems. Of the two types of alcohol problem profiles identified (i.e., Type 1 and Type 2), Type 2 appeared to have a strong genetic component, was limited to males, and comprised a minority (24%) of alcohol abusers in the sample.

Most genetic studies suffer from several methodological shortcomings that limit their contribution to understanding the nature and extent of alcohol problems. Operational definitions for alcohol problems vary across studies and often have little relation to formal diagnostic criteria (Searles, 1988). For example, Goodwin and his colleagues (1973) defined alcoholism as drinking six or more drinks consumed two or three times a month and reporting a loss of control over drinking. Even though no operational definition is perfect, the apparent uniqueness of this definition raises the possibility that these findings are due to the arbitrary threshold for alcohol problems (Murray et al., 1983). This is noteworthy because adoption studies do not show a genetic influence on likelihood of heavy drinking or mild to moderate drinking problems. Another problem with adoption studies is that the cohort studied is often young and has not passed thorough the age range of highest risk for alcohol problems (Fillmore, 1988). In the adoption study by Goodwin et al. (1973), 75% of the adopted men were under 34, and such a young cohort is typical of the other genetic studies. Because transient alcohol problems are not uncommon among young adults, it is not clear whether this genetic association holds for alcohol problems over the life span (Fillmore, 1988).

Although genetic findings are in need of replication, considerable research focuses on biochemical, neurological, and temperament differences between offspring with (FH+) and without (FH−) a family history of alcohol problems. Tarter, Alterman, and Edwards (1985) have found that FH+ subjects exhibited cognitive deficits (e.g., impulsivity, shorter attention span) compared to controls. Family history positive subjects also have an increased hyperactivity, implicating hyperactivity as an important cofactor in the development of alcohol abuse. Reduced perceived intoxication and brain wave abnormalities have also been observed among FH+ offspring, but the findings are inconsistent and their etiological role has yet to be determined (Begleiter, Porjesz, Bihari, & Kissin, 1984; Schuckit, 1980; Searles, 1988). Finn and Pihl (1988) have noted differences between offspring with multigenerational and unigenerational histories of alcohol abuse, suggesting that identifying those with a strong genetic loading may increase the consistency of findings. These findings, in combination with other data on FH+ family environment (Jacob, Krahn, & Leonard, 1991), suggest that the risk of developing an alcohol problem is a dynamic process where psychosocial and biological factors influence each other over time.

DIAGNOSTIC CONSIDERATIONS

Determining the incidence of alcohol problems in the general population has been difficult because of a continuing lack of consensus about how to define such problems (Hilton, 1991; Knupfer, 1984). Despite the lack of consensus, one thing is certain: alcohol is the most frequently used psychoactive drug among adults, and with the exception of cigarettes, the most abused psychoactive drug.

The classification of alcohol problems has evolved considerably over the past four decades. Currently, the two major diagnostic classifications of mental disorders are the *Diagnostic and Statistical Manual of Mental Disorders* (DSM) and the mental disorder section of the *International Classification of Diseases* (ICD). The first DSM (DSM-I) was published in 1952 by the American Psychiatric Association (APA) and was a variant of the ICD-6 (World Health Organization, 1948). Today, the terms in DSM-IV (APA, 1994) are compatible with both the ICD-9 and ICD-10 (World Health Organization, 1979, 1995). Although the DSM and ICD diagnostic schema are more similar today than ever before, a recent study found that "agreement between DSM-IV and ICD-10 on whether subjects were dependent or not is less than optimal" (Caetano & Tam, 1995, p. 177). According to Caetano and Tam (1995), the higher prevalence of dependence among young males in the ICD-10 is thought to be related to identifying consequences of episodic heavy drinking as signs of dependence. Despite these differences, in the United States the primary diagnostic classification schema used is DSM, and for this reason, the remainder of this section will address it.

Over the years, changes in DSM classification schema reflect both the state of knowledge and predominant attitudes at the time. The most recent version of DSM is the fourth edition (DSM-IV; APA, 1994). Whereas DSM-III-R (APA, 1987) viewed alcohol dependence as a graded phenomenon ranging from mild (enough consequences to meet criteria but no major withdrawal symptoms) to severe (several negative consequences and withdrawal symptoms), DSM-IV requires only a specification of alcohol dependence with physiological dependence (i.e., evidence of tolerance or withdrawal) or without physiological dependence (i.e., no evidence of tolerance or withdrawal). Table 5.1 lists DSM-IV criteria for alcohol dependence and alcohol abuse.

TABLE 5.1   DSM-IV Criteria for Alcohol Dependence and Alcohol Abuse

Alcohol dependence
Maladaptive pattern of alcohol use leads to clinically significant impairment or distress as evidenced by three or more of the following occurring at any time in the same 12-month period:

1. Tolerance as defined by a need for markedly increased amounts of alcohol to achieve intoxication or the desired effect or by markedly diminished effect with continued use of the same amount of alcohol.
2. Withdrawal as defined by characteristic alcohol withdrawal symptom or by alcohol use to avoid or relieve withdrawal symptoms.
3. Alcohol use in larger amounts or for a longer period of time than intended.
4. Persistent desire or unsuccessful efforts to control or reduce alcohol use.
5. Considerable time spent using alcohol, recovering from its effects or trying to obtain it.
6. Important social, occupational, or recreational activities avoided or reduced because of alcohol use.
7. Alcohol use continues despite knowledge that this could probably cause physical or psychological problems. Specify whether substance dependencies with or without physiological dependence.

Alcohol abuse
A maladaptive pattern of alcohol leading to clinically significant impairment or distress is manifested by one or more of the following occurring in a 12-month period:

1. Failure to fulfill important roles as a result of drinking (e.g., at work, school, and home).
2. Recurrent drinking in situations physically dangerous to do so (i.e., driving an automobile or operating machinery).
3. Recurrent alcohol-related legal problems.
4. Continued alcohol use despite recurrent social and interpersonal problems (e.g., loss of friends, arguments, and physical fights).

The major difference in DSM-IV between an alcohol dependence and an alcohol abuse diagnosis is that abuse is for less serious alcohol problems (i.e., no physiological dependence). Despite claims that DSM-IV is empirically based, a diagnosis of alcohol abuse is preempted by the diagnosis of alcohol dependence if the person's drinking pattern has *ever* met the criteria for dependence. Such a criterion implies that the disorder is progressive and that the condition will worsen unless an individual stops drinking. As reviewed earlier, several studies have failed to support the progressivity concept (Cahalan, 1970; Fillmore, 1988; Hasin et al., 1990), and one study (Hasin et al., 1990) has even found that some individuals initially diagnosed as alcohol dependent were later diagnosed as alcohol abusers (i.e., less severe symptoms). Other problems with the DSM-IV lacking an empirical base have been recently noted by Grant (1995).

The comorbidity of other psychiatric disorders among treated alcohol abusers has been well documented (Anthony et al., 1994; Cox, Norton, Swinson, & Endler, 1990; Drake et al., 1990; Regier et al., 1990; Ross, Glaser, & Germanson, 1988). The prevalence of psychiatric comorbidity in alcohol abusers varies from 7% to 75% (Mezzich, Arria, Tarter, Moss, & Van Thief, 1991). The two most common psychiatric problems associated with alcohol use disorders are mood and conduct disorders (Meyer & Kranzler, 1988; Ross et al., 1988; Schuckit, 1985). Based on DSM-III criteria, lifetime prevalence of an antisocial personality disorder among alcohol abusers ranges from 40% to 50% (Hesselbrock, Meyer, & Keener, 1985; Ross et al., 1988). The prevalence of major mood disorders also varies among studies. Lifetime prevalence rates range from 18% to 25% (Hesselbrock et al., 1985; Weissman & Meyers, 1980), with current rates for treated alcohol abusers ranging from 9% to 38% (Dorus, Kennedy, Gibbons, & Ravi, 1987; Keeler, Taylor, & Miller, 1979). The prevalence of anxiety disorders among alcohol abusers has been reported to range from 6% to 69% (reviewed in Kushner, Sher, & Beitman, 1990). Several surveys have also shown that of all individuals with schizophrenia or schizophreniform disorders close to half meet the lifetime criteria for an alcohol use disorder (Carey, 1996; Drake et al., 1990; Regier et al., 1990).

DIAGNOSTIC ISSUES AND PROBLEMS

Because of the high prevalence of comorbidity among alcohol abusers, diagnostic formulations are a two-step process. First, the extent and nature of the problem must be documented. This can be done with a variety of instruments that will be discussed in the assessment section of this chapter. The second step is to establish whether other psychiatric disorders (i.e., anxiety, depression) are present, and, if so, to determine whether alcohol use is the primary or secondary disorder.

As noted previously (L. C. Sobell, Sobell, Toneatto, & Shillingford, 1994; M. B. Sobell, Wilkinson, & Sobell, 1990; Sokolow, Welte, Hynes, & Lyons, 1981; Toneatto, Sobell, Sobell, & Leo, 1991), diagnostic formulations have clinical utility beyond insurance and clinical recording requirements. An accurate diagnosis is important because it allows classification of the problem in a way that can be easily communicated to other clinicians and researchers. The diagnostic formulation coupled with other assessment material provides an initial understanding of the problem behavior as well as a foundation for initial treatment planning. Diagnostic formulations also play an important role in decisions about treatment goals and intensities. Clinical issues with respect to diagnostic formulations will be discussed in the remainder of this section.

Over the past decade there have been several significant developments in the alcohol field that call for differential treatment planning. Among these developments are a growing recognition of the importance of assessing and treating alcohol abusers with dual diagnoses, whether the second disorder is a psychiatric or another substance use disorder. The high co-occurrence of psychiatric and other substance use disorders with alcohol problems has led to the suggestion alcohol abusers should be assessed for the relationship(s) that one drug or problem has with another (e.g., precipitating relapses). Unfortunately, very few empirical guidelines exist with respect to how to treat alcohol abusers who have other clinical disorders. A major question relates to whether treatments should be concurrent or sequential. The clearest example of this is with alcohol abusers who smoke cigarettes (Bobo, 1989; L. C. Sobell, Sobell, Kozlowski, & Toneatto, 1990; M. B. Sobell, Sobell, & Kozlowski, 1995). Although simultaneous treatment of drinking and smoking has been hypothesized to increase the risk of relapse, conditioning theory suggests the opposite. Because of the present lack of empirical studies, decisions regarding treating alcohol and other drug problems simultaneously or sequentially need to be made on a case-by-case basis. Also, in the absence of empirical studies it is unclear whether the same or different types of treatment (behavioral vs. pharmacological) for comorbid problems would be more effective. Although it is unclear how best to manage issues clinically, psychiatric assessment of drug comorbidity with alcohol abuse should occur before and during treatment.

For alcohol abusers who use or abuse other drugs including nicotine, it is important to gather a comprehensive profile of psychoactive substance use. Over the course of an intervention, drug use patterns may change (e.g., decreased alcohol use, increased smoking; decreased alcohol use, increased cannabis use). Further, alcohol abusers who use other drugs call into question the possibility of pharmacological synergism (i.e., a multiplicative effect of similarly acting drugs taken concurrently). Cross-tolerance (i.e., decreased effect of a drug due to previous heavy use of pharmacologically similar drugs) should also be considered when assessing alcohol abusers who use other drugs. Finally, it must be recognized that the treatment of alcohol abusers who abuse other drugs may not parallel that for individuals who abuse only alcohol (Battjes, 1988; Burglass & Shaffer, 1983; Burling & Ziff, 1988; Kaufman, 1982).

An alcohol-dependence diagnosis must also distinguish between a disorder that is secondary to other psychiatric disorders versus a primary disorder that can produce other psychiatric disorders. For example, when alcohol is chronically ingested or consumed in high doses, pharmacological effects can give rise to syndromes that mimic mood, anxiety, or psychotic disorders. In this regard, the DSM-IV (APA, 1994) provides a general discussion of the differential diagnoses of alcohol-induced disorders that resemble primary mental disorders (e.g., major depressive disorder vs. alcohol-induced mood disorder with depressive features, with onset during intoxication).

There are significant prognostic implications for alcohol abusers with comorbid psychiatric problems. Several studies have shown that alcohol abusers who have serious psychiatric problems have poorer treatment outcomes than alcohol abusers without major psychiatric symptoms (Meyer & Kranzler, 1988; Rounsaville, Dolinsky, Babor, & Meyer, 1987). Although it has been suggested that patients with serious psychiatric problems and a primary alcohol disorder should receive additional counseling, there is a lack of empirical data suggesting whether treatment of the comorbid problem reliably improves treatment outcomes. Although evidence is also lacking whether treatment for alcohol and other psychiatric problems should be concurrent or sequential and in separate or similar settings, currently most dually diagnosed clients with alcohol problems are treated in the mental health system (Carey, 1996).

One approach to the treatment of alcohol abusers with psychiatric comorbidities is to evaluate the extent to which alcohol and other psychiatric problems are functionally related. On that basis, a decision could be made to treat the disorder separately or together, because if the problems are related then the comorbidity might serve as a barrier to the resolution of the alcohol problem. For example, if individuals use alcohol to self-medicate their psychiatric symptoms (e.g., social phobia, agoraphobia), then such individuals might be reluctant to forego the use of alcohol in the absence of alternative methods of reducing anxiety. Determining the temporal patterning of the two disorders can help in formulating a treatment plan (Carey, 1996).

For alcohol abusers, diagnostic formulations may also play an important role in decisions about treatment goals and treatment intensity (M. B. Sobell & Sobell, 1987). Some research suggests that severity of alcohol dependence may interact with response to treatment goals, that is, abstinence or nonproblem drinking (Institute of Medicine, 1990; Miller, Leckman, Delaney, & Tinkcom, 1992), and different treatment intensities (Annis, 1986; Orford & Keddie, 1986). Considering the most appropriate treatment for alcohol abusers with different levels of dependence (e.g., mild vs. severe) is consistent with client-treatment matching (DiClemente, Carroll, Connors, & Kadden, 1994; Donovan et al., 1994; Mattson et al., 1994).

Because alcohol withdrawal symptoms are defining features for an alcohol dependence diagnosis, a careful history of past withdrawals is necessary. A considerable part of a client's alcohol-related history, particularly with outpatients is retrospective and based on self-report. Thus, it is important that clients understand what is meant by withdrawal symptoms. For example, a critical term that often causes alcohol abusers some confusion is delirium tremens, or "DTs" (L. C. Sobell, Toneatto, & Sobell, 1994) This term, frequently confused with minor withdrawal symptoms such as psychomotor agitation, refers to actual delirium and implies severe dependence on alcohol. A history of past withdrawal symptoms coupled with reports of recent heavy ethanol consumption should alert clinicians that withdrawal symptoms are likely to occur upon cessation of drinking. In summary, accurate diagnostic formulations are important because they often dictate differential treatment interventions.

PSYCHOLOGICAL AND BIOLOGICAL ASSESSMENT

Assessment of alcohol use and abuse has received considerable attention as evidenced by several excellent comprehensive reviews of both behavioral and biochemical measures (Addiction Research Foundation, 1993; Allen & Columbus, 1995; Allen & Litten, 1993; Allen & Mattson, 1993; Bernadt, Mumford, Taylor, Smith, & Murray, 1982; Cushman, 1992; Leigh & Skinner, 1988; Levine, 1990; Phelps & Field, 1992; L. C. Sobell, Toneatto, & Sobell, 1994). Interested readers are referred to these publications for a summary of current assessment issues and techniques.

Critical Issues in Assessment

The ideal assessment of alcohol abusers would involve behavioral observations over time while the individual is under the influence of alcohol. However, such vivo assessments are seldom possible. Consequently, in the alcohol field a significant amount of research and clinical information is obtained through self-reports (Babor, Brown, & Del Boca, 1990; L. C. Sobell & Sobell, 1990) Despite widespread skepticism among practitioners, several major reviews of the scientific literature have concluded that alcohol abusers' self-reports are generally accurate if clients are interviewed in clinical or research settings, when they are alcohol free, and when they are given assurance of confidentiality (see reviews: Babor et al., 1990; Brown, Kranzler, & Del Boca, 1992; L. C. Sobell & Sobell, 1990). The one condition when alcohol abusers' self-reports have been found to be inaccurate is when they have any alcohol in their system when interviewed (reviewed in Leigh & Skinner, 1988; M. B. Sobell, Sobell, & VanderSpek, 1979). Because all studies find some proportion, albeit small, of self-reports to be inaccurate, one way of possibly identifying inaccurate self-reports is to obtain information from multiple sources (e.g., chemical tests, self-reports, collateral reports, and official records). Data from different sources are then compared and final conclusions reached on a convergence of information (Maisto, McKay, & Connors, 1990; L. C. Sobell & Sobell, 1990).

Standardized assessments serve several critical functions. First, they provide a clinical picture of the severity of the person's alcohol problem. This picture can be used to develop treatment plans tailored to the needs of the particular individual. Second, if change is not evident during treatment, ongoing assessment information can be used to make systematic changes in the treatment plan. Third, progress during and after treatment can be compared with the initial assessment to evaluate the extent and types of changes that have occurred and to suggest when further interventions need to occur.

The depth and intensity of an assessment will be related to problem severity and the complexity of the presenting case as well as the individual needs of the clinician and researcher. With respect to the length of an assessment, intense and in-depth assessments can no longer be justified for all clients. For example, because persons with mild alcohol problems often respond well to a relatively brief intervention (reviewed in Bien et al., 1993), an assessment that is longer than the intervention cannot be justified. In contrast, severely dependent alcohol abusers may require an intensive assessment covering such areas as organic brain dysfunction, psychiatric comorbidity, and social needs. Ultimately, the assessment should be determined based on clinical judgment and current clinical needs.

The following section provides a focus on a description of the various assessment areas along with a review of different assessment instruments, scales, and questionnaires that can be used for assessing alcohol use and abuse. Readers interested in a comprehensive compilation of assessment tools for alcohol use and abuse are referred to several published directories (Addiction Research Foundation, 1993; Allen & Columbus, 1995; Lettieri, Nelson, & Sayers, 1985). In this review, only instruments that have sound psychometric properties and have clinical utility will be included. With respect to selecting an appropriate instrument it is helpful to ask "What will I learn from using the instrument and measure that I would not otherwise know from a routine clinical interview?" (L. C. Sobell, Toneatto, & Sobell, 1994, p. 540).

ASSESSMENT AREAS

Alcohol Use

Assessing alcohol consumption involves measuring the quantity and frequency of past and present use. When choosing an instrument to assess drinking, a decision must be made about the type of information desired, that is, level of precision and time frame (L. C. Sobell & Sobell, 1995, 1996; L. C. Sobell, Toneatto, & Sobell, 1994). As noted in recent reviews, there are four well established methods for assessing past alcohol consumption: 1. lifetime drinking history, hereafter LDH (Skinner & Sheu, 1982; L. C. Sobell & Sobell, 1995; L. C. Sobell, Toneatto, & Sobell, 1994); 2. quantity-frequency methods, hereafter QF (Room, 1990; Skinner & Sheu, 1982; L. C. Sobell & Sobell, 1995); 3. alcohol timeline followback, hereafter TLFB (L. C. Sobell & Sobell, 1992b, 1995, 1996); and 4. self-monitoring, SM (L. C. Sobell & Sobell, 1995; M. B. Sobell, Bogardis, Schuller, Leo, & Sobell, 1989). The first three methods are retrospective (i.e., they obtain information about alcohol use after it has occurred). The fourth, SM, asks clients to record their drinking at or about the same time that it occurred. Because several reviews have detailed the advantages and disadvantages of these drinking instruments only their key features will be noted here. Readers interested in the use of these instruments are referred to the source articles.

The LDH summarizes distinct phases and changes in a person's lifetime drinking. The LDH is a structured interview that takes 20–30 minutes to complete and requires clients to recall their drinking in discrete phases reflecting major changes in their average drinking pattern. Quantity-frequency methods are among the earliest measures used to assess drinking and require people to report their "average" consumption patterns. Although QF methods provide reliable information about overall consumption and frequency of drinking (reviewed in L. C. Sobell & Sobell, 1992b, 1995), they are unable to identify infrequent heavy drinking days which are often associated with alcohol-related problems. Because atypical drinking is important clinically, QF methods have limited clinical utility and are only useful if time is limited.

The TLFB, a drinking estimation method, was developed to aid the recall of daily drinking (L. C. Sobell & Sobell, 1992b, 1995, 1996). The method incorporates several memory aids to enhance recall and takes about 10–15 minutes to gather information for a 90-day period. It can be self-administered and is available in a paper and pencil or computer format (L. C. Sobell & Sobell, 1996). The TLFB method is recommended when more precise measures of drinking are necessary, especially when a complete picture of drinking days is needed. The TLFB method can also be used in treatment as an advice-feedback tool to help increase clients' motivation to change (L. C. Sobell & Sobell, 1996).

Self-monitoring of alcohol use which requires clients to record different aspects of their alcohol use (e.g., amount, frequency, mood, urges, and consequences) can take a variety of forms (e.g., logs, diaries). Self-monitoring has several clinical advantages: 1. it provides feedback about treatment effectiveness, 2. it can identify situations that pose a high risk of relapse, and 3. when used in an outpatient setting it gives clients an opportunity to discuss their drinking since the previous session (L. C. Sobell, Toneatto, & Sobell, 1994). When used appropriately, self-monitoring is subject to fewer memory problems than retrospective drinking methods. However, it can only be used once treatment has begun. Also, not all clients comply with instructions (Sanchez-Craig & Annis, 1982).

Consequences of Alcohol Use

One of the key defining characteristics of a DSM-IV diagnosis is alcohol-related consequences. There are several short self-administered scales that have been developed to assess psychosocial consequences and dependence symptoms related to alcohol abuse. Unfortunately, none of the scales are ideal (Davidson, 1987; L. C. Sobell, Toneatto, & Sobell, 1994). Although several scales are used for brief screening and identification of harmful and hazardous alcohol use (e.g., Alcohol Use Disorders Identification, AUDIT; Bohn, Babor, & Kranzler, 1995; Saunders, Aasland, Babor, De La Fuente, & Grant, 1993; and CAGE; Mayfield, McLeod, & Hall, 1974), in clinical settings the more commonly used scales for assessing alcohol-related consequences include the 1. Severity of Alcohol Dependence Questionnaire (SADQ and SADQ-C; Stockwell, Murphy, & Hodgson, 1983; Stockwell, Sitharthan, McGrath, & Lang, 1994), 2. Alcohol Dependence Scale (ADS; Skinner & Allen, 1982), and 3. Short Alcohol Dependence Data Questionnaire (SADD; Raistrick, Dunbar, & Davidson, 1983). These scales take about 5 minutes to administer and range from 15 to 25 items in length. The SADQ is more suited to chronic populations and is not as sensitive as the ADS, SADD, and SADQ-C for evaluating mild to moderate alcohol problems. Scales like the ADS and the SADD can also be used to screen clients for the appropriateness of a reduced drinking goal and for brief treatment (Skinner & Horn, 1984; M. B. Sobell & Sobell, 1993; Sokolow et al., 1981).

Assessing Risk Situations and Self-Efficacy

Because relapse rates among treated alcohol abusers are extremely high, assessment of high-risk situations for excessive drinking is important at assessment and during treatment (Marlatt & Gordon, 1985; M. B. Sobell & Sobell, 1993). Two instruments developed by Annis and her colleagues (Annis & Graham, 1988, 1995; Annis, Graham, & Davis, 1987) yield profiles of clients' high-risk drinking situations in the past year that can be used with clients during the course of treatment (Annis & Graham, 1995; M. B. Sobell & Sobell, 1993; Sokolow et al., 1981). The Inventory of Drinking Situations (IDS) is a 42-item scale and requires clients to rate the frequency that they drink heavily in particular situations in the past year. The Situational Confidence Questionnaire (SCQ) contains parallel items to the IDS and assesses self-efficacy by measuring how confident clients are that at the present time they would be able to resist the urge to drink heavily in particular situations. Each scale takes about 15–20 minutes to complete and contains eight subscales (e.g., unpleasant emotions, pleasant emotions, and social pressure) based on research by Marlatt and Gordon (1985).

Although the scales can be used clinically to enhance the treatment plan, they only identify generic situations or problem areas. To examine clients' individual high-risk situations or areas where they lack self-confidence, clinicians should explore specific situations with clients. Clients can be asked to describe their two or three highest risk situations for alcohol use in the past year (examples of a homework exercise for assessing high-risk situations can be found in M. B. Sobell & Sobell, 1993).

Assessment of Psychiatric Comorbidity with Alcohol Abusers

Because it is clear that a substantial number of alcohol abusers, especially those who are severely dependent, have psychiatric problems (Anthony et al., 1994; Carey, 1995; Drake et al., 1990; Regier et al., 1990), attention must be given to evaluating their presence and severity. While several diagnostic interviews and scales exist for assessing comorbidity with alcohol abusers, the comprehensiveness of assessments of individuals with comorbid disorders will depend on the resources available, degree of specificity of the information required, the treatment setting, and most importantly the skill level of the assessor (reviewed in L. C. Sobell, Toneatto, & Sobell, 1994). Among the most common instruments are 1. Structured Clinical Interview for DSM-III-R (SCID), 2. Diagnostic Interview Schedule (DIS), and 3. Composite International Diagnostic Interview (CIDI). These structured interviews help clinicians develop both a diagnosis and a treatment plan for clients.

Besides structured psychiatric interviews, several brief, more specific instruments can be useful, although not yielding formal diagnoses: 1. Beck Depression Inventory (Beck, Steer, & Garbin, 1988), 2. Beck Anxiety Inventory (Beck, Epstein, Brown, & Steer, 1988), 3. Hamilton Rating Scale for Depression (Hamilton, 1960), and 4. Symptom Checklist-90-R (Derogatis, 1983). For a brief description of the clinical utility of these instruments the reader is referred to a recent review (L. C. Sobell, Toneatto, & Sobell, 1994).

Neuropsychological Assessment

The existence of organic brain disorder as related to alcohol abuse has been thought to be an important factor for treatment planning. For example, a highly cognitive approach would not be expected to work well for alcohol abusers who have impaired abstraction ability (McCrady & Smith, 1986; Sanchez-Craig, Wilkinson, & Walker, 1987; Wilkinson & Sanchez-Craig, 1981). A neuropsychological assessment is indicated whenever damage to the central nervous system is suspected. A history of accidental falls or car accidents, common among severely dependent alcohol abusers, may increase the likelihood of neuropsychological impairment. In selecting a specific assessment strategy, a balance must be struck between a comprehensive approach, with the associated disadvantages of time and expense, and a less comprehensive approach that sacrifices breadth of assessment but is less costly (Tarter, Ott, & Mezzich, 1991).

Two tests of organic functioning, the Trail Making Test (Davies, 1968) and the Digit Symbol subscale of WAIS, are recommended as screening tests for assessing probable organic brain dysfunction due to alcohol consumption (Lezak, 1976; Miller & Saucedo, 1983; Wilkinson & Carlen, 1980). Both tests are relatively easy and quick to administer (i.e., less than 5 minutes) and are highly sensitive to brain dysfunction. Readers interested in the application and interpretation of assessing neuropsychological impairment and functioning related to alcohol problems are referred to excellent reviews of this literature (Miller & Saucedo, 1983; Parsons, 1987; Parsons & Farr, 1981).

Barriers or Potential Barriers to Change

In developing a treatment plan it is helpful to anticipate possible barriers that clients might encounter with respect to changing their behavior. Barriers can be both motivational and practical. If an individual does not feel that it is important to change, then there is probably little reason to expect that change will occur. Because many alcohol abusers are coerced into treatment (e.g., courts, significant others), it might be expected that such individuals will not have a serious interest in changing (Cunningham, Sobell, Sobell, & Gaskin, 1994). In recent years increasing attention has been given to the importance of assessing the extent to which clients believe they need to change. Two recent books discuss ways of assessing and increasing motivation in clients who are not strongly committed to change (Beck, Wright, Newman, & Liese, 1993; Miller & Rollnick, 1991).

Environmental factors also can present formidable obstacles to change. For example, individuals who are in an environment where alcohol is readily available and where a considerable number of social situations involve alcohol use might find it difficult to abstain because of the high number of environmental cues. For some individuals social avoidance strategies (e.g., never going to bars) might be the only effective alternative. Finally, clinicians should attend to individual barriers that can drastically affect a person's ability to enter and complete treatment such as child care, transportation, inability to take time off from work, and unwillingness to adopt an abstinence goal (Schmidt & Weisner, 1995).

Biochemical Measures

Because no self-report measure is error free, the use of measures complementary to self-reports is recommended, with the set of measures yielding a convergent validity approach to assessment (L. C. Sobell & Sobell, 1980). Although there has been a tendency to consider biochemical measures as "gold standards" and superior to self-report, several reviews have found that even biochemical measures suffer from validity problems (Bernadt et al., 1982; Leigh & Skinner, 1988; Levine, 1990; Maisto & Connors, 1992; O'Farrell & Maisto, 1987). Some reviews have even found self-reports to be superior to certain biochemical measures (Petersson, Trell, & Kristensson, 1983; Salaspuro, 1986).

Issues of self-report accuracy take on different meanings for clinical versus research purposes, where different levels of reporting precision are required (see discussions by Baker & Brandon, 1990; Rankin, 1990). For example, clinicians do not routinely have to obtain information to confirm their client's alcohol use unless the situation warrants it. However, in clinical trials researchers typically need to verify their clients' self-reports using an alternative measure (e.g., collateral reports).

A variety of alternative measures to self-reports of alcohol use exist. Those that will be discussed below include 1. breath tests, 2. dipsticks, 3. urinalysis, 4. sweat patches, and 5. acute liver function tests. Biochemical measures can be classified into two categories: recent/current use and use over an extended time period. Recent (i.e., past 24 hours) use of alcohol can be detected in different bodily fluids (e.g., breath, blood, and urine) and by several different detection methods. For an in-depth review of the advantages and disadvantages of different testing methods, readers are referred to several reviews (Phelps & Field, 1992; Shute, 1988; Verebey & Turner, 1991).

Breath Alcohol Tests

One of the most economical and convenient methods of assessing a person's recent use of alcohol is through breath alcohol tests. Fairly accurate and specific assessments can be made of a person's blood alcohol concentration by evidential breathalyzers. Several less specific, but nevertheless useful portable breath alcohol testers are commercially available and cost about $1 per test. Breath tests have several advantages: they are noninvasive, inexpensive, and portable and give immediate determination of breath alcohol concentration.

Alcohol Dipstick

The dipstick, a newer method of assessing alcohol use in fluids (Kapur & Israel, 1983), uses strips of filtered paper that react with carrier fluids (e.g., saliva, urine) to change color in response to different levels of ethanol. Although the dipstick has been shown to have adequate reliability and validity (Tu, Kapur, & Israel, 1992) the clinical utility of this instrument remains uncertain. Alcohol dipsticks do not seem to be as readily available as breath alcohol testers.

Urine Tests

Urinalyses can provide qualitative (i.e., different types of drugs, including alcohol) as well as quantitative (i.e., amount) information about alcohol and drug use (Schwartz, 1988). Because alcohol use can be economically and quickly detected using breath testers, urine tests are more suitable for assessing other drug use (e.g., cocaine and marijuana).

Alcohol Sweat Patch

Over a decade ago the alcohol sweat patch was introduced to provide a noninvasive technique to estimate alcohol use over a 1–10-day period (Phillips, 1992). The patch is a plastic, watertight adhesive with absorbent pads and was designed to collect transepidermal fluid at a steady rate during the time the person wore the patch. Several methodological problems render the patch unsuitable for clinical use at the present time (Leigh & Skinner, 1988; L. C. Sobell, Sobell, & Nirenberg, 1988).

Hair Analysis

Although hair analysis can detect drug use over several years and is highly accurate (Gibson & Manley, 1991; Strang, Black, Marsh, & Smith, 1993), it is also a very costly procedure. At the present time, its clinical utility is undetermined.

Liver Function Tests

Liver function tests are among the most common biochemical measures for assessing alcohol consumption over longer time periods. Several reviews have noted that elevations on different biochemical markers correlate to varying degrees with heavy drinking (Conigrave, Saunders, & Whitfield, 1995; Cushman, 1992; Leigh & Skinner, 1988; Levine, 1990). However, none of the markers alone is better at identifying heavy drinking than are self-reports or questionnaires. When two or more liver function measures are combined, their sensitivity and specificity for detecting heavy alcohol use increases (Allen & Litten, 1993; Leigh & Skinner, 1988; Levine, 1990) At present, the major utility of liver function tests is as a probable, rather than definitive, indicator of prolonged heavy drinking. Recent evidence suggests that liver function tests are more useful with severely dependent alcohol abusers than with problem drinkers (i.e., mild to moderately dependent alcohol abusers; Conigrave et al., 1995). Finally, clinicians who are not physicians and wish to use liver function tests will need to arrange for a physician to order and evaluate such tests.

TREATMENT APPROACHES

Although diagnosis should be a major determinant of the treatment of choice for any disorder, this has rarely occurred in the alcohol field. This situation is largely a result of the predominant treatments being developed in the absence of research (Callahan, Long, Pecsok, & Simone, 1987; Pattison et al., 1977). Miller et al. (1995) in a recent review of treatments for alcohol problems noted that the predominant treatments available are those lacking empirical support. In contrast, the most evaluated approaches are not readily available. Acknowledging this imbalance, this brief summary will address how diagnostics can be used in making treatment decisions. Also, it should be noted that many individuals, particularly those with mild alcohol problems, recover without any formal help or treatment (Robins, 1993; L. C. Sobell et al., 1993, 1995).

A helpful way to relate alcohol disorders to treatments is to think of the disorders as lying along a severity continuum. For individuals whose problems are not severe (i.e., who are not physically dependent), it has been well established that a brief intervention is often sufficient for recovery (Miller et al., 1995). These interventions usually emphasize motivational enhancement and assume that individuals have the skills necessary to stop drinking excessively, if they are sufficiently motivated to do so. Such interventions usually allow treatment goals of either reduced use or abstinence. For individuals whose problems are more severe or who have skills deficits, social skills training can be effective (Monti, Abrams, Kadden, & Cooney, 1989). Such an approach might also be used with individuals who do not show positive change after being treated with a brief intervention. Although skills training procedures are often conducted as part of inpatient programs, there is little support in the research literature for using inpatient treatment for alcohol use disorders. An exception may be made if environmental pressures for excessive drinking are so great that there is little likelihood of the individual improving in that environment (e.g., if the person lives with heavy drinkers who create intense social pressure to drink heavily). Use of inpatient treatment based on social needs has not been a topic of research, but it would be consistent with clinical judgment. Twelve-step treatment programs, although popular, have yet to be comparatively evaluated against less intensive or behavioral treatments, although an ongoing federally sponsored research project promises to provide valuable data in this regard (Mattson, 1993). Similarly, the effects of AA and other self-help groups have not been fairly evaluated. For example, the two existing outcome evaluations of AA used subjects who were legally coerced to attend meetings (Miller et al., 1995). Pharmacotherapy adjuncts to treatment are being actively investigated, and naltrexone, thought to counteract the rewarding effects of alcohol, has been associated with better outcomes for severely dependent individuals (O'Malley et al., 1992). The most popular pharmacotherapy, disulfiram (Antabuse™), produces an aversive reaction if alcohol is ingested. A major problem with disulfiram is that there is a very low compliance rate with taking the medication (Litten & Allen, 1991). For severe disorders, abstinence is typically the goal of treatment (M. B. Sobell & Sobell, 1995).

Earlier in this chapter it was mentioned that alcohol use disorders tend to recur, a finding that led to the development of relapse prevention approaches (Marlatt & Gordon, 1985). Relapse prevention procedures have been investigated in several studies, but the findings of controlled outcome research have been inconsistent (M. B. Sobell & Sobell, 1993).

Minorities and Treatment

To date, research on minorities has focused on the epidemiology of alcohol problems. In contrast, studies of the effectiveness of alcohol treatment for minorities have been sparse (Institute of Medicine, 1990). Moreover, ethnicity often is not reported in descriptions of treatment samples (M. B. Sobell, Brochu, Sobell, Roy, & Stevens, 1987), much less as a predictor of treatment outcome. Some research has examined barriers to treatment in order to increase the participation of minorities (McGough & Hindman, 1986). Some alcohol services have developed specific culturally sensitive programs. Preliminary evidence indicates that these programs may increase recruitment rates of minorities seeking treatment (Westermeyer, 1984).

Gender and Treatment

Current data suggest that approximately one-quarter of the alcohol treatment population are female (National Institute on Alcohol Abuse and Alcoholism, 1993). In 1992, 50% of U.S. addiction treatment units provided services especially for women compared to 23% in 1982 (Schmidt & Weisner, 1995). This increase in services is partly due to efforts to increase awareness of the incidence of fetal alcohol syndrome, a cluster of fetal abnormalities associated with heavy drinking in pregnancy. While more specialized alcohol treatment services are consistent with a treatment matching approach, female problem drinkers face different barriers to alcohol treatment (e.g., increased stigmatization, family child care demands; Collins, 1993). The social stigma associated with female problem drinkers may explain why more female problem drinkers present at mental health clinics than addiction services. Such barriers suggest that a more community-based approach to treatment may be needed to meet womens' treatment needs.

Most studies show no gender differences in treatment outcome. However, those studies that do find differences report females doing better than males (Toneatto, Sobell, & Sobell, 1992). Women have also shown a greater ability to drink moderately after treatment (Helzer, 1984; Miller & Joyce, 1979; L. C. Sobell et al., 1996). Reasons for drinking and relapse also seem to be different for women. Women were more likely to return to heavy drinking after treatment when they had fewer children at home, higher verbal IQ scores, and decreased belief in control of future drinking (Saunders, Baily, Phillips, & Allsop, 1993). Also, women in alcohol treatment were more likely to endorse reasons for drinking such as improved mood or dealing with marital conflict compared to men in treatment. Such information suggests that these factors should be explored when treating female problem drinkers.

SUMMARY

Historically, the scientific study of alcohol abuse has focused primarily on individuals who have been severely dependent on alcohol even though such persons constitute a minority of the alcohol abusing population. This chapter addresses diagnostic and assessment issues related to alcohol abusers all along the dependence continuum, ranging from those who are mildly dependent to those who are severely dependent. A thorough and careful assessment is an important part of the treatment process for individuals with all types of alcohol problems. The assessment is critical to the development of meaningful treatment plans. Accurate diagnosis of alcohol and other concurrent disorders is integral to the assessment process. The assessment can serve several critical functions: 1. It provides clinicians with an in-depth picture of a person's alcohol use and related consequences, particularly the severity of the disorder; this picture can be used to develop treatment plans tailored to the needs of each client. 2. If change is not evident during treatment, ongoing assessment information can be used to make systematic changes in the treatment plan. And 3. progress during treatment can be compared with the initial assessment to evaluate the extent and types of changes that have occurred and to suggest where further interventions are needed. The depth and intensity of an assessment will be related to problem severity and the complexity of the presenting case as well as the individual needs of the clinician or researcher. Ultimately, assessments should be determined based on clinical judgment and current clinical needs. The instruments and methods described in this chapter can be used clinically to gather information relevant to the assessment and treatment planning process. The implications of assessment data for treatment issues, such as drinking goals and treatment intensity, show how the clinical interview can significantly impact on treatment. Critical issues in assessment (e.g., self-reports, convergent data sources) are discussed as well.

REFERENCES

Adamec, D. S., & Phil, R. O. (1978). Sex differences in response to marijuana in a social setting. *Psychology of Women Quarterly, 2,* 334–353.

Adams, A. J., Brown, B., & Flom, M. C. (1976). Alcohol-induced changes in contrast sensitivity following high-intensity light exposure. *Perception and Psychophysics, 19,* 219–225.

Adams, A. J., Brown, B., Flom, M. C., & Jones, R. T. (1975). Alcohol and marijuana effects on static visual-acuity. *American Journal of Optometry and Physiological Optics, 52,* 729–735.

Adams, C. C., & Celentan, D. D. (1975). Standards for Maryland halfway house alcoholism programs. *Maryland State Medical Journal, 24,* 61.

Addiction Research Foundation. (1993). *Directory of client outcome measures for addictions treatment programs.* Toronto: Author.

Ahern, F. M. (1985). Alcohol use and abuse among four ethnic groups in Hawaii: Native Hawaiians, Japanese, Filipinos, and Caucasians. In D. L. Spiegler, D. A. Tate, S. S. Aitken, & C. M. Christian (Eds.), *Epidemiology of alcohol use and abuse among ethnic minority groups* (DHHS Publication No. ADM 89-1435, pp. 315–328). Rockville, MD: National Institute on Alcohol Abuse and Alcoholism.

Allen, J. P., & Columbus, M. (Eds.). (1995). Assessing alcohol problems: A guide for clinicians and researchers (NIAAA Treatment Handbook Series No. 4). Rockville, MD: National Institute on Alcohol Abuse and Alcoholism.

Allen, J. P., & Litten, R. Z. (1993). Psychometric and laboratory measures to assist in the treatment of alcoholism. *Clinical Psychology Review, 13,* 223–240.

Allen, J. P., & Mattson, M. E. (1993). Psychometric instruments to assist in alcoholism treatment planning. *Journal of Substance Abuse Treatment Research, 10,* 289–296.

American Psychiatric Association. (1952). *Diagnostic and statistical manual of mental disorders.* Washington, DC: Author.

American Psychiatric Association. (1987). *Diagnostic and statistical manual of mental disorders* (3rd ed., rev. ed.). Washington, DC: Author.

American Psychiatric Association. (1994). *Diagnostic and statistical manual of mental disorders* (4th ed). Washington, DC: Author.

Annis, H. A. (1986). Is inpatient rehabilitation of the alcoholic cost effective? Con position. *Advances in Alcohol and Substance Abuse, 5,* 175–190.

Annis, H. M., & Graham, J. M. (1988). *Situational Confidence Questionnaire (SCQ 39): User's guide.* Toronto: Addiction Research Foundation.

Annis, H. M., & Graham, J. M. (1995). Profile types on the Inventory of Drinking Situations: Implications for relapse prevention counseling. *Psychology of Addictive Behaviors, 9,* 176–182.

Annis, H. M., Graham, J. M., & Davis, C. S. (1987). *Inventory of Drinking Situations (IDS) user's guide.* Toronto: Addiction Research Foundation.

Anthony, J. C., Warner, L. A., & Kessler, R. C. (1994). Comparative epidemiology of dependence on tobacco, alcohol, controlled substances, and inhalants: Basic findings from the National Comorbidity Survey. *Experimental and Clinical Psychopharmacology, 2,* 244–268.

Ashley, M. J., & Rankin, J. G. (1979). Alcohol consumption and hypertension: The evidence from hazardous drinking and alcoholic populations. *Australian and New Zealand Journal of Medicine, 9,* 201–206.

Atkinson, R. M. (1994). Late onset problem drinking in older adults. *Advances in Alcoholism, 9,* 321–326.

Babor, T. F., Brown, J., & Del Boca, F. K. (1990). Validity of self-reports in applied research on addictive behaviors: Fact or fiction? *Addictive Behaviors, 12,* 5–32.

Bacon, S. D. (1973). The process of addiction to alcohol: Social aspects. *Quarterly Journal of Studies on Alcohol, 34,* 1–27.

Baker, T. B., & Brandon, T. H. (1990). Validity of self-reports in basic research. *Behavioral Assessment, 12,* 33–52.

Battjes, R. J. (1988). Smoking as an issue in alcohol and drug abuse treatment. *Addictive Behaviors, 13,* 225–230.

Beck, A. T., Epstein, N., Brown, G., & Steer, R. A. (1988). An inventory for measuring clinical anxiety: Psychometric properties. *Journal of Consulting and Clinical Psychology, 56,* 893–897.

Beck, A. T., Steer, R. A., & Garbin, M. G. (1988). Psychometric properties of the Beck Depression Inventory: Twenty-five years of evaluation. *Clinical Psychology Review, 8,* 77–100.

Beck, A. T., Wright, F. D., Newman, C. F., & Liese, B. S. (1993). *Cognitive therapy of substance abuse.* New York: Guilford.

Beckman, L. J. (1979). Reported effects of alcohol on the sexual feelings and behavior of women alcoholics and nonalcoholics. *Journal of Studies on Alcohol, 40,* 272–282.

Begleiter, H., Porjesz, B., Bihari, B., & Kissin, B. (1984). Event-related brain potentials in boys at risk for alcoholism. *Science, 225,* 1493–1496.

Bernadt, M. R., Mumford, J., Taylor, C., Smith, B., & Murray, R. M. (1982). Comparison of questionnaire and laboratory tests in the detection of excessive drinking and alcoholism. *Lancet, I,* 325–328.

Bien, T. H., Miller, W. R., & Tonigan, J. S. (1993). Brief interventions for alcohol problems: A review. *Addiction, 88,* 315–336.

Bobo, J. K. (1989). Nicotine dependence and alcoholism epidemiology and treatment. *Journal of Psychoactive Drugs, 21,* 323–329.

Bohn, M. J., Babor, T. F., & Kranzler, H. R. (1995). The Alcohol Use Disorders Identification Test (AUDIT): Validation of a screening instrument for use in medical settings. *Journal of Studies on Alcohol, 56,* 423–432.

Brown, J., Kranzler, H. R., & Del Boca, F. K. (1992). Self-reports by alcohol and drug abuse inpatients: Factors affecting reliability and validity. *British Journal of Addiction, 87,* 1013–1024.

Burglass, M. E., & Shaffer, H. (1983). Diagnosis in the addictions: I. Conceptual problems. *Advances in Alcohol and Substance Abuse, 3,* 19–34.

Burling, T. A., & Ziff, D. C. (1988). Tobacco smoking: A comparison between alcohol and drug inpatients. *Addictive Behaviors, 13,* 185–190.

Caetano, R. (1984). Ethnicity and drinking in northern California: A comparison among whites, black, and Hispanics. *Alcohol and Alcoholism, 19,* 31–44.

Caetano, R. (1985). Two versions of dependence: DSM-III and the alcohol dependence syndrome. *Drug and Alcohol Dependence, 15,* 81–103.

Caetano, R. (1989). Drinking patterns and alcohol problems in a national sample of U.S. Hispanics. In National Institute on Alcohol Abuse and Alcoholism (Ed.), *Alcohol use among U.S. ethnic minorities: Proceedings of a conference on the epidemiology of alcohol use and abuse among ethnic minority groups* (NIAAA Research Monograph No. 18, pp. 315–328). Rockville, MD: National Institute on Alcohol Abuse and Alcoholism.

Caetano, R., & Kaskutas, L. A. (1995). Changes in drinking patterns among Whites, Blacks, and Hispanics, 1984–1992. *Journal of Studies on Alcohol, 56,* 558–565.

Caetano, R., & Tam, T. W. (1995). Prevalence and correlates of DSM-IV and ICD-10 alcohol dependence: 1990 U.S. national alcohol survey. *Alcohol and Alcoholism, 30,* 177–186.

Cahalan, D. (1970). *Problem drinkers: A national survey.* San Francisco: Jossey-Bass.

Cahalan, D. (1987). Studying drinking problems rather than alcoholism. In M. Galanter (Ed.), *Recent developments in alcoholism* (Vol. 5., pp. 363–372). New York: Plenum.

Cahalan, D., & Room, R. (1974). *Problem drinking among American men.* New Brunswick, NJ: Rutgers Center of Alcohol Studies.

Callahan, E. J., Long, M. A., Pecsok, E. H., & Simone, S. (Eds.). (1987). Opiate addiction. In T. D. Nirenberg & S. A. Maisto (Eds.), *Developments in the assessment and treatment of addictive behaviors* (pp. 277–302). Norwood, NJ: Ablex.

Carey, K. B. (1996). Substance use reduction in the context of outpatient psychiatric treatment: A collaborative, motivational, harm reduction approach. *Community Mental Health, 32,* 291–306.

Clark, W. B., & Hesselbrock, M. A. (1988). A comparative analysis of U.S. and Japanese drinking patterns. In National Institute on Alcohol Abuse and Alcoholism (Ed.), *Cultural influences on drinking patterns: A focus on Hispanic and Japanese populations* (pp. 79–98). Rockville, MD: National Institute on Alcohol Abuse and Alcoholism.

Cloninger, C. R., Bohman, M., & Sigvardsson, S. (1981). Inheritance of alcohol abuse: Cross-fostering analysis of adopted men. *Archives of General Psychiatry, 38,* 861–868.

Collins, R. L. (1993). Women's issues in alcohol use and smoking. In J. S. Baer, G. A. Marlatt, & R. J. McMahon (Eds.), *Addictive behaviors across the life span: Prevention, treatment, and policy issues* (pp. 274–306). New York: Sage.

Conigrave, K. M., Saunders, J. B., & Whitfield, J. B. (1995). Diagnostic tests for alcohol consumption. *Alcohol and Alcoholism, 30,* 13–26.

Cox, B. M., Norton, R. G., Swinson, R. P., & Endler, N. S. (1990). Substance abuse and panic-related anxiety: A critical review. *Behaviour Research and Therapy, 28,* 385–393.

Cunningham, J. A., Sobell, L. C., Sobell, M. B., & Gaskin, J. (1994). Alcohol and drug abusers reasons for seeking treatment. *Addictive Behaviors, 19,* 691–696.

Cushman, P., Jr. (1992). Blood and liver markers in the estimation of alcohol consumption. In R. Z. Litten & J. Allen (Eds.), *Measuring alcohol consumption: Psychosocial and biological methods* (pp. 135–147). Totuwa, NJ: Humana.

Davidson, R. (1987). Assessment of the alcohol dependence syndrome: A review of self-report screening questionnaires. *British Psychological Society, 26,* 243–255.

Davies, A. D. M. (1968). The influence of age on trail making test performance. *Journal of Clinical Psychology, 24,* 96–98.

Dawson, D. A., & Grant, B. F. (1993). Gender effects in diagnosing alcohol abuse and dependence. *Journal of Clinical Psychology, 49,* 298–307.

De Soto, C. B., O'Donnell, W. E., & De Soto, J. L. (1989). Long-term recovery in alcoholics. *Alcoholism: Clinical and Experimental Research, 13,* 693–697.

Derogatis, L. R. (1983). *SCL-90 Revised Version Manual-1.* Baltimore: Johns Hopkins University School of Medicine.

DiClemente, C. C., Carroll, K. M., Connors, G. J., & Kadden, R. M. (1994). Process assessment in treatment matching research. *Journal of Studies on Alcohol* (Suppl. 12), 156–162.

Donovan, D. M., et al. (1994). Issues in the selection and development of therapies in alcoholism treatment matching research. *Journal of Studies on Alcohol* (Suppl. 12), 138–148.

Dorus, W., Kennedy, J., Gibbons, R. D., & Ravi, S. D. (1987). Symptoms and diagnosis of depression in alcoholics. *Alcoholism: Clinical and Experimental Research, 11,* 150–154.

Drake, R. E. et al. (1990). Diagnosis of alcohol use in schizophrenia. *Schizophrenia Bulletin, 16,* 57–67.

Fillmore, K. M. (1987). Prevalence, incidence and chronicity of drinking patterns and problems among men as a function of age: A longitudinal and cohort analysis. *British Journal of Addiction, 82,* 77–83.

Fillmore, K. M. (1988). *Alcohol use across the life course: A critical review of 70 years of international longitudinal research.* Toronto: Addiction Research Foundation.

Fillmore, K. M., Hartka, E., Johnstone, B. M., Speiglman, R., & Temple, M. T. (1988, June). *Spontaneous remission of alcohol problems: A critical review.* Paper commissioned and supported by the Institute of Medicine. Washington, DC: Institute of Medicine.

Fillmore, K. M., & Midanik, L. (1984). Chronicity of drinking problems among men: A longitudinal study. *Journal of Studies on Alcohol, 45,* 228–236.

Finn, P. R., & Pihl, R. O. (1988). Risk for alcoholism: A comparison between two different groups of sons of alcoholics on cardiovascular reactivity and sensitivity to alcohol. *Alcoholism: Clinical and Experimental Research, 12,* 742–747.

Gibson, G. S., & Manley, S. (1991). Alternative approaches to urinalysis in the detection of drugs. *Social Behavior and Personality, 19,* 195–204.

Goodwin, D. W., Schulsinger, F., Hermansen, L., Guze, S. B., & Winokur, G. (1973). Alcohol problems in adoptees raised apart from alcoholic biological parents. *Archives of General Psychiatry, 28,* 238–243.

Grant, B. F. (1995). The DSM-IV field trial for substance use disorders: Major results. *Drug and Alcohol Dependence, 38,* 71–75.

Hamilton, M. (1960). A rating scale for depression. *Journal of Neurology, Neurosurgery, and Psychiatry, 23,* 56–62.

Hasin, D. S., Grant, B., & Endicott, J. (1990). The natural history of alcohol abuse: Implications for definitions of alcohol use disorders. *American Journal of Psychiatry, 147,* 1537–1541.

Heather, N. (1990). *Brief intervention strategies.* New York: Pergamon.

Helzer, J. (1984). The impact of combat on later alcohol use by Vietnam veterans. *Journal of Psychoactive Drugs, 16,* 183–191.

Herd, D. (1989). The epidemiology of drinking patterns and alcohol-related problems among U.S. blacks. In D. Speigler, D. Tate, S. Aitken, & C. Christian (Eds.), *Alcohol use among U.S. ethnic minorities: Proceedings of a conference on the epidemiology of alcohol use and abuse among ethnic minority groups* (NIAAA research Monograph No. 18, pp. 3–50). Rockville, MD: National Institute on Alcohol Abuse and Alcoholism.

Hesselbrock, M. N., Meyer, R. E., & Keener, J. J. (1985). Psychopathology in hospitalized alcoholics. *Archives of General Psychiatry, 42,* 1050–1055.

Hill, S. Y. (1984). Vulnerability to the biomedical consequences of alcoholism and alcohol-related problems among women. In S. C. Wilsnack & L. J. Beckman (Eds.), *Alcohol problems in women: Antecedents, consequences, and intervention* (pp. 121–154). New York: Guilford.

Hilton, M. (1987). Drinking patterns and drinking problems in 1984: Results from a general population survey. *Alcoholism: Clinical and Experimental Research, 11,* 167–175.

Hilton, M. E. (1991). A note on measuring drinking problems in the 1984 national alcohol survey. In W. B. Clark & M. E. Hilton (Eds.), *Alcohol in America: Drinking practices and problems* (pp. 51–70). Albany, NY: State University of New York.

Hrubec, Z., & Omenn, G. S. (1981). Evidence of genetic predisposition to alcoholic cirrhosis and psychosis: Twin concordances for alcoholism and its biological end points by zygosity among male veterans. *Alcoholism: Clinical and Experimental Research, 5,* 207–215.

Institute of Medicine. (1990). *Broadening the base of treatment for alcohol problems.* Washington, DC: National Academy Press.

Jacob, T., Krahn, G. L., & Leonard, K. (1991). Parent-child interactions in families with alcoholic fathers. *Journal of Consulting and Clinical Psychology, 59,* 176–181.

Jellinek, E. M. (1952). Phases of alcohol addiction. *Quarterly Journal of Studies on Alcohol, 13,* 673–684.

Jellinek, E. M. (1960). *The disease concept of alcoholism.* New Brunswick, NJ: Hillhouse.

Kaij, L. (1960). *Alcoholism in twins: Studies on the etiology and sequelae of abuse of alcohol.* Stockholm: Almqvist and Wiskell.

Kapur, B. M., & Israel, Y. (1983). A dipstick methodology for rapid determination of alcohol in body fluids. *Clinical Chemistry, 29,* 1178.

Kauffman, E. (1982). The relationship of alcoholism and alcohol abuse to the abuse of other drugs. *American Journal of Drug and Alcohol Abuse, 9,* 1–17.

Keeler, M. H., Taylor, I., & Miller, W. C. (1979). Are all recently detoxified alcoholics depressed? *American Journal of Psychiatry, 136,* 586–588.

Knupfer, G. (1984). The risks of drunkenness (or Ebrietas Resurrecta). A comparison of frequent intoxication indices and of population subgroups as to problem risks. *British Journal of Addiction, 79,* 185–196.

Kushner, M. G., Sher, K. J., & Beitman, B. D. (1990). The relation between alcohol problems and the anxiety disorders. *American Journal of Psychiatry, 147,* 685–695.

Leigh, G. L., & Skinner, H. A. (1988). Physiological assessment. In D. M. Donovan & G. A. Marlatt (Eds.), *Assessment of addictive behaviors* (pp. 112–136). New York: Guilford.

Lettieri, D. J., Nelson, J. E., & Sayers, M. A. (1985). Alcoholism treatment assessment research instruments (NIAAA Treatment Research Series No. 2). Rockville, MD: National Institute on Alcohol Abuse and Alcoholism.

Levine, J. (1990). The relative value of consultation, questionnaires, and laboratory investigation in the identification of excessive alcohol consumption. *Alcohol and Alcoholism, 25,* 539–553.

Lezak, M. D. (1976). *Neuropsychological assessment.* New York: Oxford University Press.

Litten, R. Z., & Allen, J. P. (1991). Pharmacotherapies for alcoholism: Promising agents and clinical issues. *Alcoholism: Clinical and Experimental Research, 15,* 620–633.

Maisto, S. A., & Connors, G. J. (1992). Using subject and collateral reports to measure alcohol consumption. In R. Z. Litten & J. Allen (Eds.), *Measuring alcohol consumption: Psychosocial and biological methods* (pp. 73–96). Totown, NJ: Humana.

Maisto, S. A., McKay, J. R., & Connors, G. J. (1990). Self-report issues in substance abuse: State of the art and future directions. *Behavioral Assessment, 12,* 117–134.

Mandell, W. (1983). Types and phases of alcohol dependence. In M. Galanter (Ed.), *Recent developments in alcoholism* (Vol. 3, pp. 415–448). New York: Plenum.

Marlatt, G. A. (1978). Craving for alcohol, loss of control, and relapse. In P. E. Nathan, G. A. Marlatt, & T. Løberg (Eds.), *Alcoholism: New directions in behavioral research and treatment* (pp. 271–314). New York: Plenum.

Marlatt, G. A., & Gordon, J. R. (1985). *Relapse prevention.* New York: Guilford.

Mattson, M. E. (1993). Project MATCH: Rationale and methods for a multisite clinical trial matching patients to alcoholism treatment. *Alcoholism: Clinical and Experimental Research, 17,* 1130–1145.

Mattson, M. E. (1994). A chronological review of empirical studies matching alcoholic clients to treatment. *Journal of Studies on Alcohol* (Suppl. 12), 16–29.

Mayfield, D., McLeod, G., & Hall, P. (1974). The CAGE questionnaire: Validation of a new alcoholism screening instrument. *American Journal of Psychiatry, 131,* 1121–1123.

McCrady, B. S., & Smith, D. E. (1986). Implications of cognitive impairment for the treatment of alcoholism. *Alcoholism: Clinical and Experimental Research, 10,* 145–149.

McGough, D. P., & Hindman, M. (1986). *A guide to planning alcoholism treatment programs* Rockville, MD: National Institute on Alcohol Abuse and Alcoholism.

McLellan, A. T. (1986). "Psychiatric severity" as a predictor of outcome from substance abuse treatments. In R. E. Meyer (Ed.), *Psychopathology and addictive disorders* (pp. 97–139). New York: Guilford.

Meyer, R. E., & Kranzler, H. R. (1988). Alcoholism: Clinical implications of recent research. *Journal of Clinical Psychiatry, 49,* 8–12.

Mezzich, A. C., Arria, A. M., Tarter, R. E., Moss, H., & Van Thief, D. H. (1991). Psychiatric comorbidity in alcoholism: Importance of ascertaination source. *Alcoholism: Clinical and Experimental Research, 15,* 893–898.

Miller, W. R., et al. (1995). What works? A methodological analysis of the alcohol treatment outcome literature. In R. K. Hester & W. R. Miller (Eds.), *Handbook of alcoholism treatment approaches: Effective alternatives* (2nd ed., pp. 12–44). Boston: Allyn and Bacon.

Miller, W. R., & Joyce, M. A. (1979). Prediction of abstinence, controlled drinking, and heavy drinking outcomes following behavioral self-control training. *Journal of Consulting and Clinical Psychology, 47,* 773–775.

Miller, W. R., Leckman, A. L., Delaney, H. D., & Tinkcom, M. (1992). Long-term follow-up of behavioral self-control training. *Journal of Studies on Alcohol, 53,* 249–261.

Miller, W. R., & Rollnick, S. (1991). *Motivational interviewing: Preparing people to change addictive behavior.* New York: Guilford.

Miller, W. R., & Saucedo, C. F. (1983). Assessment of neuropsychological impairment and brain damage in problem drinkers. In C. J. Golden, J. J. A. Moses, J. A. Goffman, W. R. Miller, & F. Strider (Eds.), *Clinical neuropsychology: Interface with neurologic and psychiatric disorders* (pp. 141–271). New York: Grune and Stratton.

Monti, P. M., Abrams, D. B., Kadden, R. M., & Cooney, N. T. (1989). *Treating alcohol dependence.* New York: Guilford.

Murakami, S. R. (1985). An epidemiological survey of alcohol, drug, and mental health problems in Hawaii: A comparison of four ethnic groups. In D. L. Spiegler, D. A. Tate, S. S. Aitken, & C. M. Christian (Eds.), *Epidemiology of alcohol use and abuse among ethnic minority groups* (pp. 343–353). Rockville, MD: National Institute on Alcohol Abuse and Alcoholism.

Murray, R. M., et al. (1983). Current genetic and biological approaches to alcoholism. *Psychiatric Developments, 2,* 179–192.

National Institute on Alcohol Abuse and Alcoholism. (1990). *Seventh special report to the U.S. Congress on alcohol and health* (DHHS Publication No. ADM 90-1656). Washington, DC: U.S. Government Printing Office.

National Institute on Alcohol Abuse and Alcoholism. (1993). *Eighth special report to the U.S. Congress on alcohol and health.* (National Institutes of Health Publication No. 94-3699). Washington, DC: U.S. Government Printing Office.

National Institute on Drug Abuse. (1991). *National Household Survey on Drug Abuse.* Rockville, MD: U.S. Department of Health and Human Services.

Niaura, R. S., et al. (1988). Relevance of cue reactivity to understanding alcohol and smoking relapse. *Journal of Abnormal Psychology, 97,* 133–152.

O'Farrell, T. J., & Maisto, S. A. (1987). The utility of self-report and biological measures of alcohol consumption in alcoholism treatment outcome studies. *Advances in Behaviour Research and Therapy, 9,* 91–125.

O'Malley, S. S., et al. (1992). Naltrexone and coping skills therapy for alcohol dependence: A controlled study. *Archives of General Psychiatry, 49,* 881–887.

Orford, J., & Keddie, A. (1986). Abstinence or controlled drinking in clinical practice: Indications at initial assessment. *Addictive Behaviors, 11,* 71–86.

Parsons, O. A. (1987). Neuropsychological consequences of alcohol problems: Many questions—some answers. In O. A. Parsons, N. Butters, & P. E. Nathan (Eds.), *Neuropsychology of alcoholism: Implications for diagnosis and treatment* (pp. 153–175). New York: Guilford.

Parsons, O A., & Farr, S. P. (1981). The neuropsychology of alcohol and drug use. In S. Filskov & T. J. Boll (Eds.), *Handbook of clinical neuropsychology* (pp. 320–365). New York: Wiley.

Pattison, E. M., Sobell, M. B., & Sobell, L. C. (1977). *Emerging concepts of alcohol dependence.* New York: Springer.

Peele, S. (1986). The implications and limitations of genetic models of alcoholism and other addictions. *Journal of Studies on Alcohol, 47,* 63–73.

Petersson, B., Trell, E., & Kristensson, H. (1983). Comparison of g-glutamyltransferase and questionnaire test as alcohol indicators in different risk groups. *Drug and Alcohol Dependence, 11,* 279–286.

Phelps, G., & Field, P. (Eds.). (1992). Drug testing: Clinical and workplace issues. In M. F. Fleming & K. L. Barry (Eds.), *Addictive disorders* (pp. 125–142). Mosby-Year Book.

Phillips, M. (1992). Measuring alcohol consumption by transdermal dosimetry. In R. Z. Litten & J. P. Allen (Eds.), *Measuring alcohol consumption: Psychosocial and biological methods* (pp. 183–187). Totowa, NJ: Humana.

Polich, J. M., Armor, D. J., & Braiker, H. B. (1981). *The course of alcoholism: Four years after treatment.* New York: Wiley.

Raistrick, D., Dunbar, G., & Davidson, R. (1983). Development of a questionnaire to measure alcohol dependence. *British Journal of Addiction, 78,* 89–95.

Rankin, H. (1990). Validity of self-reports in clinical settings. *Behavioral Assessment, 12,* 107–116.

Regier, D. A., et al. (1990). Comorbidity of mental disorders with alcohol and other drug abuse. *Journal of the American Medical Association, 264,* 2511–2518.

Robins, L. (1991). Assessing substance abuse and psychiatric disorders: History of problems, state of affairs. In L. Harris (Ed.). *Problems of drug dependence 1990: Proceedings of the 52nd annual scientific meeting of the Committee on Problems of Drug Dependence* (NIDA Research Monograph 105, pp. 203–212). Washington, DC: NIDA.

Robins, L. N. (1993). Vietnam veterans' rapid recovery from heroin addiction: A fluke or normal expectation? *Addiction, 88,* 1041–1054.

Room, R. (1977). Measurement and distribution of drinking patterns and problems in general populations. In G. Edwards, M. M. Gross, M. Keller, J. Moser, & R. Room (Eds.), *Alcohol-related disabilities* (pp. 62–87). Geneva: World Health Organization.

Room, R. (1990). Measuring alcohol consumption in the United States: Methods and rationales. In L. T. Kozlowski, H. M. Annis, H. D. Cappell, F. B. Glaser, M. S. Goodstadt, Y. Israel, H. Kalant, E. M. Sellers, & E. R. Vingilis (Eds.), *Research advances in alcohol and drug problems* (pp. 39–80). New York: Plenum.

Ross, H. E., Glaser, F. B., & Germanson, T. (1988). The prevalence of psychiatric disorders in patients with alcohol and other drug problems. *Archives of General Psychiatry, 45,* 1023–1031.

Rounsaville, B. J., Dolinsky, Z. S., Babor, T. F., & Meyer, R. E. (1987). Psychopathology as a predictor of treatment outcome in alcoholics. *Archives of General Psychiatry, 44,* 505–513.

Russell, M. (1989). The epidemiology of drinking patterns and alcohol-related problems among U.S. blacks. In D. Speigler, D. Tate, S. Aitken, & C. Christian (Eds.), *Alcohol use among U.S. ethnic minorities: Proceedings of a conference on the epidemiology of alcohol use and abuse among ethnic minority groups* (NIAAA Research Monograph No. 18, pp. 75–94). Rockville, MD: National Institute on Alcohol Abuse and Alcoholism.

Salaspuro, M. (1986). Conventional and coming laboratory markers of alcoholism and heavy drinking. *Alcoholism: Clinical and Experimental Research, 10* (Suppl.), 5s–10s.

Sanchez-Craig, M., & Annis, H. M. (1982). "Self-monitoring" and "recall" measures of alcohol consumption: Convergent validity with biochemical indices of liver function. *British Journal of Alcohol and Alcoholism, 17,* 117–121.

Sanchez-Craig, M., Wilkinson, D. A., & Walker, K. (1987). Theory and methods for secondary prevention of alcohol problems: A cognitively based approach. In W. M. Cox (Ed.), *Treatment and prevention of alcohol problems: A resource manual* (pp. 287–331). New York: Academic Press.

Saunders, B., Baily, S., Phillips, M., & Allsop, S. (1993). Women with alcohol problems: Do they relapse for reasons different to their male counterparts? *Addiction, 88,* 1413–1422.

Saunders, J. B., Aasland, O. G., Babor, T. F., De La Fuente, J. R., & Grant, M. (1993). Development of the Alcohol Use Disorders Identification Test (AUDIT): WHO collaborative project on early detection of persons with harmful alcohol consumption: II. *Addiction, 88,* 791–804.

Schmidt, L., & Weisner, C. (1995). The emergence of problem-drinking women as a special population in need of treatment. In M. Galanter (Ed.), *Recent developments in alcoholism* (Vol. 12, pp. 309–334). New York: Plenum.

Schonfeld, L., & Dupree, L. W. (1991). Antecedents of drinking for early-onset and late-onset elderly alcohol abusers. *Journal of Studies on Alcohol, 52,* 587–592.

Schuckit, M. A. (1980). Self-rating alcohol intoxication by young men with and without family histories of alcoholism. *Journal of Studies on Alcohol, 41,* 242–249.

Schuckit, M. A. (1985). The clinical implications of primary diagnostic groups among alcoholics. *Archives of General Psychiatry, 42,* 1043–1049.

Schwartz, R. H. (1988). Urine testing in the detection of drugs of abuse. *Archives of Internal Medicine, 148,* 2407–2412.

Searles, J. S. (1988). The role of genetics in the pathogenesis of alcoholism. *Journal of Abnormal Psychology, 97,* 153–167.

Shute, P. A. (1988). Patients' alcohol drinking habits in general practice: Prevention and education. *Journal of the Royal Society of Medicine, 81,* 450–451.

Sigvardsson, S., Cloninger, C. R., & Bohman, M. (1985). Prevention and treatment of alcohol abuse: Uses and limitations of the high risk paradigm. *Social Biology, 32,* 185–193.

Skinner, H. A., & Allen, B. A. (1982). Alcohol dependence syndrome: Measurement and validation. *Journal of Abnormal Psychology, 91,* 199–209.

Skinner, H. A., & Horn, J. L. (1984). *Alcohol Dependence Scale (ADS) user's guide.* Toronto: Addiction Research Foundation.

Skinner, H. A., & Sheu, W. J. (1982). Reliability of alcohol use indices: The Lifetime Drinking History and the MAST. *Journal of Studies on Alcohol, 43,* 1157–1170.

Sobell, L. C., Cunningham, J. A., & Sobell, M. B. (1996). Natural recovery is the predominant pathway to recovery from alcohol problems: Results from two general population surveys. *American Journal of Public Health, 86,* 966–972.

Sobell, L. C., & Sobell, M. B. (1980). Convergent validity: An approach to increasing confidence in treatment outcome conclusions with alcohol and drug abusers. In L. C. Sobell, M. B. Sobell, & E. Ward (Eds.), *Evaluating alcohol and drug abuse treatment effectiveness: Recent advances* (pp. 177–185). New York: Pergamon.

Sobell, L. C., & Sobell, M. B. (1990). Self-report issues in alcohol abuse: State of the art and future directions. *Behavioral Assessment, 12,* 91–106.

Sobell, L. C., & Sobell, M. B. (1992a, July). Stability of natural recoveries from alcohol problems. Paper presented at the Second International Conference on Behavioural Medicine, Hamburg, Germany.

Sobell, L. C., & Sobell, M. B. (1992b). Timeline followback: A technique for assessing self-reported alcohol consumption. In R. Z. Litten & J. Allen (Eds.), *Measuring alcohol consumption: Psychosocial and biological methods* (pp. 41–72). Totowa, NJ: Humana.

Sobell, L. C., & Sobell, M. B. (1995). Alcohol consumption measures. In J. P. Allen & M. Columbus (Eds.), *Assessing alcohol problems: A guide for clinicians and researchers* (pp. 55–73). Rockville, MD: National Institute on Alcohol Abuse and Alcoholism.

Sobell, L. C., & Sobell, M. B. (1996). *Alcohol Timeline Followback (TLFB) users' manual.* Toronto: Addiction Research Foundation.

Sobell, L. C., Sobell, M. B., Kozlowski, L. T., & Toneatto, T. (1990). Alcohol or tobacco research versus alcohol and tobacco research. *British Journal of Addiction, 85,* 263–269.

Sobell, L. C., Sobell, M. B., & Nirenberg, T. D. (1988). Behavioral assessment and treatment planning with alcohol and drug abusers: A review with an emphasis on clinical application. *Clinical Psychology Review, 8,* 19–54.

Sobell, L. C., Sobell, M. B., Toneatto, T., & Leo, G. I. (1993). What triggers the resolution of alcohol problems without treatment? *Alcoholism: Clinical and Experimental Research, 17,* 217–224.

Sobell, L. C., Sobell, M. B., Toneatto, T., & Shillingford, J. A. (1994). Alcohol problems. In M. Hersen & S. M. Turner (Eds.), *Diagnostic interviewing* (2nd ed., pp. 155–188). New York: Plenum.

Sobell, L. C., Toneatto, T., & Sobell, M. B. (1994). Behavioral assessment and treatment planning for alcohol, tobacco, and other drug problems: Current status with an emphasis on clinical applications. *Behavior Therapy, 25,* 533–580.

Sobell, M. B., Bogardis, J., Schuller, R., Leo, G. I., & Sobell, L. C. (1989). Is self-monitoring of alcohol consumption reactive? *Behavioral Assessment, 11,* 447–458.

Sobell, M. B., Brochu, S., Sobell, L. C., Roy, J., & Stevens, J. (1987). Alcohol treatment outcome evaluation methodology: State of the art 1980–1984. *Addictive Behaviors, 12,* 113–128.

Sobell, M. B., & Sobell, L. C. (1987). Conceptual issues regarding goals in the treatment of alcohol problems. In M. B. Sobell & L. C. Sobell (Eds.), *Moderation as a goal or outcome of treatment for alcohol problems: A dialogue* (pp. 1–37). New York: Haworth.

Sobell, M. B., & Sobell, L. C. (1993). *Problem drinkers: Guided self-change treatment.* New York: Guilford.

Sobell, M. B., & Sobell, L. C. (1995). Controlled drinking after 25 years: How important was the great debate? *Addiction, 90,* 1149–1153.

Sobell, M. B., Sobell, L. C., & Kozlowski, L. T. (1995). Dual recoveries from alcohol and smoking problems. In National Institute on Alcohol Abuse and Alcoholism (Ed.), *Alcohol and tobacco: From basic science to clinical practice* (NIAAA Research Monograph No. 30, pp. 207–224). Rockville, MD: National Institute on Alcohol Abuse and Alcoholism.

Sobell, M. B., Sobell, L. C., & VanderSpek, R. (1979). Relationships between clinical judgment, self-report and breath analysis measures of intoxication in alcoholics. *Journal of Consulting and Clinical Psychology, 47,* 204–206.

Sobell, M. B., Wilkinson, D. A., & Sobell, L. C. (1990). Alcohol and drug problems. In A. S. Bellack, M. Hersen, & A. E. Kazdin (Eds.), *International handbook of behavior modification and therapy* (2nd ed., pp. 415–435). New York: Plenum.

Sokolow, L., Welte, J., Hynes, G., & Lyons, J. (1981). Multiple substance use by alcoholics. *British Journal of Addiction, 76,* 147–158.

Stockwell, T., Murphy, D., & Hodgson, R. (1983). The Severity of Alcohol Dependence Questionnaire: Its use, reliability, and validity. *British Journal of Addiction, 78,* 145–155.

Stockwell, T., Sitharthan, T., McGrath, D., & Lang, E. (1994). The measurement of alcohol dependence and impaired control in community samples. *Addiction, 89,* 167–174.

Strang, J., Black, J., Marsh, A., & Smith, B. (1993). Hair analysis for drugs: Technological breakthrough or ethical quagmire? *Addictions, 88,* 163–166.

Tarter, R. E., Alterman, A. I., & Edwards, K. L. (1985). Vulnerability to alcoholism in men: A behavior-genetic perspective. *Journal of Studies on Alcohol, 46,* 329–356.

Tarter, R. E., Ott, P. J., & Mezzich, A. C. (1991). Psychometric assessment. In R. J. Frances & S. I. Miller (Eds.), *Clinical textbook of addictive disorders* (pp. 237–267). New York: Guilford.

Toneatto, T., Sobell, L. C., & Sobell, M. B. (1992). Gender issues in the treatment of abusers of alcohol, nicotine, and other drugs. *Journal of Substance Abuse, 4,* 209–215.

Toneatto, T., Sobell, L. C., Sobell, M. B., & Leo, G. I. (1991). Psychoactive substance use disorder (Alcohol). In M. Hersen & S. M. Turner (Eds.), *Adult psychopathology and diagnosis* (2nd ed., pp. 84–109). New York: Wiley.

Tu, G. C., Kapur, B., & Israel, Y. (1992). Characteristics of a new urine, serum, and saliva alcohol reagent strip. *Alcoholism: Clinical and Experimental Research, 16,* 222–227.

Verebey, K., & Turner, C. E. (1991). Laboratory testing. In R. J. Frances & S. I. Miller (Eds.), *Clinical textbook of addictive disorders* (pp. 221–236). New York: Guilford.

Weissman, M. M., & Meyers, J. K. (1980). Clinical depression in alcoholism. *American Journal of Psychiatry, 137,* 372–373.

Welte, J. W., & Barnes, G. M. (1995). Alcohol and other drug use among Hispanics in New York state. *Alcoholism: Clinical and Experimental Research, 19,* 1061–1066.

Westermeyer, J. (1984). The role of ethnicity in substance abuse. In B. Stimmel (Ed.), *Cultural and sociological aspects of alcoholism and substance abuse* (pp. 9–18). New York: Haworth.

Wilkinson, D. A., & Carlen, P. L. (1980). Neuropsychological and neurological assessment of alcoholism: Discrimination between groups of alcoholics. *Journal of Studies on Alcohol, 41,* 129–139.

Wilkinson, D. A., & Sanchez-Craig, M. (1981). Relevance of brain dysfunction to treatment objectives: Should alcohol-related cognitive deficits influence the way we think about treatment? *Addictive Behaviors, 6,* 253–260.

Wilsnack, S. C., Klassen, A. D., Schur, B. E., & Wilsnack, R. W. (1991). Predicting onset and chronicity of women's problem drinking: A five-year longitudinal analysis. *American Journal of Public Health, 81,* 305–318.

Wilsnack, S. C., & Wilsnack, R. W. (1995). Drinking and problem drinking in US women: Patterns and recent trends. In M. Galanter (Ed.), *Recent developments in alcoholism* (Vol. 12; pp. 29–60). New York: Plenum.

World Health Organization. (1948). *International classification of diseases* (6th ed.). Geneva: Author.

World Health Organization. (1979). *International classification of diseases* (9th ed.). Geneva: Author.

World Health Organization. (1995). *International statistical classification of diseases and related health problems* (10th ed.). Geneva: Author.

Yu, E. S. H., Liu, W. T., Xia, Z., & Zhang, M. (1985). Alcohol use, abuse, and alcoholism among Chinese Americans: A review of the epidemiologic data. In D. L. Spiegler, D. A. Tate, S. S. Aitken, and C. M. Christian (Eds.), *Epidemiology of alcohol use and abuse among ethnic minority groups* (pp. 329–341). Rockville, MD: National Institute on Alcohol Abuse and Alcoholism.

CHAPTER 6

Psychoactive Substance Use Disorders: Drugs

JESSE B. MILBY, JOSEPH E. SCHUMACHER, and ROBERT D. STAINBACK

Drug use may have begun as early as 4000–7000 B.C., with use and cultivation of opium poppies (Bejerot, 1970; Brown, 1961; Maurer & Vogel, 1973). Coca use can be traced back to A.D. 600. Archeological digs have revealed South American Indian mummies buried with supplies of coca leaves. Pottery from this period has been recovered portraying the characteristic cheek bulge of the coca leaf chewer (Milby, 1981a). But cocaine, derived from coca, is just a little more than 100 years old. The variety of drugs used for recreational purposes and abuse has changed throughout the years in accordance with shifting societal standards, discovery of new compounds, and drug availability. This chapter examines drug abuse and dependence in contemporary society, including prevalence; natural history; course and etiology, especially roots of drug abuse in adolescent use; risk factor research; and some theoretical concepts of etiology. We sample current classification schemes and briefly review evolution of classification using the American Psychiatric Association's (APA) *Diagnostic and Statistical Manual of Mental Disorders* (DSM) as an illustration. We focus on DSM-IV (APA, 1994) criteria and current issues in differential diagnosis. Typical clinical pictures for various types of substance use disorders and their implications for diagnosis and assessment, are reviewed in detail. Finally, we cover the assessment of related disorders and dysfunction and briefly discuss clinical management of illustrative disorders.

EPIDEMIOLOGY

Prevalence

Prevalence and type of drug abuse are subject to period effects (changes over time regardless of age groups), age effects (maturational changes that occur consistently for all groups of individuals at the same age), and cohort effects (sustained differences among different groups). Period and cohort effects are illustrated by historical peaks in opioid dependence. It is likely that prevalence of opioid abuse and dependence in the United States peaked in the decades after the Civil War. During this period, opium and morphine could be purchased from pharmacies without prescription. Opioids were widely administered to soldiers as treatment for pain, and use often continued after the war, with addicted veterans identified as suffering the "army disease." Opioids were also found in tonics and patent medicines and used extensively by women. Brecher (1972) reviewed five studies conducted from 1880 to 1914 and found that each showed narcotics use was more common among women than men, with use estimated at 61.2% to 75.0% and average age ranging from 39.4 to 50.0 years. Kozel and Adams (1986) found that opioid abuse peaked again during the 1960s, driven by a heroin use epidemic. Sharp increases in cocaine use occurred in the mid to late 1970s. Lifetime prevalence of cocaine use among young adults and high school students increased from 5.4 million to 22.2 million between 1974 and 1985. Among adolescent substance abusers, after tobacco and alcohol, inhalants are the next most used. Inhalant abuse has steadily increased throughout the 1980s to a peak of 7% annual use reported in the survey year 1993 (O'Malley, Johnston, & Bachman, 1995).

Best estimates of national trends in drug use, especially prevalence, are provided by population-based samples completed by the National Institutes of Health. These have shown that use of illicit drugs has been steadily declining in the United States among young adults since the early 1980s. However, cocaine use has increased, and 29.2% reported use during the past year when 82.8% and 41.2% used alcohol and nicotine, respectively. For illicit drugs, 7.7% reported using cocaine and 5.3% reported using analgesics (National Institute on Drug Abuse, 1991). Among adults age 26 and older, 9.66% reported illicit drug use during the last year, and 2.5% and 1.9% use cocaine and analgesics, respectively. Clearly, illicit and legal drug abuse is ubiquitous in our society and a grave national problem. Various reports have estimated that more than half of prison inmates are incarcerated for crimes committed while they were intoxicated or crimes associated with drug abuse.

The Epidemiologic Catchment Area Study (Robins & Regier, 1991) was a large-scale study of almost 20,000 Americans (sponsored by the National Institute of Mental Health) to determine prevalence of psychiatric disorders in the United States. It used DSM-III-R (APA, 1987) diagnostic categories to determine lifetime and past year prevalence of mental disorders, including substance use disorders. It also assessed use of prescription and nonprescription drugs and found that the proportion of users who progress to meet criteria for drug abuse was consistent across all five sites at about 20% (Weissman & Johnson, 1991). See Table 6.1, which is summarized from O'Farrell (1994).

Etiology of Substance Use Disorders

Drug abuse is a multifaceted biological, pharmacologic, sociopsychological phenomenon. Animals with no previous exposure to drugs readily self-administer psychoactive drugs, and their consumatory patterns are similar to human users. This phenomenon suggests that psychoactive drugs can exert their abuse and dependence properties on a human biological system with no preexisting psychopathology or addictive liability required to establish initial use

TABLE 6.1   Lifetime and Past Year Prevalence for Alcohol and Drug Abuse/Dependence, 1991

	Lifetime	Past Year
Alcohol abuse/dependence	13.76%	6.80%
Drug abuse/dependence	6.19%	2.67%
Any substance use disorder	17.00%	No information
Alcohol abuse/dependence only	10.73%	
Drug abuse/dependence only	3.24%	
Both alcohol abuse/dependence and drug abuse/dependence	3.03%	

and self-administration. A comprehensive understanding of the etiology of substance use disorders requires recognizing the basic biological and molecular mechanisms underlying the reinforcing effects of psychoactive substances. These provide foundations for other etiological factors operating at the intrapersonal, interpersonal, and social levels and in no way diminish the importance of well-established precursors for drug abuse and variables that contribute to individual vulnerability.

Most drug abuse includes a variety of substances in any user (Wilkinson, Leigh, Cordingley, Martin, & Lei, 1987), with their use being independent, sequential, or concurrent with varying degrees of frequency and intensity. Research suggests the most vulnerable period for initiation to illicit drugs occurs before age 30 (Chen & Kandel, 1995). Meyer and Neale (1992) examined the relationship of age to first use and teenage drug use liability, using a simulated data set and three different analytic procedures, each with more complex assumptions. All three analyses yielded the same result. Age at first drug use was found to be a perfect index for subsequent drug use liability.

In a cross-sectional study of 1,108 12th graders from New York State public schools, Kandel and Yamaguchi (1993) confirmed that the developmental pattern of drug involvement identified in the 1970s still characterizes adolescent patterns of drug use progressing to abuse. Age of first use of licit drugs was a strong predictor of further progression to illicit use. There was compelling evidence for a sequential pattern of drug involvement in adolescence. The best-fitting model for males described alcohol use preceding marijuana; marijuana and cigarettes preceding cocaine and crack; and cocaine preceding crack use. It most parsimoniously classified 93.4%. A similar best-fit model for females classified 94.2% of females.

Research has shown that experimentation with many drugs is the statistical norm among U.S. adolescents (Johnston, Bachman, & O'Malley, 1982); however, most drug users do not become chronic abusers. Most individuals experiment with drugs a few times and discontinue or continue to use occasionally, so early use and use of multiple drugs is not sufficient to predict with any certainty the small proportion of early users who become chronic abusers in young adulthood.

Murray and Perry (1985) listed 12 studies conducted from 1977 to 1984 and grouped the variables studied into four general categories: demographic, social environmental, intrapersonal, and behavioral. They reported a compendium of social environmental factors associated with increased drug use: family or peer approval or tolerance for drug use, family or peers as models for use, pressure from family or peers to use drugs, greater influence by peers than parents, incompatibility between parents and peers, greater involvement in peer-related activities such as dating or parties, greater reliance on peers than parents, low educational aspiration for children by parents, lack of parental involvement in their children's activities, weak parental controls and discipline, and ready access to drugs. Correlations seem fairly constant across gender and ethnic groups. Also, many of them predict future drug usage, with their predictive strength varying as a function of the different compounds used. Thus, results from these studies of antecedents of later use and abuse suggest that future users live in an environment peopled by multiple models for drug use, where significant others tolerate or even encourage drug use, and where drugs are readily available. Adolescents who spend most of their time with peers are more likely to experience an environment which supports drug use than those who spend their free time with their families or alone.

In summary, many studies have examined correlates and risk factors for drug abuse in the United States. A major risk factor is drug availability. Risk factors related to availability are family and peer drug abuse. Others include early use of tobacco, alcohol, and other drugs; early identified problem behavior at home and school; high tendencies for sensation seeking; disturbed family relations; psychological distress and psychopathology; low self-esteem; low achievement motivation; disregard for rules and authority; and low religiosity (Blum & Richards, 1979; Bry, 1983). It appears that these risk factors, although not studied extensively in non–Western European countries, may also be precursors in other countries and cultures. Gillis, Tareen, Chaudhry, and Haider (1994) found that 10 of the 11 risk factors for U.S. substance abuse were present in their study of 60 heroin addicts who presented themselves for treatment during a 5-month period at the Mayo Hospital at Lahore, India. Addicts were compared to 60 nonusing controls who were patients' brothers or friends of similar age.

Etiological Theories

Milby (1981a, chap. 8) critically reviewed theories of addiction and found that they can be conveniently divided into two broad types: 1. circumscribed theories, which aim to explain a limited domain such as the development of heroin addiction or tolerance, and 2. comprehensive theories, which attempt to explain the broad spectrum of phenomena from initiation of use to maintenance of abuse or dependence. Types of circumscribed theories included psychoanalytic, metabolic disease, moral models, and learning theories. Since Milby's (1981a) review, several theorists have focused on the phenomenon of relapse and have postulated useful constructs from which practical interventions for relapse prevention have been derived (Carroll et al., 1994; Marlatt & Gordon, 1985). For the most part, the more rigorous scientific theories, from which testable hypotheses can be drawn, are found among circumscribed theories. The problem for the clinician is that the account of circumscribed phenomenon in drug abusing clients is of minor interest and utility. What are most useful are more general theories which try to account for the multiple phenomena of initial use, experimentation, abuse, and addiction. Fortunately, there are a few general and circumscribed theories that meet reasonable standards of scientific rigor and usefulness and that are having an important impact on the field (Koob & Bloom, 1988; Marlatt & Gordon, 1985; Solomon & Corbit, 1974; Wikler, 1973).

Most rigorous scientific theories have postulated mechanisms underlying physical dependence and tolerance and base their explanatory concepts on varieties of evidence that physical dependence and tolerance generally develop and decay on a similar time course. Tolerance and dependence have been explained by postulating opponent adaptive biological processes that seek to return the system to its predrug state. This homeostatic process opposes the drug action and becomes a disruptive state itself when drug administration ceases and it remains unopposed. Until the last decade these explanatory mechanisms remained hypothetical constructs. But recent research now indicates that tolerance and dependence are not only separable processes (Ternes, Erhman, & O'Brien, 1985) but have reliably identifiable brain sites and measurable molecular mechanisms of action. A recent comprehensive theory postulates a neurobiological basis for drug dependence that utilizes known and postulated linkages between cellular and behavioral effects of three classes of drugs: opiates, psychostimulants, and alcohol (Koob & Bloom, 1988).

Several theories associated with research on precursors of abuse in adolescence have been developed on the etiology of abuse. These focus on how drug use is initiated and maintained in adolescence, and many look to social phenomena in adolescence to explain development of abuse. Two recently proposed theories receiving considerable attention in the literature are the self-medication theory, perhaps best articulated by Khantzian (1985), and the social stress model of substance abuse, recently reviewed by Linderberg, Gendrop, and Reiskin (1993).

Although self-medication theory originally was proposed from the psychoanalytic tradition, it is also espoused by biological researchers. It proposes that individuals abuse drugs to obtain relief from aversive emotional states in an attempt to regulate (i.e., self-medicate) intolerable affect. It proposes that an individual's drug of choice is not accidental but chosen for its pharmacologic properties to relieve specific affective symptoms and feeling states. One of the theory's main attractive features is its elegantly simple explanation of abuse and dependence. Although the theory is not well articulated to yield testable hypotheses, it is compelling in that it fits with anecdotal data reported by addicted patients in treatment. Indeed, the few studies that have provided supportive evidence for it have been based on small series of patients in psychotherapy.

Detractors of the theory have criticized its reliance on anecdotal data. However, at least one large empirical study has provided mostly supportive evidence for it. Weis, Griffin, and Mirin (1992) examined a group of 494 hospitalized drug abusers, concentrating on the study of self-medication for depression. They found that 63% of patients reported drug use in response to depressive symptoms and experienced mood elevation regardless of the type of drug abused. Drug use to relieve depressive symptoms was far more likely in men if they had major depression but was equally common in women with or without major depression.

The social stress model of substance abuse was proposed to explain the contribution of variables that influence initiation of drug abuse, especially for urban adolescents (Lindenberg et al., 1993). The model proposes that the likelihood for initiation of drug abuse is a function of the stress level experienced by the individual, which is buffered by three modifier variables. These modifiers are social networks, social competencies, and community resources. Modifiers interact with each other and together buffer the impact of stress. There is considerable interest in this model. Lindenberg et al. (1993), in their recent review, found 35 studies which assessed one or more of the model's constructs. Although their review found the research marred by inconsistent operational definitions of constructs and resulting noncomparability of findings among the studies, generally findings showed a consistent relationship of the model's constructs with drug use. However, the research did not usually evaluate the contribution of individual constructs nor their interaction. The role of drug availability in the community does not seem to be posited directly by the model. However, this empirically validated high risk factor could be subsumed under the community resource construct.

Space does not permit a detailed review of these theories of etiology. Milby (1981b) counted some 63 theories, Lettieri (1985) reviewed 43, and new theories are being developed constantly. For example, see Koob and Bloom (1988) and Wise and Bozarth (1987). The interested reader will find excellent reviews in Milby (1981a) and Lettieri (1985), summaries of nine models of etiology in adolescence in Murray and Perry (1985), exposition of self-medication theory in Khantzian (1985), and a summary and review of research on the social stress model in Lindenberg et al. (1993).

CLINICAL PICTURES

Aside from the common phenomena described below there is no one clinical picture for substance use disorders. Instead, there are many clinical pictures that vary according to the pharmacological action of the substance, its legal status, and important individual differences. Limited space renders it impossible to describe clinical pictures for each type. Therefore, common characteristics usually seen in the development of most drug dependence are described, and then representative clinical pictures are described for prototypes of each pharmacological class.

Abuse usually begins with curiosity, excitement, peer pressure, or a prescription. Next, dose size, frequency, tolerance, and psychological dependence increase due to the reinforcing effects of pleasure and social or peer approval, and consequently an obsessive preoccupation with the drug occurs. The person then begins elaborate drug seeking behavior and masters drug abuse skills (e.g., drug acquisition, drug language, and drug administration).

Development of dependence begins when the initial drug effects are reduced due to tolerance. Drug craving develops and is perceived as a "need" for the drug. For most drugs, the dosage is gradually increased until the level remains fairly constant. At that point, a relatively stable dose level is maintained with dependence until something interrupts it. Periods of abstinence occur when the individual attempts to stop usage, or more frequently, when the drug source

becomes unavailable. Use is typically resumed with subsequent periods of abstinence and relapse. If physical dependence develops, tolerance or the abstinence
syndrome, or both, occur. When the drug of choice is unavailable, cross-
tolerance is manifested if drugs are substituted within the same class (e.g., valium for barbiturates). The abstinence syndrome (withdrawal) occurs when drug
use is discontinued, resulting in unpleasant physical symptoms. The user usually
becomes obsessed with drugs and spends increasing time and energy finding
and consuming drugs. Because of such obsessive preoccupation, most nondrug
interests decline.

Additional characteristics are associated with use of illegal drugs. Criminal
activities often provide money for drug acquisition, sometimes leading to incarceration and the introduction of a criminal lifestyle. When illegal activities are
undertaken to support the "habit," self-esteem frequently deteriorates along
with grooming, general hygiene, and health.

Clinical pictures are reviewed for the following prototypes: morphine (class:
opiate), barbiturates (class: barbiturate/hypnotic sedative), cocaine (class: psychostimulants), LSD (class: hallucinogens), cannabis sativa (class: cannabinols),
anabolic steroids, and inhalants. Initial dosing effects, chronic use effects, abstinence syndromes, and overdose effects are discussed. Two prototypes for concurrent dependence are discussed: 1. opiates/barbiturates and 2. barbiturates/
stimulants. Last, various types of dual diagnosis and some common patterns of
dual diagnosis are reviewed.

Opiates

Since morphine has been studied in great detail, it is chosen as our prototype
for the opiate class. Initial injections produce a "rush" sensation focused in the
abdomen, in addition to pleasurable flushing and itching of the skin. This
"rush" is followed by intense feelings of euphoria. "Nodding" (dozing in light
sleep), "driving" (purposeless motoric activity), or alternating "nodding" and
"driving" usually occur. Dry mouth, light headedness, pain relief, constipation,
and reduced appetite and sexual desire are often reported. Other symptoms
include decreased physiological responses: body temperature, heart rate, respiration, blood pressure, urination, and deep sleep (Andrews, 1943; Kay,
Eisenstein, & Jasinski, 1969; Wikler, 1973). Effects diminish in 4 to 6 hours, and
as tolerance develops, duration of euphoric effects becomes shorter.

Chronic users (multiple daily use) manifest constipation, increased urination,
decreased sex drive, impaired ejaculation, irregular menstruation, and weight
loss (Bejerot, 1970; Eisenman, Sloan, Martin, Jasinski, & Brooks, 1969). Other
effects may include lowered motivation for activity (contrasted to the "driving"
state with initial use), low social involvement, irritation with social situations,
and frequent somatic complaints (Haertzen & Hooks, 1969).

The primary phase of the abstinence syndrome occurs 5 to 6 hours after
cessation of morphine use, peaks in 36 to 48 hours, and lasts about 10 days.
Symptoms include nervousness, irritability, weakness, leg and back aches,
cramps, nausea, decreased appetite, yawns, watery eyes, runny nose, constricted
pupils, perspiration, goose flesh, and chills. After 10 days, physiological func-

tioning slowly begins to stabilize, near normal values but complete return to preaddiction baselines may take 30 weeks. While the physical distress is serious, death is seldom associated with this abstinence syndrome.

Either during the withdrawal stage or after a period of abstinence, reuse usually occurs and compulsive use resumes. Periods of abstinence before reuse are common and may occasionally occur without treatment. Such periods usually occur during and following treatment and are induced by incarceration or a period of unavailability of the drug or means to get it. Long-term follow-up studies show that before sustained abstinence is established several cycles of abstinence followed by relapse usually occur (Vaillant, 1973). Periods of abstinence are often marked by higher levels of stable functioning, then relapse occurs, associated and perhaps precipitated by increases in stress, psychosocial problems and reduced levels of functioning, and recent cocaine abuse (Kosten, Rounsaville, & Kleber, 1986; 1987). Assessments of stable abstinence in long-term follow-up studies range from about 24% after 11 years (Haastrup & Jepsen, 1988) to 42% after 20 years (Vaillant, 1973).

Most opioid addicts seek treatment, and it is important to consider the impact of such treatment on the overall clinical picture. Of course, treatment varies greatly, and what treatment an addict enters depends on his or her personal characteristics and preferences but is also a function of treatment availability and admission criteria. It is impossible to review treatment for opioid addiction given space limitations, but we think it important to remind the clinician that the most widely available treatment, methadone maintenance, is often effective (Milby, 1981, 1989). Controlled studies show that counseling and psychotherapy enhance methadone's treatment effects (Woody et al., 1983) and that psychotherapy perhaps provides the most benefit for patients with most severe psychopathology (Woody et. al., 1984). When abstinence is achieved from opioids, there tends to be concurrent improvement in many other areas of functioning: reduced criminal activity, improved medical status, social functioning, and less abuse of other drugs (Rounsaville, Kosten, & Kleber, 1987). Achieving abstinence also is related to being in a drug treatment program, especially methadone maintenance; the long-range benefits of abstinence are observed even for those addicts who have relapsed at the time of follow-up.

Opiate overdose is typified by a slowing of physical functions with pulmonary edema and respiratory distress (Millman, 1978). Death may occur due to respiratory failure and collapse of the circulatory system (Bejerot, 1970). Most of these adverse effects are from true overdoses but a portion is probably the result of: allergic reactions to the drug or dilutants, nonsterile syringes, opiate-induced arrhythmias, and failure of tolerance effects (Millman, 1978; Siegel, 1981).

Some important implications can be derived from the clinical picture. First, it should be clear that successful treatment is usually a long-term process and may involve several cycles of stability-improvement-relapse before a final level of stable adjustment, abstinence, and a functional lifestyle is achieved. Second, it is becoming increasingly clear that opioid addicts respond to active counseling and often need focused psychotherapy for concurrent disorders. Third, a program that maintains contact and rapport with the addict through multiple cycles is probably going to be in the best position to provide the sustained outpatient counseling and psychotherapy that is needed to attain stable functioning most efficiently.

Barbiturates and Hypnotic Sedatives

Barbiturates have been studied experimentally in much detail and therefore will be discussed as the prototype for the barbiturate/hypnotic sedative class. All drugs within this class are central nervous system (CNS) depressants and include both alcohol and the benzodiazapines.

Detectable effects of a single dose, for example 200 mg of secobarbital, disappear within 4–6 hours. However, if this dose is administered at 5-hour intervals, effects overlap and signs of intoxification can be seen. Addicts may stagger, slur speech, be uncoordinated, and appear drunk. They show oscillatory movement of the eyes (nystagmus) and decreased muscle tone. They may become loud, boisterous, irritable, or aggressive. Sexual inhibitions may be reduced with low doses (Millman, 1978). There is a marked variation in response to barbiturates between individuals and within an individual given the same dose repeatedly.

Chronic consumption of more than 400 mg for several weeks puts the individual at risk for addiction and produces a clinical picture marked by articulation difficulties and lack of coordination in motor acts (e.g., walking). In contrast to low doses where there may be reduced sexual inhibition, a chronic pattern of high doses leads to impaired sexual functioning and may be the etiological factor in concurrent psychosexual dysfunction. Residual effects of barbiturates, including drowsiness and irritability, may last for hours and disturbance with normal sleep patterns is common (Morin & Kwentus, 1988).

The abstinence syndrome for barbiturates, unlike opiates, can be life threatening because of the possibility of convulsions. After withdrawal of the drug for 24 hours, anxiety, restlessness, fatigue, irritability, insomnia, and nightmares frequently occur (Kales & Kales, 1974). These symptoms may be accompanied by faintness, sweating, shivering, and convulsions. There may be a delirious psychotic reaction with paranoid delusions. However, there is usually complete recovery from the psychotic reaction within 3 weeks. Many experts think hospitalization is mandatory for safe, effective treatment of barbiturate withdrawal.

Barbiturate overdose is frequent and one of the most prevalent causes of drug-related deaths. Barbiturates are often used in suicide attempts. Accidental overdose with barbiturates occurs among alcoholics, as they substitute or mix barbiturates with alcohol at bedtime to treat insomnia (thereby potentiating effects of both drugs). Memory impairment often contributes to drug automatism (i.e., the user forgets the amount consumed and ingests more, resulting in the increased possibility of overdose; Mirin, 1977). With overdose, all symptoms described earlier are exaggerated, leading to stupor and coma. Death is due to circulatory failure and respiratory collapse.

The benzodiazepines (i.e., valium and similar drugs) are frequently used for treatment of anxiety disorders. It has been common medical practice to prescribe them widely because risk of dependence was thought to be small. However, research has shown frequent normal therapeutic dose dependence with objective and measurable signs of withdrawal associated with mixed signs of tolerance (Kales & Kales, 1974; Lader, 1983; McKinnon & Parker, 1982). Appearance of a withdrawal syndrome in patients taking prescribed doses of sedatives or hypnotics may or may not indicate dysfunctional abuse-dependence meeting DSM-IV criteria. Individuals dependent on these compounds often do not recognize their dependence and are identified only when they seek treatment for some other disorder, often anxiety disorders or insomnia. For other patients more clearly dependent, a steady source of the drug is obtained from many unwary physicians, each one of whom assumes he or she is the patient's primary physician and the only one prescribing benzodiazapines. Effective treatment for the chronic insomnia or the underlying primary anxiety disorder can lead to successful treatment of the secondary drug dependence as well.

The treatment and long-term outcome for primary dependence on sedative and hypnotic drugs are hard to evaluate because of the dearth of studies available. Current data show an outcome and follow-up picture similar to, or worse than, opiate dependence. Allgulander, Borg, and Vikarder (1984) completed a 4–6-year follow-up on 50 patients originally hospitalized for primary sedative-hypnotic dependence and found that 84% resumed sedative-hypnotic use, 52% were abusing drugs at follow-up, and 42% had been readmitted for abuse. Three had experienced delirious states, and six had seizures during withdrawal. Social deterioration was observed in 48%. A recent long-term study in Sweden by Allgulander, Ljungberg, and Fisher (1987) of 221 patients admitted for dependence on sedative-hypnotics showed similar unfavorable outcomes. Poor outcomes were significantly related to primary psychiatric symptoms before first admission, concomitant alcohol abuse, familial drug and alcohol abuse, and health care occupation. Of those with primary sedative hypnotic dependence, 46% continued abuse until death or follow-up. There also were higher than expected unnatural deaths: 11% of men and 23% of the women.

Psychostimulants: Cocaine

For the psychostimulants, one prototype is described: cocaine. It is available in various forms and routes of administration. Most cocaine abusers start using drugs at an earlier age than nonusing peers and begin with alcohol and tobacco use, progressing to marijuana, with powdered cocaine use preceding crack use (Kandel & Yamaguchi, 1993). Effects of cocaine depend partly on how it is consumed: intranasally (snorted), smoked (freebasing or crack smoking), or intravenously (injected). Effects of a typical intranasal dose of pure, pharmaceutical cocaine hydrochloride (25–150 mg), include euphoria, increased energy, alertness, and sensory awareness, and decreased appetite. Crack cocaine and IV users report an intense rush of euphoria often referred to as "power" or "energy." The rush fades in seconds but the euphoria remains for several minutes.

Euphoria is followed by dysphoria, agitation, and restlessness, which prompt the user to use again. With continued use of cocaine, maladaptive cognitive and behavioral changes may occur, including grandiosity, hypervigilance, agitation, and impaired judgment. General signs of sympathetic arousal may include tachycardia, pupillary dilation, elevated blood pressure, and perspiration. Severe intoxication may be characterized by rambling speech, psychomotor agitation, anxiety, apprehension, impaired judgment, and fighting. Other symptoms might include transient ideas of reference, paranoid ideation, increased sexual interest, and visual or tactile hallucinations. Immediate abstinence effects with cocaine (the "crash") include dysphoria, craving, anxiety, tremulousness, irritability, fatigue, and depression. Beyond 24 hours of abstinence, the withdrawal syndrome may include insomnia or hypersomnia, and psychomotor agitation (APA, 1987). The minimum lethal dose of cocaine is difficult to determine because much of the street supply of the drug is adulterated. Also, death has occurred with various blood levels of cocaine in otherwise healthy individuals, prompting Smart and Anglin (1987) to suggest that "virtually no dose, however small, can be guaranteed safe for 100% of cases."

Both animal studies (Bozarth & Wise, 1985) and clinical observations (Valladares & Lemberg, 1987) attest to the toxic effects of cocaine. In reviewing emergency room visits and hospital admissions at a major metropolitan hospital, Lowenstein et al. (1987) noted acute neurologic and psychiatric symptoms as primary complaints. Neurologic complications included seizures, focal neurologic signs, headache, and transient loss of consciousness. Agitation, anxiety, depression, psychosis and paranoia, and suicidal ideation were the most frequent psychiatric symptoms. Pulmonary problems have been noted in crack smokers (Kissner, Lawrence, Selis, & Flint, 1987; Salzman, Khan, & Emory, 1987). Death associated with cocaine use is frequently due to a cardiovascular complication, such as myocardial infarction, arrhythmia, or aortic rupture (Bates, 1988).

Hallucinogens

The drug class hallucinogens contains diverse drugs with wide differences in chemical structure and mechanism of action. There is little in the literature that suggests severe dependence develops on hallucinogens. However, researchers may have ignored its dependence-inducing capacity because of the lack of classical withdrawal symptoms associated with drugs in this class. Tennant (1983), in a review of the literature, could not find one study that documented abstinence in the majority of any group of hallucinogen users for as long as 90 days following treatment. Thus, it may be that abuse of and dependence on hallucinogens is more difficult to treat than has been generally assumed.

Lysergic acid diethylamide (LSD) is our prototype. LSD has two phases of dose effects: autonomic nervous system (ANS) effects and psychological symptoms. ANS effects include pupillary dilation, decreased appetite, dizziness, increased body temperature and blood sugar, chills, restlessness, "goose flesh," nausea, vomiting, and variations in pulse and blood pressure. Psychological symptoms include euphoria, depersonalization, and body image distortion of internal stimuli (i.e., visual, auditory, tactile, olfactory, gustatory, and thermal illusions). Chronic dosage does not produce withdrawal when dosage is reduced or eliminated; however, tolerance occurs to psychological effects but not to ANS effects.

Individuals with histories of psychological disturbances, who live in insecure environments or who are undergoing crisis situations, are vulnerable to adverse reactions. Lasting adverse reactions have not been adequately documented, although anecdotal reports indicate that flashbacks and panic reactions ("bad trips") occur (McWilliams & Tuttle, 1973; Millman, 1978). One overdose death has been reported in the literature (Fysh et al., 1985). A recent review (Abraham & Aldridge, 1993) confirms continued concern over potential long-lasting adverse psychological consequences from LSD use in vulnerable individuals.

Cannabinoids

Cannabis sativa and cannabis sativa resin are the prototypes for the class cannabinoids. Although this drug is considered an hallucinogen, with usual doses hallucinations rarely occur. Thus, the drug will be considered in a separate class.

Use of cannabis sativa (marijuana) and its resin (hashish) produces physiological, perceptual, and psychological effects (Hollister, 1971). Tetrahydrocannabinol (THC) is the prevalent psychoactive ingredient in marijuana and hashish, so dosage levels refer to THC content. With low doses of 5–25 mg (one "joint" equals approximately 7.5 mg of THC), typical physiological effects include bloodshot eyes, dry mouth, unusual sensations such as tingling (parasthesias), increased appetite, and craving for sweets. Heightened senses of taste, touch, smell, sound, and vision are typical perceptual effects (Hollister, 1971). Psychological effects may include elated mood; slowed time sense; difficulties in thinking, comprehending, and expressing; poor memory; and uncontrollable laughter. Impaired performance on visuomotor and cognitive tasks, such as driving an automobile (Hollister, 1988) and piloting an aircraft (Yesavage, Leirer, Denari, & Hollister, 1985), have been reported. These effects are often not recognized by the user.

With chronic high doses of 200 mg, more intense symptoms occur. Emotional responses are magnified, sensations are distorted, and hallucinations may occur. Acute panic reactions, toxic delirium, psychosis, and transient paranoid states have occurred (Hollister, 1988; Schwartz, 1987). Chronic marijuana use may exacerbate existing mental illness, such as schizophrenia (Maycut, 1985). Decreased performance on perceptual motor tasks (Varma, Malhotra, Dang, Das, & Nehra, 1988) and reaction time, speed, and accuracy tests (Mendhiratta et al., 1988) have been associated with chronic, heavy marijuana use.

Marijuana is clearly the illicit drug most used in the United States (National Institute of Drug Abuse, 1991), and use often starts in late childhood or early adolescence. Heavy use is usually described by researchers as 1–5+ cigarettes daily or almost daily. In adolescents, regular use, especially moderate to heavy use, is associated with school adjustment and family problems, low grades, increased risk of problems with school authorities and police, and use of tobacco, alcohol, and other illicit drugs. Those who become regular users often terminate use, most often without professional help, in their 30s and 40s.

Cannabinol in marijuana is slowly metabolized and is excreted primarily in the feces, rather than in urine. It has a long half-life of 19 hours or more. Thus, those who smoke several cigarettes per day are loading their biological system and may experience more intense toxic effects. Although tolerance and reverse tolerance have been noted (Ferraro & Grisham, 1972; Hunt & Jones, 1980; Nowlan & Cohen, 1977; Weil, Zinberg, & Nelson, 1969), existence of an abstinence syndrome has been controversial. However, there is experimental evidence for an abstinence syndrome produced by repeated use of relatively high doses. The withdrawal syndrome includes nausea, sleep disturbance, tremor, perspiration, and emotional irritability and anxious mood. Its controversial status in the literature and poorly understood clinical relevance is reflected in the fact that DSM-IV describes the above symptoms but does not list the withdrawal syndrome as a diagnostic entity (APA, 1994, p. 215).

An amotivational syndrome has been described consisting of lowered activity, goalessness associated with apathy, sluggish mental and physical responses, loss of interest in personal appearance, flattening of affect, symptoms of mental confusion, and a slowed time sense (Maugh, 1974). However, its validity is controversial (Hochman & Brill, 1973). The syndrome is imprecisely defined, so its reliability and validity as a recognized clinical entity has been hard to establish. Thus, its validity as a scientifically established entity is still questioned (Gold, 1989), and it does not appear as a recognized entity in DSM-IV (APA, 1994, pp. 215–221).

Effects of chronic marijuana use on human cognition have been controversial and very difficult to study scientifically. However, a recent carefully controlled study suggests that heavy use may be associated with deficits in mathematical skills and verbal expression impairment in memory retrieval (Block & Ghoneim, 1993). Impairments depended on frequency of chronic marijuana use and "light and moderate use" defined by them as "use one to four and five to six times weekly" were not associated with deficits. This work needs to be replicated and confirmed by others before it is generally accepted that heavy use may be associated with cognitive deficits, but the findings have implications for counseling heavy users on possible risks.

Anabolic Steroids

Anabolic steroids are testosterone derivatives developed to maximize the anabolic effects of testosterone and minimize its androgenic effects. The primary anabolic effects of steroids are increases in body weight and lean muscle mass. The androgenic effects include changes in primary (increases in penis size and production of sperm) and secondary (facial hair, deepening voice) sex characteristics. The drugs have numerous medical uses (reviewed by Kochakian, 1993); however, their illicit use is the reason that they have been included in this chapter on drug abuse. Athletes are using anabolic steroids, mostly without prescription or medical supervision, to increase weight and muscle mass. Some experts feel that use of anabolic steroids is pervasive in the sports world at the elite level of competition (see review by Donahoe & Johnson, 1986). Furthermore, there is increasing evidence that their use has become more common among the general adolescent male population (Buckley, Yesalis, & Bennell, 1993).

The first reported use of anabolic steroids in athletics was by Russian weightlifters in the 1950s. American weightlifters followed their lead later in that decade. Since that time, steroid use has become increasingly popular and has spread to other sports, such as football, swimming, and track and field.

While their use is now widespread, their effect on athletic performance remains controversial. Athletes using steroids typically have strong beliefs that their performances are improved while taking the drugs. But results of controlled studies on the effects of steroids on athletic performance are mixed. In their review, Haupt and Rovere (1984) suggest that anabolic steroids yield significant strength increases in athletes intensively trained in weightlifting before and during steroid use, in those who maintain high-protein diets, and in those who compete in events where strength is measured by the single repetition-maximal weight technique. The belief that steroids will enhance strength may also play a strong role in their ultimate effect.

A second major controversy regarding steroid use is the frequency with which physical and emotional side effects occur. Athletes taking the drugs often believe side effects are not serious or permanent. The medical and scientific communities suggest otherwise, citing reports of abnormal liver function tests, reproductive system change, liver tumors, and cholesterol imbalance in chronic heavy steroid users (American College of Sports Medicine, 1984; Wright & Stone, 1985). Psychological effects of steroid use also have been reported. These effects have included mood disturbances, such as major depression and manic episodes, the latter often including aggressive behavior (Pope & Katz, 1994). Anabolic steroid use also has been associated with psychotic symptoms, including hallucinations and delusional states (Pope & Katz, 1988).

A recent concern about anabolic steroids is whether the user can become dependent on their use (Kashkin & Kleber, 1989). While steroids are not among the drugs included in the DSM-IV section on substance use disorders, recent reports in the literature suggest that some users may be at risk for dependence (Brower, Blow, Beresford, & Fuelling, 1989; Brower, Blow, Young, & Hill, 1991). Reported withdrawal symptoms have included depressed mood, restlessness, insomnia, and craving for steroids (Brower, 1993). Initial recommendations for treatment of withdrawal from high-dose anabolic steroid use have been offered by Brower (1993); however, research is needed to evaluate treatment protocols.

Controversies surrounding the effects of steroids on athletic performance, the incidence and seriousness of side effects, and dependency risk have created an unfortunate rift between the athletic and scientific communities. Added to that is the overpowering emphasis on winning in most sports settings. Under pressure to perform and without definitive knowledge of benefits and risks associated with steroid use, the athlete is left to a combination of "faith and fear" that stimulate his or her use of steroids (Donohoe & Johnson 1986). Faith that steroids will build muscle and increase strength and fear that without their use, the athlete will be at a disadvantage to steroid-using competitors. Fuller and LaFountain (1987) have suggested that athletes, when placed in these conditions, resort to defensive mechanisms to justify their use of steroids. These psychological strategies might include denial of potential health risks, condemnation of nonathletes criticizing their steroid use, and appeal to the "higher loyalties" of sport. Such justification strategies are not unlike those that might be used by other illicit drug users.

While anabolic steroids are not included in the traditionally recognized drugs of abuse, their use among athletes is cause for concern. In 1975, their use was banned in amateur athletic competition. However, there is evidence that rather than reduce steroid use, such banning has only resulted in athletes' resorting to new and improved methods of disguised use (Donohoe & Johnson, 1986). Each new method of drug testing has spawned a variety of methods to avoid detection. A reexamination of the goals of sport participation will likely be necessary before steroid use can be significantly altered.

Inhalants

Inhalants are volatile substances, a heterogenous group of mostly organic solvents that are simple hydrocarbon or substituted hydrocarbon compounds found in a variety of substances, such as gasoline, fuel gases including butane, lighter fluids, spray paints, cleaning fluids, adhesives, and typewriter correction fluid. In progressive order of vapor concentration, these compounds may be sniffed from an open container, breathed from a rag soaked in the substance, and held close to the nose or inhaled from a bag. Methods of use may imply increasing involvement with inhalant abuse (Dinwiddie, 1994). Because many of these materials contain several different chemical compounds, it is not easy to ascribe pharmacological properties or toxic effects accurately. Dinwiddie (1994) reported little evidence to suggest that tolerance to inhalants occurs; however, similarities of action to central nervous system depressants suggest that tolerance development may be possible. A withdrawal syndrome lasting 2–5 days is described in the literature (Dinwiddie, 1994). It is characterized by sleep disturbance, nausea, tremor, perfuse perspiration, irritability, abdominal, and chest discomfort, with a syndrome similar to delirium tremens reported upon cessation.

Because inhalants are low cost and readily available, without legislative control of possession and purchase, they often are the first psychoactive drug abused. Inhalant abuse is found typically among adolescents and preadolescent children, especially males, and is associated with significant mortality. Among adolescent substance abusers, after tobacco and alcohol, inhalants are the substances next most used. Inhalant abuse steadily increased throughout the 1980s to a peak of 7% annual use reported in the survey year 1993 (O'Malley et al., 1995).

Abuse seems higher among economically disadvantaged groups and among those with poor academic achievement and juvenile delinquency (Chalmers, 1991; Dinwiddie, 1994). Chalmers (1991) reported there were 121 deaths associated with volatile substance abuse in Australia from 1980 to 1987, averaging 16 deaths per year. This represented less than 1% of all drug-related deaths in Australia, but over half of them occurred in those aged 15–20. He also reported data from a review of volatile substance abuse deaths in the United Kingdom 1971–1983 that showed 24% of deaths were associated with fuel gases, 17% with aerosol propellants, and 27% with solvents in glue and other commercial products.

Concurrent Dependence

The clinical picture for concurrent dependence (i.e., dependence on two classes of drugs) is extremely complex. A typical concurrent dependence involves combined use of opiates and barbiturates. The user may substitute one drug for another and show a mixed clinical picture. For instance, instead of showing the "nod" state common to opiates, opiate/barbiturate addicts will, despite a recent dose of an opiate, show signs of barbiturate withdrawal, including anxiety, irritability, and sleep difficulty. They may show some slurring of speech, difficulty walking, keeping their balance, and general incoordination in the absence of any odor of alcohol. Frequently, the user does not realize that symptoms are from barbiturate withdrawal but attributes the effects to opiate withdrawal, the "primary" addiction. Opioid addiction is often thought of as a single class substance phenomenon, but use of opioids to exclusion of all other classes of drugs is rare (Siegal, 1981). Opioid addicts often abuse alcohol, barbiturates and synthetic hypnotics, cocaine, and other compounds (Anglin, Almog, Fisher, & Peters, 1989). Findings suggest that alcohol use during methadone treatment reflects a lifetime pattern of increased alcohol use following any decline in heroin intake.

Another typical concurrent dependence involves barbiturates and stimulants. The clinical picture is for concurrent and alternating use. To prevent aversive symptoms from chronic amphetamine dosage, barbiturates are often consumed to reduce sleeplessness and hyperexcitability. Amphetamines are used to reduce barbiturate sedation after a large dose or to reduce morning drowsiness.

Another common pattern of concurrent dependence is that of opiate and cocaine. With the widespread use of "crack" cocaine this pattern is widely seen in methadone maintenance and drug-free treated patients. (Hanbury, Sturiano, Cohen, Stimmel, & Aquillaume, 1986; Hunt, Spunt, Lipton, Goldsmith, & Strug, 1986; Strug, Hunt, Goldsmith, Lipton & Spunt, 1985). There is some evidence that depression may lead to increased vulnerability for such cocaine abuse (Kosten, Rounsaville, & Kleber, 1987).

Dual Diagnosis

Researchers find considerable comorbidity of psychiatric disorders in the general population, with comorbidity of psychiatric disorders greatest among those with a substance use disorder. It is likely that over 70% of individuals with substance abuse disorders have a diagnosed mental disorder (Kandel, 1991). Dually diagnosed patients make up a large proportion of patients in substance abuse treatment programs (Kosten & Rounsaville, 1986; Kranzler & Liebowitz, 1988; Maddux, Desmond, & Costello, 1987; Milby et al., 1996; Mirin & Weiss, 1986; Ross, Glaser, & Germanson, 1988; Rounsaville, Weissman, Crits-Christoph, Wilber, & Kleber, 1982; Rounsaville, Weissman, Kleber, & Wilber, 1982). Thus, to present a clinical picture of the dually diagnosed substance abuser would do the reader a disservice. A typical picture of the dually diagnosed patient with common characteristics would be implied. It may be more useful to review types of psychopathology that occur more frequently than others among substance abusers.

Some sense of the psychiatric comorbidity among hospitalized drug abusers is illustrated in the study by Weiss, Mirin, & Frances (1992) at a private psychiatric hospital in Massachusetts. Their study of 350 hospitalized primary drug abusers revealed 185 opioid addicts, 120 cocaine abusers, and 44 dependent on sedative-hypnotics, with a total of 52% also meeting criteria for alcohol abuse or dependence; 37% had an additional Axis I disorder. Patients received an additional diagnosis of substance abuse or dependence only if they met criteria for the additional diagnosis while drug free. The most common comorbidity was mood disorders found in 21% with major depression diagnosed in 11%.

Most studies have found that mood disorders, especially major depression and anxiety disorders, are the most likely comorbid conditions found with substance use disorders (Kranzler & Liebowitz, 1988; Milby, Sims, Khuder, et al.,

1996; Mirin & Weiss, 1986; Rounsaville, Weissman, Crits-Christoph, et al., 1982). A common clinical picture with mood and anxiety disorders is one where the individual attempts to regulate an aversive affective state(s). The drug is chosen because of its specific effect on reducing the aversive affect. Even though mood and anxiety disorders are those most commonly seen comorbid with substance use disorders, the variety of substances abused (Zeiner, Stanitis, Spurgeon, & Nichols, 1985) and other psychopathologies in dually diagnosed patients is quite varied and complex. Additional complexity is added by the increased risk substance abuse carries for repeated traumatic injuries, which have their own psychological and physiological sequelae (Cottrool & Frances, 1993) and the high likelihood that more than one substance is abused by each individual. One study of 258 alcoholics found only three who did not abuse other drugs (Zeiner et al., 1985).

Unfortunately, cyclic monthly patterns of abuse among the more dysfunctional dually diagnosed substance abusers is a clinical picture which can be observed and seems driven by monthly receipt of disability income. In a recent study of 105 schizophrenics, severity of psychiatric symptoms and urine concentrations of a cocaine metabolite were measured for 15 weeks. Cocaine use, psychiatric symptoms, and hospital admissions all peaked during the first week of each month and were highly correlated with the arrival of disability income (Shaner et al., 1995). The investigators noted irony in their results, where disability income administered to compensate for disabling effects of severe mental illness may have the opposite effect and exacerbate disability and dysfunction by enabling the availability of cocaine.

In some clinical settings dually diagnosed patients are seen as a monolithic "type" of patient with similar characteristics. This view tends to be perpetuated by the recent development of dual diagnosis treatment units. However, coexistence of one or more substance use disorders with one or more mental disorders makes for striking complexity and a variety of clinical presentations as noted above with complicated psychopathology combined with pharmacological interactions (Cushman, 1987). No amount of common assessment and interventions can force them into the same mold. There is no substitute for individualized behavioral, psychometric, and psychosocial assessment. Although such assessment is labor intensive, it provides the idiosyncratic information needed to develop the individualized and tailored treatment and aftercare plans to address unique forms of psychopathology while utilizing each person's unique strengths and assets. Without special assessment and intervention, research has shown that outcomes for dually diagnosed patients are not as favorable as for those patients with uncomplicated substance use disorders (McLellan, Woody, Luborsky, O'Brien, & Druley, 1983; Woody et al., 1983).

COURSE AND PROGNOSIS

Natural History of Drug Dependence

Even though substance use disorders are the most common mental disorders in the United States, the large Epidemiologic Catchment Area Study of almost 20,000 people found that 85%–90% of people with these disorders never received treatment (Robins & Regier, 1991). We conclude from these data that most people with such disorders, with the possible exception of those with opioid dependence, suffer without professional assistance or treatment. In the case of opioid drug dependence, it has been impossible to observe the course of addiction in a systematic way *without* intervention. One of the authors (Milby, 1981), after an extensive review of the literature, could not find one systematic study of the natural course of opioid addiction. However, much useful information can be learned from some extensive follow-up studies, some for as long as 20 years, where opioid addicts have experienced varieties of intervention (Vaillant, 1973; Robins & Murphy, 1967).

To study the extent and course of heroin addiction in a normal population, Robins and Murphy (1967) obtained a sample of African American men, ages 30–35, who had attended public school. They found 12% had been addicted to heroin, and among those addicted, 50% were still using some drug at the time of the study (i.e., at ages 30–35). Only 18% of those previously addicted were still using heroin.

Among those who abuse cocaine, a large majority have not been exposed to treatment of any kind. However, there is yet to be published a systematic study of the natural history of cocaine addiction without treatment. Fortunately, those providing treatment have examined the natural history of cocaine addiction before entering treatment.

Khalsa and Anglin (1990) studied the pretreatment history of 300 patients seeking treatment for cocaine abuse and discovered four reliable patterns for development of abuse and addiction. The first was one of stepped progression to higher and higher dosages. The second involved progression from mild to severe usage and addiction. The third was a pattern of instant severe use. The fourth included those who did not fit the first three. Progression from mild to severe abuse and addiction involved change from nasal sniffing to free-base smoking of crack cocaine. They also noted a surprising high level of maintained employment in their treatment sample. However, although subjects tended to maintain employment, they changed jobs frequently, losing and gaining new jobs in quick succession.

Initiation of drug use is most likely to occur in adolescence or young adulthood. Major risk periods for initiating cigarette, alcohol, and marijuana use typically end by age 20, and for illicit drugs, except cocaine, by age 21. Initiation of prescribed, psychoactive drug use occurs at a later age (Kandel & Logan, 1984). Young adult drug users differ from their peers along various dimensions. They typically have more difficulty making a successful transition to adult role responsibilities, engage in more deviant behavior, and become immersed in a social network supportive of their drug use (Kandel, 1984). As drug use increases, these tendencies become more pronounced and often lead to family, school, social, health, and occupational problems (Kandel, Davies, Karus, & Yamaguchi, 1986; Schwartz, Hoffman, & Jones, 1987).

The nature of drug use patterns and resulting consequences is difficult to track following young adulthood. For those who continue use, it is reasonable to assume some will become dependent on their drug(s) of choice. If these drugs are illicit, eventual legal consequences are likely (Benson & Holmberg, 1984; Hammersley & Morrison, 1987). Long-term drug abuse is associated with lower income and increased use of psychiatric, medical, and social services (Holmberg, 1985).

Outcomes of addiction are variable and difficult to predict. A small portion of addicts discontinue their habit without formal treatment (Tuchfeld, 1981; Winnick, 1962), a process that is poorly understood. Some enter treatment and make sufficient changes to terminate their use. Others respond to treatment only after repeated attempts and relapses. Finally, an unfortunate percentage continues unrelenting abuse until premature death via direct effects on health or other consequences of drug use.

Course of Drug Abuse and Dependence after Treatment

Predicting course and outcome of treatment for substance abuse is a difficult challenge. Positive outcomes occur in a variety of treatment settings (inpatient, outpatient, and therapeutic communities) and intensities (Miller & Hester, 1986a). However, high relapse rates following treatment are common across all addictions (Hunt, Barnett, & Branch, 1971). Consequences of unsuccessful treatment represent tremendous liabilities to the individual and costs to society. Therefore, understanding treatment factors associated with negative and positive outcome is imperative.

Vaillant (1973) found that opioid addicts who achieved stable abstinence after being identified in treatment increased from 10% at 5 years to 23% and 35% at 10 and 18 years, respectively. Those active in their addiction declined progressively from 53% to 41% and 25%. Percentages who died over that span were 6%, 12%, and 23%. One recent large follow-up study after treatment for cocaine dependence showed: 25% abstinent, 25% involved in daily use, and 50% with other than daily use. Over 50% of relapses occurred within 30 days after treatment (Khalsa & Anglin, 1990).

Unfavorable substance abuse treatment outcomes have been associated with primary psychiatric symptoms prior to substance abuse treatment (Allgulander et al., 1987) and with increasing severity of symptoms (McLellan et al., 1983). Early recognition of these comorbidities is important for treatment decisions and affects eventual treatment outcome.

Perhaps the most favorable prognostic indicator for substance abuse treatment is participation in aftercare following treatment. Ito and Donovan (1986) indicated that aftercare following alcoholism treatment improves treatment outcome, and its effects are independent of intake prognostic indicators. Aftercare provides a supportive structure that can assist in recovery by providing early detection of relapse episodes, development of coping skills, and an opportunity for family members to become involved constructively in the addict's recovery. Another positive prognostic indicator that seems to hold promise is the stage of change at which a given substance abuser enters treatment (Miller & Heather, 1986). Recent research is showing that those who enter treatment at the action stage rather than at the precontemplation or contemplation stages may respond best to treatment.

Continuous substance abuse results in deleterious effects. No organ system is spared. Depending on the type, frequency, and duration of abuse, neurological (Leeds, Malhotra, & Zimmerman, 1983), cardiovascular (Jaffe, 1983; Yeager,

Hobson, Padberg, Lynch, & Chakravarty, 1987), respiratory (Glassroth, Adams, & Schnoll, 1987), and musculoskeletal (Firooznia, Golimbu, Rafii, & Lichtman, 1983) problems are common. In addition, infectious complications can occur (Blanck, Ream, & Deleese, 1984), most notably evidenced by an increased probability of contracting HIV infections for intravenous drug users (D'Aquila & Williams, 1987).

FAMILIAL AND GENETIC CONSIDERATIONS

Families of drug abusers are often dysfunctional and sites of physical, emotional, and sexual abuse where the young are early exposed—if not introduced—to various forms of drug abuse by family members (Hernandez, 1992). Studies of genetic contributions to alcohol abuse and dependence liability have had to control for the influence of shared environmental factors in mono- and dizygotic twins. In one study, liability variance attributable to shared environmental factors was .50 for alcohol abuse or dependence, or both (Pickens, Svikis, McGue, Lyken, & Clayton, 1991).

The young drug abuser from a healthy, nurturant family is rare. However, there are many families who continue to struggle, against a strong environmental press of poverty, poor housing, neighborhood crime, substance abuse, and violence, to raise children and provide a wholesome family life. Such families can be strong assets and sources of social support for the drug abuser in treatment. Many such families are led by a single parent, most often a mother, but in the African American community, especially, grandmothers, aunts, sisters, and even neighbors may play this role.

Crack abuse, distribution, and related illegal activities (e.g., drug selling and prostitution), along with declining socioeconomic conditions, have severely disrupted many inner city families and households across several generations (Dunlap & Johnson, 1992). These households with drug-abusing members serve to model and perpetuate drug abuse, drug sales, and other criminal and deviant behaviors for each successive generation. Such households experience many, if not all forms of family distress identified by Kasarda (as cited in Dunlap & Johnson, 1992): low education (high school dropout), single parenthood (household head with children under age 18), poor work history, receipt of public assistance, and householder's family income from legal sources below the poverty line.

Although Wallace's (1991) study of 245 urban, African American crack smokers may not be entirely representative of the population of crack-dependent people, she observed a high rate of personal and family psychopathology. She found 91% from dysfunctional families where 51% had one or more parents with alcohol abuse or dependence, 20% with domestic violence, 22% with parental abandonment, 20% with parental separation, 14% with physical abuse, and 7% with sexual and emotional abuse. As use became compulsive and interfered with employment and family life, 18.7% of the sample were asked to leave their homes and met criteria for homelessness.

O'Donnell (1964) found that male and female opioid addicts from Kentucky who married were more likely to have multiple marriages than a population comparison group. In his 12-year follow-up of New York City opioid addicts, Vaillant (1966) found that a high percentage of addicts continued to live with their mothers or another female family member up to age 30 and observed that addicts remain unusually dependent on their families of origin.

Although attempts to link familial alcohol and drug dependence susceptibility to specific chromosomes and family inheritance patterns have not found a consistent, single, genetic locus determining abuse vulnerability, the multidetermined polygenetic contribution to drug abuse etiology is well established. The only issue still to be determined is how much of a role heritability plays in the etiology of drug abuse along with environmental risk factors. Heritability estimates for different measures of alcoholism in the same population tend to vary according to criteria for alcoholism imposed. A recent study of concordance rates for alcoholism and other drug abuse in twins suggests that 20%–35% of the vulnerability of persons who abuse or become dependent on alcohol or abuse other drugs may be genetically determined and that males have a significantly higher heritability than females (Pickens et al., 1991). When DSM-III (APA, 1980) criteria for dependence are used, the highest level of heritability observed is .59. There also is recent evidence suggesting that cigarette smoking has a heritability index around 53% (Pomerleau, 1995).

Genetic researchers are now able to utilize the known gene map location of certain markers with the technique of quantitative trait loci, chromosome mapping, to discover associations between a target trait and one or more previously mapped marker gene loci (Crabbe & Belknap, 1992). Researchers have now identified a role for a D2 dopamine receptor gene variant in persons with increased substance abuse vulnerability (Smith et al., 1992). These new genetic methods combined with pharmacological approaches may soon allow the establishment of genetic commonalities of mechanisms of action among abused drugs.

Knowledge of drug abuse genetics has implications for drug abuse assessment, treatment, and prevention when it is complemented by accurate family histories of drug abuse in presenting patients. A family history of drug abuse, especially one spanning several generations, implies a risk for drug dependence greater than that produced by the usual environmental risk factors. Such a family history implies that prevention, early identification, and treatment efforts should be targeted for persons with such histories. In the near future, multigeneration histories of substance abuse may become an important matching variable for assignment or referral to a treatment program most likely to be helpful.

DIAGNOSTIC CONSIDERATIONS

We see the process of differential diagnosis as an exercise in the logical process of scientific classification. The DSM-IV is one among many classification schemes for substance use disorders that may be divided into two types: partial and complete (Milby, 1981a). Most partial schemes organize and classify one subtype of dependence according to severity. Complete schemes attempt to organize drug dependence into a unified whole with categories typically based on the pharmacological class of drug. The most widely used complete classification scheme is the DSM-IV. Of 12 schemes compared on type of dependence, level of use in research and clinical practice, logical structure, number of organizing principles, and potential usefulness, Milby (1981a) found a third of them useless and another third of moderate or limited usefulness. Since that review several new and useful classification schemes have been added, including revision of DSM-III (DSM-III-R; APA, 1987; Cancrini, Cingolani, Compagnoni, Constantini, & Mazzoni, 1988; Wilkinson et al., 1987) and DSM-IV (APA, 1994). Recent research has supported the utility of the notion of a common dependence syndrome with psychosocial sequelae for all psychoactive drugs (Kosten, Rounsaville, Barbor, Spitzer, & Williams, 1987).

Classification in clinical science is an active rather than static process. Useful classification schemes should be in a continuous state of refinement and evolution because our understanding of substance use disorders is expanding. Type and number of psychoactive drugs available are growing. Also, modes of use and type and degree of physical and emotional dysfunction are changing. A good example of the evolution of a functional classification scheme is found in the elaboration of the APA's *Diagnostic and Statistical Manuals*. The classification scheme for substance use disorders in DSM-II (APA, 1968) was based on the pharmacological properties of the drugs and did not concern itself with degree of dysfunction. Beyond establishing a need for a certain type of drug to be employed in detoxification, it was worthless as a tool to differentially assess degree of personal and social disruption caused by drug abuse. The DSM-III, using a multiaxial classification scheme, included additional classification variables that aided in developing treatment plans and recommending modes of treatment. The DSM-III-R represented a significant advancement in diagnosis of substance use disorders. The diagnostic criteria for dependence are more consistent across substances and have been supported by reliability studies (cf. Kosten, Rounsaville, Babor, et al., 1987).

Changes from DSM-III-R to DSM-IV

The primary difference between the DSM-IV and its predecessor DSM-III-R concerns the organization of the substance-induced disorders and mental disorders due to a general medical condition. In the DSM-III-R, these conditions were identified as "organic" disorders and listed in a single section. The authors of DSM-IV did not want to imply that "nonorganic" or "functional" mental disorders were unrelated to physical or biological processes. "DSM-IV eliminated the term organic and distinguishes those mental disorders that are substance induced from those that are due to a general medical condition and those that have no specified etiology" (APA, 1994, p. 192).

DSM-IV Descriptions of the Disorders

There are 11 classes of substances of abuse identified in DSM-IV: 1. alcohol, 2. amphetamine or similarly acting sympathomimetics, 3. caffeine, 4. cannabis, 5. cocaine, 6. hallucinogens, 7. inhalants, 8. nicotine, 9. opioids, 10. phenecyclidine (PCP) or similarily acting arylcyclohexylamines, and 11. sedatives, hypnotics, or anxiolytics. For each class of substance, specific aspects of dependence, abuse, intoxication, and withdrawal are used for diagnostic purposes. Many criteria for substance dependence, abuse, intoxification, and withdrawal are applicable across classes of substances. Important features associated with each class of substance are culture, age, and gender considerations; course; impairment and complications; familial pattern; and criteria for differential diagnosis of disorders.

For each class, substance-related disorders are divided into two groups: the substance use disorders (substance dependence and substance abuse) and the substance-induced disorders (substance intoxication, substance withdrawal, substance-induced delirium, substance-induced persisting dementia, substance-induced persisting, amnesic disorder, substance-induced psychotic disorder, substance-induced mood disorder, substance-induced anxiety disorder, substance-induced sexual dysfunction, substance-induced sleep disorder, and hallucinogen persisting perception disorder [flashbacks]). Also included are polysubstance dependence and other or unknown substance-related disorders.

Substance Dependence Criteria

Substance dependence is characterized by a cluster of cognitive, behavioral, and physical symptoms associated with persistent usage despite significant substance-related functional impairment (APA, 1994). Dependence is defined as a cluster of three or more of the following symptoms occurring at any time in the same 12-month period: 1. tolerance; 2. withdrawal; 3. compulsive substance use behaviors; 4. unsuccessful efforts to decrease or discontinue use; 5. preoccupation with obtaining, using, or recovering from the substance; 6. impaired social, occupational, or recreational functioning; and 7. continued use despite knowledge of persistent or recurrent physical or psychological problems. Substance dependence can be applied with some variation to all classes of substances except caffeine.

Six course specifiers can accompany the diagnosis of dependence for most substance classes in DSM-IV. There are four remission specifiers: early full remission, early partial remission, sustained full remission, and sustained partial remission. The individual can also be specified as being on agonist therapy or in a controlled environment. Presence of tolerance and withdrawal may be specified as being with or without physiological dependence. The specifier, with perceptual disorders, may be applied to the diagnoses of alcohol withdrawal, cannabis intoxication, cocaine intoxication, opioid intoxication, phencyclidine intoxication, sedative withdrawal, hypnotic withdrawal, and anxiolytic withdrawal.

Substance Abuse Criteria

A maladaptive pattern of substance use, characterized by recurrent and significant adverse consequences related to repeated use, is the essential feature of substance abuse (APA, 1994). Criteria for a substance abuse diagnosis in DSM-IV require one or more of the following occurring within a 12-month period: 1. recurrent substance use resulting in a failure to fulfill major role obligations at work, school, or home; 2. recurrent substance use in situations in which there is physical danger; 3. recurrent substance-related legal problems; and 4. continued substance use despite having persistent or recurrent social or interpersonal problems caused or exacerbated by the effects of the substance. Symptoms present must have never met the criteria for substance dependence.

PSYCHOLOGICAL AND BIOLOGICAL ASSESSMENT

Assessment of alcohol or drug abuse requires a comprehensive knowledge of interviewing, psychometric, and diagnostic skills. Accurate assessment of alcohol and drug abuse problems must take into consideration variables like the validity of self-report, coexisting psychopathology, polydrug abuse, motivation for treatment, and gender and ethnic issues. Alcohol and drug use disorders are not static phenomena and must be viewed as constantly changing from initiation, abuse, dependency, and remission. Developmental phenomena or stages in the abuse or dependence process need to be thoroughly understood by the clinician doing a competent assessment (see Milby & Schumacher, 1994).

Assessment Strategies and Techniques

The following assessment strategies may be employed in the assessment of alcohol and drug problems: structured interviews, self-reports, direct observation, urine and blood sampling, pharmacological procedures, and psychometrics. Some combination of these strategies is likely to result in the most reliable and valid information to be obtained.

Structured Interview

A structured interview may be conducted with the patient or with a significant other. The interview should not focus solely on drug use but address numerous areas of the client's life. A structured interview may include assessments of type of drug used and pattern of use; physical health; emotional and cognitive, marital, social, vocational, and recreational functioning; and possible legal difficulties. After determining type of drug or drugs used, quantity, frequency, and duration of use (including abstinence periods) should be evaluated. Drug administration techniques are also important to assess (e.g., intravenous, intramuscular, or subcutaneous injection, inhaling, ingesting). The possibility of cross-tolerance and mixed addictions should also be assessed. Structured questioning of precipitating and maintaining factors should include the following: the social environment, emotions and cognitions, and physiological processes. Further, consequences of use (e.g., incarceration, financial costs, and interpersonal costs) should be noted. A history of intravenous use and trading sex for drugs is particularly important as an assessment of HIV/AIDS risk.

Drug abuse and dependence affect all areas of a person's life. A widely used assessment of multifunctioning is the Addiction Severity Index (ASI) introduced by McLellan and his colleagues and subsequently refined through further research (McLellan, Luborsky, Cacciola, et al., 1985; McLellan, Luborsky, O'Brien, et al., 1980). It assesses severity in seven areas: medical problems, employment and types of financial support, alcohol use, drug use, legal problems, family and social functioning, and psychiatric disorders. It yields a severity index and profile that has been shown to be sensitive to gains in treatment. Derived composite scores along with the severity index have been used in clinical outcome research for alcohol and substance use disorder studies.

Another structured interview that is useful for diagnosing other disorders in substance abusers is the National Institute on Mental Health (NIMH) Diagnostic Interview Schedule (DIS). However, its validity and utility early in treatment may be compromised in drug-dependent patients by neurological deficits and impaired recollection of their previous symptoms (Bergman, Borg, & Holm, 1980; Griffin, Weiss, Mirin, Wilson, & Bouehard-Voelk, 1987). The DSM-III-R checklist is a computer-administered semistructured diagnostic interview and is an efficient screening method for screening for establishment of research data bases. Utility and reliability of the DSM-III-R checklist have been established (see Hudziak et al., 1993).

Research has shown that structured interviews produce higher reliability than other assessment procedures, probably by controlling information variance (Helzer, Clayton, Pambakian, & Woodruff, 1978; Hesselbrock, Stabenau, Hesslebrock, & Mirkin, 1982; Mintz, Christoph, O'Brien, & Snedeker, 1980). There is evidence of robust and clinically useful levels of reliability usually obtained using structured interviews (Matarazzo, 1983).

Self-Report

When screening a patient for presence of any psychopathology, the clinician must assume within reason that information given by the client is valid and reliable. Although individual studies of self-reported data validity vary, past major reviews of the literature generally have concluded that, where there are no contingencies for reported use, self-report data are fairly accurate (Amsel, Mendell, Matthias, Mason, & Hocherman, 1976; Bale, Von Stone, Engelsing, Zarcone, & Kuldan, 1981; Bonito, Nurco, & Shaffer, 1976; Cox & Longwell, 1974; Milby & Stainback, 1991), with inconsistencies due more to faulty memory and inaccurate police records than to deliberate deception. Self-reported crack cocaine and heroin use was found to be accurate enough for measuring changes in risk behavior practices among admitted drug using, not-in-treatment, noninstitutionalized persons when assessed in a nonthreatening manner and confidentiality was assured (Weatherby et al., 1994).

However, recent studies, especially those that include cohorts of those abusing cocaine, have cast doubt on the validity of self-report. Substantial false negative classifications by self-report (i.e., denied verified use) when comparing self-reported cocaine use with urinanalysis outcomes have been associated with various mediating factors (Brown, Kranzler, & Del Boca, 1992; Falck et al., 1992; McNagny & Parker, 1992; Mieczkowski, Barzelay, Gropper, & Wish, 1991; Schumacher et al., 1995). Thus, contingencies and perhaps other mediating factors seem to impact the validity of self report. As proposed by Falck et al. (1992), need for validation of self-report data in clinical and research settings through use of urine toxicologies and further research is important to uncover more influences mediating the validity of self-report.

Direct Observation

Direct observation is extremely important in assessing the client's initial presentation to treatment personnel. Careful observation can reveal signs of withdrawal symptoms, drug-related diseases or disorders, general health and cognitive status, and quality of interpersonal skills and social support. Direct observation can be systematized and ratings derived. For example, the Objective Opiate Withdrawal scale provides an index of opiate withdrawal based on 13 physically observable signs, rated present or absent during a timed observation period (Handelsman et al., 1987).

Observational assessment strategies have been experimentally studied in controlled settings to observe, for example, the euphoric effects of heroin (Babor, Meyer, & Mirin, 1976; McNamee, Mirin, Kuhnle, & Meyer, 1976; Mirin, Meyer, & McNamee, 1976). Observational assessment has also been accomplished by allowing patients free access to a variety of substances in a lab setting (Blanchard, Libet, & Young, 1973). Elkin, Williams, Barlow, and Stewart (1974) videotaped users "shooting up" in order to later replay and assess physiological arousal. O'Brien, Testa, and O'Brien (1977) observed and measured heroin addicts' conditioned withdrawal symptoms to stimuli associated with heroin use.

Urine and Blood Samples

Urine and blood samples are frequently used in treatment of drug abuse. Toxicologic procedures are used for various therapeutic reasons: 1. to verify the abused substance in cases of acute intoxication; 2. to provide a basis for distinguishing intoxication or withdrawal from other psychopathology; 3. to prevent recent drug use from interfering with accuracy of other diagnostic tests, such as psychological testing; 4. to monitor possible drug use during rehabilitation; and 5. to serve as a therapeutic incentive to the client in treatment. Laboratory tests fall into two broad categories: competitive binding assays and chromatographic assays (Lehrer & Gold, 1986). The former include radio immunoassays and enzyme immunoassays. The latter include thin layer chromotography (TLC), gas liquid chromatography (GLC), and combined gas chromatopography and mass spectrometry (GC-MS). Commercial urine assays vary in their sensitivity and specificity (Cone, Menchen, Paul, Mell, & Mitchell, 1989; Cone & Mitchell, 1989). GC-MS is generally regarded as the most powerful analytical technique for identifying drugs, and therefore is recommended for forensic work. For clinical use, a screening test high in sensitivity (e.g., TLC) is typically used initially and positive results are confirmed with a test higher in specificity (e.g., GLC).

On-site methods like laboratory enzyme-multiple immunoassay urine toxicologies (EMIT) are good for random testing. Drugs that can be tested include amphetamine, cocaine, THC metabolites, opioids, barbiturates, benzodiazepines, methaqualone, phencyclidine, and propoxyphene. OnTrack TesTcup by Roche is an in vitro diagnostic test intended for professional use for the qualitative detection of drug or drug metabolite in urine. The OnTrack TesTcup provides only a preliminary analytical test result. A more specific alternate chemical method must be used in order to obtain confirmed analytical results when using these on-site tests.

Pharmacological Procedures

Pharmacological assessment is used to assess tolerance and dependence on opiates and barbiturates/hypnotic sedatives (Kolb, 1973; Schuckit, 1979). Opiate dependence may be determined by administration of a narcotic antagonist, such as naloxone, which will precipitate an acute abstinence state if the person is opioid dependent. To establish opiate tolerance levels, test doses of methadone are administered on a timed schedule until signs of intoxication appear. A similar procedure is used, with some short-acting barbiturates like pentobarbitol, to establish barbiturate and hypnotic sedative tolerance.

Psychometrics

Although traditional psychometric instruments have been used widely with drug abusers, in our view they have not been shown to be specifically applicable to this population or very helpful in diagnosis.

The most commonly used Minnesota Multiphasic Personality Inventory (MMPI) scale in substance abuse assessment is the MacAndrew Alcoholism scale (MacAndrew, 1965). Two new measures for assessing problems of alcohol and drug abuse with the Minnesota Multiphasic Personality Inventory-2 (MMPI-2) have been developed: the Addiction Potential scale (APS) and the Addiction Acknowledgement scale (AAS). Both new scales were shown to discriminate well between normative and psychiatric control groups and substantially better than other selected substance abuse scales (Weed, Butcher, McKenna, & Ben-Porath, 1992). Two new MMPI-2 scales for the assessment of alcohol and other drug problems for adolescents include the Alcohol/Drug Problems Acknowledgement scale (ACK) and the Alcohol/Drug Problems Proneness scale (PRO; Weed, Butcher, & Williams 1994).

Finally, the Alcohol Dependency scale (ADS; Skinner & Horn, 1984) and its parent instrument, the Alcohol Use Inventory (AUI; Horn, Wanberg, & Foster, 1983), are used to assess a multidimensional concept of alcoholism that includes several rather different styles of alcohol use and various biomedical and psychosocial consequences of excessive drinking, as well as perceived benefits from alcohol use. A general factor of alcohol dependence syndrome is measured by the following salient markers: 1. loss of behavioral control, 2. psychophysical withdrawal symptoms, 3. psychoperceptual withdrawal symptoms, and 4. obsessive-compulsive drinking style (Skinner & Horn, 1984).

GENDER AND RACIAL-ETHNIC ISSUES

Gender Differences

For alcohol and most drugs, abuse and dependence disorders are more prevalent in men than women. DSM-IV reports that alcohol abuse and dependence are more common in males than in females, with a male-to-female ratio as high as 5:1. However, this ratio varies depending on the age group. Intravenous amphetamine use has a male-to-female ratio of 3 or 4:1. The male-to-female ratio is more evenly divided among those with nonintravenous use. Cannabis use disorders appear more often in males, and hallucinogen abuse is 3 times more common in males than females. Males account for 70%–80% of inhalant-related and 75% of phencyclidine-related emergency-room visits. Males are more commonly affected by opiate addiction, with a male-to-female ratio typically being 3:1 to 4:1. Prevalence of cigarette smoking is slightly higher in males than in females. However, prevalence of smoking is reportedly decreasing more rapidly in males. Finally, caffeine use is greater in males than in females (APA, 1994).

Recently, gender has begun to receive research and clinical attention as a useful grouping variable because of increasing numbers of women presenting for alcohol and drug treatment over the last 20 years (Denier, Thevos, Latham, & Randall, 1991). Gender differences have important diagnostic and treatment implications. Legitimacy of research and treatment of substance abuse in women as a "special population" has been established (Lex, 1991).

Women have different onset and metabolic characteristics than men with respect to alcohol. DSM-IV reports the following characteristics for alcoholic females; they tend to start drinking heavily later in life; alcohol abuse or dependence may progress more rapidly; by middle age, females may have the same range of health and social problems; females tend to develop higher blood alcohol concentrations at a given dose of alcohol because of their lower percentage of body water, higher percentage of body fat, and slower metabolic rate; and females may be at greater risk than males for health-related consequences of heavy alcohol intake, such as liver damage (APA, 1994).

For drug use, women are at a higher risk for prescription abuse of drugs in the sedative, hypnotic, and anxiolytics classes (APA, 1994). Patterns of cocaine use and levels of impairment were found to be similar for men and women, with male cocaine users more likely to be polydrug abusers (APA, 1994; Denier et al., 1991). Female cocaine abusers were more likely to be diagnosed with concurrent psychiatric disorders and were more likely to report family histories of substance abuse than men (Denier et al., 1991). Women were more likely to begin, use, and maintain their use of crack cocaine in the context of more intimate opposite-sex relationships, while men were more likely to begin their use with male friends and associates and to maintain drug use with incomes from jobs and selling drugs (Henderson, Boyd, & Mieczkowski, 1994).

Women generally drink less and have lower levels of both drug and alcohol abuse and dependence (Closser & Blow, 1993; National Institute on Drug Abuse, 1991). Approximately 6% of the adult female population in the United States has serious problems with alcohol (Closser & Blow, 1993). Across age groups, educational levels, marital status, employment, religion, race, and ethnic status, differences in alcohol abuse/dependence vary (National Institute on Drug Abuse, 1991). However, among most cultural and ethnic minorities, more women than men abstain from alcohol use. One main exception to this is Native American women, who are reported to have 36 times more cirrhosis of the liver than white women (Closser & Blow, 1993). There also are significant gender differences in alcohol metabolism. Given the same volume alcohol consumed in men and women of the same body weight, women will have higher blood alcohol concentrations. These differences may be the main reason women are more susceptible to alcohol liver disease.

Closser and Blow (1993) also reported that women are more likely to report depressive symptoms and to drink in response to stress. It is well known that women receive depression diagnoses more frequently than men. Female alcoholics have substantially more psychopathology than male alcoholics. Generally, gender differences seen in treatment settings seem to be consistent with prevalence of disorders in the general population (Brady, Grice, Dustan, & Randall, 1993).

The clinician needs to be especially aware of the fetal effects of alcohol and abused drugs, and, indeed even prescribed medications. For example, benzodia-zapines may have teratogenic effects, and pregnant women should be advised of the possible effects of such drug use during pregnancy. Thus, the clinician work-ing in a substance abuse diagnostic or treatment program should be fully ap-prised of these effects of drugs and alcohol and be prepared to counsel or refer pregnant women for counseling as to these effects.

Racial-Ethnic Differences

According to DSM-IV, in the United States, whites and African Americans have nearly identical rates of alcohol abuse and dependence. Latino males reportedly have somewhat higher rates, although prevalence is lower among Latino females than among females from other ethnic groups. In a review of recent studies, however, whites were found to have higher rates of drug and alcohol use, abuse, and dependence than other racial and ethnic groups despite the perception that drug and alcohol abuse is a "minority problem" (Smith, 1993).

Cocaine use and disorders affect all race, socioeconomic, age, and gender groups in the United States. Cocaine use has shifted from more affluent individ-uals to include lower socioeconomic groups living in large metropolitan areas (APA, 1994). Since the 1920s in the United States, members of minority groups living in poverty have been overrepresented among persons with opiate depen-dence (APA, 1994). However, in the late 1800s and early 1900s, opiate depen-dence was seen more often among white middle-class individuals, suggesting that differences in use reflect the availability of opiate drugs and other social factors (APA, 1994).

It should be noted that basic subgroup or descriptive data are not sufficient and are not intended to identify underlying etiologic processes (Gfroer, 1993). Findings of race-associated differences in substance abuse research are often presented as if the person's race has intrinsic explanatory power (Lillie-Blanton, Anthony, & Schuster, 1993). In one study, race was no longer a significant pre-dictor of cocaine and other drug use when controls for socioeconomic and other variables were included in multiple logistic regression modeling (Flewelling, Rachal, & Marsden, 1992). Lillie-Blanton et al. (1993) offered strong evidence that race-specific explanations of crack cocaine use may, in fact, obscure the role that environmental and social characteristics play in the epidemiology of crack use. In their reanalysis of data from the 1988 National Household Survey of Drug Abuse, once respondents were grouped into neighborhood clusters, crack use did not differ significantly for African Americans or for Hispanic Americans as compared to white Americans. The authors called for future stud-ies of drug use prevalence that seek to include epidemiologic analyses of neigh-borhood-level social conditions. Ethnicity is a multidimensional concept. Using only one dimension, as in the case of many alcohol and drug use studies, is inadequate (Cheung, 1993). One of the major weaknesses of studies of race and substance use is the failure to recognize the presence of subcultural differences within an ethnic group (Cheung, 1993).

Iguchi and Stitzer (1991) found that race, gender, and number of opiate use episodes per week at treatment entry were significant predictors of clinical out-come as measured by urine toxicologies reflecting illicit opiate use. Although black males were found to have the greatest risk for illicit opiate use during treatment, all race and gender groups showed improvement in illicit opiate use during this brief treatment. When race, age, and gender were removed from their regression equation to derive predictors based on behavioral and environmental characteristics, number of opiate use episodes per week preceding treatment and the total number of drug-related stimulus cue exposures at baseline remained as significant, though less powerful, predictors of outcome.

CLINICAL MANAGEMENT

The Change Process

For clinicians treating drug dependence, it is important to understand that clients change their addictive behaviors for a variety of reasons and under numerous conditions. Outcomes of addictive behavior are variable and difficult to predict (Orford, 1986); positive changes occur without treatment (Saunders & Kershaw, 1979; Tuchfeld, 1981) and in a variety of treatment circumstances. In the alcoholism literature, for instance, favorable treatment outcomes have been reported with one-session "advice" giving (Edwards et al., 1977), self-help manuals (Heather, 1986), and traditional inpatient and outpatient therapy (Miller & Hester, 1986b). An influential psychological model developed to account for changes in addiction suggests six basic stages of the change process (see, e.g., Prochaska, DiClemente, & Norcross, 1992). These stages include: 1. *precontemplation,* the stage where the addict has no or limited awareness of a drug problem and has no intentions to change drug use; 2. *contemplative stage,* where the addict has awareness of a drug problem, is thinking about changing drug-related behavior, but has not generated sufficient commitment to take action; 3. *preparation,* characterized by the individual's intention to change drug use and perhaps initiate behavior change in a positive direction, but also higher inability to completely terminate the drug problem; 4. *action,* where the drug user takes overt action to resolve the drug problem, such as entry into treatment or a self-help group or various individual efforts to alter drug use; 5. *maintenance stage,* where the individual strives to prevent relapse to drug use and to strengthen adaptive behavioral changes that have been made in previous stages; and 6. *relapse,* where drug abuse is again initiated, and maintained.

The stage model of change has implications for substance abuse treatment. First, the clinician must have a basic understanding of the dynamics of each stage. A patient struggling with issues characterizing the contemplation stage (e.g., deciding whether the consequences of the addictive behavior are serious enough to change the behavior) requires different intervention strategies than a patient in the maintenance stage, when treatment generally focuses on ways to sustain progress and prevent relapse. A second implication of the stage theory is that therapeutic gains may be short-lived if extended follow-up is not provided for the patient. Challenges of the maintenance stage are significant, and positive long-term outcome depends on whether patients successfully adjust to life stressors without substance abuse. A final implication is that patients are responsible for changing their addictions. Therefore, patients should be active in making decisions about their treatment. Patients allowed this input are less likely to drop out of treatment and more likely to adhere to an established treatment plan (Parker, Winstead, & Willi, 1979; Parker, Winstead, Willi, & Fisher, 1979).

Motivation to Change

Changing addictive behavior requires a sustained high level of motivation. Where does this motivation originate, and how is it sustained? Miller (1985) operationally defined motivation for treatment as the probability of entering into, continuing in, and complying with treatment. He suggested that patient motivation primarily depends on characteristics of the patient-therapist relationship and the appropriateness of treatment alternatives offered.

In their recent edited book about preparing individuals to change addictive behavior, Miller and Rollnick (1991) suggested that certain characteristics of the patient-therapist interaction provide the basis for enhanced patient motivation for change. They have termed this style of interaction as motivational interviewing and have incorporated in this approach five basic principles to guide the therapist: 1. express sympathy, 2. enhance the patient's perceived discrepancy between the present state (e.g., current drug use) and the objective (e.g., abstinence from drug use), 3. avoid argumentation, 4. disarm resistance by encouraging the patient to evaluate new information and by suggesting new perspectives, and 5. support self-efficacy by supporting the patient's acceptance of personal responsibility for change and by providing information about a range of behavioral options.

Motivational interviewing and similar interventions intended to increase patients' motivation to change (Edwards et al., 1977; Kristenson, 1982) have been effective with problem drinkers. Miller and Rollnick's (1991) edited book broadened the application of this approach to other addictions and other health-related behaviors.

Treatment Modality Decisions

Treatment for substance abuse has been fairly standard and typically includes inpatient detoxification; individual or group therapy, or both; self-help groups; deterrent medications (e.g., disulfiram, methadone); and aftercare. Although this approach is the standard, Miller and Hester (1986a) suggested that it is, at best, modestly effective. Recent attention has been given to the idea that substance abusers could be more effectively treated if they were matched to the treatment modality most appropriate for their situation. While this "matching hypothesis" sounds reasonable and has existed in the literature for years (Ewing, 1977; Glaser & Skinner, 1981), it has had limited influence to date. This primarily is due to the fact that few studies have been done that establish the concept's validity and yield clear guidelines by which patients can be matched with treatment. In their review of the literature on matching problem drinkers with appropriate treatment, Miller and Hester (1986a) suggested that even though this literature is recent, progress is being made. For example, a prospective study of patient-treatment matching in a substance abuse population (McLellan, Woody, Luborsky, O'Brien, & Druley, 1983) found superior treatment outcome for matched versus mismatched patients.

While there are few substantial guidelines for matching patients to appropriate treatment, Miller (1989) suggested that therapists may assist clients through negotiation to self-match themselves into appropriate treatment. He provided tentative guidelines for this treatment negotiation process, which involves providing the patient with a "menu" of treatment alternatives along with information on probable outcomes of each choice. An informed, appropriate decision as to treatment is the intended outcome of this process.

Trend toward Outpatient Care

A clear trend in substance abuse treatment has been to reduce length of hospitalization, and in some cases omit it, in favor of outpatient treatment. There are obvious cost benefits to this approach, as well as evidence to suggest that outpatient treatment is as beneficial, and in some cases more beneficial, than inpatient care (Miller & Hester, 1986b). There are patients who, by the nature of their problems, require hospitalization (e.g., patients showing medical or psychiatric complications, concurrent dependencies, severe psychosocial impairment, or inability to discontinue drug use). However, long-term hospitalization is often used when less expensive, more appropriate alternatives would suffice. Various studies have suggested that brief hospitalization followed by outpatient aftercare can be equally or more effective than longer hospitalization (Page & Schaub, 1979; Pittman & Tate, 1979; Walker, Donovan, Kivlahan, & O'Leary, 1983). Some investigators have suggested that inpatient or residential treatment should be regarded as an "orientation program" (Page & Schaub, 1979) or "launching platform" (Zweben, 1986) for recovery, not the stage of treatment where major changes will occur. The reader is referred to a recent publication from the Institute of Medicine (1990) for a more extensive discussion of treatment settings and intensities.

Relapse and Aftercare

Relapse to substance use is the most frequent outcome of treatment. Hunt, Barnett, and Branch (1971) found relapse rates to be between 70%–80% at 12 months posttreatment for heroin addicts, smokers, and alcoholics. The relapse phenomenon in addictions has received much attention in the literature, particularly by Marlatt and his colleagues (Marlatt & Gordon, 1980, 1985), resulting in a well-researched relapse prevention model. A discussion of their model is beyond the scope of this chapter. However, their work has a clear implication for clinical decision making. Aftercare is an essential component of the treatment armamentarium to prevent relapse to drug use. The term "aftercare" is used to describe interventions with various intensity, scope, and length. It can be viewed as an appropriate extension of any form of primary care preceding it with a specific intention to maintain earlier treatment gains (Harmon, Lantinga, & Costello, 1982). Aftercare options for substance abusers include outpatient treatment, methadone maintenance, therapeutic communities, and halfway houses. For a complete discussion of aftercare with substance abusers, see Stainback and Walker (1990). Ito and Donovan (1986) emphasized the importance of aftercare in alcoholism treatment because they found aftercare attendance improves treatment outcome, independent from intake prognostic indicators. Aftercare is a treatment component that can be included to increase the probability of favorable long-term outcome.

SUMMARY

This chapter has examined drug abuse and dependence in contemporary society, including its epidemiology, especially roots of drug abuse in adolescent use, and theoretical concepts of etiology, and practical aspects of etiology including familial and genetic considerations and gender and racial-ethnic issues. DSM-IV diagnostic criteria are reviewed in the historical context of the evolution of classification schemes. DSM-IV criteria are reviewed in detail, as are important issues for differential diagnosis. Typical clinical pictures for various types of substance use disorders include opiates, barbiturates/hypnotic sedatives, concurrent dependence, psychostimulants/cocaine, hallucinogens, cannabinols, anabolic steroids, dual diagnosis, and inhalants. Included are some implications for assessment and diagnosis. Assessment principles and a general strategy are recommended for adaptation to specific sites with unique goals for assessment. Included is a review of various useful assessment modalities including observation, clinical and serial interviews, and psychological and biological procedures. Assessment of related disorders and dysfunctions are reviewed and put in the context of implications for treatment. Finally, a brief review of clinical management includes discussion of recent developments in the trend toward outpatient care, importance of aftercare, and findings from research on the change process and techniques for building motivation for treatment.

REFERENCES

Abraham, H. D., & Aldridge, A. M. (1993). Adverse consequences of lysergic acid diethylamide. *Addiction, 88*(10), 1327–1334.

Allgulander, C., Borg, S., & Vikander, B. (1984). A 4–6 year follow-up of 50 patients with primary dependence on sedative and hypnotic drugs. *American Journal of Psychiatry, 141*(12), 1580–1582.

Allgulander, C., Ljungberg, L., & Fisher, L. D. (1987). Long-term prognosis in addiction on sedative hypnotic drugs analyzed with the Cox regression model. *Acta Psychiatrica Scandanavica, 75,* 521–531.

American College of Sports Medicine. (1984). The use of anabolic-androgenic steroids in sports. *Sports Medicine Bulletin, 19,* 13–18.

American Psychiatric Association. (1968). *Diagnostic and statistical manual of mental disorders* (2nd ed.). Washington, DC: Author.

American Psychiatric Association. (1980). *Diagnostic and statistical manual of mental disorders* (3rd ed.). Washington, DC: Author.

American Psychiatric Association. (1987). *Diagnostic and statistical manual of mental disorders* (3rd ed., rev. ed.). Washington, DC: Author.

American Psychiatric Association. (1994). *Diagnostic and statistical manual of mental disorders* (4th ed.). Washington, DC: Author.

Amsel, Z., Mendell, W., Matthias, L., Mason, C., & Hocherman, I. (1976). Reliability and validity of self-reported illegal activities and drug use collected from narcotic addicts. *International Journal of the Addictions, 11,* 325–336.

Andrews, H. L. (1943). Changes in the electroencephalogram during a cycle of morphine addiction. *Psychosomatic Medicine, 5,* 143–146.

Anglin, M. D., Almog, I. J., Fisher, D. G., & Peters, K. R. (1989). Alcohol use by heroin addicts: Evidence for an inverse relationship. A study of methadone maintenance and drug-free treatment samples. *American Journal of Drug and Alcohol Abuse, 15*(2), 191–207.

Babor, T. F., Meyer, R. E., & Mirin, S. M. (1976). Behavioral and social effects of heroin self-administration and withdrawal. *Archives of General Psychiatry, 33,* 363–367.

Bale, R. N., Von Stone, W. W., Engelsing, T. M. J., Zacrone, V. P., Jr., & Kuldan, J. M. (1981). The validity of self-reported heroin use. *International Journal of the Addictions, 16,* 1307–1398.

Bates, C. K. (1988). Medical risks of cocaine use. *Western Journal of Medicine, 148,* 440–444.

Bejerot, N. (1970). *Addiction and society.* Springfield, IL: Thomas.

Benson, G., & Holmberg, M. B. (1984). Drug-related criminality among young people. *Acta Psychiatrica Scandinavica, 70,* 487–502.

Bergman, H., Borg, S., & Holm, L. (1980). Neuropsychological impairment and exclusive abuse of sedatives or hypnotics. *American Journal of Psychiatry, 137*(2), 215–217.

Blanchard, E. B., Libet, J. M., & Young, L. D. (1973). Apnic aversion and covert sensitization in the treatment of hydrocarbon inhalation addiction: A case study. *Journal of Behavior Therapy and Experimental Psychiatry, 4,* 383–387.

Blanck, R. R., Ream, N. W., DeLeese, J. S. (1984). Infectious complications of illicit drug use. *International Journal of the Addiction, 19,* 221–232.

Block, R. I., & Ghoneim, M. M. (1993). Effects of chronic marijuana use on human cognition. *Psychopharmacology, 110,* 219–228.

Blum, R., & Richards, L. (1979). Youthful drug use. In R. Dupont, A. Goldstein, J. O'Donnel, & B. Brown (Eds.), *Handbook on drug abuse.* Rockville, MD: National Institute on Drug Abuse.

Bonito, A. J., Nurco, D. N., & Schaffer, J. W. (1976). The veridicality of addicts' self-reports in social research. *International Journal of the Addictions, 11,* 719–724.

Bozarth, M. A., & Wise, R. A. (1985). Toxicity associated with long-term intravenous heroin and cocaine self-administration in the rat. *Journal of the American Medical Association, 254,* 81–83.

Brady, K. T., Grice, D. E., Dustan, L., & Randall, C. (1993). Gender differences in substance use disorders. *American Journal of Psychiatry, 150,* 1707–1711.

Brecher, E. M. (1972). *Licit and illicit drugs.* Boston: Little, Brown.

Brower, K. J. (1993). Anabolic steroids: Potential for physical and psychological dependence. In C. E. Yesalis (Ed.), *Anabolic steroids in sport and exercise.* Champaign, IL: Human Kinetics.

Brower, K. J., Blow, F. C., Beresford, I. P., & Fuelling, C. (1989). Anabolic-androgenic steroid dependence. *Journal of Clinical Psychiatry, 50,* 31–33.

Brower, K. J., Blow, F. C., Young, J. P., & Hill, E. M. (1991). Symptoms and correlates of anabolic-androgenic steroid dependence. *British Journal of Addiction, 86*(6), 759–768.

Brown, J., Kranzler, H. R., & Del Boca, F. K. (1992). Self-reports by alcohol and drug abuse inpatients: factors affecting reliability and validity. *British Journal of Addictions, 87,* 1013–1024.

Brown, T. T. (1961). *The enigma of drug addiction.* Springfield, IL: Thomas.

Bry, B. H. (1983) Predicting drug abuse: Review and reformulation. *International Journal of the Addictions, 18*(2), 223–233.

Buckley, W. E., Yeslis, C. E., & Bennell, D. L. (1993). A study of anabolic steroid use at the secondary school level. Recommendations for prevention. In C. E. Yesalis (Ed.), *Anabolic steroids in sport and exercise* (pp. 71–86). Champaign, IL: Human Kinetics.

Cancrini, L., Cingolani, S., Compagnoni, F., Constantini, D., & Mazzoni, S. (1988). Juvenile drug addiction: A typology of heroin addicts and their families. *Family Process, 27*(3), 261–271.

Carroll, K. M. Rounsaville, B. J., Nich, C., Gordon, L. T., Wirtz, P. W., & Gawin, F. (1994). One-year follow-up of psychotherapy and pharmacotherapy for cocaine dependence: Delayed emergence of psychotherapy effects. *Archives of General Psychiatry, 51,* 989–997.

Chalmers E. M. (1991). Volatile substance abuse. *Medical Journal of Australia, 154,* 269–274.

Chen, K, & Kandel, D. B. (1995). The natural history of drug use from adolescence to the mid-thirties in a general population sample. *American Journal of Public Health, 85,* 41–47.

Cheung, Y. W. (1993). Approaches to ethnicity: Clearing roadblocks in the study of ethnicity and substance use. *International Journal of the Addictions, 28,* 1209–1226.

Closser, M. H., & Blow, F. C. (1993). Special populations: Women, ethnic minorities, and the elderly. *Psychiatric Clinics of North America, 16,* 199–209.

Cone, E. J., Menchen, S. L., Paul, D. B., Mell, L. D., & Mitchell, J. (1989). Validity testing of commercial urine cocaine metabolite assays: I. Assay detection times, individual excretion patterns, and kinetics after cocaine administration to humans. *Journal of Forensic Sciences, 34,* 15–31.

Cone, E. J., & Mitchell, J. (1989). Validity testing of commercial urine cocaine metabolite assays: II. Sensitivity, specificity, accuracy, and confirmation by gas chromatography/mass spectrometry. *Journal of Forensic Sciences, 34,* 32–45.

Cottrol C., & Frances, R. (1993). Substance abuse, comorbid psychiatric disorder, and repeated traumatic injuries. *Hospital and Community Psychiatry, 44,* 715–716.

Cox, T. J., & Longwell, B. (1974). Reliability of interview data concerning current heroin use from heroin addicts on methadone. *International Journal of the Addictions, 9,* 161–165.

Crabbe, J. C., & Belknap, J. K. (1992). Genetic approaches to drug dependence. *Trends in Pharmacological Sciences, 13,* 212–219.

Cushman, P. (1987). Alcohol and opioids: possible interactions of clinical importance. *Advances in Alcohol and Substance Abuse, 6*(3), 33–46.

D'Aquila, R. T., & Williams, A. B. (1987). Epidemic human immunodeficiency virus (HIV) infection among intravenous drug users (IVDU). *Yale Journal of Biology and Medicine, 60,* 545–567.

Denier, C. A, Thevos, A. K., Latham, P. K., & Randall, C. L. (1991). Psychosocial and psychopathology differences in hospitalized male and female cocaine abusers: A retrospective chart review. *Addictive Behaviors, 16,* 489–496.

Dinwiddie, S. H. (1994). Abuse of inhalants: A review. *Addiction, 89,* 925–939.

Donahoe, T., & Johnson, N. (1986). *Foul play: Drug abuse in sports.* New York: Blackwell.

Dunlap, E., & Johnson, B. D. (1992). The setting for the crack era: Macro forces, micro consequences (1960–1992), *Journal of Psychoactive Drugs, 24*(4), 307–321.

Edwards, G., Orford, J., Egert, S., Guthrie, S., Hawker, A., Hensman, C., Mitcheson, M.,

Oppenheimer, E., & Taylor, C. (1977). Alcoholism: A controlled trial of "treatment" and "advice." *Journal of Studies on Alcohol, 38,* 1004–1031.

Eisenman, A. J., Sloan, J. W., Martin, W. R., Jasinski, D. R., & Brooks, J. W. (1969). Catecholamine and 17-hydroxy-corticosteroid excretion during a cycle of morphine dependence in man. *Journal of Psychiatric Research, 7,* 19–28.

Elkin, T. E., Williams, J. G., Barlow, P. H. & Stewart, W. R. (1974). *Measurement and modification of intravenous drug abuse. A preliminary study using succinyl choline.* Unpublished manuscript, University of Mississippi Medical School.

Ewing, J. (1977). Matching therapy and patients: The cafeteria plan. *British Journal of Addiction, 72,* 13–18.

Falck, R., Siegal, H. A., Forney, M. A., Wang, J., & Carlson, R. G. (1992). The validity of injection drug users self-reported use of opiates and cocaine. *Journal of Drug Issues, 22*(4), 823–832.

Ferraro, D. P., & Grishma, M. G. (1972). Tolerance to the behavioral effects of marijuana in chimpanzees. *Physiology and Behavior, 9,* 49–54.

Firooznia, H., Golimbu, C., Rafii, M., & Lichtman, E. A. (1983). Radiology of musculo-skeletal complications of drug addiction. *Seminars in Roetgenology, 18,* 198–206.

Flewelling, R. L., Rachal, J. V., & Marsden, M. E. (1992). *Socioeconomic and demographic correlates of drug and alcohol use: Findings from the 1988 and 1990 National Household Surveys on drug abuse* (DHHS Publication No. ADM 92-1889). Washington, DC: Division of Epidemiology and Prevention Research, National Institute on Drug Abuse.

Fuller, J. R., & LaFountain, M. J. (1987). Performance-enhancing drugs in sport: A different form of drug abuse. *Adolescence, 22,* 969–976.

Fysh, R. R., Oon, M. C., Robinson, K. N., Smith, R. N., White, P. C., & Whitehouse, M. J., (1985). A fatal poisoning with LSD. *Forensic Science International, 28*(2), 109–113.

Gfroerer, J. (1993). Race and crack cocaine. *Journal of the American Medical Association, 270,* 45–46.

Gillis, J. S., Tareen, I. A. K., Chaudhry, H. R., & Haider, S. (1994) Risk factors for drug misuse in Pakistan. *International Journal of the Addictions, 29*(2), 215–223.

Glaser, F. B., & Skinner, H. A. (1981). Matching in the real world: A practical approach. In E. Gottheil, A. McLellan, & K. Druley (Eds.). *Matching patient needs and treatment methods in alcoholism and drug abuse* (pp. 295–324). Springfield, IL: Thomas.

Glassroth, J., Adams, G. D., & Schnoll, S. (1987). The impact of substance abuse on the respiratory system. *Chest, 91,* 596–602.

Gold, M. S. (1989). *Marijuana.* New York: Plenum.

Griffin, M. L., Weiss, R. D., Mirin, S. M., Wilson, H., & Bouchard-Voelk, B. (1987). The use of the Diagnostic Interview Schedule in drug-dependent patient. *American Journal of Drug and Alcohol Abuse, 6*(2), 97–106.

Haastrup, S., & Jepsen, P. W. (1988). Eleven-year follow-up of 300 young opioid addicts. *Acta Psychiatrica Scandanavica, 77,* 22–26.

Haertzen, C. A., & Hooks, N. T. (1969). Changes in personality and subjective experience associated with the administration and withdrawal of opiates. *Journal of Nervous and Mental Disease, 148,* 606–614.

Hammersley, R., & Morrison, V. (1987). Effects of polydrug use on the criminal activities of heroin-users. *British Journal of Addiction, 82,* 899–906.

Hanbury, R., Sturiano, V., Cohen, M., Stimmel, B., & Aquillaume, C. (1986). Cocaine use in persons on methadone maintenance. *Advances in Alcohol and Substance Abuse 6*(2), 97–106.

Handelsman, L., Cochrane, K. J., Aronson, M. J., Ness, R., Rubenstein, K. J., & Kanof, P. D. (1987). Two new rating scales for opiate withdrawal. *American Journal of Drug and Alcohol Abuse, 13*(3), 293–308.

Harmon, S. K., Lantinga, L. J., & Costello, R. M. (1982). Aftercare in chemical dependence treatment. *Bulletin of the Society of Psychologists in Substance Abuse, 1,* 107–109.

Haupt, H. A., & Rovere, G. (1984). Anabolic steroids: A review of the literature. *American Journal of Sports Medicine, 12,* 469–483.

Heather, N. (1986). Change without therapists: The use of self-help manuals by problem drinkers. In W. Miller & N. Heather (Eds.), *Treating addictive behaviors: Processes of change* (pp. 331–359). New York: Plenum.

Helzer, J. E., Clayton, P. J., Pambakian, R., & Woodruff, R. A. (1978). Concurrent diagnostic validity of a structured psychiatric interview. *Archives of General Psychiatry, 35,* 849–853.

Henderson, D. J., Boyd, C., & Mieczkowski, T. (1994). Gender, relationships, and crack cocaine: A content analysis. *Research in Nursing and Health, 17,* 265–272.

Hernandez, J. T. (1992). Substance abuse among sexually abused adolescents and their families. *Journal of Adolescent Health, 13,* 658–662.

Hesselbrock, V., Stabenau, J., Hesselbrock, M., & Mirkin, M. (1982). A comparison of two interview schedules. *Archives of General Psychiatry, 39,* 674–677.

Hochman, J. S., & Brill, N. D. (1973). Chronic marijuana use and psychosocial adaptation. *American Journal of Psychiatry, 130,* 132.

Hollister, L. E. (1971, May). *Human pharmacology of marijuana (cannabis).* Paper presented at the American Federation for Clinical Research Symposium on Drug Abuse, Atlantic City, NJ.

Hollister, L. E. (1988). Cannabis-1988. *Acta Psychiatrica Scandinavica, 78,* 108–118.

Holmberg, M. B. (1985). Longitudinal studies of drug abuse in a fifteen-year-old population: I. Chronic drug abusers. *Acta Psychiatrica Scandinavica, 71,* 201–203.

Horn, J. L., Wanberg, K. W., & Foster, F. M. (1983). *The Alcohol Use Inventory.* Baltimore: Psych Systems.

Hudziak, J. E., Helzer, J. E., Wetzel, M. W., Kessel, K. B., McGee, B., Janca, A., & Przybeck, T. (1993). The use of the DSM-III-R Checklist for Initial Diagnostic Assessments. *Comprehensive Psychiatry, 34,* 375–383.

Hunt, C. A., & Jones, R. T. (1980). Tolerance and disposition of tetrahydrocannabinol in man. *Journal of Pharmacology and Experimental Therapeutics, 215*(1), 35–44.

Hunt, D., Spunt, B., Lipton, D., Goldsmith, D., & Strug, D. (1986). The costly bonus: Cocaine related crime among methadone treatment clients. *Advances in Alcohol and Substance Abuse, 6*(2), 107–122.

Hunt, W. A., Barnett, W., & Branch, L. G. (1971). Relapse rates in addiction programs. *Journal of Clinical Psychology, 27,* 455–456.

Iguchi, M. Y., & Stitzer, M. L. (1991) Predictors of opiate drug abuse during a 90-day methadone detoxification. *American Journal of Drug and Alcohol Abuse, 17*(3), 279–294.

Institute of Medicine. (1990). *Broadening the base of treatment for alcohol problems.* Washington, DC: National Academy Press.

Ito, J. R., & Donovan, D. M. (1986). Aftercare in alcoholism treatment: A review. In W. R. Miller & N. Heather (Eds.), *Treating addictive behaviors: Processes of change* (pp. 435–456). New York: Plenum.

Jaffe, R. B. (1983). Cardiac and vascular involvement in drug abuse. *Seminars in Roentgenology, 18,* 207–212.

Johnston, L. D., Bachman, J. G., & O'Malley, P. M. (1982). *Student drug use in America 1971–1981* (DHHS Publication No. ADM 82-1221). Washington, D.C.: U.S. Government Printing Office.

Kales, A., & Kales, J. D. (1974). Sleep disorders: Recent findings in the diagnosis and treatment of disturbed sleep. *New England Journal of Medicine, 290,* 487–499.

Kandel, D. B. (1984). Marijuana users in young adulthood. *Archives of General Psychiatry, 41,* 200–209.

Kandel, D. B. (1991). The social demography of drug use. *Millbank Quarterly, 69*(3), 366–414.

Kandel, D. B., Davies, M., Karus, D., & Yamaguchi, K. (1986). The consequences in young adulthood of adolescent drug involvement. *Archives of General Psychiatry, 43,* 746–754.

Kandel, D. B., & Logan, J. A. (1984). Patterns of drug use from adolescence to young adulthood: Periods of risk for initiation, continued use, and discontinuation. *American Journal of Public Health, 74,* 660–666.

Kandel, D., & Yamaguchi, K. (1993). From beer to crack: developmental patterns of drug involvement. *American Journal of Public Health, 83*(6), 851–855.

Kashkin, K. B., & Kleber, H. D. (1989). Hooked on hormones? An anabolic steroid addiction hypothesis. *Journal of American Medical Association, 262*(22), 3166–3170.

Kay, A., Eisenstein, R. B., & Jasinski, D. R. (1969). Morphine effects on human REM state, waking state, and NREM sleep. *Psychopharmacologia, 14,* 404.

Khalsa, H. K., & Anglin, M. D. (1990, June). *Pretreatment natural history of cocaine abuse.* Paper presented at the annual meeting of the College for Problems of Drug Dependence, Palm Beach, FL.

Khantzian, E. J. (1985). The self-medication hypothesis of addictive disorders: Focus on heroin and cocaine dependence. *American Journal of Psychiatry, 142,* 1259–1264.

Kissner, D. G., Lawrence, W. D., Selis, J. E., & Flint, A. (1987). Crack lung: Pulmonary disease caused by cocaine abuse. *American Review of Respiratory Disease, 136,* 1250–1252.

Kochakian, C. D. (1993). Anabolic-androgenic steroids: A historical perspective and definition. In C. E. Yesalis (Ed.), *Anabolic steroids in sport and exercise* (pp. 71–86). Champaign, IL: Human Kinetics.

Kolb, L. C. (1973). *Modern clinical psychiatry* (8th ed.). Philadelphia: Saunders.

Koob, G. F., & Bloom, F. E. (1988, November 4). Cellular and molecular mechanisms of drug dependence. *Science, 242*(4879), 715–723.

Kosten, T. R., & Rounsaville, B. J. (1986). Psychopathology in opioid addicts. *Psychiatric Clinics of North America, 9,* 515–532.

Kosten, T. R., Rounsaville, B. J., Babor, T. F., Spitzer, R. L., & Williams, J. B. (1987). Substance-use disorders in DSM-III-R: Evidence for the dependence syndrome across different psychoactive substances. *British Journal of Psychiatry, 151,* 834–843.

Kosten, T. R., Rounsaville, B. J., & Kleber, H. D. (1986). Antecedents and consequences of cocaine abuse among opioid addicts: A 2.5 year follow-up. *Journal of Nervous and Mental Disease, 176*(3), 176–181.

Kosten, T. R., Rounsaville, B. J., & Kleber, H. D. (1987). A 25-year follow-up of cocaine use among treated opioid addicts: Have our treatments helped? *Archives of General Psychiatry, 44*(3), 201–204.

Kozel, N. J., & Adams, E. H. (1986). Epidemiology of drug abuse: An overview. *Science, 234,* 970–974.

Kranzler, H. R., & Liebowitz, N. R. (1988). Anxiety and depression in substance abuse: Clinical implications. *Medical Clinics of North America, 72,* 867–885.

Kristenson, H. (1982). *Studies on alcohol-related disabilities in a medical intervention programme in middle aged males* (2nd ed.). Malmo, Sweden: University of Lund.

Lader, M. (1983). Dependence on benzodiazepines. *Journal of Clinical Psychiatry, 44,* 121–127.

Leeds, N. E., Malhotra, V., & Zimmerman, R. D. (1983). The radiology of drug addiction affecting the brain. *Seminars in Roentgenology, 18,* 227–233.

Lehrer, M., & Gold, M. S. (1986). Laboratory diagnosis of cocaine: Intoxication and withdrawal. *Advances in Alcohol and Substance Abuse, 6,* 123–141.

Lettieri, D. J. (1985). Drug abuse: A review of explanations and models of explanation. *Advances in Alcohol and Substance Abuse, 43*(3-4), 9–40.

Lex, B. W. (1991). Some gender differences in alcohol and polysubstance users. *Health Psychology, 10,* 121–132.

Lillie-Blanton, M., Anthony, J. C., & Schuster, C. R. (1993). Probing the meaning of racial/ethnic group comparisons in crack cocaine smoking. *Journal of the American Medical Association, 269,* 993–997.

Lindenberg, C. S., Gendrop, S. C., & Reiskin, H. K. (1993). Empirical evidence for the social stress model of substance abuse. *Research in Nursing and Health, 16,* 351–362.

Lowenstein, D. H., Massa, S. M., Rowbotham, M. C., Collins, S. D., McKinney, H. E., & Simon, R. P. (1987). Acute neurologic and psychiatric complications associated with cocaine abuse. *American Journal of Medicine, 83,* 841–846.

MacAndrew, C. (1965). The differentiation of male alcoholic outpatients from nonalcoholic psychiatric patients by means of the MMPI. *Quarterly Journal of Studies on Alcohol, 26,* 238–246.

Maddux, J. F., Desmond, D. P., & Costello, R. (1987). Depression in opioid users varies with substance use status. *American Journal of Drug and Alcohol Abuse, 13,* 275–385.

Marlatt, G. A., & Gordon, J. R. (1980). Determinants of relapse: Implications for the maintenance of behavioral change. In P. Davidson & S. Davidson (Eds.), *Behavioral medicine: Changing health lifestyles* (pp. 410–452). New York: Brunzner/Mazel.

Marlatt, G. A., & Gordon, J. R. (Eds.). (1985). *Relapse prevention: Maintenance strategies in the treatment of addictive behaviors.* New York: Guilford.

Matarazzo, J. D. (1983). The reliability of psychiatric and psychological diagnosis. *Clinical Psychology Review, 3,* 103–145.

Maugh, T. H. (1974). Marijuana (II): Does it damage the brain? *Science, 185,* 775–776.

Maurer, D. W., & Vogel, V. H. (1973). *Narcotics and narcotic addiction* (4th ed.). Springfield, IL.: Thomas.

Maycutt, M. O. (1985). Health consequences of acute and chronic marijuana use. *Progress in Neuro-psychopharmocolocy and Biological Psychiatry, 9,* 209–238.

McKinnon, G. L., & Parker, W. A. (1982). Benzodiazepine withdrawal syndrome: A literature review and evaluation. *American Journal of Drug and Alcohol Abuse, 9*(1), 19–33.

McLellan, A. T., Luborsky, L., Cacciola, J., Griffith, J., Evans, F., Barr, H. L., & O'Brien, C. P. (1985). New data from the Addiction Severity Index: Reliability and validity in three centers. *Journal of Nervous and Mental Disease, 173*(7), 412–423.

McLellan, A. T., Luborsky, L., O'Brien, C. P., & Woody, G. E. (1980). An improved diagnostic instrument for substance abuse patients: The Addiction Severity Index. *Journal of Nervous and Mental Disease, 168,* 26–33.

McLellan, A. T., Woody, G. E., Luborsky, L., O'Brien, C. P., & Druley, K. A. (1983) Increased effectiveness of substance abuse treatment: A prospective study of patient-treatment "matching." *Journal of Nervous and Mental Disease, 171,* 597–605.

McNagny, S. E., & Parker, R. M. (1992). High prevalence of recent cocaine use and the unreliability of patient self-report in an inner-city walk-in clinic. *Journal of the American Medical Association, 267,* 1106–1108.

McNamee, H. B., Mirin, S. M., Kuhnle, J. C., & Meyer, R. E. (1976). Affective changes in chronic opiate users. *British Journal of Addiction, 71,* 275–280.

McWilliams, S. A., & Tuttle, R. J. (1973). Long-term psychological effects of LSD. *Psychological Bulletin, 79,* 341–351.

Mendhiratta, S., Varma, V. K., Dang, R., Malholtra, A. K., Das, K., & Nehra, R. (1988). Cannabis and cognitive functions: A reevaluation study. *British Journal of Addiction, 83,* 749–753.

Meyer, J. M., & Neale, M. C. (1992). The relationship between age at first drug use and teenage drug use liability. *Behavior Genetics, 22*(2), 197–213.

Mieczkowski, T., Barzelay, D., Gropper, B., & Wish, E. (1991). Concordance of three measures of cocaine use in an arrestee population: Hair, urine, and self-report. *Journal of Psychoactive Drugs, 23,* 241–249.

Milby, J. B. (1981a). *Addictive behavior and its treatment.* New York: Springer.

Milby, J. B. (1981b, August). *The status of theories of addiction.* Paper presented at the annual meeting of the American Psychological Association, Los Angeles, CA.

Milby, J. B. (1989). Methadone maintenance to abstinence: How many make it? *Journal of Nervous and Mental Disease, 176*(7), 409–422.

Milby. J. B., & Schumacher, J. E. (1994). Drug abuse. In M. Hersen & S. M. Turner (Eds.), *Diagnostic interviewing* (2nd ed., pp. 189–210). New York: Plenum.

Milby, J. B., Sims, M. K., Khuder, S., Schumacher, J. E., Huggins, N., McLellan, A. T., Woody, G., & Haas, N. (1996). Psychiatric comorbidity: Prevalence in methadone maintenance treatment. *American Journal of Drug and Alcohol Abuse, 22*(1), 95–107.

Milby, J., & Stainback, R. (1991). Psychoactive substance use disorder (drugs). In M. Hersen & S. M. Turner (Eds), *Adult psychopathology and diagnosis* (2nd ed., pp. 110–148). New York: Wiley.

Miller, W. R. (1985). Motivation for treatment: A review with special emphasis on alcoholism. *Psychological Bulletin, 98,* 84–107.

Miller, W. R. (1989). Matching individuals with interventions. In R. K. Hester & W. R. Miller (Eds.), *Handbook of alcoholism treatment approaches: Effective alternatives* (pp. 261–271). Elmsford, NY: Pergamon.

Miller, W. R., & Heather, N. (Eds.). (1986). *Treating addictive behaviors: Processes of change.* New York: Plenum.

Miller, W. R., & Hester, R. K. (1986a). The effectiveness of alcoholism treatment: What research reveals. In W. Miller & N. Heather (Eds.), *Treating addictive behaviors: Processes of change* (pp. 121–174). New York: Plenum.

Miller, W. R., & Hester, R. K. (1986b). Inpatient alcoholism treatment: Who benefits? *American Psychologist, 41,* 794–805.

Miller, W. R., & Rollnick, S. (1991). *Motivational interviewing.* New York: Guilford.

Millman, R. B. (1978). Drug and alcohol abuse. In B. J. Wolman, J. Egan, & A. O. Ross (Eds.), *Handbook of treatment of mental disorders in childhood and adolescence.* Englewood Cliffs, NJ: Prentice-Hall.

Mintz, J., Christoph, P., O'Brien, C. P. & Snedeker, M. (1980). The impact of the interview method on reported symptoms of narcotic addicts. *International Journal of the Addictions, 15,* 597–604.

Mirin, S. M. (1977). Drug abuse. In E. L. Bassuk & S. C. Schoonover (Eds.), *The practitioners' guide to psycho-active drugs.* New York: Plenum.

Mirin, S. M., Meyer, R. E., & McNamee, B. (1976). Psychopathology and mood during heroin use: Acute versus chronic effects. *Archives of General Psychiatry, 33,* 1503–80.

Mirin, S. M., & Weiss, R. D. Affective illness in substance abusers. *Psychiatric Clinics of North America, 9,* 503–514 (1986).

Morin, C. M., & Kwentus, J. A. (1988). Behavioral and pharmacological treatments for insomnia. *Annals of Behavioral Medicine, 10*(3), 91–100.

Murray, D. M. & Perry, C. L. (1985). The prevention of adolescent drug abuse: Implications of etiological, developmental, behavioral, and environmental models. In C. L. Jones & R. J. Battjes (Eds.), *Etiology of drug abuse: Implications for treatment* (DHHS Publication No. ADM 85-1335) Washington, DC: U.S. Government Printing Office.

National Institute on Drug Abuse. (1991). *National survey on drug abuse: Population estimates 1990* (DGGS Publication No. ADM 91-1732).

Nowlan, R., & Cohen, S. (1977). Tolerance to marijuana: heart rate and subjective "high." *Clinical Pharmacology and Therapeutics, 22*(5), 550–556.

O'Brien, C. P., Testa, T., & O'Brien, T. J. (1977). Conditioned narcotic withdrawal in humans. *Science, 195,* 1000–1002.

O'Donnell, J. A. (1964). A follow-up of narcotice addicts: Mortality, relapse, and abstinence. *American Journal of Orthopsychiatry, 34,* 948–954.

O'Farrell, T. J. (1994). Substance abuse disorders. In V. B. Van Hasselt & M. Hersen (Eds.), *Advanced abnormal psychology* (pp. 335–358). New York: Plenum.

O'Malley, P. M., Johnston, L. D., & Bachman, J. G. (1995). Adolescent substance use: Epidemiology and implication for public policy. *Substance Abuse, 42*(2), 241–260.

Orford, J. (1986). Critical conditions for change in addictive behaviors. In W. Miller & N. Heather (Eds.), *Treating addictive behaviors: Processes of change* (pp. 91–108). New York: Plenum.

Page, R. D., & Schaub, L. H. (1979). Efficacy of a three- versus a five-week alcohol treatment program. *International Journal of the Addictions, 14,* 697–714.

Parker, M. W., Winstead, D. K., & Willi, F. J. (1979). Patient autonomy in alcohol treatment: I. Literature review. *International Journal of the Addictions, 14,* 1015–1022.

Parker, M. W., Winstead, D. K., Willi, F. J., & Fisher, P. (1979). Patient autonomy in alcohol treatment: II. Program evaluation. *International Journal of the Addictions, 14,* 1177–1184.

Pickens, R. W., Svikis, D. S., McGue, M., Lyken, D. T., & Clayton, P. J. (1991). Heterogeneity in the inheritance of alcoholism: A study of male and female twins. *Archives of General Psychiatry, 48,* 19–28.

Pittman, D. J., & Tate, R. L. (1979). A comparison of two treatment programs for alcoholics. *Quarterly Journal of Studies on Alcohol, 30,* 888–899.

Pomerleau, O. F. (1995). Individual differences in sensitivity to nicotine: Implications for genetic research on nicotine dependence. *Behavior Genetics, 25*(2), 161–177.

Pope, H. G., & Katz, D. L. (1988). Affective and psychotic symptoms associated with anabolic steroid use. *American Journal of Psychiatry, 145,* 487–490.

Pope, H. G., & Katz, D. L. (1994). Psychiatric and medical effects on anabolic-adrogenic steroid use. *Archives of General Psychiatry, 51,* 375–382.

Prochaska, J. O., DiClementi, C. C., & Norcross, J. C. (1992). In search of how people change: Applications to addictive behavior. *American Psychologist, 47,* 1102–1114.

Robins, L. N., & Murphy, G. I. (1967). Drug use in normal populations of young Negro men. *American Journal of Public Health, 57,* 1580–1596.

Robins L. N., & Regier, D. A. (Eds.). (1991). *Psychiatric disorders in American: The epidemiologic catchment area study.* New York: Free Press.

Ross, H. E., Glaser, F. B., & Germanson, T. (1988). The prevalence of psychiatric disorders in patients with alcohol and other drug problems. *Archives of General Psychiatry, 45,* 1023–1031.

Rounsaville, B. J., Kosten, T. R., & Kleber, H. D. (1987). The antecedents and benefits of achieving abstinence in opioid addicts: A 2.5-year follow-up study. *American Journal of Drug and Alcohol Abuse, 13*(3), 213–229.

Rounsaville, B. J., Weissman, M. M., Crits-Christoph, K., Wilber, C., & Kleber, H. (1982). Diagnosis and symptoms of depression in opiate addicts. *Archives of General Psychiatry, 39,* 151–156.

Rounsaville, B. J., Weissman, M. M., Kleber, H., & Wilber, C. (1982). Heterogeneity of psychiatric diagnosis in treated opiate addicts. *Archives of General Psychiatry, 39,* 161–166.

Salzman, G. A., Khan, F., & Emory, C. (1987). Pneumomediastinum after cigarette smoking. *Southern Medical Journal, 80,* 1427–1429.

Saunders, W., & Kershaw, P. (1979). Spontaneous remission from alcoholism: A community study. *British Journal of Addictions, 74,* 251–265.

Schuckit, M. A. (1979). *Drug and alcohol treatment.* New York: Plenum.

Schumacher, J. E., Milby, J. B., Raczynski, J. R., Caldwell, E., Engle, M., Carr, J., & Michael, M. (1995). Validity of self-reported crack cocaine use among homeless persons in treatment. *Journal of Substance Abuse Treatment, 12,* 335–339.

Schwartz, R. H. (1987). Marijuana: An overview. *Pediatric Clinics of North America, 34,* 305–317.

Schwartz, R. H., Hoffman, N. G., & Jones, R. (1987). Behavioral, psychological, and academic correlates of marijuana usage in adolescence. *Clinical Pediatrics, 26,* 264–270.

Shaner, A., Eckman, T. A., Roberts, L. J., Wilkins, J. N., Tucker, D., Tsuang, J. W., & Mintz, J. (1995). Disability income, cocaine use, and repeated hospitalization among schizophrenic cocaine abusers: A government sponsored revolving door? *New England Journal of Medicine, 333*(12), 777–783.

Siegal, H. A. (1981). Current patterns of psychoactive use: Some epidemiological observations. In S. E. Gardner (Ed.), *Drug and alcohol abuse: Implications for treatment.* Washington, DC: NIDA Treatment Research.

Skinner, H. A., & Horn J. L. (1984). *Alcohol Dependency Scale (ADS) users guide.* Toronto: Addiction Research Foundation.

Smart, R. G., & Anglin, L. (1987). Do we know the lethal dose of cocaine? [Letter to the editor]. *Journal of Forensic Sciences, 32,* 303–312.

Smith, E. M. (1993). Race or racism? Addiction in the United States. *Annals of Epidemiology, 3,* 165–170.

Smith, S. S., O'Hara, B. F., Persico, A. M., Gorelick, D. A., Newlin, D. B., Vlahov, D., Lolomon, L., Rickens, R., & Uhl, G. R. (1992, September). Genetic vulnerability to drug abuse: The D2 dopamine receptor Taq 1 B1 restriction fragment length polymorphism appears more frequently in polysubstance abusers. *Archives of General Psychiatry, 49,* 723–727.

Solomon, R. L., & Corbit, J. D. (1974). An opponent-process theory of motivation: I. Temporal cynamics of affect. *Psychological Review, 81*(2), 119–145.

Stainback, R. D., & Walker, C. P. (1990). Discharge planning and selection of aftercare for substance abusers. In W. D. Lerner & M. A. Barr (Eds.), *Handbook of hospital-based substance abuse treatment.* New York: Pergamon.

Strug, D. L., Hunt, D. E., Goldsmith, D. S., Lipton, D. S., & Spunt, B. (1985). Patterns of cocaine use among methadone clients. *International Journal of the Addictions, 20*(8), 1163–1175.

Tennant, F. S. (1983). Treatment of dependence upon stimulants and hallucinogens. *Drug and Alcohol Dependence, 11,* 111–114.

Ternes, J. W., Ehrman, R. N., & O'Brien, C. P. (1985). Nondependent monkeys self-administer hydromorphone. *Behavioral Neuroscience, 99*(3), 583–588.

Tuchfeld, B. S. (1981). Spontaneous remission in alcoholics: Empirical observations and theoretical implications. *Journal of Studies on Alcohol, 42,* 1981.

Vaillant, G. E. (1966). A twelve-year follow-up of New York narcotic addicts: I. The relation of treatment to outcome. *American Journal of Psychiatry, 122*(7), 727–737.

Vaillant, G. E. (1973). A 20-year follow-up of New York narcotic addicts. *Archives of General Psychiatry, 29,* 237–241.

Valladares, B. K., & Lemberg, L. (1987). The Miami Vices in the CCU: Part I. Cardiac manifestations of cocaine use. *Heart and Lung, 16,* 456–458.

Varma, V. K., Malhotra, A. K., Dang, R., Das, K., & Nehra, R. (1988). Cannabis and cognitive functions: A prospective study. *Drug and Alcohol Dependence, 21,* 147–152.

Walker, R. D., Donovan, D. M., Kivlahan, D. R., & O'Leary, M. R. (1983). Length of stay, neuropsychological performance, and aftercare: Influences on alcohol treatment outcome. *Journal of Consulting and Clinical Psychology, 51,* 900–911.

Wallace, B. C. (1991). *Crack cocaine: A practical treatment approach for the chemically dependent.* New York: Brunner/Mazel.

Weatherby, N. L, Needle, R., Cesari, H., Booth, R., McCoy, C. B., Watters, J. K., Williams, M., & Chitwood, D. D. (1994). Validity of self-reported drug use among injection drug users and crack cocaine users recruited through street outreach. *Evaluation and Program Planning, 17,* 347–355.

Weed, N. C., Butcher, J. N., McKenna, T., & Ben-Porath, Y. S. (1992). New measures for assessing alcohol and drug abuse with the MMPI-2: The APS and AAS. *Journal of Personality Assessment, 58,* 389–404.

Weed, N. C., Butcher, J. N., & Williams, C. L. (1994). Development of MMPI-A alcohol/drug problem scales. *Journal of Studies on Alcohol, 55,* 296–302.

Weil, A. T., Zinberg, N. E., & Nelson, J. M. (1969). Clinical and psychological effects of marijuana in man. *International Journal of the Addictions, 4,* 427–451.

Weis, R. D., Griffin, M. L. & Mirin, S. M. (1992). Drug abuse as self-medication for depression: an empirical study. *American Journal of Drug and Alcohol Abuse, 18*(2), 121–129.

Weis, R. D., Mirin, S. M., & Frances, R. J. (1992). The myth of the typical dual diagnosis patient. *Hospital and Community Psychiatry, 43*(2), 107–108.

Weissman, M. M. & Johnson. J. (1991). Drug use and abuse in five U. S. communities. *New York State Journal of Medicine, 91*(11), 19–23.

Wikler, A. (1973). Drug dependence. In A. B. Baker & L. H. Baker (Eds.), *Clinical neurology* (Vol. 2). Philadelphia: Harper and Row.

Wilkinson, D. A., Leigh, G. M., Cordingley, J., Martin, G. W., & Lei, H. (1987). Dimensions of multiple drug use and a typology of drug users. *British Journal of Addiction, 82,* 259–273.

Winick, C. (1962). Maturing out of narcotic addiction. *Bulletin on Narcotics, 14,* 1–7.

Wise, R. H., & Bozarth, M. A. (1987). A psychomotor theory of addiction. *Psychological Review, 94*(4), 469–492.

Woody, G. E., Luborsky, L., McLellan, A. T., O'Brien, C. P., Beck, A. T., Blaine, J., Alterman, I., & Hole, A. (1983). Psychotherapy for opiate addicts: Does it help? *Archives of General Psychiatry, 40,* 639–645.

Woody, G. E., McLellan, A. T., Luborsky, L., O'Brien, C. P., Blaine, I., Fox, S., Herman, I., & Beck, A. T. (1984). Psychiatric severity as a predictor of benefits from psychotherapy: The Penn-VA Study. *American Journal of Psychiatry, 141*(10), 1172–1177.

Wright, J. E., & Stone, M. H. (1985). NSCA statement on anabolic drug use: Literature review. *National Strength and Conditioning Association Journal, 7*(5), 45–59.

Yeager, R. A., Hobson, R. W., Padberg, F. T., Lynch, T. G., & Chakravarty, M. (1987). Vascular complications related to drug abuse. *Journal of Trauma, 27,* 305–308.

Yesavage, J. A., Leirer, V. O., Denari, M., & Hollister, L. E. (1985). Carry-over effects of marijuana intoxication on aircraft pilot performance: A preliminary report. *American Journal of Psychiatry, 142,* 1325–1329.

Zeiner, A. R., Stanitis, T., Spurgeon, M., & Nichols, N. (1985). Treatment of alcoholism and concomitant drugs of abuse. *Alcohol, 2,* 555–559.

Zweben, J. E. (1986). Treating cocaine dependence: New challenges for the therapeutic community. *Journal of Psycho-active Drugs, 18,* 239–245.

CHAPTER 7

Schizophrenia

KIM T. MUESER

Schizophrenia is the most severely debilitating of all adult psychiatric illnesses. Despite the recent trend toward community-oriented treatment, more psychiatric hospital beds are occupied by patients with schizophrenia than any other disorder. Even when patients receive optimal treatments, they usually continue to experience substantial impairments throughout most of their lives.

Since schizophrenia was first described over 100 years ago, the nature of the disorder has been hotly debated, and public misconceptions about the disorder have been commonplace. In recent years, there has been a growing consensus among clinicians and researchers to redefine the psychopathology and diagnostic features of this disorder. Once referred to as a "wastebasket diagnosis," the term *schizophrenia* is now used to describe a specific clinical syndrome. An understanding of the core clinical features of schizophrenia is a necessary prerequisite for differential diagnosis and treatment planning. After many years of struggling to improve the long-term course of schizophrenia, there is now abundant evidence that combined pharmacological and psychosocial interventions can have a major impact on improving functioning. This chapter is focused on providing readers with an up-to-date review of schizophrenia, with particular attention given to the psychopathology of the illness and its impact on other domains of functioning.

Schizophrenia is characterized by impairments in social functioning, including difficulty establishing and maintaining interpersonal relationships, problems working or fulfilling other instrumental roles (e.g., homemaker), and the inability to care for oneself (e.g., poor grooming and hygiene). These problems in daily living, in the absence of significant impairment in intellectual functioning, are the most distinguishing characteristics of schizophrenia. Consequently, many patients with the illness depend on others to meet their daily living needs. For example, estimates suggest that between 40% and 60% of patients with schizophrenia live with relatives, and an even higher percentage rely on relatives for caregiving (Goldman, 1982; Torrey, 1995). Patients without family contact typically rely on mental health, residential, and case management services. In the worst case scenario, patients who have insufficient contact with relatives and who fall between the cracks of the social service delivery system end up in jail (Torrey et al., 1992) or become homeless, with between 10% and 20% of homeless persons having schizophrenia (Susser, Stuening, & Conover, 1989).

In addition to the problems in daily living which characterize schizophrenia, patients with the illness experience a range of different symptoms and cognitive impairments. The most common symptoms include positive symptoms (e.g., hallucinations and delusions), negative symptoms (e.g., social withdrawal and apathy), and problems with mood (e.g., depression and anxiety). The specific nature of these symptoms and cognitive impairments are described in greater detail in the section titled Clinical Practice. The symptoms and cognitive impairments in schizophrenia appear to account for some, but not all, of the problems in social functioning.

The various impairments associated with schizophrenia tend to be long term, punctuated by fluctuations in severity over time. For this reason, schizophrenia has a broad impact on the family, and patients are often impeded from pursuing personal life goals. The severity of symptoms, coupled with chronic disabilities, renders most patients with schizophrenia in need of assistance throughout much of their lives. Despite the severity of the disorder, advances in the treatment of schizophrenia provide solid hope for improving the outcome.

EPIDEMIOLOGY

The lifetime prevalence of schizophrenia (including the closely related disorders of schizoaffective disorder and schizophreniform disorder) is approximately 1% (Keith, Regier, & Rae, 1991). In general, prevalence of schizophrenia is remarkably stable across a wide range of different demographic and environmental conditions, such as gender, race, religion, population density, and level of industrialization (Jablensky, 1989).

As schizophrenia frequently has an onset during early adulthood, persons with the illness are less likely to marry or remain married, particularly males (Eaton, 1975; Munk-Jørgensen, 1987). It has long been known that there is an association between poverty and schizophrenia, with patients belonging to lower socioeconomic classes (Hollingshead & Redlich, 1958; Salokangas, 1978). Historically, two theories have been advanced to account for this association. The *social drift* hypothesis postulates that the debilitating effects of schizophrenia on capacity to work result in a lowering of socioeconomic means and hence poverty (Aro, Aro, & Keskimäki, 1995). The *environmental stress* hypothesis proposes that high levels of stress associated with poverty precipitate schizophrenia in some individuals who would not otherwise develop the illness (Bruce, Takeuchi, & Leaf, 1991). Although both of these explanations may be partly true, longitudinal research on changes in socioeconomic class status and schizophrenia provides stronger support for the environmental stress hypothesis, rather than the downward drift hypothesis (Fox, 1990). The notion that environmental stress may play a role in precipitating some cases of schizophrenia is compatible with the stress-vulnerability model of the disorder, which posits an interaction between socioenvironmental stressors and biological vulnerability in determining the onset and course of the disorder (Nuechterlein & Dawson, 1984; Zubin & Spring, 1977).

CLINICAL PICTURE

Schizophrenia is characterized by two broad classes of symptoms: positive symptoms and negative symptoms. *Positive symptoms* refer to cognitions, sensory experiences, and behaviors that are present in patients, but are ordinarily absent in persons without the illness. Common examples of positive symptoms include hallucinations (e.g., hearing voices), delusions (e.g., believing that people are persecuting you), and bizarre behavior (e.g., maintaining a peculiar posture for no apparent reason). *Negative symptoms,* on the other hand, refer to the absence or diminution of cognitions, feelings, or behaviors which are ordinarily present in persons without the illness. Common negative symptoms include blunted or flattened affective expressiveness (e.g., diminished facial expressiveness), poverty of speech (i.e., diminished verbal communication), anhedonia (i.e., inability to experience pleasure), apathy, psychomotor retardation (e.g., slow rate of speech), and physical inertia.

The positive symptoms of schizophrenia tend to fluctuate over the course of the disorder and are often in remission between episodes of the illness. In addition, positive symptoms tend to be responsive to the effects of antipsychotic medication (Kane & Marder, 1993). In contrast, negative symptoms tend to be stable over time and are less responsive to antipsychotic medications (Greden & Tandon, 1991).

In addition to positive and negative symptoms, many patients with schizophrenia experience negative emotions as a consequence of their illness. Depression and suicidal ideation are common symptoms of schizophrenia, and approximately 10% of persons with this illness die from suicide (Drake, Gates, Whitaker, & Cotton, 1985; Roy, 1986). Difficulties with anxiety are common and are often due to positive symptoms, such as hallucinations or paranoid delusions (Argyle, 1990; Penn, Hope, Spaulding, & Kucera, 1994). Finally, anger and hostility may also be present, especially when the patient is paranoid.

Aside from the characteristic symptoms of schizophrenia, many patients have cognitive impairments. Cognitive deficits in areas such as attention, memory, and abstract thinking are frequently present (Frith, 1992). These impairments may interfere with patients' ability to focus for sustained periods on work or recreational pursuits, interact effectively with others, or participate in conventional psychotherapeutic interventions.

In addition to the symptoms and cognitive disturbances commonly present in schizophrenia, individuals with this diagnosis often have comorbid substance use disorders. Epidemiological surveys have repeatedly found that persons with psychiatric disorders are at increased risk for alcohol and drug abuse (Mueser, Yarnold, et al., 1990; Mueser, Yarnold, & Bellack, 1992). This risk is highest for persons with the most severe psychiatric disorders, including schizophrenia and bipolar disorder. For example, individuals with schizophrenia are more than 4 times as likely to have a substance abuse disorder than individuals in the general population (Regier et al., 1990). In general, approximately 50% of all patients with schizophrenia have a lifetime history of substance use disorder, and 25% to 35% have a recent history of such a disorder (Mueser, Bennett, & Kushner, 1995).

Presence of comorbid substance use disorders in schizophrenia has consistently been found to be associated with a worse course of the illness, including increased vulnerability to relapses and hospitalizations, housing instability and homelessness, violence, economic family burden, and noncompliance (Bartels et al., 1993; Clark, 1994; Cournos et al., 1991; Drake, Osher, & Wallach, 1989; Yesavage & Zarcone, 1983). For these reasons, recognition and treatment of substance use disorders in patients with schizophrenia is crucial to the overall management of the illness.

Another important clinical feature of schizophrenia is lack of insight and compliance with treatment (Amador, Strauss, Yale, & Gorman, 1991). Many patients with schizophrenia have little or no insight into the fact that they have a psychiatric illness, or even that they have any problems at all. Such denial of illness can lead to noncompliance with recommended treatments, such as psychotropic medications and psychosocial therapies (McEvoy et al., 1989). Furthermore, fostering insight into the illness is a difficult and often an impossible task with these patients.

Noncompliance with treatment is a related problem but can also occur due to the severe negativity often present in the illness, independent of poor insight. Medication noncompliance increases the risk of patients to relapse and is therefore a major concern to clinical treatment providers (Buchanan, 1992). Strategies for enhancing compliance involve helping the patient become a more active participant in his or her treatment and identifying personal goals of treatment that have high relevance for that individual (Corrigan, Liberman, & Engle, 1990).

COURSE AND PROGNOSIS

Schizophrenia usually has an onset in late adolescence or early adulthood, most often between the ages of 16 and 25. It is extremely rare for the first onset of schizophrenia to occur before adolescence (e.g., before the age of 12), with most diagnostic systems considering childhood-onset schizophrenia to be a different disorder than adolescent or adult onset (American Psychiatric Association [APA], 1994). More common than childhood schizophrenia, but nevertheless rare in the total population of persons with schizophrenia, are individuals who develop the illness later in life, such as after the age of 45 (Cohen, 1990). Late-onset schizophrenia is further complicated by the lack of clear-cut distinguishing characteristics that discriminates this disorder from a variety of other dimensions that develop later in old age (Howard, Almeida, & Levy, 1994).

Prior to onset of schizophrenia some, but not all persons have impairments in their premorbid social functioning (Zigler & Glick, 1986). For example, some people who later develop schizophrenia in childhood and adolescence were more socially isolated, passed fewer social-sexual developmental milestones, and had fewer friends. Aside from problems in social functioning, prior to developing schizophrenia some individuals in childhood display a maladaptive pattern of behaviors, including disruptive behavior, problems in school, and impulsivity (Baum & Walker, 1995; Hans, Marcus, Henson, Auerbach, & Mirsky, 1992). However, other patients display no unusual characteristics in their premorbid functioning.

A second moderating factor related to prognosis of schizophrenia is patient gender. Women tend to have later age of onset of the illness, spend less time in hospitals, and demonstrate better social competence and social functioning than men with the illness (Goldstein, 1988; Häfner et al., 1993; Mueser, Bellack, Morrison, & Wade, 1990). The benefits experienced by women do not appear to be explained by societal differences in tolerance for deviant behavior. A variety of different hypotheses has been advanced to account for the superior outcome of women with schizophrenia (e.g., biological differences, interactions with socioenvironmental stressors; Castle & Murray, 1991; Flor-Henry, 1985), but no single theory has received strong support.

In general, onset of schizophrenia can be described as either gradual or acute. The gradual onset of schizophrenia can take place over many months, and it may be difficult for family members and others to clearly distinguish onset of the illness. In cases of acute onset, symptoms develop rapidly over a period of a few weeks, with dramatic and easily observed changes occurring over this time.

Once schizophrenia has developed, the illness usually continues to be present at varying degrees of severity throughout most of the person's life. Schizophrenia is usually an episodic illness, with periods of acute symptom severity requiring more intensive, often inpatient, treatment interspersed by periods of higher functioning between episodes. Despite the fact that most patients with schizophrenia live in the community, it is comparatively rare, at least in the short term, for patients to return to their premorbid levels of functioning between episodes.

Although schizophrenia is a long-term and severe psychiatric illness, there is considerable interindividual variability in the course of illness (Marengo, 1994). Broadly speaking, about one-third of all persons with schizophrenia have a relatively mild course of the illness, marked by relatively few relapses and rehospitalizations, higher functioning in the community, and less day-to-day disruption from the illness. Another third of all patients have an intermediate course of the illness, including more frequent relapses and rehospitalizations, more tenuous social functioning in the community, and more persistent impairments resulting from the illness. Finally, one-third of all patients have a severe and relatively unremitting course of their illness. These patients typically experience debilitating symptoms on a daily basis, have a severely reduced capability of maintaining social relationships or work, and spend much of their time in hospitals or under close supervision.

Some general predictors of the course and outcome of schizophrenia have been identified, such as premorbid functioning, but overall the ability to predict outcome is rather poor (Avison & Speechley, 1987; Tsuang, 1986). The primary reason for this is that symptom severity and functioning are determined by the dynamic interplay between biological vulnerability, environmental factors, and coping skills (Liberman et al., 1986; Nuechterlein & Dawson, 1994). Factors such as compliance with medication (Buchanan, 1992), substance abuse (Drake et al., 1989), exposure to a hostile or critical environment (Kavanagh, 1992), availability of psychosocial programming (Bellack & Mueser, 1993), and assertive case management and outreach (Bond, McGrew, & Fekete, 1995; Mueser,

Bond, & Drake, 1995) are all environmental factors that in combination play a large role in determining outcome.

The importance of environmental factors and rehabilitation programs in determining the outcome of schizophrenia is illustrated by two long-term outcome studies conducted by Harding and her associates (DeSisto et al., 1995; Harding, Brooks, Ashikaga, Strauss, & Breyer, 1987a, 1987b). The first study was conducted in Vermont, which had a highly developed system of community-based rehabilitation programs for persons with severe mental illness. Patients in this study demonstrated surprisingly positive outcomes over the 20–40-year follow-up period. In contrast, similar patients in Maine, where more traditional hospital-based treatment programs existed, fared substantially worse over the long-term course of their illness. Thus, outcome of most cases of schizophrenia is not predetermined by specific biological factors but rather is influenced by the interaction between biological and environmental factors.

In summary, prognosis of schizophrenia is usually considered fair, and there is general agreement that it is worse than for other major psychiatric disorders, such as bipolar disorder or major depression. Despite widespread acceptance that schizophrenia is usually a lifelong disability, recent research on the long-term outcome of schizophrenia has challenged this assumption. Several long-term studies that have followed up patients 20–40 years after developing schizophrenia suggest that previous estimates of recovery from schizophrenia are overly conservative. Although definitions of "recovery" vary from one study to the next, some studies suggest as many as 20%–50% of patients fully recover from schizophrenia later in life (Ciompi, 1980; Harding et al., 1987a, 1987b).

FAMILIAL AND GENETIC CONSIDERATIONS

The etiology of schizophrenia has been a topic of much debate over the past 100 years. Kraepelin (1919/1971) and Bleuler (1911/1950) clearly viewed the illness as having a biological origin. However, from the 1920s to the 1960s, alternative theories, which speculated the disease was the result of disturbed family interactions, gained prominence (Bateson, Jackson, Haley, & Weakland, 1956). Psychogenic theories of the etiology of schizophrenia, positing that the illness was psychological in nature, rather than biological, played a dominant role in shaping the attitudes and behavior of professionals toward patients with schizophrenia and their relatives (Fromm-Reichmann, 1950; Searles, 1965). In many cases, these theories fostered poor relationships between mental health professionals and relatives (Terkelsen, 1983), which have only begun to mend in recent years (Mueser & Glynn, 1995).

Despite the intuitive appeal of these theories to many clinicians, they failed to be supported by rigorous scientific inquiry and are now being discarded. A number of factors contributed to the theories that families cause schizophrenia. First, in observational research studies, the behavior of parents interacting with an offspring with schizophrenia could often not be distinguished from their interactions with healthy offspring, raising questions as to why one child developed the illness but the other did not (Jacob, 1975; Waxler & Mishler, 1971). Second, when disturbed family relationships were present, it was difficult to rule out the possibility that these problems were secondary to the development of schizophrenia in a family member (Waxler, 1974). Third, the discovery of the beneficial effects of antipsychotic medications on the symptoms of schizophrenia raises the question of why a pharmacological intervention would have such dramatic effect on a psychological, rather than biological illness. Fourth, and perhaps most important, is the growing evidence suggesting that genetic factors play a role in the development of schizophrenia (Holzman & Matthysse, 1990).

For over a century, clinicians have often noted that schizophrenia tends to "run in families." However, clustering of schizophrenia in family members could reflect learned behavior that is passed on from one generation to the next, rather than predisposing biological factors. In the 1950s and 1960s, two paradigms were developed for evaluating the genetic contributions to the illness. The first approach, the *high risk* paradigm, involves examining the rate of schizophrenia in adopted-away offspring of mothers with schizophrenia. If the rate of schizophrenia in children of biological parents with schizophrenia is higher than in the general population, even in the absence of contact with those parents, a role for genetic factors in developing the illness is supported. The second approach, the *monozygotic/dizygotic twin* paradigm, involves comparing the concordance rate of schizophrenia in identical twins (monozygotic) compared to fraternal twins (dizygotic). Since monozygotic twins share the exact same gene pool, whereas dizygotic twins share only approximately half their genes, a higher concordance rate of schizophrenia among monozygotic twins than dizygotic twins, even reared in the same environment, would support a role for genetic factors in the etiology of schizophrenia.

Over the past 30 years, numerous studies employing either the high risk or twin paradigm have been conducted examining the role of genetic factors in schizophrenia. There has been almost uniform agreement across studies indicating that the risk of developing schizophrenia in biological relatives of persons with schizophrenia is greater than in the general population, even in the absence of any contact between the relatives (Kendler & Diehl, 1993). Thus, strong support exists for the role of genetic factors in the etiology of at least some cases of schizophrenia. For example, the risk of a woman with schizophrenia giving birth to a child who later develops schizophrenia is approximately 10%, compared to only 1% in the general population (Gottesman, 1991). Similarly, the risk of one identical twin developing schizophrenia if his or her co-twin also has schizophrenia is between 25% and 50%, compared to a risk of about 10% for fraternal twins (Walker, Downey, & Caspi, 1991).

The fact that identical twins do not have 100% concordance rate of schizophrenia, as might be expected if the disorder were purely genetic, has raised intriguing questions about the etiology of schizophrenia. Some have proposed that the development of schizophrenia might be the consequence of an interaction between genetic and environmental factors. The results of one study suggest this might be the case. Tienari (1991; Tienari et al., 1987) compared the likelihood of developing schizophrenia in three groups of children raised by adoptive families. Two groups of children had biological mothers with schizophrenia; the third group had biological mothers with no psychiatric disorder. The researchers divided the adoptive families of the children into two broad groups based on the level of disturbance present in the family: healthy adoptive families and disturbed adoptive families. Follow-up assessments were conducted to determine presence of schizophrenia and other severe psychiatric disorders in the adopted children raised in all three groups. Researchers found that children of biological mothers with schizophrenia who were raised by adoptive families with high levels of disturbance were significantly more likely to develop schizophrenia or another psychotic disorder (46%) than either similarly vulnerable children raised in families with low levels of disturbance (5%), or children with no biological vulnerability raised in either disturbed (24%) or healthy (3%) adoptive families. This study raises the intriguing possibility that some cases of schizophrenia develop as a result of the interaction between biological vulnerability and environmental stress.

Although there is strong evidence that genetic factors can play a role in the development of schizophrenia, there is also a growing body of evidence pointing to the influence of other biological, nongenetic factors playing a critical role. For example, obstetric complications, maternal exposure to the influenza virus, and other environmental-based insults to developing fetus (e.g., maternal starvation) are all associated with an increased risk of developing schizophrenia (Kirch, 1993; Rodrigo, Lusiardo, Briggs, & Ulmer, 1991; Susser & Lin, 1992; Torrey, Bowler, Rawlings, & Terrazas, 1993). Thus, there is a growing consensus that the etiology of schizophrenia may be heterogeneous, with genetic factors playing a role in the development of some cases, and early environmental-based factors playing a role in the development of other cases. Such heterogeneity may account for the fact that the genetic contribution to schizophrenia has consistently been found to be lower than the genetic contribution to bipolar disorder (Goodwin & Jamison, 1990).

DIAGNOSTIC CONSIDERATIONS

The diagnostic criteria for schizophrenia are fairly similar across a variety of different diagnostic systems. In general, diagnostic criteria specify some degree of social impairment, combined with positive and negative symptoms lasting a significant duration (e.g., 6 months or more). The diagnostic criteria for schizophrenia and schizoaffective disorder according to DSM-IV (*Diagnostic and Statistical Manual of Mental Disorders;* APA, 1994) are summarized in Tables 7.1 and 7.2.

The diagnosis of schizophrenia requires a clinical interview with the patient, a thorough review of all available records, and standard medical evaluations to rule out the possible role of organic factors (e.g., CAT scan to rule out a brain tumor). In addition, because many patients are poor historians or may not provide accurate accounts of their behavior, information from significant others, such as family members, is often critical to establish a diagnosis of schizophrenia. Because of the wide variety of symptoms characteristic of schizophrenia and variations in interviewing style and format across different clinical interviewers, the use of structured clinical interviews, such as the Structured Clinical

TABLE 7.1   DSM-IV Criteria for the Diagnosis of Schizophrenia

A. Presence of at least two of the following characteristic symptoms in the active phase for at least 1 month (unless the symptoms are successfully treated):

    1. Delusions
    2. Hallucinations
    3. Disorganized speech (e.g., frequent derailment or incoherence)
    4. Grossly disorganized or catatonic behavior
    5. Negative symptoms (e.g., affect flattening, alogia, or avolition)
    Note: only one of these symptoms is required if delusions are bizarre or hallucinations consist of a voice keeping up a running commentary on the person's behavior or thoughts, or two or more voices conversing with each other.

B. Social/occupational dysfunction: For a significant proportion of the time from the onset of the disturbance, one or more areas of functioning, such as work, interpersonal relations, or self-care, is markedly below the level achieved prior to the onset (or, when the onset is in childhood or adolescence, failure to achieve expected level of interpersonal, academic, or occupational achievement).

C. Duration: Continuous signs of the disturbance persist for at least 6 months. This 6-month period must include at least 1 month of symptoms that meet criterion A (i.e., active-phase symptoms) and may include periods of prodromal or residual symptoms. During these prodromal or residual periods, the signs of the disturbance may be manifested by only negative symptoms or by two or more symptoms listed in criterion A present in an attenuated form (e.g., odd beliefs, unusual perceptual experiences).

D. Schizoaffective and mood disorders exclusion: Schizoaffective disorder and mood disorder with psychotic features have been ruled out because either 1. no major depressive or manic episodes have occurred concurrently with the active-phase symptoms or 2. if mood episodes have occurred during active-phase symptoms, their total duration has been brief relative to the duration of the active and residual periods.

E. Substance/general medical condition exclusion: The disturbance is not due to the direct effects of a substance (e.g., drugs of abuse or medication) or a general medical condition.

Interview for DSM-IV (First, Spitzer, Gibbon, & Williams, 1995) can greatly enhance the reliability and validity of psychiatric diagnosis.

Structured clinical interviews have two main advantages over more open clinical interviews. First, structured interviews provide specific definitions of the key symptoms, agreed upon by experts, thus making explicit the specific symptoms required for diagnosis. Second, by conducting the interview in a standardized format, including a specific sequence of asking questions, variations in interviewing style are minimized, thus enhancing the comparability of diagnostic assessments across different clinicians. The second point is especially crucial considering that most research studies of schizophrenia employ structured interviews to establish diagnoses. If findings of clinical research studies are to be

TABLE 7.2   DSM-IV Criteria for the Diagnosis of Schizoaffective Disorder

A. An uninterrupted period of illness during which at some time there is either a major depressive episode (which must include depressed mood) or manic episode concurrent with symptoms that meet criterion A of schizophrenia.

B. During the same period of illness, there have been delusions or hallucinations for at least 2 weeks in the absence of prominent mood symptoms.

C. Symptoms meeting the criteria for a mood disorder are present for a substantial portion of the total duration of the active and residual periods of the illness.

D. The disturbance is not due to the direct effects of a substance (e.g., drugs of abuse or medication) or a general medical condition.

generalized into clinical practice, efforts must be taken to ensure the comparability of the patient populations and the assessment techniques employed.

The symptoms of schizophrenia overlap with many other psychiatric disorders. Establishing a diagnosis of schizophrenia requires particularly close consideration of three other overlapping disorders: substance use disorders, affective disorder, and schizoaffective disorder. We discuss issues related to each of these disorders and the diagnosis of schizophrenia below.

Substance Use Disorders

Substance use disorder, such as alcohol dependence or drug abuse, can either be a differential diagnosis to schizophrenia or a comorbid disorder (i.e., the patient can have both schizophrenia *and* a substance use disorder). With respect to differential diagnosis, substance use disorders can interfere with a clinician's ability to diagnosis schizophrenia and can lead to misdiagnosis if the substance abuse is covert (Corty, Lehman, & Myers, 1993; Kranzler et al., 1995). Psychoactive substances, such as alcohol, marijuana, cocaine, and amphetamines, can produce symptoms that mimic those found in schizophrenia, such as hallucinations, delusions, and social withdrawal (Schuckit, 1989). Since the diagnosis of schizophrenia requires presence of specific symptoms in the absence of identifiable organic factors, schizophrenia can be diagnosed in persons with a history of substance use disorder only by examining the individual's functioning during sustained periods of abstinence from drugs or alcohol. When such periods of abstinence can be identified, a reliable diagnosis of schizophrenia can be made. However, patients who have a long history of substance abuse, with few or no periods of abstinence, are more difficult to assess. For example, in a sample of 461 patients admitted to a psychiatric hospital, a psychiatric diagnosis could not be confirmed nor ruled out due to history of substance abuse in 71 patients (15%; Lehman, Myers, Dixon, & Johnson, 1994).

Substance use disorder is the most common comorbid diagnosis for persons with schizophrenia. Because substance abuse can worsen the course and outcome of schizophrenia, recognition and treatment of substance abuse in schizophrenia is a critical goal of treatment. The diagnosis of substance abuse in schizophrenia is complicated by several factors. Substance abuse, as in the general population, is often denied because of social and legal sanctions (Galletly, Field, & Prior, 1993; Stone, Greenstein, Gamble, & McLellan, 1993), a problem which may be worsened in this population because of a fear of losing benefits. Denial of problems associated with substance abuse, a core feature of primary substance use disorders, may be further heightened by psychotic distortions and cognitive impairments present in schizophrenia. Furthermore, criteria used to establish a substance use disorder in the general population are less useful for diagnosis in schizophrenia (Corse, Hirschinger, & Zanis, 1995). For example, common consequences of substance abuse in the general population of loss of employment, driving under the influence of alcohol, and relationship problems are less often experienced by people with schizophrenia, who are often unemployed or do not own cars and have limited interpersonal relationships. In addition, patients with schizophrenia tend to use smaller quantities of drugs and alcohol and rarely develop the full physical dependence syndrome that is often present in persons with the primary substance use disorder (Drake et al., 1990). Rather, patients with schizophrenia more often experience increased symptoms and rehospitalizations, legal problems, and housing instability secondary to substance abuse (Drake, Mueser, Clark, & Wallach, 1996).

Despite difficulties involved in assessing comorbid substance abuse in patients with schizophrenia, recent developments in this area indicate that if appropriate steps are taken, reliable diagnoses can be made (Drake, Rosenberg, & Mueser, 1996). The most critical recommendations for diagnosing substance abuse in schizophrenia include: 1. maintain a high index of suspicion of substance abuse, especially if a patient has a past history of substance abuse; 2. use multiple assessment techniques, including self-report instruments, interviews with patients, clinician reports, reports of significant others, and biological assays; and 3. be alert to signs that may be subtle indicators of the presence of a substance use disorder, such as unexplained symptom relapses, increased familial conflict, money management problems, and depression or suicidality. Once a substance use disorder has been diagnosed, integrated treatment that addresses both the schizophrenia and the substance use disorder is necessary to achieve a favorable clinical outcome (Drake, Bartels, Teague, Noordsy, & Clark, 1993).

Affective Disorders

Schizophrenia overlaps more prominently with the major affective disorders than any other psychiatric disorder. The differential diagnosis of schizophrenia from affective disorders is critical because the disorders respond to different treatments, particularly pharmacological interventions. Two different affective disorders can be especially difficult to distinguish from schizophrenia: bipolar disorder and major depression (APA, 1994). The differential diagnosis of these disorders from schizophrenia is complicated by the fact that affective symptoms (e.g., depression and grandiose delusions) are frequently present in persons with schizophrenia, and psychotic symptoms (e.g., hallucinations and delusions) may be present in persons with a major affective disorder.

The crux of making a differential diagnosis between schizophrenia and a major affective disorder is to determine whether psychotic symptoms are present *in the absence of* affective symptoms. If there is strong evidence that psychotic symptoms persist even when the person is not experiencing symptoms of mania or depression, then the diagnosis is either schizophrenia or the closely related disorder of schizoaffective disorder (discussed below). If, on the other hand, symptoms of psychosis are present during an affective syndrome but disappear when the person's mood is stable, the appropriate diagnosis is either major depression or bipolar disorder. For example, it is common for people with bipolar disorder to have hallucinations and delusions during the height of a manic episode but for these psychotic symptoms to subside when the person's mood becomes stable again. Similarly, persons with major depression often experience hallucinations or delusions during a depressive episode, which subside as their mood improves. If the patient experiences chronic mood problems, meeting criteria for manic, depressive, or mixed episodes, it may be difficult or impossible to establish a diagnosis of schizophrenia, since there are no sustained periods of stable mood.

Schizoaffective Disorder

Schizoaffective disorder is a diagnostic entity that overlaps the affective disorders and schizophrenia (APA, 1994). Three conditions must be met for a person to be diagnosed with schizoaffective disorder: 1. the person must meet criteria for an affective syndrome (i.e., 2-week period in which manic, depressive, or mixed affective features are present to a significant degree); 2. the person must meet criteria for the symptoms of schizophrenia during a period when they are not experiencing an affective syndrome (e.g., hallucinations or delusions in the absence of manic or depressive symptoms); and 3. the affective syndrome must be present for a substantial period of the person's psychiatric illness (i.e., a patient who experiences brief affective syndromes and who is chronically psychotic and has other long-standing impairments would be diagnosed with schizophrenia rather than schizoaffective disorder).

Schizoaffective disorder and major affective disorder are frequently mistaken for one another because it is incorrectly assumed that schizoaffective disorder simply requires the presence of both psychotic and affective symptoms. Rather, as described in the preceding section, if psychotic symptoms always coincide with affective symptoms, the person has an affective disorder, whereas if psychotic symptoms are present in the absence of an affective syndrome, the person meets criteria for either schizoaffective disorder or schizophrenia. The distinction between schizophrenia and schizoaffective disorder can be more difficult to make, because judgment must be made as to whether the affective symptoms have been present for a substantial part of the person's illness. Decision rules for determining the extent to which affective symptoms must be present to diagnose a schizoaffective disorder have not been established.

Although the differential diagnosis between schizophrenia and schizoaffective disorder is difficult, the clinical implications of this distinction are less important than between the affective disorders and either schizophrenia or schizoaffective disorder. Research on family history and treatment response suggests that schizophrenia and schizoaffective disorder are similar disorders and respond to the same interventions (Kramer, et al., 1989; Levinson & Levitt, 1987; Levinson & Mowry, 1991; Mattes & Nayak, 1984). In fact, many studies of schizophrenia routinely include patients with schizoaffective disorder and find few differences. Therefore, information provided in this chapter on schizophrenia also pertains to schizoaffective disorder, and the differential diagnosis between the two disorders is not of major importance from a clinical perspective.

PSYCHOLOGICAL AND BIOLOGICAL ASSESSMENT

Diagnostic assessment provides important information about the potential utility of interventions for schizophrenia (e.g., antipsychotic medications). However, assessment does not end with a diagnosis. It must be supplemented with additional psychological and biological assessments.

Psychological Assessment

A wide range of different psychological formulations have been proposed for understanding schizophrenia. For example, there are extensive writings about psychodynamic and psychoanalytic interpretations of schizophrenia. Although this work has made contributions to the further development of these theories, it is less certain that these formulations have improved the ability of clinicians to understand patients with this disorder, or have led to more effective interventions (Mueser & Berenbaum, 1990). Therefore, use of projective assessment techniques based on psychodynamic concepts of personality, such as the Rorschach and Thematic Aperception Tests, are not considered here.

Social Skill

An alternative to assessments based on psychodynamic models of psychological functioning is the assessment of social skill. Social skills refer to the individual behavioral components, such as eye contact, voice loudness, and the specific choice of words, which in combination are necessary for effective communication with others (Liberman, DeRisi, & Mueser, 1989). As previously described, poor social competence is a hallmark of schizophrenia. Although not all problems in social functioning are the consequence of poor social skills, many social impairments appear to be related to skill deficits (Bellack, Morrison, Wixted, & Mueser, 1990).

A number of different strategies can be used to assess social skill. Direct interviews with patients can be a good starting place for identifying broad areas of social dysfunction. These interviews can focus on answering questions such as: Is the patient lonely? Would the patient like more or closer friends? Is the patient able to stand up for his or her rights? Is the patient able to get others to respond positively to him or her? Patient interviews are most informative when combined with interviews with significant others, such as family members and clinicians who are familiar with the nature and quality of the patient's social interactions, as well as naturalistic observations of the patient's social interactions. The combination of these sources of information is useful for identifying specific areas in need of social skills training.

The last strategy for assessing social skills, which also yields the most specific type of information, involves role play assessments. Role plays involve brief simulated social interactions between the patient and a confederate taking the role of an interactive partner. During role plays patients are instructed to act as though the situation were actually happening in real life. Role plays can be as brief as 15 to 30 seconds, to assess skill areas such as initiating conversations, or can be as long as several minutes, to assess skills such as problem solving ability. Role plays can be audiotaped or videotaped and later rated on specific dimensions of social skill. Alternatively, role playing can be embedded into the procedures of social skills training, in which patients practice targeted social skills in role plays, followed by positive and corrective feedback and additional role play rehearsal. In the latter instance, assessment of social skills is integrated into the training of new skills, rather than proceeding skills training.

Recent research on the reliability and validity of social skill assessments, and the benefits of social skills training in patients with schizophrenia, has demonstrated the utility of the social skills construct. Patients with schizophrenia have consistently been found to have worse social skills than patients with other psychiatric disorders (Bellack, Morrison, Wixted, & Mueser, 1990; Bellack, Mueser, Wade, Sayers, & Morrison, 1992; Mueser, Bellack, Douglas, & Wade, 1991), and approximately half of the patients with schizophrenia demonstrate stable deficits in basic social skills compared to the nonpsychiatric population (Mueser, Bellack, Douglas, & Morrison, 1991). In the absence of skills training, social skills tend to be stable over periods of time as long as 6 months to 1 year (Mueser, Bellack, Douglas, & Morrison, 1991). Social skill in patients with schizophrenia is moderately correlated with level of premorbid social functioning, current role functioning, and quality of life (Mueser, Bellack, Morrison, & Wixted, 1990). Furthermore, role play assessments of social skill are also strongly related with social skill in more natural contexts, such as interactions with significant others (Bellack, Morrison, Mueser, Wade, & Sayers, 1990). However, social skills are only weakly related to negative symptoms and tend not to be related to positive symptoms at all (Bellack, Morrison, Wixted, & Mueser, 1990; Mueser, Douglas, Bellack, & Morrison, 1991). Patients with schizophrenia show a wide range of impairments in social skill, including areas such as conversational skill, conflict resolution, assertiveness, and problem solving (Bellack, Sayers, Mueser, & Bennett, 1994; Douglas & Mueser, 1990). Thus, ample research demonstrates that social skills are impaired with patients with schizophrenia, tend to be stable over time in the absence of intervention, and are strongly related to other measures of social functioning. Furthermore, there is growing evidence supporting the efficacy of social skills training for schizophrenia (Mueser, Wallace, & Liberman, 1995).

Family Assessment

The assessment of family functioning has high relevance in schizophrenia for two reasons. First, it has repeatedly been found that critical attitudes and high levels of emotional overinvolvement (expressed emotion, hereafter, EE) on the part of the relatives toward the patient are strong predictors of the likelihood that patients will relapse and be rehospitalized (Kavanagh, 1992). The importance of family factors is underscored by the fact that the severity of patients' psychiatric illness or their social skill impairments are not related to family EE (Mueser et al., 1993). Rather, family EE seems to act as a stressor, increasing the vulnerability of patients with schizophrenia to relapse.

The second rationale for assessing functioning of family members of patients with schizophrenia is to address problems related to the burden on relatives of caring for a mentally ill person. Family members of patients with schizophrenia typically experience a wide range of negative emotions related to coping with the illness, such as anxiety, depression, guilt, and anger (Hatfield & Lefley, 1987, 1993). Family burden may be related to levels of expressed emotion, ability to cope with the illness, and ultimately the ability of the family to successfully monitor and manage the schizophrenia in a family member (Mueser & Glynn, 1995). Therefore, assessing dimensions of coping and burden in family members may identify important targets for family intervention.

A number of specific methods can be used to assess a negative emotional climate in the family and burden of the illness. At the most basic level, interviews with individual family members, including the patient, as well as with the entire family, coupled with observation of more naturalistic family interactions, can provide invaluable information about the quality of family functioning. The vast majority of research on family expressed emotion has employed a semi-structured interview with individual family members, the Camberwell Family Interview (Brown & Rutter, 1966; Rutter & Brown, 1966). This instrument is primarily a research instrument, and it is too time consuming to be used in clinical practice. Alternatives to the Camberwell Family Interview have been proposed (e.g., Magaña et al., 1986; Mueser, Bellack, & Wade, 1992), although none have gained widespread acceptance yet. Several studies have successfully employed the Family Environment Scale (Moos & Moos, 1981), a self-report instrument completed by family members, which has been found to be related to symptoms and outcome in patients with schizophrenia (Halford, Schweitzer, & Varghese, 1991).

Many instruments have been developed for the assessment of family burden. The most comprehensive instrument, with well-established psychometric properties, is the Family Experiences Interview Schedule (Tessler & Gamache, 1995). This measure provides information regarding both dimensions of subjective burden (e.g., emotional strain) and objective burden (e.g., economic impact), as well as specific areas in which burden is most severe (e.g., household tasks).

The importance of evaluating family functioning is supported by research demonstrating clinical benefits of family intervention for schizophrenia. Over 10 long-term controlled studies of family treatment for schizophrenia have shown that family intervention has a significant impact on reducing relapse rates and rehospitalizations (Penn & Mueser, 1996). The critical elements shared across different models of family intervention are education about schizophrenia, the provision of ongoing support, improved communication skills, and a focus on helping all family members improve the quality of their lives (Glynn, 1992; Lam, 1991).

Biological Assessment

Biological assessments do not currently play a major role in the clinical management of schizophrenia, except to rule out a possible role of organic factors such as a tumor, stroke, or covert substance abuse. Urine and blood specimens are sometimes obtained in order to evaluate the presence of substance abuse. Similarly, blood samples may be obtained in order to determine whether the patient is compliant with the prescribed antipsychotic medication, although the specific level of medication in the blood has not been conclusively linked to clinical response.

Biological measures are sometimes used to characterize impairments in brain functioning associated with schizophrenia, although these assessments do not have implications for treatment of the illness at this time. For example, CAT scans of the brain indicate that between one-half and two-thirds of all patients with schizophrenia display enlarged cerebral ventricles, indicative of cortical atrophy (Liddle, 1995). Gross structural impairments in brain functioning, such as enlarged ventricles, tend to be associated with a wide range of neuropsychological impairments and negative symptoms often present in schizophrenia (Andreasen, Flaum, Swayze, Tyrrell, & Arndt, 1990; Buchanan et al., 1993; Merriam, Kay, Opler, Kushner, & van Praag, 1990).

To date, most of the advances in understanding the treatment of schizophrenia have been in the area of psychopharmacological developments. Biological assessments are still not useful for diagnosing the illness or for guiding treatment. However, the clinical utility of biological assessment is likely to increase in the years to come as advances continue to be made in the understanding of the biological roots of schizophrenia.

GENDER AND RACIAL-ETHNIC ISSUES

Several issues related to gender are important for understanding the psychopathology in the course of schizophrenia. As described in the section on course and prognosis, women tend to have a milder overall course of schizophrenia than men. The net consequence of this is that, although similar numbers of men and women have schizophrenia, men are more likely to receive treatment for the disorder. In fact, most research on the treatment of schizophrenia is conducted on samples ranging from 70% to 100% male.

Since treatment studies usually sample patients who are currently receiving treatment—often impatient treatment—the efficacy of widely studied psychosocial interventions, such as social skills training and family therapy, has been less adequately demonstrated in women. There is a need for more research on the effects of psychosocial treatments for women with schizophrenia. At the same time, further consideration needs to be given to the different needs of women with this illness. For example, women with schizophrenia are much more likely to marry and have children then are men. It is crucial, therefore, that psychosocial interventions be developed to address the relationship and parenting needs of women with schizophrenia (Apfel & Handel, 1993).

Another issue related to gender in need of further consideration is exposure to trauma. Trauma is becoming increasingly recognized as a significant contributor to adult psychopathology. Only a few studies have been conducted of the prevalence of childhood and adult sexual and physical trauma in persons with severe mental illness, but these surveys indicate that many patients are exposed to trauma (Cascardi, Mueser, DeGirolomo, & Murrin, 1996; Hutchings & Dutton, 1993; Muenzenmaier, Meyer, Struening, & Ferber, 1993). Furthermore, early traumatic exposure can lead to subsequent revictimization, and the intensification of a wide range of symptoms, including posttraumatic stress disorder (Rosenberg, Drake, & Mueser, 1996). As women are more likely to be abused than men, are more likely to sustain injuries, and are more likely to be economically dependent upon perpetrators of domestic violence, there is particular need to recognize and address trauma in the lives of women with schizophrenia. Accurate detection of trauma is further complicated by the fact that most severely mentally ill persons who have been physically or sexually assaulted deny that they have been "abused" (Cascardi et al., 1996). The development of programs that both address the cause of domestic violence and their sequelae, especially for women with schizophrenia, is a priority in this area (see Harris, 1996).

Research on the relationships between race, ethnicity, and severe psychiatric disorders demonstrates that cultural factors are critical to understanding how persons with schizophrenia are perceived by others in their social milieu, as well as the course of the illness. Although the prevalence of schizophrenia is comparable across different cultures, several studies have shown that the course of the illness is more benign in developing countries compared to industrialized nations (Lo & Lo, 1977; Murphy & Raman, 1971; Sartorius, et al., 1986). Westermeyer (1989) has raised questions about the comparability of patient samples in cross-cultural studies, but a consensus remains that the course of schizophrenia tends to be milder in nonindustrialized countries (Jablensky, 1989).

A variety of different interpretations has been offered to account for the better prognosis of schizophrenia in some cultures (Lefley, 1990). It is possible that the strong stigma and social rejection that results from severe mental illness and poses an obstacle to the ability of patients to cope effectively with their disorder and assimilate into society (Fink & Tasman, 1992), is less prominent in some cultures (Parra, 1985). Greater cultural and societal acceptance of the social deviations present in schizophrenia may enable patients to live less stressful and more productive lives. Family ties, in particular, may be stronger in developing countries or in certain ethnic minorities and less vulnerable to the disorganizing effects of mental illness (Lin & Kleinman, 1988). For example, Liberman (1994) has described how the strong functional ties of severely mentally ill persons to their families and work foster reintegration of patients back into society following psychiatric hospitalization. In contrast, until recently, families of patients with schizophrenia in many Western societies were viewed by mental health professionals as either irrelevant, or worse, as causal agents in the development of the illness (Lefley, 1990; Mueser & Glynn, 1995), thus precluding them from a role in psychiatric rehabilitation. Furthermore, the utilization of other social supports may vary across different ethnic groups or cultures, such as importance of the church to the African American community and its potential therapeutic benefits (Griffith, Young, & Smith, 1984; Lincoln & Mamiya, 1990).

Some have hypothesized that different cultural interpretations of the individual's role in society and of the causes of mental illness may interact to determine course and outcome. Estroff (1989) has suggested that the emphasis on the "self" in Western countries, compared to a more family or societally based identification, has an especially disabling effect on persons with schizophrenia, whose sense of self is often fragile or fragmented. Another important consideration is the availability of adaptive concepts for understanding mental illness. For example, *espiritsmo* in Puerto Rican culture is a system of beliefs involving the interactions between the invisible spirit world and the visible world in which spirits can attach themselves to persons (Comas-Díaz, 1980; Morales-Dorta, 1976). Spirits are hierarchically ordered in terms of their moral perfection, and the practice of espiritismo is guided by helping individuals who are spiritually ill achieve higher levels of this perfection. Troubled persons are not identified as "sick" nor are they blamed for their difficulties; in some cases, symptoms such as hallucinations may be interpreted favorably as signs that the person is advanced in his or her spiritual development, resulting in some prestige (Comas-Díaz, 1980). Thus, certain cultural interpretations of schizophrenia may promote more acceptance of persons who display the symptoms of schizophrenia, as well as avoiding the common assumption that these phenomenological experiences are the consequence of a chronic, unremitting condition.

Understanding different cultural beliefs, values, and social structures can have important implications for the diagnosis of schizophrenia. Ethnic groups may differ in their willingness to report symptoms, as illustrated by one study that reported that African American patients were less likely to report symptoms than Hispanics or non-Hispanic whites (Skilbeck, Acosta, Yamamoto, & Evans, 1984). Other studies have found that African Americans are more likely to be diagnosed with schizophrenia than other ethnic groups (e.g., Adams, Dworkin, & Rosenberg, 1984). Knowledge of cultural norms appears critical to avoid the possible misinterpretation of culturally bound beliefs and practices when arriving at a diagnosis. Several studies have shown that ethnic differences in diagnosis vary as a function of both the patient's and the interviewer's ethnicity (Baskin, Bluestone, & Nelson, 1981; Loring & Powell, 1988). Misdiagnosis of affective disorders as schizophrenia is the most common problem with the diagnosis of ethnic minorities in the United States (e.g., Jones, Gray, & Parsons, 1981, 1983).

Cultural differences are also critical in the treatment of schizophrenia, both with respect to service utilization and the nature of treatment provided. There is a growing body of information documenting that ethnic groups differ in their use of psychiatric services. Several studies have indicated that Hispanics and Asian Americans utilize fewer psychiatric services than non-Hispanic whites, whereas blacks utilize more emergency and inpatient services (Cheung & Snowden, 1990; Hough et al., 1987; Hu, Snowden, Jerrell, & Nguyen, 1991; Padgett, Patrick, Burns, & Schlesinger, 1994; Sue, Fujino, Hu, Takeuchi, & Zane, 1991). Aside from culturally based practices that may cause some individuals to seek assistance outside the mental health system (e.g., practitioners of *santeria;* González-Wippler, 1992), access to and retention in mental health services may be influenced by the proximity of mental health services (Dworkin & Adams, 1987) and by the ethnicity of treatment providers. Sue et al. (1991) reported that matching clinician and client ethnicity resulted in higher retention of ethnic minorities in mental health services. Increasing access to needed services for racial and ethnic minorities may require a range of strategies, including ensuring that services are available in the communities where clients live, working with the natural social supports in the community, awareness of relevant cultural norms, and adequate representation of ethnic minorities as treatment providers.

Cultural factors may have an important bearing on psychotherapeutic treatments provided for schizophrenia. Sue and Sue (1990) have described the importance of providing psychotherapy driven by goals that are compatible with clients' cultural norms. This requires both knowledge of subcultural norms, and familiarity with the other social support mechanisms typically available to those clients. Interventions developed for one cultural group may need substantial modification to be effective in other groups. For example, Telles et al. (1995)

reported that behavioral family therapy, which has been found to be effective at reducing relapse in schizophrenia for samples of non-Hispanic white and African American patients (Mueser & Glynn, 1995), was significantly less effective for Hispanic Americans (of Mexican, Guatemalan, and Salvadoran descent) with low levels of acculturation than more acculturated patients. These findings underscore the importance of tailoring psychosocial interventions to meet the unique needs of clients from different cultural backgrounds.

SUMMARY

Schizophrenia is a severe, long-term psychiatric illness characterized by impairments in social functioning, the ability to work, self-care skills, positive symptoms (hallucinations and delusions), negative symptoms (social withdrawal and apathy), and cognitive impairments. Schizophrenia is a relatively common illness, afflicting approximately 1% of the population, and tends to have an episodic course over the lifetime, with symptoms gradually improving over the long term. Most evidence indicates that schizophrenia is a biological illness that may be caused by a variety of factors, such as genetic contributions and early environmental influences (e.g., injuries to the developing fetus). Despite the biological nature of schizophrenia, environmental stress can either precipitate the onset of the illness or symptom relapses. Schizophrenia can be reliably diagnosed with structured clinical interviews, with particular attention paid to the differential diagnosis of affective disorders. There is a high comorbidity of substance use disorders in persons with schizophrenia, which must be treated if positive outcomes are to accrue. Psychological assessment of schizophrenia is most useful when it focuses on behavioral, rather than dynamic dimensions of the illness. Thus, assessments and interventions focused on social skill deficits and family functioning have yielded promising treatment results. Biological assessments are useful at this time primarily for descriptive, rather than clinical purposes. Finally, there are a great many issues related to gender and racial or ethnic factors that remain unexplored. Although schizophrenia remains one of the most challenging psychiatric illnesses to treat, substantial advances have been made in recent years in developing reliable diagnostic systems, understanding the role of various etiological factors, development of effective pharmacological and psychosocial treatments, and the identification of factors that mediate the long-term outcome of the illness, such as stress and substance abuse. These developments bode well for the ability of researchers and clinicians to continue to make headway in treating this serious illness.

REFERENCES

Adams, G. L., Dworkin, R. J., & Rosenberg, S. D. (1984). Diagnosis and pharmacotherapy issues in the care of Hispanics in the public sector. *American Journal of Psychiatry, 141,* 970–974.

Amador, X., Strauss, D., Yale, S., & Gorman, J. M. (1991). Awareness of illness in schizophrenia. *Schizophrenia Bulletin, 17,* 113–132.

American Psychiatric Association. (1994). *Diagnostic and statistical manual of mental disorders* (4th ed.). Washington, DC: Author.

Andreasen, N. C., Flaum, M., Swayze, II, V. W., Tyrrell, G., & Arndt, S. (1990). Positive and negative symptoms in schizophrenia: A critical reappraisal. *Archives of General Psychiatry, 47,* 615–621.

Apfel, R. J., & Handel, M. H. (1993). *Madness and loss of motherhood: Sexuality, reproduction, and long-term mental illness.* Washington, DC: American Psychiatric Press.

Argyle, N. (1990). Panic attacks in chronic schizophrenia. *British Journal of Psychiatry, 157,* 430–433.

Aro, S., Aro, H., & Keskimäki, I. (1995). Socioeconomic mobility among patients with schizophrenia or major affective disorder: A 17-year retrospective follow-up. *British Journal of Psychiatry, 166,* 759–767.

Avison, W. R., & Speechley, K. N. (1987). The discharged psychiatric patient: A review of social, social-psychological, and psychiatric correlates of outcome. *American Journal of Psychiatry, 144,* 10–18.

Bartels, S. J., Teague, G. B., Drake, R. E., Clark, R. E., Bush, P., & Noordsy, D. L. (1993). Substance abuse in schizophrenia: Service utilization and costs. *Journal of Nervous and Mental Disease, 181,* 227–232.

Baskin, D., Bluestone, H., & Nelson, M. (1981). Ethnicity and psychiatric diagnosis. *Journal of Clinical Psychology, 37,* 529–537.

Bateson, G., Jackson, D. D., Haley, J., & Weakland, J. (1956). Toward a theory of schizophrenia. *Behavioral Science, 1,* 251–264.

Baum, K. M., & Walker, E. F. (1995). Childhood behavioral precursors of adult symptom dimensions in schizophrenia. *Schizophrenia Research, 16,* 111–120.

Bellack, A. S., Morrison, R. L., Mueser, K. T., Wade, J. H., & Sayers, S. L. (1990). Role play for assessing the social competence of psychiatric patients. *Psychological Assessment, 2,* 248–255.

Bellack, A. S., Morrison, R. L., Wixted, J. T., & Mueser, K. T. (1990). An analysis of social competence in schizophrenia. *British Journal of Psychiatry, 156,* 809–818.

Bellack, A. S., & Mueser, K. T. (1993). Psychosocial treatment for schizophrenia. *Schizophrenia Bulletin, 19,* 317–336.

Bellack, A. S., Mueser, K. T., Wade, J. H., Sayers, S. L., & Morrison, R. L. (1992). The ability of schizophrenics to perceive and cope with negative affect. *British Journal of Psychiatry, 160,* 473–480.

Bellack, A. S., Sayers, M., Mueser, K. T., & Bennett, M. (1994). An evaluation of social problem solving in schizophrenia. *Journal of Abnormal Psychology, 103,* 371–378.

Bleuler, E. (1911/1950). *Dementia Praecox or the Group of Schizophrenias* (J. Zinkin, Trans.). New York: International Universities Press.

Bond, G. R., McGrew, J. H., & Fekete, D. (1995). Assertive outreach for frequent users of psychiatric hospitals: A meta-analysis. *Journal of Mental Health Administration, 22,* 4–16.

Brown, G. W., & Rutter, M. L. (1966). The measurement of family activities and relationships. *Human Relationships, 19,* 241.

Bruce, M. L., Takeuchi, D. T., & Leaf, P. J. (1991). Poverty and psychiatric status: Longitudinal evidence from the New Haven epidemiologic catchment area study. *Archives of General Psychiatry, 48,* 470–474.

Buchanan, A. (1992). A two-year prospective study of treatment compliance in patients with schizophrenia. *Psychological Medicine, 22,* 787–797.

Buchanan, R. W., Breier, A., Kirkpatrick, B., Elkashef, A., Munson, R. C., Gellad, F., &

Carpenter, W. T. (1993). Structural abnormalities in deficit and nondeficit schizophrenia. *American Journal of Psychiatry, 150,* 59–65.

Cascardi, M., Mueser, K. T., DeGirolomo, J., & Murrin, M. (1996). Physical aggression against psychiatric inpatients by family members and partners: A descriptive study. *Psychiatric Services, 47,* 531–533.

Castle, D. J., & Murray, R. M. (1991). The neurodevelopmental basis of sex differences in schizophrenia [Editorial]. *Psychological Medicine, 21,* 565–575.

Cheung, F. K., & Snowden, L. R. (1990). Community and mental health and ethnic minority populations. *Community Mental Health Journal, 26,* 277–289.

Ciompi, L. (1980). Catamnestic long-term study of life and aging in chronic schizophrenic patients. *Schizophrenia Bulletin, 6,* 606–618.

Clark, R. E. (1994). Family costs associated with severe mental illness and substance use: A comparison of families with and without dual disorders. *Hospital and Community Psychiatry, 45,* 808–813.

Cohen, C. I. (1990). Outcome of schizophrenia into later life: An overview. *Gerontologist, 30,* 790–797.

Comos-Diaz, L. (1981). Puerto Rican espiritismo and psychotherapy. *American Journal of Orthopsychiatry, 51,* 636–645.

Corrigan, P. W., Liberman, R. P., & Engle, J. D. (1990). From noncompliance to collaboration in the treatment of schizophrenia. *Hospital and Community Psychiatry, 41,* 1203–1211.

Corse, S. J., Hirschinger, N. B., & Zanis, D. (1995). The use of the Addiction Severity Index with people with severe mental illness. *Psychiatric Rehabilitation Journal, 19,* 9–18.

Corty, E., Lehman, A. F., & Myers, C. P. (1993). Influence of psychoactive substance use on the reliability of psychiatric diagnosis. *Journal of Consulting and Clinical Psychology, 61,* 165–170.

Cournos, F., Empfield, M., Horwath, E., McKinnon, K., Meyer, I., Schrage, H., Currie, C., & Agosin, B. (1991). HIV seroprevalence among patients admitted to two psychiatric hospitals. *American Journal of Psychiatry, 149,* 1225–1229.

DeSisto, M. J., Harding, C. M., McCormick, R. V., Ashikaga, T., & Brooks, G. W. (1995). The Maine and Vermont three-decade studies of serious mental illness: I. Matched comparison of cross-sectional outcome. *British Journal of Psychiatry, 167,* 331–342.

Douglas, M. S., & Mueser, K. T. (1990). Teaching conflict resolution skills to the chronically mentally ill: Social skills training groups for briefly hospitalized patients. *Behavior Modification, 14,* 519–547.

Drake, R. E., Bartels, S. B., Teague, G. B., Noordsy, D. L., & Clark, R. E. (1993). Treatment of substance abuse in severely mentally ill patients. *Journal of Nervous and Mental Disease, 181,* 606–611.

Drake, R. E., Gates, C., Whitaker, A., & Cotton, P. G. (1985). Suicide among schizophrenics: A review. *Comprehensive Psychiatry, 26,* 90–100.

Drake, R. E., Mueser, K. T., Clark, R. E., & Wallach, M. A. (1996). The course, treatment, and outcome of substance disorder in persons with severe mental illness. *American Journal of Orthopsychiatry, 66,* 42–51.

Drake, R. E., Osher, F. C., Noordsy, D. L., Hurlbut, S. C., Teague, G. B., & Beaudett, M. S. (1990). Diagnosis of alcohol use disorders in schizophrenia. *Schizophrenia Bulletin, 16,* 57–67.

Drake, R. E., Osher, F. C., & Wallach, M. A. (1989). Alcohol use and abuse in schizophrenia: A prospective community study. *Journal of Nervous and Mental Disease, 177,* 408–414.

Drake, R. E., Rosenberg, S. D., & Mueser, K. T. (1996). Assessment of substance use disorder in persons with severe mental illness. In R. E. Drake & K. T. Mueser (Eds.), *Dual diagnosis of major mental illness and substance abuse disorder: II. Recent research and clinical implications* (New Directions in Mental Health Services. No. 70, pp. 3–17). San Francisco: Jossey-Bass.

Dworkin, R. J., & Adams, G. L. (1987). Retention of Hispanics in public sector mental health services. *Community Mental Health Journal, 23,* 204–216.

Eaton, W. W. (1975). Marital status and schizophrenia. *Acta Psychiatrica Scandinavica, 52,* 320–329.

Estroff, S. E. (1989). Self, identity, and subjective experiences of schizophrenia: In search of the subject. *Schizophrenia Bulletin, 15,* 189–196.

Fink, P. J., & Tasman, A. (Eds.) (1992). *Stigma and mental illness.* Washington, DC: American Psychiatric Press.

First, M. B., Spitzer, R. L., Gibbon, M., & Williams, J. B. W. (1995). *Structured Clinical Interview for DSM-IV Axis I disorders–patient edition (SCID-I/P, Version 2.0).* New York: New York State Psychiatric Institute, Biometrics Research Department.

Flor-Henry, P. (1985). Schizophrenia: Sex differences. *Canadian Journal of Psychiatry, 30,* 319–322.

Fox, J. W. (1990). Social class, mental illness, and social mobility: The social selection-drift hypothesis for serious mental illness. *Journal of Health and Social Behavior, 31,* 344–353.

Frith, C. D. (1992). *The cognitive neuropsychology of schizophrenia.* Hove, England: Erlbaum.

Fromm-Reichmann, F. (1950). *Principles of intensive psychotherapy.* Chicago: University of Chicago Press.

Galletly, C. A., Field, C. D., & Prior, M. (1993). Urine drug screening of patients admitted to a state psychiatric hospital. *Hospital and Community Psychiatry, 44,* 587–589.

Glynn, S. M. (1992). Family-based treatment for major mental illness: A new role for psychologists. *California Psychologist, 25,* 22–23.

Goldman, H. H. (1982). Mental illness and family burden: A public health perspective. *Hospital and Community Psychiatry, 33,* 557–560.

Goldstein, J. M. (1988). Gender differences in the course of schizophrenia. *American Journal of Psychiatry, 146,* 684–689.

González-Wippler, M. (1992). *Powers of the orishas: Santeria and the worship of saints.* New York: Original Publications.

Goodwin, F. K., & Jamison, K. R. (1990). *Manic-depressive illness.* New York: Oxford University Press.

Gottesman, I. I. (1991). *Schizophrenia genesis: The origins of madness.* New York: Freeman.

Greden, J. F., & Tandon, R. (Eds.). (1991). *Negative schizophrenic symptoms: Pathophysiology and clinical implications.* Washington, DC: American Psychiatric Press.

Griffith, E. E. H., Young, J. L., & Smith, D. L. (1984). An analysis of the therapeutic elements in a Black church service. *Hospital and Community Psychiatry, 35,* 464–469.

Häfner, H., Riecher-Rössler, A., An Der Heiden, W., Maurer, K., Fätkenheuer, B., & Löffler, W. (1993). Generating and testing a causal explanation of the gender difference in age at first onset of schizophrenia. *Psychological Medicine, 23,* 925–940.

Halford, W. K., Schweitzer, R. D., & Varghese, F. N. (1991). Effects of family environment on negative symptoms and quality of life on psychotic patients. *Hospital and Community Psychiatry, 42,* 1241–1247.

Hans, S. L., Marcus, J., Henson, L., Auerbach, J. G., & Mirsky, A. F. (1992). Interpersonal behavior of children at risk for schizophrenia. *Psychiatry, 55,* 314–335.

Harding, C. M., Brooks, G. W., Ashikaga, T., Strauss, J. S., & Breier, A. (1987a). The Vermont longitudinal study of persons with severe mental illness: I. Methodology, study sample, and overall status 32 years later. *American Journal of Psychiatry, 144,* 718–726.

Harding, C. M., Brooks, G. W., Ashikaga, T., Strauss, J. S., & Breier, A. (1987b). The Vermont longitudinal study of persons with severe mental illness: II. Long-term outcome of subjects who retrospectively met DSM-III criteria for schizophrenia. *American Journal of Psychiatry, 144,* 727–725.

Harris, M. (1996). Treating sexual abuse trauma with dually diagnosed homeless women. *Community Mental Health Journal, 32,* 371–385.

Hatfield, A. B., & Lefley, H. P. (Eds.). (1987). *Families of the mentally ill: Coping and adaptation.* New York: Guilford.

Hatfield, A. B., & Lefley, H. P. (Eds.). (1993). *Surviving mental illness: Stress, coping, and adaptation.* New York: Guilford.

Hollingshead, A. B., & Redlich, F. C. (1958). *Social class and mental illness: A community study.* New York: Wiley.

Holzman, P. S., & Matthysse, S. (1990). The genetics of schizophrenia: A review. *Psychological Science, 1,* 279–286.

Hough, R. L., Landsverk, J. A., Karno, M., Burnam, A., Timbers, D. M., Escobar, J. I., & Regier, D. A. (1987). Utilization of health and mental health services by Los Angeles Mexican Americans and non-Hispanic whites. *Archives of General Psychiatry, 44,* 702–709.

Howard, R., Almeida, O., & Levy R. (1994). Phenomenology, demography, and diagnosis in late paraphrenia. *Psychological Medicine, 24,* 397–410.

Hu, T., Snowden, L. R., Jerrell, J. M., & Nguyen, T. D. (1991). Ethnic populations in public mental health: Services choices and level of use. *American Journal of Public Health, 81,* 1429–1434.

Hutchings, P. S., & Dutton, M. A. (1993). Sexual assault history in a community mental health center clinical population. *Community Mental Health Journal, 29,* 59–63.

Jablensky, A. (1989). Epidemiology and cross-cultural aspects of schizophrenia. *Psychiatric Annals, 19,* 516–524.

Jacob, T. (1975). Family interaction in disturbed and normal families: A methodological and substantive review. *Psychological Bulletin, 82,* 33–65.

Jones, B. E., Gray, B. A., & Parsons, E. B. (1981). Manic-depressive illness among poor urban blacks. *American Journal of Psychiatry, 138,* 654–657.

Jones, B. E., Gray, B. A., & Parsons, E. B. (1983). Manic-depressive illness among poor urban Hispanics. *American Journal of Psychiatry, 140,* 1208–1210.

Kane, J. M., & Marder, S. R. (1993). Psychopharmacologic treatment of schizophrenia. *Schizophrenia Bulletin, 19,* 287–302.

Kavanagh, D. J. (1992). Recent developments in expressed emotion and schizophrenia. *British Journal of Psychiatry, 160,* 601–620.

Keith, S. J., Regier, D. A., Rae, D. S. (1991). Schizophrenic disorders. In L. N. Robins, & D. A. Regier (Eds.), *Psychiatric disorders in America: The Epidemiologic Catchment Area Study* (pp. 33–52). New York: Free Press.

Kendler, K. S., & Diehl, S. R. (1993). The genetics of schizophrenia. *Schizophrenia Bulletin, 19,* 261–285.

Kirch, D. G. (1993). Infection and autoimmunity as etiologic factors in schizophrenia: A review and reappraisal. *Schizophrenia Bulletin, 19,* 355–370.

Kraepelin, E. (1919/1971). *Dementia praecox and paraphrenia* (R. M. Barclay, Trans.). New York: Krieger.

Kramer, M. S., Vogel, W. H., DiJohnson, C., Dewey, D. A., Sheves, P., Cavicchia, S., Litle, P., Schmidt, R., & Kimes, I. (1989). Antidepressants in "depressed" schizophrenic inpatients. *Archives of General Psychiatry, 46,* 922–928.

Kranzler, H. R., Kadden, R. M., Burleson, J. A., Babor, T. F., Apter, A., & Rounsaville, B. J. (1995). Validity of psychiatric diagnoses in patients with substance use disorders: Is the interview more important than the interviewer? *Comprehensive Psychiatry, 36,* 278–288.

Lam, D. H. (1991). Psychosocial family intervention in schizophrenia: A review of empirical studies. *Psychological Medicine, 21,* 423–441.

Lefley, H. P. (1990). Culture and chronic mental illness. *Hospital and Community Psychiatry, 41,* 277–286.

Lehman, A. F., Myers, C. P., Dixon, L. B., & Johnson, J. L. (1994). Defining subgroups of dual diagnosis patients for service planning. *Hospital and Community Psychiatry, 45,* 556–561.

Levinson, D. F., & Levitt, M. M. (1987). Schizoaffective mania reconsidered. *American Journal of Psychiatry, 144,* 415–425.

Levinson, D. F., & Mowry, B. J. (1991). Defining the schizophrenia spectrum: Issues for genetic linkage studies. *Schizophrenia Bulletin, 17,* 491–514.

Liberman, R. P. (1994). Treatment and rehabilitation of the seriously mentally ill in China: Impressions of a society in transition. *American Journal of Orthopsychiatry, 64,* 68–77.

Liberman, R. P., DeRisi, W. J., & Mueser, K. T. (1989). *Social skills training for psychiatric patients.* Needham Heights, MA: Allyn and Bacon.

Liberman, R. P., Mueser, K. T., Wallace, C. J., Jacobs, H. E., Eckman, T., & Massel, H. K. (1986). Training skills in the psychiatrically disabled: Learning coping and competence. *Schizophrenia Bulletin, 12,* 631–647.

Liddle, P. F. (1995). Brain imaging. In S. R. Hirsch & D. R. Weinberger (Eds.), *Schizophrenia* (pp. 425–439). Cambridge, MA: Blackwell.

Lin, K.-M., & Kleinman, A. M. (1988). Psychopathology and clinical course of schizophrenia: A cross-cultural perspective. *Schizophrenia Bulletin, 14,* 555–567.

Lincoln, E. C., & Mamiya, L. H. (1990). *The black church in the African American experience.* Durham, NC: Duke University Press.

Lo, W. H., & Lo, T. (1977). A ten-year follow-up study of Chinese schizophrenics in Hong Kong. *British Journal of Psychiatry, 131,* 63–66.

Loring, M., & Powell, B. (1988). Gender, race, and DSM-III: A study of the objectivity of psychiatric diagnostic behavior. *Journal of Health and Social Behavior, 29,* 1–22.

Magaña, A. B., Goldstein, M. J., Karno, M., Miklowitz, D. J., Jenkins, J., & Falloon, I. R. H. (1986). A brief method for assessing expressed emotion in relatives of psychiatric patients. *Psychiatry Research, 17,* 203–212.

Marengo, J. (1994). Classifying the courses of schizophrenia. *Schizophrenia Bulletin, 20,* 519–536.

Mattes, J. A., & Nayak, D. (1984). Lithium versus fluphenazine for prophylaxis in mainly schizophrenic schizoaffectives. *Biological Psychiatry, 19,* 445–449.

McEvoy, J. P., Freter, S., Everett, G., Geller, J. L., Appelbaum, P., Apperson, L. J., & Roth, L. (1989). Insight and the clinical outcome of schizophrenic patients. *Journal of Nervous and Mental Disease, 177,* 48–51.

Merriam, A. E., Kay, S. R., Opler, L. A., Kushner, S. F., & van Praag, H. M. (1990). Neurological signs and the positive-negative dimension in schizophrenia. *Biological Psychiatry, 28,* 181–192.

Moos, R. H., & Moos, B. S. (1981). *Family Environment Scale manual.* Palo Alto, CA: Consulting Psychologists Press.

Morales-Dorta, J. (1976). *Puerto Rican espiritismo: Religion and psychotherapy.* New York: Vantage.

Muenzenmaier, K., Meyer, I., Struening, E., & Ferber, J. (1993). Childhood abuse and neglect among women outpatients with chronic mental illness. *Hospital and Community Psychiatry, 44*(7), 666–670.

Mueser, K. T., Bellack, A. S., Douglas, M. S., & Morrison, R. L. (1991). Prevalence and stability of social skill deficits in schizophrenia. *Schizophrenia Research, 5,* 167–176.

Mueser, K. T., Bellack, A. S., Douglas, M. S., & Wade, J. H. (1991). Prediction of social skill acquisition in schizophrenic and major affective disorder patients from memory and symptomatology. *Psychiatry Research, 37,* 281–296.

Mueser, K. T., Bellack, A. S., Morrison, R. L., & Wade, J. H. (1990). Gender, social competence, and symptomatology in schizophrenia: A longitudinal analysis. *Journal of Abnormal Psychology, 99,* 138–147.

Mueser, K. T., Bellack, A. S., Morrison, R. L., & Wixted, J. T. (1990). Social competence in schizophrenia: Premorbid adjustment, social skill, and domains of functioning. *Journal of Psychiatric Research, 24,* 51–63.

Mueser, K. T., Bellack, A. S., & Wade, J. H. (1992). Validation of a brief version of the Camberwell Family Interview. *Psychological Assessment, 4,* 524–529.

Mueser, K. T., Bellack, A. S., Wade, J. H., Sayers, S. L., Tierney, A., & Haas, G. (1993). Expressed emotion, social skill, and response to negative affect in schizophrenia. *Journal of Abnormal Psychology, 102,* 339–351.

Mueser, K. T., Bennett, M., & Kushner, M. G. (1995). Epidemiology of substance use disorders among persons with chronic mental illnesses. In A. Lehman & L. Dixon (Eds.), *Double jeopardy: Chronic mental illness and substance abuse* (pp. 9–25). Chur, Switzerland: Harwood Academic.

Mueser, K. T., & Berenbaum, H. (1990). Psychodynamic treatment of schizophrenia: Is there a future? *Psychological Medicine, 20,* 253–262.

Mueser, K. T., Bond, G. R., Drake, R. E., & Resnick, S. G. (in press). Models of community care for severe mental illness: A review of research on case management. *Schizophrenia Bulletin.*

Mueser, K. T., Douglas, M. S., Bellack, A. S., & Morrison, R. L. (1991). Assessment of enduring deficit and negative symptom subtypes in schizophrenia. *Schizophrenia Bulletin, 17,* 565–582.

Mueser, K. T., & Glynn, S. M. (1995). *Behavioral family therapy for psychiatric disorders.* Boston: Allyn and Bacon.

Mueser, K. T., Wallace, C. J., & Liberman, R. P. (1995). New developments in social skills training. *Behaviour Change, 12,* 31–40.

Mueser, K. T., Yarnold, P. R., & Bellack, A. S. (1992). Diagnostic and demographic correlates of substance abuse in schizophrenia and major affective disorder. *Acta Psychiatrica Scandinavica, 85,* 48–55.

Mueser, K. T., Yarnold, P. R., Levinson, D. F., Singh, H., Bellack, A. S., Kee, K., Morrison, R. L., & Yadalam, K. Y. (1990). Prevalence of substance abuse in schizophrenia: Demographic and clinical correlates. *Schizophrenia Bulletin, 16,* 31–56.

Munk-Jørgensen, P. (1987). First-admission rates and marital status of schizophrenics. *Acta Psychiatrica Scandinavica, 76,* 210–216.

Murphy, H. B. M., & Raman, A. C. (1971). The chronicity of schizophrenia in indigenous tropical peoples. *British Journal of Psychiatry, 118,* 489–497.

Nuechterlein, K. H., & Dawson, M. E. (1984). A heuristic vulnerability/stress model of schizophrenic episodes. *Schizophrenia Bulletin, 10,* 300–312.

Padgett, D. K., Patrick, C., Burns, B. J., & Schlesinger, H. J. (1994). Women and outpatient mental health services: Use by black, Hispanic, and white women in a national insured population. *Journal of Mental Health Administration, 21,* 347–360.

Parra, F. (1985). Social tolerance of the mentally ill in the Mexican American community. *International Journal of Social Psychiatry, 31,* 37–47.

Penn, D., Hope, D. A., Spaulding, W. D., & Kucera, J. (1994). Social anxiety in schizophrenia. *Schizophrenia Research, 11,* 277–284.

Penn, D. L., & Mueser, K. T. (1996). Research update on the psychosocial treatment of schizophrenia. *American Journal of Psychiatry, 153,* 607–617.

Regier, D. A., Farmer, M. E., Rae, D. S., Locke, B. Z., Keith, S. J., Judd, L. L., & Goodwin, F. K. (1990). Comorbidity of mental disorders with alcohol and other drug abuse. *Journal of the American Medical Association, 264,* 2511–2518.

Rodrigo, G., Lusiardo, M., Briggs, G., & Ulmer, A. (1991). Differences between schizophrenics born in winter and summer. *Acta Psychiatrica Scandinavica, 84,* 320–322.

Rosenberg, S. D., Drake, R. E., & Mueser, K. T. (1996). New directions for treatment research on sequelae of sexual abuse. *Community Mental Health Journal, 32,* 387–400.

Roy, A. (Ed.). (1986). *Suicide.* Baltimore: Williams and Wilkins.

Rutter, M. L., & Brown, G. W. (1966). The reliability and validity of measures of family life and relationships in families containing a psychiatric patient. *Social Psychiatry, 1,* 38.

Salokangas, R. K. R. (1978). Socioeconomic development and schizophrenia. *Psychiatria Fennica,* 103–112.

Sartorius, N., Jablensky, A., Korten, A., Ernberg, G., Anker, M., Cooper, J. E., & Day, R. (1986). Early manifestations and first-contact incidence of schizophrenia in different cultures. *Psychological Medicine, 16,* 909–928.

Schuckit, M. A. (1989). *Drug and alcohol abuse: A clinical guide to diagnosis and treatment* (3rd ed.). New York: Plenum.

Searles, H. (1965). *Collected papers on schizophrenia and related subjects.* New York: International Universities Press.

Skilbeck, W. M., Acosta, F. X., Yamamoto, J., & Evans, L. A. (1984). Self-reported psychiatric symptoms among black, Hispanic, and white outpatients. *Journal of Clinical Psychology, 40,* 1184–1189.

Stone, A., Greenstein, R., Gamble, G., & McLellan, A. T. (1993). Cocaine use in chronic schizophrenic outpatients receiving depot neuroleptic medications. *Hospital and Community Psychiatry, 44,* 176–177.

Sue, S., Fujino, D. C., Hu, L.-T., Takeuchi, D. T., & Zane, N. W. S. (1991). Community mental health services for ethnic minority groups: A test of the cultural responsiveness hypothesis. *Journal of Consulting and Clinical Psychology, 59,* 533–540.

Sue, D. W., & Sue, D. C. (1990). *Counseling the culturally different: Theory and practice* (2nd ed.). New York: Wiley.

Susser, E., & Lin, S. (1992). Schizophrenia after prenatal exposure to the Dutch Hunger Winter of 1944–1945. *Archives of General Psychiatry, 49,* 983–988.

Susser, E. Struening, E. L., & Conover, S. (1989). Psychiatric problems in homeless men: Lifetime psychosis, substance use, and current distress in new arrivals at New York City shelters. *Archives of General Psychiatry, 46,* 845–850.

Telles, C., Karno, M., Mintz, J., Paz, G., Arias, M., Tucker, D., & Lopez, S. (1995). Immigrant families coping with schizophrenia: Behavioral family intervention v. case management with a low-income Spanish-speaking population. *British Journal of Psychiatry, 167,* 473–479.

Terkelsen, K. G. (1983) Schizophrenia and the family: II. Adverse effects of family therapy. *Family Process, 22,* 191–200.

Tessler, R., & Gamache, G. (1995). *Evaluating family experiences with severe mental illness: To be used in conjunction with the Family Experiences Interview Schedule (FEIS): The Evaluation Center @ HSRI toolkit* [Computer software]. Cambridge, MA: The Evaluation Center @ HSRI.

Tienari, P. (1991). Interaction between genetic vulnerability and family environment: The Finnish adoptive family study of schizophrenia. *Acta Psychiatrica Scandinavica, 84,* 460–465.

Tienari, P., Sorri, A., Lahti, I., Naarala, M., Wahlberg, K., Moring, J., Pohjola, J., & Wynne, L. C. (1987). Genetic and psychosocial factors in schizophrenia: The Finnish Adoptive Family Study. *Schizophrenia Bulletin, 13,* 477–484.

Torrey, E. F. (1995). *Surviving schizophrenia: A manual for families, consumers, and providers* (3rd ed.). New York: Harper Collins.

Torrey, E. F., Bowler, A. E., Rawlings, R., & Terrazas, A. (1993). Seasonality of schizophrenia and stillbirths. *Schizophrenia Bulletin, 19,* 557–562.

Torrey, E. F., Stieber, J., Ezekiel, J., Wolfe, S. M., Sharfstein, J., Noble, J. H., & Flynn, L. M. (1992). *Criminalizing the seriously mentally ill: The abuse of jails as mental hospitals* (Joint Report). Arlington, VA: National Alliance of the Mentally Ill; and Washington, DC: Public Citizen's Health Research Group.

Tsuang, M. T. (1986). Predictors of poor and good outcome in schizophrenia. In L. Erlenmeyer-Kimling & N. E. Miller (Eds.), *Life-span research on the prediction of psychopathology.* Hillsdale, NJ: Earlbaum.

Walker, E., Downey, G., & Caspi, A. (1991). Twin studies of psychopathology: Why do the concordance rates vary? *Schizophrenia Research, 5,* 211–221.

Waxler, N. E., & Mishler, E. G. (1971). Parental interaction with schizophrenic children and well siblings. *Archives of General Psychiatry, 25,* 223–231.

Westermeyer, J. (1989). Psychiatric epidemiology across cultures: Current issues and trends. *Transcultural Psychiatric Research Review, 26,* 5–25.

Yesavage, J. A., & Zarcone, V. (1983). History of drug abuse and dangerous behavior in inpatient schizophrenics. *Journal of Clinical Psychiatry, 44,* 259–261.

Zigler, E., & Glick, M. (1986). *A developmental approach to adult psychopathology.* New York: Wiley.

Zubin, J., & Spring, B. (1977). Vulnerability: A new view of schizophrenia. *Journal of Abnormal Psychology, 86,* 103–126.

CHAPTER 8

Mood Disorders: Depressive Disorders

PATRICIA A. AREÁN, JOHN MCQUAID, and RICARDO F. MUÑOZ

The cluster of mood disorders called depressive disorders is characterized by features such as sadness, difficulty performing daily activities, feelings of hopelessness and helplessness, and diminished interest in life. These disorders are quite common and research in this area has a long scientific history (Brown & Harris, 1978). For instance, descriptions of depressive disorders can be found in the earliest medical documents, including the Eber papyrus from ancient Egypt.

Because depressive disorders have such a long history and are so common, the term *depression* has come to describe emotional experiences ranging from the occasional periods of sadness that are common in life to the clinical syndromes we will be discussing in this chapter. It is perhaps because of the common use of the term depression that many people do not realize how serious this disorder can be. For example, one depressive condition, major depressive disorder (the most severe and most studied of depressive disorders), is consistently related to increased morbidity and physical illness (Wells, Stewart, & Hayes, 1989). Major depression has a greater impact on physical functioning, role functioning, pain, and disability than do medical illnesses such as hypertension, diabetes, and lung disease (Wells et al., 1989). Moreover, symptoms of depression increase the likelihood that its victims will attempt to take their own life: 15% of depressed individuals commit suicide (Teuting, Koslow, & Hirschfeld, 1981). In the United States, the yearly number of deaths by suicide consistently exceeds the number of deaths by homicide (U.S. Bureau of the Census, 1994).

The etiology of depressive disorders has long been debated. Thus far, we know that there are multiple causes of depression and that no one factor is solely responsible. Psychological, social, genetic, and biological factors all play a role in its development and course. Therefore, the intellectual effort dedicated to understanding and learning to control depression must be multidisciplinary. Learning to recognize and treat the different depressive disorders is a fundamental skill for any practitioner of psychology, psychiatry, or medicine to learn.

DESCRIPTION OF THE DISORDERS

Diagnostic classification systems are used to differentiate symptom patterns into diagnostic classes. Many diagnostic systems exist, but by far the most popular in this century is the fourth edition of the *Diagnostic and Statistical Manual of Mental Disorders* (DSM-IV; American Psychiatric Association [APA], 1994). DSM-IV provides a list of symptoms differentiating mood disorders under the section "Mood Disorders (Depressive Disorders)." DSM-IV lists two specific disorders and an additional, heterogeneous diagnostic category: major depressive disorder, dysthymia, and depressive disorder not otherwise specified.

All depressive disorders share clinical features from three categories. Depressive disorders are typically accompanied by vegetative symptoms. These symptoms are lack of appetite (which invariably leads to weight loss), insomnia, fatigue, social withdrawal, and agitation. Cognitive symptoms of depression include difficulty concentrating and making decisions about mundane things (such as whether to get out of bed or not); low self-esteem; negative thoughts about self, the world, and others; guilt; suicidal ideation; and in severe cases, hallucinations and delusions. The most notable group of symptoms are mood symptoms. These include feeling sad, empty, worried, hopeless, and irritable.

Major Depression

Major depressive disorder (MDD) is the most serious depressive disorder and the most widely studied. A diagnosis of MDD requires at least one major depressive episode, with no history of mania. A major depressive episode consists of at least five out of nine possible symptoms (listed in Table 8.1) being present during the same period, which must last 2 weeks or more. The symptoms must be a change from previous functioning and must be severe enough to cause "clinically significant distress" or to interfere with the individual's social or occupational functioning. At least one of the first two symptoms on the list must be present, most of the day, nearly every day, during the episode.

A number of qualifiers are used to clarify the severity, chronicity, and type of depressive symptom. For instance, MDD is different than sadness brought on by the loss of a loved one. A diagnosis is not appropriate if symptoms of depression follow bereavement and do not persist for longer than 2 months after a loss. If a manic episode (see Chap. 9 for a description) has ever been present, then the depressive episode is part of a bipolar disorder (another Axis I disorder) and is not a depressive disorder. If a medical disorder is present that is known to cause symptoms of depression (e.g., hyperthyroidism), then the symptoms are classified as depression due to a general medical condition. If substance abuse, such as alcoholism or drug abuse, is co-occurring, the official diagnosis is depression due to substance use.

MDD is further specified by four dimensions: chronicity, recurrence, severity, and remission status. MDD is considered chronic if one meets full criteria for a major depressive episode for at least 2 years. Recurrence refers to the number of separate times that an individual has had a major depressive episode. If a person has had more than one episode, then the diagnosis is MDD, recurrent. Recurrent episodes are described as with or without full interepisode recovery,

TABLE 8.1   DSM-IV Symptoms Required for Major Depressive Disorder and Dysthymia

Disorder	Symptoms
Major depressive disorder: Five of nine symptoms must be present most of the day, nearly every day, for at least 2 weeks:	1. Depressed mood 2. Diminished interest or pleasure in all, or almost all, activities (One of the above is required.) 3. Significant weight loss or weight gain or a decrease or increase in appetite 4. Insomnia or hypersomnia 5. Psychomotor agitation or retardation 6. Fatigue or loss of energy 7. Feelings of worthlessness or excessive or inappropriate guilt 8. Diminished ability to think or concentrate or to make decisions 9. Recurrent thoughts of death, suicidal ideation, plans, or attempts
Dysthymia: Depressed mood most days, for most of the week for 2 years; Two or more of these six symptoms:	1. Poor appetite or overeating 2. Insomnia or hypersomnia 3. Low energy or fatigue 4. Low self-esteem 5. Poor concentration or difficulty making decisions 6. Feelings of hopelessness

with seasonal pattern (if episodes occur regularly and only during certain seasons of the year), and with rapid cycling (if there have been at least four episodes in the previous 12 months). Severity (mild, moderate, or severe) defines how disabled the person is by the depression. This qualifier includes describing the person's ability to perform everyday activities, cognitive processes, and risk of harm to self. If someone is depressed but can continue working and going about their usual activities, then the episode is mild. If the person has difficulty getting out of bed, can no longer perform social activities and is becoming more vegetative, then the episode is moderate. If the person has thoughts of death or dying, or a plan to harm themselves, is no longer able to function, and has persecutory thoughts, including hallucinations and delusions, then the episode is severe. Another diagnostic qualifier includes the presence of psychotic features. Hallucinations or delusions can be described as either mood congruent (delusions that are consistent with symptoms of depression, such as believing in being punished by God) or mood incongruent (hallucinations and delusions that have no depressive or guilt content).

To reflect variation within depressive disorders, the DSM-IV includes several subtypes. Catatonia is relatively rare in depressive disorders. This symptom pattern includes immobility, odd and repetitive motor activity, extreme negativism or mutism, and bizarre posturing. Melancholia is characterized by lack of reactivity to pleasurable stimuli, depression regularly worse in the morning, and excessive guilt. Atypical features include brightening of mood in response to actual or potential positive events, weight gain, hypersomnia, heavy, leaden feelings in arms or legs, and interpersonal rejection sensitivity.

Dysthymia

Dysthymic disorder consists of a pattern of chronic depression (lasting 2 years or more) but is not as intense as major depression. Unlike MDD, dysthymia has only one typical presentation. Because of its relatively constant course, there is some controversy regarding whether dysthymia should be considered a specific disorder and listed under Axis I or a personality disorder and listed under Axis II. The criteria for dysthymia are listed in Table 8.1. The symptoms of dysthymia must not be absent for more than 2 months at a time during the 2-year period that defines the episode. Additionally, no major depressive episode during the first 2 years of dysthymia should have occurred, although one could be superimposed thereafter. The symptoms must not be due exclusively to other disorders (including medical conditions) or to the direct physiological effects of a substance (including medication). As in MDD, the person must not have ever met criteria for manic episode, hypomanic episode, or cyclothymic disorder. If dysthymia occurs prior to age 21, it is described as having early onset, otherwise, it is described as having late onset.

Depressive Disorder Not Otherwise Specified

This category includes several depressive conditions currently under research investigation. Clinicians do not officially accept them as discrete disorders. These include: premenstrual dysphoric disorder, a mood disorder that may be related to hormonal fluctuations in the female menstrual cycle; minor depressive disorder, depressive episodes lasting for at least 2 weeks, but with fewer than five symptoms needed to meet criteria for major depressive episode; recurrent brief depressive disorder, repeated episodes of depression that last for a period of less than 2 weeks; postpsychotic depressive disorder of schizophrenia, depression that sometimes follows a psychotic episode; major depressive episode superimposed on psychotic or delusional disorders, depression that co-occurs with a psychotic disorder; and depression due to general medical conditions, situations in which depressive disorders are thought to be present but cannot be determined to be primary, due to medical conditions, or due to substance use.

Of all of the depressive disorders, the most researched and understood disorders are MDD and, to a lesser degree, dysthymia. Because the other disorders mentioned are not well researched with regard to prevalence, course, prognosis and assessment, we will focus the remainder of this chapter on MDD and dysthymia.

EPIDEMIOLOGY

We know that depressive disorders are among the oldest psychiatric disorders. But how common, or prevalent, are they? Over the years, the measurement of psychiatric disorders has improved, and we can now, with a modicum of certainty, estimate the rates of depression. The following discussion will present the prevalence of depressive disorders in different populations. We will discuss the reports from two landmark epidemiological studies, the Epidemiological

Catchment Area Study (ECA; Regier et al., 1988; Robins & Regier, 1991) and the National Comorbidity Study (NCS; Kessler et al., 1994). These studies differ in their method of psychiatric assessment and in their method of population sampling, and therefore estimates vary between them. However, both studies provide important information regarding the prevalence of MDD and dysthymia.

Prevalence

Community Samples

Estimates of lifetime prevalence rates, or the number of persons who have *ever* experienced a major depressive episode, range from 6% (Weissman, Bruce, Leaf, Florio, & Holzer, 1991, p. 64) to 17% (Kessler et al., 1994, p. 12). These studies also indicate that in a given 12-month period, approximately 4%–10% of the general population will experience a major depressive episode (Kessler et al., 1994, p. 12; Weissman et al., 1991, p. 64).

The lifetime prevalence rates for dysthymia are lower than the rates of major depression. According to the ECA, approximately 3% of the general population have met diagnostic criteria for dysthymia in their lifetime. The NCS estimate of lifetime rates for dysthymia is 6%.

Prevalence by Gender

Both the ECA and the NCS show greater prevalence of depression in women than in men. Lifetime prevalence rates of major depression for adult women range from 7% (Weissman et al., 1991, p. 66) to 21% (Kessler et al., 1994, p. 12) and between 4% and 8% for dysthymia. For men, lifetime rates of major depression range between 3% (Weissman et al., 1991) to 13% (Kessler et al., 1994) and between 2% and 5% for dysthymia. The above differences in rates between men and women have been found repeatedly throughout the world and thus appear to be accurate reflections of true differences in the prevalence of the disorder (Klerman & Weissman, 1989). There is no consensus regarding the reason for the differences. Many theories have been put forth, including biological differences, differences in cognitive and behavioral patterns of mood control (Nolen-Hoeksema, 1987), and social influences, including differential expectations for the two genders. These issues are discussed further in the Gender, Ethnic, and Racial Issues section of this chapter.

Prevalence by Age Cohort

Age cohorts also have different prevalence rates. The ECA reports lifetime prevalence rates for major depression for four age groups: 18–29, 5.0%; 30–44, 7.5%; 45–64, 4.0%; and 65+, 1.4%. The rates of dysthymia for the same four groups are, respectively, 3.0%, 3.8%, 3.6%, and 1.7% (Weissman et al., 1991, p. 66). The NCS sampled only individuals up to age 54. They report lifetime rates for "any affective disorder" in terms of odds ratios (the greater the ratio, the greater the prevalence rate) for four age groups: 15–24, 0.85; 25–34, 0.97; 35–44, 1.06; and 45–54, 1.00.

Burke, Burke, Rae, and Regier (1991) suggest that the differences in prevalence rates are due to a cohort effect (differences due to generation). The prevalence rate of depression in the United States has increased steadily since after World War II: each 10-year cohort reports earlier onset of depression, and a higher rate throughout the life span (Klerman & Weissman, 1989). These apparent increases have been examined carefully and are found in several epidemiological databases. The reason for the increase, if it is real, cannot be due to changes in the genetic pool (the rate of change is too rapid). Other proposed explanations include increased stress in society and increased awareness of the disorder.

Treatment Utilization

An important finding of the ECA is that most patients with depressive disorders do not go to mental health professionals but to primary care settings. Primary care settings may be an important location in which to identify and intervene with major depression. Data from the ECA project indicate that only between 16% and 23% of those who meet diagnostic criteria for affective disorders go to a mental health professional for treatment (Regier et al., 1993; Shapiro, Skinner, & Kessler, 1984), but that over 75% of those meeting diagnostic criteria for depression do receive some type of health care from some physical health care provider. The result is that nearly half (48%) of persons who receive an intervention for a depressive disorder are treated by general physicians (Narrow et al., 1993). In fact, depression is currently one of the most common of disorders (not just mental disorders, but all disorders) found in primary care (Katon, 1982; Katon, Kleinman, & Rosen, 1982). This suggests that primary care settings can play an important role in the treatment, detection, and diagnosis of depressive disorders (Depression Guideline Panel, 1993). Care must be taken to ensure that mental health professionals with experience in the diagnosis and treatment of depression are involved in these efforts (Muñoz, Hollon, McGrath, Rehm, & VandenBos, 1994).

Epidemiologic Clues for the Prevention of Major Depression

The Institute of Medicine's Committee on Prevention of Mental Disorders (Mrazek & Haggerty, 1994) has suggested that epidemiological data may be useful in instituting selected preventive interventions that can target segments of the population at the age at which most individuals at risk have not yet developed the disorder to be prevented. For example, data from the ECA indicate that within the group of individuals who eventually developed a major depressive episode, 20% had their first sign or symptom by age 19 and a full-blown episode by age 25; 50% had their first sign of symptom by age 26 and a full-blown episode by age 39 (Mrazek & Haggerty, 1994, p. 91). It is clear, then, that preventive interventions that occur prior to age 25 could avert as many as 80% of cases of major depression. By age 40, over half of the cases of major depression will already have taken place. As preventive interventions in the mental health area are developed and evaluated (Muñoz & Ying, 1993) the timing and the choice of populations at risk will benefit much from epidemiological information.

CLINICAL PICTURE

The DSM-IV provides the clinician with a description of depressive disorders but does not provide a description of the depressive experience. In order to understand these disorders from the depressed person's point of view, one must go beyond the symptom pattern and familiarize oneself with how this disorder affects the person's life and with the factors that are related to being depressed. Because of the prevalence, cost, and suffering caused by depression, a great deal of research exists to help understand the factors related to these disorders.

One of the more intriguing issues of major depression is the question of etiology. These are disorders that appear to be driven by social and environmental, psychological, and biological factors. Once the disorder has begun, further changes in the above mentioned factors function to help maintain and exacerbate a current episode. Because most research into the factors that influence these disorders has been on MDD, our discussion will pertain to that particular disorder.

Social and Environmental Factors

For years, theorists have speculated about the impact social and environmental factors have on the development and maintenance of MDD. A range of variables have been identified and among the most salient factors related to MDD are positive and negative life events and social support (how many people an individual can rely on for help during troubled times).

Life Events

Most theories of depression emphasize that negative and positive life events contribute to depression. Research indicates that people who are depressed have more recent negative life events over a year prior to an episode than people who are not depressed (Paykel, 1983). Significant life events that have impact on depression include such events as poor marital functioning (Lewinsohn, Hoberman, & Rosenbaum, 1988). However, recent life events alone do not account for the onset of depression. While social stress plays an important role in the development of an initial episode, life events appear to be less influential in later episodes during the course of an illness (Post, 1992).

Early life events were also found to have a role in the etiology of depression. According to Harris, Brown, and Bifulco (1990), loss of a parent before the age of 17 years is associated with increased risk for developing a major depressive episode and for feeling helpless in stressful situations. The impact of early parental loss, however, was not substantial in the absence of a stressful, provoking agent.

A limitation to studies on life events is the fact that they tend to be retrospective; that is, we know that some people who are depressed have had an early loss or a recent stressor, but we do not know that everyone who has had an early loss or recent stressor becomes depressed. Scientists speculate that indeed not everyone who has stressful events becomes depressed. In fact, many theorists strongly believe that life events interact with other social, psychological, and biological factors to instigate an episode of depression.

Social Support

A consistent theme in depressed individuals arises: People who are depressed often report being lonely and socially isolated. A number of studies show that having a strong supportive group of friends can offset the occurrence of depression in the face of a stressful life event (Brown & Harris, 1978). For instance, Moos and colleagues have demonstrated that people who do not have 1. a supportive family (Holahan & Moos, 1987), 2. supportive social resources (Billings & Moos, 1985), 3. a large number of friends, and 4. have a number of impaired relationships (Billings, Cronkite, & Moos, 1983) are more likely to be depressed than those who have supportive family and a large number of positive relationships. Perception of support is important, too. Wethington and Kessler (1986) conducted a study to understand the relationship between perceived support (how supportive people expect their friends and family to be) and received support (subject's report of actual supportive behavior by individuals) and found that perceived support and number of severe life events in the past year predicted an increased number of symptoms of depression. Costello and Angold (1988) found that the presence of a confidant decreased the risk that a severe life event would provoke depression, which suggests that social support buffers the impact of negative life stress.

Psychological Factors

While social support and life events are important factors in depression, they are not the only important ones. Researchers have found that two types of psychological factors, namely, cognitive variables and social skills are both important factors in whether people will be depressed or not.

Cognitive Variables

A number of studies have shown that people who are depressed tend to view themselves, the world, and others in a more negative manner than nondepressed people (Beck, et al., 1979). For instance, in addition to social support and negative life events, Lewinsohn, Hoberman, and Rosenbaum (1988) found that negative cognitive factors such as poor self-esteem (one's regard for one's self), irrational beliefs (faulty beliefs about oneself, the world and others), and poor locus of control (the degree people believe they control outcomes in their life), predicted depression. Research shows that people with depression also tend to expect failure and disappointment and feel that most events in their lives merely confirm these beliefs (Elliott, 1992; Hayslip, Galt, Lopez, & Nation, 1995; Mahoney, 1993; Muran & Motta, 1993).

Recent research into the cognitive realm of depression has gone a step further to suggest that beliefs are organized around particular personality structures. Several theories of depressive etiology postulated that these cognitive vulnerabilities play a role in the onset of depression (Abramson, Metalsky, & Alloy, 1989; Beck, 1982; Blatt, Quinlan, Chevron, McDonald, & Zuroff, 1982). The general theory is that individuals have particular cognitive styles, such as being focused on achievement or interpersonal interaction. When individuals experience life events that match their vulnerability, they are at increased risk for depression. Researchers have used a variety of terms to label the cognitive vulnerabilities that are related to depression. Some individuals are hypothesized to derive self-worth from interpersonal interactions. These persons have been referred to as having interpersonal (Hammen, Ellicot, & Gitlin, 1989), sociotropic (Beck, 1982), or dependent (Blatt et al., 1982) cognitive styles. Other individuals are hypothesized to derive self-worth from their personal achievements. Researchers have described this personality style as achievement focused (Hammen et al., 1989), autonomous (Beck, 1982), or self-critical (Blatt et al., 1982).

Several researchers have demonstrated a relationship between cognitive style and vulnerability. Robins and Block (1988) found that negative interpersonal events predicted concurrent depressive symptoms in a sample of college students. In addition, they reported an interaction between interpersonal events and interpersonal (dependent) personality style. They found no effect for achievement events and no interaction with achievement-focused (autonomous) personality style. Additionally, Hammen et al. (1989) found that a match between personality style and life event predicted increased depressive symptoms. This was true for both interpersonal and achievement-focused personality styles.

Coping Skills

Other researchers have found that people who are depressed tend to have poor coping skills (Folkman, Lazarus, Pimely, & Novacek, 1987). The research on the effect of one's coping skills in dealing with problems has yielded evidence that poor or passive coping skills tend to be related to depression (Folkman et al., 1987). The research indicates that people who are depressed tend to have deficits in the area of interpersonal skills (which could account for the lack of social support depressed individuals have), and social problem-solving abilities (Heppner & Anderson, 1985; Lewinsohn, 1975; Nezu, Nezu, & Perri, 1989).

According to Lewinsohn, depression is related to the lack of positive reinforcement in one's life and a deficit in skills to enhance positive social interactions. Indeed, research has shown that depressed individuals tend to be unassertive (Sanchez & Lewinsohn, 1980), have fewer social contacts, are more socially anxious (Youngren & Lewinsohn, 1980), and are generally less socially skilled (Lewinsohn, Mischel, Chaplin, & Barton, 1980). Therefore, people who are skilled in social interactions are able to cope with interpersonal problems without becoming depressed, whereas those who are not adept at social skills are more likely to be devastated by an interpersonal problem. However, the research on cognitive vulnerabilities mentioned above seems to indicate that depression is not simply due to being socially unskilled but is due to the interaction of this lack of skill and the importance one places on socialization. Because of these recent findings, many theorists now agree that level of social skills interacts with the person's perception of the importance of social events to predict depression.

Biological Factors

The literature is replete with research into the biological determinants of depression. Among the biological theories of depression are neurotransmitter hypotheses and neuroendocrine hypotheses.

Neurotransmitter Hypotheses

Even though the role neurotransmitters (chemicals found in the central and peripheral nervous systems) play in mood regulation has long been studied, the research in this area is still ongoing and the role of these chemicals is poorly understood. Research into this area evolved from clinical observations of medications that were known to deplete certain neurotransmitters. One drug, reserpine (an antihypertensive medication), was known to deplete stores of norepinephrine and serotonin. Clinicians began to notice that the patients on this medication exhibited symptoms of depression, and hence, neurobiologists began to conduct research into the effect these two neurotransmitters have on depressed mood. Initially, these theorists believed that depression was due to a deficit in norepinephrine and serotonin. We now know that depression is due to a dysregulation of these neurotransmitters rather than a deficiency of these biochemicals. There is some evidence that depressed individuals have too many neuronal-receptor sites (areas of the neuron that absorb neurotransmitters to create or inhibit behavior) for serotonin and norepinephrine, thus diluting these neurotransmitter mood-regulating properties. There is also evidence that use of antidepressants that increase the flow of serotonin are effective, not because of an increase in these neurotransmitters, but because they decrease the number of available receptor sites. While this information is compelling, many scientists agree that neurotransmitter dysregulation is only part of the picture because neurotransmitter abnormalities such as those just described may not always lead to depressed mood.

Neuroendocrine Hypotheses

Research into neuroendocrinology is still in its infancy. There is evidence to suggest that people who are depressed have too much cortisol (a naturally occurring steroid) in their systems. For instance, one study found that about 40%–50% of patients with major depression had an abnormally high plasma, or blood, level of cortisol. Additionally, abnormalities in thyroid functions are often related to symptoms of depression, further indicating an important role for the neuroendocrine system in depression. While this preliminary evidence is compelling, the role neuroendocrines play in depression is far from established. For instance, it is still unclear whether change in neuroendocrine secretion is a function of the disorder or is a precursor of depression.

Summary

Many theorists and researchers believe that depressive disorders are primarily caused by one factor, whether biological, social, or psychological. The most likely scenario is that depression is caused by interactions among all the factors. There is growing support for the belief that people with MDD may be biologically predisposed to react in a depressed way but do not become depressed unless faced with a life stressor and are unable to cope with that stressor, either by seeking support from friends, problem-solving, or perceiving themselves as able to cope with the problem.

FAMILIAL AND GENETIC CONSIDERATIONS

Research in psychopathology has benefited greatly from the genetic revolution. Studies designed to detect the genetic contribution to depressive disorders have served to increase the complexity of our understanding of MDD. Compared to bipolar disorder or schizophrenia, the evidence for a significant genetic component to MDD is weaker. Nonetheless, MDD is influenced to some degree by genetics.

The primary approaches to studying genetic contributions to psychopathology are family studies, twin studies, and adoption studies. The belief is that researchers will be able to factor out the contribution of genetics to disease from environmental influences by comparing concordance (correlation) rates of depression in identical, or monozygotic (MZ), twins and fraternal, or dizygotic (DZ), twins. It is believed that observing rates of disorders from parents to offspring will also allow us to clarify the role genetics has in depression. While the study of genetics is far from perfect, results from such work are useful in identifying familial patterns in depressive disorders. Studies investigating the rates of depression among twins indicate that MZ twins have greater concordance rates of depression than do DZ twins (Englund & Klein, 1990). As an example of such research, MacKinnon, Henderson, and Andrews (1990) examined level of depressive symptoms and the lability of those symptoms over time in 462 twin pairs. They found that in MZ twins, the correlation between both twins having MDD was .38 while the correlation between DZ twins was significantly lower, at .13. Although these correlations suggest some genetic contribution, they are significantly smaller than those reported in studies for other Axis I disorders, such as bipolar disorder.

Family studies also lend some support for a genetic contribution to depression. Wender et al. (1986) examined the rates of psychiatric disorders in the biological and adoptive relatives of adoptees. They found that the biological relatives of adoptees who had mood disorders (either major depression, bipolar disorder, or dysthymia) had an eightfold increase in the risk for major depression and an increased risk for bipolar disorders. In addition, there was a greatly increased likelihood of suicide in biological relatives. However, there was not a significantly increased risk for dysthymia or other psychiatric disorders. Kupfer, Frank, Carpenter, and Neiswanger (1989) examined the rates for depression, alcoholism, and bipolar disorder, in first degree relatives of 179 patients with recurrent unipolar depression. They found that relatives had a 20.7% risk of MDD and that female relatives were at a higher risk for unipolar depression, while male relatives were at a higher risk for alcoholism when compared to people with no family history of depression.

The moderate relationship of genetic factors to depression has led to speculation regarding whether genetic vulnerability interacts with other factors to increase the likelihood of depression. One project has examined the interaction of genetic risk and life stress. Kendler et al. (1995) tested the hypothesis that a genetic liability interacted with life stress to provoke the onset of depression. They followed 1,030 female twin pairs (590 monozygotic, 440 dizygotic) from the Virginia Twin Registry, recording life stress and onset of depressive episode. Both siblings were interviewed regarding life stress and depression at an initial interview and a follow-up, on average 17.3 months later. Both genetic liability and stress predicted an increased risk of depression. In addition, there was an interaction effect: the increased risk produced by stress was greater for patients with a genetic vulnerability than those without. It appears that the effect of genetics on the risk for depression is due in part to an increased vulnerability to life stress.

COURSE AND PROGNOSIS

No one has ever conducted a longitudinal study of the course of untreated MDD. What we know of the course and prognosis of MDD has been learned from case studies, patient self-reports, and retrospective studies. In general, we know that MDD is a recurrent disorder in which each episode lasts for an average of 6 months. Patients who have had one episode of MDD have a 50% chance of experiencing a second. People with two previous episodes run a 70% chance of developing a third. Those who have had three episodes of MDD have a 90% chance of developing a fourth episode (DPC, 1993). Several researchers have found that *symptoms* of depression increase one's likelihood of becoming depressed. For instance, Lewinsohn et al. (1988) found that depressive symptoms predicted the onset of depression within 8 months of their onset. Dryman and Eaton (1991) found that symptoms such as diminished sex drive, worthlessness, excessive guilt, and trouble concentrating all predicted an episode of MDD.

Given early recognition and treatment with either antidepressant medication, psychotherapy, or both, MDD can be overcome. Most treatment studies find that between 40% and 60% of people in any kind of treatment recover from their episode (Kupfer et al., 1992; Shea, Elkin, et al., 1992). However, 36% of those who respond to treatment suffer a relapse (a subsequent episode of MDD) within 2 years of ending therapy (Evans, 1992; Shea, Elkin, et al., 1992). Thus, many scientists are interested in the factors that predict treatment response and relapse.

Response to Treatment

In most controlled studies, treatment responders follow a particular pattern. Most treatment responders tend to show improvement by the 8th week of treatment, tend not to have any other Axis I or II disorder, are married, and have fewer residual symptoms of depression after treatment ends (Shea, Elkin, et al., 1992; Shea, Widiger & Klein, 1992; Thase et al., 1992; Thase & Simons, 1992). Parker, Tennant, and Blignault (1985) found that a breakup of a relationship and weight loss prior to treatment were related to poorer treatment outcome and that positive life events after treatment were related to maintained improvement 20 weeks posttreatment. Monroe, Kupfer, and Frank (1992) found that severe life events before treatment, measured by interview rather than by a checklist, predicted *poorer* treatment response. An important issue in these studies is that they intentionally focused on people with recurrent depression (history of at least three prior depressive episodes); subjects in previous studies had a range of episodes. The results suggest that life events may have different implications for recurrent depressives than other patients, at least for treatment outcome. It appears, then, that those patients who respond best to treatment have fewer premorbid life events, are married, and show a relatively quick response to treatment.

Brown, Adler, and Bifulco (1988) examined the role of life events and difficulties in the recovery of a population of women experiencing depressive episodes that had lasted 12 months or more. They found that recovery from depression was predicted by decreases in difficulties (ongoing stressors of a month or more) and increases in "fresh start" events (events that promise a change for the better in a person's life). Interestingly, these effects occurred independent of whether patients were receiving treatment.

Relapse

With regard to relapse from treatment, some of the same factors related to treatment response also predict relapse. Thase et al. (1992) found that people who have residual symptoms of depression after treatment tend to have greater relapse rates than those who do not. Patients with Axis II symptoms are more likely to suffer a relapse (Shea, Elkin, et al., 1992). In a review of the literature of relapse, Belsher and Costello (1988) found that life events, social support, and cognitive vulnerabilities also predict relapse, and they concluded that there is evidence that the probability of relapsing decreases as the time since the last episode increases. Moreover, relapse is more common for patients with more extensive histories of depression.

In summary, depressive disorders tend to be recurrent but show a reasonably good response to treatment. Research is still needed to investigate the best methods for treating people who have had a long history of depression, who have Axis II disorders, and who are slow responders to treatment. Overall, people who are treated early for depression, develop strong social networks, and who respond quickly to interventions are less likely to have recurrent episodes of depression. Unfortunately, little is known about exactly how many people who seek treatment for depression fit into this category.

DIAGNOSTIC CONSIDERATIONS

The DSM-IV provides a guideline to help clinicians and researchers decide whether a person meets criteria for a particular depressive disorder. While these guidelines appear to make the diagnosis of depression a straightforward task, the presence of other medical and psychiatric disorders can complicate a diagnostic decision. As we stated in the description of depressive disorders section, before mental health professionals can make a diagnosis of any depression, they need to consider the person's physical health, the medications they are taking, family and personal history, and medical history. These considerations are important because part of the importance of diagnosis is determining the most appropriate treatment for the client. A misdiagnosis can result in mismanagement of a case.

Medical Illness

A typical issue of importance is to consider whether the person was medically ill before onset. This question is particularly salient because many medical illnesses are related to the onset of a depressive episode and treatment for these medical disorders can often alleviate depressive symptoms (Miranda, Areán, & Rickman, 1993). Endocrinological disorders like hyper- and hypothyroidism have as one of the diagnostic signs a change in affect and mood. People with chronic illnesses like diabetes mellitus have high rates of depressive disorder (Wilkinson et al., 1988). In addition, acute medical illnesses such as stroke (Starkstien et al., 1991), Parkinson's disease (Starkstein & Robinson, 1989), pancreatic cancer (Holland et al., 1986), and myocardial infarction (Fielding, 1991) have all been found to have direct and indirect causal links to increased depressive disorder. Thus, a physical examination is an important part of assessing the etiology of a depressive disorder.

Drug and Alcohol Abuse

Another important diagnostic consideration is the extent to which a person drinks alcohol or uses drugs. Often substance abuse/dependence disorders are comorbid, that is occur together, with depressive symptoms (Kessler et al., 1994; Penick et al., 1994). Current literature suggests that depressive symptoms can be a consequence of substance use and of the problems that can occur from substance abuse. This literature also suggests that using drugs or alcohol can also serve as a means of "self-medicating" symptoms of depression (Batki, 1990). Because of the common co-occurrence of substance abuse and depression, an assessment of these disorders should be conducted so that treatment for substance abuse can be implemented.

Grief and Bereavement

A third consideration is if a particular stressor, such as the death of someone close or a change in role and life functioning, has occurred recently. Two states, uncomplicated bereavement and adjustment disorder, have many symptoms of depression, such as uncontrolled crying, periods of sadness, and loss of interest in daily activities. People with these problems are not considered to have a depressive disorder and therefore may be helped best by understanding that their symptoms are common reactions to their recent stress. However, people who have lost a spouse or have suffered a major change in their life that requires adjustment to the situation can still become depressed, and therefore any symptoms of depression should be evaluated carefully. For instance, if a widow's grief is so severe that she no longer eats, sees friends, or can care for herself, then she does not have a simple case of bereavement and needs appropriate psychiatric services.

Depression Due to Other Psychiatric Disorders

Another consideration in diagnosing depressive disorders is that they share symptoms with other psychiatric disorders. All the mood disorders have some features of depression, and many people with Axis II, or personality disorders, have features of depression during an acute exacerbation of their episode. Recurrent episodes of MDD are common in bipolar disorder (please see Chap. 9 for details). People with Axis II, or personality disorders, such as dependent personality and borderline personality, often have episodes of major depression, but the current belief is that the primary problem is the personality disorder, not the depression. Many studies investigating the efficacy of short-term treatments for depression have found that participants with personality disorders were least likely to respond to treatment and most likely to relapse from treatment success (Thase & Simons, 1992). These findings suggest that the psychosocial treatments currently recommended for treating MDD may be less effective for people with personality disorders.

In summary, determining whether a person has a depressive disorder or not is not easy. Many questions must be asked in order to clarify the clinical picture so that appropriate intervention can take place.

ASSESSMENT OF DEPRESSION

A variety of devices exist which measure depression. These devices can be grouped into instruments that measure the severity of depression and those that serve to classify whether a patient meets criteria for a DSM-IV depressive disorder or not. This section focuses on the different methods for assessing depression and the manner in which one should assess for a depressive disorder.

Assessing Depressive Disorders

Before discussing the instruments to be used in assessing for a depressive disorder, it is important to discuss the details of interviewing depressed patients. First and foremost, instruments used to assess depression, whether for severity or to determine a diagnosis, should be both valid (measure the construct the instrument is meant to measure) and reliable (consistently measure the construct). Without valid and reliable measures, it would be difficult to assess with certainty the extent of people's depression, what symptoms should be targeted in treatment, and whether treatments given to depressed people are indeed effective in reducing symptoms (Vallis, Shaw, & McCabe, 1988).

Second, an interviewer must keep in mind that single symptoms do not constitute a whole disorder. For instance, improvement in mood symptoms does not mean that changes in psychosocial, biological functioning, or both have taken place. An interviewer must be sure to assess all facets of a depressed person's life. Not only should one ask about symptoms of depression but how these symptoms have affected the person's quality of life and social functioning. A thorough assessment does not use one measure of depression but incorporates into the assessment questions about daily functioning, health, and social activities.

Third, interviewing depressed patients takes experience and skill. The interviewer must pay attention not only to the patient's report of symptoms and behavior but to the patient's behavior during the interview. Often, nonverbal behavior is as important as what the patient says. Most depressed patients tend to have little eye contact, have a slumped body posture, and take a long time to respond to questions. They can often become tearful and are easily discouraged by difficult tasks or questions (Shaw et al., 1985). In addition, obtaining an understanding of depression from the point of view of the patient is also important. Sometimes patient reports may seem overly negativistic or extreme. However, given that this is the person's perspective of the world and his or her life, it is important not to argue this view or seem unbelieving of this view, as the interviewer runs the risk of alienating an already overly sensitive patient.

Often, the scope of the interview is such that the interviewer will have to interrupt the patient from time to time. People with depressive disorders tend to be overly sensitive to this kind of behavior, so it is very important to describe to the patient *before the interview starts* exactly what will happen during the course of the interview, and that at times the interviewer may interrupt the patient.

A final point: asking about suicidal ideation is extremely important. Some may feel that by asking patients if they have had thoughts of hurting themselves will put the idea into the patients' heads. *No* research has supported this particular belief. In fact, asking about and discussing suicidal ideation with patients could prevent patients who are suicidal from hurting themselves. If an interviewer never asks patients if they are suicidal, the interviewer will never have the chance to discuss alternative resources and solutions with a patient planning to kill him- or herself.

Screening Instruments

The idea of screening patients for depression comes from medical practice, where physicians routinely conduct medical tests when they suspect a patient has a particular illness. These screening tests help the doctor rule out whether further tests are needed to make a specific diagnosis. For instance, when a patient sees a doctor about symptoms of fatigue, the physician may order blood and urine tests to determine whether the fatigue is due to anemia, diabetes, or mononucleosis. Standardized screening instruments are used for similar purposes in psychiatry. Screening instruments should be highly sensitive; that is, they should ideally detect depression in *everyone* with the disorder, even if in the process, they identify some people who do not have the disorder. The most common mechanism for detecting depression is through self-report measures, such as the Beck Depression Inventory (Beck et al., 1961), the Center for Epidemiological Studies Depression Scale (Radloff, 1977), and the Geriatric Depression Scale (Yesavage et al., 1983). These instruments are completed by the patient and hand scored by the person administering the scale. A patient's score on the instrument reflects the severity of depression. These instruments are considered cost-effective and easy to administer. Patients answer questions about depressive symptoms, and the clinician adds up the answers. The problem with screening instruments is that they tend to overestimate the number of people who are depressed and therefore result in a large number of false positives (people who are depressed according to the scale but who do not meet diagnostic criteria).

To offset the problem of overidentification, brief diagnostic interviews have been developed. These instruments are similar to self-report measures, except that they are intended to be more specific; that is, they only identify someone who is truly depressed as depressed. For example, computer-assisted instruments such as the Quick Diagnostic Interview Schedule and the Computerized Diagnostic Schedule are self-report measures that specify symptoms directly related to the symptom clusters of DSM-IV. These screening devices are more accurate but unfortunately are quite expensive. Often, a computer is needed to administer the interview.

Structured and Semistructured Clinical Interviews

As in medicine, once a person is screened for depression, it is important to ascertain whether his or her reported symptoms constitute a true episode of MDD or dysthymia. This process usually involves a much lengthier interview conducted by a clinician or intake worker trained in the DSM-IV. Because of the time involved and the level of expertise needed to conduct this level of assessment, such procedures are expensive and cannot be administered to everyone presenting to a clinic.

The most common method of making a final determination of depression is to use the clinical judgment of a mental health professional such as a psychiatrist, psychologist, or social worker. While this methodology is optimal, it is also expensive. Many mental health workers do not work in settings where a depressed person is most likely to go (i.e., medical clinics) and hiring such individuals to work in these clinics can be very costly. Therefore, other mechanisms for determining a diagnosis of MDD or dysthymia have been developed. These instruments, called structured clinical interviews, were originally designed to be used in research settings but can be used in clinical practice. Below is a description of two popular interviews, the Structured Clinical Interview for DSM-IV and the Diagnostic Interview Schedule.

Structured Clinical Interview for DSM-IV (SCID)

This instrument (Spitzer, Williams, Gibbon, & First, 1992) is a semistructured clinical interview to be administered by staff trained in its use. The SCID has a long history and has been continuously reformulated to be easier and more accurate. In its current form, the interview is divided into a number of sections: a historical overview of the presenting complaint, a screening list to determine beforehand whether the patient has symptoms of MDD, alcohol or substance abuse, obsessive-compulsive disorder and anxiety disorders, and the different diagnostic modules reflecting all the Axis I diagnoses of DSM-IV. While the SCID has been used extensively in research studies, it has only fair validity and reliability. According to the SCID's creators, this instrument has only a kappa coefficient of agreement equal to .31 in nonpatient samples, indicating poor validity (ability to accurately identify a disorder; Spitzer et al., 1992). The main advantage to using the SCID is its structured nature, which decreases the amount of variation in diagnosis from clinician to clinician. However, it is still a costly instrument that requires a specially trained staff.

Diagnostic Interview Schedule for DSM-IV (DIS)

This structured and standardized instrument (Robins, Helzer, Croughan, & Ratcliff, 1981) was developed in the early 1970s to be used for the Epidemiological Catchment Area Studies. It has been amended to reflect changes in the DSMs and is now computerized so that either a lay interviewer can ask patients questions or patients can read the questions themselves. This instrumentation addresses a number of issues. First, after the initial cost to purchase the program and train the staff, the administration of the DIS is relatively cheap and convenient as a screening instrument. It is fairly valid and comes in both English and Spanish. The downside of the DIS is the initial cost (as much as $800.00 per software copy) and the cost of a computer to run the program. Also, the DIS can take anywhere from 30 minutes to 3 hours, depending on the number of symptoms the patient endorses. Because of the length, some studies have suggested that the DIS creates a tendency for the patient to deny symptoms to shorten the interview.

Summary

The assessment of depression is not easy. In order to do an accurate and thorough job an interviewer must not simply look for clusters of symptoms but also obtain a history of the disorder and the impact symptoms of depression have on the quality of life and social adjustment of the person suffering from depression. In deciding on a particular method to assess for depression (clinical interview vs. self-report measure), the choice should be based on whether the interviewer is interested in making a DSM-IV diagnosis (hence a clinical interview) or if the interviewer is interested in assessing the severity of the depressive disorder (hence a self-report measure). We believe the best method is to include *both* types of assessment in addition to assessments of quality of life, social adjustment, and daily functioning. In other words, it is important to assess the whole person, not just the symptoms he or she is experiencing.

GENDER AND ETHNIC ISSUES

Our discussion about depressive disorders has largely been informed by research conducted on primarily white and middle to upper class individuals. However, the reader should become familiar with how gender and ethnicity may affect assessment, prevention, and treatment of depressive disorders.

Gender

As described in the section on epidemiology, above, about twice as many women as men report the symptoms of depressive disorders. This finding is consistent across cultures and nations, suggesting that differential prevalence rates cannot be explained solely by societal factors (unless, of course, there are factors which have differential impacts on women and men across all, or nearly all, societies). Some theorists believe that hormonal dysregulation may account for the increased prevalence rates seen in women and that by having another diagnostic category, such as premenstrual dysphoric disorder, the rates of MDD and dysthymia will begin to resemble those of men (Steen, 1991). Others suggest that gender differences are due primarily to the fact that men and women respond differently to personal stress. For example, women may have a greater tendency to allow themselves to experience the negative mood states, while men may be more likely to use coping mechanisms that involve distracting oneself from the emotional pain. This hypothesis stems in part from the observation that, although women have higher rates of major depression, men have higher rates of substance abuse and antisocial behavior. In the ECA, men were found to have substantially greater rates in two disorders—alcohol abuse and antisocial personality. Women, on the other hand, had substantially higher rates in three disorders, major depressive episode, somatization disorder, and obsessive-compulsive disorder (Robins & Regier, 1991, p. 351). It may be possible, then, that when experiencing negative mood states, men either "medicate" their depression with drugs or strike out at others. These theorists suggest that men may have the same rates of problems with mood regulation, but that substance abuse may be masking their presence (Weissman & Klerman, 1977). Depression in women has been found to have a different course and prognosis. For instance, women tend to have longer periods of depression, have lower response rates to antidepressant medications, and have more medical comorbidity than do men (Pajer, 1995). Interestingly, men and women have similar response rates to psychotherapies like cognitive-behavioral therapy, although men are more likely than women to skip therapy sessions (Thase et al., 1994). A good review of the risk factors and treatment issues related to women (including women of color) is found in McGrath, Keita, Strickland, and Russo (1990).

Ethnicity

Much has been written about the differences in depression across different ethnic groups. These differences refer to something as basic as whether the experience of depression may actually differ subjectively, perhaps because of cultural influences (Kleinman & Good, 1985), whether there are differences in symptom pictures across cultural groups (Mezzich & Raab, 1980), whether depression measures are valid when one crosses language and cultural boundaries (Marsella, 1987), and whether even responses to pharmacological treatment may vary across ethnic groups (Lin, Poland, & Nakasaki, 1993).

The resulting data are still quite complex, and the student or practitioner should remember that what is known about depression will need to be carefully reconsidered when working with groups that have not been part of the mainstream literature on research or practice.

Rates of major depression have been found to be lower for black respondents in both the ECA and the NCS and higher for current affective disorders for Hispanics in the NCS. Specifically, ECA estimates of lifetime prevalence for whites, blacks, and Hispanics, respectively, were 5.1%, 3.1%, and 4.4% for major depression, and 3.3%, 2.5%, and 4.0% for dysthymia (Weissman et al., 1991, p.

66). The NCS lifetime rates for any affective disorders (presented in terms of odds ratios) for whites, blacks, and Hispanics were 1.00, 0.63, and 0.96, and 12-month prevalence rates were 1.00, 0.78, and 1.38 (Kessler et al., 1994, pp. 11–12). The black lifetime rate was significantly lower than the other two, and the Hispanic 12-month rate was significantly higher than the other two. The NCS also found that blacks had lower prevalences for substance abuse disorders, and that in no case were either lifetime or current prevalence rates higher among blacks than whites. These effects appear not to be due to income or educational differences. The NCS did not replicate the ECA finding of higher rates of alcohol use disorder in Hispanics than whites (Kessler et al., 1994).

It must be remembered that ethnic groups can be quite heterogenous. For example, an analysis of the rates of major depression among Mexican Americans, Cubans, and Puerto Ricans has detected greater lifetime prevalence of major depressive episode in the latter (4.2%, 3.9%, and 8.9%, respectively; Moscicki, Rae, Regier, & Locke, 1987).

Utilization of mental health services may also differ among groups. For example, ECA data from Los Angeles suggest that among individuals who meet criteria for major depression, Mexican Americans are only half as likely as non-Hispanic whites to seek mental health care (Hough et al., 1987). This utilization pattern has led to suggestions that services for ethnic minority groups should be evaluated in terms of cultural responsiveness, which has been shown to be related to length of treatment and treatment outcomes (Sue et al., 1991). Such innovations as combining prevention and treatment services may help to increase utilization and reduce the total number of depressed persons by reducing both incidence and prevalence (Muñoz, 1995).

Research into ethnic factors which affect major depression is still in its infancy. For example, a review of psychotherapy studies with Latino participants found only one randomized trial focused on depression (Navarro, 1993). The relatively small proportion of minorities in even large-scale randomized trials has prompted calls for greater attention to the recruitment and retention of low-income minorities in treatment studies (Miranda, Azocar, Organista, Muñoz, & Lieberman, in press). A similar focus on the appropriateness of assessment instruments is in order. There is considerable evidence that instruments used to detect the presence of depression are not as reliable or valid as they are in White populations (Azocar, Areán, Miranda, & Muñoz, 1993; Iwamasa, Areán, Miranda, & Muñoz, 1993; Marin & Marin, 1991). Therefore, caution should be exercised when using depression inventories in different ethnic groups. As minorities become larger segments of the population, there will be a need to obtain more detailed information on the patterns of depression across different ethnic and cultural groups. Such studies may help to shed light on the nature of depression, and on those aspects which are relatively universal, and those which can be modified by environmental and cultural influences.

SUMMARY

Depressive disorders are common and widely studied. Although we have accumulated much knowledge regarding MDD and dysthymia, research continues to address the best means of recognizing depression, of treating depression in different settings and in different cultures, and of further clarifying the etiology of these disorders. Thus far, we know that depressive disorders tend to be recurrent and are affected by a variety of factors, including life stress, biological, genetic, and psychological factors, and that once recognized, these disorders can be treated successfully. However, additional research is needed to better understand gender and ethnic differences in depressive disorders.

REFERENCES

Abramson, L. Y., Metalsky, G. L., & Alloy, L. B. (1989). Hopelessness depression: A theory-based subtype of depression. *Psychological Review, 96,* 358–372.

American Psychiatric Association. (1994). *Diagnostic and statistical manual of mental disorders* (4th ed.). Washington DC: Author.

Azocar, F., Areán, P. A., Miranda, J., & Munoz, R. (1993, July). *Differential item functioning of a Spanish translation of the Beck Depression Inventory.* Paper presented at International Congress of Psychology, Santiago, Chile.

Batki, S. L. (1990). Substance abuse and AIDS: The need for mental health services. *New Directions for Mental Health Services, 48,* 55–67.

Beck, A. T. (1982). Cognitive therapy of depression: New perspectives. In P. Clayton & J. Barrett (Eds.), *Treatment of depression: Old controversies and new approaches* (pp. 265–290). New York: Raven.

Beck, A. T., Rush, A. J., Shaw, B. E., & Emery, G. (1979). *Cognitive theory of depression.* New York: Guilford.

Beck, A. T., Ward, C. H., Mendelson, M., Mock, L., & Erbaugh, J. (1961). An inventory for measuring depression. *Archives of General Psychiatry, 4,* 561–571.

Belsher, G., & Costello, C. G. (1988). Relapse after recovery from unipolar depression: A critical review. *Psychological Bulletin, 104,* 84–96.

Billings, A. G., Cronkite, R. C., & Moos, R. H. (1983). Social-environmental factors in unipolar depression: Comparisons of depressed patients and nondepressed controls. *Journal of Abnormal Psychology, 92,* 119–133.

Billings, A. G., & Moos, R. H. (1985). Life stressors and social resources affect posttreatment outcomes among depressed patients. *Journal of Abnormal Psychology, 94,* 140–153.

Blatt, S., Quinlan, D., Chevron, E., McDonald, C., & Zuroff, D. (1982). Dependency and self-criticism: Psychological dimensions for depression. *Journal of Consulting and Clinical Psychology, 50,* 113–124.

Brown, G. W., Adler, Z., & Bifulco, A. (1988). Life events, difficulties, and recovery from chronic depression. *British Journal of Psychiatry, 152,* 487–498.

Brown, G. W., & Harris, T. (1978). *Social origins of depression.* London: Tavistock.

Burke, K. C., Burke, J. D., Rae, D. S., & Regier, D. A. (1991). Comparing age at onset of major depression and other psychiatric disorders by birth cohorts in five U.S. community populations. *Archives of General Psychiatry, 48,* 789–795.

Costello, E. J., & Angold, A. (1988). Scales to assess child and adolescent depression: Checklists, screens, and nets. *Journal of the American Academy of Child and Adolescent Psychiatry, 27,* 726–737.

Depression Guideline Panel. (1993). *Depression in primary care: Vol. 1. Detection and Diagnosis* (Clinical Practice Guideline No. 5, AHCPR Publication No. 93-0550).

Rockville, MD: Department of Health and Human Services, Public Health Service, Agency for Health Care, Policy, and Research.

Dryman, A., & Eaton, W. W. (1991). Affective symptoms associated with the onset of major depression in the community: Findings from the U.S. National Institute of Mental Health Epidemiologic Catchment Area Program. *Acta Psychiatrica Scandanavica, 84,* 1–5.

Elliott, J. E. (1992). Compensatory buffers, depression, and irrational beliefs. *Journal of Cognitive Psychology, 49,* 166–176.

Englund, S. A., & Klein, D. N. (1990). The genetics of neurotic-reactive depression: A reanalysis of Shapiro's (1970) twin study using diagnostic criteria. *Journal of Affective Disorders, 18,* 247–252.

Evans, M. D., Hollon, S., DeRubeis, R. J., Piasecki, J. M., Grove, W. M., Garvey, M. J., & Tuason, V. B. (1992). Differential relapse following cognitive therapy and pharmacotherapy for depression. *Archives of General Psychiatry, 49,* 802–808.

Fielding, R. (1991). Depression and acute myocardial infarction: A review and reinterpretation. *Social Science Medicine, 32,* 1017–1027.

Folkman, S., Lazarus, R. S., Pimely, S., & Novacek, J. (1987). Age differences in stress and coping processes. *Psychology and Aging, 2,* 171–184.

Fry, P. (1989). Mediators of perceptions of stress among community based elders *Psychological Reports, 65,* 307–314.

Golding, J., & Lipton, P. (1990). Depressed mood and major depressive disorder in two ethnic groups. *Journal of Psychiatric Research, 24,* 65–82.

Hammen, C., Ellicot, A., & Gitlin, M. (1989). Vulnerability to specific life events and prediction of course of disorder in unipolar depressed patients: Special issue. *Canadian Journal of Behavioral Sciences, 21,* 377–388.

Harris, T. O., Brown, G. W., & Bifulco, A. T. (1990). Depression and situational helplessness/mastery in a sample selected to study childhood parental loss. *Journal of Affective Disorders, 20,* 27–41.

Hayslip, B., Galt, C., Lopez, F., & Nation, P. (1995). Irrational beliefs and depressive symptoms among younger and older adults: A cross-sectional comparison. *International Journal of Aging and Human Development, 38,* 307–326.

Heppner, P. P., & Anderson, W. P. (1985). The relationship between problem-solving self-appraisal and psychological adjustment. *Cognitive Therapy and Research, 25,* 366–375.

Holahan, C. J., & Moos, R. H. (1987). Risk, resistance, and psychological distress: A longitudinal analysis with adults and children. *Journal of Abnormal Psychology, 96,* 3–13.

Holland, J. C., Korzun, A. H., Tross, S., Silberfarb, P., Perry, M., Comis, R., & Oster, M. (1986). Comparative psychological disturbance in patients with pancreatic and gastric cancer. *American Journal of Psychiatry, 143,* 982–986.

Hough, R., Landsverk, J., Karno, M., Burnam, M., Timbers, D., Escobar, J., & Regier, D. (1987). Utilization of health and mental health services by Los Angeles Mexican Americans and non-Hispanic whites. *Archives of General Psychiatry, 44,* 702–709.

Iwamasa, G., Areán, P. A., & Miranda, J. (1993, August). *Item bias in the CES-D and BDI in African Americans and Asian Americans.* Paper presented at conference of American Psychological Association, Toronto, Canada.

Katon, W. (1982). Depression: Somatic symptoms and medical disorders in primary care. *Comprehensive Psychiatry, 23,* 274–287.

Katon, W., Kleinman, A., & Rosen, G. (1982). Depression and somatization: A review, 1. *American Journal of Medicine, 72,* 127–135.

Kendler, K. S., Kessler, R. C., Walters, E. E., MacLean, C., Neale, M. C., Heath, A. C., & Eaves, L. J. (1995). Stressful life events, genetic liability, and onset of an episode of major depression in women. *American Journal of Psychiatry, 152,* 833–842.

Kessler, R. C., McGonagle, K. A., Shanyang, Z., Nelson, C. B., Hughes, M., Eshleman, S., Wittchen, H. U., & Kendler, K. S. (1994). Lifetime and 12-month prevalence of DSM-III-R psychiatric disorders in the United States: Results from the National Comorbidity Survey. *Archives of General Psychiatry, 51,* 8–19.

Kleinman, A., & Good, B. (1985). *Culture and depression.* Berkeley; CA: University of California Press.

Klerman, G. L., & Weissman, M. M. (1989). Increasing rates of depression. *Journal of the American Medical Association, 261,* 2229–2235.

Kupfer, D. J., Frank, E., Carpenter, L. L., & Neiswanger, K. (1989). Family history of recurrent depression. *Journal of Affective Disorders, 17,* 113–119.

Kupfer, D. J., Frank, E., Perel, J. M., Cornes, C., Mallinger, A. G., Thase, M. E., McEachran, A. B., & Grochocinski, V. J. (1992). Five-year outcome for maintenance therapies in recurrent depression. *Archives of General Psychiatry, 49,* 769–773.

Lewinsohn, P. M. (1975). The behavioral study and treatment of depression. In M. Hersen, R. M. Eisler, & P. M. Miller (Eds.), *Progress in behavior modification* (Vol. 1). New York: Academic Press.

Lewinsohn, P. M., Hoberman, H. M., & Rosenbaum, M. (1988) A prospective study of risk factors for unipolar depression. *Journal of Abnormal Psychology, 97,* 251–264.

Lewinsohn, P. M., Mischel, W., Chaplin, W., & Barton, R. (1980). Social competence and depression: The role of illusory self-perceptions. *Journal of Abnormal Psychology, 89,* 203–212.

Lin, K. M., Poland, R. E., & Nakasaki, G. (Eds.). (1993). *Psychopharmacology and psychobiology of ethnicity.* Washington, DC: American Psychiatric Press.

MacKinnon, A. J., Henderson, A. S., & Andrews, G. (1990). Genetic and environmental determinants of the lability of trait neuroticism and the symptoms of anxiety and depression. *Psychological Medicine, 20,* 581–590.

Mahoney, M. J. (1993). Introduction to special section: Theoretical developments in the cognitive psychotherapies. *Journal of Consulting and Clinical Psychology, 61,* 187–193.

Marín, G., & Marín, B. (1991). *Research with Hispanic populations* (Vol. 23). Newbury Park, NJ: Sage.

Marsella, A. J. (1987). The measurement of depressive experience and disorder across cultures. In A. J. Marsella, R. M. A. Hirschfeld, & M. M. Katz (Eds.), *The measurement of depression* (pp. 376–397). New York: Guilford.

McGrath, E. Keita, G. P., Strickland, B., & Russo, N. F. (Eds.). (1990). *Women and depression: Risk factors and treatment issues.* Washington, DC: American Psychological Association.

Mezzich, J. E., & Raab, E. S. (1980). Depressive symptomatology across the Americas. *Archives of General Psychiatry, 37,* 818–823.

Miranda, J., Areán, P., & Rickman, R. (1994). Relationship of mental health and medical disorders in primary care. In J. Miranda, C. Attkisson, & A. Homann (Eds.), *Mental health and primary care.* San Francisco: Jossey-Bass.

Miranda, J., Azocar, F., Organista, K. C., Muñoz, R. F., & Lieberman, A. (in press). Recruiting and retaining low-income Latinos in psychotherapy research. *Journal of Consulting and Clinical Psychology.*

Monroe, S. M., Kupfer, D. J., & Frank, E. (1992). Life stress and treatment course of recurrent depression: I. Response during index episode. *Journal of Consulting and Clinical Psychology, 60,* 718–724.

Moscicki, E. K., Rae, D. S., Regier, D. A., & Locke, B. Z. (1987). The Hispanic Health and Nutrition Examination Survey: Depression among Mexican Americans, Cuban Americans, and Puerto Ricans. In M. Gaviria & J. D. Arana (Eds.), *Health and behavior: Research agenda for Hispanics* (pp. 145–159). Chicago: University of Illinois.

Mrazek, P., & Haggerty, R. (1994). *Reducing risks for mental disorders: Frontiers for preventive intervention research.* Washington, DC: National Academy.

Muñoz, R. F. (1995). Toward combined prevention and treatment services for major depression. In C. Telles & M. Karno (Eds.), *Latino mental health: Current research and policy perspectives* (pp. 183–200). Los Angeles: UCLA Neuropsychiatric Institute.

Muñoz, R. F., Hollon, S. D., McGrath, E., Rehm, L. P., & VandenBos, G. R. (1994). On the AHCPR *Depression in Primary Care* guidelines: Further considerations for practitioners. *American Psychologist, 49,* 42–61.

Muñoz, R. F., & Ying, Y. (1993). *The prevention of depression: Research and practice.* Baltimore: Johns Hopkins University Press.

Muran, E., & Motta, R. (1993). Cognitive distortions and irrational beliefs. *Journal of Clinical Psychiatry, 49,* 166–176.

Narrow, W. E., Regier, D. A., Rae, D. S., Manderscheid, R. W., & Locke, B. Z. (1993). Use of services by persons with mental and addictive disorders: Findings from the National Institute of Mental Health Epidemiological Catchment Area Program. *Archives of General Psychiatry, 50,* 95–107.

Navarro, A. M. (1993). Efectividad de las psicoterapias con Latinos en los Estados Unidos: Una revision meta-analítica. *Interamerican Journal of Psychology, 27,* 131–146.

Nezu, A. M., Nezu, C. M. & Perri, M. G. (1989). *Social problem-solving therapy for depression: Theory, research, & practice.* New York: Wiley.

Nolen-Hoeksema, S. (1987). Sex differences in unipolar depression: Evidence and theory. *Psychological Bulletin, 101,* 259–282.

Pajer, K. (1995). New strategies in the treatment of depression in women. *Journal of Clinical Psychiatry, 56,* 30–37.

Parker, G., Tennant, C., & Blignault, I. (1985). Predicting improvement in patients with nonendogenous depression. *British Journal of Psychiatry, 146,* 132–139.

Paykel, E. S. (1983). Methodological aspects of life events research. *Journal of Psychosomatic Research, 27,* 341–352.

Penick, E. C., Powell, B. J., Nickel, E. J., Bingham, S. F., Riesny, K. R., Read, M. R., & Campbell, J. (1994). Comorbidity of lifetime psychiatric disorders among male alcoholic patients. *Alcoholism, Clinical and Experimental Research, 18,* 1289–1293.

Post, R. M. (1992). Transduction of psychosocial stress into neurobiology of recurrent affective disorder. *American Journal of Psychiatry, 149,* 999–1010.

Radloff, L. S. (1977). The CES-D scale: A self-report depression scale for research in the general population. *Applied Psychological Measurement, 1,* 385–401.

Regier, D. A., Boyd, J. H., Burke, J. D., Rae, D. S., Myers, J. K., Kramer, M., Robins, L. N., George, L. K., Karno, M., & Locke, B. Z. (1988). One-month prevalence of mental disorders in the United States. *Archives of General Psychiatry, 45,* 977–986.

Regier, D. A., Framer, M. E., Rae, D. S. Myers, J. K., Kramer, M., Robins, L. N., George, L. K., Karno, M., & Locke, B. Z. (1993). One-month prevalence of mental disorders in the United States and sociodemographic characteristics: The Epidemiological Catchment Area Study. *Acta Psychiatrica Scandinavica, 88,* 35–47.

Robins, C. J., & Block, P. (1988). Personal vulnerability, life events, and depressive symptoms: A test of a specific interactional model. *Journal of Personality and Social Psychology, 54,* 847–852.

Robins, L. N., Helzer, J. E., Croughan, J., & Ratcliff, K. S. (1981). National Institute of Mental Health–Diagnostic Interview Schedule: Its history, characteristics, and validity. *Archives of General Psychiatry, 38,* 381–389.

Robins, L. N., & Regier, D. A. (Eds.). (1991). *Psychiatric disorders in America: The Epidemiologic Catchment Area Study.* New York: Free Press.

Sanchez, V., & Lewinsohn, P. M. (1980). Assertive behavior and depression. *Journal of Consulting and Clinical Psychology, 48,* 119–120.

Shapiro, S., Skinner, E. A., & Kessler, L. G. (1984). Utilization of health and mental health service: Three Epidemiological Catchment Area sites. *Archives of General Psychiatry, 41,* 978.

Shaw, B. (1985). Closing commentary: Social cognition and depression. *Social Cognition, 3,* 135–144.

Shea, M. T., Elkin, I., Imber, S., Sotsky, S. M., Watkins, J. T., Collins, J., Pilkonis, P. A., Beckman, E., Glass, D. R., Dolan, R. T., & Parloff, M. B. (1992). Course of depressive symptoms over follow-up: Findings from the National Institute of Mental Health treatment of depression collaborative research program. *Archives of General Psychiatry, 49,* 782–787.

Shea, T., Widiger, T. A., & Klein, M. H. (1992). Comorbidity of personality disorders and depression: Implications for treatment. *Journal of Consulting and Clinical Psychology, 60,* 857–868.

Spitzer, R. L., Williams, J. B., Gibbon, M., & First, M. B. (1992). The Structured Clinical Interview for DSM-III-R (SCID): I. History, rationale, description. *Archives of General Psychiatry, 49,* 624–629.

Starkstien, S. E., Bryer, J. B., Berthier, M. L., Cohen, B., Price, T., & Robinson, R. G. (1991). Depression after stroke: The importance of cerebral hemisphere asymmetries. *Journal of Neuropsychiatry and Clinical Neuroscience, 3,* 276–285.

Starkstien, S. E., & Robinson, R. G. (1989). Affective disorders and cerebral vascular disease. *British Journal of Psychiatry, 154,* 170–182.

Steen, M. (1991). Historical perspectives on women and mental illness and prevention of depression in women, using feminist framework. *Issues in Mental Health Nursing, 12,* 359–374.

Sue, S., Fujino, D. C., Hu, L. T., Takeuchi, D. T., & Zane, N. W. S. (1991). Community mental health services for ethnic minority groups: A test of the cultural responsiveness hypothesis. *Journal of Consulting and Clinical Psychology, 59,* 533–540.

Teuting, P., Koslow, S. H., & Hirschfeld, R. M. A. (1981). Special report on depression research (DHHS Publication No. ADM 81-1085). Washington, DC: U.S. Government Printing Office.

Thase, M., Reynolds, C., Frank, E., Simons, A., McGeary, J., Fasiczka, A., Garamoni, G., Jennings, J., & Kupfer, D. (1994). Do depressed men and women respond similarly to cognitive-behavior therapy? *American Journal of Psychiatry, 151,* 500–505.

Thase, M. E., & Simons, A. D. (1992). Cognitive behavioral therapy and relapse of nonbipolar depression: Parallels with pharmacotherapy. *Psychopharmacology Bulletin, 28,* 117–122.

Thase, M. E., Simons, A. D., McGeary, J., Cahalane, J. F., Hughes, C., Harden, T., & Friedman, E. (1992). Relapse after cognitive behavior therapy for depression: Potential implications for longer course of treatment. *American Journal of Psychiatry, 149,* 1046–1052.

U.S. Bureau of Census. (1994). *Statistical abstracts of the United States* (114th ed.). Washington, DC: U.S. Government Printing Office.

Vallis, T. M., Shaw, B. F., & McCabe, S. B. (1988). The relationship between therapist compentency in cognitive therapy and general therapy skill. *Journal of Cognitive Psychotherapy, 2,* 237–249.

Weissman, M. M., Bruce, M. L., Leaf, P. J., Florio, L. P., & Holzer, C. (1991). Affective disorders. In L. N. Robins & D. A. Regier (Eds.), *Psychiatric disorders in America: The Epidemiologic Catchment Area Study* (pp. 53–80). New York: Free Press.

Weissman, M. M. & Klerman, G. L. (1977). Sex differences and the epidemiology of depression. *Archives of General Psychiatry, 34,* 98–111.

Wells, K. B., Stewart, A., & Hayes, R. D. (1989). The functioning and well-being of depressed patients: Results of the Medical Outcomes Study. *Journal of the American Medical Association, 262,* 914–919.

Wender. P. H., Kety, S. S., Rosenthal, D., Schulsinger, F., Ortmann, J., & Lunde, L. (1986). Psychiatric disorders in the biological and adoptive families of adopted individuals with affective disorders. *Archives of General Psychiatry, 43,* 923–929.

Wethington, E., & Kessler, R. C. (1986). Perceived support, received support, and adjustment to stressful life events. *Journal of Health and Social Behavior, 27,* 78–89.

Wilkinson G., Borsey, D. Q., Leslie, P., Newton, R. W., Lind, C., & Ballinger, C. B. (1988). Psychiatric morbidity and social problems in patients with insulin-dependent diabetes mellitus. *British Journal of Psychiatry, 153,* 38–43.

Yesavage, J. A., Brink, T. L., Rose, T. S., Lum, O., Huang, U., Adey, M., & Leirer, V. O. (1983). Development and validation of a geriatric screening scale: A preliminary report. *Journal of Psychiatric Research, 17,* 37–49.

Youngren, M. A. & Lewinsohn, P. M. (1980). The functional relationship between depression and problematic interpersonal behavior. *Journal of Abnormal Psychology, 89,* 333–341.

CHAPTER 9

Mood Disorders: Bipolar Disorders

BARBARA M. ROHLAND, GEORGE WINOKUR, and BRIAN L. COOK

Bipolar disorder is characterized by recurrent episodes of mania and depression. To best understand the concept of bipolar disorder, it is necessary to separate it from unipolar affective disorder, in which an individual shows only depressions and no manic episodes. Most persons with bipolar disorder have one or more episodes of both depression and mania. Occasionally, persons with bipolar illness show only manias and no depressions.

The occurrence of bipolar disorder was noted as far back as 1686 when Bonet used the term "maniacomelancholicus" in describing a group of patients. In the 1850s, Falret adopted the term "circular insanity" for the same kinds of patients, and Baillarger used the term "double-form insanity." In 1883, Kraepelin published his textbook on psychiatry, in which he separated manic-depressive illness from dementia praecox or schizophrenia on the basis of clinical descriptions and the natural history of the illnesses. The natural history of manic-depressive illness was characterized by episodes and that of schizophrenia by a chronic deteriorating course (Kraepelin, 1921). Although the original descriptions clearly noted the presence of both manias and depressions in the same patient, it was generally accepted practice to assume that those patients who had only depressions belonged in the group of manic-depressive illnesses.

DESCRIPTION OF THE DISORDER

Episodes of bipolar illness are usually discrete and show clustering of depressive or manic symptoms (Feighner et al., 1972). Common symptoms in depression are persistent complaints or observations of low mood (e.g., feelings of sadness, despondency, emptiness, or hopelessness); appetite changes with corresponding weight loss or weight gain; sleep disturbance, such as waking up early in the morning or excessive sleep; loss of energy or chronic fatigue; agitation or retardation; loss of interest in usual activities such as work or play; decrease in sexual drive; feelings of worthlessness, self-reproach or guilt; inability to concentrate or make decisions; recurrent thoughts of death or suicide; and diurnal variation (e.g., feeling worse in the morning). Although not all of these symptoms have to be present, several should be present, persistent over a 2-week period and cause significant distress or functional impairment before one would consider a diagnosis of depression.

In contrast, an episode of mania is manifested by persistence of euphoric (or irritable) mood, increased talkativity with rapid speech or push of speech, hyperactivity, perception of "racing thoughts," feelings of grandiosity, decreased need for sleep (as opposed to decreased ability to sleep), distractibility, and excessive involvement in pleasurable activity that has potential for self-harm (e.g., sexual indiscretions, spending sprees, or foolish business decisions). The onset of mania may be abrupt or may follow a prodrome of symptoms which gradually increase in severity. Symptoms do not need to persist over a specified period of time if significant impairment is present in order for a diagnosis of mania to be made.

The bipolar disorders are classified into bipolar I disorder, bipolar II disorder, cyclothymic disorder, and bipolar disorder not otherwise specified. All involve the presence (or history) of manic episodes, mixed episodes, or hypomanic episodes, usually accompanied by the presence (or history) of major depressive episodes.

Besides the presence of mania, a number of other factors separate bipolar affective disorder (manic-depressive disease) from unipolar depression (depressive disease). A recent collaborative study compared the course of 189 bipolar patients to 218 unipolar patients at 5-year follow-up (Winokur, Coryell, Endicott, & Akiskal, 1993). Bipolar patients had an earlier age of onset, more acute onset of illness, and more total episodes than persons with unipolar illness. Bipolar patients also were more likely to have shown traits of hyperactivity as children. Differences in the characteristics of patients with bipolar disorder and patients with unipolar disorder are summarized in Table 9.1.

In 1959, Leonhard suggested that the bipolar and unipolar forms of affective illness might be separate illnesses based on family history. He studied 238 bipolar and 288 unipolar patients and examined the prevalence of endogenous psychosis in parents and siblings of the probands. Of the first-degree relatives of the bipolar sample, 39.9% were ill, whereas 25.7% of the relatives of the unipolar sample were ill. Thus, the bipolar patients had endogenous psychosis in their families more frequently than did unipolar patients. This association of bipolar illness with a greater family history was confirmed by Winokur and Clayton (1967). For affective patients with a negative family history, 3.1% were manic; for affective patients who were members of a family that showed affective illness in two generations, 14.3% were manic ($p = 0.003$). In a family in which one manic patient exists, 36%–75% of ill family members will exhibit depression only; other affectively ill relatives will have manic or manic and depressive episodes over the course of their illnesses (Winokur, 1979).

In 1966, a series of findings from Sweden, Switzerland, and the United States put the bipolar-unipolar distinction on a firm basis. In that year, Angst in Switzerland and Perris in Sweden published their results, and Winokur and Clayton presented their data at the annual meeting of the Society of Biological Psychiatry in Washington, DC. Angst (1966) reported that the morbidity risk for affective disorders in the first-degree relatives of bipolar probands was higher than for those of unipolar probands. Furthermore, bipolar probands had more bipolar illness in their families than did unipolar probands. Perris (1966) in Sweden also showed that bipolar probands were more likely than unipolar probands to have bipolar illness in their families. Winokur and Clayton (1967)

TABLE 9.1   Differences in Characteristics of Probands with Bipolar Disorder and Probands with Unipolar Disorder

Characteristic	Bipolar Illness	Unipolar Illness
	Clinical Picture	
Presence of mania in proband	Yes	No
Bi- or triphasic immediate course with episodes of depression and mania	Yes	No
Age of onset in proband mean, years (SD)	24.7 (9.4)	32.1 (15.4)
Percent alcoholism in proband	46.2	16.5
Duration of illness prior to hospitalization mean, weeks (SD)	48.3 (112.9)	75.9 (121.7)
	Course of Illness	
Total number of episodes (5-year follow-up)	$m = 8.7$	$m = 4.0$
Predictors of multiple episodes	Family history of mania and/or schizoaffective mania	Early age of onset
Chronicity of illness	Males: 15% at 2 years, 3% at 5 years Females: 13% at 2 years, 4% at 5 years	Males: 17% at 2 years, 8% at 5 years Females: 21% at 2 years, 13% at 5 years
	Family Background	
Family history of bipolar illness in proband	21.7%	8.3%
Mania in relatives	4%–10%	
Affective illness in parent	51%	26%
Families having two generations of affective illness (proband parent, proband child)	54%	32%
Affective illness in parents or extended family	63%	36%
Bipolar psychosis in first-degree relatives	3.7%–10.8%	.29%–.35%
Childhood hyperactive syndrome in relatives of proband	18.9%	7.2%

showed that one-third of the first-degree relatives of bipolar patients who had an affective illness had bipolar illness. These data are presented in Table 9.2.

Despite marked differences in clinical picture, course, family history, and treatment, not all investigators accept the concept of two distinct illnesses. Gershon and colleagues (Gershon, Bunney, Leckman, van Eerdewegh, & De-Bauche, 1976; Gershon et al., 1982), in reviewing available family study data, concluded that an alternative hypothesis—that is, a common genetic diathesis—might account for both bipolar and unipolar illnesses. This viewpoint would support a kind of continuum, with nonpsychotic unipolars having the mildest type of affective disorder and bipolars with psychotic symptoms having the most severe forms of the illness. If unipolar and bipolar illness represent opposite poles of a continuum of illness severity, illness frequency and illness severity would be expected to be greater in the families of probands with illnesses of greater severity (i.e., with bipolar and bipolar with psychosis as compared to

TABLE 9.2   Initial Family Studies Supporting the Distinction between Unipolar and Bipolar Affective Disorders

| Study | Probands | First-Degree Relative Morbidity Risk (%) | |
		Unipolar	Bipolar
Angst, 1966	Unipolar	5.1	0.3
	Bipolar	13.0	4.3
Perris, 1966	Unipolar	6.4	0.3
	Bipolar	0.5	10.1
Winokur & Clayton, 1967	Bipolar	20.4	10.2

unipolar). Winokur (1984), however, presented data that showed that psychotic and nonpsychotic bipolars and unipolars (four groups) all manifested the same amount of familial affective illness. In families with mania present, 36%–75% of ill relatives will exhibit depression only; other affectively ill family members will have manic or both manic and depressive episodes over the course of their illnesses (Winokur, 1979). Research into the neurobiologic and molecular genetics of these illnesses may allow a more conclusive distinction between unipolar and bipolar disorder in the future.

Bipolar Illness and Alcoholism

The association between alcoholism and bipolar illness has become a subject of recent interest. Substance abuse and bipolar illness often co-occur. In the NIMH-ECA study, 60.7% of persons with BPAD-1 had a diagnosis of drug or alcohol abuse (Regier et al., 1990). In a 10-year follow-up study of 131 bipolar patients, Winokur et al. (1994) found that the co-occurrence of alcoholism was associated with recurrent episodes of bipolar illness in patients whose affective illness predated the onset of the alcoholism, but not in patients whose alcoholism predated the onset of their affective illness. This suggests that alcoholism seen in bipolar illness is related to the bipolar illness itself rather than being independent. It is also possible that alcoholism may precipitate a bipolar illness in a person less predisposed to develop episodes than in patients in whom the bipolar illness came first. In either case, the alcoholism may be of a different quality in bipolar patients than the alcoholism that is ordinarily seen as a separate primary illness. In a study of 445 male veterans, bipolar patients with alcoholism were compared to nonalcoholic bipolar patients on clinical and family history variables. There was no increase in the family history of alcoholism in the alcoholic/bipolar patients, which argues against separate transmission of alcoholism and bipolar illness. This does not exclude the possibility that alcoholism is secondary to the bipolar illness in some cases or that preexisting alcoholism could produce an induced "organic" bipolar picture (Winokur, Cook, Liskow, & Fowler, 1993).

EPIDEMIOLOGY

Results from epidemiological studies may be used to estimate the prevalence of bipolar illness in the general population. The lifetime prevalence of bipolar I disorder in community samples has varied from 0.4% to 1.6%. To interpret the significance of these studies, it is important to recognize that many of the epidemiological studies conducted prior to use of criteria-based psychiatric diagnoses ascertained the prevalence of psychiatric symptomatology and not of psychiatric disorder. Prevalence rates for bipolar illness may be either point prevalence (i.e., the number of individuals ill at some time in a given year) or lifetime prevalence, a potentially more meaningful piece of information.

It is becoming increasingly apparent that all forms of affective illness (unipolar plus bipolar) are more prevalent than once thought. Prior to the 1970s, meaningful data were available only from studies done outside the United States. European investigators at that time were reporting on specific psychiatric disorders, not simply symptomatology; however, their definitions for given illnesses must be carefully noted because they differ from present-day nosology. These conservative estimates of prevalence represented the state of the art of epidemiology at that time.

One European study that is often cited was conducted by Helgason (1964) in Iceland. Using the biographic method (long-term follow-up of a randomly obtained sample), Helgason reported the lifetime prevalence for manic-depressive psychosis. Again, the problem of a nosology that combines bipolar illness with some forms of unipolar illness must be considered in interpreting these data. Helgason defined manic-depressive psychosis as an illness characterized by attacks of affective disturbance, either elated or depressed, without apparent external cause and associated with psychomotor dysfunction and periods of disability. He also included involutional depression, a form of unipolar illness. Results were reported for both certain and uncertain diagnosis as a single diagnostic group.

Helgason drew his sample by identifying all Icelanders born in Iceland from 1895 to 1897 and living there on December 1, 1910. His period of observation began on that date and extended to July 1, 1957. Information was obtained on 99.4% of his probands, including those who had emigrated. Probands were followed from 13–15 years of age through 59–62 years of age. Thus, all had essentially passed through the age of risk for bipolar illness. A lifetime prevalence (certain plus uncertain diagnoses) was found to be 1.50 and 2.07 for men and women, respectively. The combined prevalence figure was 1.80%. It is impossible to determine what portion of these probands had bipolar illness and what portion had a form of unipolar illness; therefore, we can only conclude that these figures are high estimates for the true bipolar lifetime prevalence. No data exist that permit generalization of this information to other populations of European descent.

Helgason (1979) reanalyzed his data, using criteria that differentiated bipolar disorder from other affective illnesses, and reported the expectancy (morbidity risk) for bipolar illness in his probands. The resultant finding, 0.79%, is not the lifetime prevalence, but approximates this figure closely because of the protracted period of follow-up. Tsuang, Winokur, and Crowe (1980) also reported morbidity risk for bipolar illness in the relatives of their surgical controls. Their value of 0.30% is generally considered to be a conservative figure that underestimates the true lifetime risk.

A contemporary study, reported by Weissman and Myers (1978), determined illness in an urban population in the United States. These investigators interviewed 515 randomly selected adults 25 years of age or older using a structured interview. Diagnoses were made using Research Diagnostic Criteria (Spitzer, Endicott, & Robins, 1977). Weissman and Myers found a lifetime prevalence for bipolar illness (depressions associated with mania or hypomania) to be 1.2%.

The National Institute of Mental Health (NIMH) Epidemiological Catchment Area (ECA) study provides prevalence rates for criteria-based affective disorders (Weissman et al., 1988). Five urban sites in the United States were used to assess over 18,000 people. Bipolar illness was defined as depression occurring with at least one manic or hypomanic episode. The 2-week prevalence rate of bipolar disorder was 0.7%. The lifetime prevalence rate was 1.2%. Bipolar illness was found to be significantly less prevalent than unipolar depression. The study reported the prevalence rate for major depression for the 2 weeks prior to the interview to be 4.4%. In contrast to unipolar illness, bipolar disorders were also found to have an earlier age of onset and no significant sex differences for prevalence rates.

An earlier study by Robins et al. (1984) reported lifetime prevalence of psychiatric disorders in three of the ECA sites. The authors differentiated the rate for bipolar type I (mania plus depression) from bipolar type II (hypomania plus depression). Bipolar type I had a lifetime prevalence rate of 0.8%. When combined with other data, these findings suggest that approximately two-thirds of patients with bipolar disorder will have depressive disorders with at least one full manic episode (as opposed to hypomanic episodes only) at some point in their lives.

CLINICAL PICTURE

An individual experiencing an episode of bipolar affective illness may present in a manic phase, a depressed phase, or occasionally a mixed clinical state in which symptoms of both phases of the illness occur together. Thus, a description of the symptomatic behavior of bipolar illness encompasses the uniqueness of manic and hypomanic behavior, the ubiquity of depressive symptomatology, and the clinically confusing mixed state when symptoms of both mania and depression are present. Investigators delineating the clinical picture of mania and hypomania often describe the signs and symptoms of a relatively homogeneous patient population. All manic episodes are attributed to bipolar affective illness when neurological or medical etiologies are ruled out. The situation with depressive episodes is more complex. Depressed patients are diagnosed or suspected of having bipolar illness only if they have a past history of a manic episode, a familial history of mania or hypomania, or both. These individuals are the source of our clinical picture of bipolar depression. Unfortunately, this clinical picture of bipolar depression is not easily differentiated from that seen in the unipolar depressive disorders. Subtle differences exist, but none is pathognomonic.

Mania

The manic phase of bipolar illness is divided by severity into hypomania and mania, with hypomania being less severe than mania. Both of these are defined in the fourth revised edition of the *Diagnostic and Statistical Manual of Mental Disorders* (DSM-IV; American Psychiatric Association [APA], 1994) as a distinct period of abnormally and persistently elevated, expansive, or irritable mood. Hypomania is characterized by the loss of ability for goal-directed work and an incapacity to complete a definite series of thoughts. The rate of thought production is accelerated, but derailment does not occur. These individuals lack insight and do not identify themselves as ill. Their moods are cheerful, but irritability may appear at the slightest provocation. Self-confidence is high, and actions may be impulsive. Psychomotor activity is increased with a lively quality. Speech rate may be minimally increased, and these individuals are often verbose and bombastic.

A manic episode is characterized by a clustering of three or more of the following behavioral changes (APA, 1994):

1. Inflated self-esteem or grandiosity
2. Decreased need for sleep
3. More talkative than usual or pressure to keep talking
4. Flight of ideas or subjective experience that thoughts are racing
5. Distractibility
6. Increase in goal-directed activities (either socially, at work or school, or sexually) or psychomotor agitation
7. Excessive involvement in pleasurable activities that have a high potential for painful consequences (e.g., spending sprees, sexual indiscretions, foolish business decisions)

Acute mania may be heralded by a period of hypomanic signs and symptoms or begin acutely in its full form. In mania, all of the characteristics of hypomania are increased in severity. Thoughts and speech become disconnected, fleeting grandiose delusions may be present, and the individual's mood becomes expansive and exalted. Extreme irritability may appear and be associated with destructive actions. If changes in consciousness or psychotic features are present, they often dominate the clinical picture. Delusions are frequently religious in nature; visual and auditory hallucinations may occur.

Regardless of the severity of the behavioral symptoms, a patient with psychotic symptoms (delusions or hallucinations) is always classified as experiencing a manic episode. The clinical picture of a manic episode can vary considerably but most often contains the three cardinal symptoms of mania: elevated mood, flight of ideas, and psychomotor overactivity.

Depression

In his classical description of the clinical states of depression, Kraepelin (1921) defined six groups according to severity. The resulting groups were melancholia simplex, stupor, melancholia gravis, paranoid melancholia, fantastic melancholia, and delirious melancholia.

In melancholia simplex, a sense of profound inward dejection dominates the mood. The patient's view of life is markedly pessimistic and flavored with hopelessness and despair. Feelings of worthlessness are prominent, and torment from guilt is frequent. Endogenous features of decreased libido, anorexia, weight loss, and sleep disturbance with early morning awakening often are present. Energy is markedly decreased, and psychomotor retardation is demonstrated. Phobias may also be part of the clinical picture. Various combinations of these signs and symptoms characterize simple melancholia.

In depressive stupor, the prominent feature is the patient's difficulty in perceiving surroundings and assimilating these external stimuli. Apathy is readily observed, and the patient makes detached statements with confused ideas. However, the patient is most commonly observed to be mute and shows minimal physical activity. The other features of depression are present, but the stuporous quality is most striking clinically.

Melancholia gravis is characterized by the presence of ideas of sin and persecution. The patient is preoccupied with his or her present and past sins, both real and imaginary. His or her life has been without any saving grace, and damnation is viewed as the final reward. Somatic delusions concerning the rotting away of various organs may be experienced, as well as hallucinations of figures or spirits of relatives. Persecutory ideation, when present, is closely related to sinful delusions.

Paranoid melancholia is characterized by persecutory ideation centered on beliefs that the patient is being watched or spied upon. He or she often imagines being the target of others, and auditory hallucinations reflect the paranoid theme. The patient's mood is gloomy and despondent; the risk for suicide is significant.

Fantastic melancholia is characterized by multiple delusions and hallucinations. An individual patient may demonstrate delusions of guilt and persecution, bizarre somatic dysfunction, and hypochondriasis. Abundant hallucinations of spirits, the devil, monsters, and angels are present. Cognitive function appears impaired, and psychomotor activity may range from one extreme to the other. In delirious melancholia, the total clinical picture described in fantastic melancholia is present, but, in addition, cognitive function and consciousness are significantly impaired.

The currently utilized description of an episode of bipolar depression is given in DSM-IV. This reference does not differentiate the clinical picture of bipolar depression from that of unipolar (major) depression. The central feature of depression in either group is a pervasive depressed mood or loss of interest or pleasure. In the elderly, loss of interest or presence of apathy may be more prominent than complaints of sadness or discouragement. Children or adolescents often present with irritable mood, and a clinical picture mimicking a conduct disorder may confound diagnosis in this age group. To satisfy the criteria for an episode of depression, five or more of the following symptoms must be present for a consecutive 2-week period and represent a change from previous functioning; in addition, at least one of the symptoms must be either depressed mood or loss of interest or pleasure (APA, 1994):

1. Depressed mood most of the day, nearly every day as indicated by either subjective report or observation by others
2. Markedly diminished interest or pleasure in usual activities, such as hobbies, work, or sexual function

3. Significant weight loss or weight gain (e.g., a change of more than 5% of body weight in a month), or decrease or increase in appetite
4. Insomnia (classically presenting as early morning awakening) or hypersomnia
5. Changes in psychomotor activity level, manifested as either agitation or retardation of speech and movement
6. Decreased energy and a sense of sustained fatigue even in the absence of physical exertion
7. Decreased self-esteem, manifested by feelings of worthlessness, self-reproach, or excessive or inappropriate guilt
8. Diminished ability to concentrate, remember, process information, or make decisions
9. Thoughts of death or suicide

Mixed Episodes

A mixed form of bipolar illness may be seen, with both manic and depressive features. Once given little attention and thought to be rare, the patient experiencing a mixed episode is now being recognized frequently in the clinical setting. The identification of this phase of the bipolar illness is critical, since it may be the first time lithium or anticonvulsants are considered in the therapeutic management of the patient's recurring "depression."

COURSE AND PROGNOSIS

Bipolar illness starts generally before age 30. Table 9.3 presents the cumulative risk for age of onset for both males and females (Winokur, 1970). Over half the patients become ill prior to age 30, and in fact, a quarter of the patients become ill prior to age 20. Although bipolar illness frequently begins in adolescence, historically, the occurrence of early onset was interpreted by clinicians as suggesting the presence of schizophrenia.

Bipolar disorder may first manifest itself by a depression. In a recent study, 225 unipolar depressive patients were identified and then followed for as long

TABLE 9.3 Age of Onset and Age at Index Admission in Manic Patients ($N = 89$)

Age Range	Number with index admission (both sexes)	Number within age range at onset of illness			Cumulative risk (both sexes)
		Males	Females	Both sexes	
10–19	6	8	14	22	25%
20–29	16	12	13	25	53%
30–39	18	3	12	15	70%
40–49	18	5	8	13	84%
50–59	18	5	6	11	97%
60–69	11	2	1	3	100%
70–79	2	0	0	0	
Total	89	35	54	89	

as 40 years. Within the first few years after follow-up, about 4% of the patients went from unipolarity to bipolarity (Winokur & Morrison, 1973); however, in the long-term follow-up, 9.7% became bipolar (Winokur, Tsuang, & Crowe, 1982).

Episodes of bipolar illness are often biplasic or triplasic. Often, there is a short depression (few weeks), followed by a mania (2–3 months), followed in turn by a longer depression (6–9 months). Short-term follow-ups in bipolar patients are in reasonable agreement. Commonly, the patient has subsequent episodes, either superimposed on partial remission or wellness. Bratfos and Haug (1968) followed 42 patients for 6 years. They found that 7% recovered without relapse, 48% had one or more episodes, and 45% had chronic courses. Winokur, Clayton, and Reich (1969) followed 28 bipolar patients for 18–36 months after index admission. Notably, about 39% were chronically ill or only partially remitted, and 14% were well in every way. In a recent 10 year follow-up study of 131 bipolar patients (Winokur et al., 1994), chronicity from index episode to the end of the 10-year follow-up was uncommon (4%).

A large study on the course of bipolar illness was published by Angst and coworkers (1973). They evaluated 393 bipolar patients from five countries using data obtained through case histories and verbal information. Only 2 of the 393 bipolars suffered single episodes of illness. Sixty-four percent of persons with bipolar psychoses have been followed for at least 10 years and 49% for 15 years. The median number of episodes for the observation period was seven to nine, and the mean number of episodes in patients who had been observed for 40 years was not higher than in patients who had been observed for only 15 years. The authors concluded that there was a certain self-limitation in the mean number of episodes. It is important to note that these data refer to bipolars who had been treated. Between 70% and 80% of the patients had been treated in the hospital, and very few patients had received no treatment at all. The length of the episodes remains rather constant, varying only between 2.7 months in the first episode to 2.4 months in the tenth. The cycle length, or the time from the beginning of one episode to the beginning of the next, was noted to be shortened from episode to episode, but approached a certain threshold value.

More recently, Winokur et al. (1994) published a prospective and systematic evaluation of the course of bipolar illness in 131 patients over a 10-year period of follow-up from data available in the U.S. National Institute of Mental Health (NIMH) Collaborative Study of Depression. The National Institute of Mental Health Collaborative Study of the Psychobiology of Depression has been described in detail elsewhere (Coryell, Lavori, & Endicott, 1984; Katz, Secunda, & Hirschfeld, 1979; Keller, Klerman, & Lavori, 1984). In contrast to the Angst study, cycle lengths showed no systematic decrease in duration over a 10-year follow-up period. Cycle lengths in the first 5 years of follow-up were similar in length to the last 5 years of follow-up. Furthermore, the number of episodes in the first 5 years of follow-up was not correlated with the number of episodes in the last 5 years of follow-up. This was a naturalistic study, and treatment intensity was not related to decreasing episodes or to changes in cycle length. Data from this study are presented in Table 9.4.

The reasons for the differences in the findings between the Winokur and the Angst studies are not readily apparent. With a longer period of follow-up, the

TABLE 9.4   Course of Illness in Bipolar Patients at 10-Year Period Follow-Up

	Male (n = 48)	Female (n = 83)	Total (n = 131)
Percentage chronically ill (never had an 8-week period of wellness)	2.1	4.8	3.8
Number of manic, schizoaffective manic episodes (mean)	2.2	3.0	
Number of depressive episodes (mean)	2.0	2.5	
Total number of affective episodes	2.8	3.1	
Percentage with only one episode (i.e., no further episodes of illness)	12.8	10.1	11.1
Percentage with no further hospitalizations	25.5	21.5	23.0

Angst findings may turn out to be accurate. Marked differences in the methods of the Winokur and the Angst study exist and may explain some of the differences. The assessment of episodes in the Angst study was dependent on hospitalization, whereas in the Winokur study, assessment of an episode depended on the development of a set of symptoms with or without hospitalization or any other medical care. Therefore, the episodes in the Angst study probably were more severe. It also is possible that the cycle length is not decreased or that the number of episodes is increased in bipolar illness, but that there is a decrease in cycle length for episodes that meet the criteria of severity leading to hospitalization. Finally, the Angst study was largely historical (hospitalizations and records) and the period of observation has to do with the beginning of the illness to the end of the time of follow-up. In contrast, the surveillance of the Winokur study was more intense in that it provided systematic follow-up of every patient on an individual basis, for the same period of time, and with the same methods.

The data presented by Angst and Winokur in regard to the proportion of persons who have only one episode of illness are not consistent with data presented by Pollock in the early part of the century (1909–20). Pollock (1931) reported that about 55% of manic patients had only one recorded episode as opposed to Angst, who reported single episodes in 3/393 patients, and Winokur, who reported single episodes in 14/126 bipolar patients. Like the Angst study, Pollock's study also depended on hospital admissions. More recently, Fukuda, Etoh, and Iwandate (1983) followed 100 bipolars in Japan for 12 years and reported a much higher percentage (39%) of patients who had only one or two episodes. The reasons for the differences between the modern Japanese study and Angst's study, as well as the reasons for the differences in the material from today and Pollock's material, are not apparent.

Family History as Predictor of Illness Severity

Family history has been evaluated as a predictor of the course of illness. While it has been demonstrated that persons with bipolar disorder are more likely than unipolar patients to have affective illness in parents or extended family (Winokur, 1973), family history of all affective illness does not predict a multiple episode course in either bipolar or unipolar illness (Winokur, Coryell, Keller,

Endicott, & Akiskal, 1993). A family history of mania, however, in bipolar patients was associated with more episodes at 10-year follow-up than if such a family history were absent. (Winokur et al., 1994).

Bipolar Illness and Suicidal Behavior

In any follow-up of bipolar disorder, it is necessary to evaluate the consequences of the illness. Although suicide is the major concern, increased mortality in bipolar patients from natural causes has been reported. Tsuang, Woolson, and Fleming (1980) reported data from the "Iowa 500" on follow-up of patients admitted to the hospital in the 1930s. They found excessive death from unnatural causes in both primary unipolar depressives and manics. The unnatural deaths, mainly suicides, were higher in the unipolar depressives, but manic patients experienced excessive natural death.

In a large modern study of hospitalized patients with affective disorders, excessive death from natural causes was found in female bipolar depression and in male and female manics who had concurrent organic mental disorders or serious medical illness (Black, Winokur, & Nasrallah, 1987). In the absence of these conditions, however, natural death was not excessive. Alternately, unnatural deaths, mainly suicides, were significantly increased. Taken together (bipolars of both sexes admitted for either depression or mania), no increased natural death rate was found after the patients with organic medical disorders were omitted; however, unnatural deaths (mainly suicides) were significantly increased, mainly in males. The increase in the unnatural death rate of bipolars was not as large as that in unipolars. A reasonable conclusion is that bipolar illness causes an increased suicide rate, but the increased natural death rate is the result of patients with two diseases, bipolar illness and serious medical disease.

FAMILIAL AND GENETIC CONSIDERATIONS

Family studies, twin studies, and adoption studies all suggest that genetic factors are important in bipolar illness, but a distinct mode of transmission has not been conclusively demonstrated. Linkage studies have described potential associations between bipolar illness and genes localized to chromosomes X, 11, 18, and 21.

Family Studies

In a study of 57 bipolar probands, the morbidity risk for parents was 34% plus or minus 4.6, and for siblings 35% plus or minus 5.0 (Winokur et al., 1969). In that study, no male proband had an ill father, which suggested the possibility of X chromosome linkage. Females, on the other hand, had ill fathers and ill mothers. In the relatives of the probands, females were much more likely to be affected than males. Of 99 male first-degree relatives at risk, 19 had an affective disorder, and of 100 female relatives at risk, 50 had an affective disorder.

Twin Studies

A modern twin study was reported from Denmark. Bartlesen, Harvald, and Hauge (1977) showed a concordance rate of 74% in bipolar monozygotic twins and 17% in dizygotic twins, which clearly suggests a genetic factor in bipolar illness.

Adoption Studies

Mendlewicz and Rainer (1977), in a study of adoptees with bipolar illness, reported that 31% of biological parents and 12% of adopted parents of hospitalized bipolar adoptees had an affective disorder. The percentage in biological parents was comparable to the risk reported in parents of nonadopted bipolar patients. Those data also present strong evidence that a genetic factor is present in bipolar illness.

Gene Linkage Studies (Chromosome X)

Reich, Clayton, and Winokur (1969) provided support for the transmission of bipolar illness via a dominant gene on the X chromosome in two families. Mendlewicz, Linkowski, and Wilmotte (1980) studied a large family with bipolar illness in Israel and reported that the illness was specifically linked to the G6PD region of the X chromosome; however, results of several are somewhat contradictory. Gershon, Targum, Mattysse, and Bunney (1979) published results for linkage with red-green color blindness and concluded that bipolar illness is not transmitted by a single gene close to the region on the X chromosome that transmits color blindness. Del Zompo, Bocchetta, Goldin, and Corsini (1984) presented data that supported linkage between bipolar illness and the color blindness–G6PD region of the X chromosome in two Sardinian pedigrees. Baron et al. (1987) reported a positive finding of linkage between bipolar disorders and X chromosome markers. However, reevaluation of pedigree data has shown greatly diminished support for linkage to Xq28 (Baron et al., 1993). Bocchetta, Piccardi, and Del Zompo (1994) have suggested that an X-linked gene, perhaps G6PD itself, may contribute to the susceptibility of bipolar illness in some ethnic groups.

The role of X-linked inheritance in the transmission of bipolar illness remains unclear. Many cases of male-to-male transmission have been reported, and the results of recent studies have been conflicting. It is clear that X-linked inheritance alone cannot account for the transmission of bipolar illness and cannot account for it in all cases of illness.

Gene Linkage Studies (Chromosome 11)

A finding of an autosomal linkage was reported by Egeland and her coworkers (1987) in a large Amish pedigree, in whom the linkage was to the Harvey-ras locus and the insulin gene locus, both on chromosome 11. However, reanalysis of a large lateral extension of the original pedigree excluded this linkage (Kelsoe et al., 1989). More recently, De bruyn et al. (1994) examined linkage in 14 bipolar families with several candidate genes on chromosome 11, including the c-Harvey-ras-oncogene and the insulin gene. Results of this investigation excluded close linkage of bipolar illness to each candidate gene.

Gene Linkage Studies (Chromosome 18)

Berrettini et al. (1994) evaluated 22 manic-depressive families for linkage to 11 loci on chromosome 18. Although the overall logarithm odds score analysis was not significant, several families yielded logarithm odds scores consistent with linkage under dominant or recessive modes. These results are consistent with the hypothesis that a susceptibility gene in the pericentromeric region of chromosome 18 with a complex mode of inheritance may exist. Furthermore, two plausible candidate genes, a corticotropin receptor and the alpha subunit of a GTP binding protein, have been localized to this region.

Gene Linkage Studies (Chromosome 21)

Straub et al. (1994) published findings which suggest the presence of a gene on chromosome 21 predisposing at least one family to bipolar disorder.

DIAGNOSTIC CONSIDERATIONS

The clinical pictures of unipolar and bipolar depressive episodes generally share a broad range of affective symptomatology. While characteristics that differentiate the unipolar depressive from the bipolar depressive may have some validity in distinguishing groups of patients, application to an individual patient is of little clinical value. The wise clinician will attempt to differentiate one from the other by utilizing information on the course of the patient's illness and the family history of affective illness and not by eliciting subtle behavioral differences in depressive symptomatology. Many researchers have reported subtle differences; however, other investigators reported no differences between bipolar and unipolar depressive episodes when cross-sectional symptoms were compared (Abrams & Taylor, 1980). The literature summarized below suggests that symptomatic differences exist between bipolar and unipolar depression; however, further research is needed in this area given that considerable overlap exists on most variables.

Psychomotor Activity

Prolonged periods of psychomotor retardation characterize the bipolar depressed patient (Bunney & Murphy, 1973). Psychomotor agitation, in contrast, is more frequent and severe in the unipolar patient (Beigel & Murphy, 1971).

Psychotic Symptoms

Delusions, hallucinations, or catatonia may be seen during episodes of bipolar or unipolar depression and do not differentiate unipolar from bipolar illness. However, the likehood of bipolar disease in persons who manifest psychotic symptoms is greatly increased and is estimated to be between 20% and 30%. This percentage is about twice that predicted by epidemiological data. Bipolar psychotically depressed patients also are characterized by childhood or adolescent age of onset, profound psychomotor retardation, antidepressant-induced periods of mania or hypomania, and a strong family history of affective illnesses, often in three consecutive generations.

Sleep Disturbance

Detre et al. (1972) found that the type of sleep disturbance a patient is experiencing may be associated with the classification of the depressive episode. Bipolar depressive patients more frequently have hypersomnia, whereas unipolar patients more commonly have hyposomnia.

Somatic Manifestations

Beigel and Murphy (1971) also reported that unipolar patients had significantly higher ratings for somatic complaints than did matched bipolar patients.

Anger

Beigel and Murphy (1971) reported that bipolar depressives rarely experience anger directed inward or displaced outward toward others.

Anxiety

The presence or absence of anxiety does not appear to differentiate the two groups.

Feelings of Guilt

Winokur and Wesner (1987) found a high incidence of reproach and guilt in bipolar depression, a higher incidence than that seen in unipolar depression.

In summary, unipolar depressed patients appear to have more anger directed at self or others, to present more frequently with multiple somatic complaints as part of their depression, to experience hyposomnia, and to have higher levels of psychomotor agitation. In contrast, bipolar depressed patients have minimal anger, few somatic complaints, more hypersomnia, and more psychomotor retardation.

While the differential diagnosis between bipolar depression and unipolar depression represents the most frequent diagnostic challenge, other diagnostic considerations may also present clinical confusion. The distinction between schizoaffective disorder and bipolar disorder in a patient with both affective symptoms and psychosis can be particularly problematic. Studies using the research diagnostic criteria (RDC) definition of schizoaffective disorder have shown that in persons with bipolar disorder, the manic states are similar to those in schizoaffective manics, although the schizoaffective manic probably has an earlier age of onset and a more malignant course (Clayton, 1987). Previous episodes of mania or depression without psychosis and family history of bipolar illness make bipolar illness more likely than schizoaffective disorder in patients who present with both affective and psychotic symptoms. Distinguishing bipolar illness from schizophrenia can be difficult if the patient's history and family history are unknown. It may not be possible to distinguish psychotic illness from affective illness in the initial presentation of patients who do not have a family history of either schizophrenia or bipolar illness. Finally, patients with certain personality disorders (e.g., antisocial or borderline personality disorders) and patients with alcohol and drug abuse can present with symptoms of hypomania or, in extreme cases, mania; these conditions must be considered in the differential diagnosis of bipolar illness.

PSYCHOLOGICAL AND BIOLOGICAL ASSESSMENT

Abnormalities and variability in biochemical, neuroendocrine, and second messenger system function in persons with bipolar illness have been described, but as of yet, the cause of illness has not been determined. Probably the most popular concept is the "biogenic amine hypothesis," which states that, in depression, a functional deficit of either norepinephrine or serotonin occurs at critical synapses in the central nervous system. This theory implies that an excess of these amines may be present in mania. Other biogenic amines, such as dopamine, have also been implicated. Other neurotransmitters or neuromodulators such as the cholinergic system, the GABAergic system, and the endorphin system may be important in bipolar disorder. Janowski et al. (1983) suggested that an affective state may be relevant to a balance between central cholinergic and adrenergic neurotransmitters with depression a disorder of cholinergic predominance and mania a disorder of adrenergic predominance. However, no unchallenged body of evidence supports any of these theories. Furthermore, there is no evidence that mania and depression are opposites of each other in regard to their neurobiologic correlates.

Laboratory findings in manic episodes include polysomnographic abnormalities, increased cortisol secretion, and absence of dexamethasone nonsuppression. While some of these findings have been used to suggest insight into the physiologic etiology of bipolar disorder, it is difficult to distinguish course from effect in persons who exhibit symptoms of illness and the central defect in bipolar illness has not been determined. There also appear to be no laboratory features that distinguish major depressive episodes found in major depressive disorder from those in bipolar I disorder.

Abnormalities in endocrine parameters have been reported. Schlesser, Winokur, and Sherman (1980) presented evidence of inability to suppress serum cortisol after administration of dexamethasone the night before. Eighty-five percent of bipolar depressives were abnormal suppressors. On the other hand, manics suppressed normally the morning after dexamethasone administration. This has not been replicated by everyone. The implication of the finding is that a hypothalamic-pituitary-adrenal abnormality exists in bipolar patients, as well as in some unipolar patients. In the sleep laboratory, bipolar depressed patients have shortened rapid eye movement (REM) latency, higher REM density, and problems with sleep continuity (Kupfer, 1983).

Secondary mania has been described in cases where symptoms of mania are precipitated by organic or neurologic factors. As suggested by Clayton (1994), "induced mania" may be a preferable term since "secondary mania" describes a temporal and not necessarily a causal relationship. As summarized by Clayton, causes of induced mania include neurologic conditions such as neoplasm, epilepsy, head injury, and cerebrovascular lesions. Drugs which have been associated with acute symptoms of mania include corticosteroids, methamphetamine, cocaine, and L-dopa. Finally, metabolic or endocrine disturbances, infections, or other systemic conditions can also precipitate manic symptoms. Unlike most bipolar patients, patients with secondary or induced mania have a negative family history (Krauthammer & Klerman, 1978). Such reports may have value for their heuristic reasons (i.e., they may suggest studies of more specific pathophysiology and etiology).

Traditional psychological testing has not proved very useful in the diagnosis or treatment of bipolar disorder (Klerman, Keller, Andreason, & Clayton, 1986). However, there is a literature documenting the usefulness of neuropsychological testing. These tests have revealed many hemispheric (usually right) deficiencies among bipolar patients (Powell & Miklowitz, 1994).

Therapy in Bipolar Disorder

Treatment of bipolar illness must incorporate strategies that address the management of acute episodes as well as prevent recurrent episodes of illness. In addition, treatment must address both the manic and depressive symptoms of the illness, a task which becomes particularly challenging when manic and depressive symptoms occur concurrently or cycle in rapid succession. Current approaches to the treatment of bipolar illness emphasize somatic therapies (i.e., pharmacotherapy and ECT). Family and psychosocial factors also appear to be important in the outcome of lithium-maintained bipolar patients (O'Connell et al., 1991), and comprehensive treatment of bipolar patients should also address these issues. Pharmacological management of bipolar illness has been described elsewhere (Perry, Alexander, & Garvey, 1994). Lithium carbonate remains the drug of first choice for the treatment of bipolar illness. Lithium therapy is associated with improvement in 76% of patients and reduces the rate of relapse by 50%. Recurrences, when they occur, are less severe. Illness which does not respond to lithium treatment has spurred intensive research directed toward finding alternate interventions. Carbamazepine, an anticonvulsant, has emerged as the primary alternative therapy when lithium proves ineffectual or in patients who cannot tolerate lithium because of adverse effects. In responsive individuals, carbamazepine has a rapid onset of action, which is comparable to that seen with neuroleptics. If combined with lithium, benefits may be better than those of either agent alone. Carbamazepine has a low risk for bone marrow suppression (its most notorious adverse effect), and other side effects are usually well tolerated. Valproic acid is another anticonvulsant that appears to be an effective antimanic agent and is regarded as a third-line treatment for mania.

Treatment of Acute Mania

In the acute treatment of manic episodes, the primary pharmacological therapy is lithium. If a fulminant manic psychosis is present, adjunctive therapy with antipsychotic medications of the phenothiazine or butyrophenone classes is often required. These drugs have potent sedating effects and are effective in achieving rapid control of symptoms of hyperactivity and excitement in the acutely manic patient. Unlike the specific antimanic effect of lithium carbonate, however, antipsychotic agents do not appear to have a specific antimanic effect, and lithium alone should be used in patients who are manageable without antipsychotics. The benzodiazepines, specifically lorazepam and clonazepam, have been suggested as possessing specific antimanic effects while being less likely to induce the intolerable side effects often seen with antipsychotics. Thus, they are often utilized along with lithium in the acute treatment. As control of the episode is obtained, the antipsychotic or other adjunctive medication is tapered and ultimately discontinued while the lithium is continued for maintenance and prophylactic therapy.

It has been estimated that approximately 40% of manic patients present with a dysphoric or mixed-mania state. These patients often do not benefit from lithium, and alternate therapies such as anticonvulsants (carbamazepine and valproic acid) and the benzodiazepines (clonazepam and lorazepam) are often used. The beneficial activity from these agents appears to arise from their anticonvulsant properties.

Electroconvulsive therapy (ECT) is a very effective treatment for acute mania and may be the treatment of choice if the illness is life threatening and rapid resolution of manic symptoms is imperative. ECT has been demonstrated to be particularly effective in rapid resolution of the catatonic syndrome, a life-threatening condition that can occur in either the manic or depressive phases of bipolar illness (Rohland, Carroll, & Jacoby, 1993). With increasing availability of effective pharmacological management, ECT is infrequently used for the acute management of mania. ECT is also effective in the treatment of depressive symptoms in bipolar illness (see below).

Treatment of Acute Depression

Acute depressive episodes are most commonly treated with antidepressant medications. The 1950s saw the development of the first drugs with truly effective antidepressant properties. Two classes of antidepressants, monoamine oxidase inhibitors (MAOIs) and tricyclic antidepressants, were serendipitously discovered during this period. The MAOIs came from research in drug therapy for tuberculosis, whereas the tricyclics were derived from work with the neuroleptic antipsychotics. Since that time, other heterocyclic antidepressants have been developed and recent additions include bupropion and the serotonin specific reuptake inhibitors (fluoxetine, paroxetine, and sertraline). These drugs may indeed possess unique therapeutic benefits, but their roles in the specific treatment of bipolar depressive disorder remain unclear. The tricyclics and MAOIs treat acute depression but do not stabilize the mood as do lithium and the anticonvulsants. Some clinical observations suggest that antidepressants may precipitate mania or induce more frequent episodes of illness (rapid cycling), but the issue as to whether or not antidepressants induce mania or cause rapid cycling remains an unresolved controversy. The generic names for various drugs identified by major class are shown in Table 9.5.

ECT as an organic treatment in psychiatry dates back to 1938 when Cerletti first reported its use. Its introduction was a refinement in artificially induced convulsive therapy in use at that time. Although schizophrenia was the illness that was thought to benefit by convulsive therapy, it soon became apparent that ECT's most dramatic effects were in affective disorder, most commonly depression. Early reports were anecdotal in nature, but, as scientific methodology improved in psychiatry, well-designed, controlled studies demonstrated the efficacy of this treatment modality for depression. The therapeutic response of depressive signs and symptoms to ECT appears not to be a function of diagnosis (unipolar vs. bipolar illness). An APA Task Force reviewed the literature and practice of ECT, and the following conclusions were drawn (APA Task Force Report, 1978): ECT is clinically indicated for the treatment of major depressive episodes if the patient has proven unresponsive to antidepressant medication or has serious suicidal risk or if the depression is especially severe as demonstrated by a profound degree of weight loss or psychotic thought content.

The safety of ECT was increased dramatically by the introduction of two

TABLE 9.5   Major Classes of Commonly Used Antidepressants

Generic (Brand) Name	Daily Dose Range (oral, in milligrams)
Category: Tricyclic Antidepressants (TCAs)	
Amitriptyline (Elavil)	50–300
Amoxapine (Asendin)	100–600
Desipramine (Norpramin)	75–300
Doxepin (Adapin, Sinequan)	75–300
Imipramine (Tofranil)	50–300
Nortriplyline (Pamelor, Aventyl)	20–150
Category: Monoamine Oxidase Inhibitors (MAOIs)	
Isocarboxazid (Marplan)	10–50
Phenelzine (Nardil)	15–90
Tranylcypromine (Parnate)	20–40
Category: Serotonin Specific Reuptake Inhibitors (SSRIs)	
Fluoxetine (Prozac)	20–80
Paroxetine (Paxil)	20–80
Sertaline (Zoloft)	50–200
Category: Other Second-Generation Antidepressants	
Bupropion (Wellbutrin)	300–450
Trazadone (Desyrel)	300–800
Venlafaxine (Effexor)	225–375
Nefazodone (Serzone)	300–600

methodological advances in the 1950s. A short-acting hypnotic and a muscle relaxant are administered prior to the production of the seizure; thus, a modified convulsion is produced. The most recent advance is the use of brief pulse wave stimulation to produce seizures. This technique minimizes transient memory impairment and confusion that was previously observed in ECT treatment. Pharmacotherapy remains the mainstay for the treatment of severe depression, but ECT retains indications under certain clinical situations.

Maintenance Therapy

Because bipolar disorder is an episodic illness characterized by recurrence, prevention of future manic and depressive episodes is central to therapy. The Consensus Development Panel (1985) concluded that studies addressing the prevention of recurrence of bipolar episodes support the determination that lithium carbonate possesses prophylactic properties. It is estimated, however, that 50% or more of bipolar patients receive incomplete or no preventive benefit from lithium. Clinical practice suggests that the anticonvulsants that are beneficial for acute mania may also possess preventive properties, either alone or in combination with lithium. Current clinical research is attempting to validate these observations. Maintenance ECT has been used to prevent manic and depressive episodes in some bipolar patients. The evidence for its usefulness is mainly anecdotal.

Psychosocial interventions may modify the course of bipolar illness when combined with pharmacologic maintenance treatment. In a 9-month study of the longitudinal course of bipolar manic patients following hospital discharge,

Miklowitz, Goldstein, Nuechterlein, Snyder, and Mintz (1988) found that the emotional atmosphere of the family during the postdischarge period appeared to be an important predictor of the clinical course of bipolar disorder. Patients who return to homes with high levels of expressed emotion are at increased risk for relapse following hospitalization compared to patients who return to homes where expressed emotion is low. Behavioral family management has been used to reduce family stress in bipolar patients and their family members by enhancing communication and problem solving skills (Miklowitz & Goldstein, 1990). Hence, behavioral family management (BFM) may be a useful adjunct to pharmacologic treatment in enhancing clinical and social outcome in bipolar patients.

GENDER AND RACIAL-ETHNIC ISSUES

Gender

Recent epidemiologic studies in the United States indicate that bipolar I disorder is equally common in men and women. This is in contrast to major depressive disorder, which is more common in women. Gender, in persons with bipolar illness, appears to be related to the order of appearance of manic and major depressive episodes. In males, the first episode is more likely to be a manic episode, whereas in females, the first episode is more likely to be depression. In a prospective follow-up of the NIMH Collaborative Study of Depression, there was no difference in the number of manic or depressive episodes or hospitalizations between male and female bipolar patients in 131 bipolar patients at 2-year and 5-year follow-up (Winokur et al., 1994). Analysis of the data at 10-year follow-up found that the total number of affective episodes was higher in the 83 women than in the 48 men who were studied; women were older at the time of index admission and had been ill for a longer period of time. However, the age at first affective illness was not significantly different. Some women have their first episode of illness during the postpartum period and women with bipolar I disorder have an increased risk of developing subsequent episodes (often psychotic) in the immediate postpartum period. The premenstrual period may be associated with worsening of an ongoing major depressive, manic, mixed, or hypomanic episode.

Racial-Ethnic Issues

There are no reports of differential incidence of bipolar I disorder based on race or ethnicity. Cultural difference, however, can affect the experience and communication of symptoms of both manic and depressive phases of bipolar illness. For example, complaints of "nerves" and headaches (in Latin and Mediterranean culture); weakness, tiredness, or "imbalance" (in Chinese and Asian cultures); problems of the "heart" (in Middle Eastern cultures); or of being "heartbroken" (among Hopi) may be variable expressions of depressive symptoms. In some cultures, depression may be experienced largely in somatic terms, rather than subjective cognitive symptoms of sadness or guilt. Furthermore, cultures may differ in their perception of the seriousness of certain emotions.

There is a growing body of evidence which suggests that kinetic and dynamic response to medications may be influenced by ethnicity. Several studies, reviewed by Lin, Poland, & Lesser (1986), suggested that Asian bipolar patients respond clinically to lower lithium blood levels as compared to Caucasians. Because neuroleptics and benzodiazepines are used in the management of acute manic episodes, and antidepressants are used in the treatment of acute depressive episodes, possible interethnic variations in response to these drugs also is important to consider. Lin et al. (1986) reported that in general, Asians reported significantly higher extrapyramidal side effects than Caucasians or African Americans, but African Americans experienced a greater number than Caucasians. Similar findings with Korean Americans for clozapine were reported by Matsuda et al. (1996). With respect to tricyclic antidepressants and benzodiazepines, African Americans, Asians, and Hispanics have been reported to respond to lower doses than Caucasians (Lin et al., 1986; Marcos & Cancro, 1982; Yamamoto et al., 1979; Ziegler & Biggs, 1977). As discussed in their review of cross-cultural considerations in the practice of psychopharmacology, ethnic variation in dosage requirements is most likely to be due to a complex interaction of cultural, environmental, and genetic factors. Factors related to ethnicity may include differential considerations of body weight and fat distribution, as well as ethnically or genetically based differences in the enzyme systems that metabolize drugs and variation in receptor mediated responses. Differences in diet related to ethnicity could potentially affect drug plasma levels. Furthermore, culturally related habits such as smoking, alcohol, and drug ingestion may affect the metabolism of psychotropic agents. Finally, responses to medication may be affected by cultural variation in symptom expression.

SUMMARY

Bipolar illness is an illness characterized by remissions and exacerbations. The lifetime prevalence of bipolar I disorder in community samples has varied from 0.4% to 1.6%. Roughly 90% of individuals who have a single episode will have future episodes. Although the majority of individuals with bipolar I disorder return to a fully functional level between episodes, 20%–30% of persons with this illness continue to display mood lability (usually depressive) and interpersonal or occupational difficulties between episodes of mania or depression (APA, 1994). The clinical picture, course of illness, and the familial backgrounds of persons with bipolar disorder distinguish this disorder from unipolar affective illness. Some evidence exists, however, which suggests that bipolar and unipolar disorders represent a continuum of severity rather than two distinct illnesses. This controversy remains unresolved and is a subject of ongoing study. Family studies, twin studies, adoption studies, and molecular studies all suggest that genetic factors are important in bipolar illness; however, the mode of inheritance is uncertain. Treatment, effective in the resolution and prevention of symptoms of mania and depression, does not appear to alter the natural history of bipolar illness. Long-term follow-up studies provide the best information about the natural history of bipolar patients and will continue to be important in providing insight into the etiology, pathophysiology and effectiveness of treatment in bipolar patients. These studies provide important information for patients and their families in understanding their illness and its likely course in addition to providing clinicians with a reliable baseline for the effects of controlled treatment.

REFERENCES

Abrams, R., & Taylor, M. A. (1980). A comparison of unipolar and bipolar depressive illness. *American Journal of Psychiatry, 137,* 1084–1087.

American Psychiatric Association. (1978). *The APA Task Force report on electroconvulsive therapy.* Washington, DC: Author.

American Psychiatric Association. (1994). *Diagnostic and statistical manual of mental disorders* (4th ed.). Washington, DC: Author.

Angst, J. (1966). *Etiologie und nosologie endogener depressiver psychogen.* Berlin: Springer.

Angst, J., Baastrup, P., Grof, P., Hippius, H., Poldinger, W., & Weis, P. (1973). The course of monopolar depression and bipolar psychoses. *Psychiatrica Neurologia, Neurochirurgia, 76,* 489–500.

Baron, M., Freimer, N. F., Risch, N., Lerer, B., Alexander, J. R., Straub, R. E., Asokan, S., Das, K., Person, A., Amos, J., Endicott, J., Ott, J., & Gilliam, T. C. (1993). Diminished support for linkage between manic depressive illness and X-chromosome markers in three Israeli pedigrees. *Nature Genetics, 3,* 49–55.

Baron, M., Risch, M., Hamburger, R., Mandel, B., Kushner, S., Newman, M., Drumer, D., & Belmaker, R. (1987). Genetic linkage between X-chromosome markers and affective illness. *Nature, 326,* 289–292.

Bartelsen, A., Harvald, B., Hauge, N. (1977). A Danish twin study of manic depressive disorders. *British Journal of Psychiatry, 130,* 330–351.

Beigel, A., & Murphy, D. (1971). Unipolar and bipolar affective illness: Differences in clinical characteristics accompanying depression. *Archives of General Psychiatry, 24,* 215–220.

Berrettini, W. H., Ferraro, T. N., Goldin, L. R., Weeks, D. E., Detera-Wadleigh, S., Burnberger, J. I., & Gershon, E. S. (1994). Chromosome 18 DNA markers and manic-depressive illness: Evidence for a susceptibility gene. *Proceedings of the National Academy of Science, USA, 91,* 5918–5921.

Black, D., Winokur, G., & Nasrallah, A. (1987). Is death from natural cause still excessive in psychiatric patients? *Journal of Nervous and Mental Disease, 1975,* 674–680.

Bocchetta, A., Piccardi, M. P., & Del Zompo, M. (1994). Is bipolar disorder linked to Xq28? [Correspondence]. *Nature Genetics, 6,* 224.

Bratfos, O., & Haug, J. (1968). The course of manic-depressive psychosis. *Acta Psychiatrica Scandinavica, 44,* 89–112.

Bunney, W., & Murphy, D. (1973). The behavioral switch process and psychopathology. In J. Mendels (Ed.), *Biological psychiatry.* New York: Wiley.

Clayton, P. J. (1987). Bipolar and schizoaffective disorder. In G. Tischler (Ed.), *Diagnosis and classification in psychiatry.* Cambridge: Cambridge University Press.

Clayton, P. J. (1994). Bipolar illness. In G. Winokur & P. Clayton (Eds.), *The medical basis of psychiatry.* (2nd ed.). Philadelphia: Saunders.

Consensus Development Panel. (1985). Mood disorders: Pharmacologic prevention of recurrence. *American Journal of Psychiatry, 142,* 469–476.

Coryell, W., Lavori, P., Endicott, J., Keller, M., & VanEerdewegh, M. (1984). Outcome in schizoaffective psychotic and nonpsychotic depression. *Archives of General Psychiatry, 120,* 787–791.

De bruyn, A., Mendelbaum, K., Sandkuijl, L. A., Delvenne, V., Hirsch, D., Staner, L., Mendlewicz, J., & Van Broeckhoven, C. (1994). Nonlinkage of bipolar illness to tyrosine hydroxylase, tyrosinase, and D2 and D4 dopamine receptor genes on chromosome 11. *American Journal of Psychiatry, 151,* 102–106.

Del Zompo, M., Bocchetta, A., Goldin, L., & Corsini, G. (1984). Linkage between X-chromosome markers and manic depressive illness. *Acta Psychiatrica Scandinavica, 70,* 282–287.

Detre, T., Himmelhoch, J., Swartzburg, M., Anderson, C., Byck, R., & Kuper, D. (1972). Hypersomnia and manic-depressive disease. *American Journal of Psychiatry, 128,* 1303–1305.

Egeland, J., Gerhard, D., Pauls, D., Sussex, J., Kidd, K., Allen, C., Hostetter, A., & Houseman, D. (1987). Bipolar affective disorders linked to DNA markers on chromosome 11. *Nature, 325,* 783–787.

Feighner, J., Robins, E., Guze, S., Woodruff, R., Winokur, G., & Munoz, R. (1972). Diagnostic criteria for use in psychiatric research. *Archives of General Psychiatry, 26,* 57–63.

Fukuda, L., Etoh, T., & Iwandate, T. (1983). The course and prognosis of manic-depressive psychosis: A quantitative analysis of episodes and intervals. *Journal of Experimental Medicine, 139,* 299–307.

Gershon, E., Bunney, W., Leckman, J., van Eerdewegh, N., & DeBauche, B. (1976). The inheritance of affective disorders: A review of data and hypothesis. *Behavior Genetics, 6,* 227–261.

Gershon, E., Hamovit, J., Guroff, J., Dibble, E., Leckman, J., Sceery, W., Targum, S., Nurnberger, J., Goldin, L., & Bunney, W. (1982). The family study of schizoaffective bipolar I, bipolar II, unipolar, and normal control probands. *Archives of General Psychiatry, 39,* 1157–1167.

Gershon, E., Targum, S., Mattysse, S., & Bunney, W. (1979). Color blindness not closely linked to bipolar illness. *Archives of General Psychiatry, 36,* 1423–1430.

Helgason, T. (1964). Epidemiology of mental disorders in Iceland. *Acta Psychiatrica Scandinavica, 40* (Suppl. 173), 11–251.

Helgason, T. (1979). Epidemiological investigations concerning affective disorders. In M. Schou & E. Stromgren (Eds.), *Origin, prevention, and treatment of affective disorders.* New York: Academic Press.

Hirschfeld, R., Klerman, G., Keller, M., Andreason, N., & Clayton, P. J. (1986). Personality of recovered patients with bipolar affective disorder. *Journal of Affective Disorders, 11,* 81–89.

Janowski, D., Risch, S., Judd, L., Parker, D., Kalin, N., & Huey, L. (1983). Behavioral and neuroendocrine effects of physostigmine in affective disorder patients. In P. Clayton & J. Barrett (Eds.), *Treatment of depression, old controversies and new approaches.* New York: Raven.

Katz, M., Secunda, S., Hirschfeld, R., & Koslow, S. (1979), NIMH Clinical Research Branch collaborative program on the psychobiology of depression. *Archives of General Psychiatry, 36,* 765–771.

Keller, M., Klerman, G., Lavori, P., Coryell, W., Endicott, J., & Taylor, J. (1984). Long-term outcome of episodes of major depression. *Journal of the American Medical Association, 252,* 788–792.

Kelsoe, J. R., Ginns, E. I., Egeland, J. A., Gerhard, D. S., Goldstein, A. M., Bale, S. J., Pauls, D. L., Long, R. T., Kidd, K. K., Conte, G., Housman, D. E., & Paul, S. M. (1989). Reevaluation of the linkage relationship between chromosome 11p loci and the gene for bipolar affective disorder in the Old Order Amish. *Nature, 342,* 238–242.

Kraepelin, E. (1921). *Manic depressive insanity and paranoia.* Edinburgh: Livingstone.

Krauthammer, C., & Klerman, G. (1978). Secondary mania. *Archives of General Psychiatry, 35,* 1333–1339.

Kupfer, D. (1983). Application of sleep EEG in affective disorders. In J. Davis & J. Haas (Eds.), *The affective disorders.* Washington, DC: American Psychiatric Press.

Leonhard, K. (1959). *Aufterlung der Endogenen Psychosen* (2nd ed.). Berlin: Academie.

Lewis, D., & McChesney, C. (1985). Tritiated imipramine binding distinguishes among subtypes of depression. *Archives of General Psychiatry, 42,* 485–488.

Lin, K., Poland, K. E., & Lesser, I. M. (1986). Ethnicity and psychopharmacology. *Culture, Medicine, and Psychiatry, 10,* 151–165.

Marcos, L. R., & Cancro, R. (1982). Pharmacotherapy of Hispanic depressed patients: Clinical observations. *American Journal of Psychotherapy, 36,* 505–512.

Matsuda, K. T., Cho, M. C., Lin, K. M., Smith, M. W., Yong, A. S., & Adams, J. A. (1996). Clozapine dosage, serum levels, efficacy and side-effect profiles: A comparison of Korean American and Caucasian patients. *Psychopharmacology Bulletin, 32,* 253–257.

Mendlewicz, J., Linkowski, P., & Wilmotte, J. (1980). Linkage between glucose-6-phosphate dehydrogenase deficiency and manic depressive psychosis. *British Journal of Psychiatry, 137,* 337–342.

Mendlewicz, J., & Rainer, J. (1977). Adoption studies supporting genetic transmission in manic-depressive illness. *Nature, 268,* 327–329.

Miklowitz, D. J., & Goldstein, M. J. (1990). Behavioral family treatment for patients with bipolar affective disorder. *Behavior Modification, 14,* 457–489.

Miklowitz, D. J., Goldstein, M. J., Nuechterlein, K. H., Snyder, K. S., & Mintz, J. (1988). Family factors and the course of bipolar affective disorder. *Archives of General Psychiatry, 45,* 225–231.

O'Connell, R. A., Mayo, J. A., & Flatow, L. (1991). Outcome of bipolar disorder on long-term treatment with lithium. *British Journal of Psychiatry, 159,* 123–129.

Perris, C. (1966). A study of bipolar (manic-depressive) and unipolar recurrent depressive psychoses. *Acta Psychiatrica Scandinavica, 42(Suppl. 194),* 7–184.

Perry, P. J., Alexander, B., & Garvey, M. J. (1994). Clinical psychopharmacology and other somatic therapies. In G. Winokur & P. Clayton (Eds.), *The medical basis of psychiatry* (2nd ed.). Philadelphia: Saunders.

Pollock, H. (1931). Recurrence of attacks in manic-depressive psychoses. *American Journal of Psychiatry, 22,* 567–574.

Powell, K. B., & Miklowitz, D. J. (1994). Frontal lobe dysfunction in the affective disorders. *Clinical Psychology Review, 14,* 525–546.

Regier, D. A., Farmer, M. E., Rae, D. S., Locke, B. Z., Keith, S. J., Judd, L. L., & Goodwin, F. K. (1990). Comorbidity of mental disorders with alcohol and other drug abuse. *Journal of the American Medical Association, 264,* 2511–2518.

Reich, T., Clayton, P., & Winokur, G. (1969). Family history studies: V. The genetics of mania. *American Journal of Psychiatry, 125,* 358–360.

Robins, L., Helzer, J., Weissman, M., Orvaschel, H., Gruenberg, E., Burke, J., & Regier,

D. (1984). Lifetime prevalence of psychiatric disorders in three sites. *Archives of General Psychiatry, 41,* 949–958.

Rohland, B. M., Carroll, B. T., & Jacoby, R. G. (1993). ECT in the treatment of the catatonic syndrome. *Journal of Affective Disorder, 29,* 255–261.

Schlesser, M., Winokur, G., & Sherman, B. (1980). Hypothalamic-pituitary-adrenal axis activity in depressive illness. *Archives of General Psychiatry, 37,* 737–743.

Spitzer, R., Endicott, J., & Robins, E. (1977). *Research diagnostic criteria: Rationale and reliability.* Paper presented at the Annual Meeting of the American Psychiatric Association, Toronto.

Straub, R. E., Lehner, T., Luo, Y., Loth, J. E., Shao, W., Sharpe, L., Alexander, J. R., Das, K., Simon, R., Fieve, R. R., Lerer, B., Endicott, J., Ott, J., Gilliam, T. C., & Baron, M. (1994). A possible vulnerability locus for bipolar affective disorder on chromosome 21q22.3. *Nature Genetics, 8,* 291–296.

Tsuang, M., Winokur, G., & Crowe, R. (1980). Morbidity risk of schizophrenia and affective disorders among first-degree relatives of patients with schizophrenia, mania, depression, and surgical conditions. *British Journal of Psychiatry, 137,* 497–504.

Tsuang, M., Woolson, R., & Fleming, J. (1980). Causes of death in schizophrenia and manic depression. *British Journal of Psychiatry, 136,* 239–242.

Weissman, M., Leaf, P., Tischler, G., Blazer, D., Karno, M., Bruce, M., & Florio, L. (1988). Affective disorder in five United States communities. *Psychological Medicine, 18,* 141–153.

Weissman, M., & Myers, J. (1978). Affective disorders in a U.S. urban community. *Archives of General Psychiatry, 35,* 1304–1311.

Winokur, G. (1970). Genetic findings and methodological considerations in manic-depressive disease. *British Journal of Psychiatry, 117,* 267–274.

Winokur, G. (1973). The types of affective disorders. *Journal of Nervous and Mental Disease, 156,* 82–97.

Winokur, G. (1979). Unipolar depression, is it divisible into autonomous subtypes? *Archives of General Psychiatry, 36,* 47–52.

Winokur, G. (1984). Psychosis in bipolar and unipolar affective illness with special reference to schizoaffective disorder. *British Journal of Psychiatry, 145,* 236–242.

Winokur, G., & Clayton, P. (1967). Family history studies: Two types of affective disorder separated according to genetic and clinical factors. In J. Wortis (Ed.), *Recent advances in biological psychiatry.* New York: Plenum.

Winokur, G., Clayton, P., & Reich, T. (1969). *Manic depressive illness.* St. Louis: Mosby.

Winokur, G., Cook, B., Liskow, B., & Fowler, R. (1993). Alcoholism in manic depressive (bipolar) patients. *Journal on Studies on Alcohol, 54,* 574–576.

Winokur, G., Coryell, W., Akiskal, H. S., Endicott, J., Keller, M., & Mueller, T. (1994). Manic-depressive (bipolar) disorder: The course in light of a prospective ten-year follow-up of 131 patients. *Acta Psychiatrica Scandinavica, 89,* 102–110.

Winokur, G., Coryell, W., Endicott, J., & Akiskal, H. (1993). Further distinctions between manic-depressive illness (bipolar disorder) and primary depressive disorder (unipolar depression). *American Journal of Psychiatry, 150,* 1176–1181.

Winokur, G., Coryell, W., Keller, M., Endicott, J., & Akiskal, H. (1993). A prospective follow-up of patients with bipolar and primary unipolar affective disorder. *Archives of General Psychiatry, 50,* 457–465.

Winokur, G., & Morrison, J. (1973). The Iowa 500: Follow-up of 225 depressives. *British Journal of Psychiatry, 123,* 543–548.

Winokur, G., Tsuang, M., & Crowe, R. R. (1982). The Iowa 500: Affective disorder in relatives of manic and depressed patients. *American Journal of Psychiatry, 139,* 209–212.

Winokur, G., & Wesner, R. (1987). From unipolar depression to bipolar illness: Twenty-nine who changed. *Acta Psychiatrica Scandinavica, 73,* 59–63.

Yamamoto, J., Fung, D., Lo, S., & Reece, S. (1979). To proof: *Psychopharmacology Bulletin, 15,* 29–31.

Ziegler, V. E., & Biggs, J. T. (1977). Tricyclic plasma levels-effects of age, race, sex, and smoking. *Journal of the American Medical Association, 238,* 2167–2169.

CHAPTER 10

Anxiety Disorders

DEBORAH C. BEIDEL and SAMUEL M. TURNER

The past 15 years have witnessed a remarkable period of scientific development in the study of anxiety disorders. The third edition of the *Diagnostic and Statistical Manual of Mental Disorders* (DSM-III; American Psychiatric Association [APA], 1980) radically altered the conceptualization of these disorders. Rather than three broad categories (phobic neurosis, obsessive-compulsive neurosis, or anxiety neurosis), nine different diagnoses were introduced. In 1987, further classificatory changes were made, including subsuming agoraphobia under panic disorder (DSM-III-R, APA, 1987). The most recent revision (DSM-IV; APA, 1994) made only minor changes in much of the existing diagnostic schema but added three new diagnostic categories (acute stress disorder, anxiety disorder due to a general medical condition, substance-induced anxiety disorder). This attention is well justified as the data indicate clearly that anxiety disorders constitute the most common psychiatric problems in the United States, with the exception of substance abuse disorders (Blazer et al., 1985; Burnam et al., 1987; Kessler, 1994; Robins et al., 1984).

DESCRIPTION OF THE DISORDERS

Panic Attacks

The most significant change in DSM-IV was the clear acknowledgment that panic attacks occur in the context of many different anxiety states as well as nonanxiety disorders. Although not a codable disorder, criteria for panic attacks are now listed separately in the diagnostic schema. A panic attack consists of a discrete period of intense fear or discomfort in which four (or more) somatic and cognitive symptoms develop abruptly and reach a peak within 10 minutes (DSM-IV, p. 395). Symptoms include palpitations; pounding heart or accelerated heart rate; sweating; trembling or shaking; sensations of shortness of breath or smothering; feelings of choking; chest pain or discomfort; nausea or abdomina distress; feeling dizzy, unsteady, lightheaded, or faint; derealization or depersonalization; fear of losing control or going crazy; fear of dying; paresthesias; chills or hot flushes.

There are three characteristic types of panic attacks: 1. unexpected (uncued): onset is not associated with a situational trigger; 2. situationally bound (cued): the attack occurs immediately upon exposure to or in anticipation of exposure to the anxiety-producing stimulus; or 3. situationally predisposed: the attack is more likely to occur upon exposure although not immediately upon exposure and not necessarily every time the individual is exposed to the event. Uncued attacks are more characteristic of panic disorder and frequently occur in generalized anxiety disorder (GAD) patients, whereas situationally bound attacks are more characteristic of specific and social phobia. However, there is not a one-to-one relationship between type of attack and particular disorder. Furthermore, although not specifically mentioned in the DSM-IV, patients with obsessive-compulsive disorder often report panic attacks. In the general population, about 15% of individuals reported occurrence of panic attacks at some time in their lives, and 3% reported a panic attack in the previous month (Eaton, Kessler, Wittchen, & Magee, 1994). Finally, it is important to note that criteria for defining a panic attack did not change in DSM-IV and have remained essentially the same since DSM-III.

Panic Disorder without Agoraphobia

One of the most significant changes in DSM-III that remains in DSM-IV was the addition of panic disorder as a discrete category. The work of Klein and his associates is usually credited with differentiating panic from other forms of anxiety. Klein and Fink (1962) reported that antidepressants were effective in decreasing phobic inpatients' episodic anxiety or panic attacks but were ineffective for ameliorating anticipatory anxiety or avoidance. On the other hand, benzodiazepines were effective for anticipatory anxiety. Through a semantic drift, anticipatory anxiety became synonymous with generalized anxiety (Turner, Beidel, & Jacob, 1988). This pharmacological dissection strategy was thought to have delineated two distinct types of anxiety. However, several recent studies have shown that imipramine is effective for GAD patients (e.g., Kahn et al., 1981), and the newer high-potency benzodiazepines appear to be effective for treating panic disorder, thus calling into question this early model (Lydiard, Roy-Byrne, & Ballenger, 1988).

Panic disorder is defined by occurrence of a panic attack. To meet diagnostic criteria, attacks must be recurrent and unexpected, and at least one attack must be followed by 1. persistent worry or concern about having another attack, 2. worry about the implications of the attack or its consequences, or 3. a significant change in behavior related to the attacks. There is no evidence of behavioral avoidance (agoraphobia).

Panic Disorder with Agoraphobia

Agoraphobia, considered to be a complication of panic disorder, is a fear of being in public places or situations where escape might be difficult or where help may be unavailable in case a panic attack occurs. However, a recent study (Jacob, Furman, Durrant, & Turner, 1996) indicates that this conceptualization may not be correct (see psychological and biological assessment section). Despite the precursor, patients with agoraphobia avoid (or endure with marked distress) certain situations. In the most severe form, patients may refuse to travel any distance from home or even leave the house. Thus, this disorder includes presence of panic attacks and behavioral avoidance of situations that are associated with their potential onset. Places commonly feared by agoraphobics include crowded places, such as supermarkets, shopping malls, restaurants, churches, theaters, riding in buses, cars, or planes, and traveling over bridges or through tunnels. Some individuals with agoraphobia will enter these situations but only with a trusted companion.

Agoraphobia without History of Panic

Some agoraphobics report fear and avoidance of public places but apparently have never had panic attacks. Thus, although their behavior is similar to those suffering from panic disorder with agoraphobia, they have never experienced the sudden, unexpected onset of panic. According to DSM-IV, such patients are usually afraid of the occurrence of incapacitating or extremely embarrassing physical symptoms or limited symptom attacks (anxiety that consists of no more than three panic attack symptoms). These patients also may fear dizziness or falling, loss of bowel or bladder control, or vomiting (APA, 1994). Interestingly, for some patients, symptoms they fear have never occurred, at least not in public places that they fear. This also apparently differentiates the disorder from panic disorder with agoraphobia, where sudden onset of panic constitutes the first stage of the disorder. Agoraphobia without history of panic is seen only rarely in clinic settings and thus has not been the subject of much empirical study. Recent evidence suggests that some agoraphobics without history of panic (those who fear losing control of their bodily functions) possess some clinical characteristics reminiscent of obsessive-compulsive disorder and may actually fall within the obsessional realm (Beidel & Bulik, 1990; Jenike, Vitagliano, Rabinowitz, Goff, & Baer, 1987). Weissman, Leckman, Merikangas, Gammon, and Prusoff (1984) reported a prevalence rate of 2.9% in the general population, but a recalculation revealed a more modest 1% prevalence rate (Jacob & Turner, 1988). More recently, individuals who were diagnosed with agoraphobia without panic attacks were reassessed by clinicians using standard interview schedules. Most individuals were discovered to have specific phobias rather than agoraphobia without panic attacks (APA, 1994). Therefore, the nature and proper classification of this condition must await further study.

Social Phobia

Although fears when in the presence of others have been noted back to the days of the Hippocratic Corpus (Marks, 1985) and have been addressed in the literature since at least 1970 (Marks, 1970), social phobia was not introduced into the American psychiatric nomenclature until 1980. Social phobia refers to a marked and persistent fear of social or performance situations in which embarrassment may occur (APA, 1994). Exposure almost invariably provokes an anxiety response, which can result in a situationally bound or situationally predisposed panic attack. Social or performance situations are avoided or endured with significant distress. Individuals with this disorder may feel uncomfortable performing certain activities in the presence of others, such as speaking, eating, drinking, or writing; fearing that he or she may do something which will

cause humiliation or embarrassment, such as forgetting a speech, mispro-
nouncing a word, or shaking uncontrollably. Some social phobics also fear that
others will detect their nervousness by observing signs of somatic distress such
as blushing or trembling. For some, the fear is not limited to circumscribed
social situations but is present in most social interactions, including one to one
conversations. Those social phobics who fear a broad range of social situations
are considered to have the "generalized" subtype. Since the subtype distinction
was introduced, the results of several investigations (Herbert, Hope, & Bellack,
1992; Holt, Heimberg, & Hope, 1992; Turner, Beidel, & Townsley, 1992) indicate
that the generalized subtype is associated with more severe anxiety, depression,
social inhibition, fear of negative evaluation, avoidance, fearfulness, and self-
consciousness. Generalized social phobia may be related to an earlier age of
onset (Herbert et al., 1992; Holt et al., 1992). Stemberger, Turner, Beidel, and
Calhoun (1995) found that the generalized subtype was more neurotic, more
frequently shy as children, and more introverted than the specific subtype.

Many social phobics (86%) avoid at least some social situations (Turner,
Beidel, Dancu, & Keys, 1986), although strict avoidance is not necessary for the
diagnosis. With respect to social functioning, Liebowitz, Gorman, Fyer, and
Klein (1985) and Turner et al. (1986) report that inability to work, incomplete
educational attainment, lack of career advancement, and severe social restrictions were common features of this disorder. Lost productivity is also common
(Van Amerigen, Mancini, & Streiner, 1993). Finally, social phobics in a community sample were more dependent on others and relied more heavily on public
assistance (Schneier, Johnson, Hornig, Liebowitz, & Weissman, 1992).

Specific Phobia

A significant change made in DSM-IV was the renaming of simple phobia as
specific phobia. Specific phobia refers to a marked and persistent fear of clearly
discernible, circumscribed objects or situations (APA, 1994). When confronted
with the feared situation, specific phobics experience internal emotional reactions and may have panic attacks that are situationally bound or situationally
predisposed. The situations are either avoided or endured with significant distress. In the general population, common specific phobias include fears of animals such as dogs, snakes, insects, and mice, as well as fears of blood-injury,
heights and enclosed spaces (Agras, Sylvester, & Oliveau, 1969; APA, 1994). In
clinical settings, claustrophobia (fear of closed spaces) and acrophobia (fear of
heights) are those most commonly encountered (Emmelkamp, 1988).

The renaming of these phobic conditions from simple to specific phobia is a
clear recognition that these disorders are not necessarily minor abreactions.
Data collected from the large-scale ECA survey revealed that a significant percentage of the general population suffers from some type of specific phobia, but
this disorder accounts for a very small percentage of those treated in anxiety
disorders clinics (Barlow, DiNardo, Vermilyea, Vermilyea, & Blanchard, 1986).
Those who do seek treatment are rarely "simple," often presenting with additional Axis I or II conditions, or both (Barlow, 1988).

New to DSM-IV is the subtyping of specific phobias: animal type, if the fear
is cued by animals or insects; natural environment type, if cued by objects or

events in the environment such as storms, heights, or water; blood/injection/ injury type if cued by blood, injuries, or needles; or situational type if cued by a specific situation such as public transportation, tunnels, bridges, elevators, flying, driving, or enclosed places (APA, 1994). There is also an "other" type that is used if the fear is related to any other stimuli. In clinical settings, the situational subtype is most frequent, followed by natural environment, blood-injury-illness, and animal.

Obsessive-Compulsive Disorder

Obsessive-compulsive disorder (OCD) is characterized by presence of intrusive thoughts, often coupled with repetitive behaviors that are elaborate and time consuming and that create significant distress for the individual or significant others (APA, 1994). Obsessions are recurrent and persistent thoughts, impulses, or images that are experienced as intrusive and inappropriate and that cause marked anxiety or distress. In most cases, the irrationality of obsessions is recognized by the individual, and there is an attempt to ignore or suppress the intrusive thoughts by neutralizing them with other thoughts or actions. Furthermore, individuals recognize that the obsessions are a product of their own mind and that they are not imposed externally. This is important because this distinction separates obsessions from delusions. Delusional individuals do not recognize the irrationality of their thoughts and frequently view them as having been imposed externally. Those with OCD attempt to ignore or suppress the obsessions or neutralize them with other thoughts or actions. The most common forms of obsessions are doubts, thoughts, impulses, fears, images, and urges. The most common content areas include dirt and contamination, aggression, inanimate-interpersonal (e.g., locks, bolts, other safety devices, and orderliness), sex, religion, and what was referred to as a miscellaneous category (Akhtar, Wig, Verna, Pershod, & Verna, 1975; Khanna & Channabasavanna, 1988).

Compulsions are repetitive behaviors or mental acts that the person feels driven to perform in response to obsessions or according to rules that must be applied rigidly (APA, 1994). Compulsions are designed to prevent occurrence of a future event, or to neutralize the after effects of an event which may have occurred, such as coming into contact with "germs." Similar to obsessions, the purposelessness of these actions most often is recognized, but the person nonetheless feels compelled to carry out the ritual to completion. Completing the ritual may be negatively reinforcing because it provides a temporary decrease in anxiety for most patients, although a few individuals do report increased anxiety (e.g., Walker & Beech, 1969). Common forms of compulsions are hand-washing and bathing, cleaning, checking, counting, and ordering. Repetitive cleaning behaviors often are seen with contamination fears, while checking behaviors are common in those who experience self-doubt or dread the onset of some future event (Turner & Beidel, 1988). However, it also is common for more than one type of obsession or compulsion, or both, to be present. In addition, patients often develop elaborate avoidance strategies to avoid contact with feared objects or situations, thereby lessening their daily distress and limiting the necessity to engage in ritualistic behaviors. OCD is considered to have the most chronic course among the anxiety disorders.

Posttraumatic Stress Disorder

Posttraumatic stress disorder (PTSD) was introduced with the 1980 revision of the DSM (APA, 1980). In the DSM-IV, those with PTSD are defined as individuals who have been exposed to a traumatic event in which 1. the person experienced, witnessed, or was confronted with actual or threatened death or serious injury, or a threat to the physical integrity of self or others, and 2. the person's response involved intense fear, helplessness, or horror. This latter criterion is new to the diagnostic criteria. Examples of such events include combat experiences, assault, rape, or observing the serious injury or violent death of another person. Patients with this diagnosis report that they "reexperience" the event in one of the following ways: recurrent and intrusive recollections, recurrent and intrusive dreams, suddenly acting or feeling as if the event were recurring, intense psychological or physical reactivity, and distress when exposed to events that symbolize or resemble some aspect of the trauma. As a result of the trauma, there is an attempt to avoid stimuli associated with the event including thoughts, feelings, activities, or situations, and there might be difficulty recalling important aspects of the event. Furthermore, patients usually describe numbing of general emotions, including diminished interest in activities, feeling of detachment or estrangement from others, restricted range of affect, and a sense of a foreshortened future. Occurrence of general and persistent autonomic arousal also is a component of the disorder and may include difficulty sleeping, irritability or anger, difficulty concentrating, hypervigilance, exaggerated startle responses, and physiologic reactivity upon exposure to stimuli associated with the event (APA, 1994).

The symptoms must persist for at least 1 month, and the disorder has two subtypes: acute, if the duration of symptoms is less than 3 months, and chronic, if symptom duration is 3 months or more. There is also a delayed onset specifier, if the onset occurs at least 6 months after the event. Historically, PTSD has been used to apply to persons who had participated in combat, but also is used for those who experience natural disasters, assault or rape (Kilpatrick et al., 1989), or a host of other noncombat-related events. Community studies reveal variable rates for the disorder, ranging from 1% to 14%, depending on the method of assessment and the type of population involved (APA, 1994). Davidson, Hughes, Blazer, and George (1991) reported a 1.3% lifetime prevalence rate and a 0.44% 6-month prevalence rate for PTSD in a community sample. Epidemiological estimates of combat-related PTSD vary, but most studies report a lifetime prevalence of between 15% and 30% of combat veterans (Center for Disease Control, 1988; Kulka et al., 1988).

Acute Stress Disorder

Acute stress disorder is a new diagnostic category introduced in the DSM-IV, but the criteria are similar to those of PTSD. In fact, the description of the stress-inducing event and the individual's reaction is the same as for PTSD; only a duration requirement separates the two. Individuals with this disorder report a subjective sense of numbing, detachment, or absence of emotion; a reduction in awareness of surroundings, derealization, depersonalization, or dissociative amnesia. Symptoms of reexperiencing, avoidance of the stimuli, and symptoms of anxiety or arousal are identical to those for PTSD. In addition, there must be clinically significant distress or functional impairment. The disturbance lasts for a minimum of 2 days and a maximum of 4 weeks. The short symptom duration (maximum = 4 weeks) for this condition makes it unclear if someone with this disorder would require treatment. If the symptoms persist for longer than 4 weeks, a diagnosis of PTSD would be warranted. Because of recent introduction of this category, its epidemiology is uncertain.

Generalized Anxiety Disorder

In DSM-III, GAD was reserved for those who did not meet criteria for any other anxiety disorder (Barlow, 1988), but reported persistent worry and perhaps accompanying somatic distress lasting for a 1-month period. Basically, it was a residual diagnostic category and was quite controversial. For a review of its subsequent evolution, see Barlow (1988). Currently in DSM-IV, the essential feature of this disorder is excessive anxiety and worry occurring more days than not for a period of at least 6 months about a number of events or activities (APA, 1994). Individuals report that it is difficult to control the worry that is associated with the following somatic and cognitive symptoms: muscle tension, restlessness or feeling keyed up or on edge, easy fatigability, difficulty concentrating or mind going blank, sleep disturbance, and irritability. In DSM-IV, the number of cognitive and somatic complaints was reduced by 66% (from 18 to 6) as a result of attempts to validate the presence of these symptoms (Brown, Barlow, & Liebowitz, 1994). The focus of the anxiety is not confined to the features of any other Axis I disorder, and the anxiety, worry, or physical symptoms must cause clinically significant distress or functional impairment.

Other Anxiety Disorders

Anxiety disorders can be the result of a general medical condition (anxiety disorder due to a general medical condition) or resulting from the ingestion of or withdrawal from certain substances (substance-induced anxiety disorder). Symptoms induced by either of these conditions can include panic attacks, anxiety, obsessions, compulsions, and phobias. Thus, prior to assigning one of the above diagnoses, it is necessary to carefully rule out general medical disorders including endocrine, cardiovascular, respiratory, metabolic, and neurological conditions. Jacob and Turner (1988) noted a number of medical conditions that may be related to presence of panic disorder. These include mitral valve prolapse, other cardiovascular conditions, vestibular abnormalities, hyperthyroidism, hypothyroidism, hypoglycemia, partial complex seizures, pheochromocytoma, hypoparathyroidism, hyperparathyroidism, and Cushing's syndrome. The challenge to the clinician in deriving a diagnosis is to determine if the anxiety state results from one of these general medical conditions. For example, temporal order of the disease and the anxiety symptoms may assist in determining a relationship between the two conditions. Similarly, presence of anxiety symptoms only during an episode of the physical illness or an atypical age of onset for the anxiety disorder may suggest an etiological role for the medical condition (APA, 1994). Prior to beginning any intervention for anxiety, the patient's medical condition should be evaluated, and treated if necessary, by a physician.

Anxiety symptoms can be induced by ingestion of or withdrawal from a number of substances including alcohol, "recreational drugs," or caffeine. Substances specifically listed by the DSM-IV include alcohol, amphetamine, caffeine, cannabis, cocaine, hallucinogen, inhalants, phencyclidine, sedatives, hypnotics, or anxiolytics. Also included are medications, such as anesthetics, analgesics, sympathomimetics, anticholinergics, insulin, thyroid preparations, oral contraceptives, antihistamines, anti-Parkinsonian medications, corticosteroids, antihypertensive and cardiovascular medications, anticonvulsants, lithium carbonate, antipsychotic medications, and antidepressant medications. Another class of anxiety precipitants includes heavy metals and toxins (e.g., gasoline, organophosphate insecticides, and carbon monoxide). If anxiety is due to any one of these conditions, treatment for the medical disorder should also result in a remediation of the anxiety symptoms. If not, other additional causes should be considered (APA, 1994).

Epidemiology

Data from the NIMH Epidemiological Catchment Area (ECA) survey provided some initial estimates of prevalence. Six-month rates (adjusted to control for slight variations in the age and sex distributions across the five ECA sites) for the combined anxiety/somatoform categories ranged from 6.6%, 7.2%, and 7.4% (St. Louis, Los Angeles, and New Haven sites) to 14.8% (Baltimore and Piedmont sites) of the general adult population (Burnam et al., 1987). Somatoform disorders contributed only minimally to these prevalence rates (less than 0.4%). A more recent study by Kessler et al. (1994) suggests that the previous ECA data were an underestimate. According to results from the National Comorbidity Survey (NCS), 24.9% of the general population reported the lifetime occurrence of an anxiety disorder, and 17.2% of the sample reported the presence of an anxiety disorder in the past 12 months. This 12-month prevalence rate for anxiety was higher than for any other diagnostic category, and the lifetime prevalence rate was second only to the rate for substance abuse disorders. This suggests that anxiety disorders affect a substantial part of the general population. Data for lifetime and 12-month prevalence rates are presented in Table 10.1.

Different rates of disorders between the two epidemiological surveys are likely due, at least in part, to methodological differences. The NCS study used a national sample, concentrated on a younger age range than previous surveys

TABLE 10.1   Lifetime and 12-Month Prevalence Rates for Anxiety Disorders

Disorder	Lifetime	12 Month
Panic disorder	3.5	2.3
Agoraphobia without panic	5.3	2.8
Social phobia	13.3	7.9
Specific phobia	11.3	8.8
Generalized anxiety disorder	5.1	3.1
Any anxiety disorder	24.9	17.2

(ages 15–54), used a correction weight to adjust for nonresponse bias, and based diagnoses on DSM-III-R rather than DSM-III (Kessler et al., 1994).

CLINICAL PICTURE

The differentiation of "normal" anxiety from the clinical syndromes included in the diagnostic nomenclature is based not only on symptom severity but also on the degree of functional interference. The specific inclusion of a functional impairment criterion is presented more clearly in DSM-IV than in any previous version of DSM. Consideration of impairment is most important in determining whether symptoms actually are disorders. For example, although 61% of a telephone survey sample reported they are much or somewhat more anxious than others in social situations, only 18.7% reported at least moderate interference or distress. This percentage dropped to 7.1% when strict DSM-III-R criteria were applied and further dropped to 1.9% when only "at least moderate impairment" was considered (Stein, Walker, & Forde, 1994).

Anxiety is a multidimensional construct, commonly conceptualized as a tripartite system (Lang, 1977). Anxiety responses usually are divided into three dimensions: subjective distress (self-report), physiological response, and avoidance or escape behavior (overt behavioral response). Consistent with the transient "fight or flight" response, the somatic complaints of anxiety patients are characterized primarily by sympathetic nervous system activation. Thus, complaints of tachycardia, tremulousness, dizziness, lightheadedness, parasthesias, and dyspnea are common. Certain types of anxiety disorder patients differentially experience somatic symptomatology. Amies, Gelder, and Shaw (1983) reported that dizziness, difficulty breathing, weakness in limbs, fainting episodes, and buzzing or ringing in the ears were endorsed significantly more often by agoraphobics than social phobics, whereas patients with social phobia were significantly more likely to endorse blushing and muscle twitching than agoraphobics. Page (1994) reported that patients with panic disorder were more likely than social phobics to endorse parasthesias, choking or smothering, feeling dizzy or lightheaded, feeling faint as well as worrying that they might die, collapse, or go crazy. Individuals with GAD sometimes report gastrointestinal distress including indigestion, nausea, constipation, diarrhea, and urinary urgency and frequency. Others have noted a predominant central nervous system hyperarousal (Noyes et al., 1992). In DSM-IV, muscle tension is the primary somatic complaint. Finally, the reaction of needle/blood/injury phobics is defined by parasympathetic (rather than sympathetic) activation manifested by bradycardia and hypotension (Ost, 1996), which is clearly different from the somatic responses found in other phobic states.

Cognitive symptoms of anxiety usually entail worry about specific events involving the possibility of danger or harm to one's self or to others. Although most often experienced as specific thoughts, cognitive symptoms also may occur in the form of ideas, images, or impulses. Occurrence of the fearful event, although a possibility, is usually of very low probability, thus fear is out of proportion to situational demand. Anxiety patients are usually aware that the fear is excessive or unreasonable, yet such knowledge does little to assuage the overly aroused emotional state.

In specific or social phobias, the thought usually has a specific theme and is most often triggered by actual or anticipated contact with the feared stimulus. On the other hand, those with more pervasive anxiety states such as GAD present with a broader constellation of anxious cognitions, termed "worry," which encompasses several thematic areas, has the characteristics of mental problem solving, and the possibility of at least one negative outcome (Borkovec, Robinson, Pruzinsky, & DePress, 1983, p. 10). A final category of cognitive phenomena are obsessions that consist of intrusive unwanted thoughts, images, or impulses that are often horrific and are perceived by the patient as uncontrollable, yet always as a product of one's own mind and not the work of outside forces. Differentiation among the types of anxious cognitions can be quite subtle and may be tied to the severity of the specific disorder. That is, the more chronic and disabling the condition, the more likely that the thoughts are consistent. A recent attempt to differentiate worry from obsessionality (Turner, Beidel, & Stanley, 1992) highlighted several distinguishing characteristics, including thematic content (GAD patients do not often report excessive concern with dirt, contamination, aggressive impulses, or horrific images), form of the cognition (GAD patients do not report images or impulses but primarily conceptual, verbal linguistic activity as described by Borkovec & Shadick, 1989, p. 22), and intrusive quality (worry is perceived as less intrusive and less ego-dystonic than obsessions). Thus, although there are some similarities, there are important differences as well.

The characteristic behavior of anxiety patients is escape from or avoidance of the feared stimulus. Many patients devise elaborate strategies, often engaging the cooperation of others in order to avoid the feared object or situation. In severe cases of panic disorder with agoraphobia, avoidance may become so restrictive that the affected individual becomes "housebound." In the case of OCD, avoidance is usually accompanied by occurrence of ritualistic behaviors, such as washing or checking, which serve to "undo" or prevent occurrence of the feared event. Although escape or avoidance is almost always present, it is not necessary for an anxiety disorder diagnosis to be made if the individuals suffer great distress when in various situations. In addition, behavioral avoidance is sometimes manifested in subtle ways that may not be readily apparent to the patient but can be detected by a trained clinician.

Other aspects of the clinical presentation often include appetite or sleep disturbances, and concentration and memory difficulties. Suicidal ideation and suicide attempts have been noted to occur in patients with panic disorder or social phobia. Cox, Direnfeld, Swinson, and Norton (1994) reported that 31% of patients with panic disorder and 34% of patients with social phobia reported suicidal ideation in the past year. Only one panic patient and two social phobic patients actually had made suicidal attempts in the past year, and 18% of panic patients and 12% of social phobia patients reported lifetime occurrence of suicide attempts. An important factor was that patients who made suicide attempts were more likely to report past psychiatric hospitalizations and treatment for depression and those with current ideation had higher scores on a depression inventory. Thus, one cannot discount the role of depression as a mediating factor in the relationship of suicidality and anxiety disorders. Even if not significantly depressed, anxiety patients often present with a dysphoric mood, usually attributed to the impairment that results from their disorder (i.e., depression mostly is secondary). Many of these additional symptoms are similar to those experienced by primarily depressed patients, making it sometimes difficult to differentiate these two affective states. In addition, certain patients may present with a mixed symptom picture (to be discussed in the Diagnostic Considerations section).

COURSE AND PROGNOSIS

In this section, behavioral and cognitive theories of etiology, age of onset, course, and prognosis (treated or untreated) will be discussed. Biological theories of etiology will be discussed in the Familial and Genetic Considerations section.

Behavioral Theories of Etiology

Studies investigating the mode of onset for certain anxiety disorders indicate that conditioning experiences play an important role in etiology. Conditioning experiences were reported to be instrumental in the onset of agoraphobia (76.7%–84%), claustrophobia (66.7%), and dental phobias (68.4%; Ost, 1987; Ost & Hugdahl, 1983). Although still evident, conditioning experiences appear less significant in the onset of social phobia (58%), animal phobias (48%), and blood phobias (45%; Ost, 1987). In the case of the latter two specific phobias, vicarious conditioning accounts for the fear onset in approximately 25% of the cases. Behavioral theories enjoy a prominent role in explaining the acquisition of anxiety and phobic states. However, it is clear that no single theory can adequately explain the onset or nature of these disorders. In the ensuing paragraphs, behavioral theories used to account for the acquisition and maintenance of the anxiety disorders will be discussed. In light of the voluminous literature on the subject, this review will touch briefly on important perspectives and highlight some of the more recent formulations.

The earliest accounts of fear acquisition, exemplified by the case of Little Albert (Watson & Rayner, 1920), were based on a strict Pavlovian model. Delprato and McGlynn (1984) provided a summary of 25 studies that support Pavlovian conditioning as a mechanism for fear acquisition. Also, a combination of classical and operant conditioning is inherent in the two-factor theory (e.g., Mowrer, 1947): a model frequently used to explain anxiety. However, traditional conditioning models have been subject to a variety of criticisms. First, despite instances where conditioning is evident in the case histories of anxiety patients, there are almost an equivalent number of instances where there appears to be no direct conditioning experience. Second, there are certain individuals who, under even the most ideal traumatic conditioning situations, fail to acquire fear (Rachman, 1990). Third, types of learning other than classical conditioning can effectively explain the acquisition of fear (Bandura, 1969). Rachman (1977) proposed a "three-pathway" hypothesis in which classical conditioning is considered to be one method through which fear may be acquired. According to the theory, other mechanisms include vicarious learning and transmission via information, instruction, or both.

Another problem for traditional conditioning models is that they do not adequately explain the unequal distribution of fears in the general population (Agras et al., 1969). For example, a significant proportion of the population endorsed fears of heights or snakes, yet few actually have had traumatic conditioning experiences. To account for this, Seligman (1971) proposed the notion of preparedness. Essentially, preparedness theory postulated that the unequal distribution of fears in the general population stems from a biological bias, such that certain fears are more easily acquired, inasmuch as they enhance the species' survival. Nonhuman primate studies provided some support for preparedness theory. For example, Cook and Mineka (1989) reported that fearful reactions were more easily acquired when laboratory-reared monkeys observed other monkeys behaving fearfully in the presence of fear relevant stimuli such as snakes or lizards than when they behaved fearfully in the presence of rabbits or flowers.

Although Seligman (1971) argued that biological preparedness accounts for phobia characteristics such as rapid acquisition, irrationality, belongingness, and high resistance to extinction, and initial laboratory studies (e.g., Ohman, 1986; Ohman, Eriksson, & Olafsson, 1975; Ohman, Fredikson, Hugdahl, & Rimmo, 1976) appeared to provide some initial support, McNally's (1987) comprehensive and thoughtful review argued persuasively that the entire body of experimental evidence for preparedness is equivocal. Only enhanced resistance to extinction of laboratory conditioned electrodermal responses has been demonstrated consistently, whereas data supporting ease of acquisition, belongingness, and irrationality have received only minimal support (McNally, 1987).

Conditioning theories also must address the issue of previously acquired information. The observer monkeys in the Cook and Mineka (1989) study had no prior information about any of the stimuli as dangerous or safe, yet conditioning was more evident for those objects feared "naturally" by wild-bred monkeys. Other studies provide further evidence that prior information and experience may be significant mediating factors. Mineka and Cook (1986) demonstrated that monkeys could be immunized against snake fear by prior observational learning. Laboratory-bred monkeys first observed other monkeys behaving nonfearfully in the presence of a toy snake, then monkeys who behaved fearfully when confronted with the same snake. When the observer monkeys were exposed to the toy snake, they failed to acquire a fear response, suggesting that prior exposure to nonfearful models "immunized" the observer monkeys against the later acquisition of fear. These data suggest that prior positive environmental experiences may explain why only some individuals acquire fear after a traumatic event. Also, conditioning experiences can be cumulative (Mineka, Davidson, Cook, & Heir, 1985), and there are factors before, within, and following the conditioning experience that are relevant (Mineka & Zinbarg, 1991).

In summary, behavioral theories have evolved from simple straightforward classical conditioning theories toward more complex conceptualizations. First, as has been noted by Rachman (1977), fear may be acquired as a result of vicarious conditioning, information transmission, or classical conditioning. Vicarious conditioning may be a particularly powerful mechanism for fear acquisition. In Cook and Mineka's studies, learning occurred within a very brief period of time (8 minutes) and produced strong emotional responses that were easily observable and approximately equivalent in intensity to those of the models. Although extant family studies often have attributed strong familial prevalence rates to a biological etiology, the vicarious conditioning literature clearly indicates that other pathways may be equally important, or that some combination of biological and psychological-environmental parameters might be essential. However, behavioral theories may never fully account for the acquisition or maintenance of fear. Even under the strictest environmental controls, not all rhesus monkeys acquired a fear of snakes. Thus, it is likely that multiple mechanisms are involved, and we turn now to an examination of some other possible contributors.

Cognitive Theories of Etiology

The cognitive theory of Beck and Emery (1985) utilizes an information-processing model in which the basic elements of cognitive organization are cognitive schemas. Schemas are organized into cognitive constellations (cognitive sets). When a set is activated, the content directly influences the person's perceptions, interpretations, associations, and memories, which in turn assign meaning to the stimuli. Cognitive sets contain rules. For the anxiety disorders, rules relate to the estimations of danger, vulnerability, and capacity for coping. If there is a perception of high vulnerability, the rules result in conclusions that one is incapable of dealing with the situation. Unlike the rules for depression which are absolute, rules for anxiety disorders have a conditional form such as the following: If A happens, it may (rather than will) have a negative result. Thus, according to Beck and Emery (1985), the crux of an anxiety disorder is "a cognitive process that may take the form of an automatic thought or image that appears rapidly, as if by reflex, after the initial stimulus that seems plausible (e.g., shortness of breath), and that is followed by a wave of anxiety" (pp. 5–6). If a specific thought or image cannot be identified, it is still possible to infer that a cognitive set with a meaning relevant to danger has been activated. The schemata themselves appear to develop as a result of removing maladaptive cognition from a primary etiological function to one that might function to maintain the disorder. Thus, cognitive theory does not appear to have a unique explanatory role in illuminating etiology or in treatment outcome (Beidel & Turner, 1986; Brewin, 1985).

Two other cognitive theories which attempt to explain the onset of anxiety disorders are the "fear of fear" model (Goldstein & Chambless, 1978) and the expectancy model and its associated construct of anxiety sensitivity (Reiss, 1991; Reiss & McNally, 1985). Fear of fear posits that an individual who has experienced panic attacks may, through the process of interoceptive conditioning, learn to fear any change in physiological state that could signal the onset of panic. In effect, low-level bodily sensations become a conditioned stimulus that triggers fear and worry regarding the onset of panic. Of course, this is not a purely cognitive model because interoceptive conditioning has a central role. Fear of fear seems to be a particularly important characteristic of individuals with panic disorder, and interventions built on the fear of fear hypothesis typically involve exposure treatment where the individual not only is exposed to places where panic might occur but also to the physical sensations of panic itself. More recently, however, Reiss and his colleagues have proposed an elaboration of the fear of fear hypothesis by introducing the construct of "anxiety sensitivity." Anxiety sensitivity is defined as an individual difference variable consisting of beliefs that the experience of anxiety causes illness, embarrassment, or additional anxiety (Reiss & McNally, 1985; Reiss, Peterson, Gursky, & McNally, 1986). According to Reiss et al. (1986), anxiety sensitivity builds upon the original fear of fear hypothesis, yet departs from it. Although Goldstein and Chambless (1978) regarded the emergence of fear of fear as a consequence of panic attacks, Reiss and McNally (1985) consider fear of fear to result from several factors: panic attacks, biological predisposition, and personality needs to avoid embarrassment or illness or to maintain control (see Reiss, 1991, for a full discussion of the expectancy model of anxiety). Anxiety sensitivity is the quantification of belief that anxiety causes illness or embarrassment and, like fear of fear, is thought to be more prevalent in patients with agoraphobia.

Empirical investigations by Reiss and his colleagues (Holloway & McNally, 1987; Maller & Reiss, 1987; McNally & Lorenz, 1987; Peterson & Heilbronner, 1987; Reiss et al., 1986) suggest that the Anxiety Sensitivity Inventory assesses a dimension other than general anxiety, anxiety symptoms, or fear of fear. However, the studies have been criticized from a methodological as well as a theoretical perspective by Lilienfeld, Jacob, and Turner (1989) and Lilienfeld, Turner, and Jacob (1993). Furthermore, Lilienfeld, Turner, and Jacob (1993, 1996) have pointed out that current data suggest that anxiety sensitivity might be best viewed as not distinct from trait anxiety (or other constructs such as negative affect), but a lower order facet of one or more of these constructs. In this conceptualization, anxiety sensitivity is one manifestation of a much broader construct or set of anxiety vulnerability features.

In the past 10 years, cognitive theories have achieved a major place in etiological theories of anxiety. McNally (1995) noted that a core assumption of this approach is that those with disorders process information about threats differently than those without the disorder. Furthermore, the assumption is that the cognitive biases figure in the maintenance, and perhaps the etiology, of anxiety disorders. To fit the theory, these thoughts must fit the definition of automatic; that is, they must be capacity free, unconscious, and involuntary. Capacity free refers to the fact that the processing of information does not consume resources (i.e., the thoughts are produced effortlessly). In reviewing the body of literature on cognitive processing, McNally (1995) concluded that cognitive biases are involuntary, may sometimes be unconscious, but are not capacity free. The most parsimonious explanation for these data is that they must be driven by some other function. Thus, these thoughts may be maintained by pathological anxiety (i.e., emotion), but they do not appear to play a primary etiological role.

In summary, cognitive theories of anxiety have allowed the clinician to examine more directly the role of beliefs and cognitions in the etiology and maintenance of these disorders. The empirical evidence to date indicates that although these variables are important syndromal phenomena and may be important in maintaining fear and avoidance, their role as primary catalysts in the onset of the disorders remains uncertain. High-risk studies may well be necessary in order to resolve the issue of primacy or secondary status for cognitive features of anxiety.

Age of Onset

Among the anxiety disorders, specific phobias have the earliest age of onset, usually appearing during early childhood. Interestingly, ages of onset for certain specific phobias mirror developmental stages established for "normal" childhood fears. Developmentally, animal fears are common in preschool children, and two studies reported that specific animal phobias first appear between the ages of 4.4 and 6.9 years (Marks & Gelder, 1966; Ost, 1987), while in a third, 100% of a sample of animal and insect phobics had an age of onset prior to age 10 (McNally & Steketee, 1985). Similarly, younger elementary children commonly fear natural events such as lightning and thunder and health-related concerns, while fear of injury is seen in older elementary school children (Barrios, Hartmann, & Shigatomi, 1981). With respect to phobias, Liddell and Lyons (1978) reported that age of onset for a small sample of thunderstorm phobics was 11.9 years, age of onset for blood phobics was 8.8 years, and for dental phobics, 10.8 years. Studies of normal fears in children often are fraught with methodological limitations including data based almost solely on parental report rather than child self-report or behavioral observation. Thus, it is unclear how many of these normal fears may have been the initial expression of a specific phobia. Furthermore, it is tempting to speculate that certain constitutional or environmental characteristics may be pivotal in the differentiation of normal fear from specific phobia. Certainly, the relationship between normal childhood fears and age of onset for specific phobias is deserving of further investigation.

Certain specific phobias (especially claustrophobia) appear to have a much later average age of onset, ranging from 16.1 to 22.7 years (Marks & Gelder, 1966; Sheehan, Sheehan, & Minichiello, 1981; Thyer, Parrish, Curtis, Nesse, & Cameron, 1985). Age of onset for claustrophobia in the Ost (1987) investigation also was later than for other specific phobias (20.2 years). Interestingly, these ages are more similar to the age of onset for panic disorder (see below) than for other specific phobias, supporting the hypothesis proposed by Klein (1981), and discussed by Ost (1987), that claustrophobia may be a restricted but functional and descriptive equivalent of panic disorder with agoraphobia.

The generally accepted age of onset for panic disorder usually is during early adulthood. Ost (1987) compiled data from 13 samples of panic and agoraphobic patients, reporting an age of onset ranging from 19.7 to 32 years of age, with a mean of 26.5 years across all studies. Although some researchers have described a bimodal age distribution with the first period occurring during late adolescence and the second around age 30 (Marks & Gelder, 1966), others found a unimodal distribution (Ost, 1987; Thorpe & Burns, 1983).

Age of onset for social phobia falls somewhere between those for specific phobias and panic disorder with agoraphobia, usually occurring during adolescence. The typical age of onset ranges from 15.7 to 20.0 years (Amies et al., 1983; Liebowitz et al., 1985; Marks & Gelder, 1966; Ost, 1987; Thyer et al.,

1985; Turner et al., 1986), although it is likely that the critical period is early adolescence (Turner & Beidel, 1989a). Adolescence has been noted to be the crucial period for acquisition of social fearfulness (Ohman, 1986). The importance of peer groups and the necessity of establishing one's place within a social system is an important stage of adolescent development and likely accounts for the onset of social phobia during this period. For those with anxious temperaments (e.g., Kagan, Reznick, Clarke, Snidman, & Garcia-Coll, 1984), environmental demands which emerge during adolescence may provide the onset trigger (Turner & Beidel, 1989a). However, it should be noted that social phobia has been diagnosed in children as young as age 8 (Beidel & Turner, 1988).

For OCD, typical age of onset ranges from late adolescence to early adulthood (e.g., Rasmussen & Tsuang, 1986; Turner & Beidel, 1988). In addition, OCD is one of the few anxiety disorders whose symptoms are identical in children and adults, and the frank onset of this disorder has been witnessed in those as young as age 4 (Turner & Beidel, 1988). Furthermore, although actual onset may be around age 20, retrospective reports from OCD patients indicate that vestiges of the disorder often are present at a much earlier age.

A review of the literature did not reveal any figures for a "typical" age of onset for GAD or PTSD. Noyes et al. (1992) reported an age of onset of 23.6 years for a small sample of GAD patients. In the case of PTSD, given that the disorder is triggered by a traumatic event, the onset of the disorder can be expected to occur at any age.

Course and Complications

Anxiety disorders tend to have a chronic course. For example, Breier, Charney, and Heninger (1986) reported that agoraphobia was chronic and unremitting. Similarly, a sample of 22 outpatients with severe animal phobias reported that once established, their fear intensity remained constant or gradually increased over subsequent years (McNally & Steketee, 1985). A similar pattern has been noted for OCD, which is described as a chronic condition with periodic exacerbations (Rasmussen & Tsuang, 1986). In a multicenter study of the parameters of panic disorder, panic disorder with agoraphobia, and agoraphobia without panic disorder (Goisman et al., 1994), there was a .42 probability that a panic disorder patient would be symptom free for 8 weeks. Probabilities for the two groups with agoraphobia were .15, indicating that these latter groups were very unlikely to have symptom-free periods. Similar figures were reported for Keller et al. (1994), who found a .39 probability of full remission (8 weeks symptom free) at 1-year follow-up for uncomplicated panic disorder and a .17 probability of full remission for panic disorder with agoraphobia. At 18 months, the probabilities increased to .49 and .20, respectively. However, there was a high rate of relapse (within 1 year) after remission. Probability of relapse rates were .31 for panic disorder patients and .35 for panic disorder with agoraphobia. Comorbidity of Axis II disorders may play a role in chronicity, as Pollack, Otto, Rosenbaum, and Sachs (1992) reported 59% of those without a personality disorder had a 2-month period of remission compared to 29% of those with a comorbid personality disorder. Although over 80% of these patients received pharmacological treatment and 75% received psychological treatment as well, interpretation of the study results is difficult because of 1. the mixed method of treatment and 2. psychological treatment that primarily consisted of nonspecific dynamic intervention rather than the highly efficacious behavioral and cognitive-behavioral treatments.

Davidson (1993) reported that onset of social phobia prior to age 11 was predictive of nonrecovery in adulthood. A prospective follow-along study of social phobia (Reich, Goldenberg, Goisman, Vasile, & Keller, 1994) reported that no demographic (gender or age) or clinical variables (age of onset, duration of illness, comorbidity, or level of functioning) accurately predicted outcome 65 weeks after intake. Noyes et al. (1992) reported that compared to panic patients, those with GAD were significantly more likely to describe a gradual onset for their disorder. Like panic patients, those with GAD had an unremitting course of illness. In a follow-up study of GAD, 44 patients were interviewed an average of 15.7 months after completing a clinical drug trial (Mancuso, Townsend, & Mercante, 1993). Among those patients, 50% continued to meet criteria for GAD, whereas 50% did not. Interestingly, there were an equal number of "treatment responders" (designated at the end of the clinical trial) in each group. However, those who continued to have GAD symptoms were also more likely to have concurrent diagnoses of dysthymia, social phobia, or both, as well as a higher prevalence of Axis II cluster B and C personality disorders.

The few empirical data that do exist, along with our clinical experience, lead us to draw the following tentative conclusions. First, symptom exacerbation is often correlated with onset of significant life stressors (Klein & Fink, 1962; Turner & Beidel, 1988). Second, once the disorder is established, behavioral avoidance often functions to reduce general emotional distress, but this is associated with social impairment, and symptoms tend to reemerge or worsen when contact with the phobic environment is initiated. Third, it is likely that a subset of anxiety disorders patients do overcome their disorder without professional intervention, but the personality or environmental characteristics that might be associated with these successful outcomes are currently unknown.

Anxiety disorders can result in significant life complications. Schneier et al. (1992) reported that social phobics were significantly more likely to be receiving disability and welfare payments than normal controls (22% vs. 11%). Similarly, Goisman et al. (1994) noted that only 50% of those with panic disorder, agoraphobia, or both were receiving some form of financial assistance (unemployment, disability, welfare, or social security payments).

Treatment Outcome

Pharmacological Treatments

Pharmacological treatments for anxiety disorders primarily consist of antidepressant, benzodiazepines, or beta-blocking agents. It is beyond the scope of this chapter to provide a thorough review for each pharmacological agent with each disorder. Thus, we will comment on the efficacy of the various classes of agents and factors that may predict treatment outcome. The reader is encouraged to keep in mind, however, that what constitutes improvement in pharmacological treatment studies in many cases differs from outcome measures used in behavioral and cognitive-behavioral studies. Thus, comparisons of outcome across behavioral and pharmacological treatment are fraught with limitations.

There is no evidence for efficacy of any drug in the treatment of specific phobia (Lydiard et al., 1988). Panic disorder and panic disorder with agoraphobia have been treated successfully with tricyclic antidepressants such as imipramine (Ballenger, 1986; Liebowitz, 1985) and the benzodiazepine, alprazolam (Ballenger, 1990; Ballenger et al., 1988; Cross-National Collaborative Panic Study Second Phase Investigation, 1992). Curtis et al. (1993) note that the benzodiazepines may have a more rapid effect at the initiation of treatment, but that within a month, the antidepressants "catch up," such that differences were no longer apparent, and 8 months later, outcome for the two drugs appears equal. More recently, fluvoxamine, one of a new class of antidepressants known as *selective* serotonin reuptake inhibitors (SSRIs) also has been reported to be effective when compared to placebo (Hoehn-Saric, McLeod, & Hipsley, 1993). The bulk of the evidence at this time does not indicate that beta blockers are effective in the treatment of any anxiety disorder (Fyer & Sandberg, 1988; Gorman et al., 1983).

The pharmacological treatment of social phobia has a shorter history than that of panic disorder and agoraphobia; however, a number of studies have appeared over the past 15 years. The efficacy of SSRIs has been reported primarily in case reports or open clinical trials. Outcome for buspirone is equivocal; an open trial indicated some efficacy (Munjack et al., 1991), but the only placebo-controlled trial (Clark & Agras, 1991) did not report a difference between buspirone and placebo and found that the combination of buspirone and cognitive-behavioral treatment did more poorly than cognitive-behavioral treatment alone. Phenelzine, a monoamine oxidase inhibitor (MAOI), has been found to be effective in treating social phobia, particularly the generalized subtype (Liebowitz et al., 1988). In contrast, the beta blocker atenolol does not appear to be more effective than placebo (Liebowitz et al., 1988; Turner, Beidel, & Jacob, 1994). Finally, Davidson et al. (1993) reported efficacy of clonazepam (a benzodiazepine) when compared to placebo. However, clonazepam has a very high relapse rate.

Antidepressants (older and newer compounds) have a history of use to treat OCD and the results of recent studies support that, particularly for the SSRIs (Stanley & Turner, 1995). In summarizing the literature on clomipramine (a potent serotonin inhibitor), Goodman, McDougle, and Price (1992) noted that there appears to be a consistent pattern: antidepressant drugs that are less serotonergic than clomipramine are generally not effective for the treatment of OCD. The next generation of serotonin-reuptake inhibitors (SSRIs) such as fluvoxamine, fluoxetine, sertraline, and paroxetine have reported success rates of between 40%–60%, although only fluvoxamine has shown strong positive effects in a placebo-controlled trial (Goodman et al., 1992). A multicenter trial of sertraline indicated that it was more effective than placebo, but these effects were less than what is typically found for clomipramine or fluvoxamine (Goodman et al., 1992).

Benzodiazepines have been widely used for treating GAD (Ballenger, 1984). Beta blockers have been used by primary care physicians to treat GAD (Lydiard et al., 1988), but they are rarely more effective than placebo (Noyes, 1985). Rickels and colleagues (Rickels, Downing, Schweizer, & Hassman, 1993) reported that 73% of patients treated with imipramine, 69% of patients treated with trazedone, 66% of patients treated with diazepam, and 47% of patients treated with placebo were judged as moderately to markedly improved. This high placebo response rate has been noted in many recent drug trials. Although the reason for it is unclear, one likely explanation is that assessment of treatment outcome in drug trials relies heavily on clinician judgment, ratings which are known to be more susceptible to placebo effects than behavioral or self-report inventories (Turner, Beidel, & Jacob, 1994).

There only are a few controlled trials of treatment for PTSD. These studies have been reviewed by Davidson (1992), who reported positive treatment outcome for amitriptyline or imipramine but not for desipramine. Outcome for MAOIs is equivocal, with only one of two studies reporting a positive outcome. Fluoxetine also has been reported to be effective in decreasing the specific symptoms of arousal and numbing (van der Kolk et al., 1994).

The positive outcome from these studies must be tempered by acknowledgment that withdrawal of these medications has produced relapse rates ranging from 23% to 86% (Fontaine & Chouinard, 1986; Pato, Zohar-Kadouch, Zohor, & Murphy, 1988). Furthermore, many of these studies, and particularly the earlier ones, suffer from methodological confounds, such as the almost total reliance upon clinician and patient rating scales.

Even if the overall outcome for pharmacological treatments is positive, not all patients respond to these interventions. Relapse rates have been noted above. In addition, attention to patient factors that might predict positive outcome would be desirable. Only two studies have addressed this issue. As noted earlier, a naturalistic study of panic disordered patients indicated that panic-free periods were more likely to occur in patients without comorbid Axis I or II disorders (Pollack et al., 1992). Although a host of possible predictor variables for OCD has been the subject of discussion (e.g., schizotypal personality, fixidity of beliefs), no clear findings have been reported to date (Stanley & Turner, 1995).

Behavioral and Cognitive-Behavioral Treatments

Although numerous psychosocial interventions exist, more than 20 years of empirical data are so compelling that there can be no doubt that behavioral and cognitive-behavioral interventions are the psychosocial treatments of choice (Beidel, Turner, & Ballenger, in press). Although engineered differently, all of the interventions, behavioral or cognitive-behavioral, share a common element: exposure to the anxiety-producing stimulus (e.g., Hoffart, 1993; Turner, Cooley-Quille, & Beidel, 1996). After a brief review of the outcome literature, patient factors that appear to affect treatment outcome will be examined.

Panic Disorder

For panic disorder with agoraphobia, in vivo exposure (with or without the concomitant use of medication) appears to be the treatment of choice (Clum, 1989; Craske, Rapee, & Barlow, 1992; Lydiard et al., 1988). In a recent comprehensive review of the panic treatment literature, Ballenger, Lydiard, and Turner (1995) concluded that exposure-based interventions produce improvement in the 60%–70% range. Positive results usually are achieved in 10 to 20 sessions. Treatment effects last at least up to 9 years, and many patients show further improvement (without additional treatment) during the follow-up period. Furthermore, gradual or intensive approaches appear to be equally effective (Craske et al., 1992). The empirical evidence for adding coping or cognitive strategies to standard exposure procedures is equivocal. One recent review concluded that it does increase effectiveness (Clum, 1989), but others have reported that addition of cognitive components does not generate improvement rates that are higher than exposure alone (Jansson, Jerremalm, & Ost, 1986; Michelson, Mavissakalian, & Marchione, 1985). However, use of cognitive strategies does appear to reduce number of drop-outs compared to exposure alone (Clum, 1989).

Cognitive-behavioral treatment (e.g., cognitive restructuring, respiratory training) may be effective for those with uncomplicated panic disorder (Beck, 1988; Clark, Salkovskis, & Chalkley, 1985). Panic Control Therapy (Barlow, Craske, Cerney, & Klosko, 1989) incorporates exposure to somatic symptoms. A wait-list controlled investigation comparing the merging of the exposure treatment with cognitive therapy (Beck & Emery, 1985) to relaxation training and a combination group consisting of all three elements found that only the two groups containing exposure to somatic cues were superior to the control group in terms of the percentage of patients who were panic free at posttreatment. Focused cognitive therapy (Beck, Sokol, & Clark, 1992) also has been reported to be effective when compared to supportive therapy or applied relaxation (e.g., Beck et al., 1992). The findings are not surprising given the central role of exposure in each intervention.

Specific Phobia

Although few individuals with specific phobias seek treatment (Myers et al., 1984), available outcome data indicate that behavioral interventions, such as systematic desensitization, imaginal and in vivo flooding, graduated in vivo exposure, participant modeling, and applied tension are effective. In a review of the literature, Ost (1996) noted that positive treatment rates are quite high (averaging about 80% improvement) with very minimal treatment lengths (1.9–9.0 hours depending upon the particular phobia). For animal phobias, therapist-directed exposure or participant modeling are the treatments of choice. Flying phobias appear to respond to self-instructional training, applied relaxation, and various methods of exposure. Participant modeling and guided mastery are effective for acrophobia. The biphasic physiological response of blood/illness/injury phobias (an initial increase in blood pressure and heart rate, then a rapid drop so sharp that readings often fall below resting baseline levels) requires special consideration. Fainting on the part of the patient needs to be prevented to eliminate the possibility of injury and also to allow the exposure to take place. Applied tension (tensing during the exposure sessions; see Ost, 1996, for details) has been markedly successful in the treatment of these phobias.

Social Phobia

Social phobia has been successfully treated by standard behavioral procedures and cognitive-behavioral interventions (see Turner, Cooley-Quille, & Beidel,

1996, for a review). As noted earlier, the key ingredient appears to be the exposure (imaginal or in vivo) to the fear producing stimuli. Social skills training also has been demonstrated to be effective (Wlazlo, 1990), and Social Effectiveness Therapy (which combines exposure and social skills training; Turner, Beidel, & Cooley, 1994) appears to be particularly promising, especially for the generalized subtype. Cognitive-behavioral group therapy combines exposure with cognitve restructuring and has shown some degree of efficacy (Heimberg et al., 1990). Recently, the preponderance of evidence from substantive reviews (Turner, Cooley-Quille, & Beidel, 1996), dismantling studies (Hope, Heimberg, & Bruch, 1995), and meta-analyses (Feske & Chambless, 1995; Taylor, 1996) indicates clearly that addition of cognitive procedures does not produce superior outcome to that of exposure alone for this disorder. Follow-up data indicate that effects of behavioral or cognitive-behavioral treatment are maintained for up to 5 years posttreatment (Heimberg, Salzman, Holt, & Blendell, 1993).

Generalized Anxiety Disorder

There are few controlled trials documenting efficacy of behavioral treatments for GAD, although systematic desensitization, in vivo desensitization, stress inoculation, social skills training, problem solving strategies, cognitive therapy, and cognitive restructuring are considered to be useful (Craske et al., 1992). Butler, Fennell, Robson, and Gelder (1991) reported that cognitive-behavioral therapy (Beck's cognitive therapy) was consistently superior to a wait-list control, whereas there were fewer differences between behavior therapy (relaxation, graduated exposure, and pleasant events scheduling) and a wait-list group. In a recent review of the literature, outcome data were collapsed across five controlled studies that included three behavioral and five cognitive interventions (Durham & Allan, 1993). An average reduction of 50% for somatic symptoms on the Hamilton Anxiety Scale and 25% reduction on the State-Trait Anxiety Inventory Trait subscale was reported. Comparison average improvement rates were 14% for the treated group and 11% for the wait-list control using the Hamilton scores, and 11% for the treated group and 4% for the wait-list control group for the trait subscale. These data suggest that although individuals who receive treatment do better than those who do not, change is minimal and more efficacious interventions need to be developed.

Obsessive-Compulsive Disorder

For OCD, the psychosocial treatment of choice is exposure combined with response prevention (see Stanley & Turner, 1995, for an extended review of the literature). Graduated exposure strategies appear less effective than a more intensive procedure (Turner & Beidel, 1988). Recent reviews (Stanley & Turner, 1995) confirm estimates of Foa, Stekekee, and Ozarow (1985) that 51% of patients achieve at least a 70% reduction in symptoms. The most conservative estimates (adjusting for dropout and refusal rates that account for about 20% of the patients seeking behavioral treatment), 72% of patients benefit from exposure and response prevention. Positive treatment outcome is maintained over time (79% remain improved or much improved 1 to 6 years later; Stanley & Turner, 1995).

Posttraumatic Stress Disorder

Treatment outcome data for PTSD are based primarily on combat-related veterans. Even within that subgroup, controlled studies are few, but intensive exposure (flooding) appears to be effective when outcome is compared to wait list controls, problem-solving training, or supportive treatment. Treatment gains appear to be maintained for up to 6 months but longer term outcome data are not available (Frueh, Turner, & Beidel, 1995). With respect to noncombat PTSD, case reports suggest effectiveness of cognitive behavior therapy and stress inoculation training. Foa, Rothbaum, Riggs, and Murdock (1991) reported that both stress inoculation training and prolonged exposure were effective for rape victims with PTSD, although follow-up data suggested superiority for the exposure intervention.

Combined Pharmacological and Psychosocial Treatments

Several recent studies have compared behavioral and cognitive-behavioral procedures with pharmacological treatment for panic disorder. A comparison of alprazolam and panic control therapy (PCT) revealed that only PCT was more effective than placebo and wait-list controls (Klosko, Barlow, Tassinari, & Cerny, 1990). Percentages of patients who were free from panic disorder at posttreatment were 87% for the PCT group, 50% for alprazolam, 36% for placebo, and 33% for wait-list control. Although current data do not consistently show a synergistic effect for the combination of pharmacological and behavioral treatments for panic disorder, one study (Hegel, Ravaris, & Ahles, 1994) reported that 1 year after the cessation of cognitive-behavioral treatment and alprazolam withdrawal, 76% of the sample was medication free, and 85% remained panic free. Furthermore, the positive outcome suggests that use of alprazolam in combination with cognitive behavioral treatment was not contraindicated, as had been considered previously. Finally, ability to enhance the effects of exposure treatment by first treating the patients with either fluvoxamine or psychological panic management was examined in a group of panic patients (DeBeurs, van Balkom, Lange, Koele, & van Dyck, 1995). The combination of fluvoxamine and exposure in vivo was significantly superior (and had twice as large an effect size) when compared to psychological panic management plus exposure in vivo, placebo plus exposure in vivo, or exposure in vivo alone on self-reported agoraphobic avoidance. There were no other differences among groups, indicating that psychological panic management combined with exposure in vivo was not superior to exposure in vivo alone. Finally, behavioral and cognitive behavioral treatments have been used successfully to aid in the withdrawal of patients from benzodiazepines (Otto et al., 1993).

Flooding (an intensive exposure procedure) is more effective than atenolol (a beta blocker) in the treatment of social phobia (Turner, Beidel, & Jacob, 1994). Only one study (Falloon, Lloyd, & Harpin, 1981) addressed the combination of pharmacological and behavioral treatment for social phobia. The results indicated that propranolol did not result in superior outcome over exposure treatment alone. Other studies are ongoing.

A meta-analysis examining behavioral and pharmacological treatment for OCD indicated that on self- and assessor ratings of obsessive-compulsive symptoms, both serotonin antidepressants (clomipramine, fluoxetine, and fluvoxamine) and behavioral therapy were significantly superior to placebo (Christensen, Hadzi-Pavlovic, Andrews, & Mattick, 1987). On assessor ratings, there was no difference in effect sizes between two classes of active treatments. However, on self-report ratings, behavior therapy was significantly more effective than the pharmacological agents.

Predictors of Treatment Outcome

Numerous demographic and clinical factors have been examined in an attempt to predict positive treatment outcome from behavioral and cognitive-behavioral treatments. In short, across all disorders (with the exception of specific phobia) poorer treatment outcome is predicted by more severe psychopathology. This severity may be in the primary anxiety disorder (Basoglu et al., 1994; Castle et al., 1994; Keijsers, Hoogduin, & Schaap, 1994; Steketee & Shapiro, 1995; Turner, Beidel, Wolff, Spaulding, & Jacob, 1996), comorbid affective and anxiety states (Albus & Scheibe, 1993; Brown, Antony, & Barlow, 1995; Keijsers, Hoogduin, & Schaap, 1994; Steketee & Shapiro, 1995; Turner et al., 1996), or comorbid Axis II disorders (AuBuchon & Malatesta, 1994; Stanley & Turner, 1995; Turner et al., 1996).

FAMILIAL AND GENETIC CONSIDERATIONS

As with other areas of psychopathology, there has been increased interest in biological factors in the anxiety disorders, and the possibility of biological etiology has been pursued through twin studies and family or family history studies. Family and family history studies reveal an increased morbidity rate among first-degree relatives of patients with an anxiety disorder. Data consistently demonstrate higher lifetime prevalence rates of panic disorder in relatives of patient probands (7.7 to 20.5/100) compared to relatives of normal controls (0.8 to 7.7/ 100; Weissman, 1993). Fyer (1993) reported that rates of social phobia in first-degree relatives of social phobia probands were higher than in first-degree relatives of normal controls (16% vs. 5%), whereas rates for other disorders were not different between groups. Similarly, Fyer et al. (1990) reported higher rates of specific (simple) phobia among first-degree relatives of specific (simple) phobic probands compared to rates among relatives of normal control probands (31% vs. 11%). Again, rates of other disorders did not differ between the groups. Two family studies of OCD have produced inconsistent findings. Black, Noyes, Goldstein, and Blum (1992) did not find a higher prevalence of OCD among relatives of OCD probands when compared to normal controls. They did, however, find a higher prevalence of anxiety disorders in general among relatives of OCD probands, primarily due to presence of GAD. When OCD was more broadly defined to include subclinical levels of OCD, there was a higher prevalence among parents of OCD probands compared to normal controls (16% vs.

3%). Based on a larger sample of patients, rates of OCD and subthreshold OCD were significantly higher among OCD probands than normal controls (10.3% vs. 1.9% for OCD and 7.9% vs. 2.0% for subthreshold OCD; Pauls, Alsobrock, Goodman, Rasmussen, & Leckman, 1995).

In addition to their ability to document familial relationships, two family studies have provided data to support validity of GAD as a distinctive diagnosis. Weissman (1990) reported results of three family studies which indicated that 1. rates of panic disorder were not different among relatives of GAD patients compared to normal controls; 2. rates of GAD were not different among relatives of panic patients versus controls; and 3. rates of GAD were higher among relatives of GAD patients (19.5/100) compared to relatives of panic patients (5.4/100) or normal controls (5.3/100). Noyes et al. (1992) compared the familial aggregation of panic disorder and GAD in probands with one of these two disorders. There was a higher frequency of GAD in families of GAD patients when compared to families of panic disorder patients. In contrast, there was more panic disorder in families of panic disorder patients than in families of GAD patients.

The majority of these studies assessed all of the available first-degree relatives of anxiety patients. Other investigations have attempted to examine the issue of increased familial prevalence by focusing more specifically on the parent-child relationship. These studies are one of two types: 1. those where a child with an anxiety disorder is the proband and the rates of anxiety disorders in the parents are assessed, and 2. those where the proband is an adult with an anxiety disorder and the investigator seeks to establish the incidence and prevalence of anxiety disorders in the patients' children.

Studies of Children of Patients with Anxiety Disorders

Among studies that have assessed the children of patients with an anxiety disorder, Sylvester, Hyde, and Reichler (1988) reported that children of normal control parents were significantly less anxious and depressed when compared to offspring of panic patients or depressed patients, whereas there were few differences between children of the two patient groups. However, there were two findings that suggested at least some specificity between parent diagnosis and child symptoms. First, offspring of panic patients reported higher trait anxiety than any other group. Second, children of depressed parents reported fewer pleasurable experiences and more depression than normal controls.

Weissman, Leckman, Merikangas, Gammon, and Prusoff (1984) compared children of probands with major depression, with or without an additional anxiety disorder, to children of a normal control group. Children whose parents had both depression and an anxiety disorder were at greater risk for a psychiatric disorder and more likely to have been referred for treatment. This initial study did not include a parent group with only an anxiety disorder. However, more recent studies have included a group of panic only patients (Warner, Mufson, & Weissman, 1995). The results indicate that anxiety disorders were more common in children whose parents had early-onset major depression disorder than in children of normal controls. There was no difference in rates of anxiety disorder in offspring among children with panic disorder and depression, panic disorder without depression, and normal controls. In summarizing the data, the authors noted that the risk for offspring to have any type of anxiety disorder was increased by proband recurrent early-onset major depression and by impaired functioning in the coparent. Furthermore, the relationship between major depression in the parent and panic spectrum disorders in the offspring was largely due to the family's chaotic environment. The authors' definition of anxiety disorder included subthreshold conditions such as limited symptom attacks, near-panic attacks, and situational panic attacks. When rates for DSM-IV anxiety disorders were compared across the groups, the only difference was that offspring of panic plus major depression patients had higher rates of separation anxiety disorder than offspring of normal controls. Thus, although findings from this study potentially are important, they must be interpreted cautiously.

Rosenbaum et al. (1988) compared rates of "behavioral inhibition" in the offspring of four groups: panic disorder patients with or without comorbid major depression, major depression alone, and a psychiatric control group. The term "behavioral inhibition" (Kagan, 1982, see below) describes a child's degree of sociability as displayed by behaviors ranging along an approach-withdrawal dimension. Briefly, inhibited children are those who consistently emit few spontaneous vocalizations when in the presence of a stranger and cry and cling to their mothers rather than approach other children in play settings. These behaviors resemble those of individuals who consider themselves "shy or socially phobic" although empirical studies relating these constructs have yet to be conducted. Using the assessment procedures developed by Kagan, Reznick, and Snidman (1987), Rosenbaum et al. (1988) reported that 86% of the panic disorder offspring were judged to be "behaviorally inhibited," compared to 70% of the anxious and depressed group, 50% in the major depression only group, and 15% in the psychiatric control group. More recent studies from this group of investigators started with "behaviorally inhibited children" and examined psychopathology in the parents. Results of those studies will be discussed below.

Turner, Beidel, and Costello (1987) compared offspring of anxious adults to two control groups: children of dysthymic patients and normal controls. Results indicated that children of anxiety probands were 1. almost 3 times as likely to have one of several DSM-III disorders as the children of dysthymic patients, 2. twice as likely as the children of dysthymic parents to have a DSM-III anxiety disorder, and 3. over 9 times as likely to have a DSM-III disorder as the children of normal parents. In a replication sample, rates of anxiety disorders were 33% for children of anxious parents, 37% for children of depressed parents, 31% for children of anxious and depressed parents, and 8% for children of normal control parents (Beidel & Turner, 1996). Thus, rates of anxiety disorders are higher in children with parents with emotional disorders but not specifically just parents with anxiety disorders.

Studies of the Relatives of Children Who Have Anxiety Disorders

Several studies of familial relationships have addressed the incidence and prevalence of anxiety disorders in the relatives of children with a DSM-III disorder. Last and her colleagues (Last, Hersen, Kazdin, Francis, & Grubb, 1987; Last, Hersen, Kazdin, Orvaschel, & Ye, 1990) conducted an extensive family investigation of the first- and second-degree relatives of child probands diagnosed with an anxiety disorder. In addition to the anxiety probands, relatives of children with attention deficit hyperactivity disorder and normal controls were included in the latest study (Last et al., 1990). Results indicated an increased risk for anxiety disorders in the first- and second-degree relatives of children with anxiety disorders when compared to relatives of normal control children. Similarly, there was a trend for increased risk for anxiety disorders in the first- and second-degree relatives of children with anxiety disorders when compared to relatives of children with attention deficit disorder.

Behavioral Inhibition and Anxiety Disorders

Rosenbaum and Biederman and their colleagues (Biederman et al., 1990; Rosenbaum et al., 1991; Rosenbaum et al., 1992) have reported on parental pathology of "behaviorally inhibited" children. Results indicated that there was higher rate of parental anxiety disorders among the children who were behaviorally inhibited, but primarily among those children *who also had an anxiety disorder.* Rates of parental pathology were not higher among children who only had behavioral inhibition (e.g., Rosenbaum et al., 1992). As noted by Turner, Beidel, and Wolff (1996), there are methodological limitations to each of these investigations that require cautious interpretation of the findings. For a extended review and discussion of these studies, the interested reader is referred to Turner, Beidel, and Wolff (1996).

Twin Studies

In addition to family studies, twin studies also provide important data to test hypotheses about genetic contributions. Torgersen (1983) reported that the proband-wise concordance rate for any anxiety disorders category, with the exception of GAD, was higher for monozygotic (MZ) than dizygotic (DZ) twins. The overall concordance rate for the MZ twins was 34% compared to 17% for the DZ twins, but no co-twin had the same anxiety disorder as the proband, and concordance rates for GAD were higher for DZ than MZ twins. Thus, the data did not support the one-to-one genetic transmission. Andrews, Stewart, Allen, and Henderson (1990) reached similar conclusions. Kendler, Neale, Kessler, Heath, and Eaves (1992a, 1992b), based on a study of 1,033 female-female twin pairs, reported that GAD is a moderately familial disorder with heritability estimates of about 30%. Rasmussen (1993) noted that twin studies of OCD patients also support the heritability of a neurotic anxiety factor, but support for the heritability of an OCD factor was equivocal. In a study of 4,042 twin pairs from the Vietnam Era Twin registry, True et al. (1993) demonstrated that heritability plays a substantial role in the susceptibility for PTSD symptoms. Using 2,163 personally interviewed female twins from a population-based registry, Kendler and his colleagues (Kendler et al., 1992a, 1992b) reported that the familial aggregation of agoraphobia, social phobia, situational phobics, and specific phobia was consistent with "phobia proneness," with heritability estimates indicating that "genetic factors play a significant but by no means overwhelming role in the etiology of phobias" (1992b, p. 279). Individual-specific environmental effects appeared to account for twice as much variance in liability as did the genetic factors. Thus, all of these studies are consistent in noting evidence for the heritability of some general factor, but not necessarily for a specific anxiety disorder.

In summary, there are some general trends that appear to be consistent across all studies that have used family or twin designs in the search for a genetic etiology. First, significantly higher rates of anxiety disorders appear in the families of anxiety probands when compared to families of normal controls. However, when families of probands with other types of psychopathology are included in the investigation (e.g., a psychiatric control group), the outcome becomes less clear. Significant differences among psychiatric groups for familial prevalence or morbidity risks are not always evident. At this time, twin studies do not support the direct transmission of a particular anxiety disorder. Therefore, there are several other factors that warrant consideration in explaining the observed familial pattern: 1. the increased prevalence rates among the probands' families could reflect the stress of coping with a psychiatrically ill individual within the family structure, or 2. that there is some underlying vulnerability that is manifested in different fashions dependent upon environmental circumstances.

PSYCHOLOGICAL AND BIOLOGICAL ASSESSMENT

The issue of vulnerability is one that has been noted consistently throughout this chapter. Numerous investigators have attempted to shed light on this concept from several different perspectives. Nonhuman primate studies of individual differences in anxiety have significant implications for the study of vulnerability in humans. There are substantial individual differences both in the intensity and extent of anxiety-like behaviors in infant and juvenile rhesus monkeys (Suomi, 1986). When in novel situations or when separated from familiar surroundings, some infant monkeys show evidence of behavioral, autonomic, and endocrinological signs of fearfulness, while others respond with exploratory or play behaviors (Suomi, Kraemer, Baysinger, & Delizio, 1981). Longitudinal studies indicate that these characteristics remain stable throughout adolescence and young adulthood. Furthermore, it appears that environmental conditions cannot alter completely constitutional vulnerability. When faced with challenging situations, biological monkey siblings "adopted away" at birth and raised in adoptive families continued to show greater similarity in both cortisol levels and behavioral fear scores than the similarity between adopted siblings (Suomi, 1986).

Kagan and his associates (Kagan, 1982; Kagan et al., 1987; Kagan, Reznick, Snidman, Gibbons, & Johnson, 1988; Reznick et al., 1986) identified a temperamental factor called behavioral inhibition (BI). From an initial pool of 300 children, these investigators identified 60 children who consistently displayed inhibited or uninhibited behaviors in the presence of novel events (Kagan, 1982). Inhibited children were those who cried, clung to their mothers when approached by a stranger, were reluctant to interact with their peers in a play situation, and emitted few spontaneous vocalizations when in the presence of an unknown investigator. When placed in these situations, the inhibited children had higher heart rates and less heart-rate variability than the noninhibited children. The preponderance of evidence supports the usefulness of the behavioral inhibition construct. However, although BI is a stable pattern of behavior for some children, others become less inhibited with increasing age. Thus, as noted by Turner, Beidel, and Wolff (1996), the specific behaviors defining the BI construct do not appear to be immutable even if they have a biological basis. However, the *tendency* to react in an inhibited fashion, under particular environmental circumstances might be biologically based (see Turner, Beidel, & Wolff, 1996, for an extended discussion of BI and its relationship to anxiety disorders).

Another study which addressed the issue of biological vulnerability in anxiety disorders was that of Turner, Beidel, and Epstein (1991). Skin conductance responses of children with an anxiety disorder were compared to normal controls when presented with novel or fear-producing stimuli including a 100 db tone and a picture of a snake appearing ready to "strike." For the specific details of this investigation, as well as the exact assessment protocol, the reader is referred to Turner, Beidel, and Epstein (1991). Although the small number of children in this investigation (11 normal controls and 8 anxious children) precludes broad generalizations, results indicate that when exposed to the tone or the snake, anxious children have a significantly higher mean response amplitude, indicative of increased arousal. In addition, anxious children have a five-fold increase in spontaneous fluctuations during baseline and tone condition, and twice the number of spontaneous fluctuations during the snake condition. Furthermore, habituation rates are significantly lower among the anxious children than normal controls. Interestingly, both groups of children report only minimal levels of subjective distress during the assessment. A more recent investigation (Turner & Beidel, 1996) attempted to replicate these results using a group of children who did not have an anxiety disorder but were the offspring of a patient with a disorder (i.e., a high-risk sample). The results indicated that children without an anxiety diagnosis but who were the offspring of a parent with a diagnosis had significantly more spontaneous fluctuations than children of normal controls or children of depressed parents. In addition, these children were less likely to habituate to repeated presentations of the same stimulus, whereas the offspring of normal control parents habituated rapidly. Unlike the pilot study, where these differences may have been attributed to the child's psychopathology, results of this second study suggest that children of anxious parents who do not themselves have a disorder show similar psychophysiological characteristics as those who have a disorder when exposed to fearful or novel stimuli. This suggests that these children might have "vulnerability" features that could predispose them to develop maladaptive anxiety.

The studies reviewed to this point have focused on vulnerability in the general sense of the term. Although the results indicate that certain individuals may be more prone or vulnerable to anxiety reactions, only Hirshfeld et al. (1992) reported on the long-term outcome of children initially identified as vulnerable (i.e., behaviorally inhibited). Results of that investigation indicated that children who maintained a stable pattern of behavioral inhibition (over a 5–6-year period) were significantly more likely to have anxiety disorders, and in particular, phobic disorders. However, none of these studies provided any indication about the exact nature of the vulnerability. In the following sections, other research investigations that have sought to determine if specific structures or neurochemicals are related to the anxiety disorders will be discussed.

Structural and Neurochemical Abnormalities in the Anxiety Disorders

Historically, most studies addressing these biological parameters, and the two areas which have focused on structural abnormalities, have been directed at panic disorder. During the late 1970s and early 1980s, a high prevalence of mitral valve prolapse in patients with panic attacks was reported (e.g., Gorman, Fyer, Glicklich, King, & Klein, 1981), but subsequent studies found that the prevalence rate was no higher than in the general population (e.g., Kathol et al., 1980; Shear, Devereaux, Kranier-Fox, Mann, & Frances, 1984).

The vestibular system has also been the subject of investigation as a correlate of panic disorder. For example, Jacob, Moller, Turner, and Wall (1985) reported that 67% of 21 panic disorder or agoraphobic patients had some type of vestibular abnormality. In 39% of the patients with abnormal tests, results were consistent with a peripheral vestibular lesion. This study was replicated using a much larger sample of patients, including those with panic disorder and no to mild agoraphobia ($n = 30$), panic disorder with moderate to severe agoraphobia ($n = 29$), anxiety disorders but no panic attacks ($n = 28$), depression ($n = 13$), and normal controls ($n = 45$; Jacob, Furman, Durrant, & Turner, 1996). The results indicated that although vestibular laboratory abnormalities were common in all groups, they were most prevalent in the patients with panic disorder with moderate to severe agoraphobia. The laboratory dysfunction was associated with presence of vestibular symptoms between panic attacks and with ratings of space and motion discomfort. Furthermore, these results could not be explained by higher subjective distress on the part of the patients during the tasks, because subjective ratings were not different between the groups. These findings suggest that many agoraphobics rely on visual or proprioceptive cues for spatial orientation to compensate for their disordered vestibular system. Thus, they tend to avoid or be fearful in situations such as heights, open spaces, long corridors, tunnels or shopping malls because the visual spatial cues in these situations are misleading or absent (Jacob et al., 1996). The findings from this study hold significant implications for theories of the etiology of agoraphobia.

Another series of investigations has attempted to evaluate biochemical changes that may occur when panic is produced in a laboratory setting. Induction of panic in the laboratory was seen as a method by which to examine the pathophysiology of panic (Carr & Sheehan, 1984). Initial studies focused on inducing panic by infusing panic patients with lactate (e.g., Pitts & McClure, 1967). However, over the subsequent years, numerous challenge paradigms have been developed. Substances that appear to induce panic in panic patients include lactate, bicarbonate, CO_2, caffeine, yohimbine, tricyclic antidepressants, isoprenaline, noradrenaline, chlorimipramine, mCPP, flumazenil, cholecystokinin, and hypoglycemia (Nutt & Lawson, 1992). In addition, panic can be induced by hyperventilation and through behavioral methods such as putting claustrophobics in enclosed places (Rachman, 1988). Only lactate and flumazenil appear to induce panic only in panic patients and not other anxiety patients. Reactivity to so many different substances suggests many different neurochemical and neurobiological systems, several of which contradict each other. There is also the problem of expectancy effects (see Turner, Beidel, & Jacob, 1988). Furthermore, Margraf, Ehlers, and Roth (1986) noted that these studies have serious methodological limitations, including 1. inadequate criteria for defining panic attacks, 2. strict reliance on patient report that a panic attack was occurring, 3. use of only single-blind criteria, and 4. failure to account for group differences in baseline anxiety levels. When these baseline differences are taken into account, there appear to be no differences in the responses of panic patients compared to other diagnostic or control groups (see Margraf et al., 1986, for a complete discussion of the literature's methodological deficiencies). In summarizing the empirical literature on laboratory-induced panic, there are so many methodological confounds that it is difficult to conclude that these data clearly indicate biological vulnerability for the onset of panic disorder, and it appears likely that the findings of the laboratory studies are influenced by nonbiological factors present in the individual or the environment. Of late, there appears to be little interest in further pursuing this line of research.

Other investigators have pursued the potential etiological role of catecholamine, norepinephrine, and serotonin. Although the relationship between increased catecholamine levels and "stress" are well documented, there is little conclusive evidence that levels of catecholamines are higher in chronically anxious patients when compared to normal controls. Findings of no differences between anxiety patients and normal controls (Liebowitz, Fyer, Gorman, et al., 1985; Mathew, Ho, Francis, Taylor, & Weinman, 1982) have been reported as often as those that have found differences (Ballenger et al., 1984; Nesse, Cameron, Curtis, McCann, & Huber-Smith, 1984).

A recent review by Tancer (1993) found few data to support a biological basis for social phobia. Laboratory infusions of lactate or epinephrine did not produce social phobic symptoms in social phobic patients. Although caffeine induced anxiety symptoms in social phobic patients, the symptoms were not those experienced by social phobic patients in social settings. There does not appear to be any global dysfunction in either the hypothalamic-pituitary-adrenal (HPA) or hypothalamic-pituitary-thyroid (HPT) endocrine axes (Tancer, 1993). Catecholamine responses when giving a speech did not differ between social phobics and normal volunteers (Levin et al., 1989). Finally, neuroendocrine challenges for the noradrenergic, serotonergic, and dopaminergic systems indicate that there may be some dysregulation in serotonergic transmission but activity in the noradrenergic and dopaminergic systems remains normal (Tancer, 1993). However, this latter finding was found in a small group of social phobic patients ($n = 21$) and thus requires further replication.

In recent years, there has been increased interest in the relationship between serotonin functioning and the anxiety disorders. A thorough review of this literature can be found in Kahn, Van Praag, Wetzler, and Barr (1988). In brief, much of the interest in serotonin is derived from the successful results of pharmacological investigations that have administered drugs with potent serotonergic effects to patients with anxiety disorders, particularly patients with OCD. Evidence of the effectiveness of these compounds has led investigators (correctly or incorrectly) to hypothesize abnormal serotonin functioning as an etiological determinant of the disorder (see treatment section for a review of biological treatment studies). In a recent review of the neurobiology of OCD, Rapoport (1991) proposed that the current data support basal ganglia dysfunction and disorder in the serotonin system. The strongest data to suggest a serotonin dysfunction come from pharmacological treatment studies where selective serotonin reuptake inhibitors appear to be effective in the treatment of this disorder. However, it always is dubious to attempt determination of causality from treatment outcome data. Early studies reported decreased number of platelet serotonin uptake sites in blood platelets (Weizman, Carmi, & Hermesh, 1986), but the findings were not replicated (Bastani, Arora, & Meltzer, 1991; Insel, Mueller, Gillin, Siever, & Murphy, 1985). Similarly, one study reported an increase in cerebrospinal fluid 5-HIAA (serotonin) in OCD patients (Insel et al., 1985); however, these findings also have not been replicated (Insel & Winslow, 1992). Finally, laboratory studies using mCPP challenges have produced mixed results; some studies have reported exacerbation of OCD symptomatology after oral administration, whereas other studies have not (Rapoport, 1991). However, the evidence for serotonin abnormalities is stronger for OCD than for any other anxiety disorder (Insel & Winslow, 1992).

More recent neurobiological studies have addressed the question of basal ganglia dysfunction in this disorder. Rapoport (1991) proposed that dysfunction of the basal ganglia-thalamic frontal cortical loops produce symptoms, such as excessive grooming, checking, and doubting behaviors found in OCD. Data from clinical trials of trichotillomania, nail biting, and canine acral lick dermatitis demonstrated that clomipramine was superior to desipramine in remediating each of these behaviors. Furthermore, a second study with fluoxetine treatment for canine acral lick dermatitis also resulted in decreased grooming behaviors. Based on these data, Rapoport (1991) proposed that the basal ganglia is a repository for species-typical behavior and the frontal cortex-basal ganglia-thalamic circuit is the center for phylogenetic self-protective behaviors such as grooming or checking. In those with OCD, trichotillomania, nailbiting, or dogs with acral lick dermatitis, this system has gone awry (see Rapoport, 1991, for an extensive discussion of this issue). Although intriguing, this hypothesis is not without its difficulties. First, no specific dysregulation or neuroanatomical abnormality has been identified (although neuroimaging studies described below suggest some possibilities). Second, as noted by Rapoport (1991), this model cannot account for the efficacy of behavioral treatment. Third, anatomically, existence of these basal ganglia "loops" is still undetermined.

Recent PET and SPECT neuroimaging studies do provide some support for a basal ganglia dysfunction. Baxter (1992), in his review of the area, concluded that the preponderance of the data provide evidence of abnormalities in the orbital prefrontal cortex. The caudate nucleus also may be involved although the data are less consistent. Three studies have noted that effective treatment of OCD (either with medication or behavior therapy) reduced the abnormalities, although not all studies have noted decreases in the same regions. This area of research is in its infancy and further research is necessary.

In summary, the results of endocrine and neuroendocrine studies to date provide minimal support for an etiological role of these factors in anxiety disorders.

Like the laboratory-induction procedures, there are serious methodological limitations (see Turner et al., 1988). For example, measurement of bioamine activity often is limited to peripheral assessment, even though 1. its mechanism of action may be on the central nervous system and 2. the relationship between the concentration of these elements in the peripheral nervous system compared to the central nervous system is unknown. Finally, newer studies using neuroimaging techniques show promise, but as noted by Baxter (1992), more studies using more specific tracers (in order to detect the role of specific neurotransmitters) are needed.

DIAGNOSTIC CONSIDERATIONS

As noted, a clear advancement of the DSM-IV was acknowledgment (long known by experienced clinicians) that individuals with anxiety disorders *other* than panic disorder also have panic attacks. Thus, one diagnostic consideration when assessing a primary complaint of panic attacks pertains to the stimuli under which the attacks occur. Similarly, presenting complaints of specific phobias of knives (Barlow, 1988) or thunderstorms (Turner & Beidel, 1988) may indicate presence of a more pervasive anxiety disorder, such as OCD. Patients with extensive washing rituals often present at dermatology clinics with contact dermatitis. Similarly, the OCD-related condition of dysmorphophobia often is found in the plastic surgeon's office (Rasmussen & Eisen, 1992).

Differential diagnosis often is difficult because of the substantial comorbidity among the anxiety disorders. For example, Brown and Barlow (1992) reported that 50% of anxiety patients with a principal anxiety disorder had at least one other clinically significant anxiety or depressive disorder. Among panic disordered patients, 20% had secondary GAD, whereas 36% of panic disordered patients with mild agoraphobia also had secondary GAD. Nine percent of social phobics also had secondary panic disorder, and 29% of patients with primary GAD had secondary social phobia, as did 24% of OCD patients. Seventeen percent of OCD patients had a lifetime prevalence of eating disorders (Rasmussen & Eisen, 1992). Finally, there is the issue of GAD. Those presenting at anxiety disorders clinics typically do not have a singular diagnosis of GAD. Only 26% of primary GAD patients had GAD as the sole diagnosis (Brawman-Mintzer et al., 1993). The most common comorbid diagnoses were social phobia (23%) and specific phobia (21%). Forty-two percent of GAD patients had a major depressive episode in their lifetime. Prevalence of GAD across all of the other diagnostic categories led some investigators to suggest that it may not be a distinct disorder, but perhaps the basis from which other disorders arise, and the residual state often remaining following treatment for other specific disorders (Turner & Beidel, 1989a, 1989b). A recent review by Brown et al. (1994) provided some evidence for validity of GAD, but diagnostic unreliability and high rates of comorbidity continue to plague this diagnostic category.

In addition to comorbidity among the anxiety disorders, anxiety and depressive states share many symptoms, leading some investigators to suggest that many anxiety disorders, most specifically obsessive-compulsive disorder and panic disorder, are merely variants of depressive disorder. However, the bulk of the evidence, based on actual symptoms, childhood characteristics and childhood events, differential predictors of outcome, personality characteristics, and analysis of genetic models based on large samples of twin data support the hypothesis that anxiety and depression are indeed different disorders (e.g., Kendler, Heath, Martin, & Eaves, 1987). Kendler et al. (1987) examined anxiety and depressive symptoms in an unselected sample of twins (3,798 pairs). The results, based on factor analysis, indicated that symptoms of anxiety and depression tend to form separate symptom clusters (depression-distress and general anxiety) and that it was the environment rather than any specific genetic influences which were depressogenic or anxiogenic.

Although depression and anxiety may be separate disorders, the clinician is still confronted with distinguishing between these affective states that often have a high rate of concordance. One method for drawing distinctions has been to examine the disorder's etiology and designate as "primary" the one that had the earliest onset. Thus, secondary depression would be defined as depression that occurs after the onset of the anxiety disorder. Secondary depression is common among anxiety patients, with estimates ranging from 17.5% to 60%, and averaging approximately 30%–35% for panic disorder and agoraphobic patients (Barlow et al., 1986; Breier, Charney, & Heninger, 1984; Lesser et al., 1988; Uhde et al., 1985; Van Valkenberg, Akiskal, Puzantian, & Rosenthal, 1984). Using epidemiological data, Andrade, Eaton, and Chilcoat (1994) reported that 2.1% of their total sample was comorbid for panic attacks and major depression. However, 62% of those with panic attacks reported presence of a dysphoric mood.

Another method of determining primacy is to determine the longitudinal course of the disorders. Breier et al. (1984) examined the course of depression in 60 patients with agoraphobia or panic disorder. Seventy percent had an episode of depression, with 43% reporting that depression occurred before the first panic attack. The average time between remission of the depression and the subsequent onset of the panic attack was 4 years. In contrast, 57% of those patients who had both anxiety and depressive disorders reported that the depression occurred following the onset of the panic. For those patients, symptoms of panic, anticipatory anxiety, and generalized anxiety were chronic and unremitting, while symptoms of depression were episodic in nature, with 63% of those patients having remissions of depression which lasted for 1 year or more (Breier et al., 1986). In such cases, the depressive disorder would clearly be seen as secondary to the anxiety disorder.

Depression also is common in OCD, where the majority of patients may experience at least some dysphoric mood (Barlow et al., 1986). Again, the most common distinction has been based on the etiological onset of the disorders. Depression that occurs after the onset of OCD is considered to be secondary. Even though considered secondary, presence of significant depression in a patient with OCD could have important treatment implications.

Often it is necessary to differentiate between patients with anxiety that is but one symptom of a primary Axis II personality disorder, and those who truly manifest comorbid Axis I and II disorders. For example, although individuals with paranoid personality disorder are often anxious when in the company of others, their anxiety is due to concern about the motives of others, as opposed to social phobics who fear doing something to humiliate or embarrass themselves.

However, even with careful diagnosis and the use of hierarchical diagnostic rules, there will be a subset of individuals with anxiety disorders and personality disorders. Several investigators (Mavissakalian & Hammen, 1986, 1988; Pollack et al. 1992; Reich & Noyes, 1987; Rennenberg, Chambless, & Gracely, 1992) all reported Axis II disorders in approximately 30%–56% of panic patients, primarily histrionic, dependent, avoidant, and obsessive-compulsive subtypes. Turner et al. (1991) found that 41% of a socially phobic sample met criteria for a personality disorder, most commonly avoidant personality disorder or obsessive-compulsive personality disorder. Cluster C (anxious) personality disorders were identified in 17% of patients with GAD, whereas 2% of GAD patients had cluster B (unstable) personality disorder. The most common Axis II disorders in OCD patients are avoidant, histrionic, and paranoid personality disorders (Sciuto et al., 1991), and there is evidence that those with OCD and comorbid schizotypal symptoms, which may account for up to 20% of obsessive-compulsive patients, have a significantly poorer prognosis than those without such features (Jenike, Baer, Minichiello, Schwartz, & Carey, 1986; Stanley, Turner, & Borden 1990).

In summary, differential diagnosis is necessary to fully understand these conditions. Moreover, certain treatments that may be effective for one disorder may be relatively ineffective for another. Although differentiation is possible, it can be complicated because a substantial percentage of anxiety patients are comorbid for an additional anxiety disorder, a depressive disorder, or a personality disorder. In the majority of cases, patients with additional diagnoses appear to be more symptomatic (Jenike et al., 1986; Mavissakalian & Hammen, 1988; Turner & Beidel, 1989a, 1989b) and may have a poorer treatment prognosis (Mavissakalian & Hammen, 1988).

GENDER, RACIAL, AND ETHNIC ISSUES

The Epidemiological Catchment Area Survey (ECA) reported that African Americans had a higher lifetime prevalence than whites for simple phobia and agoraphobia (Blazer et al., 1985; Robins et al., 1984). However, the data are difficult to interpret because the sampling strategy overincluded severely disadvantaged African Americans (Baltimore and St. Louis sites) and elderly African Americans, underincluded low-income African American males, and virtually excluded middle-class African Americans. The lifetime prevalence for panic disorder was 1.2% for African Americans and 1.4% for whites. There were no differences in clinical presentation, except that African Americans reported a higher mean number of symptoms during their worst episode. The more recent National Comorbidity Study (NCS; Kessler et al., 1994) reported that African Americans had anxiety disorder prevalence rates that were no different from those of whites. Thus, the NCS findings are consistent with the ECA findings on panic disorder but not for specific phobia and agoraphobia. Hispanics in the ECA study consisted of Mexican Americans in the Los Angeles area. There were no differences in prevalence of anxiety disorders between Mexican Americans and non-Hispanic whites. The NCS data also did not find any differences between Hispanics and whites for any anxiety disorder.

Panic disorder without agoraphobia occurs twice as often in women as in men (Eaton et al., 1994). According to the DSM-IV, panic disorder with agoraphobia occurs three times as often in women as in men. Those with panic disorder and agoraphobia constitute over 50% of the patients seeking treatment at anxiety disorders clinics (Barlow et al., 1986; Chambless, 1982). Epidemiological data suggest that social phobia is more common in women, but the genders are equally represented in clinic samples. Among individuals with situations, animal, and natural environment phobia types, 75%–90% are female (except for heights, where 55%–70% are female). Among blood/injection/injury subtypes, 55%–70% are female. Obsessive-compulsive disorder affects men and women in equal proportions (Turner & Beidel, 1989b). In epidemiological samples, about 3% of the population meets criteria for GAD, two-thirds of whom are women. In clinical samples, approximately 55%–60% of patients are women.

The data indicate that there likely are no differences in the rates of anxiety disorders with respect to various ethnic groups. There may be some differences, however, in the symptomatic expression of these disorders or in other conditions that covary with them. For example, *ataque de nervios* ("attack of nerves") is a description used by Hispanics to describe presence of a group of symptoms that bears some similarities to panic disorder. In addition to many of the same features of panic, ataque de nervios includes becoming hysterical, screaming, hitting oneself or others, breaking things, nervousness, and feeling depressed before or after the episode. These episodes typically occur in stressful situations, such as funerals or family disputes. Liebowitz et al. (1994) examined presence of ataque de nervios and panic symptoms in 156 Hispanic patients seeking treatment for anxiety disorders. Results indicated that 70% of the subjects reported at least one episode of ataque de nervios in their lifetime; 80% of those patients were female. Among those reporting ataque de nervios, 41.3% had panic disorder as their primary diagnosis. Within this subgroup, 80% of the patients referred to their panic attacks as ataque de nervios. However, like the current reconceptualization of panic attacks, ataque de nervios was present in individuals with a variety of anxiety disorders as well as major depression, and common symptoms in that group included increased rates of sweating, depersonalization, fear of going crazy, and fear of losing control. These findings suggest that ataque de nervios constitutes a condition that is broader than just panic disorder. It remains unclear if it is a separate condition or whether it is a culturally specific manifestation of the same vulnerabilities associated with panic.

In their seminal article, Neal and Turner (1991) reviewed the literature on anxiety disorders in African Americans and noted the paucity of empirical data. There has been some improvement since that review, and studies are beginning to emerge addressing the epidemiology, clinical presentation, and treatment outcome for African Americans with anxiety disorders. As noted above, the best epidemiological data suggest that prevalence rates are about the same for African Americans and whites. Likewise, the clinical presentation of the anxiety disorders appears to be similar in African Americans as it is in white patients.

Although the core features of anxiety disorders appear to be essentially the same for all racial and ethnic groups, secondary features or other syndromes may covary with them and complicate the diagnostic process. Bell and Jenkins (1994) conducted substantial research on the phenomenon of isolated sleep paralysis. As described by these investigators, sleep paralysis, lasting from several seconds to a few minutes, is a state of consciousness that occurs while falling asleep or upon awakening, during which time the individual is unable to move. The individual is fully conscious of the experience, which can be accompanied by terrifying hallucinations (hypnopompic or hypnagogic) and a sense of acute danger. After the paralysis passes, the individual may experience panic symptoms and the realization that the distorted perceptions were false. Sleep paralysis that occurs in the absence of narcolepsy is referred to as isolated sleep paralysis. Isolated sleep paralysis (ISP) appears to be far more common and recurring among African Americans than among white Americans or Nigerian Blacks (Bell, Hildreth, Jenkins, & Carter, 1988). Among a group of African American patients receiving treatment at a local health center, 41% reported occurrence of at least one episode of ISP (Bell & Jenkins, 1994). This is higher than the 15% that had been reported for whites (Hufford, 1982). Furthermore, among African American patients who experience episodes of ISP, 36% reported the occurrence of panic attacks and 16% met criteria for panic disorder (Bell, Dixie-Bell, & Thompson, 1986). Bell and his colleagues have hypothesized that panic disorder in African Americans may be manifested differently than in white Americans, with recurrent isolated sleep paralysis and increased frequency of panic attacks as the core features. Alternatively, ISP could be a culturally specific manifestation of the same underlying vulnerability responsible for panic. In fact, Bell and Jenkins (1994) have proposed a stress-response hypothesis to explain the relationship of panic, ISP, and high rates of essential hypertension in African Americans.

With respect to treatment-seeking behavior, Neighbors (1985) found that 87% of a sample of African Americans experiencing psychological distress sought help from some informal network. Among the 48% who sought help from a professional, 22% went to emergency rooms, 22% went to a general physician, and 19% went to ministers. Only 9% went to a mental health clinician. Thus, it does not appear that most African Americans seek help from mental health professionals.

Treatment outcome data are few. Chambless and Williams (1995) reported that both African American and white patients with agoraphobia benefitted from an in vivo exposure program. However, African Americans were more severely phobic at pretreatment. At posttreatment, although both groups improved, African American patients were still more symptomatic. At follow-up, differences were less evident. It is unclear from these data, however, if these differences could reflect symptom severity rather than racial group differences. Culturally sensitive factors were reported as important in the treatment outcome of an African American social phobic treated with Social Effectiveness Therapy (Fink, Turner, & Beidel, 1996). The treatment package used in this study was effective, but only when racial factors, central to the development of the disorder, specifically were included in the exposure program. This suggests that in certain cases, specifically addressing ethnicity or racial factors might be critical to achieving a positive treatment outcome.

Although relatively few psychotropic drug treatment studies report efficacy data for ethnic and racial groups, and still fewer studies are conducted to directly address this issue (Turner & Cooley-Quille, 1996), there is a growing number of studies demonstrating that various racial/ethnic groups respond differently to these drugs (Lin, Poland, & Silver, 1993). Asians consistently require smaller doses of tricyclic antidepressants (TCAs) than Caucasians to achieve the same therapeutic effect (Lin, Poland, & Lesser, 1986; Yamamoto et al., 1979). Similarly, lower dosages of lithium and benzodiazepines are required in Asians to achieve the same results required by higher dosages in Caucasians. Similarly, African Americans and Hispanics appear to respond to lower doses of TCAs than do Caucasians (Marcos & Cancro, 1982; Ziegler & Biggs, 1977).

It is important to note that emerging data indicate that Hispanics and African Americans experience greater side effects than Caucasians from various pharmacological compounds, which suggests a difference in pharmacokinetics among various racial and ethnic groups (Lin et al., 1986; Matsuda, Cho, Lin, & Smith, 1995; Sellwood & Tarrier, 1994). It appears, then, that ethnicity and racial factors need to be considered when various psychotropic drugs are used in the treatment of anxiety, and the control of these factors in drug treatment studies is essential to allow unambiguous interpretation of outcome and to make recommendations for use in treatment.

SUMMARY

Over the past decade, conceptualization of the anxiety disorders has undergone a radical evolution. Increased attention to classification and diagnostic differentiation, along with the high prevalence of these conditions in the general population, clearly has contributed to a burgeoning interest in the area. Questions of etiology are emerging as central to our further understanding of the nature of these disorders and will no doubt intensely occupy the attention of researchers over the next decade. Currently, it seems clear that the anxiety disorders are familial, but the exact nature of this familial factor is poorly understood. Emerging human and nonhuman primate data suggest that the high likelihood of early temperamental factors are related to increased vulnerability to anxiety in some individuals. In order to fully address the issue of vulnerability, longitudinal studies with those considered to be at high risk will be necessary. However, based on the extant literature, the nature of this vulnerability is likely to be complex, encompassing biological, psychological, and environmental parameters.

Although many questions remain, there are now a number of treatment interventions (behavioral and drug) with demonstrated efficacy. Questions of efficacy for ethnic minority groups, however, are just now beginning to be addressed. Although the treatment for some of the anxiety disorders is better understood than others, in our opinion, such treatment of these disorders has evolved to the point where few additional advances are likely possible without increased understanding of the basic psychopathology and the further elucidation of the mechanisms of change.

REFERENCES

Agras, W. S., Sylvester, D., & Oliveau, D. (1969). The epidemiology of common fear and phobia. *Comprehensive Psychiatry, 10,* 151–156.

Akhtar, S., Wig, N. H., Verna, V. K., Pershod, D., & Verna, S. K. (1975). A phenomeno-logical analysis of symptoms in obsessive-compulsive neuroses. *British Journal of Psychiatry, 127,* 342–348.

Albus, M., & Scheibe, G. (1993). Outcome of panic disorder with or without concomitant depression: A two-year prospective follow-up study. *American Journal of Psychiatry, 150,* 1878–1880.

American Psychiatric Association. (1980). *Diagnostic and statistical manual of mental disorders* (3rd ed.). Washington, DC: Author.

American Psychiatric Association. (1987). *Diagnostic and statistical manual of mental disorders* (3rd ed., rev. ed.). Washington, DC: Author.

American Psychiatric Association. (1994). *Diagnostic and statistical manual of mental disorders* (4th ed.). Washington, DC: Author.

Amies, P. L., Gelder, M. G., & Shaw, P. M. (1983). Social phobia: A comparative clinical study. *British Journal of Psychiatry, 142,* 174–179.

Andrade, L., Eaton, W. W., & Chilcoat, H. (1994). Lifetime comorbidity of panic attacks and major depression in a population-based study: Symptom profiles. *British Journal of Psychiatry, 165,* 363–369.

Andrews, G., Stewart, G., Allen, R., & Henderson, A. S. (1990). The genetics of six anxiety disorders: A twin study. *Journal of Affective Disorders, 19,* 23–29.

AuBuchon, P. G., & Malatesta, V. J. (1994). Obsessive-compulsive patients with comorbid personality disorder: Associated problems and response to a comprehensive behavior therapy. *Journal of Clinical Psychiatry, 55,* 448–453.

Ballenger, J. C. (1984). Psychopharmacology of the anxiety disorders. *Psychiatric Clinics of North America, 7,* 757–771.

Ballenger, J. C. (1986). Pharmacotherapy of the panic disorders. *Journal of Clinical Psychiatry, 47* (Suppl. 6), 27–32.

Ballenger, J. C. (1990). Efficacy of benzodiazepines in panic disorder and agoraphobia. *Journal of Psychiatric Research, 24* (Suppl. 2), 15–25.

Ballenger, J. C., Burrows, G. D., DuPont, R. L., Lesser, I. M., Noyes, R., Jr., Pecknold, J. C., Rifkin, A., & Swinson, R. P. (1988). Alprazolam in panic disorder and agoraphobia: Results from a multicenter trial. *Archives of General Psychiatry, 45,* 413–422.

Ballenger, J. C., Lydiard, R. B., & Turner, S. M. (1995). The treatment of panic disorder and agoraphobia. In G. O. Gabbard, (Ed.-in-Chief), *Treatment of psychiatric disorders* (2nd ed., pp. 1422–1452). Washington, DC: American Psychiatric Press.

Ballenger, J. C., Peterson, G. A., Laraia, M., Hucek, A., Lake, C. R., Jimerson, D., Cox, D. J., Trockman, C., Shipe, J. R., & Wilkinson, C. (1984). A study of plasma catecholamines in agoraphobia and the relationship to serum. In J. C. Ballenger (Ed.), *Biology of agoraphobia* (pp. 27–63). Washington, DC: American Psychiatric Press.

Bandura, A. (1969). *Principles of behavior modification.* New York: Holt, Rinehart, and Winston.

Barlow, D. H. (1988). *Anxiety and its disorders.* New York: Guilford.

Barlow, D. H., Craske, M. G., Cerny, J. A., & Klosko, J. S. (1989). Behavioral treatment of panic disorder. *Behavior Therapy, 20,* 261–282.

Barlow, D. H., DiNardo, P. A., Vermilyea, B. B., Vermilyea, J. A., & Blanchard, E. B. (1986). Comorbidity and depression among the anxiety disorders: Issues in diagnosis and classification. *Journal of Nervous and Mental Disease, 174,* 63–72.

Barrios, B. A., Hartman, D. B., & Shigetomi, C. (1981). Fears and anxieties in children. In E. J. Mash & L. G. Terdal (Eds.), *Behavioral assessment of childhood disorders* (pp. 259–304). New York: Guilford.

Basoglu, M., Marks, I. M., Kilic, C., Swinson, R. P., Noshirvani, H., Kuch, K., & O'Sullivan, G. (1994). Relationship of panic, anticipatory anxiety, agoraphobia, and global improvement in panic disorder with agoraphobia treated with alprazolam and exposure. *British Journal of Psychiatry, 164,* 647–652.

Bastani, B., Arora, R., & Meltzer, H. (1991). Serotonin uptake and imipramine binding in the blood platelets of obsessive-compulsive disorder patients. *Biological Psychiatry, 30,* 13–139.

Baxter, L. R. (1992). Neuroimaging studies of obsessive-compulsive disorder. *Psychiatric Clinics of North America, 15,* 871–884.

Beck, A. T. (1988). Cognitive approaches to panic disorder: Theory and therapy. In S. Rachman & J. D. Maser (Eds.), *Panic: Psychological perspectives.* Hillsdale, NJ: Erlbaum.

Beck, A. T., & Emery G. (1985). *Anxiety disorders and phobias: A cognitive perspective.* New York: Basic Books.

Beck, A. T., Sokol, D., & Clark, D. A. (1992). A crossover study of focused cognitive therapy for panic disorder. *American Journal of Psychiatry, 149,* 778–783.

Beidel, D. C., & Bulik, C. M. (1990). Flooding and response prevention as a treatment for bowel obsessions. *Journal of Anxiety Disorders, 4,* 247–256.

Beidel, D. C., & Turner, S. M. (1986). A critique of the theoretical bases of cognitive behavior theories and therapies. *Clinical Psychology Review, 6,* 177–197.

Beidel, D. C., & Turner, S. M. (1988). Comorbidity of test anxiety and other anxiety disorders in children. *Journal of Abnormal Child Psychology, 16,* 275–287.

Beidel, D. C., & Turner, S. M. (1996). At risk for anxiety: I. Psychopathology in the offspring of anxious parents. Manuscript under review.

Beidel, D. C., Turner, S. M., & Ballenger, J. C. (in press). Psychosocial treatments for anxiety disorders. In D. Dunner (Ed.), *Current psychiatric therapy* (Vol. 2). Philadelphia: Saunders.

Bell, C. C., Dixie-Bell, D. D., & Thompson, B. (1986). Further studies on the prevalence of isolated sleep paralysis in black subjects. *Journal of the National Medical Association, 78,* 649–659.

Bell, C. C., Hildreth, C. J., Jenkins, E. J., & Carter, C. (1988). The relationship of isolated sleep paralysis and panic disorder to hypertension. *Journal of the National Medical Association, 80,* 289–294.

Bell, C., & Jenkins, E. J. (1994). Isolated sleep paralysis and anxiety disorders. In S. Friedman (Ed.) *Anxiety disorders in African Americans* (pp. 117–127). New York: Springer.

Biederman, J., Rosenbaum, J. F., Hirshfeld, D. R., Faraone, S. V., Bolduc, E. A., Gersten, M., Meminger, S. R., Kagan, J., Snidman, N., & Reznick, J. S. (1990). Psychiatric correlates of behavioral inhibition in young children of parents with and without psychiatric disorders. *Archives of General Psychiatry, 47,* 21–26.

Black, D. B., Noyes, R., Goldstein, R. B., & Blum, N. (1992). A family study of obsessive-compulsive disorder. *Archives of General Psychiatry, 49,* 362–368.

Blazer, D., George, L. K., Landerman, R., Pennybacker, M., Melville, M. L., Woodbury, M., Manton, K. G., Jordan, K., & Locke, B. (1985). Psychiatric disorders: A rural-urban comparison. *Archives of General Psychiatry, 42,* 651–656.

Borkovec, T. D., Robinson, E., Pruzinsky, T., & DePress, J. A. (1983). Preliminary exploration of worry: Some characteristics and processes. *Behaviour Research and Therapy, 21,* 9–16.

Borkovec, T. D., & Shadick, R. (1989). *The nature of normal versus pathological worry.* Paper prepared for the DSM-IV Task Force.

Brawman-Mintzer, Lydiard, R. B., Emmamuel, N., Payeur, R., Johnson, M., Roberts,

J., Jarrell, M. P., & Ballenger, J. C. (1993). Psychiatric comorbidity in patients with generalized anxiety disorder. *American Journal of Psychiatry, 150,* 1216–1218.

Breier, A., Charney, D. S., & Heninger, G. R. (1984). Major depression in patients with agoraphobia and panic disorder. *Archives of General Psychology, 41,* 1129–1135.

Breier, A., Charney, D. S., & Heninger, G. R. (1986). Agoraphobia with panic attacks. *Archives of General Psychology, 43,* 1029–1036.

Brewin, C. R. (1985). Depression and causal attributions: What is their relation? *Psychological Bulletin, 98,* 297–309.

Brown, T. A., Antony, M. M., & Barlow, D. H. (1995). Diagnostic comorbidity in panic disorder: Effect on treatment outcome and course of comorbid diagnoses following treatment. *Journal of Consulting and Clinical Psychology, 63,* 408–418.

Brown, T. A., & Barlow, D. H. (1992). Comorbidity among anxiety disorders: Implications for treatment and DSM-IV. *Journal of Consulting and Clinical Psychology, 60,* 835–844.

Brown, T. A., Barlow, D. H., & Liebowitz, M. R. (1994). The empirical basis of generalized anxiety disorder. *American Journal of Psychiatry, 151,* 1272–1280.

Burnam, M. A., Hough, R. L., Escobar, J. I., Karno, M., Timbers, D. M., Telles, C. A., & Locke, B. Z. (1987). Six-month prevalence of specific psychiatric disorders among Mexican Americans and Non-Hispanic whites in Los Angeles. *Archives of General Psychiatry, 44,* 687–694.

Butler, G., Fennell, M., Robson, P., & Gelder, M. (1991). Comparison of behavior therapy and cognitive behavior therapy in the treatment of generalized anxiety disorder. *Journal of Consulting and Clinical Psychology, 59,* 167–175.

Carr, D. B., & Sheehan, D. V. (1984). Evidence that panic disorder has a metabolic cause. In J. D. Ballenger (Ed.), *Biology of agoraphobia* (pp. 99–111). Washington, DC: American Psychiatric Press.

Castle, D. J., Deale, A., Marks, I. M., Cutts, F., Chadhoury, Y., & Stewart, A. (1994). Obsessive-compulsive disorder: prediction of outcome from behavioural psychotherapy. *Acta Psychiatrica Scandinavica, 89,* 393–398.

Center for Disease Control (1988). Health status of Vietnam veterans. *Journal of the American Medical Association, 259,* 2701–2724.

Chambless, D. L. (1982). Characteristics of agoraphobia. In D. L. Chambless & A. J. Goldstein (Eds.), *Agoraphobia* (pp. 1–18). New York: Wiley.

Chambless, D. L., & Williams, K. E. (1995). A preliminary study of African Americans with agoraphobia: Symptom severity and outcome of treatment with in vivo exposure. *Behavior Therapy, 26,* 501–515.

Christensen, H., Hadzi-Pavlovic, D., Andrews, G., & Mattick, R. (1987). Behavior therapy and tricyclic medication in the treatment of obsessive-compulsive disorder: A quantitative review. *Journal of Consulting and Clinical Psychology, 55,* 701–711.

Clark, D. B., & Agras, S. (1991). The assessment and treatment of performance anxiety in musicians. *American Journal of Psychiatry, 148,* 598–605.

Clark, D., Salkovskis, P., & Chalkley, A. (1985). Respiratory control as a treatment for panic attacks. *Journal of Behavior Therapy and Experimental Psychiatry, 16,* 23–30.

Clum, G. (1989). Psychological interventions versus drugs in the treatment of panic disorder. *Behavior Therapy, 20,* 429–457.

Cook, M., & Mineka, S. (1989). Observational conditioning of fear to fear-relevant versus fear-irrelevant stimuli in rhesus monkeys. *Journal of Abnormal Psychology, 98,* 448–459.

Cox, B. J., Direnfeld, D. M., Swinson, R. P., & Norton, G. R. (1994). Suicidal ideation and suicide attempts in panic disorder and social phobia. *American Journal of Psychiatry, 151,* 882–887.

Craske, M. M., Rapee, R. M., & Barlow, D. H. (1992). Cognitive-behavioral treatment of panic disorder, agoraphobia and generalized anxiety disorder. In S. M. Turner, K. S. Calhoun, & H. E. Adams (Eds.), *Handbook of clinical behavior therapy* (2d ed., pp. 39–66). New York: Wiley.

Cross National Collaborative Panic Study Second Phase Investigation. (1992). Drug treatment of panic disorder: Comparative efficacy of alprazolam, imipramine, and placebo. *British Journal of Psychiatry, 160,* 191–202.

Curtis, G. C., Massana, J., Udina, C., Ayuso, J. L., Cassanos, G. B., & Perugi, G. (1993). Maintenance drug therapy of panic disorder. *Journal of Psychiatric Research, 27,* 127–142.

Davidson, J. R. T. (1992). Drug therapy of posttraumatic stress disorder. *British Journal of Psychiatry, 160,* 309–314.

Davidson, J. R. T. (1993, March). Childhood histories of adult social phobics. Paper presented at the Anxiety Disorders Association of America Annual Convention. Charleston, SC.

Davidson, J. R. T., Hughes, D., Blazer, D. G., & George, L. K. (1991). Posttraumatic stress disorder in the community: An epidemiological study. *Psychological Medicine, 21,* 713–721.

Davidson, J. R. T., Potts, N., Ruchichi, E., Krishnan, R., Ford, S. M., Smith, R., & Wilson, W. (1993). Treatment of social phobia with clonazepam and placebo. *Journal of Clinical Psychopharmacology, 13,* 423–428.

DeBeurs, E., van Balkom, A. J. L. M., Lange, A., Koele, P., & van Dyck, R. (1995). Treatment of panic disorder with agoraphobia: Comparison of fluvoxamine, placebo, and psychological panic management combined with exposure and of exposure in vivo alone. *American Journal of Psychiatry 152,* 683–691.

Delprato, D. J., & McGlynn, F. D. (1984). Behavioral theories of anxiety disorders. In S. M. Turner (Ed.), *Behavioral theories and treatment of anxiety* (pp. 1–49). New York: Plenum.

Durham, R. C., & Allan, T. (1993). Psychological treatments of generalized anxiety disorder: A review of the clinical significance of results in outcome studies since 1980. *British Journal of Psychiatry, 156,* 19–26.

Eaton, W. W., Holzer, C. E. III, Von Korff, M., Anthony, J. C., Helzer, J. E., George, L., Burnam, M. A., Boyd, J. H., Kessler, L. G., & Locke, B. Z. (1984). The design of the epidemiologic catchment area surveys. *Archives of General Psychiatry, 41,* 942–948.

Eaton, W. W., Kessler, R. C., Wittchen, H. U., & Magee, W. J. (1994). Panic and panic disorder in the United States. *American Journal of Psychiatry, 151,* 413–420.

Emmelkamp, P. M. G. (1988). Phobic disorders. In C. G. Last & M. Hersen (Eds.), *Handbook of anxiety disorders* (pp. 66–86). New York: Pergamon.

Falloon, I. R. H., Lloyd, G. G., & Harpin, R. E. (1981). The treatment of social phobia: Real life rehearsal with nonprofessional therapists. *Journal of Nervous and Mental Disease, 169,* 180–184.

Feske, U., & Chambless, D. (1995). Cognitive-behavioral versus exposure treatment for social phobia: A meta-analysis. *Behavior Therapy, 26,* 695–720.

Fink, C. M., Turner, S. M., & Beidel, D. C. (1996). Culturally relevant factors in the behavioral treatment of social phobia: A case study. *Journal of Anxiety Disorders, 10,* 201–209.

Foa, E. B., Steketee, G. A., & Ozarow, B. J. (1985). Behavior therapy with obsessive-compulsives: From theory to treatment. In M. Mavissakalian, S. M. Turner, & L. Michelson (Eds.), *Obsessive-compulsive disorder: Psychological and pharmacological treatments* (pp. 49–120). New York: Plenum.

Foa, E. B., Rothbaum, B. O., Riggs, D. S., & Murdock, T. B. (1991). Treatment of post-traumatic stress disorder in rape victims: A comparison between cognitive-behavioral procedures and counseling. *Journal of Consulting and Clinical Psychology, 59,* 715–723.

Fontaine, R., & Chouinard, G. (1986). An open clinical trial of fluoxetine in the treatment of obsessive-compulsive disorder. *Journal of Clinical Psychopharmacology, 6,* 98–101.

Frueh, B. C., Turner, S. M., & Beidel, D. C. (1995). Exposure therapy for combat-related PTSD: A critical review. *Clinical Psychology Review, 15,* 799–818.

Fyer, A. J. (1993). Heritability of social anxiety: A brief review. *Journal of Clinical Psychiatry, 54,* 10–12.

Fyer, A. J., Mannuzza, S., Gallops, M. S., Martin, L. Y., Aaronson, C., Gorman, J. M., Liebowitz, M. R., & Klein, D. F. (1990). Familial transmission of simple phobias and fears: A preliminary report. *Archives of General Psychiatry, 47,* 252–256.

Fyer, A. J., & Sandberg, D. (1988). Pharmacologic treatment of panic disorder. In A. J. Francis & R. E. Hales (Eds.), *Review of psychiatry* (Vol. 7, pp. 88–137). Washington, DC: American Psychiatric Press.

Goisman, R. M., Warshaw, M. G., Peterson, L. G., Rogers, M. P., Cuneo, P., Hunt, M. F., Tomlin-Albanese, J. M., Kazim, A., Gollan, J. K., Epstein-Kaye, T., Reich, J. H., & Kellar, M. B. (1994). Panic, agoraphobia, and panic disorder with agoraphobia: Data from a multicenter anxiety disorders study. *Journal of Nervous and Mental Disease, 182,* 72–79.

Goldstein, A. J., & Chambless, D. L. (1978). A reanalysis of agoraphobia. *Behavior Therapy, 9,* 47–59.

Goodman, W. K., McDougle, C. J., & Price, L. H. (1992). Pharmacotherapy of obsessive-compulsive disorder. *Journal of Clinical Psychiatry, 53,* 29–37.

Gorman, J., Fyer, A. F., Glicklich, J., King, D., & Klein, D. F. (1981). Effect of imipramine on prolapsed mitral valves of patients with panic disorder. *American Journal of Psychiatry, 138,* 977–978.

Gorman, J. M., Levy, G. F., Liebowitz, M. R., McGrath, P., Appleby, I. L., Dillon, D. J., Davies, S. O., & Klein, D. F. (1983). Effect of acute b-adrenergic blockade of lactate-induced panic. *Archives of General Psychiatry, 40,* 1079–1082.

Hegel, M. T., Ravaris, C. L., & Ahles, T. A. (1994). Combined cognitive-behavioral and time-limited alprazolam treatment of panic disorder. *Behavior Therapy, 25,* 183–195.

Heimberg, R. G., Dodge, C. S., Hope, D. A., Kennedy, C. R., Zollo, L., & Becker, R. E. (1990). Cognitive behavioral treatment of social phobia: Comparison to a credible placebo control. *Cognitive Therapy and Research, 14,* 1–23.

Heimberg, R. G., Salzman, D. G., Holt, C. S., & Blendell, K. A. (1993). Cognitive-behavioral group treatment of social phobia: Effectiveness at five-year follow-up. *Cognitive Therapy and Research, 17,* 325–339.

Herbert, J. D., Hope, D. A., & Bellack, A. S. (1992). Validity of the distinction between generalized social phobia and avoidant personality disorder. *Journal of Abnormal Psychology, 104,* 332–339.

Hirshfeld, D. R., Rosenbaum, J. F., Biederman, J., Bolduc, E. A., Faraone, S. V., Snidman, N., Reznick, J. S., & Kagan, J. (1992). Stable behavioral inhibition and its association with anxiety disorder. *Journal of the American Academy of Child and Adolescent Psychiatry, 31,* 103–111.

Hoehn-Saric, R., McLeod, D. R., & Hipsley, P. A. (1993). Effect of fluvoxamine on panic disorder. *Journal of Clinical Psychopharmacology, 13,* 321–326.

Hoffart, A. (1993). Cognitive treatments of agoraphobia: A critical evaluation of theoretical bases and outcome evidence. *Journal of Anxiety Disorders, 7,* 75–91.

Holloway, W., & McNally, R. J. (1987). Effects of anxiety sensitivity on the response to hyperventilation. *Journal of Abnormal Psychology, 96,* 330–334.

Holt, C. S., Heimberg, R. G., & Hope, D. A. (1992). Avoidant personality disorder and the generalized subtype of social phobia. *Journal of Abnormal Psychology, 101,* 318–325.

Hope, D. A., Heimberg, R. G., & Bruch, M. A. (1995). Dismantling cognitive-behavioral therapy for social phobia. *Behaviour Research and Therapy, 33,* 637–650.

Hufford, D. (1982). *The terror that comes in the night.* Philadelphia: University of Pennsylvania Press.

Insel, T. R., Mueller, E. A., Gillin, C., Siever, L. J., & Murphy, D. L. (1985). Tricyclic response in obsessive-compulsive disorder. *Progress in Neurological-Psychopharmacology and Biological Psychiatry, 9,* 25–31.

Insel, T. R., & Winslow, J. T. (1992). Neurobiology of obsessive-compulsive disorder. *Psychiatric Clinics of North America, 15,* 813–824.

Jacob, R. G., Furman, J. M., Durrant, J. D., & Turner, S. M. (1996). Panic, agoraphobia, and vestibular dysfunction. *American Journal of Psychiatry, 153,* 503–512.

Jacob, R. G., Moller, M. B., Turner, S. M., & Wall, C. (1985). Otoneurological examination in panic disorders and agoraphobia with panic attacks: A pilot study. *American Journal of Psychiatry, 142,* 715–720.

Jacob, R. G., & Turner, S. M. (1988). Panic disorder: Diagnosis and assessment. In A. J. Frances & R. E. Hales (Eds.), *Review of psychiatry* (pp. 67–87). Washington, DC: American Psychiatric Press.

Jansson, L., Jerremalm, A., & Ost, L. G. (1986). Follow-up of agoraphobic patients treated with exposure in-vivo or applied relaxation. *British Journal of Psychiatry, 149,* 486–490.

Jenike, M. A., Baer, L., Minichiello, W. E., Schwartz, C. E., & Carey, Jr., R. J. (1986). Concomitant obsessive-compulsive disorders and schizotypal personality disorder. *American Journal of Psychiatry, 143,* 530–532.

Jenike, M. A., Vitagliano, H. L., Rabinowitz, J., Goff, D. C., & Baer, L. (1987). Bowel obsessions responsive to tricyclic antidepressants in four patients. *American Journal of Psychiatry, 144,* 1347–1348.

Kagan, J. (1982). Heart rate and heart rate variability as signs of a temperamental dimension in infants. In C. E. Izard (Ed.), *Measuring emotions in infants and children* (pp. 38–66). Cambridge: Cambridge University Press.

Kagan, J., Reznick, J. S., Clarke, C., Snidman, N., & Garcia-Coll, C. (1984). Behavioral inhibition to the unfamiliar. *Child Development, 55,* 2212–2225.

Kagan, J., Reznick, J. S., & Snidman, N. (1987). The physiology and psychology of behavioral inhibition in children. *Child Development, 58,* 1459–1473.

Kagan, J., Reznick, J. S., Snidman, N., Gibbons, J., & Johnson, M. O. (1988). Childhood derivatives of inhibition and lack of inhibition to the unfamiliar. *Child Development, 59,* 1580–1589.

Kahn, R. J., McNair, D. M., Covi, L., Downing, R. W., Fisher, S., Lipman, R. S., Rickels, K., & Smith, V. (1981). Effects of psychotropic agents on high anxiety subjects. *Psychopharmacology Bulletin, 17,* 97–100.

Kahn, R. S., Van Praag, H. M., Wetzler, G. M., & Barr, G. (1988). Serotonin and anxiety revisited. *Biological Psychiatry, 23,* 189–208.

Kathol, R. G., Noyes, R., Slyman, D. J., Crowe, R. R., Clancy, J., & Kerber, R. E. (1980). Propranolol in chronic anxiety disorders. *Archives of General Psychiatry, 37,* 1361–1365.

Keijsers, G. P. J., Hoogduin, C. A. L., & Schapp, C. P. D. R. (1994a). Predictors of treatment outcome in the behavioral treatment of obsessive-compulsive disorder. *British Journal of Psychiatry, 165,* 781–786.

Keijsers, G. P. J., Hoogduin, C. A. L., & Schapp, C. P. D. R. (1994b). Prognostic factors in the behavioral treatment of panic disorder with and without agoraphobia. *Behavior Therapy, 25,* 689–708.

Keller, M. B., Yonkers, K. A., Warshaw, M. G., Pratt, L. A., Gollan, J. K., Massion, A. O., White, K., Swartz, A. R., Reich, J., & Lavori, P. W. (1994). Remission and relapse in subjects with panic disorder and panic with agoraphobia. *Journal of Nervous and Mental Disease, 182,* 290–296.

Kendler, K. S., Heath, A. C., Martin, N. G., & Eaves, L. J. (1987). Symptoms of anxiety and symptoms of depression: Same genes, different environments. *Archives of General Psychiatry, 44,* 451–457.

Kendler, K. S., Neale, M. C., Kessler, R. C., Heath, A. C., & Eaves, L. J. (1992a). Generalized anxiety disorder in women: A population-based twin study. *Archives of General Psychiatry, 49,* 267–272.

Kendler, K. S., Neale, M. C., Kessler, R. C., Heath, A. C., & Eaves, L. J. (1992b). The genetic epidemiology of phobias in women: The interrelationship of agoraphobia, social phobia, situational phobia, and simple phobia. *Archives of General Psychiatry, 49,* 273–281.

Kessler, R. C., McGonagle, K. A., Zhao, S., Nelson, C. B., Hughes, M., Eshleman, S., Wittchen, H. U., & Kendler, K. S. (1994). Lifetime and 12-month prevalence of DSM-III-R psychiatric disorders in the United States: Results from the national comorbidity survey. *Archives of General Psychiatry, 51,* 8–19.

Khanna, S., & Channabasavanna, S. M. (1988). Phenomenology of obsessions in obsessive-compulsive neurosis. *Psychopathology, 21,* 12–18.

Kilpatrick, D. G., Saunders, B. E., Amick-McMullan, A., Best, C. L., Veronen, L. J., & Resnick, H. S. (1989). Victim and crime factors associated with the development of crime-related posttraumatic stress disorder. *Behavior Therapy, 20,* 199–214.

Klein, D. F. (1981). Anxiety reconceptualized. In D. F. Klein & J. R. Rabkin (Eds.), *Anxiety: New research and changes concepts* (pp. 235–263). New York: Raven.

Klein, D. F., & Fink, M. (1962). Psychiatric reaction patterns to imipramine. *American Journal of Psychiatry, 119,* 432–438.

Klosko, J. S., Barlow, D. H., Tassinari, R., & Cerney, J. A. (1990). A comparison of alprazolam and behavior therapy in treatment of panic disorder. *Journal of Consulting and Clinical Psychology, 58,* 77–84.

Kulka, R. A., Schlenger, W. E., Fairbank, J. A., Hough, R. L., Jordan, B. K., Marmar, C. R., & Weiss, D. S. (1988). *National Vietnam Veterans Readjustment Study (NVVRS): Description, current status, and initial PTSD prevalence estimates, final report.* Washington, DC: Veterans Administration.

Lang, P. J. (1977). Physiological assessment of anxiety and fear. In J. D. Cone & R. P. Hawkins (Eds.), *Behavioral assessment: New directions in clinical psychology* (pp. 178–195). Brummer/Mazel.

Last, C. G., Hersen, M., Kazdin, A. E., Francis, G., & Grubb, H. J. (1987). Psychiatric illness in the mothers of anxious children. *American Journal of Psychiatry, 144,* 1580–1583.

Last, C. G., Hersen, M., Kazdin, A. E., Orvaschel, H. & Ye, W. (1990). *Anxiety disorders in children and their families.* Unpublished manuscript, Nova University.

Lesser, I. M., Rubin, R. T., Pecknold, J. C., Rifkin, A., Swinson, R. P., Lydiard, R. B., Burrows, G. D., Noyes, R., Jr., & DuPont, R. L. (1988). Secondary depression in panic disorder and agoraphobia. *Archives of General Psychiatry, 45,* 437–443.

Levin, A. P., Sandberg, D., Stein, J., Cohen, B., Strauman, T., Gorman, J. M., Fyer, A. J., Crawford, R., & Liebowitz, M. R. (1989). *Responses of generalized and limited social phobics during public speaking.* Unpublished manuscript, Columbia University.

Liddell, A., & Lyons, M. (1978). Thunderstorm phobias. *Behaviour Research and Therapy, 16,* 306–308.

Liebowitz, M. R., Fyer, A. J., Gorman, J. M., Dillon, D., Davies, S., Stein, J. M., Cohen, B. S., & Klein, D. F. (1985). Specificity of lactate infusions in social phobia versus panic disorders. *American Journal of Psychiatry, 142,* 947–950.

Liebowitz, M. R., Gorman, J. M., Fyer, A. J., Campeas, R., Levin, A. P., Sandberg, D., Hollander, E., Papp, L., & Goetz, D. (1988). Pharmacotherapy of social phobia: A placebo-controlled comparison of phenelzine and atenolol. *Journal of Clinical Psychiatry, 49,* 252–257.

Liebowitz, M. R., Gorman, J. M., Fyer, A. J., & Klein, D. F. (1985). Social phobia. *Archives of General Psychiatry, 42,* 729–736.

Liebowitz, M. R., Salman, E., Jusino, C. M., Garfinkel, R., Street, L., Cardenas, D. L., Silvestre, J., Fyer, A. J., Carrasco, J. L., Davies, S., Guarnaccia, P., & Klein, D. F. (1994). *Ataque de nervios* and panic disorder. *American Journal of Psychiatry, 151,* 871–875.

Lilienfeld, S. O., Jacob, R. G., & Turner, S. M. (1989). Comment on Holloway and McNally's (1987) "Effects of anxiety sensitivity on the response to hyperventilation." *Journal of Abnormal Psychology, 98,* 100–102.

Lilienfeld, S. O., Turner, S. M., & Jacob, R. G. (1993). Anxiety Sensitivity: An examination of theoretical and methodological issues. *Advances in Behaviour Research and Therapy, 15,* 147–183.

Lilienfeld, S. O., Turner, S. M., & Jacob, R. G. (1996). Further comments on the nature and measurement of anxiety sensitivity: A reply to Taylor (1995b). *Journal of Anxiety Disorders, 10,* 411–424.

Lin, K. M., Poland, R. E., & Lesser, I. M. (1986). Ethnicity and psychopharmacology. *Culture, Medicine, and Psychiatry, 10,* 151–165.

Lin, K. M., Poland, R. E., & Silver, B. (1993). The interface between psychobiology and ethnicity. In K. M. Lin, R. E. Poland, and G. Nakasaki (Eds.), Psychopharmacology and psychobiology of ethnicity (pp. 11–35). Washington, DC: American Psychiatric Press.

Lydiard, R. B., Roy-Byrne, P. P., & Ballenger, J. C. (1988). Recent advances in psychopharmacological treatment of anxiety disorders. *Hospital and Community Psychiatry, 39,* 1157–1165.

Maller, R. G., & Reiss, S. (1987). A behavioral validation of the Anxiety Sensitivity Index. *Journal of Anxiety Disorders, 1,* 265–272.

Mancuso, D. M., Townsend, M. H., & Mercante, D. E. (1993). Long-term follow-up of generalized anxiety disorder. *Comprehensive Psychiatry, 34,* 441–446.

Marcos, L. R., & Cancro, R. (1982). Pharmacotherapy of Hispanic depressed patients: Clinical observations. *American Journal of Psychotherapy, 36,* 505–512.

Margraf, J., Ehlers, A., & Roth, W. T. (1986). Sodium lactate infusions and panic attacks: A review and critique. *Psychosomatic Medicine, 48,* 23–51.

Marks, I., & Gelder, M. G. (1966). Different onset ages in varieties of phobias. *American Journal of Psychiatry, 123,* 218–221.

Marks, I. M. (1970). The classification of phobic disorders. *British Journal of Psychiatry, 116,* 377–386.

Marks, I. M. (1985). Behavioral treatment of social phobia. *Psychopharmacology Bulletin, 21,* 615–618.

Mathew, R. J., Ho, B. T., Francis, D. J., Taylor, D. L., & Weinman, M. L. (1982). Catacholamines and anxiety. *Acta Psychiatrica Scandinavica, 65,* 142–147.

Matsuda, K. T., Cho, M. C., Lin, K. M., & Smith, M. W. (1995, May). Clozapine dosage, efficacy, side-effect profiles: A comparison of Asian and Caucasian patients. Presented at the New Clinical Drug Evaluation Unit (NCDEU) Annual Meeting, Orlando.

Mavissakalian, M., & Hamann, S. (1986). DSM-III personality disorder in agoraphobia. *Comprehensive Psychiatry, 27,* 471–479.

Mavissakalian, M., & Hammen, M. S. (1988). Correlates of DSM-III personality disorder in panic disorder and agoraphobia. *Comprehensive Psychiatry, 29,* 535–544.

McNally, R. J. (1987). Preparedness and phobias: A review. *Psychological Bulletin, 101,* 283–303.

McNally, R. J. (1995). Automaticity and the anxiety disorders. *Behaviour Research and Therapy, 33,* 747–754.

McNally, R. J., & Lorenz, M. (1987). Anxiety sensitivity in agoraphobics. *Journal of Behavior Therapy and Experimental Psychiatry, 18,* 3–11.

McNally, R. J., & Steketee, G. S. (1985). The etiology and maintenance of severe animal phobias. *Behaviour Research and Therapy, 23,* 431–435.

Michelson, L., Mavissakalian, M., & Marchione, K. (1985). Cognitive and behavioral treatments of agoraphobia: Clinical, behavioral, and psychophysiological outcomes. *Journal of Consulting and Clinical Psychology, 53,* 913–925.

Mineka, S., & Cook, M. (1986). Immunization against the observational conditioning of snake fear in rhesus monkeys. *Journal of Abnormal Psychology, 95,* 307–318.

Mineka, S., Davidson, M., Cook, M., & Heir, R. (1985). Observational conditioning of snake fear in rhesus monkeys. *Journal of Abnormal Psychology, 93,* 355–372.

Mineka, S., & Zinbarg, R. (1991). Animal models of psychopathology. In C. E. Walker (Ed.), *Clinical psychology: Historical and research foundations* (pp. 51–86). New York: Plenum.

Mowrer, O. H. (1947). On the dual nature of learning: A reinterpretation of "conditioning" and "problem-solving." *Harvard Education Review, 17,* 102–148.

Munjack, D. J., Bruns, J., Baltazar, P. L., Brown, R., Leonard, M., Nagy, R., Koek, R., Crocker, B., & Shafer, S. (1991). A pilot study of buspirone in the treatment of social phobia. *Journal of Anxiety Disorders, 5,* 87–98.

Myers, J. K., Weissman, M. M., Tischler, G. L., Holzer, C. E., Leaf, P. J., Orvaschel, H., Anthong, J. C., Boyd, J. H., Burke, J. D., Kramer, M., & Stoetzman, R. (1984), Six-month prevalence of psychiatric disorders in three communities. *Archives of General Psychiatry, 41,* 287–292.

Neal, A. M., & Turner, S. M. (1991). Anxiety disorders research with African Americans: Current status. *Psychological Bulletin, 109,* 400–410.

Neighbors, H. W. (1985). Seeking help for personal problems: Black Americans' use of health and mental health services. *Community Mental Health Journal, 21,* 156–166.

Nesse, R. M., Cameron, O. G., Curtis, G. C., McCann, D. S., & Huber-Smith, M. J. (1984). Adrenergic function in patients with panic anxiety. *Archives of General Psychiatry, 41,* 771–776.

Noyes, R., Jr. (1985). Beta-adrenergic blocking drugs in anxiety and stress. *Psychiatric Clinics of North America, 8*, 119–132.

Noyes, R., Woodman, C., Garvey, M. J., Cook, B. L., Suelzer, M., Clancy, J., & Anderson, D. J. (1992). Generalized anxiety disorder versus panic disorder: Distinguishing characteristics and patterns of comorbidity. *Journal of Nervous and Mental Disease, 180*, 369–378.

Nutt, D., & Lawson, C. (1992). Panic attacks: A neurochemical overview of models and mechanisms. *British Journal of Psychiatry, 160*, 165–178.

Ohman, A. (1986). Face the beast and fear the face: Animal and social fears as prototypes for evolutionary analyses of emotion. *Psychophysiology, 23*, 123–145.

Ohman, A., Eriksson, A., & Olafsson, C. (1975). One-trial learning and superior resistance to extinction of autonomic responses conditioned to potentially phobic stimuli. *Journal of Comparative and Physiological Psychology, 88*, 619–627.

Ohman, A., Fredrikson, M., Hugdahl, K., & Rimmo, P. A. (1976). The premise of equipotentiality in human classical conditioning: Conditioned electrodermal responses to potentially phobic stimuli. *Journal of Experimental Psychology: General, 105*, 313–337.

Ost, L. G. (1987). Age of onset in different phobias. *Journal of Abnormal Psychology, 96*, 223–229.

Ost, L. G. (1996). Long-term effects of behavior therapy for specific phobia. In M. Mavissakalian and R. F. Prien (Eds.), *Long-term treatments of anxiety disorders* (pp. 121–170).

Ost, L. G., & Hugdahl, K. (1983). Acquisition of phobias and anxiety response patterns in clinical patients. *Behaviour Research and Therapy, 21*, 623–631.

Otto, M. W., Pollack, M. H., Sachs, G. S., Reiter, S. R., Meltzer-Brody, S., & Rosenbaum, J. R. (1993). Discontinuation of benzodiazepine treatment: Efficacy of cognitive-behavioral therapy for patients with panic disorder. *American Journal of Psychiatry, 150*, 1485–1490.

Page, A. C. (1994). Distinguishing panic disorder and agoraphobia from social phobia. *Journal of Nervous and Mental Disease, 182*, 611–617.

Pato, M. T., Zohar-Kadouch, R., Zohar, J., & Murphy, D. L. (1988). Return of symptoms after discontinuation of clomipramine in patients with obsessive-compulsive disorder. *American Journal of Psychiatry, 145*, 1521–1525.

Pauls, D. L., Alsobrook, J. P., Goodman, W., Rasmussen, S., & Leckman, J. F. (1995). A family study of obsessive-compulsive disorder. *American Journal of Psychiatry, 152*, 76–84.

Peterson, R. A., & Heilbronner, R. L. (1987). The Anxiety Sensitivity Index: Construct validity and factor analytic structure. *Journal of Anxiety Disorders, 1*, 117–121.

Pitts, F. N., Jr., & McClure, J. N., Jr. (1967). Lactate metabolism in anxiety neuroses. *New England Journal of Medicine, 277*, 1328–1336.

Pollack, M. H., Otto, M. W., Rosenbaum, J. F., & Sachs, G. S. (1992). Personality disorders in patients with panic disorder: Association with childhood anxiety disorders, early trauma, comorbidity, and chronicity. *Comprehensive Psychiatry, 33*, 78–83.

Rachman, S. (1988). Panics and their consequences: A review and prospect. In S. Rachman & J. D. Maser (Eds.), Panic: Psychological perspectives (pp. 259–303). Hillsdale, NJ: Erlbaum.

Rachman, S. J. (1977). The conditioning theory of fear-acquisition. A critical examination. *Behaviour Research and Therapy, 15*, 375–387.

Rachman, S. (1990). *Fear and courage* (2nd ed.) New York: Freeman.

Rachman, S., & Hodgson, R. (1980). *Obsessions and compulsions.* Englewood Cliffs, NJ: Prentice-Hall.

Rapoport, J. L. (1991). Recent advances in obsessive-compulsive disorder. *Neuropsychpharmacology, 5,* 1–10.

Rasmussen, S. (1993). Genetic studies of obsessive-compulsive disorder. *Annals of Clinical Psychiatry, 5,* 241–248.

Rasmussen, S., & Eisen, J. L. (1992). The epidemiology and differential diagnosis of obsessive compulsive disorder. *Journal of Clinical Psychiatry, 53,* 4–10.

Rasmussen, S. A., & Tsuang, M. T. (1986). Clinical characteristics and family history in DSM-III obsessive-compulsive disorder. *American Journal of Psychiatry, 143,* 317–322.

Reich, J., Goldenberg, I., Goisman, R., Vasile, R., & Keller, M. (1994). A prospective, follow-along study of the course of social phobia: II. Testing for basic predictors of course. *Journal of Nervous and Mental Disease, 182,* 297–301.

Reich, J. H., & Noyes, R., Jr. (1987). A comparison of DSM-III personality disorders in acutely ill panic and depressed patients. *Journal of Anxiety Disorders, 1,* 123–131.

Reiss, S. (1991). Expectancy theory of fear, anxiety, and panic. *Clinical Psychology Review, 11,* 141–153.

Reiss, S., & McNally, R. J. (1985). The expectancy model of fear. In S. Reiss & R. R. Bootzin (Eds.), *Theoretical issues in behavior therapy* (pp. 107–121). New York: Academic Press.

Reiss, S., Peterson, R. A., Gursky, D. M., & McNally, R. J. (1986). Anxiety sensitivity, anxiety frequency, and the prediction of fearfulness. *Behaviour Research and Therapy, 24,* 1–8.

Rennenberg, B., Chambless, D. L., & Gracely, E. J. (1992). Prevalence of SCID-diagnosed personality disorders in agoraphobic outpatients. *Journal of Anxiety Disorders, 6,* 111–118.

Reznick, J. S., Kagan, J., Sniderman, N., Gersten, M., Boak, K., & Rosenberg, A. (1986). Inhibited and uninhibited children: A follow-up study. *Child Development, 57,* 660–680.

Rickels, K., Downing, R., Schweizer, E., & Hassman, H. (1993). Antidepressants for the treatment of generalized anxiety disorder: A placebo-controlled comparison of imipramine, trazodone, and diazepam. *Archives of General Psychiatry, 50,* 884–895.

Robins, L. N., Helzer, J. E., Weissman, M. M., Orvaschel, H., Greenberg, E., Burke, J. D., Jr., & Regier, D. A. (1984). Lifetime prevalence of specific psychiatric disorders at three sites. *Archives of General Psychiatry, 41,* 949–958.

Rosenbaum, J. R., Biederman, J., Gersten, M., Hirshfeld, D. R., Meminger, S. R., Herman, J. B., Kagan, J., Reznick, J. S., & Snidman, N. (1988). Behavioral inhibition in children of parents with panic disorder and agoraphobia. *Archives of General Psychiatry, 45,* 463–470.

Rosenbaum, J. F., Biederman, J., Bolduc, E. A., Faraone, S. V., Hirshfeld, D. R., & Kagan, J. (1992). Comorbidity of parental anxiety disorders at risk for childhood-onset anxiety in inhibited children. *American Journal of Psychiatry, 149,* 475–481.

Rosenbaum, J. F., Biederman, J., Hirshfeld, D. R., Bolduc, E. A., Kagan, J., Snidman, N., & Reznick, J. S. (1991). Further evidence of an association between behavioral inhibition and anxiety disorders: Results from a family study of children from a nonclinical sample. *Journal of Psychiatric Research, 25,* 49–65.

Schenier, F. R., Johnson, J., Hornig, C. D., Liebowitz, M. R., & Weissman, M. M. (1992). Social phobia: Comorbidity and morbidity in an epidemiological sample. *Archives of General Psychiatry, 49,* 282–288.

Sciuto, G., Diaferia, G., Battaglia, M., Perna, G., Gabriele, A., & Bellodi, L. (1991). DSM-III-R personality disorders in panic and obsessive-compulsive disorder: A comparison study. *Comprehensive Psychiatry, 32,* 450–457.

Seligman, M. (1971). Phobias and preparedness. *Behavior Therapy, 2,* 307–320.

Sellwood, W., & Tarrier, N. (1994). Demographic factors associated with extreme noncompliance in schizophrenia. *Social Psychiatry and Epidemiology, 29,* 172–177.

Shear, M. K., Devereux, R. B., Kranier-Fox, R., Mann, J. J., & Frances, A. (1984). Low prevalence of mitral valve prolapse in patients with panic disorder. *American Journal of Psychiatry, 141,* 302–303.

Sheehan, D. V., Sheehan, K. E., & Minichiello, W. E. (1981). Age of onset of phobic disorders. *Comprehensive Psychiatry, 22,* 544–553.

Stanley, M. A., & Turner, S. M. (1995). Current status of pharmacological and behavioral treatment of obsessive-compulsive disorder. *Behavior Therapy, 26,* 163–186.

Stanley, M. A., Turner, S. M., & Borden, J. W. (1990). Schizotypal features in obsessive-compulsive disorder. *Comprehensive Psychiatry, 31,* 511–518.

Stein, M. B., Walker, J. R., & Forde, D. R. (1994). Setting diagnostic thresholds for social phobia: Considerations from a community survey of social anxiety. *American Journal of Psychiatry, 151,* 408–412.

Steketee, G., & Shapiro, L. J. (1995). Predicting behavioral treatment outcome for agoraphobia and obsessive-compulsive disorder. *Clinical Psychology Review, 15,* 317–346.

Stemberger, R. T., Turner, S. M., Beidel, D. C., & Calhoun, K. (1995). Social phobia: An analysis of possible developmental factors. *Journal of Abnormal Psychology, 104,* 526–531.

Suomi, S. J. (1986). Anxiety in young nonhuman primates. In R. Gittelman (Ed.), *Anxiety disorders of childhood* (pp. 1–23). New York: Guilford.

Suomi, S. J., Kraemer, G. U., Baysinger, C. M., & Delizio, R. D. (1981). Inherited and experiential factors associated with individual differences in anxious behavior displayed by rhesus monkeys. In D. Klein & J. Rabkin (Eds.), *Anxiety: New research and changing concepts* (pp. 179–200). New York: Raven.

Sylvester, C. E., Hyde, T. S., & Reichler, R. J. (1988). Clinical psychopathology among children of adults with panic disorder. In D. L. Dunner, E. S. Gershon, & J. E. Barrett (Eds.), *Relatives at risk for mental disorder* (pp. 87–98). New York: Raven.

Tancer, M. E. (1993). Neurobiology of social phobia. *Journal of Clinical Psychiatry, 54,* 26–30.

Taylor, S. (1996). Meta-analysis of cognitive-behavioral treatments for social phobia. *Journal of Behavior Therapy and Experimental Psychiatry, 27,* 1–9.

Thorpe, G. L., & Burns, L. E. (1983). *The agoraphobic syndrome.* New York: Wiley.

Thyer, B. A., Parrish, R. T., Curtis, G. E., Nesse, R. M., & Cameron, O. G. (1985). Age of onset of DSM-III anxiety disorders. *Comprehensive Psychiatry, 26,* 113–121.

Torgersen, S. (1983). Genetic factors in anxiety disorders. *Archives of General Psychiatry, 40,* 1085–1089.

True, W. R., Rice, J., Eisen, S. A., Heath, A. C., Goldberg, J., Lyons, M. J., & Nowak, J. (1993). A twin study of genetic and environmental contributions to liability for posttraumatic stress symptoms. *Archives of General Psychiatry, 50,* 257–264.

Turner, S. M., & Beidel, D. C. (1988). *Treating obsessive-compulsive disorder.* New York: Pergamon.

Turner, S. M., & Beidel, D. C. (1989a). Social phobia: Clinical syndrome, diagnosis, and comorbidity. *Clinical Psychology Review, 9,* 3–18.

Turner, S. M., & Beidel, D. C. (1989b). *On the nature of obsessional thoughts and worry: Similarities and dissimilarities.* Paper prepared for the DSM-IV Task Force.

Turner, S. M., & Beidel, D. C. (1996). Children at risk for anxiety disorders: Psychophysiological correlates. Manuscript in preparation.

Turner, S. M., Beidel, D. C., Borden, J. W., Stanley, M. A., & Jacob, R. G. (1991). Social phobia: Axis I and II correlates. *Journal of Abnormal Psychology, 100,* 102–106.

Turner, S. M., Beidel, D. C., & Cooley, M. R. (1994). *Social Effectiveness Therapy: A Program for Overcoming Social Anxiety and Phobia.* Mount Pleasant, SC: Turndel.

Turner, S. M., Beidel, D. C., & Costello, A. (1987). Psychopathology in the offspring of anxiety disorders patients. *Journal of Consulting and Clinical Psychology, 55,* 229–235.

Turner, S. M., Beidel, D. C., Dancu, C. V., & Keys, D. J. (1986). Psychopathology of social phobia and comparison to avoidant personality disorder. *Journal of Abnormal Psychology, 95,* 389–394.

Turner, S. M., Beidel, D. C., & Epstein, L. H. (1991). Vulnerability and risk for anxiety disorders. *Journal of Anxiety Disorders, 5,* 151–166.

Turner, S. M., Beidel, D. C., & Jacob, R. G. (1988). Assessment of panic. In S. Rachman & J. D. Maser (Eds.), *Panic: Psychological perspectives* (pp. 37–50). Hillsdale, NJ: Erlbaum.

Turner, S. M., Beidel, D. C., & Jacob, R. G. (1994). Behavioral and pharmacological treatment of social phobia. *Journal of Consulting and Clinical Psychology, 62,* 350–358.

Turner, S. M., Beidel, D. C., & Stanley, M. A. (1992). Are obsessional thoughts and worry different cognitive phenomena? *Clinical Psychology Review, 12,* 257–270.

Turner, S. M., Beidel, D. C., & Townsley, R. M. (1992). Social phobia: A comparison of specific and generalized subtypes and avoidant personality disorder. *Journal of Abnormal Psychology, 101,* 326–331.

Turner, S. M., Beidel, D. C., & Wolff, P. (1996). Behavioral inhibition: Relationship to anxiety disorders. *Clinical Psychology Review, 16,* 157–172.

Turner, S. M., Beidel, D. C., Wolff, P., & Spaulding, S. (1996). Clinical features affecting treatment outcome in social phobia. *Behaviour Research and Therapy, 34,* 795–804.

Turner, S. M., & Cooley-Quille, M. R. (1996). Socioecological and sociocultural variables in psychopharmacological research: Methodological considerations. *Psychopharmacology Bulletin, 32,* 183–192.

Turner, S. M., Cooley-Quille, M. R., & Beidel, D. C. (1996). Behavioral and pharmacological treatment of social phobia: Long-term outcome. In M. Mavissakalian & R. Prien (Eds.), *Anxiety disorders: Psychological and pharmacological treatments* (pp. 291–300). Washington, DC: American Psychiatric Press.

Uhde, T. W., Boulenger, J. P., Roy-Byrne, P. P., Geraci, M. F., Vittone, B. J., & Post, R. M. (1985). Longitudinal course of panic disorder: Clinical and biological considerations. *Progress in Neuro-Psychopharmacology and Biological Psychiatry, 9,* 39–51.

Van Amerigan, M., Mancini, C., & Streiner, D. (1993). Fluoxetine efficacy in social phobia. *Journal of Clinical Psychiatry, 54,* 27–32.

van der Kolk, B. A., Dreyfuss, D., Michaels, M. Shera, D., Berkowitz, R., Fisler, R., & Saxe, G. (1994). Fluoxetine in posttraumatic stress disorder. *Journal of Clinical Psychiatry, 55,* 517–523.

Van Valkenberg, C., Akiskal, H. G., Puzantian, V., & Rosenthal, T. (1984). Anxious depressions: Clinical, family history, and naturalistic outcome-comparisons with panic and major depressive disorders. *Journal of Affective Disorders, 6,* 67–82.

Walker, V. J., & Beech, H. R. (1969). Mood states and the ritualistic behavior of obsessional patients. *British Journal of Psychiatry, 150,* 1261–1268.

Warner, V. Mufson, L., & Weissman, M. M. (1995). Offspring at high and low risk for depression and anxiety: Mechanisms of psychiatric disorder. *Journal of the American Academy of Child and Adolescent Psychiatry, 34,* 786–797.

Watson, J. B., & Rayner, R. (1920). Conditional emotional reactions. *Journal of Experimental Psychology, 3,* 1–14.

Weissman, M. M. (1990). Panic and generalized anxiety: Are they separate disorders? *Journal of Psychiatric Research, 24,* 157–162.

Weissman, M. M. (1993). Family genetic studies of panic disorder. *Journal of Psychiatric Research, 27,* 69–78.

Weissman, M. M., Bland, R. G., Canino, G. J., Greenwald, S., Hwu, H. G., Lee, C. K., Rubio-Stipec, M., Wickramaratne, P. J., Wittchen, H. U., & Yeh, E. K. (1994). The cross-national epidemiology of obsessive-compulsive disorder. *Journal of Clinical Psychiatry, 55,* 5–10.

Weissman, M. M., Leckman, J. F., Merikangas, K. R., Gammon, G. D., & Prusoff, B. A. (1984). Depression and anxiety disorders in parents and children. *Archives of General Psychiatry, 41,* 845–852.

Weizman, A., Carmi, M., & Hermesh, H. (1986). High affinity imipramine binding and serotonin uptake in platelets of eight adolescent and ten adult obsessive-compulsive patients. *American Journal of Psychiatry, 143,* 335–339.

Wlazlo, A., Schroeder-Hartwig, K., Hand, I., Kaiser, G., & Munchau, N. (1990). Exposure in vivo versus social skills training for social phobia: Long-term outcome and differential effects. *Behaviour Research and Therapy, 28,* 181–193.

Yamamoto, J., Fung, D., Lo, S., & Reece, S. (1979). Psychopharmacology for Asian Americans and Pacific Islanders. *Psychopharmacology Bulletin, 15,* 29–31.

Ziegler, V. E., & Biggs, J. T. (1977). Tricyclic plasma levels-effects of age, race, sex, and smoking. *Journal of the American Medical Association, 238,* 2167–2169.

CHAPTER 11

Somatoform Disorders

LAURENCE J. KIRMAYER and SUZANNE TAILLEFER

The somatoform disorders are a group of conditions in which people suffer from somatic symptoms or worry about bodily illness or deformity that cannot be accounted for by an organic medical condition or another psychiatric disorder such as depression or anxiety. Although "psychosomatic diseases" are no longer recognized as distinct disorders because psychological and behavioral factors may affect any medical condition, the somatoform disorders retain the implication of being wholly or predominantly caused by psychological processes. As we shall see, in some cases this presumption may be unwarranted.

The DSM-IV (*Diagnostic and Statistical Manual of Mental Disorders;* American Psychiatric Association [APA], 1994) category of somatoform disorders emerged out of earlier notions of hysteria (Hyler & Spitzer, 1978) and includes seven related disorders: somatization disorder (formerly Briquet's syndrome or hysteria), conversion disorder, pain disorder (formerly psychogenic or somatoform pain disorder), hypochondriasis, body dysmorphic disorder, and two residual categories for patients who do not meet full criteria for any of the previously mentioned disorders, undifferentiated somatoform disorder and somatoform disorder not otherwise specified.

Despite many conceptual problems, the somatoform disorders survive as a useful set of diagnoses in the DSM-IV largely because of their relevance to Western health care systems where patients with medically unexplained somatic symptoms or bodily distress in excess of what can be explained by organic pathophysiology present a common clinical problem. The diagnosis of a somatoform disorder serves to label and situate patients who would otherwise fall through the cracks of a diagnostic system increasingly oriented around laboratory tests and biological treatments for specific pathophysiology.

The somatoform disorders are diagnoses that reproduce two fundamental dualisms that are deeply embedded in Western medicine, health psychology, and indeed, in the everyday concept of the person (Kirmayer, 1988). The first is that mind and body are distinct realms, so that there is something noteworthy or even exceptional about people who express in somatic terms problems that a professional would situate in the psychological or social realm. The second is that what is physical is somehow more real, substantial, and ultimately, more legitimate as illness than what is psychological. Somatoform disorders emerge from this dualistic conception, contribute to it, and, in consequence, are part and parcel of social processes that challenge the legitimacy and reality of people's suffering. The obverse of somatization might be considered to be psychologization: the tendency to attribute to psychological factors symptoms that others see as fundamentally somatic in nature. Many mental health practitioners tend to be psychologizers, confidently attributing somatic distress to psychological conflicts, personality traits, or social stressors even when physiological explanations are available.

Keeping in mind this cultural construction of the category, in this chapter we will review what is known about the somatoform disorders. We will argue that, just as the notion of "psychophysiological disorder" has been replaced by that of "psychological factors affecting medical condition"—a shift from a categorical, disorder-based scheme to one of diagnosing specific situations—so too should the somatoform disorders be reconceptualized as symptoms or patterns of illness behavior that interact with other medical and psychiatric conditions. As illness behavior, somatoform disorders can be best typified and understood in terms of dimensions rather than categories, processes rather than symptoms and signs, and social contexts rather than isolated behaviors. We think this social approach to somatization not only fits the research data better than the individual psychopathology oriented perspective, it also has very useful implications for clinical assessment and treatment. Rethinking the category of somatoform disorders from a social and cultural perspective will allow us to avoid some of the negative attitudes and stigmatization that plague patients who receive these diagnoses.

DESCRIPTION OF THE DISORDERS

The DSM-IV somatoform disorders share two features: 1. they involve predominately somatic symptoms or bodily preoccupation and 2. they are based on the idea that the focus on the body cannot be fully explained by any known medical disease or substance use. In addition to these features, the diagnostic criteria generally stipulate that symptoms are not due to faking or malingering or another psychiatric disorder. A fourth criterion, that symptoms are associated with psychological factors, is not always made explicit. To warrant diagnosis, these symptoms must result in significant distress, medical help-seeking, impairment of functioning in work or other social roles, or all of the above.

Somatization disorder (SD) is characterized by a pattern of multiple somatic symptoms recurring over a period of several years. Criterion A stipulates that symptoms must begin before age 30 and result in medical help-seeking or lead to significant social or occupational impairment. Based on clinical reports and a field trial, DSM-IV has simplified the criteria B found in DSM-III-R to require four different types of symptoms: 1. a history of pain related to at least four different anatomical sites or functions; 2. a history of at least two gastrointestinal symptoms other than pain (e.g., nausea, bloating, vomiting other than during pregnancy, diarrhea, or multiple food intolerance); 3. at least one sexual or reproductive symptom other than pain; 4. at least one pseudoneurological (conversion) symptom not related to pain (APA, 1994). A third criterion (C) requires that either there be no medical condition that can fully explain the symptoms or that the distress and disability are in excess of what can be medically explained. The simplified DSM-IV criteria show high concordance with the DSM-III (APA, 1980) and III-R (APA, 1987) diagnostic criteria based on longer explicit symptom lists (Yutsy et al., 1995).

Undifferentiated somatoform disorder is a broad category that includes patients who do not reach criteria for SD because their symptoms are fewer in number or less severe. Undifferentiated SD simply requires one or more medically unexplained physical complaints lasting at least 6 months and resulting in "clinically significant" distress or impairment of functioning. This category includes neurasthenia or chronic fatigue syndrome, as well as other functional somatic symptoms and syndromes without widely accepted medical explanations.

Conversion disorder involves one or more symptoms that affect the voluntary motor or sensory systems and that mimic a neurological or other medical condition. The diagnostic criteria stipulate that psychological factors (i.e., conflicts or "other stressors") are judged to be associated with the symptom because they antecede its onset or exacerbation. Conversion disorder may be subtyped as *with motor symptom or deficit* (e.g., paralyses, ataxia, aphonia, difficulty swallowing, or "globus hystericus" [lump in throat], *with sensory symptom or deficit* (e.g., paresthesias, diplopia, blindness, deafness, or hallucinations), *with seizures or convulsions* (pseudoepilepsy), or *with mixed presentation.*

Pain disorder involves any clinically significant pain that causes distress or impaired functioning for which "psychological factors are judged to have an important role in the onset, severity, exacerbation or maintenance of the pain." Pain due to mood, anxiety, or psychotic disorders and dyspareunia (painful intercourse in women) are specifically excluded from the category. Pain disorder is subtyped as associated exclusively with psychological factors or with both psychological factors and a medical condition. In each case it may be acute or chronic. If no psychological factors are associated with the pain, it is not given a somatoform diagnosis.

Hypochondriasis is characterized by at least 6 months of preoccupation with fears of having, or the idea that one has, a serious disease "based on the person's misinterpretation of bodily symptoms." This preoccupation, fear, or idea must persist despite "appropriate medical evaluation and reassurance." Hypochondriasis is distinguished from delusional disorder and other somatoform and anxiety disorders. If the person generally does not recognize the excessive or unreasonable nature of their illness worry but the disease conviction does not reach delusional intensity, the diagnosis may be qualified as "with poor insight."

Body dysmorphic disorder involves a "preoccupation with an imagined defect in appearance" or, if a mild physical anomaly is present, a preoccupation markedly in excess of what is reasonable or appropriate. Dissatisfaction with overall body shape and anorexia nervosa are explicitly excluded.

Somatoform disorder not otherwise specified is a residual category for people with clusters of symptoms that do not meet full criteria for any specific somatoform disorder. The illustrative examples given in DSM-IV are 1. pseudocyesis ("hysterical pregnancy"), 2. nonpsychotic hypochondriacal symptoms of less than 6 months duration (i.e., acute or transient hypochondriacal worry), and 3. unexplained physical symptoms of less than 6 months duration.

The *International Classification of Diseases* (ICD-10: World Health Organization [WHO], 1992) uses a very similar nosology but adds the category of *somatoform autonomic dysfunction,* which involves "psychogenic" bodily symptoms in organs regulated by the autonomic nervous system. These autonomic syndromes are subdivided by system into heart and cardiovascular (e.g., cardiac neurosis), upper gastrointestinal tract (functional dyspepsia and aerophagia), lower gastrointestinal tract (irritable bowel syndrome), respiratory system (psychogenic hyperventilation, hiccup, and cough), genitourinary system (frequent micturation and dysuria), and other organ or system. ICD-10 also includes neurasthenia (chronic mental or physical fatigue) as a distinct diagnosis under the rubric of "other neurotic disorders"; many isolated functional somatic symptoms and culture-related somatic syndromes would also be classified under this rubric. To a greater degree than DSM-IV, the ICD criteria conflate symptoms and somatic preoccupation, thus making hypochondriacal anxiety more closely related to functional symptoms.

The status of the common functional somatic syndromes remains ambiguous in DSM-IV because of continuing controversy over the validity of medical diagnoses. Thus, irritable bowel syndrome (abdominal pain relieved by defecation or alteration of bowel habits, usually accompanied by sensations of abdominal bloating or distension) is presumed to reflect disturbed gut motility; to date, however, it has not been possible to reliably demonstrate the motility disturbance. Over the last 20 years, fibromyalgia syndrome (diffuse muscular aches and pains with extreme tenderness on palpation at specific bony prominences or anatomical "tender points") has gone from being a "wastebasket" diagnosis viewed with skepticism by many clinicians to wide acceptance as a discrete rheumatological disorder; yet, no definite organic pathology has been identified. At present, chronic fatigue syndrome (greater than 6 months of debilitating fatigue with many associated somatic and psychological symptoms of malaise) continues to be a hotly contested diagnosis for which no organic markers or definite etiology has been found. For these and most other functional somatic syndromes, diagnosis remains a process of excluding other organic medical explanations. Since this process of exclusion is never complete, uncertainty about diagnosis remains. Indeed, uncertainty about diagnosis, and the self-doubt and social ambiguity that ensue, are central to patients' experience of somatoform disorders.

EPIDEMIOLOGY

Somatoform disorder is the single most frequent class of problem in primary care medicine. Medically unexplained symptoms—especially pain, fatigue, and generalized malaise—constitute from 25% to 60% of family medicine practice (Kirkwood et al., 1982). Every medical specialty has its own collection of "idiopathic" (unexplained) or functional somatic syndromes that reflect the limitations of current medical knowledge more than any identified psychopathology (see Table 11.1). These syndromes occupy a large portion of clinicians' time and effort and account for substantial health care costs. Still, patients who present to the clinic with somatoform disorders represent a fraction of those in the general population with functional somatic syndromes. Many people cope with

TABLE 11.1   Symptoms and Syndromes of Uncertain Etiology in Medical Specialties

Specialty and Symptom	Reference
Ear, Nose, and Throat	
Burning tongue or mouth	Van Houdenhove & Joostens, 1995
Intractable sneezing	Fochtmann, 1995
Stridor	Lacy & McManis, 1994
Tinnitus	Sullivan et al., 1988
Cardiology	
Chest pain with normal angiogram	Eifert, 1991
Endocrinology	
Pseudocyesis	Starkman et al., 1985
Gastroenterology	
Dysphagia (difficulty swallowing)	Kim et al., 1996
Irritable bowel	Thompson & Pigeon-Reesor, 1990
Nonulcer dyspepsia	Wilhelmsen, Haug, Ursin, & Berstad, 1995
Gynecology	
Chronic pelvic pain	Walker et al., 1988
Dysmenorrhea	Whitehead et al., 1986
Dyspareunia	Meana & Binik, 1994
Hyperemesis gravidarum	Katon, Ries, Bokan, & Kleinman, 1980
Premenstrual tension	Kuczmierczyk, Labrum, & Johnson, 1995
Vaginismus	Meana & Binik, 1994
Vulvidynia	McKay & Farrington, 1995
Infectious Disease and Immunology	
Chronic fatigue	Abbey & Garfinkel, 1991
Environmental sensitivity	Göthe, Molin & Nilsson, 1995
Multiple or "total" allergy	Simon, Katon & Sparks, 1990
Neurology	
Conversion	Toone, 1990
Pseudoseizures	Savard, 1990
Paralysis	Fishbain & Goldberg, 1991
Paresthesias	
Sensory loss	Rada, Meyer & Kellner, 1978
Dizziness	O'Connor, Hallam, Beyts, & Hinclife, 1988
Headache	Blanchard, 1992
Post-concussion syndrome	Lishman, 1988
Syncope	Kapoor, Fortunato, Hanusa, & Schulberg, 1995
Pulmonology	
Dyspnea (shortness of breath)	Bass, 1992
Rheumatology	
Fibromyalgia	Bennett, 1981
Myofascial pain syndromes	Merskey, 1993
Repetitive strain injury	Sinclair, 1988
Urology	
Interstitial cystitis	Ratliff, Klutke, & McDougall, 1994

these problems without medical help. Patients who do come to the clinic often are prompted by coexisting problems like depression, anxiety, or life stresses. Studies then find much higher rates of psychiatric comorbidity among patients with somatoform disorders in clinical settings compared to community samples. This comorbidity may partially reflect the cumulative effect of multiple problems on help seeking rather than an intrinsic connection between the mood and anxiety disorders and common functional symptoms. This tendency for clinical studies to overestimate the strength of the association in the general population (a form of "Berkson's bias" in epidemiology) points to the need for community studies to establish the causes of somatoform disorders. Unfortunately, community epidemiological studies are hampered by the necessity for medical evaluation to rule out organic explanations before the diagnosis of somatoform disorders can be made with confidence.

The Epidemiologic Catchment Area (ECA) studies in the United States assessed the prevalence of somatization disorder (SD) in the general population using the Diagnostic Interview Schedule, a structured interview administered by trained lay interviewers (Robins & Regier, 1991). The somatization disorder section of the DIS lists 38 somatic symptoms and includes a set of probes to assess severity as well as inclusion and exclusion criteria for scoring each symptom as meeting criteria. The DIS probes ask patients if they have seen a doctor for each symptom and if they were given a medical explanation or diagnosis. In the ECA studies, the somatization disorder section of the DIS was edited by physicians to improve the recognition of medically unexplained symptoms.

The prevalence of SD varied across the five ECA sites from 0% (Los Angeles) to 0.44% (Durham, NC) with a mean of 0.13% (Swartz, Landerman, George, Blazer, & Escobar, 1991). SD was approximately 10 times more common among women than men. Prevalence rates also varied across ethnic groups from 0.08% of Hispanics, 0.1% of non-Hispanic whites and 0.45% of blacks.

In the ECA study, every respondent with SD also met criteria for at least one other psychiatric disorder. The most common coexisting disorders were phobias (69%), major depression (55%), panic disorder (38%), alcohol abuse (23%), schizophrenia (21%), and dysthymia (19%). Only 5% of respondents with SD met criteria for antisocial personality disorder, contrary to previous research and theory linking the two disorders (Lilienfeld, 1992). In the ECA study, people with both somatization disorder and major depression usually met criteria for SD before the onset of depression. Panic disorder was more closely associated with the onset of SD, which suggests that it plays a stronger role in the evolution of SD. The diagnoses most closely associated with SD, as indicated by their relative risk ratios, were panic disorder, schizophrenia, mania, obsessive-compulsive disorder, and major depression. In general, respondents were equally divided among those with onset of SD before a coexisting psychiatric disorder and those with SD following the disorder. Thus, SD cannot be understood as simply due to an underlying affective or anxiety disorder.

While no study has explicitly addressed the epidemiology of undifferentiated somatoform disorder, there have been surveys of a wide range of related functional somatic symptoms and conditions (Mayou, Bass, & Sharpe, 1995). The DIS provides a count of medically unexplained somatic symptoms and this allowed Escobar, Rubio-Stipec, Canino, and Karno (1989) to construct a measure of an abridged somatization syndrome (SS), which required a lifetime occurrence of four medically unexplained symptoms for men and six for women. Somatization syndrome approximates the combined prevalence of undifferentiated somatoform disorder and somatoform disorder NOS. In two large community samples from Los Angeles and Puerto Rico, the lifetime rates of SS identified by these criteria were 11.6% (ranging from 4.4% to 20%); 4% of the sample met criteria for "active" SS based on symptoms within the past year.

SD, SS, and the somatic symptom count were not significantly associated with age in the ECA study but were associated with female gender and lower levels of education. Divorced, separated, and widowed individuals had higher rates of current SS and symptom counts. SD and SS are associated with high levels of utilization of both medical and mental health services. Both are associated with work and social disability and with lower income, lower occupational status, or unemployment.

Most studies of the prevalence of conversion disorder have relied on clinical samples, particularly patients referred to psychiatry (Folks, Ford, & Regan, 1984). Although the dramatic nature of many conversion symptoms ensures they come to medical attention, referral samples may, nonetheless, underestimate both community and primary care prevalence. A history of conversion symptoms has been found in anywhere from 5% to 24% of psychiatric outpatients (Guze, Woodruff, & Clayton, 1971; Stefansson, Messina, & Meyerowitz, 1976) and from less than 1% to 3% of patients seen in medical or neurological clinics and hospitals (Toone, 1990). Studies of hospital referrals from a fixed catchment area have yielded estimates of community prevalence of 0.3% or less (Stefansson et al., 1976). The rates are much higher in some other parts of the world; for example, 8%–10% of all outpatient referrals to psychiatry in Libya and Sudan (Hafeiz, 1980; Pu, Mohamed, Iman, & El-Roey, 1986). In general, conversion symptoms have been thought to be more common in rural regions, and in those of lower socioeconomic class and with less formal education (Folks et al., 1984; Lazare, 1981); however, recent data find higher rates in some urban populations (Swartz, Landerman, Blazer, & George, 1989). Several authors have described a decline in the prevalence of conversion disorder in Britain and the United States over the last half century (Leff, 1988). However, because most studies are based on referral populations, it remains unclear as to what extent this apparent decrease simply represents changes in symptoms and patterns of help-seeking.

The prevalence of hypochondriasis in the general population is unknown, but it affects 4%–8% of patients in primary care (Barsky, Wyshak, Klerman, & Latham, 1990; Kirmayer & Robbins, 1991b). Primary care patients with hypochondriasis have high rates of other Axis I disorders. In one study of 63 patients, 43% had a lifetime history of major depression, 45% dysthymia, and 17% panic disorder (Barsky, Wyshak, & Klerman, 1992).

Pain disorder is common in the United States; from 15% to 33% of the population between the ages of 25–74 suffers from some form of chronic musculoskeletal pain (Magni, Caldieron, Rigatti-Luchini, & Merskey, 1990; Magni, Marchetti, Moreschi, Merskey, & Rigatti Luchini, 1993). In one large survey, more than 80% of respondents had sought medical help for their chronic pain. Up to 10%–15% of adults in the United States have some degree of work disability from back pain alone (Von Korff, Dworkin, LeResche, & Kruger, 1990).

The community prevalence of body dysmorphic disorder (BDD) is unknown. A survey among college students found high rates of dissatisfaction and preoccupation with appearance and up to 28% with sufficient symptoms to meet diagnostic criteria (Fitts, Gibson, Redding, & Deister, 1989); however, anorexia nervosa was not ruled out so that this is likely an overestimate. In a clinical sample of patients with anxiety disorders and major depression, BDD was most prevalent among patients with social phobia (11%) and obsessive-compulsive disorder (Brawman-Mintzer et al., 1995). In a clinical sample of patients with obsessive-compulsive disorder, 12% met DSM-IV criteria for BDD (Simeon, Hollander, Stein, Cohen, & Aronowitz, 1995). The majority of patients with milder forms of BDD are seen by plastic surgeons, dermatologists, or other medical specialists, and may never come to psychiatric attention.

No global prevalence can be given for somatoform disorder NOS because it is an ill-defined residual category. Pseudocyesis is a rare condition; sporadic functional symptoms, on the contrary, are exceedingly common. About 4% of primary care patients have a transient form of hypochondriasis that will resolve spontaneously or with a doctor's reassurance (Barsky, Cleary, Sarnie, & Klerman, 1993; Robbins & Kirmayer, 1996).

CLINICAL PICTURE

The clinical picture of the somatoform disorders varies with the social and cultural background of patients, their specific somatic symptoms, and the clinical context in which patients are seen. Most patients with somatoform disorders seek medical care and are referred to mental health practitioners when medical diagnosis and treatment prove ineffective. As a result of this failure of conventional treatment, patients may seek many alternative forms of care. By the time the mental health practitioner sees these patients they may be frustrated and angry about the care they have received. Patients are often made to feel "it's all in your head." Clinicians, in turn, feel frustrated that ordinary reassurances or symptomatic treatments have been ineffective. The mutual disappointment and blaming of patient and physician sometimes erupts into hostility. In this context, it is easy for the consultant to misattribute anxious, hostile, or paranoid thoughts and behavior in the patient to personality traits when such behavior is, at least in part, a response to circumstances.

Somatization Disorder

Although the age of onset of somatization disorder is required to be before age 30 by definition, in the ECA study 55% of cases reported an onset before age 15 (Swartz, 1991, p. 231). This points to a development of SD in early adolescence or childhood. The most common symptoms in SD include: chest pain, palpitations, abdominal bloating, depressed feelings, dizziness, weakness, quitting work because of poor health, shortness of breath without exertion, headache, and fatigue (Smith, Monson, & Ray, 1986b). This list, however, does not capture the richness of patients' language of suffering.

> *Case 1.* A 31-year old man was referred to a behavioral medicine clinic by an internist for treatment of abdominal pain. He arrived with a carefully written list of his current symptoms ranked by the degree of distress they caused him (from most to least): "constant ringing in the ears; dizziness and lightheadedness; headaches with numbness in the face, squeezing at the temples with bands of pressure and fuzzy head; pain in the lower right abdomen; jerking sensations in the throat, chest, and stomach; rapid, steady throbbing throughout the entire body; pains in the middle back, left shoulder, and arm; numbness in the left forearm and hand (right forearm and hand less often); spots before eyes—occasionally; hard-to-breathe feeling; rapid irregular heartbeat and pounding slow heartbeat both usually accompanied by nausea and lasting several hours." He denied any personal or emotional problems and said that all was well with his work and homelife save that his wife and daughter were upset that his many illnesses prevented them from ever having a family vacation. Treatment focused on developing coping strategies for the four most distressing symptoms with the goal of being able to take a family vacation. He was able to accomplish this after six sessions of cognitive behavioral therapy with hypnosis for relaxation. Three months later, he went to another emergency room where his recurrent abdominal pain was diagnosed as irritable bowel syndrome. He felt relieved to have a diagnosis and embarked on a program to control his symptoms through dietary changes. (Kirmayer, 1986)

In addition to their somatic complaints, patients with SD commonly suffer from the gamut of psychological symptoms and often meet criteria for mood and anxiety disorders (Wetzel, Guze, Cloninger, & Martin, 1994). It is misleading, therefore, to view SD patients as having predominately somatic problems. Over 70% of patients with SD also meet criteria for personality disorder (Stern, Murphy & Bass, 1993). Although SD was classically related to histrionic personality (Slavney, 1990), the most commonly associated personality disorders are avoidant, paranoid, self-defeating, and obsessive-compulsive (Smith, Golding, Kashner, & Rost, 1991).

Undifferentiated Somatoform Disorder

The number and diversity of somatic symptoms may identify subgroups of patients with undifferentiated somatoform disorder: 1. a "diversiform" group that reports many different symptoms in different systems, particularly pain complaints that approximate somatization disorder, and 2. an "asthenic" group that reports fewer and less diverse symptoms, mainly fatigue, weakness, and minor illnesses such as upper respiratory tract infections, and resembles neurasthenia or chronic fatigue syndrome (Bohman, Cloninger, von Knorring, & Sigvardsson, 1984; Cloninger, Sigvardsson, von Knorring & Bohman, 1984; Sigvardsson, Bohman, von Knorring, & Cloninger, 1986). In general, patients with isolated functional symptoms or functional somatic syndromes resemble patients with other medical disorders in having elevated rates of depression, anxiety, and other psychological problems which may be both contributors to and consequences of their somatic illness (Kirmayer & Robbins, 1991a).

Conversion Disorder

Conversion disorder occurs across the lifespan and tends to affect women more frequently than men. By definition, patients with conversion disorder have symptoms resembling a neurological disorder. The most common symptoms include: gait disturbances, pseudoseizures, episodes of fainting (syncope) or loss of consciousness; muscle tremors, spasms, weakness, or paralysis; sensory changes, including paresthesias or anesthesia, speech disturbances (aphonia), and visual disturbances, such as blindness and diplopia (Folks et al., 1984; Tomasson, Dent & Coryell, 1991; Toone, 1990; Watson & Buranen, 1979a). Among the symptoms classically described as hysterical conversion, the main exception to these pseudoneurological symptoms is pseudocyesis ("hysterical pregnancy") which, in DSM-IV, is classified as somatoform disorder NOS (Martin, 1996). Pseudocyesis may be associated with endocrine disturbances, which sets it apart from other conversion symptoms (Small, 1986; Starkman, Marshall, La Ferla, & Kelch, 1985).

> *Case 2.* A 52-year woman old presented to the general hospital emergency room with the sudden onset of paralysis of her left arm and the inability to straighten her torso, walking and sitting bent over at the waist (a symptom termed *camptocormia*). She described the symptoms as having started abruptly while she was working at her typewriter in the office where she was employed as a secretary. She feared she had suffered a stroke. Initially, she could give no precipitating stressful event. On later questioning by her regular family physician, she revealed that she had discovered that morning that her employer had promoted a coworker with less seniority, with whom he was having an affair, to a more senior position. She initially felt shocked, angry, and betrayed, but these feelings were forgotten when her alarming paralysis suddenly developed. She accepted an explanation from this trusted physician of the symptoms as a stress reaction and connected the intensity of the reaction to her childhood experience of witnessing of the sexual abuse of a sibling. The symptoms gradually resolved over the next 2 weeks with two sessions of counselling in her doctor's office to validate her feelings, identify other stressors, and plan an appropriate response to her predicament at work.

Although patients with conversion symptoms were classically described as blandly indifferent to their symptoms (termed *"la belle indifférence"*), clinical experience suggests they are more often concerned and distressed. This distress, however, may be muted because there are other even more distressing recent events from which the conversion symptoms serve as a distraction. The form of conversion symptoms may have symbolic meaning in some situations but usually is more readily attributed to available models of illness (Slavney, 1994). For example, patients with epilepsy may develop pseudoseizures. About 70% of unilateral conversion symptoms affect the left side of the body, which may reflect neuropsychological, symbolic, or pragmatic factors (Axelrod, Noonan, & Atanacio, 1980).

Hypochondriasis

Patients with hypochondriasis show varying degrees of concern, worry, fear, and preoccupation with the notion that they have an illness. They remain concerned or convinced that something is wrong despite medical reassurance. At times this conviction may reach near delusional intensity and the boundary with delusional disorder remains somewhat arbitrary. More typically, patients have anxieties that they view as irrational but find they cannot rid themselves of bodily preoccupation and catastrophizing thoughts.

> *Case 3.* A 24-year old man presented to the mental health clinic with depression and the persistent fear that he had cancer or another mortal illness. Since the age of 12, when he learned of the sudden death of a cousin, he had suffered from frequent worries about his health. His parents had responded to his fears by taking him on frequent visits to a pediatrician where his hyperventilation was misdiagnosed at first as asthma. He viewed himself as vulnerable to illness and was preoccupied with symptoms of weakness, malaise, and a chronically stuffy nose for which he had become dependent on decongestant spray. He described sporadic panic attacks, usually triggered by events that should have made him angry. During these attacks he feared that he would lose his mind or die of a heart attack. Afterward, he was left feeling still more worried that he had a physical illness. Over many sessions of cognitive-behavioral therapy, it became apparent that he misidentified the bodily concomitants of strong emotions like anger, fear, or even intense happiness as possible symptoms of illness. Learning to reattribute these somatic symptoms to specific emotions and to the effects of physiological arousal resolved his hypochondriacal worries but did not entirely eliminate his panic attacks.

Hypochondriacal fears commonly accompany depression and anxiety disorders but may have a life of their own, enduring even when mood and other anxiety symptoms are not present (Noyes et al., 1994). Hypochondriacal preoccupation often has an obsessional quality and may occur with other symptoms of obsessive-compulsive disorder (Starcevic, 1990). A sense of bodily vulnerability may be associated with more pervasive feelings of fragility of the self or with fears of loss of control.

Body Dysmorphic Disorder

Patients with body dysmorphic disorder are preoccupied with the notion that some aspect of their body is misshapen and ugly. This bodily defect is imagined or grossly exaggerated. The most common complaints involve the face (e.g., wrinkles, complexion, facial hair, asymmetric or disproportionate features), hair, nose, and skin, but any body part can be the focus of preoccupation (Phillips, 1991). Patients engage in frequent checking in the mirror to monitor their "defect" and may attempt to camouflage it, usually without success. They are convinced that others are reacting negatively to them and commonly have ideas or delusions of reference. They fear embarrassment and avoid social situations, sometimes to the point of being housebound. As a result, the condition may result in severe social disability.

> *Case 4.* A 34-year old married mother of four was referred to the mental health clinic by a concerned friend. She complained of a 5-year history of increasing social isolation caused by an intense fear of offending others with her physical appearance. She believed that her nose had been gradually growing and her eyes shrinking in size, leading to such profound ugliness that no one could stand to

look at her. She had isolated herself from neighbors and family. She shopped only in stores in a part of town where she would not encounter people who knew her. She parked her car outside her children's school but would not go inside to pick them up. She never left her home unless she had a specific errand to run.

She dated the onset of her "physical change" to the birth of her youngest child, at which time the family moved to a new city so that she could care for her elderly parents. Over the 3 months prior to consulting the clinic, she had become increasingly distressed and hopeless about her appearance. When others reassured her that her appearance was, in fact, attractive, she thanked them for their kindness but was left completely unconvinced. She asked for therapy to be conducted by telephone so that the therapist would not be offended by her appearance and so that she would not have to travel in public to get to appointments.

In a series of 30 cases of BDD referred to a psychiatry clinic, all but two cases had mood disorders, mainly major depression (Phillips, McElroy, Keck, Pope, & Hudson, 1993). Anxiety disorders were the next most common current and lifetime diagnoses including 50% with social phobia and 37% with obsessive-compulsive disorder. Fully 77% had a history of psychotic symptoms either associated with a mood disorder (43%) or as a primary psychotic disorder (33%). Given the predominance of obsessive thinking and compulsive behaviors, BDD may be related to obsessive-compulsive disorder and respond to similar pharmacological and behavioral treatments (Hollander, Neville, Frenkel, Josephson, & Liebowitz, 1992). As with OCD, BDD patients' symptoms range along a spectrum of severity from obsession to delusion (Phillips, Kim, & Hudson, 1995).

Somatic Presentations of Other Psychiatric Disorders

The DSM-IV somatoform disorders leave out a group of patients commonly described as "somatizing" who have underlying psychiatric disorders (mainly depression, anxiety, or personality disorders but sometimes also psychotic disorders) but who make exclusively somatic clinical presentations. The majority of these somatizers are willing to acknowledge a psychosocial contribution to their distress provided it is not presented as an explanation that excludes somatic factors (Kirmayer, Robbins, Dworkind, & Yaffe, 1993). As a group, "presenting" somatizers tend to be less depressed than patients who "psychologize," show less social dissatisfaction, have a more negative attitude toward mental illness and are more likely to have been a medical inpatient (Bridges, Goldberg, Evams, & Sharpe, 1991). They make more normalizing and fewer psychologizing attributions for common somatic symptoms, are less introspective and less likely to seek help if they are anxious or depressed (Kirmayer & Robbins, 1996).

COURSE AND PROGNOSIS

There is wide variation in course, disability, and outcome across the somatoform disorders. In general, psychiatric comorbidity contributes to chronicity for the range of somatoform disorders (Rief, Hiller, Geissner, & Fichter, 1995). Nevertheless, recent research demonstrates that cognitive behavioral interventions can significantly reduce symptomatology, distress, disability, and excessive or inappropriate health care utilization (Sharpe et al., 1996; Speckens et al., 1995).

SD is defined as a chronic condition, and patients generally accrue the requisite number of symptoms over a period of several years. The ECA study found that of patients with a lifetime diagnosis of SD, fully 90% had symptoms in the past year, yielding a remission rate of less than 8% (Swartz et al., 1991, p. 227). Patients are liable to continue to experience multiple somatic symptoms in shifting functional systems. They are at risk for iatrogenic illness due to complications of invasive diagnostic procedures, and unnecessary medication or surgery.

For patients with SD, a simple intervention consisting of a consultation letter to the patient's primary care physician has been shown to significantly reduce expenditures for health care and improve health outcomes (Rost, Kashner, & Smith, 1994). The letter includes information on the diagnosis of SD and suggestions for the frequency of scheduled visits, reduction of investigations of new symptoms, and avoidance of hospitalization and surgery unless clearly indicated. Similar benefits have been demonstrated for psychiatric consultations with primary care patients with undifferentiated somatoform disorder or subsyndromal somatization (Smith, Rost, & Kashner, 1995).

Bass and Benjamin (1993) have outlined a general approach to the clinical management of the chronic somatizing patient geared to general practitioners. They include the following strategies: 1. in the initial interview identify psychosocial issues but avoid direct confrontation; 2. provide unambiguous information about medical findings; 3. plan time for gradual discussion of psychosocial issues; 4. work out a problem list and negotiate an agenda with the patient; 5. set limits for diagnostic investigations. Additional efforts at psychological support and reattribution training may further improve outcome (Barsky, Geringer, & Wool, 1988; Goldberg, Gask, & O'Dowd, 1989).

Conversion disorder tends to be an acute, self-limited condition. Conversion symptoms usually have an abrupt onset in relation to some acute stressor, cause substantial impairment and resolve spontaneously or respond to a wide variety of suggestive therapeutics (Ford & Folks, 1985; Hafeiz, 1980). Patients who progress to chronicity have greater psychiatric comorbidity, intractable social circumstances, and a broader propensity to experience and report multiple somatic symptoms through which they eventually reach criteria for SD (Couprie, Wijdicks, Rooijmans, & van Gijn, 1995; Kent, Tomasson, & Coryell, 1995). Longitudinal studies of patients with conversion disorders find that from 10% to 50% are eventually diagnosed with an organic disease that may have accounted for their conversion symptoms (Cloninger, 1987; Slater, 1965; Watson & Buranen, 1979b). In one study, about 20% of patients with conversion disorder seen in general hospital psychiatric consultation met criteria for somatization disorder on 2-year follow-up (Kent et al., 1995; Tomasson et al., 1991). The link between conversion disorder and somatization disorder is overstated in DSM-IV, however, because in the general population, sporadic conversion symptoms are much more common than somatization disorder.

Although hypochondriasis is defined as a chronic condition, about 50% of patients with high levels of hypochondriacal worry in primary care have their anxiety at least temporarily resolved with standard reassurance and so have "transient" hypochondriasis (Barsky, Wyshak, & Klerman, 1990b). Medical illness or other life events may give rise to transient hypochondriasis (Barsky et al., 1993). Previous or coexisting psychiatric disorder, including Axis I disorders and personality disorders, predispose a person to the development of persistent hypochondriasis (Barsky et al., 1992; Robbins & Kirmayer, 1996). Psychoeducational and cognitive-behavioral approaches to reduce hypochondriacal anxiety can improve the prognosis in this group with persistent worry (Barsky, 1996; Warwick & Salkovskis, 1990). Similar results have been reported for patients with body dysmorphic disorder (Rosen, Reiter, & Orosan, 1995b).

As noted above, up to 33% of the adult population in the United States suffer from some form of chronic pain. An 8-year follow-up study suggests that about one-third of people with chronic musculoskeletal pain will recover while two-thirds continue to be symptomatic (Magni et al., 1993). Patients with multiple, anatomically unrelated pains differ from those with discrete, localized chronic pain in having greater psychiatric comorbidity. Data from the ECA study suggest the total number of pain complaints is more predictive of associated psychopathology and utilization of health care services than the specific location, duration, severity or medical explanation of the pain complaints (Dworkin, Von Korff, & LeResche, 1990; Von Korff, Wagner, Dworkin, & Saunders, 1991). People with single pain complaints did not differ from those with no history of pain in rates of psychiatric disorders and health service utilization. Psychological factors contribute to the risk of acute pain becoming a chronic condition. In a study of patients with acute herpes zoster (shingles), patients who went on to develop chronic pain had higher state and trait anxiety, more depressive symptoms, lower life satisfaction, and greater disease conviction at the time of their initial assessment (Dworkin et al., 1992).

ETIOLOGICAL CONSIDERATIONS

Studies of somatoform disorders have considered the role of personality, psychodynamic, cognitive, and social factors in shaping symptom experience. In this section we will consider putative etiological factors in terms of temperamental differences; personality and psychiatric comorbidity; sensory-perceptual mechanisms; cognitive-evaluative processes; emotion suppression or inhibition; and social-interactional factors. Finally, we will discuss the role of specific development experiences including trauma and present an integrative model of somatization.

Temperament, Personality, and Psychiatric Comorbidity

The tendency to experience high levels of both somatic symptoms and emotional distress may reflect underlying temperamental traits, particularly the trait that has been termed neuroticism or negative affectivity in factorial studies of the dimensions of personality (Pennebaker & Watson, 1991). Individuals high on negative affectivity are prone to experience affective and anxiety disorders which give rise to somatic symptoms. Lower levels of dysphoria may also give rise to significant somatic symptoms through physiological mechanisms like hyperventilation or sleep disturbance (Sharpe & Bass, 1992). Individuals with high levels of negative affectivity may also experience more frequent, intense, and distressing bodily sensations due to the dysregulation of autonomic or pain control systems even in the absence of dysphoric mood.

The majority of patients with SD meet criteria for personality disorders (Stern et al., 1993). Indeed, it has been suggested that SD itself is best conceptualized as a personality disorder based on an interaction between temperamental traits of negative affectivity and family experiences that model and reinforce the sick role (Kirmayer, Robbins, & Paris, 1994). First-degree relatives of patients with SD have elevated rates of SD, antisocial personality disorder, major depression, and alcoholism (Cloninger, Martin, Guze, & Clayton, 1986). Cross-fostering adoption studies of SD provide evidence for both heritable pathophysiological mechanisms and family environment in somatization (Bohman et al., 1984; Sigvardsson et al., 1986).

In a classic paper, Engel (1959) introduced the notion of the "pain-prone personality" characterized by perfectionistic striving and minimization or denial of emotional distress. Blumer and Heilbronn (1982) later expanded this notion to include "ergomania" or "workaholism" and a familial tendency toward depression. Personality factors may play a role in aggravating pain whatever its origins but do not reliably distinguish patients with clear-cut medical explanations for pain from those whose problems are more complicated and obscure. Turk and Melzack (1992) concluded that "the search for a 'pain-prone personality' . . . or psychogenic pain has proved futile."

Studies of clinical populations with pain show high levels of comorbid Axis I disorders. Depression is the most common diagnosis and is found in 25% to 50% of hospital patients with acute pain referred to psychiatric evaluation and from 10% to 100% of patients with chronic pain (Blumer & Heilbronn, 1982; Romano & Turner, 1985). However, earlier claims that chronic pain was essentially a variant of major depressive disorder (Blumer, 1984; Blumer & Heilbronn, 1982) have not been borne out by more recent studies showing that many chronic pain patients have little or no evidence of depressed mood (Ahles, Yunus, & Masi, 1987) and that major depression is somewhat more likely to be a consequence of chronic pain than an antecedent (Brown, 1990; Magni, Moreschi, Rigatti Luchini, & Merskey, 1994). Specific types of pains may be associated with other specific psychiatric disorders; for example, up to one-third of patients with noncardiac chest pain have concurrent panic disorder (Beitman, Mukerji, Flaker, & Basha, 1988).

Somatic Perception, Attention, and Amplification

Mechanic and others have studied the effect of "introspectiveness" on the increased reporting of both psychological and somatic symptoms (Hansell & Mechanic, 1986; Mechanic, 1979). Individual differences in the tendency to focus attention on the self and on bodily sensations are associated with elevated symptom reporting in the laboratory and in epidemiological studies (Pennebaker, 1982; Robbins & Kirmayer, 1986, 1991b). While self-focused patients tend to report both somatic and psychological symptoms, patients who preferentially attend to the body may be more likely to report somatic rather than cognitive or emotional symptoms.

Barsky and Klerman (1983) introduced the notion of *somatic amplification:* a hypothesized tendency for individuals to experience bodily sensations as intense, noxious, and disturbing. Related concepts include augmenting-reducing and perceptual sensitivity. Amplification may involve sensory, perceptual, and cognitive-evaluative processes. The background level of everyday bodily discomfort (a sort of bodily "white noise") as well as the higher levels of distress that ordinarily accompany illness or injury may be selectively focused on and amplified by some individuals giving rise to more varied and intense symptom reports and hypochondriacal worry.

To test this hypothesis, Barsky, Wyshak, and Klerman (1990a) developed the Somatosensory Amplification Scale (SSAS), an 11-item self-report questionnaire with adequate internal consistency and test-retest reliability. Higher levels on the SSAS were found in hypochondriacal patients as well as in patients making frequent use of medical care (Barsky, 1992; Barsky, Cleary, & Klerman, 1992). Unfortunately, despite its name, the SSAS does not really tap underlying perceptual processes of amplification. It includes many symptom experience items that represent the outcome of hypochondriacal cognitions. There is a need for longitudinal studies to determine the direction of causality between hypochondriasis and less symptom-based measures of amplification.

While selective attention and preoccupation with the body may lead to amplified somatic sensations, conversion symptoms seem to involve a different deployment of attention, in which the affected body part, function or sensory system is selectively ignored. This form of selective inattention or alternate control is usually subsumed under the construct of dissociation (Kihlstrom, 1992). Evidence that conversion disorders are related to dissociative mechanisms comes from observations of their frequent occurrence in patients with dissociative identity disorder (Putnam, Guroff, Silberman, Barban, & Post, 1986), high levels of hypnotic susceptibility in patients with conversion symptoms (Bliss, 1984), the ability to create laboratory models of conversion symptoms with hypnosis (Sackeim, Nordlie, & Gur, 1979), and a dramatic therapeutic response to hypnosis (Williams, Spiegel, & Mostofsky, 1978).

Dissociative mechanisms may also contribute to other somatic symptoms to the extent that individuals high on hypnotizability or openness to absorbing experiences may be more likely to become intensely focussed on and absorbed by bodily sensations. Wickramasekera (1995) has suggested that there are two groups of somatizing patients: one with high levels of hypnotizability and the tendency to become absorbed by their symptoms and the other with unusually low levels and the inability to block out noxious sensations.

Cognitive Evaluation, Attribution, and Coping

Attention is guided by cognitive schemas that indicate potential sources of threat (Cioffi, 1991; Lazarus & Folkman, 1984). Somatizers may be primed by preexisting schemas or beliefs about their own vulnerability to disease to interpret the generalized malaise and symptoms that accompany affective or anxiety disorders as indicating serious physical illness. The literature on hypochondriasis and abnormal illness behavior has demonstrated the role of worry, fear, disease conviction, and self-rated bodily sensitivity or intolerance to noxious stimuli as important correlates of somatic symptom reporting (Barsky, Goodson, Lane, & Cleary, 1988; Barsky & Klerman, 1983; Pilowsky, 1967). Hypochondriacal worry often accompanies depression and anxiety disorders and, when sufficiently intense, may overshadow other symptoms (Barsky et al., 1992; Kenyon, 1976).

A lack of effective coping with common bodily symptoms or illnesses may result in greater anxiety about the body, increased body focus, persistent symptoms, and hypochondriacal worry. Hypochondriacal college women (as indicated by high scores on the MMPI hypochondriasis scale) tend to spend more time on health-related pursuits than those who are less symptomatic (Karoly & Lecci, 1993). This preoccupation with efforts to assess and maintain one's health interacts with more specific thoughts linking bodily sensations to illness. Hypochondriacal patients are prone to catastrophizing thoughts in which they equate specific bodily sensations or events with the idea that they are sick (Salkovskis, 1989). For example, a patient may think, "This tightness in my chest is not normal. It's probably from my heart. Maybe I'm going to have a heart attack." These thoughts create more anxiety and focus attention on the chest area. Both the anxiety and the attentional focus may increase muscle tension in the chest wall leading to more symptoms which, in turn, increase the conviction that one is ill. The more dire the symptom interpretation, the greater the anxiety, tension, and distress.

Somatic amplification affects both somatic and emotional distress and so cannot account for the denial of coexisting emotional problems found in some somatizing patients. The selective emphasis on somatic symptoms and explanations for distress may have more to do with attributional style, defense style, or structural factors influencing help-seeking and stigmatization. An unwillingness or inability to attribute the bodily concomitants of emotional arousal or affective disorder to psychosocial causes may lead patients to present clinically with somatic symptoms while minimizing underlying emotional distress (Kleinman, 1980; Robbins & Kirmayer, 1986, 1991a; Stoeckle & Barsky, 1980).

Robbins and Kirmayer (1991a) developed the Symptom Interpretation Questionnaire (SIQ), a self-report measure that asks respondents to rate the extent to which they would attribute common somatic symptoms to each of three types of hypothetical causes: *somatic* (physical disorder or disease); *psychological* (emotional distress or problem); and *normalizing* (environmental or other ordinary external event; e.g., "If I felt fatigued, I would probably think that it is because 1. I'm emotionally exhausted or discouraged; 2. I'm anemic or my blood is weak; and 3. I've been overexerting myself or not exercising enough"). Among family medicine patients, the SIQ has been found to predict somatizing or psychologizing clinical presentations of depression and anxiety (Kirmayer & Robbins, 1996; Robbins & Kirmayer, 1991a). Patients with psychiatric disorders are more likely to attribute common somatic symptoms to psychological causes on the SIQ (Wise & Mann, 1995). A subset of items of the SIQ predicted the tendency for primary care patients with fatigue associated with an acute viral illness to subsequently develop chronic fatigue (Cope, David, Pelosi, & Mann, 1994). Patients who are high-frequency users of medical care are less able to generate normalizing explanations for common somatic symptoms (Sensky, MacLeod & Rigby, 1996).

Bridges, Goldberg, Evans, and Sharpe (1991) found that patients who make somatized presentations of depression or anxiety in primary care have more hostile attitudes toward mental illness than those who make psychosocial presentations. Somatizers may live in familial or cultural contexts where mental illness is stigmatized. These negative attitudes toward mental illness extend to a greater hesitancy among somatizers to talk to a doctor about any emotional problem and a greater reluctance to seek specialty mental health care (Kirmayer & Robbins, 1996).

Attributions of distress to physical illness may also act to limit the dysphoria and loss of self-esteem that would otherwise result when distress is attributed to personal character or emotional weakness. Bridges and colleagues (1991) suggest that insisting on a physical illness explanation for symptoms and holding the doctor responsible for missing the correct organic diagnosis removes personal blame from the somatizer. The blame-avoidance function of somatization may explain why patients who make somatic presentations of depression or anxiety in primary care tend to report lower levels of dysphoria than do psychosocial presenters (Bridges et al., 1991; Kirmayer & Robbins, 1996; Powell, Dolan, & Wessely, 1990; Verhaak & Tijhuis, 1994).

The interaction between anxiety, attention, and attributions is well demonstrated by the phenomenon of "medical students' disease" (Mechanic, 1972). A substantial proportion of medical students experience transient hypochondriasis during their training. The pressures of study, sleep loss, and apprehension about examinations lead to anxiety. Inundated by information about pathophysiology, students scan their bodies and misinterpret benign sensations as signs and symptoms of disease. The hypochondriacal worry that results usually resolves when the stress of examinations passes and when students acquire additional information to clarify that their unusual sensations do not fit the pattern of any disease. To the extent that this is a useful model of transient hypochondriasis, the factors that lead to chronicity must be added to explain clinical hypochondriasis.

Emotion Suppression, Inhibition, and Denial

There is limited empirical support for an earlier generation of psychodynamic hypotheses about the relationship of intrapsychic conflict, personality, and defense mechanisms to somatization. Much of this literature assumed an "either/or" relationship between somatization and psychological-mindedness in which distress was either adequately cognized and expressed in symbolic terms through the language of psychology or suppressed, repressed, and converted into physiological distress. This "either/or" theory has not been borne out in large-scale epidemiological studies where somatic and emotional distress are found to be highly positively correlated rather than inversely correlated as psychodynamic theory might suggest (Simon & Von Korff, 1991). However, these epidemiological studies have not attempted to separate out a subgroup for whom emotional and somatic distress might be inversely correlated, nor can they deal with the possibility that self-reports are not accurate reflections of underlying distress or psychological disturbance. It is possible that epidemiological studies based on self-report questionnaires or lay interviewers incorrectly classify as healthy some people who deny emotional distress or somatic symptoms (Shedler, Mayman, & Manis, 1993). Study of the consequences of this type of "illusory" mental health requires careful clinical observation and measures of dysfunction that are independent of self-report.

A group of related concepts—including *repression-sensitization, alexithymia, levels of emotional awareness,* and *level of thinking*—involve the tendency to suppress emotional expression or the inability to cognitively elaborate emotional conflict. The relevance of these concepts for somatization derives from the theory that suppression or "hypocognition" of strong emotions will lead to more prolonged emotional arousal which in turn may result in higher levels of somatic symptoms and distress (Pennebaker, 1995).

Some support for the notion of somatization versus verbalization as "either/ or" phenomena comes from studies of repressive coping style (Schwartz, 1990). There is evidence that while individuals who are "repressors" initially report less emotional distress in response to an acute stressor, they show more prolonged levels of physiological arousal and increased depressive and somatic symptomatology over the long run (Bonanno & Singer, 1990). Similarly, suppressing or not telling one's story of stress or trauma may lead to persistent somatic symptoms. Conversely, telling one's story can relieve symptoms (Pennebaker, 1990).

It often has been claimed that somatizing patients lack "psychological mindedness"; that is, the ability to label, symbolize, and describe their emotions, fantasies, conflicts, or other aspects of their inner life. Efforts have been made to operationalize the definition and measurement of this deficit through the concept of *alexithymia,* a term coined by Sifneos (1973) to mean "no words for feeling." Alexithymic individuals are said to lack the ability to discriminate feelings and bodily sensations, tend not to express their psychological states, think in a concrete and action-oriented rather than a reflective way about the world, and lack a rich fantasy life. The Toronto Alexithymia Scale (TAS) is currently the most psychometrically sound self-report measure of alexithymia (Taylor, Bagby, Ryan & Parker, 1990). Versions of the TAS have three or four distinct dimensions that correlate differently with symptom and personality measures (Hendryx, Haviland, Gibbons, & Clark, 1992; Hendryx, Haviland & Shaw, 1991; Kirmayer & Robbins, 1993). Scores on the TAS also are significantly affected by level of education (Kauhanen, Kaplan, Julkunen, Wilson, & Salonen, 1993; Kirmayer & Robbins, 1993).

While there is some preliminary evidence that high scores on the TAS may be predictive of chronicity among somatizing patients (Bach & Bach, 1995), at present the TAS has little utility in clinical settings and should not be used to exclude patients from psychotherapy because they are deemed "not psychologically minded," since this is likely to be a state secondary to preoccupation with somatic symptoms that can change as these symptoms are directly addressed through techniques of behavioral medicine (Wise, Mann, Mitchell, Hryniak, & Hill, 1990). In fact, alexithymia is more closely related to measures of depressive symptoms than to somatization (Cohen, Auld, & Brooker, 1994). Depression or dysphoria may be associated with a range of confusing sensations that cannot be clearly separated into emotions and bodily symptoms. In some cases, the inability or reluctance of mental health practitioners to address patients' somatic symptoms and concerns may lead to a breakdown in communication that is attributed to psychological deficits in the patient (Kirmayer, 1987).

Family, Social, and Developmental Factors

Developmental experiences of reinforcement and modeling of illness behavior play a role in shaping adult illness behavior (Whitehead, Busch, Heller, & Costa, 1986; Whitehead, Winget, Fedoravicius, Wooley, & Blackwell, 1982; Wilkinson, 1988). Somatization is common among children and adolescents (Campo & Fritsch, 1994). Exaggerated parental concerns with illness, pathologizing of normal sensations (or misattribution of bodily concomitants of emotional distress) and medical help-seeking may predispose children to develop bodily preoccupation and anxiety as adults (Benjamin & Eminson, 1992). For example, childhood reinforcement of illness behavior in response to menstruation correlates with adult premenstrual symptoms and associated disability; similarly, reinforcement of illness behavior in response to colds predicts adult levels of symptomatology and disability with colds (Whitehead et al., 1994). These effects are specific to illness and independent of the effects of life stress and neuroticism. A lack of parental protection in childhood may also increase the likelihood of high rates of health care utilization for somatoform symptoms in adulthood (Craig, Drake, Mills, & Boardman, 1994).

There has been increasing recognition of the role of childhood trauma and sexual abuse in somatization (Walker, Gelfand, Gelfand, Koss, & Katon, 1995; Walker, Katon, Neraas, Jemelka, & Massoth, 1992). Traumatic experiences in adulthood, such as domestic violence or state violence experienced by refugees, may also lead to persistent somatic problems (McCauley et al., 1995; Westermeyer, Bouafuely, Neider, & Callies, 1989).

Along with dissociative disorders and somatization disorder, conversion symptoms may be associated with high rates of childhood sexual abuse (Alper, Devinsky, Perrine, Vazquez, & Luciano, 1993; Coryell & Norten, 1981; Morrison, 1989). However, the association is nonspecific since histories of trauma and abuse are found among patients with a wide range of psychological disorders. A more specific link may exist between suppression or inhibition of verbal response to trauma and subsequent somatic distress (Pennebaker, 1985, 1990).

An Integrative Model

The physiological, psychological, and social factors discussed above may interact in a series of nested vicious cycles to give rise to persistent somatoform disorders. Figure 11.1 depicts some of these loops. Bodily sensations arise from everyday physiological disturbances or common illness, such as viral infections, or from emotional arousal or major mood or anxiety disorders. These sensations may be more or less insistent, capturing attention despite efforts to ignore them, but even mild sensations can become magnified once attention is focused on the affected region of the body. Selective attention to the body or to specific sensations is guided by cognitive-interpretive processes that make use of symptom and illness schemas. These include attributional processes by which sensa-

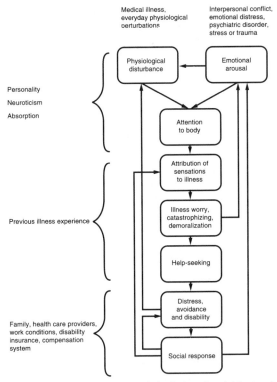

FIGURE 11.1   A model of physiological, psychological, and social factors in somatization.

tions may be interpreted as symptoms or signs of an illness. Once an illness schema is accessed it may guide subsequent attention to identify further symptoms confirmatory of the illness out of the background noise of bodily sensations (Arkes & Harkness, 1980). More or less neutral sensations may also be reevaluated as uncomfortable and threatening. To the extent that the ensuing thoughts and images represent the putative illness as serious, cognitive-evaluation will lead to illness worry, catastrophizing, and demoralization. The identification of a potentially worrisome symptom leads to the search for a remedy, and, if it persists, to adoption of the sick role with restrictions in activity. The responses of care providers may validate the sick role or question the reality of the person's symptoms and suffering.

Specific traits and external factors may act at many levels in this evolution of illness cognition and behavior. Constitutional or acquired differences in autonomic and emotional reactivity may make some individuals more prone to experience uncomfortable bodily sensations due to physiological dysregulation or dysphoric mood. Differences in attentional set, attributional style, and coping will influence the tendency to minimize, ignore, or explain symptoms away on the one hand, or become absorbed in sensations and convince oneself that they are symptoms of a serious illness.

All of these processes are normal aspects of the response to any illness. They may reach disabling levels for some individuals either because of the intensity of specific factors or because of runaway feedback loops. Only some of these potential loops have been drawn in the diagram. One loop involves feedback from illness, worry, and catastrophizing to emotional arousal, which in turn generates more symptoms. This loop is the focus of the cognitive assessment and treatment of hypochondriasis (Warwick & Salkovskis, 1990). Another loop from social response to emotional arousal signifies that the response of significant others to illness worry may also exacerbate bodily preoccupation or hypochondriasis (Robbins & Kirmayer, 1996). A third loop runs from sick role behavior back to physiological disturbance; this occurs, for example, when restriction or avoidance of activity leads to physical deconditioning with consequent feelings of fatigue, weakness, and muscular discomfort. This loop has been postulated to play a key role in the genesis of chronic fatigue syndrome and cognitive-behavioral interventions aimed at modifying this cycle have proven therapeutically efficacious (Wessely & Sharpe, 1995).

Finally, two additional loops are drawn to underscore the importance of social processes in exacerbating and maintaining somatization. There is much evidence that the response of family members, employers, health care professionals, and the larger society to a person's illness behavior may either aggravate or resolve somatoform disorders (McDaniel, Hepworth, & Doherty, 1992). Many of these studies involve patients with chronic pain. Couple and family response is known to influence the intensity and disability associated with chronic pain (Block, Kremer & Gaylor, 1980).

The course of somatoform disorders is strongly influenced by the response of care providers and the health care system. Excessive and invasive diagnostic investigations may increase patients' worry and conviction that they are ill, heighten body consciousness, and lead to the reporting of more somatic symptoms. Conversely, realistic reassurance and opportunities to receive support and clinical care without the need to present fresh somatic symptoms as a "ticket" to see the doctor can reduce the intensity of somatic distress, health care utilization, and costs, and the risk of iatrogenic illness (Smith, Monson, & Ray, 1986a). The single best predictor of return to work after back injury is preinjury level of job satisfaction (Kleinman, Brodwin, Good, & Good, 1992).

Wider societal attitudes and cultural notions about specific illnesses and vulnerabilities may also contribute to the emergence of specific syndromes. This was observed in the sudden rise in repetitive strain injury syndrome in Australia in response to insurance and disability coverage (Hall & Morrow, 1988). Similar stories could be told about environmental sensitivity syndrome, hypoglycemia, chronic candidiasis, and other recently popular diagnoses that may be promoted by mass media (Shorter, 1994). Chronic fatigue syndrome may be an example of an enduring problem that is undergoing a renaissance, in part, as a result of media coverage (Abbey & Garfinkel, 1991). In the case of chronic fatigue, the influence from social responses also runs back to attributions. Patients who find their illness doubted or discounted by health care providers may become more insistent on a disease explanation for their distress in an effort to gain legitimacy and counteract the stigma associated with psychological and psychiatric problems (Wessely, 1994). Clinicians' power to ratify illness is a double-edged sword. There is evidence, for example, that primary care patients with acute viral illnesses who are intensively investigated are more likely to go on to develop chronic fatigue (Cope et al., 1994). It is particular important to reassess these social loops when problems do not respond to interventions focused exclusively at an individual level.

DIAGNOSTIC CONSIDERATIONS

The category of somatoform disorders arises from the assumption that medically unexplained somatic distress and worry can be attributed to psychopathology. In fact, this determination is often difficult to make (Kirmayer, 1994). The diagnostic criteria for somatoform disorders raise a number of thorny diagnostic problems including: 1. When is a symptom medically unexplained? 2. When is worry or distress excessive? 3. When can a symptom be said to be "psychogenic," that is, predominately caused by psychological factors?

The notion that a symptom is medically unexplained is based on efforts to rule out identifiable organic causes. The extent of the medical investigation depends on available technology and clinical practices. The offering of a plausible explanation for symptoms, even in the absence of definite laboratory confirmation, depends on current medical knowledge. New theories and technology allow further investigations and provide new explanations for previously obscure symptoms. To some extent, the decision that a symptom or syndrome is idiopathic or unexplained reflects diagnostic conventions within the medical community, which are, in turn, influenced by larger social forces.

For many patients and practitioners, calling a syndrome "unexplained" is tantamount to saying that symptoms are imaginary. However, there are many types of physiological perturbation that can give rise to significant somatic distress (Sharpe & Bass, 1992). For example, unnoticed hyperventilation can give rise to feelings of faintness, shortness of breath, paresthesias, and other unusual sensations. Our ability to measure abnormalities in the functioning of many physiological systems is still quite rudimentary. It is likely that many functional symptoms and syndromes are due to subtle disturbances of physiological process rather than gross structural abnormalities and hence will lie beyond the power of clinical and laboratory measures to resolve for some time to come.

In the case of hypochondriasis, there is a diagnostic assumption that worry and emotional distress are greater than appropriate for the severity or likelihood of organic disease. However, there are no established norms for how much distress is appropriate to a given condition so that clinical judgments that distress is exaggerated may be influenced by factors other than the relative level of patients' worry. The diagnostic criteria for hypochondriasis also include the notion that the patient's illness worry does not respond to appropriate medical reassurance. But how much reassurance is enough? Do most patients given the label hypochondriacal actually receive adequate reassurance? When assessed in primary care, each laboratory investigation the clinician conducts causes apprehension and uncertainty, so the clinician's ultimate declaration that "nothing is wrong" may be met with some doubt. When hypochondriacal patients are evaluated and treated by mental health practitioners, they may find that a sudden shift to focus on their anxiety and related psychological or social problems conflicts with the experiential primacy of their somatic distress. In either case, the assumption that they have been "adequately" reassured may not be justified as features of the clinical encounter may aggravate hypochondriacal concerns. The observation that many hypochondriacal patients respond well to systematic reassurance and reattribution training points to the limitations of their earlier encounters with physicians (Kellner, 1992; Warwick, 1992).

It is a short segue from the notion that symptoms are medically unexplained or amplified by patients' anxieties to the assumption that symptoms are caused by psychological factors. Given the epistemological constraints of the clinical setting, however, this assumption often is difficult to support with concrete data. The difficulty of ascertaining psychological causation was openly acknowledged in the DSM-III-R criteria for somatoform pain disorder where there was a retreat from the causal imputations of "psychogenic pain" to the judgment that pain simply persists too long or is too intense. DSM-IV pain disorder reinstates a judgment of whether pain is entirely or partially due to medical or psychological factors as a diagnostic qualifier but this faces the same epistemological difficulties. Melzack and Wall (1983) have noted the low correlation between size of tissue injury and severity of pain. Indeed, such observations are basic to their theory of pain, which emphasizes the ability of central cognitive evaluative processes to regulate somatic pain no matter what its origin. This problem is compounded by the fact that observers are not able to reliably discriminate individual differences in style of expression or coping with pain from actual pain experience (Poole & Craig, 1992). In practice, any distinction between "psychogenic" and organic pain reflects patients' style of self-presentation, credibility, and the larger functioning of the hospital ward or health care team as a system in which the patient is made to carry the brunt of diagnostic uncertainty and treatment failure.

In DSM-II, conversion disorder was classified as "hysterical neurosis, conversion type" and characterized by "involuntary psychogenic loss or disorder of function" involving the special senses or voluntary motor system. This definition was broadened in DSM-III to include any symptom that involved "a loss of, or alteration in," attributed to "an expression of a psychological conflict or need." The notion of psychogenic causation has proved difficult to operationalize and of limited use in discriminating conversion symptoms from symptoms that ultimately are found to have organic causation (Cloninger, 1987; Watson & Buranen, 1979b).

"Medically explained," "exaggerated distress," and psychogenic causation are not easy criteria to apply, and these diagnostic judgments remain liable to clinician bias and other extraneous factors (Kirmayer, 1988). It may be more useful, therefore, to approach somatoform disorders in terms of psychosocial factors that shape the reporting of all distress—although whether these will prove sufficient to explain the extreme variants that form the prototypical definitions of the DSM remains to be seen.

DSM-IV stipulates that to receive a diagnosis of somatoform disorder, symptoms must not be due to another psychiatric disorder. In many cases, however, symptoms of somatoform disorder are clearly secondary to another antecedent or underlying psychiatric disorder. Somatic symptoms commonly accompany mood and anxiety disorders. Pain, fatigue, and a wide range of other "vegetative" symptoms are among the most frequent symptoms of major depression. Palpitations, feelings of faintness or dizziness, and other symptoms of autonomic hyperarousal are cardinal signs of panic disorder and other anxiety disorders. Hypochondriacal worry and disease conviction also are common in depression and anxiety disorders. It has been claimed that many somatizing patients have "masked" depressions in which the emotional and cognitive symptoms are muted, hidden, or denied. More commonly, the emotional distress is quite evident, but patients insist that it is secondary to their original somatic illness. A somatoform diagnosis serves to acknowledge the prominence of physical symptoms and patients' own somatic causal attributions.

All symptoms should be treated as having both physiological and psychosocial dimensions and should be investigated and treated at multiple levels. This integrative approach avoids the danger that, in labeling symptoms as "psychogenic," clinicians will no longer search for or discount evidence of underlying organic disease that requires medical attention (see Table 11.3).

Case 5. A 22-year Laotian man, who had immigrated to Canada 4 years earlier, was brought to the hospital emergency room by his brothers and mother. Several hours earlier while comfortably watching TV and experiencing no distress, he had the sudden onset of pain in his lower back, radiating forward through his buttocks. This was followed by a paralysis affecting all four limbs. His trunk was unaffected and he had no difficulty breathing. In the emergency room, he appeared to be in little distress, answering the doctor's questions in good humour and seeming to be only mildly worried about his dramatic symptoms. His physical examination was inconsistent. He had some power in his extremities though deep tendon reflexes could not be elicited. He stated that these symptoms had occurred several times in the last year and always subsided after a few hours. He had stopped working several months earlier and was living with his parents because of fear of recurrent symptoms. A psychiatric consultation was requested to "rule out conversion disorder."

The psychiatric consultant was unable to elicit any history of emotional trauma or stress that might account for the acute onset of symptoms. He considered the impact of migration and the possibility of a poor social adjustment but felt this was too remote to account for increasing symptoms over the last year. He attempted hypnosis to assess the availability of dissociative mechanisms for symptom production, but while the patient relaxed and appeared to enjoy the experience, his paralysis persisted.

On hearing the history of the symptoms, an astute neurologist made the diagnosis of familial periodic hypokalemic paralysis (Stedwell, Allen, & Binder, 1992). The diagnosis was confirmed by the finding of a low serum potassium level, which returned to normal as the patient's paralysis spontaneously resolved over the next few hours.

The determination that symptoms are medically unexplained can involve extensive investigation to rule out occult or obscure diseases. Many chronic illnesses, like asthma or hypothyroidism, have systemic effects resulting in fatigue and other somatic symptoms. The manifestations and course of these diseases have a high degree of individual variability, and often it remains uncertain whether patients' somatic symptoms are due to a pathophysiological process.

TABLE 11.2   Diseases That May Be Mistaken for Conversion Symptoms

Basilar artery migraine	Temporal lobe epilepsy
Brain tumors	Torsion dystonia
Creutzfeldt-Jakob disease	Toxic neuropathy
Diabetic neuropathy	Porphyria
Drug-induced dystonic reactions	Sensory seizures
Endocrine disorders (e.g., Addison's disease)	Spinal cord tumors
Hypokalemic periodic paralysis	Parkinson's disease
Multiple sclerosis	Wilson disease
Myasthenia gravis	

Note. See Jefferson & Marshall (1981).

Table 11.2 lists some of the many uncommon diseases that give rise to symptoms that are readily mistaken for conversion symptoms. In some cases, laboratory tests or diagnostic maneuvers can elicit physical signs that distinguish between conversion and organic disease.

Psychological factors contributing to somatic distress should be assessed whatever the evidence for or against organic disease. From the illness behavior perspective, the same cognitive and social factors that affect functional illness also influence the symptoms and course of organic illness. The principal difference is the social response to illness based on whether it is viewed as medically validated or remains ambiguous. This underscores the fact that the making of a diagnosis is itself an intervention. Diagnostic terms carry personal and social meanings that have immediate implications for patients' wellness, self-esteem, interpretation of subsequent sensations, and potential stigmatization. Diagnostic labels may also function as metaphors that influence subsequent illness experience, coping, and self-image (Kirmayer, 1994).

PSYCHOLOGICAL AND BIOLOGICAL ASSESSMENT

Assessment of patients with somatoform disorders occurs in the context of outpatient or hospital management, disability or compensation evaluation, and research. Depending on context, the goals of assessment include 1. ruling out coexisting medical disorders; 2. making a psychiatric diagnosis that can guide clinical treatment planning and intervention; 3. determining the level and types of symptoms, illness impact, and disability; 4. predicting outcome or prognosis; and 5. assessing mediating processes relevant to research or clinical intervention (Barsky, 1996; Bass & Benjamin, 1993; Creed & Guthrie, 1993; Warwick, 1995). The diagnosis of a somatoform disorder does not indicate the specific symptoms, their meaning and impact for the patient, or their interaction with other psychological, medical, and social problems. Assessment must go well beyond the mere establishment of a diagnosis to include a clinically rich and useful picture of the person's pathology, resources, and lifeworld.

Establishing a collaborative relationship with somatizing patients can pose special challenges (Bass & Benjamin, 1993; McDaniel, Campbell, & Seaburn, 1989). Patients who fear their own emotional vulnerability or who have experienced rejection and stigmatization by doctors, employers, and others may vigor-

TABLE 11.3   An Outline for the Assessment of Somatizing Patients

Medical comorbidity
Psychiatric comorbidity
Symptom characteristics
   Type
      Location
      Intensity
      Sensory qualities
   Temporal pattern
      Frequency
      Duration
      Contours of onset and resolution
Amplifying factors
   Attention
      Body-focus
      Self-focus (introspectiveness)
      Hypnotizability
   Cognition
      Symptom attributions
      Perception of vulnerability and risk
      Catastrophizing thoughts
Coping strategies
Symptom context
   Recent life events
   Chronic stressors
   Marital and family adjustment
   Economic situation
   Work satisfaction
   Social supports

ously resist any implication that their problems are psychological in nature. This may reflect both psychological defensiveness and an effort to avoid further stigmatization and negation of the seriousness of their symptoms. The clinician can offer him- or herself as a consultant who is expert in assessing the psychosocial factors that can aggravate any physical illness and in teaching strategies to improve coping with illness. The clinician cannot arbitrate the ontological distinction between "real" organic disease and "imaginary" psychological disorder but must focus instead on factors that maintain symptoms and that are relevant to treatment. It is important to start from the assumption that all pain and other somatic symptoms are "real" regardless of the relative contribution of physiological and psychological, or peripheral and central, processes. Even pain from identifiable physical lesions is always the outcome of psychological processes (Merskey, 1991). What is at stake in the psychological assessment and "diagnosis" of somatic symptoms is the identification, for each individual in a specific life context, of factors that exacerbate or maintain symptoms and that may be modified to reduce suffering and disability.

Situating the evaluation process in a medical setting may help avoid some of the implicit message that the patients' problems are essentially psychological. In general, somatizing patients are not averse to considering a psychosocial dimension to their problem but rightly reject the implication that their problems are entirely psychological or "all in their head." Frequently, as patients see that the clinician is interested in the details of their somatic symptoms, they will volunteer information about emotional distress, social problems, and psychological issues. Sometimes this opening does not occur until the clinician has succeeded in helping the patient to reduce symptoms. Wickramasekera (1989) argued for a more frontal approach in which the links between emotional distress and conflict and somatic symptoms are directly demonstrated to patients with biofeedback monitoring during a stress-inducing interview in the clinician's office.

Assessment usually begins with the collection of detailed information on the presenting symptoms, their intensity, quality, temporal characteristics, and impact on the patient's life. Using the symptoms as a focus, it is possible to collect detailed information about other aspects of psychological and social functioning, which are introduced in terms of their possible impact on somatic distress, or as areas of functioning where somatic illness may be having disruptive effects. It is often useful to obtain a symptom diary in which the patient records each occurrence of major symptoms, their characteristics, the situations or context in which they occur, the associated cognitive, emotional, and behavioral responses as well as the responses of others. This diary involves a form of self-monitoring that may have immediate therapeutic effects and sets the stage for subsequent cognitive and family interventions.

Although for most clinical purposes simple visual analog scales suffice, there are a number of self-report or interview-based measures for assessing the intensity and quality of specific somatic symptoms including pain (Melzack, 1975), nausea (Melzack, Rosberger, Hollingsworth, & Thirlwell, 1985), and fatigue (Smets, Garssen, Bonke, & De Haes, 1995). These provide sensitive indicators of level of distress as well as various qualitative dimensions and can be used to monitor treatment progress.

Psychiatric Diagnosis

Several screening interviews and self-report measures for SD have been devised based on the assumption that common "nonspecific" somatic symptoms are more likely to be an indication of underlying psychiatric disorder than of organic medical illness, particularly when symptoms involve many different functional physiological systems. Othmer and de Souza (1985) found seven symptoms that highly discriminated SD patients from a sample of other psychiatric outpatients: vomiting, pain in the extremities, shortness of breath without exertion, amnesia, difficulty swallowing, a burning sensation of the genitals or rectum, and painful menstruation. A similar 11-item index was developed by Swartz and colleagues (1986) based on statistical analysis of data from the Epidemiologic Catchment Area Study (Robins & Regier, 1991). The discriminating symptoms included: a history of feeling sickly most of one's life, abdominal pain and gas, nausea, diarrhea, dizziness, chest pain, fainting spells, pain in the extremities, vomiting, and weakness. Both indices are useful for screening in epidemiological surveys or clinical settings (Smith & Brown, 1990). In DSM-IV, a simplified set of criteria have been introduced and validated in a field trial (Yutsy et al., 1995). Clinical screening based on these criteria first ascertains whether patients have a lifetime history of at least four separate pain complaints;

if not, the diagnosis of SD can be excluded. Otherwise, the clinician proceeds to inquire about gastrointestinal, sexual, or reproductive symptoms and conversion symptoms. If at least one of each is identified, the patient meets DSM-IV criteria for SD.

A variety of structured diagnostic interviews have been devised to assess psychiatric diagnoses in community and clinical populations by standardized criteria. The Diagnostic Interview Schedule (DIS) has been the most widely used instrument of this type (Robins, Helzer, & Orvaschel, 1985). Despite this wide use, the DIS has been criticized by many authors (Bass & Murphy, 1990). Robins (1982) found low concordance between psychiatrist and lay interviewers for the diagnosis of somatization disorder using the DIS and a sensitivity of only 41%. The DIS asks about lifetime occurrence of symptoms, and patient's memory may be poor for details of remote illnesses. In addition, some patients suffering with somatoform disorders may conceal information in the fear that the physicians will not take their current symptoms seriously. Nonphysician interviewers may have difficulty recognizing SD because they are less able to reject implausible medical explanations offered by patients.

The Composite International Diagnostic Interview (CIDI) is a standardized diagnostic instrument based on the DIS and the Present State Examination (PSE) that assesses mental disorders according to both DSM-III-R and ICD-10 criteria (Robins et al., 1989). The CIDI assesses more somatoform disorders than the DIS including somatization disorder, conversion disorder, somatoform pain disorder, and hypochondriasis. It is available in 16 languages and incorporates some efforts to make distinctions relevant to cross-cultural diagnosis. The CIDI has been used in a recent cross-national study of somatoform disorders (Janca, Isaac, Bennett, & Tacchini, 1995).

Barsky and colleagues (1992) developed the Structured Diagnostic Interview for Hypochondriasis (SDIH), a clinician-administered diagnostic interview for hypochondriasis modeled on the Structured Clinical Interview for DSM-III-R (SCID; Spitzer, Williams, Gibbon, & First, 1990). In a sample of general medical clinic patients, the SDIH had an interrater agreement on the diagnosis of 96%, and there was high concordance between the interview and the Whiteley Index of hypochondriasis (Pilowsky, 1967) and physician's rating of patients as hypochondriacal. Similar findings were reported by Noyes and colleagues (1993).

Pope and Hudson (1991) developed a structured interview modeled on the SCID to diagnose several common functional somatic syndromes which the authors hypothesized were variant forms of "affective spectrum disorder." Although these authors have not published psychometric characteristics of their interview, they have used it to examine the overlap between functional syndromes and their relationship to major depression (Hudson, Goldenberg, Pope, Keck, & Schlesinger, 1992). Robbins and colleagues (Kirmayer, Robbins, Taillefer, & Helzer, 1995) developed the Diagnostic Interview for Functional Syndromes (DIFS), modeled on the DIS for use by trained lay interviewers to estimate the prevalence of the three most common functional syndromes by currently accepted criteria: fibromyalgia (FMS), irritable bowel (IBS), and chronic fatigue (CFS) syndromes. However, there was substantial discrepancy between clinician and interview-based diagnoses. This may reflect inconsistencies in clinicians' diagnostic practices and the waxing and waning of symptoms in functional syndromes, as well as inherent limitations of the instrument.

Associated Factors: Personality, Amplification, and Coping

Determination of the intensity, duration, and quality of specific symptoms allows diagnosis of somatoform disorders and other possibly comorbid conditions by standardized criteria. However, DSM-IV diagnosis is only one aspect of the clinical evaluation. In addition to diagnosis, the clinical assessment of patients with somatization disorders requires attention to illness cognitions and coping skills, somatic amplification, attributional biases, and related personality traits, as well as the family system, work, and larger social contexts of suffering. These domains can be explored with clinical interviews that start from the nature of somatic symptoms and inquire about the patients' cognitive response as well as their impact on others.

Psychological testing using standard instruments must be adapted to the experience of patients with predominately somatic symptomatology. Test results may be subject to "physiogenic invalidity": misinterpreting symptoms that arise from the disturbed physiology of disease as evidence of psychopathology.

Neuropsychological testing has limited utility but should be considered where there is a history or signs suggestive of dementia or other organic mental disorder. On formal cognitive testing, chronic fatigue syndrome patients have mild cognitive impairments that usually are correlated with depressive symptomatology and cannot account for the magnitude of their subjective complaints (Cope, Pernet, Kendall, & David, 1995; DeLuca, Johnson, Beldowicz, & Natelson, 1995; Krupp, Sliwinski, Masur, Friedberg, & Coyle, 1994; McDonald, Cope, & David, 1993).

The Minnesota Multiphasic Personality Inventory (MMPI) in both its original and second generation versions (MMPI-2) generates several scales relevant to the assessment of somatizing patients (Hathaway & McKinley, 1989). The hypochondriasis scale consists of 32 items, all of which deal with somatic preoccupation or general physical functioning. The standard interpretation of the MMPI suggests that patients with high scores on hypochondriasis have excessive bodily concern, may have conversion disorder or somatic delusions, are likely to be diagnosed as having somatoform, somatoform pain, depressive, or anxiety disorders, are not good candidates for psychotherapy and tend to be critical of therapists and may terminate therapy prematurely when therapists suggest psychological reasons for symptoms. The MMPI does not provide an adequate assessment of specific hypochondriacal beliefs for which more specialized instruments are needed.

The 60-item MMPI hysteria scale identifies individuals who tend to react to stress by demonstrating physical symptoms such as headaches, stomach discomfort, chest pains, weakness, and somatic symptoms that do not fit the pattern of any known organic disorder. The typical high scorer is said to be someone who avoids responsibility through the development of physical symptoms, is self-centered, narcissistic and egocentric, psychologically immature, and resistant to psychological interpretations. The hysteria scale has been divided into two subscales: items that primarily address denial of psychological problems (DH) and items relating to admission of physical problems (AD; McGrath & O'Malley, 1986).

In addition to individual scale scores, the MMPI yields profiles based on multiple scales. A high score on both hypochondriasis and hysteria scales may indicate the presence of a somatoform disorder, particularly if the score on the depression scale is low (the "conversion V" pattern). With few exceptions, however, more recent studies with the MMPI have shown that it is not able to reliably distinguish patients with symptoms due to organic disease and those with medically unexplained symptoms (Blakely et al., 1991; Kim, Hsu, Williams, Weaver, & Zinsmeister, 1996; Pincus, Callahan, Bradley, Vaughn, & Wolfe, 1986). MMPI profile patterns also have not been shown to consistently predict treatment outcome among chronic pain patients (Chapman & Pemberton, 1994). Patients' specific beliefs regarding pain are better predictors of satisfaction and response to treatment (Deyo & Diehl, 1988). This points to the need for more specific inventories that assess cognitions involved in coping with somatic distress (DeGood & Shutty, 1992).

The Whiteley Index (WI) is a self-report measure of hypochondriacal beliefs (Pilowsky, 1967). The WI has good test-retest reliability and internal consistency and contains 14 items tapping three factors: 1. *bodily preoccupation* (e.g., "Are you bothered by many pains and aches?"); 2. *disease phobia* (e.g., "If a disease is brought to your attention [through radio, television, newspapers, or someone you know], do you worry about getting it yourself?"); and 3. *conviction of the presence of disease with nonresponse to reassurance* (e.g., "If you feel ill and someone tells you that you are looking better, do you become annoyed?"). The WI has been widely used in studies of hypochondriasis and provides a useful screening measure (Pilowsky, 1990). Although it might be thought to measure "illness worry" rather than hypochondriasis, in fact, it has a low correlation with estimates of the severity of disease and seems to reflect patient characteristics more than disease burden (Robbins & Kirmayer, 1996).

Expanding on the WI, Pilowsky and colleagues (Pilowsky, Murrell, & Gordon, 1979; Pilowsky & Spence, 1983; Pilowsky, Spence, Cobb, & Katsikitis, 1984) developed the Illness Behavior Questionnaire (IBQ) to assess forms of "abnormal illness behavior" (Pilowsky, 1978). The IBQ is a 62-item self-report instrument measuring patients' attitudes, ideas, affects, and attributions in relation to illness. It generates scores on seven factors of illness behavior, including general hypochondriasis, disease conviction, and denial. While there is a lack of information regarding the IBQ's internal and test-retest reliability (Bradley, Prokop, Gentry, Van der Heide, & Prieto, 1981), an interview form of the questionnaire has been shown to have adequate interrater reliability, with a mean percentage of agreement of 88% (Pilowsky & Spence, 1983).

Several studies have shown that patients with diverse chronic pain syndromes or pain symptoms without organic cause have elevated scores on relevant IBQ scales (Bradley, McDonald Haule, & Jaworski, 1992). However, a study of outpatients visiting a gastroenterology clinic having a primary complaint of upper abdominal pain found that among the patients with no organic cause for their pain, only patients with a psychiatric diagnosis had indications of abnormal illness behavior on the IBQ (Colgan, Creed, & Klass, 1988). Other studies have found little difference between patients with chronic fatigue syndrome and multiple sclerosis (Trigwell, Hatcher, Johnson, Stanley, & House, 1995). Despite its questionable use to discriminate somatoform disorders from other medical conditions, the IBQ remains a useful clinical and research tool to systematically assess a range of important illness cognitions.

The IBQ measures beliefs and attitudes rather than behaviors. One of the few attempts to develop an instrument that taps illness behavior is the Illness Behavior Inventory (IBI), developed by Turkat and Pettegrew (1983). The IBI is a 20-item self-report questionnaire assessing two dimensions of illness-related behaviors: *work-related illness behavior* (9 items pertaining to work and activity when feeling ill; e.g., "I work fewer hours when I'm ill") and *social illness behavior* (11 items concerning illness behaviors in social situations; e.g., "Most people who know me are aware that I take medication"). The IBI has good internal consistency and concurrent validity with the McGill Pain Questionnaire (Melzack, 1980), but has been little used in subsequent research.

The Illness Attitude Scale (IAS) is a 21-item self-report questionnaire measuring seven components of hypochondriasis including generic worry about illness, concern about pain, health beliefs, and bodily preoccupation (Kellner, Abbott, Winslow, & Pathak, 1987). The IAS reflects the authors' hypothesis that the most distinctive characteristic of hypochondriasis is not the fact that patients worry about health but that their fears are not eliminated by a satisfactory medical examination and they are resistant to medical reassurance (Fava & Grandi, 1991). The IAS differentiates between patients with DSM-III hypochondriasis and various other clinical groups (Hitchcock & Mathews, 1992).

Instruments also have been devised for the assessment of body image disturbances as found in BDD. For example, the Body Dysmorphic Disorder Examination assesses self-consciousness, preoccupation with appearance, overvalued ideas about the importance of appearance to self-worth, and body image avoidance and checking behaviors (Rosen, Reiter, & Orosan, 1995a).

Beyond these research and screening tools, the clinical assessment of symptom and illness meanings and attributions follows standard cognitive therapy strategies developed for work with anxiety and depressive disorders (Salkovskis, 1989; Sharpe, Peveler, & Mayou, 1992; Warwick, 1995). Assessment involves eliciting automatic thoughts and images, exploring cognitive and behavioral coping strategies and testing alternative thoughts and behaviors. This type of assessment typically is woven into ongoing treatment.

The Social Context of Illness

Assessment of the social context of illness should be a routine part of the assessment of all individual psychopathology. In addition to recent life events, chronic stressors, and social supports, couple and family interviews may reveal crucial interactions that aggravate or maintain symptoms—or uncover important resources to aid the clinician in devising treatment strategies (Griffith & Griffith, 1994; McDaniel et al., 1989; Rolland, 1987). DSM-IV provides an outline for a cultural formulation in Appendix I that should be part of the assessment of all patients with somatoform disorders. When there is significant cultural distance between patient and clinician, other family and community members, culture brokers, and anthropologists can be consulted to explore the local meanings of the symptoms and appropriate treatment approaches.

GENDER AND CULTURAL ISSUES

As discussed earlier in this chapter, somatization disorder is 10 times more common among women than men in the general population of North America. Similarly, the most common forms of undifferentiated somatoform disorder (e.g., the functional somatic syndromes of fibromyalgia, irritable bowel, and chronic fatigue) are diagnosed from two to nine times more frequently among women than men (Toner, 1995). In contrast, hypochondriasis is equally represented across the genders and somatized presentations of depression and anxiety may actually be proportionately more common among men (Kirmayer & Robbins, 1991b).

Potential explanations for these gender differences in prevalence include (Toner, 1995; Wool & Barsky, 1994): 1. a higher prevalence of related psychiatric disorders among women (i.e., mood and anxiety disorders), which secondarily give rise to somatoform disorders; 2. differences in illness behavior and help-seeking; 3. differential exposure to sexual and physical abuse; 4. social stresses and psychological conflicts associated with gender roles; 5. hormonal or other physiological differences; and 6. gender bias in the diagnostic process.

1. The prevalence of major depression (Nolen-Hoeksma, 1995) and several anxiety disorders (Yonkers & Gurguis, 1995) is higher among women than men. As noted above, patients with somatoform disorders often have underlying mood or anxiety disorders that may account, in part, for their symptoms. A higher prevalence of these disorders among women could give rise to part of the gender difference in prevalence of somatoform disorders. However, many patients with somatoform disorders do not have identifiable mood or anxiety disorders. Further, the gender difference in somatoform disorders is much greater than that for mood or anxiety, which suggests that other factors must be involved.

2. Women may have a greater tendency to focus on their bodies and, hence, notice and report more symptoms (Pennebaker & Watson, 1991). In addition, women may be more likely to seek help because they are more willing than men to admit distress and acknowledge the need for assistance (Verbrugge, 1985). In some circumstances, women may be more able to seek help because they are less constrained than men by full-time employment. More commonly, however, women face considerable barriers to help-seeking due to heavy work and family responsibilities. Indeed, Ginsburg and Brown (1982) found that many women with postpartum depression presented their babies to the pediatrician for minor somatic complaints in a sort of "somatization-by-proxy" both because they could not justify taking time for themselves to seek help and because other around them normalized their seriously depressed mood as ordinary "baby-blues."

3. A number of recent studies have demonstrated high prevalences of sexual or physical abuse among women with somatoform disorders including irritable

bowel and other functional gastrointestinal disorders as well as chronic pelvic pain (Walker et al., 1988; Walker, Gelfand, Gelfand & Katon, 1995). Women are generally more likely than men to experience sexual and physical abuse, and although somatization is only one possible outcome (Walker et al., 1992), this could account for some of the differential prevalence. Childhood and domestic violence are common contributors to a wide range of somatic and psychological forms of distress.

4. Gender roles may subject women to increased social stressors causing elevated levels of both emotional and somatic distress (Verbrugge, 1985). Women may face narrow standards and rigid expectations for physical attractiveness and reproductive fitness that may make them preoccupied with their bodies and prone to somatoform disorders (Cash & Pruzinsky, 1990).

5. Physiological differences between men and women may result in differential rates and patterns of functional somatic symptoms. Female sex hormones have effects on smooth muscle throughout the gut and other organ systems and may contribute directly to a higher prevalence of irritable bowel syndrome among women (Talley, 1991). The menstrual cycle itself may be associated with a wide range of somatic symptoms and with the intensification of preexisting functional somatic syndromes to a level that prompts help-seeking and clinical attention (Whitehead et al., 1986).

6. Finally, there may be gender bias in the diagnostic process itself, whereby clinicians are more likely to attribute symptoms to psychosocial causes for women than for men (Kirmayer, 1988). Such a gender bias has been found for the diagnosis of histrionic personality (Chodoff, 1982; Fernbach, Winstead, & Derlega, 1989; Warner, 1978; Winstead, 1984), although the diagnostic criteria themselves are not obviously gender biased, at least when applied by a standardized diagnostic interview (Nestadt et al., 1990). To the extent that women are more forthcoming about psychosocial problems and emotions in the clinician-patient interaction, clinicians may be more likely to view women as emotionally distressed or histrionic. Women may be more likely, then, to have their medically unexplained or functional symptoms explicitly labeled as a somatoform disorder (Slavney, Teitelbaum, & Chase, 1985).

Although somatoform disorders are common worldwide, they show great variation in form and prevalence across geographical regions and ethnocultural groups (Kirmayer, 1984a, 1984b). Indeed, the gender ratio itself differs markedly across cultures, giving some evidence of the importance of sociocultural factors in shaping illness experience. A review of cultural aspects of the somatoform disorders for DSM-IV identified three major issues for existing nosology: 1. the overlap between somatoform, affective, and anxiety disorders; 2. cultural variations in symptomatology; and 3. the use of somatic symptoms as idioms of distress (Kirmayer & Weiss, 1996).

Most basically, cross-cultural work challenges the separation of affective, anxiety, dissociative, and somatic categories in the DSM. The requirement that patients with somatoform disorders not have another disorder that explains their symptoms seems overly restrictive since somatic symptoms may be such a prominent part of depressive and anxiety disorders. Further, syndromes resembling depression or anxiety but without prominent mood symptoms are common. Neurasthenia may represent an example of this overlap that is not well captured by existing nosology (Ware & Weiss, 1994).

A wealth of clinical observations and anthropological field work demonstrates that there are many culture-specific symptoms. For example, feelings of heat in the head or body are common in equatorial regions, as are peppery feelings and the sensations of "worms crawling in the head." In South Asia, men may complain of losing semen in their urine. There have been several attempts to develop expanded symptom inventories with items tapping culture-specific somatic symptoms but these have not been widely used (Ebigbo, 1982; Mumford et al., 1991). Some of the symptoms that appear culture-specific may, in fact, occur in other places but lack salience in terms of local illness categories and so are rarely noticed or reported.

The preferential use of a bodily idiom to express suffering has been linked to cognitive factors in symptom expression, as well as to social, familial, and cultural responses to distress (Angel & Thoits, 1987; Kirmayer, 1986; Kleinman, 1986). In Appendix I, DSM-IV lists a variety of cultural idioms of distress with prominent somatic symptoms, including *ataques de nervios, bilis* or *colera, brain fag, dhat, falling out* or *blacking out, hwa-byung, koro, nervios, shenjing shuairuo,* and *shenkui.* Many of these terms refer to illness causes or explanations rather than to discrete syndromes. They direct attention to the links between social circumstances and somatic distress. They are tied to ethnophysiological notions about how the body works and to local ways of talking about everyday problems. Worldwide, sociosomatics is a more common mode of illness experience and explanation than psychosomatics—that is, people see the connections between untoward social situations and bodily distress and put more emphasis on this than on an individual's psychological characteristics. Within a somatic idiom of distress, bodily symptoms may serve to communicate one's plight to others.

Anthropological research suggests several potential ways in which symptoms may have meaning (Table 11.4). Symptoms may be direct indices of underlying disease or physiological disturbance, occurring as one manifestation of abnormalities in structure or process. To the extent that this meaning is available to the patient, it may play a role in exacerbating illness worry and somatic distress.

Symptoms may also be indices of underlying psychopathology, as when, for example, conversion symptoms are taken to indicate dissociative pathology. The classical psychoanalytic interpretation of somatic symptoms understood them

TABLE 11.4   Levels of Potential Meaning of Somatic Symptoms

1. Index of disease or physiological disorder
2. Index of psychopathology
3. Symbolic representation of psychological conflict
4. Representation of illness model
5. Metaphor for experience
6. Cultural idiom of distress
7. Act of positioning in a local world
8. Form of social commentary or protest

Note. Adapted from Kirmayer, Dao, and Smith, in press.

as symbolic expressions of underlying (unconscious) conflicts which they either represented through analogy or displacement. More recent clinical experience suggests that symptoms more often are related to available illness models in the individual's local world (Slavney, 1990).

Somatic symptoms may also have meaning as metaphors for other domains of experience. These may be idiosyncratic to the individual or drawn from common cultural idioms. This communicative meaning of symptoms may be conscious and explicit or hidden and implicit to patients and their entourage.

Finally, symptoms may function as moves in a local system of power, serving to position the individual and providing more or less explicit social commentary, criticism, or protest. For example, in many families, a woman who suffers persistent physical complaints may be able to command more resources for help and gain more control over her time and activities than one who tries to criticize her spouse directly.

These meanings are not intrinsic to somatic symptoms but arise from how they are used by patients, their families, and others. In fact, the epistemological limitations of the clinical situation are such that the meaning of symptoms remains largely indeterminate (Kirmayer, 1994). The interpretation of a symptom as having symbolic meaning or as a rhetorical strategy on the part of a patient should always be made because it will be helpful to the patient rather than simply because it gives the clinician a satisfying feeling of closure or the license to blame the patients for the limitations of current therapeutics.

SUMMARY AND CONCLUSION

The DSM-IV category of somatoform disorder implies that persistent complaints of somatic distress in the absence of a medical explanation represents a distinctive form of psychopathology. Somatic symptoms, however, can arise from a wide range of physiological perturbations, as well as being a normal concomitant of emotional distress. Milder forms of somatoform disorders then do not represent a distinctive type of psychopathology. More severe forms (e.g., somatization disorder) may reflect the generalized effects of intense emotional distress, as well as other psychological and social factors that contribute to chronicity and disability.

While the DSM-IV somatoform disorder diagnoses have utility for research purposes, they may be misleading in clinical contexts: they reify patterns of illness behavior that cut across other psychiatric disorders as discrete conditions; they situate interactional problems inside the person and so promote biological and psychological reductionism; they ignore the social context of suffering and so point away from exactly those social contingencies that explain the onset of symptoms and that hold clues to their alleviation.

An approach in terms of dimensions of illness cognition and behavior may be more fruitful in terms of assessing the psychological factors that contribute to somatic distress and help-seeking. In this view, there are three basic forms of somatization: 1. functional somatic symptoms, which arise from a wide range of different physiological and psychological mechanisms, including autonomic dysregulation, hyperventilation, cognitive-attentional amplification, and dissociation (this category includes undifferentiated somatoform disorder and conversion disorder); 2. hypochondriacal illness worry, which has similar roots to other anxiety disorders including panic and generalized anxiety disorder with pathologizing attributions and catastrophizing cognitions that specifically invoke the threat of disease or deformity (dysmorphophobia also fits this model); and 3. somatic presentations of depression, anxiety, and other psychiatric disorders or psychosocial distress, which reflect patients' efforts to avoid the stigma of psychiatric illness and present the doctor with an appropriate somatic complaint.

A broader social focus on family, work, disability, and health care systems may provide explanations for persistent distress and functional impairment that appear inexplicable at purely physiological or even psychological levels. From this perspective, symptoms have potential meanings that may be taken up by patients, their families, and others in ways that either reinforce illness or serve to further invalidate the afflicted person. To the extent that patients must struggle to prove the reality of their suffering to skeptical physicians and incredulous family and friends, they may be forced into a rigid position that exacerbates their illness. For this reason, we have emphasized the importance of understanding the physical and social roots of somatic distress as an entree into the lifeworld of the patient.

REFERENCES

Abbey, S. E., & Garfinkel, P. E. (1991). Neurasthenia and chronic fatigue syndrome: The role of culture in the making of a diagnosis. *American Journal of Psychiatry, 148,* 1638–1646.

Ahles, T. A., Yunus, M. B., & Masi, A. T. (1987). Is chronic pain a variant of depressive disease? The case of primary fibromyalgia syndrome. *Pain, 29,* 105–111.

Alper, K., Devinsky, O., Perrine, K., Vazquez, B., & Luciano, D. (1993). Nonepileptic seizures and childhood sexual and physical abuse. *Neurology, 43*(10), 1950–1953.

American Psychiatric Association. (1980). *Diagnostic and statistical manual of mental disorders* (3rd ed.). Washington, DC: Author.

American Psychiatric Association. (1987). *Diagnostic and statistical manual of mental disorders* (3rd ed., rev. ed.). Washington, DC: Author.

American Psychiatric Association. (1994). *Diagnostic and statistical manual of mental disorders* (4th ed.). Washington, DC: Author.

Angel, R., & Thoits, P. (1987). The impact of culture on the cognitive structure of illness. *Culture, Medicine, and Psychiatry, 11,* 465–494.

Arkes, H. R., & Harkness, A. R. (1980). Effect of making a diagnosis on subsequent recognition of symptoms. *Journal of Experimental Psychology, 6,* 568–575.

Axelrod, S., Noonan, M., & Atanacio, B. (1980). On the laterality of psychogenic somatic symptoms. *Journal of Nervous and Mental Disease, 168*(9), 517–528.

Bach, M., & Bach, D. (1995). Predictive value of alexithymia: A prospective study in somatizing patients. *Psychotherapy and Psychosomatics, 64*(1), 43–48.

Barsky, A. J. (1992). Amplification, somatization, and the somatoform disorders. *Psychosomatics, 33*(1), 28–34.

Barsky, A. J. (1996). Hypochondriasis: Medical management and psychiatric treatment. *Psychosomatics, 37*(1), 48–56.

Barsky, A. J., Cleary, P. D., & Klerman, G. L. (1992). Determinants of perceived health status of medical outpatients. *Social Science and Medicine, 10,* 1147–1154.

Barsky, A. J., Cleary, P. D., Sarnie, M. K., & Klerman, G. L. (1993). The course of transient hypochondriasis. *American Journal of Psychiatry, 150*(3), 484–488.

Barsky, A. J., Cleary, P. D., Wyshak, G., Spitzer, R. L., Williams, J. B. W., & Klerman, G. L. (1992). A structured diagnostic interview for hypochondriasis: A proposed criterion standard. *Journal of Nervous and Mental Disease, 180*(1), 20–27.

Barsky, A. J., Geringer, E., & Wool, C. A. (1988). A cognitive-educational treatment for hypochondriasis. *General Hospital Psychiatry, 10,* 322–327.

Barsky, A., Goodson, J. D., Lane, R. S., & Cleary, P. D. (1988). The amplification of somatic symptoms. *Psychosomatic Medicine, 50,* 510–519.

Barsky, A. J., & Klerman, G. L. (1983). Overview: Hypochondriasis, bodily complaints, and somatic styles. *American Journal of Psychiatry, 140*(3), 273–283.

Barsky, A. J., Wyshak, G., & Klerman, G. L. (1990a). The Somatosensory Amplification Scale and its relationship to hypochondriasis. *Journal of Psychiatry Research, 24*(4), 323–334.

Barsky, A. J., Wyshak, G., & Klerman, G. L. (1990b). Transient hypochondriasis. *Archives of General Psychiatry, 47*(8), 746–753.

Barsky, A. J., Wyshak, G., & Klerman, G. L. (1992). Psychiatric comorbidity in DSM-III-R hypochondriasis. *Archives of General Psychiatry, 49,* 101–108.

Barsky, A. J., Wyshak, G., Klerman, G. L., & Latham, K. S. (1990). The prevalence of hypochondriasis in medical outpatients. *Social Psychiatry and Psychiatric Epidemiology, 25,* 89–94.

Bass, C. (1992). Chest pain and breathlessness: Relationship to psychiatric illness. *American Journal of Medicine, 92*(Suppl. 1A), 12–15.

Bass, C., & Benjamin, S. (1993). The management of chronic somatisation. *British Journal of Psychiatry, 162,* 472–480.

Bass, C. M., & Murphy, M. R. (1990). Somatization disorder: Critique of the concept and suggestions for further research. In C. M. Bass & R. H. Cawley (Eds.), *Somatization: Physical symptoms and psychological illness* (pp. 301–332). Oxford: Blackwell.

Beitman, B. D., Mukerji, V., Flaker, G., & Basha, I. M. (1988). Panic disorder, cardiology patients, and atypical chest pain. *Psychiatric Clinics of North America, 11*(2), 387–397.

Benjamin, S., & Eminson, D. M. (1992). Abnormal illness behaviour: Childhood experiences and long-term consequences. *International Review of Psychiatry, 4,* 55–70.

Bennett, R. M. (1981). Fibrositis: Misnomer for a common rheumatic disorder. *Western Journal of Medicine, 134,* 405–413.

Blakely, A. A., Howard, R. C., Sosich, R. M., Murdoch, J. C., Menkes, D. B., & Spears, G. F. (1991). Psychiatric symptoms, personality, and ways of coping in chronic fatigue syndrome. *Psychological Medicine, 21*(2), 347–62.

Blanchard, E. B. (1992). Psychological treatment of benign headache disorders. *Journal of Consulting and Clinical Psychology, 60*(4), 537–551.

Bliss, E. L. (1984). Hysteria and hypnosis. *Journal of Nervous and Mental Disease, 172*(4), 203–206.

Block, A. R., Kremer, E. F., & Gaylor, M. (1980). Behavioral treatment of chronic pain: the spouse as a discriminative cue for pain behavior. *Pain, 9,* 243–252.

Blumer, D., & Heilbronn, M. (1982). Chronic pain as a variant of depressive disease: The pain-prone disorder. *Journal of Nervous and Mental Disease, 170*(7), 381–406.

Blumer, D., & Heilbronn, M. (1984). Chronic pain as a variant of depressive disease: a rejoinder. *Journal of Nervous and Mental Disease, 172*(7), 405–407.

Bohman, M., Cloninger, C. R., von Knorring, A.-L., & Sigvardsson, S. (1984). An adoption study of somatoform disorders: III. Cross-fostering analysis and genetic relationship to alcoholism and criminality. *Archives of General Psychiatry, 41,* 863–871.

Bonanno, G. A., & Singer, J. L. (1990). Repressive personality style: Theoretical and methodological implications for health and pathology. In J. L. Singer (Ed.), *Repression and dissociation: Implications for personality theory, psychopathology, and health* (pp. 435–470). Chicago: University of Chicago Press.

Bradley, L. A., McDonald Haule, J., & Jaworski, T. M. (1992). Assessment of psychological status using interviews and self-report instruments. In D. C. Turk & R. Melzack (Eds.), *Handbook of pain assessment.* London: Guilford.

Bradley, L. A., Prokop, C. K., Gentry, W. D., Van der Heide, L. H., & Prieto, E. J. (1981). Assessment of chronic pain. In C. K. Prokop & L. A. Bradley (Eds.), *Medical psychology: Contributions to behavioral medicine* (pp. 91–117). New York: Academic Press.

Brawman-Mintzer, O., Lydiard, R. B., Phillips, K. A., Morton, A., Czepowicz, V., Emmanuel, N., Villareal, G., Johnson, M., & Ballenger, J. C. (1995). Body dysmorphic disorder in patients with anxiety disorders and major depression: A comorbidity study. *American Journal of Psychiatry, 152*(11), 1665–7.

Bridges, K., Goldberg, D., Evams, B., & Sharpe, T. (1991). Determinants of somatization in primary care. *Psychological Medicine, 21,* 473–483.

Brown, G. K. (1990). A causal analysis of chronic pain and depression. *Journal of Abnormal Psychology, 99*(2), 127–137.

Campo, J. V., & Fritsch, S. L. (1994). Somatization in children and adolescents. *Journal of the American Academy of Child and Adolescent Psychiatry, 33*(9), 1223–1235.

Cash, T. F., & Pruzinsky, T. (Eds.). (1990). *Body images: Development, deviance, and change.* New York: Guilford.

Chapman, S. L., & Pemberton, J. S. (1994). Prediction of treatment outcome from clinically derived MMPI clusters in rehabilitation for chronic low back pain. *Clinical Journal of Pain, 10*(4), 267–76.

Chodoff, P. (1982). Hysteria and women. *American Journal of Psychiatry, 139,* 545–551.

Cioffi, D. (1991). Beyond attentional strategies: A cognitive-perceptual model of somatic interpretation. *Psychological Bulletin, 109*(1), 25–41.

Cloninger, C. R. (1987). Diagnosis of somatoform disorders: A critique of DSM-III. In G. L. Tischler (Ed.), *Diagnosis and classification in psychiatry: A critical appraisal of DSM-III.* New York: Cambridge University Press.

Cloninger, C. R., Martin, R. L., Guze, S. B., & Clayton, P. J. (1986). A prospective follow-up and family study of somatization in men and women. *American Journal of Psychiatry, 143*(7), 873–878.

Cloninger, C. R., Sigvardsson, S., von Knorring, A.-L., & Bohman, M. (1984). An adoption study of somatoform disorders: II. Identification of two discrete somatoform disorders. *Archives of General Psychiatry, 41,* 863–871.

Cohen, K., Auld, F., & Brooker, H. (1994). Is alexithymia related to psychosomatic disorder and somatizing? *Journal of Psychosomatic Research, 38*(2), 119–127.

Colgan, S., Creed, F., & Klass, H. (1988). Symptom complaints, psychiatric disorder and abnormal illness behaviour in patients with upper abdominal pain. *Psychological Medicine, 18,* 887–892.

Cope, H., David, A., Pelosi, A., & Mann, A. (1994). Predictors of chronic "postviral" fatigue. *Lancet, 344,* 864–868.

Cope, H., Pernet, A., Kendall, B., & David, A. (1995). Cognitive functioning and magnetic resonance imaging in chronic fatigue. *British Journal of Psychiatry, 167,* 86–94.

Coryell, W., & Norten, S. (1981). Briquet's syndrome (somatization disorder) and primary depression: Comparison of background and outcome. *Comprehensive Psychiatry, 22*(3), 249–255.

Couprie, W., Wijdicks, E. F., Rooijmans, H. G., & van Gijn, J. (1995). Outcome in conversion disorder: A follow-up study. *Journal of Neurology, Neurosurgery, and Psychiatry, 58*(6), 750–752.

Craig, T. K. J., Drake, H., Mills, K., & Boardman, A. P. (1994). The South London Somatisation Study: II. Influence of stressful life events, and secondary gain. *British Journal of Psychiatry, 165,* 248–258.

Creed, F., & Guthrie, E. (1993). Techniques for interviewing the somatising patient. *British Journal of Psychiatry, 162,* 467–471.

DeGood, D. E., & Shutty, M. S. J. (1992). Assessment of pain beliefs, coping, and self-efficacy. In D. C. Turk & R. Melzack (Eds.), *Handbook of pain assessment.* New York: Guilford.

DeLuca, J., Johnson, S. K., Beldowicz, D., & Natelson, B. H. (1995). Neuropsychological impairments in chronic fatigue syndrome, multiple sclerosis, and depression. *Journal of Neurology, Neurosurgery, and Psychiatry, 58*(1), 38–43.

Deyo, R. A., & Diehl, A. K. (1988). Psychosocial predictors of disability in patients with low back pain. *Journal of Rheumatology, 15,* 1557–1564.

Dworkin, R. H., Hartstein, G., Rosner, H. L., Walther, R. R., Sweeney, E. W., & Brand, L., (1992). A high-risk method for studying psychosocial antecedents of chronic pain: The prospective investigation of herpes zoster. *Journal of Abnormal Psychology, 101*(1), 200–205.

Dworkin, S. F., Von Korff, M., & LeResche, L. (1990). Multiple pains and psychiatric disturbance: An epidemiologic investigation. *Archives of General Psychiatry, 47,* 239–244.

Ebigbo, P. O. (1982). Development of a culture specific (Nigeria) screening scale of somatic complaints indicating psychiatric disturbance. *Culture, Medicine and Psychiatry, 6,* 29–43.

Eifert, G. (1991). Cardiophobia: A paradigmatic behavioural model of heart-focused anxiety and nonanginal chest pain. *Behaviour Research and Therapy, 30*(4), 329–345.

Engel, G. E. (1959). "Psychogenic" pain and the pain-prone patient. *American Journal of Medicine, 26,* 899–918.

Escobar, J. L., Rubio-Stipec, M., Canino, G., & Karno, M. (1989). Somatic Symptom Index (SSI): A new and abridged somatization construct. *Journal of Nervous and Mental Disease, 177*(3), 140–146.

Fava, G. A., & Grandi, S. (1991). Differential diagnosis of hypochondriacal fears and beliefs. *Psychotherapy and Psychosomatics, 55*(2-4), 114–119.

Fernbach, B. E., Winstead, B. A., & Derlega, V. J. (1989). Sex differences in diagnosis and treatment recommendations for antisocial personality and somatization disorders. *Journal of Social and Clinical Psychology, 8*(3), 238–255.

Fishbain, D. A., & Goldberg, M. (1991). The misdiagnosis of conversion disorder in a psychiatric emergency service. *General Hospital Psychiatry, 13*(3), 177–181.

Fitts, S. N., Gibson, P., Redding, C. A., & Deister, P. J. (1989). Body dysmorphic disorder: Implications for its validity as a DSM-III-R disorder. *Psychological Reports, 64,* 655–658.

Fochtmann, L. J. (1995). Intractable sneezing as a conversion symptom. *Psychosomatics, 36*(2), 103–12.

Folks, D. G., Ford, C. V., & Regan, W. M. (1984). Conversion symptoms in a general hospital. *Psychosomatics, 25*(4).

Ford, C. V., & Folks, D. G. (1985). Conversion disorders: An overview. *Psychosomatics, 26*(5), 371–383.

Ginsburg, S., & Brown, G. W. (1982). No time for depression: A study of help-seeking among mothers of preschool children. In D. Mechanic (Ed.), *Symptoms, illness behavior, and help-seeking* (pp. 87–114). New York: Neale Watson.

Goldberg, D., Gask, L., & O'Dowd, T. (1989). The treatment of somatization: Teaching techniques of reattribution. *Journal of Psychosomatic Research, 33*(6), 689–695.

Göthe, C.-J., Molin, C., & Nilsson, C. G. (1995). The environmental somatization syndrome. *Psychosomatics, 36*(1), 1–11.

Griffith, J. L., & Griffith, M. E. (1994). *The body speaks: Therapeutic dialogues for mind-body problems.* New York: Basic Books.

Guze, S. B., Woodruff, R. A., & Clayton, P. J. (1971). A study of conversion symptoms in psychiatric outpatients. *American Journal of Psychiatry, 128*(5), 643–646.

Hafeiz, H. B. (1980). Hysterical conversion: A prognostic study. *British Journal of Psychiatry, 136,* 548–551.

Hall, W., & Morrow, L. (1988). "Repetition Strain Injury": An Australian Epidemic of Upper Limb Pain. *Social Science and Medicine, 27*(6), 645–649.

Hansell, S., & Mechanic, D. (1986). The socialization of introspection and illness behavior. In S. McHugh & T. M. Vallis (Eds.), *Illness behavior* (pp. 253–260). New York: Plenum.

Hathaway, S. R., & McKinley, J. C. (1989). *Minnesota Multiphasic Personality Inventory-2: Manual for administration.* Minneapolis: University of Minnesota Press.

Hendryx, M. S., Haviland, M. G., Gibbons, R. D., & Clark, D. C. (1992). An application of item response theory to alexithymia assessment among abstinent alcoholics. *Journal of Personality Assessment, 58*(3), 506–515.

Hendryx, M. S., Haviland, M. G., & Shaw, D. G. (1991). Dimensions of alexithymia and their relationships to anxiety and depression. *Journal of Personality Assessment, 56*(2), 227–237.

Hitchcock, P. B., & Mathews, A. (1992). Interpretation of bodily symptoms in hypochondriasis. *Behaviour Research and Therapy, 30*(3), 223–234.

Hollander, E., Neville, D., Frenkel, M., Josephson, S., & Liebowitz, M. R. (1992). Body dysmorphic disorder: Diagnostic issues and related disorders. *Psychosomatics, 33*(2), 156–165.

Hudson, J. I., Goldenberg, D. L., Pope, H. G., Jr., Keck, P. E., Jr., & Schlesinger, L. (1992). Comorbidity of fibromyalgia with medical and psychiatric disorders. *American Journal of Medicine, 92,* 363–367.

Hyler, S. E., & Spitzer, R. L. (1978). Hysteria split asunder. *American Journal of Psychiatry, 135*(12), 1500–1503.

Janca, A., Isaac, M., Bennett, L. A., & Tacchini, G. (1995). Somatoform disorders in different cultures: A mail questionnaire survey. *Social Psychiatry and Psychiatric Epidemiology, 30,* 44–48.

Jefferson, J. W., & Marshall, J. R. (1981). *Neuropsychiatric Features of Medical Disorders.* New York: Plenum.

Kapoor, W. N., Fortunato, M., Hanusa, B. H., & Schulberg, H. C. (1995). Psychiatric illnesses in patients with syncope. *American Journal of Medicine, 99*(5), 505–512.

Karoly, P., & Lecci, L. (1993). Hypochondriasis and somatization in college women: A personal projects analysis. *Health Psychology, 12*(2), 103–109.

Katon, W. J., Ries, R. K., Bokan, J. A., & Kleinman, A. (1980). Hyperemesis gravidarum: A biopsychosocial perspective. *International Journal of Psychiatry in Medicine, 10*(2), 151–162.

Kauhanen, J., Kaplan, G. A., Julkunen, J., Wilson, T. W., & Salonen, J. T. (1993). Social factors in alexithymia. *Comprehensive Psychiatry, 34*(5), 330–335.

Kellner, R. (1992). The case for reassurance. *International Review of Psychiatry, 4,* 71–80.

Kellner, R., Abbott, P., Winslow, W. W., & Pathak, D. (1987). Fears, beliefs, and attitudes in DSM-III hypochondriasis. *Journal of Nervous and Mental Disease, 175*(1), 20–25.

Kent, D. A., Tomasson, K., & Coryell, W. (1995). Course and outcome of conversion and somatization disorders. *Psychosomatics, 36,* 138–144.

Kenyon, F. E. (1976). Hypochondriacal states. *British Journal of Psychiatry, 129,* 1–14.

Kihlstrom, J. F. (1992). Dissociation and conversion disorders. In D. J. Stein, J. Young, & F. L. Orlando (Eds.), *Cognitive science and clinical disorders* (pp. 247–270). New York: Academic Press.

Kim, C. H., Hsu, J. J., Williams, D. E., Weaver, A. L., & Zinsmeister, A. R. (1996). A prospective psychological evaluation of patients with dysphagia of various etiologies. *Dysphagia, 11*(1), 34–40.

Kirkwood, C. R., Clure, H. R., Brodsky, R., Gould, G. H., Knaak, R., Metcalf, M., & Romeo, S. (1982). The diagnostic content of family practice: 50 most common diagnoses recorded in the WAMI community practices. *Journal of Family Practice, 15*(3), 485–492.

Kirmayer, L. J. (1984a). Culture, affect, and somatization. Part 1. *Transcultural Psychiatric Research Review, 21*(3), 159–188.

Kirmayer, L. J. (1984b). Culture, affect, and somatization. Part 2. *Transcultural Psychiatric Research Review, 21*(4), 237–262.

Kirmayer, L. J. (1986). Somatization and the social construction of illness experience. In S. McHugh & T. M. Vallis (Eds.), *Illness behavior: A multidisciplinary perspective* (pp. 111–133). New York: Plenum.

Kirmayer, L. J. (1987). Languages of suffering and healing: Alexithymia as a social and cultural process. *Transcultural Psychiatric Research Review, 24,* 119–136.

Kirmayer, L. J. (1988). Mind and body as metaphors: Hidden values in biomedicine. In M. Lock & D. Gordon (Eds.), *Biomedicine examined* (pp. 57–92). Dordrecht: Kluwer.

Kirmayer, L. J. (1994). Improvisation and authority in illness meaning. *Culture, Medicine, and Psychiatry, 18*(2), 183–214.

Kirmayer, L. J., Dao, T. H. T., & Smith, A. (in press). Somatization and psychologization: Understanding cultural idioms of distress. In S. Okpaku (Ed.), *Clinical methods in transcultural psychiatry.* Washington, DC: American Psychiatric Press.

Kirmayer, L. J., & Robbins, J. M. (1991a). Functional somatic syndromes. In L. J. Kirmayer & J. M. Robbins (Eds.), *Current concepts of somatization: Research and clinical perspectives* (pp. 79–106). Washington, DC: American Psychiatric Press.

Kirmayer, L. J., & Robbins, J. M. (1991b). Three forms of somatization in primary care: Prevalence, co-occurrence and sociodemographic characteristics. *Journal of Nervous and Mental Disease, 179*(11), 647–655.

Kirmayer, L. J., & Robbins, J. M. (1993). Cognitive and social correlates of the Toronto Alexithymia Scale. *Psychosomatics, 34*(1), 41–52.

Kirmayer, L. J., & Robbins, J. M. (1996). Patients who somatize in primary care: A longitudinal study. *Psychological Medicine, 26,* 937–951.

Kirmayer, L. J., Robbins, J. M., Dworkind, M., & Yaffe, M. (1993). Somatization and the recognition of depression and anxiety in primary care. *American Journal of Psychiatry, 150*(5), 734–741.

Kirmayer, L. J., Robbins, J. M., & Paris, J. (1994). Somatoform disorders: Personality and the social matrix of somatic distress. *Journal of Abnormal Psychology, 103*(1), 125–136.

Kirmayer, L. J., Robbins, J. M., Taillefer, S., & Helzer, J. (1995). *Development of a structured diagnostic interview for functional somatic syndromes* (Working Paper No. 5). Sir Mortimer B. Davis–Jewish General Hospital, Montréal, Department of Psychiatry, Culture and Mental Health Research Unit.

Kirmayer, L. J., & Weiss, M. G. (1996). Cultural considerations on somatoform disorders. In T. A. Widiger, A. J. Frances, H. A. Pincus, R. Ross, M. B. First, & W. W. Davis (Eds.), *DSM-IV sourcebook* (Vol. 3). Washington, DC: American Psychiatric Press.

Kleinman, A. (1980). *Patients and healers in the context of culture.* Berkeley: University of California Press.

Kleinman, A. (1986). *Social Origins of Distress and Disease.* New Haven, CT: Yale University Press.

Kleinman, A., Brodwin, P. E., Good, B. J., & Good, M. J. D. (1992). Pain as a human experience: An introduction. In M. J. D. Good, P. E. Brodwin, B. J. Good, & A. Kleinman (Eds.), *Pain as human experience: Anthropological perspectives.* Berkeley: University of California Press.

Krupp, L. B., Sliwinski, M., Masur, D. M., Friedberg, F., & Coyle, P. K. (1994). Cognitive functioning and depression in patients with chronic fatigue syndrome and multiple sclerosis. *Archives of Neurology, 51*(7), 705–10.

Kuczmierczyk, A., Labrum, A. H., & Johnson, C. C. (1995). The relationship between mood, somatization, and alexithymia in premenstrual syndrome. *Psychosomatics, 36,* 26–32.

Lacy, T. J., & McManis, S. E. (1994). Psychogenic stridor. *General Hospital Psychiatry, 16,* 213–223.

Lazare, A. (1981). Conversion symptoms. *New England Journal of Medicine, 305,* 745–748.

Lazarus, R., & Folkman, S. (1984). *Stress, appraisal, and coping.* New York: Springer.

Leff, J. (1988). *Psychiatry around the globe: A transcultural view.* London: Gaskell.

Lilienfeld, S. O. (1992). The association between antisocial personality and somatization disorders: A review and integration of theoretical models. *Clinical Psychology Review, 12,* 641–662.

Lishman, W. A. (1988). Physiogenesis and psychogenesis in the "postconcussional syndrome." *British Journal of Psychiatry, 153,* 460–469.

Magni, G., Caldieron, C., Rigatti-Luchini, S., & Merskey, H. (1990). Chronic musculoskeletal pain and depressive symptoms in the general population. An analysis of the first National Health and Nutrition Examination Survey data. *Pain, 43,* 299–307.

Magni, G., Marchetti, M., Moreschi, C., Merskey, H., & Rigatti Luchini, S. (1993). Chronic musculoskeletal pain and depressive symptoms in the National Health and Nutrition Examination: I. Epidemiologic follow-up study. *Pain, 53,* 163–168.

Magni, G., Moreschi, C., Rigatti Luchini, S., & Merskey, H. (1994). Prospective study on the relationship between depressive symptoms and chronic musculoskeletal pain. *Pain, 56,* 289–297.

Martin, R. L. (1996). Conversion disorder, proposed autonomic arousal disorder, and pseudocyesis. In T. A. Widiger, A. J. Frances, H. A. Pincus, R. Ross, M. B. First, & W. W. Davis (Eds.), *DSM-IV sourcebook* (Vol. 2, pp. 893–914). Washington, DC: American Psychiatric Press.

Mayou, R., Bass, C., & Sharpe, M. (1995). Overview of epidemiology, classification, and aetiology. In R. Mayou, C. Bass, & M. Sharpe (Eds.), *Treatment of functional somatic symptoms* (pp. 42–65). Oxford: Oxford University Press.

McCauley, J., Kern, D. E., Kolodner, K., Dill, L., Schroeder, A. F., Dechant, H. K., Ryden, J., Bass, E. B., & Derogatis, L. R. (1995). The battering syndrome: Prevalence and clinical characteristics of domestic violence in primary care internal medicine practices. *Annals of Internal Medicine, 123*(10), 737 ff.

McDaniel, S. H., Campbell, T., & Seaburn, D. (1989). Somatic fixation in patients and physicians: A biopsychosocial approach. *Family Systems Medicine, 7*(1), 5–16.

McDaniel, S. H., Hepworth, J., & Doherty, W. J. (1992). *Medical family therapy.* New York: Basic Books.

McDonald, E., Cope, H., & David, A. (1993). Cognitive impairment in patients with chronic fatigue: A preliminary study. *Journal of Neurology, Neurosurgery, and Psychiatry, 56*(7), 812–815.

McGrath, R. E., & O'Malley, W. B. (1986). The assessment of denial and physical complaints: The validity of the Hy Scale and associated MMPI signs. *Journal of Clinical Psychology, 42*(5), 754–760.

McKay, M., & Farrington, J. (1995). Vulvodynia: Chronic vulvar pain syndromes. In A. Stoudemire & B. S. Fogel (Eds.), *Medical-psychiatric practice* (Vol. 3, pp. 381–414). Washington, DC: American Psychiatric Press

Meana, M., & Binik, Y. M. (1994). Painful coitus: A review of female dyspareunia. *Journal of Nervous and Mental Disease, 182*(5), 264–272.

Mechanic, D. (1972). Social psychologic factors affecting the presentation of bodily complaints. *New England Journal of Medicine, 286*(21), 1133–1139.

Mechanic, D. (1979). Development of psychological distress among young adults. *Archives of General Psychiatry, 36,* 1233–1239.

Melzack, R. (1975). The McGill Pain Questionnaire: Major properties and scoring methods. *Pain, 1,* 277–299.

Melzack, R. (1980). Psychological aspects of pain. In J. J. Bonica (Ed.), *Pain.* New York: Raven.

Melzack, R., Rosberger, Z., Hollingsworth, M. L., & Thirlwell, M. (1985). New approaches to measuring nausea. *Canadian Medical Association Journal, 133,* 755–759.

Melzack, R., & Wall, P. D. (1983). *The challenge of pain.* New York: Basic Books.

Merskey, H. (1991). The definition of pain. *European Psychiatry, 6,* 153–159.

Merskey, H. (1993). The classification of fibromyalgia and myofascial pain. In H. Vaerøy & H. Merskey (Eds.), *Progress in fibromyalgia and myofascial pain* (pp. 191–194). New York: Elsevier.

Morrison, J. (1989). Childhood sexual histories of women with somatization disorder. *American Journal of Psychiatry, 146,* 239–241.

Mumford, D. B., Bavington, J. T., Bhatnagar, K. S., Hussain, Y., Mirza, S., & Naeaghi, M. M. (1991). The Bradford Somatic Inventory: A multiethnic inventory of somatic symptoms reported by anxious and depressed patients in Britain and the Indo-Pakistan subcontinent. *British Journal of Psychiatry, 158,* 379–386.

Nestadt, G., Romanoski, A. J., Chahal, R., Merchant, A., Folstein, M. F., Gruenberg, E. M., & McHugh, P. R. (1990). An epidemiological study of histrionic personality disorder. *Psychological Medicine, 20*(2), 413–422.

Nolen-Hoeksma, S. (1995). Epidemiology and theories of gender differences in unipolar depression. In. M. V. Seeman (Ed.), *Gender and psychopathology* (pp. 63–87). Washington, DC: American Psychiatric Press.

Noyes, R., Jr., Kathol, R. G., Fisher, M. M., Philips, B. M., Suelzer, M. T., & Holt, C. S. (1993). The validity of DSM-III-R hypochondriasis. *Archives of General Psychiatry, 50,* 961–970.

Noyes, R., Jr., Kathol, R. G., Fisher, M. M., Phillips, B. M., Suelzer, M. T., & Woodman, C. L. (1994). Psychiatric comorbidity among patients with hypochondriasis. *General Hospital Psychiatry, 16,* 78–87.

O'Connor, K. P., Hallam, R., Beyts, J., & Hinclife, R. (1988). Dizziness: Behavioural, subjective, and organic aspects. *Journal of Psychosomatic Research, 32*(3), 291–302.

Othmer, E., & DeSouza, C. (1985). A screening test for somatization disorder (hysteria). *American Journal of Psychiatry, 142*(10), 1146–1149.

Pennebaker, J. W. (1982). *The psychology of physical symptoms.* New York: Springer.

Pennebaker, J. W. (1985). Traumatic experience and psychosomatic disease: Exploring the roles of behavioral inhibition, obsession, and confiding. *Canadian Psychology, 26,* 82–95.

Pennebaker, J. W. (1990). *Opening up: The healing power of confiding in others.* New York: Morrow.

Pennebaker, J. W. (Ed.). (1995). *Emotion, disclosure, and health.* Washington, DC: American Psychological Association.

Pennebaker, J. W., & Watson, D. (1991). The psychology of somatic symptoms. In L. J. Kirmayer & J. M. Robbins (Eds.), *Current concepts of somatization.* Washington, DC: American Psychiatric Press.

Phillips, K. A. (1991). Body dysmorphic disorder: The distress of imagined ugliness. *American Journal of Psychiatry, 148,* 1138–1149.

Phillips, K. A., Kim, J. M., & Hudson, J. I. (1995). Body image disturbance in body dysmorphic disorder and eating disorders. Obsessions or delusions? *Psychiatric Clinics of North America, 18*(2), 317–334.

Phillips, K. A., McElroy, S. L., Keck, P. E., Pope, H. G., & Hudson, J. L. (1993). Body dysmorphic disorder: 30 cases of imagined ugliness. *American Journal of Psychiatry, 150,* 302–309.

Pilowsky, I. (1967). Dimensions of hypochondriasis. *British Journal of Psychiatry, 113,* 89–93.

Pilowsky, I. (1978). A general classification of abnormal illness behaviours. *British Journal of Medical Psychology, 51,* 131–137.

Pilowsky, I. (1990). The concept of abnormal illness behavior. *Psychosomatics, 31*(2), 207–213.

Pilowsky, I., Murrell, G. C., & Gordon, A. (1979). The development of a screening method for abnormal illness behaviour. *Journal of Psychosomatic Research, 23,* 203–207.

Pilowsky, I., & Spence, N. D. (1983). *Manual for the Illness Behaviour Questionnaire (IBQ).* Adelaide, South Australia: University of Adelaide.

Pilowsky, I., Spence, N., Cobb, J., & Katsikitis, M. (1984). The illness behavior questionnaire as an aid to clinical assessment. *General Hospital Psychiatry, 6,* 123–130.

Pincus, T., Callahan, L. F., Bradley, L. A., Vaughn, W. K., & Wolfe, F. (1986). Elevated MMPI scores for hypochondriasis, depression, and hysteria in patients with rheumatoid arthritis reflect disease rather than psychological status. *Arthritis and Rheumatism, 29*(12), 1456–1466.

Poole, G. D., & Craig, K. D. (1992). Judgments of genuine, suppressed, and faked facial expressions of pain. *Journal of Personality and Social Psychology, 63*(5), 797–805.

Pope, H. G., Jr., & Hudson, J. I. (1991). A supplemental interview for forms of "affective spectrum disorder." *International Journal of Psychiatry in Medicine, 21*(3), 205–232.

Powell, R., Dolan, R., & Wessely, S. (1990). Attributions and self-esteem in depression and chronic fatigue syndromes. *Journal of Psychosomatic Research, 34*(6), 665–673.

Pu, T., Mohamed, E., Iman, K., & El-Roey, A. (1986). One hundred cases of hysteria in Eastern Libya: A sociodemographic study. *British Journal of Psychiatry, 148,* 606–609.

Putnam, F. W., Guroff, J. J., Silberman, E. K., Barban, L., & Post, R. M. (1986). The clinical phenomenology of multiple personality disorder. *Journal of Clinical Psychiatry, 47*(6), 285.

Rada, R. T., Meyer, G. G., & Kellner, R. (1978). Visual conversion reaction in children and adults. *Journal of Nervous and Mental Disease, 166*(8), 580–587.

Ratliff, T. L., Klutke, C. G., & McDougall, E. M. (1994). The etiology of interstitial cystitis. *Urologic Clinics of North America, 21*(1), 21–30.

Rief, W., Hiller, W., Geissner, E., & Fichter, M. M. (1995). A two-year follow-up study of patients with somatoform disorders. *Psychosomatics, 36,* 376–386.

Robbins, J. M., & Kirmayer, L. J. (1986). Illness cognition, symptom reporting and somatization in primary care. In S. McHugh & T. M. Vallis (Eds.), *Illness behavior: A multidisciplinary model* (pp. 283–302). New York: Plenum.

Robbins, J. M., & Kirmayer, L. J. (1991a). Attributions of common somatic symptoms. *Psychological Medicine, 21,* 1029–1045.

Robbins, J. M., & Kirmayer, L. J. (1991b). Cognitive and social factors in somatization. In L. J. Kirmayer & J. M. Robbins (Eds.), *Current concepts of somatization: Research and clinical perspectives* (pp. 107–141). Washington, DC: American Psychiatric Press.

Robbins, J. M., & Kirmayer, L. J. (1996). Transient and persistent hypochondriacal worry in primary care. *Psychological Medicine, 26,* 575–589.

Robins, L. N. (1982). Validity of the Diagnostic Interview Schedule, Version II: DSM-III diagnoses. *Psychological Medicine, 12,* 855–870.

Robins, L. N., Helzer, J. E., & Orvaschel, H. (1985). The Diagnostic Interview Schedule. In W. W. Eaton & L. G. Kessler (Eds.), *Epidemiologic field methods in psychiatry* (pp. 143–170). Orlando, FL: Academic Press.

Robins, L. N., & Regier, D. (1991). *Psychiatric disorders in America: The Epidemiologic Catchment Area study.* New York: Free Press.

Robins, L. N., Wing, J., Wittchen, H.-U., Helzer, J. E., Babor, T. F., Burke, J., Farmer, A., Jablinsky, A., Pickens, R., Regier, D. A., Sartorius, N., & Towle, L. H. (1989). The Composite International Diagnostic Interview: An epidemiologic instrument suitable for use in conjunction with different diagnostic systems and in different cultures. *Archives of General Psychiatry, 45,* 1069–1077.

Rolland, J. S. (1987). Chronic illness and the life cycle: A conceptual framework. *Family Process, 26*(2), 203–222.

Romano, J. M., & Turner, J. A. (1985). Chronic pain and depression: Does the literature support a relationship? *Psychological Bulletin, 97,* 18–34.

Rosen, J. C., Reiter, J., & Orosan, P. (1995a). Assessment of body image in eating disorders with the body dysmorphic disorder examination. *Behaviour Research and Therapy, 33*(1), 77–84.

Rosen, J. C., Reiter, J., & Orosan, P. (1995b). Cognitive-behavioral body image therapy for body dysmorphic disorder. *Journal of Consulting and Clinical Psychology, 63*(2), 263–9; erratum, *63*(3), 437.

Rost, K., Kashner, T. M., & Smith, G. R., Jr. (1994). Effectiveness of psychiatric intervention with somatization disorder patients: Improved outcomes at reduced cost. *General Hospital Psychiatry, 16,* 381–387.

Sackeim, H. A., Nordlie, J. W., & Gur, R. C. (1979). A model of hysterical and hypnotic blindness: Cognition, motivation, and awareness. *Journal of Abnormal Psychology, 88*(5), 474–489.

Salkovskis, P. M. (1989). Somatic problems. In K. Hawton, P. M. Salkovskis, J. Kirk, & D. M. Clark (Eds.), *Cognitive behaviour therapy for psychiatric problems* (pp. 235–276). Oxford: Oxford University Press.

Savard, G. (1990). Convulsive pseudoseizures: A review of current concepts. *Behavioral Neurology, 3*(3), 133–141.

Schwartz, G. E. (1990). Psychobiology of repression and health: A systems approach. In J. L. Singer (Ed.), *Repression and dissociation: Implications for personality theory, psychopathology, and health* (pp. 405–434). Chicago: University of Chicago Press.

Sensky, T., MacLeod, A. K., & Rigby, M. F. (1996). Causal attributions about common somatic symptoms among frequent general practice attenders. *Psychological Medicine, 26*(3), 641–646.

Sharpe, M., & Bass, C. (1992). Pathophysiological mechanisms in somatization. *International Review of Psychiatry, 4,* 81–97.

Sharpe, M., Hawton, K., Simkin, S., Surawy, C., Hackmann, A., Klimes, I., Peto, T., Warrell, D., & Seagroatt, V. (1996). Cognitive behaviour therapy for the chronic fatigue syndrome: A randomised controlled trial. *British Medical Journal, 312,* 22–26.

Sharpe, M. J., Peveler, R., & Mayou, R. (1992). The psychological treatment of patients with functional somatic symptoms: A practical guide. *Journal of Psychosomatic Research, 36*(6), 515–529.

Shedler, J., Mayman, M., & Manis, M. (1993). The illusion of mental health. *American Psychologist, 48*(11), 1117–1131.

Shorter, E. (1994). *From the mind into the body: The cultural origins of psychosomatic symptoms.* New York: Free Press.

Sifneos, P. E. (1973). The prevalence of "alexithymic" characteristics in psychosomatic patients. *Psychotherapy and Psychosomatics, 22,* 255–262.

Sigvardsson, S., Bohman, M., von Knorring, A. L., & Cloninger, C. R. (1986). Symptom patterns and causes of somatization in men: I. Differentiation of two discrete disorders. *Genetic Epidemiology, 3*(3), 153–69.

Simeon, D., Hollander, E., Stein, D. J., Cohen, L., & Aronowitz B. (1995). Body dysmorphic disorder in the DSM-IV field trial for obsessive-compulsive disorder. *American Journal of Psychiatry, 152*(8), 1207–1209.

Simon, G. E., Katon, W. J., & Sparks, P. J. (1990). Allergic to life: Psychological factors in environmental illness. *American Journal of Psychiatry, 147*(7), 901–908.

Simon, G. E., & Von Korff, M. (1991). Somatization and psychiatric disorder in the NIMH Epidemiologic Catchment Area study. *American Journal of Psychiatry, 148*(11), 1494–1500.

Sinclair, D. S. (1988). Repetitive strain syndrome: An Australian experience. *Journal of Rheumatology, 15*(11), 1729–1730.

Slater, E. (1965). Diagnosis of "hysteria." *British Medical Journal, 279,* 1395–1399.

Slavney, P. R. (1990). *Perspectives on Hysteria.* Baltimore: Johns Hopkins University Press.

Slavney, P. R. (1994). Pseudoseizures, sexual abuse, and hermeneutic reasoning. *Comprehensive Psychiatry, 35*(6), 471–477.

Slavney, P. R., Teitelbaum, M. L., & Chase, G. A. (1985). Referral for medically unexplained somatic complaints: The role of histrionic traits. *Psychosomatics, 26*(2), 103–109.

Small, G. W. (1986). Pseudocyesis: An overview. *Canadian Journal of Psychiatry, 31,* 452–457.

Smets, E. M., Garssen, B., Bonke, B., & De Haes, J. C. (1995). The Multidimensional

Fatigue Inventory (MFI) psychometric qualities of an instrument to assess fatigue. *Journal of Psychosomatic Research, 39*(3), 315–25.

Smith, G., Monson, R., & Ray, D. (1986a). Psychiatric consultation in somatization disorder: A randomized controlled study. *New England Journal of Medicine, 314,* 1407–1413.

Smith, G. R., & Brown, F. W. (1990). Screening Indexes in DSM-III-R Somatization Disorder. *General Hospital Psychiatry, 12,* 148–152.

Smith, G. R., Golding, J. M., Kashner, T. M., & Rost, K. (1991). Antisocial personality disorder in primary care patients with somatization disorder. *Comprehensive Psychiatry, 32*(4), 367–372.

Smith, G. R., Monson, R. A., & Ray, D. C. (1986b). Patients with multiple unexplained symptoms: Their characteristics, functional health, and health care utilization. *Archives of Internal Medicine, 146,* 69–72.

Smith, G. R., Jr., Rost, K., & Kashner, M. (1995). A trial of the effect of a standardized psychiatric consultation on health outcomes and costs in somatizing patients. *Archives of General Psychiatry, 52,* 238–243.

Speckens, A. E., van Hemert, A. M., Spinhoven, P., Hawton, K. E., Bolk, J. H., & Rooijmans, H. G. (1995). Cognitive behavioural therapy for medically unexplained physical symptoms: A randomised controlled trial. *British Medical Journal, 311*(7016), 1328–1332.

Spitzer, R. L., Williams, J. B. W., Gibbon, M., & First, M. B. (1990). *Structured Clinical Interview for DSM-III-R. Nonpatient edition.* Washington, DC: American Psychiatric Press.

Starcevic, V. (1990). Relationship between hypochondriasis and obsessive compulsive disorder: Close relatives separated by nosological schemes? *American Journal of Psychotherapy, 44*(3), 340.

Starkman, M. N., Marshall, J. C., La Ferla, J., & Kelch, R. P. (1985). Pseudocyesis: Psychologic and neuroendocrine interrelationships. *Psychosomatic Medicine, 47*(1), 46–57.

Stedwell, R. E., Allen, K. M., & Binder, L. S. (1992). Hypokalemic paralyses: a review of the etiologies, pathophysiology, presentation, and therapy. *American Journal of Emergency Medicine, 10*(2), 143–148.

Stefansson, J. D., Messina, J. A., & Meyerowitz, S. (1976). Hysterical neurosis, conversion type: Clinical and epidemiological considerations. *Acta Psychiatrica Scandinavica, 53,* 119–138.

Stern, J., Murphy, M., & Bass, C. (1993). Personality disorders in patients with somatization disorder: A controlled study. *British Journal of Psychiatry, 363,* 785–789.

Stoeckle, J. D., & Barsky, A. J. (1980). Attributions: Uses of social science knowledge in the doctoring of primary care. In L. Eisenberg & A. Kleinman (Eds.), *The relevance of social science for medicine* (pp. 223–240). Dordrecht: Reidel.

Sullivan, M. D., Katon, W., Dobie, R., Sakai, C., Russo, J., & Harrop-Griffiths, J. (1988). Disabling tinnitus: Association with affective disorder. *General Hospital Psychiatry, 10,* 285–291.

Swartz, M., et al. (1986). Developing a screening index for community studies of somatization disorder. *Journal of Psychiatric Research, 20,* 335–343.

Swartz, M., Landerman, R., Blazer, D., & George, L. (1989). Somatization symptoms in the community: A rural/urban comparison. *Psychosomatics, 30*(1), 44–53.

Swartz, M., Landerman, R., George, L. K., Blazer, D. G., & Escobar, J. (1991). Somatization disorder. In L. N. Robins & D. A. Regier (Eds.), *Psychiatric disorders in*

America: The Epidemiologic Catchment Area study (pp. 220–257). New York: Free Press.

Talley, N. J. (1991). Diagnosing an irritable bowel: Does sex matter? *Gastroenterology, 110,* 834–837.

Taylor, G. J., Bagby, R. M., Ryan, D. P., & Parker, J. D. A. (1990). Validation of the alexithymia construct: A measurement-based approach. *Canadian Journal of Psychiatry, 35,* 290–297.

Thompson, W. G., & Pigeon-Reesor, H. (1990). The irritable bowel syndrome. *Seminars in Gastrointestinal Disease, 1*(1), 57–73.

Tomasson, K., Dent, D., & Coryell, W. (1991). Somatization and conversion disorders: Comorbidity and demographics at presentation. *Acta Psychiatrica Scandinavica, 84,* 288–293.

Toner, B. B. (1995). Gender differences in somatoform disorders. In M. V. Seeman (Ed.), *Gender and psychopathology* (pp. 287–310). Washington, DC: American Psychiatric Press.

Toone, B. K. (1990). Disorders of hysterical conversion. In C. M. Bass & R. H. Cawley (Eds.), *Somatization: Physical symptoms and psychological illness* (pp. 207–234). Oxford: Blackwell.

Trigwell, P., Hatcher, S., Johnson, M., Stanley, P., & House, A. (1995). "Abnormal" illness behaviour in chronic fatigue syndrome and multiple sclerosis. *British Medical Journal, 311*(6996), 15–18.

Turk, D. C., & Melzack, R. (Eds.). (1992). *Handbook of pain assessment.* New York: Guilford.

Turkat, I. D., & Pettegrew, L. S. (1983). Development and validation of the Illness Behavior Inventory. *Journal of Behavioral Assessment, 5*(1), 35–47.

Van Houdenhove, B., & Joostens, P. (1995). Burning mouth syndrome: Successful treatment with combined psychotherapy and pharmacotherapy. *General Hospital Psychiatry, 17,* 385–388.

Verbrugge, L. M. (1985). Gender and health: An update on hypotheses and evidence. *Journal of Health and Social Behavior, 26,* 156–182.

Verhaak, P. F. M., & Tijhuis, M. A. R. (1994). The somatizing patient in general practice. *International Journal of Psychiatry in Medicine, 24*(2), 157–177.

Von Korff, M., Dworkin, S. F., LeResche, L., & Kruger, A. (1990). An epidemiologic comparison of pain complaints. *Pain, 32,* 173–183.

Von Korff, M., Wagner, E. H., Dworkin, S. F., & Saunders, K. W. (1991). Chronic pain and use of ambulatory health care. *Psychosomatic Medicine, 53,* 61–79.

Walker, E. A., Gelfand, A. N., Gelfand, M. D., & Katon, W. J. (1995). Psychiatric diagnoses, sexual and physical victimization, and disability in patients with irritable bowel syndrome or inflammatory bowel disease. *Psychological Medicine, 25,* 1259–1267.

Walker, E. A., Gelfand, A. N., Gelfand, M. D., Koss, M. P., & Katon, W. J. (1995). Medical and psychiatric symptoms in female gastroenterology clinic patients with histories of sexual victimization. *General Hospital Psychiatry, 17,* 85–92.

Walker, E. A., Katon, W. J., Hansom, J., Harrop-Griffiths, J., Holm, L., Jones, M. L., Hickok, L., & Jemelka, R. P. (1992). Medical and psychiatric symptoms in women with childhood sexual abuse. *Psychosomatic Medicine, 54,* 658–664.

Walker, E., Katon, W., Harrop-Griffiths, J., Holm, L., Russo, J., & Hickok, L. R. (1988). Relationship of chronic pelvic pain to psychiatric diagnosis and childhood sexual abuse. *American Journal of Psychiatry, 145,* 75–80.

Walker, E. A., Katon, W. J., Neraas, K., Jemelka, R. P., & Massoth, D. (1992). Dissociation in women with chronic pelvic pain. *American Journal of Psychiatry, 149*(4), 534–537.

Ware, N. C., & Weiss, M. G. (1994). Neurasthenia and the social construction of psychiatric knowledge. *Transcultural Psychiatric Research Review, 31*(2), 101–124.

Warner, R. (1978). The diagnosis of antisocial and hysterical personality disorders: An example of sex bias. *Journal of Nervous and Mental Disease, 166,* 839–845.

Warwick, H. (1992). Provision of appropriate and effective reassurance. *International Review of Psychiatry, 4,* 76–80.

Warwick, H. (1995). Assessment of hypochondriasis. *Behaviour Research and Therapy, 33*(7), 845–853.

Warwick, H. C., & Salkovskis, P. M. (1990). Hypochondriasis. *Behaviour Research and Therapy, 28,* 105–117.

Watson, C. G., & Buranen, C. (1979a). The frequencies of conversion reaction symptoms. *Journal of Abnormal Psychology, 88*(2), 209–211.

Watson, C. G., & Buranen, C. (1979b). The frequency and identification of false positive conversion reactions. *Journal of Nervous and Mental Disease, 167,* 243–247.

Wessely, S. (1994). Neurasthenia and chronic fatigue: Theory and practice in Britain and America. *Transcultural Psychiatric Research Review, 31*(2), 173–208.

Wessely, S., & Sharpe, M. (1995). Chronic fatigue, chronic fatigue syndrome, and fibromyalgia. In R. Mayou, C. Bass, & M. Sharpe (Eds.), *Treatment of functional somatic symptoms* (pp. 285–312). Oxford: Oxford University Press.

Westermeyer, J., Bouafuely, M., Neider, J., & Callies, A. (1989). Somatization among refugees: An epidemiologic study. *Psychosomatics, 30,* 34–43.

Wetzel, R. D., Guze, S. B., Cloninger, C. R., & Martin, R. L. (1994). Briquet's syndrome (hysteria) is both a somatoform and a "psychoform" illness: A Minnesota Multiphasic Personality Inventory study. *Psychosomatic Medicine, 56*(6), 564–569.

Whitehead, W. E., Busch, C. M., Heller, B. R., & Costa, P. T. (1986). Social learning influences on menstrual symptoms and illness behavior. *Health Psychology, 5,* 13–23.

Whitehead, W. E., Crowell, M. D., Heller, B. R., Robinson, J. C., Schuster, M. M., & Horn, S. (1994). Modeling and reinforcement of the sick role during childhood predicts adult illness behavior. *Psychosomatic Medicine, 56,* 541–550.

Whitehead, W. E., Winget, C., Fedoravicius, A. S., Wooley, S., & Blackwell, B. (1982). Learned illness behavior in patients with irritable bowel syndrome and peptic ulcer. *Digestive Diseases and Sciences, 27*(3), 202–208.

Wickramasekera, I. (1989). Enabling the somatizing patient to exit the somatic closet: A high risk model. *Psychotherapy, 26*(4), 530–544.

Wickramasekera, I. (1995). Somatization: Concepts, data, and predictions from the high risk model of threat perception. *Journal of Nervous and Mental Disease, 183*(1), 15–23.

Wilhelmsen, I., Haug, T. T., Ursin, H., & Berstad, A. (1995). Discriminant analysis of factors distinguishing patients with functional symptoms from patients with duodenal ulcer. Significance of somatization. *Digestive Diseases and Sciences, 40*(5), 1105–1111.

Wilkinson, S. R. (1988). *The child's world of illness: The development of health and illness behaviour.* Cambridge: Cambridge University Press.

Williams, D. T., Spiegel, H., & Mostofsky, D. I. (1978). Neurogenic and hysterical seizures: Differential diagnostic and therapeutic considerations. *American Journal of Psychiatry, 135*(1), 82–86.

Winstead, B. A. (1984). Hysteria. In C. S. Widom (Ed.), *Sex roles and psychopathology* (pp. 73–100). New York: Plenum.

Wise, T. N., & Mann, L. S. (1995). The attribution of somatic symptoms in psychiatric outpatients. *Comprehensive Psychiatry, 36*(6), 407–410.

Wise, T. N., Mann, L. S., Mitchell, J. D., Hryniak, M., & Hill, B. (1990). Secondary alexithymia: An empirical validation. *Comprehensive Psychiatry, 31*(4), 284–285.

Wool, C. A., & Barsky, A. J. (1994). Do women somatize more than men? Gender differences in somatization. *Psychosomatics, 35*(5), 445–452.

World Health Organization. (1992). *The ICD-10 classification of mental and behavioural disorders: Clinical descriptions and diagnostic guidelines.* Geneva: World Health Organization.

Yonkers, K. A., & Gurguis, G. (1995). Gender differences in the prevalence and expression of anxiety disorders. In M. V. Seeman (Ed.), *Gender and psychopathology* (pp. 113–130). Washington, DC: American Psychiatric Press.

Yutsy, S. H., Cloninger, C. R., Guze, S. B., Pribor, E. F., Martin, R. L., Kathol, R. G., Smith, G. R., & Strain, J. J. (1995). DSM-IV field trial: Testing a new proposal for somatization disorder. *American Journal of Psychiatry, 152*(1), 97–101.

CHAPTER 12

Dissociative Disorders: Phantoms of the Self

ETZEL CARDEÑA

> I look at my reflection in the window, and find myself to be strange, novel. For a moment I was almost afraid of the image the window pane returned to me—of this phantom of myself.
>
> L. Dugas and F. Moutier (1911), cited in Nemiah, 1995

Few categories of psychopathology are as controversial as the dissociative disorders. Detractors find some of these disorders, particularly dissociative identity disorder, suspect if not outright iatrogenic; supporters maintain that the former disregard of dissociation has condemned many patients to inadequate diagnosis and treatment. Leaving aside for a moment this debate, it is undeniable that the study of the dissociative disorders has grown exponentially in the last few years, after a considerable neglect since the beginning of the century. Besides a specialized journal, *Dissociation,* and a professional society, International Society for the Study of the Dissociative Disorders (ISSDD), there have been a number of volumes dedicated to clinical and theoretical issues, including three comprehensive anthologies (Lynn & Rhue, 1994; Michelson & Ray, 1996; D. Spiegel, 1994).

The rise of systematic research on dissociation has been fostered by recent cognitive models consistent with dissociative theories and by the development of specific measures of dissociation, including paper-and-pencil questionnaires of trait dissociation (e.g., Dissociative Experiences Scale, or DES; Carlson & Putnam, 1993; the Questionnaire of Experiences of Dissociation, or QED; Riley, 1988) and state dissociation (e.g., the Stanford Acute Stress Reaction Questionnaire, or SASRQ; Cardeña, Koopman, Classen, & Spiegel, 1993; the Peritraumatic Dissociative Experiences Questionnaire, or PDEQ; Marmar et al., 1994). Structured clinical interviews have also been developed (e.g., the Dissociative Disorders Interview Schedule or DDIS; Ross, 1991; Structured Clinical Interview of Dissociative Disorders, or SCID-D; Steinberg, 1993). Carlson & Armstrong (1994) have written a good review of the DES and of clinical interviews, but they almost completely ignore dissociation questionnaires other than the DES.

Loewenstein (1991b) has developed a systematic office mental status examination that includes questions on identity, amnesia, autohypnotic phenomena, posttraumatic stress disorder (PTSD), and somatoform and affective symptoms. Also, more general tests such as the MMPI and the Rorschach have been used with this population.

Despite these developments, there is no consensus on what "dissociation" actually means. The term has been used for such different phenomena as the running of behavioral subroutines (e.g., driving while focusing on a conversation), a lack of mental contents (e.g., "blanking out"), the apparent recovery of traumatic memories, experiences in which the phenomenal self seems to be located outside of the physical body (i.e., out-of-body experiences), the seeming independence between explicit and implicit forms of memory, the apparently painless piercing of flesh in some rituals, and intrusive and realistic recollections ("flashbacks"), among others. Dissociation has been used as a descriptive term or as a hypothetical construct, sometimes synonymous with repression, sometimes as a distinct defense mechanism.

In a recent chapter, Erdelyi (1994) subsumed the notion of the "unconscious" under the idea of dissociation, which he defined as the discrepancy between two indicators of information (e.g., conscious experience of tranquility, concurrent with physiological indicators of distress) or as memories that while inaccessible at one point may be later recovered. Besides these, other uses of the term include an alteration of consciousness characterized by estrangement from the self or the environment, and a mechanism of defense to ward off the emotional impact of traumatic events and memories (Cardeña, 1994).

The concept of dissociation according to the DSM-IV (*Diagnostic and Statistical Manual of Mental Disorders;* American Psychiatric Association [APA], 1994) is narrower and, arguably, a descriptive rather than an explanatory term (although, in the same context, Nemiah, 1995, uses "dissociation" as a mental process that gives rise to the dissociative disorders). DSM-IV defines the dissociative disorders as a "disruption in the usually integrated functions of consciousness, memory, identity, or perception of the environment" (APA, 1994, p. 477) that is distressing or impairs basic areas of functioning. Of course, to qualify as "dissociative" such discrepancies cannot be the product of malingering or other forms of conscious deception.

Although the DSM-IV does not assume that these disorders develop as the result of a defense mechanism invoked to cope with ongoing trauma, it nonetheless asserts that these disorders are commonly linked to traumatic events. There is reason to believe that while traumatic events are related to the dissociative disorders, they are not sufficient by themselves to explain these conditions. Otherwise, every seriously traumatized individual would end up having a dissociative disorder, which is clearly not the case. The proposed predisposing factors for the development of pathological dissociativity include an inborn disposition to dissociate (e.g., Braun, 1993), the similar notion of high hypnotizability (e.g., Stutman & Bliss, 1985), repeated exposure to trauma in an inescapable situation, at least among children (cf. Terr, 1991), and an early chaotic family environment (Tillman, Nash, & Lerner, 1994).

While "repression" and "dissociation" have been frequently used to refer to the same manifestations (e.g., the inability to remember a traumatic event), some authors differentiate "repression," defined as a defense mechanism to ward off internal pressures, from "dissociation," defined as an alteration in consciousness to deflect the overwhelming impact of ongoing trauma. This distinction, while problematic and not consensually accepted, does make some reference to the historical fact that Pierre Janet, the originator of the term "dissociation," saw it as a lack of integration produced by the impact of trauma on a psychologically deficient system, whereas Freud saw it more as the product of conflict among psychological structures. Be that as it may, one can use "dissociation" as a descriptive term to encompass disorders centered on the lack of integration among psychological processes such as memory or identity, or as an experienced disconnection with the self or the environment, without having to endorse either Janet's or Freud's explanations.

The effort to define the dissociative disorders by observable characteristics follows the move of the DSM taxonomy from a psychoanalytic characterization in its first two editions to the more descriptive model adopted in later versions. However, some changes in the dissociative nosology have been controversial. Foremost among them, conversion disorder was moved from the dissociative to the somatoform category.

Critics of this taxonomic change have invoked historical, conceptual, and empirical arguments. Clearly, many of the "hysterical" cases described at the turn of the century involved conversion and dissociative phenomena such as alterations of consciousness and identity (Kihlstrom, 1994). Of greater importance, dissociation as a discrepancy or lack of integration between behaviors and conscious experience would fit the nature of conversion and related disorders in which complaints of pain or lack of function parallel the absence of pathophysiology. There is also accumulating data on the substantial comorbidity of somatization disorders with traumatic history and dissociative symptomatology (e.g., Pribor, Yutzi, Dean, & Wetzel, 1993; Saxe et al., 1994).

Another clarification about the dissociative disorders is that they refer to conditions with an environmental and psychological etiology rather than a neurological one. As a result, the DSM-IV does make a distinction between the presumed psychological etiology of dissociative amnesia and the biological etiology of, for example, alcohol amnestic syndrome. This distinction may be somewhat lost now, after some of these disorders were renamed in the last edition; for instance, "psychogenic" amnesia became "dissociative" amnesia. The presumption of a psychological etiology does not, of course, imply absence of biological underpinnings in these conditions (APA, 1994; Brown, 1994).

In accord with the distinction between psychological and medical etiology, Cardeña et al. (1996) proposed the diagnosis of "secondary dissociative disorder due to a nonpsychiatric medical condition," but the DSM Committee did not endorse that recommendation. That rejection notwithstanding, there is ample evidence that dissociative experiences are associated with various medical conditions and biological factors including damage to the central nervous system, prescription and nonprescription drugs, and seizure disorders (Good, 1993). The reader should be aware that some authors use the term "dissociation" to address neurologically based conditions such as "blindsight," in which there is a discrepancy between conscious experience and behavior (Farthing, 1992).

Even within the strict province of psychogenic conditions a final clarification must be made. Some dissociative phenomena, although they may be present as part of a clinical condition, are also found among normal individuals and, in fact, may be associated with personal development practices such as meditation. However, there is reason to question the notion that the dissociative disorders are just extreme instances of a continuum (cf. Braun, 1993). Waller, Putnam, &

Carlson (1996) have presented evidence that dissociation should be analyzed in terms of types rather than as a continuum. Whereas some dissociative phenomena (e.g., absorption) overlap in clinical and nonclinical populations, others seem to distinguish nonpathological from pathological conditions (e.g., severe depersonalization, amnesia). We need to further clarify the various types of dissociative phenomena, what contextual factors trigger them, and how mental control and organization predict which manifestations become pathological. It should be borne in mind that, according to the DSM, dissociative disorders have to produce distress or impairment, or both, in areas such as social or professional life.

All of the previous considerations apply to our culture and do not even address the fact that cultural beliefs and practices can pathologize or normalize diverse gaps in experience (Kirmayer, 1994), an issue I will cover more extensively when describing the proposed new diagnosis of "trance dissociative disorder."

The new diagnosis of acute stress disorder (ASD), initially proposed as "brief reactive dissociative disorder" (D. Spiegel & Cardeña, 1991), and posttraumatic stress disorder (PTSD) also involve substantial dissociative symptomatology, but they will not be discussed here. The DSM-IV mentions dissociative symptomatology as a possible constituent in somatization disorders and panic attacks. Diagnosis of a dissociative disorder or a dual diagnosis depends on the constellation and presentation of symptoms.

The following sections address dissociative disorders in adults, by far the most studied group. The dissociative disorders are usually manifested in early to middle adulthood. Nonetheless, reports of childhood dissociative disorders can be traced at least to the 18th century. Their assessment is particularly difficult because some manifestations (e.g., spontaneous staring spells, imaginary companions) are normal in some age groups. Putnam (1994) provides an authoritative introduction to the diagnosis and treatment of the dissociative disorders in children and adolescents.

EPIDEMIOLOGY

Epidemiological studies have rarely used instruments that evaluate dissociative disorders (e.g., Kessler et al., 1994). An exception is the study by Mezzich, Fabrega, Coffman, and Haley (1989), who reported that these disorders, using DSM-III (APA, 1980) criteria, were rare in a psychiatric sample. More recently, it has been found that dissociative symptomatology is more common during or shortly after a disaster than previously thought (Cardeña & Spiegel, 1993; D. Spiegel & Cardeña, 1991).

Ross (1991) has provided specific information on the epidemiology of dissociative disorders in clinical and nonclinical samples. Using DSM-III-R (APA, 1987) criteria (which are different in some important ways from the current DSM-IV criteria), he found that approximately between 20% and 40% of psychiatric patients also fulfilled criteria for dissociative disorders (5% to 14% fulfilled criteria for DID). For a nonclinical Canadian population (n = 454), Ross reported the following rates: 7% dissociative amnesia, 3.1% dissociative identity disorder (DID), 2.4% depersonalization disorder, .2% dissociative fugue, .2% of dissociative disorders not otherwise specified (DDNOS; 11.2%, a dissociative disorder of some type). There are some important qualifications to these data. The 3.1% prevalence of DID in the general population seems very high, but Ross himself commented that it included individuals who were high functioning, and the DSM-III-R criteria he used did not include the requirements for amnesia or for the symptoms to be clinically distressing or produce maladjustment. Thus, the 3.1% of DID likely included individuals who might experience alternative personalities while "channeling" or doing similar activities without a pathological implication—individuals who would not count as DID with the new criteria. The description by Ross of a pathological type of DID in about 1% of his sample is likely to be closer to the actual prevalence of this condition.

On the other hand, the DSM-IV criteria for fugue and amnesia are more lenient than those Ross used, so it is likely that some individuals diagnosed as DDNOS by Ross would receive an amnesia or fugue diagnosis with the new criteria. A brief report by Silva and Ward (1993) with British nonclinical volunteers who completed the DES found rates of dissociativity similar to those of Ross.

Studies of the prevalence of dissociative disorders among clinical populations are reviewed by Gleaves (1996). The rate of dissociative disorders among various clinical populations ranged from a low of 10% among obsessive-compulsive disorder patients, to a high of 88% among women reporting sexual abuse.

ETHNICITY, GENDER, AND CULTURE

A number of studies in the United States and Europe (see Vanderlinden, van der Hart, & Varga, 1996) suggest that at least among nonclinical populations dissociativity reaches its peak somewhere in early adolescence and then gradually declines with age. It is of interest that hypnotizability has a similar age distribution (Hilgard, 1968).

There is scant information on the impact of socioeconomic status or ethnicity on the incidence of dissociative pathology. In a recent study, dissociative symptoms (not necessarily disorders) were more common among "minorities" but when socioeconomic status was controlled, that difference disappeared (Zatzick, Marmar, Weiss, & Metzler, 1994). Nor have European studies found that ethnicity affects dissociativity (Vanderlinden et al., 1996), but an important caveat is that these studies have been conducted only in Western technological societies. Dissociative phenomena and disorders seem to have a different presentation in some societies (see below). With respect to the so-called culture-bound syndromes with a dissociative component, both pathological spirit possession and *ataque de nervios* are predominantly found among women of lower socioeconomic status, while *amok, berserk,* and similar "assault" conditions are mostly found among men (Lewis-Fernández, 1994; Simons & Hughes, 1985).

It is fair to say that, other than for some culture-bound syndromes and dissociative identity disorder (DID), we do not have consistent findings as to the gender distribution of other dissociative disorders (e.g., Vanderlinden et al., 1996). Some proponents of a strong skeptic position affirm that dissociative identity disorder is mostly a condition of affluent Caucasian women in the United States, but research shows that this condition is found in other countries (e.g., Coons, Bowman, Kluft, & Milstein, 1991). It also is the case that in the United States, DID does not affect only Caucasian or affluent women (or men). For instance, Coons, Bowman, and Milstein (1988) published a paper of 50 cases, 40 of whom came from a state psychiatric hospital and could not afford private care. The largest occupational level (28%) of these clients was clerical/sales/technician (P.M. Coons, personal communication, 1996). Another therapist with a heavy load of dissociative patients also reported that a substantial amount of his DID patients were non-Caucasian of lower socioeconomic strata (P. Barach, personal communication, 1996).

What remains true is that, at least in the United States, dissociative identity disorder is found at much higher rates among women than among males. As Kluft (1996) maintains, however, the ratio of about 9 : 1 female to male found in many studies may be excessive because some males with DID end up being part of the legal system and are not assessed in epidemiological studies.

DISSOCIATIVE AMNESIA

This disorder is important for its own sake and because it serves as the basis for two other dissociative disorders: dissociative fugue and dissociative identity disorder. According to the DSM-IV, dissociative amnesia (previously called "psychogenic") is characterized by one or more instances of amnesia for important personal information that cannot be explained by ordinary forgetfulness, by the common developmental amnesia for the first years of life, or by an organic condition.

Dissociative amnesia is closely related to severe stress or exposure to trauma, including experiences of combat, natural disaster, being the victim of violence, or childhood abuse. Legal problems, financial disaster, severe marital problems, depression, and suicide attempts have also precipitated this disorder (Coons & Milstein, 1992; Kopelman, 1987; Loewenstein, 1991a).

Although this is not the proper forum to cover it in detail, mention should be made of the skepticism (e.g., Loftus, 1993) concerning reports of apparently recovered memories, particularly concerning early abuse, which could be interpreted as denying the existence of dissociative amnesia. There is good reason to question the view that false memories are easily or commonly produced by psychotherapists (Brown, 1995); more important, evidence for the reality of dissociative amnesia has accumulated for decades and in contexts independent of therapy or early abuse, including combat trauma, torture, traumatic loss, and crime (van der Hart & Nijenhuis, 1995).

At this stage, the debate should no longer be about whether most recovered memories are completely accurate or inaccurate, perhaps untenable positions given the evidence, but about the individual and social characteristics that facilitate or hinder accurate retrieval. Even in less controversial examples than early abuse, an evaluation of the validity of the amnesia is likely to be more complex than has been usually considered. For example, Kopelman, Christensen, Puffett, and Stanhope (1994) did a thorough study of a case of functional retrograde amnesia in which there was a probable mixture of actual amnesia and simulation. The authors proposed that dissociative amnesia involves different levels of awareness for different memories in accord with current models of memory and cognition that go well beyond a simple conscious-nonconscious dichotomy.

Dissociative amnesia typically involves loss of explicit or declarative memory (that is, awareness of personal information or previous experience), whereas implicit memory (i.e., general knowledge, such as language, and habits, conditioned responses, and such) is usually preserved (Kihlstrom, 1987).

The precipitating event(s) for dissociative amnesia can be complex and involve idiosyncratic elements. I recently observed a psychologically immature soldier who had been found in an airport bathroom with profound generalized amnesia. For days he was unable to remember his identity, personal history, and so on. Even after most of the amnesia and anxiety symptoms, such as severe stuttering, had cleared after a few days, he was unable to remember what exactly had happened in that bathroom then (there was no evidence of a sexual attack or of an organic condition) or at a 5-month follow-up. The only obvious external event before the amnesia episode was the impending sale of his childhood home (which seemed to have a greater personal impact for him than for most individuals), but forgotten fantasies about that event or about something else might have played an equal or more important role.

A more typical precursor involved a Gulf War veteran with PTSD who, after hearing a cannon shot, slid under a parked car. Even weeks after the incident he had no memory whatsoever of the period from the moment of the shooting to the time when other soldiers eventually got him from under the car. Not uncharacteristically, he had been unresponsive to his colleagues' promptings for a few minutes.

The presentation of amnesia can vary according to frequency of episodes, extent of amnesia, and temporal parameters. With regard to frequency, patients can have one or very few episodes of amnesia, or have a chronic condition. The first type of presentation has been dramatized in a number of movies in which the character suddenly forgets everything about his or her life, often after a severe traumatic event such as a bloody battle. In contrast with this presentation, Coons and Milstein (1992) described a group of patients, typically with reported history of early abuse, with chronic forms of amnesia. They reported one or more of the following: episodes of "missing time," unexplainable forgetfulness, and chronic amnesia for periods that should be remembered (e.g., not remembering any event that occurred when the person was 13 years of age).

Amnesia episode(s) can be characterized as generalized, selective, or localized. Generalized amnesia involves amnesia for all or most personal information, including name, personal history, identity of relatives and friends, and so forth. In the case mentioned above, the soldier found in the bathroom was initially unable to remember who he was, his previous personal history, or where he was going to or coming from, nor could he recognize relatives or friends.

Localized amnesia is defined as amnesia for a certain period of time, be it hours, days, or longer. The amnesic patient cannot remember what transpired during a certain period but remembers previous and subsequent events. Selective amnesia is forgetfulness for memories related to a particular event or person, as would happen to someone who, in the midst of a very difficult divorce, forgets who his or her spouse is, the marriage ceremony, for example, while preserving other types of information. Schacter, Wang, Tulving, and Freedman (1982) correctly pointed out that dissociative amnesia is organized more according to emotional than temporal parameters. In a recent systematic study of dissociative amnesia and fugue with 25 patients, Coons and Milstein (1992) found that more than 76% of the amnesias were for selective information.

A final dimension is whether the amnesia is retrograde or anterograde to its onset. In the case of dissociative amnesia after a traumatic event, the loss of memory is typically retrograde in the sense that the patient does not remember part or all of the traumatic or surrounding events, while she or he usually has no problem with learning new material or remembering what occurred after the trauma. This presentation is in sharp contrast with a number of organic amnesias (e.g., various dementias or alcohol amnestic syndrome) in which the amnesia is anterograde; that is, the patient is unable to remember events occurring after the onset of amnesia, although the person may preserve older memories and may show implicit, but not explicit, memory for new material (cf. Kihlstrom, 1987).

Depression, anxiety, episodes of depersonalization (see below), and "trance" (e.g., apparent unawareness of the surroundings) frequently predate or are associated with dissociative amnesia. In cases with a history of early and chronic abuse, a more complex syndrome that may also include self-injurious behavior, substance abuse, sexual problems, and so on, is likely (cf. Cardeña & Spiegel, 1996).

When dissociative amnesia is not chronic and follows a traumatic event, the prognosis is usually good. Once the client is in a safe environment therapy can gradually bring a complete or substantial recovery of the memories in a matter of days or weeks; there can also be spontaneous recovery of material without therapeutic intervention. Chronic and recurrent episodes of amnesia, on the other hand, are much more complex and typically require longer therapy and have a less certain outcome.

Differential diagnosis of this condition includes other dissociative disorders that are superordinate to amnesia (dissociative fugue and dissociative identity disorder), acute stress disorder, posttraumatic stress disorder, and somatization. There also are a number of medical conditions that can produce amnesias, among them transient global amnesia or TGA, a transient amnestic episode involving confusion, probably caused by temporary vascular insufficiency (Rollinson, 1978), amnestic alcohol, or Korsakoff's syndrome, head injury, epilepsy, dementia, amnesic stroke, postoperative amnesia, postinfectious amnesia, alcoholic "black-out," and anoxic amnesia (Benson, 1978; Keller and Shaywitz, 1986; Kopelman, 1987). Dissociative amnesia must be differentiated also from the amnesia produced by various drugs, especially alcohol. In a legal context, the clinician should also consider the possibility of malingering.

Usually the presentation of the amnesia (i.e., selective, retrograde, associated with depression or anxiety) and the surrounding circumstances (i.e., precipitating trauma or severe stress without head injury) give an indication of the likely diagnosis (Sivec & Lynn, 1995). A detailed clinical history and laboratory analyses can usually rule out other possibilities.

As with the other dissociative disorders, at present there are no biological techniques to evaluate dissociative amnesia, although cognitive procedures are being developed to distinguish real from simulated amnesia (e.g., Kopelman et al., 1994). The clinician has to be mindful that amnesia may not be a presenting problem. There are a number of reasons for this; among them, patients may have amnesia for the amnestic episodes; that is, they may be aware of suddenly finding themselves in a place without knowing how they got there, but may later forget that this event occurred or they may assume that these episodes of "forgetfulness" are shared by everybody else.

Assessment for this and other dissociative disorders may include one or more of the questionnaires and clinical interviews mentioned above. At the very least, if the clinician suspects amnesia, a number of areas should be investigated, including "gaps" of memory in everyday life, whether the client can give an account of at least the salient episodes from late childhood onward, whether the client has found items that must have recently been bought but for which he or she has no memory, and so on (cf. Loewenstein, 1991b). Although the earlier reports of dissociative amnesia and fugue concentrated on male soldiers in time of war, more recent work (e.g., Coons & Milstein, 1992) has reported a preponderance of females.

Dissociative Fugue

Dissociative fugue is defined by the sudden wandering away from home, place of employment, and so forth; amnesia for one's past; and confusion about personal identity or adoption of a new identity. It is not surprising that generalized amnesia and personal confusion would be associated with leaving one's customary surroundings. To what extent dissociative fugue should be considered more than an extreme case of generalized amnesia is debatable.

Before the current edition of the DSM, the diagnosis was circumscribed to adopting a different identity than the original one. This form was probably immortalized by William James's description of the Reverend Ansel Bourne, who left his hometown and adopted a new name and profession only to, at a later point, "wake up" to the knowledge of his previous identity (James, 1890/1923; see also Kenny, 1986). It is not too uncommon to read in newspapers of modern day "Bournes."

More recent studies show that it is more common by far to find a presentation in which the person is at least initially confused about his or her identity (Loewenstein, 1991a; Riether & Stoudemire, 1988). It is possible that an undetected and unresolved case of identity confusion may resolve into a new identity.

The nature of this confusion of identity is not clear at present, but a number of authors have concurred in defining it as some type of consciousness alteration. William James (1890/1923) saw fugue as a long-lasting "trance." Stengel (1941, p. 255, cited in Loewenstein, 1991a) defined it as "states of altered or narrowed consciousness with the impulse to wander." These definitions are consistent with Pierre Janet's view of dissociation as involving a focusing and narrowing of consciousness (van der Kolk & van der Hart, 1989). While there are no studies that directly evaluate this hypothesis, nonclinical groups exposed to the 1989 San Francisco Bay Area earthquake reported that their attention was significantly narrower and more focused during the earthquake week than 4 months afterward (Cardeña & Spiegel, 1993), a finding consistent with laboratory studies (e.g., Christianson & Loftus, 1987). Other authors question the existence of a dissociative alteration of consciousness and propose other constructs such as strategic self-presentation and a culturally prescribed "idiom of distress" (Kenny, 1986; Spanos, 1994).

As in the case of dissociative amnesia, traumatic events and severe stress are the common precipitants of this condition. Older references on dissociative amnesia and fugue centered on soldiers at time of war. Grinker and Spiegel (1945, p. 372) wrote that "the psychotic reactions seen mostly in ground troops were due to a negation of reality by the process of dissociation." While the aftereffects of war continue producing dissociative symptomatology, most fugue patients seen in hospitals are civilians fleeing the terrors of urban life.

Loewenstein (1991a) maintains that in our nomadic modern societies some patients have a "nonclassic" presentation in which they do not complain of fugue unless queried about it. He maintains that, in our cities, isolated or abused individuals may have episodes of fugue without anybody noticing, much less bringing this fact to official agencies. Some may become homeless people; others, particularly teenagers having a fugue episode after abuse, may be easily lured or forced into illegal activities. For these reasons, the current estimates of the prevalence of fugue, which have targeted sedentary samples, probably underestimate this condition.

The symptoms associated with dissociative fugue are the same as those for dissociative amnesia. If the fugue is part of a DID, the DSM nosology makes the latter superordinate because episodes of fugue are common in DID.

Differential diagnoses of fugue include complex partial seizures involving postictal episodes of aimless wandering, amnesia, and disorientation, also known as "poriomania" (Mayeux et al., 1979). Episodes of poriomania tend to be short-lived, usually a matter of minutes, in contrast to the longer duration of a fugue; the latter is also more responsive to hypnosis and similar techniques (Sivec & Lynn, 1995).

Other diagnoses to consider are manic or schizophrenic episodes accompanied by traveling, organic, nonepileptic factors such as brain tumors, and alcohol- and drug-related loss of memory and wandering (cf. Akhtar & Brenner, 1979). Generally, the characteristic symptoms of other diagnoses (e.g., the grandiosity and impulsivity in mania) can easily differentiate the conditions. Nonetheless, clinicians unfamiliar with the dissociative disorders may easily conclude that they are dealing with a psychosis.

In a community health center in México a few years ago, I consulted on the case of a woman who had wandered from her hometown to Mexico City. She had traveled to the city after she had arrived home from jogging and had found the door to her house open. Her immediate thought was that her daughter had been raped, which was not the case but was not an unrealistic assumption in their circumstances. She nonetheless became very confused and started traveling to the capital. She had a very sketchy recollection of that trip. Although she fulfilled criteria for a dissociative disorder and had no history of psychosis, a physician in another hospital diagnosed her condition as schizophrenia and prescribed a large amount of neuroleptics that induced both muscular rigidity and akathisia (restlessness and inability to stand still). The neuroleptics were tapered off and the iatrogenic symptoms disappeared, without the irruption of any schizophrenic symptoms.

Dissociative Identity Disorder

The possibility that two or more very different individuals coexist in one body has intrigued scientists and writers for a number of centuries. At the turn of the century, William James, Morton Prince, Pierre Janet, and other eminent clinicians described this phenomenon (Kenny, 1986). Although long regarded as an exotic and extremely rare curiosity, recent years have seen a great increase in the study and incidence of this condition.

DID is the new label for what used to be called "multiple personality disorder." According to the DSM-IV, the defining features are the presence within the person of two or more identities with characteristic behaviors, moods, and so on, that recurrently take control of the individual. The other essential feature is that the individual is unable to recall personal information. In the case of DID, the issue of amnesia is more complex than in pure dissociative amnesia, because an alter may claim to have memory for events that another alter is amnesic about. The diagnosis requires that the symptoms produce distress or impairment.

The DSM-IV made more changes to the diagnostic criteria of this condition than to any other dissociative disorder. There were two main reasons to change the name from "multiple personality disorder" to "dissociative identity disorder." One was that the older term emphasized the concept of "many" personalities, whereas the current view is that the main problem of these individuals is not having a number of personalities, but failing to have the sort of complex, multifaceted but unified personality that most of us have. Another way of stating this is that the many aspects of our personality, acquiescent or aggressive, playful or serious, are not integrated in these patients, but remain as isolated and personalized nuclei. The ISSD (1994) states it this way: "The DID patient is a single person who experiences him/herself as having separate parts of the mind that function with some autonomy. The patient is not a collection of separate people sharing the same body."

Another reason for the name change is that the term "personality" is usually held for the characteristic pattern of thoughts, feelings, moods, behaviors, and so on, of the whole individual. From this perspective, the fact that DID patients consistently switch between different identities, behavior styles, and so forth, constitutes their characteristic personality. This is also the main reason why the current phraseology of the DSM refers to "distinct identities or personality states," rather than to personalities. Other phrasing changes in diagnostic criteria clarified that while alters may be personalized by the individual, they are not to be considered as having an objective, independent existence.

The DSM-IV readopted the criterion of amnesia, which had been abandoned by the DSM-III-R (APA, 1987). Their rationale had been that, even though amnesia may indeed be an essential characteristic of the condition, patients might fail to report this symptom either because they might not remember their own amnesic episodes, or for other reasons (Kluft, Steinberg, & Spitzer, 1988). Analysis of various publications and data sets revealed, however, that an increase in false negative diagnoses with the readoption of the new criterion is very unlikely since amnesia was a symptom in almost all DID patients who had been thoroughly evaluated by different authors (cf. Cardeña et al., 1996). These data confirmed that amnesia is a central component of the condition.

It is generally considered that DID is the most severe of the dissociative disorders, and it is certainly the most studied one. Although originally only a few authors could account for most of the research in this area, there has been a steady growth in the number of contributors to the field. While it is still probably true that the majority of clinicians have not treated a DID patient, acceptance of the diagnosis among psychologist and psychiatrists is considerable (Dunn, Paolo, Ryan, & van Fleet, 1994).

DID is the most controversial of all dissociative disorders, not the least by the recent increase in its diagnosis (Boor, 1982). Positions range from those who believe that the condition is mostly or completely iatrogenic (e.g., Aldridge-Morris, 1989), produced by naive therapists and the media, through those who state that the condition is not necessarily iatrogenic but is molded by cultural expectations and social roles and strategies (e.g., Spanos, 1994), to those who believe that DID is a valid and specific diagnosis (e.g., Putnam, 1989).

Proponents of the iatrogenic explanation point out that DID patients show significantly higher hypnotizability than other clinical groups and normal individuals (Frischholz, Lipman, Braun, & Sachs, 1992) and are thus prone to follow explicit or subtle suggestions provided by hypnotists probing for possible hidden "personalities" or alters. At least two studies (Putnam, Guroff, Silberman, Barban, & Post, 1986; Ross, Norton, & Fraser, 1989) have answered this objection by showing that neither the use of hypnosis nor other proposed therapist characteristics can account for who gets a DID diagnosis. Also, if the majority of DID patients were just following clinicians' suggestions, they would have adopted other diagnoses since the vast majority of them have received a number of other previous diagnoses (Coons et al., 1988; Putnam et al., 1986; Ross, Norton, & Wozney, 1989).

The fact remains, however, that DID is more frequently diagnosed in the United States than in other countries, although there is growing transcultural evidence for its validity and reliability (e.g., Boon & Draijer, 1991; Coons, Bowman, Kluft, & Milstein, 1991; Martinez-Taboas, 1991; Tutkun, Yargic, & Sar, 1995). There are a number of possible explanations for this phenomenon. One of them is that the characteristics and method of evaluation of this condition have just recently become part of the clinician's awareness in the United States, and other countries are lagging behind. This possibility became distinctly real for me recently, while teaching a course in Spain on dissociative disorders. In the midst of the course, three independent clinicians without a previous knowledge of dissociative disorders described patients from their practice who were almost textbook descriptions of these disorders and did not fit very well the clinicians' alternative diagnoses.

Another explanation is that early chronic abuse is a causal factor of DID, and the United States may have a greater incidence of abuse than other countries. The link between early abuse and DID is not devoid of its own controversies. Some authors have rightly pointed out that there is little to no evidence for many reports of abuse, particularly "satanic" abuse. In the particular case of DID patients, however, a number of studies have found independent corroboration (e.g., medical or legal records, corroboration from family members) for the patients' reports of abuse (Coons, 1994; Coons & Milstein, 1986; Hornstein & Putnam, 1992). This does not mean, of course, that all reports, or all details of every report, are valid or accurate, but it shows that at least a significant proportion of DID patients have verifiable histories of abuse. Whether childhood abuse in the United States has a higher incidence or differs in any other important way from that in other countries is, however, not proved at this point.

There have been sociocultural explanations for the modality or incidence of DID in the United States. Different cultures vary in how they define and interpret psychological and psychopathological experience, including discontinuities in experience (Kirmayer, 1994), and provide "idioms of distress" to allow for the expression of psychological suffering. Kenny (1986) and Spanos (1994) have correctly drawn attention to the sociocultural and historical variables that mediate the expressions of multiplicity in this and other cultures and eras, although their appeal to abandon the "disease theory" of DID is, in my view, unwarranted. Or at least no more warranted than abandoning the "disease theories" for depression, eating disorders, substance abuse disorders, and other conditions that show cultural variation and for which there are expectable cultural roles.

That DID, as well as our nonpathological sense of self, is mediated by cultural notions of identity, personal consistency, and the like, is a different issue than whether DID is an iatrogenic condition. Clearly, the high hypnotic susceptibility of DID patients coupled with the incompetent use of hypnosis or other suggestive techniques by some practitioners increases the possibility of iatrogenicity. The skeptics of the diagnosis, however, have not proved that this process can account for a significant number of DID diagnoses. In a balanced overview of the DID controversy, Horevitz (1994, p. 447) stated that "critics who claim MPD is nonexistent, rare, iatrogenic, or overdiagnosed may be right or they may be wrong. However, no data at present exists to directly support these contentions." More recently, Gleaves (1996) reviewed the literature and concluded that there is no empirical support for the iatrogenesis of DID.

Therapists can, nonetheless, unwittingly reinforce a lack of integration. The *Guidelines for Treating Dissociative Identity Disorder* from the ISSD (1994) explicitly state that it is "counterproductive" to try to create new alters, give names to unnamed ones, or to in other ways enhance the lack of integration of the individual.

The clinical presentation of these patients can vary widely. Even among DID patients, there is a wide range of symptom severity, level of adaptation, and so on, with some patients being able to perform adequately in various areas of functioning (Kluft, 1994). Symptom presentation can vary across time in the same patient, sometimes fulfilling all the criteria for DID, sometimes fulfilling criteria only for DDNOS (dissociative disorders not otherwise specified; see below). Besides the "textbook" or classical presentation, Kluft (1991) provides an extensive list of DID presentations, including epochal or sequential (i.e., switches are rare), latent (alters are manifested only at times of stress), posttraumatic DID, and others.

The course and prognosis depends on symptom severity and characterological fragility of the patient, and there is a recent study showing a wide variety of therapy trajectories even while maintaining a number of therapy variables constant (Kluft, 1994). Nonetheless, it is widely accepted that therapy for these patients will typically take a number of years (Putnam & Loewenstein, 1993).

The DSM-IV (APA, 1994, p. 486) maintains that DID is more common among first-degree biological relatives, but there is no current information on whether this relationship is caused by genetic or environmental factors or, more likely, an interaction of both. Theories of the development of DID (e.g., Braun, 1993) generally propose that DID requires a predisposition to have dissociative experiences, coupled with a history of traumatic events. There is indirect support for heritability of at least a propensity to dissociate if we consider research on the heritability of hypnotizability (Morgan, 1973) and of absorption (Tellegen et al., 1988), both of which have been found to be positively correlated with dissociativity, although these relationships have been questioned recently (Whalen & Nash, 1996).

Putnam et al. (1986) and Coons et al. (1988) found that DID patients had received on average about four previous diagnoses before the final DID diagnosis. They mostly included depression and other affective disorders, personality disorders, and schizophrenia. Later studies have found substantial comorbidity between DID and depression and affective lability (including self-injury attempts), anxiety, conversion and other somatoform disorders (headaches are almost always found among DIDs), personality disorders (especially borderline), and first-rank symptoms. Substance abuse and eating disorders are not infrequent in DID either (cf. Cardeña & Spiegel, 1996).

By definition, DID includes dissociative amnesia. DID patients also commonly present other dissociative disorders including dissociative fugue, depersonalization, "trance" states, and so on. While DIDs report some first-rank symptoms such as auditory hallucinations, they typically have adequate reality testing outside of specific events such as fugues or flashbacks and do not present the negative symptoms of schizophrenia.

Because DID patients are multisymptomatic and often have other diagnoses, a thorough evaluation is essential. A careful differential diagnosis of DID should rule out other dissociative disorders, dissociative symptoms produced by epilepsy, psychotic states, some personality disorders, transient effects of medications and drugs, malingering, conversion and somatization disorders, depression, and psychosexual disorders (cf. Coons, 1984). As with other disorders, the clinician should also consider malingering and factitious disorder as possible diagnoses (Coons & Milstein, 1994).

In most cases, thorough assessment with a systematic interview and one or more of the instruments mentioned above can provide enough information for a diagnosis. While a questionnaire such as the DES can provide valuable information, more specific instruments such as the SCID-D are recommended for a clinical diagnosis. The *Guidelines for Treating Dissociative Identity Disorder* of ISSD (1994) explicitly recommend that hypnosis and amytal interviews not be used during evaluation unless there is uncertainty as to diagnosis after other procedures have been used or in case of emergency, and even then caution should be exercised not to provide leading or suggestive questions. Considering the high suggestibility of these patients, these cautions are warranted.

DEPERSONALIZATION

The DSM-IV defines depersonalization as persistent or recurrent experiences of feeling detached from one's mental processes or body, without loss of reality testing. It involves a perception or experience in which the usual sense of one's reality is temporarily lost or altered. The person may experience a sense of being unreal, of being dead or unfeeling. The range of phenomena under the umbrella of depersonalization is very broad, and there have been very few attempts to establish the extent to which it is valid to cluster all of these manifestations together. One of the exceptions is a study that proposed five different types of depersonalization: inauthenticity, self-negation, self-objectification, derealization, and body detachment (Jacobs & Bovasso, 1992). Self-objectification was more closely related to psychological disorganization than the other factors, but since only students participated it is unknown to what extent this finding would generalize to actual depersonalization disorder.

Feeling estranged from bodily or psychological processes is not unusual, although it is not a common topic of conversation. A number of writers (e.g., Poe, Trakl, and Villaurrutia) have centered their poems or stories on these experiences. Perhaps the most extreme form of depersonalization is autoscopy, where a person encounters a self-image outside of the body. The experience of a "double" of oneself was studied by the psychoanalyst Otto Rank and was described by Poe ("William Wilson") and Dostoevsky, among others. The scientific literature on the phenomenon has not been as prolific as the literary one.

Depersonalization experiences are distinguished from psychotic beliefs in that the former describe *experiences* of alienation with intact reality testing, whereas psychotic episodes involve delusional beliefs. A depersonalized individual may feel like a robot or as if body movements are mechanical; a psychotic, on the other hand, would hold delusional beliefs that she or he may have actual mechanical implants, is turning into metal, and so forth.

The four most common features of depersonalization are 1. an altered sense of self (e.g., "my body doesn't belong to me"); 2. a precipitating event (e.g., an accident, marijuana use); 3. a sense of unreality or a dreamlike state (e.g., "nothing seems real," "I'm not real"); and 4. sensory alterations (e.g., "colors are less vibrant," "voices sound strange"; Kubin, Pakianathan, Cardeña, & Spiegel, 1989).

Depersonalization *syndrome* should be distinguished from depersonalization as an isolated or transient symptom. The syndrome involves depersonalization as the predominant disturbance with recurrent and chronic episodes that cause distress or maladjustment. Depression and anxiety are frequently present in depersonalization syndrome.

Isolated depersonalization symptoms are the third most common psychiatric symptoms and are present in about 40% of psychiatric patients (Steinberg,

1990). Depersonalization symptoms are frequent in other dissociative disorders and in panic attacks. When depersonalization occurs exclusively in the presence of another psychological disorder, the latter is the superordinate diagnosis.

Depersonalization episodes are not that uncommon among nonclinical populations and frequently occur during or shortly after a traumatic event (Koopman, Classen, Cardeña, & Spiegel, 1995; Noyes & Kletti, 1977). They can also occur as a byproduct of meditation (Lazarus, 1976) or psychedelic ingestion, and some hypnotic suggestions are specifically geared to producing a sense of disconnection with one's movements or sensations (Cardeña & Spiegel, 1991).

Depersonalization and derealization are terms often used interchangeably, but the DSM makes a distinction between them. Whereas depersonalization involves detachment from, or sense of unreality about, oneself, in derealization this sense of detachment or unreality refers to the external world. A good example is what a PTSD patient told me during a meeting. When commenting on a session with his therapist he mentioned feeling as if he were seeing the therapist "through a fog . . . as if it were a dream." It is rare to find a case of chronic depersonalization without derealization, or vice versa.

Derealization as a dissociative symptom is different from a psychotic symptom. In derealization, the person would experience that his or her relatives were not quite real but would know them to be real; a psychotic would actually hold the belief that the relatives had been exchanged by impostors (i.e., "l'illusion des sosies"; Reed, 1972).

Patients may not report depersonalization initially but present only with depression, general anxiety, or fear of becoming mad. They may lack the language to describe how they feel or may confuse their experiences with incipient psychosis. Because of this communication problem, the clinician should consider using direct queries on whether the person may have chronic episodes of disconnections with the body or emotions, out of body experiences, sensations of the world being unreal at times, and so forth.

Differential diagnoses include other conditions in which depersonalization is one but not the central symptom (e.g., dissociative identity disorder, panic attacks), depression, obsession, and hypochondriasis. Other conditions to rule out include schizophrenia, borderline personality disorder, substance abuse disorders, organic illness, and medication side effects. The diagnostician should be particularly careful to rule out seizure disorders, particularly temporal lobe epilepsy, which often includes depersonalization episodes (Litwin & Cardeña, 1993).

DISSOCIATIVE DISORDERS NOT OTHERWISE SPECIFIED (DDNOS)

The dissociative disorders not otherwise specified include dissociative pathologies of consciousness, identity, memory, or perception that do not fulfill the criteria of the disorders described so far. A substantial proportion of dissociative patients fall under this category. In a large general psychiatric sample ($n =$ 11,292) Mezzich et al. (1989) found the majority (57%) of dissociative disorder diagnoses to be atypical (a pre–DSM-IV designation of DDNOS). This figure is very similar (60%) to the one obtained by Saxe and collaborators (1993) in a subgroup of general psychiatric patients reporting clinical levels of dissociation. However, the epidemiological study by Ross (1991), who used a thorough evaluation of dissociativity, did not confirm this pattern. Diagnostic criteria have changed, and new epidemiological studies with detailed evaluation of dissociation are needed to clarify this issue.

Lynn and Rhue (1988), H. Spiegel (1974), and Hartmann (1984) have respectively described subgroups of high fantasizers, hypnotic "virtuosos," and "thin boundaried" individuals who are vulnerable to distressing fantasies, excessive suggestibility, and uncontrolled loss of boundaries, which seems to increase their risk for psychopathology. Uncontrolled and disorganized fluctuations of consciousness seem to increase the risk of pathology in this and other cultures (Cardeña, 1992). What little evidence we have also suggests that the majority of dissociative patients in other cultures have different presentations than the ones described so far (Cardeña et al., 1996; Saxena & Prasad, 1989).

The DSM-IV contains the following as examples of DDNOS:

1. Cases similar to DID that do not fulfill all its criteria—for instance, an individual presenting with two or more identities but without amnesia. The instances of identity alteration without amnesia, and typically with a greater overall integration of personality have been called "ego states."
2. Derealization without depersonalization (e.g., sensing oneself as "normal" but the world as not quite real or as diffuse). This example is specific to adults. Children without any pathology might nonetheless blur the distinction between their fantasy and consensual reality.
3. Dissociative states in individuals who have been subjected to chronic forms of coercion, suggestion, "brainwashing," and so on. West and Martin (1994) have described the presentation of captivity and cult victims. Among the phenomena they describe are an emotionally and intellectually restricted "pseudoidentity," which at least temporarily substitutes for the previous identity, episodes of unawareness, and disorientation, emotional unresponsiveness and lack of motivation, and so forth.
4. Dissociative trance disorder (see below).
5. Loss of consciousness, being stuporous or comatose without a medical reason.
6. Ganser's syndrome, or the giving of approximate answers (e.g., "a car has three wheels") that cannot be explained by dementia, psychosis, or malingering. Ganser's syndrome is typically accompanied by other dissociative phenomena such as time alteration. The DSM-IV considers dissociative amnesia and fugue as superordinate diagnoses to Ganser's syndrome. Coons (1992) has described also different personality states associated with gender identity disorder.

The assessment of DDNOS is the same as that for the other dissociative disorders. Its prognosis depends on such factors as the severity of the disorder and its chronicity and history.

Differential diagnosis should include dissociative-like phenomena occurring as the byproduct of medication (e.g., Finestone & Manly, 1994), and seizure or other medical conditions (cf. Cardeña et al., 1996; Good, 1993). It should be borne in mind also that, as with the other dissociative disorders, DDNOS can be diagnosed only when there is evidence of clinical levels of distress or maladjustment.

Dissociative Trance Disorder

One of the examples of DDNOS is dissociative trance disorder, which includes some cases of trance or spirit possession. Cardeña et al. (1996) proposed that dissociative trance disorder should be taken out of the list of the DDNOS and considered a dissociative disorder in its own right. This action would enhance the cross-cultural applicability of the DSM taxonomy because there is evidence that many, if not most, of the dissociative manifestations in other cultures might fall under this rubric. The DSM-IV included the proposal of a "trance dissociative disorder" in an appendix for "further study."

Although we do not have as yet a cross-cultural database to compare dissociative manifestations in other cultures, there are indications that they often differ in important ways from the criteria used by the DSM-IV. For instance, Saxena and Prasad (1989) reported that 90% of clinic outpatients in India with a dissociative diagnosis had "atypical dissociative disorder," or DDNOS according to DSM-III criteria; many of those patients specifically complained of distressing or maladjusting forms of spirit possession.

The word "trance" has been used in many, often inconsistent, ways. In the DSM-IV it is defined as a consciousness state characterized by a narrow focus of consciousness or stereotypical behaviors experienced as alien to the subject, or both. The notion of trance usually entails a diminution of the temporal, spatial, and mnestic contexts for the self, or what Shor called "generalized reality orientation" (Shor, 1959), and a decrease in reflective awareness (cf. Cardeña & Spiegel, 1991). Examples of "trance" include a patient who suddenly becomes unaware of or unresponsive to the therapist (because the individual either has no apparent mental contents or is fully absorbed in a memory or a fantasy), and a patient who starts writing lines on a paper and becomes temporarily unable to stop the scribbling on the paper. Although amnesia has been focused on as a central component of most dissociative disorders, lack of reflective consciousness and control of behavior are often seen in the clinical context and are central to modern views of dissociation (Hilgard, 1994; Woody & Bowers, 1994).

Spirit possession is defined by the DSM-IV as an alteration of identity and consciousness characterized by the replacement of the individual's usual identity by a different identity, commonly believed to be that of an ancestor or other noncorporeal being; it is frequently accompanied by amnesia. Spirit possession in this sense is different from the *belief* that illnesses or other occurrences are caused by metaphysical forces. It might be tempting to conclude that spirit possession is nothing but a metaphysical explanation for what we call dissociative identity disorder. At this point such conclusion is unwarranted. In contrast with dissociative identity disorder, pathological spirit possession has not been associated with a history of early abuse, the possessing entity is experienced as external to the individual and generally conforms to a specific religious pantheon, and the disorder seems to be more reactive to a current stressor and less chronic than DID.

Alterations of consciousness that we could characterize as spirit possession or trance are frequently a common aspect of cultural and religious practices in many parts of the world (Bourguignon, 1976), and the proposal of a dissociative trance disorder explicitly states that such culturally accepted practices and experiences are outside the pale of this disorder.

Examples of culture-bound pathological manifestations with a central dissociative component include 1. cases of long-lasting and uncontrolled spirit possession involving identity substitution, harming or self-harming acts, amnesia, and so on; 2. *ataque de nervios,* a condition characterized by feelings of fear, grief, and so on, after exposure to trauma, somatic complaints and paresthesias, unawareness of the surroundings, partial or total amnesia for the event, etc.; 3. *latah* and other startle syndromes in which the victim, after a sudden fright, may start mimicking others without apparent control; 4. *amok, berserk,* and similar phenomena in which, after "losing face," the experiencer may brood for a while, have narrowing of consciousness, and then go on an apparently automatic killing rampage until stopped (cf. Cardeña et al., 1996; Simons & Hughes, 1985).

Assessment of general dissociative alterations in our culture may be done through the instruments mentioned, but an evaluation of a dissociative manifestation in a member from another culture or subculture requires that clinicians be conversant at least with the semantic network of disease and health of that group. As the APA states (1995, p. 76), diagnostic evaluation "must be sensitive to the patient's ethnicity and place of birth, gender, social class, sexual orientation, and religious and spiritual beliefs," a principle that is even more poignant in the evaluation of experiential and behavioral phenomena that may be acceptable in other cultures. Bias or lack of knowledge about the client's culture indicates the need for a consultant. There is no systematic database on which to evaluate the prognosis of trance dissociative disorder, but we have considerable anthropological literature on the efficacy of indigenous treatment for some of these manifestations.

CONCLUSIONS

The previous sections give an overview of dissociative disorders that have been accepted, and others that remain in consideration. Considering the brief span in which systematic research on dissociation and the dissociative disorders has been conducted, it is likely that our conception of, and diagnostic criteria for, these disorders will change in the future, and there are some areas such as consideration of cultural variations where we have at most skimmed the surface. The dissociative disorders have been, and will probably remain, mired in controversy for a number of years, but actual empirical investigation is gradually replacing uninformed speculation. It is now established, for example, that traumatic events are commonly associated with dissociative phenomena and symptomatology, that dissociative disorders are more common than used to be thought, and that dissociative disorders can be present at an early age. Many other areas remain open for debate, among them, what personal characteristics predispose individuals to react to trauma with dissociativity rather than with other symptoms, how DID alters should be considered (personalized psychophysiological states, role enactments, etc.), whether traumatic events are encoded differently than other processes, and what neurophysiological and perceptual processes underlie dissociative experiences.

Whatever the outcome of some of these debates, we now have valid and reliable instruments to measure dissociativity, but many more theoretical and empirical developments need to occur before we can actually say that we have really gone beyond the ideas of such brilliant thinkers as Janet or James. Nevertheless, it seems that the dissociative disorders, in some shape or another, are here to stay.

REFERENCES

Akhtar, S., & Brenner, I. (1979). Differential diagnosis of fugue-like states. *Journal of Clinical Psychiatry, 9,* 381–385.

Aldridge-Morris, R. (1989). *Multiple personality: An exercise in deception.* Hillside, NJ: Erlbaum.

American Psychiatric Association. (1980). *Diagnostic and statistical manual of mental disorders* (3rd ed.). Washington, DC: Author.

American Psychiatric Association. (1987). *Diagnostic and statistical manual of mental disorders* (3rd ed., rev. ed.). Washington, DC: Author.

American Psychiatric Association. (1994). *Diagnostic and statistical manual of mental disorders* (4th ed.). Washington, DC: Author.

American Psychiatric Association. (1995). Practice guidelines for psychiatric evaluation of adults. *American Journal of Psychiatry, 152* (Suppl.), 67–80.

Benson, D. F. (1978). Amnesia. *Southern Medical Journal, 71,* 1221–27.

Boon, S., & Draijer, N. (1991). Diagnosing dissociative disorders in the Netherlands: A pilot study with the Structured Clinical Interview for the DSM-III-R Dissociative Disorders. *American Journal of Psychiatry, 148,* 458–462.

Boor, M. (1982). The multiple personality epidemic. *Journal of Nervous and Mental Disease, 170,* 302–304.

Bourguignon, E. (1976). *Possession.* San Francisco: Chandler.

Braun, B. G. (1993). Multiple personality disorder and posttraumatic stress disorder. In J. P. Wilson & B. Raphael (Eds.), *International handbook of traumatic stress syndromes* (pp. 35–47). New York: Plenum.

Brown, D. (1995). Pseudomemories, the standard of science and the standard of care in trauma treatment. *American Journal of Clinical Hypnosis, 37,* 1–24.

Brown, P. (1994). Toward a psychobiological model of dissociation and posttraumatic stress disorder. In S. J. Lynn & J. Rhue (Eds.), *Dissociation* (pp. 94–122). New York: Guilford.

Cardeña, E. (1992). Trance and possession as dissociative disorders. *Transcultural Psychiatric Research Review, 29,* 287–300.

Cardeña, E. (1994). The domain of dissociation. In S. J. Lynn & J. Rhue (Eds.), *Dissociation* (pp. 15–31). New York: Guilford.

Cardeña, E., Koopman, C., Classen, C., & Spiegel, D. (1993). *Stanford Acute Stress Reaction Questionnaire.* Typescript (available from the author).

Cardeña, E., Lewis-Fernández, R., Beahr, D., Pakianathan, I., & Spiegel, D. (1996). Dissociative disorders. In *Sourcebook for the DSM-IV* (Vol. 2, pp. 973–1005). Washington, DC: American Psychiatric Press.

Cardeña, E., & Spiegel, D. (1991). Suggestibility, absorption, and dissociation: An integrative model of hypnosis. In J. F. Schumaker (Ed.), *Human suggestibility: Advances in theory, research, and application* (pp. 93–107). New York: Routledge.

Cardeña, E., & Spiegel, D. (1993). Dissociative reactions to the Bay Area Earthquake. *American Journal of Psychiatry, 150,* 474–478.

Cardeña, E., & Spiegel, D. (1996). Diagnostic issues, criteria and comorbidity of dissociative disorders. In L. Michelson & W. Ray (Eds.), *Handbook of dissociation: Theoretical, empirical, and clinical perspectives* (pp. 227–250). New York: Plenum.

Carlson, E. B., & Armstrong, J. (1994). The diagnosis and assessment of dissociative disorders. In S. J. Lynn & J. Rhue (Eds.), *Dissociation* (pp. 159–174). New York: Guilford.

Carlson, E. B., & Putnam, F. W. (1993). An update on the dissociative experiences scale. *Dissociation, 6,* 16–27.

Christianson, S. A., & Loftus, E. F. (1987). Memory for traumatic events. *Applied Cognitive Psychology, 1,* 225–239.

Coons, P. M. (1984). The differential diagnosis of multiple personality. *Psychiatric Clinics of North America, 7,* 51–67.

Coons, P. M. (1992). Dissociative disorders not otherwise specified: A clinical investigation of 50 cases with suggestions for typology and treatment. *Dissociation, 5,* 187–195.

Coons, P. M. (1994). Confirmation of childhood abuse in child and adolescent cases of multiple personality and dissociative disorder not otherwise specified. *Journal of Nervous and Mental Disease, 182,* 461–464.

Coons, P. M., Bowman, E. S., Kluft, R. P., & Milstein, V. (1991). The cross-cultural occurrence of MPD: Additional cases from a recent survey. *Dissociation, 4,* 124–128.

Coons, P. M., Bowman, E. S., & Milstein, V. (1988). Multiple personality disorder: A clinical investigation of 50 cases. *Journal of Nervous and Mental Disorder, 176,* 519–527.

Coons, P. M., & Milstein, V. (1992). Psychogenic amnesia: A clinical investigation of 25 cases. *Dissociation, 5,* 73–79.

Coons, P. M., & Milstein, V. (1994). Factitious or malingered multiple personality disorder: Eleven cases. *Dissociation, 7,* 81–85.

Dunn, G. E., Paolo, A. M., Ryan, J. J., & van Fleet, J. N. (1994). Belief in the existence of multiple personality disorder among psychologists and psychiatrists. *Journal of Clinical Psychology, 50,* 454–457.

Erdelyi, M. E. (1994). Dissociation, defense, and the unconscious. In D. Spiegel (Ed.), *Dissociation: Culture, mind, and body* (pp. 3–20). Washington, DC: American Psychiatric Press.

Farthing, G. W. (1992). *The psychology of consciousness.* Englewood Cliffs, NJ: Prentice-Hall.

Finestone, D. H., & Manly, D. T. (1994). Dissociation precipitated by propalonol. *Psychosomatics, 35,* 83–87.

Frischholz, E. J., Lipman, L. S., Braun, B. G., & Sachs, R. G. (1992). Psychopathology, hypnotizability, and dissociation. *American Journal of Psychiatry, 149,* 1521–1525.

Gleaves, D. H. (1996). The sociocognitive model of dissociative identity disorder: A reexamination of the evidence. *Psychological Bulletin, 120,* 42–59.

Good, M. I. (1993). The concept of an organic dissociative disorder: What is the evidence? *Harvard Review of Psychiatry, 1,* 145–157.

Grinker, R. R., & Spiegel, J. P. (1945). *Men under stress.* Philadelphia: Blakiston.

Hartmann, E. (1984). *The nightmare.* New York: Basic Books.

Hilgard, E. R. (1968). *The experience of hypnosis.* New York: Harcourt, Brace, and World.

Hilgard, E. R. (1994). Neodissociation theory. In S. J. Lynn & J. Rhue (Eds.), *Dissociation* (pp. 32–51). New York: Guilford.

Horevitz, R. (1994). Dissociation and multiple personality: Conflicts and controversies. In S. J. Lynn & J. Rhue (Eds.), *Dissociation* (pp. 434–461). New York: Guilford.

Hornstein, N. L., & Putnam, F. W. (1994). Clinical phenomenology of child and adolescent dissociative disorders. *Journal of the American Academy of Child and Adolescent Psychiatry, 31,* 1077–1085.

International Society for the Study of Dissociation (ISSD). (1994). *Guidelines for treating dissociative identity disorder.* Chicago: Author.

Jacobs, J. R., & Bovasso, G. B. (1992). Toward the clarification of the construct of depersonalization and its association with affective and cognitive dysfunctions. *Journal of Personality Assessment, 59,* 352–365.

James, W. (1890/1923). *Principles of psychology.* New York: Holt.

Keller, R., & Shaywitz, B. A. (1986). Amnesia or fugue state: A diagnostic dilemma. *Developmental and Behavioral Pediatrics, 7,* 131–132.

Kenny, M. G. (1986). *The possession of Ansel Bourne: Multiple personality in American culture.* Washington, DC: Smithsonian Institution Press.

Kessler, R. C., McGonagle, K. A., Zhao, S., Nelson, C. B., Hughes, M., Eshleman, S., Wittchen, H. U., & Kendler, K. S. (1994). Lifetime and 12-month prevalence of DSM-III-R psychiatric disorders in the United States. *Archives of General Psychiatry, 51,* 8–19.

Kihlstrom, J. F. (1987). The cognitive unconscious. *Science, 237,* 1445–1452.

Kihlstrom, J. F. (1994). One hundred years of hysteria. In S. J. Lynn & J. W. Rhue. (Eds.), *Dissociation: Clinical and theoretical perspectives* (pp. 365–394). New York: Guilford.

Kirmayer, L. J. (1994). Pacing the void: Social and cultural dimensions of dissociation. In D. Spiegel (Ed.), *Dissociation: Culture, mind, and body* (pp. 91–122). Washington, DC: American Psychiatric Press.

Kluft, R. (1991). Clinical presentations of multiple personality disorder. *Psychiatric Clinics of North America, 14,* 605–629.

Kluft, R. P. (1994). Treatment trajectories in multiple personality disorder. *Dissociation, 7,* 63–76.

Kluft, R. P. (1996). Dissociative identity disorder. In L. K. Michelson & W. J. Ray (Eds.), *Handbook of dissociation: Theoretical, empirical, and clinical perspectives* (pp. 337–366). New York: Plenum.

Kluft, R., Steinberg, M., & Spitzer, R. L. (1988). DSM-III-R revisions in the dissociative disorders: Exploration of their derivation and rationale. *Dissociation, 1,* 39–46.

Koopman, C., Classen, C., Cardeña, E., & Spiegel, D. (1995). When disaster strikes, acute stress disorder may follow. *Journal of Traumatic Stress, 8,* 29–46.

Kopelman, M. D. (1987). Amnesia: Organic and psychogenic. *British Journal of Psychiatry, 150,* 428–442.

Kopelman, M. D., Christensen, H., Puffett, A., & Stanhope, N. (1994). The great escape: A neuropsychological study of psychogenic amnesia. *Neuropsychologia, 32,* 675–691.

Kubin, M., Pakianathan, I., Cardeña, E., & Spiegel, D. (1989). *Depersonalization disorder.* Unpublished manuscript.

Lazarus, A. (1976). Psychiatric problems precipitated by transcendental meditation. *Psychological Reports, 10,* 39–74.

Lewis-Fernández, R. (1994). Culture and dissociation. A comparison of *ataque de nervios* among Puerto Ricans and possession syndrome in India. In D. Spiegel (Ed.), *Dissociation: Culture, mind, and body.* Washington, DC: American Psychiatric Press.

Litwin, R. G., & Cardeña, E. (1993). *Dissociation and reported trauma in organic and psychogenic seizure patients.* Paper presented at the 101st annual convention of the American Psychological Association, Toronto.

Loewenstein, R. J. (1991a). Psychogenic amnesia and psychogenic fugue: A comprehensive review. In A. Tasman & S. M. Goldfinger (Eds.), *Review of psychiatry* (Vol. 10, pp. 189–222). Washington, DC: American Psychiatric Press.

Loewenstein, R. J. (1991b). An office mental status examination for chronic complex dissociative symptoms and dissociative identity disorder. *Psychiatric Clinics of North America, 14,* 567–604.

Loftus, E. F. (1993). The reality of repressed memories. *American Psychologist, 48,* 518–537.

Lynn, S. J., & Rhue, J. W. (1988). Fantasy proneness: Hypnosis, developmental antecedents, and psychopathology. *American Psychologist, 43,* 35–44.

Lynn, S. J., & Rhue, J. W. (1994). *Dissociation.* New York: Guilford.

Marmar, C. R., Weiss, D. S., Schlenger, W. E., Fairbank, J. A., Jordan, B. K., Kulka, R. A., & Hough, R. L. (1994). Peritraumatic dissociation and posttraumatic stress in male Vietnam theater veterans. *American Journal of Psychiatry, 151,* 902–907.

Martinez-Taboas, A. (1991). Multiple personality in Puerto Rico: Analysis of fifteen cases. *Dissociation, 4,* 189–192.

Mayeux, R., Alexander, M. P., Benson, F., Brandt, J., & Rosen, J. (1979). Poriomania. *Neurology, 29,* 1616–1619.

Mezzich, J. E., Fabrega, H., Coffman, G. A., & Haley, R. (1989). DSM-III disorders in a large sample of psychiatric patients: Frequency and specificity of diagnoses. *American Journal of Psychiatry, 146,* 212–219.

Michelson, L. K., & Ray, W. J. (Eds.), (1996). *Handbook of dissociation: Theoretical, empirical, and clinical perspectives.* New York: Plenum.

Morgan, A. H. (1973). The heritability of hypnotic susceptibility in twins. *Journal of Abnormal Psychology, 82,* 55–61.

Nemiah, J. C. (1995). Dissociative disorders. In H. I. Kaplan & B. J. Sadock (Eds.), *Comprehensive textbook of psychiatry/VI* (pp. 1281–1293). Baltimore: Williams and Wilkins.

Noyes, R., & Kletti, R. (1977). Depersonalization in response to life-threatening danger. *Comprehensive Psychiatry, 18,* 375–384.

Pribor, E. E., Yutzi, S. H., Dean, T. J., & Wetzel, R. D. (1993). Briquet's syndrome, dissociation, and abuse. *American Journal of Psychiatry, 150,* 1507–1511.

Putnam, F. (1989). *Diagnosis and treatment of multiple personality disorder.* New York: Guilford.

Putnam, F. W. (1994). Dissociative disorders in children and adolescents. In S. J. Lynn & J. Rhue (Eds.), *Dissociation* (pp. 175–189). New York: Guilford.

Putnam, F. W., Guroff, J. J., Silberman, E. K., Barban, L., & Post, R. M. (1986). The clinical phenomenology of multiple personality disorder: Review of 100 recent cases. *Journal of Clinical Psychiatry, 47,* 285–293.

Putnam, F. W., & Loewenstein, R. J. (1993). Treatment of multiple personality disorder: A survey of current practices. *American Journal of Psychiatry, 150,* 1048–1052.

Reed, G. (1972). The psychology of anomalous experience. London: Hutchinson University.

Riether, A. M., & Stoudemire, A. (1988). Psychogenic fugue states: A review. *Southern Medical Journal, 81,* 568–571.

Riley, K. C. (1988). Measurement of dissociation. *Journal of Nervous and Mental Disease, 176,* 449–450.

Rollinson, R. D. (1978). Transient global amnesia- A review of 213 cases from the literature. *Australian and New Zealand Journal of Medicine, 8,* 547–549.

Ross, C. A. (1991). Epidemiology of multiple personality and dissociation. *Psychiatric Clinics of North America, 14,* 503–517.

Ross, C. A., Norton, G. R., & Fraser, G. A. (1989). Evidence against the iatrogenesis of multiple personality disorder. *Dissociation, 2,* 61–65.

Ross, C. A., Norton, G. R., & Wozney, K. (1989). Multiple personality disorder: An analysis of 236 cases. *Canadian Journal of Psychiatry, 34,* 413–418.

Saxe, G. N., Chinman, G., Berkowitz, R., Hall, K., Lieberg, G., Schwartz, J., & van der Kolk, B. A. (1994). Somatization in patients with dissociative disorders. *American Journal of Psychiatry, 151,* 1329–1334.

Saxe, G. N., van der Kolk, B. A., Berkowitz, R., Chinman, G., Hall, K., Lieberg, G., & Schwartz, J. (1993). Dissociative disorders in psychiatric patients. *American Journal of Psychiatry, 150,* 1037–1042.

Saxena, S., & Prasad, K. V., (1989). DSM-III subclassification of dissociative disorders applied to psychiatric outpatients in India. *American Journal of Psychiatry, 146,* 261–262.

Schacter, D. L., Wang, P. L., Tulving, E., & Freedman, M. (1982). Functional retrograde amnesia: A quantitative case study. *Neuropsychologia, 20,* 523–532.

Shor, R. E. (1959). Hypnosis and the concept of the generalized reality-orientation. *American Journal of Psychotherapy, 13,* 582–602.

Silva, P. de, & Ward, A. J. (1993). Personality correlates of dissociation. *Personality and Individual Differences, 14,* 857–859.

Simons, R. C., & Hughes, C. C. (Eds.). (1985). *The culture-bound syndromes.* Dordrecht: Reidel.

Sivec, H. J., & Lynn, S. J. (1995). Dissociative and neuropsychological symptoms: The question of differential diagnosis. *Clinical Psychology Review, 15,* 297–316.

Spanos, N. P. (1994). Multiple identity enactments and multiple personality disorder: A sociocognitive perspective. *Psychological Bulletin, 116,* 143–165.

Spiegel, D. (Ed.). (1994). *Dissociation: Culture, mind, and body.* Washington, DC: American Psychiatric Press.

Spiegel, D., & Cardeña, E. (1991). Disintegrated experience: The dissociative disorders revisited. *Journal of Abnormal Psychology, 100,* 366–378.

Spiegel, H. (1974). The grade 5 syndrome: The highly hypnotizable person. *International Journal of Clinical and Experimental Hypnosis, 22,* 303–319.

Steinberg, M. (1990). The spectrum of depersonalization: Assessment and treatment. In A. Tasman & S. M. Goldfinger (Eds.), *Review of psychiatry* (Vol. 10, pp. 223–247). Washington, DC: American Psychiatric Press.

Steinberg, M. (1993). *The structured clinical interview for DSM-IV dissociative disorders.* Washington, DC: American Psychiatric Press.

Stengel, E. (1941). On the aetiology of the fugue states. *Journal of Mental Sciences, 87,* 572–599.

Stutman, R. K., & Bliss, E. I. (1985). Posttraumatic stress disorder, hypnotizability, and imagery. *American Journal of Psychiatry, 142,* 741–743.

Tellegen, A., Lykken, D. T., Bouchard, T. J., Wilcox, K. J., Segal, N. L., & Rich, S. (1988). Personality similarity in twins reared apart and together. *Journal of Personality and Social Psychology, 54,* 1031–1039.

Terr, L. C. (1991). Childhood traumas: An outline and overview. *American Journal of Psychiatry, 148,* 10–20.

Tillman, J. G., Nash, M. R., & Lerner, P. M. (1994). Does trauma cause dissociative pathology? In S. J. Lynn & J. W. Rhue (Eds.), *Dissociation: Clinical and theoretical perspectives* (pp. 395–414). New York: Guilford.

Tutkun, H., Yargic, L. I., & Sar, V. (1995). Dissociative identity disorder: A clinical investigation of 20 cases in Turkey. *Dissociation, 8,* 3–9.

van der Hart, O., & Nijenhuis, E. (1995). Amnesia for traumatic experiences. *Hypnos, 22,* 73–86.

van der Kolk, B. A., & van der Hart, O. (1989). Pierre Janet and the breakdown of adaptation in psychological trauma. *American Journal of Psychiatry, 146,* 1530–1540.

Vanderlinden, J., van der Hart, O., & Varga, K. (1996). European studies of dissociation. In L. K. Michelson & W. J. Ray (Eds.), *Handbook of dissociation: Theoretical, empirical, and clinical perspectives* (pp. 25–49). New York: Plenum.

Waller, N. G., Putnam, F. W., & Carlson, E. B. (1996). Types of dissociation and dissociative types: A taxometric analysis of dissociative experiences. *Psychological Methods, 3,* 300–321.

West, L. J., & Martin, P. R. (1994). Pseudo-identity and the treatment of personality change in victims of captivity and cults. In S. J. Lynn & J. Rhue (Eds.), *Dissociation* (pp. 268–288). New York: Guilford.

Whalen, J. E., & Nash, M. R. (1996). Hypnosis and dissociation. In L. K. Michelson & W. J. Ray (Eds.), *Handbook of dissociation: Theoretical, empirical, and clinical perspectives* (pp. 191–206). New York: Plenum.

Woody, E. Z., & Bowers, K. S. (1994). A frontal assault on dissociated control. In S. J. Lynn & J. Rhue (Eds.), *Dissociation* (pp. 52–79). New York: Guilford.

Zatzick, D. F., Marmar, C. R., Weiss, D. S., & Metzler, T. (1994). Does trauma-linked dissociation vary across ethnic groups? *Journal of Nervous and Mental Disease, 182,* 576–582.

CHAPTER 13

Sexual and Gender Identity Disorders

NATHANIEL MCCONAGHY

Sexual and gender identity disorders are classified in the DSM-IV (*Diagnostic and Statistical Manual of Mental Disorders;* American Psychiatric Association [APA], 1994) as sexual dysfunctions, paraphilias, and gender identity disorders. The dysfunctions, stated to be characterized by disturbance in sexual desire and in the psychophysiological changes that characterize the sexual response cycle, are further classified into seven categories. Sexual desire disorders include hypoactive sexual desire disorder, deficient (or absent) sexual fantasies and desire for sexual activity; and sexual aversion disorder, extreme aversion to and avoidance of all or almost all genital sexual contact with a partner. Presumably this DSM-IV diagnosis could not be used for those women who accept genital contact but have an aversion to their breasts being fondled or to touching their partners' genitals. Sexual arousal disorders include female sexual arousal disorder, inability to attain or maintain an adequate genital lubrication-swelling response of sexual excitement until completion of the sexual activity, and male erectile disorder, inability to attain or maintain an adequate erection until completion of the sexual activity. Orgasm disorders include female and male orgasmic disorders and premature ejaculation. Female orgasmic disorder is delay or absence of orgasm following a normal sexual excitement phase. It is pointed out that women vary widely in the type or intensity of stimulation that trigger orgasm and that the diagnosis should be based on the clinician's judgment that the woman's orgasmic capacity is less than would be reasonable for her age, sexual experience, and the adequacy of sexual stimulation she receives. Male orgasmic disorder is delay or absence of orgasm following a normal sexual excitement phase during sexual activity that the clinician, taking into account the person's age, judges to be adequate in focus, intensity, and duration. Orgasmic disorder in men is commonly an inability to reach orgasm by ejaculation in the vagina, orgasm being possible with other types of stimulation. The DSM-IV criteria for premature ejaculation include ejaculation with minimal sexual stimulation before, upon, or shortly after penetration, and before the person wishes it. The clinician must take into account factors that affect duration of the excitement phase, such as age, novelty of the sexual partner or situation, and frequency of sexual activity.

The fourth category of dysfunctions, sexual pain disorders, includes dyspareunia, genital pain in either males or females before, during, or after sexual intercourse; and vaginismus, involuntary spasm of the musculature of the outer third of the vagina that interferes with sexual intercourse. Vaginismus usually prevents penetration of any object above a certain size into the vagina, including the subject's finger or a tampon. If intercourse is attempted, vaginismus is commonly accompanied by spasm of the adductor muscles of the thighs preventing their separation. Vaginismus does not prevent women from experiencing sexual arousal and orgasm with other activities than coitus. To receive the diagnosis of sexual disorder in the above four categories, the DSM-IV criterion A requires that the condition is recurrent or persistent, and criterion B requires that the disturbance causes marked distress or interpersonal difficulty. Criterion B presumably allows absence of orgasmic capacity to be considered not a dysfunction in at least some of the women who reported in many surveys that they enjoyed intercourse very much, although they did not reach orgasm (McConaghy, 1993). Criterion C is that the dysfunction does not occur exclusively during, or is not better accounted for by another Axis 1 disorder, and is not due exclusively to the direct physiological effect of a substance or a general medical condition. These dysfunctions are classified separately. The number of issues left to the judgment of the individual clinician by the DSM-IV criteria makes it unlikely that reliability of the diagnoses made by different clinicians using these criteria will be high.

The terms "paraphilias" and "gender identity disorders" are used in the DSM-IV for conditions previously referred to as sexual deviations (behaviors seen as deviating from those currently socially acceptable). With recent changes in social values, masturbation and homosexuality have ceased to be classified as deviations. Essential features of paraphilias are stated to be recurrent, intense sexually arousing fantasies, sexual urges, or behaviors generally involving 1. nonhuman objects, 2. suffering or humiliation of oneself or one's partner, or 3. children or other nonconsenting persons, that occur over a period of at least 6 months (criterion A). The behaviors, sexual urges, or fantasies cause significant distress or impairment in social, occupational, or other important areas of functioning (criterion B). DSM-IV provides a series of specific criteria A for some of the more common paraphilias. The criterion for exhibitionism is that it involves exposure of one's genitals to an unsuspecting stranger; and for fetishism, that it involves use of nonliving objects (e.g., female undergarments). Frotteurism, involving the touching and rubbing against a nonconsenting person, is classified but not rape or sexual assault of a nonconsenting person. Pedophilia, involving sexual activity with a prepubescent child or children (generally age 13 years or younger) by a person who is at least 16 years old and 5 years older, is classified; hebephilia, sexual activity of adults with pubertal or immediately postpubertal subjects, is not. Sexual masochism involves the act (real, not simulated) of being humiliated, beaten, bound, or otherwise made to suffer; and sexual sadism involves acts (real, not simulated) in which the psychological or physical suffering (including humiliation) of the victim is sexually exciting. Transvestic fetishism involves cross-dressing, and voyeurism, the act of observing an unsuspecting person, who is naked, in the process of disrobing or engaged in sexual activity.

DSM-IV requires for the diagnosis of gender identity disorder as criterion A, a strong and persistent cross-gender identity, manifested in children by four or more of the features: 1. desire to be, or the insistence that one is, of the other sex; 2. cross-dressing; 3. preference for cross-sex roles in play or fantasy; 4.

intense desire to participate in opposite-sex games and pastimes; and 5. strong preference for opposite sex playmates; and in adolescents and adults by the stated desire to be, to live, or to be treated as of the opposite sex, frequent passing as the other sex, or the conviction that he or she has the typical feelings and reactions of the other sex. Criterion B is persistent discomfort or sense of inappropriateness with his or her sex; C, that the disturbance is not concurrent with a physical intersex condition; and D, that the disturbance causes clinically significant distress or impairment in social, occupational, or other important areas of functioning.

EPIDEMIOLOGY

Spector and Carey (1990) reviewed over 20 studies investigating prevalence of dysfunctions in community samples, few of which were representative. They expressed regret at the failure of the National Institute of Mental Health Epidemiologic Catchment Area (ECA) Program study of the prevalence of psychiatric disorders to provide data concerning the prevalence of specific sexual dysfunctions. The ECA study carried out in St. Louis, using Diagnostic Interview Schedules administered by lay interviewers, reported a prevalence of all psychosexual dysfunctions of 24%. This was the most common diagnosis after tobacco use disorder. Among the highest prevalences found were in the study by Frank, Anderson, and Rubinstein (1978) of 100 predominantly white, well-educated, happily married couples; 65% of the women and 40% of the men reported dysfunctions. However, 85% of both men and women stated that their sexual relations were very or moderately satisfying. Therefore, they would be unlikely to receive a DSM-IV diagnosis of dysfunction, in view of criterion B that the disturbance causes marked distress or interpersonal difficulty. The most common dysfunctions were, for women, difficulty getting excited (48%) and difficulty reaching orgasm (44%), and for men, ejaculating too quickly (36%) and difficulty getting (7%) and maintaining (9%) an erection.

Community studies, as summarized by Spector and Carey (1990), reported prevalences in women of inhibited female orgasm, 5%–20%; of sexual arousal disorder, 11%–48%; of hypoactive sexual desire disorder, 34%; and of dyspareunia, 8%–23%. Prevalence rates in men were for erectile difficulty, 3%–9%; for premature ejaculation, 36%–38%; for hypoactive sexual desire disorder, 16%; and for inhibited male orgasm, 1%–10%. In an earlier review, Nathan (1986) reanalyzed 22 general population sex surveys applying DSM-III criteria (APA, 1980). Although only 6 of the 22 were included in Spector and Carey's review, prevalence rates were in the same range. Spector and Carey concluded that inhibited orgasm was one of the least common dysfunctions in men, both in community and clinical samples. Hunt (1974) was critical of Kinsey, Pomeroy, and Martins's (1948) statement that husbands achieved orgasm in virtually 100% of their occasions of martial coitus, pointing out that the Kinsey study did not obtain detailed data concerning this. In Hunt's nonrepresentative sample, 8% of married men aged 45 or more missed orgasm from occasional to most coital experiences, and he added that, surprisingly, 15% of men aged under 25 years missed orgasm in at least 25% of such experiences. Hunt considered this due in most cases to erectile failure produced by anxiety, and in some to attempts being made too soon after having reached orgasm. Twenty-one percent of the adolescent boys in Sorensen's (1973) study had masturbated in the previous month without reaching orgasm. Varying over the age range, from 19% to 30% of a 78% representative sample of 18–59-year-old subjects in the United States reported that they did not always have an orgasm during sex with their primary partners (Laumann, Gagnon, Michael, & Michaels, 1994).

As stated previously, several studies reported that some women commonly enjoy intercourse although they do not reach orgasm (McConaghy, 1993). The possibility that this also is true of some men does not seem to have been investigated. In a 60% representative sample of British men and women aged 16 to 59, 50% of women and 34% of the men disagreed with the statement that sex without orgasm or climax cannot be really satisfying for a person of their sex (Johnson, Wadsworth, Wellings, Field, & Bradshaw, 1994). No community studies appear to have investigated prevalence of sexual dysfunctions in homosexual activities. Weinrich (1991) stated that premature ejaculation is arguably very uncommon in homosexual men but gave no supporting data. Nathan (1986) cited Bell and Weinberg as finding a rate of 27% in homosexual men, which she pointed out was substantially lower than the 35% found consistently in surveys of married men. She commented that this might be attributable to the difference in what is defined as premature in homosexual and heterosexual relations.

Due largely to lack of the relevant data in the studies reviewed, Spector and Carey (1990) did not report prevalence of dysfunctions in relation to the subjects' ages, which appears to be the most important determinant of the major dysfunctions of inhibited female orgasm and male erectile disorders. In his study of a representative sample of adolescents, Sorensen (1973) found that over 50% of the girls rarely or never reached orgasm in sexual relationships. This was reported by 25% of women in their first year of marriage, but 11% or less in their 20th year (Hunt, 1974; Kinsey, Pomeroy, Martin, & Gebhart, 1953). A similar but weaker trend was evident in the study of Laumann et al. (1994). They asked their subjects whether in the previous 12 months there had ever been a period of several months or more when they experienced particular sexual dysfunctions. Lack of interest in having sex was reported by 16% of men and 33% of women; being unable to come to a climax (8% and 24%); coming to a climax too quickly (28% and 10%); experiencing physical pain during intercourse (3% and 14%); not finding sex pleasurable (8% and 21%); feeling anxious about their ability to perform sexually (17% and 11%); and (for men) having trouble achieving or maintaining erection (10%) and (for women) having trouble lubricating (19%). In general, all these dysfunctions as defined decreased with increasing age in women, except lack of interest in sex (which reached 37% in those aged 55–59) and having trouble lubricating (which was experienced by 21%–24% of women aged 45–59). Other studies have found decline in women's sexual interest commencing from the perimenstrual period. In an investigation of a representative sample of 497 women living with their husbands, hypoactive sexual desire disorder was reported by 4% of those aged 38, 3% of those aged 46, 9% of those aged 50, and 21% of those aged 54 (Hallstrom & Samuelsson, 1990). At follow-up 6 years later, prevalence in the four groups was 0%, 7%, 16%, and 29%—a significant increase in the older women. Of the sexual dysfunctions in men investigated by Laumann et al. (1994), only having trouble achieving or maintaining erection showed a clear relationship with age, being reported by over 20% of men aged 50–59. Prevalence rates in community studies of men for complete inability to attain erection were 1% at 30, 2% at 40, 7% at 50, 18% at 60, 27% at 70, 55% at 75, and 76% at 80 years of age (Kinsey, Pomeroy, & Martin, 1948; Weizman & Hart, 1987). Prevalence in men of the same age is markedly lower in healthy than in unhealthy subjects (McConaghy, 1993). Prevalence of difficulty in achieving erection without manual stimulation of the penis, experienced with increasing age, does not appear to have been documented.

Only a small percentage of subjects diagnosed as having sexual dysfunctions seek treatment for them, suggesting that the disturbance may not be causing the marked distress or interpersonal difficulty required to receive a diagnosis with DSM-IV criteria. Of a community sample of 436 women in the United Kingdom (Osborn, Hawton, & Gath, 1988), 142 reported at least one of four operationally defined dysfunctions: impaired sexual interest (17%), vaginal dryness (17%), infrequency of orgasm (16%), and dyspareunia (8%). Only 32 of the 142 considered that they had a sexual problem, as did a further 10 with no dysfunctions. Of the total of 42 women who considered that they had a problem, 16 said they would wish treatment if it were available, and one was receiving it. Of 1,080 men attending a medical outpatient clinic, 401 on questioning admitted to having erectile dysfunction (Slag et al., 1983). Prior to the inquiry only six had been identified as having the dysfunction. The authors commented that subjects were reluctant to call attention to their dysfunction but were eager to discuss and seek evaluation when the physicians broached the topic. In fact, only 188, slightly less than half, accepted the offer of evaluation. Their mean age was 59 years; the mean age of those who refused evaluation was 67 years. Forty percent of 103 men aged 51 considered that they suffered from some kind of sexual dysfunction, but only 7% considered the problem abnormal for their age and only 5% planned to consult a therapist (Solstad & Hertoft, 1993). Martin (1981) reported that of 188 60–79-year-old male volunteers of a Baltimore study of aging, only 10% of the 88 with potency problems had sought medical advice for the condition. He considered that the majority were uninterested, due to low sexual motivation.

Spector and Carey (1990) pointed out prevalence of dysfunctions in subjects who seek professional help may not reflect prevalence in the population. However, in the literature they reviewed, prevalences of sexual dysfunctions diagnosed by practitioners mainly paralleled those reported in community studies. In women, prevalences of hypoactive sexual desire, sexual arousal, and inhibited orgasm disorders were fairly equivalent, and markedly higher than that of dyspareunia. Snyder and Berg (1983a) found, in 45 couples presenting with sexual dissatisfaction, about 70% of the women reported each of the former three dysfunctions and 20% reported dyspareunia. Citing a finding that dyspareunia was a common problem reported to medical practitioners, Spector and Casey suggested that women may interpret pain as a medical symptom and seek help from a general practitioner or gynecologist. They found erectile disorder to be the most common complaint in men seeking treatment in the 1970s. It was reported by about 40%; 20% reported premature ejaculation. The erectile disorder reported was usually secondary or acquired, with primary or lifelong erectile disorder being infrequent. Inhibited male orgasm was also infrequent, being reported by less than 8% of subjects. Spector and Carey concluded that complaints of hypoactive sexual desire in men increased markedly in the 1980s, reaching over 50% and outnumbering the percentage of women with this complaint in some studies. Such apparent increase in prevalence in men may have reflected lack of representativeness of the few studies available for their review. It was not present in two unreviewed studies. Only 13 of 113 dysfunctional men reported impaired sexual interest; 62 had erectile dysfunction, and 26 had premature ejaculation; 72 of the 117 dysfunctional women reported impaired sexual interest (Catalan, Hawton, & Day, 1990). Stuart, Hammond, and Pett (1987) restricted their investigation of inhibited sexual desire to women because of the limited number of men who reported it.

In his discussion of the concept of retarded ejaculation, Apfelbaum (1989) suggested that a number were autosexual rather than heterosexual or homosexual and made up only a small part of the total number of autosexual men, most of whom may make no effort to have an orgasm with a partner, including those who simply pursue their solitary masturbatory ways. There does not seem to have been any attempt to determine prevalence of such autosexuality. Johnson et al. (1994) did not investigate masturbatory activities but reported that 0.8% of men and 0.7% of women reported never feeling sexually attracted to anyone at all.

Information about prevalence of perpetrators of paraphilias is rarely sought in community surveys of mental disorder in representative community samples. In the representative sample investigated by Laumann et al. (1994), 2.8% of men and 1.5% of women reported forcing a person of the opposite sex to do something sexual they did not want to do; only 0.1% of women and 0.2% of men reported forcing persons of the same sex. However, 22% of women and 1.7% of men reported being forced by a person of the opposite sex, and 0.8% of women and 2.3% of men reported being forced by a person of the same sex. In contrast, women were assailants in 25% of sexual assaults of adults in a supplementary study of the Los Angeles NIMH ECA survey (Sorenson, Stein, Siegel, Golding, & Burnam, 1987). In her 3-year study of a national sample of adolescents, Ageton (1983) found that 10% of the males reported having forced females into sexual behavior that involved contact with the sexual parts of the body. Yearly, over the same 3 years, 1 adolescent male in 200 was arrested for forcible rape. Ageton did not report sexually assaultive behavior by women. Certainly, women rarely seek treatment for or are charged with sexual assault or pedophilia, possibly in part because male child partners of women do not usually regard the experience negatively. Russell's decision (1986) that pedophilic activity was abusive, whether or not the children considered their reactions neutral or positive, appears to be generally applied only to adult sexual activity with female children. Women were convicted of 1% of sexual offenses and 1.5% of acts of indecency against children in Britain (O'Connor, 1987). As pointed out earlier, coercive sex with adolescents and adults, apart from frotteurism, is not classified as a paraphilia in DSM-IV. Laumann et al. (1994) did not question their subjects about having been perpetrators of pedophilic acts; 17% of women and 12% of men reported that they had been sexually touched before the age of 12 or 13 by someone over age 14. The sexual behaviors experienced were vaginal intercourse in 14% of women and anal sex in 18% of men with male perpetrators, and vaginal intercourse in 42% of the men with female perpetrators. Oral sexual contact was reported by 30% of men and 10% of women with male perpetrators and 10% of men with female perpetrators. In their study, the median age of abuse was 9.9 for boys and girls.

Finkelhor, Hotaling, Lewis, and Smith (1990) reported the first national survey. Chosen from a randomly generated sample of all residential phone numbers in the United States, 1,145 men and 1,481 women (76% of those requested) answered four questions concerning experiences they had when children (indicated to be age 18 or younger) that they would now consider sexual abuse. Someone trying or succeeding in having any kind of sexual intercourse, or anything like that, was reported by 14.6% of women and 9.5% of men. When anything like touching, grabbing, kissing, or rubbing against their bodies; having nude photos taken; being exhibited to or having a sex act performed in their presence; or oral sex or sodomy were added, 27% of women and 16% of men reported at least one of these experiences. Force was used in 15% of the incidents against boys and 19% of those against girls. Perpetrators in the Finkelhor et al. study were men in 98% of the offenses against girls and 83% of those against boys. In the Laumann et al. study (1994) they were men only, women only, and both in 91%, 4%, and 4%, respectively, of the offenses against girls; and 38%, 54%, and 7%, respectively, of the offenses against boys. Perpetrators were relatives for 52% and strangers for 7% of the women, and relatives for 19% and strangers for 4% of the men. Most of the remainder were family friends. In the study by Finkelhor et al., perpetrators were relatives for 29% and strangers for 21% of the women, and relatives for 11% and strangers for 40% of the men. Discrepancies in the findings of these studies are due in part to differences in diagnostic criteria (see Diagnostic Considerations, below). The studies agreed in finding that prevalence of child-adult sexual experiences reported by subjects of different ages does not support the belief that there had been an increase in the wake of the "sexual revolution" of the 1960s. Clinical and forensic data indicate that many men who molest boys do so on one occasion with hundreds of victims, whereas those who molest girls typically do so repeatedly with at most a few victims (McConaghy, 1993). McConaghy estimated in regard to the prevalence of offenders against girls that as a pedophile has on average one to two female victims, if it were accepted that 90% of pedophiles are male, that 30% of women are their victims, and that there are about four times as many adults as children in the population, about 5% of men and 0.5% of women would molest girls. As fewer boys are molested than girls and the number molested by one offender is higher, the percentage of men who molest boys should be considerably lower than 5%. About 15% of male and 2% of female university students in the United States and Australia reported some likelihood of having sexual activity with a prepubertal child if they could do so without risk (Malamuth, 1989; McConaghy, Zamir, & Manicavasagar, 1993).

Person, Terestman, Myers, Goldberg, and Salvadori (1989) investigated the sexual activities of university students. Men reported that over the previous 3 months 4% had exhibited in public; 4% watched others make love; 3% were tied or bound during sexual activities; 2% whipped or beat a partner; 1% degraded and 1% tortured a partner; 1% were forced to submit; 1% dressed in the clothes of the opposite sex; and 1% were whipped or beaten or degraded by a partner. Twenty-one percent reported a lifetime prevalence of having exhibited in public; the lifetime prevalence of the other practices were not stated. Women reported that 6% were forced to submit to sexual acts; 4% were tied or bound during sex activities; 4% were sexually degraded; 1% were tortured by a partner; 1% were whipped or beaten by a partner; and 1% tortured a sexual partner. Activities were described as sadomasochistic, implying that the subjects being hurt or humiliated consented to them. This was consistent with the prevalence and nature of the students' reported fantasies. In a national survey of 2,000 subjects (Hunt, 1974), sexual pleasure was obtained by 4.8% of men and 2.1% of women by inflicting pain and by 2.5% of men and 4.6% of women by receiving pain. Templeman and Stinnett (1991) found that 65% of 57 male undergraduates had engaged in some form of sexual misconduct, although only two had been arrested for sexual offenses. Two others had been in trouble with parents, school, or employers for their sexual behavior. Voyeurism was the most common offense, reported by 42%; frottage was reported by 35%, and making obscene phone calls by 8%. Only one subject reported exhibitionism, which appears inconsistent with the evidence that it is the most common sexual offense (McConaghy, 1993). Thirty percent of 500 women in Albuquerque reported being victims of exhibitionists, compared with 8% who reported being victims of obscene phone calls, and 4% victims of voyeurs (DiVasto et al., 1984). Students in Templeman and Stinnett's study were raised and educated in primarily rural environments, where exhibitionism may be more rarely carried out as the possibility of the offender's being recognized would be greater than in urban environments. Three (5%) reported coercive sexual behaviors, consistent with the percentage of male students reporting the use of some physical force to obtain sexual acts in the United States and Australia (McConaghy, 1993). Two reported sexual contacts with girls under age 12, and a further three reported sexual contact with girls aged 13–15 when they were over age 20 years.

It would seem that as many as half the male population have carried out occasional paraphilic practices. This could account for the finding that the majority of sex offenders reported multiple paraphilias of unstated frequencies (Abel & Rouleau, 1990). My clinical experience with offenders seeking treatment is that the majority report having carried out mainly the same deviant behavior, and if they were charged repeatedly, it was usually for the same form of deviation (McConaghy, Blaszczynski, Armstrong, & Kidson, 1989). Knight, Prentky, and Circe (1994) found that 81% of 59 incarcerated rapists reported having engaged in some paraphilic behavior more than twice; the clinical records of 74.6% of the same sample did not contain any evidence of paraphilias. Consistent with prevalence of deviant behaviors, regular use of deviant sexual fantasies appears common. In Hunt's (1974) study, masturbatory fantasies of forcing someone to have sex were reported by 13% of men and 3% of women, and of being forced to have sex by 10% of men and 19% of women. The coital fantasy of being overpowered or forced to surrender was the second most prevalent fantasy in 50% of married upper class New York women (Hariton & Singer, 1974). Over 30% of normal men reported sexual fantasies of tying up and of raping a woman, and 10%–20% of torturing or beating up a woman (Crepault &

Couture, 1980; Person et al., 1989). A significant percentage of normal men are aroused by descriptions of rape in which the woman experiences pain or is humiliated (Malamuth & Check, 1983; Pfaus, Myronuk, & Jacobs, 1986). Penile circumference assessment of paraphilias in 66 normal controls demonstrated clinically significant tendencies to sadism, defined as nonsexual violence against fully clothed females in 5%, pedophilia in 18%, and at least one paraphilia in 28% (Fedora et al., 1992).

Prevalence of gender identity disorders in children has not been investigated in community studies. Zuger and Taylor (1969) compared incidence of feminine behaviors (dressing in female clothes, wearing lipstick, etc., preferring girl play-mates, desire to be female, feminine gesturing, doll-play, and aversion to boys' games) in 95 schoolboys and 26 patients who showed marked effeminacy likely to be diagnosed as gender identity disorder using DSM-IV criteria. Overlap in frequency of behaviors occurred with six schoolboys and one patient. Zuger and Taylor decided that the patient may have been incorrectly diagnosed, en-abling them to conclude that the behavior of the patients was clearly differenti-ated from that of the schoolboys. Although their results indicated that a fourth of the schoolboys showed some feminine behaviors, Zuger and Taylor did not attribute any significance to this. They thus retained the accepted belief that opposite-sex–linked behaviors of interest to sex researchers were extreme and categorical, present in only 1 or 2 boys in 1,000. This view was maintained without discussion in the monograph "The 'Sissy Boy Syndrome' and the Devel-opment of Homosexuality" (Green, 1987). The 12% or more of subjects cur-rently aware of the presence of some homosexual feelings compared to the remainder reported an increased incidence of opposite-sex behaviors and wish to be of the opposite sex in childhood and adolescence. The degree to which these behaviors were shown correlated with the current ratio of homosexual to heterosexual feelings experienced by the men and degree of opposite-sex iden-tity in both men and women (McConaghy, 1987; McConaghy, Buhrich, & Si-love, 1994). Several studies in addition to that of Zuger and Taylor have found that a percentage of normal children show some degree of opposite-sex–linked behaviors (McConaghy, 1993).

The DSM-IV classification of gender identity disorders in adolescents and adults abandoned the distinction, discussed subsequently (see Clinical Picture, below), between transvestism and transsexualism, which has been generally ac-cepted until the present. Prevalence of transvestism has not been investigated in representative community samples, although Schott (1995) cited an estimate of as many as 1 million for the population of transvestic males in the United States. Person et al. (1989) found that 4% of female and 1% of male university students reported dressing in the clothes of the opposite sex in the previous 3 months. The motivation for the behavior was not reported, but 3% of the men and 2% of the women reported recent sexual fantasies of dressing in clothes of the oppo-site sex. Fifteen of 138 male medical students but none of 58 female medical students reported they had obtained sexual arousal from dressing in the external or underclothes of the opposite sex (McConaghy, 1982). Reported prevalence of transsexualism has steadily increased since the condition was recognized. Estimated rates for male-to-female and female-to-male transsexualism, respec-tively, were one in 100,000 and 400,000 in the United States in 1968; one in

37,000 and 100,000 in Sweden in 1968 and in the United Kingdom in 1974; one in 45,000 and 200,000 in the Netherlands in 1980; one in 26,000 and 100,000 in the Netherlands in 1983; and one in 18,000 and 54,000 in the Netherlands in 1986 (Eklund, Gooren, & Bezemer, 1988). The highest figure as yet reported was a prevalence of one in 2,900 for male and in 8,300 for female Singapore-born transsexuals (Tsoi, 1988). Eklund et al. pointed out the ratio of male-to-female as compared to female-to-male transsexuals tended to remain consistent at about three to one. There was no trend for the age of subjects seeking treatment to be younger in the more recent studies, which Eklund et al. argued would be the case if the true prevalence of transsexualism had risen. They considered that more transsexuals were seeking sex conversion due to the increasingly benevolent social climate concerning the procedure.

CLINICAL PICTURE

Investigations have failed to find consistent associations between subjects' sexual dysfunctions and psychological adjustment (Stuart et al., 1987). This could be due in part to insufficient attention being given to differences in dysfunctions. Subjects with premature ejaculation since the beginning of their sexual lives compared to those in whom it developed after years of satisfactory sexual functioning were significantly more likely to report high levels of anxiety during coitus and on an anxiety rating scale (Cooper, Cernovsky, & Colussi, 1993). In their study of happily married couples, Frank et al. (1978) investigated the prevalence not only of sexual dysfunctions but what they termed sexual difficulties, problems related to the emotional tone of sexual relations. The most common in women were inability to relax (47%), too little foreplay before intercourse (38%), disinterest (35%), partner choosing an inconvenient time (31%), and being turned off (28%); and in men, attraction to persons other than the spouse and too little foreplay before intercourse (21%), too little tenderness after intercourse (17%), and disinterest and partner choosing an inconvenient time (16%). Frank et al. found these sexual difficulties to be not only more prevalent than dysfunctions but also more significant, in that their presence correlated more highly with subjects' and their spouses' lack of sexual satisfaction than did the presence of dysfunctions. In the case of men, correlations between presence of dysfunctions and lack of sexual satisfaction were not statistically significant. In reporting a similar finding in older men, Schiavi, Schreiner-Engel, Mandeli, Schanzer, and Cohen (1990) considered that as older healthy couples continued to engage in satisfying sexual intercourse in the face of significant decrements in erectile function, it may be as important to focus attention on attitudinal factors and coping strategies as on mechanisms involved in erectile capacity. Although the functional controls in the study of Heiman, Gladue, Roberts, and LoPiccolo (1986) were selected on the basis that at initial interview they reported not experiencing any notable sexual difficulty, 24% of the men and 42% of the women reported on the subsequently administered personal history questionnaire that they had a dysfunction. Only 2% of the men and 6% of the women reported sexual dissatisfaction. Nettelbladt and Uddenberg (1979) found no association between presence of the dysfunctions of premature ejaculation or erectile difficulties and men's and their female partners' sexual satisfaction. Also, the couples' sexual satisfaction was related to their emotional relationship rather than their sexual function. Snyder and Berg (1983a) reached the same conclusion from findings in a clinical population, couples presenting with sexual dissatisfaction to a sexual dysfunctions clinic. Dysfunctions were common complaints of both men and women, but none reported by the women correlated with their sexual dissatisfaction, and only failure to ejaculate during intercourse correlated with that of men. Dissatisfaction correlated strongly in both sexes with the partner's lack of response to sexual requests and the frequency of intercourse being too low. Despite consistent evidence of the importance of sexual difficulties rather than dysfunctions in couples' sexual satisfaction, most subjects seeking treatment for sexual problems tend to report dysfunctions rather than reduced satisfaction, which accounts for the focus on dysfunctions in the treatment literature. However, the importance of relationship factors rather than sexual dysfunctions in the sexual satisfaction of these subjects could account for the common finding of outcome studies that despite minimal improvement of the specific dysfunction with which they presented, many subjects reported increased sexual interest and enjoyment following psychological treatment (Adkins & Jehu, 1985; De Amicis, Goldberg, LoPiccolo, Friedman, & Davies, 1985; Hawton, Catalan, Martin, & Fagg, 1986). Hawton et al. pointed out that improvement in a couple's general relationship was a frequently reported outcome of therapy for sexual problems and could result from the equally frequently reported improvement in their communication.

Stuart et al. (1987) noted that it was commonly believed that a variety of interpersonal difficulties influence the development and maintenance of sexual dysfunctions, such as couples' power struggles, poor or destructive communication, and lack of respect and affection, but these beliefs relied heavily on clinical impression. They found only one study that compared women with normal sexual functioning and women with a disorder of sexual desire. Ninety-one percent of the former but only 35% of the latter rated their communication with their partners as good or very good. In their own study of 90 married women who presented to a sex and marital therapy clinic, 59 met their criteria for inhibited sexual desire (ISD); 21 of the remaining 31 had normal sexual functioning while their husbands experienced sexual dysfunctions. Women with ISD and their spouses, compared to the remainder, were significantly less satisfied with the way couple conflict was resolved and with their spouses' listening ability; they reported a less satisfactory marital adjustment as assessed by the Diadic Adjustment Scale. Baxter and Wilmot (1985) found that in close relationships, explicit discussion of the relationship was the most taboo topic, reported by 66% of undergraduates in cross-sex relationships. If this is true of sexually dysfunctional couples, the possibility for most of improving their communication without therapy would seem low. Heiman et al. (1986) found that sexually functional women were distinguished from sexually dysfunctional women by greater arousal, pleasure, and sexual interest, a positive reaction to their current partner's body (touch, smell, genitals, and physical appearance), and less emotional involvement with the partner in first coitus. Sexually functional as compared to dysfunctional men were more likely to obtain pleasure from varied sexual activities, to attach less importance to emotional closeness, holding, and expression of care during sex, to have more frequent oral and coital sex, and to use fantasy in partner sex, including atypical and deviant fantasy. Dysfunctional subjects would appear to have a more romantic and less physical attitude to sexual activity.

The sexual functioning of the partner appears to play an important role in maintaining the sexual activity of both men and women. Partners of men with psychogenic as opposed to organic erectile dysfunctions reported more relationship problems but also higher levels of vaginismus and dyspareunia, which usually preceded the erectile dysfunctions (Speckens, Hengeveld, Lycklama a Nijeholt, van Hemert, & Hawton, 1995). Absence or inability of a partner to perform sexually is the most common cause of the cessation of intercourse in older women (McConaghy, 1993). Anorgasmia was reported to decline greatly over the first year of marriage in a series of studies (Nathan, 1986), all of which were carried out before 1956. Nathan also cited studies reporting that only 1%–3% of men and married women but 15%–20% of unmarried heterosexual women claimed never to have any desire for sex. The increase from age 15 to middle age in the ability of women to reach orgasm in sexual relationships suggests that learning is strongly involved (McConaghy, 1993). Mead (1950) pointed out that adolescent girls are expected to restrict the limits of sexual relationships, and boys to extend them. This is likely to result in girls' attempting to limit their sexual arousal in physical relationships and experiencing anxiety if it increases. When they no longer need to restrain their arousal, they have to learn to relinquish the control they have regularly practiced, and to lose their anxiety at becoming aroused. Women who consistently experienced orgasm during coitus compared to those who did not were found to be more likely to report inability to control their thinking or movements as they approached orgasm. They also obtained higher scores on a hypnotic susceptibility scale (Bridges, Critelli, & Loos, 1985). This was considered to reflect a greater ability to suspend effortful, controlled cognitive processes.

In Hunt's (1974) U.S. survey of sexual behavior in the 1970s, women emphasized the role of men in helping them to learn to become aroused: "A man . . . taught me how to move my body, how to feel my own rhythms." "I talked it over a lot with two of them (her lovers), hoping to work it out and become a better and more exciting woman." "A man . . . got me to read several books on peak experiences and joy . . . to blow my mind" (pp. 164, 165). The men emphasized the importance of arousing their partners: "She let me know what it was that I did that got to her." "You try to create something in your partner." "I began to learn . . . how to make a woman rise up higher and higher." "I really work at getting the girl so hot" (pp. 162–163). Darling and Davidson (1986) found that opinions of clinicians differed concerning the prevalent practice of men asking their partners immediately after intercourse whether the partners had experienced orgasm. They pointed out that women may believe men are seeking confirmation of their skill as lovers, in which case women could feel pressure to pretend to orgasm in future. Hunt (1974) reported this reaction in some of the women in his survey, one of whom commented that "men seem to be so hung-up about making the woman have an orgasm—so I often fake it, and go ape, and tell them they were fantastic." Studies have consistently found that 60% of women pretend to reach orgasm on occasion (McConaghy, 1993). Steiner (1981) commented that male pretense of orgasm had not been investigated and found that 36% of male junior college students reported it. Hunt (1974) considered that some men who failed in attempts to reach orgasm shortly after having done so could pretend they were successful. If this is correct, it suggests that both men and women fake orgasm to satisfy male expectations.

The apparent importance of the role of men in helping women learn to become sexually aroused could seem at variance with Morokoff's (1978) statement that she found little evidence to support a relationship between male sexual technique and female orgasm. However, it could be that having learned to reach orgasm, women no longer depend on the technique of the male. Also, the type of learning suggested by the statements of the women in Hunt's survey does not appear to involve physical techniques as much as psychological factors. This is compatible with failure of evidence to support the commonly held belief that inadequate duration of genital stimulation in sexual relationships is an important determinant of women's inability to reach orgasm (McConaghy, 1993). Huey, Kline-Graber, and Graber (1981) found no difference in duration of foreplay or intromission reported by 153 women who did not experience orgasm with coitus or other sexual activities, 114 women who reached orgasm with other sexual activities apart from coitus, and 24 women who experienced orgasm with coitus and usually with other sexual activities. Consistent with the concept that orgasmically inadequate women are those who fear losing control, and that it is not the male's sexual technique as such, but his encouraging the woman to let her feelings of sexual arousal take over, which enables her to learn to reach orgasm, Morokoff (1978) believed that in our culture sexual arousal and orgasm in women are associated with a letting-go, a loosening. Supporting the role of learning in women's achieving the ability to experience orgasm in sexual relationships, Morokoff cited a number of studies that found this ability strongly developed in societies where women were expected to possess it and weakly developed or absent in societies where they were not. Culturally determined changes concerning female sexuality were considered the likely explanation for the higher frequency of orgasm in women in the United States born later in the present century (Hunt, 1974; Kinsey et al., 1953) and for the disappearance in Hunt's later study of the association between orgasmic responsiveness and higher socioeconomic class found by Kinsey et al. Mead (1958) concluded that the human female's capacity for orgasm was much more a potentiality that may or may not be developed by a given culture, or in the specific life history of an individual, than an inherent part of a woman's full humanity.

In view of the failure to find significant clinical psychopathology in subjects with sexual dysfunctions, Wolpe's (1958) concept that these dysfunctions are due to anxiety directly concerning sexual activity and performance has been generally accepted by clinicians. Wolpe considered that such anxiety could be conditioned by faulty cognitions, including expectations about performance, and by experiences occurring at any stage of life, not merely the first 5 years as advanced in psychoanalytic theory. Such anxiety could partially or totally inhibit the subject's sexual responsiveness. Hale and Strassberg (1990) provided evidence that anxiety about sexual performance is a factor in erectile dysfunctions in men and pointed out that earlier studies that had demonstrated that anxiety did not consistently impair sexual arousal had not investigated anxiety over sexual activity.

Biological factors may also play a causal role in sexual dysfunctions. There would appear to be a weaker biological basis for female than for male orgasm throughout mammalian species. Although orgasm has been observed in individual female dogs, rabbits, cats of all species, and a variety of female primates, the majority of females of these species were considered not to reach orgasm, and no evidence of orgasm was reported in any females of most infrahuman species (Kinsey, et al., 1953). Women with late menarche (from age 16 onward) were less able to achieve orgasm than those with menarche from age 11 (Raboch & Raboch, 1986). Investigators of women's sexual behavior have commonly concluded that women differ biologically in their ability to learn to reach orgasm (Mead, 1950) and that some women seem unable to do so (Kaplan, 1974). Martin (1981) reviewed studies indicating that frequencies of current sexual activity reported by men in their 40s and over were highly related to the frequencies they reported for their adolescence and early adulthood. He found this to be the case also among the 60–79-year-old men he studied. As experiential factors could be expected to have varied markedly over the subjects' lives, these findings suggest that biological factors could play an important role in determining frequencies of men's sexual activities throughout their postpubertal lives. If this is so, biological factors involved would seem also to be involved in determining prevalence of sexual dysfunctions, independent of the important effect of aging. Martin found, in regard to his elderly subjects' levels of sexual activity throughout their lives, that 75% of the least active, 46% of the moderately active, and 19% of the most active were partially or totally impotent; 21% of the least active as compared with 8% of the most active had experienced a long-term problem with premature ejaculation.

As with investigations of subjects with sexual dysfunctions, traditional measures of personality and psychopathology have yielded inconsistent results when administered to sex offenders (Knight, et al., 1994). Offenders studied were mainly those incarcerated, most of whom are rapists and child molesters (Henn, Herjanic, & Vanderpearl, 1976). Few were charged with exhibitionism. Many incarcerated sex offenders would not be regarded as paraphiliacs by the DSM-IV, which does not classify hebephiles and most rapists as sexually disordered. Herman (1990) concluded that convicted sex offenders, comprising less than 10% of all offenders, were a highly skewed population, in which those who attack strangers, use extreme force, and lack the social skills to avoid detection were overrepresented. They were far more likely to look abnormal than undetected offenders in the normal population. She considered that many convicted sex offenders met the diagnostic criteria for sociopathic, schizoid, paranoid, and narcissistic personality disorders. Her statement that there was no evidence that these disorders were more common in undetected sexually aggressive males than in the total male population was incorrect. Males who had committed sexual assaults compared to the remainder of a representative sample of adolescents were found to be basically delinquent youths (Ageton, 1983). Sexual aggression of male college students was associated with family violence in childhood, current use of alcohol, and peer relationships that reinforced highly sexualized views of women (Koss & Dinero, 1988), consistent with the presence of antisocial personality traits. Additional evidence of the possible relation of alcohol use to sex offenses were findings that police and victims confirmed alcohol intoxication in 70% of rapists (Marshall & Barbaree, 1990a). In Ageton's (1983) study, about half the males who reported carrying out sexual assaults reported that they had been drinking or taking drugs prior to the event. Victims considered the offender's intoxication to be a major factor precipitating the assault.

As the majority of rapists and child molesters are not reported to authorities and those reported are frequently not incarcerated, features specific to the incarcerated group may account for findings Knight, Rosenberg, and Schneider (1985) considered most surprising. For example, marked similarities were present between convicted rapists and child molesters, and the two groups were similar to the general prison population. Several studies had described both groups as deficient in social skills and accomplishments. These findings were not replicated when the offenders were compared with socioeconomically matched community controls (Stermac, Segal, & Gillis, 1990). Other similarities found by Knight et al. included low socioeconomic status, high rate of school failure or drop-out, subsequent unstable employment record of an unskilled nature, and previous convictions for nonsexual offenses. It seems likely that these features contribute to the detection and conviction both of incarcerated sex offenders and the rest of the prison population and characterize less well the majority of perpetrators whose offenses are not reported or who are charged but not convicted. This is consistent with the finding of Knight et al. that defendants referred for evaluation as possible child molesters had less extensive criminal histories than the convicted group. Bard et al. (1987) commented about investigations of incarcerated offenders that the only distinction that received consistent empirical scrutiny was that between rapists and child molesters. Rapists were younger than child molesters, who were more evenly distributed throughout the age span. U.S. Department of Justice studies were cited by Herman (1990) as consistently finding that about 25% of rapists were under 18 years of age. Knight et al. found that a number of studies reported a higher incidence of mental retardation and organic brain syndrome in child molesters. As could be expected, rapists were more likely to show behavioral excesses, to err by being overassertive or explosive, and to have greater heterosexual experience.

In reviewing classifications of incarcerated rapists, Knight et al. (1985) commented that few empirical data exist as to their reliability or validity. The distinction between anger and power rapists (Groth, Burgess, & Holmstrom, 1977) has received widespread acceptance. Power rapists were the more common. They did not desire to harm their victims but to control them so that they had no say in the matter. Anger rapists expressed anger, rage, contempt, and hatred for their victims by abusing them in profane language, beating them, sexually assaulting them, and forcing them to perform or submit to additional degrading acts. They used more force than was necessary simply to subdue the victims, who suffered physical violence to all parts of their bodies. Knight and Prentky (1990) found the distinction made in the DSM-III-R (APA, 1987) between nonsadistic rapists, who used no more aggression than necessary to ensure compliance, and sadistic rapists, who used excessive aggression, difficult to substantiate. The differentiation by Burgess and Holmstrom (1980) between "blitz" and "confidence" rapes was replicated by Bowie, Silverman, Kalick, and Edbril (1990). They found that the same two types of rape predominated in their study of 1,000 consecutive rape victims seen at a Boston rape crisis intervention program over a 10-year period. Blitz rapes were sudden surprise attacks by an unknown assailant. Confidence rapes involved some nonviolent interaction between the rapist and the victim before the attacker's intention to commit rape emerged. Incidents could be classified as blitz rapes in 60% of cases and confidence rapes in 36% (Silverman, Kalick, Bowie, & Edbril, 1988). Blitz rapes generally occurred in settings the victims assumed to be secure, significantly more occurring in their homes. Blitz rape victims were more likely to have experienced actual threats to their lives and were twice as likely as confidence rape victims to have seen a weapon or had the presence of one implied by the assailant. Blitz victims resisted their assailants less frequently than confidence victims and attempted to flee the situation only half as often. Confidence rape victims were 3 times more likely than blitz victims to have consumed alcohol or other drugs, to have spent some time with the assailant in a public or private place, or to have been in transit with him prior to the assault. The rape was more likely to have taken place in the rapist's home or automobile. Confidence victims reported feeling more anger during the incident. They waited significantly longer before seeking medical attention or help from the crisis program. Some, particularly victims of date rapes, were unclear that the assault or forced sexual encounter to which they were subjected constituted rape. Confidence rape assailants were more likely to be of the same race as their victim, to have known the victim's name or address, to have consumed alcohol or other drugs before committing the rape, and to have prolonged the incident beyond 5 hours.

In Ageton's (1983) study of sexual assault in adolescents, most of the offenders were boyfriends or dates in the age range of the victims; less than 20% were unknown to the victims. Only 5% of the assaults were reported to the police; they were mainly blitz rapes carried out by unknown or multiple assailants and involved threats or employment of violence. Over half those reported were completed assaults, compared with 20% of uncompleted assaults. Ageton suggested that, consistent with features of confidence rapes, attempted nonviolent assaults by dates or boyfriends may not be defined by the victims as legitimate sexual assaults for purposes of reporting to officials. The assaultive compared with nonassaultive males matched for age and class were alienated from home and school, showing a wide variety of delinquent behaviors, including physical assaults, and greater exposure to delinquent peers who supported delinquent and sexually aggressive behaviors. Data obtained 2 years prior to the subjects' sexually assaultive behaviors revealed that they were then more committed to a delinquent peer group than were the controls. Ageton concluded that all her results pointed to the fact that sexual assault offenders were basically delinquent youths. She suggested that research should be directed to determining differences between sexually assaultive and nonassaultive delinquents.

Pedophilia, unlike sexual assault or hebephilia, is classified as a paraphilia in the DSM-IV. Most pedophiles are male and offend against only male or only female children. The homosexual offenders, like hebephiles, commonly commence their deviant activity in adolescence. In adulthood, when they seek treatment or are charged, a number report having had many victims who were strangers or casual acquaintances. The majority of male homosexual pedophiles and hebephiles, although commonly of average or above average intelligence, report an inability to be socially or sexually interested in adults of either sex. The offenses of heterosexual pedophiles commonly commence in adulthood, and they have one or a few victims who are related or well known to them. Male heterosexual pedophiles are more likely to be heavy drinkers, to be of lower socioeconomic class, to have had little schooling, and to have committed other criminal offenses (McConaghy, 1993). Some brain-damaged or developmentally delayed men are drawn to the company of children of both sexes who are at their intellectual or emotional level. Sexual activity may be initiated by these men, or they may be regularly approached for such activity by one or more young adolescent males for monetary or other gains. In Laumann et al.'s (1994) representative sample, men who touched girls or boys aged 13 or less were typically over age 18 with victims aged 7–10. Women who touched boys were typically age 14–17 and their partners were age 11–13; these women would not be diagnosed as pedophiles according to DSM-IV criteria, which require that the subjects be at least 16 years old and 5 years older than the child.

Exhibitionism, which appears to be the commonest sex offense and paraphilia, rarely results in incarceration. It typically takes the form of the unsolicited genital exposure by postpubertal males to one or a few females, usually strangers around the age of puberty. The behavior commonly commences in adolescence, when it is experienced as sexually exciting. Adult subjects seek treatment when they find themselves unable to cease the behavior in situations where they have previously carried it out. They usually report that the excitement is largely nonsexual but rather a state of heightened arousal approaching panic. It is rarely carried out by women (McConaghy, 1993). Voyeurism appears to be a related paraphilia that is also extremely rare in women and commences in adolescence when it is experienced as sexually exciting. In adulthood, it becomes compulsive and the excitement is largely nonsexual. Its best-known form has been termed "peeping," the looking by males into a private area to observe a partially or completely nude woman without her consent. Forms of voyeurism less likely to come to attention are the observing by heterosexual men of heterosexual couples having intercourse in parked automobiles and by homosexual men of homosexual activity in public lavatories or steam baths. When exhibitionists and voyeurs present for treatment in adulthood, most are in satisfactory sexual relationships, report a stable work history, and appear to show no obvious personality problems (Langevin & Lang, 1987; Smukler & Schiebel, 1975). Frotteurism is limited by some workers to the pressing of the subject's penis against the body of an unknown woman and toucheurism to the intimate touching of an unknown woman (Freund, 1990). Both are carried out in public, with frotteurism usually in crowded situations. Presumably because of the resultant difficulty in identifying and charging frotteurs they rarely come to attention, but it would seem likely that their behavior develops a compulsive quality similar to that of toucheurs, who are charged and referred for treatment. Clinical assessment does not provide evidence of marked psychopathology apart from the deviant behavior.

Masochism and sadism rarely lead to seeking of treatment or criminal charges, and information concerning it is largely obtained by investigating members of "S and M" clubs. Recent studies have found that 20%–30% of members were female. The women were more likely to be bisexual, and most of the men predominantly heterosexual (Breslow, Evans, & Langley, 1985; Moser & Levitt, 1987). Over 50% of the men and 21% of the women were aware of sadomasochistic interest by age 14. Beating, bondage, and fetishistic practices were common, and more extreme and dangerous practices rare. Members of sadomasochistic clubs were of above average intelligence and social status and most wished to continue sadomasochistic activities. In view of the rarity with which practicing sadomasochists seek medical treatment, few must suffer significant physical damage. The statement in DSM-IV that the severity of the sadistic acts usually increases over time would appear to require support. However, the majority of subjects identifying as sadomasochists by joining a club would not be classified as having the paraphilia in DSM-IV, as they are not distressed by their behavior.

Fetishists are almost invariably male. In childhood they commonly experience a strong interest in particular objects, most frequently clothing or footwear. At puberty the interest is associated with sexual arousal disproportionate to that produced by the secondary sexual characteristics of women or men. When the fetish is a body part, such as hair, feet, or hands, or a deformity or mutilation, the condition is termed "partialism" in the DSM-IV. If the fetishist wears the clothing of the opposite sex his condition is termed "transvestic fetishism." At least in some pubertal and adolescent boys, transvestic fetishism will be followed by the adult form of transvestism. This is characterized by reduction or in some cases reported loss of sexual arousal with cross-dressing, as it increasingly produces feelings of relaxation, of relief from responsibility, and of sensuality, elegance, and beauty (Buhrich, 1977). If at this stage the subjects resist the desire to cross-dress, which can arise when they are alone or see women's clothes, they experience increased tension, which appears responsible for the behavior's becoming compulsive. Transvestites are predominantly heterosexual and usually marry. Periodic cross-dressing to feel masculine appears not to have been reported in women.

Development of an operation to convert male to female genitalia led to recognition of the separate clinical condition of transsexualism. An increasing number of men with the urge to cross-dress, usually since childhood, made strong efforts to obtain the operation and live permanently as women. They and the smaller number of women who in general made less strong efforts to obtain some degree of sex conversion to live permanently as men were termed "transsexuals." Male transsexuals, who had never experienced fetishistic arousal with cross-dressing and sought sex conversion in early adulthood, like almost all female transsexuals, were typically attracted to members of their biological sex. They were termed classical transsexuals to distinguish them from fetishistic transsexuals, men who gave a history of fetishistic transvestism in that they were predominantly attracted to women and married (Buhrich & McConaghy, 1978). However, compared to nuclear transvestites, who had no desire to alter their bodily appearance by taking female hormones or having surgery, fetishistic transsexuals report having stronger opposite-sex identity and homosexual feelings since childhood, leading to their seeking sex conversion in middle age (McConaghy, 1993). The rare women who sought sex conversion to live as gay males were considered to be at the end of a continuum of men and women attracted to or idealizing homosexual persons of the opposite sex, a condition termed "transhomosexuality" by Clare and Tully (1989). Only one of nine female-to-male transsexuals who regard themselves as homosexual or bisexual report any fetishism with cross-dressing (Coleman, Bockting, & Gooren, 1993). Transvestites tend to be of higher socioeconomic class than transsexuals and more stable in their relationships and occupation as compared to male but not female transsexuals (McConaghy, 1993).

Presence of marked wishes to be of the opposite sex accompanied by extreme opposite-sex behavior in childhood—in boys, dressing in female clothes, using cosmetics and jewelry, and walking and posturing like girls and, in girls, marked tomboyism—is termed gender identity disorder of childhood. In adulthood, the majority of these boys identify as homosexual (Zuger, 1966, 1984). Less information is available about the outcome of girls with the disorder. As discussed earlier, gender identity disorder is considered, probably incorrectly, to be categorically different from the milder forms of opposite-sex–linked behaviors termed "sissiness" and "tomboyism," which correlate in boys with their ratio of homosexual to heterosexual feelings, and in both boys and girls with their degree of opposite-sex identity in adulthood (McConaghy, 1987; McConaghy, Buhrich, & Silove, 1994).

COURSE AND PROGNOSIS

Information concerning the course of most sexual dysfunctions with or without treatment is limited, so that only the marked changes in their prevalence with age in both men and women discussed earlier (see Epidemiology, above) can be regarded as established. Thirty-six (7%) of a representative sample of middle-aged married women ($N = 497$) reported absence of desire; 6 years later half of the 36 had regained desire without treatment, 70% to a weak and 30% to a moderate extent (Hallstrom & Samuelsson, 1990). Of 50 men mainly over age 50 with erectile dysfunction who took no action following recommendation for treatment, 4 reported being much better and 4 slightly better at 2-year follow-up (Tiefer & Melman, 1987). Tiefer and Melman also cited a finding that 30% of men with erectile dysfunction who did not accept or who dropped out of behavioral treatment were asymptomatic by 6–12 months. De Amicis et al. (1984) were able to follow up 49 of 155 couples (mean age about 35 years), 3 years after they had a single evaluation at a sexual therapy clinic (i.e., not offered or declined treatment). Women but not men reported a significant increase in sexual satisfaction. In regard to dysfunctions, apart from the 11 with dyspareunia, more women reported improvement than stayed the same or got worse; more men stayed the same or got worse than reported improvement, although 6 of 16 with premature ejaculation and 7 of 16 with erectile dysfunction improved. Half the subjects received treatment elsewhere before follow-up, but this did not appear to modify the outcome. Six of 8 diabetic women and 8 of 14 diabetic men who had sexual dysfunctions at initial assessment when their average age was 35 had recovered 6 years later (Jensen, 1986). Eight of the 14 women and men who recovered had a new partner. Four of the remainder attributed the recovery to improvement in their emotional and social security. Five of the 14 had objective signs of peripheral and autonomic neuropathy at both interviews.

As for the effect of treatment on the course of sexual dysfunctions, Masters and Johnson (1970) reported a failure rate of about 20%, one of the best in the literature. This report was severely criticized by Zilbergeld and Evans (1980), on the grounds that the subjects were much more highly motivated than those treated in most studies, that those less likely to respond were screened out, that it was not clear that subjects who dropped out of or were asked to leave therapy were counted as failures, and that outcome was reporting as number of failures to initiate reversal of the basic symptomatology. A successful outcome would not necessarily mean that subjects' dysfunctions were reversed, but rather that they felt less guilty about sex, became less performance-oriented during sex, or enjoyed sex more. Zilbergeld and Evans pointed out that other studies have not found such a low relapse rate as Masters and Johnson reported at the 5-year follow-up (7% of those who were not treatment failures), citing a rate of 54% in subjects treated by two psychiatrists trained by Masters and Johnson. When results comparable to those of Masters and Johnson have been reported by other therapists, they have been open to some of the same criticisms. LoPiccolo and Stock (1986) treated 150 women for orgasmic dysfunction with a behavioral desensitization program, including directed masturbation. Following treatment, 95% were able to reach orgasm with self-masturbation, 85% with genital stimulation from their partners, and 40% with penile-vaginal intercourse. No information was provided as to whether any patients dropped out of therapy.

Reported dropout rates vary remarkably, from almost half of the 70% of 133 couples who accepted the offer of sex therapy (Catalan et al., 1990) to only 49 (4%) of 1,225 couples who attended a medical school sex clinic over 15 years (Renshaw, 1988). Renshaw reported an 80% reversal of symptoms in the completors of her 7-week program, but details of the reversal were not given. Forty percent of 140 couples assessed by Hawton et al. (1986) as suitable for treatment did not complete it. One to 6 years later, follow-up of 76% of the 140 couples, including 61% of those who had completed treatment, revealed recurrence or continuing difficulty with the presenting problem in 64 (75%) of the 86 couples whose relationships were still intact. This caused little or no concern to 22 (34%), and only 11 had sought further help. Nine couples (10%) reported that a new sexual problem had developed. Slightly over 50% of both the men and women reported that they were very or moderately happy with their sexual relationships. Significant improvement in the couples' general relationships had been found at termination of therapy and was still present at follow-up.

Milan, Kilmann, and Boland (1988) investigated women with secondary orgasmic dysfunction 2 to 6 years after they and their partners had been randomly allocated to active treatment or a series of didactic lectures planned to act as a placebo. Their mean age at intake was 33.3 years. When the patients who had received the active treatment showed no greater improvement in orgasmic frequency than did those who received the lectures, it was decided that the latter group had not improved spontaneously, but that the lectures were an effective treatment. As discussed earlier, orgasmic frequency increases with age in women, so it was possible the improvement reported in the women in all groups would have occurred without treatment. At posttreatment and follow-up, on average the women reached orgasm on less than 50% of occasions of coitus, and the frequency of intercourse at follow-up was below pretreatment levels, a change that also occurs spontaneously with aging. Munjack et al. (1976) randomly allocated 22 anorgasmic women, most of whom were happily married, either to immediate or delayed treatment with an education, communication, and desensitization program. Following treatment, a third of the treated women were orgasmic on at least 50% of sexual relations, whereas there was no change in the untreated group. Untreated groups cannot be regarded as a satisfactory comparison group, as they almost invariably show a markedly poorer response than those treated with placebo psychological therapies, possibly due to low motivation to change while awaiting treatment (McConaghy, 1993).

Of the various dysfunctions, hypoactive sexual desire disorder is generally considered to have the worst prognosis with therapy (Schover & Leiblum, 1994). The major exception appears to be the report of Renshaw (1988). She found an 80% reversal of symptoms in over 1,000 couples, of whom 442 of the women and 250 of the men showed no interest in sex. Hawton et al. (1986), in their 1- to 6-year follow-up, found that although 70% of women with impaired sexual interest reported its resolution at termination of therapy, at the 1- to 6-year follow-up over half had relapsed, comparable to the spontaneous remission after 6 years of half the women in a community sample who reported absence of sexual desire (Hallstrom & Samuelsson, 1990). De Amicis, Goldberg, LoPiccolo, Friedman, and Davies (1985) found regression to worse than pretherapy levels at 3-year follow-up in both men and women treated at a sexual dysfunctions clinic for sexual desire disorder, and Kaplan (1977) reported limited success in women with this condition. Munjack and Kanno (1979), in their review, found inadequate but suggestive evidence that retardation, and particularly absence of ejaculation, may also respond poorly to treatment. The good response at termination of treatment in men with premature ejaculation and with erectile dysfunction was maintained at follow-up only by the latter group (De Amicis et al., 1985; Hawton et al., 1986). De Amicis et al. found that the good immediate response of women with anorgasmia persisted at 3-year follow-up. Vaginismus has also been consistently found to respond well to treatment. Success, usually defined as ability to have coitus, was the immediate outcome in 80% of cases in 37 studies reviewed by van de Weil, Jasper, Schultz, and Gal (1990). Persistence of response was found at 1- to 6-year follow-up in 18 of 20 female patients (Hawton et al., 1986).

Of the characteristics of sexually dysfunctional patients that affect their acceptance of and response to treatment, as expected from the earlier discussion (Clinical Picture), a hostile relationship with the partner has consistently been found to predict a poor response (Snyder & Berg, 1983b; Takefman & Brender, 1984). Segraves, Schoenberg, Zarins, Camic, and Knopf (1981) found that 27% of 46 men with erectile dysfunction who self-referred to a sexual dysfunction clinic, but 56% of 47 men referred from a urology department, declined the offer of behavioral sex therapy. Of those who accepted treatment, all the self-referred patients completed six or more sessions; 57% of the urology-referred men dropped out before six sessions. Segraves et al. found urology-referred patients much less willing than self-referred patients to accept a possible role of psychological factors in their dysfunction. They pointed out that the current models of behavioral sex therapy were developed on a highly sophisticated self-referred population. Catalan et al. (1990) found that couples who dropped out, as compared to those who completed sex therapy, had shown less initial motivation for treatment and more marked relationship and marital problems, and the presenting person had shown greater anxiety. Hawton et al. (1986) found a history of psychiatric disorder, particularly in the female partner, to be the major pretreatment predictor of poor outcome at 1- to 5-year follow-up. Couples who rated themselves before treatment as able to communicate anger showed a better response, which the authors considered reflected their general ability to communicate with each other.

Comparing the format of psychological treatments on the course of sex dysfunctions, Libman, Fichten, and Brender (1985) found equal effectiveness whether administered by therapists to individuals, couples, or groups, or as bibliotherapy—that is, by the subject's use of self-help treatment books combined with minimal therapist contact. LoPiccolo and Stock (1986) reported use of a self-treatment book and film for women to become orgasmic combined with limited therapist contact was as effective as a complete program of therapist-administered sex therapy. Libman et al. (1985) found bibliotherapy alone to be ineffective, leading Rosen (1987) to criticize the commercialization of psychotherapy involved in the publication and recommendation for use without therapist supervision of self-help treatment books for sex dysfunctions. Libman et al. (1985) found no empirical support for the frequently expressed beliefs that cotherapists are more effective than single therapists or that gender of the therapists affects treatment outcome.

Review of studies comparing different components of sex therapy revealed that in the treatment of orgasmic dysfunction in women, directed masturbation for primary anorgasmia was more effective than sensate focusing combined with supportive psychotherapy, and there were few differences between sensate focusing, systematic desensitization, and communication training (Fichten, Libman, & Brender, 1983). Auerbach and Kilmann (1977) reported that group systematic desensitization combined with relaxation produced improvement of over 40% in frequency of successful intercourse in men with secondary erectile dysfunction; relaxation alone produced improvement of 3%. No adequate placebo-controlled studies or studies comparing recommended psychological treatments appear to have been carried out in recent years, Schover and Leiblum (1994) concluding that there has been a stagnation of sex therapy. As pointed out earlier, consistent with the low correlation between presence of dysfunctions and sexual satisfaction discussed earlier, a common finding of outcome studies has been that despite minimal improvement of the specific dysfunction with which they presented, many subjects reported increased sexual interest and enjoyment following psychological treatment (Adkins & Jehu, 1985; De Amicis et al., 1985; Hawton et al., 1986). This finding led LoPiccolo, Heiman, Hogan, and Roberts (1985) to conclude that treatment was more effective in changing the way people think and feel about their sexual lives than in totally eliminating presenting complaints, emphasizing that a good sexual relationship involved more than just an erect penis or an orgasm and encouraged patients to enjoy the sexual process rather than to strive for results. Although this conclusion would seem relevant for subjects who seek and persist in psychological treatment for sexual dysfunctions, it may not be for those individuals mentioned earlier who seek physical treatment and if referred for psychological treatment are unlikely to persist with it. Recognition of the existence of these patients may in part account for the shift Schover and Leiblum (1994) noted from the belief in the 1970s that almost all sexual problems were psychogenic to the current belief that they usually have an organic cause. Schover and Leiblum termed this behavior "shopping in the organic market" for chemical means to improve the course of dysfunctions. They pointed out that enhancing erections has become a lucrative industry for urologists, pharmaceutical companies who market the drugs used in intracavernous (IC) injection therapy, and manufacturers of penile prostheses. Schover and Leiblum believed that urologists often prescribe IC injection therapy or vacuum erection devices for men with psychogenic sexual dysfunction because the patients refuse to see a mental health professional. At the same time they suggested that a combination of IC injections with sex therapy could possibly improve the outcome of erectile dysfunction. They also reported that some urologists used IC injections or vacuum injection therapy for premature ejaculation, either believing that the treatment will delay orgasm or telling the patient he will be able to go on thrusting after orgasm. Schover and Leiblum said that men invariably told them that such thrusting is a chore.

Rosen and Ashton (1993) reviewed studies of response to oral medications, which they referred to as "prosexual drugs," or "aphrodisiacs." These terms suggest that these drugs increase sexual desire, but most studies have used them for erectile disorder. Rosen and Ashton concluded that no single drug has proved to be clinically safe and reliably effective for human use, but that further research was justified. However, there seemed to be sufficient evidence from controlled trials to justify the recommendation of Morales, Condra, Owen, Surridge, Fenemore, and Harris (1987) that due to its ease of administration, safety, and modest effect, yohimbine could be used in patients with organic erectile dysfunction who would not accept more invasive methods. Some open trials have reported successful treatment of erectile disorder by use of topical applications of yohimbine or nitroglycerin ointment to the subject's penis (McConaghy, 1996). A number of uncontrolled and a few placebo-controlled studies reported reduction of premature ejaculation with selective serotonin reuptake inhibitors. Significantly greater clinical improvement was reported with paroxetine 20–40 mg per day for 5 weeks than placebo (Waldinger, Hengeveld, & Zwinderman, 1994) and 20 patients with premature ejaculation estimated average time to ejaculation after vaginal penetration increased to 6.1 minutes with clomipramine 25 mg and 8.4 minutes with clomipramine 50 mg. These were both significantly greater than the estimated time on placebo (Segraves, Saran, Segraves, & Maguire, 1993). Rosen and Ashton (1993) criticized the dearth of studies of the effects of prosexual drugs in women.

Investigations of the course of untreated sex offenders have reported widely varying rates of reoffending (Marshall & Barbaree, 1990a). Incest offenders showed the lowest rates, from 4% to 10%. Those for rapists were 7%–35%, for nonfamilial molesters of girls, 10%–29%, and for nonfamilial molesters of boys, 13%–40%. Those for exhibitionists were the highest for all sex offenders, 41%–

71%. The outcome of treated offenders also showed variability marked enough to cause Furby, Weinrott, and Blackshaw (1989) to warn that using it for comparison with that of untreated offenders would allow one to conclude anything one wanted. Some programs exclude offenders considered at high risk of reoffending (i.e., the severely brain damaged and those convicted of sex offenses who deny they have a problem). Probably all exclude patients while they are actively psychotic. Some programs discharge patients who appear to be failing to respond, and others report high dropout rates. Many need to charge their clients to continue to operate and so exclude a number of offenders, although few studies report the cost of the programs. Marshall and Barbaree (1990a) found that reported rates of reoffending in treated exhibitionists ranged from 7% to 48%, and that some programs appeared to be more effective with homosexual and others with heterosexual child molesters. Rapists were found to be the least responsive to treatment. However, in view of the high percentage of youthful rapists referred to earlier, most must cease offending in the long term. In 3,795 (76%) of 5,000 outpatient offenders treated in a fee-for-service cognitive behavioral program and followed up for 1–17 years (65% over 3 years), Maletzky (1991) reported response rates of 94.7% for heterosexual ($N = 2,865$), 86.4% for homosexual ($N = 855$), and 75.7% for bisexual pedophiles, 93.1% for exhibitionists ($N = 770$), and 73.5% for rapists ($N = 145$). Despite the high rate of reported reoffending of untreated exhibitionists (41%–71%), my experience is that they and voyeurs are among the least likely to relapse of the offenders treated in my program, less than 5% reoffending. Both findings are consistent with the clinical impression that exhibitionism and voyeurism are the most compulsive of sex offenses, since the program focuses on treating patients' compulsive urges. Kroth (1979) found that heterosexual pedophiles, particularly incest offenders, rarely reoffended following treatment, an average of 2% being reported. This could be in part due to reduced opportunities of incest offenders following detection of their offense, or because, as in the Giarretto program, they are treated when the mean age of the victim is 12–13 years (Kroth, 1979), close to the age when incestuous abuse usually ceases (Faller, 1989; Herman, 1985). The mean age of incest victims in population samples is well below this (Russell, 1983). In my experience, fetishists are somewhat more resistant to treatment and commonly require addition of medroxyprogesterone to cognitive-behavioral procedures. Homosexual pedophiles and hebephiles, who lack social or sexual interest in adults, rarely develop this with treatment and also commonly require such addition to resist forming relationships with boys.

Apart from type of offense treated, length of follow-up was of major importance in evaluating outcome. As expected, the longer the follow-up, the higher the rate of reoffending. Marshall and Barbaree (1990a) considered periods of less than 2 years inadequate. In regard to other factors affecting prognosis, Maletzky (1991) reported that not living with or being well known to the victim, having more than one victim, totally denying the crime, using force, having multiple paraphilias, and having histories of unstable employment or social relationships significantly predicted poor outcome. Stermac (1993) wondered about the effect of selection criteria based on the ability of clients to pay for services or to have insurance. In my program, for which subjects are not charged, those who are sufficiently organized to be in stable employment and hence could pay show a better response. Adolescent as compared to adult offenders were found to require more intensive treatment independent of the nature of their offense (McConaghy et al., 1989).

Despite the large number of uncontrolled factors which would appear to make meaningful determination of the relative efficacy of existing programs impossible, Marshall and Barbaree (1990a) concluded that these programs varied in effectiveness in dealing with different types of offense, and that therapists conducting them could benefit by more closely examining the others. It seems unlikely that such post hoc comparison of the outcome of unmatched groups of offenders selected by different criteria would provide useful information. Few comparisons randomly allocating offenders to different programs or techniques have been carried out and would seem urgently required if cost-effective programs are to be developed to provide treatment for the large number of offenders who currently receive none. However, such studies may not prove useful. No North American workers have attempted to replicate findings of the comparison studies using random allocation carried out by me and my colleagues (McConaghy, Armstrong, & Blaszczynski, 1981, 1985; McConaghy, Armstrong, Blaszczynski, & Allcock, 1983), which demonstrated the superiority of nonaversive systematic desensitization (alternative behavior completion; McConaghy, 1993) to electric shock and covert sensitization aversive therapies. The two forms of aversive therapy remain the major behavioral methods used to modify sexually offensive behaviors in North America (Quinsey & Earls, 1990). Quinsey and Marshall (1990) were disturbed that the literature concerning electrical aversive therapy appears to have dried up since 1983. They found no controlled studies of electrical aversion which investigated its effectiveness in reducing inappropriate sexual arousal. They also commented that evidence for the efficacy of covert sensitization was not overwhelming and that a variety of techniques have been shown to reduce penile circumference response (see Psychological and Biological Assessment). However, it was not yet known which techniques were most efficacious or what procedural details were the most important. This latter finding would also seem disturbing. Comparison studies if acknowledged would provide valuable information about relative cost effectiveness of the various techniques presently in use.

In a comparison study of alternative behavior completion, low-dosage medroxyprogesterone therapy, and the two combined, 28 of 30 sex offenders ceased deviant behavior at 1 year following commencement of treatment. Two of the 28 had required the addition of electric shock aversive therapy (McConaghy, Blaszczynski, & Kidson, 1988). Three relapsed in the following 2–5 years but responded to the reinstitution of MPA. All subjects who requested treatment were accepted. These results were comparable with those of multimodal programs that required much longer periods of staff-patient contact. In an uncontrolled study, 89% of 44 treated sex offenders contacted after 6 months and 79% of 19 contacted after 12 months reported no further deviant activity (Travin, Bluestone, Coleman, Cullen, & Melella, 1986). Failure to randomly allocate subjects to treatment or no treatment rendered uninterpretable comparison studies in which 25% of 68 treated and 60% of 58 untreated child molesters reoffended after 4 years (Marshall & Barbaree, 1988), 39% of 23 treated and 57% of 21 untreated exhibitionists reoffended after 8 years, and 23% of 17 exhibitionists treated with a multimodal procedure that shifted the major focus from sexual deviance to changing cognitions reoffended after 4 years (Marshall, Eccles, & Barbaree, 1991). A similar failure also rendered uninterpretable the recidivism rates at 6-year follow-up of 50 child molesters, who received a multimodal program incorporating electric shock aversive therapy and 86 child molesters who did not (Rice, Quinsey, & Harris, 1991). In this study, the authors stated that they had doubts about the comparability of the two nonrandomly selected groups.

Lack of critical interest in empirical evaluations of treatments for sex offenders was most evident in relation to the study of Marques, Day, Nelson, and West (1994). This appears to be the only study so far to have published outcome findings on incarcerated sex offenders randomly allocated to treatment or no treatment. The treatment employed was an intensive form of relapse prevention, the therapy Marshall (1996) considers the most significant innovation and an integral and standard part of treatment of sex offenders. Marques et al. (1994) reported that at an average follow-up of 3 years, of the 83 child molesters who commenced treatment and the 79 who were denied it, 8 in both groups carried out further sexual crimes. Of the 23 rapists who commenced treatment and the 18 who were denied it, 3 in the former group and 5 in the latter group carried out further sexual crimes. Marques et al. did not discuss the possible negative effects of denying subjects treatment, particularly after the subjects had volunteered to accept it. Meta-analyses of evaluations of psychological treatments have consistently found that untreated groups have significantly poorer outcomes than those treated with placebo (McConaghy, 1990). Marques et al. included a comparison group of offenders who did not want treatment, matched to the treated group on variables they considered important. Of these untreated rapists who did not have the negative experience of being denied treatment, 2 of 18 carried out further sexual crimes, consistent with the possibility that denial of treatment may have had a negative effect. This study of Marques provided strong evidence that relapse prevention, at least for incarcerated offenders, is ineffective in reducing the likelihood that treated child molesters will carry out further sexual crimes and at best has a minimal effect on rapists.

Marshall and Pithers (1994) stated that they "cannot see how any ethically concerned researcher would suggest a random design treatment outcome study for sex offenders" (p. 24), which means they considered the appropriate design a matched comparison group, the strategy employed in Marshall's own studies. Yet in their discussion of the study by Marques et al., Marshall and Pithers ignored the finding that untreated rapists in the matched comparison group were slightly less likely than the treated subjects to commit further sexual crimes and concluded that the study data indicated a significant treatment effect with rapists. The findings of this study might have been expected to result in a major reappraisal of the relapse prevention model for treatment of sex offenders and at least to stimulate attempts to evaluate it in comparison with more cost-effective procedures. In contrast, the study has been cited as demonstrating that the model is effective in reducing recidivism (Bumby, 1996; Schlank & Shaw, 1996).

The study did provide evidence that personality of sex offenders was a major factor determining outcome. Those with prior felony convictions were significantly more likely to reoffend. Only 1 of 26 offenders who initially volunteered for treatment but then did not accept it committed a further sexual offence—the best response of any group. The reasons for their refusal were realistic, suggesting they were emotionally mature. Three of 8 subjects who commenced treatment but withdrew or were terminated within 1 year committed a further sexual offence—the worst response of any group. Marques et al. considered these subjects to be the most impulsive with the least self-control.

DSM-IV states that the severity of sadistic acts usually increases over time, and individuals with sexual sadism, when severe and especially when associated with antisocial personality disorder, may seriously injure or kill their victims. This may be meant to apply to the rare sadistic or sexual murderers, whose condition seems different from that of subjects who identify as masochists and sadists by joining clubs (McConaghy, 1993).

FAMILIAL AND GENETIC CONSIDERATIONS

The importance of children's parental relationships in the first few years of their lives in determining their later behavior, including their sexual behavior, is a major tenet of psychoanalytic theory. Investigation of factors determining married women's ability to attain orgasm in sexual activity provided little support for the theory in relation to female orgasmic disorder. Degree of attachment to, or conflict with their mothers or fathers, resemblance of their husbands to their fathers, childhood happiness, type of childhood discipline, and amount of punishment were all unrelated (Terman, 1938, 1951). Morokoff (1978) cited a 1973 study of Fisher's which found no relationship between women's attainment of orgasm and parental attitudes of permissiveness or repressiveness concerning sex or nudity, or the subjects' attitudes toward their mothers. Overall quality of home life, parental attitudes and openness about sex, early religious attitudes, parental strictness, and family abuse did not enter a discriminant analysis which distinguished sexually dysfunctional from functional women (Heiman et al., 1986). While not distinguishing the functional from the nonfunctional, perception of a poor mother-daughter relationship in childhood distinguished women who sought sexual therapy from those who did not. However, of 90 married women presenting because of their or their husbands' problems, the 59 diagnosed as having inhibited sexual desire in the study by Stuart et al. (1987) rated their perception of their parents' attitudes toward sex and demonstrations of affection significantly more negatively than did the remaining women, most of whom were sexually functional.

Knight et al. (1985) found incarcerated sex offenders to resemble the total incarcerated population in having poor and alcoholic families of origin. Prentky et al. (1989), in a study of 82 incarcerated sex offenders, found that caregiver inconstancy, sexual deviation within the family, and sexual abuse of the subject were related to severity of sexual aggression. Childhood and juvenile institutional history and physical abuse and neglect were associated with severity of nonsexual aggression. Severity of aggression rather than frequency of crimes was predicted by the subjects' developmental history. These childhood experiences were interpreted as causal of the later deviant behaviors. Early exposure to family violence, along with childhood sexual abuse, and early age of sexual initiation predicted later sexually aggressive behaviors in the national sample of 2,972 male students investigated by Koss and Dinero (1988). Marshall and Barbaree (1990b) reported that poor socialization, and in particular exposure to parental violence in the sex offender's childhood, facilitated his use of aggression as well as cutting him off in adolescence from access to more appropriate sociosexual interactions. Also, family backgrounds of sex offenders were similar to those of people with antisocial personalities. As this personality disorder is in part inherited (Schulsinger, 1972), genetic factors as well as modeling of the disturbed childhood relationships may have contributed to the later aggression of offenders. Of 5,000 treated sex offenders, 27% reported having first-degree relatives with a history of sexual offences, and 44% first-degree relatives with a history of alcoholism (Maletzky, 1991). Alcoholism also has been shown to be in part genetically determined.

Watkins and Bentovim (1992) cited evidence that a higher percentage of pedophiles than rapists reported histories of childhood sexual victimization: 57% versus 23% in one study and 56% versus 5% in another. Adult sex offenders who carried out offenses in adolescence compared to those who had not were more likely to report having been sexually abused in childhood, the abuse being more serious and occurring at an earlier age (Knight & Prentky, 1993). The hypothesis that subjects sexually abused in their childhood become sex offenders through "identification with the aggressor" was criticized by Herman (1990) as based on retrospective reports of identified offenders, who were not representative of the much larger undetected population of offenders. Also, most studies supporting the theory lacked appropriate comparison groups and employed a vague definition of childhood sexual abuse. It has also been argued that sex offenders, particularly child molesters, could report being victimized in childhood to obtain the sympathy of the interviewer or more lenient legal treatment, or unconsciously exaggerate remembered events to reduce feelings of guilt (Freund, Watson, & Dickey, 1990). The hypothesis is not applicable to all pedophiles; even when child molesters who did not show penile volume plethysmography evidence of an erotic preference for children were excluded, only a minority of the remaining pedophiles (43.9% and 49.4%) reported having been molested by an adult male or female (over age 17) prior to ages of 12 and 16, respectively (Freund & Kuban, 1994). Significantly more sex offenders against adult women and control men with erotic preference for adult women reported having been seduced between ages 12 and 15 by physically mature women than did the pedophiles, a finding the authors considered should be pursued further. Clinical studies of nonincarcerated sex offenders seeking treatment have reported that subjects with evidence of congenital or acquired brain damage are overrepresented (Berlin & Meinecke, 1981; McConaghy et al., 1988).

DIAGNOSTIC CONSIDERATIONS

As pointed out, reliability of DSM-IV diagnoses of sexual dysfunctions is likely to be low in view of the number of issues left to the judgment of the individual clinician. Nathan (1986) noted that most surveys of inhibited female orgasm asked only about orgasm during intercourse, whereas DSM-III did not set any requirements for the technique, gender, or even presence of a partner during the sexual activity that leads to orgasm. Also, most surveys ask about frequency of orgasm but not about ease, whereas DSM-III defined a dysfunction if either parameter was compromised. Frank et al. (1978) found that whereas 15% of their female sample reported inability to have orgasms, 46% reported difficulty in achieving them. Nathan's comments apply also to the DSM-IV diagnosis. Premature ejaculation is defined in DSM-IV as persistent or recurrent ejaculation with minimum stimulation before or shortly after penetration and before the person wishes it. Commenting on Masters and Johnson's (1970) definition of early ejaculation as the male ejaculating before the female is orgasmic at least 50% of the time, McCarthy (1989) pointed out that some clinicians base the diagnosis not on time, movement, or partner response, but on the male's sense of voluntary control over the ejaculatory process. Criteria of 7 minutes or less latency to ejaculation combined with 4 or less on an 8-point ejaculatory control scale classified 24% of 110 heterosexual male undergraduates as rapid ejaculators; 2 minutes or less latency plus little or no control classified none, although 4% had latencies of less than 2 minutes and 8% reported no control (Grenier & Byers, in press). The students' concern with ejaculating faster than desired did not correlate significantly with their estimated latency to ejaculation and not strongly ($r = 0.27$) with perceived ejaculatory control. The authors considered that assessment of premature ejaculation required a multivariate approach.

Apfelbaum (1989) found the standard concept of retarded ejaculation diagnostically ambiguous and in actuality referred to male coital anorgasmia. This is, of course, consistent with its classification as male orgasmic disorder in DSM-IV, although Apfelbaum regarded the condition as due to lack of desire, either for sexual activity generally, when its subjects masturbated to orgasm only with difficulty, or for sexual partners, in subjects who were autosexual so that only their own touch was sexually arousing. Apfelbaum suggested that masturbatory and partner anorgasmia are apt terms for these two conditions. Lack of arousal in partner anorgasmia was masked by presence of facile and sustained erections, which he believed almost suggested priapism, in that they were maintained far beyond the ordinary range without erotic arousal. He related such erections to those of men who were successfully raped by women and to those which were sustained under stress. Men with retarded ejaculation may confess, although only privately, that they were unwilling to impregnate their partner or that they were repulsed by them and enjoyed denying them the satisfaction of seeing the subjects have coital orgasms. Apfelbaum considered that patients mainly sought treatment because their partners wanted to be impregnated. This is not the author's experience. Apfelbaum also stated that too much is made of the concept that these patients fear impregnating their partners and that retarded ejaculation occurs in anal intercourse and may even have a higher incidence in gay men. Apfelbaum seemed to believe that men with retarded ejaculation experience a need to satisfy their partners by themselves reaching orgasm and do not wish to reach orgasm for themselves. He also emphasized that the partners are usually multiorgasmic and enjoy rather than feel oppressed by the patients' prolonged attempts to reach orgasm. Apfelbaum's formulation led him to reject as coercive the standard treatment, which he identified as a demand strategy. Here, the patient begins to masturbate, and his partner then takes over and is required to stimulate his penis in an aggressive and forceful way until he is near the point of ejaculatory inevitability, when he suddenly switches to intromission. As Apfelbaum pointed out, the number of subjects presenting with the condition is very low, so that impressions concerning the condition have not been empirically tested.

Clinicians' judgments about degree of deficiency or absence of sexual fantasies and desire for sexual activity necessary to diagnose hypoactive or inhibited sexual desire have appeared arbitrary. In one study, women were given this diagnosis who had engaged in premarital intercourse significantly more often and showed no difference in frequency or duration of intercourse or duration of foreplay compared to those not so diagnosed (Stuart et al., 1987). In another, men who received the diagnosis reported a frequency of masturbation 20% higher than that of men reporting a healthy sex life (Nutter & Condron, 1985). In making the diagnosis, it should be established that subjects who report acceptable frequencies of sexual activity are having intercourse out of obligation to their partners rather than out of sexual desire (Wincze & Carey, 1991), and that those who report low frequencies are not avoiding sexual activity because of dissatisfaction with their sexual relationships rather than reduced desire (Nutter & Condron, 1985).

Diagnosis of sexual dysfunctions requires that the health professional inquire directly concerning them. Such inquiry revealed erectile dysfunction in 401 of 1,080 men attending a medical outpatient clinic; only six had been identified prior to the inquiry (Slag et al., 1983), Buvat et al. (1985) found that none of 26 impotent diabetics aged 21–55 reported the dysfunction until they were directly questioned about it. Forty-three percent of male and 21% of female patients who attended a Boston University medical outpatient clinic reported that the doctor had not discussed their sexual functioning (Ende, Rockwell, & Glasgow, 1984). The importance attached to the DSM definitions of sexual disorders over the past decade may have encouraged health professionals to ignore sexual behaviors that are not classified as disorders. In relation to the 12 million cases of sexually transmitted disease diagnosed each year in the United States, including 40,000 new infections with HIV, Seidman and Rieder (1994) pointed out that behavioral change among sexually active persons is the most effective preventive measure. Their review of studies of sexual behavior in the United States indicated that most 18–24-year-olds have multiple, serial sex partners and do not consistently use condoms. They cited a 1990 report of the Department of Health and Human Services that charged all health care providers with taking complete sexual and drug use histories on all adolescent and adult patients and with giving advice and counseling concerning strategies for avoiding infection and unwanted pregnancies. Studies indicated that only 11%–37% of primary care physicians routinely took sexual histories from new patients, and Seidman and Rieder believed many psychiatrists (and presumably psychologists) were ill at ease with taking explicit sexual histories.

Seidman and Rieder also pointed out that, despite the fact that male-to-female transmission of HIV was 5 times as likely with anal as with vaginal intercourse, and was practiced by a substantial proportion of women, it was rarely discussed in the medical literature and was apparently a topic of extreme sensitivity for many individuals, including physicians. Bolling and Voeller (1987) stated that a fourth of American women occasionally engaged in anal intercourse, and about 10% did so regularly for pleasure; however, most of the women only revealed this after repeated personal interviews and development of strong trust in the interviewer, so that it would be unlikely to be revealed in standard medical or field interviews. In fact, such studies have revealed incidences not far below that reported by Bolling and Voeller (McConaghy, 1993). However, as Seidman and Rieder (1994) pointed out, in some of the few population studies that have investigated this behavior there was potential for confusion with rear-entry vaginal intercourse. In taking sexual histories from adolescents, awareness is necessary that most will not reveal sexual activities or feelings considered deviant, an awareness not always shown even by experienced sexuality researchers. Studies of the effects of exposure to altered levels of sex hormones in utero accepted as valid the reports of 62 child, adolescent, and young adult subjects and 48 controls that only one (a control) experienced some degree of homosexual feelings. Prevalence of homosexual feelings and activity particularly in adolescence is established to be considerably higher than 1% (McConaghy, 1993).

The DSM-IV diagnosis of paraphilia requires both that the behavior, sexual urges, or fantasies were present over a period of at least 6 months and that they cause clinically significant distress or impairment in social, occupational, or other important areas of functioning. At the same time it states that many individuals with these disorders assert that the behavior causes them no distress and that their only problem is social dysfunction as a result of the reaction of others to their behavior. Investigations of prevalence of child-adult sexual activity indicate that the majority of perpetrators have not been detected (McConaghy, 1993) and therefore have not been exposed to the reaction of others. When some are detected some time after the offense they appear to have shown no clinically significant distress or impairment in social, occupational, or other important areas of functioning. This would also appear true of many adult transvestites and subjects involved in sadism and masochism (McConaghy, 1993). Some adult sex offenders against children report an isolated act or acts without awareness of recurrent, intense sexually arousing fantasies or sexual urges concerning prepubescent children. Marshall and Eccles (1991) commented that many rapists, incest offenders, exhibitionists, and a substantial number of nonfamilial child molesters do not display or report deviant sexual preferences, and yet they persistently engage in sexually offensive behaviors, so that most clinicians tend to ignore DSM diagnoses.

Sexual assault, the offense which along with child molestation most commonly results in incarceration, is not classified in the DSM-IV as a paraphilia. The DSM-III-R classified as sadists those rapists who were considered to inflict suffering on the victims far in excess of that necessary to gain compliance and in whom the visible pain of the victim was sexually arousing. This was believed to apply to less than 10% of rapists. The DSM-III-R further stated that some rapists are sexually aroused by coercing or forcing a nonconsenting person to engage in intercourse and can maintain sexual arousal while observing the victim's suffering, but unlike persons with sexual sadism they do not find the victim's suffering sexually arousing. As pointed out earlier, Knight and Prentky (1990) were unable to substantiate these subtle distinctions in sex offenders. The claim should not mislead assessors into regarding as markedly deviant or uncommon presence of sexual arousal in men to visual stimuli or fantasies of the infliction of pain or suffering on women (Crepault & Couture, 1980; Person et al., 1989) or in women to fantasies of having pain or suffering inflicted upon themselves or of being raped (Hariton & Singer, 1974; Person et al., 1989). Investigation and management of victims' rape fantasies has been considered important in their treatment (McCombie & Arons, 1980). DSM-IV acknowledges the marked prevalence of sexually arousing fantasies commonly regarded as deviant, emphasizing that a paraphilia must be distinguished from the nonpathological use of sexual fantasies, behaviors, or objects as a stimulus for sexual excitement, which are paraphilic only when they lead to clinically significant distress or impairment. It states in regard to sadists that some act on their sadistic sexual urges with nonconsenting victims, possibly allowing retention of the concept of sadistic rapists advanced in the DSM-III-R.

Differences in diagnostic criteria would appear to produce marked discrepancies in findings concerning adult-child sexual relations. As pointed out earlier, studies of representative samples of the United States population found child molesters to be male for 98% of girl and 83% of boy victims (Finkelhor et al., 1990); and to be male, female, and both for 91%, 4%, and 4% of girl and 38%, 54%, and 7% of boy victims, respectively (Laumann et al., 1994). Strangers were molesters of 40% and 4% of boys in the two studies, respectively. Finkelhor et al. asked subjects about experiences they would now consider sexual abuse, and Laumann et al. asked subjects whether they had been touched sexually by anyone before puberty; cases were restricted to those with molesters over age 14. In the latter study, 45% of men but 70% of women considered that the experiences had affected their lives, almost always negatively. As the majority of men did not regard prepubertal sexual experiences with older usually female subjects as negative, they would be unlikely to consider them as sexual abuse and so would not report them in the study by Finkelhor et al. Laumann et al. agreed with their male subjects' assessments, stating that contacts between boys and older women appear to be less likely to be victim-offender situations than the behavior of sexually precocious boys with girls who are only somewhat older than they. Yet in their report of the subjects' adult adjustment, both men and women touched sexually in childhood were relatively equally impaired in comparison to those not touched; both groups were less happy and healthy in the previous year and more sexually dysfunctional. The finding that victims of childhood sexual experiences with adults report greater psychological dysfunction in adulthood has been the major reason advanced for considering these experiences sexually abusive (McConaghy, 1993).

Conditions of transvestism and transsexualism are no longer classified as such in the DSM-IV, although there is substantial evidence that they exist as clinical entities, with fetishistic transsexualism as an intermediate state (McConaghy, 1993). DSM-IV provides for transvestism to be diagnosed only as transvestic fetishism, emphasizing the fetishistic aspect of the behavior. In a discussion of this form of fetishism it points out that sexual arousal with cross-dressing diminishes or disappears in some individuals, but in regard to the differential diagnosis of gender identity disorder it states that transvestic fetish-ism occurs in heterosexual (or bisexual) men for whom cross-dressing behavior is for the purpose of sexual excitement. As pointed out earlier, most adult trans-vestites do not cross-dress for sexual excitement, and indeed many prefer not to acknowledge any fetishistic aspect to their behavior (McConaghy, 1993). DSM-IV includes the condition of transsexualism with cross-gender identification in children as gender identity disorder. It states that gender identity disorder of childhood is not meant to describe a child's nonconformity to stereotypic sex role behavior, as, for example, "tomboyishness" in girls or "sissyish" behavior in boys. Rather, it represents a profound disturbance of the normal sense of identity with regard to maleness and femaleness. It would appear that no scien-tific terms have been felt necessary to replace the lay terms "sissy" and "tom-boy". These are not restricted to extreme opposite-sex–linked behaviors. Sissy is applied to boys who avoid rough and tumble play and contact sports and who show interest in housework or artistic activities, and tomboy to girls who show the opposite behaviors. The degree to which sissy and tomboyish behaviors are shown in childhood correlates in later adolescence and adulthood with the de-gree to which boys experience homosexual feelings and girls report masculine personality traits (McConaghy, 1987; McConaghy & Zamir, 1995a). Neverthe-less, the DSM-IV reflects the generally accepted position that these opposite-sex–linked behaviors are not on a continuum with gender identity disorder of childhood, which as reported earlier is likely to be followed in adulthood by predominant homosexuality. Inquiry concerning presence of these sex-linked behaviors in childhood and adolescence may be indicated when a subject's bal-ance of homosexual to heterosexual feelings and sex role are relevant.

Concern has recently been expressed that interviewers may, with or without use of hypnosis, unconsciously influence the recall of patients, particularly in relation to what have been classified as repressed memories, usually of child-hood sexual abuse. Croyle and Loftus (1993) pointed out the difficulty in as-sessing accuracy of memories of past sexual behavior in view of the absence of independent data. They cited evidence that people tend to rehearse more vivid experiences, such as victimizations in assaults, accidents, and hospitalizations, and that when people are exposed to new relevant information during rehearsal, the new information can contaminate the original memory. They pointed out the need to avoid leading questions, while stressing that such avoidance cannot undo earlier contaminations of memory. In a review that stimulated a prolonged correspondence, Crews (1994) criticized the acceptance of the extraordinary vividness and precision of recovered memories as evidence of their validity, stat-ing that people had been convicted on this basis without supportive evidence. He also criticized a notion he attributed to the retrievers of the memories: that the memories were videotaped records of events stored in a special part of the brain and then suddenly yielded up. He emphasized the lack of research valida-tion supporting the views advanced by Terr (1994) that trauma sets up new rules for memory and that investigations of memory in university students do not duplicate in any way clinicians' observations.

Clinicians need to determine the policy to adopt concerning behaviors as-sessed as legally mandatory to report. A U.S. national survey indicated that 40% of professionals mandated to report suspected abuse failed to do so (Thompson-

Cooper, Fugere, & Cormier, 1993). Adler (1995) wondered how many patients would accept treatment or feel able to disclose anything that could be even vaguely incriminating if they were asked to complete a consent form that stated that confidentiality will be maintained unless the clinician has reasonable grounds to believe that clients might be a danger to themselves or others. In regard to the major problems associated with mandatory reporting, including the incompatibility of punitive and therapeutic goals, Thompson-Cooper et al. (1993) argue that therapists should be given discretion not to report cases if patients are responding appropriately to therapy.

PSYCHOLOGICAL AND BIOLOGICAL ASSESSMENT

The unstructured interview still appears to be the most common method of psychological assessment of subjects with sexual disorders. It enables the clinician to determine the nature of their disorder while assessing their personality and commencing to establish appropriate therapeutic relationships, which will maximize the likelihood of their cooperating with the chosen therapy (McConaghy, in press). Use of structured interviews by clinicians would add considerably to the time taken to adequately assess subjects. Although it should enhance diagnostic agreement with other clinicians, provided all use the same interview, such agreement is of no advantage in the treatment of individual patients unless it leads to selection of more appropriate treatment. Currently, there is no evidence that this is the case. Morganstern (1988) pointed out that often the highest treatment priority needs to be given to a problem other than the one of which the client initially complained. The therapist is likely to realize this only in the course of an unstructured interview. Catania, Gibson, Chitwood, and Coates (1990) concluded that, in regard to data about which subjects have privacy concerns, current evidence suggests that self-administered questionnaires reduce measurement error compared to face-to-face interviews. However, of 100 51-year old men who accepted being interviewed after having completed a questionnaire, 7 said at interview that they had erectile dysfunction more than occasionally, whereas none had reported this by questionnaire (Solstad & Hertoft, 1993). Although inventories completed by the subjects avoid the criticism that they have been influenced by the interviewer, the influence of the context remains. AuBuchon and Calhoun (1985) found a negative relationship between menstruation and checklist-assessed mood in women who were informed that a possible relationship between behavior and menstrual cycles was being investigated. This relationship was not present in those not informed. The difference was attributed to social expectancy and demand characteristics of the experiment. Few studies have investigated the test-retest reliability of questionnaire assessments of sexual behaviors. Responses of 116 homosexual men who completed retest questionnaires after 2–18 weeks showed high reliability (kappa values greater than .8) for demographic data, smoking history, and sexual orientation, but moderate reliability (kappa values .41–.6) for 6-month number of steady and nonsteady partners and frequency of various sexual practices (Saltzman, Stoddard, McCusker, Moon, & Mayer, 1987). The authors speculated that social desirability effects could have been responsible for the shifts, which were toward more safe-sex behaviors. Clark and Tifft (1966) retested 45 male sociology students prior to their undergoing a polygraph examination which they believed would detect falsehoods. If the responses to the second questionnaire are accepted as valid, in the initial questionnaire percentages of over- and underreporting were nearly equal (15% and 17.5%) for vaginal intercourse; 15% underreported and 5% overreported homosexual contacts; and 30% underreported masturbation, 95% admitting it in their final responses.

Level of motivation is of importance in relation to compliance with regular self-reporting by diary. Reading (1983) randomly allocated paid male volunteers to report their sexual behaviors either by interview after 1 and 3 months ($N = 21$); interviews after 1, 2, and 3 months ($N = 18$); or diary cards completed daily and returned every 3 days in addition to interviews at 1, 2, and 3 months ($N = 29$). Dropout occurred in 14%, 16%, and 34% of the three procedures, respectively. A further three dropped out prior to the first month with the last procedure, as they considered that completing diary cards caused potency difficulties. Frequency of urges of pedophiles for sexual contact with children reported by daily diary card did not differ in those receiving the male sex-hormone reducing chemical medroxyprogesterone from those receiving placebo (Wincze, Bansal, & Malamud, 1986), indicating that the diary card assessment lacked validity. In addition to the clinical evidence of the efficacy of the chemical in reducing such urges (McConaghy, 1993), reduction (to which they were blind) in sex offenders' testosterone levels produced by medroxyprogesterone correlated highly with their global assessment of the degree of reduction of their deviant urges by questionnaire (McConaghy, Blaszczynski, & Kidson, 1988). Patients' self-report of behaviors in inventories can of themselves produce changes in behaviors. LoPiccolo and Steger (1974) found test-retest reliabilities of subjects' scores on the Sexual Interaction Inventory lower than expected. They related this to evidence that self-recording of sexual activity led to marked changes in activity. It would appear that if such inventories are used to assess response to treatment they need to be administered a number of times prior to initiation of treatment, for such reactivity to stabilize. Also, subjects' behavior may change following cessation of their self-recording, so that their final response to treatment cannot be judged from the final inventory.

Wincze and Carey (1991) pointed out that behavioral inventories have not been widely used in clinical sexuality assessments and cited Conte's (1983) suggestion that one reason was that many inventories were developed for specific research purposes and had limited clinical utility. They also pointed out that their use could be time consuming and inconvenient in a busy practice. Nevertheless, they stated that they had used a number of self-report questionnaires in assessing patients with sexual dysfunctions and suggested Conte's (1983) review and the compendium of Davis, Yarber, and Davis (1988) as sources for other measures which could be useful. A further such source is the *Dictionary of Behavioral Assessment Techniques* (Hersen & Bellack, 1988). Jacobson, Follette, and Revenstorf (1984) pointed out that scores on scales of marital satisfaction between subjects who received active and placebo marital therapy could be statistically significant when the changes were clinically trivial. They recommended comparing treated subjects' individual scores with norms of functionally well subjects on the same scales. With this procedure the mean improvement rate with behavioral marital therapy was about 35%, considerably less than was generally believed (Jacobson et al., 1984).

Assessment of sexual behaviors and feelings as categorical can produce misleading findings. Sexual or gender identity was first identified in relation to transsexualism (McConaghy, 1993). Transsexuals were conceptualized as identifying totally as members of the biologically opposite sex. The possibility that in nontranssexuals sexual identity could be dimensional was not considered. In investigating girls exposed to increased levels of androgens in utero, Ehrhardt and Baker (1974) commented that 35% were undecided or thought that they might have chosen to be boys, but that "none had a conflict with their female gender identity" (p. 43). However, McConaghy and Armstrong (1983) found that when students were given the opportunity to report their sexual identity dimensionally by rating the degrees to which they ever feel uncertain of their identity as a member of their sex, their strength of identity as a member of their sex, and the strength with which they feel like a member of the opposite sex, their responses to these items correlated at most about .5. Correlations were stronger in subjects who reported some awareness of homosexual feelings, with these subjects reporting a greater degree of opposite-sex identity. Fifty-nine percent of lesbian, 32% of bisexual, and 22% of heterosexual women reported that as children they felt like boys or men (Phillips & Over, 1995). Some male transvestites report a male identity when dressed as men and a female identity when dressed as women (Buhrich & McConaghy, 1977).

The randomized response technique was introduced to obtain nonanonymous self-reports of socially unacceptable behaviors. Finkelhor and Lewis (1988) used it in a phone survey to determine the number of child molesters in the general population. Subjects were asked to answer "Yes" if either or both of two questions was correct. The questions were "Have you ever sexually abused a child" and "Do you rent the place where you live?" By independently determining the percentage of subjects who rent, the percentage of child molesters could be estimated from the percentage who answered "Yes." Failure to obtain consistent results was attributed to the nature of the questions used. Also, Catania et al. (1990) cited studies where the randomized response technique did not appear to enhance reporting. However, the technique seems worthy of further evaluation.

In relation to the obtaining of reliable data, Catania et al. (1990) pointed out that it meant little if the behavior measured is a pale reflection of actual sexual behavior. They considered the frequently investigated correlations between partners' reports of their sexual behaviors to be at best weak validity estimates requiring validation against some objective index, though of interest in their own right as mutual perceptions. Catania et al. pointed out that such objective indices as have been employed (e.g., sexually transmitted disease rates, condom sales, urine analysis for sperm) did not achieve one-to-one correspondence with self-reports of sexual behavior and concluded that although such indices were useful, development of more exacting measures remained a major challenge.

Physiological assessment of men's sexual arousal by measurement of their penile volume responses (PVRs) to pictures of male and female nudes of 13-second duration was validated by Freund's (1963) demonstration that it classified correctly the majority of individual subjects who reported relatively ex-clusively heterosexual or homosexual feelings or behaviors. McConaghy (1967) replicated this finding using a simpler apparatus for measuring PVRs to a brief standardized presentation of moving pictures of nude men and nude women of 10-second duration. Subsequently, a strain gauge measuring penile circumfer-ence (PC) used to assess penile tumescence during sleep was also used to mea-sure sexual arousal, as it was assumed that PC and PV changes were identical. Zuckerman (1971) accepted this in his widely cited review of physiological mea-sures of sexual arousal. He decided that use of PCRs was preferable on the grounds that the circumference gauge was easier to apply, simpler to calibrate, and did not stimulate as large an area of the penis. Without validation being considered necessary, use of strain gauges to measure sexual arousal in men was adopted by researchers apart from Freund and McConaghy. Comparison of PCRs and PVRs of individual subjects to the standardized presentation of films of nudes revealed that though the two responses could be reasonably equivalent they could also be largely mirror images (McConaghy, 1974). It was suggested the mirror-image responses occurred in subjects whose initial penile tumescence was associated with a rapid elongation of the penis, such that the increase in blood flow necessary to maintain elongation was not sufficient to also maintain an increase in circumference (the response measured by PCR). In these subjects PVR increases were paralleled either by no change or by decrease in PCR, the latter then being a mirror image of the PVR. PVRs, therefore, measure the initial stage of penile tumescence more accurately than PCRs, which can only accu-rately measure the later stage after 2 minutes or more (Freund, 1971). This could account for the greater sensitivity of PVRs in assessing sexual orientation, as the initial stage may more accurately reflect sexual arousal, the later stage of tumescence possibly being more influenced by hemodynamic factors determin-ing erection.

PVRs and PCRs continue to be treated as equivalent, even after it has been shown that the PCRs to pictures of a nude young woman failed to discriminate as groups six homosexual from six heterosexual men (Mavissakalian, Blanch-ard, Abel, & Barlow, 1975), and PCRs to heterosexual, homosexual, and lesbian slides did not distinguish as groups eight homosexual from eight heterosexual men (Sakheim, Barlow, Beck, & Abrahamson, 1985). Sakheim et al. found that to correctly identify most heterosexual and homosexual men as individuals us-ing PCRs, it was necessary to use the more powerful erotic stimuli of moving films of men and women involved in homosexual (but not heterosexual) activity. By that time PCRs to pictures of single male and female nudes had been adopted for use in single-case studies as the major outcome measure of change in individual subjects' heterosexual and homosexual feelings (McConaghy, 1993). The findings of these single-case studies remain the only evidence that such widely used techniques as masturbatory satiation and aversive procedures modify deviant sexual arousal. They continue to be cited in this respect (Laws & Marshall, 1991), despite the demonstrated lack of validity of PCRs to such stim-uli as measures of individuals' sexual arousal. When PCR assessment with use of the more powerful stimulus of movies of sexual activity failed to distinguish bisexual from homosexual men, Tollison, Adams, and Tollison (1979) questioned the existence of bisexuality, claiming that there was to that date no physiological evidence for bisexual arousal except as a by-product of sexual reorientation therapy. In fact, PVR assessments had provided such evidence (McConaghy, 1993).

Findings of early studies reporting that pedophiles and rapists could be distinguished from control subjects by their PCRs to audio- or videotaped descriptions of sexual activities or pictures of male and female nudes of various ages have led to the widespread use of these responses in diagnosis and assessment of treatment outcome. Subsequent studies showed inconsistent results (McConaghy, 1988, 1993), possibly due to 1. the lower sensitivity of PCRs compared to PVRs as measures of arousal, 2. the ability of subjects to learn to modify their PCRs with the prolonged time these responses require for assessment, and 3. the significant percentage of normal controls who show evidence of arousal to stimuli of children or acts of sexual aggression (McConaghy, in press). Lalumiere and Quinsey (1994), using meta-analysis of studies investigating the PCRs of rapists, demonstrated that the assessment did discriminate rapists from nonrapists as groups. The fact that it was necessary to combine results of several studies by meta-analysis to obtain convincing statistical evidence that PCR assessment discriminated the two groups would seem to show that assessment should be used only to investigate groups, not individuals. Nevertheless, the authors considered that the result supported its use to identify an individual offender's treatment needs and risk of recidivism. In reviewing evidence that changes in PCRs with treatment fail to predict such risks, Marshall and Barbaree (1990a) commented that if behaviorists are to maintain their exaggerated faith in erectile measurements, they must solve the experimental riddle of demonstrating the relevance of changing such indices to the maintenance of offensive behavior and, particularly, to the issue of treatment benefits. Ethical concerns regarding the forcing of uninformed subjects to see or hear pornographic material contributed to the termination of the use of PCRs in prison treatment programs in Utah (Card & Dibble, 1995).

Presumably, because of the small number of women sex offenders, their genital physiological responses do not appear to have been investigated. Changes in sexually functional and dysfunctional women's vaginal, clitoral, or labial blood flow with exposure to erotic stimuli were measured either by the associated temperature changes using a thermistor or by vaginal color changes using a photoplethysmograph. Clitoral responses have also been assessed using a strain gauge. Rosen and Beck (1988) concluded that photoplethysmograph assessment of vaginal pulse amplitude (VPA) was the most widely used and most sensitive measure of arousal in distinguishing the responses of groups of women to erotic as compared to nonerotic stimuli, but its correlation with subjectively assessed arousal was insignificant in the majority of women studied. Hatch (1981) found no consistent reports of differences in physiologically assessed genital arousal to erotic stimuli of sexually functional and dysfunctional women, or of changes in the arousal of the dysfunctional women following treatment. However, Palace and Gorzalka (1990, 1992) demonstrated that these negative findings were due to differences in stimuli and assessment procedures, including use of VPA rather than vaginal blood volume (VBV), which they considered the more sensitive indicator of sexual arousal. They provided replicated evidence that sexually dysfunctional women showed less VBV response and subjective arousal to erotic films, but found few significant correlations between genital and subjective measures of sexual arousal.

Men with hypoactive sexual desire and those whose erectile disorder is not situational (and hence not obviously psychogenically determined) require biological assessment. Situational erectile disorder is that which occurs with some but not all partners, or with all partners but not in private masturbation where no pressure to produce an erection is experienced. Physical examination is indicated to exclude such conditions as Peyronie's disease and hypogonadism, and blood and urine screening to exclude diabetes, hyperprolactinaemia (raised levels of the pituitary hormone prolactin, HPRL), and thyroid dysfunction. Presumably reflecting differences in patient samples, the percentage of impotent men reported to show hormone abnormalities varies markedly between studies, as do conclusions about what hormones should be investigated. Some studies have recommended that in initial evaluation only testosterone levels be measured, and prolactin estimations be carried out only in patients whose testosterone levels are low, as the presence of pituitary tumors associated with elevation of prolactin is rare. However, Buvat et al. (1985) found that 10 of 850 men with erectile dysfunction showed marked HPRL (above 35 ng/ml), and 6 of the 10 showed radiologic evidence of a pituitary adenoma. Five of the 10 had testosterone levels within the normal range. It would seem possible that failure to estimate prolactin levels and perhaps diabetes and thyroid dysfunction in men with erectile disorder or hypoactive sexual desire could have medicolegal consequences. Although the level of testosterone necessary to maintain erectile function is markedly below that necessary to maintain sexual interest (McConaghy, 1993), testosterone levels are usually routinely investigated in men with nonsituational erectile disorder, whether or not they show physical signs of hypogonadism.

Assessment of nocturnal penile tumescence (NPT) by PCR remains widely used in the differential diagnosis of psychogenic and organic erectile dysfunction. Wincze and Carey (1991) stated that its use, usually in a full sleep laboratory, has been considered the gold standard of this diagnosis but is well beyond the financial means of most clients. Indeed, clinicians might want to consider more affordable and perhaps more valid psychophysiological assessments. Meisler and Carey (1990) considered that it may misdiagnose as many as 20% of the subjects investigated. Cheaper alternatives to sleep laboratory assessment of NPT include assessing subjects' NPT in their own homes, using a ring of stamps or a snap gauge around the penis, which bursts if tumescence occurs, or the Rigiscan portable monitoring instrument. NPT investigation is routine for medicolegal purposes in patients complaining of erectile disorder secondary to compensatible accidents or injuries.

In opposition to the belief of the 1970s that most cases of erectile disorder were entirely psychogenically determined (LoPiccolo, 1982), it is now generally accepted that organic factors, usually impairment in penile blood flow, commonly contribute to their etiology (Meuleman et al., 1992). Such impairment is assessed by determination of the penile-brachial index (PBI), the ratio of the blood pressure in the penile arteries, commonly measured by Doppler ultrasound probe, and conventionally measured blood pressure in the brachial artery in the arm. Erectile dysfunction is almost invariable in men with ratios of 0.6, although ratios of 0.7–0.9 do not exclude this (Metz & Bengtsson, 1984). Reliance of clinicians on NPT and PBI assessment in impotence was questioned by Saypol, Peterson, Howards, and Yazel (1983). They reported close agreement between diagnoses of the psychiatrist and urologist reached by clinical examination alone and diagnoses reached on the basis of the patients' fasting blood sugar and testosterone levels and their PBI and NPT assessments. They suggested that expensive tests be reserved for patients about whom the psychiatrist and urologist disagree or cannot determine the diagnosis.

Pharmacological erection tests are increasingly being used to assess penile vascular supply in erectile dysfunction. Vasodilating chemicals—papaverine alone or with phentolamine, prostaglandin E1 alone, or a mixture of all three—are injected into one of the cavernous sinuses of the subject's penis. McMahon (1994) noted that development of a rigid, well-sustained erection within 10 minutes suggests that no major vascular abnormality exists; a slow onset as assessed by Rigiscan indicates presence of some degree of arterial disease, and rapid detumescence, a venous leak. Failure to develop a full erectile response can be due to the inhibiting effect of the test setting, which may be overcome by prolongation of the observation period and addition of manual or visual stimulation (Meuleman et al., 1992). When the pharmacological erection test indicates presence of vascular pathology, further physical investigations are necessary to determine its nature. Also, assessment of neurogenic factors producing impotence is indicated if the patient has a history of diabetes, pelvic pathology, or radical prostatectomy or if physical examination reveals the absence of the cremasteric or bulbocavernosal reflex or reduced lower limb reflexes (McConaghy, in press).

Physical and laboratory examinations are more rarely carried out on women with sexual dysfunctions. Although, as for men, it is necessary to exclude illness, medications, or substances as responsible for reduced sexual interest or ability to reach orgasm, the effects of neurological and vascular disease and of medications and drugs of abuse on the sexuality of women are much more poorly documented. Physical examination is necessary to investigate dyspareunia, but hormone studies are not routine in the investigation of sexually dysfunctional women in the absence of evidence of hormonal imbalance, such as excessive hirsutism. Significant hormonal fluctuations that occur throughout the menstrual cycle have not been demonstrated to be accompanied by consistent fluctuations in sexual behaviors (McConaghy, 1993).

Serum testosterone levels are of value in monitoring the response of paraphilic men to androgen-reducing chemical therapy, with percentage reduction from pretreatment levels correlating highly with subjects' reported degree of reduction of paraphilic urges (McConaghy et al., 1988). Reduction to 30% of pretreatment level produces sufficient reduction in deviant arousal without impairing erectile responses in acceptable sexual activities. A number of studies have reported differences in hypothalamic nuclei in men and women, in homosexual compared to heterosexual subjects, and in male-to-female transsexuals compared to control males (Swaab, Zhou, & Hofman, 1995).

GENDER AND RACIAL-ETHNIC ISSUES

Gender issues are of course of major importance in every area of sexuality. However, there are evident biases in the degree of attention paid to them. Biological factors determining women's as compared to men's normal and dysfunctional sexual activities are poorly researched, supporting the impression that women's sexuality is much more determined by social factors (McConaghy, 1993). Schover (1989) suggested that a possible reason older women seemed far less concerned with staying sexually active than were older men with comparable medical problems is our youth-oriented ideal of female sexuality. This gender difference may diminish when future cohorts of women with greater expectation of sexual pleasure reach their 50s or 60s. Another contributing factor could be the higher percentage of heterosexual older women as compared to men who lack a partner. As pointed out earlier, presence of a partner plays an important role in the maintenance of sexual interest. Another interesting difference in older subjects that requires explanation is the finding of Eklund et al. (1988) that almost all female-to-male transsexuals presented before the age of 50, whereas a number of male-to-female transsexuals presented after that age. Despite the marked increase in reported prevalence of transsexualism since it was first recognized, Eklund et al. pointed out the ratio of male-to-female as compared to female-to-male transsexuals has tended to remain consistent at about three to one.

Earlier studies of victims of sexual aggression investigated only female subjects. Koss and Oros (1982) developed a sexual experiences survey to investigate the concept that rape represented an extreme behavior on a continuum with normal male sexual behavior. Men could report sexually coercive behaviors only as perpetrators and women only as victims. Use of the questionnaire modified to allow men and women to report coercive behaviors as both perpetrators and victims demonstrated that with less forceful behaviors investigated, percentage of male victims approached that of female victims and reported perpetration of sexual coercion correlated with masculine behavior in both men and women (McConaghy & Zamir, 1995b). As pointed out earlier, the Los Angeles ECA study found 13% of women and 7% of men reported having been sexually assaulted in adulthood (Sorenson et al., 1987). The most recent assault involved a male assailant in 75% of cases, who acted alone in 90%, and was acquainted with but not related to the victim in 77%. Thirteen percent of assaults of women were by spouses and 13% by lovers; 6% of assaults of men were by spouses and 18% by lovers. Sex of the victims of the 25% of women assailants was not reported. The fact that women rarely seek treatment or are diagnosed or charged with sexual assault or pedophilia appears in part due to the tendency of male children not to regard experiences with older women negatively. Also most male children who report being touched sexually by an older person report women, unlike men, to be only a few years older (Laumann et al., 1994). The definition of pedophilic activity as abusive, whether or not the children considered their reactions neutral or positive, is applied only to sexual activity of postpubertal subjects with girl children.

Adoption of safe sex practices of women at risk have not matched those of homosexual men, resulting in a rapid increase in heterosexual and maternal-fetal HIV transmission in the United States, particularly among minority women. In pointing this out, Nelson (1991) argued that present public health strategies are incomplete and recommended "sexual self-defense," a female-targeted strategy.

Ethnic issues related to sexual and gender disorders have been investigated mainly in relation to sexual assault, risk of adolescent pregnancy, and more recently safe sex practices, reflecting the desire to reduce the incidence of HIV infection. Most studies investigating sexual behavior do not appear to have considered whether interviewers and respondents should be matched for race. The failure to do so in the study by Laumann et al. (1994) was one aspect Lewontin (1995) emphasized in his trenchant criticism. He commented satirically on the authors' recognition that race was an important variable organizing the pattern of social relationships: "Apparently being interviewed about your sex life is not part of social relationships" (p. 28). However, Laumann et al. had pointed out lack of empirical data concerning the importance in research interviews of matching interviewers with the respondents on such variables as gender or race. Ostrow, Kessler, Stover, and Peqegnat (1993) considered that in investigating the sexual behavior of communities, use of community members as interviewers might facilitate access but also might reduce respondents' honesty if they felt their confidentiality could be violated. Stevenson, De Moya, and Boruch (1993) considered use of informants experienced with the population essential both to identify and obtain the cooperation of subjects and to select and develop appropriate questions. They believed that distrust between investigators of sexual behavior and the African American community could be a major stumbling block for AIDS researchers. They advised that this be reduced by such strategies as obtaining endorsement from respected African American leaders.

No significant race or social-class differences were found in the total sample of adolescent female victims of sexual assault in Ageton's (1983) study, although urban girls were more vulnerable. Those who reported violent sexual assaults were typically black, lower class urban adolescents, characteristic of victims of reported rape. Parker (1991) pointed out that on the basis of the National Crime Survey (NCS) figures, 11% of black and 8% of white women will be victims of attempted or completed rape at least once during their lifetimes. Correlates of rates of rape in standard metropolitan statistical areas were poverty, percentage black, and percentage divorced. In regard to arrests for forcible rape, as with most arrests, blacks are overrepresented. In 1986, when a little over 12% of the U.S. population was counted as black, 47% of men arrested for rape were black. Such overrepresentation did not appear due to police racism, as it was present in victims' reports in the NCS data of the perceived characteristics of their aggressors (Harris, 1991). A consistent finding concerning male rape in institutional settings was the disproportionate number of black aggressors and white victims both in prisons and juvenile corrective-training schools (King, 1992). King suggested that coerced sexual assault in all-male institutions may be part of personalized ethnic power struggle, reflecting a deep-seated resentment of lower class blacks against middle-class whites. It was also pointed out that the findings might be influenced by the racial prejudice of researchers. They could of course also reflect differences in the readiness of black and white victims to report assaults. Fewer Hispanics compared to non-Hispanic white men and women in the Los Angeles ECA project reported having been sexually assaulted (Sorenson et al., 1987).

A mid-1980s National Research Council study (Hacker, 1987) found that 40% of black and 20% of white teenagers became pregnant, approaching half the number who were sexually active and indicating the inadequate use of contraception. Differences in the outcome of the pregnancies of the black and white girls were not great. Respectively, 35% and 40% arranged abortions, and 51% and 46% delivered the baby, of whom 99% and 92% subsequently reared their child. The annual birth rate per 1,000 unmarried girls aged 15–19 was 87 for blacks and 19 for whites, giving the United States the highest rate of out-of-wedlock childbirth among developed countries, even among the white teenagers (Hacker, 1987). The United States also had one of the highest rates of abortion for adolescents (Furstenberg et al., 1989).

Easterbrook et al. (1993) pointed out the need to take into account behavioral differences that exist between white and minority racial and ethnic groups in relation to the excess prevalence of HIV infection among U.S. black and Hispanic homosexuals. From 1981 through 1991, 24%–30% of the reported morbidity from gonorrhea and 10%–12% of the reported morbidity from primary and secondary syphilis in the United States affected adolescents. Differences in reported rates of both infections between white, black, and Hispanic adolescents increased during the latter half of the 1980s (Webster et al., 1993).

Ethnic differences may contribute to differences in the reported prevalence of transsexualism between and within countries. Tsoi (1990) suggested, in relation to the markedly higher prevalence of transsexualism he found in Singapore-born men and women as compared with that in most Western countries, that the greater availability of sex-conversion surgery may have drawn out the Singapore transsexuals earlier. Also, Singaporese had a stronger need for sex conversion since homosexuality was not accepted by society there. He reported 200 male transsexuals in Singapore who could not be differentiated from male homosexuals from their earlier sexual behavior until they started to cross-dress and sought sex conversion. None had ever married or experienced heterosexual intercourse. Absence among his subjects of fetishistic transsexuals, who are usually predominantly heterosexual and have married, requires explanation. Ninety percent of the transsexual prostitutes investigated by MacFarlane (1984) in Wellington, New Zealand, were half or quarter-caste Maoris, who made up only 9% of the population. Lothstein and Roback (1984) reported that black women were grossly underrepresented among applicants for sex conversion to their clinic in Cleveland, Ohio. They considered that the few who did apply were borderline or frankly schizophrenic.

SUMMARY

DSM-IV definition of sexual and gender identity disorders are summarized and studies of their prevalence reviewed. The importance of age in relation to prevalence of dysfunctions is pointed out. The most common complaints appear to be erectile dysfunction in men and impairment of sexual interest in women. However, the majority of subjects with dysfunctions do not seek treatment for them. Data as to prevalence of subjects who commit paraphilic or sexually coercive or assaultive acts are reviewed, and the high percentage of normal subjects who have sexual fantasies of carrying out or being victims of these acts is noted. The issue of whether gender identity disorder of childhood is on a continuum with or categorically different from sissiness and tomboyism is raised; all three are followed by increasing likelihood of experiencing homosexual feelings in adulthood or a degree of opposite-sex identity, or both. Sexual dysfunctions have not been found to be associated with subjects' impaired psychological adjustment and to be only weakly associated with their sexual satisfaction. Sexual satisfaction was related to subjects' sexual difficulties which reflect the emotional tone of sexual relationships. Psychological treatment may be successful by reducing sexual difficulties rather than dysfunctions. Reduction of difficulties would seem to involve improving couples' communication and the quality of their relationships. This quality may be less significant to sexually functional subjects. Presence of a sexually active partner appears to be of importance in developing and maintaining subjects' sexual functioning. Learning would appear to play a major role in women's achieving orgasm, although biological differences may also be involved, as they may be with level of men's sexual interest and erectile and ejaculatory function.

Results of traditional personality assessment of sex offenders have been inconsistent, although a significant percentage of sexually assaultive men show delinquent or antisocial personality features. Most committed their offenses while under the influence of alcohol. Convicted rapists and child molesters were similar to the general prison population in many behavioral features. Classifications of anger and power, sadistic and nonsadistic, and blitz and confidence rapists are described, as are differences between heterosexual and homosexual pedophiles. Postpubertal women who sexually touch prepubertal boys are usually too young to be classified as pedophiles. The paraphilias of exhibitionism, voyeurism, frotteurism, sadism, masochism, fetishism, and transvestic fetishism are described. Failure of DSM-IV to separately classify the adult form of transvestic fetishism, previously regarded as a gender identity disorder, is noted, as is its failure to retain the related term "transsexualism."

Evidence of the course of sexual dysfunctions with and without treatment is reviewed. No placebo-controlled studies evaluating psychological treatment appear to have been carried out in recent years. The good immediate outcome of anorgasmia and vaginismus but not premature ejaculation appears to persist. A hostile relationship with the partner was consistently found to be associated with a poor prognosis of sexual dysfunction. A significant percentage of men with erectile dysfunction refuse behavioral sex therapy, possibly related to increased acceptance that organic factors frequently contribute to the condition and that physical treatment is required. The outcome of both treated and untreated sex offenders was found to be too varied to provide meaningful evidence that any treatment was effective. Random allocation of incarcerated sex offenders to relapse prevention or no treatment demonstrated treatment to be virtually ineffective. No placebo-controlled trials have been carried out, although systematic desensitization, based on a behavior completion model, was demonstrated to be superior to aversive electric shock and covert sensitization aversive therapy in random allocation controlled studies. On the basis of this model, a much lower dose of medroxyprogesterone than that generally used was introduced and shown to be effective in allowing subjects to control deviant sexual urges.

Women's ability to attain orgasm in sexual activity was found to be unrelated to the nature of their parental relationships. Marked pathology was found in the families of incarcerated sex offenders, who were also more likely to report childhood sexual victimization. Problems with current definitions of sexual dysfunctions and paraphilias were noted, and the need was emphasized for health professionals to inquire about their subjects' sexual activity, including anal intercourse (while avoiding the use of leading questions that might contaminate their memories). Assessment of sexual behavior by unstructured and structured interviews, questionnaires, and diaries was discussed. Penile response assessment is not sufficiently sensitive to discriminate sex offenders from nonoffenders as individuals, but only as groups. Vaginal blood volume responses of sexually functional and dysfunctional women differed significantly but did not correlate with their reported awareness of sexual arousal. Physical, hormonal, nocturnal penile tumescence, and pharmacological erection test assessments of sexually dysfunctional men were discussed. Monitoring of serum testosterone levels of offenders treated with medroxyprogesterone is of value. The low number of female as compared to male sex offenders would appear to have led earlier investigators of sexual aggression to consider only male aggressors and female victims. The focus of awareness of ethnic issues in sexual disorders has mainly been on prevalence of sexual assault, adolescent pregnancy, and safe sex practices; such issues may be of significance in the prevalence of transsexualism.

REFERENCES

Abel, G. G., & Rouleau, J. L. (1990). The nature and extent of sexual assault. In W. L. Marshall, D. R. Laws, & H. E. Barbaree (Eds.), *Handbook of sexual assault: Issues, theories, and treatment of the offender* (pp. 9–21). New York: Plenum.

Adkins, E., & Jehu, D. (1985). Analysis of a treatment program for primary orgastic dysfunction. *Behaviour Research and Therapy, 23,* 1219–126.

Adler, R. (1995). To tell or not to tell: The psychiatrist and child abuse. *Australian and New Zealand Journal of Psychiatry, 29,* 190–198.

Ageton, S. S. (1983). *Sexual assault among adolescents.* Lexington: Lexington Books.

American Psychiatric Association. (1980). *Diagnostic and statistical manual of mental disorders* (3rd ed.). Washington, DC: Author.

American Psychiatric Association. (1987). *Diagnostic and statistical manual of mental disorders* (3rd ed., rev. ed.). Washington, DC: Author.

American Psychiatric Association. (1994). *Diagnostic and statistical manual of mental disorders* (4th ed.). Washington, DC: Author.

Apfelbaum, B. (1989). Retarded ejaculation: a much-misunderstood syndrome. In S. R. Leiblum & R. C. Rosen (Eds.), *Principles and practice of sex therapy* (pp. 168–206). New York: Guilford.

AuBuchon, P. G., & Calhoun, K. S. (1985). Menstrual cycle symptomatology: The role of social expectancy and experimental demand characteristics. *Psychosomatic Medicine, 47,* 35–45.

Auerbach, R., & Kilmann, P. R. (1977). The effects of group systematic desensitization on secondary erectile failure. *Behavior Therapy, 8,* 330–339.

Bard, L. A., Carter, D. L., Cerce, D. D., Knight, R. A., Rosenberg, R., & Schneider, B. (1987). A descriptive study of rapists and child molesters: Developmental, clinical, and criminal characteristics. *Behavioral Sciences and the Law, 5,* 203–220.

Baxter, L. A., & Wilmot, W. W. (1985). Taboo topics in close relationships. *Journal of Social and Personal Relationships, 2,* 253–269.

Berlin, F. S., & Meinecke, C. F. (1981). Treatment of sex offenders with antiandrogenic medication: Conceptualization, review of treatment modalities, and preliminary findings. *American Journal of Psychiatry, 138,* 601–607.

Bolling, D. R., & Voeller, B. (1987). AIDS and heterosexual anal intercourse. *Journal of the American Medical Association, 258,* 474.

Bowie, S. I., Silverman, D. C., Kalick, S. M., & Edbril, S. D. (1990). Blitz rape and confidence rape: Implications for clinical intervention. *American Journal of Psychotherapy, 44,* 180–188.

Breslow, N., Evans, L., & Langley, J. (1985). On the prevalence and roles of females in the sadomasochistic subculture: Report of an empirical study. *Archives of Sexual Behavior, 14,* 303–319.

Bridges, C. F., Critelli, J. W., & Loos, V. E. (1985). Hypnotic susceptibility, inhibitory control, and orgasmic consistency. *Archives of Sexual Behavior, 14,* 373–376.

Buhrich, N. (1977). *Clinical study of heterosexual male transvestism.* Unpublished doctoral disseration. Sydney: University of New South Wales.

Buhrich, N., & McConaghy, N. (1977). The clinical syndromes of femmiphilic transvestism. *Archives of Sexual Behavior, 6,* 397–412.

Buhrich, N., & McConaghy, N. (1978). Two clinically discrete syndromes of transsexualism. *British Journal of Psychiatry, 133,* 73–76.

Bumby, K. M. (1996). Assessing the cognitive distortions of child molesters and rapists: Development and validation of the MOLEST and RAPE scales. *Sexual Abuse: A Journal of Research and Treatment, 8,* 37–54.

Burgess, A. W., & Holmstrom, L. L. (1980). Rape typology and the coping behavior of rape victims. In S. L. McCombie (Ed.), *Rape crisis intervention handbook* (pp. 27–42). New York: Plenum.

Buvat, J., Lemaire, A., Buvat-Herbaut, M., Guieu, J. D., Bailleul, J. P., & Fossati, P. (1985). Comparative investigations in 26 impotent and 26 nonimpotent diabetic patients. *Journal of Urology, 133,* 34–38.

Card, R. D., & Dibble, A. (1995). Predictive value of the Card/Farrall stimuli in discriminating between gynephilic and pedophilic sexual offenders. *Sexual Abuse: A Journal of Research and Treatment, 7,* 129–141.

Catalan, J., Hawton, K., & Day, A. (1990). Couples referred to a sexual dysfunction clinic psychological and physical morbidity. *British Journal of Psychiatry, 156,* 61–67.

Catania, J. A., Gibson, D. R., Chitwood, D. D., & Coates, T. J. (1990). Methodological problems in AIDS behavioral research: Influences on measurement error and participation bias in studies of sexual behavior. *Psychological Bulletin, 108,* 339–362.

Clare, E., & Tully, B. (1989). Transhomosexuality, or the dissociation of sexual orientation and sex object choice. *Archives of Sexual Behavior, 18,* 531–536.

Clark, J. P., & Tifft, L. L. (1966). Polygraph and interview validation of self-reported deviant behavior. *American Sociological Review, 31,* 516–523.

Coleman, E., Bockting, W. O., & Gooren, L. (1993). Homosexual and bisexual identity in sex-reassigned female-to-male transsexuals. *Archives of Sexual Behavior, 22,* 37–50.

Conte, H. R. (1983). Development and use of self-report techniques for assessing sexual functioning: A review and critique. *Archives of Sexual Behavior, 12,* 555–576.

Cooper, A. J., Cernovsky, Z. Z., & Colussi, K. (1993). Some clinical and psychometric characteristics of primary and secondary premature ejaculators. *Journal of Sex and Marital Therapy, 19,* 276–288.

Crepault, C., & Couture, M. (1980). Men's erotic fantasies. *Archives of Sexual Behavior, 9,* 565–581.

Crews, F. (1994, November 17). The revenge of the repressed. *New York Review of Books,* pp. 54–60.

Croyle, R. T., & Loftus, E. F. (1993). Recollection in the kingdom of AIDS. In D. G. Ostrow & R. C. Kessler (Eds.), *Methodological issues in AIDS behavioral research* (pp. 163–180). New York: Plenum.

Darling, C. A., & Davidson, J. K. (1986). Enhancing relationships: Understanding the feminine mystique of pretending orgasm. *Journal of Sex and Marital Therapy, 12,* 182–196.

Davis, C. M., Yarber, W. L., & Davis, S. L. (1988). *Sexuality-related measures: A compendium.* Lake Mills, IA: Graphic Publishing.

De Amicis, L. A., Goldberg, D. C., LoPiccolo, J., Friedman, J., & Davies, L. (1984). Three-year follow-up of couples evaluated for sexual dysfunction. *Journal of Sex and Marital Therapy, 10,* 215–228.

De Amicis, L. A., Goldberg, D. C., LoPiccolo, J., Friedman, J., & Davies, L. (1985). Clinical follow-up of couples treated for sexual dysfunction. *Archives of Sexual Behavior, 14,* 467–489.

DiVasto, P. V., Kaufman, L. R., Jackson, R., Christy, J., Pearson, S., & Burgett, T. (1984). The prevalence of sexually stressful events among females in the general population. *Archives of Sexual Behavior, 13,* 59–67.

Easterbrook, P. J., Chmeil, J. S., Hoover, D. R., Saah, A. J., Kaslow, R. A., Kinglsey, L. A., & Detels, R. (1993). Racial and ethnic differences in human immunodeficiency virus type 1 (HIV-1) seroprevalence among homosexual and bisexual men. *American Journal of Epidemiology, 138,* 415–429.

Ehrhardt, A. A., & Baker, S. W. (1974). Fetal androgens, human central nervous system differentiation, and behavior sex differences. In R. C. Friedman & R. M. Richart (Eds.), *Sex differences in behavior* (pp. 33–51). New York: Wiley.

Eklund, P. L. E., Gooren, L. J. G., & Bezemer, P. D. (1988). Prevalence of transsexualism in the Netherlands. *British Journal of Psychiatry, 152,* 638–640.

Ende, J., Rockwell, S., & Glasgow, M. (1984). The sexual history in general medicine practice. *Archives of Internal Medicine, 144,* 558–581.

Faller, K. C. (1989). Characteristics of a clinical sample of sexually abused children: How boys and girl victims differ. *Child Abuse and Neglect, 13,* 281–291.

Fedora, O., Reddon, J. R., Morrison, J. W., Fedora, S. K., Pascoe, H., & Yeudall, L. T. (1992). Sadism and other paraphilias in normal controls and aggressive and nonaggressive sex offenders. *Archives of Sexual Behavior, 21,* 1–15.

Fichten, C. S., Libman, E., & Brender, W. (1983). Methodological issues in the study of sex therapy: Effective components in the treatment of secondary orgasmic dysfunction. *Journal of Sex and Marital Therapy, 9,* 191–202.

Finkelhor, D., Hotaling, G., Lewis, I. A., & Smith, C. (1990). Sexual abuse in a national survey of adult men and women: Prevalence, characteristics, and risk factors. *Child Abuse and Neglect, 14,* 19–28.

Finkelhor, D., & Lewis, I. A. (1988). An epidemiologic approach to the study of child molestation. *Annals of the New York Academy of Sciences, 528,* 64–78.

Frank, E., Anderson, B., & Rubinstein, D. (1978). Frequency of sexual dysfunction in "normal" couples. *New England Journal of Medicine, 299,* 111–115.

Freund, K. (1963). A laboratory method of diagnosing predominance of homo- or hetero-erotic interest in the male. *Behaviour Research and Therapy, 12,* 355–359.

Freund, K. (1971). A note on the use of the phallometric method of measuring mild sexual arousal in the male. *Behavior Therapy, 2,* 223–228.

Freund, K. (1990). Courtship disorder. In W. L. Marshall, D. R. Laws, & H. E. Barbaree (Eds.), *Handbook of sexual assault* (pp. 195–207). New York: Plenum.

Freund, K., & Kuban, M. (1994). The basis of the abused abuser theory of pedophilia: A further elaboration on an earlier study. *Archives of Sexual Behavior, 23,* 553–563.

Freund, K., Watson, R., & Dickey R. (1990). Does sexual abuse in childhood cause pedophilia? An exploratory study. *Archives of Sexual Behavior, 19,* 557–568.

Furby, L., Weinrott, M. R., & Blackshaw, L. (1989). Sex offender recidivism: A review. *Psychological Bulletin, 105,* 3–30.

Furstenberg, F. F., Jr., Brooks-Gunn, J., & Chase-Lansdale, L. (1989). Teenaged pregnancy and childbearing. *American Psychologist, 44,* 313–320.

Green, R. (1987). *The "sissy boy syndrome" and the development of homosexuality.* New Haven, CT: Yale University Press.

Grenier, G., & Byers, E. S. (in press). Ejaculatory control, ejaculatory latency, and attempts to prolong heterosexual intercourse: Trying to make a good thing better. *Archives of Sexual Behavior.*

Groth, A. N., Burgess, A. W., & Holmstrom, L. L. (1977). Rape: power, anger, and sexuality. *American Journal of Psychiatry, 134,* 1239–1243.

Hacker, A. (1987). American apartheid. *New York Review of Books, 37,* 26–33.

Hale, V. E., & Strassberg, D. S. (1990). The role of anxiety on sexual arousal. *Archives of Sexual Behavior, 19,* 569–581.

Hallstrom, T., & Samuelsson, S. (1990). Changes in women's sexual desire in middle life: The longitudinal study of women in Gothenburg. *Archives of Sexual Behavior, 19,* 259–268.

Hariton, E. B., & Singer, J. L. (1974). Women's fantasies during sexual intercourse. *Journal of Consulting and Clinical Psychology, 42,* 313–322, 1974.

Harris, A. R. (1991). Race, class, and crime. In J. F. Sheley (Ed.), *Criminology* (pp. 95–119). Belmont, CA: Wadsworth.

Hatch, J. P. (1981). Psychophysiological aspects of sexual dysfunction. *Archives of Sexual Behavior, 10,* 49–64.

Hawton, K., Catalan, J., Martin, P., & Fagg, J. (1986). Long-term outcome of sex therapy. *Behaviour Research and Therapy, 24,* 665–675.

Heiman, J. R., Gladue, B. A., Roberts, C. W., & LoPiccolo, J. (1986). Historical and current factors discriminating sexually functional from sexually dysfunctional married couples. *Journal of Marital and Family Therapy, 121,* 163–174.

Henn, F. A., Herjanic, M., & Vanderpearl, R. H. (1976). Forensic psychiatry: Profiles of two types of sex offenders. *American Journal of Psychiatry, 133,* 694–696.

Herman, J. L. (1985). Father-daughter incest. In A. W. Burgess (Ed.), *Rape and sexual assault* (pp., 83–96). New York: Garland.

Herman, J. L. (1990). Sex offenders: A feminist perspective. In W. L. Marshall, D. R. Laws, & H. E. Barbaree (Eds.), *Handbook of sexual assault* (pp. 177–193). New York: Plenum.

Hersen, M., & Bellack, A. S. (1988). *Dictionary of behavioral assessment techniques.* New York: Pergamon.

Huey, C. J., Kline-Graber, G., & Graber, B. (1981). Time factors and orgasmic response. *Archives of Sexual Behavior, 10,* 111–118.

Hunt, M. (1974). *Sexual behavior in the 1970s.* New York: Dell.

Jacobson, N. S., Follette, W. C., & Revenstorf, D. (1984). Psychotherapy outcome research: Methods for reporting variability and evaluating clinical significance. *Behavior Therapy, 15,* 336–352.

Jacobson, N. S., Follette, W. C., Revenstorf, D., Baucom, D. H., Hahlweg, K., & Margolin, G. (1984). Variability in outcome and clinical significance of behavioral marital therapy: A reanalysis of outcome data. *Journal of Consulting and Clinical Psychology, 53,* 497–504.

Jensen, S. B. (1986). Sexual dysfunction in insulin-treated diabetics: A six-year follow-up study of 101 patients. *Archives of Sexual Behavior, 15,* 271–283.

Johnson, A. M., Wadsworth, J., Wellings, K., Field, J., & Bradshaw, S. (1994). *Sexual attitudes and lifestyles.* Oxford: Blackwell.

Kaplan, H. S. (1974). *The new sex therapy.* New York: Brunner/Mazel.

Kaplan, H. S. (1977). Hypoactive sexual desire. *Journal of Sex and Marital Therapy, 3,* 3–9.

King, M. B. (1992). Male rape in institutional settings. In G. C. Mezey & M. B. King (Eds.), *Male victims of sexual assault* (pp. 67–74). Oxford: Oxford University Press.

Kinsey, A. C., Pomeroy, W. B., & Martin, C. E. (1948). *Sexual behavior in the human male.* Philadelphia: Saunders.

Kinsey, A. C., Pomeroy, W. B., Martin, C. E., & Gebhard, P. H. (1953). *Sexual behavior in the human female.* Philadelphia: Saunders.

Knight, R. A., & Prentky, R. A. (1990). Classifying sexual offenders. In W. L. Marshall, D. R. Laws & H. E. Barbaree (Eds.), *Handbook of sexual assault* (pp. 23–52). New York: Plenum.

Knight, R. A., & Prentky, R. A. (1993). Exploring characteristics for classifying juvenile sex offenders. In H. E. Barbaree, W. L. Marshall, & S. M. Hudson (Eds.), *The juvenile sex offender* (pp. 45–83). New York: Guilford.

Knight, R. A., Prentky, R. A., & Cerce, D. D. (1994). The development, reliability, and validity of an inventory for the multidimensional assessment of sex and aggression. *Criminal Justice and Behavior, 21,* 72–94.

Knight, R. A., Rosenberg, R., & Schneider, B. A. (1985). Classification of sexual offenders; perspectives, methods, and validation. In A. W. Burgess (Ed.), *Rape and sexual assault* (pp. 222–293). New York: Garland.

Koss, M. P., & Dinero, T. E. (1988). Predictors of sexual aggression among a national sample of male college students. *Annals of the New York Academy of Sciences, 528,* 133–147.

Koss, M. P., & Oros, C. J. (1982). Sexual experiences survey: A research instrument investigating sexual aggression and victimization. *Journal of Consulting and Clinical Psychology, 50,* 455–457.

Kroth, J. A. (1979). Family therapy impact on intrafamilial child sexual abuse. *Child Abuse and Neglect, 3,* 297–302.

Lalumiere, M. L., & Quinsey, V. L. (1994). The discriminability of rapists from non-sex offenders using phallometric measures: A meta-analysis. *Criminal Justice and Behavior, 21,* 150–175.

Langevin, R., & Lang, R. A. (1987). The courtship disorders. In G. D. Wilson (Ed.), *Variant sexuality: Research and theory* (pp. 202–228). London: Croom Helm.

Laumann, E. O., Gagnon, J. H., Michael, R. T., & Michaels, S. (1994). *The social organization of sexuality.* Chicago: University of Chicago Press.

Laws, D. R. (Ed.). (1989). *Relapse prevention with sex offenders.* New York: Guilford.

Laws, D. R., & Marshall, W. L. (1991). Masturbatory reconditioning with sexual deviates: An evaluative review. *Advances in Behavior Research and Therapy, 13,* 13–25.

Lewontin, R. C. (1995, April 20). Sex, lies, and social science. *New York Review of Books,* pp. 24–29.

Libman, E., Fichten, C. S., & Brender, W. (1985). The role of therapeutic format in the treatment of sexual dysfunction: A review. *Clinical Psychology Review, 5,* 103–117.

LoPiccolo, J. (1982). Book review. *Archives of Sexual Behavior, 11,* 277–279.

LoPiccolo, J., Heiman, J. R., Hogan, D. R., & Roberts, C. W. (1985). Effectiveness of single therapists versus cotherapy teams in sex therapy. *Journal of Consulting and Clinical Psychology, 53,* 287–294.

LoPiccolo, J., & Steger, J. C. (1974). The sexual interaction inventory: A new instrument for assessment of sexual dysfunction. *Archives of Sexual Behavior, 3,* 585–595.

LoPiccolo, J., & Stock, W. E. (1986). Treatment of sexual dysfunction. *Journal of Consulting and Clinical Psychology, 54,* 158–167.

Lothstein, L. M., & Roback, H. (1984). Black female transsexuals and schizophrenia: A serendipitous finding. *Archives of Sexual Behavior, 13,* 371–390.

MacFarlane, D. F. (1984). Transsexual prostitution in New Zealand: Predominance of persons of Maori extraction. *Archives of Sexual Behavior, 13,* 301–309.

Malamuth, N. M. (1989). The attraction to sexual aggression scale: Part two. *Journal of Sex Research, 26,* 324–354.

Malamuth, N. M., & Check, J. V. P. (1983). Sexual arousal to rape depictions: Individual differences. *Journal of Abnormal Psychology, 92,* 55–67.

Maletzky, B. M. (1991). *Treating the sexual offender.* Newbury Park, CA: Sage.

Marques, J. K., Day, D. M., Nelson, C., & West, M. A. (1994). *Criminal Justice and Behavior, 21,* 28–54.

Marshall, W. L. (1996). Assessment, treatment, and theorizing about sex offenders. *Criminal Justice and Behavior, 23,* 162–199.

Marshall, W. L., & Barbaree, H. E. (1988). The long-term evaluation of a behavioral treatment program for child molesters. *Behaviour Research and Therapy, 26,* 499–511.

Marshall, W. L., & Barbaree, H. E. (1990a). Outcome of comprehensive cognitive-behavioral treatment programs. In W. L. Marshall, D. R. Laws & H. E. Barbaree (Eds.), *Handbook of sexual assault* (pp. 363–385). New York: Plenum.

Marshall, W. L., & Barbaree, H. E. (1990b). An integrated theory of the etiology of sexual offending. In W. L. Marshall, D. R. Laws, & H. E. Barbaree (Eds.), *Handbook of sexual assault* (pp. 257–275). New York: Plenum.

Marshall, W. L., & Eccles, A. (1991). Issues in clinical practice with sex offenders. *Journal of Interpersonal Violence, 6,* 68–93.

Marshall, W. L., Eccles, A., & Barbaree, H. E. (1991). The treatment of exhibitionists: A focus on sexual deviance versus cognitive and relationship features. *Behaviour Research and Therapy, 29,* 129–1135.

Marshall, W. L., & Pithers, W. D. (1994). A reconsideration of treatment outcome with sex offenders. *Criminal Justice and Behavior, 21,* 6–9.

Martin, C. E. (1981). Factors affecting sexual functioning in 60–79-year-old married males. *Archives of Sexual Behavior, 10,* 399–420.

Masters, W. H., & Johnson, V. E. (1970). *Human sexual inadequacy.* Boston: Little, Brown.

Mavissakalian, M., Blanchard, E. B., Abel, G. G., & Barlow, D. H. (1975). Responses to complex erotic stimuli in homosexual and heterosexual males. *British Journal of Psychiatry, 126,* 252–257.

McCarthy, B. M. (1989). Cognitive-behavioral strategies and techniques in the treatment of early ejaculation. In S. R. Leiblum & R. C. Rosen (Eds.), *Principles and practice of sex therapy* (pp. 141–167). New York: Guilford.

McCombie, S. L., & Arons, J. H. (1980). Counselling rape victims. In S. L. McCombie (Ed.), *The rape crisis intervention handbook* (pp. 145–171). New York: Plenum.

McConaghy, N. (1967). Penile volume change to moving pictures of male and female nudes in heterosexual and homosexual males. *Behaviour Research and Therapy, 5,* 43–48.

McConaghy, N. (1982). Sexual deviation. In A. S. Bellack, M. Hersen, & A. E. Kazdin (Eds.), *International handbook of behavior therapy and modification* (pp. 683–716). New York: Plenum.

McConaghy, N. (1987). Heterosexuality/homosexuality: Dichotomy or continuum? *Archives of Sexual Behavior, 16,* 411–424.

McConaghy, N. (1988). Sexual dysfunction and deviation. In A. S. Bellack & M. Hersen (Eds.), *Behavioral assessment: A practical handbook* (3rd ed., pp. 490–541). New York: Pergamon.

McConaghy, N. (1990). Can reliance be placed on a single meta-analysis? *Australian and New Zealand Journal of Psychiatry, 24,* 405–415.

McConaghy, N. (1993). *Sexual behavior: Problems and management.* New York: Plenum.

McConaghy, N. (1996). Treatment of sexual dysfunctions. In V. B. Van Hasselt & M. Hersen (Eds.), *Sourcebook of psychological treatment manuals for adult disorders* (pp. 333–373). New York: Plenum.

McConaghy, N. (in press). Assessment of sexual dysfunction and deviation. In A. S. Bellack & M. Hersen (Eds.), *Behavioral assessment: A practical handbook* (4th ed.). Needhom Heights, MA: Allyn & Bacon.

McConaghy, N., & Armstrong, M. S. (1983). Sexual orientation and consistency of sexual identity. *Archives of Sexual Behavior, 12,* 317–327.

McConaghy, N., Armstrong, M. S., & Blaszczynski, A. (1981). Controlled comparison of aversive therapy and covert sensitization in compulsive homosexuality. *Behaviour Research and Therapy, 19,* 425–434.

McConaghy, N., Armstrong, M. S., & Blaszczynski, A. (1985). Expectancy, covert sensitization, and imaginal desensitization in compulsive sexuality. *Acta Psychiatrica Scandinavica, 72,* 1176–187.

McConaghy, N., Armstrong, M. S., Blaszczynski, A., & Allcock, C. (1983). Controlled comparison of aversive therapy and imaginal desensitization in compulsive gambling. *British Journal of Psychiatry, 142,* 366–372, 1983.

McConaghy, N., Blaszczynski, A., Armstrong, M. S., & Kidson, W. (1989). Resistance to treatment of adolescent sexual offenders. *Archives of Sexual Behavior, 18,* 97–107.

McConaghy, N., Blaszczynski, A., & Kidson, W. (1988). Treatment of sex offenders with imaginal desensitization and/or medroxyprogesterone. *Acta Psychiatrica Scandinavica, 77,* 199–206.

McConaghy, N., Buhrich, N., & Silove, D. (1994). Opposite sex-linked behaviors and homosexual feelings in the predominantly heterosexual male majority. *Archives of Sexual Behavior, 23,* 565–577.

McConaghy, N., & Zamir, R. (1995a). Sissiness, tomboyism, sex-role, sex identity, and orientation. *Australian and New Zealand Journal of Psychiatry, 29,* 278–283.

McConaghy, N., & Zamir, R. (1995b). Heterosexual and homosexual coercion, sexual orientation, and sexual roles in medical students. *Archives of Sexual Behavior, 24,* 489–502.

McConaghy, N., Zamir, R., & Manicavasagar, V. (1993). Nonsexist sexual experiences survey and scale of attraction to sexual aggression. *Australian and New Zealand Journal of Psychiatry, 27,* 686–693.

McMahon, C. G. (1994). Management of impotence: Part 2. diagnosis. *General Practitioner, CME Files, 2,* 83–85.

Mead, M. (1950). *Male and female.* London: Gollancz.

Meisler, A. W., & Carey, M. P. (1990). A critical reevaluation of nocturnal penile tumescence monitoring in the diagnosis of erectile disorder. *Journal of Nervous and Mental Disease, 178,* 78–89.

Meuleman, E. J. H., Bemelmans, B. L. H., Doesburg, W. H., van Asten, W. N. J. C., Skotnicki, S. H., & Debruyne F. M. J. (1992). Penile pharmacological duplex ultrasonography: A dose-effect study comparing papaverine, papaverine/phentolamine, and prostaglandin E1. *Journal of Urology, 148,* 63–66.

Metz, P., & Bengtsson, J. (1984). Penile blood pressure. *Scandinavian Journal of Urology and Nephrology, 15,* 161–164.

Milan, R. J., Kilmann, P. R., & Boland, J. P. (1988). Treatment outcome of secondary orgasmic dysfunction: A two- to six-year follow-up. *Archives of Sexual Behavior, 17,* 463–480.

Morales, A., Condra, M., Owen, J. A., Surridge, D. H., Fenemore, J., & Harris, C. (1987). Is yohimbine effective in the treatment of organic impotence? Results of a controlled trial. *Journal of Urology, 137,* 1168–1172.

Morganstern, K. P. (1988). Behavioral interviewing. In M. Hersen & A. S. Bellack (Eds.), *Behavioral assessment: A practical handbook* (3rd ed., pp. 86–118). New York: Pergamon.

Morokoff, P. (1978). Determinants of female orgasm. In J. LoPiccolo & L. LoPiccolo (Eds.), *Handbook of sex therapy* (pp. 147–165). New York: Plenum.

Moser, C., & Levitt, E. E. (1987). An exploratory-descriptive study of a sadomasochistically oriented sample. *Journal of Sex Research, 23,* 322–337.

Munjack, D., Cristol, A., Goldstein, A., Phillips, D., Goldberg, A., Whipple, K., Staples, F., & Kanno, P. (1976). Behavioral treatment of orgasmic dysfunction: A controlled study. *British Journal of Psychiatry, 129,* 497–502.

Nathan, S. (1986). The epidemiology of the DSM-III psychosexual dysfunctions. *Journal of Sex and Marital Therapy, 12,* 267–281.

Nelson, E. W. (1991). Sexual self-defense versus the liaison dangereuse: a strategy for AIDS prevention in the '90s. *American Journal of Preventative Medicine, 7,* 146–149.

Nettelbladt, P., & Uddenberg, N. (1979). Sexual dysfunction and sexual satisfaction in 58 married Swedish men. *Journal of Psychosomatic Research, 23,* 141–147.

Nutter, D. E., & Condron, M. K. (1985). Sexual fantasy and activity patterns of males with inhibited sexual desire and males with erectile dysfunction versus normal controls. *Journal of Sex and Marital Therapy, 11,* 91–98.

O'Connor, A. A. (1987). Female sex offenders. *British Journal of Psychiatry, 150,* 615–620.

Osborn, M., Hawton, K., & Gath, D. (1988). Sexual dysfunctions among middle-age women in the community. *British Medical Journal, 296,* 959–962.

Ostrow, D. G., Kessler, R. C., Stover, E., & Peqegnat, W. (1993). In D. G. Ostrow & R. C. Kessler (Eds.), *Methodological issues in AIDS behavioral research* (pp. 1–16). New York: Plenum.

Palace, E. M., & Gorzalka, B. B. (1990). The enhancing effects of anxiety on arousal in sexually dysfunctional and functional women. *Journal of Abnormal Psychology, 99,* 403–411.

Palace, E. M., & Gorzalka, B. B. (1992). Differential patterns of arousal in sexually functional and dysfunctional women: physiological and subjective components of sexual response. *Archives of Sexual Behavior, 21,* 135–159.

Parker, R. N. (1991). Violent crime. In J. F. Sheley (Ed.), *Criminology* (pp. 143–158). Belmont, CA: Wadsworth.

Person, E. S., Terestman, N., Myers, W. A., Goldberg, E. L., & Salvadori, C. (1989). Gender differences in sexual behaviors and fantasies in a college population. *Journal of Sex and Marital Therapy, 15,* 187–198.

Pfaus, J. G., Myronuk, L. D. S., & Jacobs, W. J. (1986). Soundtrack contents and depicted sexual violence. *Archives of Sexual Behavior, 15,* 231–237.

Phillips, G., & Over, R. (1995). Differences between heterosexual, bisexual, and lesbian women in recalled childhood experiences. *Archives of Sexual Behavior, 24,* 1–20.

Prentky, R. A., Knight, R. A., Sims-Knight, J. E., Straus, H., Rokous, F., & Circe, D. (1989). Developmental antecedents of sexual aggression. *Development and Psychopathology, 1,* 153–169.

Quinsey, V. L., & Earls, C. M. (1990). The modification of sexual preferences. In W. L. Marshall, D. R. Laws, & H. E. Barbaree (Eds.), *Handbook of sexual assault* (pp. 279–295). New York: Plenum.

Raboch, J., & Raboch J., Jr. (1986). Some factors influencing women's ability to achieve orgasm. *Geburtschilfe Faruenheilkd, 46,* 817–820.

Reading, A. E. (1983). A comparison of the accuracy and reactivity of methods of monitoring male sexual behavior. *Journal of Behavioral Assessment, 5,* 11–23.

Renshaw, D. C. (1988). Profile of 2376 patients treated at Loyola sex clinic between 1972 and 1987. *Sexual and Marital Therapy, 3,* 111–117.

Rice, M. E., Quinsey, V. L., & Harris, G. T. (1991). Sexual recidivism among child molesters released from a maximum security psychiatric institution. *Journal of Consulting and Clinical Psychology, 59,* 381–386.

Rosen, G. M. (1987). Self-help treatment books and the commercialization of psychotherapy. *American Psychologist, 42,* 46–51.

Rosen, R. C., & Ashton, A. K. (1993). Prosexual drugs: Empirical status of the "new aphrodisiacs." *Archives of Sexual Behavior, 22,* 521–543.

Rosen, R. C., & Beck, J. G. (1988). *Patterns of sexual arousal.* New York: Guilford.

Russell, D. E. H. (1983). The incidence and prevalence of intrafamilial and extrafamilial sexual abuse of female children. *Child Abuse and Neglect, 7,* 133–146.

Russell, D. E. H. (1986). *The secret trauma: Incest in the lives of girls and women.* New York: Basic Books.

Sakheim, D. K., Barlow, D. H., Beck, J. G., & Abrahamson, D. J. (1985). A comparison of male heterosexual and male homosexual patterns of sexual arousal. *Journal of Sex Research, 21,* 183–198.

Saltzman, S. P., Stoddard, A. M., McCusker, J., Moon, M. W., & Mayer, K. H. (1987). Reliability of self-reported sexual behavior risk factors for HIV infection in homosexual men. *Public Health Reports, 102,* 692–697.

Saypol, D. C., Peterson, G. A., Howards, S. S., & Yazel, J. J. (1983). Impotence: Are the newer diagnostic methods a necessity? *Journal of Urology, 130,* 260–262.

Schiavi, R. C., Schreiner-Engel, P., Mandeli, J., Schanzer, H., & Cohen, E. (1990). Healthy aging and male sexual function. *American Journal of Psychiatry, 147,* 766–771.

Schlank, A. M., & Shaw, T. (1996). Treating sexual offenders who deny their guilt: A pilot study. *Sexual Abuse: A Journal of Research and Treatment, 8,* 17–23.

Schott, R. L. (1995). The childhood and family dynamics of transvestites. *Archives of Sexual Behavior, 24,* 309–327.

Schover, L. R. (1989). Sexual problems in chronic illness. In S. R. Leiblum & R. C. Rosen (Eds.), *Principles and practice of sex therapy* (pp. 319–351). New York: Guilford.

Schover, L. R., & Leiblum, S. R. (1994). Commentary: The stagnation of sex therapy. *Journal of Psychology and Human Sexuality, 6,* 5–30.

Schulsinger, F. (1972). Psychopathy heredity and environment. *International Journal of Mental Health, 1,* 190–206.

Segraves, R. T., & Segraves, K. A. (1992). Aging and drug effects on male sexuality. In R. C. Rosen & S. R. Leiblum (Eds.), *Erectile disorders assessment and treatment* (pp. 96–138). New York: Guilford.

Segraves, R. T., Saran, A., Segraves, K., & Maguire, E. (1993). Clomipramine versus placebo in the treatment of premature ejaculation: A pilot study. *Journal of Sex and Marital Therapy, 19,* 198–200.

Segraves R. T., Schoenberg, H. W., Zarins, C. K., Camic, P., & Knopf, J. (1981). Characteristics of erectile dysfunction as a function of medical care system entry point. *Psychosomatic Medicine, 43,* 227–234.

Seidman, S. N., & Rieder, R. O. (1994). A review of sexual behavior in the United States. *American Journal of Psychiatry, 151,* 330–341.

Silverman, D. C., Kalick, S. M., Bowie, S. I., & Edbril, S. D. (1988). Blitz rape and confidence rape: A typology applied to 1,000 consecutive cases. *American Journal of Psychiatry, 145,* 1438–1441.

Slag, M. F., Morley, J. E., Elson, M. K., Trence, D. L., Nelson, C. J., Nelson, A. E., Kinlaw, W. B., Beyer, H. S., Nuttall, F. Q., & Shafer, R. B. (1983). Impotence in medical clinic outpatients. *Journal of the American Medical Association, 249,* 1736–1740.

Smukler, A. J., & Schiebel, D. (1975). Personality characteristics of exhibitionists. *Diseases of the Nervous System, 36,* 600–603.

Snyder, D. K., & Berg, P. (1983a). Determinants of sexual dissatisfaction in sexually distressed couples. *Archives of Sexual Behavior, 12,* 237–246.

Snyder, D. K., & Berg, P. (1983b). Predicting couples' response to brief directive sex therapy. *Journal of Sex and Marital Therapy, 9,* 114–120.

Solstad, K., & Hertoft, P. (1993). Frequency of sexual problems and sexual dysfunction in middle-aged Danish men. *Archives of Sexual Behavior, 22,* 51–58.

Sorensen, R. C. (1973). *Adolescent sexuality in contemporary America.* New York: World.

Sorenson, S. B., Stein, J. A., Siegel, J. M., Golding, J. M., & Burnam, M. A. (1987). The prevalence of adult sexual assault. *American Journal of Epidemiology, 126,* 1154–1164.

Speckens, A. E. M., Hengeveld, M. W., Lycklama a Nijeholt, G., van Hemert, A. M., & Hawton, K. E. (1995). Psychosexual functioning of partners of men with presumed nonorganic erectile dysfunction: Cause or consequence of the disorder? *Archives of Sexual Behavior, 24,* 157–172.

Spector, I. P., & Carey M. P. (1990). Incidence and prevalence of the sexual dysfunctions: A critical review of the empirical literature. *Archives of Sexual Behavior, 19,* 389–408.

Steiner, A. E. (1981). Pretending orgasm by men and women: An aspect of communication in relationships. *Dissertation Abstracts International, 42,* 2553B.

Stermac, L. (1993). Review. *Archives of Sexual Behavior, 22,* 78–81.

Stermac, L. E., Segal, Z. V., & Gillis, R. (1990). Social and cultural factors in sexual assault. In W. L. Marshall, D. R. Laws & H. E. Barbaree (Eds.), *Handbook of sexual assault* (pp. 143–159). New York: Plenum.

Stevenson, H. C., De Moya, D., & Boruch, F. R. (1993). Ethical issues and approaches in AIDS research. In D. G. Ostrow & R. C. Kessler (Eds.), *Methodological issues in AIDS behavioral research* (pp. 19–51). New York: Plenum.

Stuart, F. M., Hammond, D. C., & Pett, M. A. (1987). Inhibited sexual desire in women. *Archives of Sexual Behavior, 16,* 91–106.

Swaab, D. F., Zhou, J. N., & Hofman, M. A. (1995, May). *Sexual differentiation of the human hypothalamus.* Paper presented at the International Behavioral Development Symposium, Minot State University, ND.

Takefman, J., & Brender, W. (1984). An analysis of the effectiveness of two components in the treatment of erectile dysfunction. *Archives of Sexual Behavior, 13,* 321–340.

Templeman, T. L., & Stinnett, R. D. (1991). Patterns of sexual arousal and history in a "normal" sample of young men. *Archives of Sexual Behavior, 20,* 137–150.

Terman, L. M. (1938). *Psychological factors in marital happiness.* New York: McGraw-Hill.

Terman, L. M. (1951). Correlates of orgasm adequacy in a group of 556 wives. *Journal of Psychology, 32,* 115–172.

Terr, L. (1994). *Unchained memories: True stories of traumatic memories, lost and found.* New York: Basic Books.

Thompson-Cooper, I., Fugere, R., & Cormier, B. M. (1993). The child abuse reporting laws: An ethical dilemma for professionals. *Canadian Journal of Psychiatry, 38,* 557–562.

Tiefer, L., & Melman, A. (1987). Adherence to recommendations and improvement over time in men with erectile dysfunction. *Archives of Sexual Behavior, 16,* 301–309.

Tollison, C. D., Adams, H. E., & Tollison, J. W. (1979). Cognitive and physiological indices of sexual arousal in homosexual, bisexual, and heterosexual males. *Journal of Behavioral Assessment, 1,* 305–314.

Travin, S., Bluestone, H., Coleman, E., Cullen, K., & Melella, J. (1986). Pedophile types and treatment perspectives. *Journal of Forensic Sciences, 31,* 614–620.

Tsoi, W. F. (1988). The prevalence of transsexualism in Singapore. *Acta Psychiatrica Scandinavica, 78,* 501–504.

Tsoi, W. F. (1990). Developmental profile of 200 male and 100 female transsexuals in Singapore. *Archives of Sexual Behavior, 19,* 595–605.

van de Wiel, H. B. M., Jaspers, J. P. M., Schultz, W. C. M., & Gal J. (1990). Treatment of vaginismus: A review of concepts and treatment modalities. *Journal of Psychosomatic Obstetrics and Gynaecology, 11,* 1–18.

Waldinger, M. D., Hengeveld, M. W., & Zwinderman, A. H. (1994). Paroxetine treatment of premature ejaculation: A double-blind, randomized, placebo-controlled study. *American Journal of Psychiatry, 151,* 1377–1379.

Watkins, B., & Bentovim, A. (1992). In G. C. Mezey & M. B. King (Eds.), *Male victims of sexual assault* (pp. 27–66). Oxford: Oxford University Press.

Webster, L. A., Berman, S. M., & Greenspan, J. R. (1993). Surveillance for gonorrhea and primary and secondary syphilis among adolescents, United States: 1981–1991.

Weinrich, J. D. (1991). Review. *Archives of Sexual Behavior, 20,* 326–329.

Weizman, R., & Hart, J. (1987). Sexual behavior in healthy married elderly men. *Archives of Sexual Behavior, 16,* 39–44.

Wincze, J. P., Bansal, S., & Malamud, M. (1986). Effects of medroxyprogesterone acetate on subjective arousal, arousal to erotic stimulation, and nocturnal penile tumescence in male sex offenders. *Archives of Sexual Behavior, 15,* 293–305.

Wincze, J. P., & Carey, M. P. (1991). *Sexual dysfunction.* New York: Guilford.

Wolpe, J. (1958). *Psychotherapy by reciprocal inhibition.* Stanford, CA: Stanford University Press.

Zilbergeld, B., & Evans, M. (1980). The inadequacy of Masters and Johnson. *Psychology Today, 14,* 29–43.

Zuckerman, M. (1971). Physiological measures of sexual arousal in the human. *Psychological Bulletin, 75,* 297–329.

Zuger, B. (1966). Effeminate behavior present in boys from early childhood: I. The clinical syndrome and follow-up studies. *Journal of Pediatrics, 69,* 1098–1107.

Zuger, B. (1984). Early effeminate behavior in boys: Outcome and significance for homosexuality. *Journal of Nervous and Mental Disease, 172,* 90–97.

Zuger, B., & Taylor, P. (1969). Effeminate behavior present in boys from early childhood: II. Comparison with similar symptoms in non-effeminate boys. *Pediatrics, 44,* 375–380.

CHAPTER 14

Eating Disorders

BILL N. KINDER

Anorexia nervosa was first described by Morton in 1694 and bulimia nervosa was identified in 1892 by Osler; however, these disorders have become a major focus of clinicians and scientists only recently (Shapiro, 1988). The identification of these "new" psychopathological states has posed some problems, even as basic as what should these conditions be called and what are their specific diagnostic characteristics. For example, various names have been given to bulimia nervosa, including anorexia bulimia nervosa (Ehrensing & Weitzman, 1970), subclinical anorexia nervosa (Button & Whitehouse, 1981), binge eating syndrome (Wardle, 1980), compulsive eating (Ondercin, 1979), and bulimarexia (Boskind-Lodohl & White, 1978).

DESCRIPTION OF THE DISORDER

The specific diagnostic criteria for these disorders have evolved significantly in the last two decades. In DSM-II (American Psychiatric Association [APA], 1968), anorexia nervosa was to be coded (with no definition given) under the classification of "Feeding Disturbance." In DSM-III (APA, 1980), more specific criteria were presented which were further modified in DSM-III-R (APA, 1987). Bulimia first achieved the status of a separate syndrome in the DSM-III in 1980, and the name was changed to bulimia nervosa in the DSM-III-R, along with changes in the diagnostic criteria compared to the DSM-III.

Some changes in the diagnostic criteria for eating disorders are apparent in DSM-IV (APA, 1994). In DSM-III-R, anorexia nervosa and bulimia nervosa were included in the section "Disorders Usually First Evident in Infancy, Childhood, or Adolescence." In DSM-IV, they are listed in a new section titled "Eating Disorders," recognizing that research has shown eating disorders may have an outset at any age (Pryor, 1995).

Minor changes in the criteria for anorexia nervosa appear in DSM-IV, primarily for sake of clarity. For example, the low body weight criterion has been further defined as less than 85% of expected body weight. The criterion regarding body image disturbance has been expanded to include the "denial of the seriousness of the current body weight." Moreover, the major change in diagnostic criteria for anorexia nervosa in DSM-IV is a subtyping based on the presence or absence of binging or purging. Anorexics are subtyped as "restricting type" if they do not regularly binge or purge and are subtyped as "binge eating/purging type" if they regularly binge or purge during an episode of anorexia nervosa. This change in criteria seems to reflect data from research which has indicated significant clinical differences in these two types of anorexics. Specifically, anorexics who binge or purge tend to be older, to have been ill longer, and to be heavier and have more impulse control problems compared to restricting type anorexics (DaCosta & Halmi, 1992; Pryor, 1995).

Several changes in the diagnostic criteria for bulimia nervosa also are apparent in DSM-IV. As with anorexia nervosa, the criteria for bulimia nervosa now require subtyping based on compensatory behaviors; individuals who compensate by purging (e.g., vomiting, taking laxatives) are subtyped as "purging type," while individuals who engage in nonpurging compensatory behaviors (e.g., fasting, excessive exercise) are subtyped "nonpurging type." Additionally, DSM-IV criteria require that both the binge eating and the inappropriate compensatory behaviors must occur on average at least twice a week for a period of 3 months.

The most significant change in criteria for bulimia nervosa in DSM-IV is the addition of a criterion stating that "the disturbance does not occur exclusively during episodes of anorexia nervosa." What has been suggested by many workers in the field of eating disorders is thus recognized by this additional criterion: the diagnosis of anorexia nervosa overrides bulimia nervosa (Pryor, 1995).

Because of the changes in the specific diagnostic criteria over the years, the scientific literature is sometimes confusing and often contradictory. Many researchers have not adhered to these criteria in the diagnosis of individuals to be included in their studies. Shapiro (1988) reviewed 18 studies investigating personality correlates of bulimia. It was reported in 11 of these studies that the DSM-III definition of bulimia was used; however, closer examination revealed that this definition was modified in some way in all of these studies. DSM-III criteria state that the bulimic episodes must not be due to anorexia nervosa, yet three studies included individuals with a history of anorexia nervosa. Two other studies operationalized the DSM-III criteria by means of a questionnaire that had not been validated. Shapiro (1988) was able to find only one study of the 18 that appeared to follow the criteria as stated in DSM-III. This lack of clear-cut and consistent definitions is a serious limitation in a number of studies.

EPIDEMIOLOGY

Anorexia nervosa is primarily a disorder of young women. The usual age of onset is during the adolescent period and the early 20s, although the disorder is occasionally seen in prepubescence. One early attempt at a set of diagnostic criteria for this disorder included that the age of onset must be prior to 25 (Feighner et al., 1972); however, most view this criterion as too restrictive, and no age restrictions are mentioned in the DSM-IV.

Anorexia nervosa occurs predominately in females, with most reports indicating that only between 4% and 10% of reported cases are male (Eckert, 1985). Data concerning the prevalence vary greatly. Jones, Fox, Babigian, and Hutton (1980) reviewed data from Monroe County, New York, from 1960 to 1976 and reported 0.35 to 0.64 cases per 100,000 population per year. In a study of over 10,000 households, Robins et al. (1984) found a lifetime prevalence rate of 0.0%–0.1% in three major U.S. metropolitan areas. DSM-IV cites prevalence rates of 0.5%–1.0% for presentations meeting full criteria for anorexia nervosa among females in late adolescence and early adulthood. It also appears that anorexia nervosa has become more common in the last two decades, although Eckert (1985) suggests this may be because of increased case finding due to greater public and medical awareness of the disorder. One study (Nasser, 1988) reviewed prevalence data on eating disorders in non-Western cultures and suggested that the reported increases in prevalence were related to recent identification with Western norms in relation to body weight and thinness among females.

Similar findings have been reported for bulimia nervosa. Like anorexia nervosa, bulimia nervosa appears to be predominately a disorder of young females, usually beginning in late adolescence or early adult life. Stangler and Printz (1980) reviewed the records of 500 students seen consecutively for emotional problems at a university student health service and found that 3.8% had received a diagnosis of bulimia (5.3% of the females). Other studies have suggested even higher prevalence rates. DSM-IV cites prevalence rates of 1.0%–3.0% among adolescent and young adult females and notes that the occurrence of this disorder among males is approximately one-tenth that of females.

Mitchell and Pyle (1985) drew several conclusions from the existing epidemiological data. First, binge eating episodes are relatively common in young college populations, but their presence does not represent a serious eating disorder in most cases. Second, between 8% and 14% of young women and between 1% and 10% of young men meet DSM-III criteria for bulimia, but lower prevalence rates are reported if more stringent criteria are used. Third, Mitchell and Pyle indicated that the eating behaviors seen in bulimic patients may represent the extreme end of a spectrum of abnormal eating behaviors. Finally, they concluded that, like anorexia nervosa, bulimia nervosa may be increasing in the general population and further suggested that cultural preoccupations with physical attractiveness and thinness may be related to this phenomenon.

Some of the conclusions of Mitchell and Pyle (1985) are supported by a study by Drewnowski, Hopkins, and Kessler (1988). In a survey using a national probability sample of 1,007 male and female college students from a stratified sample of 53 universities and colleges in the continental United States, binge eating was found to be relatively common, with 6.1% of females and 10.0% of males reporting at least two eating binges per week on the average during the preceding 3 months. However, when the entire DSM-III-R criteria were applied, only 1.0% of women and 0.2% of men in the entire sample were classified as bulimic. The probable diagnosis of bulimia nervosa was most prevalent (2.2%) among undergraduate women living in group housing on campus. The results of this well-designed study suggest that previous estimates of bulimia nervosa may in fact be somewhat inflated, at least among college populations. In a later review of studies on the epidemiology of bulimia nervosa, Fairburn and Beglin (1990) found higher mean prevalence rates in studies in which the diagnosis of bulimia nervosa was based only on self-report questionnaire data (9.0%) compared to more sophisticated studies using interview data (1.5%). These somewhat differing incidence and prevalence rates may well be due to the inconsistent definitions of these disorders across studies.

CLINICAL PICTURE

The essential feature of anorexia nervosa is a refusal to maintain body weight over a minimal normal weight for height and age. Earlier criteria required this weight loss to be at least 25% below expected weight (APA, 1980), which most investigators found as too restrictive (Eckert, 1985). DSM-IV criteria require the weight to be less than 85% of that expected. The term *anorexia* literally means a loss of appetite and as such is somewhat of a misnomer since actual loss of appetite is relatively rare in anorexic individuals.

Anorexics have an intense, irrational fear of gaining weight or becoming fat, even when they may be quite significantly underweight. These individuals often go to great lengths to lose weight and to maintain a low body weight, usually by significantly reducing total food intake. Because there is often family and peer pressure to eat, they may engage in a variety of devious behaviors such as hiding food in napkins which can later be disposed of in the trash or toilet (Eckert, 1985). The use of laxatives, diuretics, or both also is common (Crisp, Hsu, & Harding, 1980), as is extensive exercising. Self-induced vomiting and binge eating also have been reported in 10%–47% of anorexic patients (Eckert, 1985).

Anorexia nervosa patients deny their eating disturbance or minimize the severity of their symptoms, failing to acknowledge their thinness. They minimize associated secondary symptoms such as amenorrhea, nutritional deficiencies, and chronic fatigue. Because of this extreme denial, anorexics do not view themselves as physiologically "abnormal" and are thus often quite resistant to therapeutic interventions. Evidence suggests that the severity of this denial is related to the severity of the disorder and to subsequent treatment outcome. For example, Goldberg et al. (1980) found a significant inverse relationship between degree of denial and weight gain at the end of a 35-day inpatient treatment program.

Another significant aspect of anorexia nervosa is a disturbance in body image. Anorexics claim to "feel fat" even when they may be quite emaciated. A poor self-image and specifically a poor attitude toward the body is essentially universal among these individuals. These cognitive distortions appear to be accompanied by actual perceptual distortions as anorexics tend to overestimate their body size. The empirical findings in this area have, however, been controversial.

The consensus is that anorexics overestimate the size of their various body parts to a significant degree. Slade (1985) reviewed the available studies and computed average overestimation ratios, finding that anorexics' mean overestimation was 24% compared to an average of 16% for control populations.

The specificity and clinical meaning of these results, however, have been challenged on several grounds. Individuals with bulimia nervosa also overestimate their body size (Wilmuth, Leitenberg, Rosen, Fondacaro, & Gross, 1985) to an equal or greater extent than anorexics (Thompson, Berland, Linton, & Weinsier, 1986). In developing the adjustable light beam procedure to measure body size estimation, Thompson and Thompson (1986) found that asymptomatic females and males also overestimated the size of four body sites. Several review articles have addressed this lack of specificity of size overestimation in eating-disordered patients (e.g., Cash & Brown, 1987), and Hsu (1982) questioned the clinical significance in anorexic patients because the overestimation phenomenon also has been documented in normal adolescents and college students, obese patients, pregnant women, and schizophrenics. Coovert, Thompson, and Kinder (1988) reported that not only do undergraduate female college students overestimate body size, they also overestimate the size of inanimate objects, in this case "body size" estimates for a mannequin and a ball. Thus, body size overestimation may be only a part of a general perceptual process, not specifically related to eating-disordered patients.

Individuals with bulimia nervosa share some characteristics with anorexics, but there also are major differences. Like anorexics, bulimics show a marked concern about their weight and make frequent attempts at controlling it. Most bulimics, however, maintain weight within the average range for their age and height, although frequent fluctuations in weight may be seen due to alternating binges and fasts.

The essential feature of bulimia nervosa is recurrent episodes of binge eating (consuming large amounts of food in a relatively brief period of time). Food consumed during a binge often has a high caloric content and is of the type and texture to facilitate rapid eating. Mitchell, Pyle, and Eckert (1981) had subjects record what was eaten during a binge and found that the average caloric intake per binge was 3,415 calories with a range of 1,200 to 11,500. These same investigators reported a mean duration of 1.18 hours per binge with a range of 15 minutes to 8 hours. During binges, food is consumed as inconspicuously as possible or in secret. Many bulimics induce vomiting after a binge. Others try to compensate for the large amount of calories consumed during binges by repeated strict dieting, vigorous exercise, or the use of laxatives or diuretics. Bulimics also feel a tremendous lack of control over their eating during binges, followed by feelings of low self-worth and depression after a binge.

COURSE AND PROGNOSIS

Anorexia nervosa usually consists of a single episode, although the disorder may be episodic or unremitting until death; mortality rates are reported to be between 5% and 18%. A recent review (Herzog, Keller, & Lavori, 1988) reporting on relapse found rates ranging from 4% to 9%. Mortality rates ranged from 0% to 22%, with over half of the studies reporting rates of 4% or less. Of the reported deaths, the cause was anorexia nervosa or its medical complications in 50% of the patients, with 24% from suicide.

The most serious complications in anorexia nervosa are a variety of medical conditions, some of which are potentially fatal if untreated or uncorrected. Most of the symptoms resemble those found in starved or semistarved normals, and most return to normal after a return to more normal eating patterns and subsequent weight gain. The frequency of these symptoms often varies greatly across studies, partly because of the different diagnostic criteria used (Mitchell, 1985). Amenorrhea is invariably present, and the absence of three consecutive menstrual cycles when otherwise expected is a part of the DSM-IV criteria for females. A variety of hematological and renal complications have been reported (Mitchell, 1985) as have metabolic problems, including increased serum cholesterol and elevated serum carotene levels. Several coronary abnormalities have been reported in approximately half of anorexic patients (Palossy & Oo, 1977), and case reports have appeared (e.g., Powers, 1982) documenting cardiac failure during treatment. It has been suggested that certain of these coronary irregularities are associated with serum potassium abnormalities but not with other variables including admission weight, medications, or the severity of anorexic symptoms (Kay, Hoffman, Boswick, Rockwell, & Ellinwood, 1988). Gastrointestinal problems including constipation, delayed gastric emptying, and decreased gastric fluid output have been reported (Mitchell, 1985) as well as dental pathology, most likely related to high carbohydrate intake and repeated vomiting (Stege, Visco-Dangler, & Rye, 1982).

However, many of the studies that have investigated nutritional factors in anorexia nervosa have reported inconsistent or even contradictory findings. While the importance of nutritional rehabilitation seems evident, there have been few controlled studies that have examined the efficacy of the various dietary regimes that are commonly prescribed (Rock & Curran-Celentano, 1994).

Less is known about the possible medical complications associated with bulimia nervosa. Fluid and electrolyte abnormalities appear to be relatively common, as do dental problems. Renal, endocrine, gastrointestinal, and neurological findings are reported less frequently (Mitchell, 1985).

A variety of psychological symptoms have been reported to occur with anorexia nervosa and bulimia nervosa. Herzog et al. (1988) reported that 27 of 33 articles mentioned psychiatric disorders in anorexic patients at follow-up, the most common of which were depression, obsessive-compulsive characteristics, and schizophrenia. These findings are difficult to interpret, however, due to the generally nonstandardized methods of evaluation; for example, explicit diagnostic criteria for the diagnosis of a psychiatric disorder were used in only three of the studies reviewed. Depression appears to be the most common symptom, being reported in 15%–36% of subjects.

Similar findings were reported by Mizes (1985) in his review of symptomatology in bulimics. Negative mood states, most notably depression and anxiety, were often reported. Bulimic individuals have been characterized in some studies as more irritable, passive, weak, and constrained compared to normal controls.

The major treatment modalities for anorexia nervosa and bulimia nervosa have been pharmacological, psychotherapeutic (usually with a behavioral or cognitive emphasis), or some combination of these approaches. Pharmacological approaches have been used most extensively with bulimia nervosa; less work has been done pharmacologically with anorexic subjects.

Pharmacological Treatments

Most studies with bulimic populations have used either tricyclic antidepressants or MAO inhibitors. For example, Barlow, Blouin, Blouin, and Perez (1988) administered desipramine in a double-blind cross-over design to 47 normal weight bulimics. At the end of 16 weeks of treatment, this medication was significantly more effective than a placebo in reducing the weekly frequency of binging and vomiting, although the effect was modest and the drug had no effect on depressive symptomatology. In a similar vein, Agras, Dorean, Kirkley, Arnow, and Bachman (1987) administered imipramine to 10 bulimic women and compared them to 10 bulimics receiving a placebo in a double-blind study over a 16-week period. Participants receiving the medication demonstrated a significantly greater reduction in purging (self-induced vomiting and laxative use) compared to participants receiving the placebo. However, only one-third of subjects receiving imipramine had completely stopped. The antidepressant agent buproprion was found superior to a placebo in reducing binge eating and purging in another study by Horne et al. (1988) in a group of nondepressed bulimics.

These three studies are representative of the recent investigations of pharmacological treatments of bulimia nervosa and of the general findings in this area. The results typically favor the drug treatment over placebos; however, the effects are modest at best. Mitchell (1988) reviewed the studies addressing pharmacological approaches to the management of bulimia nervosa and concluded that they do offer a promising short-term treatment of the disorder. He questioned the long-term efficacy of these medications, however, since follow-up data are rarely available for periods of more than a few weeks or months. Also high relapse rates occur upon withdrawal of the drug, frequent changes of medications are required over time, and dropout rates during the active stages of these studies is often very significant (ranging from 18% to 53% in the studies reviewed). Finally, in reviewing many studies of this nature, it is apparent that other treatment modalities often are combined with a pharmacological component. The exact nature of these nonpharmacological treatments is often not well explained, and usually no attempts are made to separate out the potential differential effects of the various treatment modalities.

In summary, controlled trials of pharmacological approaches for both anorexia nervosa and bulimia nervosa have demonstrated the short-term efficacy of a number of different medications; however, the long-term effectiveness of these pharmacological approaches remains uncertain (Jimerson, Herzog, & Brotman, 1993; Mitchell, Raymond, & Specker, 1993).

Nonpharmacological Treatments

Psychological treatments for anorexia nervosa frequently involve some form of operant conditioning. One of two criteria are generally chosen to be reinforced: specific eating behaviors (e.g., size of portions, number of mouthfuls, caloric contents of foods) or weight gain (Bemis, 1987). A fixed interval schedule is common, with intervals varying from 1 to 7 days. Typical positive reinforcers are freedom of movement within and outside of the hospital, access to various recreational activities, and visiting privileges. Negative consequences have included bed rest, restriction to hospital room or seclusion, and tube feeding.

Bemis (1987) concluded that the data indicate that operant methods have been found "equal or superior to psychotherapy, milieu treatment, intensive nursing regimes, pharmacotherapy, and hyperalimentation in experimental and quasi-experimental comparisons" (p. 445). However, long-term follow-up is rarely reported, and the effects of these treatments on other variables such as changes in mood rarely have been investigated. Chiodo (1985) was particularly critical of the reliance upon short-term weight gain as the sole independent variable in many of these studies.

Several different behavioral treatment methods have been used with bulimic patients. Rosen and Leitenberg (1982) used exposure plus response prevention with six bulimic patients. The first component exposed subjects to the feared stimulus (e.g., eating certain foods or certain amounts of foods) in the presence of a therapist. The second component consisted of preventing the escape response, in this case vomiting. Rosen and Leitenberg (1982) reported varying outcomes across subjects: the average reduction in vomiting was 89% while one of the six subjects showed no improvement. Similar findings were reported by Giles, Young, and Young (1985), who added a cognitive restructuring component to exposure plus response prevention with 34 bulimics. Fifty-nine percent of subjects attained an 80% or greater reduction in vomiting at the end of treatment; 63% of the improved subjects were still abstinent from vomiting at follow-up (1 1/4 years).

Rosen (1987) reviewed studies using behavioral treatments of bulimia nervosa and concluded that these are effective techniques for this disorder. Reduction in vomiting ranged from 20% to 96% (mean reduction of 70%) across studies. Rosen noted, however, a high dropout rate in these studies and concluded more research is called for before asserting that these modalities are the treatment of choice for bulimic patients.

Cognitive-behavioral therapies also have been used in the treatment of eating disorders with generally positive results. Typical of these approaches is the work described by Fairburn (1985), which features three stages of treatment that are problem oriented and focused primarily on the present and future. Stage 1 is mostly educational, focusing on the maintenance and treatment of eating disorders from the cognitive viewpoint. Self-monitoring is initiated for assessing situations that may trigger binge eating or purging. In stage 2, other cognitive techniques are introduced for resisting binge eating. Modeled after Beck's (1976) cognitive therapy for depression, patients are taught to identify and modify dysfunctional attitudes and thoughts regarding eating, body, weight, and shape. The focus in stage 3 is on the use of relapse prevention strategies.

Across several studies, the mean percentage reductions in binge eating or purging have ranged from 73% to 94% (Wilson & Pike, 1993). Some studies also have reported reasonably good maintenance of change at follow-up. For example, Fairburn, Jones, Pevler, Hope, and O'Connor (1993) reported a decline of over 90% in binge eating and purging at 1 year follow-up, with 36% of patients having ceased all binging and purging. It also has been suggested that cognitive-behavioral treatments may have a broader effect on associated psychopathology such as improvements in depression, self-esteem, and measures of personality disorders (Wilson & Pike, 1993). The specific mechanisms underlying these improvements associated with cognitive-behavioral strategies, however, remain unclear (Wilson & Fairburn, 1993; Wilson & Pike, 1993).

Despite these promising results for several treatment modalities with anorexics and bulimics, few definitive data exist regarding prognostic indicators with respect to these disorders. Herzog et al. (1988) concluded that in the 24 studies of anorexia nervosa that reported on predictors of therapeutic outcome, the data were often contradictory. For example, one study found 17 predictors of outcome while another could find no predictors. Across all studies, the variables found to be predictive most consistently were duration of the disorder, presence of associated personality disorders, disturbed parent-child relationships, and presence of vomiting. In the studies of prognostic factors in bulimia nervosa, no one factor was found predictive of outcome consistently across studies. This lack of a consistent relationship between specific prognostic indicators and outcome has been reported in an adolescent population as well (Steinhousen & Seidel, 1993). Finally, Laessle, Zoettl, and Pirke (1987) conducted a meta-analysis of 25 outcome studies of bulimia nervosa, considering the relative effectiveness of pharmacological and psychological treatments. Psychological treatments in general were superior to drug therapy (mean effect sizes = 1.14 and 0.60, respectively), especially when combined with some form of dietary management (mean effect size = 1.30).

FAMILIAL AND GENETIC CONSIDERATIONS

Several theories have been proposed regarding the etiology of anorexia nervosa. From a biological and genetic perspective, increased risk of anorexia nervosa in the first-degree biological relatives of individuals with this disorder has been reported (APA, 1994). However, the data are far from conclusive, and a number of the twin and family studies are isolated case reports. One review (Nowlin, 1983) noted that approximately 50% of sets of monozygotic twins were concordant for the disorder while another review (Vandereycken & Pierloot, 1981) concluded there was no substantial support for the notion that genetic factors play a significant role in the etiology of anorexia nervosa.

Nongenetic family variables have been suggested as potential determinants in the development of anorexia nervosa. Bruch (1973, 1978) argued that the disorder develops as a function of impaired mother-child relationships and suggested that the anorexic individual is controlled, and even exploited, by those in the immediate environment as a child. (The discussion of childhood sexual abuse in anorexics will be undertaken later in this chapter.) Systems theories suggest this disorder develops because of distorted family interaction patterns. Some support for these ideas can be found in the research of Minuchin, Rosman, and Baker (1978). These investigators found families of anorexics to appear superficially overly good or nice and grossly unable to manage conflict situations. These families were described as extremely overprotective of family members, characterized by enmeshment (inappropriate extreme intermember involvement), and rigidly resistant to family change.

Less theorizing has taken place regarding the etiology of bulimia nervosa, although several researchers (e.g., Bruch, 1978; Minuchin et al., 1978) have extended some of their notions regarding anorexia nervosa to bulimics. Possible genetic or biological factors have been suggested, mostly based upon the close association between depression and bulimia nervosa; however, these data are open to differing interpretations (Hinz & Williamson, 1987). DSM-IV indicated increased frequency of bulimia nervosa, mood disorders, and substance abuse/dependence in first-degree biological relatives of individuals with this disorder.

In summary, various genetic and familial variables have been implicated in the genesis of eating disorders, and there are data supporting each to varying degrees. However, these data are open to several interpretations, and no one factor has emerged as the most significant of these potential etiological variables to date.

DIAGNOSTIC CONSIDERATIONS

In individuals with anorexia nervosa or bulimia nervosa, two additional diagnostic considerations often are of importance. First is the issue of dual diagnosis or comorbidity, as many eating-disordered patients will be found to have other diagnosable conditions as well. Second, prior sexual or physical abuse may be an issue for a number of eating-disordered individuals.

Depression is a common symptom in anorexia nervosa. Eckert (1985) found the proportion of anorexics reported as clinically depressed in several studies ranged from 35% to 85%. Often these patients were reported to be depressed before the acute stage of their illness. Biological markers thought to be related to affective disorders such as dexamethasone nonsuppression and high plasma cortisol levels have been reported in anorexics (Gerner & Gwirtsman, 1981; Walsh, 1982), although these abnormalities tend to disappear with subsequent weight gain.

There also have been repeated findings of pervasive depressive symptomatology accompanying bulimia nervosa. Abraham and Beaumont (1982) reported that 70% of their subjects reported suicidal ideation following binges, and Hatsukami, Eckert, Mitchell, and Pyle (1984) found that 44% of their bulimic subjects met the DSM-III criteria for an affective disorder at some time in their lives. Bulimics also have been found to score high on various standardized measures of depression and often obtain abnormal dexamethasone suppression test results.

It has been reported that bulimics are more likely than normals to engage in impulsive behaviors such as shoplifting (Mitchell & Pyle, 1985) and to have a high incidence of substance abuse. Walfish, Stenmark, Sarco, Shealy, and Krone (1992) found that 14% of 100 consecutive women entering a residential substance abuse program met DSM-III-R criteria for bulimia nervosa, with cocaine abusers having the highest incidence (19%). Hatsukami, Owen, Pyle, and Mitchell (1982) suggested there are several commonalities between alcohol abuse and the abuse of food seen in bulimics, including secretiveness and social isolation, preoccupation with the abuse, and use of the substance (alcohol or food) to deal with stress or negative feelings.

Comorbidity of eating disorders and personality disorders has been reported in a number of studies; however, the results of this research are inconsistent at best (Skodol et al., 1993). The rate of one or more personality disorders among eating-disordered groups has varied from 27% to 93%. It has been suggested (Skodol et al., 1993) that much of this variability is related to the different diagnostic methods used across studies. These same researchers found bulimia nervosa to be associated with borderline personality disorder and anorexia nervosa with avoidant personality disorder. Finally, eating-disordered individuals with a personality disorder diagnosis were characterized by chronicity and low levels of overall functioning compared to eating-disordered individuals without a personality disorder diagnosis (Skodol et al., 1993).

It has been suggested that anorexics are psychosexually immature and that anorexia nervosa may represent a rejection of adult femininity as a refusal to accept the inevitability of becoming a sexually mature woman. In a recent review, however, Scott (1987) found little or no evidence supporting these claims. Similar findings were reported in another review (Coovert, Kinder, & Thompson, 1989); however, these investigators did report that two trends are apparent in the studies reviewed. So-called bulimic anorexics (those who binge or purge) tended to be more sexually active than anorexics who controlled their weight by food intake restriction. Second, in spite of the continued appearance in the literature of case studies reporting a high incidence of sexual abuse among eating-disordered patients, the empirical data did not support this conclusion.

Several recent studies have suggested that the association between eating disorders and sexual or physical abuse is a more complicated issue. For example, Hall, Tice, Beresford, Wooley, and Hall (1989) reported on 158 consecutive first admissions to an eating disorders inpatient facility. Fifty percent of patients diagnosed with anorexia nervosa or bulimia nervosa reported some type of sexual abuse, with fathers being the most frequent perpetrators (30% of all cases). One-third of the instances occurred prior to adolescence. Further, these authors identified three specific eating patterns that they suggest may be related to previous sexual assaults. One group reported that their bulimic symptoms were specifically triggered by anger toward male authority figures. Another group of anorexics reported trying to lose so much weight in an attempt to "disgust" the individual who had assaulted them sexually. A third group of obese women reported gaining considerable amounts of weight so that they could become essentially "nonsexual."

Women who report more recent abuse have been found to show greater body image disturbance (Waller, Hamilton, Rose, Sumra, & Baldwin, 1993), although Schaaf and McCanne (1994) found no association between physical or sexual abuse and body image disturbance or eating disorder symptomatology. A strong relationship was found between prior sexual abuse and purging behavior (Waller, Halek, & Crisp, 1993), yet no relationship was found between abuse and treatment outcome in a group of bulimic patients (Fallon, Sadik, Saoud, & Garfinkle, 1994).

Sexual abuse does not appear to be a risk factor specific to eating disorders but rather a risk factor for psychiatric disorders in general (Welch & Fairburn, 1994). Thus, it appears prudent to consider the possibility of prior sexual or physical abuse in the evaluation and treatment of individuals with eating disorders (Rorty, Yager, & Rossotto, 1994).

PSYCHOLOGICAL AND BIOLOGICAL ASSESSMENT

Two scales have been developed for use specifically with eating-disordered individuals. The Eating Disorder Inventory (EDI; Garner & Olmsted, 1984) is a 64-item self-report measure of the psychological characteristics and behaviors associated with eating disorders. There are eight subscales: Drive for Thinness, bulimia, Body Dissatisfaction, Ineffectiveness, Perfectionism, Distrust, Lack of Interoceptive Awareness, and Maturity Fears. The Eating Attitudes Test (EAT-26; Garner, Olmsted, Bohr, & Garfinkle, 1982) is a 26-item scale measuring a broad range of behaviors and attitudes associated with anorexia nervosa. Both of these scales are sound from a psychometric perspective and have been used extensively with eating-disordered individuals.

More traditional psychological assessment instruments have been used less extensively with bulimics or anorexics. For example, the Rorschach has been used to study ego boundary disturbances in adolescents (Strober & Goldenberg, 1981) and young adults (Sugarman, Quinlan, & Devenis, 1982) with anorexia nervosa.

Mizes (1985) reviewed the studies using the Minnesota Multiphasic Personality Inventory (MMPI) with bulimics. For females, consistent elevations have been found on scales 2 (Depression), 4 (Psychopathic Deviant), 7 (Psychasthenia), and 8 (Schizophrenia) with notably low scores on scale 5 (Masculinity-Femininity). These findings are representative of significant depression, anxiety, and worry, rumination, impulsivity, and feelings of alienation often seen in bulimics (Mizes, 1985).

Similar patterns of scale elevations have been reported recently with a group of 116 eating-disordered patients (Pryor & Wiederman, 1996). Additionally, these authors found no significant differences in the patterns of anorexics compared to bulimics, and there were no differences between diagnostic subtypes (e.g., restricting anorexics vs. binging/purging anorexics and purging bulimics versus nonpurging bulimics).

Both anorexia nervosa and bulimia nervosa, particularly in their chronic forms, can lead to numerous and often serious physical conditions that require medical attention (APA, 1994). These need to be assessed with a thorough physical exam that includes blood chemistry studies and electrocardiography.

GENDER AND RACIAL-ETHNIC ISSUES

Both anorexia nervosa and bulimia nervosa are disorders primarily affecting females, with at least 90% of all individuals receiving either of these diagnoses being women (Eckert, 1985; Stangler & Printz, 1980). Both disorders are more prevalent in industrialized countries, especially those where, for females at least, being considered attractive is associated with being thin.

Little research has been conducted to date with nonwhite groups. For bulimia nervosa, it has been suggested that the prevalence is much less among nonwhites compared to whites (Fairburn & Beglin, 1990). These suggestions are supported by the data of Robins et al. (1984), where the proportion of African American responding households ranged from 10% to 32% across the three study cities (based on $n = 2,674$) for the diagnosis of anorexia nervosa. Across all three samples, the lifetime prevalence of anorexia nervosa was determined to be 0.0%. On the one hand, it may be that many previous studies simply have not reported data on racial differences in eating disorders. On the other hand, the few extant data suggest that the prevalence and incidence of eating disorders is very small in the African American population. However, preliminary data have suggested that eating disorders are becoming more prevalent among nonwhites (Hsu, 1987). Hsu was able to document in the published literature a total of only 18 cases of anorexia nervosa among African Americans in North America and Europe. He then reports on seven cases of African Americans referred for treatment at only two hospitals within a 42-month period, representing 4% of all referrals during that time.

SUMMARY

Clinical and scientific interest in eating disorders has increased greatly in the past 20 years and an extensive amount of research has appeared relatively quickly. For example, the review by Hinz and Williamson (1987) of a very limited area of eating disorder research (i.e., Is bulimia simply a variant of affective disorders?) cites almost 100 references, the vast majority of which were published between 1980 and 1985. This explosion of research has continued in the last decade.

However, there are serious methodological weaknesses in many studies, including diagnostic criteria that have varied greatly, relatively low n's (with case reports abounding), and inadequate comparison groups. Standardized interview schedules or psychological tests are lacking in many cases. There has been overreliance on single outcome measures such as decrease in purging or weight gain, and follow-up periods are usually only a few weeks to a few months. Long-term or longitudinal data are rare.

Nevertheless, some tentative conclusions can be reached. Eating disorders primarily are conditions of adolescence and early adulthood in females, and the medical complications associated with both anorexia nervosa and bulimia nervosa are often serious and potentially life-threatening without intervention. Both anorexic and bulimic patients evidence significant cognitive distortions about themselves and their body image and a variety of other psychological symptoms, most notably depression, are frequently noted in both disorders. There are several theories regarding the etiology of eating disorders and limited support can be found for each in the literature. The same can be said about treatment efforts, which have usually been behavioral or pharmacological in nature. With continued improvements and refinements in research methodology, future research should lead to a significant increase in our factual knowledge concerning anorexia nervosa and bulimia nervosa.

REFERENCES

Abraham, S. R., & Beaumont, P. J. V. (1982). How patients describe bulimia or binge eating. *Psychological Medicine, 12,* 625–635.

Agras, W. S., Dorian, B., Kirkley, B. G., Arnow, B., & Bachman, J. (1987). Imipramine in the treatment of bulimia: A double-blind controlled study. *International Journal of Eating Disorders, 6,* 29–38.

American Psychiatric Association (1968). *Diagnostic and statistical manual of mental disorders* (2nd ed.). Washington, DC: Author.

American Psychiatric Association. (1980). *Diagnostic and statistical manual of mental disorders* (3rd ed.). Washington, DC: Author.

American Psychiatric Association. (1987). *Diagnostic and statistical manual of mental disorders* (3rd ed., rev. ed.). Washington, DC: Author.

American Psychiatric Association. (1994). *Diagnostic and statistical manual of mental disorders* (4th ed.). Washington, DC: Author.

Barlow, J., Blouin, J., Blouin, A., & Perez, E. (1988). Treatment of bulimia with desipramine: A double-blind crossover study. *Canadian Journal of Psychiatry, 33,* 129–133.

Beck, A. T. (1976). *Cognitive therapy and the emotional disorders.* New York: International Universities Press.

Bemis, K. M. (1987). The present status of operant conditioning for the treatment of anorexia nervosa. *Behavior Modification, 11,* 432–463.

Boskind-Lodahl, M., & White, W. C. (1978). The definition and treatment of bulimarexia in college women: A pilot study. *Journal of the American College of Health Associations, 27,* 84–97.

Bruch, H. (1973). *Eating disorders: Obesity, anorexia nervosa, and the person within.* New York: Basic Books.

Bruch, H. (1978). *The golden cage.* Cambridge, MA: Harvard University Press.

Button, E. J., & Whitehouse, A. (1981). Subclinical anorexia nervosa. *Psychological Medicine, 11,* 509–516.

Cash, T. F., & Brown, T. A. (1987). Body image in anorexia nervosa and bulimia nervosa: A review of the literature. *Behavior Modification, 11,* 487–521.

Chiodo, J. (1985). The assessment of anorexia nervosa and bulimia. *Progress in Behavior Modification, 19,* 255–292.

Coovert, D. L., Kinder, B. N. & Thompson, J. K. (1989). The psychosexual aspects of anorexia nervosa and bulimia nervosa: A review of the literature. *Clinical Psychology Review, 9,* 169–180.

Coovert, D. L., Thompson, J. K., & Kinder, B. N. (1988). Interrelationships among multiple aspects of body image and eating disturbance. *International Journal of Eating Disorders, 7,* 495–502.

Crisp, A. H., Hsu, L. K. G., & Harding, B. (1980). Clinical features of anorexia nervosa: A study of a consecutive series of 102 female patients. *Journal of Psychosomatic Research, 24,* 179–191.

DaCosta, M., & Halmi, K. A. (1992). Classification of anorexia nervosa: Question of subtypes. *International Journal of Eating Disorders, 11,* 305–313.

Drewnowski, A., Hopkins, S. A., & Kessler, R. C. (1988). The prevalence of bulimia nervosa in the U.S. college student populations. *American Journal of Public Health, 78,* 1322–1325.

Eckert, E. D. (1985). Characteristics of anorexia nervosa. In J. E. Mitchell (Ed.), *Anorexia nervosa and bulimia: Diagnosis and treatment* (pp. 3–28). Minneapolis: University of Minnesota Press.

Ehrensing, R. H., & Weitzman, E. L. (1970). The mother-daughter relationship in anorexia nervosa. *Psychosomatic Medicine, 32,* 201–208.

Fairburn, C. G. (1985). Cognitive-behavioral treatment for bulimia. In D. M. Garner &

P. E. Garfinkle (Eds.), *Handbook of psychotherapy for anorexia nervosa and bulimia* (pp. 160–192). New York: Guilford.

Fairburn, C. G., & Beglin, S. J. (1990). Studies of the epidemiology of bulimia nervosa. *American Journal of Psychiatry, 147,* 401–408.

Fairburn, C. G., Jones, R., Peveler, R. C., Hope, R. A., & O'Conner, M. E. (1993). Psychotherapy and bulimia nervosa: The long-term effects of interpersonal psychotherapy, behavior therapy, and cognitive behavior therapy for bulimia nervosa. *Archives of General Psychiatry, 50,* 419–428.

Fallon, B. A., Sadik, C., Saoud, J. B., & Garfinkle, R. S. (1994). Childhood abuse, family environment, and outcome in bulimia nervosa. *Journal of Clinical Psychiatry, 55,* 424–428.

Feighner, J. P., Robins, E., Guze, S. P., Woodruff, R. A., Winokur, G., & Munoz, R. (1972). Diagnostic criteria for use in psychiatric research. *Archives of General Psychiatry, 26,* 57–63.

Garner, D. M. & Olmsted, M. P. (1984). *Manual for the Eating Disorder Inventory.* Odessa, FL: Psychological Assessment Resources.

Garner, D. M., Olmsted, M. P., Bohr, Y., & Garfinkle, P. E. (1982). The Eating Attitudes Test: Psychometric features and correlates. *Psychological Medicine, 12,* 871–878.

Gerner, R. H., & Gwirtsman, H. E. (1981). Abnormalities of dexamethasone suppression text and urinary MHPG in anorexia nervosa. *American Journal of Psychiatry, 138,* 650–653.

Giles, T. R., Young, R. R., & Young, D. E. (1985). Clinical studies and clinical replication series: Behavioral treatment of severe bulimia. *Behavior Therapy, 16,* 393–405.

Goldberg, S. C., Halmi, K. A., Eckert, E. D., Casper, R. C., Davis, J. M., & Roper, M. (1980) Attitudinal dimensions in anorexia nervosa. *Journal of Psychiatric Research, 15,* 239–251.

Hall, R. C., Tice, L., Beresford, T. P., Wooley, B., & Hall, A. K. (1988). Sexual abuse in patients with anorexia nervosa and bulimia. *Psychosomatics, 30,* 73–79.

Hatsukami, D., Owen, P., Pyle, R., & Mitchell, J. (1982). Similarities and differences on the MMPI between women with bulimia and women with alcohol or drug abuse problems. *Addictive Behavior, 7,* 435–439.

Hatsukami, D., Eckert, E., Mitchell, J. E., & Pyle, R. (1984). Affective disorder and substance abuse in women with bulimia. *Psychological Medicine, 23,* 701–704.

Herzog, D. B., Keller, M. B., & Lavori, P. W. (1988). Outcome in anorexia nervosa and bulimia nervosa: A review of the literature. *Journal of Nervous and Mental Disease, 176,* 131–143.

Hinz, L. D., & Williamson, D. A. (1987). Bulimia and depression: A review of the affective variant hypothens. *Psychological Bulletin, 102,* 150–158.

Horne, R. L., Ferguson, J. M., Pope, H. G., Hudson, J. I., Lineberry, C. G., Ascher, J., & Cato, A. (1988). Treatment of bulimia with buproprion: A multicenter controlled trial. *Journal of Clinical Psychiatry, 49,* 262–266.

Hsu, L. K. G. (1982). Is there a disturbance in body image in anorexia nervosa? *Journal of Nervous and Mental Disease, 17,* 305–307.

Hsu, L. K. G. (1987). Are the eating disorders becoming more common in blacks? *International Journal of Eating Disorders, 6,* 113–124.

Jimerson, D. C., Herzog, D. B., & Brotman, A. W. (1993). Pharmacolic approaches in the treatment of eating disorders. *Harvard Review of Psychiatry, 1,* 82–93.

Jones, D. J., Fox, M. M., Babigian, H. M., & Hutton, H. E. (1980). Epidemiology of anorexia nervosa in Monroe County, New York: 1960–1976. *Psychosomatic Medicine, 42,* 551–558.

Kay, G. N., Hoffman, G. W., Boswick, J., Rockwell, K., & Ellenwood, E. H. (1988). The electrocardiogram in anorexia nervosa. *International Journal of Eating Disorders, 7,* 791–795.

Laessle, R. G., Zoettl, C., & Pirke, K. (1987). Meta-analysis of treatment studies for bulimia. *International Journal of Eating Disorders, 6,* 647–653.

Minuchin, S., Rosman, B. L., & Baker, L. (1978). *Psychosomatic families: Anorexia nervosa in context.* Cambridge, MA: Harvard University Press.

Mitchell, J. E. (1985). Medical complications of anorexia nervosa and bulimia. In J. E. Mitchell (Ed.), *Anorexia nervosa and bulimia: Diagnosis and treatment* (pp. 48–77). Minneapolis: University of Minnesota Press.

Mitchell, J. E., & Pyle, R. L. (1985). Characteristics of bulimia. In J. E. Mitchell (Ed.), *Anorexia nervosa and bulimia: Diagnosis and treatment* (pp. 29–47). Minneapolis: University of Minnesota Press.

Mitchell, J. E., Pyle, R. L., & Eckert, E. D. (1981). Frequency and duration of binge-eating episodes in patients with bulimia. *American Journal of Psychiatry, 138,* 835–836.

Mitchell, J. E., Raymond, N., & Specker, S. (1993). A review of the controlled trials of pharmacotherapy and psychotherapy in the treatment of bulimia nervosa. *International Journal of Eating Disorders, 14,* 229–247.

Mizes, J. S. (1985). Bulimia: A review of its symptomatology and treatment. *Advances in Behavioral Research and Therapy, 7,* 91–142.

Nasser, M. (1988). Eating disorders: The cultural dimension. *Social Psychiatry and Psychiatric Epidemiology, 23,* 184–187.

Nowlin, N. S. (1983). Anorexia nervosa in twins: Case report and review. *Journal of Clinical Psychiatry, 44,* 101–105.

Ondercin, P. (1979). Compulsive eating in college women. *Journal of College Student Personnel, 20,* 153–157.

Palossy, B., & Oo, M. (1977). ECG alteration in anorexia nervosa. *Annals of Cardiology, 19,* 280–282.

Powers, P. S. (1982). Heart failure during treatment of anorexia nervosa. *American Journal of Psychiatry, 139,* 1167–1170.

Pryor, T. (1995). Diagnostic criteria for eating disorders: DSM-IV revisions. *Psychiatric Annals, 25,* 40–44.

Pryor, T., & Wiederman, M. W. (1996). Use of the MMPI-2 in the outpatient assessment of women with anorexia nervosa or bulimia nervosa. *Journal of Personality Assessment, 66,* 363–373.

Robins, L. M., Helzer, J. E., Weissman, M. M., Orvaschel, H., Burlie, J. E., & Reiger, D. A. (1984). Lifetime prevalence of specific psychiatric disorders in three sites. *Archives of General Psychiatry, 41,* 949–958.

Rock, C. L., & Curran-Celentano, J. (1994). Nutritional disorder of anorexia nervosa: A review. *International Journal of Eating Disorders, 15,* 187–203.

Rorty, M., Yager, J., & Rossotto, E. (1994). Childhood sexual, physical, and psychological abuse in bulimia nervosa. *American Journal of Psychiatry, 151,* 1122–1126.

Rosen, J. C. (1987). A review of behavioral treatments for bulimia nervosa. *Behavior Modification, 11,* 464–486.

Rosen, J. C., & Leitenberg, H. (1982). Bulimia nervosa: Treatment with exposure and response prevention. *Behavior Therapy, 13,* 117–124.

Schaaf, K. K., & McCanne, T. R. (1994). Childhood abuse, body image disturbance, and eating disorders. *Child Abuse and Neglect, 18,* 607–615.

Scott, D. W. (1987). The involvement of psychosexual factors in the causation of eating disorders: Time for a reappraisal. *International Journal of Eating Disorders, 6,* 199–213.

Shapiro, S. (1988) Bulimia: An entity in search of definition. *Journal of Clinical Psychology, 44,* 491–498.

Skodol, A. E., Oldham, J. M., Hyler, S. E., Kellman, H. D., Doidge, N., & Davies, M. (1993). Comorbidity of DSM-III-R eating disorders and personality disorders. *International Journal of Eating Disorders, 14,* 403–416.

Slade, P. D. (1985). A review of body-image studies in anorexia nervosa and bulimia nervosa. *Journal of Psychiatric Research, 19,* 255–265.

Stangler, R. S., & Printz, A. M. (1980). DSM-III: Psychiatric diagnosis in a university population. *American Journal of Psychiatry, 137,* 937–940.

Stege, P., Visco-Dangler, L., & Rye, L. (1982). Anorexia nervosa: Review including oral and dental manifestations. *Journal of the American Dental Association, 104,* 648–652.

Steinhousen, H. C., & Seidel, R. (1993). Outcome in adolescent eating disorders. *International Journal of Eating Disorders, 14,* 487–496.

Strober, M., & Goldenberg, I. (1981). Ego boundary disturbance in juvenile anorexia nervosa. *Journal of Clinical Psychology, 37,* 433–438.

Sugarman, A., Quinlan, D. M., & Devenis, L. (1982). Ego boundary disturbance in anorexia nervosa. *Journal of Personality Assessment, 46,* 455–461.

Thompson, J. D., Berland, N. W., Linton, P. H., & Weinsier, R. (1986). Assessment of body distortion via a self-adjusting light beam in seven eating disorder groups. *International Journal of Eating Disorders, 5,* 113–120.

Thompson, J. K., & Thompson, C. M. (1986). Body size distortion and self-esteem in asymptomatic, normal weight males and females. *International Journal of Eating Disorders, 5,* 1061–1068.

Vandereycken, W., & Pierloot, R. (1981). Anorexia nervosa in twins. *Psychotherapy and Psychosomatics, 35,* 55–63.

Walfish, S., Stennmark, D. E., Sarco, D., Shealy, J. S., & Drove, A. M. (1992). Incidence of bulimia in substance misusing women in residential treatment. *International Journal of the Addictions, 27,* 425–433.

Waller, G., Halek, C., & Crisp, A. H. (1993). Sexual abuse as a factor in anorexia nervosa: Evidence from two separate case series. *Journal of Psychosomatic Research, 37,* 837–879.

Waller, G., Hamilton, K., Rose, N., Sumra, J., & Baldwin, G. (1993). Sexual abuse and body-image distortion in the eating disorders. *British Journal of Clinical Psychology, 32,* 350–352.

Walsh, B. T. (1982). Endocrine disturbances in anorexia nervosa and depression. *Psychosomatic Medicine, 44,* 85–91.

Wardle, J. (1980). Dietary restraint and binge eating. *Behavioral Analysis and Modification, 4,* 201–209.

Welch, S. L., & Fairburn, C. G. (1994). Sexual abuse and bulimia nervosa: Three integrated case control comparisons. *American Journal of Psychiatry, 151,* 402–407.

Wilmuth, M. E., Leitenberg, H., Rosen, J. C., Fondacaro, K. M., & Gross, J. (1985). Body size distortion in bulimia nervosa. *International Journal of Eating Disorders, 4,* 71–78.

Wilson, G. T., & Fairburn, C. G. (1993). Cognitive treatment for eating disorders. *Journal of Consulting and Clinical Psychology, 61,* 261–269.

Wilson, G. T., & Pike, K. M. (1993). Eating disorders. In D. H. Barlow (Ed.), *Clinical handbook of psychological disorders: A step-by-step treatment manual* (2nd ed., pp. 278–317). New York: Guilford.

CHAPTER 15

Sleep Disorders: Evaluation and Diagnosis

CHARLES M. MORIN and JACK D. EDINGER

Sleep disorders are common and debilitating conditions that contribute to emotional distress, social and occupational dysfunction, increased risks for injury, and, in some instances, serious medical illnesses. Despite their prevalence and clinical significance, sleep disorders have traditionally received little attention in health provider training programs. This chapter is designed to familiarize readers with those sleep disorders most likely to be encountered in their practices. Specifically, this chapter reviews the diagnostic classification, clinical characteristics, natural course, and prognosis of various sleep disorder subtypes and explores the epidemiology of sleep pathology in modern society. In addition, the contributions of heredity, gender, and ethnicity in the development of sleep disorders are considered, and common methods for assessing patients' sleep complaints are described.

CLASSIFICATION

Whereas various nosologies are available for sleep disorder classification, the *International Classification of Sleep Disorders* (ICSD; American Sleep Disorders Association, 1990) and the "Sleep Disorders" section of the *Diagnostic and Statistical Manual of Mental Disorders* (DSM-IV; American Psychiatric Association [APA], 1994) currently enjoy the widest use. The ICSD delineates clinical features and diagnostic criteria for more than 80 highly specific sleep disorders. As such, this system is best suited for sleep specialists. In contrast, the DSM-IV describes a smaller number of global diagnostic subtypes, many of which subsume several ICSD diagnoses. Although there is considerable overlap between these two nosologies, the DSM-IV is likely more familiar and available to psychologists and other mental health practitioners. Thus, the DSM-IV system for sleep disorders classification is considered at length herein.

As illustrated in Table 15.1, the DSM-IV delineates a variety of discrete diagnostic subtypes of sleep-wake disturbances that are grouped into four broader categories on the basis of their presumed etiologies. *Primary sleep disorders* include various sleep-wake disturbances arising from abnormalities in the biological sleep-wake system and complicated by such factors as conditioned arousal at bedtime, poor sleep hygiene practices, and the development of secondary medical illnesses. Included within this broad category are several *dyssomnias*

TABLE 15.1   DSM-IV Sleep Disorders Classification

I. Primary sleep disorders
   A. Dyssomnias
      1. Primary insomnia
      2. Narcolepsy
      3. Breathing-related sleep disorders
      4. Primary hypersomnia
      5. Circadian rhythm sleep disorders
      6. Other dyssomnias
   B. Parasomnias
      1. Nightmare disorder
      2. Sleepwalking disorder
      3. Sleep terror disorder
      4. Other parasomnias
II. Sleep disorder related to another mental disorder
   A. Insomnia subtype
   B. Hypersomnia subtype
   C. Parasomnia subtype
   D. Mixed subtype
III. Sleep disorder related to a general medical condition
   A. Insomnia subtype
   B. Hypersomnia subtype
   C. Parasomnia subtype
   D. Mixed subtype
IV. Substance-induced sleep disorder
   A. Insomnia subtype
   B. Hypersomnia subtype
   C. Parasomnia subtype
   D. Mixed subtype

caused by abnormalities in the timing, amount, or quality of sleep and *parasomnias* characterized by abnormal events (nightmares) or unusual behaviors (e.g., sleepwalking) arising out of sleep. In contrast, *sleep disorders related to another mental disorder* involve a prominent sleep complaint attributable to a coexisting mental disorder such as a mood or anxiety disorder. Similarly, *sleep disorders due to a general medical condition* include disturbances arising directly from the effects (pain, seizures, etc.) of an active medical illness. Finally, *substance-induced sleep disorders* are presumed to arise from inappropriate use of medications, illicit drugs, stimulants, or alcohol.

Of the various sleep disorders listed in Table 15.1, only those classified as primary sleep disorders may occur independently of a coexisting psychiatric, medical, or substance use problem. Moreover, the remaining diagnoses are assigned only as codiagnoses among individuals who present a prominent sleep-wake complaint that warrants separate clinical attention. For example, a patient who presents a clinically central complaint of insomnia that is determined to arise from a recurrent *major depressive disorder* would be assigned both a diagnosis of *major depressive disorder, recurrent* and a diagnosis of *sleep disorder related to mood disorder, insomnia subtype.* The ensuing discussion provides descriptions of the various diagnostic subgroups listed in Table 15.1. Inasmuch as the reader is likely to have less knowledge of the primary sleep disorder subtypes, more extensive descriptions of these disorders are provided.

Primary Sleep Disorders

Dyssomnias

Primary insomnia. Primary insomnia, characterized by difficulty initiating or maintaining sleep or persistent poor-quality sleep, is a relatively common form of sleep disturbance that cannot be attributed to an underlying psychiatric, medical, or substance abuse problem. However, the diagnosis of primary insomnia does not imply total absence of psychiatric or medical disorders but rather a sleep disturbance that is viewed as independent of any other coexisting conditions. Indeed, individuals suffering from primary insomnia often complain of mild anxiety, mood disturbances, concentration or memory dysfunction, somatic concerns, and general malaise, but such clinical findings are viewed as common symptoms rather than as causes of their sleep disturbances.

The development and persistence of this condition has been ascribed to a myriad of psychological, behavioral, and physiological anomalies. As suggested by some writers (Hauri & Fisher, 1986; Spielman, 1986), primary insomnia, like many other forms of sleep disturbance, arises from a special confluence of endogenous *predisposing characteristics,* sleep-disruptive *precipitating events,* and *perpetuating behaviors or circumstances.* Vulnerabilities, such as proneness to worry, repression of disturbing emotion, physiological hyperarousal, or innate propensity toward light and fragmented sleep—or all of the above—may predispose certain individuals to a primary sleep disturbance. Among such individuals, insomnia may develop given sufficient stress or disruption from a precipitating event (e.g., loss of a loved one, undergoing a painful medical procedure, frequent disruption of sleep-wake schedule). Subsequently, primary insomnia persists when conditioned environmental cues and maladaptive habits serve to perpetuate sleep disturbance long after the initial precipitating circumstances are resolved.

Many primary insomniacs report intense preoccupation with sleep and heightened arousal as bedtime approaches (Hauri & Fisher, 1986). Indeed, such patients frankly report that they view bedtime as the worst time of day. A vicious cycle often emerges in which repetitive unsuccessful sleep attempts reinforce the insomniac's sleep-related anxiety, which, in turn, contributes to a continued pattern of sleep difficulty. Through their repetitive association with unsuccessful sleep efforts, the bedroom environment and presleep rituals often become cues or stimuli for poor sleep. Moreover, in some cases, formerly benign habits, such as watching television, eating, or reading in bed may also reduce the stimulus value of the bed and bedroom for sleep and may further enhance the primary insomniac's sleep problem. As a result, it is not unusual for primary insomniacs to report improved sleep in novel settings where conditioned environmental cues are absent and usual presleep rituals are obviated.

Primary insomniacs are prone to many poor sleep hygiene practices that initially may emerge as a means of combating their sleep disturbances. For example, poor sleep at night may lead to daytime napping or sleeping late on weekends in efforts to catch up on lost sleep. Alternatively, such individuals may lie in bed for protracted periods trying to *force* sleep only to find themselves becoming more and more awake. Such findings are particularly common among middle-aged and older adults due to an increase in sleep fragmentation and shortening of their natural biological sleep-wake rhythm due to aging (Bliwise, 1993). In addition, other practices, such as routinely engaging in physically or mentally stimulating activities shortly before bed or failing to adhere to a regular sleep-wake schedule, may emerge as a function of lifestyle choices or perceived social obligations and also contribute to sleep difficulty. Dysfunctional sleep cognitions, such as unrealistic expectations and amplification of the consequences of insomnia, can exacerbate or perpetuate what might otherwise have been a transient sleep problem (Morin, 1993).

Narcolepsy. Narcolepsy is a relatively rare (prevalence = 1 : 10,000–20,000) hereditary sleep disorder resulting in moderate to severe daytime dysfunction. Classic narcolepsy is defined by a tetrad of symptoms including 1. *excessive daytime sleepiness* and unintended sleep episodes occurring during situations (e.g., driving, at work, during conversations) when normals typically are able to remain awake; 2. *cataplexy,* which consists of an abrupt and reversible decrease or loss of muscle tone (without loss of consciousness) precipitated by such emotions as laughter, anger, surprise, or exhilaration; 3. *sleep paralysis,* which involves awakening from nocturnal sleep with an inability to move; and 4. *hypnogogic hallucinations* consisting of vivid images and dreams, usually just as sleep develops, but sometimes intruding into wakefulness (Guilleminault, 1994; Karacan & Howell, 1988).

Individuals with narcolepsy complain of frequent overwhelming episodes throughout the day during which they feel compelled to sleep despite having obtained a seemingly adequate amount of sleep during the previous night (Parks, 1985). Although daytime naps are often viewed as momentarily restorative, excessive sleepiness may return shortly thereafter. As the syndrome progresses, naps may lose their restorative value, and even nocturnal sleep may become disturbed (Parks, 1985). Because unrelenting sleepiness and cataplectic paralysis may severely compromise quality of life and personal safety, patients suspected of narcolepsy should be referred to a sleep specialist to assure a proper evaluation and subsequent effective management.

Breathing-related sleep disorders. A variety of breathing-related sleep disorders (BRSDs) may produce significant nocturnal sleep disruption and result in sleep-wake complaints. Patients suffering form *obstructive sleep apnea* experience repetitive partial (hypopneas) or complete (apneas) obstructions of their upper airways during sleep despite continued diaphragmatic effort to breathe. Other patients may show repeated episodes of increased breathing difficulty or *upper airway resistance* during sleep. In contrast, patients suffering from *central sleep apnea* experience sleep disruption as a result of repeated events during which both airflow and respiratory efforts cease. Finally, patients with *central alveolar hypoventilation syndrome* experience sleep-related worsening of their daytime proneness to hypoventilate. Whatever their exact form, such BRSDs lead to repeated arousals from sleep (to restart normal breathing) and consequent diminution in sleep's quality and restorative value.

Although some patients with BRSDs complain of insomnia, most report excessive daytime sleepiness and unintentional sleep episodes occurring while watching television, reading, or even driving. Additional symptoms may include loud snoring, gasping for breath during sleep, frequent dull headaches upon awakening, and *automatic behaviors* (i.e., carrying out activities without, at the moment, being aware of one's actions). BRSDs may result in such psychological consequents as dysphoria, irritability, and concentration and memory problems. In addition, they may produce serious medical consequents, including hypertension, arrhythmias, cardiac arrest, sexual dysfunction, and nocturnal enuresis (Guilleminault, 1989). Because of the potential seriousness of these conditions, patients suspected of BRSDs should always be referred to a sleep specialist for evaluation and management.

Primary hypersomnia. Primary hypersomnia is a sleep-wake disorder characterized by excessive daytime sleepiness that cannot be attributed to a BRSD, presence of narcolepsy, or a medical, psychiatric, or substance abuse problem. Individuals with this condition present complaints of severe daytime drowsiness that interferes with work performance, social functioning, and general quality of life. Daytime somnolence leads to frequent naps that are not refreshing. Nocturnal sleep is long, undisturbed, and without respiratory impairment. Moreover, there is no evidence of sleep paralysis or cataplexy. Awakening in the morning is often difficult and accompanied by excessive grogginess or *sleep drunkenness* (Parks, 1985).

Circadian rhythm sleep disorder. Individuals with circadian rhythm sleep disorders (CRSDs) experience persistent or recurrent sleep-wake difficulties as a result of a mismatch between their endogenous, circadian sleep-wake rhythms and the sleep-wake schedules imposed on them by occupational or social demands. Alterations of the usual sleep-wake pattern due to jet lag, rotating shift work, or social and recreational pursuits may all lead to CRSDs. In some individuals, CRSDs are intermittent or recurrent as a function of frequently changing work or travel schedules. For others, aberrant bedtimes may, over a period of time, lead to a persistent shift (either advance or delay) in the underlying circadian mechanisms that regulate the timing of when sleep occurs.

These individuals typically complain that their sleep is disrupted or does not occur at a time that is consistent with their desired sleep-wake schedule. In addition, they often report insomnia at certain times of day and excessive sleepiness at other times. Among individuals engaged in rotating shift work, alterations in chosen sleep-wake schedules between workdays and days off may perpetuate the sleep-wake complaints. In other cases, the person appears to obtain a normal amount of sleep if it is allowed to occur ad lib and not at the time chosen in response to actual or perceived external demands (Edinger & Erwin, 1992; Weitzman et al., 1981). Whatever the cause, such individuals usually require interventions designed to resynchronize their endogenous and exogenous sleep-wake rhythms.

Parasomnias

Nightmare disorder. Nightmare disorder is characterized by repeated awakenings from nocturnal sleep or daytime naps precipitated by disturbing dreams. Typically such dreams involve threats to the individual's physical, psychological, and emotional well-being. Upon awakening, the individual appears fully alert, oriented, and cognizant of the arousing dream's content. Whereas anxiety and depressed mood may develop as secondary features of the nightmares, such emotional symptoms do not meet criteria for a major psychiatric disturbance. Moreover, inasmuch as nightmares are common to children, college students, and many noncomplaining normal adults (Hartman, 1994), nightmare disorder is diagnosed only when recurrent disturbing dreams cause obvious impairment of emotional, social, or occupational functioning.

Individuals with nightmare disorder complain of repeated disturbing dreams that arouse them from their sleep. Since nightmares arise during rapid eye movement (REM) sleep, individuals with nightmare disorder typically report nightmare-induced awakenings during the latter half of the night, when REM episodes typically become longer and more vivid. Careful interview also usually reveals dream content that reflects a recurrent theme reflective of underlying conflicts, characteristic fears, or more general personality characteristics (Kales, Soldatos, Caldwell, Charney, et al., 1980). For example, individuals with obsessive-compulsive traits often report recurrent nightmares during which they find themselves repeatedly unable to finish an important assignment despite their persistent efforts to do so. In addition, individuals with nightmare disorder usually complain of anxiety and sleep disturbance caused by the nightmares as well as resultant disruption of their normal day-to-day functioning.

Sleepwalking and sleep terror disorders. In approximately 15% of all patients presenting to sleep centers, aberrant nocturnal behaviors disrupt normal sleep (Coleman et al., 1982). Among the more common of these are sleepwalking and night terrors. Both phenomena occur early in the sleep period and appear to represent incomplete arousals from the deepest stages of sleep known as slow-wave sleep (Gastaut & Broughton, 1965). Individuals with *sleepwalking disorder* arise from bed in a stuporous state and amble about their homes but may also walk out of doors (Kales, Soldatos, Caldwell, Kales, et al., 1980). Typically such sleepwalking episodes involve behaviors that are relatively routine or of low complexity, such as using the bathroom, eating, talking, or walking aimlessly about the home. In contrast, individuals with *night terror disorder* display episodes during which they suddenly emit a shrill scream, usually after sitting up in bed. Since neither of these conditions is associated with REM sleep, the affected individual usually does not report dream content in association with the event. Moreover, the patient is usually difficult to arouse from the episode and may have no recall of the event the next morning. Since more SWS occurs in younger age groups, these events are observed most commonly in children, although they also may develop in adults. At a minimum, such events cause individual embarrassment and may contribute to avoidance of certain situations (e.g., going on trips, overnight visits to friends' homes). However, both sleepwalking and night terror episodes may result in injury to the affected individual or to a bed partner, and in such cases, referral to a specialty sleep disorders clinic would be indicated.

Sleep Disorders Related to Another Mental Disorder

Sleep-wake complaints are extremely common among DSM-IV Axis I and Axis II psychiatric disorders (Nofzinger, Buysse, Reynolds, & Kupfer, 1993). However, a small subset of individuals with psychiatric disorders either minimizes the importance of other symptoms or reports disturbances of sleep and wakefulness as the most salient concerns. In such cases the diagnosis of sleep disorder related to another mental condition would be assigned in addition to the diagnosis for the contributing psychiatric condition.

Several clinical case series (Buysse et al., 1994; Coleman et al., 1982; Edinger et al., 1989; Tan, Kales, Kales, Soldatos, & Bixler, 1984) have shown that mood disorders are more prevalent than other psychiatric conditions among patient groups who present to sleep disorders centers. Among such groups, those suffering from depression typically complain of insomnia characterized by sleep-onset difficulty, early morning awakenings, and nonrefreshing, fragmented sleep. Nocturnal sleep recordings generally corroborate these difficulties and, in addition, show a reduced latency to the onset of the first REM period, an increase in the number of eye movements during REM episodes (particularly early in the night), a reduction in deep or slow-wave sleep, and an increase in both lighter sleep stages and arousals (Reynolds & Kupfer, 1987). Conversely, patients with bipolar disorder show a cyclic pattern of insomnia and hypersomnia corresponding to their manic-depressive *swings,* but such individuals most often complain of hypersomnia and fatigue during their depressive periods. Finally, individuals with atypical mood disorders (e.g., seasonal depression) complain of hypersomnia, which is manifested by extended nocturnal sleep periods, frequent napping, and feelings of fatigue and lethargy (Walsh, Moss, & Sugerman, 1994).

Anxiety disorders also frequently contribute to sleep disturbances, but proportionately account for a lower percentage of sleep disorder diagnoses than do the mood disorders (Buysee et al., 1994; Tan et al., 1984). Most commonly, anxiety disorders result in a complaint of insomnia characterized by sleep initiation difficulty and occasionally sleep maintenance problems (Reynolds, Shaw, Newton, Coble, & Kupfer, 1983). Among individuals with phobic or obsessive-compulsive disorders, sleep disturbance may emerge in response to troublesome stimuli or situations, whereas those with generalized anxiety disorders and post-traumatic stress disorders may experience a more pervasive and unrelenting insomnia problem (Walsh et al., 1994). Alternatively, some patients with panic disorder complain of sleep disturbances caused by nocturnal panic attacks occurring during non-REM sleep (Hauri, Friedman, & Ravaris, 1989).

In addition to mood and anxiety disorders, a number of other psychiatric conditions may occasionally give rise to a predominant sleep-wake complaint. Insomnia is not uncommon among individuals with somatoform disorders, likely because of their tendencies to somatize emotional or psychological conflicts (Walsh et al., 1994). In contrast, insomnia problems arise among some Axis II personality disorders as a result of their chaotic lifestyles and irregular sleep-wake schedules. Insomnia and *night wandering* commonly accompany dementia, likely as a result of associated anomalies in the biological sleep-wake system (Bliwise, 1993). Finally, marked sleep disturbance is common to schizophrenia and other psychoses, but individuals with such disorders rarely report sleep difficulties as their primary or sole complaint.

Sleep Disorder Due to a General Medical Condition

Sleep-wake disturbances arise in the context of medical disorders that are too numerous to consider herein. However, most such medical conditions do not warrant a separate sleep disorder diagnosis, inasmuch as sleep complaints do not dominate their clinical presentation. Nevertheless, a subset of patients with medical conditions complains of sleep difficulties to such a degree that such complaints warrant separate clinical attention. A diagnosis of sleep disorder due to a general medical condition is made in such cases.

Individuals with sleep disorders due to a general medical condition may suffer from an insomnia type, hypersomnia type, parasomnia type, or a mixture (mixed type) of these forms of sleep-wake disturbances. Insomnia may arise from a variety of medical conditions including vascular headaches, cerebrovascular disease, hyperthyroidism, chronic bronchitis, degenerative neurological conditions, and pain accompanying rheumatoid arthritis. In contrast, conditions such as hypothyroidism, viral encephalitis, and chronic fatigue syndrome may all result in hypersomnia complaints (Wooten, 1994). Among patients with medically based parasomnia, those with sleep-related epileptic seizures constitute the largest subgroup. Regardless of their presenting sleep difficulties, individuals with a medically based sleep disorder require intervention for their contributing medical conditions in order to realize sleep-wake improvements.

Substance-Induced Sleep Disorder

A variety of medications, illicit drugs, and other substances in common use may contribute to sleep-wake disturbances. Many of these substances produce insomnia, hypersomnia, parasomnias, or a mixture of these symptoms, either while in use or during periods of withdrawal and abstinence. When such sleep-wake disturbances are presented as a predominant clinical complaint, a diagnosis of substance-induced sleep disorder would be warranted as a codiagnosis in addition to the DSM-IV diagnosis descriptive of the substance use problem. Most commonly, such a diagnosis would be associated with excessive use of alcohol, sedating hypnotic medications, and stimulants.

Although the exact prevalence of alcohol-related sleep disorders is unknown, such conditions are likely to be relatively common since 10% of men and 3%–5% of women develop significant alcohol dependence/abuse problems (Shuckit & Irwin, 1988). Alcohol ingestion may facilitate sleep onset but usually leads to sleep maintenance difficulties due to sleep fragmentation caused by metabolic withdrawal effects occurring amid the sleep period. Also, heavy alcohol consumption may result in variety of parasomnias, such as bedwetting, sleep terrors, and sleepwalking. Moreover, given alcohol's pronounced suppressant effects on REM sleep, vivid, disturbing dreams may emerge during alcohol withdrawal due to an *REM rebound effect* (Gillin, 1994). Among chronic alcohol abusers, insomnia may persist through even extended periods of abstinence (Adamson & Burdick, 1973) and serve as the primary catalyst for relapse.

Like alcohol, sedating prescription medications and sedative-hypnotics in particular may contribute to a substance-induced sleep disorder. Although most sedating medications used as sleep aids are effective for transient sleep disturbances, most such medications lose their effectiveness with continued use. Individuals who frequently use sedating medications for sleep usually experience a return of their insomnia as they become tolerant to such drugs. In turn, hypersomnia complaints may emerge among those who increase medication dosages to reestablish drug efficacy. In addition, abrupt withdrawal of some sedating medications with short *half-lifes* may lead to a period of *rebound insomnia* during which sleep disturbances worsen (Gillin, 1994). Clinical observations suggest that such withdrawal effects often contribute to loss of self-efficacy in regard to sleep and encourage many individuals to continue use of hypnotics long after such drugs lose their effectiveness.

In contrast, stimulants such as amphetamines, cocaine, caffeine, and nicotine increase daytime alertness and may disrupt nighttime sleep. As a result, insomnia complaints may arise during periods of use. Conversely, complaints of hypersomnia may emerge during periods of withdrawal and abstinence. However, paradoxical symptoms, such as insomnia during nicotine withdrawal and hypersomnia during periods of heavy caffeine use, have also been observed (Gillin, 1994; Regestein, 1989). Whatever their exact characteristics, stimulant-related sleep disorders often may persist for prolonged periods given the addictive properties of many of the substances that perpetuate them.

EPIDEMIOLOGY

Prevalence

Various surveys have suggested high prevalence of intermittent and chronic sleep-wake complaints in modern society. For example, most studies suggest that insomnia is an intermittent or chronic problem for almost one-third of the adult population in industrialized countries (Gallup Organization, 1991; Lugaresi, Zucconi, & Bixler, 1987; Mellinger, Balter, & Uhlenhuth, 1985). Somewhat less prevalent but still relatively common are hypersomnia complaints, which are presented by 3% to 5% of the adult populations in Western nations (Ford & Kamerow, 1989; Lugaresi et al., 1987). Less is known about the prevalence of parasomnias, but limited data suggest prevalences of 1% to 5% for current nightmares and night terrors and approximately 1% for sleepwalking (Lugaresi et al., 1987).

Unfortunately, prevalences of most specific sleep disorder diagnoses remain unknown. Most previous population surveys have queried respondents about general sleep symptoms (insomnia, hypersomnia, loud snoring, etc.) and have not included questions that would allow the establishment of specific sleep disorder diagnoses. In addition, surveys are subject to reporting biases that may confound prevalence estimates. Moreover, as discussed later in the chapter, some primary and medically related sleep disorders (e.g., breathing-related sleep disorders, narcolepsy, and nocturnal seizures) require confirmatory laboratory tests that have not been included in most epidemiological investigations. Additional well-controlled and time-consuming studies are required before the relative prevalences of the various sleep disorder diagnoses can be firmly established.

Psychological and Medical Consequents

Little is currently known about the psychological and medical consequents of specific sleep disorders, but growing evidence suggests a robust relationship between sleep complaints and both mental and physical health problems. For example, both insomnia and hypersomnia complaints, in the absence of other psychiatric symptoms, increase the risk for subsequent depressive disorders (Ford & Kamerow, 1989; Lugaresi et al., 1987). Moreover, persistent sleep disturbances have been implicated in the development or exacerbation of various other forms of psychiatric disturbance, including anxiety disorders, substance abuse problems, and even psychoses (National Commission on Sleep Disorders Research, 1993). In addition, several studies have implicated BRSDs in the development of such serious medical conditions as hypertension, cardiac arrhythmias, myocardial infarction, stroke, and some forms of dementia, all of which increase risk of mortality. Furthermore, both psychiatric and medical complaints may arise from chronic sleep disruption due to shift work and other causes of circadian disorders (National Commission on Sleep Disorders Research, 1993).

Sleep disorders may also increase risk of injury. Presumably due to their relative fatigue and loss of alertness, insomniacs report twice as many traffic accidents as do noncomplaining, normal sleepers (National Commission on Sleep Disorders Research, 1993). One study found that as many as 27% of all traffic accidents are caused by a driver's falling asleep behind the wheel, and such occurrences accounted for 83% of all observed fatalities (Parson, 1986). Although it is difficult to ascertain the exact cause of sleepiness in such cases, sleep loss due to sleep disorders and improper sleep scheduling is a likely factor in many such events (Mitler et al., 1988). Along with their potential contribution to driver errors, sleep disorders and sleep loss have been implicated in serious railroad and maritime accidents as well as in accidents in the workplace (Mitler et al., 1988).

COURSE AND PROGNOSIS

Insomnia can begin at any time during the course of the life span, but onset of the first episode is more common in young adulthood (Kales & Kales, 1984). It is often triggered by stressful life events, with the most common precipitants involving separation or divorce, death of a loved one, occupational stress, and interpersonal conflicts (Healy et al., 1981; Vollrath, Wicki, & Angst, 1989). In a small subset of cases, insomnia begins in childhood, in the absence of psychological or medical problems, and persists throughout adulthood (Hauri & Olmstead, 1980). Insomnia is a frequent problem among women during menopause and often persists even after other symptoms (e.g., hot flashes) have resolved. The first episode of insomnia can also occur in late life, although it must be distinguished from normal age-related changes in sleep patterns and from sleep disturbances due to medical problems or prescribed medications.

For the large majority of insomnia sufferers, sleep difficulties are transient in nature, lasting a few days, and resolving themselves once the initial precipitating event has subsided. Its course may also be intermittent, with repeated brief episodes of sleep difficulties following a close association with the occurrence of stressful events (Vollrath et al., 1989). Even when insomnia has developed a chronic course, typically there is extensive night-to-night variability in sleep patterns, with an occasional restful night's sleep intertwined with several nights of poor sleep. The subtype of insomnia (i.e., sleep onset, maintenance, or mixed insomnia) may also change over time (Hohagen et al., 1994).

There are many risk factors for insomnia, including female gender, advancing age, emotional factors, and hyperarousal. A history of insomnia itself also increases the risk for future episodes of sleep difficulties (Klink, Quan, Kaltenborn, & Lebowitz, 1992). This pattern of recurrence is present in both primary insomniacs and in patients whose sleep difficulties are associated with affective or anxiety disorders (Vollrath et al., 1989). The prognosis for insomnia can also be complicated by prolonged usage of hypnotic drugs.

In narcolepsy, primary symptoms of excessive daytime sleepiness and irresistible sleep attacks usually develop during late adolescence, although onset of the syndrome may occur at any time between childhood and the fifth decade of life (Parks, 1985). Cataplexy, sleep paralysis, and hypnagogic hallucinations almost always follow rather than precede onset of daytime sleepiness, and some features may not develop at all. Although drug therapy can provide some relief for sleep attacks and cataplexy, narcolepsy is a lifelong disorder. Excessive daytime sleepiness may worsen over time, and nighttime sleep can become impaired as a result of stimulant medications used to stay awake during the day. Other symptoms may decrease or fluctuate in intensity over the life span.

The most common form of BRSDs, obstructive sleep apnea, can occur at any age. It is, however, much more prevalent among middle-aged obese males. When left untreated, its course is usually progressive, and, in most severe cases, it can lead to significant daytime impairments (sleepiness, memory and concentration difficulties) and severe medical complications (e.g., hypertension, heart failures). Onset of primary hypersomnia usually occurs between ages 15 and 30, and symptoms develop gradually over several weeks or months (Edinger & Erwin, 1992).

CRSDs due to jet lag and shift work have a recurrent course that is directly linked to the frequency of traveling or schedule change. Following a transmeridian flight, it takes approximately 1 day for each time zone crossed for the circadian rhythm to become resynchronized with local time. Likewise, after a week of work on the night shift, it takes up to 10 days to become fully reacclimated to working in the daytime and sleeping at night. Adjustment to frequent changes in sleep schedules are more difficult with advancing age. Shift workers tend to consume more stimulants to stay awake and more hypnotics to sleep than those working regular day shifts. Working on shifts for several years may increase risk of sleep difficulties when returning to a regular daytime shift.

Most parasomnias tend to occur first in childhood. Sleep terror and sleepwalking have a typical onset between ages 5 and 12 and tend to resolve spontaneously by midadolescence, suggesting a developmental/maturation course to these conditions. Their persistence, and especially onset, in adulthood have been associated with greater likelihood of concomitant psychopathology (Kales, Kales, et al., 1980; Kales, Soldatos, Caldwell, et al., 1980). Sleepwalking is more common than sleep terrors, but their co-occurrence is also frequent. In some individuals, both conditions may develop at the same time, whereas in others they may develop at different times. Following sleep deprivation, there is an increase in the amount of deep sleep during the recovery period. As such, sleep deprivation can increase incidence of sleep terror and sleepwalking, which originate from deep sleep (stages 3–4). Fever and sleeping in an unfamiliar environment have also been associated with higher risks for these parasomnias. Nightmares can occur at any age, but their first occurrence is usually between 3 and 5 years of age. Frequency and course of nightmares are highly variable. Frequent and chronic nightmares affect less than 1% of the population. Emotional stress can trigger nightmares in both children and adults, although they can also be isolated phenomena, independent of anxiety (Wood & Bootzin, 1990).

Sleep pathologies due to mental, medical, or substance abuse disorder tend to closely parallel the temporal course of the underlying disorder. Conditioning factors may contribute to or perpetuate a sleep problem, especially insomnia, even after the underlying condition has resolved. For example, sleep disturbances associated with major depression may persist long after the depression has lifted (Hauri, Chernik, Hawkins, & Mendels, 1974; Rush et al., 1986). Likewise, sleep difficulties associated with chronic use of benzodiazepine-hypnotics or with alcohol abuse may continue even after complete withdrawal from the substance.

FAMILIAL AND GENETIC CONSIDERATIONS

Familial and genetic factors may predispose some individuals to the development of certain sleep disorders. For instance, individuals suffering from a sleep disorder often report a positive family history for a similar condition. Also, twin studies indicate that monozygotic twins have a higher concordance of sleep habits and sleep difficulties than dizygotic twins (Heath, Kendler, Eaves, & Martin, 1990). Although some clinical evidence suggests that the complaint of insomnia runs in families, it is unclear whether this is strictly due to genetic predisposition, influence of familial and social learning factors, or a combination of both. Narcolepsy is the only sleep disorder for which there is strong evidence of genetic transmission (Guilleminault, 1994). Studies of human leukocyte antigens (HLA) have traced two antigens (DR2 and DQw1) in 90%–100% of narcoleptic patients. These antigens are also present in up to 35% of nonnarcoleptic individuals as well as in other autoimmune diseases (e.g., lupus and multiple sclerosis). Nonetheless, first-degree relatives of a narcoleptic proband are eight times more likely to have a disorder of excessive daytime sleepiness than are individuals in the general population. Some evidence also suggests familial predisposition to sleep terrors and sleepwalking (Kales, Soldatos, Bixler, et al., 1980). Risk of sleepwalking increases to 45% when one parent is affected and to 60% when both are affected. Prevalence of these conditions is up to 10 times greater in first-degree relatives of an affected individual than in the general population. The association of nightmares to familial and genetic factors has not been documented.

Except for narcolepsy, relatively few studies have examined the role of familial and genetic factors as predisposing factors to sleep disorders. It may be that hereditary factors predispose some individuals to develop sleep disorders, but the actual manifestation of the disorder may be influenced by psychological and environmental factors as well.

DIAGNOSTIC CONSIDERATIONS

This section outlines the most important issues to consider in making a differential diagnosis. As a starting point, we refer to the four broad categories of sleep-wake complaints likely to be encountered in clinical practice and review the distinguishing features leading to various sleep disorder diagnoses.

Insomnia

The clinical features of insomnia involve a subjective complaint of difficulty initiating or maintaining sleep, or nonrestorative sleep that causes significant distress or impairments in social or occupational functioning. DSM-IV does not provide specific operational criteria to define insomnia severity. In clinical research, insomnia is generally defined as a sleep-onset latency or wake after sleep onset (or both) greater than 30 minutes per night for a minimum of three nights per week (Lacks & Morin, 1992), with a corresponding sleep efficiency (ratio of time asleep to time spent in bed) of less than 85%. Sleep duration alone is not always useful to diagnose insomnia because of individual differences in sleep needs. Some people may function well with as little as 5–6 hours of sleep and would not necessarily complain of insomnia; conversely, others needing 9–10 hours may still complain of inadequate sleep. Thus, the patient's subjective complaint is crucial in establishing a diagnosis of primary or secondary insomnia.

Numerous factors can produce a subjective complaint of insomnia: emotional, medical, pharmacological, and environmental. The main differential diagnosis is usually between primary insomnia and insomnia related to another mental disorder. This distinction is not always easily made. There is a high rate of comorbidity between sleep and psychiatric disorders in general, and more specifically between insomnia, depression, and anxiety conditions (Morin & Ware, 1996). A difficult issue is that insomnia is a feature of several psychiatric disorders. Problems falling asleep are often linked to anxiety conditions and early morning awakenings to major depression. Nonetheless, many insomnia patients may present concurrent features of anxiety, depression, or both, that do not meet criteria for a psychiatric disorder. In the presence of coexisting insomnia and anxiety or depression, it is essential to clarify the relative onset and course of each disorder to determine which condition is primary and which is secondary in nature. The diagnosis of primary insomnia is made when its onset and course are independent of a mental disorder. Conversely, a diagnosis of insomnia associated with psychopathology is indicated when onset of the sleep problem coincided with, and its subsequent course occurred exclusively in association with, psychopathology. Data from clinical case series suggest that between 35% and 44% of patients presenting to a sleep clinic with a primary complaint of insomnia receive a diagnosis of insomnia related to another mental disorder (Buysse et al., 1994; Coleman et al., 1982).

Insomnia can also result from another sleep disorder. Restless legs syndrome, a condition characterized by an unpleasant and creeping sensation in the calves of the legs, can produce severe sleep-onset insomnia. Periodic limb movements is a related condition characterized by stereotyped and repetitive leg twitches that can produce sleep maintenance difficulties. Some breathing-related sleep disorders, especially central sleep apnea, can also produce difficulties maintaining sleep. Obstructive sleep apnea more typically leads to a complaint of excessive daytime sleepiness. The clinical history combined with daily monitoring of sleep-wake schedules is usually sufficient to determine whether insomnia is related to an underlying circadian rhythm disorder. Some parasomnias, especially nightmares, can cause awakenings, but the main diagnostic focus is the nightmare. Insomnia might also arise from various medical conditions (e.g., hyperthyroidism, pain, congestive heart failure, pulmonary disease) or from use or withdrawal of prescribed medications (e.g., steroids, bronchodilators), sedative-hypnotics, alcohol, or illicit stimulants (e.g., cocaine). In those instances, the primary diagnosis would be, respectively, a sleep disorder associated with a medical condition or a substance-induced sleep disorder.

Even when insomnia is secondary to psychiatric, medical, or substance abuse disorders, psychological factors are almost always involved in perpetuating sleep difficulties over time. Whereas treatment should focus on the underlying condition, it may not always bring about sleep improvements. In such cases, treatment may need to target both the insomnia and the presumed underlying cause.

Hypersomnia

The main sleep disorders with a predominant complaint of excessive daytime sleepiness are narcolepsy, breathing-related sleep disorders, and primary hypersomnia. The differential diagnosis among those conditions is based on history, clinical features, nocturnal sleep recordings, and objective measurement of daytime sleepiness. Frequently, daytime sleepiness is caused by the practice of allotting too little time for sleep on most nights. Such volitional sleep restriction should be the first consideration in making a differential diagnosis. This possibility is suggested when a person reports fewer than 6 or 7 hours of sleep per night and by evidence of adequate daytime alertness when sleep duration is extended to 8 or 9 hours. Such presentation is more likely among chronically sleep-deprived individuals with highly demanding occupational and family schedules. When time is available to catch up on sleep, such as on weekends, daytime alertness is much improved. Conversely, individuals with narcolepsy, breathing-related sleep disorders, and primary hypersomnia experience daytime sleepiness regardless of the amount of nocturnal sleep they obtain. Several additional symptoms help to distinguish among those conditions (see Table 15.2).

The most prominent symptoms in breathing-related sleep disorders, especially obstructive sleep apnea, include loud snoring and pauses in breathing. These symptoms are typically witnessed by a bed partner. In narcolepsy, the main clinical features are repeated and irresistable sleep attacks throughout the day with or without accompanying symptoms of cataplexy, hypnagogic halluci-

TABLE 15.2   Symptoms Associated with Sleep Apnea, Narcolepsy, and Primary Hypersomnia

Symptom	Apnea	Narcolepsy	Primary hypersomnia
Snoring	+	−	−
Breathing lapses	+	−	−
Sleep attacks	−	+	−
Cataplexy	−	+	−
Hypnagogic hallucinations	−	+	−
Sleep paralysis	−	+	−
Restless sleep	+	+	−
Excessive daytime sleepiness	+	+	+
Sleep drunkenness	+	−	+
Automatic behaviors	+	+	+

nations, and sleep paralysis. A short latency to REM sleep is a diagnostic feature of narcolepsy. In both apnea and narcolepsy, sleep continuity is impaired and the proportion of time spent in stages 3–4 sleep is significantly reduced. Conversely, nocturnal sleep is usually long, deep, and undisrupted in primary hypersomnia. However, in the absence of classic symptoms, this latter diagnosis is often made by default. Daytime napping is refreshing in narcoleptics but not in patients with apnea or primary hypersomnia. Sleep drunkenness, which is characterized by difficult arousal and disorientation, is more often associated with primary hypersomnia and apnea than with narcolepsy. Onset of the disorder can provide additional clues for the differential diagnosis; narcolepsy typically occurs early in life (i.e., late adolescence), whereas sleep apnea is much more prevalent among middle-aged obese males. Patients suspected of sleep apnea, narcolepsy, or primary hypersomnia should always be referred to a sleep disorders center for nocturnal polysomnography and daytime multiple sleep-latency test, two assessment procedures essential to confirm these diagnoses.

However, before making a sleep center referral, other explanations for the patient's hypersomnia should be considered. In shift workers, a complaint of excessive sleepiness is typically due to the underlying desynchronization of circadian rhythms. Hypersomnia may also occur in the context of another mental disorder. This is more common in major affective disorder, especially in bipolar patients. Hypersomnia is usually part of the depressive phase, whereas insomnia is predominant during the manic phase. Several medical conditions (e.g., hypothyroidism and chronic fatigue syndrome) and prescribed drugs (e.g., antihypertensives) may cause hypersomnia. Use or withdrawal from substances (e.g., alcohol and sedative-hypnotics) can also impair daytime wakefulness. Individuals with primary insomnia often report fatigue and tiredness, but they are not necessarily sleepy during the day.

Circadian Rhythm Sleep Disorders

Most circadian rhythm sleep disorders (CRSDs) can produce insomnia, hypersomnia, or a combination of both. The main feature distinguishing CRSDs from other sleep disorders is a poor timing of sleep and wake episodes with reference to the desired schedule. In jet lag and shift work, sleep and wake-fulness are compromised by frequently changing schedules or traveling across several time zones. Insomnia due to a delayed sleep phase is characterized by intractable difficulty falling asleep until early in the morning (e.g., 3:00 a.m.). There is usually no difficulty staying asleep once sleep has been achieved. More common in younger people, particularly college students, this condition is pre-sumed to arise from an endogenous delay in the biological clock (Weitzman et al., 1981), but it may also be exacerbated by irregular sleep schedules and a natural tendency to stay up late. The main differential diagnosis is with primary sleep-onset insomnia, which is more strongly associated with sleep-anticipatory anxiety and concomitant psychological symptomatology. In the phase advance syndrome, the presenting complaint involves a compelling difficulty in staying awake during the evening (e.g., after 8:00 or 9:00 p.m.), followed by early morn-ing awakening (e.g., 4:00 a.m.). Total sleep duration is not shortened. More frequent in older adults, this condition must be distinguished from early morn-ing awakening, which is also a common form of sleep maintenance insomnia in both depression and in late life. Duration of the previous sleep episode must be considered instead of relying exclusively on the actual clock time of the final awakening. In true early morning awakening, the final awakening is premature regardless of bedtime on the previous night.

Parasomnias

The main differential diagnosis among parasomnias involves sleep terrors and nightmares. The former is characterized by a piercing scream, confusion, exces-sive autonomic arousal, and only partial awakening. There is no recollection of disturbing dreams or of the incident upon awakening in the morning. In con-trast, nightmares trigger a full awakening, followed by a quick return to con-sciousness and vivid recall of a disturbing dream. The timing of the abnormal or distressful event is critical to make an accurate diagnosis. Sleep terrors origi-nate from stage 3–4 sleep, which occur almost exclusively in the first third of the night, whereas nightmares arise from REM sleep, which is more predomi-nant and more intense in the last third of the night. The distinction between sleepwalking and sleep terrors can be more difficult. These conditions often occur together and are considered by some as manifestations of the same under-lying arousal disorder with varying intensity. Parasomnias do not necessarily lead to a complaint of insomnia or hypersomnia, although in the most severe forms either of these difficulties may be present.

Since parasomnias may accompany other primary sleep disorders such as narcolepsy and breathing-related sleep disorders, those conditions should be excluded before a diagnosis of parasomnia is made. Nightmare is also a com-mon symptom of posttraumatic stress disorder (Ross, Ball, Sullivan, & Caroff, 1989) and major depressive episodes, so it is important to exclude such psychiat-ric conditions from consideration as well. Nocturnal panic attack may present similar features to sleep terrors and nightmares. Unlike in sleep terror, nocturnal panic attack leads to a full awakening, and unlike nightmares, there is no recol-lection of disturbing dreams. A seizure disorder is the most common medical condition producing symptoms similar to those of parasomnias. Finally, the introduction (L-dopa compounds and certain antihypertensive drugs) and withdrawal (antidepressants and benzodiazepines) of certain medications may lead to transient increases in nightmare activity (Hartmann, 1994), but such medications are not indicative of a nightmare disorder.

PSYCHOLOGICAL AND BIOLOGICAL ASSESSMENT

Accurate diagnosis of sleep disorders rests on thorough evaluation. This principle applies to all psychiatric disorders but is even more relevant to sleep disorders because sleep is affected by a host of psychological, medical, pharmacological, and circadian factors. The differential diagnosis of sleep disorders requires detailed and multifaceted evaluation involving a clinical interview, psychological and physical examinations, daily sleep monitoring, and, for some disorders, more specialized laboratory procedures.

Clinical History

A detailed clinical history is the most important diagnostic tool for evaluation of sleep disorders. The clinical history should elicit type of complaint (insomnia, hypersomnia, unusual behaviors during sleep), chronology, and course; exacerbating and alleviating factors; and responses to previous treatments. In particular, it is important to inquire about life events, psychological disorders, substance use, and medical illnesses at the time of onset of the sleep problem to help establish its etiology. Two interviews are available to gather this information in a structured format: the *Structured Interview for Sleep Disorders* (Schramm et al., 1993), designed according to DSM-III-R criteria, is helpful to establish a preliminary differential diagnosis among the different sleep disorders, and the *Structured Interview for Insomnia* (Morin, 1993) is more specifically geared for patients with a suspected diagnosis of primary or secondary insomnia.

Determining whether the course of the disorder has been chronic or intermittent is crucial in the diagnosis of some disorders. For instance, patients with narcolepsy have persistent daytime sleepiness, whereas patients with hypersomnia related to depression have more intermittent symptoms. Duration and course of insomnia can be transient, intermittent, or chronic; these distinctions can have important implications for diagnosis and treatment planning. For example, transient insomnia may require an intervention that focuses directly on precipitating conditions, whereas chronic insomnia will almost always require an intervention that also targets perpetuating factors (e.g., maladaptive sleep habits and dysfunctional cognitions). In light of the high comorbidity between sleep disturbances and psychiatric disorders, the history should identify relative onset and course of each condition in order to establish whether the sleep disorder is primary or secondary in nature.

A careful functional analysis of exacerbating and alleviating factors also can be quite useful diagnostically. For insomnia patients, detailed analysis of the following factors is crucial: sleeping environment; activities leading up to bedtime; patient's cognitions at bedtime or in the middle of the night; perceived impact of sleep disruptions on mood, performance, and relationships; coping strategies; and secondary gains. Interviewing the bed partner can yield most valuable diagnostic information about a patient suspected of sleep apnea or some forms of parasomnia. Patients may be unaware of their own snoring or breathing pauses in their sleep, and they may deny or underestimate their degree of daytime sleepiness. Patients suffering from sleepwalking or sleep terrors typically have no recollection of such events, and the bed partner (or parents) represent a most important source of clinical information.

Daily Self-Monitoring

Prospective daily sleep diary monitoring is extremely useful for establishing a diagnosis of some sleep disorders, especially for insomnia. A typical sleep diary includes entries for bedtime, arising time, sleep latency, number and duration of awakenings, sleep duration, naps, use of sleep aids, and various indices of sleep quality and daytime functioning (Morin, 1993). These data provide information about a patient's sleep habits and schedules, the nature of the sleep problem, and its frequency and intensity, all of which may vary considerably from the patient's global and retrospective report during a clinical interview. Despite some discrepancies between subjective and objective measurements of sleep parameters, daily morning estimates of specific sleep parameters represent a useful index of insomnia (Coates et al., 1982). The sleep diary is a practical and economical assessment tool for prospectively tracking sleep patterns over long periods of time in the home environment. Self-monitoring is also helpful to establish a baseline prior to initiating treatment and to monitor progress as the intervention unfolds. Because of the extensive night-to-night variability in sleep patterns of insomniacs, it is recommended that baseline data for at least 1 or 2 weeks be obtained (Lacks & Morin, 1992). Self-monitoring can be helpful not only for elucidating insomnia complaints, but also for diagnosing circadian rhythm sleep disorders or even for distinguishing daytime sleepiness due to insufficient sleep from that due to other sleep pathologies. Recording the timing of unusual events in sleep can also assist the clinician in differentiating between a sleep terror or a nightmare.

Psychological Assessment

Clinical indications for psychological assessment vary according to the specific sleep disorders. Although any sleep disorder can be associated with comorbid psychopathology, and chronic sleep disturbances of any kind can produce psychological symptoms, such findings are less probable when the presenting complaint is hypersomnia or the suspected diagnosis is circadian rhythm sleep disorders. Psychopathology is also rare among children with parasomnias, whereas its incidence is more variable among adults. Psychological assessment should be an integral component in the evaluation of insomnia. At the very least, a screening assessment is indicated because insomnia is frequently associated with psychopathology, and even when formal criteria for specific psychiatric disorders are not met, clinical features of anxiety and depression are extremely common among patients with insomnia complaints (Setia, Doghramji, Hauri, & Morin, 1996).

Although the Minnesota Multiphasic Personality Inventory (MMPI) has been extensively used to document rate of psychopathology and predict outcome among insomnia patients (Edinger, Stout, & Hoelscher, 1988), a more cost-effective approach is to use brief screening instruments that target specific psychological features (e.g., emotional distress, anxiety, and depression) most commonly associated with insomnia complaints. Instruments such as the Brief Symptom Inventory (Derogatis & Melisatros, 1983), the Beck Depression Inventory, and the State-Trait Anxiety Inventory can yield valuable screening data. As for all self-report measures, these instruments are subject to bias resulting from denial or exaggeration of symptoms and should never be used in isolation to confirm a diagnosis. Psychometric screening should always be complemented by a more in-depth clinical interview.

Numerous other self-report measures tapping various dimensions of insomnia can also yield useful information. Some instruments are used as global measures of quality (Pittsburgh Sleep Quality Index; Buysse, Reynolds, Monk, Berman, & Kupfer, 1989), satisfaction (Coyle & Watts, 1991), or impairment of sleep (Morin, 1993). Other scales are designed to evaluate mediating factors of insomnia, such as state (Pre-Sleep Arousal Scale; Nicassio, Mendlowitz, Fussell, & Petras, 1985) and trait arousal (Arousal Predisposition Scale; Coren, 1988), dysfunctional sleep cognitions (Beliefs and Attitudes about Sleep Scale; Morin, 1994), sleep-incompatible activities (Sleep-Behavior Self-Rating Scale; Kazarian, Howe, & Csapa, 1979), and sleep hygiene principles (Sleep Hygiene Awareness and Practice Scale; Lacks & Rotert, 1986). These measures are particularly useful for designing individually tailored insomnia interventions.

Behavioral Assessment Device

Of several behavioral assessment devices available to monitor sleep, wrist actigraphy is increasingly being used for ambulatory data collection. This activity-based monitoring system uses a microprocessor to record and store wrist activity along with actual clock time. Data are processed through microcomputer software, and an algorithm is used to estimate sleep and wake based on wrist activity. Despite some limitations in assessing specific sleep parameters (e.g., sleep latency), wrist actigraphy is a cost-effective method for confirming the diagnosis of insomnia and some circadian rhythm sleep disorders and for evaluating their treatment outcome (Sadeh, Hauri, Kripke, & Lavie, 1995).

Sleep Laboratory Evaluation

Polysomnography. Nocturnal polysomnography (PSG) involves monitoring of electroencephalogram (EEG), electro-oculogram (EOG), and electromyogram (EMG) readings. These three parameters are sufficient to distinguish sleep from wake and to quantify the proportion of time spent in various stages of sleep. Several additional variables—respiration, EKG, oxygen saturation, and leg movements—are usually monitored to detect other sleep-related abnormalities (e.g., breathing pauses and leg twitches) not recognized by the sleeping person. Nocturnal PSG is essential for the diagnosis of sleep apnea, narcolepsy, and periodic limb movements. It can yield useful data to document the severity of insomnia, especially in light of discrepancies between subjective complaints and objective findings. However, its clinical utility in the assessment and differential diagnosis of insomnia is more controversial. Some authors (Kales & Kales, 1984) claim that clinical evaluation is sufficient and reliable to diagnose insomnia, whereas others (Edinger et al., 1989; Jacobs, Reynolds, Kupfer, Lovin, & Ehrenpreis, 1988) argue that laboratory findings can significantly alter initial diagnostic impressions. Whether information gained from one night of PSG evaluation is of sufficient clinical value to improve treatment recommendations and outcome is still a matter of debate. The high cost of PSG remains a major deterrent to its routine use. Most insurance companies do not cover the cost of a sleep study for a suspected diagnosis of insomnia, whereas they reimburse for sleep apnea or narcolepsy.

Multiple sleep latency test (MSLT). Assessment of daytime sleepiness should be an integral component of the evaluation process when daytime alertness is compromised by a sleep disorder. The MSLT is a daytime assessment procedure in which a person is offered five or six 20-minute nap opportunities at 2-hour intervals throughout the day. Latency to sleep onset provides an objective measure of physiological sleepiness. Individuals who are well rested and without sleep disorders take 10 minutes or more to fall asleep or do not fall asleep at all. A mean sleep latency of less than 5 minutes is considered pathological and is associated with increased risks of falling asleep at inappropriate times or places, such as while driving. The MSLT is also a diagnostic test for narcolepsy in that patients with this condition enter REM sleep in two or more of the scheduled naps whereas normal sleepers rarely get into REM sleep during daytime naps. The MSLT is performed almost exclusively on patients with a presenting complaint of excessive daytime sleepiness. Although insomnia patients may complain about daytime tiredness, typically they do not display pathological sleepiness on the MSLT.

Two self-report measures of daytime sleepiness can provide useful screening data on daytime sleepiness: the Epworth Sleepiness Scale (Johns, 1991), a global and retrospective measure assessing the likelihood (on a 4-point scale) of falling asleep in several situations (e.g., watching TV, or riding in a car); and the Stanford Sleepiness Scale (Hoddes, Zarcone, Smythe, Phillips, & Dement, 1973), a 7-point Likert-type scale measuring subjective sleepiness at a specific moment in time.

Combining nocturnal PSG and daytime MSLT provides the most comprehensive assessment of sleep disorder inasmuch as these procedures are recognized by many as the "gold standards" in assessing sleep and its disorders. These laboratory-based procedures are clinically indicated when the presenting complaint is excessive daytime sleepiness and when symptoms suggestive of breathing-related disorders, narcolepsy, and periodic limb movements are present (Reite, Buysse, Reynolds, & Mendelson, 1995). The diagnosis of insomnia, particularly sleep-onset insomnia in younger patients, can be established fairly reliably through careful clinical evaluation complemented by daily sleep diaries. A clinician can always initiate treatment, and if the patient is unresponsive, a PSG evaluation can still be conducted to screen for another disorder that was missed during the clinical evaluation. A sleep study may have a higher yield of diagnostically useful information in older patients, especially those with a subjective complaint of sleep maintenance insomnia, because this segment of the population is at increased risk for several sleep pathologies (Edinger et al., 1989). Patients with circadian rhythm sleep disorders usually do not require PSG evaluation. These disorders can be reliably established by clinical history, sleep diary monitoring, and, possibly, with ambulatory monitoring of rest-activity cycles using a wrist-actigraphy device. PSG is usually not indicated for patients with most parasomnias such as sleepwalking, sleep terrors, or night-mares. Because these conditions rarely occur on a nightly basis, a single night of sleep monitoring is unlikely to capture the disorder. However, PSG may be warranted if other disorders (e.g., seizures) are suspected.

AGE, GENDER, AND RACIAL-ETHNIC ISSUES

Insomnia complaints are twice as common among women as among men, and such complaints increase across the life span. Persistent insomnia affects 9% to 15% of younger adults, but more than 25% of people age 65 or older (Gallup Organization, 1991; Mellinger et al., 1985). The nature of insomnia complaints also changes with aging. Sleep-onset insomnia is more common among younger people, whereas difficulties maintaining sleep, such as nocturnal or early morn-ing awakenings, are more prevalent in middle-aged and older people. Although women report more sleep difficulties, their sleep pattern is apparently better preserved with aging. Among noncomplaining older adults, men display more sleep pathologies than women (Reynolds et al., 1985). Breathing-related sleep disorders also increase with aging, but unlike insomnia, obstructive sleep apnea is much more prevalent in men than in women. After menopause, women may have a higher predisposition to central apnea. Some limited data suggest that in adults, nightmares are more common in females, whereas in children, sleep terrors are more frequent in boys (Kales, Kales, Soldatos, et al., 1980; Kales, Soldatos, Caldwell, et al., 1980). There are no data on age, gender, or cultural differences in circadian rhythm sleep disorders; however, older adults may have more difficulties adjusting to schedule changes. Aside from a suspected higher incidence of isolated sleep paralysis in African Americans, there is no evidence of racial or ethnic differences in any of the sleep disorders.

SUMMARY

Sleep disorders are extremely prevalent in the general population and even more so in patients with psychiatric and medical disorders. Consequences of sleep disorders are numerous, impairing daytime functioning, diminishing quality of life, and even posing significant health and public safety hazards. Increasing evidence suggests that sleep disturbances may increase vulnerability to psychiat-ric disorders and, perhaps, prevent or delay recovery (see Billard, Partinen, Roth, & Shapiro, 1994; Morin & Ware, 1996). Unless a systematic inquiry about sleep-wake complaints is integrated in a clinical evaluation, many of those disor-ders can go unrecognized and remain untreated. A detailed sleep history is often sufficient to make a preliminary diagnosis. When a more medically based sleep disorder (e.g., sleep apnea or narcolepsy) is suspected, referral to a sleep disorders center is essential to confirm the diagnosis and initiate appropriate treatment. Mental health practitioners are more likely to encounter patients with a primary sleep disorder such as insomnia or sleep complaints co-occurring with psychopathology. An accurate differential diagnosis has important implications for treatment planning. When sleep disturbance is a core symptom of underlying psychopathology, treatment should focus on the basic psychopathology. If on the other hand, the sleep disorder is primary in nature, treatment should be primarily sleep focused. At times, sleep and psychological symptomatology coexist without clear evidence of a specific cause-effect relationship. In such a case, multifocused interventions targeting both symptom clusters may be required to optimize treatment outcome.

REFERENCES

Adamson, J., & Burdick, J. A. (1973). Sleep of dry alcoholics. *Archives of General Psychiatry, 28,* 146–149.

American Psychiatric Association. (1994). *Diagnostic and statistical manual of mental disorders* (4th ed.). Washington, DC: Author.

American Sleep Disorders Association. (1990). *International classification of sleep disorders (ICSD).* Diagnostic and Classification Steering Committee, M. J. Thorpy (Chairman). Rochester, MN: Author.

Billard, M., Partinen, M., Roth, T., & Shapiro, C. (1994). Sleep and psychiatric disorders. *Journal of Psychosomatic Research, 38* (Suppl. 1), 1–2.

Bliwise, D. L. (1993). Sleep in normal aging and dementia. *Sleep, 16,* 40–81.

Buysse, D. J., Reynolds, C. F., Kupfer, D. J., Thorpy, M. J., Bixler, E., Manfredi, R., Kales, A., Vgontzas, A., Stepanski, E., Roth, T., Hauri, P., & Mesiano, D. (1994). Clinical diagnoses in 216 insomnia patients using the International Classification of Sleep Disorders (ICSD), DSM-IV, and ICD-10 categories: A report from the APA/NIMH DSM-IV field trial. *Sleep, 17,* 630–637.

Buysse, D. J., Reynolds, C. F., Monk, T. H., Berman, S. R., & Kupfer, D. J. (1989). The Pittsburgh Sleep Quality Index: A new instrument for psychiatric practice and research. *Psychiatry Research, 28,* 193–213.

Coates, T. J., Killen, J. D., George, J., Marchine, E., Silverman, S., & Thoresen, C. (1982). Estimating sleep parameters: A multitrait multimethod analysis. *Journal of Consulting and Clinical Psychology, 50,* 345–352.

Coleman, R. M., Roffwarg, H. P., Kennedy, S. J., Guilleminault, C., Cinque, J., Cohn, M. A., Karacan, I., Kupfer, D. J., Lemmi, H., Miles, L. E., Orr, W. C., Phillips, E. R., Roth, T., Sassin, J. F., Schmidt, H. S., Weitzman, E. D., & Dement, W. C. (1982). Sleep-wake disorders based on a polysomnographic diagnosis. A national cooperative study. *Journal of the American Medical Association, 247,* 997–1003.

Coren, S. (1988). Prediction of insomnia from arousability predisposition scores: Scale development and cross-validation. *Behaviour Research and Therapy, 26,* 415–420.

Coyle, K., & Watts, F. N. (1991). The factorial structure of sleep dissatisfaction. *Behaviour Research and Therapy, 29,* 513–520.

Derogatis, L. R., & Melisaratos, N. (1983). The Brief Symptom Inventory: An introductory report. *Psychological Medicine, 13,* 595–605.

Edinger, J. D., & Erwin, C. W. (1992). Common sleep disorders: Overview of diagnosis and treatment. *Clinician Reviews, 60–88.*

Edinger, J. D., Hoelscher, T. J., Webb, M. D., Marsh, G. R., Radtke, R. A., & Erwin, C. W. (1989). Polysomnographic assessment of DIMS: Empirical evaluation of its diagnostic value. *Sleep, 12,* 315–322.

Edinger, J. D., Stout, A. L., & Hoelscher, T. J. (1988). Cluster analysis of insomniacs' MMPI profiles: Relation of subtypes to sleep history and treatment outcome. *Psychosomatic Medicine, 50,* 77–87.

Ford, D. E., & Kamerow, D. B. (1989). Epidemiologic study of sleep disturbances and psychiatric disorders: An opportunity for prevention? *Journal of the American Medical Association, 262,* 1479–1484.

Gallup Organization. (1991). *Sleep in America.* Princeton, NJ: Author.

Gastaut, H., & Broughton, R. J. (1965). A clinical and polygraphic study of episodic phenomena during sleep. *Biological Psychiatry, 7,* 197–221.

Gillin, J. C. (1994). Sleep and psychoactive drugs of abuse and dependence. In M. H. Kryger, T. Roth, & W. C. Dement (Eds.), *Principles and practice of sleep medicine* (2nd ed., pp. 934–942). Philadelphia: Saunders.

Guilleminault, C. (1989). Clinical features and evaluation of obstructive sleep apnea. In M. H. Kryger, T. Roth, & W. C. Dement (Eds.), *Principles and practice of sleep medicine* (pp. 552–558). Philadelphia: Saunders.

Guilleminault, C. (1994). Narcolepsy syndrome. In M. H. Kryger, T. Roth, & W. C. Dement (Eds.), *Principles and practice of sleep medicine* (2nd ed., pp. 549–561). Philadelphia: Saunders.

Hartman, E. (1994). Nightmares and other dreams. In M. H. Kryger, T. Roth, & W. C. Dement (Eds.), *Principles and practice of sleep medicine* (2nd ed., pp. 407–410). Philadelphia: Saunders.

Hauri, P. J., Chernik, D., Hawkins, D., & Mendels, J. (1974). Sleep of depressed patients in remission. *Archives of General Psychiatry, 31,* 386–391.

Hauri, P. J., & Fisher, J. (1986). Persistent psychophysiological (learned) insomnia. *Sleep, 9,* 38–53.

Hauri, P. J., Friedman, M., & Ravaris, C. L. (1989). Sleep in patients with nocturnal panic attacks. *Sleep, 12,* 323–337.

Hauri, P. J., & Olmstead, E. M. (1980). Childhood-onset insomnia. *Sleep, 3,* 59–65.

Healy, E. S., Kales, A., Monroe, L. J., Bixler, E. O., Chamberlin, K., & Soldatos, C. R. (1981). Onset of insomnia: Role of life-stress events. *Psychosomatic Medicine, 43,* 439–451.

Heath, A. C., Kendler, K. S., Eaves, L. J., & Martin, N. G. (1990). Evidence for genetic influences on sleep disturbance and sleep pattern in twins. *Sleep, 13,* 318–335.

Hoddes, E., Zarcone, V., Smythe, H., Phillips, R., & Dement, W. C. (1973). Quantification of sleepiness: A new approach. *Psychophysiology, 10,* 431–436.

Hohagen, F., Kappler, C., Schramm, E., Riemann, D., Weyerer, S., & Berger, M. (1994). Sleep onset insomnia, sleep maintaining insomnia and insomnia with early morning awakening: Temporal stability of subtypes in a longitudinal study on general practice attenders. *Sleep, 17,* 551–554.

Jacobs, E. A., Reynolds, C. F., Kupfer, D. J., Lovin, P. A., & Ehrenpreis, A. B. (1988). The role of polysomnography in the differential diagnosis of chronic insomnia. *American Journal of Psychiatry, 145,* 346–349.

Johns, M. W. (1991). A new method for measuring daytime sleepiness: The Epworth Sleepiness Scale. *Sleep, 14,* 540–545.

Kales, A., & Kales, J. D. (1984). *Evaluation and treatment of insomnia.* New York: Oxford University Press.

Kales, J. D., Kales, A., Soldatos, C. R., Caldwell, A. B., Charney, D. S., & Martin E. D. (1980). Night terrors: Clinical characteristics and personality patterns. *Archives of General Psychiatry, 37,* 1413–1417.

Kales, A., Soldatos, C. R., Bixler, E. O., Ladda, R. L., Charney, D. S., Weber, G., & Schweitzer, P. K. (1980). Hereditary factors in sleepwalking and night terrors. *British Journal of Psychiatry, 137,* 111–118.

Kales, A., Soldatos, C. R., Caldwell, A. B., Charney, D. S., Kales, J. D., Markel, D., & Cadieux, R. (1980). Nightmares: Clinical characteristics and personality patterns. *American Journal of Psychiatry, 137,* 1197–1201.

Kales, A., Soldatos, C. R., Caldwell, A. B., Kales, J. D., Humphrey, F. J., Charney, D. S., & Schweitzer, P. K. (1980). Somnambulism: Clinical characteristics and personality patterns. *Archives of General Psychiatry, 37,* 1406–1410.

Karacan, I., & Howell, J. W. (1988). Narcolepsy. In R. L. Williams, I. Karacan, & C. A. Moore (Eds.), *Sleep disorders: Diagnosis and treatment* (pp. 87–108). New York: Wiley.

Kazarian, S. S., Howe, M. G., & Csapo, K. G. (1979). Development of the sleep behavior self-rating scale. *Behavior Therapy, 10,* 412–417.

Klink, M. E., Quan, S. F., Kaltenborn, W. T., & Lebowitz, M. D. (1992). Risk factors associated with complaints of insomnia in a general adult population: Influence of previous complaints of insomnia. *Archives of Internal Medicine, 152,* 1572–1575.

Lacks, P., & Morin, C. M. (1992). Recent advances in the assessment and treatment of insomnia. *Journal of Consulting and Clinical Psychology, 60,* 586–594.

Lacks, P., & Rotert, M. (1986). Knowledge and practice of sleep hygiene techniques in insomniacs and poor sleepers. *Behaviour Research and Therapy, 24,* 365–368.

Lugaresi, E., Zucconi, M., & Bixler, E. O. (1987) Epidemiology of sleep disorders. *Psychiatric Annals, 17,* 446–453.

Mellinger, G. D., Balter, M. B., & Uhlenhuth, E. H. (1985). Insomnia and its treatment. *Archives of General Psychiatry, 42,* 225–232.

Mitler, M. M., Carskadon, M. A., Czeisler, C. A., Dement, W. C., Dinges, D. F., & Graeber, R. C. (1988). Catastrophes, sleep, and public policy: Consensus report. *Sleep, 11,* 100–109.

Morin, C. M. (1993). *Insomnia: Psychological assessment and management.* New York: Guilford.

Morin, C. M. (1994). Dysfunctional beliefs and attitudes about sleep: Preliminary scale development and description. *Behavior Therapist, 17,* 163–164.

Morin, C. M., & Ware, C. (1996). Sleep and psychopathology. *Applied and Preventive Psychology, 5,* 211–224.

National Commission on Sleep Disorders Research. (1993). *Wake up America: A national sleep alert.* Washington, DC: Author.

Nicassio, P. M., Mendlowitz, D. R., Fussell, J. J., & Petras, L. (1985). The phenomenology of the presleep state: The development of the presleep arousal scale. *Behaviour Research and Therapy, 23,* 263–271.

Nofzinger, E. A., Buysse, D. J., Reynolds, C. F., & Kupfer, D. J. (1993). Sleep disorders related to another mental disorder (Nonsubstance/Primary): A DSM-IV literature review. *Journal of Clinical Psychiatry, 54,* 244–255.

Parks, J. D. (1985). *Sleep and its disorders.* London: Saunders.

Parson, M. (1986). Fits and other causes of loss of consciousness while driving. *Quarterly Journal of Medicine, 58,* 295–303.

Regestein, Q. R. (1989). Pathologic sleepiness induced by caffeine. *American Journal of Medicine, 87,* 586–588.

Reite, M., Buysse, D., Reynolds, C., & Mendelson, W. (1995). The use of polysomnography in the evaluation of insomnia. *Sleep, 18,* 58–70.

Reynolds, C. F., & Kupfer, D. J. (1987). Sleep research in affective illness: State of the art circa 1987. *Sleep, 10,* 199–215.

Reynolds, C. F., Kupfer, D. J., Taska, L. S., Hoch, C. C., Sewitch, D. W., & Spiker, D. G. (1985). The sleep of healthy seniors: A revisit. *Sleep, 8,* 20–29.

Reynolds, C. F., Shaw, D. M., Newton, T. F., Coble, P. A., & Kupfer, D. J. (1983). EEG sleep in outpatients with generalized anxiety: A preliminary comparison with depressed outpatients. *Psychiatric Research, 8,* 81–89.

Ross, R. J., Ball, W. A., Sullivan, K. A., & Caroff, S. N. (1989). Sleep disturbance as the hallmark of posttraumatic stress disorder. *American Journal of Psychiatry, 146,* 697–707.

Rush, A. J., Erman, M. K., Giles, D. E., Schlesser, M. A., Carpenter, G., Vasavada, N., & Roffwarg, H. P. (1986). Polysomnographic findings in recently drug-free and clinically remitted depressed patients. *Archives of General Psychiatry, 43,* 878–884.

Sadeh, A., Hauri, P., Kripke, D. F., & Lavie, P. (1995). The role of actigraphy in the evaluation of sleep disorders. *Sleep, 18,* 288–302.

Schramm, E., Hohagen, F., Grasshoff, U., Rieman, D., Hujak, G., Weeb, H.-G., & Berger, M. (1993). Test-retest reliability and validity of the structured interview for sleep disorders according to DSM-III-R. *American Journal of Psychiatry, 150,* 867–872.

Schuckit, M. A., & Irwin, M. (1988) Diagnosis of alcoholism. *Medical Clinics of North America, 72,* 1133–1153.

Setia, M., Doghramji, K., Hauri, P., & Morin, C. (1996). *Evaluation of insomnia.* Manuscript under editorial review.

Spielman, A. J. (1986). Assessment of insomnia. *Clinical Psychology Review, 6,* 11–25.

Tan, T., Kales, J. D., Kales, A., Soldatos, C. R., & Bixler, E. O. (1984). Biopsychobehavioral correlates of insomnia: IV. Diagnoses based on DSM-III. *American Journal of Psychiatry, 141,* 356–362.

Vollrath, M., Wicki, W., & Angst, J. (1989). The Zurich study: VIII. Insomnia: Association with depression, anxiety, somatic syndromes, and course of insomnia. *European Archives of Psychiatry and Neurological Sciences, 239,* 113–124.

Walsh, J. K., Moss, K. L., & Sugerman, J. (1994). Insomnia in adult psychiatric disorders. In M. H. Kryger, T. Roth, & W. C. Dement (Eds.), *Principles and practice of sleep medicine* (2nd ed., pp. 500–508). Philadelphia: Saunders.

Weitzman, E. D., Czeisler, C. A., Coleman, R. M., Spielman, A. J., Zimmerman, J. C., Dement, W. C., Richardson, G. S., & Pollack, C. P. (1981). Delayed sleep phase syndrome: A chronological disorder with sleep onset insomnia. *Archives of General Psychiatry, 38,* 737–746.

Wood, J. M., & Bootzin, R. R. (1990). The prevalence of nightmares and their independence from anxiety. *Journal of Abnormal Psychology, 99,* 64–68.

Wooten, V. (1994). Medical causes of insomnia. In M. H. Kryger, T. Roth, & W. C. Dement (Eds.), *Principles and practice of sleep medicine* (2nd ed., pp. 509–522). Philadelphia: Saunders.

CHAPTER 16

Personality Disorders

W. L. MARSHALL and R. SERIN

The primary criteria identified in DSM-IV (*Diagnostic and Statistical Manual of Mental Disorders;* American Psychiatric Association [APA], 1994) for diagnosing personality disorders include "an enduring pattern of inner experience and behavior that deviates markedly from the expectations of an individual's culture, [that] is pervasive and inflexible, has an onset in adolescence or early adulthood, is stable over time, and leads to distress or impairment" (p. 629). It is important to note, however, that many, if not most, individuals deemed to have a personality disorder are not themselves distressed by the disorder, although their lives may be objectively determined to be impaired. For many of these people, their personality functioning is egosyntonic, and this, of course, presents a problem in securing their cooperation in treatment. Research, for example, has revealed that 80% or more of people with personality disorder never seek treatment for their problems (Drake & Vaillant, 1985).

As we will see, there are reasons for concern about possible cultural and gender biases in diagnostic practices. However, these are simply aspects of the larger problems concerning the reliability and validity of personality disorder diagnoses, problems that have beset these disorders since they were first included in the diagnostic manual. Indeed, the defining criteria introduced with DSM-III (APA, 1980), and subsequently modified in DSM-III-R (APA, 1987) and DSM-IV (APA, 1994), were meant to reduce diagnostic unreliability, but there is little evidence to suggest that they have been successful. The early field trials with DSM-III (APA, 1980) revealed rather poor reliability for the personality disorders (overall kappa of .56), and subsequent examinations have not encouraged optimism concerning the reliability of these diagnoses (Dahl, 1986). However, either expanding the breadth of information collected (Zimmerman, Pfohl, Stangl, & Corenthal, 1986) or using structured interviews (Loranger, Oldham, Russakoff, & Susman, 1987) appears to increase reliability.

Other than the considerable, and as yet unresolved, problem of the poor reliability of most of the personality disorders, the issue of diagnostic overlap or comorbidity appears to be central to these conditions. The heterogeneity of symptoms displayed by patients diagnosed as having each particular type of personality disorder encouraged the authors of recent versions of the diagnostic manual to permit the use of multiple diagnoses. This strategy was meant to avoid the problem presented by previous editions of the diagnostic manual that forced the clinician to decide which diagnosis was primary and to exclude all others. However, this solution, although it has many benefits, does cause confusion for researchers in particular, who need to identify subjects whose diagnosis is clear. Furthermore, the heterogeneity of symptoms manifest by persons having personality disorders means that the boundary between disorders is vague and certain to confuse diagnosticians. Indeed, the problem of diagnostic overlap, and the related issue of comorbidity, presents a serious obstacle to adequate research on these disorders. For example, Morey (1988) found that eight of the personality disorders diagnosed according to DSM-III-R overlapped with other diagnoses by 50% and this represented a marked increase in overlap from DSM-III. Two-thirds of patients who receive one diagnosis of personality disorder will meet criteria for at least one other personality disorder (Clarkin, Widiger, Frances, Hurt, & Gilmore, 1983). Obviously, this overlap will cause problems for researchers and will no doubt confuse clinicians.

It has been suggested (Livesley, 1989; Livesley, Schroeder, Jackson, & Jang, 1994; Widiger & Costa, 1994) that the solution to many of these problems would be to adopt a dimensional rather than categorical system of classification. Some authors (Livesley, Jackson, & Schroeder, 1992; Millon, 1983) have suggested that 10 or more dimensions may be necessary to classify patients with personality disorders. If true, this would present practical difficulties for diagnosticians because that many dimensions would involve considerably more complexity of interpretation than would the simpler categorical systems. However, at least two research projects have suggested that as few as three or at most five dimensions are sufficient to identify all features of the diverse personality disorders (Widiger & Trull, 1992; Widiger, Trull, Hurt, Clarkin, & Frances, 1987; Wiggins & Pincus, 1989). Although a dimensional system was considered for both DSM-III-R and DSM-IV, agreement among committee members was not achieved (Widiger, Frances, Spitzer, & Williams, 1988), so the manual retained the categorical approach.

DSM-IV identifies 10 distinct personality disorders (and one nonspecific category), which are grouped into three clusters: A. odd and eccentric disorders (paranoid, schizoid, and schizotypal); B. dramatic, emotional, or erratic disorders (antisocial, borderline, histrionic, and narcissistic); and C. anxious and fearful disorders (avoidant, dependent, and obsessive-compulsive). While two of these clusters (A and C) appear to have sufficient features in common for the clusters to make sense, cluster B is a rather confusing grouping (Widiger & Costa, 1994). In fact, there is little in the way of evidence to support the identity of any of these clusters (Frances, 1985), and there seems to be no clinical utility to them.

PREVALENCE

Studies of the prevalence of personality disorders have examined rates among inpatient samples, outpatients, and in the community at large. Depending on the sample chosen, prevalence rates vary quite considerably. Data in Table 16.1 describe the results of a community study conducted in the United States. Similar studies in Europe reveal different rates with the lifetime prevalence for most disorders being somewhat lower than that observed in the United States (Maier,

TABLE 16.1   Lifetime Prevalence

Disorder	Percentage
Cluster A	
Paranoid	0.4
Schizoid	0.7
Schizotypal	3.0
Cluster B	
Antisocial	3.0
Borderline	1.7
Histrionic	3.0
Narcissistic	0.0
Cluster C	
Avoidant	1.3
Dependent	1.7
Obsessive-compulsive	1.7

Note. Adapted from Zimmerman & Coryell (1990).

Lichtermann, Klingler, Heun, & Hallmayer, 1992). Comparisons of these and other findings suggest that approximately 6% to 9% of the population will have one or more personality disorders during their lives (Merikangas & Weissman, 1986).

Widiger and his colleagues (Widiger & Frances, 1989; Widiger & Rogers, 1989) reviewed prevalence studies and found that, generally speaking, the rates were higher among inpatient psychiatric patients than among outpatients. For example, borderline personality disorder, which was the most commonly diagnosed personality disorder among patients in treatment, was reported in 11% of outpatients and 19% of inpatients (Widiger & Frances, 1989). Similarly, outpatient prevalence figures for schizotypal personality disorder range between 10% and 15% (Bornstein, Klein, Malon, & Slater, 1988), while among inpatients the rates vary between 20% and 30% (Widiger & Rogers, 1989). For antisocial personality disorder the rates differ depending on whether psychiatric patients or prisoners are surveyed. In psychiatric outpatients the prevalence rates for antisocial personality disorder are near 5%, in psychiatric inpatients the rates are 12% to 37%, while in prison populations the rates range from 30% to 70% (Widiger & Rogers, 1989). The quite variable rates for prisoners reflect differences in the diagnostic criteria used and apparently in the particular population of prisoners that were sampled.

COMORBIDITY AND DIAGNOSTIC OVERLAP

These two terms "comorbidity" and "overlap" are often used as synonyms in the literature when, in fact, they refer to two conceptually distinct features of diagnosis. Comorbidity should be used to describe the co-occurrence in the same person(s) of two or more diagnostically distinct disorders. Overlap, on the other hand, refers to the similarity of symptoms in two or more different disorders (i.e., the disorders overlap for diagnostic criteria). Insofar as the diagnostic criteria for different disorders are distinct, overlap should not occur. However, criteria for the personality disorders remain sufficiently vague, or require significant inferential skill by the diagnostician, that overlap seems certain to occur.

Comorbidity of personality disorders and Axis I disorders and overlap between the various personality disorders remain issues of concern despite the sensible attempts by the authors of DSM-III-R and DSM-IV to resolve the problem by encouraging the use of multiple diagnoses. While the DSM solution has advantages for clinical practice, it causes problems for researchers in identifying homogenous samples, and it has produced debate regarding the true nature of the various disorders.

In particular, borderline personality disorder has been the focus of considerable debate. Patients diagnosed as borderline have been commonly found to have schizotypal features (Davis & Akiskal, 1986; George & Soloff, 1986), and considerable overlap has been observed between borderline diagnosis and other personality disorders (Clarkin et al., 1983; Pfohl, Coryell, Zimmerman, & Stangl, 1986). For example, it was observed in one study (Widiger, Frances, & Trull, 1987) that 47% of borderlines met the criteria for antisocial personality disorder and 57% met the criteria for histrionic disorder. Most problematic, and the source of considerable debate, is the observed comorbidity between borderline personality disorder and affective disorders (Andrulonis & Vogel, 1984; Gunderson & Elliott, 1985; McManus, Lerner, Robbins, & Barbour, 1984; Perry, 1985). Nakdimen (1986) interpreted these observations to mean that borderline disorder should be classified as a subtype of affective disorder.

Also, avoidant disorder patients manifest symptoms (e.g., social inadequacy and hypersensitivity to negative evaluations) that are remarkably similar to those that identify social phobia (an Axis I disorder). Reich, Noyes, and Troughton (1987), for example, found that phobic patients were far more likely than nonphobics to meet the criteria for a cluster C personality disorder, and Turner, Beidel, Dancu, and Keys (1986) reported that social phobics and avoidant patients displayed the same physiological reactivity, and the content of their cognitions was similar. In fact, both DSM-III-R and DSM-IV explicitly note the overlap in these two disorders but suggest that the solution is to apply both diagnoses. This suggestion will not help researchers, and no differential treatment approaches are described by the authors of the diagnostic manuals.

GENDER AND CULTURAL ISSUES

The diagnostic manual insists that clinicians determine, in the case of recent immigrants or members of minority groups, that the client's functioning, while differing from the expectations of his or her current or broader society, is not reflective of appropriate responding in the client's society of origin or minority group. Recent immigrants, or members of minority cultures, may be susceptible to misdiagnosis unless the diagnostician makes the effort to determine which attitudes and behaviors are appropriate for a person from a distinct culture. The same is true of gender biases in the diagnosis of personality disorders. As Pantony and Caplan (1991) and Widiger and Spitzer (1991) noted, the influence of sex-role stereotypes on diagnostician's determination of presence or absence of personality disorders has not been clearly determined but is evidently present.

For example, clinicians have been shown to be reluctant to diagnose males as having histrionic personality disorder and loath to consider females as having antisocial personality disorder (Widiger & Spitzer, 1991).

Prevalence studies also have found that personality disorders occur more frequently in urban populations than in rural residents and that they are differentially distributed according to gender (Merikangas & Weissman, 1986). Schizoid and schizotypal disorders are more frequently diagnosed in males, as is antisocial personality disorder, whereas histrionic and borderline disorders are identified more commonly in women. All the disorders in cluster C (primarily anxieties and fearful symptoms) are diagnosed most frequently in women. However, some authors have suggested that these apparent differential rates for males and females are the product of sex-role stereotype biases reflected in both the diagnostic criteria and their application (Brown, 1992). In the case of histrionic personality disorder, diagnoses among patients reveal significantly higher prevalence rates for women, whereas an epidemiological survey of over 3,000 community adults revealed approximately the same prevalence (2.2%) in males and females (Nestadt et al., 1990).

Sensitivity to cultural norms and differences in the expression of the features of antisocial personality disorder is particularly important. Also, the emphasis on aggressivity in the prerequisite diagnosis of conduct disorder may yield underdiagnosis in females because of gender differences in the prevalence and expression of aggression.

With respect to diagnosis of psychopathy using the PCL-R with male offenders, there appear to be differences between African Americans and Caucasians, with African Americans scoring significantly higher. Whether this reflects true differences between these two groups or whether it more likely results from differences in social circumstances and opportunities remains to be seen. Economically disadvantaged African Americans living in inner cities can be expected to learn as children self-interested strategies in order to survive, and these strategies may, in the eyes of a privileged clinician, appear to reveal a psychopathic character. There are also PCL-R norms for female offenders (Loucks, 1995; Neary, 1990) that reveal lower rates in females than males.

Together, these studies suggest that, at a minimum, there are cultural and gender differences in the ways psychopathy is expressed (Hare, 1991) and perhaps in the ways certain features may be recorded as evidence for or against psychopathic traits in an examinee.

Henry and Cohen (1983) suggested that clinicians typically overdiagnosed borderline personality disorder in women. Widiger and Trull (1993) responded to this contention by pointing to the results of 75 prevalence studies estimating the percentage of women diagnosed as borderline. They compared studies that used semistructured interviews to those that used unstructured interviews. If gender biases were operating, Widiger and Trull argued, we should expect higher prevalence rates in unstructured studies since these would have allowed for greater personal biases on the part of diagnosticians than would structured approaches. That is exactly the opposite of what Widiger and Trull observed in their review, although it must be said that prevalence differences derived by the two approaches, even though statistically significant, were not remarkable: an average of 80% of the subjects identified as borderline by structured interview were women, with a figure of 73% using the unstructured method. In both cases, the figures reveal that a high proportion of persons diagnosed as borderline were women. While Widiger and Trull's observations may reduce concerns about the application of diagnostic criteria, they do not address the more basic concern that gender biases may have led to the identification of diagnostic criteria that are more likely to identify women as disordered.

In an early review of what was then called "hysterical" personality (now identified as histronic personality disorder), Chodoff and Lyons (1958) wrote that, given the history of the concept of "hysteria," it was inevitable that gender biases in diagnosis would emerge. They suggested that even the traits said to characterize the disorder are no more than features of the traditional female stereotype. Since the descriptions were made predominantly, if not entirely, by male psychiatrists, the responses they elicited from interviews, so Chodoff and Lyons suggested, "might not have been obtained by a woman examiner" (p. 738). Furthermore, the description that emerged of hysterical personality, so Chodoff and Lyons claimed, was "a picture of women in the words of men" that "amounts to a caricature of femininity!" (p. 738). Changing the name of the disorder to "histrionic" rather than "hysterical" in DSM-III was meant, at least in part, to diminish these biases, but the impact does not seem to have been profound. Histrionic personality disorder is still diagnosed much more commonly in females than in males (Kass, Spitzer, & Williams, 1983; Reich, 1987), and studies that ask subjects to rate the diagnostic criteria indicate that most people view the features of the disorder as decidedly feminine (Sprock, Blashfield, & Smith, 1990).

In an interesting examination of gender bias, Warner (1978) had 175 mental health professionals make a diagnosis after reading a case history. The patient was described as a woman in half the cases and as a male in the other half, but the case description remained the same. Of those clinicians who were given the "female" case, 76% diagnosed the patient as suffering from a hysterical personality disorder, while only 49% applied that diagnosis when the patient was described as a man. Ford and Widiger (1989) also examined these issues, but looked at gender bias both in the diagnostic criteria and in the application of the overall diagnosis of histrionic personality disorder. They found no influence of gender of the patient for the individual criteria, but a noticeable influence of gender in the assignment of the diagnosis. These problems of gender bias do not appear to have disappeared with the subsequent revisions of the diagnostic manual.

Kaplan (1983) claimed that diagnostic criteria for dependent personality disorder represented no more than the male concept of females as submissive, passive, and inadequate. Therefore, the diagnosis, Kaplan suggested, would simply identify women who had adopted an extreme version of the traditional patriarchal notion of femininity, or men who had failed to live up to the social expectations of what constitutes a "real man."

Some subsequent studies did not, however, appear to support Kaplan's ideas. Reich (1987), for example, used both a structured interview and two self-report measures completed by patients and found that the rates for dependent personality disorder were the same for males and females. Morey and Ochoa (1989) had clinicians indicate both their diagnoses of the patients they were seeing and whether DSM-III-R diagnostic criteria were present in these patients. Overdiagnosis occurred when the clinician assigned a diagnosis but appropriate criteria were not present, and underdiagnosis occurred when criteria were present but the diagnosis was not applied. Gender of the patient did not predict either under- or overdiagnosis of dependent personality, contrary to what we might expect from Kaplan's (1983) view.

However, there are problems concerning the relevance of these studies to Kaplan's position, not the least of which is the artificial circumstances under which the diagnoses were applied, and it seems likely that any tendency to be either biased or diagnostically sloppy would be reduced under these conditions of scrutiny. A more relevant study (Sprock et al., 1990) had undergraduates place DSM-III-R personality disorder diagnostic criteria on a dimension of masculinity-femininity. Criteria for dependent disorder received the highest femininity ratings of any of the personality disorders. Apparently, this issue has not been resolved to everyone's satisfaction, and more careful studies, perhaps removed from day-to-day diagnostic practices, are needed.

ETIOLOGY

Several authors have suggested that personality disorders have their origin in childhood due to a failure in attachment bonds with parents (see Marshall & Barbaree, 1991, for an elaboration of this view). Attachment bonds with parents provide the developing child with a template for later relationships (Bowlby, 1977). If attachments are poor then the child will typically develop adult relationship styles that are characterized by ambivalence, fear, or avoidance (Bartholomew, 1990). In addition, poor attachments will fail to instill in the child the self-confidence and social skills needed to develop appropriate intimacy (Marshall, 1989; Marshall, Hudson, & Hodkinson, 1993). Such disadvantaged individuals can be expected to adopt various maladaptive ways of dealing with interpersonal relations, and failure to function effectively in such relationships has been said to characterize the personality disorders (Marshall & Barbaree, 1984). In fact, in the study by Widiger, Trull, et al. (1987), two of the three dimensions that emerged from their analysis of personality disorder symptoms were "social involvement" and "assertion/dominance." The fact that personality disorders are understood to typically emerge during late adolescence, when the demands for social interaction and interpersonal relationships become preeminent, strengthens these suggestions concerning the origins of personality disorders and the nature of the problems of these patients. Consistent with these claims, Goldberg, Mann, Wise, and Segall (1985) found that personality-disordered patients typically described their parents as either uncaring, overprotective, or both.

SPECIFIC DISORDERS

Two specific personality disorders have received the bulk of research attention over the past several years: antisocial personality disorder and borderline personality disorder. Accordingly, the primary focus of our discussion of the specific disorders will be on these two. We will provide far briefer descriptions of the remaining disorders.

Cluster A: Odd and Eccentric Disorders

Paranoid Personality Disorder

Pervasive suspiciousness regarding the motives of other people and a tendency to interpret what others say and do as personally meaningful in a negative way are the primary features of paranoid patients. Such patients consistently misread the actions of others as threatening or critical, and they expect other people to exploit them. Consequently, paranoid personalities tend to be hypervigilant and take extreme precautions against potential threats from others. They believe that other people intend to hurt them, and they are reluctant to share anything personal for fear it might be used against them. In addition, they are typically humorless and eccentric and are seen by others as hostile, preoccupied with power and control, and jealous. Not surprisingly, they have considerable problems in relationships, as most people cannot tolerate their need to control and particularly their destructive jealousy. Frequently, paranoid patients become socially isolated, and this seems only to add to their persecutory ideas.

These features, identified in both diagnostic criteria and in clinical reports, have been confirmed in research. For example, Turkat and his colleagues have found that, compared with normal subjects, paranoid personalities experienced far more paranoid thoughts both currently and during their school days (Turkat & Banks, 1987), had greater difficulty in dealing with ambiguity, were more suspicious (Thompson-Pope & Turkat, 1988), and were more likely to misread social cues as evidence of hostility by others (Turkat, Keene, & Thompson-Pope, 1990).

Kendler, Masterson, and Davis (1985) reported that paranoid personality occurs quite commonly in the relatives of schizophrenics, which suggests the possibility that paranoid personality might be a subtype of schizophrenia or that there is a genetic link between the two disorders. However, paranoid personality disorder overlaps more significantly with avoidant and borderline personality disorders than it does with schizophrenia (Morey, 1988).

In a large-scale study of prevalence and stability of personality disorder among adolescents in upstate New York communities, Bernstein et al. (1993) identified the presence of moderate or severe forms of the various disorders on two occasions separated by a 2-year interval. They found that paranoid disorder was one of the four most persistent types of personality disorder.

Schizoid Personality Disorder

Individuals with this condition seem determined to avoid intimate involvement with others, and they display little in the way of emotional responsiveness. These clients often indicate that they rarely experience intense emotions and may be puzzled by the enthusiasms of others. Schizoid clients are typically loners who are cold and indifferent toward others and display social indifference. In fact, they seem not to enjoy relationships of any type with others, apparently preferring to be alone. They enjoy solitary activities and do not seek or seem to desire sexual relations. There seems little doubt that most lack the skills necessary for effective social interaction, but they also appear uninterested in acquiring such skills.

Morey's (1988) examination of the impact on diagnostic practices of changes from DSM-III to DSM-III-R revealed that the frequency of schizoid diagnoses increased significantly (from 1.4% of patients to 11.0%). This apparently was due to a shift in the diagnosis from schizotypal to schizoid as a result of changes in diagnostic criteria. Unfortunately, this makes it difficult to compare research on schizoid personality that was conducted prior to and after the publication of DSM-III-R.

One of the main problems with this diagnostic category is that so little methodologically sound research has been done on the problem. As a consequence, we know little more about it than we did several years ago, and clinical speculations remain unfettered by data. Those studies that do appear in the literature frequently confound schizoid and schizotypal features and do not, therefore, permit any reasonable conclusions.

Schizotypal Personality Disorder

The major presenting feature of these patients is eccentricity of thought and behavior. Many schizotypal patients are extremely superstitious. Their ideation and behavior are peculiar, and these features tend to turn other people away so that schizotypal patients are typically socially isolated. No doubt this isolation from others increases the likelihood that they will have unusual thoughts and perceptions, since they have little opportunity to check the sense of their cognitions. Their thinking tends to be magical and full of odd beliefs and ideas of reference. They typically believe in paranormal phenomena such as telepathy and clairvoyance.

Although their beliefs, perceptual experiences, speech, and behaviors are quite odd and tend to isolate them from others, they are not considered to be so eccentric as to meet criteria for delusional or hallucinatory experiences. There is, however, considerable disagreement on this issue. For example, McGlashan (1987) claimed that transient psychoses characterize these patients, and Kendler (1985) concluded that schizotypal disorder is simply a subtle form of schizophrenia. Research examining biological features has found strong similarities between schizotypal patients and schizophrenics (Baron, Levitt, Gruen, Kane, & Asnis, 1984; Siever, 1985), and many family members of schizophrenics exhibit schizotypal symptoms (Kendler, 1985). Indeed, Widiger and Shea (1991) suggested that schizotypal disorder may be a prodromal or residual stage of schizophrenia. This obviously is an issue that deserves greater attention, although diagnostic overlap with borderline personality disorder is also considerable (Morey, 1988), and this also warrants further research. Finally, the long-term prognosis for schizotypal patients is poor.

Cluster B: Dramatic, Emotional, or Erratic Disorders

As we noted earlier, this cluster does not seem to have as much in common as is implied by grouping these four disorders. While histrionic and borderline disorders may be seen as dramatic, it is hard to see what this descriptor has to do with antisocial personality disorder (APD). Indeed, except for a limited range of emotional expression, none of the descriptors of cluster B seem to fit antisocial patients. In fact, it might be better to consider antisocial patients as belonging to a separate category of personality disorder.

Antisocial Personality Disorder

Development of DSM-IV criteria. The purpose of this section is to review the DSM-IV changes in diagnostic criteria for APD, providing a context for current assessment and treatment issues regarding this population. Distinct from other personality disorders, the essential feature of APD is a "pervasive pattern of disregard for, and violation of, the rights of others that begins in childhood or early adolescence and continues into adulthood" (APA, 1994). It is important to note that alternative diagnostic strategies such as Hare's Psychopathy Check-list–Revised (PCL-R; Hare, 1991) are gaining prominence in the forensic literature and will therefore be included in this review.

With respect to the revisions to DSM-IV, the goal of the Task Force was to simplify and shorten the DSM-III-R criteria for APD without sacrificing reliability of diagnosis. In reviewing DSM-III-R criteria, the DSM-IV Task Force considered correlation with overall criteria, complexity, prevalence, and interrater reliability. Widiger and Corbitt (1993) summarized arguments by various authors (Hare, Hart, & Harpur, 1991; Millon, 1981) for greater emphasis on personality traits and the need for a briefer, simpler criterion set. They also commented on the generally acceptable degree of inclusiveness and validity of the DSM-III-R criteria, although this has been disputed (Rogers, Duncan, Lynett, & Sewell, 1994).

The reliance on behavioral indices of the disorder since DSM-II has raised concerns regarding the relation of DSM criteria to clinical conceptions of a related construct, that of psychopathy (Hare et al., 1991; Wulach, 1983). The relatively few criteria reflecting affective and interpersonal processes (Millon, 1981) and recent prototypicality studies (Rogers et al., 1994) comparing DSM-IV and other measures of APD (PCL-R, ICD-10, dyssocial personality disorder) underscore this concern.

DSM-IV criteria for the diagnosis of APD present seven exemplars reflecting the violation of the rights of others, nonconformity, callousness, deceitfulness, irresponsibility, irritability, and recklessness. Three or more of these must be met. These criteria represent a reduced and simplified version of the DSM-III-R criterion set. Three items from the DSM-III-R criteria—parental irresponsibility, failure to sustain a monogamous relationship, and inconsistent work—were all dropped as they failed to meet acceptable levels of association with APD, prevalence, interrater reliability, or all of these (Widiger & Corbitt, 1993; Rogers et al., 1994). Widiger and Corbitt (1993) reached the important conclusion that DSM-IV diagnostic criteria had 98% concordance with the DSM-III-R diagnosis.

DSM-IV (APA, 1994) cautions clinicians to ensure that in the assessment of antisocial traits, the social and economic context be carefully considered. For instance, antecedents or motivation for antisocial behavior may be significantly different among individuals. Clinicians must therefore ensure that this behavior is not exclusively in response to trauma or part of a broader protective strategy (Herman, 1992).

A final concern expressed (Rogers et al., 1994) is the temporal instability of the diagnosis of APD. Because of the early onset and long course of the disorder, diagnostic inconsistency over time with DSM-III is disconcerting (Helzer, Spitznagel, & McEnvoy, 1987). It remains to be seen whether DSM-IV criteria reflect greater temporal stability.

Prevalence. DSM-IV reported prevalence rates for APD of approximately 3% in males and 1% in females, for community samples. These results are comparable to the National Comorbidity Survey (Kessler et al., 1994), which reported prevalence rates of 5.8% in males and 1.2% in females.

Incidence in forensic and correctional settings will understandably be higher, yet contemporary estimates are unavailable for DSM-IV. Estimates in Great Britain are that approximately 25%–33% of patients in special hospitals are psychopathic, which is quite high, presumably because those offenders considered treatable are diverted to these special hospitals while those considered untreatable are simply imprisoned (Chiswick, 1992). Hare (1983, 1985) reported higher estimates using DSM-III-R, where approximately 40% of Canadian prisoners would be diagnosed as APD. Similar data for a correctional sample were provided by Hart and Hare (1989), reflecting the relative overdiagnosis of DSM-III (50% incidence of APD) compared with an early version PCL (12.5% incidence of psychopathy). These rates are slightly lower than estimates provided by Côté and Hodgins (1990), who used yet another assessment strategy, the Diagnostic Interview Schedule (DIS; Robins, Helzer, Croughan, & Ratcliff, 1981). In a random sample of 495 male inmates in Quebec, 61.5% were diagnosed as APD using DIS criteria.

Description of the disorder. The description of a persistent pattern of antisocial behavior has a long clinical tradition (Pinel, 1809) that is clearly described by Cleckley (1976). Individuals thus identified have been referred to as psychopaths, sociopaths, or dyssocial personalities, with these terms sometimes being used interchangeably (Schlesinger, 1980). In correctional settings psychopathy and APD have been used interchangeably, albeit incorrectly, given research over the past decade. Some authors (Harding, 1992) have suggested that the reluctance to use the term psychopathic stems from its pejorative connotation. Psychopathy, however, is a resilient term and has enjoyed a relative resurgence in use in correctional and forensic settings, notably in North America, with the emergence of Hare's (1991) checklist. The PCL-R has been demonstrated to be a reliable and more specific construct than APD (Hare, 1983) and has greater predictive validity (Hare, 1991; Harris, Rice, & Quinsey, 1993). For example, psychopaths, as defined by the PCL-R, have a greater number and variety of criminal offenses than do nonpsychopaths (psychopaths and nonpsychopaths are defined as approximately the top and bottom 15% of the distribution of PCL-R scores; Kosson, Smith, & Newman, 1990). Use of the PCL-R in Britain (Raine, 1985) and Scotland (Cooke, 1994a, 1994b) yielded similar factor structures to North American studies (Hare et al., 1990) but noticeably lower mean scores.

The APD versus psychopathy debate has led to some confusion, possibly obscuring theoretical advances and improvements in the identification of treatment targets (Lilienfeld, 1994). Central to this issue is whether existing assessment strategies (DSM-IV), with fixed indicators of a trait, sufficiently reflect the *personality* domain of the disorder. Employing essentially behavioral criteria may increase diagnostic reliability but also yield a group of antisocial individuals who are markedly heterogeneous in terms of personality traits (Blackburn, 1992; Lilienfeld, 1994; Millon, 1981). At the same time, those patients whose personality structure is representative of the disorder, but whose behavior is not specifically antisocial, are excluded (Hare et al., 1991; Lilienfeld, 1994). Overinclusiveness refers to the overdiagnosis of individuals with a particular disorder because the criteria are too broad, particularly for specific settings, such as prisons. Underinclusiveness refers to the missed diagnosis of individuals who reflect the core personality traits, but lack the behavioral referents, for example, socialized psychopaths (Widom, 1978). Proponents of the PCL-R have argued that other diagnostic strategies possess both of these limitations (Hare et al., 1991; Lilienfeld, 1994).

Consistent with factor-analytic studies of the PCL-R, it has been proposed that two factors, personality traits and lifestyle instability, should be *necessary* and *sufficient* for a diagnosis of APD (Hare et al., 1991; Rogers et al., 1994). Such an approach may address concerns regarding the over- and underinclusiveness of existing criteria (Lilienfeld, 1994) and might eventually yield a more dimensional model of APD (Rogers et al., 1994). Meloy (1995) attempted to address this difficulty by describing psychopathic versus nonpsychopathic APD. This distinction may be helpful for correctional and forensic applications but may confuse rather than illuminate all but the highly informed clinician. This proposal, however, highlights the present conundrum for clinicians in these settings—that is, using existing diagnostic nosology (APD), which is overinclusive in their setting and has limited predictive or prognostic utility, versus adopting the highly reliable PCL-R with its wealth of empirical literature in the area of risk assessment (Harris, Rice, & Quinsey, 1993; Hart, Kropp, & Hare, 1988; Serin & Amos, 1995; Steadman et al., 1993; Webster, Eaves, Douglas, & Wintrup, 1995). Specific guidelines for the forensic use of the PCL-R are also now available to inform those who choose to use it clinically (Gacono & Hutton, 1994; Hare, 1991).

Clinical picture. Notwithstanding this debate over the most preferred assessment strategy, there is consensus regarding the clinical picture presented by those broadly diagnosed as APD. APD individuals have been described as failing to comply with societal norms and repeatedly performing acts that are grounds for arrest; disregarding the wishes, rights, and feelings of others; being frequently deceitful and manipulative in order to gain personally; displaying a pattern of impulsivity through a failure to plan ahead or acting without due regard to the consequences; irritable and aggressive for nondefensive situations; reckless; irresponsible in various aspects of their lives; displaying little remorse for their behavior; and indifferent and quick to rationalize. It is important that callousness, contempt for others, and inflated self-appraisals are also indisputable characteristics of this group, but they are not specifically reflected in DSM-IV criteria. Such descriptors, however, are central to, or prototypical of, clinicians' formulations of APD (Rogers et al., 1994) and are represented in ICD-10 criteria for dyssocial personality.

Course and prognosis. Robins and Regier (1991) reported the average duration of APD (DSM-III) to be 19 years, from first to last symptom. This remittance over time of symptoms has been described as the "burn-out" factor, with expectations of symptom alleviation by the fourth decade of life. Harpur and Hare (1994) presented cross-sectional data suggesting that personality style, as reflected by Factor 1 of the PCL-R, does not appreciably diminish with age. Accordingly, a diagnosis of psychopathy may be less "age dependent" than APD (Harpur & Hare, 1994). These data are consistent with views that psychopathy is a taxon (Harris, Rice, & Quinsey, 1994). Further, various case studies exist that refute the burn-out hypothesis, at least for persistent offenders.

While onset of antisocial behavior as an adolescent is requisite, much is to be gained from an appreciation of the developmental literature, particularly on conduct disorder. This should not be surprising, since some of these youths become APD adults. Moffitt (1993) provided a model for understanding developmental antecedents of adult psychopathology and developmental trajectories of antisocial behavior. The pattern and pervasiveness of antisocial behavior by the individuals she described as "life-course persistent" are important markers for adult difficulties in a broad range of societal and relationship interactions. Kazdin (1987, 1993) presented a *contextual* evaluation of treatment considerations for conduct-disordered youth, with emphasis on problem-solving skills training *and* parent management training. He described impediments to treatment compliance and the need for prescriptive intervention that is broad based and multifaceted. Failure to attend to this literature will greatly limit the utility of assessment and treatment initiatives for adults. Kazdin's (1993) analogy of a chronic care model is important because it provides for shared responsibility of the disorder and its sequelae. Treatment, then, becomes management and symptom reduction, not cure. This view is consistent with recent suggestions in the adult literature (Joseph, 1992; Meloy, 1995; Quinsey & Walker, 1992).

Treatment considerations. Reviews of the empirical literature on treatment efficacy for APD patients, and for psychopaths in particular, have been unequivocally pessimistic (Suedfeld & Landon, 1978; Wong & Elek, 1990), leading to conclusions of therapeutic impotence (Harding, 1992). Many earlier studies, however, suffered from poor methodology. Further, programs delivered in previous decades did not reflect contemporary knowledge of effective treatment programs for resistant clients (Gendreau, in press; Miller & Rollnick, 1991). Unfortunately, however, recent treatment studies have been no more encouraging. Psychopaths tend to exploit unstructured programs, masking their resistance with verbal skills, and may in fact do poorer when provided inappropriate intervention (Rice, Harris, & Cormier, 1992). Attrition from treatment programs is also high (Ogloff, Wong, & Greenwood, 1990) and has proved to be of prognostic value (Marques, Day, Nelson, & West, 1994). Last, in substance abuse treatment, APD patients fare less well than non-APD patients (Alterman & Cacciola, 1991; Poldrugo & Forti, 1988).

Surprisingly, as Meloy (1995) noted, therapeutic hope has not vanished. Approximately two-thirds of psychiatrists think that psychopaths are sometimes treatable (Tennent, Tennent, Prins, & Bedford, 1993). Despite a poor response to hospitalization, prognosis is improved for APD patients if there is a treatable anxiety or depression (Gabbard & Coyne, 1987) or a demonstration of therapeutic alliance (Gerstley et al., 1989).

Treatment of other groups of resistant clients (Miller & Rollnick, 1991) suggests that the noncompliance of APD patients may be a responsivity factor. That is, treatment must be responsive or matched to a particular patient's needs and interpersonal style. Poor treatment performance may, in part, be influenced by an intervention that is of insufficient intensity (Gendreau, in press) or viewed by patients as irrelevant (Miller & Rollnick, 1991) or involuntary (Gabbard & Coyne, 1987). Several of these issues have been specifically considered in the context of provision of treatment (Templeman & Wollersheim, 1979), yet they remain untested hypotheses. Newman and Wallace (1993) provided an analogy between psychopathy and learning disability to emphasize how to make intervention more responsive for this group of patients. They extended this point by providing laboratory evidence in support of their hypothesis that psychopaths have specific information-processing deficits that must be considered in the delivery of treatment programs.

Perhaps because of the present state of theory regarding APD and psychopathy (Lilienfeld, 1994) and the recognized heterogeneity of APD patients (Blackburn, 1992), strategies to measure treatability and treatment gain are relatively unsophisticated (Serin, 1995). Overviews of relevant treatment needs and models for delivering such programs are presently available (Blackburn, 1993a; Rice, Harris, & Quinsey, 1996), but there is little evidence that these are prescriptively applied. Furthermore, programs vary according to the extent that personality and criminality are emphasized, and yet a "problems-based" approach may enhance compliance and efficacy (Nezu & Nezu, 1993; Rice et al., in press; Templeman & Wollersheim, 1978). Cognitive models of intervention predominate (Beck et al., 1990; Blackburn, 1993b), but there is still strong interest in alternative psychotherapeutic approaches (Gallwey, 1992) despite rather scant empirical support for their efficacy. A recent outcome study of a cognitively based treatment program, however, is encouraging (Robinson, 1995). Similar programs for juveniles have yielded good treatment gains, but with limited generalization of effects (Guerra & Slaby, 1990).

While treatment targets for forensic and correctional samples have obscured the distinction between criminality and antisocial personality, they typically include some combination of aggressive and antisocial attitudes and beliefs, impulsivity or poor self-regulation, social skills, anger, assertiveness, substance abuse, empathy, problem solving, and moral reasoning (Rice et al., 1996; Serin & Kuriychuk, 1994). For many of these targets there exist structured program materials; however, assessment technology to measure treatment gain remains relatively unsophisticated (Rice et al., 1996). Further, overreliance on self-report assessment methods is problematic for a population whose candor is suspect (Serin & Kuriychuk, 1994).

Another management strategy for antisocial or acting-out behavior, particularly in closed settings, has been pharmacotherapy. Short-term use of psychopharmacologic agents is most often used to manage difficult or threatening behavior (Rice, Harris, Varney, & Quinsey, 1989). However, problems of side effects of long-term drug use and noncompliance have been noted in forensic patients (Harris, 1989). While short-term use of antipsychotic, antianxiety, and sedative medications is not uncommon (Tupin, 1987), symptom alleviation is rarely sustained, and patients are typically provided no new skills to improve their ability to deal with future situations. For some patients, medication may reduce arousal level sufficiently for them to more fully participate in cognitive-behavioral treatment (Rice & Harris, 1993).

Familial, biological, and genetic considerations. The developmental literature (Moffitt, 1993), at the very least, confirms that familial and genetic risk factors are present in many disordered youth, contributing to present and future difficulties and various diagnoses. How these factors interact to increase the risk of subsequent diagnosis, however, is unclear (Moffitt, 1993). Nonetheless, the presence of neuropsychological damage or difficulties (e.g., emotional reactivity, temperament, impulse control, and cognitive abilities) and familial or environmental factors (e.g., criminogenic environments, neglect, or physical abuse, and poor parenting skills) are predispositional factors that contribute to increased risk. In combination, these markers appear to make children particularly vulnerable to psychopathology. Improved identification of behavioral or neuropsychological markers (White et al., 1994) and intervention strategies (Kazdin, 1993) are important in promotion of a preventative perspective for adult APD.

Previous reviews by Rutter et al. (1990) disputed genetic influences on juvenile delinquency and, hence, antisocial behavior. Raine (1993), however, noted there is stronger support when self-reported delinquency is considered versus legal definitions (Grove et al. 1990). For instance, he summarized twin study analyses, citing that 51.5% of MZ twins are concordant for crime compared to 20.6% for DZ twins, yet conceded that adoption studies also highlight the importance of environmental variables and their crucial interaction effect.

Summaries of biochemical influences on crime and antisocial behavior have been completed recently where antisocials are characterized by reduced central serotonin and norepinephrine, with no effect for dopamine (Schalling, 1993; Virkkunen & Linnoila, 1993). These conclusions are also supported by meta-analyses of 29 recent studies summarized by Raine (1993). He further noted that norepinephrine was only reduced in those antisocials who also displayed affective stability and alcoholism. Raine (1993) concluded that these biochemical findings support a behavioral disinhibition theory of antisocial behavior, yet there remains no singular pharmacologic intervention guided by such research (Bond, 1993).

Comorbidity of disorders. Meta-analytic reviews of studies comparing substance abuse disorder and APD have suggested a strong association (Schubert, Wolf, Patterson, Grande, & Pendelton, 1988). But Gerstley, Alterman, McLellan, & Woody (1990) cautioned that the lack of independence between substance use disorders and APD may lead to an overdiagnosis of APD in substance use patients. At issue is whether the antisocial behavior is independent of the need to obtain drugs (Research Diagnostic Criteria; Spitzer, Endicott, & Robbins,

1978). DSM-IV criteria for substance dependence and substance abuse are explicit regarding dependency and abuse, but this does not appear to preclude a diagnosis of APD if criteria are met because of patients' addictions. The suggestion by Gerstley et al. (1990) to use the PCL-R to focus on personality traits is similar to Meloy's (1995) proposal—that is, make certain accommodations for particular settings or comorbid disorders.

When APD and substance use are comorbid in a community sample, treatment response is poorer (Gerstley et al., 1990). In a related vein, postrelease performance is also poorer in those offenders released to the community with both disorders, using DIS criteria (Porporino & Motiuk, 1995). It is important to note that Porporino and Motiuk found that neither the presence of an Axis I diagnosis nor alcohol abuse alone affected recidivism. Alcohol plus APD was only marginally more indicative of recidivism than APD alone.

Millon (1996) presented an overview of the likelihood of specific comorbid diagnoses within DSM-IV personality disorders, although this is a rationally derived model. For instance, he rank-ordered diagnoses in order of likelihood of comorbidity with APD. In ascending order they are sadistic personality, narcissistic personality, and substance abuse. Furthermore, he provided a concise clinical description of unique features for each potentially overlapping disorder that will assist clinicians to more accurately distinguish among a rather heterogeneous group of patients. For instance, in distinguishing from antisocial personality, he noted narcissistic individuals are egocentric but tend not to be impulsive. Similarly, relative to antisocial patients, the manipulative behavior of borderlines tends not to be aggrandizing or intended to gain power. These descriptions highlight pervasiveness, severity, motivation, and personality style, emphasizing that a diagnosis should be much more than a simple compilation of behaviors or symptoms.

Summary. The goal of the DSM-IV Task Force to develop simplified yet reliable criteria for APD appears to have been met. These changes, however, have not served to bridge the conceptual differences between divergent views regarding the preferred assessment. It is important that alternative strategies to DSM, such as the PCL-R and ICD-10, yielded the most prototypical items, as reported by experienced clinicians (Rogers et al., 1994). In part, the setting and the time available to the clinician might dictate the approach taken, as the PCL-R requires more specific training, use of a semistructured interview and collateral collaborative information, and, perhaps, greater time. Some clinicians in community settings, for whom APD is a less frequent and therefore less prognostic diagnosis, may choose DSM-IV criteria. Rogers et al. (1994) proposed a screening model, with DSM-IV acting as a triage for the more intensive PCL-R strategy. It seems such suggestions, while sensitive to the present reality, fail to address the fundamental issue of whether the nosology sufficiently reflects the assessment technology and theory of the constructs of APD or psychopathy.

In the meantime, treatment initiatives can only partly be guided by theory. Prognosis, even after treatment, remains relatively poor for APD patients, yet conceptualizing treatment as a management strategy rather than a cure is perhaps a more helpful framework, likely to insulate clinicians from undue optimism. This, however, should not be equated with therapeutic nihilism.

Furthermore, improved treatment responsivity for APD patients may yield enhanced treatment efficacy, but this remains an empirical question.

Borderline Personality Disorder

Fluctuations in mood, an unstable sense of their own identity, and instability in their relationships characterize borderline patients. This overriding instability in all aspects of their functioning makes borderlines unpredictable and impulsive, and along with their irritability and argumentative style, these features tend to seriously interfere with their relationships. However, they seem unable to tolerate being alone and, accordingly, display desperateness regarding relationships, although they typically alternate between idealizing and devaluing their partners.

Millon (1992) and Widiger, Miele, and Tilly (1992) described the origins of the present conceptualization of borderline personality disorder. Perry and Klerman (1978) examined four influential reports on what was variously called "borderline personality organization" (Kernberg, 1967), "the borderline syndrome" (Grinker, Werble, & Drye, 1968), "borderline states" (Knight, 1953), and simply "borderline patients" (Gunderson & Singer, 1975). Perry and Klerman found that of the 104 different criteria identified in these four reports, 55 appeared in only one of the reports. In fact, only one of the criteria (the patient's behavior at interview is adaptive and appropriate) appeared in all four reports. After reviewing the literature, Spitzer, Endicott, and Gibbon (1979) concluded that the label "borderline" had been used up to that time to identify two different constellations of symptoms: 1. instability and vulnerability and 2. a set of features described by Kety, Rosenthal, Wender, and Schulsinger (1971) as "borderline schizophrenia." The former constellation provided the basis for identifying borderline personality disorder in DSM-III, while the latter became schizotypal personality disorder. Perhaps not surprisingly, there have been consistent observations ever since of considerable overlap and even confusion between these two disorders (Jacobsberg, Hymowitz, Barasch, & Frances, 1986; McGlashan, 1983; Rosenberger & Miller, 1989; Serban, Conte, & Plutchik, 1987). Oddly enough, the DSM-III characteristic (intolerance of being alone) that most accurately distinguished borderlines from schizotypals (McGlashan, 1987; Plakun, 1987) has been dropped from the diagnostic criteria in DSM-III-R and DSM-IV.

Borderline disorder has a lifetime occurrence in approximately 2% of the population and is said to be more common in women than in men (Swartz, Blazer, George, & Landerman, 1986), although claims about gender differences in personality disorders have, as we noted earlier, been seriously challenged (Brown, 1992). Borderline disorder, which typically onsets in adolescence (McGlashan, 1983), has been shown to display reasonable stability over time (Barasch, Frances, Hurt, Clarkin, & Cohen, 1985; Pope, Jonas, Hudson, Cohen, & Gunderson, 1983). However, Stone (1993) reported that of patients diagnosed during early adulthood as borderline, only 25% still met the diagnostic criteria in middle age.

Debate continues concerning the nature of borderline disorders with Millon (1986), Kernberg (1984), and Gunderson and Zanarini (1987), in particular, expressing strong disagreement regarding the appropriate diagnostic criteria. Widiger et al. (1992) reviewed the various alternative perspectives on the diagnosis and found considerable inconsistencies in the results of research aimed at evaluating the diagnostic formulations they examined. They attribute these inconsistencies in findings to differences in research samples across different settings and, most important, to variability in interpretations of diagnostic criteria. This latter observation is consistent with the observed low reliability of the diagnosis of borderline using DSM criteria (Hurt, Clarkin, Koenigsberg, Frances, & Nurmberg, 1986; Widiger, Hurt, Frances, Clarkin, & Gilmore, 1984). In fact, a field trial of DSM-III criteria revealed very poor reliability ($r = .29$) for this diagnosis (Mellsop, Varghese, Joshua, & Hicks, 1982).

These disagreements about the appropriate criteria for borderlines, and the unreliability of the application of diagnostic criteria, of course challenge the value of attempting to integrate research findings. It is no surprise that inconsistencies typify the results of research with these patients. Consistent with this, raters have been found to vary in their identification of the presence or absence of each of the diagnostic criteria (Angus & Marziali, 1988; Skodol, Rosnick, Kellman, Oldham, & Hyler, 1988). When researchers report satisfactory interrater reliabilities, it is apparently due to establishing clear but local operational definitions that unfortunately vary across settings (Widiger et al., 1992). Once again, reliability has been shown to be superior when dimensional ratings rather than categorical distinctions are used (Widiger et al., 1992), and the use of various rating scales and structured interviews facilitate this approach (Reich, 1992).

The etiology of borderline disorder has been debated for many years with different views emphasizing childhood experiences, biological factors, psychodynamic processes, or social learning. Certainly the evidence strongly implicates disruptions in the family of origin and childhood abuse and neglect as very significant factors in the development of borderline disorder (Links, 1992; Marziali, 1992). Borderline patients typically recall their parents as either neglectful (Goldberg, et al., 1985; Paris & Frank, 1989) or abusive (Bryer, Nelson, Miller, & Krol, 1987). However, retrospective studies present problems of interpretation when there is no available check on the accuracy of recall. In fact, problems of distorted recall of parental behaviors may be even more problematic with borderline patients than with other populations. Briere and Zaidi (1989), in the examination of 100 females seen at an emergency service, found that among sexually abused females a diagnosis of borderline personality disorder was 5 times more likely to have been given than to female patients who were not sexually abused. Physical abuse by parents has also been found to be typical of the childhoods of borderlines (Zanarini, Gunderson, Marino, Schwartz, & Frankenburg, 1989).

Despite problems with some of these studies, the findings suggest that attachment problems with parents may be a significant etiological factor in borderline disorder. Borderline patients, as we have seen, have very significant problems with adult relationships, and this may be understood to result from a fear of, or ambivalence about, intimacy. People who have problems with adult intimacy are considered to have developed these difficulties as a result of poor parent-child attachments (Berman & Sperling, 1994), which fail to instill the self-confidence and skills necessary for effective intimacy (Batholomew, 1989) and fail to provide an adequate template for adult intimate relationships (Bowlby, 1988). The features of borderline disorder may then be seen as attempts to adjust to their distrust of intimacy.

Murray (1979) suggested an association between minimal brain dysfunction (MBD) and the development of borderline disorder. He suggested that the distorting effects of MBD on perceptual processes may interfere with effective parent-child relationships and that these effects may continue to disrupt relationships throughout the life span. Confused perceptions, emotional instability, and poor impulse control typical of MBD were said to lead to the development of borderline behavior. Research that has examined this claim has generally supported the idea that a subset of borderlines have soft neurological signs (Marziali, 1992), but the evidence is certainly not convincing.

Available evidence suggests a relatively high incidence of borderline features in first-degree relatives of borderline patients (Links, 1992), and this has been taken by some to suggest familial transmission of the disorder (Baron, Risch, Levitt, & Gruen, 1985; Loranger, Oldham, & Tulis, 1983). Torgensen (1984) examined the genetic contribution to the development of both borderline disorder and schizotypal disorder using Norwegian twins. Diagnoses were done by a clinician blind to the zygosity of the subjects. The results did not offer support for a genetic etiology because none of the three monozygotic twins were concordant for borderline disorder and only two of the seven dizygotic twins were. Clearly, however, this was a limited examination of the issue given that the number of subjects was quite small.

Histrionic Personality Disorder

Attention-seeking behaviors distinguish people with this disorder. They are overly dramatic in their emotional displays, are self-centered, and constantly attempt to be the center of attention.

The flamboyant displays characteristic of histrionics are apparently intended to have others focus on them as they seem unable to tolerate being ignored. Associated with this tendency is the overresponsiveness of histrionic patients to what others might consider insignificant events. Their insincerity and shallowness, however, make it difficult for histrionics to hold other people's attention for long, and as a consequence, they typically have few friends. Because of their very strong need for attention, they tend to be very demanding and inconsiderate when they are involved in relationships, and not surprisingly, their relationships are often short-lived and emotionally tumultuous. Again, as a result of needing to be the center of attention, histrionic patients are often flirtatious, and they seem unable to develop any degree of intimacy in relationships. Their behavior causes considerable distress to themselves and to others with whom they become involved.

Histrionic patients are frequently depressed and often suffer from poor health (Nestadt et al., 1990). The primary problem of overlap with other disorders, however, is with borderline personality disorder (Pfohl et al., 1986; Pope et al., 1983). Widiger et al. (1987), for example, found that 57% of borderline patients also met criteria for histrionic personality disorder.

Narcissistic Personality Disorder

Narcissistic patients grandiosely consider themselves to have unique and out-standing abilities. They have an exaggerated sense of self-importance, and indeed, egocentricity is the hallmark of narcissistic patients. They are so preoc-cupied with their own interests and desires that they typically have difficulty feeling any concern for others, although they are themselves easily hurt. Simi-larly, their self-esteem is readily shattered by negative feedback from others, presumably because they desire only admiration and approval (Kernberg, 1975). The self-absorption of these patients frequently leads to obsession with unrealis-tic fantasies of success. They expect, and demand, to be treated as special, and this, along with their lack of empathy, leads them to exploit others. Like histri-onic patients, the typical behaviors of narcissists alienate others, and they are frequently lonely and unhappy individuals.

Ronningstam and Gunderson (1990) claimed that research had validated these features as characteristic of narcissistic personality disorder. However, while Morey (1988) reported a remarkable increase (from 6.2% of patients to 22%) in the application of the diagnosis from DSM-III to DSM-III-R, Zimmer-man and Coryell (1989) could find no cases of narcissistic personality disorder in a sample of 800 community subjects. When it is diagnosed, there is consider-able overlap with borderline personality disorder (Morey, 1988).

Cluster C: Anxious and Fearful Disorders

Although avoidant and dependent disorders appear to share anxieties and fears as primary features, the obsessive-compulsive patient seems to be more charac-terized by preoccupation with orderliness and rules. Again, there seems to be little value in clustering these disorders in the same category.

Avoidant Personality Disorder

A pervasive pattern of avoiding interpersonal contacts and extreme sensitivity to criticism and disapproval characterize the avoidant client. They actively avoid intimacy with others, although they clearly desire affection. As a result, they frequently experience emotional loneliness. Social discomfort and fear of being evaluated negatively are common features of these patients. Avoidant clients are afraid of criticism, and so they restrict the range of their social interactions to those people they trust not to denigrate them, but even with these people, they refrain from getting too close. These fears cause problems for them not only in interpersonal relationships but also in their choice of jobs, academic pursuits, and leisure activities. Their avoidance of intimacy also distresses other people who may wish to form a close relationship with the avoidant person.

People with avoidant styles were identified in the literature for many years prior to the inclusion of this personality disorder in the diagnostic manual. For instance, Horney (1945) pointed out that there were people who found interper-sonal relationships of any kind to be such an intolerable strain that "solitude becomes primarily a means of avoiding it" (p. 73). Millon (1969) was the first to use the term "avoidant personality" to describe people who actively avoided social interactions. He (Millon, 1981) suggested that a child rejected by his or her parents would lack self-confidence and would, as a consequence, avoid others for fear of further rejection. This notion fits with the extensive literature on parent-child attachments and the consequences for adult relationships of parental rejection (Bartholomew, 1989, 1990; Berman & Sperling, 1994). Children who have poor parental bonds typically grow up to be afraid of intimate relationships and carefully avoid any depth in whatever relationships they form. These are just the characteristics that identify avoidant personality clients.

Trull, Widiger, and Frances (1987) found considerable overlap between avoidant personality disorder and dependent disorder, and Morey (1988) reported overlap with borderline disorder. As we have noted earlier, there is also a problem concerning the distinction between avoidant disorder and social phobia. In particular, Turner, Beidel, Dancu, and Keys (1991) found considerable overlap between these two disorders, and they appear to differ only in the severity of their symptoms (Holt, Heimberg, & Hope, 1992).

Dependent Personality Disorder

These patients appear to be afraid to rely on themselves to make decisions. They seek advice and direction from others, need constant reassurance, and seek out relationships where they can adopt a submissive role to their partner. Dependent patients not only allow other people to assume responsibilities for important aspects of their lives, they seem to desperately need others to do so. They seem unable to function independently and typically ask their spouses or partners to decide what jobs they should seek or what clothes they should purchase, and indeed, they defer to others for all the decisions in their lives. Dependent personality patients subordinate their needs to those of other people in their lives, even people they hardly know. This style often gets them involved in abusive relationships or destroys relationships with partners who could be beneficial to their lives.

Reich (1990) observed that the relatives of male dependent patients were likely to experience depression whereas the relatives of female dependents were more likely to have panic disorder. Panic-disordered patients have also been found to have comorbidity with various personality disorders, including the dependent disorder (Johnson, Weissman, & Klerman, 1990).

Obsessive-Compulsive Personality Disorder

Inflexibility and perfection characterize this disorder. It is the centrality of these two features and the absence of obsessional thoughts and compulsive behaviors that distinguish this personality disorder from Axis I obsessive-compulsive disorder. Preoccupation with rules and order make these patients rigid and inefficient as a result of focusing too much on the details of a problem. Obsessive-compulsive personality patients also attempt to ignore feelings since they consider emotions to be unpredictable. They tend to be moralistic and judgmental, and this causes them problems in dealing with others.

Turkat and Levin (1984) could find no reports in the literature that they considered at all helpful in understanding obsessive-compulsive personality disorder. Most of the research they reviewed was concerned with the psychoanalytic notion of the anal retentive character, which was thought to be related to obsessive-compulsive personality. It is not clear, however, that the results of this research are helpful in understanding the personality disorder. Very little research on this disorder has emerged over the years since DSM-III-R was published, except that which concerned distinguishing this personality disorder from obsessive-compulsive disorder. Studies using objective measures have found a clear independence, whereas those using projective techniques or clinical interviews find co-occurrence of the two disorders (Cawley, 1974; Coursey, 1984; Slade, 1974). In fact, Joffe, Swinson, and Regan (1988) found that other personality disorders (e.g., avoidant, dependent, and schizotypal) were more likely to co-occur with obsessive-compulsive disorder than was obsessive-compulsive personality disorder.

TREATMENT

As Gorton and Akhtar (1990) observed, there are two important factors that make it difficult to evaluate treatment with the personality disorders: 1. many of these patients are not themselves upset by their characteristic personality style and so do not seek treatment, and 2. the dropout rates from treatment among these patients is extremely high (Kelly et al., 1992). There is no doubt that these patients constitute a serious challenge for the therapist. All of them have considerable difficulties with relationships, and this affects the therapeutic alliance. Also most have problems maintaining focus between sessions on the therapeutic process. Even when the focus in treatment is on an Axis I disorder, patients who also have a personality disorder do poorer than those who are free of such problems (Reich & Green, 1991). In recent years, however, far more effort has been devoted to developing treatment programs for these patients, although to date outcome data are limited.

Essentially three approaches have been developed: 1. object-relations therapy, 2. cognitive-behavioral approaches, and 3. the use of medications.

Object-Relations Therapy

The leading proponents of object-relations therapy have been Kernberg (1975, 1984) and Kohut (1977). In their view, treatment should be aimed at correcting flaws in the self that have resulted from unfortunate formative experiences. The transference relationship between patient and therapist serves as a vehicle for confronting, in a supportive way, the patient's defenses and distortions. This process is slow and, if successful, produces gradual changes. Thus treatment is seen as necessarily long term.

In the only controlled evaluation of this approach that we could find, Stevenson and Meares (1992) treated, then followed-up for 1 year, 30 borderline patients. At follow-up, 30% of the patients no longer met DSM criteria for borderline personality disorder. Single case reports of similar treatment programs with narcissistic patients have provided encouraging results (Ackerman, 1975; Kinston, 1980), but we await more extensive and more rigorous evaluations.

Although Stone (1985) and Walsh (1990) have suggested that a psychotherapeutic approach emphasizing a supportive relationship and aimed at enhancing social skills may be useful with schizotypal patients, as long as the goals are limited, there have, as yet, not been any controlled evaluations of such an approach.

Cognitive-Behavioral Approaches

Beck (Beck et al., 1990) has extended his cognitive analyses to personality disorders and has suggested that treatment must correct cognitive distortions of these patients in order to be successful. Beck's treatment is directed at challenging core schemas and beliefs that are thought to underlie the problems of these patients. Cognitive restructuring techniques provide bases for change, along with skills training and behavioral practices. To date, however, adherents of this promising approach have not produced controlled evaluations. This appears to be at least partly explained by the relatively recent development of this approach and because Beck et al. (1990) have claimed that, unlike the application of cognitive therapy to other problems, treatment of personality disorders will take far longer.

Linehan and Heard (1992) developed what they call "dialectical behavior therapy." To date, this approach has been used only with borderline patients, but there does not seem to be any reason why it cannot be adapted to the problems of other personality disorders. One of the main features of this approach is acceptance by the therapist of the patient's demanding and manipulative behaviors. In addition, several standard behavioral procedures are used, such as exposure to external and internal cues that evoke distress, skills training approaches, contingency management, and cognitive restructuring. The dialectical process describes "both the coexisting multiple tensions . . . and the thought processes and styles used and targeted in the treatment strategies" (Linehan & Heard, 1992, p. 249).

Linehan, Armstrong, Suarez, Allmon, and Heard (1991) compared the treatment outcome of 22 female borderline patients randomly assigned to dialectical behavior therapy with 22 patients randomly assigned to "treatment as usual." At the end of 1 year of treatment, those assigned to dialectical behavior therapy had made fewer suicidal attempts and had spent less time in hospital than those allocated to the other treatment program. An important additional observation was that while only 17% of the dialectically treated patients dropped out, almost 60% of the other group withdrew prior to treatment termination. Although both groups displayed less depression and hopelessness after treatment, there were no group differences on these measures. A second study (Linehan, Heard, & Armstrong, 1993) produced similar positive results.

Behavioral approaches employing social skills training and desensitization have been effective in ameliorating the problems of avoidant personality-disordered patients (Alden, 1989; Renneberg, Goldstein, Phillips, & Chambless, 1990; Stravynski, Lesage, Marcouiller, & Elie, 1989). However, the benefits of these programs have not been evaluated at long-term follow-up, and Alden (1989) observed that most of these patients remained socially uncomfortable.

Pharmacologic Interventions

Borderline patients have been successfully treated with a variety of pharmacologic agents, including amitriptyline (Soloff et al., 1986), thiothixene (Goldberg et al., 1986), and carbemazepine (Gardner & Cowdry, 1986). It has been suggested that different subtypes of borderline patients may be differentially responsive to either antipsychotics or antidepressant medications. Goldberg et al. (1986), for example, found antipsychotics to be most effective with borderlines displaying psychotic-like features, while Cole, Saloman, Gunderson, Sunderland, and Simmonds (1984) found maximal improvements for antidepressants with those patients who also met criteria for major depression. In addition, Waldinger and Frank (1989) indicated that medications may facilitate psychotherapy with borderline patients.

Goldberg et al. (1986) and Schulz (1986) also found low doses of thiothixene to be beneficial with schizotypal-disordered patients. Also schizotypals seem to respond to antidepressants (Markowitz, Calabrese, Schulz, & Meltzer, 1991); however, the benefits of any medications with schizotypal disorder are modest at best (Gitlin, 1993).

CONCLUSIONS

Other than the rather extensive research on borderline and antisocial personality disorders, and to a lesser extent on schizotypal patients, the personality disorders remain a neglected domain in the field of psychopathology. There is no doubt that diagnostic problems continue to hamper progress in this field. Whether switching from a categorical classification to a dimensional system is the best solution to this problem is not clear, although research focusing on dimensional analyses seems most likely to enhance our understanding of these disorders. As long as the authors of the diagnostic manual insist on pursuing a categorial system, problems of heterogeneity, comorbidity, and overlap will make research difficult.

Whatever decision is made on classification, clinicians and researchers must give greater emphasis to developing and properly evaluating treatment programs for the personality disorders. Controlled, long-term outcome studies of large numbers of patients are required to determine effectiveness of treatment. Of course, for the low-incidence personality disorders such studies may not be feasible, but this should not deter researchers from making the best effort they can within the restrictions imposed by these low frequencies.

REFERENCES

Ackerman, P. H. (1975). Narcissistic personality disorder in an identical twin. *International Journal Psychoanalytic Psychotherapy, 4,* 389–409.

Alden, L. (1989). Short-term structured treatment for avoidant personality disorder. *Journal of Consulting and Clinical Psychology, 57,* 756–764.

Alterman, A. I., & Cacciola, J. S. (1991). The antisocial personality disorder diagnosis in substance abusers. *Journal of Nervous and Mental Disease, 179,* 401–409.

American Psychiatric Association. (1980). *Diagnostic and statistical manual of mental disorders* (3rd ed.). Washington, DC: Author.

American Psychiatric Association. (1987). *Diagnostic and statistical manual of mental disorders* (3rd ed., rev. ed.). Washington, DC: Author.

American Psychiatric Association. (1994). *Diagnostic and statistical manual of mental disorders* (4th ed.). Washington, DC: Author.

Andrulonis, P. R., & Vogel, N. G. (1984). Comparison of borderline personality subcategories to schizophrenic and affective disorders. *British Journal of Psychiatry, 144,* 358–363.

Angus, L. E., & Marziali, E. (1988). A comparison of three measures for the diagnosis of borderline personality disorder. *American Journal of Psychiatry, 145,* 1453–1454.

Barasch, A., Frances, A., Hurt, S., Clarkin, J., & Cohen, S. (1985). Stability and distinctness of borderline personality disorder. *American Journal of Psychiatry, 142,* 1484–1486.

Baron, M., Levitt, M., Gruen, R., Kane, J., & Asnis, L. (1984). Platelet monoamine oxidase activity and genetic vulnerability to schizophrenia. *American Journal of Psychiatry, 141,* 836–842.

Baron, M., Risch, N., Levitt, M., & Gruen, R. (1985). Familial transmission of schizotypal and borderline personality disorders. *American Journal of Psychiatry, 142,* 927–934.

Bartholomew, K. (1989). *Attachment styles in young adults: Implications for self-concept and interpersonal functioning.* Unpublished doctoral dissertation, Stanford University.

Bartholomew, K. (1990). Avoidance of intimacy: An attachment perspective. *Journal of Personal and Social Relationships, 7,* 147–178.

Beck, A. T., Freeman, A., Pretzer, J., Davis, D. D., Fleming, B., Ottaviani, R., Beck, J., Simon, K. M., Padesky, C., Meyer, J., & Trexler, L. (1990). *Cognitive therapy of personality disorders.* New York: Guilford.

Berman, W. H., & Sperling, M. B. (1994). The structure and function of adult attachment. In M. B. Sperling & W. H. Berman (Eds.), *Attachment in adults: Clinical and developmental perspectives* (pp. 3–28). New York: Guilford.

Bernstein, D. P., Cohen, P., Velez, C. N., Schwab-Stone, M., Siever, L. J., & Shinsato, L. (1993). Prevalence and stability of the DSM-III-R personality disorders in a community-based survey of adolescents. *American Journal of Psychiatry, 50,* 1237–1243.

Blackburn, R. (1992). Criminal behaviour, personality disorder, and mental confusion: The origins of confusion. *Criminal Behaviour and Mental Health, 2,* 66–77.

Blackburn, R. (1993a). Clinical programs with psychopaths. In K. Howells & C. Hollins (Eds.), *Clinical approaches to the mentally disordered offender* (pp. 179–208). Chichester, England: Wiley.

Blackburn, R. (1993b). *The psychology of criminal conduct.* Chichester, England: Wiley.

Bond, A. J. (1993). Prospects for antiaggressive drugs. In C. Thompson & P. Cowen (Eds.), *Violence: Basic and clinical services* (pp. 147–170). London: Butterworth Heineman.

Bornstein, R. F., Klein, D. N., Mallon, J. C., & Slater, J. F. (1988). Schizotypal personality disorder in an outpatient population: Incidence and clinical characteristics. *Journal of Clinical Psychology, 44,* 322–325.

Bowlby, J. (1977). The making and breaking of affectional bonds: I. Aetiology and psychopathology in the light of attachment theory. *British Journal of Psychiatry, 30,* 301–210.

Bowlby, J. (1988). *A secure base: Parent-child attachment and health human development.* New York: Basic Books.

Briere, J., & Zaidi, L. Y. (1989). Sexual abuse histories and sequelae in female psychiatric emergency room patients. *American Journal of Psychiatry, 146,* 1602–1606.

Brown, L. S. (1992). A feminist critique of the personality disorder. In L. S. Brown & M. Ballou (Eds.), *Personality and psychopathology: Feminist reappraisals* (pp. 176–189). New York: Guilford.

Bryer, J. B., Nelson, B. A., Miller, J. B., & Knol, P. K. (1987). Childhood sexual and physical abuse as factors in adult psychiatric illness. *American Journal of Psychiatry, 144,* 1426–1430.

Cawley, R. (1974). Psychotherapy and obsessional disorders. In H. R. Beech (Ed.), *Obsessional states* (pp. 259–290). London: Methuen.

Chiswick, D. (1992). Compulsory treatment of patients with psychopathic disorder: An abnormally aggressive or seriously irresponsible exercise. *Criminal Behavior and Mental Health, 2,* 106–113.

Chodoff, P., & Lyons, H. (1958). Hysteria, the hysterical personality and "hysterical" conversion. *American Journal of Psychiatry, 114,* 734–740.

Clarkin, J. F., Widiger, T. A., Frances, A. J., Hurt, S. W., & Gilmore, M. (1983). Prototypic typology and the borderline personality disorder. *Journal of Abnormal Psychology, 92,* 263–275.

Cleckley, H. (1976). *The mask of sanity* (5th ed.). St. Louis: Mosby.

Cole, J. O., Saloman, M., Gunderson, J., Sunderland, P., & Simmonds, P. (1984). Drug therapy for borderline patients. *Comprehensive Psychiatry, 25,* 249–254.

Cooke, D. J. (1994a). *Psychopathic disturbance in the Scottish Prison Population: The cross-cultural generalisability of the Hare Psychopathy Checklist.* Unpublished manuscript.

Cooke, D. J. (1994b). *Cross-cultural perspectives on psychopathy.* Unpublished manuscript.

Côté, G., & Hodgins, S. (1990). Co-occurring mental disorders among criminal offenders. *Bulletin of the American Academy of Psychiatry and Law, 18,* 271–281.

Coursey, D. (1984). The dynamics of obsessive-compulsive disorder. In T. R. Insel (Ed.), *New findings in obsessive-compulsive disorder* (pp. 104–121). Washington, DC: American Psychiatric Association.

Dahl, A. R. (1986). Some aspects of DSM-III personality disorder illustrated by a consecutive sample of hospitalized patients. *Acta Psychiatrica Scandinavica, 73,* 61–67.

Davis, G. C., & Akiskal, H. S. (1986). Descriptive, biological, and theoretical aspects of borderline personality disorder. *Hospital and Community Psychiatry, 37,* 685–692.

Drake, R. E., & Vaillant, G. E. (1985). A validity study of axis II of DSM-III. *American Journal of Psychiatry, 142,* 553–558.

Ford, M. R., & Widiger, T. A. (1989). Sex bias in the diagnosis of histrionic and antisocial personality disorders. *Journal of Consulting and Clinical Psychology, 57,* 301–305.

Frances, A. (1985). Validating schizotypal personality disorders: Problems with the schizophrenic connection. *Schizophrenia Bulletin, 11,* 595–597.

Gabbard, G. O., & Coyne, L. (1987). Predictors of response of antisocial patients to hospital treatment. *Hospital and Community Psychiatry, 38,* 1181–1185.

Gacono, C. B., & Hutton, H. E. (1994). Suggestions for the clinical and forensic use of the Hare Psychopathy Checklist-Revised (PCL-R). *International Journal of Law and Psychiatry, 17,* 303–317.

Gallwey, P. (1992). The psychotherapy of psychopathic disorder. *Criminal Behaviour and Mental Health, 2,* 159–168.

Gardner, D. L., & Cowdry, R. W. (1986). Positive effects of carbamazepine on behavioral dyscontrol in borderline personality disorder. *American Journal of Psychiatry, 143,* 519–522.

Gendreau, P. (in press). The principles of effective intervention with offenders. In A. J. Harland (Ed.), *Choosing correctional options that work: Defining the demand and evaluating the supply*. Thousand Oaks, CA: Sage.

George, A., & Soloff, P. M. (1986). Schizotypal symptoms in patients with borderline personality disorder. *American Journal of Psychiatry, 143*, 212–215.

Gerstley, L. J., Alterman, A. I., McLellan, A. T., & Woody, G. E. (1990). Antisocial personality disorder in patients with substance abuse disorders: A problematic diagnosis? *American Journal of Psychiatry, 147*, 173–178.

Gerstley, L. J., McLellan, A. T., Alterman, A. I., Woody, G. E., Luborsky, L., & Prout, M. (1989). Ability to form an alliance with the therapist: A possible marker of prognosis for patients with antisocial personality disorder. *American Journal of Psychiatry, 146*, 508–512.

Gitlin, M. J. (1993). Pharmacotherapy of personality disorders: Conceptual framework and clinical strategies. *Journal of Clinical Psychopharmacology, 13*, 343–353.

Goldberg, R. L., Mann, L. S., Wise, T. N., & Segall, E. R. (1985). Parental qualities as perceived by borderline personality disorder. *Hillside Journal of Clinical Psychiatry, 7*, 134–140.

Goldberg, S. C., Schulz, S. C., Schulz, P. M., Resnick, R. J., Hamer, R. M., & Friedel, R. O. (1986). Borderline and schizotypal personality disorder treated with low-dose thiothixene versus placebo. *Archives of General Psychiatry, 43*, 680–686.

Gorton, G., & Akhtar, S. (1990). The literature on personality disorders, 1985–1988: Trends, issues, and controversies. *Hospital and Community Psychiatry, 41*, 39–51.

Grinker, R. R., Werble, B., & Drye, R. C. (1968). *The borderline syndrome*. New York: Basic Books.

Grove, W. M., Eckert, E. D., Heston, L., Bouchard, T. J., Segal, N., & Lykken, D. T. (1990). Heritability of substance abuse and antisocial behavior: A study of monozygotic twins reared apart. *Biological Psychiatry, 27*, 1293–1304.

Guerra, N. G., & Slaby, R. G. (1990). Cognitive mediators of aggression in adolescent offenders: 2. Intervention. *Developmental Psychology, 26*, 269–277.

Gunderson, J. G., & Elliott, G. R. (1985). The interface between borderline personality disorder and affective disorder. *American Journal of Psychiatry, 142*, 277–288.

Gunderson, J. G., & Singet, M. T. (1975). Defining borderline patients: An overview. *American Journal of Psychiatry, 132*, 1–10.

Gunderson, J. G., & Zanarini, M. C. (1987). Current overview of borderline diagnosis. *Journal of Clinical Psychiatry, 43*, 5–11.

Harding, T. W. (1992). Psychopathic disorder: Time for a decent burial of a bad legal concept? *Criminal Behavior and Mental Health, 2*, vi–ix.

Hare, R. D. (1983). Diagnosis of antisocial personality disorder in two prison populations. *American Journal of Abnormal Psychiatry, 140*, 887–890.

Hare, R. D. (1985). A comparison of procedures for the assessment of psychopathy. *Journal of Consulting and Clinical Psychology, 53*, 7–16.

Hare, R. D. (1991). *The Hare Psychopathy Checklist–Revised*. Toronto: Multihealth Systems.

Hare, R. D., Harpur, T. J., Hakstian, A. R., Forth, A. E., Hart, S. D., & Newman, J. P. (1990). The Revised Psychopathy Checklist: Reliability and factor structure. *Psychological Assessment: A Journal of Consulting and Clinical Psychology, 2*, 338–341.

Hare, R. D., Hart, S. D., & Harpur, T. J. (1991). Psychopathy and DSM-IV criteria for antisocial personality disorder. *Journal of Abnormal Psychology, 100*, 391–398.

Harpur, T. J., & Hare, R. D. (1994). The assessment of psychopathy as a function of age. *Journal of Abnormal Psychology, 103*, 604–609.

Harris, G. T. (1989). The relationship between neuroleptic drug dose and the performance of psychiatric patients in a maximum security token economy program. *Journal of Behavior Therapy and Experimental Psychiatry, 20,* 57–67.

Harris, G. T., Rice, M. E., & Quinsey, V. L. (1993). Violent recidivism of mentally disordered offenders: The development of a statistical prediction instrument. *Criminal Justice and Behaviour, 20,* 315–335.

Harris, G. T., Rice, M. E., & Quinsey, V. L. (1994). Psychopathy as a taxon: Evidence that psychopaths are a discrete class. *Journal of Consulting and Clinical Psychology, 62,* 387–397.

Hart, S. D., & Hare, R. D. (1989). Discriminant validity of the Psychopathy Checklist in a forensic psychiatric population. *Psychological Assessment: A Journal of Consulting and Clinical Psychology, 1,* 211–218.

Hart, S. D., Kropp, P. R., & Hare, R. D. (1988). Performance of male psychopaths following conditional release from prison. *Journal of Consulting and Clinical Psychology, 56,* 227–232.

Helzer, J. E., Spitznagel, E. L., & McEnvoy, L. (1987). The predictive validity of lay Diagnostic Interview Schedule diagnoses in the general population: a comparison with physician examiners. *Archives of General Psychiatry, 44,* 1069–1077.

Henry, K., & Cohen, C. (1983). The role of labeling in diagnosing borderline personality disorder. *American Journal of Psychiatry, 140,* 1527–1529.

Herman, J. L. (1992). *Trauma and recovery.* New York: Basic Books.

Holt, C. S., Heinberg, R. G., & Hope, D. A. (1992). Avoidant personality disorder and the generalized subtype of social phobia. *Journal of Abnormal Psychology, 101,* 318–325.

Horney, K. (1945). *Our inner conflicts.* New York: Norton.

Hurt, S. W., Clarkin, J. F., Koenigsberg, H. W., Frances, A., & Nurmberg, H. G. (1986). Diagnostic Interview for Borderlines: Psychometric properties and validity. *Journal of Consulting and Clinical Psychology, 54,* 256–260.

Jacobsberg, L. B., Hymowitz, P., Barasch, A., & Frances, A. J. (1986). Symptoms of schizotypal personality disorder. *American Journal of Psychiatry, 143,* 1222–1227.

Joffe, R. T., Swinson, R. P., & Regan, J. J. (1988). Personality features of obsessive-compulsive disorder. *American Journal of Psychiatry, 145,* 1127–1129.

Johnson, J., Weissman, M. M., & Klerman, G. L. (1990). Panic disorder and suicide attempts. *Archives of General Psychiatry, 47,* 805–808.

Joseph, P. (1992). Noncustodial treatment: Can psychopaths be treated in the community? *Criminal Behaviour and Mental Health, 2,* 192–201.

Kaplan, M. (1983). A woman's view of DSM-III. *American Psychologist, 38,* 786–792.

Kass, F., Spitizer, R., & Williams, J. (1983). An empirical study of the issue of sex bias in the diagnostic criteria of DSM-III Axis II personality disorders. *American Psychologist, 38,* 799–801.

Kazdin, A. E. (1987). Treatment of antisocial behavior in children: Current status and future directions. *Psychological Bulletin, 102,* 187–203.

Kazdin, A. E. (1993). Treatment of conduct disorder: Progress and directions in psychotherapy research. *Development and Psychopathology, 5,* 277–310.

Kelly, T., Soloff, P. H., Cornelius, J., George, A., Lis, J. A., & Ulrich, R. (1992). Can we study (treat) borderline patients? Attrition from research and open treatment. *Journal of Personality Disorders, 6,* 417–433.

Kendler, K. S. (1985). Diagnostic approaches to schizotypal personality disorder: A historical perspective. *Schizophrenia Bulletin, 11,* 538–553.

Kendler, K. S., Masterson, C. C., & Davis, K. L. (1985). Psychiatric illness in first-degree relatives of patients with paranoid psychosis, schizophrenia, and medical controls. *British Journal of Psychiatry, 147,* 524–531.

Kernberg, O. F. (1967). Borderline personality organization. *Journal of the American Psychoanalytic Association, 15,* 641–685.

Kernberg, O. F. (1975). *Borderline conditions and pathological narcissism.* New York: Jason Aronson.

Kessler, R. C., McGonagle, K. A., Zhao, S., Nelson, L. B., Hughes, M., Eslheman, S., Wittchen, H., & Kendler, K. (1994). Lifetime and 12-month prevalence of DSM-III-R psychiatric disorders in the United States: Results from the National Comorbidity Study. *Archives of General Psychiatry, 51,* 8–19.

Kety, S. S., Rosenthal, D., Wender, P. H., & Schulsinger, F. (1971). Mental illness in the biological and adoptive families of adopted schizophrenics. *American Journal of Psychiatry, 128,* 302–306.

Kinston, W. (1980). A theoretical and technical approach to narcissistic disturbance. *International Journal of Psychoanalysis, 61,* 383–393.

Knight, R. (1953). Borderline states. *Bulletin of the Menninger Clinic, 17,* 1–12.

Kohut, H. (1977). *The restoration of the self.* New York: International Universities Press.

Kosson, D. S., Smith, S. S., & Newman, J. P. (1990). Evaluation of the construct validity of psychopathy in black and white male inmates: Three preliminary studies. *Journal of Abnormal Psychology, 99,* 250–259.

Lilienfeld, S. O. (1994). Conceptual problems in the assessment of psychopathy. *Clinical Psychology Review, 14,* 17–38.

Linehan, M. M., Armstrong, H. E., Suarez, A., Allmon, D., & Heard, H. L. (1991). Behavioral treatment of chronically parasuicidal borderline patients. *Archives of General Psychiatry, 48,* 1060–1064.

Linehan, M. M., & Heard, H. L. (1992). Dialectical behavior therapy for borderline personality disorder. In J. F. Clarkin, E., Marziali, & H. Munroe-Blum (Eds.), *Borderline personality disorder: Clinical and empirical perspectives* (pp. 248–267). New York: Guilford.

Linehan, M. M., Heard, H. L., & Armstrong, H. E. (1993). Naturalistic follow-up of a behavioral treatment for chronically parasuicidal borderline patients. *Archives of General Psychiatry, 50,* 971–974.

Links, P. S. (1992). Family environment and family psychopathology in the etiology of borderline personality disorder. In J. F. Clarkin, E. Marziali, & H. Munroe-Blum (Eds.), *Borderline personality disorder: Clinical and empirical perspectives* (pp. 45–66). New York: Guilford.

Livesley, W. J. (1989). Classifying personality disorders: Ideal types, prototypes, or dimensions? *Psychiatric Clinics of North America, 12,* 531–539.

Livesley, W. J., Jackson, D. N., & Schroeder, M. L. (1992). Factorial structure of traits delineating personality disorders in clinical and general population samples. *Journal of Abnormal Psychology, 101,* 432–440.

Livesley, W. J., Schroeder, M. L., Jackson, D. N., & Jang, K. L. (1994). Categorical distinctions in the study of personality disorder: Implications for classification. *Journal of Abnormal Personality, 103,* 6–17.

Loranger, A., Oldham, J., Russakoff, L. M., & Susman, V. (1987). Structured interviews and borderline personality disorder. *Archives of General Psychiatry, 41,* 565–568.

Loranger, A., Oldham, J., & Tulis, E. H. (1983). Familial transmission of DSM-III borderline personality disorders. *Archives of General Psychiatry, 40,* 975–799.

Loucks, A. (1995). *Criminal behaviour, violent behaviour, and prison maladjustment in federal female offenders.* Unpublished doctoral dissertation, Queens University, Kingston, Ontario.

Maier, W., Lichtermann, D., Klingler, T., Heun, R., & Hallmayer, J. (1992). Prevalence of personality disorders (DSM-III-R) in the community. *Journal of Personality Disorders, 6,* 1987–196.

Markowitz, P. J., Calabrese, J. R., Schulz, C. S., & Meltzer, H. Y. (1991). Fluoxetine in the treatment of borderline and schizotypal personality disorders. *American Journal of Psychiatry, 148,* 1067–1067.

Marques, J. K., Day, D. M., Nelson, C., & West, M. A. (1994). Effects of cognitive-behavioral treatment on sex offender recidivism: Preliminary results of a longitudinal study. *Criminal Justice and Behavior, 21,* 28–54.

Marshall, W. L. (1989). Intimacy, loneliness, and sexual offenders. *Behaviour Research and Therapy, 27,* 491–503.

Marshall, W. L., & Barbaree, H. E. (1984). Disorders of personality, impulse, and adjustment. In S. M. Turner & M. Hersen (Eds.), *Adult psychopathology: A behavioral perspective* (pp. 406–449). New York: Wiley.

Marshall, W. L., & Barbaree, H. E. (1991). Personality, impulse control, and adjustment disorders. In M. Hersen & S. M. Turner (Eds.), *Adult psychopathology and diagnosis* (2nd ed., pp. 360–391). New York: Wiley.

Marshall, W. L., Hudson, S. M., & Hodkinson, S. (1993). The importance of attachment bonds in the development of juvenile sex offending. In H. E. Barbaree, W. L. Marshall, & S. M. Hudson (Eds.), *The juvenile sex offender* (pp. 164–181). New York: Guilford.

Marziali, E. (1992). The etiology of borderline personality disorder: Developmental factors. In J. F. Clarkin, E. Marziali, & H. Munroe-Blum (Eds.), *Borderline personality disorder: Clinical and empirical perspectives* (pp. 27–44). New York: Guilford.

McGlashan, T. M. (1983). The borderline syndrome: I. Testing three diagnostic systems. *Archives of General Psychiatry, 40,* 1311–1318.

McGlashan, T. M. (1987). Testing DSM-III symptom criteria for schizotypal and borderline personality disorders. *Archives of General Psychiatry, 44,* 143–148.

McManus, M., Lerner, H. D., Robbins, D., & Barbour, C. (1984). Assessment of borderline symptomatology in hospitalized adolescents. *Journal of the American Academy of Child Psychiatry, 23,* 685–694.

Mellsop, G., Varghese, F., Joshua, S., & Hicks, A. (1982). The reliability of Axis II of DSM-III. *American Journal of Psychiatry, 139,* 1360–1361.

Meloy, J. R. (1995). Treatment of antisocial personality disorder. In G. Gabbard (Ed.), *Treatments of psychiatric disorders: The DSM-IV Edition* (pp. 2273–2290). Washington, DC: American Psychiatric Press.

Merikanges, K. R., & Weissman, M. M. (1986). Epidemiology of DSM-III Axis II personality disorders. In A. J. Frances & R. E. Hales (Eds.), *The American Psychiatric Association Annual Review* (pp. 49–74). Washington, DC: American Psychiatric Press.

Miller, W. R., & Rollnick, S. (1991). *Motivational interviewing.* New York: Guilford.

Millon, T. (1969). Modern psychopathology: *A biosocial approach to maladaptive learning and functioning.* Philadelphia: Saunders.

Millon, T. (1981). *Disorders of personality: DSM-III: Axis II.* New York: Wiley.

Millon, T. (1983). An integrative theory of personality and psychopathology. In T. Millon (Ed.), *Theories of personality and psychopathology* (pp. 3–19). New York: Holt, Rinehart, and Winston.

Millon, T. (1986). Personality prototypes and their diagnostic criteria. In T. Millon & G. L. Klerman (Eds.), *Contemporary directions in psychopathology* (pp. 671–712). New York: Guilford.

Millon, T. (1992). The borderline construct: Introductory notes on its history, theory, and empirical grounding. In J. F. Clarkin, E. Marziali, & H. Munroe-Blum (Eds.), *Borderline personality disorder: Clinical and empirical perspectives* (pp. 3–23). New York: Guilford.

Millon, T. (1996). *Disorders of personality: DSM-IV and beyond* (2nd ed.). New York: Wiley.

Moffitt, T. E. (1993). Adolescence-limited and life-course-persistent antisocial behavior: A developmental taxonomy. *Psychological Review, 100,* 674–701.

Morey, L. C. (1988). Personality disorders in DSM-III and DSM-III-R: Convergence, coverage, and internal consistency. *American Journal of Psychiatry, 145,* 573–577.

Morey, L. C., & Ochoa, E. (1989). An investigation of adherence to diagnostic criteria: Clinical diagnosis of the DSM-III personality disorders. *Journal of Personality Disorders, 3,* 180–192.

Murray, M. E. (1979). Minimal brain dysfunction and borderline personality adjustment. *American Journal of Psychotherapy, 33,* 391–403.

Nakdimen, K. A. (1986). A new formulation for borderline personality disorder? *American Journal of Psychiatry, 143,* 1069.

Neary, A. (1990). *DSM-III and Psychopathy Checklist assessment of antisocial personality disorder in Black and White female felons.* Unpublished doctoral dissertation, University of Missouri, St. Louis.

Nestadt, G., Romanoski, A. J., Chahal, R., Merchant, A., Folstein, J. F., Gruenberg, E. M., & McHugh, P. R. (1990). An epidemiological study of histrionic personality disorder. *Psychological Medicine, 20,* 413–422.

Newman, J. P., & Wallace, J. F. (1993). Psychopathy and cognition. In K. S. Dobson & P. C. Kendall (Eds.), *Psychopathology and cognition* (pp. 293–349). Orlando, FL: Academic Press.

Nezu, A. M., & Nezu, C. M. (1993). Identifying and selecting target problems for clinical interventions. A problem-solving model. *Psychological Assessment, 5,* 254–263.

Ogloff, J. P. R., Wong, S., & Greenwood, A. (1990). Treating criminal psychopaths in a therapeutic community program. *Behavioral Sciences and the Law, 8,* 81–90.

Pantony, K., & Caplan, P. J. (1991). Delusional dominating personality disorder: A modest proposal for identifying some consequences of rigid masculine socialization. *Canadian Psychology, 32,* 120–135.

Paris, J., & Frank, H. (1989). Perceptions of parental bonding in borderline patients. *American Journal of Psychiatry, 146,* 1498–1499.

Perry, J. C. (1985). Depression in borderline personality disorder: Lifetime prevalence at interview and longitudinal course of symptoms. *American Journal of Psychiatry, 142,* 152–21.

Perry, J. C., & Klerman, G. L. (1978). The borderline patient: A comparative analysis of four sets of diagnostic criteria. *Archives of General Psychiatry, 35,* 141–150.

Pfohl, B., Coryell, W., Zimmerman, M., & Stangl, D. (1986). DSM-III personality disorders: Diagnostic overlap and internal consistency of individual DSM-III criteria. *Comprehensive Psychiatry, 27,* 21–34.

Pinel, P. (1809). *Traite medico-phiosophique sur l'alienation mentale* (2nd ed.). Paris: Chez J. Ant Brosson.

Plakun, E. M. (1987). Distinguishing narcissistic and borderline personality disorders using DSM-III criteria. *Comprehensive Psychiatry, 28,* 437–443.

Poldrugo, F., & Forti, B. (1988). Personality disorders and alcoholism treatment outcome. *Drug and Alcohol Dependence, 21,* 171–176.

Pope, H. G., Jonas, J. M., Hudson, J. I., Cohen, B. M., & Gunderson, J. G. (1983). Borderline personality disorder: A phenomenologic, family history, treatment response, and long-term follow-up study. *Archives of General Psychiatry, 40,* 23–30.

Porporino, F. J., & Motiuk, L. L. (1995). The prison careers of mentally disordered offenders. *International Journal of Law and Psychiatry, 18,* 29–44.

Quinsey, V. L., & Walker, W. D. (1992). Dealing with dangerousness: Community risk management strategies with violent offenders. In D. V. Peters, R. J. McMahon, & V. L. Quinsey (Eds.), *Aggression and violence throughout the lifespan* (pp. 244–262). Newbury Park, CA: Sage.

Raine, A. (1985). A psychometric assessment of Hare's checklist for psychopathy in an English prison population. *British Journal of Clinical Psychology, 24,* 247–258.

Raine, A. (1993). *The psychopathology of crime: Criminal behavior as a clinical disorder.* San Diego: Academic Press.

Reich, J. (1987). Sex distribution of DSM-III personality disorders in psychiatric outpatients. *American Journal of Psychiatry, 144,* 485–488.

Reich, J. (1990). Comparison of males and females with DSM-III dependent personality disorder. *Psychiatry Research, 33,* 207–214.

Reich, J. (1992). Measurement of DSM-III and DSM-III-R borderline personality disorder. In J. F. Clarkin, E. Marziali, & H. Munroe-Blum (Eds.), *Borderline personality disorder: Clinical and empirical perspectives* (pp. 116–148). New York: Guilford.

Reich, J., & Green, A. I. (1991). Effect of personality disorders on outcome of treatment. *Journal of Neurons and Mental Disease, 179,* 74–82.

Reich, J., Noyes, R., & Troughton, E. (1987). Dependent personality disorder associated with phobic avoidance in patients with panic disorder. *American Journal of Psychiatry, 144,* 323–326.

Renneberg, B., Goldstein, A. J., Phillips, D., & Chambless, D. L. (1990). Intensive behavioral group treatment of avoidant personality disorder. *Behavior Therapy, 21,* 363–377.

Rice, M. E., & Harris, G. T. (1993). Treatment for prisoners with mental disorder. In J. H. Steadman & J. J. Cocozza (Eds.), *Mental illness in America's prisons* (pp. 91–130). Seattle, WA: National Coalition for the Mentally Ill in the Criminal Justice System.

Rice, M. E., Harris, G. T., & Cormier, C. (1992). Evaluation of a maximum security therapeutic community for psychopaths and other mentally disordered offenders. *Law and Human Behavior, 16,* 399–412.

Rice, M. E., Harris, G. T., & Quinsey, V. L. (1996). Treatment of forensic patients. In B. Sales & S. Shah (Eds.), *Mental health and the law: Research, policy, and practice* (pp. 141–190) New York: Carolina Academic Press.

Rice, M. E., Harris, G. T., Varney, G. W., & Quinsey, V. L. (1989). *Violence in institutions: Understanding, prevention, and control.* Toronto: Hans Huber.

Robins, L. N., Helzer, J. E., Croughan, J., & Ratcliff, K. S. (1981). National Institute of Mental Health Diagnostic Interview Schedule. Its history, characteristics, and validity. *Archives of General Psychiatry, 38,* 381–389.

Robins, L. N., & Regier, D. A. (1991). *Psychiatric disorders in America.* New York: Free Press.

Robinson, D. (1995). The impact of cognitive skills training on postrelease recidivism among Canadian Federal Offenders. *Research Report R-34.* Ottawa: Correctional Service of Canada.

Rogers, R., Duncan, J. C., Lynett, E., & Sewell, K. E. (1994). Prototypical analysis of antisocial personality disorder: DSM-IV and beyond. *Law and Human Behavior, 18,* 471–484.

Ronningstan, E., & Gunderson, J. G. (1990). Identifying criteria for narcissistic personality disorder. *American Journal of Psychiatry, 147,* 918–922.

Rosenberger, P. H., & Miller, G. A. (1989). Comparing borderline definitions: DSM-III borderline and schizotypal disorders. *Journal of Abnormal Psychology, 92,* 161–169.

Rutter, M., Boltin, P., Harrington, R., Le Couteur, A., Macdonald, H., & Simonoff, E. (1990). Genetic factors in child psychiatric disorders: I. A review of research strategies. *Journal of Child Psychology and Psychiatry, 31,* 5–37.

Schalling, D. (1993). Neurochemical correlates of personality, impulsivity, and disinhibitory suicidality. In S. Hodgins (Ed.), *Mental disorder and crime* (pp. 208–226). Newbury Park, CA: Sage.

Schlesinger, L. B. (1980). Distinctions between psychopathic, sociopathic, and antisocial personality disorders. *Psychological Reports, 47,* 15–21.

Schubert, D. S., Wolf, A. W., Patterson, M. B., Grande, T. P., & Pendelton, L. (1988). A statistical evaluation of the literature regarding the associations among alcoholism, drug abuse, and antisocial personality disorder. *International Journal of the Addictions, 23,* 797–808.

Schulz, S. C. (1986). The use of low-dose neuroleptics in the treatment of "schizo-obsessive" patients. *American Journal of Psychiatry, 143,* 1318–1319.

Serban, G., Conte, H. R., & Plutchik, R. (1987). Borderline and schizotypal personality disorders: Mutually exclusive or overlapping? *Journal of Personality Assessment, 5,* 15–22.

Serin, R. C. (1995). Treatment responsivity in criminal psychopaths, *Forum on Corrections Research, 7,* 23–26.

Serin, R. C., & Amos, N. L. (1995). The role of psychopathy in the assessment of dangerousness. *International Journal of Law and Psychiatry, 18,* 231–238.

Serin, R. C., & Kuriychuk, M. (1994). Social and cognitive processing deficits in violent offenders: Implications for treatment. *International Journal of Law and Psychiatry, 17,* 431–441.

Siever, L. J. (1985). Biological markers in schizotypal personality disorders. *Schizophrenia Bulletin, 11,* 564–575.

Skodol, A. E., Rosnick, L., Kellman, D., Oldham, J. M., & Hyler, S. E. (1988, May). *The validity of structured assessments of Axis II.* Paper presented at the 141st Annual Meeting of the American Psychiatric Association, Montreal, Quebec.

Slade, P. D. (1974). Psychometric studies of obsessional illness and obsessional personality. In H. R. Beech (Ed.), *Obsessional states* (pp. 95–112). London: Methuen.

Soloff, P. H., George, A., Nathan, R. S., Schulz, P. M., Ulrich, R. F., & Perel, J. M. (1986). Progress in pharmacotherapy of borderline disorders. *Archives of General Psychiatry, 43,* 691–697.

Spitzer, R. L., Endicott, J., & Gibbon, M. (1979). Crossing the border into borderline personality and borderline schizophrenia. *Archives of General Psychiatry, 36,* 17–24.

Spitzer, R. L., Endicott, J., & Robins, L. N. (1978). Research diagnostic criteria for the use in psychiatric research. *Archives of General Psychiatry, 35,* 773–782.

Sprock, J., Blashfield, R. K., & Smith, B. (1990). Gender weighting of DSM-III-R personality disorder criteria. *American Journal of Psychiatry, 147,* 586–590.

Steadman, H. J., Monahan, J., Robins, P. C., Applebaum, P., Grisso, T., Klassen, D., Mulvey, E. P., & Roth, L. (1993). From dangerousness to risk assessment: Implications for appropriate research strategies. In S. Hodgins (Ed.), *Mental disorder and crime* (pp. 39–62). Newbury Park, CA: Sage.

Stevenson, J., & Meares, R. (1992). An outcome study of psychotherapy for patients with borderline personality disorder. *American Journal of Psychiatry, 149,* 358–362.

Stone, M. (1985). Schizotypal personality: Psychotherapeutic aspects. *Schizophrenia Bulletin, 11,* 576–589.

Stone, M. (1993). Long-term outcome in personality disorders. *British Journal of Psychiatry, 162,* 299–313.

Stravynski, A., Lesage, A., Marcouiller, M., & Elie, R. (1989). A test of the therapeutic mechanism in social skills training with avoidant personality disorder. *Journal of Neurons and Mental Disease, 177,* 739–744.

Suedfeld, P., & Landon, P. B. (1978). Approaches to treatment. In R. D. Hare & D. Schalling (Eds.), *Psychopathic behavior: Approaches to research* (pp. 347–276). Chichester, England: Wiley.

Swartz, M., Blazer, I., George, L., & Landerman, R. (1986). Somatization disorder in a community population. *American Journal of Psychiatry, 143,* 1403–1408.

Torgersen, S. (1984). Genetic and nosological aspects of schizotypal and borderline personality disorders. *Archives of General Psychiatry, 41,* 546–554.

Templeman, T. L., & Wollersheim, J. P. (1979). A cognitive-behavioral approach to the treatment of psychopathy. *Psychotherapy: Theory, Research, and Practice, 16,* 132–139.

Tennent, G., Tennent, D., Prins, H., & Bedford, A. (1993). Is psychopathic disorder a treatable condition? *Medicine, Science, and the Law, 33,* 63–66.

Thompson-Pope, S. K., & Turkat, I. D. (1988). Reactions to ambiguous stimuli among paranoid personalities. *Journal of Psychopathology and Behavioral Assessment, 10,* 21–32.

Trull, T. J., Widiger, T. A., & Frances, A. (1987). Covariation of criteria for avoidant, schizoid, and dependent personality disorders. *American Journal of Psychiatry, 144,* 767–771.

Tupin, J. P. (1987). Psychopharmacology and aggression. In L. H. Roth (Ed.), *Clinical treatment of the violent person.* New York: Guilford.

Turkat, I. D., & Banks, D. S. (1987). Paranoid personality and its disorder. *Journal of Psychopathology and Behavioral Assessment, 9,* 295–304.

Turkat, I. D., Keane, S. P., & Thompson-Pope, S. K. (1990). Social processing in paranoid personalities. *Journal of Psychopathology and Behavioral Assessment, 12,* 263–269.

Turkat, I. D., & Levin, R. A. (1984). Formulation of personality disorders. In H. E. Adams & P. B. Sutker (Eds.), *Comprehensive handbook of psychotherapy* (pp. 495–522). New York: Plenum.

Turner, S. M., Beidel, D.C., Dancu, C. V., & Keys, D. J. (1986). Psychopathology of social phobia and comparison to avoidant personality disorder. *Journal of Abnormal Psychology, 95,* 389–397.

Turner, S. M., Beidel, D.C., Dancu, C. V., & Keys, D. J. (1991). Social phobia: Axis I and II correlates. *Journal of Abnormal Psychology, 100,* 102–106.

Virkkunen, M., & Linnoila, M. (1993). Serotonin in personality disorders with habitual violence and impulsivity. In S. Hodgins (Ed.), *Mental disorder and crime* (pp. 194–207). Newbury Park, CA: Sage.

Waldinger, R. J., & Frank, A. F. (1989). Transference and the vicissitudes of medication use by borderline patients. *Psychiatry, 52,* 416–427.

Walsh, J. (1990). Assessment and treatment of the schizotypal personality disorder. *Journal of Independent Social Work, 4,* 41–59.

Warner, R. (1978). The diagnosis of antisocial and hysterical personality disorders: An example of sex bias. *Journal of Nervous and Mental Disease, 166,* 839–845.

Webster, C. D., Eaves, D., Douglas, K., & Wintrup, A. (1995). The *HCR-20 Scheme: The assessment of dangerousness and risk.* Simon Fraser University and Forensic Psychiatric Services Commission of British Columbia. Vancouver, BC: Simon Fraser University Press.

White, J. L., Moffitt, T. E., Caspi, A., Bartusch, B. J., Needles, D. J., & Stouthamer-Loeber, M. D. (1994). Measuring impulsiveness and examining its relationship to delinquency. *Journal of Abnormal Psychology, 103,* 192–205.

Widiger, T. A., & Corbitt, E. M. (1993). Antisocial personality disorder: Proposals for DSM-IV. *Journal of Personality Disorders, 7,* 63–77.

Widiger, T. A., & Costa, P. T. (1994). Personality and personality disorders. *Journal of Abnormal Psychology, 103,* 78–91.

Widiger, T. A., & Frances, A. J. (1989). Epidemiology, diagnosis, and comorbidity of borderline personality disorder. In A. Tasman, R. E. Hales, & A. J. Frances (Eds.), *Review of psychiatry* (Vol. 8, pp. 8–24). Washington, DC: American Psychiatric Press.

Widiger, T. A., Frances, A. J., Spitzer, R. L., & Williams, J. B. W. (1988). The DSM-III personality disorder: An overview. *American Journal of Psychiatry, 145,* 786–795.

Widiger, T. A., Frances, A. J., & Trull, T. J. (1987). A psychometric analysis of the social-interpersonal and cognitive-perceptual items for the schizotypal personality disorder. *Archives of General Psychiatry, 44,* 741–745.

Widiger, T. A., Hurt, S. W., Frances, A. J., Clarkin, J. F., & Gilmore, M. (1984). Diagnostic efficiency and DSM-III. *Archives of General Psychiatry, 41,* 1005–1012.

Widiger, T. A., Miele, G. M., & Tilly, S. M. (1992). Alternative perspectives on the diagnosis of borderline personality disorder. In J. F. Carkin, E. Marziali, & H. Munroe-Blum (Eds.), *Borderline personality disorder: Clinical and empirical perspectives* (pp. 89–115). New York: Guilford.

Widiger, T. A., & Rogers, J. H. (1989). Prevalence and comorbidity of personality disorders. *Psychiatric Annals, 19,* 132–136.

Widiger, T. A., & Shea, T. (1991). Differentiation of Axis I and Axis II disorders. *Journal of Abnormal Psychology, 100,* 399–406.

Widiger, T. A., & Spitzer, R. L. (1991). Sex bias in the diagnosis of personality disorders: Conceptual and methodological issues. *Clinical Psychology Review, 11,* 1–22.

Widiger, T. A., & Trull, T. J. (1992). Personality and psychopathology: An application of the five-factor model. *Journal of Personality, 60,* 363–393.

Widiger, T. A., & Trull, T. J. (1993). Borderline and narcissistic personality disorders. In P. B. Sutker & H. E. Adams (Eds.), *Comprehensive handbook of psychopathology* (2nd ed., pp. 371–397). New York: Plenum.

Widiger, T. A., Trull, T. J., Hurt, S. W., Clarkin, J. F., & Frances, A. J. (1987). A multidimensional scaling of the DSM-III personality disorders. *Archives of General Psychiatry, 44,* 557–563.

Widom, C. S. (1978). A methodology for studying noninstitutionalized psychopaths. In R. D. Hare & D. Schalling (Eds.), *Psychopathic Behavior: Approaches to Research* (pp. 71–84). Chichester, England: Wiley.

Wiggins, J. S., & Pincus, A. L. (1989). Conceptions of personality disorders and dimensions of personality. *Psychological Assessment: A Journal of Consulting and Clinical Psychology, 1,* 305–316.

Wong, S., & Elek, D. (1990). *The treatment of psychopathy: A review.* Unpublished manuscript, Regional Psychiatric Centre, Saskatoon, Saskatchewan.

Wulach, J. S. (1983). Diagnosing the DSM-III antisocial personality disorder. *Professional Psychology-Research and Practice, 14,* 330–340.

Zanarini, M. C., Gunderson, J. G., Marino, M. F., Schwartz, E. O., & Frankenburg, F. R. (1989). Childhood experiences of borderline patients. *Comprehensive Psychiatry, 30,* 18–25.

Zimmerman, M., & Coryell, W. (1989). DSM-III personality disorder diagnoses in a nonpatient sample. *Archives of General Psychiatry, 46,* 682–689.

Zimmerman, M., & Coryell, W. (1990). Diagnosing personality disorder in the community: A comparison of self-report and interview measures. *Archives of General Psychiatry, 47,* 527–531.

Zimmerman, M., Pfohl, B., Stangl, D., & Corenthal, C. (1986). Assessment of DSM-III personality disorders: The importance of interviewing an informant. *Journal of Clinical Psychiatry, 47,* 261–263.

PART THREE

Special Topics

CHAPTER 17

Motor Activity and DSM-IV

WARREN W. TRYON

There are theoretical and practical clinical reasons why psychologists should be interested in motor activity. The first purpose of this chapter is to provide a developmental rationale for theoretical interest in activity. The second purpose is to provide practical clinical reasons why psychologists should extend their assessment practices to include activity measurement. A primary reason being that DSM-IV (*Diagnostic and Statistical Manual of Mental Disorders;* American Psychiatric Association [APA], 1994), like its predecessors, lists abnormal activity levels (e.g., agitation and psychomotor retardation) in many of its inclusion and exclusion criteria. Special attention will be devoted to how wrist activity can be used to diagnose several sleep disorders, thereby extending behavioral assessment into a new domain. The ability to obtain comprehensive, objective, quantitative, reliable, and valid naturalistic behavioral samples pertinent to child and adult psychopathology through unobtrusive, cost-effective technology allows psychologists to carefully monitor progress throughout treatment regardless of theoretical orientation or whether treatment is psychologically or pharmacologically based. The first clinical contributions by psychologists were in terms of assessment. Recent technological advances in activity measurement (Tryon & Williams, 1996) have enabled psychologists to substantially extend their clinical practices and research interests.

Activity is a remarkable life-span developmental variable because consistent individual differences can be discerned during gestation, through infancy, childhood, adolescence, and adulthood, into elderly and late life. Because activity is relevant to all developmental stages, it also pertains to psychopathology at all developmental stages. This chapter begins by briefly reviewing the developmental evidence for theoretical interest in activity and then considers the role activity measurement plays in DSM-IV diagnoses.

DEVELOPMENTAL EVIDENCE

Eaton and Saudino (1992) reviewed 14 studies showing that mothers can reliably and validly detect fetal activity beginning with the 28th week of gestation. Fetal activity appears to increase to a peak at around week 34 and then decrease through week 39. Consistent individual differences in prenatal activity level have been documented. Prenatal activity differences therefore constitute the earliest, first, behavioral trait.

Every theoretical description and account of infant temperament recognizes activity as a fundamental dimension of individual difference (Goldsmith et al., 1987). It is extremely unusual for psychologists to completely agree on anything, but this is the case with regard to activity and infant temperament. Perhaps it is because infants do not possess language and because their behavioral repertoire is so limited that differences in activity are so consistently noticed by all investigators.

Activity is considered to be a heritable trait because individual differences in activity are so clearly in evidence both prenatally and in young infants. Zuckerman (1991, pp. 7–8) reported that by age 9, activity is among the temperament facets with the highest heritability ratios. Buss and Plomin (1984, table 9.2) reported an identical twin activity correlation of .62 and a fraternal twin correlation of −.13 based on 228 identical and 172 fraternal twins whose average age was 61 months. Their table 9.4 presented mean identical/fraternal twin concordance rates for activity of 45/26, 88/59, 78/54, and 75/57. Their table 9.6 reported MZ/DZ twin correlations of .24/.11 at 6 months, .33/.28 at 12 months, .43/.14 at 18 months, and .58/.14 at 24 months in the same longitudinally studied subjects. These data strongly support the conclusion that activity is a prominent heritable aspect of temperament.

The robust presence of activity as a major dimension of stable individual difference prenatally through infancy leads to the strong expectation that it will continue into, and modify, latter developmental periods including the emergence of adult personality (Buss, 1989). Considerable evidence exists that personality can be described by five factors (the Big Five): Neuroticism, Extraversion, Openness, Agreeableness, and Conscientiousness (Costa & McCrae, 1980, 1992, 1994, 1995; Digman, 1990; 1994; Goldberg, 1990; Goldberg & Rosolack, 1994). Neuroticism entails self-piety, anxiety, insecurity, timidity, passivity, and immaturity. Its opposite pole is emotional stability. Extraversion entails being lively, talkative, sociable, spontaneous, adventurous, energetic, conceited, vain, nosey, and sensual. Its opposite pole is introversion. Openness refers to willingness to try new experiences, toleration, and appreciation of the unfamiliar. Curious, creative, imaginative, and untraditional describe this pole. Conventional and narrow-minded describe the other pole. Agreeableness entails trust, amiability, generosity, agreeableness, tolerance, courtesy, altruism, warmth, and honesty. The opposite pole on this dimension involves vindictiveness, criticism, disdain, antagonism, aggressiveness, dogmatism, temper, distrust, greed, and dishonesty. Conscientiousness entails industry, order, self-discipline, consistency, grace, reliability, formality, foresight, maturity, and thrift. Its opposite pole entails negligence, inconsistency, rebelliousness, irreverence, and intemperance.

Factor analytic studies have consistently demonstrated that activity is a facet of extraversion. Digman (1994) refactored two data sets collected on first- and second-grade children more than 30 years ago and found striking support for the current five-factor model. The differences from the results first obtained are attributed to changes in factor analytic procedures. Van Lieshout and Haselager (1994) had 937 parents and 899 teachers administer a Dutch translation of the

California Child Q-Set (Block & Block, 1980) to 1,836 children aged 3 to 14 years over six studies. They reported that the first five principal components corresponded to the Big Five personality factors.

Disagreement remains regarding the exact number of factors needed to characterize adult personality (Block, 1995), but certainty exists across investigators that extraversion and neuroticism must be included in any final personality taxonomy because they are so well documented (Eysenck 1991, 1994). Costa and McCrae (1992) describe the activity (E4) extraversion facet as follows: "A high Activity score is seen in rapid tempo and vigorous movement, in a sense of energy, and in a need to keep busy. Active people lead fast-paced lives. Low scorers are more leisurely and relaxed in tempo, although they are not necessarily sluggish or lazy" (p. 17). Reference to rapid and vigorous movements, keeping busy, and living a fast-paced life are just the kind of behaviors that activity-sensing devices respond to.

Halverson, Kohnstamm, and Martin (1994) edited a book entitled *The Developing Structure of Temperament and Personality from Infancy to Adulthood*, which attempted to give further insight into how personality develops from temperament. Section II was entitled "Emerging Conceptions of the Childhood Precursors of Personality Structure." Martin, Wisenbaker, and Huttunen (1994) reviewed factor analytic studies of temperament measures based on the work of Thomas and Chess (1977) and Thomas, Chess, and Birch (1968). The authors presented the results of 12 large factor analytic studies. Their table 8.2 consistently revealed an activity factor. The authors concluded that the activity factor develops into a facet of adolescent and adult extraversion. Figure 12.2 of Hagekull (1994) diagramed infant activity as making two contributions to childhood. First, infant activity contributes to childhood activity and to any external behavior problems that may develop during childhood. Second, activity and approach-withdrawal infant temperaments combine to form adolescent shyness, which is also related to internal behavior disorders that develop during adolescence. Both childhood activity and adolescent shyness are thought to develop into adult extraversion/introversion. Hagekull (1994) also theorized that infant activity influences childhood sociability, which helps determine adult agreeableness (friendliness/hostility).

Negative emotionality in childhood entails anger, fussing, loudness, and general irritability stemming from a low frustration tolerance. Martin, Wisenbaker, and Huttunen (1994) viewed negative emotionality as a precursor to adult agreeableness and neuroticism. Task persistence in childhood is viewed as a precursor of adult conscientiousness. Adaptability in childhood is thought to relate positively with adult agreeableness and negatively with adult neuroticism. Social inhibition in childhood seems related to extraversion in adulthood.

Another approach to the emergence of temperament is to determine the earliest age at which the five-factor solution consistently emerges. Section III of Halverson et al. (1994) focused on "Deriving the Five-Factor Model from Parental Ratings of Children and Adolescents." Robins, John, and Caspi (1994) provided evidence that five factors can be recovered from Block and Block's (1980) California Child Q-Set as adapted for use by laypersons (Caspi et al., 1992). However, evidence of two additional factors also is found. One factor is activity, the other irritability.

Inactivity is a health risk for cardiovascular disease (Fox, Naughton, & Haskell, 1971; Leon, Connett, Jacobs, & Rauramaa, 1987; Morris, Everitt, Pollard, Chave, & Semmence, 1980; Oberman, 1985; Paffenbarger & Hale, 1975; Paffenbarger, Hyde, Wing, & Steinmetz, 1984; Powell, Thompson, Caspersen, & Kendrick, 1987), colon cancer (Gerhardsson, Norell, Kiviranta, Pedersen, & Ahlbom, 1986; Slattery, Schumacher, Smith, West, & Abd-Elghany, 1988; Vena et al., 1985), diabetes mellitus, hypertension, and osteoporosis (Siscovick, La-Porte, & Newman, 1985). Activity reduces the risk of all causes of mortality (Blair et al., 1989; Paffenbarger, Hyde, Wing, & Hsieh, 1986). Consequently, the inclination or conscious decision to adopt an active lifestyle partly determines who survives to late life. This selective factor tends to remove inactive persons from the population over time. Unfortunately, several chronic diseases (e.g., chronic obstructive pulmonary disease and coronary heart disease) diminish activity level and restore and augment the lower tail of the activity dimension in later life (Tryon, 1991a, pp. 209–220).

Palmore (1970) suggested that exercise is the single health practice most strongly associated with longevity in the elderly. Elderly people evaluate their own health, and the health of others, largely in terms of activity (Burnside, 1978; Gueldner & Spradley, 1988), with more active persons perceived as healthier. McAuley, Courneya, and Lettunich (1991) reported that self-efficacy increases following exercise in older persons. Stewart, King, and Haskell (1993) reported increased quality of life as a result of endurance exercise training in 50–65-year-old adults. Taylor (1991) reviewed other psychological benefits of regular exercise. Some evidence supports the view that aerobic exercise improves neuropsychological function in older individuals by increasing cerebral metabolism (Dustman et al., 1984).

The purpose of this section has been to contextualize why activity is of theoretical and practical interest to psychologists. That activity is a prominent life-span developmental variable and that psychopathology alters developmental expression explains why psychopathology alters activity and therefore why activity excesses and deficits are entailed in many DSM inclusion and exclusion criteria.

DSM-IV

Tryon (1986) reviewed activity-related inclusion and exclusion criteria for DSM-I, DSM-II, and DSM-III. Tryon (1991b) analyzed DSM-III-R. This chapter provides a comprehensive analysis of DSM-IV inclusion and exclusion criteria relating to activity. Important issues include: 1. the reliability and validity of the instrument used to measure activity; 2. the site of attachment chosen; 3. the content validity of the behavioral sample taken, that is, its representativeness of natural situations and circumstances; 4. the duration or extent of the behavioral sample obtained; and 5. the interpretation of the inclusion and exclusion criteria.

Comprehensive reviews of the operating characteristics of activity-measuring instruments and their reliability and validity have been published previously by Tryon (1985; 1991a, pp. 23–63). A comprehensive analysis of a new fully proportional instrument capable of accurately measuring and storing the intensity of physical activity every minute of the day and night (there are 1,440 minutes in 24 hours) for 22 days is presented by Tryon and Williams (1996).

Site of attachment also has been discussed (Tryon, 1991a, pp. 8, 42–43). The waist (trunk) and wrist are the two most common sites of attachment. They are not equally active at all times. The dominant and nondominant wrists may be differentially active. Waist movements expend more energy because they entail displacement of the body's center of gravity. Wrist movements are greater than waist movements during sleep and have been the preferred site of attachment for sleep-wake discriminations for this reason. The ability to discriminate sleep from wake using wrist activity has been documented (Sadeh, Hauri, Kripke, & Lavie, 1995; Tryon, 1991a, pp. 149–184).

Behavioral samples are content valid to the extent that they are representative of the behavior being assessed, just as psychometric tests are content valid if they adequately survey the domain being measured (Anastasi, 1988, p. 140; Linehan, 1980; Tryon 1993). Behavioral observations made under office or laboratory conditions may or may not validly represent behavior displayed at home or school. Test developers and behavioral assessors bear the burden of proof regarding content validity. Generalization must be demonstrated rather than assumed. Content validity depends upon the duration of assessment as well as the conditions under which assessment occurs. DSM-IV often refers to 2 weeks as the relevant duration. Regarding activity measurement, 2 weeks has the advantage of replicating each day of the week once. We do not all engage in the same activities each day of the week. Our behavior often differs on the weekend from that during the week.

The main focus of this chapter is on interpreting the activity-related diagnostic inclusion and exclusion criteria. Complete diagnostic criteria are tabled so that the reader can better evaluate their description in the text. We begin our coverage with sleep disorders for at least two reasons. First, many psychologists are surprised to learn that several important aspects of sleep can be evaluated in the home using unobtrusive wrist activity monitors. Second, the Standards of Practice Committee (1995) of the American Sleep Disorders Association recently published "Practice Parameters for the Use of Actigraphy in the Clinical Assessment of Sleep Disorders." This event marks the clinical maturity of an important technology of which most psychologists are unaware. Understanding the role of actigraphy in the evaluation of sleep disorders requires an understanding of the sleep-onset process to which we now turn.

BEHAVIORAL SLEEP MEASUREMENT

Sleep Onset Spectrum

Going to sleep is not a discrete or simple process but entails an orderly progression of behavioral and physiological events. Harsh and Ogilvie (1994) and Ogilvie and Wilkinson (1988) refer to this as a sleep onset period (SOP). Tryon (1991a) used the term sleep onset spectrum (SOS) to emphasize the orderly sequence of events associated with sleep onset. This process begins with lying quietly, followed by decreased muscle tone and EEG changes, and culminates in an increased auditory threshold.

Although sleep was initially studied behaviorally (Tryon, 1995a, 1995b), now it is primarily studied in terms of electroencephalography (EEG) and polysomnography (PSG). Kryger, Roth, and Dement's (1994) recent 95-chapter second edition of their comprehensive sleep medicine text exclude all but EEG and PSG approaches to sleep. EEG sleep scoring criteria (Rechtschaffen & Kales, 1968) distinguished several stages of sleep versus one waking stage. It is important to note that criteria for EEG stage 1 sleep, and therefore sleep onset, were derived from the behavioral "gold standard" that hand-held objects are dropped upon going to sleep because muscle tone decreases (cf. Blake, Gerard, & Kleitman, 1939; Perry & Goldwater, 1987; Snyder & Scott, 1972). Rechtschaffen (1994) and Tryon (1995a, 1995b) reviewed other behaviorally oriented sleep studies. Rechtschaffen (1994) stated that "physiological measures derive their value as indicators of sleep from their correlations with the behavioral criteria, not from any intrinsic ontological or explanatory superiority" (p. 5). He further concluded that "any scientific definition of sleep that ignores the behaviors by which sleep is generally known unnecessarily violates common understanding and invites confusion" (Rechtschaffen, 1994, p. 4).

Wrist Actigraphic Sleep Assessment

Webster, Messin, Mullaney, and Kripke (1982) attached accelerometers to both wrists and both ankles and found that the left wrist was the single most active site. Van Hilten, Middelkoop, Kuiper, Kramer, and Roos (1994) recorded wrist and waist activity (cf. Middelkoop, 1994). They found the wrists to be equally active but more active than the waist. Sadeh, Sharkey, and Carskadon (1994) attached miniature wrist actigraphs (Model AMA-32, Ambulatory Monitoring, Inc., Ardsley, NY) to both wrists of 20 normal adults and 16 adolescents for two nights in a sleep laboratory. Recording activity every 30 seconds, they found that mean activity was significantly greater at the dominant than at the nondominant wrist during PSG-determined sleep (6.84 vs. 6.16 activity counts) as well as during wakefulness (25.8 vs. 22.3 activity counts). The mean values obtained during sleep are actually quite similar, which may explain why the authors also reported that when data for the dominant wrist were submitted to the sleep-wake scoring algorithm developed for the nondominant wrist, and vice versa, agreement rates ranged from 93% to 99% across all 36 subjects. Wrist actigraphy detects PSG-determined sleep with 93%–99% accuracy regardless of which wrist is used. In conclusion, the wrist is the preferred site of attachment for discriminating sleep from wake, but it does not seem to matter which wrist is used.

Tryon (1995a, 1995b) reviewed the literature validating wrist actigraphy against polysomnography. In brief, Webster, Kripke, Messin, Mullaney, and Wyborney (1982) developed and prospectively validated and cross-validated wrist actigraphy, reporting 96% agreement with PSG. Zomer et al. (1987) reported a correlation of $r(13) = .94$, $p < .0001$ with wrist actigraphy. Sadeh, Alster, Urbach, and Lavie (1989) reported 91% agreement between wrist actigraphy and

PSG. Cole and Kripke (1989) and Cole, Kripke, Gruen, Mullaney, and Gillin (1992) reported 88% agreement with PSG. Mason et al. (1992) reported that wrist actigraphy estimated total sleep time correlated $r(8) = .823, p < .005$ with PSG. In sum, wrist actigraphy both correlates highly and agrees well in terms of number of minutes with PSG estimates of total sleep time, number of awakenings, and time awake after going to sleep in normal and pathological sleepers. Sadeh et al. (1994) reported that PSG-determined sleep could be correctly detected from 93% to 99% of the time with wrist actigraphy. Sadeh et al. (1995) recently reviewed the actigraphy literature and concluded that "actigraphy provides a cost-effective method for longitudinal, natural assessment of sleep-wake patterns" (p. 300).

The one area where discrepant findings consistently emerge is in estimating initial sleep-onset latency. While a period of quiescence precedes PSG-defined stage 1 sleep, some patients with sleep disorders such as insomnia lie motionless for up to 45 minutes prior to the onset of EEG stage 1 sleep. This discrepancy usually has been interpreted as *entirely* due to wrist actigraphy *error*. Several facts argue against this interpretation. First, no measurement procedure is without error including PSG. Ogilvie and Wilkinson (1988) reported that interrater EEG sleep scoring agreement values range from 80% to 98%. Spiegel (1981, p. 62) reported that the reliability of scoring stage 1 sleep can be as low as 60%, whereas the reliability of scoring stage 2 sleep is approximately 90%. Hence, up to 40% of EEG stage 1 scoring, and therefore sleep-wake scoring and PSG versus actigraphy differences, can be questioned. Second, the multidimensional character of sleep onset led Rechtschaffen (1994) to conclude that

> despite these and other significant relationships between behavioral sleep measures and physiological indicators, there appears to be no hope of defining a precise behavioral or physiological point of sleep onset, except by arbitrary criteria. This is not a new sentiment. It was expressed by Davis et al. (1937) in one of the earliest empirical studies of sleep onset; Kleitman (1963) said as much in the opening sentence of his chapter on sleep onset; and it has more recently been reiterated by Ogilvie and Wilkinson (1988). (p. 7)

One cannot therefore reasonably take one point, EEG sleep stage 1, as a gold standard and disparage all other multidimensional facets of sleep onset as being in error.

If the onset of EEG sleep stage 1 is *arbitrarily* selected as a reference point, one can behaviorally predict this event using a "deadman" device like the one described by Ogilvie, Wilkinson, and Allison's (1989), and a similar device described by Tryon, Gruen, and Reitman (1995), because the onset of EEG stage 1 sleep was validated using the "gold standard" that people drop handheld objects due to decreased muscle tone associated with sleep onset (cf. Blake, Gerard, & Kleitman, 1939; Perry & Goldwater, 1987; Snyder & Scott, 1972). Subjects are instructed to maintain closure of a 90 g hand-held microswitch while in bed attempting to sleep. A battery-powered electric clock will continue to run as long as the switch remains closed. The switch opens when muscle tone decreases as a part of EEG stage 1 sleep onset, thereby stopping the clock and documenting the time or latency of sleep onset.

SLEEP DISORDERS

DSM-IV distinguished four major sleep disorders: 1. primary sleep disorders (dyssomnias and parasomnias), 2. sleep disorders related to another mental disorder, 3. sleep disorder due to a general medical condition, and 4. substance-induced sleep disorder.

Primary Sleep Disorders

Primary Sleep Disorders are "presumed to arise from endogeneous abnormalities in sleep-wake generating or timing mechanisms, often complicated by conditioning factors" (APA, 1994, p. 551).

Dyssomnias

Dyssomnias are "characterized by abnormalities in the amount, quality, or timing of sleep" (p. 551).

Primary insomnia (307.42). The five primary DSM-IV criteria that define this disorder are listed in Table 17.1. The patient has substantial difficulty *initiating or maintaining sleep for at least 1 month* that cannot be explained by narcolepsy, breathing-related sleep disorder, circadian rhythm sleep disorder, a parasomnia, major depressive disorder, generalized anxiety disorder, delirium, prescription drugs, drug abuse, or a general medical condition. The clinical impact (criterion B) must necessarily rely on clinical judgment, patient self-report, and spouse or family report. Excluding other possible diagnoses entails evaluating the extent to which their diagnostic inclusion and exclusion criteria are met as discussed elsewhere in this chapter. Difficulty initiating and maintaining sleep for at least 1 month has traditionally been evaluated exclusively by self-report in that 30 consecutive nights of sleep laboratory assessment or home monitoring has not been done and will not be done for several reasons. It is prohibitively expensive and patients would not likely comply. Wrist actigraphy (cf. Hauri & Wisbey, 1992), supplemented by hand pressure estimates of initial sleep-onset latency, is a cost-effective practical method of monitoring sleep-onset and maintaining sleep after initial onset in the patient's home for a month.

The 1 month criterion is meant to distinguish temporary from chronic complaints. Continuous difficulty initiating or maintaining sleep is implied but greater specificity is lacking because there has not been a practical method of quantifying sleep onset and wake after sleep onset prior to actigraphy. The consistency with which primary insomniacs have difficulty initiating and maintaining sleep over 30 consecutive nights remains unknown because the relevant research has not yet been conducted. This is an instance of where the theoretical definition of a disorder exceeds quantitative evaluation by standard methods. Wrist actigraphy provides a practical cost-effective method for obtaining this information (cf. Pollak, Perlick, & Linsner, 1992).

Probably it is the case that a 1-week behavioral sample will accurately predict a 1-month behavioral sample thereby allowing a positive diagnosis to be based on seven consecutive nights of data collection plus self-report that the measured week is representative of at least the previous 3 weeks. The 1-week behavioral

TABLE 17.1   DSM-IV Diagnostic Criteria for Sleep Disorders

Dyssomnias

I. Primary Insomnia (307.42, p. 557)

   A. *"The predominant complaint is difficulty initiating or maintaining sleep, or nonrestorative sleep, for at least 1 month."*

   B. "The sleep disturbance (or associated daytime fatigue) causes clinically significant distress or impairment in social, occupational, or other important areas of functioning."

   C. "The sleep disturbance does not occur exclusively during the course of Narcolepsy, Breathing-Related Sleep Disorder, Circadian Rhythm Sleep Disorder, or a Parasomnia."

   D. "The disturbance does not occur exclusively during the course of another mental disorder (e.g., Major Depressive Disorder, Generalized Anxiety Disorder, a delirium)."

   E. "The disturbance is not due to the direct physiological effects of a substance (e.g., a drug of abuse, a medication) or a general medical condition."

II. Primary Hypersomnia (307.44, p. 562)

   A. *"The predominant complaint is excessive sleepiness for at least 1 month (or less if recurrent) as evidenced by either prolonged sleep episodes or daytime sleep episodes that occur almost daily."*

   B. "The excessive sleepiness causes clinically significant distress or impairment in social, occupational, or other important areas of functioning."

   C. "The excessive sleepiness is not better accounted for by insomnia and does not occur exclusively during the course of another Sleep Disorder (e.g., Narcolepsy, Breathing-Related Sleep Disorder, Circadian Rhythm Sleep Disorder, or a Parasomnia) and cannot be accounted for by an inadequate amount of sleep."

   D. "The disturbance does not occur exclusively during the course of another mental disorder."

   E. "The disturbance is not due to the direct physiological effects of a substance (e.g., a drug of abuse, a medication) or a general medical condition."

III. Narcolepsy (347, p. 567)

   A. *"Irrestible attacks of refreshing sleep that occur daily over at least 3 months."*

   B. "The presence of one or both of the following:

     1. Cataplexy (i.e., brief episodes of sudden bilateral loss of muscle tone, most often in association with intense emotion).

     2. Recurrent intrusions of elements of rapid eye movement (REM) sleep into the transition between sleep and wakefulness, as manifested by either hypnopompic or hypnagogic hallucinations or sleep paralysis at the beginning or end of sleep episodes."

   C. "The disturbance is not due to the direct physiological effects of a substance (e.g., a drug of abuse, a medication) or another general medical condition."

IV. Breathing-Related Sleep Disorder (780.59, p. 573)

   A. *"Sleep disruption, leading to excessive sleepiness or insomnia, that is judged to be due to a sleep-related breathing condition* (e.g., obstructive or central sleep apnea syndrome or central alveolar hypoventilation syndrome)."

   B. "The dusturbance is not better accounted for by another mental disorder and is not due to the direct physiological effects of a substance (e.g., a drug of abuse and a medication) or another general medical condition (other than a breathing-related disorder)."

V. Circadian Rhythm Sleep Disorder (307.45, p. 578)

   A. *"A persistent or recurrent pattern of sleep disruption leading to excessive sleepiness or insomnia that is due to a mismatch between the sleep-wake schedule required by a person's environment and his or her circardian sleep-wake pattern."*

   B. "The sleep disturbance causes clinically significant distress or impairment in social, occupational, or other important areas of functioning."

   C. "The disturbance does not occur exclusively during the course of another Sleep Disorder or other mental disorder."

   D. "The disturbance is not due to the direct physiological effects of a substance (e.g., a drug of abuse, a medication) or a general medical condition."

TABLE 17.1   (*Continued*)

Parasomnias

I. Nightmare Disorder (307.47, p. 583)

    A. "*Repeated awakenings from the major sleep period or naps* with detailed recall of extended and extremely frightening dreams, usually involving threats to survival, security, or self-esteem. The awakenings generally occur the *second half of the sleep period.*"

    B. "On awakening from the frightening dreams, the person rapidly becomes oriented and alert (in contrast to the confusion and disorientation seen in Sleep Terror Disorder and some forms of epilepsy)."

    C. "The dream experience, or sleep disturbance resulting from the awakening, causes clinically significant distress or impairment in social, occupational, or other important areas of functioning."

    D. "The nightmares do not occur exclusively during the course of another mental disorder (e.g., a deliruim, Posttraumatic Stress Disorder) and are not due to the direct physiological effects of a substance (e.g., a drug of abuse or a medication) or a general medical condition."

II. Sleep Terror Disorder (307.46, p. 587)

    A. "*Recurrent episodes of abrupt awakening from sleep, usually occurring during the first third of the major sleep episode* and beginning with a panicky scream."

    B. "Intense fear and signs of autonomic arousal such as tachycardia, rapid breathing, and sweating during each episode."

    C. "Relative unresponsiveness to efforts of others to comfort the person during the episode."

    D. "No detailed dream is recalled and there is *amnesia for the episode.*"

    E. "The episodes cause clinically significant distress or impairment in social, occupational, or other important areas of functioning."

    F. "The disturbance is not due to the direct physiogical effects of a substance (e.g., a drug of abuse, a medication) or a general medical condition."

III. Sleepwalking Disorder (307.46, p. 591)

    A. "*Repeated episodes of rising from bed during sleep and walking about, usually occurring during the first third of the major sleep episode.*"

    B. "While sleepwalking, the person has a blank, staring face, is relatively unresponsive to the efforts of others to communicate with him or her, and can be awakened only with great difficulty."

    C. "On awakening (either from the sleepwalking episode or the next morning), the person has *amnesia for the episode.*"

    D. "Within several minutes after awakening from the sleepwalking episode, there is no impairment of mental activity or behavior (although there may initially be a short period of confusion or disorientation)."

    E. "The sleepwalking causes clinically significant distress or impairment in social, occupational, or other important areas of functioning."

    F. "The disturbance is not due to the direct physiological effects of a substance (e.g., a drug of abuse and a medication) or a general medical condition."

Note. Italic entries concern activity.

sample will probably provide a comprehensive baseline evaluation against which one can evaluate the effectiveness of whatever therapeutic intervention is implemented.

Primary hypersomnia (307.44). The five primary DSM-IV criteria defining this disorder are listed in Table 17.1. The patient *sleeps too long or sleeps during the day* over a period of *at least 1 month* to the point where it compromises social or occupational functioning, or both, and cannot be explained by insomnia, another sleep disorder, another mental disorder, licit or illicit drugs, a general medical condition, or *insufficient sleep.* While impact on social and occupational functioning remains a clinical judgment, one must have data showing the times the patient slept during each 24-hour period for 30 consecutive days. Standard methods cannot provide these data and consequently, this diagnosis is never reached on empirical grounds. Wrist actigraphy could be sleep scored over each 24-hour period for 1 month to provide the necessary empirical support. These data could be inspected for when the patient went to sleep at night, when they awoke, if they slept during the day, and if so for how long. It could be determined if daytime sleeping was responsive to inadequate nighttime sleep and if daytime napping occurred when the patient was at work or home.

Narcolepsy (347). The DSM-IV criteria for narcolepsy are presented in Table 17.1. The patient has uncontrollable periods of *diurnal sleep over a period of at least 3 months* that may be associated with cataplexy or intrusions of REM sleep during sleep-wake transitions that cannot be explained by a drug or general medical condition. Sleep laboratory or home PSG analysis is capable of detecting REM sleep during sleep-wake transitions. The problem is the degree to which this phenomenon occurs nightly and the maximum number of nights the patient can spend in the sleep laboratory. Standard methods do not provide information on diurnal sleep over at least 3 months' time.

Wrist actigraphy records could be continuously scored for sleep to detect instances of daytime sleeping over a 3-month period. It may well be that a 1- or 2-week behavioral sample would accurately predict a 3-month behavioral sample. In this case, a reduced behavioral sample in combination with self-report that the measured period is representative of at least the prior 3 months would provide an empirical basis for reaching this diagnosis.

Breathing-related sleep disorder (780.59). The two primary criteria for this disorder are given in Table 17.1. *Abnormal breathing disrupts that patient's sleep* and leads to excessive daytime sleepiness or *insomnia* that cannot be explained by another mental disorder and is not due to a drug or other general medical condition. Generally abnormal breathing is evaluated in the sleep laboratory or with home PSG. However, Tryon (1991a, p. 189) described the use of abdominal actigraphy to detect spasmodic breathing which results as patients come out of an obstructive sleep apnea (OSA) episode. Normal breathing causes the abdominal actigraph to rise and fall so sligthly and smoothly that little activity is recorded by the internal accelerometer. However, sudden movements of the diaphragm entail high degrees of acceleration despite relatively short movements. This activity causes clear spikes to occur in the actigraph record at the time this event occurs. Such information allows one to count the frequency with which OSA events occur and to specify the time of their occurrence with an accuracy of 1 minute or better if a shorter recording epoch is chosen. A 1-second epoch is the shortest epoch that users can select with current software.

Wrist actigraphy can be used to determine if OSA events disturbed sleep by synchronizing the internal clocks of both the wrist and abdominal actigraphs. Wrist actigraphy can also be supplemented with the previously described hand pressure device to determine initial sleep-onset latency to evaluate whether OSA events lead to insomnia. All of these analyses can be conducted in the patient's home over as many nights as desired.

Circadian rhythm sleep disorder (307.45). The four inclusion criteria for this DSM-IV disorder are provided in Table 17.1. The patient experiences clinically significant *persistent or recurrent sleep disruption* leading to excessive sleepiness or *insomnia* because of a mismatch between their internal sleep-wake schedule and environmental demands that cannot be explained by another sleep disorder, a drug, or a general medical condition. Data documenting sleep disruption over an unspecified number of consecutive nights and the concurrent possibility of delayed sleep onset, insomnia, are not presently available by standard methods. Wrist actigraphy supplemented with hand pressure sleep-onset timing can supply the desired information (cf. Brown, Smolensky, D'Alonzo, & Redman, 1990; Mason & Tapp 1992; Sodeh, 1994).

Four subtypes are acknowledged. *Delayed sleep phase type* is defined by "a persistent pattern of late sleep onset and late awakening times, with an inability to fall asleep and awaken at a desired earlier time" (APA, 1994, p. 578). Hand pressure monitoring can determine sleep onset. Wrist actigraphy can document the time of awakening that can be compared to the patients' target awakening time to verify the extent to which they cannot wake up at a chosen earlier time.

Jet lag type is defined by "*sleepiness* and alertness that occur at an inappropriate time of day relative to local time, occurring after repeated travel across more than one time zone" (p. 578). Sleepiness is usually evaluated by a Multiple Sleep Latency Test (MLST; Carskadon, 1994). Because sleep latency is calculated from lights out until the first epoch scored sleep, sleep-onset latency can be accurately estimated by the hand pressure device mentioned above. Carskadon indicated that MSLTs are generally conducted at least 4 times at 2-hour intervals beginning 1.5–3 hours after the end of nocturnal sleep; generally beginning about 0900 or 1000 hours. The test is discontinued after 20 minutes if the subject does not fall asleep. The standard MSLT continues for 15 minutes after sleep onset. The simplicity of the handheld pressure device means that patients can self-administer this test in their own homes. Awakening at home can be achieved by a preset alarm clock. Normal sleep onset occurs within 10–20 minutes. Sleep onset in 5 minutes or less indicates sleepiness.

Shift work type is defined as "*insomnia during the major sleep period* or *excessive sleepiness during the major wake period* associated with night shift work or frequency changing shift work" (APA, 1994, p. 578). Insomnia and daytime sleepiness can be evaluated by previously described handheld pressure and wrist actigraphic methods.

Parasomnias

Parasomnias are "characterized by *abnormal behavioral* or physiological events occurring in association with sleep, specific sleep stages, or sleep-wake transitions" (p. 551). Sleep is associated with very little activity. Abnormal behaviors entail substantial movement which wrist actigraphy can detect.

Nightmare disorder (370.47). The four criteria constituting this sleep disorder are presented in Table 17.1. Patients experience distress or dysfunction because they *repeatedly awaken* and become alert during their *major sleep period* due to frightening dreams that cannot be explained by another mental disorder, a drug, or a general medical condition. Wrist actigraphy can clearly discriminate a highly vigilant, alert state from sleep. The emotional distress due to the very frightening dream will produce motor activity far in excess of that associated with quiet sleep. Actigraphy documents the time of onset to an accuracy of 1 minute or better if a nonstandard epoch length is chosen.

DSM-IV requires a repeated pattern of such events without specifying their frequency. Wrist actigraphy could provide normative data by studying patients thought to have this disorder while they sleep at home over a month or two. Perhaps a 1-week behavioral sample would accurately predict a 1-month sample and therefore would be sufficient to empirically establish this diagnosis.

Sleep terror disorder (307.46). The six criteria used to diagnose this disorder are presented in Table 17.1. The patient experiences clinically significant stress or occupational dysfunction because of *abrupt awakening* from sleep due to intense fear that cannot be explained by a drug or general medication. The patient may *not remember* these events. Actigraphy can document the time of abrupt awakening with an accuracy of 1 minute or better if a nonstandard epoch is chosen. An objective record of nocturnal awakening is especially important given that the patient can have amnesia for these episodes. This factor is especially critical if they live alone and no one is available to document the frequency of these events or if the person lives with an uncooperative or often absent spouse.

Sleepwalking disorder (307.46). The six DSM-IV criteria for this disorder are found in Table 17.1. The patient *repeatedly rises from bed during sleep and walks about* but may have *no recollection* of doing so the next morning. Wrist actigraphy will detect awakening and is probably sufficient to detect ambulation. An additional waist actigraph will decisively detect ambulation. That the patient may have no recollection of these events makes it important to have an objective record of their occurrence. Actigraphy can document the time these events occurred to an accuracy of 1 minute or better if a nonstandard epoch is chosen.

Sleep Disorders Related to Another Mental Disorder

The essential feature of this disorder "is the presence of either insomnia or hypersomnia that is judged to be related temporally and causally to another mental disorder" (APA, 1994, p. 592).

Insomnia related to another mental disorder (307.42). The ability of wrist actigraphy, supplemented by hand pressure monitoring, to quantify insomnia makes it relevant to evaluating insomnia due to another mental disorder.

Hypersomnia related to another mental disorder (307.44). The ability of wrist actigraphy, supplemented by hand pressure monitoring, to quantify hypersomnia makes it relevant to evaluating hypersomnia due to another mental disorder.

Sleep Disorder Due to a General Medical Condition (780.xx)

Some medical disorders can produce insomnia, hypersomnia, or a parasomnia (cf. Redeker et al. 1994). Wrist actigraphy supplemented with hand pressure monitoring is capable of quantifying all of these conditions as described above. The subtypes of this disorder are insomnia type, hypersomnia type, parasomnia type, and mixed type. The latter is diagnosed when multiple sleep problems exist but no single type predominates.

Substance-Induced Sleep Disorder

The subtypes of this disorder also are insomnia type, hypersomnia type, parasomnia type, and mixed type. Actigraphy and hand pressure monitoring are relevant to all three as previously stated.

Two specifiers exist. The first is "with onset during intoxication" indicating that symptoms developed as a result of intoxication. The "with onset during withdrawal" specifier is used if the sleep disorder begins after discontinuing a substance.

MOOD DISORDERS

The use of actigraphy to quantify mood disorders has been reviewed by Teicher (1995) and Tryon (1985, 1986, 1991a, 1991b). Aronen et al. (1996) reported that activity correlated significantly with clinical ratings of depressive severity across several mood disorders and concluded that actigraphy provides an objective measure of depressive severity. Teicher et al. (1995) used actigraphy to identify abnormal rest-activity circadian rhythms in patients with seasonal affective disorder (SAD).

The DSM-IV distinguishes "unipolar" depressive disorder from bipolar disorder. Both of these disorders are distinguished from mood disorder due to a general medical condition and from substance-induced mood disorder. These disorders presume a definition of major depressive episode, manic episode, mixed episode, and hypomanic episode to which we now turn.

Episode Definitions

Major depressive episode. Table 17.2 presents the DSM-IV definition of a major depressive episode (MDE). A patient must have five or more of the nine listed characteristics to qualify as having a MDE. Three of these criteria concern activity. Item four specifies "insomnia or hypersomnia nearly every day" (APA, 1994, p. 327). Wrist actigraphy supplemented by hand pressure monitoring can document the presence of insomnia and hypersomnia. Item five specifies "psychomotor agitation or retardation nearly every day (observable by others, not merely subjective feelings of restlessness or being slowed down)" (p. 327). The parenthetical admonition insists on noticeable change, and activity monitors will clearly measure such changes (cf. Raoux et al., 1994). Because the emphasis is on change rather than absolute level, the most relevant point of comparison is a 1- or 2-week activity measurement taken as part of a comprehensive physical examination prior to the onset of the MDE. The rationale is the same as having a healthy electrocardiogram on file when diagnosing heart disease. Unfortunately, behavioral specimens are not presently obtained as part of routine physi-

TABLE 17.2   Episode Definitions

I. Major Depressive Episode (p. 327)
  A. "Five (or more) of the following symptoms have been present during the same 2-week period and represent a change from previous functioning; at least one of the symptoms is either 1. depressed mood or 2. loss of interest or pleasure."
    1. "Depressed mood most of the day, nearly every day, as indicated by either subjective report (e.g., feels sad or empty) or observation made by others (e.g., appears tearful)."
    2. "Markedly diminished interest or pleasure in all or almost all, activities most of the day, nearly every day (as indicated by either subjective account or observation made by others)."
    3. "Significant weight loss when not dieting or weight gain (e.g., a change of more than 5% of body weight in a month), or decrease or increase in appetite nearly every day."
    4. "*Insomnia or hypersomnia nearly every day.*"
    5. "*Psychomotor agitation or retardation nearly every day (observable by others, not merely subjective feelings of restlessness or being slowed down).*"
    6. "*Fatigue or loss of energy nearly every day.*"
    7. "Feelings of worthlessness or excessive or inappropriate guilt (which may be delusional) nearly every day (not merely self-reproach or guilt about being sick)."
    8. "Diminished ability to think or concentrate, or indecisiveness, nearly every day (either by subjective account or as observed by others)."
    9. "Recurrent thoughts of death (not just fear of dying), recurrent suicidal ideation without a specific plan, or a suicide attempt or a specific plan for committing suicide."
  B. "The symptoms do not meet criteria for a Mixed Episode."
  C. "The symptoms cause clinically significant distress or impairment in social, occupational, or other important areas of functioning."
  D. "The symptoms are not due to the direct physiological effects of a substance (e.g., a drug of abuse or a medication) or a general medical condition (e.g., hypothyroidism)."
  E. "The symptoms are not better accounted for by bereavement, i.e., after the loss of a loved one, the symptoms persist for longer than 2 months or are characterized by marked functional impairment, morbid preoccupation with worthlessness, suicidal ideation, psychotic symptoms, or psychomotor retardation."
II. Manic Episode (p. 332)
  A. "A distinct period of abnormally and persistently elevated, expansive, or irritable mood, lasting at least 1 week (or any duration if hospitalization is necessary)."
  B. "During the period of mood disturbance, three (or more) of the following symptoms have persisted (four if the mood is only irritable) and have been present to a significant degree."
    1. "Inflated self-esteem or grandiosity."
    2. "*Decreased need for sleep (e.g., feels rested after only 3 hours of sleep).*"
    3. "More talkative than usual or pressure to keep talking."
    4. "Flight of ideas or subjective experience that thoughts are racing."
    5. "Distractibility (i.e., attention too easily drawn to unimportant or irrelevant external stimuli)."
    6. "*Increase in goal-directed activity (either socially, at work or school, or sexually) or psychomotor agitation.*"
    7. "Excessive involvement in pleasurable activities that have a high potential for painful consequences (e.g., engaging in unrestrained buying sprees, sexual indiscretions, or foolish business investments)."
  C. "The symptoms do not meet criteria for a Mixed Episode."
  D. "The mood disturbance is sufficiently severe to cause marked impairment in occupational functioning or in usual social activities or relationships with others, or to necessitate hospitalization to prevent harm to self or others, or there are psychotic features."
  E. "The symptoms are not due to the direct physiological effects of a substance (e.g., a drug of abuse, a medication, or other treatment) or a general medical condition (e.g., hyperthyroidism)."

TABLE 17.2   (*Continued*)

III. Mixed Episode (p. 335)
    A. "*The criteria are met both for a Manic Episode and for a Major Depressive Episode (except for duration) nearly every day during at least a 1-week period.*"
    B. "The mood disturbance is sufficiently severe to cause marked impairment in occupational functioning or in usual social activities or relationships with others, or to necessitate hospitalization to prevent harm to self or others, or there are psychotic features."
    "The symptoms are not due to the direct physiological effects of a substance (e.g., a drug of abuse, a medication, or other treatment) or a general medical condition (e.g., hyperthyroidism)."
IV. Hypomanic Episode (p. 338)
    A. "A distinct period of persistently elevated, expansive, or irritable mood, lasting throughout at least 4 days, that is clearly different from the usual nondepressed mood."
    B. "During the period of mood disturbance, three (or more) of the following symptoms have persisted (four if the mood is only irritable) and have been present to a significant degree:
      1. "Inflated self-esteem or grandiosity."
      2. "*Decreased need for sleep (e.g., feels rested after only 3 hours of sleep).*"
      3. "More talkative than usual or pressure to keep talking."
      4. "Flight of ideas or subjective experience that thoughts are racing."
      5. "Distractibility (i.e., attention too easily drawn to unimportant or irrelevant external stimuli)."
      6. "*Increase in goal-directed activity (either socially, at work or school, or sexually) or psychomotor agitation.*"
      7. "Excessive involvement in pleasurable activities that have a high potential for painful consequences (e.g., the person engages in unrestrained buying sprees, sexual indiscretions, or foolish business investments)."
    C. "*The episode is associated with an unequivocal change in functioning that is uncharacteristic of the person when not symptomatic.*"
    D. "*The disturbance in mood and the change in functioning are observable by others.*"
    E. "The episode is not severe enough to cause marked impairment in social or occupational functioning, or to necessitate hospitalization, and there are no psychotic features."
    F. "The symptoms are not due to the direct physiological effects of a substance (e.g., a drug of abuse, a medication, or other treatment) or a general medical condition (e.g., hyperthyroidism)."

Note. Italic entries concern activity.

cal examinations but perhaps may be included in the future given the connection between exercise and health. The next best comparison is with a friend, co-worker, or family member who most closely matches the patient's premorbid lifestyle. A 1- or 2-week behavioral sample could be obtained from this person as proxy for the patient's probable premorbid activity level. Futterman and Tryon (1994) found evidence of psychomotor retardation when comparing depressed and control subjects. Barkley and Tryon (1995) demonstrated psychomotor retardation within a college sample that varied widely in depression.

Item six specifies "fatigue or loss of energy nearly every day." Unless occupational or other necessity forces the person to remain active, fatigue should be reflected in a less active lifestyle that can be tracked by activity measurement. People who elect to watch TV rather than take a walk, elect to stay home rather than shop, will be less active. It is especially important to use fully proportional actigraphy when attempting to measure fatigue to separate small or weak movements from normally energetic ones.

Manic episode. Table 17.2 indicates that three of seven criteria must be met if mood is expansive but four of seven criteria must be met if mood is only irritable. Two of these seven criteria entail activity. Item two specifies "decreased need for sleep (e.g., feels rested after only 3 hours of sleep)" (p. 332). Wrist actigraphy supplemented by hand pressure monitoring can document total sleep time and thereby determine if the patient is sleeping as little as 3 hours.

Item 6 specifies "increase in goal-directed activity (either socially, at work or school, or sexually) or psychomotor agitation" (p. 332). Combining psychomotor agitation with goal-directed activity means that both inappropriate and appropriate activity increases qualify. Actigraphy cannot distinguish between goal-directed activity and psychomotor agitation but fortunately item 6 does not require this discrimination to be made. Hence, actigraphy is very suitable for evaluating item 6. Site of attachment remains an issue. Waist activity consumes more calories than wrist or ankle activity because it is associated with the body's center of gravity. The waist is usually active only during ambulation. Hence, increased waist activity is probably a more conservative indicator of item 6 than is wrist or ankle activity.

Mixed episode. Criteria for both an MDE and a manic episode must be met for at least 1 week as described above. The requirement of a 1-week behavioral sample can easily be met with actigraphy in between the intake and the first treatment session.

Hypomanic episode. The criteria are the same for hypomania as for mania, but duration need only extend to 4 rather than 7 days. The "decreased need for sleep (e.g., feels rested after only 3 hours of sleep)" and "increase in goal-directed activity (either socially, at work or school, or sexually) or psychomotor agitation" (p. 338) can be evaluated by actigraphy supplemented with hand pressure monitoring. These alterations must be unequivocal and observable by others; not merely self-reported.

Depressive Disorders

All depressive disorders entail meeting the criteria for an MDE, as defined above, for which actigraphy and hand pressure monitoring can be informative as previously described.

Major depressive disorder, single episode (292.2x). DSM-IV requires the presence of a single MDE, as defined above, that cannot be "better accounted for by schizoaffective disorder and is not superimposed on schizophrenia, schizophreniform disorder, delusional disorder, or psychotic disorder not otherwise specified" (p. 344). No history of a manic, hypomanic, or mixed episode is allowed. This exclusion does not apply if all the maniclike symptoms are due to drugs or a general medical condition.

Major depressive disorder, recurrent (296.3x). Two or more MDEs are required. At least two months must transpire during which the MDE inclusion criteria are not met for two incidents to be considered separate. The same exclusions apply as for diagnosing a single episode.

Dysthymic disorder (300.4). The inclusion criteria (cf. DSM-IV; APA, 1994, p. 349) require depressed mood, self-report or observable by others, for at least 2 years except in adolescents, where duration must be at least 1 year. Presence of at least two of six criteria is required including "insomnia or hypersomnia" and "low energy or fatigue," for which actigraphy can be informative. Symptoms cannot be absent for longer than 2 months. Exclusion criteria entail not qualifying for an MDE, never having had a manic episode, a hypomanic episode, or a mixed episode; not meeting criteria for a psychotic or delusional disorder; not due to a drug or medical condition, and that the symptoms produce "clinically significant distress or impairment" (p. 349).

Bipolar Disorders

Bipolar I disorder. Having one or more manic or mixed episodes is the essential defining feature of Bipolar I disorder. Patients may have had previous MDEs or substance-induced mood disorders. Exclusion criteria include not being better accounted for by schizoaffective disorder or delusional disorder.

Bipolar I disorder, single manic episode (296.0x). Patients qualify for a manic episode without ever having had an MDE. Symptoms cannot be better explained "by schizoaffective disorder and is not superimposed on schizophrenia, schizophreniform disorder, delusional disorder, or psychotic disorder not otherwise specified" (p. 355).

Bipolar I disorder, most recent episode hypomanic (296.40). The patient is currently in or most recently had a hypomanic episode and has a history with at least one prior manic or mixed episode. The same exclusion criteria apply.

Bipolar I disorder, most recent episode manic (296.4x). The patient is currently in or most recently had a manic episode and has a history with at least one prior MDE, manic or mixed episode. The same exclusion criteria apply.

Bipolar I disorder, most recent episode mixed (296.6x). The patient is currently in or most recently had a mixed episode and has a history with at least one prior manic or mixed episode. The same exclusion criteria apply.

Bipolar I disorder, most recent episode depressed (296.5x). The patient is currently in or most recently had an MDE and has a history with at least one prior MDE. The same exclusion criteria apply.

Bipolar I disorder, most recent episode unspecified (296.7). The patient has symptoms of a manic, hypomanic, or mixed episode or for an MDE but does not meet the duration criteria. The patient has had at least one prior manic or mixed episode.

Bipolar II disorder. "The essential feature of bipolar II disorder is a clinical course that is characterized by the occurrence of one or more major depressive episodes accompanied by at least one hypomanic episode" (p. 359).

Bipolar II disorder (296.89). "Presence (or history) of one or more major depressive episodes," "presence (or history) of at least one hypomanic episode," "there has never been a Manic Episode or a Mixed Episode" (p. 362). The same exclusion criteria apply as for bipolar I disorders. Two specifiers are used—hypomanic and depressed—depending on the current clinical condition.

Cyclothymic disorder (301.13). Hypomanic symptoms are experienced over the past 2 years, 1 year for children and adolescents, and not asymptomatic for more than 2 consecutive months. Patients have not had an MDE or a manic or mixed episode during the first 2 years of their illness.

Melancholic Features Specifier

DSM-IV provides for the specifier "with melancholic features" under the following conditions. First, either of the following criteria are met during a current or most recent episode: 1. "loss of pleasure in all, or almost all activities" and 2. "lack of reactivity to usually pleasurable stimuli (does not feel much better, even temporarily, when something good happens)" (APA, 1994, p. 384). Second, three or more of the following six features must apply: 1. "distinct quality of depressed mood (i.e., the depressed mood is experienced as distinctly different from the kind of feeling experienced after the death of a loved one)," 2. "depression regularly worse in the morning," 3. "early morning awakening (at least 2 hours before usual time of awakening)," 4. "marked psychomotor retardation or agitation," 5. "significant anorexia or weight loss," and 6. "excessive or inappropriate guilt" (p. 384). Actigraphy can clearly document the time of awakening with an accuracy of 1 minute and therefore empirically determine if awakening is occurring at least 2 hours before usual. Psychomotor changes are said to be "nearly always present and are observable by others" (p. 383). Actigraphy can quantify this frequently occurring symptom far more precisely and definitely more objectively than it can be self-reported or rated.

Mood Disorder Due to a General Medical Condition (293.83)

This condition is diagnosed when patients meet criteria for an MDE, manic, hypomanic, or mixed episode because of a general medical condition. Actigraphy is as relevant to evaluating the psychological correlates of medical disorders as to primary psychological disorders.

Substance-Induced Mood Disorder

This disorder is diagnosed if symptoms of an MDE, manic, hypomanic, or mixed episode occur within 1 month of intoxication or withdrawal from a substance.

Attention-Deficit Hyperactivity Disorder

DSM-IV provides the following six facets of hyperactivity: 1. "often fidgets with hands or feet or squirms in seat," 2. "often leaves seat in classroom or in other situations in which remaining seated is expected," 3. "often runs about or climbs excessively in situations in which it is inappropriate (in adolescents or adults, may be limited to subjective feelings of restlessness), 4. "often has difficulty playing or engaging in leisure activities quietly," 5. "is often 'on the go' or often acts as if 'driven by a motor,'" and 6. "often talks excessively" (p. 84). Three impulsivity facets are also defined.

Attention-deficit hyperactivity disorder, predominantly hyperactive-impulsive type (314.01). This condition is diagnosed when six of the nine combined hyperactivity-impulsivity facets are documented but fewer than six of the inattention facets are found. Computer-based actigraphs typically record activity over 1-minute epochs. Knowing the times that a child is in situations where gross motor movements are inappropriate, one can inspect the record for evidence of hyperactivity. Leaving one's seat, running, and climbing produce levels of waist activity that would far exceed that associated with seated children. Always being on the go and driven as if by a motor will produce activity measurements containing few periods of immobility or low activity levels. In addition to inspecting actigraph records for the presence of hyperactivity, one should also determine if there is a relative absence of inactivity. Normal children can be inactive for more than a few minutes. Failure to find quiescent periods may be more important than excessively high levels of activity in these children. Fidgeting with feet can probably be detected since relatively little foot movement is prompted by teachers of seated children. Fidgeting with hands may not be distinguishable from the constructively active child. Teicher, Ito, Glod, and Barber (1996) used an infrared motion analysis system to track the position of four markers placed on a cap, shoulder, back, and right elbow 50 times a second with a resolution of 0.04 mm (measurement error = 0.001%). ADHD boys were 2.3 to 3.8 times as active during a continuous performance test as control boys.

Attention-deficit hyperactivity disorder, predominantly inattentive type (314.00). This condition is diagnosed when the inattention criteria are satisfied and the hyperactivity-impulsivity criteria are not. Not satisfying criteria always raises questions regarding the thoroughness of the examination because the easiest way to not satisfy a criterion is to not assess it carefully or comprehensively. Tryon and Pinto (1994) found important exceptions between teacher-rated and measured activity despite high overall correlations between the two data sets. Some children rated as hyperactive were not measurably more active than some control children. This is especially important because teacher ratings are part of the reasons cited for prescribing medication.

Two behavioral sampling issues are pertinent. The first issue is whether observational data derive from the natural environment or were obtained during testing in an office setting or other evaluation environment. One must assess behaviors in their natural context or provide evidence that observations made under clinic or laboratory conditions generalize to natural settings. The second issue concerns the size of the behavioral sample taken. Brief samples are more likely to overlook or minimize hyperactivity that becomes irritable to teachers and parents over weeks and months.

Attention-deficit hyperactivity disorder, combined type (314.01). This condition is diagnosed when both inattention and hyperactive-impulsive criteria are met.

Attention-deficit hyperactivity disorder, not otherwise specified (314.9). This condition is diagnosed when prominent symptoms of inattention or hyperactivity exist but the full criteria for either subtype are not met.

Anxiety Disorders

Actigraphy can be used to quantify certain correlates of anxiety.

Generalized anxiety disorder (300.02). Among other symptoms, patients must exhibit three or more of the following six: 1. "restlessness or feeling keyed up or on edge," 2. "being easily fatigued," 3. "difficulty concentrating or mind going blank," 4. "irritability," 5. "muscle tension," and 6. "sleep disturbance (difficulty falling or staying asleep, or restless unsatisfying sleep)" (APA, 1994, p. 436). Only one symptom is needed for children. Restlessness may result in pacing or other agitated behavior that actigraphy would easily detect. Fatigue can result in lifestyle changes favoring inactivity. Patients who curtail or avoid activities that they previously engaged in regularly reduce their 24-hour activity output. Difficulty initiating or maintaining sleep can be documented using wrist actigraphy supplemented by hand pressure monitoring.

Posttraumatic stress disorder (309.81). In addition to other criteria, patients must have two of the following five persistent symptoms: 1. "difficulty falling or staying asleep," 2. "irritability or outbursts of anger," 3. "difficulty concentrating," 4. "hypervigilance," and 5. "exaggerated startle response" (p. 428). Actigraphy, supplemented by hand pressure monitoring, can provide objective data regarding problems with sleep onset and sleep maintenance. Sadeh, Lavie, Scher, Tirosh, and Epstein (1991) demonstrated that 4.45 nights of wrist actigraphy can discriminate between sleep-disturbed and control children. Glod, Teicher, Hartman, and Harakal (in press) used 72 hours of continuous wrist actigraphy to show that 19 prepubertal children with documented abuse were twice as active at night as normal and depressed children. Abused children have more difficulty falling asleep and staying asleep.

Schizophrenia and Other Psychotic Disorders

Schizophrenia: catatonic type (295.20). A schizophrenic receives this diagnosis if their clinical presentation is dominated by at least two of the following five features: 1. "motoric immobility as evidenced by catalepsy (including waxy flexibility) or stupor," 2. "excessive motor activity (that is apparently purposeless and not influenced by external stimuli)," 3. "extreme negativism (an apparently motiveless resistance to all instructions or maintenance of a rigid posture against attempts to be moved) or mutism," 4. "peculiarities of voluntary movement as evidenced by posturing (voluntary assumption of inappropriate or bizarre postures), stereotyped movements, prominent mannerisms, or prominent grimacing," and 5. "echolalia or echopraxia" (p. 289). Actigraphy can quantify the first two features. Immobility and stupor will result in hypoactivity. Actigraphy can also document excessive motor activity, but observational data are needed to determine whether elevated activity levels are purposeless or not influenced by external stimuli.

Schizoaffective disorder (295.70). This diagnosis is given when criteria for a major depressive, manic, or mixed episode are met concurrently with criterion A for schizophrenia (cf. DSM-IV; APA, 1994, pp. 285–286). Subtypes include bipolar type if a manic or mixed episode occur along with an MDE and depressive type if only an MDE is involved.

Catatonic disorder due to a general medical condition (293.89). Actigraphy is as informative when catatonia is induced by a general medical condition as when it is the primary illness.

Substance-Related Disorders

The following disorders entail psychomotor agitation or retardation as one of their inclusion criteria: amphetamine intoxication (292.89), amphetamine withdrawal (292.0), cocaine intoxication (292.89), cocaine withdrawal (292.0). Psychomotor agitation, but not retardation, is associated with alcohol withdrawal (291.8), caffeine intoxication (305.90), and sedative, hypnotic, or anxiolytic withdrawal (292.0).

Insomnia is associated with alcohol withdrawal (291.8), amphetamine withdrawal (292.0), caffeine intoxication (305.90), nicotine withdrawal (292.0), opioid withdrawal (292.0), and sedative, hypnotic, or anxiolytic withdrawal (292.0). Hypersomnia is characteristic of amphetamine withdrawal (292.0) or cocaine withdrawal (292.0).

Medication-Induced Movement Disorders

Neuroleptic-induced Parkinsonism (332.1). This condition can result within a few weeks of initiating or increasing the dose of neuroleptic medication. Van Hilten, Middelkoop, Kerkhof, and Roos (1991) demonstrated that it is possible to detect the 4–6 Hz tremor characteristic of Parkinson's disease (PD) using a Geweiler wrist-worn actigraph (Sing Medical, Homberectikon, Switzerland) with a 0.1 g threshold and a bandpass filter of 0.25–3.0 Hz. Apparently, the bandpass window is not sharply defined, thereby enabling partial tremor detection. The authors recommend the construction of a 4–6 Hz sensitive device.

Van Someren et al. (1993) constructed an accelerometer-based, wrist-worn tremor sensitive actigraph sensitive to the 3–12 Hz range. They were aware that normal arm movements produce transient 3–12 Hz vibrations that could be mistaken for 4–6 Hz Parkinsonian tremor. To distinguish valid tremor from these transients, the computer scored tremor only when at least six full waves of 2.94–12.5 Hz signal were detected. All signal not scored tremor was scored activity. They obtained wrist data on 8 patients with PD before and after a tremor relieving thalamotomy and 10 aged-matched and 10 young control subjects. Their data clearly discriminated between preoperative patients and control subjects and between pre- and postoperative patients. Clearly, this type of device can be used to monitor patients as they first receive neuroleptic medication and when the dosage of such medication is increased to detect tremor onset early.

Medication-induced postural tremor (331.1). This condition can occur in response to the administration of lithium, antidepressants, and valproate (DSM-IV; APA, 1994, p. 680). Wrist tremography, described above, could also be used to evaluate the onset of postural tremor.

Neuroleptic-induced tardive dyskinesia (333.82). This condition may also be detected using a modified wrist actigraph given the work of Tryon and Pologe (1987) on the accelerometric assessment of tardive dyskinesia.

Neuroleptic-induced acute akathesia (333.99). This condition causes restless movements of the leg, fidgeting, pacing, and the inability to sit or stand still. It is a form of drug-induced movement, and patients feel that they must move to obtain relief. Movement does not bring relief, yet they continue to feel the necessity to move. Wrist, waist, and ankle actigraphy will clearly reveal the presence of akathesia. Tryon (1991a, pp. 202–205) described a protocol for evaluating akathesia. Essentially, the patient is asked to sit quietly in a chair for a chosen duration, perhaps while watching television. Actigraphs on all four limbs monitor their ability to remain motionless.

Criteria Sets and Axes Provided for Further Study

Postconcussional disorder entails disordered sleep for which actigraphy supplemented by hand pressure monitoring could be informative (p. 705), especially if longitudinal evaluations are desired to evaluate variability in sleep parameters.

Caffeine withdrawal entails "marked fatigue or drowsiness" (p. 709). Fatigue may well be reflected in low-energy lifestyle choices. Drowsiness may be evaluated by conducting the modified Multiple Sleep Latency Test using hand pressure monitoring described above.

Postpsychotic depressive disorder of schizophrenia requires that criteria for a major depressive episode be superimposed on the residual phase of schizophrenia (p. 712).

Premenstrual dysphoric disorder includes insomnia or hypersomnia among its 11 inclusion criteria (p. 717). Actigraphy supplemented by hand pressure monitoring may be informative here.

Minor depressive disorder entails "insomnia or hypersomnia nearly every day," "psychomotor agitation or retardation nearly every day (observable by others, not merely subjective feelings of restlessness or being slowed down)," and "fatigue or loss of energy nearly every day" (p. 720). The primary difference between this disorder and MDE is that it requires fewer (at least two but fewer than five) criteria to be met. However, all of the activity-related criteria are included.

Recurrent brief depressive disorder requires that all MDE criteria B be met over a period of at least 2 days but less than 2 weeks (p. 723). Depressive periods must occur at least once per month for the last year and not be associated with the menstrual cycle. Actigraphy makes the same contributions here as when diagnosing MDE.

Mixed anxiety-depressive disorder entails "sleep disturbance (difficulty falling or staying asleep, or restless unsatisfying sleep)" and "fatigue or low energy" (p. 724). Wrist actigraphy supplemented with hand pressure monitoring can quantify sleep-onset latency. Actigraphy can determine if sleep is maintained once initiated. Fatigue may result in selecting a less energetic lifestyle which will lower 24-hour activity levels.

ANOREXIA NERVOSA

Epling and Pierce (1991) and Pierce and Epling (1994) described an animal model of anorexia nervosa with close human parallels in which activity plays a central role. The primary observation is that when food availability is restricted to one meal per day, and when access is given to an activity wheel, adolescent male as well as female rats will increase their activity and decrease their food intake until they die! Running typically increases to 15 km per day, which is a lot for humans and enormous for the much smaller rat. The authors hypothesized that restricting food intake to one meal per day simulates famine conditions. Evolution apparently has favored continuous migration, with very little time spent feeding, to a region where food is more plentiful. Hence, food restriction can set the occasion for sustained activity and heightened anorexia to facilitate migration. Because the rats cannot go anywhere in their activity wheel and because the experimenter does not increase the frequency of food presentation, the animals never arrive at a more plentiful food supply but continue migrating until death. Self-imposed food restriction and exercise opportunity result in equally futile conditions for humans. Food restriction both increases activity, which burns more calories and strengthens anorexia thereby further reducing caloric intake. This artificial famine escape migration state is maintained until exhaustion or death results. Activity increases are integral to this disorder but are not yet reflected in the inclusion criteria for anorexia nervosa (307.1, pp. 544–545). Perhaps DSM-V will correct this omission.

MINORITIES AND GENDER

Sex

Women have routinely been included in activity research, but sex has not been used as an independent variable. Eaton and Enns (1986) performed a meta-analysis of 90 studies involving 127 independent estimates of sex difference of persons aged 2 months to 30 years (median = 55.5 months = 4.6 years) based on sample sizes ranging from 7 to 25,000 (median = 68) using a variety of methodologies. They reported boys to be more active than girls by $d = 0.49$ standard deviations on average. Tryon (1991a, pp. 93–101) restricted his review of the developmental evidence to studies that actually measured activity level. Boys were found to be more active than girls by 6 to 8 months of age and to remain more active up until about 10 years of age. By 12 years of age, boys' activity declined to the point where within-sex variability was as large as between-sex differences, precluding a significant difference. This finding is consistent with Eaton and Yu's (1989) report of an age-related activity decrease where older normal children are rated as less active than younger ones. Sex differences in measured activity have not been reported in teenagers or adults but could be easily accomplished. Two experimental designs could be used. The simplest approach is to use actigraphs (Tryon, 1991a; Tryon & Williams, 1996) to obtain minute-by-minute activity measurements 24 hours per day for 2, 3, or 4 weeks. In addition to analyzing these data for mean level, circadian rhythm analyses can be performed to determine whether men and women distribute their activity similarly. A second approach is to use actigraphs to measure activity in one or more specific test situations. One should be careful to obtain an adequate behavioral sample and to limit conclusions to situations similar to those tested.

Sex effects regarding activity may largely reflect cultural preferences in how one spends leisure time. If boys prefer active outdoor sports and girls passive indoor activities, then a sex difference will emerge that may have nothing to do with biology. Another possibility is that activity differences may reflect social roles. Caring for young children or delivering mail on foot probably occasions more activity than working as a secretary or accountant.

Race

Racial composition of subjects participating in activity studies is not consistently reported, and no known study has examined racial activity differences. No hypotheses have been suggested that a racial activity difference exists, and consequently no tests of such hypotheses have been published as far as this author can tell. The same two research designs recommended for the study of sex effects could be used to explore racial effects. Any racial effect found may reflect cultural differences in how leisure time is spent or in chosen occupations as mentioned above.

CONCLUSIONS

All observable behaviors have a measurable activity or energy level ranging from zero to beyond the maximum level current devices can accurately record. Individual differences in energy level begin prenatally, are clearly evident during infancy and childhood, become part of extraversion in adult personality, and reflect important individual differences during late life. Behavior disorders alter normal activity patterns. Wrist- and waist-worn activity monitors objectively quantify the physical forces associated with behavior, and the more sophisticated computerized devices accumulate and record these measurements every minute of the day and night for up to 22 consecutive days before filling memory. The history of medicine is a history of measurement in that modern medicine defines and diagnoses disease in terms of physical and chemical laboratory analyses of biological specimens. Actigraphy provides psychology and psychiatry with the opportunity to objectively collect and analyze behavioral specimens (samples) from the natural environment and under controlled laboratory conditions. This article articulates the relevance of activity measurements to many DSM-IV disorders of sleep and waking behaviors. Actigraphy can be used to evaluate change over time and therefore provide objective evidence of therapeutic efficacy for both behavioral and pharmacological interventions. Actigraphy is a cost-effective extension of behavioral assessment having broad applicability for clinicians as well as investigators.

The objectives of good clinical practice are similar to those of good research. The clinician's need for high-quality information upon which to base diagnostic and treatment decisions is just as great as the researcher's need for high-quality information upon which to evaluate theoretical hypotheses. Both clinicians and psychotherapy investigators are concerned with therapeutic efficacy, and both are entitled to the same quality of information. Clinicians often supplement client self-report with psychological testing regarding questions of anxiety, depression, and personality disorder but are reluctant to obtain instrumented behavioral samples of activity, preferring to rely exclusively on self-report for this information. No evidence exists that clients can self-report activity more accurately than other aspects of their behavior and personality for which psychological testing is routinely ordered. Activity is ideally suited for instrumented measurement and a broad range of devices are available from simple pedometers and step counters up to sophisticated but easy to use computerized actigraphs. Activity monitoring is especially suitable for continuous measurement over time and therefore is able to objectively quantify change throughout treatment and follow-up.

REFERENCES

American Psychiatric Association. (1994). *Diagnostic and statistical manual of mental disorders* (4th ed.). Washington, DC: Author.

Anastasi, A. (1988). *Psychological testing* (6th ed.). New York: Macmillian.

Aronen, E. T., Teicher, M. H., Geenens, D., Curtin, S., Glod, C. A., & Pahlavan, K. (1996). Motor activity and severity of depression in hospitalized prepubertal children. *Journal of the American Academy of Child and Adolescent Psychiatry., 35,* 752–763.

Barkley, T. J., & Tyron, W. W. (1995). Psychomotor retardation found in college students seeking counseling. *Behaviour Research and Therapy, 33,* 977–984.

Blair, S. N., Kohl, H. W., Paffenbarger, R. S., Clark, D. G., Cooper, K. H., & Gibbons, L. W. (1989). Physical fitness and all-cause mortality: A prospective study of healthy men and women. *Journal of the American Medical Association, 262,* 2395–2401.

Blake, H., Gerard, R. W., & Kleitman, N. (1939). Factors influencing brain potentials during sleep. *Journal of Neurophysiology, 2,* 48–60.

Block, J. (1995). A contrarian view of the five-factor approach to personality description. *Psychological Bulletin, 117,* 187–215.

Block, J., & Block, J. H. (1980). *The California Child Q-Set.* Palo Alto, CA: Consulting Psychologists Press. (Original work published 1969).

Brown, A. C., Smolensky, M. H., D'Alonzo, G. E., & Redman, D. P. (1990). Actigraphy: A means of assessing circadian patterns in human activity. *Chronobiology International, 7,* 125–133.

Burnside, I. M., (1978). *Working with the elderly.* North Scituate, MA: Duxbury.

Buss, A. (1989). Temperaments as personality traits. In G. A. Kohnstamm, J. E. Bates, & M. K. Rothbart (Eds.), *Temperament in childhood* (pp. 49–58). New York: Wiley.

Buss, A., & Plomin, R. (1984). *Temperament: Early developing personality traits.* Hillsdale, NJ: Erlbaum.

Carskadon, M. A. (1994). Measuring daytime sleepiness. In M. H. Kryger, T. Roth, & W. C. Dement (Eds.), *Principles and practice of sleep medicine* (2nd ed., pp. 961–966). Philadelphia: Saunders.

Caspi, A., Block, J., Block, J. H., Klopp, B., Lynam, D., Moffitt, T. E., & Stoughamer-Loeber, M. (1992). A "common language" version of the California Child Q-Set for personality assessment. *Psychological Assessment, 4,* 512–523.

Cole, R. J., & Kripke, D. F. (1989). Progress in automatic sleepwake scoring by wrist actigraph. *Sleep Research, 18,* 331.

Cole, R. J., Kripke, D. F., Gruen, W., Mullaney, D. J., & Gillin, J. C. (1992). Automatic sleep/wake identification from wrist activity. *Sleep, 15,* 461–469.

Costa, P. T., Jr., & McCrae, R. R. (1980). Still stable after all these years: Personality as a key to some issues in adulthood and old age. In P. B. Baltes & O. G. Brim (Eds.), *Life-span development and behavior.* New York: Academic Press.

Costa, P. T., Jr., & McCrae, R. R. (1992). *Revised NEO Personality Inventory (NEO PI-R) and NEO Five-Factor Inventory (NEO-FFI): Professional manual.* Odessa, FL: Psychological Assessment Resources.

Costa, P. T., Jr., & McCrae, R. R. (1994). Stability and change in personality from adolescence through adulthood. In C. F. Halverson, Jr., G. A. Kohnstamm, & R. P. Martin (Eds.), *The developing structure of temperament and personality from infancy to adulthood* (pp. 139–150). Hillsdale, NJ: Erlbaum.

Costa, P. T., Jr., & McCrae, R. R. (1995). Solid ground in the wetlands of personality: A reply to Block. *Psychological Bulletin, 117,* 216–220.

Davis, H., Davis, P. A., Loomis, A. L., Harvey, E. N., & Hobart, G. (1937). Changes in human brain potentials during the onset of sleep. *Science, 86,* 448–450.

Digman, J. M. (1990). Personality structure: Emergence of the five-factor model. *Annual Review of Psychology, 41,* 417–440.

Digman, J. M. (1994). Child personality and temperament: Does the five-factor model embrace both domains? In C. F. Halverson, Jr., G. A. Kohnstamm, & R. P. Martin (Eds.), *The developing structure of temperament and personality from infancy to adulthood* (pp. 323–338). Hillsdale, NJ: Erlbaum.

Dustman, R. E., Ruhling, R. O., Russell, E. M., Shearer, D. E., Bonekat, W., Shigeoka, J. W., Wood, J. S., & Bradford, D. C. (1984). Aerobic exercise training and improved neuropsychological function of older individuals. *Neurobiology of Aging, 5,* 35–42.

Eaton, W. O., & Enns, L. R. (1986). Sex differences in human motor activity level. *Psychological Bulletin, 100,* 19–28.

Eaton, W. O., & Saudino, K. J. (1992). Prenatal activity level as a temperament dimension? Individual differences and developmental functions in fetal movement. *Infant Behavior and Development, 15,* 57–70.

Eaton, W. O., & Yu, A. P. (1989). Are sex differences in child motor activity level a function of sex differences in maturational status? *Child Development, 1989, 60,* 1005–1011.

Epling, W. F., & Pierce, W. D. (1991). *Solving the anorexia puzzle: A scientific approach.* Toronto: Hogrefe and Huber.

Eysenck, H. J. (1991). Dimensions of personality: Sixteen, 5, or 3?—Criteria for a taxonomic paradigm. *Personality and Individual Differences, 12,* 773–790.

Eysenck, H. J. (1994). The Big Five or Giant Three: Criteria for a paradigm. In C. F. Halverson, Jr., G. A. Kohnstamm, & R. P. Martin (Eds.), *The developing structure of temperament and personality from infancy to adulthood* (pp. 37–51). Hillsdale, NJ: Erlbaum.

Fox, S. M., Naughton, J. P., & Haskell, W. L. (1971). Physical activity and the prevention of coronary heart disease. *Annals of Clinical Research, 3,* 404–432.

Futterman, C. S., & Tryon, W. W. (1994). Psychomotor retardation found in depressed outpatient women. *Journal of Behavior Therapy and Experimental Psychiatry, 25,* 41–48.

Gerhardsson, M., Norell, S. E., Kiviranta, H., Pedersen, N. L., & Ahlbom, A. (1986). Sedentary jobs and colon cancer. *American Journal of Epidemiology, 123,* 775–780.

Glod, C. A., Teicher, M. H., Hartman, C. R., & Harakal, T. (in press). Increased nocturnal activity and impaired sleep maintenance in abused children. *Journal of the American Academy of Child and Adolescent Psychiatry.*

Goldberg, L. R. (1990). An alternative "description of personality": The Big Five factor structure. *Journal of Personality and Social Psychology, 59,* 1216–1229.

Goldberg, L. R., & Rosolack, T. K. (1994). The Big Five factor structure as an integrative framework: An empirical comparison with Eysenck's P-E-N model. In C. F. Halverson, Jr., G. A. Kohnstamm, & R. P. Martin (Eds.), *The developing structure of temperament and personality from infancy to adulthood* (pp. 7–35). Hillsdale, NJ: Erlbaum.

Goldsmith, H. H., Buss, A. H., Plomin, R., Rothbart, M. K., Thomas, A., Chess, S., Hinde, R. A., & McCall, R. B. (1987). Roundtable: What is temperament? Four approaches. *Child Development, 58,* 505–529.

Gueldner, S. H., & Spradley, J. (1988). Outdoor walking lowers fatigue. *Journal of Gerontological Nursing, 14,* 6–12.

Hagekull, B. (1994). Infant temperament and early childhood functioning: Possible relations to the Five-Factor Model. In C. F. Halverson, Jr., G. A. Kohnstamm, & R. P. Martin (Eds.), *The developing structure of temperament and personality from infancy to adulthood* (pp. 227–240). Hillsdale, NJ: Erlbaum.

Halverson, C. F., Jr., Kohnstamm, G. A., & Martin, R. P. (1994). *The developing structure of temperament and personality from infancy to adulthood.* Hillsdale, NJ: Erlbaum.

Harsh, J. R., & Ogilvie, R. D. (1994). Introduction: A first sketch. In R. D. Ogilvie & J. R. Harsh (Eds.), *Sleep onset: Normal and abnormal processes* (pp. xvii–xxviii). Washington, DC: American Psychological Association.

Hauri, P. J., & Wisbey, J. (1992). Wrist actigraphy in insomnia. *Sleep, 15,* 293–301.

Kryger, M. H., Roth, T., & Dement, W. C. (1994). *Principles and practice of sleep medicine* (2nd ed.). Philadelphia: Saunders.

Leon, A. S., Connett, J., Jacobs, D. R., Jr., & Rauramaa, R. (1987). Leisure-time physical activity levels and risk of coronary heart disease and death: The Multiple Risk Factor International Trial. *Journal of the American Medical Association, 258,* 2388–2395.

Linehan, M. M. (1980). Content validity: Its relevance to behavioral assessment. *Behavioral Assessment, 2,* 147–159.

Martin, R. P., Wisenbaker, J., & Huttunen, M. (1994). In C. F. Halverson, Jr., G. A. Kohnstamm, & R. P. Martin (Eds.), *The developing structure of temperament and personality from infancy to adulthood* (pp. 157–172). Hillsdale, NJ: Erlbaum.

Mason, D. J., & Tapp, W. (1992). Measuring circadian rhythms: Actigraph versus activation checklist. *Western Journal of Nursing Research, 14,* 358–379.

Mason, W. J., Ancoli-Israel, S., Kripke, D. F., Jones, D. W., Parker, L., Fell, R. L., Almendarez, L., & Goldberg, J. (1992). Reliability of actillume recordings in nursing home patients. *Sleep Research, 21,* 349.

McAuley, E., Courneya, K. S., & Lettunich, J. (1991). Effects of acute and long-term exercise on self-efficacy responses in sedentary, middle-aged males and females. *The Gerontologist, 31,* 534–542.

Middelkoop, H. A. M. (1994). (Ed.), *Actigraphic assessment of sleep and sleep disorders.* Delft, The Netherlands: Eburon.

Morris, J. N., Everitt, M. G., Pollard, R., Chave, S. P. W., & Semmence, A. M. (1980). Vigorous exercise in leisure time: Protection against coronary heart disease. *Lancet, 2,* 1207–1210.

Oberman, A. (1985). Exercise and the primary prevention of cardiovascular disease. *American Journal of Cardiology, 55,* 10D–20D.

Ogilvie, R. D., & Wilkinson, R. T. (1988). Behavioral versus EEG-based monitoring of all-night sleep/wake patterns. *Sleep, 11,* 139–155.

Ogilvie, R. D., Wilkinson, R. T., & Allison, S. (1989). The detection of sleep onset: Behavioral, physiological, and subjective convergence. *Sleep, 12,* 458–474.

Paffenbarger, R. S., Jr., & Hale, W. E. (1975). Work activity and coronary heart mortality. *New England Journal of Medicine, 292,* 545–550.

Paffenbarger, R. S., Jr., Hyde, R. T., Wing, A. L., & Hsieh, C. C. (1986). Physical activity, all-cause mortality, and longevity of college alumni. *New England Journal of Medicine, 314,* 605–613.

Paffenbarger, R. S., Jr., Hyde, R. T., Wing, A. L., & Steinmetz, C. H. (1984). A natural history of athleticism and cardiovascular health. *Journal of the American Medical Association, 252,* 491–495.

Palmore, E. (1970). Health practices and illness among the aged. *The Gerontologist, 10,* 313–316.

Perry, T. J., & Goldwater, B. C. (1987). A passive behavioral measure of sleep onset in high-alpha and low-alpha subjects. *Psychophysiology, 24,* 657–665.

Pierce, W. D., & Epling, W. F. (1994). Activity anorexia: An interplay between basic and applied behavior analysis. *The Behavior Analyst, 17,* 7–23.

Pollak, C. P., Perlick, D., & Linsner, J. P. (1992). Daily sleep reports and circadian rest-activity cycles of elderly community residents with insomnia. *Biological Psychiatry, 32,* 1019–1027.

Powell, K. E., Thompson, P. D., Caspersen, C. J., & Kendrick, J. S. (1987). Physical activity and the incidence of coronary heart disease. *Annual Review of Public Health, 8,* 253–287.

Raoux, N., Benoit, O., Dantchev, N., Denise, P., Franc, B., Allilaire, J. F., & Widlocher, D. (1994). Circadian pattern of motor activity in major depressed patients undergoing antidepressant therapy: Relationship between actigraphic measures and clinical course. *Psychiatric Research, 52,* 85–98.

Rechtschaffen, A. (1994). Sleep onset: Conceptual issues. In R. D. Ogilvie & J. R. Harsh (Eds.), *Sleep onset: Normal and abnormal processes* (pp. 3–17). Washington, DC: American Psychological Association.

Rechtschaffen, A., Hauri, P., & Zeitlin, M. (1966). Auditory awakening thresholds in REM and NREM sleep stages. *Perceptual and Motor Skills, 22,* 927–942.

Rechtschaffen, A., & Kales, A. (1968). *A manual of standard terminology, techniques and scoring system for sleep states of human subjects* (NIH Publication No. 204). Washington, DC: Superintendent of Documents, Book 1–62; or Los Angeles: UCLA Brain Information Service/Brain Research Institute, University of California.

Redeker, N. S., Mason, D. J., Wykpisz, E., Glica, B., & Miner, C. (1994). First postoperative week activity patterns and recovery in women after coronary artery bypass surgery. *Nursing Research, 43,* 168–173.

Robins, R. W., John, O. P., & Caspi, A. (1994). Major dimensions of personality in early adolescence: The Big Five and beyond. In C. F. Halverson, Jr., G. A. Kohnstamm, & R. P. Martin (Eds.), *The developing structure of temperament and personality from infancy to adulthood* (pp. 267–291). Hillsdale, NJ: Erlbaum.

Sadeh, A. (1994). Assessment of intervention for infant night wakening: Parental reports and activity-based home monitoring. *Journal of Consulting and Clinical Psychology, 62,* 63–68.

Sadeh, A., Alster, J., Urbach, D., & Lavie, P. (1989). Actigraphically based automatic bedtime sleep-wake scoring: Validity and clinical applications. *Journal of Ambulatory Monitoring, 2,* 209–216.

Sadeh, A., Hauri, P. J., Kripke, D. F., & Lavie, P. (1995). The role of actigraphy in the evaluation of sleep disorders. *Sleep, 18,* 288–302.

Sadeh, A., Lavie, P., Scher, A., Tirosh, E., & Epstein, R. (1991). Actigraphic home-monitoring sleep-disturbed and control infants and young children: A new method for pediatric assessment of sleep-wake patterns. *Pediatrics, 87,* 494–499.

Sadeh, A., Sharkey, M., & Carskadon, M. A. (1994). Activity-based sleep-wake identification: An empirical test of methodological issues. *Sleep, 17,* 201–207.

Siscovick, D. S., LaPorte, R. E., & Newman, J. M. (1985). The disease-specific benefits and risks of physical activity and exercise. *Public Health Reports, 100,* 180–188.

Slattery, M. L., Schumacher, M. C., Smith, K. R., West, D. W., & Abd-Elghany, N. (1988). Physical activity, diet, and risk of colon cancer in Utah. *American Journal of Epidemiology, 128,* 989–999.

Snyder, F., & Scott, J. (1972). The psychology of sleep. In N. S. Greenfield and R. A. Sternback (Eds.), *Handbook of psychophysiology* (pp. 645–708). Toronto: Holt, Rinehart and Winston.

Spiegel, R. (1981). *Sleep and sleeplessness in advanced age.* New York: SP Medical and Scientific Books.

Standards of Practice Committee. (1995). Practice parameters for the use of actigraphy in the clinical assessment of sleep disorders. *Sleep, 18,* 285–287.

Stewart, A. L., King, A. C., & Haskell, W. L. (1993). Endurance exercise and health-related quality of life in 50–65 year-old adults. *The Gerontologist, 33,* 782–789.

Taylor, S. E. (1991). *Health psychology* (pp. 119–123). New York: McGraw-Hill.

Teicher, M. H. (1995). Actigraphy and motion analysis: New tools for psychiatry. *Harvard Review of Psychiatry, 3,* 18–35.

Teicher, M. H., Ito, Y., Glod, C. A., & Barber, N. I. (1996). Objective measurement of hyperactivity and attentional problems in ADHD. *Journal of the American Academy of Child and Adolescent Psychiatry, 35,* 334–342.

Thomas, A., & Chess, S. (1977). *Temperament and development.* New York: Brunner/Mazel.

Thomas, A., Chess, S., & Birch, H. (1968). *Temperament and behavior: Disorders in children.* New York: New York University Press.

Tryon, W. W. (1985). The measurement of human activity. In W. W. Tryon (Ed.), *Behavioral assessment in behavioral medicine* (pp. 200–256). New York: Springer.

Tryon, W. W. (1986). Motor activity measurements and DSM-III. *Progress in Behavior Modification, 20,* 35–66.

Tryon, W. W. (1991a). *Activity measurement in psychology and medicine.* New York: Plenum.

Tryon, W. W. (1991b). Motoric assessment and DSM-III-R. In M. Hersen & S. M. Turner (Eds.), *Adult psychopathology and diagnosis* (pp. 413–440). New York: Wiley.

Tryon, W. W. (1993). The role of motor excess and instrumented activity measurement in Attention-Deficit Hyperactivity Disorder. *Behavior Modification, 17,* 371–406.

Tryon, W. W. (1996). Nocturnal activity and sleep assessment. *Clinical Psychology Review, 16,* 197–213.

Tryon, W. W., Gruen, W., & Reitman, M. (1995). *A simple hand-held device for measuring sleep-onset latency.* Manuscript in preparation.

Tryon, W. W., & Pinto, L. P. (1994). Comparing activity measurements and ratings. *Behavior Modification, 18,* 251–261.

Tryon, W. W., & Pologe, B. (1987). Accelerometric assessment of tardive dyskinesia. *American Journal of Psychiatry, 144,* 1548–1587.

Tryon, W. W., & Williams, R. (1996). Fully proportional actigraphy: A new instrument. *Behavior Research Methods Instruments & Computers, 28,* 392–403.

van Hilten, J. J., Middelkoop, H. A. M., Kerkhof, G. A., & Roos, R. A. C. (1991). A new approach in the assessment of motor activity in Parkinson's disease. *Journal of Neurology, Neurosurgery, and Psychiatry, 54,* 976–979.

van Hilten, J. J., Middelkoop, H. A. M., Kuiper, S. I. R., Kramer, C. G. S., & Roos, R. A. C. (1994). Where to record motor activity: An evaluation of commonly used sites of placement for activity monitors. In H. A. M. Middelkoop (Ed.), *Actigraphic assessment of sleep and sleep disorders* (pp. 39–48). Delft, The Netherlands: Eburon. Also published in *Electroencephalography and Clinical Neurophysiology, 89,* 359–362.

van Lieshout, C. F. M., & Haselager, G. J. T. (1994). The Big Five personality factors in Q-sort descriptions of children and adolescents. In C. F. Halverson, Jr., G. A. Kohnstamm, & R. P. Martin (Eds.), *The developing structure of temperament and personality from infancy to adulthood* (pp. 293–318). Hillsdale, NJ: Erlbaum.

van Someren, E. J. W., van Gool, W. A., Vonk, B. F. M., Mirmiran, M., Speelman, J. D., Bosch, D. A., & Swaab, D. F. (1993). Ambulatory monitoring of tremor and other movements before and after thalamotomy: A new quantitative technique. *Journal of the Neurological Sciences, 117,* 16–23.

Vena, J. E., Graham, S., Zielezny, M., Swanson, M. K., Barnes, R. E., & Nolan, J. (1985). Lifetime occupational exercise and colon cancer. *American Journal of Epidemiology, 122,* 357–365.

Webster, J. B., Kripke, D. F., Messin, S., Mullaney, D. J., & Wyborney, G. (1982). An activity-based sleep monitor system for ambulatory use. *Sleep, 5,* 389–399.

Webster, J. B., Messin, S., Mullaney, D. J., & Kripke, D. F. (1982). Transducer design and placement for activity recording. *Medical and Biological Engineering and Computing, 20,* 741–744.

Zomer, J., Pollack, I., Tzischinsky, O., Epstein, R., Alster, J., & Lavie, P. (1987). *Computerized assessment of sleep time by wrist actigraphy.* Poster paper 528, 5th International Congress of Sleep Research.

Zuckerman, M. (1991). *Psychobiology of personality.* Cambridge: Cambridge University Press.

CHAPTER 18

DSM-IV and Multidimensional Assessment Strategies

RONALD ACIERNO, MICHEL HERSEN, and VINCENT B. VAN HASSELT

Diagnosis is not an end in itself. Although a classification system is essential for any science, its ultimate purpose is to optimize applied activities within that science. Indeed, a diagnostic conclusion, if it is to be useful, should strongly predict responses to given variables (e.g., treatment) introduced into the system. Unfortunately, the extent to which current psychological assessment devices such as the DSM-IV (*Diagnostic and Statistical Manual of Mental Disorders;* American Psychiatric Association [APA], 1994) fulfill this role is questionable. In large part, this is because DSM-IV classification is made almost exclusively on the basis of only one of several factors that determine treatment response: namely, symptomatology. As a result of such simplification, diagnoses assigned by the DSM-IV are highly reliable; however, their predictive validities are less impressive. That is, the "treatment utility" (Hayes, Nelson, & Jarrett, 1987) of the DSM-IV and preceding DSMs, or their usefulness in guiding selection and implementation of focused psychological interventions characterized by intentionally circumscribed effects, is less than optimal. In support of this point, consider existing research bases of treatment-outcome and meta-analytic studies that utilize DSM-based classification schemes but have failed to demonstrate differential treatment effectiveness with general psychopathology (e.g., Luborsky, Singer, & Luborsky, 1975). Clinical experience alone is sufficient to dispel the frequently resulting, albeit incorrect, conclusion that all treatments are "equal." A far more likely explanation for a noted lack of superiority of one treatment over another is that outcome results are confounded by uncontrolled heterogeneity of patients comprising diagnostic groups assumed to be homogeneous in these studies. Indeed, it is "an uncritical and simplistic reliance on diagnostic labels and subject selection criteria . . . based on the erroneous assumption that once persons have been assigned a diagnostic label, they are sufficiently similar to be randomly assigned to different treatment conditions" (Eifert, Evans, & McKendrick, 1990, p. 164) that is responsible for the failure to obtain results indicative of differential treatment efficacy. Ultimately, the DSM classification systems have failed to sufficiently address all *relevant* indicators of subtypes within diagnostic classes of psychopathology. Consequently, outcome studies employing these psychodiagnostic assessment schemes suffer from a loss of experimental control (Beutler, 1991; Eifert et al., 1990; Hayes et al., 1987;

Wolpe, 1977, 1986, 1990). This is not to say that the DSM-IV does not attempt to address differences within diagnoses. For example, five classes of bipolar disorder and several types of major depressive disorder (e.g., melancholic and recurrent) are outlined. Unfortunately, these subgroups are also almost exclusively defined in terms of observable or, more frequently, self-reported symptomatology and as such contribute only somewhat to predictions of treatment outcome. This criticism of DSM-IV is reminiscent of our earlier critique regarding DSM-III (APA, 1980) and DSM-III-R (APA, 1987). In commenting on DSM construction in the previous edition of this book, we noted: "In most branches of therapeutics, some relationship between diagnosis and treatment is apparent. . . Strangely enough, however, this was not . . . the case in psychiatry" (Hersen & Turner, 1991, p. 464). Simply stated, assignment of a DSM-IV diagnosis does not regularly imply that a specific treatment is indicated, and in the few cases where one form of an intervention has been found to be more appropriate than another (Task Force on Promotion and Dissemination of Psychological Procedures, 1995), treatment efficacy is lower than expected.

Development of the multiaxial system used in the DSM-IV was justified by its developers on the basis that it provided "a convenient format for organizing and communicating clinical information, for capturing the complexity of clinical situations, *and for describing the heterogeneity of individuals presenting with the same diagnosis*" (APA, 1994, p. 25, italics added). This last point is by far most critical. As mentioned, the primary deficiency of DSM-based diagnoses is no longer reliability. However, validity, measured in terms of the relationship between a diagnosis and its impact on treatment selection, is still questionable. Apparently, the multiaxial system is not doing its job in specifying heterogeneous pathology subtypes. While Axes I, II, and III are conceptually relevant and, to some extent, empirically supported, Axes IV and V contribute minimally to diagnostic processes. It is important to note that their lack of value is evident in their uniform absence from subject description sections of all assessment and controlled treatment outcome and literatures. Indeed, investigators conducting group studies rarely make reference to subjects' psychosocial and environmental stressors or global levels of functioning as part of their diagnostic formulation. Instead, only Axes I or II, and occasionally Axis III, descriptions are provided. Moreover, DSM-IV's use of Axis IV to simply list probable stressors, with no provision for illustrating causal relationships between these stressors and presenting psychopathology, is disappointing and ironic, particularly when considering that it is precisely these relationships that form the basis of most successful psychological interventions.

Overall, then, it appears that the DSM-IV possesses strong psychometric qualities of reliability, with diagnoses frequently (but not consistently) based on empirical evidence. It does not, however, differentiate subjects into diagnostically homogeneous subgroups. As a result, its contribution to treatment selection (e.g., its treatment utility) is often quite minimal. Although Axes IV and V were proposed to allow classification along alternate dimensions of psychopathology, thereby identifying heterogeneous subgroups of patients, they appear entirely too unstructured to assist in this manner (note that we made similar criticisms about DSM-III and DSM-III-R).

Fortunately, direction for constructing useful diagnostic axes along which psychopathological relationships to environmental factors can be enumerated comes from behavioral and medical researchers, who have historically attended closely to two areas in addition to symptomatology when conducting assessment. These include 1. specification of pathologic etiology and 2. analysis of functional aspects that serve to maintain pathology. Of course, assessment of symptoms also remains important; however, the prescriptive nature of many contemporary interventions demands multidimensional diagnostic specification in excess of that provided by the symptom-oriented DSM-IV. Note that a proposition to employ alternate axes of diagnostic assessment is not wholly unique. For example, Lazarus (1973) and Maier, Philipp, and Heuser (1986) offered means by which to identify dimensional aspects of psychopathology in addition to those given by the DSM. However, variables listed above are those that have received most empirical attention and appear to account for the greatest amount of variance in predicting treatment outcome. The following pages illustrate successful empirical demonstrations of such multidimensional prescriptive assessment along these proposed alternative axes.

ALTERNATIVE AXIS: TRIPARTITE ASSESSMENT OF SYMPTOMS

The DSM-IV's reliable evaluation and specification of symptoms is perhaps its greatest strength (of course, this is expected in light of the fact that the DSM-IV regularly confines itself to symptoms when defining diagnosis). However, even more thorough multivariate assessment of symptoms is easily accomplished and has been shown to possess increased predictive validity. It is widely agreed that *comprehensive* measurement of symptoms requires measurement of motoric behavior, cognition, and physiology, through behavioral observation, self-report, and physiological monitoring (see Bellack & Hersen, in press, for coverage of specific techniques). Such multilevel symptom assessment potentiates greater treatment efficiency, particularly when implementing contemporary prescriptive interventions. The utility of comprehensive symptom assessment has recently been realized in the area of substance abuse treatment. For example, several researchers have demonstrated advantages of subclassifying individuals who abuse alcohol as either "internalizers" or "externalizers" on the basis of specific cognitive and behavioral markers. Characteristics of externalizers include impulsivity, sociopathy, interpersonal dysfunction, episodic binge drinking, aggressiveness, increased negativity, and an external locus of control. By contrast, symptoms of internalizing drinkers include relative independence, low aggressiveness and impulsivity, increased self-reflection and anxiety, and an internal locus of control. Employing this symptom-based subclassification scheme, Cooney, Kadden, Litt, and Getter (1991) found that internalizers improved to a relatively greater extent following interpersonally based treatment while externalizers (possessing, by definition, impaired interpersonal functioning) responded best to highly structured cognitive-behavioral treatment. This treatment by symptom-subgroup interaction effect was also impressively demonstrated at the 2-year follow-up point. Using a similar classification scheme, Kadden, Cooney, Getter, and Litt (1989) compared specific group skills training, including problem solving, relaxation, and relapse prevention, to interactional group therapy, involving attention to in-session group dynamics. Subjects were classified as either high or low in global psychopathology (i.e., as externalizers or internalizers, respectively). The investigators hypothesized that, for those subjects high in global psychopathology, a directive skills training intervention would be most beneficial, relative to individuals low in global psychopathology, for whom interpersonally based treatment was thought to be more appropriate. Results consistent with those of Cooney et al. (1991) were obtained and were in accord with hypothesized interactions.

Annis and Davis (1989) offered an additional symptom-based dimension upon which to base substance abuse diagnosis that further enhanced predictive validity. Specifically, these researchers utilized self-report measures to identify subjects possessing "generalized" or "differentiated" drinking patterns, defined in terms of their ability to identify specific situations in which alcohol consumption occurred. After classification in this manner, patients were treated by either traditional substance abuse counseling or by relapse prevention techniques. A subtype by treatment interaction was identified in which those with nonspecific drinking patterns responded to both interventions equally well, while those with differentiated drinking patterns evinced relatively greater improvement following relapse prevention therapy, a treatment regimen specifically aimed at altering behavior in clearly defined "risk" situations. Once again, level of assessment specificity provided by the DSM-IV would not have been sufficient to identify these subgroups or to reveal these interactions.

One dimension of substance use disorders the DSM-IV does address is drug-use class. In support of differentiating diagnosis on the basis of drug class, Vaglum and Fossheim (1980) found that adolescents abusing psychedelic drugs evinced dissimilar treatment responses compared to youth using opiates or stimulants. It is interesting to note that in the former group of drug users, improvement was associated with increased levels of family and individual therapy and reduced amounts of confrontational milieu therapy. In contrast, enhanced treatment gains in the latter group of opiate or stimulant using youth were most strongly predicted by increased levels of confrontational milieu therapy. In this case, then, differing DSM-based substance abuse classes had implications for alternative treatment delivery strategies.

Similar symptom-based subtypes, validated by their differential treatment response, have been identified within DSM-defined categories of somatic disorders. For example, Martelli, Auerbach, Alexander, and Mercuri (1987) successfully identified cognitive subtypes of fearful patients preparing to undergo dental surgery. In this experiment, individuals were classified, according to their coping style, as either problem focused or emotion focused. In the former group, a preference for information and education about forthcoming medical procedures was evident, whereas no such preference was demonstrated by patients in the latter group. Prior to their presentation for dental surgery, subjects in both groups received either a "problem-focused" or an "emotion-focused" intervention. Problem-focused treatment entailed provision of information regarding probable sensory events and surgical procedures, as well as training in specific problem analysis and solution strategies. Emotion-focused treatment involved primarily palliative measures applied to dysphoric states elicited by aversive situations, with no emphasis on problem solving or solution skill training. Results supported the validity of this method of subtyping and revealed an interaction between patients' cognitive styles and treatment that would not have been identified through standard DSM-IV symptom assessment. Specifically, pain and treatment satisfaction ratings made by patients, and adjustment to surgery ratings made by physicians, were greater when treatment was matched with preferred cognitive coping styles. Moreover, "responses were relatively poor when mismatches occurred" (Martelli et al., 1987, p. 201).

Analogous symptom-based subtypes of affective disorders within DSM-IV diagnostic categories also appear to exist. The strongest support for this contention comes from studies of subjective and physiological correlates of anxiety in depressed patients. Although ignored as a relevant measure of mood disorder, subclassification by the DSM-IV, anxiety level appears to predict treatment response for a significant proportion of depressed patients (McKnight, Nelson, Hayes & Jarrett, 1984; Paykel et al., 1973; Wolpe, 1977, 1979, 1986). Most important, anxiety may provide a reliable means by which to identify and discriminate endogenous from nonendogenous forms of depression, in that endogenous depressives evince significantly lower levels of anxiety than their nonendogenous counterparts (Heerlein, Lauer, & Richter, 1989; Wolpe, 1986) and respond at a significantly greater rate to several somatic forms of treatment (MAOI treatment excepted; Brown & Shuey, 1980; McKnight et al., 1984; Prusoff, Weissman, Kleiman, & Rounsaville, 1980; Woggon, 1993). It is important that this endogenous/nonendogenous distinction is supported along physiological behavioral symptom lines through the sedation threshold test. Specifically, depressed patients with anxiety (i.e., nonendogenous depressives) evince above average sedation thresholds, as do anxiety-disordered patients. By contrast, endogenous depressed patients demonstrate *below* average sedation thresholds, indicating that these two groups of depressives are qualitatively, as opposed to merely quantitatively, different and likely have dissimilar treatment requirements and responses. Indeed, Conti, Placidi, Dell'Osso, Lenzi, and Cassano (1987) found that depressed patients with low levels of anxiety (i.e., endogenous depressives) in their sample required only antidepressant medication to improve, while anxious depressives responded no better to pharmacotherapy than to placebo. It is obvious that the DSM-IV's failure to include anxiety level as a variable in the diagnosis of endogenous/melancholic depression severely limits usefulness of this subtype. Indeed, it is widely agreed that the DSM does not effectively discriminate endogenous from nonendogenous depression (de Jonghe, Ameling, & Assies, 1988; Robbins, Block, & Peselow, 1989; Zimmerman, Stangle, & Coryell, 1985). And although several empirically supported core symptoms other than anxiety level are considered in the DSM-IV diagnosis of melancholic depression, including guilt, disinterest in people, early morning insomnia, psychomotor retardation, and lack of appetite (de Jonghe et al., 1988; Gunther, Gunther, Streck, Romig, & Rodel, 1988; Musa, 1986; Robbins et al., 1989), the category appears to be a measure of depressive severity, a factor that, in isolation, does not reliably differentiate endogenous from nonendogenous depression (Gallagher-Thompsen et al., 1992; Robbins et al., 1989; Willner, Wilkes, & Orwin, 1990).

In addition to support for depressive subtypes obtained through physiological (e.g., sedation threshold) and behavioral (e.g., psychomotor retardation) symptom assessment, Simons, Lustman, Wetzel, and Murphy (1985) provided evidence for existence of affective-disordered subgroups that could be differentiated along cognitive lines. In this investigation, subjects were rated in terms of their "learned resourcefulness," defined as their ability to monitor, control, and change unpleasant internal events. Those assessed as low in learned resourcefulness evinced relatively more favorable responses to pharmacological treatment, while those rated high in this area achieved greatest gains with a cognitively oriented intervention, thereby illustrating an interaction between coping style and treatment type.

It is clear that thorough symptom assessment, conducted in accord with existing empirical findings and in greater depth than that specified by the DSM-IV, facilitates selection of optimally effective interventions by enabling clinicians to match their treatments and treatment modalities to each patient's presenting psychopathology. The aforementioned examples outlined areas in which DSM-IV symptom assessment falls short and may be improved. Such a notion of comprehensive, tripartite symptom assessment is not extremely novel (Lang, 1968), and its potential usefulness in increasing effective and efficient application of psychological interventions should be obvious. Rarely, however, does the DSM-IV (or controlled group outcome studies) clarify intradiagnostic distinctions on the basis of simultaneous measurement of cognition, physiology, and behavior (excepting specific diagnostic classes: e.g., panic disorder), or in the empirically supported manners outlined above, leading to increased variability of subjects given identical diagnostic labels. Furthermore, comprehensive symptom assessment is only one of the important diagnostic axes that must be considered. Indeed, the "treatment utility" of diagnosis is advanced even further over existing DSM-IV standards by measurement of contextual factors that serve to maintain psychopathology.

ALTERNATIVE AXIS: ASSESSMENT OF MAINTAINING FACTORS

The clinical utility of any diagnostic system is dramatically enhanced when factors that serve to elicit or perpetuate pathology are formally delineated. Such specification is accomplished through a functional analysis of psychopathology in which contextual contingencies of reinforcement or conditioned discriminitive stimuli in the environment are systematically identified. The value of this level of assessment is apparent when considering that two individuals diagnosed with the same DSM-IV disorder, but whose pathological behavior is maintained by disparate elements, will necessarily require differing forms of treatment in order to achieve lasting improvement. Additionally, assessment of factors that maintain pathology often provides valuable "insight" into parameters of problem behaviors. For example, phobic avoidance of interpersonal contact in response to fear elicited by previous social failures is distinguished from social fears that do not have a basis in skills deficits. Treatment for the second class of phobia may very likely require only exposure to feared situations, whereas treatment for the first social phobia should involve some form of skills training in addition to exposure strategies (Wolpe, 1990). As implied earlier, effective measurement of factors that maintain psychopathology entails 1. specification of antecedents and consequents (i.e., contingencies) within which problem be-haviors exist, 2. specification of effects problem behaviors have on significant others, and 3. delineation of environmental stimuli that vary as a function of problem behaviors. The manner and complexity of a functional assessment of maintaining factors will vary widely across disorders and is determined, in large part, by the symptom presentation of the patient. It is most frequently the case, however, that functional assessment of childhood psychopathology is less difficult than assessment of adult problem behavior.

Azrin et al. (1994) demonstrated the clinical utility of complementing DSM-IV assessment with functional analysis of maintaining factors in their controlled evaluation of two treatments for drug abuse. Specifically, standard supportive counseling was compared to a behaviorally oriented intervention characterized by a thorough and individualized identification of stimuli that reliably elicited drug use, followed by specific skills training to decrease the amount of time spent in the presence of those stimuli. Moreover, existing contingency patterns of drug use reinforcement were outlined for each patient and intentionally al-tered so that drug use resulted in high levels of response cost, while abstinence resulted in increased levels of social reinforcement. Note that both associative (i.e., conditioned stimuli that elicited drug use) and instrumental (i.e., contin-gencies of drug use reinforcement) components of learned pathological behav-ior were addressed by this intervention. Predictably, subjects receiving the highly individualized behavioral treatment that specifically emphasized assessment of maintaining factors used drugs to a significantly lesser extent than their counter-parts receiving standard substance abuse counseling. Furthermore, these differential treatment effects were maintained at the 9-month follow-up (Azrin et al., 1996).

While individual functional assessment cannot be practically specified by a classification system such as the DSM-IV, notation of general categories, or even the presence or absence of conditioned stimuli and operant contingencies that reinforce problem behavior, is easily accomplished. Support for this point is also provided through single-case controlled research, in which subject vari-ables, pathology, and maintaining factors are regularly described in greater de-tail than is typically provided in group research designs. Illustrative is the study by Kallman, Hersen, and O'Toole (1975) in which a 42-year-old male with non-neurological paralysis was treated in a behavioral format. For 5 years preceding his presentation for treatment, the patient experienced several episodes of paral-ysis during which he could not move his legs. These periods lasted for 1–2 weeks. It is interesting that symptom onset was concomitant with the patient's forced retirement and reluctant acceptance of his wife's household duties. Inpatient treatment was initiated and involved differential contingent reinforcement of standing and walking behaviors by female research assistants. Following this treatment, both ambulatory behaviors returned and the patient was discharged from the hospital. However, he experienced relapse after only 4 weeks and was again hospitalized. Functional assessment along the parameters outlined above revealed discriminative stimuli that reliably elicited problem behavior (e.g., fam-ily discord) as well as contingencies that perpetuated the behavior (e.g., positive reinforcement through family attention and negative reinforcement through re-lief from household duties). In light of these additional data, familial contingencies were altered so that members reinforced only appropriate ambulatory behavior and extinguished paralytic behavior. This more comprehensive intervention, based on an active consideration of maintaining factors, resulted in lasting therapeutic gain.

Assessment of maintaining factors is routinely given attention by most clinicians. It is all the more ironic, therefore, that the DSM-IV lacks such a means of diagnostic specification, increasing the likelihood that diagnostic classes are composed of heterogeneous groups of patients. This is distressing when considering that DSM specification is the sine qua non of contemporary empirical research. Moreover, identification of both instrumental and associative relationships that serve to maintain psychopathology facilitates increasingly effective and enduring clinical interventions. Axis IV of the DSM-IV was advanced to fulfill a similar role. However, simply listing psychosocial stress events that co-occur with onset of psychopathology provides little or no relevant information concerning the relationship between these stressors and the disorder at hand and, as such, does not contribute to treatment selection. Therefore, an axis addressing the relationship between possible maintaining factors and pathology should, in the least, attempt to identify and classify learned problem behavior as having operant or associative (or both) sustaining properties, followed by operational definitions of how these contingencies and discriminative stimuli maintain problem behavior. While this introduces some theoretical speculation into the diagnostic process, such activity is justifiable and useful when based on previous empirical research. As mentioned, however, assessment should not end with maintaining factors. Indeed, the path by which psychopathology developed regularly provides essential direction to the course a treatment should take (Eifert, et al., 1990; Hersen, 1981; Wolpe, 1986).

ALTERNATIVE AXIS: ETIOLOGY

Current psychological and pharmacological interventions are characterized by a high degree of effect specificity. As such, they require multifaceted, yet conceptually consistent diagnostic procedures. Such diagnostic accuracy is provided by complementing measurement of symptoms and maintaining factors with assessment of etiology (Agras, 1987; Eifert, et al., 1990; Hersen, 1981; Wolpe, 1986). Traditionally, etiological speculation was confined to theoretical orientations of given therapists or investigators, lacking any form of empirical verification. As a result, the DSM-III and later versions removed referents to psychopathological etiology in almost all diagnostic categories as a means to avoid theory specific bias. It appears, however, that in its effort to remain "ideologically neutral," the DSM has ignored a potentially essential form of information. Indeed, etiological assessment is regularly performed in the applied practices of clinicians from all perspectives, where it plays a pivotal role in treatment selection. That is, the "what" given by symptom measurement must often be complemented by the "how" delineated through etiological assessment in order to maximize treatment efficacy. Therefore, it is extremely distressing to note that, despite its probable relevance to treatment, etiology is not even considered (i.e., experimentally controlled) in almost all existing treatment-outcome studies employing DSM-based diagnosis (Hersen, 1981; Wolpe, 1977, 1979, 1990). As a result, all noted effects in these studies are potentially confounded by etiological differences within diagnostic groups, and conclusions are "rendered nugatory by the imprecision of the data" (Wolpe, 1977). Because DSM-IV diagnostic criteria now serve as the standard basis for nearly all subject selection and identification in proposed grant-funded and published empirical projects, it is essential that an axis be formulated that permits measurement of etiology.

The necessity of etiological assessment in clarifying results of empirical investigations and enhancing treatment efficacy is clearly demonstrated by the large base of existing affective disorder research with endogenous and nonendogenous depression (e.g., Conti et al., 1987; Kupfer & Thase, 1983). Admittedly, evaluations of the utility of conducting etiological assessment with depressed patients have produced mixed results. Apparently, the not-infrequent lack of an interaction effect between etiology and treatment is a direct result of weak etiological assessment strategies, which themselves are based wholly on overt symptom assessment. For example, Gallagher-Thompsen et al. (1992) compared diagnostic agreement of the DSM-III, DSM-III-R, Research Diagnostic Criteria (RDC; 1975), and Newcastle Index and concluded that the sections of these instruments used to assign a diagnosis of endogenous depression were measuring different constructs. The RDC classification of endogenous depression has also been the target of specific criticisms by de Jonghe et al. (1988), Young et al. (1987), Zimmerman, Coryell, & Black (1990), and Zimmerman et al. (1985). Other symptom-based scales for endogenous depression appear to be equally problematic. For example, when comparing the Newcastle I, Newcastle II, and Michigan Indices, Davidson and Pelton (1988) obtained diagnostic agreement for only 30% of subjects. Relatively more distressing was the wide range of subjects classified as endogenous depressives by the three scales, from a low of 23% with the Newcastle II Index to a high of 78% for the Michigan Index. Obviously, with such imprecise reference measures, valid etiological assessment is impossible and determination of treatment by etiology interaction is precluded. In support of this point, Davidson and Pelton (1988) demonstrated that treatment by etiological subtype interactions that existed when classification was made by one system was obliterated when categorization was made on the basis of a second system. This point was made particularly poignant by the fact that no between-group (main) effects of the two compared treatments (low-dose and high-dose MAOIs) were revealed by any scales, leading to the erroneous conclusion that both dosage levels were equally effective.

Although experimenters have repeatedly identified several symptoms of endogenous depression (e.g., early morning insomnia, increased negative affect in morning, poor appetite, psychomotor disturbance, and low anxiety; Robbins, Alessi, & Colfer, 1989; Zimmerman et al., 1985), relatively more objective methods of diagnostic classification have been advanced as a means to complement these overt measures. Perhaps the best known and somewhat controversial indicator of endogenous depression is nonsuppression on the dexamethasone suppression test (DST; Chadhury, Valdiya, & Augustine, 1989; Robbins, Alessi, & Colfer, 1989; Zimmerman, et al., 1985; Zimmerman et al., 1990). The controversy over the DST arises from its intermittent failure to predict depressive group membership (e.g., Klein & Berger, 1987). However, the sometimes poor showing of this test is inextricably linked to inconsistent use of reference criteria to set diagnosis across settings and investigators. When other symptom-based reference systems are discarded and the DST is used as the primary criterion of classification, a homogenous subgroup of depressives is identified. Moreover, even when using external reference criteria such as those supplied by the RDC, diagnostic agreement with the DST is good if narrow versions of RDC definitions are employed, whereas no such relationship is apparent when broad versions of RDC criteria are used (Zimmerman et al., 1990). Logically, if the reference criteria are unreliable or invalid, then the specificity and sensitivity of the test being evaluated will also appear questionable.

Two other biologically based methods of identifying endogenous and nonendogenous depression have been reported in the recent past, providing convergent validation for this affective disorder subtype. Bertschy et al. (1989) reported that cardiac beta-adrenergic sensitivity was significantly lower in endogenous depressives, and that this association was independent of depressive severity. Along slightly different lines, Maes, DeRuyter, and Suy (1987) employed several biologically based predictors, including age, the DST, l-tryptophan: competing amino acid ratio, and the 3-methoxy-4-hydroxyphenylglycol flow in 24-hour urine to classify, with 85% accuracy, subjects as nonendogenous or endogenous depressives. Combinations of these objective measures and aforementioned symptom indicators of endogenous depression may form a reliable and valid means by which to classify depressive subgroups according to etiology (although the requirement that a physician perform some of these objective tests may cause them to be adopted with less than unbridled enthusiasm).

Of course, classification according to etiology is justified only if the effort expended results in improved treatment efficacy and efficiency. Evidence to this effect has been provided by several sources and has been available for the past two decades. For example, Paykel et al. (1973) classified their depressed subjects, prior to treatment, as anxious, psychotic, hostile, or personality-disordered and found that greater initial severity of depression predicted greatest treatment response to amitriptyline. However, this relationship *did not* hold for those depressed patients who also exhibited anxiety (i.e., nonendogenous depressives). In fact, these individuals responded to pharmacotherapy with the least improvement of any group. Similarly, Kiloh, Ball, and Garside (1977) demonstrated that endogenous depressives maintained gains following antidepressant medication treatment regimens at a significantly greater level than nonendogenous depressives given the same intervention. It is interesting to note that Raskin and Crook (1970) found that while antidepressant medication and placebo produced very similar treatment gains in nonendogenous depressed patients, patients with endogenous depression responded only to the active medication. Robbins, Alessi, and Colfer (1989) also reported evidence in support of specific treatment indications when patients present with endogenous depression. In their study of 38 depressed adolescents, over half did not respond to a psychosocial intervention for depression. These nonresponders were then treated by a combination of psychosocial therapy and tricyclic antidepressants, to which 92% responded with improvement. It is important that DST nonsuppression, indicative of endogenous depression, was associated with a failure to respond to psychological treatment alone. Similar treatment by depressive subtype interactions have been found by Bech, Gram, Reisby, and Raphaelson (1980), Brown and Shuey (1980), Davidson and Pelton (1988), McKnight, Nelson, Hayes, and Jarrett (1984), Prusoff et al. (1980), and Woggon (1993). Moreover, the diagnostic value of the endogenous versus nonendogenous distinction is also clear from a long-term study by Buckholtz-Hansen, Wang, and Sorensen (1993). These investigators followed pharmacologically treated depressed patients for 10 years and found that suicidality in nonendogenous depressives was 100 times that of a normal reference group compared to endogenous depressives, whose suicide rate was only 20 times that of normals. Obviously, alternative therapeutic considerations are in order when conducting pharmacotherapy with nonendogenous and endogenous depressives. Consequences of ignoring this subclassification (as is the case with the DSM-IV) are potentially extreme.

Etiologically based subtypes of nonendogenous depression also appear to exist (Craighead, 1980; Hersen, 1981; Wolpe, 1990) and are validated by their differential treatment response. Specifically, nonendogenous depression may be produced by social skill deficits leading to reduced interpersonal reinforcement, prolonged anxiety, marital discord, and so on. Along these lines, Heiby (1986) utilized a cross-over design to evaluate the relative efficacy of self-control training and social skills training with four depressed subjects low in either self-control or social skill. As hypothesized, treatment that was matched to patient-defined deficit was more effective than treatment that was not otherwise matched. In another well-known study, McKnight, et al., (1984) demonstrated that depressed subjects presenting with clear skill deficits responded well to skills training as opposed to cognitive therapy, while depressed patients presenting primarily with depressogenic cognitions improved most following cognitive treatment.

Overall, the utility of subclassifying affective disorders according to etiological origin is great, both in terms of immediate treatment selection and long-term clinical outcome. Therefore, it is essential that some formalized consideration of etiology be incorporated into DSM structure. This will have the dually beneficial consequence of improving psychological treatments with this class of pathology, as well as controlling the confounding effects produced by diagnostic heterogeneity in any treatment-outcome study employing DSM-based diagnoses.

Analogous findings of etiological heterogeneity have been noted within DSM diagnostic categories of anxiety disorders. Wolpe (1981), Öst and Hugdahl (1983), Rachman (1977), and Kleinknecht (1994) have all noted potential benefits of differentiating conditioned from cognitively based specific phobias. Similarly, Trower, Yardley, Bryant, and Shaw (1978) demonstrated that etiological subtypes of social phobia also exist and evidence differential treatment response. Moreover, etiological subtypes of panic also exist. Russell, Kushner, Bertman, and Bartels (1991) reported on an intriguing sample of panickers for whom attacks were not accompanied by fear. These individuals had very large and uniform responses to both actual and placebo challenge tests, as well as pharmacotherapy (none experienced an attack during placebo challenge, all during real challenge, and all improved significantly with drug treatment), strongly implicating a biological basis for the disorder. Along slightly different lines, Ley (1992) has outlined several additional subtypes of panic with primarily psychological origins, including hyperventilatory, cognitive, and conditioned. These subgroups are not differentiated by the DSM and very likely require alternative forms of intervention.

Obviously, etiological assessment is of great potential usefulness in selecting and implementing focused or prescriptive treatments. Indeed, most clinicians routinely attempt to identify how their patients developed their pathology in order to both select treatment and prevent future recurrences of problem behavior. It is unfortunate and distressing, therefore, that the DSM, and as a consequence contemporary treatment-outcome studies, largely ignores this area of assessment. This oversight has the effect of severely confounding and minimizing obtained experimental results. Indeed, the variance accounted for by etiology is potentially great, and an axis devoted to its measurement is warranted.

SUMMARY

Enhanced treatment efficacy is the ultimate purpose of assessment and diagnosis in psychology. Accordingly, those aspects of measurement that most strongly predict response to a given therapeutic strategy or intervention should be central components of definitive and useful diagnostic tools. That is, effective assessment procedures should be structured so that their "treatment utility" is maximized. Therefore, consistent with the nature of most psychopathology, diagnostic endeavors should be multidimensional. Unfortunately, contemporary psychology's primary diagnostic instrument, the DSM-IV, appears not to possess the quality of multidimensionality and is instead largely confined to delineation of overt symptomatology. Admittedly, this focus has had the effect of dramatically increasing diagnostic reliability. However, the validity of many DSM-IV defined disorders is suspect because individuals with similar diagnoses, presumed to be part of a homogeneous group, do not necessarily share common etiological characteristics. While their overt symptom presentations may be nearly identical, differences may exist along other dimensions that are particularly relevant to treatment, including factors that serve to maintain pathology as well as those that contribute to pathological etiology, in addition to symptomatology.

The benefits of investigating these additional areas of assessment lie, of course, in their ability to clarify differential treatment responses of patient subgroups. For the past 20 years, attempts to evaluate relative effectiveness of several psychological treatments for depression and other forms of mental illness have produced somewhat disappointing results, leading some to claim that most, if not all, treatments are of nearly equal potency. In large part, however, these studies employed assessment strategies that failed to control for differences in etiology and maintaining factors among subjects within experimental groups. That is, these experiments utilized heterogeneous groups of subjects presumed to be homogeneous. Under such conditions, differential treatment effects are predictably lost to aggregate averages. Obviously, accurate validation of differential treatment efficacy presupposes accurate processes of classification that control for all major sources of treatment-outcome variance (i.e., symptoms, maintaining factors, and etiology).

Substance abuse researchers have provided support for the value of conducting multivariate symptom assessment beyond that specified by the DSM-IV. Specific diagnostic parameters have included classification of patients on the basis of cognitive and behavioral symptoms as internalized and externalized drinkers, generalized and differentiated drinkers, and so on. Although still in its nascent stages, subclassification along these lines has revealed that the effects of several existing treatments may be even greater than previously thought with some patients and less than expected with others. Subclassification on the basis of multivariate assessment of symptoms with other forms of psychopathology (e.g., depression, anxiety) has also been characterized by increased "treatment utility." However, comprehensive evaluation of the advantages produced by simultaneous measurement of cognition, physiology, and behavior requires complex experimental designs with large sample sizes and has not been adequately accomplished with any disorder.

While assessment of symptoms traditionally occupies a position of central import in any diagnostic system, identification of those factors that serve to maintain pathology is also extremely helpful in guiding selection and implementation of therapeutic techniques. Most research in this area has been undertaken by behaviorally oriented investigators working with clearly defined behavior-based psychopathologies. It is important to note, though, that assessment of maintaining factors has also proved valuable in treating relatively more complex forms of pathology, such as substance abuse, marital discord, and depression. Moreover, it is typically advantageous for clinicians to collect some data that detail why psychopathology persists. Indeed, this is standard procedure in the practices of most clinicians.

A third area of potential relevance to treatment outcome is psychopathological etiology. To date, most research in this area has been conducted with depressive disorders and has produced only mixed results. However, existing etiological assessment techniques appear to rely, to an inappropriate extent, on overt symptomatology and, as such, produce subgroups of questionable validity. Obviously, if classification is error prone, then outcome evaluated on the basis of this classification will be irrelevant. Multidimensional methods of etiological measurement reveal treatment by subtype interactions that are not apparent when using DSM assessment techniques. This is distressing when considering that almost all current treatment-outcome research employs subject selection criteria that are in whole, or in large part, based on the DSM-IV, a diagnostic system that purposely ignores etiological factors.

In sum, addition of two diagnostic axes and modification of a third existing axis have been proposed as a means to augment and enhance the treatment utility of DSM-based diagnoses. These axes have been chosen and outlined on the basis of existing empirical data that suggest that they account for the greatest variance in treatment outcome. Furthermore, failure to distinguish psychopathology on the basis of each of these axes increases the risk that experimental results will be confounded through the use of heterogeneous samples of subjects presumed to be homogeneous. Initial attempts at multidimensional assessment are outlined.

REFERENCES

Agras, W. S. (1987). So where do we go from here? *Behavior Therapy, 18,* 203–217.

American Psychiatric Association. (1980). *Diagnostic and statistical manual of mental disorders* (3rd ed.). Washington, DC: Author.

American Psychiatric Association. (1987). *Diagnostic and statistical manual of mental disorders* (3rd ed., rev. ed.). Washington, DC: Author.

American Psychiatric Association. (1994). *Diagnostic and statistical manual of mental disorders* (4th ed.). Washington, DC: Author.

Annis, H., & Davis, L. (1989). Relapse prevention. In R. Hester & W. Miller (Eds.), *Handbook of alcoholism treatment approaches.* New York: Pergamon.

Azrin, N. H., Acierno, R., Kogan, E. S., Donohue, B., Besalel, V., & McMahon, P. (1996). Follow-up results of supportive versus behavioral therapy for illicit drug use. *Behaviour Research and Therapy., 34,* 41–46.

Azrin, N. H., McMahon, P., Donohue, B., Besalel, V., Lapinski, K., Kogan, E., Acierno, R., & Galloway, E. (1994). Behavior therapy for drug abuse: A controlled treatment-outcome study. *Behaviour Research and Therapy, 32,* 857–866.

Bech, P., Gram, L. F., Reisby, N., & Rafaelsen, O. J. (1980). The WHO depression scale: Relationship to the Newcastle scales. *Acta Psychiatrica Scandinavica, 62,* 140–147.

Bellack, A. S., & Hersen, M. (in press). *Behavioral assessment: A practical handbook* (4th ed.). New York: Pergamon.

Bertschy, G., Vandel, S., Puech, A., Vandel, B. Sandoz, M., & Allers, G. (1989). Cardiac beta-adrenergic sensitivity in depression: Relation with endogenous subtype and desipramine response. *Neuropsychobiology, 21,* 177–181.

Beutler, L. E. (1991). Have all won and must all have prizes? Revisiting Luborsky et al.'s verdict. *Journal of Consulting and Clinical Psychology, 59,* 226–232.

Brown, W. A., & Shuey, I. (1980). Response to dexamethasone and subtype of depression. *Archives of General Psychiatry, 37,* 747–751.

Buchholtz-Hansen, P. E., Wang, A. G., & Sorensen, P. (1993). Mortality in major affective disorder: Relationship to subtype of depression. *Acta Psychiatrica Scandinavica, 87,* 329–335.

Chadhury, S., Valdiya, P. S., & Augustine, M. (1989). The dexamethasone suppression test in endogenous depression. *Indian Journal of Psychiatry, 31,* 296–300.

Conti, L., Placidi, G. R., Dell'Osso, L., Lenzi, A., & Cassano, G. B. (1987). Therapeutic response in subtypes of major depression. *New Trends in Experimental and Clinical Psychiatry, 3,* 101–107.

Cooney, N. L., Kadden, R. M., Litt, M. D., & Getter, H. (1991). Matching alcoholics to coping skills or interactional therapies: Two-year follow up results. *Journal of Consulting and Clinical Psychology, 59,* 598–601.

Craighead, W. C. (1980). Away from a unitary model of depression. *Behavior Therapy, 11,* 122–128.

Davidson, J. R., & Pelton, S. (1988). A comparative evaluation of three discriminant scales for endogenous depression. *Psychiatry Research, 23,* 193–200.

de Jonghe, F., Ameling, E., & Assies, J. (1988). An elaborate description of the symptomatology of patients with research diagnostic criteria endogenous depression. *Journal of Nervous and Mental Disease, 176,* 475–479.

Eifert, G. H., Evans, I. M., & McKendrick, V. G. (1990). Matching treatments to client problems not diagnostic labels: A case for paradigmatic behavior therapy. *Journal of Behavior Therapy and Experimental Psychiatry, 21,* 163–172.

Gallagher-Thompson, D., Futterman, A., Hanley-Peterson, P., Zeiss, A., Fronson, G., & Thompson, L. (1992). Endogenous depression in the elderly: Prevalence and agreement among measures. *Journal of Consulting and Clinical Psychology, 60,* 300–303.

Gunther, W., Gunther, R., Streck, P., Romig, H., & Rodel, A. (1988). Psychomotor disturbances in psychiatric patients as a possible basis for new attempts at differential diagnosis and therapy: III. Cross validation study on depressed patients: The psychotic motor syndrome as a possible state marker for endogenous depression. *European Archives of Psychiatry and Neurological Sciences, 237,* 65–73.

Hayes, S. C., Nelson, R. O., & Jarrett, R. B. (1987). The treatment utility of assessment: A functional approach to evaluating assessment quality. *American Psychologist, 42,* 963–974.

Heiby, E. M. (1986). Social versus self-control skills deficits in four cases of depression. *Behavior Therapy, 17,* 158–169.

Heerlein, A., Lauer, G., & Richter, P. (1989). Alexithymia and affective expression in endogenous and nonendogenous depression. *Nervenarzt, 60,* 220–225.

Hersen, M. (1981). Complex problems require complex solutions. *Behavior Therapy, 12,* 15–29.

Hersen, M., & Turner, S. M. (1991). DSM-III, DSM-III-R, and behavior therapy. In M. Hersen & S. M. Turner (Eds.), *Adult psychopathology and diagnosis* (2nd ed., pp. 463–481). New York: Wiley.

Kadden, R. M., Cooney, N. L., Getter, H., & Litt, M. D. (1989). Matching alcoholics to coping skills or interactional therapies: Posttreatment results. *Journal of Consulting and Clinical Psychology, 57,* 698–704.

Kallman, W. M., Hersen, M., & O'Toole, D. H. (1975). The use of social reinforcement in a case of conversion reaction. *Behavior Therapy, 6,* 411–413.

Kiloh, L. G., Ball, J. R., & Garside, R. F. (1977). Depression: A multivariate study of Sir Aubrey Lews's data on melancholia. *Australian and New Zealand Journal of Psychiatry, 11,* 149–156.

Klein, H. E., & Berger, M. (1987). The pitfalls of the dexamethasone suppression test: A biological marker of endogenous depression? *Human Psychopharmacology Clinical and Experimental, 2,* 85–103.

Kleinknecht, R. A. (1994). Aquisition of blood, injury, and needle fears and phobias. *Behaviour Research and Therapy, 32,* 817–823.

Kupfer, D. L., & Thase, M. F. (1983). The use of the sleep laboratory in the diagnosis of affective disorders. *Psychiatric Clinics of North America, 6,* 3–25.

Lang, P. J. (1968) Fear reduction and fear behavior: Problems in treating a construct. In J. M. Shlien (Ed.), *Research in psychotherapy* (Vol. 3). Washington, DC: American Psychological Association.

Lazarus, A. (1973). Multimodal behavior therapy and treating the basic id. *Journal of Nervous and Mental Disease, 156,* 404–411.

Ley, R. (1992). The many faces of Pan: Psychological and physiological differences among three types of panic attacks. *Behaviour Research and Therapy, 30,* 347–357.

Luborsky, L., Singer, B., & Luborsky, L. (1975). Comparative studies of psychotherapy: Is it true that "Everyone has won and all must have prizes?" *Archives of General Psychiatry, 32,* 995.

Maes, M. H., de Ruyter, M., & Suy, E. (1987). Prediction of subtype and severity of depression by means of dexamethasone suppression test, 1-tryptophan: Competing amino acid ration, and MHPG flow. *Biological Psychiatry, 22,* 177–188.

Maier, W., Philipp, M., & Heuser, I. (1986). Dimensional assessment of endogenous depression based on a polydiagnostic approach. *Psychopathology, 19,* 267–275.

Martelli, M. F., Auerbach, S. M., Alexander, J., & Mercuri, L. G. (1987). Stress management in the health care setting: Matching interventions with patient coping styles. *Journal of Consulting and Clinical Psychology, 55,* 201–207.

McKnight, D., Nelson, R., Hayes, S., & Jarrett, R. (1984). Importance of treating individually assessed response classes of depression. *Behavior Therapy, 15,* 315–335.

Musa, M. N. (1986). Higher steady-state plasma concentration of imipramine in endogenous compared to nonendogenous depression. *Research Communications in Psychology, Psychiatry, and Behavior, 11,* 11–22.

Öst, L. G., & Hugdahl, K. (1983). Acquisition of agoraphobia, mode of onset and anxiety response patterns. *Behaviour Research and Therapy, 21,* 623–631.

Paykel, E. S., Prusoff, B. A., Klerman, G. L., Haskell, D., & Dimascio, A. (1973). Clinical response to amitriptyline among depressed women. *Journal of Nervous and Mental Disease, 156,* 149–165.

Prusoff, B. A., Weissman, M. M., Klerman, G. L., & Rounsaville, B. J. (1980). Research diagnostic criteria subtypes of depression. *Archives of General Psychiatry, 37,* 796–801.

Rachman, S. (1977). The conditioning theory of fear-acquisition: A critical examination. *Behaviour Research and Therapy, 15,* 375.

Raskin, A., & Crook, T. H. (1976). The endogenous-neurotic distinction as a predictor of response to antidepressant drugs. *Psychological Medicine, 6,* 59–70.

Robbins, D. R., Alessi, N. E., Colfer, M. V. (1989). Treatment of adolescents with major depression: Implications of the DST and the melancholic clinical subtype. *Journal of Affective Disorders, 17,* 99–104.

Robbins, C. J., Block, P., & Peselow, E. D. (1989). Specificity of symptoms in RDC endogenous depression. *Journal of Affective Disorders, 16,* 243–248.

Russell, J. L., Kushner, M. G., Beitman, B. D., & Bartels, K. M. (1991). Nonfearful panic disorder in neurology patients validated by lactate challenge. *American Journal of Psychiatry, 148,* 361–364.

Simons, A. D. Lustman, P. J., Wetzel, R. D., & Murphy, G. E. (1985). Predicting response to cognitive therapy of depression: The role of learned resourcefulness. *Cognitive Therapy and Research, 9,* 79–89.

Spitzer, R., Endicott, J., & Robins, E. (1978). Research diagnostic criteria: Rationale and reliability. *Archives of General Psychiatry, 35,* 773–782.

Task Force on Promotion and Dissemination of Psychological Procedures. (1995). *The Clinical Psychologist, 48,* 3–23.

Trower, P., Yardley, K., Bryant, B., & Shaw. (1978). The treatment of social failure: A comparison of anxiety reduction and skills aquisition procedures for two social problems. *Behavior Modification, 2,* 41–60.

Vaglum, P., & Fossheim, I. (1980). Differential treatment of young abusers: A quasi-experimental study of a "therapeutic community" in a psychiatric hospital. *Journal of Drug Issues, 10,* 505–516.

Willner, P., Wilkes, M., & Orwin, A. (1990). Attributional style and perceived stress in endogenous and reactive depression. *Journal of Affective Disorders, 18,* 281–287.

Woggon, B. (1993). The role of moclobemide in endogenous depression: A survey of recent data. Third International Symposium: RIMAs in subtypes of depression: Focus on moclobemide. *International Clinical Psychopharmacology, 7,* 137–139.

Wolpe, J. (1977). Inadequate behavior analysis: The Achilles' heel of outcome research in behavior therapy. *Journal of Behavior Therapy and Experimental Psychiatry, 8,* 1–3.

Wolpe, J. (1979). The experimental model and treatment of neurotic depression. *Behaviour Research and Therapy, 17,* 555–565.

Wolpe, J. (1981). The dichotomy between classically conditioned and cognitively learned anxiety. *Journal of Behavior Therapy and Experimental Psychiatry, 12,* 35–42.

Wolpe, J. (1986). The positive diagnosis of neurotic depression as an etiological category. *Comprehensive Psychiatry, 27,* 449–460.

Wolpe, J. (1990). *The practice of behavior therapy* (4th ed.). New York: Pergamon.

Young, M. A., Keller, M. B., Lavori, P. W., Scheftner, W. A., Fawcett, J., Endicott, J., & Hirschfeld, R. (1987). Lack of stability of the RDC endogenous subtype in consecutive episodes of major depression. *Journal of Affective Disorders, 12,* 139–143.

Zimmerman, M., Coryell, W. H., & Black, D. W. (1990). Variability in the application of contemporary diagnostic criteria: Endogenous depression as an example. *American Journal of Psychiatry, 147,* 1173–1179.

Zimmerman, M., Stangle, D., & Coryell, W. (1985). The research diagnostic criteria for endogenous sepression and the dexamethasone suppression test: A discriminant function analysis. *Psychiatry Research, 14,* 197–208.

Author Index

Abbey, S. E., 354
Abbott, P., 364
Abd-Elghany, N., 550
Abel, G. G., 416, 445
Abraham, H. D., 170
Abraham, S. R., 474
Abrahamson, D. J., 445
Abrams, D. S., 145
Abrams, R., 269
Abramson, L. Y., 237
Acierno, R., 584
Ackerman, P. H., 529
Acosta, F. X., 220
Adam, C., 130
Adamec, D. S., 130
Adams, A. J., 130
Adams, E. H., 160
Adams, G. D., 178
Adams, G. L., 220
Adams, H. E., 445
Adams, J. A., 276
Adamson, J., 490
Addiction Research
    Foundation, 93, 138, 139
Adey, M., 245
Adkins, E., 419, 430
Adler, L., 242
Adler, N., 9
Adler, R., 442
Ageton, S. S., 414, 422, 423,
    450
Agras, W. S., 285, 293, 299,
    471, 585
Ahern, F. M., 132
Akhtar, S., 286, 393, 529
Akiskal, H. S., 257, 259, 265,
    266, 267, 275, 315, 511
Albus, M., 304
Alden, L., 530
Aldridge-Morris, R., 395
Alessi, N. E., 586, 587

Alexander, B., 272
Alexander, J., 581, 582
Alexander, J. R., 268, 269
Alexander, M. P., 393
Allan, T., 302
Allcock, C., 433
Allen, B. A., 141, 145, 146
Allen, C., 268
Allen, C. R., 175
Allen, D. N., 106
Allen, J. P., 138, 139
Allen, K. M., 357
Allen, R., 307
Allers, G., 587
Allgulander, C., 168, 177
Allilaire, J. F., 560
Allison, S., 553
Allmon, D., 530
Alloy, L. B., 237
Allstop, S., 147
Almedia, O., 206
Almog, I. J., 174
Alper, K., 352
Alsobrock, S. P., 305
Alster, J., 552
Alterman, A. I., 107, 133,
    520, 521, 522, 523
Alterman, I., 166, 175
Amador, X., 206
Ameling, E., 582, 586
American College of Sports
    Medicine, 172
American Psychiatric
    Association, 3, 4, 5, 6, 7,
    8, 9, 10, 11, 12, 13, 14,
    16, 17, 18, 25, 32, 40, 68,
    72, 75, 90, 104, 129, 130,
    134, 137, 160, 169, 171,
    175, 180, 181, 185, 186,
    187, 206, 210, 213, 214,
    231, 262, 263, 276, 282,

284, 285, 286, 287, 288,
289, 333, 334, 335, 385,
387, 394, 402, 465, 468,
473, 476, 483, 508, 517,
547, 554, 558, 559, 564,
565, 568, 578, 579
Amies, P. L., 290, 296
Amos, J., 268
Amos, N. L., 519
Amsel, Z., 183
Anastasi, A., 551
An Der Heiden, W., 207
Anderson, B., 411, 418, 437
Anderson, C., 269
Anderson, D. J., 290, 297,
    298, 299, 305
Anderson, M. A., 89
Anderson, W. P., 238
Andrade, L., 314
Andreason, N. C., 24, 31,
    218, 271
Andreoli, A., 45, 46, 47
Andres, H. L., 165
Andrews, G., 48, 240, 304,
    307
Andrulonis, P. R., 511
Angel, R., 367
Anglin, L., 169
Anglin, M. D., 174, 176, 177
Angold, A., 237
Angst, J., 7, 257, 492, 493
Angus, L. E., 525
Anker, M., 219
Anlborn, A., 550
Annis, H., 581
Annis, H. A., 138, 140, 141
Anthony, J. C., 34, 131, 135,
    141, 187, 301
Anthony, M. M., 304
Apfel, R. S., 218
Apfelbaum, B., 414, 437

Appelbaum, P., 206
Apperson, L. J., 206
Appleby, I. L., 299
Apter, A., 212
Arean, P., 243, 249
Argyle, N., 205
Arias, M., 220
Arkes, H. R., 353
Armor, D. J., 131
Armstrong, H. E., 530
Armstrong, J., 384
Armstrong, M. S., 416, 433, 444
Arndt, S., 218
Arnow, B., 471
Arntz, A., 50, 51
Aro, S., 204
Aronen, E. T., 560
Aronowitz, B., 340
Arons, J. H., 440
Aronson, M. J., 184
Arora, R., 312
Arria, A. M., 135
Asche, J., 471
Ashikaya, T., 208
Ashles, T. A., 303, 347
Ashley, J. J., 132
Ashton, A. K., 431
Asnis, L., 516
Asokan, S., 268
Assie, J., 582, 586
Atanacio, B., 342
Atkinson, J. H., 7, 89
Atkinson, R. M., 131
Aubert, J. L., 13
Aubuchon, P. G., 304, 442
Auerbach, J. G., 206
Auerbach, R., 430
Auerbach, S. M., 581, 582
Augustine, M., 586
Auld, F., 351
Avison, W. R., 207
Axelrod, S., 342
Ayuso, J. L., 299
Azocar, F., 249
Azrin, N. H., 584

Babigian, H. M., 466
Babor, T. F., 137, 138, 141, 180, 184, 212, 361
Bach, D., 351
Bachman, J., 471
Bachman, J. D., 160, 161
Bachman, J. G., 173
Bacon, S. D., 128
Baer, L., 284, 315
Bagby, R. M., 351
Bailleul, J. P., 438

Baily, S., 147
Baker, L., 473
Baker, S. W., 444
Baker, T. B., 143
Baldwin, G., 475
Bale, R. N., 183
Bale, S. J., 268
Ball, J. R., 587
Ball, W. A., 498
Ballenger, C. B., 243
Ballenger, J. C., 299, 300, 311, 313, 340
Baltazar, P. L., 50, 57, 299
Balter, M. B., 491
Balter, M. D., 503
Bandura, A., 292
Bansal, S., 443
Barach, P., 389
Barasch, A., 524
Barban, L., 348, 395, 397
Barbaree, H. E., 423, 431, 432, 433, 434, 436, 446, 514
Barbour, C., 511
Bard, L. A., 423
Barkley, T. J., 562
Barlow, D. H., 7, 184, 285, 288, 300, 301, 302, 303, 304, 313, 316, 445
Barlow, J., 471
Barnes, G. M., 132
Barnes, R. E., 550
Barnett, W., 177, 190
Baron, M., 268, 269, 516
Barr, G., 311
Barrachlough, B., 78
Barrios, B. A., 296
Barsky, A. J., 339, 340, 345, 346, 348,
Bartels, K. M., 588
Bartels, S. B., 213
Bartels, S. J., 206
Bartholomew, K., 514, 525, 528
Bartlesen, A., 267
Barton, R., 238
Barton, S., 4
Bartusch, B. J., 522
Barzelay, D., 183
Basha, I. M., 347
Baskin, D., 220
Basoglu, M., 304
Bass, C., 338, 341, 345, 346, 347, 355, 358, 361
Bass, E. B., 352
Bass, S. M., 34
Bastani, B., 312
Bates, C. K., 169

Bates, G. W., 44
Bateson, G., 208
Batki, S. L., 243
Battjes, R. J., 137
Baum, K. M., 206
Bavington, J. T., 367
Baxter, L. A., 419
Baxter, L. R., 312, 313
Baysinger, C. M., 308
Beahr, D., 386, 395, 400, 401, 402
Beardsley, G., 9
Beasalel, V., 584
Beaumont, R. J. U., 474
Bech, P., 588
Beck, A. T., 25, 38, 142, 143, 166, 175, 237, 238, 245, 294, 301, 471, 521, 530
Beck, J., 521, 530
Beck, J. G., 445, 446
Beckman, E., 241, 242
Beckman, L. J., 132
Bedford, A., 521
Beech, H. R., 286
Beers, S. R., 99
Begleiter, H., 107, 134
Beglin, S. J., 467, 476
Beidel, D. C., 11, 12, 194, 283, 284, 285, 286, 291, 297, 298, 299, 300, 301, 302, 303, 304, 306, 307, 309, 311, 313, 315, 316, 317, 511, 528
Beigel, A., 269, 270
Beitman, B. D., 136
Beitmann, B. D., 347, 588
Bejerot, N., 160
Beldowick, D., 362
Belknapp, J. K., 179
Bell, C., 316, 317
Bellack, A. S., 205, 206, 207, 215, 216, 217, 285, 443, 580
Bellack, M., 24
Belmaker, R., 268
Bemelmans, B. L. H., 447, 448
Bemis, K. M., 471–472
Bengtsson, J., 448
Benjamin, L. S., 16
Benjamin, S., 345, 352, 358
Bennell, D. L., 171
Bennett, L. A., 361
Bennett, M., 205, 216
Benoit, O., 560
Ben-Porath, Y. S., 184
Benson, D. F., 391, 393
Benson, G., 176

Benton, A., 114
Benton, A. L., 95, 99, 114
Bentovim, A., 436
Berchick, R. J., 38
Berenbaum, H., 215
Beresford, I. P. 172
Beresford, T. P., 475
Berg, P., 413, 419, 429
Berg, S., 67
Bergeman, C. S., 67
Berger, M., 493, 499, 586
Berger, P., 45, 46, 47
Bergman, H., 183
Berkowitz, R., 300, 386, 400
Berland, N., 469
Berlin, F. S., 436
Berman, S. M., 451
Berman, S. R., 501
Berman, W. H., 526, 527
Bernadt, M. R., 133, 143, 207
Bernstein, D. P., 515
Berrettini, W. H., 268
Berthier, M. L., 243
Bertschy, G., 587
Beutler, L. E., 578
Beyer, H. S., 413, 438
Bezemer, P. D., 418, 449
Bhatnagar, K. S., 367
Bickel, W. K., 7
Biederman, J., 306, 307, 309
Bien, T. H., 129, 131, 139
Bifulco, A. T., 236, 243
Biggs, J. T., 276, 318
Bigler, E. D., 124
Bihari, B., 107, 134
Biles, J. K., 34
Billard, M., 503
Billings, A. G., 237
Bin, T. H., 145
Binder, L. S., 357
Bingham, S. F., 243
Birch, H., 549
Bixler, E., 489, 496
Bixler, E. O., 489, 491, 492
Black, D., 267
Black, D. B., 304
Black, D. W., 586, 587
Black, J., 144
Blackburn, R., 519, 521
Blacker, D., 11, 13, 16, 17
Blackshaw, L., 432
Blackwell, B., 352
Blaine, J., 166, 175
Blair, S. N., 550
Blake, H., 552, 553
Blakely, A. A., 363
Blanchard, E. B., 184, 285, 314, 445

Blanck, R. R., 178
Blashfield, R., 42
Blashfield, R. K., 513
Blass, J. P., 107
Blaszezynski, A., 416, 433, 436, 443
Blatt, S., 237, 238
Blazer, D., 261, 282
Blazer, D. G., 287, 315, 338, 339, 340, 345, 360
Blazer, I., 524
Blendell, K. A., 302
Bleuler, E., 208
Blignault, I., 241
Bliss, E. I., 385
Bliwise, D. L., 486, 489
Block, A. R., 354
Block, J., 549
Block, J. H., 549
Block, P., 238, 582
Block, R. I., 171
Bloom, F. E., 163, 164
Blouin, A., 471
Blouin, A. G., 32, 34
Blouin, J., 471
Blouin, J. H., 32, 34
Blow, F. C., 172, 186
Bluestone, H., 220, 433
Blum, N., 41, 42, 43, 304
Blum, R., 162
Blumer, D., 347
Boak, K., 308
Boardman, A. P., 352
Bobo, J. K., 136
Bocchetta, A., 268
Bochting, W. O., 427
Bogardis, J., 140
Bohman, M., 69, 72, 73, 75, 79, 107, 129, 133, 341, 347
Bohn, M. J. 141
Bohr, Y., 476
Boland, J. P., 428
Bolduc, E. A., 306, 307, 309
Bolk, J. H., 345
Boller, F., 117
Bolling, D. R., 439
Bolk, J. H., 345
Boller, F., 117
Bolling, D. R., 439
Bonanno, G. A., 351
Bond, A. J., 522
Bond, G. R., 207
Bonekat, W., 550
Bonilla, E., 89
Bonito, A. J., 183
Bonke, B., 360
Boon, S., 395
Boor, M., 395
Booth, R., 183
Bootzin, R. R., 494

Borden, J. W., 315
Borg, S., 168, 183
Boring, E. G., 92, 93
Borkovec, T. D., 291
Borsey, D. Q., 243
Boruch, F. R., 450
Borus, J., 35, 39, 49
Bosch, D. A., 568
Boskind-Lodohl, M., 465
Boswick, J., 470
Botlin, P. 522
Bouchard, T. J., 67, 69, 71, 72, 397, 522
Bouafuely, M., 352
Bouehard-Voelk, B., 183
Boulenger, J. P., 314
Bourguignon, E., 402
Bovasso, G. B., 398
Bowers, K. J., 172
Bowers, K. S., 401
Bowers, W., 41, 43
Bowie, S. I., 424
Bowlby, J., 514, 526
Bowler, A. E., 210
Bowman, E. S., 389, 395, 397
Boyd, C., 186
Boyd, J. H., 234, 235, 301
Bozarth, M. A., 164, 169
Bradford, D. C., 550
Bradley, B. P., 5
Bradley, L. A., 363
Bradshaw, S., 412, 414
Brady, K. T., 186
Braiker, H. B., 131
Branch, L. G., 177
Branch, L. J., 190
Brand, L., 346
Brandson, T. H., 143
Brandt, J., 393
Bratfos, O., 265
Braun, B. G., 385, 386, 395, 397
Brawman-Mintzer, O., 313, 340
Brecher, E. M., 160
Breier, A., 208, 218, 297, 314
Brender, W., 429, 430
Brenner, I., 393
Brent, D. A., 44
Breslow, N., 426
Brewin, C. R., 294
Bridges, C. F., 420
Bridges, K., 344, 350
Briere, J., 525
Briggs, G., 210
Brill, N. D., 171
Brink, T. L., 245
Broca, P., 92

Brochu, S., 146
Brockington, I. F., 34
Brodsky, R., 336
Brodwin, P. E., 354
Brooker, H., 351
Brooks, G. W., 208
Brooks, J. W., 165
Brooks, R. B., 50, 51
Brooks-Gunn, J., 451
Brotman, A. W., 471
Broughton, R. J., 488
Brower, K. J., 172
Brown, A. C., 558
Brown, B., 130
Brown, C. H., 34
Brown, D., 389
Brown, G., 39, 142
Brown, G. G., 120
Brown, G. K., 347
Brown, G. W., 217, 230, 236, 237, 242, 365
Brown, J., 138, 183
Brown, J. M., 145
Brown, L. S., 512, 524
Brown, P., 386
Brown, R., 299
Brown, R. V., 44
Brown, R. W., 360
Brown, T. A., 288, 313, 469
Brown, T. T., 160
Brown, W. A., 582
Bruce, M., 261
Bruce, M. L., 204, 234, 248
Bruch, H., 473, 474
Bruch, M. A., 302
Bruns, J. R., 50, 51
Bry, B. H., 162
Bryant, B., 588
Bryer, J. B., 243, 525
Brynjolfsson, J., 78
Buchanan, A., 206
Buchanan, R. W., 207, 218
Buchleim, P., 45, 46, 47
Bucholz, K., 360
Bucholz, K. K., 32
Buckholtz-Hansen, P. E., 588
Buckley, W. E., 171
Budman, S., 48, 67
Buhrich, N., 417, 426, 444
Bukstein, O., 44
Bulik, C. M., 284
Bumby, K. M., 434
Bunney, W., 258, 268, 269
Buranen, C., 342, 345, 356
Burdick, J. A., 490
Burgess, A. N., 423, 424
Burgett, T., 416
Burglass, M. E., 137

Burke, J., 261, 361
Burke, J. D., 234, 235
Burke, J. D., Jr., 282, 301
Burke, K. C., 234
Burks, J. S., 106
Burleson, J. A., 212
Burlie, J. E., 467, 476
Burling, T. A., 137
Burnam, A., 220
Burnam, M., 249
Burnam, M. A., 282, 289, 414, 449, 451
Burns, B. J., 220
Burns, J., 299
Burns, L. E., 296
Burnside, I. M., 550
Burrows, G. D., 299, 314
Busch, C. M., 352
Bush, P., 206
Buss, A., 548
Buss, A. H., 548
Butcher, J. N., 185
Butler, G., 302
Butters, N., 119
Button, E. J., 465
Buvat, J., 438, 447
Buvat-Herbaut, M., 438, 447
Buysse, D., 502
Buysse, D. J., 488, 489, 495, 501
Byck, R., 269
Byers, E. S., 437

Cacciola, J., 182
Cacciola, J. S., 520
Cadieux, R., 493, 494, 503
Cadoret, R. J., 69, 72, 79
Caetano, R., 132, 134
Cahalan, D., 129, 131, 132, 135
Cahalane, J. F., 242
Caine, E. D., 8, 122
Calabrese, J. R., 531
Caldieron, C., 339
Caldwell, A. B., 488, 493, 494, 503
Caldwell, E., 183
Calhoun, K. S., 442
Callahan, E. J., 145
Callahan, L. F., 363
Callies, A., 352
Cameron, O. G., 296, 311
Camic, P., 429
Campbell, J., 243
Campbell, T., 358, 364
Campeas, R., 299
Campo, J. V., 352
Cancrini, L., 180

Cancro, R., 276, 318
Canino, G., 339
Cantor, N., 15
Caplan, P. J., 6, 10, 511
Card, R. D., 446
Cardeña, E., 7, 12, 384, 385, 386, 387, 391, 393, 395, 397, 398, 399, 400, 401, 402
Cardenas, D. L., 316
Carey, K. B., 136, 137, 141
Carey, M. A., 315
Carey, M. P., 411, 412, 413, 414, 438, 443, 447
Carlen, P. L., 142
Carlson, E. B., 384, 387
Carlson, R. G., 183
Carmi, M., 312
Caroff, S. N., 498
Carol, K. M., 138
Caron, C., 3, 11
Carpenter, L. L., 240, 241
Carr, D. B., 310
Carrasco, J. L., 316
Carroll, B. T., 273
Carroll, K. M., 162
Carskadon, M. A., 492, 552, 558
Carter, C., 317
Carter, D. L., 423
Cascardi, M., 218, 219
Cash, T. F., 366, 469
Casper, R. C., 463
Caspi, A., 209, 522, 549
Cassano, G. B., 582, 586
Cassanos, G. B., 299
Castle, D. J., 207, 304
Catalan, J., 414, 419, 428, 429, 430
Catania, J. A., 442, 444
Cato, A., 471
Caveness, W. F., 99
Cawley, R., 529
Celentan, D. D., 130
Centerwall, B. S., 69
Cerce, D. D., 416, 420, 423
Cermak, L. S., 119
Cerney, J. A., 301, 303
Cernovsky, Z. Z., 418
Cesari, H., 183
Chadhoury, Y., 304
Chadhury, S., 586
Chahal, R., 34, 366, 512, 526
Chakravarty, M., 178
Chalkleyk, A., 301
Chalmers, E. M., 173
Chamberlin, K., 492
Chambless, D., 302

Chambless, D. L., 530
Channabasavanna, S. M., 45, 46, 47, 286
Chaplin, W., 238
Chapman, S. L., 363
Charney, D. S., 297, 314, 488, 493, 494, 503
Chase, G. A., 366
Chase-Lansdale, L., 451
Chaudhry, H. R., 162
Chave, S. P. W., 550
Check, J. V. P., 417
Chelune, G. J., 111
Chen, K., 161
Chernik, D., 494
Chess, S., 548, 549
Cheung, F. K., 220
Cheung, V. W., 187
Chevron, E., 237, 238
Chilcoat, H., 314
Chinman, G., 386, 400
Chiodo, J., 472
Chipuer, H. M., 67
Chiswick, D., 518
Chitwood, D. O., 442, 444
Chmeil, J. S., 451
Cho, M. C., 276, 318
Chodoff, P., 366, 513
Chouinard, G., 300
Christensen, H., 304, 389, 392
Christianson, S. A., 393
Christoph, P., 183
Christy, J., 416
Cingolani, S., 180
Cinque, J., 488, 489, 496
Cioffi, D., 348
Ciompi, L., 208
Circe, D., 435
Clancy, J., 290, 297, 298, 299, 305, 310
Clare, E., 427
Clark, D. B., 299, 301
Clark, J. P., 443
Clark, L. A., 3, 7
Clark, R. E., 206, 213
Clark, W. B., 132
Clarke, C., 297
Clarkin, J., 524
Clarkin, J. F., 509, 511, 514, 525
Clarkin, J. K., 525
Classen, C., 384, 399
Clayton, P., 265, 267, 268, 270, 271
Clayton, P. J., 178, 179, 183, 257, 339, 347
Cleary, P., 340, 346

Cleary, P. D., 348, 349
Cleckley, H., 518
Clifford, C., 133, 138, 143, 207
Clod, C. A., 560
Cloninger, C. R., 68, 72, 73, 75, 79, 107, 129, 341, 345, 347, 356, 360
Closser, M. H., 186
Clow, A., 133, 138, 143, 207
Clum, G., 300, 301
Clure, H. R., 336
Coates, T. J., 442, 444, 500
Cobb, J., 363
Coble, P. A., 489, 503
Cochrane, K. J., 184
Coffman, G. A., 387, 399
Cohen, B., 243, 311
Cohen, B. M., 524, 526
Cohen, B. S., 296, 311
Cohen, C., 512
Cohen, C. I., 206
Cohen, E., 418
Cohen, K., 351
Cohen, L., 340
Cohen, M. A., 488, 489, 496
Cohen, P., 515
Cohen, S., 170, 524
Coid, B., 45, 46, 47
Cole, J. O., 531
Cole, M., 117
Cole, R. J., 552, 553
Coleman, E., 427, 433
Coleman, R. M., 488, 489, 496, 498
Colfer, M. V., 586, 587
Colgan, S., 363
Collins, J., 241, 242
Collins, R. L., 132, 146
Collins, S. D., 169
Columbus, M., 138, 139
Coluss, K., 418
Comas-Diaz, L., 219, 220
Comis, R., 243
Compagnoni, F., 180
Condra, M., 431
Condron, M. K., 438
Cone, E. J., 184
Conigrave, K. M., 144, 145
Conneally, P. M., 89
Connett, J., 549
Connors, G. J., 138, 139, 143
Conover, S., 203
Consensus Development Panel, 274
Constantini, D., 180
Conte, G., 268
Conte, H. R., 443, 524

Conti, L., 582, 586
Conway, C. G., 4
Cook, B., 259
Cook, B. L., 290, 297, 298, 299, 305
Cook, M., 293, 294
Cooke, D. J., 318
Cooley-Quille, M. R., 300, 301, 302, 317
Cooney, N. L., 580, 581
Cooney, N. T., 145
Coons, P. M., 389, 390, 391, 396, 397, 400
Cooper, A. J., 418
Cooper, J. E., 219
Coovert, D. L., 469, 475
Cope, H., 349, 355, 362, 363,
Corbit, J. D., 163
Corbitt, E. M., 7, 517
Cordingley, J., 161
Coren, S., 501
Corenthal, C., 41, 43, 508
Cormier, B. M., 442
Cormier, C., 520, 522
Cornelius, S., 529
Corrigan, P. W., 206
Corse, S. J., 212
Corsini, G., 268
Corty, E., 212
Coryell, W., 257, 259, 265, 266, 267, 295, 342, 345, 352, 511, 526, 527, 582, 586, 587
Costa, P. T., 16, 67, 352, 509
Costa, P. T., Jr., 548
Costello, A., 306
Costello, E. J., 237
Costello, R., 174
Costello, R. M., 190
Côtè, G., 518
Cottler, L. B., 32
Cotton, P. G., 205
Cottrool, C., 175
Couprie, W., 345
Courneya, K. S., 550
Cournos, F., 206
Coursey, D., 529
Couture, M., 417, 440
Covi, L., 283
Cowdry, R. W., 531
Cox, B. J., 291
Cox, B. M., 135
Cox, T. J., 183
Coyle, K., 501
Coyle, P. K., 362
Coyne, L., 521
Crabbe, J. C., 179
Craig, K. D., 356

Craig, T. K. J., 352
Craighead, W. C., 588
Craske, M. M., 300, 301, 302
Crawford, R., 311
Creed, F., 358, 363
Crepault, C., 416, 440
Crews, F., 441
Crisp, A. H., 468, 475
Cristol, A., 429
Critchley, M., 99
Critell, J. W., 420
Crits-Christoph, K., 175
Crocker, B., 299
Cronkite, R. C., 237
Crook, T. H., 587
Cross-National Collaborative
    Panic Study Second
    Phase Investigation, 92,
    299
Croughan, J., 32, 33, 35, 247,
    518
Crowe, R. R., 69, 310
Croyle, R. T., 441
Csapa, K. G., 501
Cullen K., 433
Cuneo, P., 297, 298
Cunningham, J. A., 129, 143
Curran-Celentano, J., 470
Curtin, S., 560
Curtis, G. C., 296, 299, 311
Curtis, G. E., 296
Cushman, P., 144, 175, 238
Czeisler, C. A., 492, 498
Czepowicz, V., 340

DaCosta, M., 466
Dadlesten, K., 78
D'Aquila, R. T., 178
Dahl, A., 45, 46, 47
Dahl, A. R., 508
Dalgard, O. S., 68, 69
Danahoe, T., 171
Dancu, C. V., 285, 297, 511,
    528
Dang, R., 170
Dantchev, N., 560
Darling, C. A., 420
Das, K., 170, 268, 269
David, A., 349, 355, 362
Davidson, J. K., 420
Davidson, J. R., 586, 588
Davidson, J. R. T., 13, 287,
    298, 299, 300
Davidson, M., 293
Davidson, R., 141
Davies, A. D. M., 142
Davies, L., 419, 427, 429,
    430

Davies, M., 35, 39, 49, 176,
    475
Davies, S., 296, 311, 316
Davis, C. M., 443
Davis, C. S., 141
Davis, D. D., 521, 530
Davis, G. C., 511
Davis, H., 553
Davis, J. M., 468
Davis, K. L., 12, 515
Davis, L., 581
Davis, P. A., 553
Davis, S. L., 443
Davis, W. W., 3, 6
Dawson, D. A., 132
Dawson, M. E., 204, 207
Day, A., 414, 428, 430
Day, D. M., 434, 435, 520
Day, R., 219
Deale, A., 304
De Amicis, L. A., 419, 427,
    429, 430
Dean, R. S., 96
Deant, J., 386
De Bouche, B., 258
De Beurs, E., 303
Debruyne, F. M. J., 447, 448
Dechant, H. K., 352
De Faire, U., 67
De Giroloma, J., 218, 219
De Good, D. E., 363
De Haes, J. C., 360
Deister, P. J., 340
de Jonghe, F., 582, 586
Delaney, H. D., 138
Del Boca, F. K., 138, 183
Deleese, J. S., 178
Delizio, R. D., 308
Dell'Osso, L., 582, 586
Delprato, D. J., 292
DeLuca, J., 362
Delvin, M. G., 7
Del Zompo, M., 268
Demby, A., 48, 67
Dement, W. C., 488, 489,
    492, 496, 498, 502
De Moya, D., 450
Denari, M., 170
Denier, C. A., 186
Denise, P., 560
Dent, D., 342, 345
De Press, J. A., 291
Depression Guideline Panel,
    235, 241
DeRisi, W. J., 215
Derlega, V. J., 366
Derogatis, L. R., 352, 501
DeRubeis, R. J., 241

de Ruyter, M., 587
de Silva, P., 388
DeSisto, M. S., 208
Desmond, D. P., 174
DeSota, C. B., 131
DeSota, S. L., 131
de Souza, C., 360
Detels, R., 451
Detera-Wadleigh, S., 268
Detre, T., 269
Devereaux, R. B., 310
Deveris, L., 476
Devinsky, O., 352
Deyo, R. A., 363
Dibble, A., 446
Dibble, E., 258
Dickey, R., 436
Diclemente, C. D., 138, 188
Diehl, A. K., 363
Diehl, S. R., 209
Diekstra, R. F. W., 45, 46, 47
Digman, J. M., 548
Dillon, D., 296, 311
Dillon, D. J., 299
Dimascio, A., 582, 587
DiNardo, P. A., 285, 314
Dinero, T. E., 423, 436
Dinges, D. F., 492
Dinwiddie, S. H., 173
Direnfeld, D. M., 291
DiVasto, P. V., 416
Dixie-Bell, D. D., 317
Dixon, L. B., 212
Dobbs, M., 78
Dodrill, C. B., 111
Doesburg, W. H., 447, 448
Doghramji, K., 500
Doherty, W. J., 354
Doidge, N., 475
Dolan, R., 350
Dolan, R. T., 241, 242
Dolinsky, Z. S., 137
Donohoe, T., 172
Donohue, B., 584
Donovan, D. M., 138, 190
Dorean, B., 471
Dorus, W., 136
Douglas, K., 519
Douglas, M. S., 216
Downey, G., 209
Downing, R., 299
Downing, R. W., 283
Draijer, N., 395
Drake, H., 352
Drake, R. E., 135, 136, 141,
    205, 206, 207, 208, 213,
    218, 518
Drewnowski, A., 467

Dreyfuss, D., 300
Druley, K. A., 175, 177, 189
Drumer, D., 268
Dryman, A., 241
Dunbar, G., 14
Duncan, J. C., 517, 518, 519, 520
Dunlap, E., 178
Dunn, G. E., 395
Du Pont, R. L., 299, 314
Dupree, L. W., 131
Durham, R. C., 302
Durrant, J. D., 310
Dustan, L., 186
Dustman, R. E., 550
Dutton, D. G., 48
Dutton, M. A., 218
Dworkin, R. H., 346
Dworkin, R. J., 220
Dworkin, S. F., 340, 346
Dworkind, M., 344

Earhardt, A., 444
Earls, C. M., 433
Easterbrook, P. J., 451
Eaton, W. O., 547, 570
Eaton, W. W., 204, 241, 283, 313, 314, 316
Eaves, D., 519
Eaves, L. J., 70, 71, 72, 73, 75, 78, 79, 240, 307, 314, 494
Ebigbo, P. O., 367
Eccles, A., 434, 439
Eckert, E. D., 69, 71, 72, 466, 467, 468, 469, 474, 476, 522
Eckman, T. A., 175
Edbril, S. D., 424
Edigner, J. D., 487, 489, 493, 501, 502, 503
Eduardsen, I., 68, 70, 77, 80
Edwards, G., 188, 189
Edwards, J., 44
Edwards, K. L., 133
Egeland, J. A., 75, 268
Egert, S., 188, 189
Ehlers, A., 311
Ehrensing, R. H., 465
Eifert, G. H., 578, 585
Eisen, J. L., 313
Eisen, S. A., 74, 307
Eisenberg, H. J., 99
Eisenman, A. J., 165
Eisenstein, R. B., 165
Elek, D., 520
Eklund, P. L. E., 418, 449
Elias, M. F., 104
Elie, R., 530

Elkashef, A., 218
Elkin, I., 241, 242
Elkin, T. E., 184
Ellicot, A., 238
Elliott, D. J., 10
Elliott, G. R., 511
Elliott, J. E., 237
Ellinwood, E. H., 470
El-Roey, A., 339
Elson, M. K., 413, 438
Emery, G., 237, 294, 301
Eminson, D. M., 352
Emmanuel, N., 313, 340
Emmelkamp, P. M. G., 285
Emory, C., 169
Ende, J., 438
Endicott, J., 24, 25, 26, 29, 30, 31, 32, 35, 131, 135, 257, 259, 261, 265, 266, 267, 269, 275, 522, 524, 586
Endlers, N. S., 135
Engel, G. E., 347
Engelsing, T. M., 183
Engelsing, T. M. J., 183
Engle, J. D., 206
Engle, M., 183
Englund, S. A., 240
Enns, L. R., 570
Epling, W. F., 570
Epstein, L. H., 308
Epstein, N., 142
Epstein, R., 552, 567
Epstein-Kaye, T., 297, 298
Erbaugh, J., 245
Erbaugh, J. K., 25
Erdelyi, M. E., 385
Erdman, H. P., 32, 34
Erhman, R. N., 163
Eriksson, A., 293
Ernberg, G., 219
Erwin, C. W., 487, 489, 493
Escobar, J., 249, 338, 340, 345
Escobar, J. I., 220, 282, 289
Escobar, L. S., 339
Eshleman, S., 234, 243, 249, 282, 289, 290, 315, 387, 518
Estroff, S. E., 219
Ethrenpres, A. B., 502
Etoh, T., 266
Eussen, M., 51
Evans, B., 344, 350
Evans, F., 182
Evans, I. M., 578, 585
Evans, L., 426
Evans, L. A., 220

Evans, M., 428
Evans, M. D., 241
Everett, G., 206
Everitt, M. G., 550
Ewing, J., 189
Eysenck, H. J., 549
Ezekiel, J., 203

Fabrega, H., 387, 399
Fagg, J., 419, 428, 429, 430
Fairbank, J. A., 287, 384
Fairburn, C. G., 467, 472, 473, 475, 476
Falck, R., 183
Faller, K. C., 432
Fallon, B. A., 475
Falloon, I. R. H., 217, 303
Faraone, S. V., 306, 307, 309
Farmer, A., 34, 361
Farmer, A. E., 76, 78
Farmer, M. E., 259
Farr, S. P., 142
Farthing, G. W., 386
Fasiczka, A., 248
Fätkenheuer, B., 207
Fava, G. A., 364
Fawcett, J., 586
Fedora, O., 417
Fedora, S. K., 417
Fedoravicius, A. S., 352
Feighner, J., 256, 466
Fekete, D., 207
Fenemore, J., 431
Fennell, M., 302
Fenton, W. S., 16
Ferber, J., 218
Ferguson, B., 45, 46, 47
Ferguson, J. M., 471
Fernbach, B. E., 366
Ferraro, D. P., 170
Ferraro, T. N., 268
Feske, U., 302
Fichten, C. S., 430
Fichter, M. M., 344
Field, C. D., 212
Field, J., 412, 414
Field, P., 138, 143
Fielding, R., 243
Fieve, R. R., 269
Fillmore, K. M., 129, 130, 131, 132, 133, 135
Finestone, D. H., 400
Fink, C. M., 283, 298, 317
Fink, P. J., 219
Finkelhor, D., 415, 440, 444
Finn, P. R., 134
Firooznia, H., 178
First, C. D., 211

First, M. B., 3, 5, 6, 8, 9, 13, 15, 35, 36, 38, 39, 40, 48, 49, 51, 246, 361
Fisher, D. G., 174
Fisher, J., 485
Fisher, L. D., 168, 177
Fisher, M. M., 343, 361
Fisher, P., 189
Fisher, S., 283
Fistbein, A., 36
Fitts, S. N., 340
Flaker, G., 347
Flatow, L., 272
Flaum, M., 218
Fleiss, J. L., 27
Fleming, B., 521, 530
Fleming, J., 267
Flewelling, R. L., 187
Flint, A., 169
Floderins-Myrhed, B., 71
Flom, M. C., 130
Flor-Henry, P., 207
Florio, L., 261
Florio, L. P., 234, 248
Flynn, L. M., 203
Foa, E. B., 13, 302, 303
Fogelson, D. L., 50
Folkman, S., 238, 348
Folks, D. G., 339, 342, 345
Follette, W. C., 443, 444
Folstein, J. F., 512, 526
Folstein, M., 34
Folstein, M. F., 366
Fondacaro, K. M., 469
Fontaine, R., 300
Ford, C. V., 339, 342, 345
Ford, D. E., 491, 492
Ford, M. R., 513
Ford, S. M., 299, 300
Forde, D. R., 290
Forney, M. A., 183
Forti, B., 520
Fossati, P., 438, 447
Fossheim, I., 581
Fowler, K., 259
Fox, J. W., 204
Fox, M. M., 466
Fox, S., 166, 175
Fox, S. M., 550
France, B., 560
France, R., 175
Frances, A., 28, 310, 509, 524, 525
Frances, A. J., 3, 5, 6, 8, 9, 10, 13, 14, 15, 509, 510, 511, 524, 525, 526, 528
Frances, R. J., 174
Francis, D. J., 311

Francis, G., 306
Frank, A. F., 531
Frank, D., 411, 418, 437
Frank, E., 240, 241, 248
Frank, G., 24
Frank, H., 525
Frankenburg, F. R., 525
Franklin, G. M., 89, 106
Fraser, G. A., 395
Fredikson, M., 293
Freedman, M., 391
Freimer, N. F., 268
Frenkel, M., 11
Freter, S., 206
Freund, K., 425, 436, 444, 445
Friberg, L., 71
Friedberg, F., 362
Friedel, R. O., 530
Friedman, E., 242
Friedman, J., 419, 427, 429, 430
Friedman, M., 489, 492
Frischholz, E. J., 395
Frith, C. D., 205
Fritsch, S. L., 352
Fromm-Reichmann, F., 208
Fronson, G., 582, 586
Frueh, B. C., 302
Fuelling, C., 172
Fugere, R., 442
Fujino, D. C., 220, 249
Fukuda, L., 266
Fuller, J. R., 172
Fung, D., 276
Furby, L., 432
Furman, J. M., 310
Furstenberg, F. F., Jr., 451
Futterman, A., 582, 586
Futterman, C. S., 562
Fyer, A. F., 310
Fyer, A. J., 285, 296, 299, 311, 316

Gabbard, G. O., 521
Gacono, C. B., 519
Gagnon, J. H., 412, 413, 414, 415, 425, 440, 449, 450
Gal, J., 429
Gallagher-Thompson, D., 582, 586
Gallant, S. J., 6, 10
Galletly, C. A., 212
Galloway, E., 584
Gallup Organization, 491, 503
Gallwey, P., 521
Galt, C., 237
Gamache, G., 217

Gamble, G., 212
Gammon, G. D., 284, 304, 305
Gans, M., 6, 10
Garamoni, G., 248
Garcia-Coll, C., 297
Gardner, D. L., 531
Garfinkel, P. E., 354
Garfinkel, R., 316
Garfinkle, R. S., 475, 476
Garner, D. M., 476
Garside, R. F., 587
Garssen, B., 360
Garvey, M. J., 241, 272, 290, 297, 298, 299, 305
Gask, L., 345
Gaskins, J., 143
Gastaut, H., 109, 488
Gates, C., 205
Gath, D., 413
Gaylor, M., 354
Gazis, J., 44
Gebhart, P. H., 412
Geenens, D., 560
Geissner, E., 344
Gelder, M., 302
Gelder, M. G., 290, 296
Gelfand, A. N., 352, 366
Gelfand, M. D., 352, 366
Gellad, F., 218
Geller, J. L., 206
Gendreau, P., 521
Gendrop, S. C., 163
Genero, N., 15
George, A., 511, 529, 530
George, J., 500
George, L., 339, 360, 524
George, L. K., 282, 287, 338, 340, 345
Geraci, M. F., 314
Gerardi, R. W., 552, 553
Gerdeman, B., 117
Gerhard, D., 268
Gerhard, D. S., 75, 268
Gerhardsson, M., 550
Geringer, E., 345
Germanson, T., 135
Gerner, R. H., 474
Gershon, E., 258, 268
Gersten, M., 307, 308
Gerstley, L. J., 521, 522, 523
Geschwind, N., 92
Getter, H., 580, 581
Gfroere, J., 187
Ghoneim, M. M., 171
Gibbon, M., 35, 36, 38, 39, 40, 48, 49, 51, 211, 246, 361, 524

Gibbons, J., 308
Gibbsons, R. D., 136
Gibson, D. R., 442, 444
Gibson, G. E., 107
Gibson, G. S., 144
Gibson, P., 340
Giles, T. R., 472
Gilliam, T. C., 269
Gillin, C., 312
Gillin, J. C., 490, 491, 553
Gillis, J. S., 162
Gillis, R., 423
Gilmore, M., 509, 511, 525
Ginns, E. I., 268
Ginsburg, S., 365
Gitlin, M., 238
Gitlin, M. J., 531
Gladue, B. A., 418, 419, 435
Glaser, F. B., 135, 189
Glasgow, M., 438
Glass, D. R., 241, 242
Glassroth, J., 178
Gleaves, D. H., 388, 396
Glica, B., 559
Glick, M., 206
Glicklich, J., 310
Glod, C. A., 567
Glynn, S. M., 208, 217, 219, 221
Goethe, K. E., 99
Goetz, D., 299
Goff, D.C., 284
Goisman, R. M., 297, 298
Gold, J. H., 10
Gold, M. S., 171, 184
Goldberg, D., 344, 345, 350
Goldberg, D. C., 419, 427, 429, 430,
Goldberg, E. L., 415, 417, 440
Goldberg, J., 74, 307
Goldberg, L. R., 548
Goldberg, R. L., 514, 525
Goldberg, S. C., 468, 530
Goldenberg, D. L., 361
Goldenberg, I., 298, 476
Goldin, L., 258, 268
Goldin, L. R., 268
Golding, J. M., 414, 449, 451
Goldman, H. H., 203
Goldring, E., 32
Goldsmith, D., 174
Goldsmith, D. S., 174
Goldsmith, H. H., 548
Goldstein, A., 429
Goldstein, A. J., 268, 294, 295, 530
Goldstein, G., 107, 113

Goldstein, J. M., 207
Goldstein, K., 93, 94, 104
Goldstein, M. G., 9
Goldstein, M. J., 217, 275
Goldstein, R. B., 304
Goldwater, B. C., 552, 553
Golimbu, C., 178
Gollan, J. K., 297, 298
Gonzalez-Wippler, M., 220
Good, B., 248
Good, B. J., 354
Good, M. I., 386, 401
Good, M. J., 354
Goodman, A., 5
Goodman, S., 50
Goodman, W. K., 299, 305
Goodson, J. D., 349
Goodwin, D. W., 16, 107, 133
Goodwin, F. R., 210, 259
Gooren, L., 427
Gooren, L. J. G., 418, 449
Gordon, A., 363
Gordon, J. R., 131, 141, 146, 162, 163, 190
Goreczny, A. J., 106
Gorelick, A., 36
Gorenstein, E., 5, 6, 8, 18
Gorman, J. M., 206, 285, 296, 299, 310, 311
Gorton, G., 529
Gorzalka, B. B., 446
Gottesman, I. I., 69, 76, 77, 78, 209
Gould, G. H., 336
Goulding, J. M., 341
Graber, B., 421
Gracely, E. J., 50, 315
Graham, J. M., 141
Graham, S., 550
Gram, L. F., 588
Grande, T. P., 522
Grandi, S., 364
Grant, B. F., 131, 132, 135
Grant, I., 7, 89
Grasshoff, M. A., 499
Grasshoff, U., 499
Gray, B. A., 220
Greden, J. F., 205
Green, A. I., 529
Green, R., 417
Greenberg, E., 282
Greenspan, J. R., 451
Greenstein, R., 212
Greenwood, A., 520
Greist, J. H., 32, 34
Grenier, G., 437
Grice, D. E., 186
Griffin, M. L., 163, 183

Griffith, E. E. H., 219
Griffith, J., 182
Griffith, J. L., 364
Griffith, M. E., 364
Grisham, M. G., 170
Grinker, R. R., 393, 524
Gropper, B., 183
Gross, J., 469
Groth, A. N., 423
Grove, W., 24, 25, 27, 31, 52, 69, 71, 72, 241, 522
Grubb, H. J., 306
Gruen, R., 516, 526
Gruen, W., 553
Gruenberg, A. M., 77, 80
Gruenberg, E., 261
Gruenberg, E. M., 34, 366, 512, 526
Gruling, H., 78
Guarnaccia, P., 316
Gueldner, S. H., 550
Guerra, N. G., 521
Guieu, J. D., 438, 447
Guilleminault, C., 486, 488, 489, 494, 496
Gunderson, D., 531
Gunderson, J. G., 11, 511, 524, 525, 526, 527
Gunther, W., 582
Gur, R. C., 348
Gurguis, G., 345
Gurling, H. M. D., 133, 138, 143, 207
Guroff, J., 258
Guroff, J. J., 348, 395, 397
Gursky, D. M., 295
Gusella, J. F., 89
Guthrie, E., 358
Guthrie, S., 188, 189
Gutierrez, R., 7
Guze, B. B., 339
Guze, S., 256
Guze, S. B., 15, 32, 79, 107, 133, 341, 347, 360
Guze, S. P., 466
Gwitsman, H. E., 474

Haas, G., 216
Haas, N., 174
Haastrup, S., 165
Hacker, A., 451
Hackmann, A., 345
Hadzi-Paulovic, D., 304
Haertzen, C. A., 165
Hafeiz, H. B., 339, 345
Häfner, H., 207
Hagekull, B., 549
Haggerty, R., 235

Haider, S., 162
Hajak, G., 499
Hale, V. E., 421
Hale, W. E., 550
Halek, C., 475
Haley, J., 208
Haley, R., 387, 399
Halford, W. K., 217
Hall, A. K., 475
Hall, K., 386, 400
Hall, P., 141
Hall, R. C., 475
Hall, W., 354
Hallmayer, J., 510
Hallowell, E. M., 101
Hallstrom, T., 412, 427, 429
Halmi, K. A., 466, 468
Halstead, W. C., 93
Halverson, C. F., Jr., 549
Hamburger, M., 32
Hamburger, R., 268
Hamburger, S. D., 101
Hamer, R. M., 530
Hamilton, J. A., 6, 10
Hamilton, K., 475
Hamilton, M., 142
Hammen, C., 238
Hammen, M. S., 315
Hammersley, R., 176
Hammond, D. C., 414, 418,
    419, 435, 438
Hamovit, J., 258
Hanbury, R., 174
Hand, I., 302
Handel, M. H., 218
Handelsman, L., 184
Handmaker, N., 145
Hanley-Peterson, P., 582, 586
Hans, S. L., 206
Hansell, S., 347
Harakal, T., 567
Harden, T., 242
Harding, B., 468
Harding, C. M., 208
Harding, T. W., 518, 520
Hare, R. D., 512, 517, 518,
    519, 520
Hariton, E. B., 416, 440
Harkness, A. R., 353
Harmon, S. K., 190
Harpin, R. E., 303
Harpur, T. J., 517, 519
Harrington, R., 522
Harris, A. R., 450
Harris, C., 431
Harris, G. T., 434, 518, 519,
    520, 521, 522
Harris, M., 219
Harris, M. E., 522

Harris, T., 230, 237
Harris, T. O., 236
Harrop-Griffiths, J., 366
Harsh, J. R., 551
Hart, J., 413
Hart, S. D., 58, 517, 518, 519
Hartka, E., 129
Hartman, C. R., 567
Hartman, D. B., 296
Hartman, E., 400, 488, 499
Hartstein, G., 346
Harvald, B., 267
Harvey, E. N., 553
Haseiager, G. J. T., 548
Hasin, D., 7
Hasin, D. S., 131, 135
Haske, W. L., 550
Haskell, D., 582, 587
Hassman, H., 299
Hatch, J. P., 446
Hatchers, S., 364
Hatfield, A. B., 216
Hathaway, S. R., 362
Hatsukoni, D., 474
Haug, J., 265
Hauge, N., 267
Haupt, H. A., 172
Hauri, P. J., 485, 489, 492,
    494, 496, 501, 551, 554
Haviland, M. G., 351
Hawker, A., 188, 189
Hawkins, D., 494
Hawton, K., 345, 413, 414,
    419, 428, 429, 430
Hawton, K. E., 420
Hayes, R. D., 230
Hayes, S., 582, 588
Hayes, S. C., 598
Hayslip, B., 237
Healey, E. S., 492
Heape, C. L., 48
Heard, H. L., 530
Heath, A. C., 68, 70, 71, 72,
    73, 74, 75, 78, 79, 240,
    307, 314, 494
Heather, N., 177, 188
Heaton, R. K., 89, 106
Heerlein, A., 582
Hegedus, A., 107
Hegel, M., 303
Heiby, E. M., 588
Heilbronn, M., 347
Heilbronner, R. L., 295
Heilman, K. M., 112, 122
Heiman, J. R., 418, 419, 430,
    435
Heimberg, R. G., 285, 302,
    528
Heir, R., 293

Helgason, T., 260
Heller, B. R., 352
Helzer, J., 261, 282, 361
Helzer, J. E., 7, 15, 32, 33, 34,
    35, 146, 183, 247, 361,
    467, 476, 518
Henderson, A. S., 240, 307
Henderson, D. J., 186
Hendryx, M. S., 351
Hengeveld, M. W., 420, 431
Heninger, G. R., 297, 314
Henn, F. A., 422
Henry, K., 512
Hensman, C., 188, 189
Henson, L., 206
Heppner, P. P., 238
Hepworth, J., 354
Herbert, J. D., 285
Herd, D., 132
Herjanic, M., 422
Herman, I., 166, 175
Herman, J. L., 422, 423, 432,
    436, 518
Hermansen, L., 107, 133
Hermesh, H., 312
Hernandez, J. T., 178
Hersen, M., 24, 25, 38, 39,
    40, 306, 307, 443, 579,
    580, 584, 585, 586, 588
Hertoft, P., 412, 442
Herzog, D. B., 467, 470, 471,
    473
Hesselbrock, M. A., 132
Hesselbrock, M. N., 135
Hesselink, J. R., 89
Hester, R. K., 145, 177, 188,
    189, 190
Heston, L., 69, 71, 72, 522
Hett, G., 78
Heun, R., 510
Heuser, I., 580
Hewitt, J. K., 68
Hickok, L. R., 366
Hicks, A., 28, 41, 52, 525
Higgins, S. T., 7
Hildreth, C. J., 317
Hilgard, E. R., 388, 401
Hill, B., 351
Hill, E. M., 172
Hill, S. Y., 107, 132
Hiller, W., 344
Hilton, M., 130, 134
Himmelhoch, J., 269
Hinde, R. A., 548
Hindman, M., 146
Hirschfeld, R., 265, 586
Hirschfeld, R. M. A., 11, 31,
    45, 46, 47, 230
Hirschinger, N. B., 212

Hirshfeld, D. R., 306, 307, 309
Hinz, L. D., 474, 477
Hispsley, P. A., 299
Hitchcock, P. B., 364
Ho, B. T., 311
Hobart, G., 553
Hoberman, H. M., 236, 237, 241
Hobson, R. W., 178
Hocherman, I., 183
Hochman, J. S., 171
Hoddes, E., 502
Hodgins, S., 518
Hodgson, R., 141
Hodkinson, S., 514
Hoehn-Saric, R., 299
Hoekstra, R., 51
Hoelscher, T. J., 489, 501, 502, 503
Hoffart, A., 300
Hoffman, G. W., 470
Hoffman, N. G., 176
Hofman, M. A., 448
Hogan, D. R., 430
Hogg, B., 44
Hohagen, F., 449, 493, 500
Holahan, C. J., 237
Hole, A., 166, 175
Holland, J. C., 243
Hollander, E., 11, 299, 340
Hollingshead, A. B., 204
Hollingsworth, M. L., 360
Hollister, L. E., 170
Hollon, S. D., 7, 235, 241
Holloway, W., 295
Holm, L., 183, 366
Holmberg, M. B., 176, 177
Holmberg, R., 176
Holmstrom, L. L., 423, 424
Holt, G. S., 285, 302, 361, 528
Holzer, C., 234, 248
Holzer, C. E., 301
Holzman, P. S., 209
Hoogduin, C. A. L., 304
Hooks, N. T., 165
Hoover, D. R., 451
Hope, D. A., 205, 285, 302, 528
Hope, R. A., 472
Hopkins, S. A., 467
Horevitz, R., 396
Horn, J. L., 141, 185
Horne, R. L., 471
Horney, K., 257
Hornig, C. D., 285, 298
Hornstein, N. L., 396
Hostetter, A., 75, 268

Hotaling, G., 415, 440
Hough, R., 220, 249
Hough, R. L., 282, 287, 289, 384
House, A., 364
Houseman, D., 268
Housman, D. E., 75, 268
Howard, C. C., 363
Howard, G. S., 4
Howard, R., 206
Howards, S. S., 448
Howe, M. G., 501
Howell, J. W., 485
Howes, M. J., 35, 39, 49
Hoyer, E. B., 7
Hrubec, Z., 133
Hryniak, M., 351
Hsieh, C. C., 550
Hsu, J. J., 363
Hsu, L. K. G., 468, 469, 477
Hu, L. T., 220, 249
Huang, U., 245
Huber-Smith, M. J., 311
Hudson, J. I., 344, 361, 471, 524, 526
Hudson, S. M., 514
Hudziak, J. E., 183
Huey, C. J., 421
Huey, L., 271
Hufford, D., 317
Hugdahl, K., 293, 588
Huggins, N., 174
Hughes, C., 242
Hughes, D., 287, 360
Hughes, J., 234, 243, 249, 282, 289, 290, 315, 387, 388, 402, 518
Hughes, J. R., 7
Hunt, C., 48
Hunt, C. A., 170
Hunt, D., 174
Hunt, D. E., 174
Hunt, M., 411, 412, 416, 420, 421
Hunt, M. F., 297, 298
Hunt, W. A., 177, 190
Hurt, S., 524
Hurt, S. W., 509, 511, 514, 525
Hussain, Y., 367
Hutchings, P. S., 218
Hutton, H. E., 466, 519
Huttunen, M., 549
Hyde, R. T., 550
Hyde, T. S., 305
Hyler, S. E., 47, 51, 333, 475, 525
Hymowitz, F., 524
Hynes, G., 136, 141

Iguchi, M., 187
Iman, K., 339
Imber, S., 241, 242
Insel, T. R., 312
Institute of Medicine, 129, 130, 138, 146, 190
International Society for the Study of Dissociation (ISSD), 394, 396, 397
Irwin, M., 490
Israel, A. C., 3, 14, 16
Israel, Y., 144
Issac, M., 361
Ito, J. R., 190
Iwamasa, G., 249
Iwandate, T., 266

Jablensky, A., 204, 219, 361
Jackson, D. D., 208
Jackson, D. N., 14, 17, 67, 68, 509
Jackson, H. J., 44
Jackson, J. H., 93
Jackson, R., 416
Jacob, R. G., 283, 284, 288, 295, 299, 300, 303, 310, 311, 313
Jacob, T., 134, 209
Jacobs, D. R., Jr., 549
Jacobs, E. A., 502
Jacobs, J. R., 398
Jacobs, W. J., 417
Jacobsberg, L. B., 45, 46, 47, 524
Jacobson, N. S., 443, 444
Jacoby, R. G., 273
Jaffe, R. B., 177
James, W., 392
Jamison, K. R., 210
Janca, A., 183, 361
Jang, K. L., 14, 17, 67, 68, 509
Janowski, D., 271
Jansson, L., 301
Jarrell, M. P., 313
Jarrett, R., 582, 578, 588
Jasinski, D. R., 165
Jaworski, T. M., 363
Jefferson, J. W., 358
Jehu, D., 419, 430
Jellinek, E. M., 128, 129, 131
Jemelka, R. P., 352, 366
Jenike, M. A., 284, 315
Jenkins, E. J., 316, 317
Jenkins, I., 217
Jennings, J., 248
Jensen, S. B., 427
Jerrell, J. M., 220
Jerremalm, A., 301

Jervis, G. A., 109
Jessen, P. W., 165
Jimeson, D.C., 471
Joffe, R. T., 529
John, O. P., 549
Johns, M. W., 503
Johnson, A. M., 412, 414
Johnson, B. D., 178
Johnson, J., 160, 285, 298, 528
Johnson, J. L., 212
Johnson, M., 313, 340, 364
Johnson, M. O., 308
Johnson, N., 172
Johnson, S. K., 362
Johnson, V. E., 428, 437
Johnston, L. D., 160, 161, 173
Johnstone, B. M., 129
Jonas, J. M., 524, 526
Jones, B. E., 220
Jones, D. J., 466, 472
Jones, R., 176
Jones, R. T., 170
Jordan, B. K., 287, 384
Jordan, K., 382
Joschke, K., 34
Joseph, P., 520
Josephson, S., 11
Joshua, S., 28, 41, 52, 525
Judd, L., 271
Judd, L. L., 259
Julkunen, J., 351
Jusino, C. M., 316
Joyce, M. A., 146
Joynt, R. J., 95

Kabacoff, R. I., 39, 40
Kadden, R. M., 138, 145, 212, 580, 581
Kagan, J., 297, 306, 307, 308, 309
Kahn, R. S., 283, 311
Kaij, L., 133
Kaiser, G., 302
Kaiser, S., 34
Kales, A., 488, 489, 492, 496, 502, 552
Kales, J. D., 167, 168, 493, 494, 502, 503
Kalick, S. M., 424
Kalin, N., 271
Kallman, W. M., 584
Kaltenborn, W. T., 493
Kamerow, D. S., 491, 492
Kandel, D., 161
Kandel, D. B., 161, 168, 176
Kane, J., 35, 39, 49, 516
Kane, J. M., 205

Kanner, L., 101
Kanno, P., 429
Kanof, P. D., 184
Kanton, W., 366
Kanton, W. S., 352
Kaplan, G. A., 351
Kaplan, H. S., 422, 429
Kaplan, M., 513, 514
Kappler, C., 493
Kaprio, J., 71
Kapur, B. M., 144
Karacan, I., 485
Karno, M., 217, 220, 234, 235, 249, 261, 282, 289, 339
Karoly, P., 349
Karus, D., 176
Kashkin, K. B., 172
Kashner, M., 345
Kashner, T. M., 341, 345
Kaskutas, L. A., 132
Kaslow, R. A., 451
Kass, F., 513
Kathol, R. G., 310, 343, 360, 361
Katon, W., 235
Katon, W. J., 352, 366
Katsikitis, M., 363
Katz, D. L., 172
Katz, M., 265
Kaufman, E., 137
Kaufman, L. R., 416
Kauhanen, J., 351
Kavanagh, D. J., 207, 216
Kay, A., 165
Kay, G. N., 470
Kay, S. R., 36, 218
Kazarian, S. S., 50
Kazdin, A. E., 306, 520, 522
Kazdin, R. T., 306, 307
Kazim, A., 297, 298
Keck, P. E., 344, 361
Keddie, A., 138
Keeler, M. H., 136
Keene, S. P., 515
Keener, J. J., 135
Keijsers, G. P. J., 304
Keita, G. P., 248
Keith, S. J., 204, 259
Kelch, R. P., 342
Keller, M. B., 24, 31, 257, 259, 265, 266, 267, 275, 297, 298, 469, 470, 473, 586
Keller, R., 391
Kellman, D., 525
Kellman, H. D., 47, 51, 475
Kellner, R., 356, 364
Kelly, T., 529

Kelsoe, J. R., 268
Kendall, B., 362
Kendell, R. C., 3, 15, 16
Kendler, H. S., 77, 80
Kendler, K., 9, 518
Kendler, K. S., 16, 68, 70, 71, 72, 73, 75, 77, 78, 79, 209, 234, 240, 243, 249, 282, 289, 290, 307, 314, 315, 387, 494, 515, 516
Kennedy, C. J., 89
Kennedy, J., 136
Kennedy, S. J., 488, 489, 496
Kenny, M. G., 392, 393, 394, 396
Kent, D. A., 345
Kenyon, F. E., 349
Kerber, T. E., 310
Kerkhof, G. A., 568
Kern, D. E., 352
Kernberg, O. F., 524, 527, 529
Kershaw, P., 188
Keskimäki, I., 204
Kessel, K. B., 183
Kessler, L. G., 235
Kessler, R. C., 71, 72, 73, 75, 78, 79, 131, 135, 141, 234, 237, 240, 243, 249, 282, 283, 289, 290, 307, 315, 316, 387, 450, 467, 518
Kety, S. S., 240, 524
Keys, D. J., 285, 297, 511, 528
Khalsa, H. K., 176, 177
Khan, F., 169
Khanna, S., 286
Khantzian, E. J., 163, 164
Khuder, S., 174
Kidd, K. K., 75, 268
Kidson, W., 416, 433, 436, 443
Kihlstrom, J. F., 11, 348, 386, 390, 391
Kilic, C., 304
Killen, J. D., 500
Kilmann, P. R., 428, 430
Kiloh, L. G., 587
Kim, C. H., 363
Kim, J. M., 344
Kinder, B. N., 469, 475
King, A. C., 550
King, D., 310
King, H. E., 104
King, M. B., 450
King, S. A., 10
Kingsley, L. A., 451
Kinlaw, W. B., 413, 438

Kinney, D. K., 77, 80
Kinsey, A. C., 411, 412, 413, 421, 422
Kinston, W., 529
Kirch, D. G., 210
Kirkley, B. G., 471
Kirkmayer, L. J., 333, 339, 340, 341, 344, 346, 347, 349, 350, 351, 352, 354, 355, 356, 358, 363, 366, 367, 368
Kirkpatrick, B., 218
Kirkwood, C. R., 336
Kissin, B., 107, 134
Kissner, D. G., 169
Kivlahan, D. R., 190
Kivranta, H., 550
Klass, H., 363
Klassen, A. D., 131
Kleber, H. D., 165, 166, 172, 174
Kleiman, G. L., 582, 588
Klein, D. F., 283, 285, 296, 298, 299, 310, 311, 316
Klein, D. N., 3, 17, 240
Klein, H. E., 586
Klein, M. H., 32, 34, 241
Kleinknecht, R. A., 588
Kleinman, A., 235, 248, 349, 354, 367
Kleinman, A. M., 219
Kleitman, N., 552, 553
Klerman, G., 265, 271
Klerman, G. L., 234, 235, 248, 339, 340, 345, 346, 348, 349, 528, 582, 587
Kletti, R., 399
Klimes, I., 345
Kline-Graber, G., 421
Klinger, T., 510
Klink, M. E., 493
Klopp, B., 549
Klosko, J. S., 301, 303
Klove, H., 110
Kluft, R. P., 389, 395, 396, 397
Klutke, C. G., 337
Knaak, R., 336
Knight, R. W., 416, 422, 423, 435, 436, 440
Knopf, J., 429
Knupfer, G., 134
Koch, G. G., 28
Kochakian, C. D., 171
Koek, R., 299
Koele, P., 303
Koenigsberg, H. W., 525
Kogan, E., 584
Kogan, E. S., 584

Kohnstamm, G. A., 549
Kohut, H., 529
Kolb, L. C., 184
Kolodner, K., 352
Koob, G. F., 163, 164
Koopman, C., 384, 399
Kopelman, M. D., 389, 391, 392
Korten, A., 219
Korzun, A. H., 243
Koskenuno, M., 71
Koslow, S., 265
Koslow, S. H., 230
Koss, M. P., 352, 423, 436, 449
Kosson, D. S., 518
Kosten, T. R., 165, 166, 174, 180
Kozel, N. J., 160
Kozlowski, L. T., 136
Kraepelin, E., 208, 256, 262
Krahn, G. L., 134
Kramer, C. G. S., 552, 568
Kramer, G. U., 308
Kramer, M., 34, 234, 235, 301
Kranier-Fox, R., 310
Kranzler, H. R., 135, 137, 138, 141, 174, 183, 212
Krauthammer, C., 271
Kremer, E. F., 354
Kringlen, E., 39, 68, 69, 70, 76, 77, 78, 80
Kripke, D. F., 501, 552, 553, 551
Krishnan, R., 299, 300
Kristenson, H., 189
Kristensson, H., 143
Krol, P. K., 525
Krone, A. M., 474
Kropp, P. R., 519
Kroth, J. A., 432
Kruger, A., 340
Krupp, L. B., 362
Kuban, M., 436
Kubin, M., 398
Kucera, J., 205
Kuch, K., 304
Kuhnle, J. C., 184
Kuiper, S. I. R., 552, 568
Kuldan, J. M., 183
Kulka, R. A., 287, 384
Kupfer, D. J., 240, 241, 248, 269, 271, 488, 489, 496, 501, 502, 503, 586
Kuriychu, K. M., 521
Kushner, M. G., 136, 205, 588
Kushner, S., 268

Kushner, S. F., 218
Kwentus, J. A., 167

Lacks, P., 495, 500, 501
Lader, M., 168
Ladha, N., 47
Laessie, R. G., 473
La Ferla, J., 342
La Fountain, M. J., 172
Lahey, B. B., 11
Lahti, I., 209
Lalumiere, M. L., 446
Lam, D. H., 217
Landerman, R., 282, 338, 339, 340, 345, 360, 524
Landis, J. R., 28
Landon, P. B., 520
Landsuerk, J. A., 220, 249
Lane, R. S., 349
Lang, E., 141
Lang, P. J., 290, 583
Lang, R. A., 425
Lange, A., 303
Langevin, R., 425
Langinvaino, H., 71
Langley, J., 426
Lantinga, L. J., 190
Lapinski, K., 584
LaPorte, R. E., 550
Lashley, K. S., 94
Last, C. G., 306, 307
Lathan, K. S., 339
Lathan, P. K., 186
Lauer, G., 582
Laumann, E. O., 412, 413, 414, 415, 425, 440, 449, 450
Lavie, P., 501, 551, 552, 567
Lavori, P. W., 265, 297, 469, 470, 473, 586
Lawrence, W. D., 169
Laws, D. R., 445
Lawson, C., 310
Lazare, A., 339
Lazarus, A., 399, 580
Lazarus, R. S., 238, 348
Leaf, P. J., 204, 234, 248, 261, 301
Lebowitz, M. D., 493
Leckkman, A. L., 138
Leckman, J. F., 258, 284, 304, 305
Le Couteur, A., 522
Leeds, N. E., 177
Leff, J., 339
Lefley, H. P., 216, 219
Lehman, A. F., 212
Lehner, T., 269
Lehrer, M., 184

Lei, H., 161
Leiberg, G., 386, 400
Leiblum, S. R., 429, 430, 431
Leigh, G. L., 130, 143, 144, 145
Leigh, G. M., 161
Leirer, V. O., 170, 245
Leitenberg, H., 469, 472
Lemaire, A., 438, 447
Lemberg, L., 169
Lenzi, A., 582, 586
Leo, G. I., 136, 140
Leon, A. S., 549
Leonard, K., 134
Leonard, M., 299
Lerer, B., 268, 269
LeResche, L., 340, 346
Lerner, H. D., 511
Lerner, P. M., 385
Lesage, A., 530
Lesieur, H. R., 5
Leslie, P., 243
Lesser, I. M., 276, 299, 314, 318
Lettieri, D. J., 139, 164
Lettunich, J., 550
Levin, A. P., 299, 311
Levin, H. S., 99
Levin, R. A., 528
Levine, J., 138, 143, 144, 145
Levinson, D. F., 214
Levitt, E., 426
Levitt, M., 516, 526
Levitt, M. M., 214
Levy, G. F., 299
Levy, R., 206
Lewinsohn, P. M., 236, 237, 238, 241
Lewis, F. R., 386, 388, 395, 400, 401, 402
Lewis, I. A., 415, 440, 444
Lewontin, R. C., 450
Lex, B. W., 186
Ley, R., 589
Lezak, M. D., 142
Lia, W. T., 132
Libman, E., 430
Liberman, R. P., 206, 207, 215, 216, 219
Libet, J. M., 184
Lichtermann, D., 510
Lichtman, E. A., 178
Liddle, P. F., 218
Lieberman, A., 249
Liebowitz, M. R., 11, 12, 13, 174, 285, 288, 298, 299, 311, 316
Liese, B. S., 143

Lilienfeld, S. O., 3, 14, 16, 18, 295, 338, 519, 521
Lillie, B. M., 187
Lin, K. M., 210, 219, 248, 276, 318
Lincoln, E. C., 219
Lind, C., 243
Linderberg, C. S., 163, 164
Lineberry, L. G., 471
Linehan, M. M., 530, 551
Linkowski, P., 268
Links, P. S., 525, 526
Linnoila, M., 522
Linsner, J. P., 554
Linton, P. H., 469
Lipman, L. S., 395
Lipman, R. S., 283
Lipson, D. S., 174
Lis, J. A., 529
Liskow, B., 259
Litt, M. D., 580, 581
Litten, R. Z., 138, 145, 146
Litwin, R. G., 399
Livesley, W. J., 14, 17, 67, 68, 509
Ljungberg, L., 168, 177
Lloyd, G. G., 303
Lo, S., 276
Lo, T., 219
Lo, W. H., 219
Locke, B. Z., 234, 235, 249, 259, 282, 289
Loeber, R. T., 11
Loenwenstein, R. J., 384, 389, 392, 393, 397
Löffler, W., 207
Loftus, E. F., 389, 393, 441
Logan, J. A., 176
Long, M. A., 145
Long, R. T., 268
Longwell, B., 183
Loomis, A. L., 553
Loos, V. E., 420
Lopez, F., 237
Lopez, S., 220
LoPiccolo, J., 418, 419, 427, 428, 429, 430, 435, 443, 447
Loranger, A. W., 45, 46, 47, 508, 526
Lorenz, M., 295
Loring, M., 220
Lorna, B., 35, 49, 51
Loth, J. E., 269
Lothstein, L. M., 451
Loucks, A., 512
Lovin, P. A., 502
Lowenstein, D. H., 169

Luborsky, L., 166, 175, 177, 182, 189, 578
Luciano, D., 352
Luckie, L. S., 145
Lugaresi, E., 491, 492
Lum, O., 245
Lund, I., 75
Lunde, L., 240
Luo, Y., 269
Luria, A. R., 94
Lusiardo, G., 210
Lustman, P. J., 583
Lycklama a Nijeholt, G., 420
Lydiard, R. B., 299, 300, 313, 314, 340
Lykken, D. T., 67, 69, 71, 72, 178, 179, 397, 522
Lynam, D., 549
Lynch, T. G., 178
Lynett, E., 517, 518, 519, 520, 523
Lynn, S. J., 384, 391, 393, 400
Lyons, H., 513
Lyons, J., 136, 141
Lyons, M. J., 74, 307

MacAndrew, C., 185
Macdonald, H., 522
MacFarlane, D. F., 451
Machfinger, P. E., 34
MacKinnon, A. J., 240
MacLean, C., 340
MacLeod, A. K., 349
Maddux, J. F., 174
Maes, M. H., 587
Magaña, A. B., 217
Magee, W. J., 283, 316
Magni, G., 339, 346, 347
Magnusson, D., 26
Maguire, E., 431
Mahoney, M. J., 237
Maier, W., 509, 580
Maisto, S. A., 139, 143
Malatesta, V. J., 304
Maletzky, B. M., 432, 436
Malhotra, A. K., 170
Maller, R. G., 295
Malmud, M., 443
Malmuth, N. M., 415, 417
Malow, R. M., 50
Mamiya, L. H., 219
Mancini, C., 285
Mancuso, D. M., 298
Mandel, B., 268
Mandeli, J., 418
Manderscheid, R. W., 235
Manfredi, R., 489, 496

Manicavasagar, V., 415
Manley, S., 144
Manis, M., 351
Manly, D. T., 400
Mann, A., 349, 351, 355
Mann, L. S., 514, 525
Mann, J. J., 310
Manton, K. G., 282
Marchbanks, R. M., 78
Marchetti, M., 339, 346
Marchine, E., 500
Marchione, K., 301
Marcos, L. R., 276, 318
Marcus, S., 32
Marcouiller, M., 530
Marcus, J., 206
Marder, S. R., 305
Marengo, J., 207
Margraf, J., 311
Marin, B., 249
Marino, L., 17, 18
Marino, M. F., 525
Markel, D., 493, 494, 503
Markowitz, P. J., 531
Marks, I. M., 284, 296, 304
Marlatt, G. A., 129, 131, 141, 146, 162, 163, 190
Marmar, C. R., 287, 384, 388
Marques, J. K., 434, 435, 520
Marsden, M. E., 187
Marsella, A. J., 248
Marsh, A., 144
Marsh, G. R., 489, 502, 503
Marshall, J. C., 342
Marshall, J. R., 358
Marshall, W. L., 422, 431, 432, 433, 434, 436, 439, 445, 446, 514
Martelli, M. F., 581, 582
Martin, C. E., 411, 412, 413, 421, 422
Martin, G. W., 161
Martin, J. B., 89
Martin, N. G., 68, 70, 314, 494
Martin, P. R., 400, 419, 428, 429, 430
Martin, R. L., 341, 342, 347, 360
Martin, R. P., 551, 549
Martin, W. R., 165
Martinez-Taboas, A., 395
Marziali, E., 525, 526
Masi, A. T., 347
Mason, C., 183
Mason, D. J., 558, 559
Massa, S. M., 169
Massana, J., 299

Massion, A. O., 297
Massoth, D., 352, 366
Masters, W. H., 428, 437
Masterson, C. C., 515
Masur, D. M., 362
Matarazzo, J. D., 183
Mathews, A., 364
Matsuda, K. T., 276, 318
Mattes, J. A., 214
Matthews, C. G., 110
Matthews, K., 9
Matthias, L., 183
Matthysse, S., 209
Mattick, R. J., 304, 311
Mattson, M. E., 138
Mattysse, S., 268
Maurer, D. W., 160
Maurer, K., 207
Mavissakalian, M., 301, 315, 445
Maycut, M. O., 170
Mayfield, D., 141
Mayer, K. H., 442
Mayeux, R., 393
Mayman, M., 351
Mayo, J. A., 272
Mayou, R., 338, 364
Mazzoni, S., 180
McAuley, E., 550
McCabe, S. B., 244
McCann, D. S., 311
McCanne, T. R., 475
McCall, R. B., 548
McCarthy, B. M. 437
McCauley, J., 352
McClean, C. J., 71
McClearn, G. E., 67, 72
McClure, J. H., Jr., 310
McCombie, S. L., 440
McConaghy, N., 410, 412, 413, 415, 416, 417, 420, 421, 425, 426, 427, 429, 431, 433, 434, 435, 436, 439, 440, 441, 442, 443, 444, 445, 446, 447, 448, 449
McCormick, R. V., 208
McCough, D. P., 146
McCoy, C. B., 183
McCrady, B. S., 142
McCrae, R. R., 67, 548
McCue, M., 71, 77, 101, 113
McCurdy-Myers, J., 6, 10
McCusker, J., 442
McCutchan, J. A., 89
McDaniel, S. H., 354, 358, 364
McDonald, C., 237, 238

McDonald, E., 362
McDonald, S. P., 24, 31
McDonald Haule, J., 363
McDougall, E. M., 337
McDougle, C. J., 299
McDowell, D. E., 50, 51
McElroy, S. L., 344
McEnvoy, L., 518
McEvoy, J. P., 206
McEvoy, L., 32, 34
McGee, B., 183
McGlashan, T., 16
McGlashan, T. M., 516, 524
McGlynn, F. D., 292
McGonagle, K. A., 234, 243, 249, 282, 289, 290, 315, 387, 518
McGrath, D., 141
McGrath, E., 7, 235, 248
McGrath, P., 299
McGrath, R. E., 363
McGrew, J. H., 207
McGue, M., 178, 179
McGuffin, P., 69, 78
McGuire, M., 77
McGullin, P., 76
McHugh, P. R., 366, 512, 526
McKay, J. R., 139
McKendrick, V. G., 578, 585
McKenna, T., 184
McKinley, J. C., 362
McKinney, H. E., 169
McKinnon, G. L., 168
McKnight, D., 582, 588
McLellan, A. T., 131, 166, 174, 175, 177, 182, 189, 212, 521, 522, 523
McLeod, D. R., 299
McLeod, G., 141
McMahon, C. G., 448
McMahon, P., 584
McManus, M., 511
McNagny, S. E., 183
McNair, D. M., 83
McNally, R. J., 293, 294, 295, 296, 297
McNamara, M. E., 9
McNamee, H. B., 184
McWilliams, S. A., 170
Mead, M., 420, 421, 422
Meares, R., 529
Mechanic, D., 347, 350
Mednick, S. A., 101
Meeh, P. E., 17
Meinecke, C. F., 436
Melella, J., 433
Melisatros, N., 501
Mell, L. D., 184

Mellinger, G. D., 491, 503
Mellsop, G., 28, 52, 525
Melman, A., 427
Meloy, J. R., 519, 520, 523
Meltzer, B. S., 303
Meltzer, H., 312, 531
Melville, M. L., 282
Melzack, R., 356, 360, 364
Meminger, S. R., 307
Menchen, S. L., 184
Mendell, W., 183
Mendelson, M., 25, 245
Mendelson, W., 502
Mendlewicz, J., 268
Menkes, D. B., 363
Mercante, D. E., 298
Merchant, A., 34, 366, 512,
    526
Mercuri, L. G., 581, 582
Merikangas, K. R., 7, 284,
    304, 305, 512
Merriam, A. E., 281
Merry, J., 48, 67
Merskey, H., 339, 346, 347,
    359
Mesiano, D., 489, 496
Messin, S., 552
Messina, J. A., 339
Mesulam, M. M., 94
Metalsky, G. L., 237
Metcal, M., 336
Metz, P., 448
Metzler, T., 388
Meuleman, E. J. H., 447, 448
Meyer, I., 218
Meyer, J. M., 161
Meyer, R. E., 135, 137, 180,
    184
Meyerowitz, S., 339
Meyers, J. K., 135
Mezzich, A. C., 135, 142
Mezzich, J. E., 248, 387, 399
Michael, R. T., 412, 413, 414,
    415, 425, 440, 449, 450
Michaels, M., 183, 300
Michaels, S., 412, 413, 414,
    415, 425, 449, 450
Michelson, L., 301, 384
Midanik, L., 131
Middelkoop, H. A. M., 552,
    568
Mieczkowski, T., 183, 186
Miele, G., 3, 6, 8, 523, 525
Miklowitz, D. J., 217, 272,
    275
Milan, R. J., 428
Milby, J. B., 160, 162, 164,

166, 174, 176, 179, 180,
    182, 183
Mill, K., 352
Miller, E. N., 89
Miller, G. A., 524
Miller, J. B., 525
Miller, J. P., 32, 44
Miller, R. E., 104
Miller, T., 521
Miller, W. C., 136
Miller, W. R., 129, 131, 138,
    142, 143, 145, 146, 177,
    188, 189, 190
Millman, R. B., 165, 167
Millon, T., 509, 517, 519,
    523, 524, 527
Milstein, V., 389, 390, 391,
    392, 393, 396, 397
Mineka, S., 293, 294
Miner, C., 559
Minichiello, W. E., 296, 315
Minshew, N. J., 101
Mintz, J., 175, 183, 220, 275
Minuchin, S., 473, 474
Miranda, J., 243, 249
Mirin, S. M., 163, 174, 175,
    180, 183, 184
Mirmiran, M., 568
Mirsky, A. F., 111, 206
Mirza, S., 367
Mischel, W., 238
Mishler, E. G., 209
Mitchell, J. D., 184, 351
Mitchell, J. E., 467, 469, 470,
    471, 474
Mitcheson, M., 188, 189
Mitler, M. M., 492
Mizes, J. S., 470, 476
Mock, J. E., 25
Mock, L., 245
Moffitt, T. E., 520, 522, 549
Mohamed, E., 339
Moller, M. B., 310
Mombour, W., 45, 46, 47
Monk, T. H., 501
Monroe, L. J., 492
Monroe, S. M., 241
Monson, R., 354
Monson, R. A., 341
Montgomery, H. A., 145
Monti, P. M., 145
Moon, M. W., 442
Moos, B. S., 217
Moos, R. H., 217, 237
Morales, A., 431
Morales, D. S., 219
Moran, J., 9

Moreschi, C., 339, 346,
    347
Morey, L. C., 14, 509, 513,
    515, 516, 527
Morgan, A. H., 397
Morganstern, K. P., 442
Morin, C. M., 486, 495, 499,
    500, 501
Moring, J., 209
Morley, J. E., 414, 438
Morokoff, P., 421, 435
Morris, J. N., 550
Morrison, J., 265, 352, 417
Morrison, R. L., 207, 215,
    216
Morrison, V., 176
Morrow, L., 354
Morton, A., 340
Moscicki, E. K., 249
Moser, C., 426
Moss, H., 135
Moss, K. L., 489
Mostofsky, D. I., 348
Motiuk, L. L., 523
Motta, R., 237
Mowrer, O. H., 292
Mowry, B. J., 214
Mrazek, P., 235
Mueller, E. A., 312
Mueller, T., 257, 259, 265,
    267, 275
Muenzenmaier, K., 218
Mueser, K. T., 205, 206, 207,
    208, 213, 215, 216, 217,
    218, 219, 221
Mufsor, L., 305
Mukerjji, V., 347
Mullaney, D. J., 552, 553
Mumford, D. B., 367
Mumford, J., 138, 143
Munchau, J., 301
Munjack, D. J., 50, 51, 299,
    429
Munk-Jøgensen, P., 204
Munoz, R., 7, 32, 235, 249,
    256, 466
Munson, R. C., 218
Murakami, S. R., 132
Muran, E., 237
Murdoch, J. C., 363
Murdock, T. B., 303
Murphy, C. E., 583
Murphy, D., 141, 161, 164,
    269, 270, 300, 312
Murphy, G. I., 176
Murphy, H. B. M., 219
Murphy, M., 341, 347, 361

Murray, M. I., 526
Murray, R. M., 133, 138, 143, 207
Murrell, G. C., 363
Murrin, M., 218, 219
Musa, M. N., 582
Myers, C. P., 212
Myers, J. K., 234, 235, 240, 301
Myers, W. A., 415, 417, 440
Myronuk, L. D. S., 417
Myslobodsky, M. S., 111

Naeaghi, M. M., 367
Nagy, R., 299
Nakasaki, G., 248
Nakdiem, K. A., 511
Narrow, W. E., 235
Nash, M. R., 385, 397
Nasrallah, A., 267
Nasser, M., 467
Natelson, B. H., 362
Nathan, R. S., 530
Nathan, S., 411, 412, 420, 436
Nation, P., 237
National Commission on Sleep Disorders Research, 492
National Comorbidity Study, 234
National Household Survey of Drug Abuse, 187
National Institute on Alcohol Abuse and Alcoholism, 130, 132, 140
National Institute of Drug Abuse, 132, 160, 170, 186
National Institute of Mental Health, 160, 261, 265
Naughton, J. P., 550
Navarro, A. M., 249
Nayak, D., 214
Naylor, S. L., 89
Nazikian, H., 44
Neal, A. M., 316
Neale, M. C., 70, 71, 72, 73, 75, 78, 79, 161, 240, 307
Neary, A., 512
Needle, R., 183
Needles, D. J., 522
Neese, R. M., 296, 311
Nehra, R., 170
Neider, J., 352
Neils, J., 117
Neiswanger, K., 240, 241

Nelson, A. E., 413, 438
Nelson, B. A., 525
Nelson, C. B., 234, 243, 249, 282, 289, 290, 315, 434, 435, 520
Nelson, C. J., 413, 438
Nelson, E. W., 450
Nelson, J. E., 139
Nelson, J. M., 170
Nelson, L. B., 518
Nelson, L. M., 89, 106
Nelson, M., 220
Nelson, R., 578, 582, 588
Nemiah, J. C., 384, 385
Neraas, K., 352, 366
Ness, R., 184
Nesselroade, J. R., 67
Nestadt, G., 34, 366, 512, 526
Nettlebladt, P., 418
Neville, D., 11
Newlove, T., 48
Newman, C. F., 143
Newman, J. P., 518, 521
Newman, J. M., 550
Newman, M., 268
Newton, T. F., 489, 503
Newton, R. W., 243
Nezu, A. M., 238, 521
Nguyen, T. D., 220
Niaura, R. S., 9, 129
Nichols, N., 175
Nickel, E. J., 243
Nijenhuis, E., 389
Nirenbergs, T. D., 144
Noble, J. H., 203
Nofzinger, E. A., 488
Nolan, J., 550
Nolen-Hoeksema, S., 234, 365
Noonan, M., 342
Noordsy, D. L., 206, 213
Norcross, J. C., 188
Nordlie, J. W., 348
Norell, S. E., 550
Norten, S., 352
Norton, G. R., 291, 395
Norton, R. G., 135
Noshirvani, H., 304
Novacek, J., 238
Nowak, J., 74, 307
Nowlan, R., 170
Nowlin, N. S., 473
Noyes, R., Jr., 290, 297, 298, 299, 304, 305, 314, 315, 343, 361, 399, 511
Nuechterlein, K. H., 50, 204, 207, 275

Nurco, D. N., 183
Nurmberg, H. G., 525
Nurnberger, J., 258
Nussbaum, P. D., 122
Nutt, D., 310
Nuttall, F. Q., 413, 428
Nutter, D. E., 438

Oberman, A., 550
O'Boyle, M., 50, 51
O'Brien, C. P., 163, 166, 175, 177, 182, 183, 184, 189
O'Brien, T. J., 183, 184
Obsenski, K., 71
Ochoa, E., 513
O'Connell, R. A., 272
O'Conner, A. A., 414
O'Connor, M. E., 472
O'Donnell, J. A., 178
O'Donnell, W. E., 131
O'Dowd, T., 345
O'Farrell, T. J., 143, 160
Ogilvie, R. D., 551, 553
Ogloff, J. P. R., 520
O'Hare, A., 77
Ohman, A., 293, 297
Olafsson, C., 293
Oldham, J., 508, 526
Oldham, J. M., 45, 47, 51, 475, 525
O'Leary, M. R., 190
Oliveau, D., 285, 293
Oliveto, A. H., 7
Olmstead, E. M., 492
Olmstead, M. P., 476
O'Malley, P. M., 160, 161, 173
O'Malley, S. S., 146
O'Malley, W. P., 363
Omenn, G. S., 133
Ondercin, P., 465
Ono, Y., 45, 46, 47
Onstad, S., 39, 68, 70, 76, 77, 78, 80
Oo, M., 470
Opler, L. A., 36, 218
Oppenheimer, E., 188
Oreman, J., 75
Orford, J., 138, 188, 189
Organista, K. C., 249
Oros, C. J., 449
Orosan, P., 346, 364
Ortmann, J., 240
Orvaschel, H., 261, 282, 301, 306, 307, 361, 467, 476
Orwin, A., 582
Osborn, M., 413

Osher, F. C., 206, 207
Ost, L. G., 290, 296, 301, 558
Oster, M., 243
Ostrow, D. G., 450
O'Sullivan, G., 304
Othmer, E., 360
O'Toole, D. H., 584
Ott, J., 269
Ott, P. J., 142
Ottaviani, R., 521, 530
Ottina, K., 89
Otto, M. W., 297, 300, 303, 315
Over, R., 444
Owen, J. A., 431
Owen, P., 474
Ozarow, B. J., 302

Padberg, F. T., 178
Padesky, C., 52, 530
Padgett, D. K., 220
Paffenbarger, R. S., Jr., 550
Page, A. C., 290
Page, R. D., 190
Pahlavan, K., 560
Pajer, K., 248
Pakianaathan, I., 386, 395, 398, 400, 401, 402
Palace, E. M., 446
Palmore, E., 550
Palossy, B., 470
Pambakian, R., 183
Paolo, A. M., 395
Papp, L., 299
Paris, J., 347, 358, 525
Parker, D., 271
Parker, G., 241
Parker, J. D., 351
Parker, M. W., 189
Parker, R. M., 183
Parker, R. N., 450
Parker, W. A., 168
Parkinson, A., 44
Parks, J. D., 486, 487, 493
Parloff, M. B., 241, 242
Parra, F., 219
Parrish, B. A., 296
Parrish, R. T., 296
Parson, M., 492
Parsons, E. B., 220
Parsons, O. A., 107, 142
Partinen, M., 503
Pascoe, H., 417
Pathak, D., 364
Pato, M. T., 300
Patrick, C., 220
Patterson, M. B., 522

Pattison, E. M., 128, 129, 145
Paul, D. B., 184
Paul, S. M., 268
Pauls, D., 268
Pauls, D. L., 75, 268, 305
Payeur, R., 313
Paykel, E. S., 236, 582, 587
Payton, J. B., 101
Paz, G., 220
Pearson, S., 416
Pecknold, J. C., 299, 314
Pecsok, E. H., 145
Pederson, N. L., 67, 71, 550
Peele, S., 5, 133
Pelosi, A., 349, 355
Pelton, S., 586, 588
Pemberton, J. S., 363
Pendelton, L., 522
Penick, E. C., 243
Penn, D. L., 205
Penn, P., 217
Pennebaker, J. W., 346, 347, 351, 352, 365
Pennybacker, M., 282
Peqegnat, W., 450
Perel, J. M., 530
Perez, E., 471
Perez, E. L., 32, 34
Perlick, P., 554
Pernet, A., 362
Perri, M. G., 238
Perrine, K., 352
Perris, C., 257
Perry, C. L., 161, 164
Perry, J. C., 511
Perry, M., 243
Perry, P. J., 272
Perry, T. J., 552, 553
Pershod, D., 286
Person, A., 268
Person, E. S., 415, 417, 440
Perugi, G., 299
Peselow, E. D., 582
Peters, K. R., 174
Peterson, C., 4
Peterson, G. A., 448
Peterson, L. G., 297, 298
Peterson, R. A., 295
Pett, M. A., 414, 418, 419, 435, 438
Petterew, L. S., 364
Petersson, B., 143
Petterson, A., 78
Peveler, R., 364
Pevler, R. C., 472
Peyser, J. J., 106
Pfaus, J. G., 417

Pfister, H., 34
Pfohl, B., 41, 42, 43, 508, 511, 526
Phelps, G., 138, 143
Phil, R. O., 130
Philipp, M., 580
Phillips, B. J., 343, 361
Phillips, D., 429, 530
Phillips, G., 444
Phillips, K. A., 11, 340, 343, 344
Phillips, M., 144, 147
Phillips, R., 502
Piasecki, J. M., 241
Pickens, R., 71, 361
Pickens, R. W., 178, 179
Pierce, W. D., 570
Pierloot, R., 173
Pihl, R. O., 134
Pike, K. M., 472, 473
Pilkonis, P. A., 48, 241, 242
Pilowsky, I., 349, 361, 363
Pimely, S., 238
Pincus, A. L., 509
Pincus, H. A., 3, 5, 6, 8, 9, 13, 15
Pincus, T., 363
Pinel, P., 518
Pinto, L. P., 566
Pirke, K., 473
Pithers, W. D., 434
Pittman, P. J., 190
Pitts, F. N., Jr., 310
Placidi, G. R., 582, 586
Plakun, E. M., 524
Plomin, R., 67, 71, 548
Plutchik, R., 524
Pohjola, J., 209
Poiland, K. E., 276
Poland, R. E., 248, 318
Poldrugo, F., 520
Polich, J. J., 131
Pollack, C. P., 498, 554
Pollack, H., 266
Pollack, I., 552
Pollack, M. H., 297, 300, 303, 315
Pollard, R., 550
Pomerleau, O. F., 179
Pomeroy, W. B., 411, 412, 413, 421, 422
Poole, G. D., 356
Pope, H. G., 35, 39, 49, 172, 344, 361, 471, 524, 526
Pope, H. G., Jr., 361
Porchaska, J. O., 188
Porjesz, B., 107, 134

Porporino, F. J., 523
Poser, C. M., 106
Post, P. M., 348
Post, R. M., 236, 314, 395, 397
Potter, M., 78
Potts, N., 299, 300
Powell, B., 220
Powell, B. J., 243
Powell, K. B., 272
Powers, P. S., 470
Prasad, K. V., 400, 401
Pratt, L. A., 297
Prentky, R. A., 416, 422, 535, 436, 440
Pretzer, J., 521, 530
Pribor, E. E., 386
Pribor, E. F., 360
Price, L. H., 299
Price, T., 243
Prieto, E. J., 363
Prins, H., 521
Printz, A. M., 467, 476
Prior, M., 212
Prokop, C. K., 363
Prusoff, B. A., 284, 304, 305, 582, 587, 588
Pruzinsky, T., 291, 366
Pryor, T., 465, 466, 476
Przybeck, T., 183
Pu, T., 339
Puech, A., 587
Puffett, A., 389, 392
Pull, C., 45, 46, 47
Putnam, F. W., 348, 384, 386, 387, 395, 396, 397
Ppuzantian, V., 315
Pyle, R. L., 467, 469, 474

Quan, S. F., 493
Quinlan, D., 237, 238
Quinlan, D. M., 476
Quinsey, V. L., 433, 434, 446, 510, 518, 519, 521

Raab, E. S., 248
Rabinowitz, J., 284
Raboch, J., 422
Raboch, J., Jr., 422
Rachal, J. V., 187
Rachlin, H., 4
Rachman, S., 310, 588
Rachman, S. J., 292, 293
Raczynski, J. R., 183
Radloff, L. S., 245
Radtke, R. A., 489, 502, 503

Rae, D. S., 204, 234, 235, 249, 259
Rafil, M., 178
Raine, A., 518, 522
Rainer, J., 268
Raistrick, D., 141
Raman, A. C., 219
Randall, C., 186
Randall, C. L., 186
Rankin, H., 143
Rankin, J. G., 132
Rao, D. C., 77
Raoux, N., 560
Rapee, R. M., 300, 301, 302
Raphaelson, O. J., 588
Rapoport, J. L., 312
Rasmussen, S., 297, 305, 307, 313
Ratcliff, K. S., 32, 33, 34, 35, 247, 518
Ratey, J. J., 101
Ratliff, T. L., 337
Rauramaa, R., 549
Ravaris, C. L., 303, 489, 492
Ravi, S. D., 136
Rawlings, R., 210
Ray, D., 354
Ray, D. C., 341
Ray, W. J., 384
Raymond, N., 471
Rayner, R., 292
Read, M. R., 243
Reading, A. E., 443
Ream, N. W., 178
Rechtschaffen, A., 552, 553
Redding, C. A., 340
Reddon, J. R., 417
Redeker, N. S., 559
Redlich, F. C., 204
Redman, D. P., 558
Reece, S., 276
Reed, G., 399
Regan, J. J., 529
Regan, W. M., 339, 342
Regestein, Q. R., 491
Regier, D., 338, 360
Regier, D. A., 361, 467, 476, 520
Rehm, L. P., 7, 235
Reich, J., 43, 52, 511, 513, 525, 528, 529
Reich, J. H., 297, 298, 315
Reich, T., 79, 267, 268
Reichler, R. J., 305
Reiger, D. A., 45, 46, 47, 131, 135, 136, 141, 160, 176,

204, 205, 220, 234, 235, 248, 249, 259, 261, 282
Reisby, N., 588
Reiskin, H. K., 163
Reiss, S., 294, 295
Reite, M., 502
Reiter, J., 346, 364
Reitman, M., 553
Rennenberg, B., 50, 315, 530
Renshaw, D. C., 428, 429
Resnick, R. J., 530
Revenstorf, D., 443, 444
Reynolds, C., 248, 502
Reynolds, C. F., 488, 489, 495, 501, 502, 503
Reynolds, S., 3, 7
Reznick, J. S., 297, 306, 307, 308, 309
Rhue, J. W., 384, 400
Rice, J., 74, 307
Rice, M. E., 434, 518, 519, 520, 521, 522
Rich, S., 67, 397
Richards, L., 162
Richardson, G. S., 498
Richman, D. D., 89
Richter, P., 582
Rickels, K., 283, 299
Rickman, R., 243
Riecher-Rössler, A., 207
Rieder, R. O., 438, 439
Rief, W., 344
Riemann, D., 493, 499
Riesny, K. R., 243
Riether, A. M., 392
Rifkin, A., 299, 314
Rigatti-Luchini, S., 339, 347
Rigby, M. F., 349
Riggs, D. S., 303
Riley, K. C., 384
Risch, S., 271
Risckind, J. H., 39
Riso, L. P., 17
Roback, H., 451
Robbins, D., 511
Robbins, D. R., 582, 586, 587
Robbins, J. M., 339, 340, 344, 346, 347, 349, 350, 351, 354, 358, 361, 365, 366
Roberts, C. W., 418, 419, 430, 435
Roberts, J., 313
Roberts, L. J., 175
Robin, C. J., 238
Robinette, C. D., 69
Robins, E., 24, 25, 26, 29, 31,

32, 33, 34, 35, 256, 261, 466
Robins, L. M., 467, 476
Robins, L. N., 132, 145, 160, 176, 234, 235, 247, 248, 261, 282, 315, 338, 360, 361, 518, 522, 528
Robins, R. W., 549
Robinson, D., 521
Robinson, E., 291
Robinson, R. G., 243
Robson, P., 302
Rock, C. L., 470
Rockwell, K., 470
Rockwell, S., 438
Rodel, A., 582
Rodrigo, G., 210
Roffwarg, H. P., 488, 489, 496
Rogers, J. H., 510
Rogers, M. D., 297, 298
Rogers, R., 517, 518, 519, 520, 523
Rohland, B. M., 273
Rokous, F., 435
Rolland, J. S., 364
Rollinson, R. D., 391
Rollnick, S., 143, 189, 521
Romanoski, A. J., 34, 366, 512, 526
Romeo, S., 334
Romig, H., 582
Ronningstam, E., 527
Rooijmans, H. G., 345
Room, R., 131, 132, 140
Roos, R. A. C., 552, 568
Roper, M., 468
Rorty, M., 475
Rosberger, Z., 360
Rose, N., 475
Rose, R. J., 71
Rose, T. S., 245
Rosen, G., 235
Rosen, G. M., 430
Rosen, J., 393
Rosen, J. C., 346, 364, 469, 472
Rosen, R. C., 431, 446
Rosenbaum, J. F., 297, 300, 306, 307, 309, 315
Rosenbaum, J. R., 303
Rosenbaum, M., 236, 237, 241
Rosenberg, R., 423, 435
Rosenberg, S. D., 218, 220, 308, 313
Rosenberger, P. H., 524
Rosenthal, D., 75, 240, 521

Rosenthal, R. L., 5
Rosenthal, T., 315
Rosman, B. L., 473
Rosner, H. L., 346
Rosnick, L., 47, 51, 525
Rosolack, T. K., 548
Ross, H. E., 135
Ross, R., 10
Ross, R. J., 498
Rossotto, E., 475
Rost, K., 341, 345
Rotert, M., 501
Roth, L., 39, 206
Roth, T., 488, 489, 496, 501
Roth, W. T., 311
Rothbart, M. K., 548
Rothbaum, B. O., 303
Rouleau, J. L., 416
Rounsaville, B., 35, 39, 49
Rounsaville, B. J., 137, 165, 166, 174, 175, 180, 312, 582, 588
Rourke, B. P., 120
Rovere, G., 172
Rowbotham, M. C., 169
Roy, A., 205
Roy, J., 146
Roy-Byrne, P. P., 299, 300, 314
Rubenstein, K. J., 184
Rubin, R. T., 314
Rubinstein, D., 411, 418, 437
Rubio-Stipec, M., 339
Ruchichi, E., 299, 300
Rudd, R. P., 44
Ruddy, J., 48
Ruhling, R. O., 550
Rumsey, J. M., 101
Rush, A. J., 13, 237
Russakoff, L. M., 45, 47, 508
Russell, D. E. H., 414, 432
Russell, E. M., 550
Russell, J. L., 588
Russell, M., 132
Russo, N. F., 248
Rutter, M., 3, 11, 522
Rutter, M. L., 217
Ryan, C. F., 40
Ryan, D. P., 351, 352
Ryan, J. J., 395
Rye, L., 470

Saah, A. J., 451
Sabshin, M., 5
Sachs, G. S., 297, 300, 303, 315
Sachs, R. G., 395

Sackeim, H. A., 348
Sadeh, A., 501, 551, 552, 553, 558, 567
Sadik, C., 475
Sakaguchi, A. Y., 89
Sakheim, D. K., 445
Salaspuro, M., 143
Salkovskis, P., 301
Salkovskis, P. M., 346, 354, 364
Sallaerts, S., 51
Salman, E., 316
Salokangas, R. K. R., 204
Saloman, M., 531
Salomen, J. T., 351
Saltzman, S. P., 442
Salvadori, C., 415, 417, 440
Salzman, D. G., 302
Salzman, G. A., 169
Samuelsson, S., 412, 427, 429
Sanchez, V., 238
Sanchez-Craig, M., 140, 142
Sandberg, D., 299, 311
Sanderson, C. J., 7, 14
Sandoz, M., 587
Saoud, J. B., 475
Saran, A., 431
Sarco, D., 474
Sargeant, M., 78
Sarnie, M. K., 340, 346
Sartorius, N., 45, 46, 47, 219, 361
Sassin, J. F., 488, 489, 496
Satz, P., 89, 94, 100
Saucedo, C. F., 142
Saudino, K. J., 547
Saunders, J. B., 141, 144, 145, 147
Saunders, K. W., 346
Saunders, W., 188
Sav, V., 395
Saxe, G., 300
Saxe, G. N., 386, 400
Saxena, S., 400, 401
Sayers, M., 216
Sayers, M. A., 139
Sayers, S. L. 216
Saypool, D. C., 448
Sceery, W., 258
Schaaf, K. K., 475
Schacter, D. L., 391
Schaeffer, K. W., 107
Schaffer, J. W., 183
Schalling, D., 522
Schanzer, H., 418
Schaub, L. H., 190
Scheerer, K., 93

Scheftner, W. A., 586
Scheibe, G., 304
Scher, A., 567
Schiavi, R. C., 418
Schiebel, D., 425
Schlank, A. M., 434
Schlenger, W. E., 287, 384
Schlesinger, H. J., 220
Schlesinger, L., 361
Schlesinger, L. B., 518
Schlesser, M., 271
Schmidt, H. S., 488, 489, 496
Schmidt, L., 146
Schneider, B. A., 423, 435
Schneier, F. R., 285, 298
Schnoll, S., 178
Schoenberg, H. W., 429
Schonfeld, L., 131
Schott, R. L., 417
Schover, L. R., 429, 430, 431, 449
Schramm, E., 493, 499
Schreiner-Engel, P., 418
Schroeder, A. F., 352
Schroeder, M. L., 14, 17, 509
Schroeder-Hartwig, K., 302
Schubert, D. S., 522
Schukit, M. A., 134, 135, 184, 212
Schuller, R., 140
Schulsinger, F., 107, 133, 240, 436, 524
Schultz, C. S., 531
Schultz, W. C. M., 429
Schulz, P. M., 530
Schulz, S. C., 530, 531
Schumacher, J. E., 174, 182, 183
Schumacher, M. C., 550
Schur, B. E., 131
Schuster, C. R., 187
Schwab-Stone, M., 515
Schwartz, C. E., 315
Schwartz, E. O., 525
Schwartz, J., 386, 400
Schwartz, R. H., 144, 170, 176
Schweitzer, P. K., 488
Schweitzer, R. D., 217
Schweizer, E., 299
Scott, D. W., 475
Scott, J., 552, 553
Seaburn, D., 358, 364
Seagraves, K., 431
Seagraves, R. T., 429, 431
Seagroatt, V., 345
Searles, H., 208

Searles, J. S., 133, 134
Secunda, S., 265
Segal, D. L., 38, 39, 40
Segal, N., 67, 69, 71, 72, 522
Segal, N. L., 397
Segal, Z. V., 423
Segall, E. R., 514, 525
Seidel, R., 473
Seidman, S. N., 438, 439
Seinler, G., 34
Self, D., 50, 51
Seligman, M., 293
Selis, J. E., 169
Sellwood, W., 318
Semmence, A. M., 550
Sensky, T., 349
Serban, G., 524
Serin, R. C., 529
Serrao, P., 48
Setia, M., 500
Severino, S., 10
Sewell, K. E., 517, 518, 519, 520, 523
Seyfried, W., 33, 34
Shadick, R., 291
Shafer, R. B., 413, 438
Shafer, S., 299
Shaffer, H., 137
Shalzinger, F., 75
Shaner, A., 175
Shanyang, Z., 234, 243, 249
Shao, W., 269
Shapiro, C., 501
Shapiro, L. J., 296, 304
Shapiro, R. W., 24, 31, 34
Shapiro, S., 235, 465, 466
Sharfstein, J., 203
Sharkey, M., 552
Sharpe, L., 269
Sharpe, M., 338, 346, 354, 355, 364
Sharpe, M. J., 345
Sharpe, T., 344, 350
Shaw, B., 588
Shaw, B. E., 237
Shaw, B. F., 244
Shaw, D. G., 352
Shaw, D. M., 290, 296, 489, 503
Shaw, T., 434
Shaywitt, B. A., 391
Shea, M. T., 241, 242
Shea, T., 516
Shealy, J. S., 474
Shear, M. K., 310
Shearer, D. E., 550
Shedler, J., 351

Sheehan, D. V., 296, 310
Sheehan, K. E., 296
Shelly, C., 107
Sher, K. J., 3, 17, 34, 136
Shera, D., 300
Sherman, B., 271
Sherrington, R., 78
Sheu, W. J., 140
Shigatomi, C., 296
Shigeoka, J. W., 550
Shillingford, J. A., 136
Shinsato, L., 515
Shor, R. E., 401
Shorter, E., 354
Shoulson, I., 89
Shuckit, M. A., 490
Shuey, I., 582
Shute, P. A., 143
Shutty, M. S. J., 363
Siegel, H. A., 165, 174, 183
Siegel, J. M., 414, 449, 451
Siever, L. J., 12, 312, 515, 516
Sifneos, P. E., 351
Sigvardsson, S., 72, 73, 75, 79, 107, 129, 133, 347
Silberfarb, P., 243
Silberman, E. K., 348, 395, 397
Silove, D., 417, 427
Silver, B., 318
Silverman, D. C., 424
Silverman, S., 500
Silvestre, S., 316
Simeon, D., 340
Simkin, S., 345
Simmonds, P., 531
Simon, G. E., 350
Simon, K. M., 521, 530
Simon, R., 269
Simon, R. P., 169
Simone, S., 145
Simonoff, E., 522
Simons, A. D., 241, 242, 244, 248, 583
Simons, R. C., 402
Simpson, T. L., 145
Sims, M. K., 174
Sims-Knight, J. E., 435
Singer, B., 578
Singer, J. L., 351, 416, 440
Siscovick, D. S., 550
Sivan, A. B., 114
Sivec, H. J., 391, 393
Skare, S., 32
Skilbeck, W. M., 219
Skinner, E. A., 235

Skinner, H. A., 138, 140, 141, 143, 144, 145, 185, 189
Skodol, A. E., 11, 13, 475, 525
Skotnicki, S. H., 447, 448
Skre, I., 47, 51, 68, 70, 76, 77, 78, 80
Slaby, R. G., 521
Slade, P. D., 468, 529
Slag, M. F., 413, 438
Slater, E., 345
Slattery, M. L., 550
Slavney, P. R., 341, 342, 366, 368
Sliwinski, M., 362
Sloan, J. W., 165
Slotnick, H. B., 50
Slyman, D. J., 310
Small, G. W., 342
Smart, R. G., 169
Smets, E. M., 360
Smith, B., 138, 143, 144, 513
Smith, C., 415, 440
Smith, D. E., 142
Smith, D. L., 219
Smith, E. M., 187
Smith, G., 354, 360
Smith, G. R., 341
Smith, G. R., Jr., 345
Smith, G. T., 5
Smith, K. R., 550
Smith, L. E., 11
Smith, M., 318
Smith, M. W., 276
Smith, R., 299, 300
Smith, S. S., 179, 518
Smith, V., 283
Smithartan, T., 141
Smolensky, M. H., 558
Smukler, A. J., 425
Smythe, H., 502
Snedeker, M., 183
Snidman, N., 297, 306, 307, 308, 309
Snowden, L. R., 220
Snyder, D. K., 413, 419, 429
Snyder, F., 552, 553
Snyder, K. S., 275
Sobell, L. C., 128, 129, 130, 131, 136, 138, 139, 140, 141, 142, 143, 144, 145, 146
Sobell, M. B., 128, 129, 130, 131, 136, 138, 139, 140, 141, 142, 143, 144, 145, 146
Sokol, D., 301
Sokolow, L., 136, 141

Soldatos, C. R., 488, 492, 489, 493, 494, 503
Soldz, S., 48, 67
Soloff, P. H., 529, 530
Soloff, P. M., 511
Solomon, R. L., 163
Solstad, K., 413, 442
Sorensen, P., 588
Sorensen, R. C., 412
Sorenson, S. B., 414, 449, 451
Sorri, A., 209
Sosich, R. M., 363
Sotsky, S. M., 241, 242
Spanos, N. P., 393, 395, 396
Spaulding, S., 304
Spaulding, W. D., 205
Spears, C. F., 363
Speckens, A. E. M., 420
Speckens, S. E., 345
Specker, S., 471
Spector, I. P., 411, 412, 413, 414
Spector, S. A., 89
Speechley, K. N., 207
Speelman, J. D., 568
Speigel, J., 393
Speiglman, R., 129
Spence, N. D., 363
Sperling, M. B., 526, 527
Spiegel, D., 7, 12, 384, 386, 387, 391, 393, 395, 397, 398, 399, 400, 401, 402
Spiegel, H., 348, 400
Spielman, A. J., 485, 498
Spinhoven, P., 345
Spitzer, R., 261, 513
Spitzer, R. L., 24, 25, 26, 28, 29, 30, 31, 32, 35, 36, 38, 39, 40, 44, 47, 48, 49, 51, 180, 211, 246, 333, 361, 395, 509, 511, 512, 522, 524
Spitznagel, E. L., 34, 518
Spradley, J., 550
Spreen, O., 101
Spring, B., 204
Sprock, J., 513, 514
Spunt, B., 174
Spurgeon, M., 175
Stainback, R. D., 190
Standage, K., 47
Standards of Practice Committee, 551
Stangl, D., 41, 42, 43, 511, 526
Stangle, D., 582, 586
Stangler, R. S., 467, 476
Stanhope, N., 390, 392

Stanitis, T., 175
Stanley, M. A., 291, 298, 300, 302, 303, 304, 315
Stanley, P., 364
Staples, F., 429
Starcevic, V., 343
Starkman, M. N., 342
Starkstien, S. E., 243
Starvynski, A., 530
Stedwell, R. E., 357
Steen, M., 248
Steer, R. A., 39, 142
Stefansson, J. D., 339
Stege, P., 470
Steger, J. C., 443
Stein, D. J., 340
Stein, J., 311
Stein, J. A., 414, 449, 451
Stein, J. M., 311
Stein, M. B., 290
Stein, N., 10
Steinberg, M., 384, 395, 398
Steiner, A. E., 421
Steinhauer, S. R., 107
Steinhouser, H. C., 473
Steinmetz, C. H., 550
Stekekee, G. A., 302
Steketee, G., 296, 297, 304
Stemberger, R. T., 285
Stenmark, D. E., 474
Stepanski, E., 489, 496
Stermac, L., 432
Stermac, L. E., 423
Stern, J., 341, 347
Stevens, J., 146
Stevenson, H. C., 450
Stevenson, J., 529
Stewart, A., 230
Stewart, A. L., 550
Stewart, G., 307
Stewart, M. A., 69, 72, 79
Stewart, W. R., 184
Stieber, J., 203
Stinnett, R. D., 416
Stitzer, M. L., 187
Stock, W. E., 428, 430
Stockwell, T., 141
Stoddard, A. M., 442
Stoetzman, R., 301
Stolttman, R., 32, 34
Stone, A., 212
Stone, M., 524, 529
Stone, M. H., 172
Stoudemire, A., 9, 392
Stout, A. L., 501
Stouthamer-Loeber, M. D., 522, 549
Stover, E., 450

Strain, J. J., 10
Strang, J., 144
Strassberg, D. S., 421
Straub, R. E., 268, 269
Strauman, T., 311
Straus, H., 435
Strauss, A., 93
Strauss, D., 206
Strauss, J. S., 208
Stravynski, A., 530
Streck, P., 582
Street, L., 316
Streetan, D. H. P., 104
Streiner, D., 285
Streiner, D. L., 44
Strickland, B., 248
Strober, M., 476
Struening, E., 218
Strug, D., 174
Strug, D. L., 174
Stuart, F. M., 414, 418, 419,
    435, 438
Stuening, E. L., 203
Stunkard, A. J., 4
Stutman, R. K., 385
Suarez, A., 530
Subotnik, K. L., 50
Sue, D. C., 220
Sue, D. W., 220
Sue, S., 220, 249
Suedfeld, P., 520
Suelzer, M., 290, 297, 298,
    299, 305
Suelzer, M. T., 343, 361
Sugarmon, A., 476
Suterman, J., 489
Sullivan, K. A., 498
Sumra, J., 475
Sunderland, P., 531
Suomi, S. J., 308
Surawy, C., 345
Surridge, D. H., 431
Susman, V., 508
Susman, V. L., 45, 47
Susser, E., 203, 210
Susser, J. N., 75
Sussex, J., 268
Sutker, P. B., 50
Suy, E., 587
Svikis, D., 71
Svikis, D. S., 178, 179
Swaab, D. F., 448, 568
Swanson, M. K., 550
Swartz, A. R., 297
Swartz, M., 338, 339, 340,
    345, 360, 524
Swartzburg, M., 269
Swayze, V. W., II, 218

Sweeney, E. W., 346
Swift, W. J., 50
Swinson, R. P., 135, 199, 291,
    304, 314, 529
Sylvester, C. E., 305
Sylvester, D., 285, 293

Tacchini, G., 361
Takefman, J., 429
Takeuchi, D. T., 204, 220
Tallefer, S., 361
Talley, N. J., 366
Taloric, S. A., 50
Tam, T. W., 134
Tan, T., 489
Tancer, M. E., 311
Tandon, R., 205
Tanzi, R. E., 89
Tapp, W., 558
Tareen, I. A. K., 162
Targum, S., 258, 268
Tarrier, N., 318
Tarter, R. E., 101, 106, 107,
    133, 135, 142
Task Force on DSM-IV, 12,
    14
Task Force on Promotion
    and Dissemination of
    Psychological
    Procedures, 579
Tasman, A., 219
Tassinari, R., 303
Tate, R. L., 190
Taylor, C., 138, 143, 188
Taylor, D. L., 311
Taylor, G. J., 351
Taylor, I., 136
Taylor, J., 265
Taylor, M. A., 13, 269
Taylor, P., 417
Taylor, S., 302
Taylor, S. E., 550
Teague, G. B., 206, 213
Teicher, M. H., 560, 567
Teitelbaum, M. L., 366
Tellegen, A., 67, 397
Telles, C., 220
Telles, C. A., 282, 289
Temple, M. T., 129
Templeman, T. L., 416, 521
Tennant, C., 241
Tennent, D., 521
Tennant, F. S., 169
Tennent, G., 521
Terestman, N., 415, 417, 440
Terkelsen, K. G., 208
Terman, L. M., 435
Ternes, J. W., 163

Terr, L., 441
Terr, L. C., 385
Terrazas, A., 210
Tessler, R., 217
Testa, T., 183, 184
Teuber, H. L., 94
Teuting, P., 230
Thase, M. F., 586
Thevos, A. K., 186
Thirlwell, M., 360
Thoits, P., 367
Thomas, A., 548, 549
Thomas, C., 11
Thompson, B., 317
Thompson, C. M., 469
Thompson, D. S., 89, 106
Thompson, J. D., 469
Thompson, J. K., 469, 475
Thompson, L., 582, 586
Thompson-Cooper, I., 442
Thompson-Pope, S. K., 515
Thoresen, C., 500
Thorpe, G. L., 296
Thorpy, M. J., 10, 489, 496
Thyer, B. A., 296
Tice, L., 475
Ticnari, P., 209
Tidmarsh, S., 78
Tiefer, L., 427
Tierney, A., 216
Tifft, L. L., 443
Tijhuis, M. A. R., 350
Tillman, J. G., 385
Tilly, S., 3, 6, 8
Tilly, S. M., 523, 525
Timbers, D., 249
Timbers, D. M., 220, 282,
    289
Tinkcom, M., 138
Tirosh, E., 567
Tischler, G. L., 261, 301
Tollison, C. D., 445
Tollison, J. W., 445
Tomasson, K., 342, 345
Tomlin-Albanese, J. M., 297,
    298
Toneatto, T., 136, 138, 139,
    140, 141, 142, 146
Toner, B. B., 365
Tonigan, J. S., 129, 131, 145
Toone, B. K., 339, 342
Topham, A., 133, 138, 142,
    207
Torgersen, S., 39, 68, 70, 72,
    73, 74, 76, 77, 78, 80,
    307, 526
Torrey, E. F., 203, 210
Towle, L. H., 361

Townsend, M. H., 298
Townsley, R. M., 12, 285
Travin, S., 433
Trell, R., 143
Trence, D. L., 413, 438
Trexler, L., 521, 530
Trief, P. M., 10
Trigwell, P., 364
Tross, S., 243
Troughton, E., 511
Trower, P., 588
True, W. R., 74, 307
Truett, K. R., 70
Trull, T. J., 3, 4, 5, 17, 18, 67,
    509, 511, 512, 514, 526,
    528
Tryon, W. W., 547, 550, 551,
    552, 553, 557, 560, 562,
    566, 569, 570, 571
Tsoi, W. F., 418, 451
Tsuang, J. W., 175
Tsuang, M., 267
Tsuang, M. T., 11, 13, 15, 17,
    207, 297
Tuason, V. B., 241
Tuchfeld, B. S., 177, 188
Tucker, D., 175, 220
Tucker, G., 9
Tullis, E. H., 526
Tully, B., 427
Tulving, E., 391
Tupin, J. P., 522
Turkat, I. D., 364, 515, 528
Turkheimer, E., 124
Turley, B., 44
Turner, C. E., 143
Turner, S. M., 11, 12, 283,
    284, 285, 286, 288, 291,
    294, 295, 297, 298, 299,
    300, 301, 302, 303, 304,
    306, 307, 309, 310, 311,
    313, 315, 316, 317, 511,
    528, 579, 585, 586, 588
Tutkum, H., 395
Tuttle, R. J., 170
Tyrell, G., 218
Tzischinsky, O., 552

Uddenberg, N., 418
Udina, C., 299
Uhde, T. W., 314
Uhlenhuth, E. H., 492, 503
Ulmer, A., 210
Ulrich, R. F., 529, 530
Urbach, D., 552
U.S. Bureau of the Census,
    230

Vaglum, P., 581
Vaillant, G. L., 165, 176, 177,
    179, 508
Valdiya, P. S., 586
Valenstein, E., 112, 122
Vallaldares, B. K., 169
Vallis, T. M., 244
Van Amerigan, C., 285
van Asten, W. N. J. C., 447,
    448
Van Balkom, A. J. L. M., 303
Van Beijsterveldt, B., 50, 51
Vandel, B., 587
Vandel, S., 587
VandenBos, G. P., 7
VandenBos, G. R., 235
Vandereycher, W., 473
Vander Hart, O., 388, 389,
    392
Van der Heide, L. H., 363
Van der Kolk, B. A., 300,
    386, 392, 400
Vanderlinden, J., 388
Vanderpearl, R. H., 422
VanderSpek, R., 139
Van de Weil, H. B. M., 429
Vandiver, T., 34
Van Dyck, R., 303
Van Eerdewegh, N., 258
Van Fleet, J. N., 395
Van Gijn, J., 345
Van Gool, W. A., 568
Van Gorp, W. G., 89
Van Hasselt, V. B., 38, 39, 40
Van Hemert, A. M., 345, 420
Van Hilten, J. J., 552, 568
Van Lieshout, C. F. M., 548
Van Praag, H. M., 218, 311
Van Someren, E. J. W., 568
Van Thief, D. H., 13
Van Valkenberg, C., 315
Varga, K., 388
Varghese, F., 28, 41, 52, 525
Varghese, F. N., 217
Varma, V. K., 170
Varney, G. W., 522
Vasile, R., 298
Vaughn, W. K., 363
Vazquez, B., 352
Velez, C. N., 515
Vena, J. E., 550
Verbrugge, L. M., 365, 366
Verebey, K., 143
Verhaak, P. F. M., 350
Vermilyea, B. B., 285, 314
Vermilyea, J. A., 285, 314
Verna, S. K., 286

Verna, V. K., 286
Vernon, P. A., 67, 68
Vgontzas, A., 489, 496
Vidkander, B., 168
Viken, R., 71
Villareal, G., 340
Virkkunen, M., 522
Visco, Dangler, L., 470
Visscher, B., 89
Vitagliano, H. L., 284
Vittone, B. J., 314
Voeller, B., 439
Vogel, N. G., 511
Vogel, V. H., 160
Vollrath, M., 492, 493
von Crannach, M., 34
von Gieso, T., 34
Vonk, B. F. M., 568
von Knorring, A., 341
von Knorring, A. L., 73, 75,
    79, 347
Von Korf, M. R., 34
Von Korff, M., 340, 346, 350
Von Stone, W. W., 183

Wade, J. H., 207, 216, 217
Wadsworth, J., 412, 414
Wagner, L. C., 346
Wahlberg, K., 209
Wakefield, J., C., 5, 18
Waldinger, M. D., 431
Waldinger, R. J., 531
Waldman, I. D., 3, 14, 16
Walfish, S., 474
Walker, A. F., 99
Walker, C. P., 190
Walker, E., 209
Walker, E. A., 352, 366
Walker, E. F., 206
Walker, J. R., 290
Walker, K., 142
Walker, R. D., 190
Walker, V. J., 286
Walker, W. D., 520
Wall, C., 310
Wall, P. D., 356
Wallace, B. C., 178
Wallace, C. J., 216
Wallace, J. F., 521
Wallace, M. R., 89
Wallach, M. A., 206, 207,
    213
Waller, G., 475
Waller, N. G., 386
Walsh, B. T., 7, 11, 474
Walsh, J., 529
Walsh, J. K., 489

Walters, E. E., 70, 79, 240
Walther, R. R., 346
Wanag, A. G., 588
Wang, J., 183
Wang, P. L., 391
Ward, A. J., 388
Ward, C. H., 25, 245
Wardle, J., 465
Ware, C., 495, 501
Ware, N. C., 367
Warner, L. A., 131, 135, 141
Warner, R., 366, 513
Warner, V., 305
Warrell, D., 345
Warshaw, M. G., 297, 298
Warwick, H., 346, 354, 356, 358, 364
Watkins, B., 436
Watkins, J. T., 241, 242
Watkins, P. C., 89
Watson, C. G., 342, 345, 356, 365
Watson, D., 3, 7, 346
Watson, J. B., 292
Watson, R., 436
Watters, J. K., 183
Watts, F. N., 501
Waxler, N. E., 209
Weakland, J., 208
Weatherby, N. L., 183
Weaver, A. L., 363
Webb, M. D., 489, 502, 503
Weber, G., 488
Webster, C. D., 519
Webster, J. B., 552
Webster, L. A., 451
Weeb, H. G., 499
Weed, N. C., 185
Weeks, D. E., 268
Weil, A. T., 170
Weinman, M. L., 311
Weinrich, J. D., 412, 413
Weinrott, M. R., 432
Weinsier, R., 469
Weis, R. D., 163, 174, 183
Weisner, C., 146
Weiss, D. S., 287, 384, 388
Weiss, M. G., 366, 367
Weiss, R. E., 175
Weissman, M. M., 135, 160, 175, 234, 235, 248, 260, 261, 282, 284, 285, 298, 301, 304, 305, 467, 476, 512, 528, 582, 588
Weitzman, E. D., 488, 489, 496, 498
Weitzman, E. L., 465

Weizman, A., 312
Welch, S. L., 475
Wellings, K., 412, 414
Wells, C. E., 122
Wells, K. B., 230
Welte, J., 132, 136, 141
Wender, P. H., 75, 240, 524
Werble, B., 524
Werner, H., 93
Wernicke, C., 92
Wesner, R., 270
Wessley, S., 350, 354
West, D. W., 550
West, J. A., 50
West, L. J., 400
West, M. A., 434, 435, 520
Westermeyer, J., 146, 352
Wethington, E., 237
Wetzel, M. W., 183
Wetzel, R. D., 341, 386
Wetzel, R. O., 583
Wetzler, G. M., 311
Wexler, N. S., 89
Weyerer, S., 493
Whalen, J. E., 397
Whatley, S., 78
Whipple, K., 429
Whitaker, A., 205
White, J. L., 522
White, K., 297
Whitehead, W. E., 352, 366
Whitehouse, A., 465
Whitfield, J. B., 144, 145
Wick, W., 492, 493
Wickramasekera, I., 348, 360
Widiger, T. A., 3, 4, 5, 6, 7, 8, 10, 12, 14, 16, 17, 18, 241, 509, 510, 511, 512, 513, 514, 516, 517, 523, 525, 526, 528
Widlocher, D., 560
Widom, C. S., 519
Wiederman, M. W., 476
Wig, V. K., 286
Wiggins, J. S., 509
Wijdicks, E. F., 345
Wikinson, R. T., 551, 553
Wikler, A., 163, 165
Wilcox, K. J., 67, 397
Wilkes, M., 582
Wilkins, J. N., 175
Wilkinson, D. A., 136, 161
Wilkinson, G., 243
Wilkinson, S. C., 142
Wilkson, D. A., 142
Wilkson, S. R., 352
Wilkson, W., 299, 300

Willi, F. J., 189
Williams, A. B., 178
Williams, C. J., 71
Williams, C. L., 184
Williams, D. E., 363
Williams, D. T., 348
Williams, J., 513
Williams, J. B. W., 6, 7, 9, 11, 13, 35, 36, 38, 39, 40, 48, 49, 51, 180, 184, 211, 246, 361, 509
Williams, J. L., 50
Williams, K. E., 317
Williams, M., 183
Williams, R., 547, 551, 571
Williamson, D. A., 474, 477
Willner, P., 582
Wilmot, W. W., 419
Wilmotte, J., 268
Wilmuth, M. E., 469
Wilsnack, S. C., 131, 132
Wilson, G. T., 11, 472, 473
Wilson, H., 183
Wilson, T. W., 351
Wincze, J. P., 438, 443, 447
Wing, A. L., 550
Winget, C., 352
Wings, J., 361
Winick, C., 177
Winokur, G., 32, 107, 133, 256, 257, 259, 265, 266, 267, 268, 270, 271, 275, 466
Winslow, J. T., 312
Winslow, W. W., 364
Winstead, B. A., 366
Winstead, D. K., 189
Wintrup, A., 519
Wisbey, J., 554
Wise, R. A., 169
Wise, R. H., 164
Wise, T. N., 349, 351, 514, 525
Wisenbaker, J., 549
Wish, E., 183
Wittchen, H., 518
Wittchen, H. U., 34, 39, 234, 243, 249, 282, 283, 289, 290, 315, 316, 361, 387
Wixted, J. T., 215, 216
Wlazlo, A., 302
Woggon, B., 582, 588
Wolf, A. W., 522
Wolfe, F., 363
Wolfe, S. M., 203
Wolff, P., 304, 307, 309
Wollersheim, J. P., 521

Wolpe, J., 421, 579, 582, 583, 585, 586, 588
Wonderlich, S. A., 50
Wong, S., 520
Wood, J. M., 494
Wood, J. S., 550
Woodbury, M., 282
Woodman, C., 290, 297, 298, 299, 300, 305
Woodman, C. L., 343
Woodruff, R. A., 32, 183, 256, 339, 347, 466
Woodworth, G., 72, 79
Woody, E. Z., 401
Woody, G., 174
Woody, G. E., 166, 175, 177, 182, 189, 521, 522, 523
Wool, C. A., 345, 365
Wooley, B., 475
Wooley, S., 352
Woolson, R., 267
Wooten, V., 490
Works, J., 32
World Health Organization (WHO), 45, 134, 335
Wozney, K., 395
Wright, F. D., 143
Wright, J. E., 172
Wyborney, G., 552
Wykpisz, E., 559
Wynne, L. C., 209
Wysjal, G., 330, 345, 347, 349, 361

Xia, Z., 132

Yaffe, M., 344
Yager, J., 475

Yale, S., 206
Yamaguchi, K., 161, 168, 176
Yamamoto, J., 220, 276
Yarber, W. L., 443
Yardley, K., 588
Yargic, I., 395
Yarnold, P. R., 205
Yates, W. R., 72, 79
Yazel, J. J., 448
Ye, W., 306, 307
Yeager, R. A., 177
Yeo, R. A., 124
Yesalis, C. E., 171
Yesavage, J. A., 170, 206, 245
Yeudall, L. T., 417
Ying, Y., 235
Yohman, J. R., 107
Yong, A. S., 276
Yonkers, K. A., 297, 365
Young, A. B., 89
Young, D. E., 472
Young, J. L., 219
Young, L. D., 184
Young, M. A., 586
Young, J. P., 172
Young, R. R., 472
Youngren, M. A., 238
Yu, A. P., 571
Yu, E., 132
Yunus, M. B., 347
Yutsy, S. H., 360
Yutzi, S. H., 386

Zaidi, L. Y., 523
Zamir, R., 415, 441, 449
Zanarini, M. C., 524, 525
Zane, N. W. S., 220, 249
Zanis, D., 212

Zarcone, V., 206, 502
Zarcone, V. P., Jr., 183
Zarins, C. K., 429
Zatzick, D. F., 388
Zaudig, M., 34
Zeiner, A. R., 175
Zeiss, A., 582, 586
Zelenak, J. P., 44
Zhang, M., 132
Zhao, S., 282, 289, 290, 315, 387, 518
Zhou, J. N., 448
Ziegler, V. E., 276, 318
Zielezny, M., 550
Ziff, D. C., 137
Zigler, E., 206
Zilbergeld, B., 428
Zimmerman, M., 41, 42, 43, 68, 508, 511, 526, 527, 582, 586, 587
Zimmerman, R. D., 177
Zinbarg, R., 293
Zingbarg, R. E., 7
Zinberg, N. E., 170
Zinsmeister, A. R., 362
Zoettl, C., 473
Zohar-Kadoch, R., 300
Zohor, J., 300
Zomer, J., 552
Zubin, J., 107, 204
Zucconi, M., 491, 492
Zuckerman, M., 445, 548
Zuger, B., 417, 427
Zuroff, D., 237, 238
Zweben, J. E., 190
Zwinderman, A. H., 431

Subject Index

Acute stress disorder, 7, 12–13, 287–288
AIDS dementia, 89–90, 104, 109
Alcohol Dependency scale, 185
Alcohol disorders, 4, 106–107, 119
  alcohol amnestic disorder, 107
  Alcohol Dependence Scale, 141
  alcoholic Korsakoff's syndrome, 119
  Alcoholics Anonymous, 128
  alcoholism, 106–107
  alcohol timeline followback, 140
  assessment, 138–145
  clinical picture, 130–131
  course and prognosis, 131
  diagnostic considerations, 134–138
  epidemiology, 130
  gender differences, 132–133, 146–147
  genetic influences, 133–134
  Inventory of Drinking Situations, 141
  lifetime drinking history, 140
  minorities, 131–132, 146
  quantity-frequency methods, 140
  Severity of Alcohol Dependence
    Questionnaire, 141
  Short Alcohol Dependence Data
    Questionnaire, 141
  treatment approaches, 145
Alcohol Use Inventory, 185
Alexithymia, 251
Alzheimer's disease, 89, 104–105, 109,
  116–118
Amnestic disorder, 7, 9, 118–120
Anabolic steroid abuse, 4
Anorexia nervosa, 4, 11, 570
Anxiety disorders, 11, 282–318, 567
  acute stress disorder, 287–288
  agoraphobia without history of panic, 284
  assessment, 308–313
  clinical picture, 290–292
  course and complications, 297–298
  diagnostic considerations, 313–315

epidemiology, 289–290
etiological theories, 292–296
familial and genetic considerations,
  304–308
gender, racial, and ethnic issues, 315–318
generalized anxiety disorder, 283, 288,
  290–291, 297–299, 302, 304–305, 307,
  313, 315
obsessive-compulsive disorder, 283, 286,
  291, 297, 299, 302–305, 307, 313–315
onset, 296–297
panic attacks, 282–283
panic disorder with agoraphobia, 283–284,
  296, 300–301
panic disorder without agoraphobia, 283,
  300–301
posttraumatic stress disorder, 287, 297,
  303, 307
social phobia, 283, 284–285, 296–297,
  301–302
specific phobia, 283, 285–286, 296, 301
treatment outcome, 298–304
Attention-deficit disorder, 11
Attention-deficit hyperactivity disorder, 6, 19,
  69, 566–567
Avoidant personality disorder, 12, 511,
  527–528
Axes, DSM-IV, 8, 24, 29, 35–36

Beck Anxiety Inventory, 142
Beck Depression Inventory, 142, 245
Behavioral family management, 275
Binge eating disorder, 7
Bipolar disorder, 11, 17, 256–277, 564–565
  assessment, 270–272
  clinical picture, 261–264
  course and prognosis, 264–267
  description, 256–259
  diagnostic considerations, 269–270
  epidemiology, 259–261

Bipolar disorder (*continued*)
  familial and genetic considerations,
    267–269, 272
  gender and racial-ethnic issues, 275–276
  treatment, 272–275
Body dysmorphic disorder, 11, 14, 335, 340,
    343–344
Body Dysmorphic Disorder Examination,
    364
Brain malformations, 100–101
Brain tumors, 99–100
Breathing-related sleep disorder, 11
Brief depressive disorder, 17
Brief reactive dissociative disorder, 12–13
Broca's aphasia, 92, 113
Bulimia nervosa, 4, 7, 11

Caffeine dependence, 7
Center for Epidemiological Studies
    Depression Scale, 245
Circulatory system diseases, 101–104
  arteriovenous malformations, 102–103
  stroke, 102–103
  transient ischemic attack, 102
Classification, dimensional vs. categorical,
    3–19
Clinical significance, 5–6
Cocaine abuse, 4
Cognitive decline, age-related, 7, 8
Communicative disorders, 112–113
  acalculia, 113
  agraphia, 113
  alexia, 113
  aphasia, 112–113
Comorbidity, 3, 14
Composite International Diagnostic
    Interview, 142, 361
Computerized Diagnostic Schedule, 246
Conduct disorder, 11
Control, 4–5
Conversion disorder, 11, 14, 335, 342, 356
Cyclothymia, 17

Degenerative and demyelinating diseases,
    104–106
  AIDS-related dementia, 104
  Alzheimer's disease, 104–105
  Creutzfeldt-Jakob disease, 104
  Huntington's disease, 104–105
  multiple sclerosis, 104–106
  Parkinson's disease, 104
  Pick's disease, 104
Delirium, 7, 9
Dementia, 7, 8, 9
Depressive disorders, 10, 230–250, 262–264,
    563–564
  assessment, 244–247

biological factors, 238–239
  course and prognosis, 241–242
  depressive disorders not otherwise
    specified, 10, 233
  diagnostic considerations, 242–244
  epidemiology, 233–236
  familial and genetic considerations,
    240–241
  gender and ethnic issues, 247–249
  psychological factors, 237–238
  social and environmental factors, 236–237
Depressive personality disorder, 11
Deviance, statistical, 6
Diagnostic Interview Schedule, 29, 32–35, 38,
    142, 246–247, 338, 361, 523
Dictionary of Behavioral Assessment
    Techniques, 443–444
Disorders due to general medical condition,
    9
Disorders not otherwise specified, 7, 10
Dissociative amnesia, 12, 389–392
Dissociative disorders, 7, 11, 384–403
  depersonalization, 398–399
  dissociative amnesia, 12, 389–392
  dissociative disorders not otherwise
    specified, 396, 399–401
  dissociative fugue, 392–394
  dissociative identity disorder, 12, 387–389,
    393–398, 402–403
  dissociative trance disorder, 401–402
  epidemiology, 387–388
  ethnicity, gender and culture, 388–389
  Guidelines for Treating Dissociative
    Identity Disorder, 396–398
  multiple personality disorder, 396
Dissociative Disorders Interview Schedule,
    384
Dissociative Experiences Scale, 384, 397
Dissociative identity disorder, 12, 387–389,
    393–398, 402–403
DSM-I, 25
DSM-II, 25
DSM-III, 25, 29, 32, 34–35, 39–40, 104
DSM-III-R, 25, 35, 38, 41–42, 44–45, 90,
    102, 104
DSM-IV, 25, 29, 32, 35–36, 38, 40–42, 44–45,
    90–91, 106
DSM-IV and multidimensional assessment
    strategies, 578–590
  alternative axis: assessment of maintaining
    factors, 583–585
  alternative axis: etiology, 585–589
  alternative axis: tripartite assessment of
    symptoms, 580–583
Double depression, 17
Dyscontrol , 4–5
Dysthymia, 11, 233

Eating disorders, 465–477
    anorexia nervosa, 465–477
    assessment, 476
    bulimia nervosa, 465–477
    clinical picture, 468–469
    course and prognosis, 469–473
    descriptions, 465–466
    diagnostic considerations, 474–475
    epidemiology, 466–468
    familial and genetic considerations,
        473–474
    gender and racial-ethnic issues, 476–477
    treatment, 471–473
Electroconvulsive therapy, 273–274
Epidemiological Catchment Area Program,
    32, 338–340, 411, 414, 449
Epilepsy, 109–111
Equipotentiality, 94

Family History Research Diagnostic Criteria,
    31
Family Informant Schedule and Criteria, 31

Gender issues, 122–123
Generalized anxiety disorder, 14, 283, 288
Genetic basis and psychopathology, 58–81
    adoption method, 65–66
    anxiety disorders, 73–74
    basic premises, 59–60
    family method research, 62–72
    linkage methods, 66–67
    mood disorders, 74–76
    quantitative genetics, 61–62
    schizophrenia, 76–78
    somatoform disorders, 72–73
    substance abuse studies, 71–72
    twin method, 64–65,
    Virginia Twin Study, 71–76
Geriatic Depression Scale, 245

Hamilton Anxiety Scale, 302
Hamilton Rating Scale for Depression, 142
Head trauma, 97–99
    posttraumatic amnesia, 98
HIV, 450–451
Huntington's disease, 89, 104–105, 116–117
Hypochondriasis, 13–14, 335, 339–340,
    342–243

Illness Attitude Scale, 364
Illness Behavior Questionnaire, 363–364
Impairment, 5–8
Insomnia, 7
Intelligence, 18
Intermittent explosive disorder, 4
International Classification of Disease, 10th
    edition, 44–45, 335–336, 361, 519–520,
    523

International Classification of Sleep
    Disorders, 483
International Personality Disorder
    Examination, 45–48, 51
    reliability and validity, 47
International Society for the Study of the
    Dissociative Disorders, 384
Interview development, 24–25

Jet lag syndrome, 7

Kleptomania, 4

Lithium carbonate, 272

Magnetic resonance imaging, 92, 96, 117
Magnetic resonance spectroscopy, 96
Major depressive disorder, 7, 231–232
Male erectile disorder, 10
Mania, 261–262
Melancholia, 263
Mental retardation, 18
Mild neurocognitive disorder, 7
Millon Clinical Multiaxial Inventory, 44
Minimal brain dysfunction, 526
Minnesota Multiphasic Personality
    Inventory, 43, 185, 349, 362–363, 384,
    501
Minor depressive disorder, 7
Mixed anxiety-depressive disorder, 7, 11
Mood disorders, 7, 10, 13
Morbidity risk, 63
Motor activity and DSM-IV, 547–572
    anorexia nervosa, 570
    anxiety disorders, 567
    attention-deficit hyperactivity disorder,
        566–567
    bipolar disorders, 564–565
    depressive disorders, 563–564
    developmental evidence, 547–550
    dysomnias, 554–558
    DSM-IV, 550–551
    medication-induced movement disorders,
        568–569
    minorities and gender, 570–571
    mood disorder due to a general medical
        condition, 565
    mood disorders, 560–570
    parasomnias, 558–559
    primary sleep disorders, 554–559
    schizophrenia and other psychotic
        disorders, 567–568
    sleep disorders due to a general medical
        condition, 559–560
    sleep disorders related to another mental
        disorder, 559
    sleep onset spectrum, 551–552

Motor activity and DSM-IV (*continued*)
 substance-induced mood disorder, 565
 substance-induced sleep disorder, 560
 substance-related disorders, 568
 wrist actigraphic sleep assessment, 552–553
Multiple sleep latency test, 502–503
Multithreshold model, 61

National Institute of Mental Health, 32, 265, 289, 411, 414
Nicotine dependence, 4
Normality, 4

Obsessive-compulsive disorder, 11, 14, 283, 286
Oppositional defiant disorder, 6, 11
Organic disorders , 9
Organic mood disorder, 9, 10
Organic personality disorder, 9

Pain disorder, 9–10, 14, 335, 339
Pathological gambling, 4, 5
Pedophilia, 4
Perception and motility disorders, 113–116
 apraxia, 115–116
 autotopognosia, 114
 finger agnosia, 114
 neglect, 115
 paralysis, 114
 paresis, 114
 right-left disorientation, 114
 visual agnosia, 114–115
Peritraumatic Dissociative Experiences Questionnaire, 384
Personality disorders, 7, 14, 19, 67–68, 508–531
 antisocial personality disorder, 511–515, 517–524
 avoidant personality disorder, 511, 527–528
 borderline personality disorder, 511–516, 524–526
 comorbidity, 510–511
 dependent personality disorder, 513–514, 528
 etiology, 514
 gender and cultural issues, 511–514
 histrionic personality disorder, 511–513, 516, 526
 narcissistic personality disorder, 527
 obsessive-compulsive personality disorder, 528–529
 paranoid personality disorder, 515
 prevalence, 509–510
 schizoid, 512, 515–516
 schizotypal personality disorder, 512, 516
 treatment, 529–531
Personality Disorders Advisory Committee (DSM-III-R), 14

Personality Disorders Work Group (DSM-IV), 14
Pharmacologic intervention, 12
Physical disorders, 8–11, 17, 18
Pluripotentiality, 94
Polysomnography, 501–502
Positive emission tomography, 92
Postpsychotic depressive disorder of schizophrenia, 11
Posttraumatic stress disorder, 7, 12, 13, 287, 384
Premenstrual dysphoric disorder, 6, 10
Premenstrual syndrome, 6, 10
Psychoactive substance use disorders, 159–191
 anabolic steroids, 171–172
 assessment, 182
 barbituates and hypnotic sedatives, 167–168
 cannabinoids, 170–171
 clinical management, 188–191
 clinical picture, 164–175
 course and prognosis, 175–178
 diagnostic considerations, 179–182
 etiology, 160–164
 familial and genetic considerations, 178–179, 185
 hallucinogens, 169–170
 inhalants, 173
 opiates, 165–167
 prevalence, 159–160
 psychostimulants, 168–169
 racial-ethnic considerations, 187–188
Psychological factors affecting a medical condition, 9–10

Questionnaire of Experiences of Dissociation, 384
Quick Diagnostic Interview Schedule, 246

Racial-ethnic considerations, 123, 187–188
Recurrent brief depressive disorder, 7
Research Diagnostic Criteria, 29–30
Rorschach, 384

Schedule for Affective Disorders and Schizophrenia, 29–31, 38, 43
Schizoaffective disorder, 13, 214
Schizophrenia, 13, 15, 19, 203–221, 567–568
 assessment, biological, 217–218
 assessment, psychological, 214–217
 clinical picture, 205–206
 comorbidity, 212–214
 course and prognosis, 206–208
 diagnostic considerations, 210–214
 epidemiology, 204
 familial and genetic considerations, 208–210
 gender and racial-ethnic issues, 218–221

Schizotypal personality disorder, 71, 512, 516
Selective mating, 61
Sexual and gender identity disorders,
     409–453
  assessment, 442–448
  clinical picture, 418–427
  course and prognosis, 427–435
  diagnostic considerations, 436–442
  dyspareunia, 409–410, 420
  epidemiology, 411–418
  exhibitionism, 410, 422, 425, 432
  familial and genetic considerations,
     435–436
  female orgasmic disorder, 409, 428–429,
     435
  female sexual arousal disorder, 409
  fetishism, 410
  frotteurism, 410, 425
  gender and racial-ethnic issues, 449–451
  gender identity disorder, 410–411, 417,
     427, 441
  hebephilia, 424
  hypoactive sexual desire disorder, 409, 429
  inhibited sexual desire, 419
  male erectile disorder, 409, 427, 430–431,
     438, 443
  male orgasmic disorder, 409, 437
  nocturnal penile tumescence, 447–448
  paraphilias, 410
  pedophilia, 410, 424–425, 436, 439–440,
     443, 446
  penile volume response, 444–447
  premature ejaculation, 409, 418, 429, 431,
     437
  retarded ejaculation, 437
  sexual assault, 422–424, 431–436, 439–440,
     446, 450
  sexual aversion disorder, 409
  sexual masochism, 410, 425, 439
  sexual sadism, 410, 425, 439
  transsexualism, 417–418, 426–427,
     440–441, 444, 451
  transvestic fetishism, 410, 417, 426–427,
     439–441
  vaginal blood volume, 446–447
  vaginal pulse amplitude, 446–447
  vaginismus, 410, 420, 429
  voyeurism, 425, 432
Sexual arousal disorder, 10
Simplicity, in diagnosis, 15
Sleep disorders, 483–504
  age, gender, and racial-ethnic issues, 503
  assessment, 499–503
  breathing-related sleep disorders, 486–487,
     492–493, 557
  circadian rhythm sleep disorder, 487, 493,
     497–498, 558
  classification, 483–491

  course and prognosis, 492–494
  diagnostic considerations, 495–499
  dyssomnias, 484–487, 554–558
  epidemiology, 491–492
  familial and genetic considerations,
     494–495
  narcolepsy, 486, 493–494, 496–497, 557
  nightmare disorder, 487–488, 558–559
  parasomnias, 484, 487–488, 493, 498–499,
     558–559
  primary hypersomnia, 487, 496–497,
     556–557
  primary insomnia, 485–486, 492–493,
     495–496, 554–556
  sleep disorders related to another mental
     disorder, 484, 488–489, 494, 559
  sleep disorders related to a general medical
     condition, 484, 489–490, 494, 559–560
  sleep disorders related to a mood disorder,
     484, 494
  sleepwalking and sleep terror disorders,
     488, 493–494, 559
  substance-induced sleep disorders, 484,
     490–491, 560
Sleep-wake schedule disorder, 7
Social phobia, generalized, 11–12, 283–285
Somatosensory Amplification Scale, 348
Somatization disorders, 13–14, 333–369
  assessment, 358–365
  body dysmorphic disorder, 335, 340,
     343–344
  conversion disorder, 335, 342, 356
  course and prognosis, 344–346
  diagnostic considerations, 355–358
  epidemiology, 336–340
  etiological considerations, 346–355
  gender and cultural issues, 365–368
  hypochondriasis, 335, 339–340, 342–343
  pain disorder, 335, 339
  pseudocyesis, 340
  somatization disorder, 13–14, 334–335,
     340–341, 356
  somatoform autonomic dysfunction, 336
  somatoform disorder not otherwise
     specified, 335, 340
  undifferentiated somatoform disorder, 335,
     341
Specific phobias, 14, 283, 285–286
Stanford Acute Stress Reaction
     Questionnaire, 384
State-Trait Anxiety Inventory, 302
Structured Clinical Interview of Dissociative
     Disorders, 384, 397
Structured Clinical Interview for DSM-IV,
     29, 35–40, 43, 142, 246–247, 361–362
  nonpatient version, 36
  patient version, 36
  reliability, 38–40

Structured Diagnostic Interview for
    Hypochondriasis, 361
Structured interview, 24–29
    development, 24–25
    LEAD, 28–29, 44, 47–48, 51
    reliability and validity, 25–29
Structured Interview for DSM-IV Axis II,
    46–52
    reliability and validity, 49–51
Structured Interview for DSM-IV
    Personality, 41–45
    reliability and validity, 43–44
Structured Interview for Insomnia, 499
Structured Interview for Sleep Disorders, 499
Substance-related disorders, 4
Symptom Checklist-90-R, 142
Symptom Interpretation Questionnaire, 349

Toronto Alexithymia Scale, 351–352
Toxic, infectious, and metabolic illnesses,
    107–109
    Creutzfeldt-Jakob disease, 109
    encephalitis, 108–109

herpes simplex, 109
kuru, 109
meningitis, 108
neurosyphylis, 109
phenylketonuria, 108
Tay-Sachs disease, 108
Tradition, in diagnosis, 15
Trail Making Test, 142
Transvestic fetishism, 4, 6
Trichotillomania, 11

Unipolar disorder, 11
U.S. Alcohol, Drug Abuse, and Mental
    Health Administration, 45
Utility, in diagnosis, 15

Validity, in diagnosis, 15

Wechsler Adult Intelligence Scale, 142
Wernicke-Korsakoff's syndrome, 107
Wernicke's aphasia, 92, 113
World Health Organization, 45–46